Resting Places

SECOND EDITION

Resting Places

*The Burial Sites of Over
10,000 Famous Persons*

Second Edition

SCOTT WILSON

Volume 2
Lewis, Sheldon – Z (entries 5498–10113);
bibliography; index

McFarland & Company, Inc., Publishers
Jefferson, North Carolina, and London

2

LIBRARY OF CONGRESS CATALOGUING-IN-PUBLICATION DATA

Wilson, Scott, 1953–
Resting places : the burial sites of over 10,000 famous persons /
Scott Wilson.— 2nd ed.
p.   cm.
Includes bibliographical references and index.

ISBN-13: 978-0-7864-2896-0 (2 volume set)
(softcover : 50# alkaline paper) ∞

1. Celebrities — Biography — Dictionaries.
2. Celebrities — Tombs — Dictionaries.   I. Title.
CT105.W573   2007   920.02 — dc22   2006038118

British Library cataloguing data are available

Cover photograph ©2007 Corbis Images

Manufactured in the United States of America

McFarland & Company, Inc., Publishers
Box 611, Jefferson, North Carolina 28640
www.mcfarlandpub.com

Contents

5498. Lewis, Sheldon (April 20, 1869–May 7, 1958) Philadelphia born silent screen actor best known for his updated 1919 Metro version of *Dr. Jekyll and Mr. Hyde* (with a cheater finale), overshadowed by the John Barrymore version filmed a few months later. Other films include *Orphans of the Storm* (1921), *Seven Footprints to Satan* (1929), *The Monster Walks* (1932). He retired in 1936 and died in San Gabriel at 89. Married to actress Virginia Pearson. Unmarked. Block L, sec. 942, lot 25, 90' in from curb 940, Valhalla Memorial Park, North Hollywood, CA.

5499. Lewis, Sinclair (Feb. 7, 1885–Jan. 10, 1951) Novelist from Sauk Centre, Minnesota, published his first book debunking the harmonious American small town myth, *Main Street*, in 1920. *Babbitt* followed in 1922, *Arrowsmith* (1925) earned a Pulitzer Prize, which he declined. *Dodsworth* appeared in 1929 and in 1930 Lewis became the first American to receive the Nobel Prize in Literature. He died from heart and lung ailments in the Villa Electra nursing home in Rome, Italy, telling the Franciscan nuns who attended him "God bless you all" before he expired. He was returned to Sauk Centre, where his ashes were scattered in the grave during a committal service on January 28, 1951, a winter wind blowing some of them off into the air. The urn remains in the Sinclair Lewis Interpretive Center in town. Flush plaque in his parents' lot, near front of cemetery and left of entrance drive. Greenwood Cemetery, Sauk Centre, MN.

5500. Lewis, Ted (Theodore Leopold Friedman, June 6, 1891–Aug. 25, 1971) Band leader and showman with tilted, battered top hat, slow delivery (*When My Baby Smiles at Me, Me and My Shadow*) and the trademark line "Is everybody happy?" appeared in nightclubs, a few films, and continued throughout his career to promote his home town of Circleville, Ohio, which today houses the Ted Lewis Museum. He died in New York. After services at Temple Rodeph Shalom there, he was returned home, where a white monument in the Friedman lot bears an engraving of his tilted top hat and cane. Main drive in entrance and around to the left; lot down road on right. Sec. 7, Forrest Cemetery, Circleville, OH.

5501. Lewis, Vera (Vera Mackey, June 10, 1873–Feb. 8, 1956) Hawk faced New York born actress in films 1914–1947, including *Intolerance* (1916), *The Merry-Go-Round* (1919), *Stella Dallas* (1925), *King Kong, Nothing Sacred, Angels With Dirty Faces, The Roaring Twenties, The Return of Dr. X, The Smiling Ghost, The Cat Creeps* (1946). She died in Woodland Hills, California. Sec. A, lot 485, grave 4, Holy Cross Cemetery, Culver City, CA.

5502. Lewis, Walter "Furry" (March 6, 1893–Sept. 14, 1981) Memphis Blues singer and guitarist from the 1920's achieved a following in the 1960's and 70's based on his recordings forty plus years later; he was equally adept at Ragtime. Sec. 7, div. 2, row 15, grave 16, Hollywood Cemetery, Memphis, TN.

5503. Lewton, Val (Vladimir Leventon, May 7, 1904–March 14, 1951) Russian born writer-producer, nephew of Nazimova, grew up at Tarrytown, New York. A handful of RKO horror films he supervised from 1942–46 have become genre classics and given legend to his flair for suspense and atmosphere, his personal involvement in their quality despite a low budget an almost unheard of feat for a studio producer (*Cat People, I Walked With a Zombie, The Seventh Victim, The Leopard Man, The Ghost Ship, Curse of the Cat People, The Body Snatcher, Isle of the Dead, Bedlam*). A driven man, he died from a heart attack at 46. His eulogy was spoken by actor Alan Napier, with cremation at Westwood Memorial Park through Gates, Kingsley and Gates, who picked up the ashes. As his hobby had been sailing his boat, the *Nina*, named for his mother, his family and a few friends went out on the *Nina* and scattered Lewton's ashes into the Pacific. His mother Nina Lewton (Dec. 10, 1874–Feb. 26, 1967), Nazimova's sister, is in the Iris Columbarium, niche 28619, Great Mausoleum, Forest Lawn, Glendale, CA.

5504. Leyendecker, J.C. (Joseph C. Leyendecker, March 21, 1874–July 25, 1951) Noted artist from Germany did magazine covers and ads for men's clothing. The Arrow collar man was his companion of many years, Charles A. Beach. Beach lived with Leyendecker and his brother, artist **F.X. Leyendecker** on Mount Tom Road in New Rochelle, New York. Frank (F.X.) died from a drug overdose at 45 on April 19, 1924. J.C. survived him by twenty seven years, leaving everything to Beach, who died in his New Rochelle home June 22, 1954. The brothers are buried together. White Oak sec., near intersection of White Oak and Forest. Woodlawn Cemetery, the Bronx, N.Y.C.

5505. Liberace (Wladzu Valentino Liberace, May 16, 1919–Feb. 4, 1987) Flamboyant Milwaukee born pianist used a candelabra, an abundance of jewels, and a sense of humor about himself in his act. He made a few films, but was primarily a concert favorite until the year before his death. Terminally ill with viral pneumonia and HIV, he fought charges of homosexuality publicized by the media. Surrounded by his favorite tapes and foods, he died in his Palm Springs home, refusing medication and holding a rosary. Interred with his mother and brother, orchestra leader and violinist **George Liberace** (July 31, 1911–Oct. 16, 1983). White sarcophagus and statue, inscribed with their names and his candelabra, piano and signature, with the epitaph *Sheltered Love*. Right side, Courts of Remembrance, Forest Lawn Hollywood Hills, Los Angeles.

5506. Lido, Bob (Robert Freda, Sept. 21, 1915–Aug. 9, 2000) Violinist and vocalist with Lawrence Welk's orchestra 1952–1979, a prominent feature on the long running television show. Cremated through J.T. Oswald mortuary, Los Angeles. Ashes to his son at Dumont, NJ.

5507. Liddle, Don (Donald Eugene Liddle, May

25, 1925–June 5, 2000) Major league pitcher with the New York Giants threw what became one of the most famous offerings ever in the first game of the 1954 world series, belted by Cleveland's Vic Wertz far into the outfield and caught, to the amazement of everyone, by Willie Mays in an over the shoulder grab that remains among the most fabled fielding feats in baseball history. Liddle, sent in to relieve Sal Maglie against Wertz, was immediately replaced by Marv Grissom, to whom he remarked as he left the mound "I got my man." Sec. MIV, lot 78, space 1, Highland Memorial Cemetery, College Drive, Mount Carmel, IL.

5508. Lieb, Robert (Robert P. Lieb, Sept. 15, 1914–Sept. 28, 2002) Pelham, New York, born actor on Broadway and numerous television shows, including a running part as George Baxter's brother-in-law on *Hazel* and as Officer Flaherty in the 1960 *Twilight Zone* episode *Night of the Meek*. Films include *Angel in My Pocket* (1968), *Myra Breckenridge* (1970) *and Dangerous Heat* (1994). He died in Los Angeles of pneumonia following multiple strokes. Cremated through Angeleno Valley mortuary. Ashes scattered at sea October 1 off the coast of Los Angeles County.

5509. Liebling, Abbott J. *see* **Jean Stafford.**

5510. Lifar, Serge (April 2, 1904–Dec. 15, 1986) Russian star of the *Ballets Russes* helped revitalize French dance through leadership of the Paris Opera and founded the *Institut Choreographique* in Paris in 1947. Black monument with a gold Russian cross. Sainte-Geneviève-des-Bois (Russian Cemetery), Paris.

5511. Light, Enoch (Aug. 18, 1905–July 31, 1978) Developer of stereophonic sound. Umpawag Burial Ground, Redding, CT.

5512. Lightner, Winnie (Winifred Reeves, Sept. 17, 1899–March 5, 1971) Stage comedienne from George White's Scandals of 1923 in several early sound musical comedies, retiring in 1934, the wife of director Roy Del Ruth, with whom she is buried. Sec. D, lot 259, grave 3, San Fernando Mission Cemetery, Mission Hills, CA.

5513. Lightoller, Charles *see* **Titanic.**

5514. Likens, Sylvia (Sylvia Marie Likens, Jan. 3, 1949–Oct. 26, 1965) The center of a notorious Hoosier murder case was a teenager from Lebanon, Indiana, left in the care of Gertrude Baniszewski at her makeshift foster home in the 3800 block of East New York St., Indianapolis, in July 1965, soon became the prime object of her guardian's wrath, encouraging other teens to beat and rape her as she kept her confined in a basement until she died at 16. Baniszewski served twenty years, was paroled, moved to Iowa, changed her name and died from lung cancer in 1990. The Likens girl was returned to her home town. Sec. 34, lot 33, Oak Hill Cemetery, Lebanon, IN.

5515. Liliuokalani, Lydia (Sept. 2, 1838–Nov. 11, 1917) Queen of Hawaii from 1891 was a proponent of "Hawaii for Hawaiians" but was unseated in the January Revolution of 1893. U.S. President Benjamin Harrison, long interested in Hawaii (and about to leave office) sent marines in to protect American lives, meanwhile proclaiming Hawaii a U.S. protectorate and annexing it. Queen Liliuokalani was also a poetess and composed the song *Aloha Oe*. Kalakaua Tomb, Royal Mausoleum, Honolulu, HI.

5516. Lillie, Beatrice (May 29, 1894–Jan. 20, 1989) English stage comedienne since 1914, the daughter of a government official. Friend to Coward, Shaw, Chaplin, and the toast of both London and Broadway, Bea Lillie's few films failed to capture her wide appeal to live audiences. As Lady Peel, widow of Lord Peel, she retired to her home Peel Fold at Henley-on-Thames. Her upright gray double stone reads *She gave the gift of laughter to many*. New section, parish churchyard at Harpsden, near Henley-on-Thames.

5517. Lillie, "Pawnee Bill" (Gordon William Lillie, Feb. 14, 1860–Feb. 3, 1942) Showman and Indian agent from Bloomington, Indiana, was appointed to lead homesteaders into Oklahoma during the 1889 land rush. He later wrote of his experience with that and living among the Pawnee, as well as his efforts to save the buffalo. A partner of Buffalo Bill Cody 1908–1913. Family mausoleum, Highland Cemetery, Pawnee, OK.

5518. Lilly, Eli (July 8, 1838–June 6, 1898) Established the pharmaceutical company beginning with gelatin capsules as opposed to tablets. His son **Eli Lilly** (April 1, 1885–Jan. 24, 1977) was president 1932–1948 and directed the Lilly Endowment Fund, which established libraries and philanthropic organizations. Colonel Lilly (Lilly Sr.) has a mausoleum shaped as an arched chapel; his son adjacent him has a large statue. Opposite end of the section with Booth Tarkington and Benjamin Harrison. Sec. 13, Crown Hill Cemetery, Indianapolis, IN.

5519. Lincoln, Abraham (Feb. 12, 1809–April 15, 1865) 16th President of the United States 1861–65, the homespun Kentucky born politician known for both his compassion and holding the union together at any cost looms larger in American history and legend than any other individual. His death is an equally familiar story. Lee had surrendered to Grant on Sunday, April 9, ending the Confederate cause and the Civil War. That event launched actor John Wilkes Booth and his band of conspirators on his plan to murder (originally to kidnap) Lincoln. The following Friday evening, April 14, the president and first lady and their guests, Clara Harris and Major Henry Rathbone, were at Ford's Theatre in Washington watching Laura Keene in *Our American Cousin*. When the guard stepped out, Booth crept up behind Lincoln, shooting him in the back of the head and attacking Rathbone with a knife. As he leapt onto the stage, his boot was caught in the American flag, injuring his leg. Shouting "Sic semper tyrannis!" (Thus to all tyrants!) he limped across the stage and out the door. While the army began tracking Booth, Lincoln was carried across 10th St. into the Peterson house and laid on a bed, where he died the next morning. When their young son **William Wallace "Willie" Lincoln** (Dec. 21, 1850–Feb. 20, 1862) died in the White House, Lincoln had taken the offer of his friend Thomas Carroll and placed the boy in the Carroll mausoleum on a steep hillside, vault 292 on a ledge high above Rock Creek in Oak Hill Cemetery, Georgetown. There Lincoln would go and sit with the coffin, on two occasions reputedly having it opened so he could look on the face again. After the assassination, Willie was removed from Oak Hill and placed aboard the funeral train, which made a slow journey to twenty cities before arriving back in their hometown, Springfield, Illinois, for the funeral on May 4, attended by only his eldest son Robert and a Hanks cousin from Kentucky among relatives. His wife Mary, prostrated by grief, remained in Washington. The coffins rested in a receiving vault built into a hillside at Oak Ridge Cemetery in Springfield from May 4 through December 21, 1865, when they were moved into a temporary tomb on a hillside northeast of the present tomb. The spot is now marked by an uninscribed rough hewn stone. The temporary tomb was removed in 1871 and the bodies of the president, Willie and **Edward Baker "Eddie" Lincoln** (March 10, 1846–Feb. 1, 1850, removed from Hutchinson Cemetery in Springfield) were placed in the partially completed permanent tomb. It was dedicated October 15, 1874. In 1876 a gang of grave robbers had removed the slab over the crypt and were pulling out the coffin when they were foiled by secret service agents. From then on the body was moved at various times, particularly during the renovation from November 1899 through June 1901 after twenty five years deterioration.

The first lady, Lexington, Kentucky born **Mary Todd Lincoln** (Dec. 13, 1818–July 16, 1882), after years of depression and a period of confinement in a mental institution, had lost her husband and three of her sons by the time of her death in Springfield. Their youngest son **Thomas "Tad" Lincoln** (April 4, 1853–July 15, 1871) died at eighteen. Upon their deaths both were placed with the president and two younger sons in a tomb at Oak Ridge in Springfield. The **Todd** family, southerners who sent sons to war against the federal government and bore great animosity toward Lincoln, are buried at Lexington Cemetery, Lexington, Kentucky. On April 24, 1901, Lincoln's remains and those of his wife were placed in a marble tomb and cemented inside the monument, but their son Robert visited the site disguised as a workman and was dissatisfied with the security, calling for it to be more heavily guarded and cemented against theft. Accordingly, on September 26, 1901, the casket of the president was locked in a steel cage and buried ten feet below the floor in the interior of the tomb, surrounded by six feet of solid cement. Before that final reburial, the coffin was opened one last time, reportedly for identification purposes. In 1962, Fleetwood Lindley, a seventy five year old Springfield florist, recalled the

scene he had witnessed as a boy of fourteen: "His face was readily recognizable; it seemed to be covered with a moss like mold, the color of frost. Father had seen it once before, in 1888. He said then it was about as dark as an old saddle." Although another renovation of the structure was required by 1931, the body of Lincoln was undisturbed. It remained sealed far below the oval chamber in the rear interior of the tomb. The exterior was designed by Larkin G. Mead, Jr., built of white brick and Quincy granite, with an obelisk rising in the air above a large circular base with a bronze statue of Lincoln and four groupings of military statues, all by Mead. The bust on a pedestal before the entrance (the nose repeatedly rubbed by visitors for luck) is by Gutzon Borglum. On the wall behind the brown marble block cenotaph (with Lincoln's name and dates) inside the burial chamber are the words of Edwin M. Stanton upon Lincoln's death: *Now he belongs to the ages.* Lincoln is buried 30" north of the cenotaph; his wife and sons, whose names are inscribed in the wall, are in crypts south of the cenotaph. The elaborate structure of Lincoln's Tomb is matched in size among the presidents only by the mammoth monuments to Grant, Garfield, McKinley and Harding. Oak Ridge Cemetery, Springfield, IL.

5520. Lincoln, Elmo (Otto Elmo Linkenhelter, Feb. 6, 1889–June 27, 1952) Silent screen and stage actor was the first screen Tarzan, in *Tarzan of the Apes* (1918). A native of Rochester, Indiana, he died in Los Angeles of a heart attack. His ashes were placed in an unmarked communal niche in the colonnade of the Chapel of the Psalms at Hollywood Cemetery with no marker for thirty-nine years. In the summer of 1991 the Fulton County Historical Society of Rochester, Indiana, had a name plate affixed to the wall near where the ashes are stored. Colonnade, north wall, Chapel of the Psalms, Hollywood Forever Cemetery, Hollywood (Los Angeles), CA.

5521. Lincoln, Evelyn (June 25, 1909–May 11, 1995) Secretary to John F. Kennedy from his election to the senate in 1953 until his death in Dallas a decade later. She published two volumes of reminiscences and was one of the original seven charter founders of the JFK Library and Museum in Boston. She died following cancer surgery in Chevy Chase, Maryland, at 85. Columbarium Court 4, sec. A, stack 16, niche 3, Arlington National Cemetery, Arlington, VA.

5522. Lincoln, Nancy Hanks (Feb. 5, 1784–Oct. 5, 1818) The mother of Abraham Lincoln was from Campbell County, Virginia. She and her husband Thomas Lincoln moved their family from Kentucky to the Little Pigeon Creek settlement, now the Lincoln Boyhood Home, near Gentryville, Indiana, in the southwestern part of the state. In 1818 the "milk sick" swept the settlement and she died at 34. She was buried just south of the cabin, but the current tombstone was not erected until 1879, and the site of her grave (which is only approximate) as it appears today with the clean white marker and iron fence around the plot date to 1938, when the boyhood home was opened. Lincoln Boyhood Home, Gentryville, IN.

5523. Lincoln, Robert Todd (Aug. 1, 1843–July 25, 1926) The eldest of Abraham and Mary Todd Lincoln's four sons was the only one to live to adulthood. His life had many ironies: in early 1865 he lost his footing in front of an approaching train but was pulled back to safety — by Edwin Booth. He served in the Civil War and as Secretary of War under Presidents Garfield and Arthur (1881–85). To his dismay and depression, he was at his father's deathbed *and* at the general scene when both Garfield and McKinley were fatally shot. He became a wealthy railroad executive and owned an estate at Manchester, Vermont, where he died. In another of history's tricks, because of the constant stream of visitors at his father's tomb in Springfield, he chose (as a Civil War veteran) to be buried in a quiet, out of the way spot in Arlington, where, just over the hill, the fourth assassinated president, John Kennedy, was buried in 1963. Streams of visitors en route to and from Kennedy's gravesite pass by Robert Lincoln's lot every day. Sec. special site 13, Arlington National Cemetery, Arlington, VA.

5524. Lincoln, Thomas (Jan. 6, 1778–Jan. 17, 1851) and **Sarah Bush Johnston Lincoln** (Dec. 12, 1788–April 10, 1869) After Nancy Hanks Lincoln's death, Thomas remarried Sarah Bush Johnston and settled in Coles County, Illinois. Never close, Abraham Lincoln declined to visit his father Thomas during his last illness, but remained affectionately fond of his stepmother Sarah. Upon her death at 80, she was buried in the dress her step-son had bought her on his last visit there, in 1861. An obelisk inscribed *Thomas Lincoln, father of our martyred president* was put over the graves in 1880, and is in a fence near the graves where, n 1923, a larger granite monument was unveiled, inscribed *Thomas and Sarah Bush Lincoln*, their dates of birth and death and *Father and stepmother of our martyred president. Their humble but worthy home gave to the world Abraham Lincoln.* Shiloh Cemetery, near Charleston, Coles County, IL.

5525. Lind, Jenny (Oct. 6, 1820–Nov. 2, 1887) Stockholm born Swedish Nightingale began touring in 1844 with noted appearances at Castle Garden in Battery Park, Manhattan. She married the conductor Goldschmidt in Boston in 1852, residing afterward in Dresden and then in London. Her last appearance was at Dusseldorf in 1870. Madame Goldschmidt died at their home at Malvern Hills, England. Their graves are marked by a monument of Swedish granite with a cross on top in the cemetery at Great Malvern, Worcestershire.

5526. Lindbergh, Anne Morrow (June 22, 1906– Feb. 7, 2001) Daughter of New Jersey Senator Dwight Morrow and wife of Charles A. Lindbergh from 1929. In 1933, a year after the kidnapping and murder of their son, she helped her husband chart commercial air routes, chronicled in *North to the Orient* (1935) and *Listen! The Wind* (1938). Her several later published memoirs and letters include *Gift From the Sea* (1955), *Hour of Gold, Hour of Lead* (1973), *Locked Rooms and Open Doors* (1974), *The Flower and the Nettle* (1976). An intimate biography was published shortly before her death at 94 in the St. Johnsbury, Vermont, home she shared with her daughter Reeve Tripp. She also had a home at Darien, Connecticut. Cremated through Ricker mortuary, Woodsville, New Hampshire, at Mt. Pleasant Crematory, St. Johnsbury, Vermont. In her memoir *No More Words* (2001), her daughter Reeve Lindbergh mused that she was likely to want to be scattered — rather than buried — over her husband's grave and favorite places; in Vermont, Connecticut, Maine, Switzerland, though this was not stated as fact.

5527. Lindbergh, Charles Augustus (Feb. 4, 1902–Aug. 26, 1974) Lucky Lindy became an international hero by flying his Spirit of St. Louis nonstop from New York to Paris in May 1927, the first non-stop solo trans–Atlantic flight. He was later the center of media attention again with the kidnapping and murder of his baby son in 1932 and because of his pacifist sentiments just prior to American involvement in World War II, though he served with the Air Force once the U.S. was at war. Diagnosed with lymphatic cancer in N.Y. in the summer of 1974, he was flown on August 17 back to his favorite home to die: a frame cottage at Kipahulu on Maui. He lived only nine days, requesting daily reports on the digging of the grave, hewn from rock. He was buried in work clothes in a eucalyptus coffin. At the four corners of the grave, plumera plants mark the graves of gibbons he had owned. He chose his own epitaph, inscribed beneath his name and dates on the flat marker surrounded by stones: *If I take the wings of morning and dwell in the uttermost parts of the sea.* Congregational Church Cemetery, Kipahulu, Maui, HI.

5528. Lindbergh, Charles Augustus III (June 22, 1930–March 1?, 1932) The Lindbergh Baby, eldest son of Colonel Charles A. and Anne Morrow Lindbergh, was kidnapped from his crib in their home near Hopewell, New Jersey, on the night of March 1, 1932. After over nine weeks of negotiating with the alleged kidnapper(s) and delivering marked ransom money through meetings by an intermediary at two cemeteries in the Bronx, and despite assurances that "Cemetery John" to Lindbergh's representative John F. Condon that the baby was safe, the body was found in a field not far from the house on May 12. Evidence indicated he had died from a blow to the head, probably on the night of the abduction. Not until September 1934 was an arrest made, with the execution of Bruno Richard Hauptmann following in April 1936. In 1932 the Lindbergh Law went into effect, making kidnapping a federal offense punishable by death. The day after the baby was found, Lindbergh identified the body at the Swayze mortuary in Trenton. He then had it cremated the same afternoon at Rose Hill Cemetery in Linden, New Jersey, supposedly at the suggestion of State Police Chief H. Norman Schwarzkopf (Sr.), who advised them a grave would become a tourist attraction. Lindbergh flew out by himself and scattered the ashes over the Atlantic from his plane on June 10, 1932. The same day the child's ashes were scattered at sea, the English maid **Violet Sharpe**, employed at the Morrow home (Anne Lindbergh's parents) "Next Day Hill" in Englewood, New Jersey, drank bichloride of mercury and died after reportedly being badgered by police about suspected complicity in the kidnapping. She was buried in Brookside Cemetery across the road from the large Morrow lot, unmarked and the location not given out per a 1932 order. The Morrow lot contains three flat pink granite slabs. In the center is **Dwight Whitney Morrow** (Jan. 11, 1873–Oct. 5, 1931), Ambassador to Mexico and U.S. Senator, **Elizabeth Cutter Morrow** (dec. 1955) on the right and on the left their eldest daughter **Elisabeth Reeve Morrow Morgan** (March 17, 1904–Dec. 3, 1934), who died in Pasadena at 30 from heart disease. She was the subject of *Lindbergh, The Crime* (1994) by Noel Behn. East sec. lot 39–45, Brookside Cemetery, Englewood, NJ. See also Condon, Hauptmann, Hoffman, Schwarzkopf.

5529. Linden, Eric (Sept. 15, 1909–July 14, 1994) Actor played troubled youths in films 1931–41 (*Are These Our Children?, The Crowd Roars, Ah, Wilderness*). He died in Laguna Beach, California. Cremated July 18 by the Neptune Society. Ashes scattered at sea July 19 off Newport Beach, CA.

5530. Linder, Max (Gebriel Leuvielle, Dec. 16, 1883–Oct. 31, 1925) Joyous Max, 5'2" French silent screen comedian from Bordeaux. His well dressed, silk toppered boulevard bon vivant met with perpetual misfortune, the basis for portions of Chaplin's work and others. A 1919 film *Seven Years Bad Luck*, made in America, featured the prototype of the mirror scene later re-done in *Duck Soup*. He did some 360 films for Pathé 1907–1915 but his career declined after service in World War I, when he was wounded twice and hospitalized for nervous depression. He and his young wife were found in their Paris hotel room with their wrists slit in an alleged suicide pact in which her participation and enthusiasm was unclear. Both died the next day. Linder is buried in the village cemetery at Saint Loubes, where he was born, app. 20 km. from Bordeaux. The wife, **Helene Peters Linder**, is in the 95th div. at Pere Lachaise Cemetery, Paris.

5531. Lindgren, Astrid (Astrid Ericsson, Nov. 14, 1907–Jan. 28, 2002) Swedish author of over one hundred works, best known for the free-spirited *Pippi Longstocking*, who first appeared in 1945. She died in Stockholm at 94. Burial near her parents in the town cemetery at Vimmerby, Sweden.

5532. Lindh, Anna (Anna Maria Lindh, June 19, 1957–Sept. 11, 2003) Swedish foreign minister, a Social Democrat in government from 1982, was strongly favoring a "Ja" vote on the Euro — the common European Union currency — only four days away, when she was stabbed while shopping without bodyguards at a store in Stockholm, and died the next morning at 46. Prime Minister Olaf Palme had been similarly killed in 1986 and his assailant never caught, but the tightened security only extended to the prime minister and the king. The wife of politician Bo Holmberg, her memorial service was held in Stockholm September 19, and private burial the next day. Monument by artist Annie Winblad Jakubowski, set c. May 2004. Grave 1503, Katarina Kyrkogård, Stockholm.

5533. Lindley, Audra (Sept. 24, 1918–Oct. 16, 1997) Actress played Mrs. Roper in the TV series *Three's Company* 1977–79 and the spinoff *The Ropers*, as well as many other TV and film appearances. She died from leukemia in L.A. at 79. Cremated through Forest Lawn Hollywood Hills, her ashes are buried with her father **Bert Lindley** (Dec. 3, 1873–Sept. 17, 1953). Block 18, lot 141, grave D, Woodlawn Cemetery, Santa Monica, CA.

5534. Lindsay, Howard (March 29, 1889–Feb. 11, 1968) Playwright long in collaboration with Russell Crouse wrote *Arsenic and Old Lace* (1941). He also cowrote and starred in the play *Life With Father* (1939). Like Crouse, his ashes were scattered at sea.

5535. Lindsay, John V. (Nov. 24, 1921–Dec. 19, 2000) Mayor of New York City 1966–1973 was originally a Republican, but by the primaries in 1969 he switched to the Liberal Party, having alienated the GOP with his opposition to the Vietnam War, and by 1972 was running as a Democrat. Lindsay routinely turned up in shirtsleeves in the roughest sections of the city, and was noted for his walk through Harlem after the 1968 assassination of Rev. Martin Luther King. He died at 79 in Hilton Head, South Carolina. Cremated through the Island Funeral Home there, his ashes were returned to the family.

5536. Lindsay, Margaret (Margaret Kies, Sept. 19, 1910–May 8, 1981) Iowa born actress often in British roles (*Cavalcade* 1933) and in many stylish B films of the 30's and 40's (*G Men* 1935, *The House of the Seven Gables* 1940). She died from emphysema. Sec. P, lot 415, Holy Cross Cemetery, Culver City, CA.

5537. Lindsay, Vachel (Nicholas Vachel Lindsay, Nov. 10, 1879–Dec. 5, 1931) Illinois poet from Springfield who declaimed his work. His best known poem was *Lincoln Walks at Midnight*, until the 1970's inscribed on a plaque on the fence at Lincoln's Springfield home. Lindsay had become unbalanced and suicidal and his death, although covered up for many years, resulted from drinking a bottle of Lysol. Buried along a drive atop a hill behind Lincoln's tomb. Block 13, Oak Ridge Cemetery, Springfield, IL.

5538. Lindstrom, Fred (Frederick Charles Lindstrom, Nov. 21, 1905–Oct. 4, 1981) Versatile infielder, outfielder and third baseman with the New York Giants 1924–1932, six straight .300 seasons, .379 average. Hall of Fame 1976. Sec. 4, block 9, lot 10, All Saints Cemetery, Des Plaines, IL.

5539. Lingan, James McCubbin (May 13, 1751–

July 28, 1812) Soldier in the American Revolution was, with Lighthorse Harry Lee, defending Alexander Hanson from a mob after Hanson denounced in print a call to arms against England, when Lingan was beaten to death in the ensuing frenzy. Hanson survived, as did Lee, though Lee was blinded by hot wax poured in his eyes. A lesser known martyr in the history of the First Amendment than Zenger or Lovejoy, Lingan was removed from a Georgetown cemetery in 1908 and reburied, one of only eleven Revolutionary veterans at Arlington. Sec. 1, grave 89, Arlington National Cemetery, Arlington, VA.

5540. Lingle, Jake (Alfred P. Lingle, 1891–June 9, 1930) *Chicago Tribune* reporter in the 1920's was an encyclopedia of the city's underworld, friend to the police commissioner and Capone alike, he was sought by figures on both sides of the law to use his influence. In debt from gambling, he attempted to extort money from both Capone and Bugs Moran's men. While entering the train station from Michigan Avenue, he was shot in the head by a man dressed as a priest. The *Tribune* declared war on gangsters, but gradually Lingle's connections were revealed. Thousands lined the streets from Our Lady of Sorrows Church to watch the long funeral procession. Sec. B, block 5, Mt. Carmel Cemetery, Hillside, IL.

5541. Link, Arthur S. (Arthur Stanley Link, Aug. 8, 1920–March 26, 1998) Historian catalogued, edited and annotated the papers of Woodrow Wilson in 69 volumes from 1958–1983, published by Princeton University Press, (using the same desk Wilson had used as president of Princeton). He also taught at Princeton and authored over thirty books, including a five volume biography of the 28th president. He died from lung cancer at 77 in Advance, North Carolina. Ashes interred at Shallowford Presbyterian Church columbarium, Lewisville, NC.

5542. Linville, Larry (Sept. 29, 1939–April 10, 2000) Actor from Ojai, California, known for his role as inept Frank Burns on TV's "M.A.S.H." 1972–77. He died from cancer at 60 in Sloane Kettering Hospital, Manhattan. Service through John Kirtl mortuary. Several of Linville's relatives are in Nordoff Cemetery at Ojai. There was no service in New York; the ashes were taken to California, to the Los Angeles area, by his wife.

5543. Linville, Robert (Aug. 15, 1936–Nov. 3, 2001) One of Buddy Holly's Crickets sang back-up on *It's So Easy, Think It Over,* etc. Garden of the Christus, lot 165-C, space 1, Lawn Haven Memorial Gardens, Clovis, NM.

5544. Lippmann, Walter (Sept. 23, 1889–Dec. 14, 1974) New York born journalist from the famed Harvard class of 1909 was a political commentator of varying stands. He founded *The New Republic* in 1914, later a columnist with the *New York World* and the *New York Herald Tribune.* His book *The Public Philosophy* (1955) was considered the epitome of the "new conservatism," yet he backed Kennedy and Johnson until breaking with the administration over policy in Vietnam. Pulitzer Prize in Journalism 1958 and 1962. He died in New York City. Ashes scattered off the coast of Maine.

5545. Lipscomb, Eugene A. "Big Daddy" (Aug. 9, 1931–May 10, 1963) Defensive lineman for the Rams 1953–55, the Colts 1956–60 and the Steelers 1960–62. Football on flush plaque. Sec. B, row 1, grave 13, Lincoln Memorial Cemetery, Mt. Clemens, near Warren (north Detroit), MI

5546. Lister, Joseph Baron (April 5, 1827–Feb. 10, 1912) Surgeon and scientist in Glasgow, Edinburgh and London, inspired by Pasteur, was a pioneer in antiseptic medicine. His principles of sterilization, keeping bacteria from gaining entry into the operation wound, remains the first principle of surgery. Above ground sarcophagus, Hampstead Cemetery, Fortune Green Road, London.

5547. Liston, Sonny (Charles Liston, May 8, 1932–c. Dec 29, 1970) Heavyweight boxing champion won the title from Floyd Patterson in 1962 and lost it to Cassius Clay (Muhammad Ali) in 1964. He was found dead in a Las Vegas hotel room, the date of death only guessed at and the causes undetermined, on January 5, 1971. His plaque reads *Charles "Sonny" Liston 1932–1970. A Man.* Garden of Peace, Paradise Memorial Gardens, Las Vegas, NV.

5548. Liszt, Franz (Oct. 22, 1811–July 31, 1886) Hungarian pianist and composer, father-in-law of Richard Wagner. Liszt died in Bayreuth, Germany, from pneumonia and despite his wish that he be buried in a Franciscan monastery after a mass, was buried by a Lutheran minister in a local cemetery. A Wagner festival was in progress at the time of his death and his funeral received little attention or respect. Chapel-vault in Statfriedhof, Bayreuth.

5549. Litel, John (Dec. 30, 1892–Feb. 3, 1972) Fatherly figure from Albany, Wisconsin, in B films of the 30's and 40's, many at Warner Brothers. He died in Woodland Hills, California. Cremated February 8 at Ivy Lawn Cemetery in Ventura, his ashes were scattered at sea.

5550. Little, Cleavon (June 1, 1939–Oct. 22, 1992) Oklahoma born actor with extensive stage and screen credits, best remembered as Sheriff Bart in Mel Brooks' 1974 comedy *Blazing Saddles.* He died at 53 from colon cancer in his Sherman Oaks, California, home. Services were held at the Apostolic Church in Inglewood, with the ashes sent October 28 by Aftercare to spread in New York Harbor.

5551. Little, Little Jack (John J. Leonard, May 30, 1899 or May 28, 1900–April 9, 1956) London born songwriter (*Jealous, In a Shanty in Old Shanty Town*) and bandleader of the 1920's and 30's. He was seriously ill with hepatitis when he took his own life at 56 in a hotel at 2549 Washington St., Hollywood, Florida. Catholic Garden 1, lot 97, space 1, Lauderdale Memorial Gardens (now Forest Lawn Central), Fort Lauderdale, FL.

5552. Little Turtle (c. 1752–July 14, 1812) Miami chief during the battles of the Northwest Territory was a guiding force against William Henry Harrison at Fallen Timbers and Greeneville, and signed the Treaty of Grouseland. His grave is in a lot in Fort Wayne, discovered by workmen in 1911. Marked by a stone often used as second base by neighborhood children until a planned renovation c. 1993. By 2002, a plaque and boulders line the walkway to the park and his statue. The plaque reads *Chief Little Turtle 1752–1812 Me-She-Kin-No-Quah, Chief of the Miami Indians, Teacher of his people, Friend of the United States. His endeavors toward peace should serve as an inspiration for future generations. This plot of ground, the last resting place of Chief Little Turtle, is dedicated to the children of America and made a public park in 1959 ... under the auspices of the Allen County–Fort Wayne Historical Society.* Among other inscribed boulders lining the walk into the park is one with his words: *"I have been the last to sign this treaty. I will be the last to break it" Spoken at the signing of the Treaty of Greenville August 3, 1795.* Lawton Place, Fort Wayne, IN.

5553. Littlefield, Lucien (Aug. 16, 1895–June 4, 1960) Versatile character actor in hundreds of films beginning in 1913 (*The Cat and the Canary* 1927, *Tom Sawyer* 1930) also wrote some screenplays including *Early to Bed* (1936). Whispering Pines sec., lot 720, Forest Lawn, Glendale, CA.

5554. Litvak, Anatole (May 10, 1902–Dec. 15, 1974) Ukrainian born film director in Germany, France, and Hollywood for over thirty years, married to Miriam Hopkins 1937–39, long at Warner Brothers (*Tovarich, The Amazing Dr. Clitterhouse, Confessions of A Nazi Spy, City For Conquest, Out of the Fog, Sorry Wrong Number, The Snake Pit*), later directed *Anastasia* (1956), *Night of the Generals* (1967). He died at Neuilly-sur-Seine. Ashes in columbarium niche 15994, Pere Lachaise Cemetery, Paris, until their removal June 19, 1978, to Nice.

5555. Liveright, Horace (Dec. 10, 1883–Sept. 24, 1933) New York publisher from Osceola Mills, Pennsylvania, was a bond salesman in Philadelphia and New York until publishing from 1917, including the works of Eugene O'Neill, drawing fire from the Society for the Suppression of Vice, etc. The publishing company eventually went bankrupt and he produced for the stage from 1925, including *The Firebrand, Hamlet in Modern Times, An American Tragedy* and *Dracula*. He died from pneumonia in his New York home at 49. Eulogy at the Universal Chapel delivered by Upton Sinclair. Mt. Sinai Cemetery, Philadelphia, PA.

5556. Livermore, Mary (Dec. 19, 1820–May 23, 1905) Chicago minister's wife and a leader in the women's suffrage movement. During the Civil War she organized Midwestern volunteer groups into some 3,000 chapters, so that it was said "a line of vegetables connected Chicago and Vicksburg." Lot 5½, Wyoming Cemetery, Melrose, MA.

5557. Livingston, Jay (March 28, 1915–Oct. 17, 2001) Composer and lyricist from McDonald, Pennsylvania, collaborated with Ray Evans on film songs including *To Each His Own* (1946), *Silver Bells* (1951), *Tammy, Dear Heart,* many others. They won Oscars for *Buttons and Bows* (1948, from *Paleface*), *Mona Lisa* (1950, from *Captain Carey U.S.A.*) and *Que Sera Sera* (1956, from *The Man Who Knew Too Much*), their 64 year partnership included seven Oscar nominations, TV themes including *Bonanza* and *Mr. Ed*, and extended to the new millennium, including the songs used in *The Godfather III* (1990). Livingston died at 86 in Los Angeles. Crypt at top tier corner, Wall of Memories, Westwood Memorial Park, west Los Angeles, CA.

5558. Livingston, Margaret (Nov. 25, 1895–Dec. 13, 1984) Silent screen actress played the temptress from the city in Murnau's *Sunrise* (1927). Married to bandleader Paul Whiteman. She died at Warrington, Pennsylvania, and was entombed with Whiteman in their mausoleum. First Presbyterian Church Cemetery of Ewing, Trenton, NJ.

5559. Livingston, Philip (Jan. 15, 1716–June 12, 1778) Signer of the Declaration of Independence from New York. He also founded Kings College (Columbia University). Brother of William Livingston. Sec. A, lot 524, Prospect Hill Cemetery, York, PA.

5560. Livingston, Robert (Nov. 27, 1746–Feb. 26, 1813) Member of the Second Continental Congress 1775–76 and the congress under the Articles of Confederation 1784–85. Chancellor of New York 1777–1801, he administered the oath to Washington in 1789. As minister to France he organized with James Monroe the purchase of Louisiana 1801–1803. Buried with his son **Edward** (1764–1836), representative and senator from Louisiana and a member of Jackson's cabinet. St. Paul's Episcopal Church cemetery, Tivoli, NY.

5561. Livingston, William (Nov. 30, 1723–July 25, 1790) Federalist colonial New York lawyer and writer, brother of Philip Livingston, funded Alexander Hamilton's education near his estate at Elizabethtown (Elizabeth), New Jersey. A member of the Continental Congress, he did not sign the Declaration, having returned to New Jersey to lead the militia and serve as Governor 1776–1790. He was a delegate to the Constitutional Convention in 1787. Buried at Elizabethtown, his body was removed the next winter to the vault of his son **Brockholst** (1757–1823) in New York; both were moved again. Obelisk over vault, sec. 98, lot 564/565, Greenwood Cemetery, Brooklyn, N.Y.C.

5562. Livingstone, David (March 19, 1813–May 1, 1873) Scottish medical missionary, the subject of Stanley's long search through Africa and his famed greeting "Dr. Livingstone, I presume?" Livingstone died in Africa from dysentery and intestinal disease, a victim of his tireless efforts there to fight illness. His body was heavily wrapped and sent back to England, where it was buried April 18, 1874, beneath a black marble slab in the nave of Westminster Abbey, London.

5563. Livingstone, Mary *see* **Jack Benny.**

5564. Llewelyn, Desmond (Sept. 12, 1914–Dec. 19, 1999) British actor for six decades played "Q," James Bond's gadget man, in the *007* films from their debut in 1963. He died at 85 in a head-on crash in southern England while on his way to meet his biographer. A memorial service was held in St. Mary's (St. Mary the Virgin) Church at Battle, East Sussex, southern England, to be followed by private cremation.

5565. Lloyd, Doris (Hessy Doris Lloyd, July 3, 1896–May 21, 1968) Liverpool born stage actress in endless small roles in films for over forty years, including many melodramas at Universal and elsewhere in the 1930's and early 1940's (*Waterloo Bridge* 1931, *Tarzan the Ape Man, Back Street* 1932, *Oliver Twist* 1933, as Nancy, *Peter Ibbetson, Kind Lady* (both 1935 and 1951), *Mary of Scotland, The Black Doll, The Wolfman, Night Monster, Frankenstein meets the Wolf-Man, The Invisible Man's Revenge, The Lodger* 1944, *The Verdict, The Time Machine*). She died in Santa Barbara. Buried under her full name. Wee Kirk Churchyard, lot 228, Forest Lawn, Glendale, CA.

5566. Lloyd, Frank (Feb. 2, 1888–Aug. 10, 1960) Scottish born director of many films from the early silents won the first best director Oscar in 1928 for *The Divine Lady, Weary River* and *Drag*. Best known for *Cavalcade* (1933), *Berkeley Square* (1933) and *Mutiny on the Bounty* (1935). At his best in English settings. Garden of Ascension, lot 8436/38, Forest Lawn, Glendale, CA.

5567. Lloyd, Gladys (Oct. 11, 1895–June 6, 1971) Yonkers born wife of actor Edward G. Robinson played small roles in his early talkies (*Little Caesar, Five Star Final, Two Seconds, The Hatchet Man*). Upon their divorce, she obtained or forced the sale of much of his art collection. Ashes scattered at sea.

5568. Lloyd, Harold (April 20, 1893–March 8, 1971) Comedian of the 1920's silents with a pair of fake glasses specialized in acrobatics despite the loss of part of one hand, best known for *Safety Last* (1923), hanging from the hands of a clock high above a city street. He lived at his estate Greenacres in Beverly Hills, devoting much of his time to his several hobbies and Shriner's Activities. He died from cancer at 77. Service at the Scottish Rite Temple in L.A. with entombment beside his wife, actress **Mildred Davis** (Feb. 22, 1901–Aug. 18, 1969) and (three months later) his son **Harold Jr.** (Jan. 25, 1931–June 8, 1971). Behind an ornate iron gate marked Lloyd. Begonia Corridor, crypts 767–772, Begonia Terrace, Great Mausoleum, Forest Lawn, Glendale, CA.

5569. Lloyd, John Henry "Pop" (April 25, 1884–March 19, 1965) Star of the Negro Leagues 1906–1932, masterful shortstop and manager of several teams. In 1924 he hit over .400 with the Bacharach Giants at age 40. Hall of Fame 1977. A new marker with a bronze plaque bearing his image and noting his career was placed at his grave May 16, 1998. Sec. S, lot 910–912, Atlantic City Cemetery, Pleasantville, NJ.

5570. Lloyd, Marie (Matilda Alice Victoria Wood, Feb. 12, 1870–Oct. 7, 1922) The foremost London music hall artist of the 19th century, known for the then popular Cockney low comedy sympathetic to the common man, with no small amount of ribald humor and fun poking at the upper classes. Monument with a Celtic cross, Hampstead Cemetery, Fortune Green Road, London.

5571. Lloyd-George, David, 1st Earl of Dwyfor (Jan. 17, 1863–March 26, 1945) English statesman was twice Prime Minister (1916–1922), a major participant in the Paris Peace Talks at Versailles in 1919. A memorial is in the nave of Westminster Abbey. A stone was dedicated July 27, 1970 at his grave along the River Dwyfor at Llanystumdwy, Gwynedd, Wales.

5572. Lobert, Hans (John Henry Lobert, Oct. 18, 1880–Sept. 14, 1968) Speed king of the National League circled the bases in 1910 from a standing start in 13.8 seconds. He began as a third baseman with Pittsburgh in 1903 and over fifteen years played for the Cubs, Reds, Phillies and Giants, with whom he was still listed as a scout upon his death 65 years later in Philadelphia at 87. Family stone marked *Smith*. American Mechanics sec., A-AMC-A16-38, Philadelphia Memorial Park, Frazer, PA.

5573. Locke, David Ross ("Petroleum V. Nasby") (Sept. 20, 1833–Feb. 15, 1888) American satirist from Toledo was a newspaper favorite of the 19th century around the same period as "Mr. Dooley." Nasby wrote with a decidedly northern slant, attacking slavery, copperheads and carpetbaggers, always with the trademark poor English and improper diction of the wise fool. His lot has a monument with a gothic canopy. Sec. 14, lot 6, Woodlawn Cemetery, Toledo, OH.

5574. Locke, John (Aug. 29, 1632–Oct. 28, 1704) English philosopher of the Age of Reason known for his *Essay Concerning Human Understanding*. He was also an experimental scientist and helped establish the Bank of England. He died at Essex and was buried against the south wall of the church at High Laver.

5575. Lockhart, Frank (c.1901–April 25, 1928) Race driver from Dayton, Ohio, raised in Los Angeles, won the 1926 Indianapolis 500 at 94.63 m.p.h., the prize then $40,000. He was killed two years later in a race at Daytona Beach, Florida, thrown from the car and landing at his wife's feet. An article dated May 3 said a brother had gone to Indianapolis to bring the body back to Los Angeles, but the family was destitute. The ashes of Frank S. Lockhart, 27, were interred Sept. 9, 1930. Columbarium of Faith, urn in niche 5938, Corridor of Vistas, Dahlia Terrace, Great Mausoleum, Forest Lawn, Glendale, CA.

5576. Lockhart, Gene (July 18, 1891–April 1, 1957) Cherub faced character actor and playwright, husband of actress **Kathleen Lockhart** (Aug. 9,

1894–Feb. 17, 1978) and father of actress June Lockhart. His many appearances include *A Christmas Carol* (1938, as Bob Cratchit, and featuring his wife and daughter as his wife and daughter), *The Sea Wolf, Going My Way, Miracle on 34th St.* He also co-wrote the song *The World is Waiting for the Sunrise.* He died from a heart attack in Santa Monica at 65. His widow survived him by just under 21 years. Sec. D, lot 279 and 280,, Holy Cross Cemetery, Culver City, CA.

5577. Locklear, Ormer (Oct. 28, 1891–Aug. 2, 1920) Texas born World War I aviator and barnstorming stunt pilot, the first to jump from the wing of one plane to another in midair, made several daredevil film appearances in Hollywood in 1920. While filming *The Skywayman* before a large crowd at night in Los Angeles, he did a dramatic tailspin lit by floodlights for filming from below. Either the flares he dropped to signal the start of filming lit the plane on fire or — more likely — the lights were not turned off (as he had instructed) in time for him to judge his distance, and blinded him. The resulting crash incinerated him and his longtime flying partner **Milton Elliot.** Both funeral corteges were showered with flowers dropped from above by a plane. Lt. Elliot was buried at Gadsden, Alabama. Lt. Locklear had services in Hollywood and in Fort Worth. Sec. 9, lot 89, space E, Greenwood Memorial Park, Fort Worth, TX.

5578. Lockridge, Ross (April 25, 1914–March 6, 1948) Author of *Raintree County* (1948), set in Henry County, Indiana, and filmed in 1957 with Montgomery Clift and Elizabeth Taylor. He committed suicide at 33, just as his book was on the best seller lists. Sec. O, lot 103, Rose Hill Cemetery, Bloomington, IN.

5579. Lockwood, Margaret (Margaret Mary Day, Sept. 15, 1916–July 15, 1990) English actress in numerous films 1935–1976, mother of actress Julia Lockwood. She is best known opposite Michael Redgrave in Alfred Hitchcock's *The Lady Vanishes* (1938). She died in London at 73. Cremated at Putney Vale Cemetery, Kingston Road, London. Ashes removed.

5580. Loden, Barbara (July 8, 1932–Sept. 5, 1980) Actress, writer and director from Marion, North Carolina, played Betty in *Wild River* (1960) and wayward Ginny Stamper in *Splendor in the Grass* (1961), for Elia Kazan, with whom she began a relationship, marrying him in 1967. Tony Award for *After the Fall.* She also wrote, directed and starred in *Wanda* (1971) and directed plays prior to her death from breast cancer at 48 in Manhattan. Kazan took her ashes from Garden State Crematory to their New York home and placed them on a shelf in the room where she had meditated.

5581. Lodge, Henry Cabot (May 12, 1850–Nov. 9, 1924) Republican senator from Massachusetts and chairman of the Senate Foreign Relations Committee in 1918 began a campaign staunchly opposing President Wilson's Fourteen Point program for entry into the League of Nations as part of the Treaty of Versailles. Lodge successfully led the isolationists, including William Borah and Hiram Johnson, and Wilson refused to bend, thus defeating American entry into the League. The two men continued to hate one another. Upon Wilson's death in February 1924, his wife sent Lodge a note requesting that he not attend the services. Lodge himself did not live out the year. He suffered a stroke on November 5 and died at Charlesgate Hospital in Cambridge four days later. An appropriate hymn *The Strife is O'er, the Battle Done* was sung at the Episcopal services at Christ Church, Cambridge. Interment in the family's red sandstone family vault, built into the hillside on Oxalis Path facing Auburn Lake, Mount Auburn Cemetery, Cambridge, MA.

5582. Lodge, Henry Cabot (July 5, 1902–Feb. 27, 1985) Grandson of Sen. Henry Cabot Lodge, Republican senator from Massachusetts in the 1940's (losing to John Kennedy in 1952), vice presidential candidate with Richard Nixon in 1960, ambassador to South Vietnam 1963–67 and to Germany in 1968, and headed the U.S. delegation at the Paris Peace talks over Vietnam in 1969. Entombed in the family vault along with his grandfather. Oxalis Path facing Auburn Lake, Mount Auburn Cemetery, Cambridge, MA.

5583. Lodge, John Davis (Oct. 20, 1903–Oct. 29, 1985) Grandson of Henry Cabot Lodge and brother of his namesake was an actor in films (*The Scarlet Empress, Murders in the Zoo*) before serving as Republican rep. from Ct. 1947–51, Governor 1951–55 and ambassadorships under Eisenhower (Spain), Nixon (Argentina) and Reagan (Switzerland). He died in Manhattan while giving a speech. Sec. 30, Arlington National Cemetery, Arlington, VA.

5584. Loeb, Philip (March 28, 1891–Sept. 2, 1955) Actor in several films (*Room Service* 1938, *A Double Life* 1947, as Max Lasker). On radio in *The Goldbergs* as Jake, reprised in the 1950 film. A suicide in New York at 64; he had been blacklisted in the HUAC witch hunts. Handled through The Riverside. Loeb lot, facing road. Sec. 11, lot 2007, Mt. Sinai Cemetery, Philadelphia, PA.

5585. Loeb, Richard (June 11, 1905–Jan. 28, 1936) Partner in crime with Nathan Leopold, Jr. in the murder for sport of fourteen year old Bobby Franks in Chicago in May 1924. Saved from the gallows by Clarence Darrow's impassioned words against the death penalty, Loeb never lived to be paroled as Leopold did. Serving a life sentence at Northern Illinois Penitentiary at Stateville, outside Joliet, he was cut to death in the shower by a prisoner he had allegedly assaulted. Cremated at Oakwoods Cemetery in Chicago, his ashes were taken by his brother Allan on July 21, 1936. They were reportedly placed unmarked (and unrecorded) in the family plot of his father Albert, who died in October 1924. Sec. U, lot 4, Rosehill Cemetery, Chicago, IL.

5586. Loesser, Frank (Henry Frank Loesser, June 29, 1910–July 28, 1969) Composer and lyricist, with songs showcased in films from the 1930's through the 60's, including *Three Smart Girls, Cocoanut Grove, Thanks for the Memory* (in *The Big Broadcast of 1938*), *Destry Rides Again* (lyricist), *St. Louis Blues* (1939), *Johnny Apollo, Sweater Girl, Praise the Lord and Pass the Ammunition, Spring Will Be A Little Late This Year* (from *Christmas Holiday* 1944), *I Wish I Didn't Love You So* (AA nom., from *The Perils of Pauline* 1947), *Baby It's Cold Outside* (from *Neptune's Daughter* 1949), *Guys and Dolls* (lyricist), many others. He died from cancer in New York at 59. Ashes scattered.

5587. Loew, Marcus (May 7, 1870–Sept. 5, 1927) Founder with Samuel Goldwyn and Louis B. Mayer (who ran the studio) of M-G-M studios in 1924. Loew controlled the distribution and owned a vast chain of theaters. Epitaph on crypt, left side, reads *A man everyone knew and loved.* Family mausoleum, sec. 11, Maimonides Cemetery, Brooklyn, N.Y.C.

5588. Loewe, Frederick (June 10, 1901–Feb. 14, 1988) Austrian born composer with Alan J. Lerner wrote dozens of Broadway's popular tunes through the 1950's and 60's for shows including *Brigadoon, My Fair Lady, Gigi* and *Camelot.* A line from *Thank Heaven For Little Girls* (from *Gigi*) is on his plaque, inscribed *Thank Heaven for Frederick Loewe.* Sec. B-8, lot 89, Desert Memorial Park, Cathedral City (Palm Springs), CA.

5589. Loft, Arthur (May 25, 1897–Jan. 1, 1947) Character actor in many films of the 1930's and 40's. Eventide sec., lot 479, Forest Lawn, Glendale, CA.

5590. Loftin, Carey (William Carey Loftin, Jan. 31, 1914–March 4, 1997) Actor and stuntman in films from the 1930's did part of the driving in the famed car chase in *Bullitt* (1968), was the homicidal truck driver — never seen — in *Duel* (1971) and did the stunt driving in *Vanishing Point* the same year, many others. Sheltering Hills, lot 112, space 2, Forest Lawn Hollywood Hills, Los Angeles.

5591. Lofting, Hugh (Jan. 14, 1886–Sept. 26, 1947) English born author of *Doctor Doolittle* and other children's books; the famed character who could talk to the animals was created in letters to his children during World War I. *Quis sparabit* (Who shall separate us). Evergreen Cemetery, Killingworth, CT.

5592. Loftus, Cecilia "Cissie" (Oct. 22, 1876–July 12, 1943) Stage and vaudeville actress born in Scotland made only a few films (*The Old Maid, The Blue Bird, The Black Cat* 1941), billed as Cissie Loftus. She died from a heart attack in New York. Actors Fund of America plot at Kensico Cemetery, Valhalla, NY.

5593. Logan, Ella (Ina Allan, March 6, 1913–May 1, 1969) Scottish singer-actress in the Broadway production of *Finian's Rainbow* (1947), known for her distinctive rendition of *How Are Things in Glocca Morra?, That Old Devil Moon, Look to the Rainbow* etc. She died of cancer in Burlingame, California, at 56. Sec. P, lot 415, grave 4, Holy Cross Cemetery, Culver City, CA.

5594. Logan, Jacqueline (Jacquelin Medura Logan, Nov. 29, 1904–April 4, 1983) Silent screen actress from Corsicana, Texas (Mary Magdalene in *King of Kings* 1927, many others). She died in Melbourne, Florida, at 81. Block 12, lot 13, grave 4, Greenwood Cemetery, Decatur, IL.

5595. Logan, John A. (Feb. 9, 1826–Dec. 26, 1886) Democratic congressman from Illinois and Union general in the Civil war helped found the Grand Army of the Republic organization and through it began Memorial Day in 1868, the concept stemming from Confederate Decoration Day. Logan ran for vice president on the losing GOP ticket in 1884 (having switched parties). He died in Washington, D.C. and was buried in Rock Creek Cemetery, removed in 1888 to a mausoleum in the adjacent Soldiers Home National Cemetery, Washington, D.C.

5596. Logan, Joshua (Oct. 5, 1908–July 12, 1988) Acclaimed Broadway director from Texarkana, Texas, also frequently produced and co-wrote. Among his hits were *South Pacific, Mr. Roberts, Picnic,* the film versions of *Sayonara* and *Camelot,* many others. Autobiography *Josh* 1976. Logan suffered for years from debilitating super nuclear palsy. He died in his Manhattan home at 79. Buried with his wife Nedda Harrigan (*q.v.*) and daughter in St. Matthew's Episcopal Church Cemetery, Bedford (Village), eastern Westchester County, NY.

5597. Lollar, Sherm (John Sherm Lollar, Jr., Aug. 23, 1924–Sept. 24, 1977) A.L. catcher from Durham, Arkansas, played from 1946–1963, with the Chicago White Sox 1952–63, seven time All Star and Golden Glove winner 1958 and 1959, when they won the pennant. Veterans sec. C, lot 43, Rivermonte Memorial Gardens, Springfield, MO.

5598. Lolordo, Patsy (Pasqualino Lolordo, c. 1885–Jan. 8, 1929) Briefly president of the Unione Sicilione in Chicago, Capone's friend was shot to death in his own home by visitors, allegedly three of Moran's men (Clark and the Gusenbergs), the fifteenth Capone ally killed in three months and theoretically the impetus for the St. Valentine's Day Massacre. The death certificate lists burial January 12 at Mt. Carmel Cemetery, Hillside, Illinois, though there is no record of him there.

5599. Lomax, John Avery (Sept. 23, 1867–Jan. 26, 1948) Mississippi born folklorist accumulated and published many purely American folk songs with his brother as well as promoting blues great Ledbelly. Sec. 2, lot 477, Oakwood Cemetery, Austin, TX.

5600. Lombard, Carole (Jane Peters, Oct. 6, 1908–Jan. 16, 1942) Blonde film star of the 1930's from Fort Wayne, Indiana, did many dramas but is best remembered for her "screwball comedies" including *Twentieth Century* (1933), *My Man Godfrey* (1936, with her ex-husband William Powell), *Nothing Sacred* (1937), and *To Be or Not to Be* (1942, released posthumously). Married to Clark Gable from 1939, she was among the first to launch a war bond tour after the bombing of Pearl Harbor. She had wound up a rally in Indianapolis just before boarding a plane back to Los Angeles with her mother Bessie. The TWA twin engine DC-3 crashed into Table Rock Mountain near Las Vegas and burst into flames, killing all aboard. Gable, who joined the search parties at the crash site, refused national and military honors and followed her will, which specified she be clothed in white, viewed only by her family, and placed in a crypt at Forest Lawn in Glendale, California. Entombed as specified next to her mother, Gable was interred to her right in 1960, and his widow Kay placed in the row below them in 1983. Left side, Sanctuary of Trust, Memorial Terrace, Great Mausoleum, Forest Lawn, Glendale, CA.

5601. Lombardi, Ernie (April 6, 1908–Sept. 26, 1977) Oakland, California, born catcher with the Cincinnati Reds in the 30's and 40's. Slow of foot but a power hitter, he batted .306 over seventeen seasons, ten times over .300. He won batting titles in 1938 and 1942, and the N.L. MVP 1938. Hall of Fame 1986. Exterior crypt. Garden Mausoleum 2, crypt 342, tier 5, Mountain View Cemetery, Oakland, CA.

5602. Lombardi, Vince (June 11, 1913–Sept. 3, 1970) Football coach with the Green Bay Packers from 1959, known for his statement "Winning isn't everything; it's the only thing." Under Lombardi the Packers won Super Bowls I and II in 1967 and '68, and five league championships. Sec. 30 beside road, Mount Olivet Cemetery, Red Bank, NJ.

5603. Lombardo, Guy (June 19, 1902–Nov. 5, 1977) Bandleader with his Royal Canadians from the late 1920's brought his "sweetest music this side of Heaven" to TV audiences every New Year's Eve, becoming the king of *Auld Lang Sine*. He died following heart surgery in Houston. Mass at Our Holy Redeemer Catholic Church at Freeport, Long Island. Interred next to his brothers **Carmen Lombardo** (July 16, 1903–April 12, 1971), who played saxophone and sang with the band, **Lebert** Lombardo (Feb. 11, 1905–June 16, 1993), their trumpeter, and near Count Basie (1984). Wall crypt, second tier, Forsythia Court (south), Pinelawn Memorial Park, Farmingdale, Long Island, NY.

5604. Lombardo, Tony (Antonio Lombardo, Nov. 23, 1881–Sept. 7, 1928) Capone sponsored president of the Unione Siciliano was the fourth in that office to be assassinated. He had only recently succeeded Frankie Yale when he was shot in the head four times with dum-dum bullets on a Chicago street, the hit done by the Aiello gang opposing Capone. While the death certificate lists him as 37, the dates on his crypt indicate he was 46. Mausoleum, sec. M, Mt. Carmel Cemetery, Hillside, IL.

5605. Lon Nol (Nov. 11, 1913–Nov. 17, 1985) Cambodian general and political leader was premier under Sihanouk 1966–7 and in 1970 led the coup that deposed him and assumed control of the government. His efforts to suppress the Communist Khmer Rouge failed, led to civil war in which he lost power, regained it in 1972 but was forced out of the country in 1975 by the Khmer Rouge. He settled in Hawaii. Black upright monument with his picture on it. Roselawn sec., Loma Vista Memorial Park, Fullerton, CA.

5606. London, Jack (John Griffith Chaney, Jan. 12, 1876–Nov. 22, 1916) American author from San Francisco lived the life of a sailor and hobo and traveled the country, becoming a Marxist in 1894, and going to the Klondike with the Gold Rush of 1897–98. His best known works, reflecting his travels, were *The Call of the Wild* (1903), *The Sea Wolf* (1904) and *White Fang* (1906), all written at his ranch in Glen Ellen, California. Smoking up to five packs of cigarettes a day and beset by alcoholism, he committed suicide at 40 with an overdose of morphine. Cremated at Oakland, his ashes were buried beneath a boulder at his ranch with the epitaph *The stone the builders rejected*. Jack London Ranch, Glen Ellen, Sonoma County, CA.

5607. London, Julie (Julie Peck, Sept. 26, 1926–Oct. 18, 2000) Singer-actress from Santa Clara, California, married to Jack Webb 1945–53 and to Bobby Troup for over thirty years until his death, appeared in over two dozen films from 1944, but was best known for her recordings, particularly *Cry Me A River*, which sold three million copies in 1955. Her last album was in 1967, and her last acting work as Nurse Dixie McCall in TV's *Emergency!*, produced by Webb and co-starring Troup. She died at 74, five years after suffering a stroke which left her in declining health. Columbarium of Providence, niche 68415 — moved to niche 64716 in 2003 — with Troup, Courts of Remembrance, Forest Lawn Hollywood Hills, Los Angeles.

5608. Lonergan, Richard "Peg Leg" (dec. Dec. 26, 1925) Chief of Brooklyn's Irish White Hand gang controlled dock labor from 1923 in direct opposition to the Unione Sicilione. Lonergan was shot through the head, allegedly by Al Capone on a visit to Brooklyn in a free-for-all at the Adonis Club just after midnight on Christmas night 1925, as a favor to Frankie Yale. Unmarked in his family plot. Sec. 28, range 2, plot J, grave 19, (3rd) Calvary Cemetery, Woodside, Queens, N.Y.C.

5609. Long, Earl K. (Aug. 26, 1895–Sept. 5, 1960) Brother of Huey, Governor of Louisiana 1939–40, 1948–52, 1956–60. Buried beneath his monument and statue. Earl K. Long Memorial Park, Maple and Valley Streets, Winnfield, LA.

5610. Long, Huey (Huey Pierce Long, Jr., Aug. 30, 1893–Sept. 10, 1935) Flamboyant, powerful, dictatorial Governor of Louisiana, The Kingfish ran the state from 1928–1932 before becoming senator, promoting his "share the wealth" and "every man a king" theories. On Sunday evening, September 8, 1935, he was in the state capitol in Baton Rouge where his friend the governor had called a special session to gerrymander against an anti–Long judge, Benjamin H.

Pavey. While surrounded by bodyguards in a hall corridor, Long was shot twice, allegedly by Dr. Carl A. Weiss, Pavey's son-in-law, who was riddled with sixty one bullets. Long was taken to Our Lady of the Lake Hospital, where he died from a hemorrhage resulting from a kidney wound that had been overlooked. He lay in state in the state capitol building and was buried on the grounds in a sunken garden, where a large pedestal and bronze statue of him stand over the grave. The book and film *All the King's Men* was based on the life and death of Long, but Robert Penn Warren's reasons for the assassination of Willie Stark differed from the perceived cause of Long's killing. Louisiana State Capitol grounds, Baton Rouge, LA.

5611. Long, Lotus (Lotus Pearl Knott, July 18, 1909–Sept. 14, 1990) Japanese-Hawaiian actress in a dozen Hollywood efforts 1929–49, including *Mr. Wong* entries and the title role in *Tokyo Rose* (1946). Sec. B, tier 29, grave 67, San Fernando Mission Cemetery, Mission Hills, CA.

5612. Long, Richard (Dec. 17, 1927–Dec. 21, 1974) Juvenile of the 1940's turned leading man of the 1950's and 60's in films ranging from *Tomorrow is Forever* (1945), *The Stranger* (1946) and *The Egg and I* (1947) to *House on Haunted Hill* (1958). TV series included *Bourbon Street Beat* and *Seventy Seven Sunset Strip* (in both as Rex Randolph, 1959–61), and as Jarrod in *The Big Valley* (1965–69). He died from a heart ailment at 47. Cremated at Grandview Memorial Park in Glendale, California, his ashes were scattered at sea.

5613. Long, Russell B. (Nov. 3, 1918–May 9, 2003) Son of Huey Long influenced American tax laws over nearly four decades in the U.S. Senate. First elected in 1948 at one day under 30, the minimum age, he served until 1986. On the Senate Finance Committee from 1953 and the head of it 1966–1981, he pushed through the earned income credit, the provision allowing $1 of taxes to go for presidential campaign financing, and the 1975 provision giving a tax break to businesses helping workers buy a share of the company. He died in Washington at 84. Sec. B, lot 298, Rose Lawn Memorial Park, Baton Rouge, LA.

5614. Long, Walter (March 5, 1879–July 4, 1952) Burly silent and talkies actor usually in brutish parts, including numerous Huns in World War I films, a black in *Birth of a Nation* (1915), a thug in *Intolerance* (1916), later a frequent foil for Laurel & Hardy, *Moby Dick* (1930), as Miles Archer in *The Maltese Falcon* (*Dangerous Female*, 1931). World War I and II flush veteran's marker. Sec. 6, lot 527, Hollywood Forever Cemetery, Hollywood (Los Angeles), CA.

5615. Longfellow, Henry Wadsworth (Feb. 27, 1807–March 24, 1882) New England poet born at Portland, Maine and a graduate of Bowdoin College. Professor of Languages at Harvard from 1836, among his best known works were *Evangeline* (1847), *The Song of Hiawatha* (1855), *The Courtship of Miles Standish* (1858) and *Paul Revere's Ride* (1863). A widower

at his mansion "Craigie" in Cambridge, Massachusetts, since 1861, he caught a chill and was diagnosed with peritonitis, which proved fatal. The first American man of letters to be honored with a memorial bust in the Poets Corner, Westminster Abbey, London. His large gray granite monument is marked only *Longfellow* in the center of the lot; his wife and children buried all around his central monument, each with a plaque, on a ridge accessible by a sidewalk. Indian Ridge Path, lot 580, above Fountain Avenue, Mount Auburn Cemetery, Cambridge, MA.

5616. Longstreet, James (Jan. 8, 1821–Jan. 2, 1904) Confederate lieutenant general in the Civil War, commander of the First Corps, Army of Northern Virginia 1862–65, balked at Lee's orders to attack at both Little Round Top and Cemetery Ridge at Gettysburg but gave the orders as Lee instructed, to his regret, and was blamed with Lee for not taking full advantage of their potential there to bring about the beginning of the end for the Army of the Potomac. He continued as a major general throughout the war, afterward serving as a diplomat under Grant and as commissioner of Pacific Railways. Monument with sculpted crossed flags. Lot 3, block 36, Alta Vista Cemetery, Gainesville, GA.

5617. Longworth, Alice Roosevelt (Feb. 12, 1884–Feb. 20, 1980) Socialite daughter of President Theodore Roosevelt and his first wife, Alice Hathaway Lee, who died two days after their daughter was born. She became a national figure as her father ascended to the presidency in 1901. Known for her acid tongued wit and irreverence, to her were attributed many caustic observations on various powerful people. She married Nicholas Longworth, the future Speaker of the House of Representatives, in the White House in 1906 and lived at his family home in Cincinnati when not in Washington. She returned to D.C. permanently shortly after his death in 1931 and took up her long residence at her Massachusetts Avenue home in what she called "detached malevolence." Her last gesture before her death at 96 was reportedly to stick out her tongue at her granddaughter's husband. She was cremated and buried at the grave of her daughter Paulina, who died from cancer in 1957. Sec. F, lot 51, Rock Creek Cemetery, Washington, D.C.

5618. Longworth, Nicholas (Nov. 5, 1869–April 9, 1931) Ohio congressman and Speaker of the House from 1925 until his death was considered a contender for the 1932 presidential nomination but died from pneumonia while in South Carolina. His wife, Theodore Roosevelt's daughter Alice, returned to Washington, D.C. after his death. A tall spire marks his family lot; his parents are marked by a boulder and his grave by a small marker. Sec. 24, lot 1, Spring Grove Cemetery, Cincinnati, OH.

5619. Loo, Richard (Oct. 1, 1903–Nov. 20, 1983) Hawaiian born actor of Chinese ancestry in dozens of films from 1932, often as Oriental soldiers or spies, ranging from *The Bitter Tea of General Yen* (1932) and

West of Shanghai (1938) to *The Sand Pebbles* (1966). Sec. F, lot 28, grave 8, San Fernando Mission Cemetery, Mission Hills, CA.

5620. Loos, Anita (April 26, 1888/89–Aug. 18, 1981) American playwright, screenwriter 1912–1958 (from *The New York Hat* to *Gigi*) and novelist whose works include *Gentleman Prefer Blondes* and *The Women* also authored two novels and reminiscences including *The Talmadge Girls* (1978), her last book. Residing for many years on West 57th St. in New York, across from Carnegie Hall, she died at Doctors Hospital in Manhattan at 93. A memorial service of a joyous nature, as she requested, was held at the Frank E. Campbell mortuary. She wished to be cremated and her ashes scattered over the Trinity and Cascade mountain ranges at Mount Shasta (formerly Sissons), California. Her cremains were buried by her niece, marked by a flat plaque, with her parents, siblings, and intermittent husband John Emerson in the Smith lot, Etna Cemetery, Etna, Siskiyou County, CA.

5621. Lopat, Eddie (Edmund W. Lopat, June 21, 1918–June 15, 1992) Dreaded pitcher for the New York Yankees at the height of their dominance in the 1950's. Slanted stone area. Sec. 12-A, row 25, lot 6, grave 1, St. Mary Cemetery, Greenwich, CT.

5622. Lopatnikoff, Nikolai (March 16, 1903–Oct. 7, 1976) Russian born composer and pianist in the U.S. from 1939 taught music at the Carnegie Institute in Pittsburgh. His stone bears the epitaph *Peace Attend Thee*. Sec. 9-9, lot 272, Homewood Cemetery, Pittsburgh, PA.

5623. Lopes, Lisa "Lefteye" (May 27, 1971–April 25, 2002) Singer with TLC for a decade prior to her death in an auto crash when her rented sport utility vehicle rolled off a highway north of Tegucigalpa in the northern Honduras. Grave-length bronze plaque. Hillandale Memorial Gardens, Lithonia (suburban Atlanta), GA.

5624. Lopez, Al (Alfonso Ramon Lopez, Aug. 20, 1908–Oct. 30, 2005) Catcher 1930–49 with various teams hit .261 with 51 runs and 652 RBIs, setting a record — later broken — for the most games caught at 1,918. As a manger with Cleveland 1951–56 went to the world series in 1954 and with the Chicago White Sox returned in 1959, the only American League manager to twice beat the Yankees out of pennant flags from 1949–64. Hall of Fame 1977; with his death at 97 in Tampa he was its oldest living member and — until the week before his death — the last manager to land Chicago in a world series for forty-six years. Mausoleum, project A, unit 1, sec. C, Garden of Memories, Tampa, FL.

5625. Lopez, Isidro "El Indio" (May 17, 1929–Aug. 16, 2004) Tejano music pioneer, alto sax player and vocalist, best known for *Besame y Olvidame*. Seaside Memorial Park, Corpus Christi, TX.

5626. Lopez, Vincent (Dec. 10, 1895–Sept. 20, 1975) Orchestra leader from the 1920's to the 1950's played for several years at the Taft Hotel in New York.

He died in Miami, where his crypt plaque bears his trademark greeting *Lopez speaking*. East Court Mausoleum, unit 3, crypt 236, bottom tier, Southern Memorial Park, Miami, FL.

5627. Lorch, Ted (Theodore Lorch, Sept. 29, 1880–Nov. 11, 1947) Character actor in many films may be best remembered as Professor Sedletz in The Three Stooges two reeler *Half Wits' Holiday* (1947). Columbarium of Confidence, niche 21226, Great Mausoleum, Forest Lawn, Glendale, CA.

5628. Lord, Del (Delmar Lord, Oct. 7, 1894–March 23, 1970) One of the original Keystone Kops known for his sense of timing, went on to direct many Three Stooges two reelers at Columbia. Sec. R, grave 260, Olivewood Cemetery, Riverside, CA.

5629. Lord, Jack (John Joseph Patrick Ryan, Dec. 30, 1920–Jan. 21, 1998) New York born actor famed as Steve McGarrett in TV's *Hawaii Five-O* 1968–1980, with the frequent signature end line "Book 'em, Danno" (to James MacArthur). Beset in later years with an Alzheimer's related debilitating illness, he died of heart failure at 77 in his home in Hawaii, where he remained after the series. Cremated January 22, with no funeral at his request. His wife Marge reportedly planned to scatter the ashes on Oahu.

5630. Lord, Pauline (Aug. 13, 1890–Oct. 11, 1950) Stage actress (*Anna Christie*) from California made a few films, notably as *Mrs. Wiggs of the Cabbage Patch* (1934). She died from asthma and a heart ailment at Alamogordo, New Mexico. Ashes buried with her family. Sec. 6, lot 7397, Kensico Cemetery, Valhalla, NY.

5631. Lord, Robert (Robert Henry Lord, May 1, 1900/1901–April 5, 1976) Writer-producer from Chiago in Hollywood from the 1920's, notably at Warners in the 1930's, including *Little Caesar, The Finger Points* (adaptation), *Five Star Final* (adaptation), *One Way Passage* (story), *Frisco Jenny, 20,000 Years in Sing Sing* (adaptation), *Bordertown* (story), *Dr. Socrates, Black Legion* (1937). He produced at Warners as well 1932–42, and later for Humphrey Bogart's Santana Productions (*Tokyo Joe, Knock on Any Door, In A Lonely Place, Sirocco*). Dead from a heart attack at Midway Hospital, Los Angeles, at 74, (per Herrick file) he was cremated with no services April 8 through Pierce Bros. Hollywood at Chapel of the Pines Crematory, Los Angeles. Ashes scattered at sea May 18, 1976.

5632. Lord, Captain Stanley *see* **Titanic.**

5633. Lord, Walter (Oct. 8, 1917–May 19, 2002) Baltimore born, New York based author and historian was writing tax manuals when he published *A Night to Remember*, the prototype in studies of the sinking of the Titanic, in 1955. He had collected interviews with some sixty survivors in preparing the pioneer combination of journalistic narrative and history. Among his other works were *Day of Infamy* (1957), *The Good Years, 1900–1914* (1960), *The Dawn's Early Light* (1972), and *The Night Lives On* (1986), in part an updating of *A Night to Remember*. Beset in later years by Parkinson's Disease, Lord never married and left no survivors upon his death in his Manhattan home. A memorial service was held June 10 at the National Historic Society. Direct cremation through Frank E. Campbell mortuary, where the ashes were held until the executor had them buried in June. There is a bench in his memory in his mother's lot, with his name, *author* and *historian* on the front and on the top the names of many of his books. Marked by a monument with a bronze plaque. Yew, lot 19½, Green Mount Cemetery, Baltimore, MD.

5634. Loredo, Linda (June 20, 1907–Aug. 11, 1931) Arizona born actress of Mexican ancestry in Laurel and Hardy shorts at Hal Roach Studios 1928–1931, when she died in Queen of Angels Hospital, Los Angeles, from peritonitis complications following an appendectomy on June 11. Burial August 13. Sec. K, tier 16, grave 119, Calvary Cemetery, East Los Angeles.

5635. Lorimer, Louise (July 14, 1898–Aug. 12, 1995) All purpose character actress in films and television, died in Newton, Massachusetts, at 97. Cremated at Newton Centre Cemetery, the ashes were returned to Eaton-McKay mortuary, partially kept by a great nephew and part to be buried or scattered in Maine.

5636. Lorne, Marion (Aug. 12, 1888–May 9, 1968) Actress on stage and screen (Robert Walker's mother in Hitchcock's *Strangers on a Train* 1951) best known as ditzy Aunt Clara on TV's *Bewitched* 1964–68. Cremated at Ferncliff May 13, her ashes were interred August 16, 1968. Unit 3, niche panel EE, niche 10, second floor, main mausoleum, Ferncliff Cemetery, Hartsdale, NY.

5637. Lorraine, Lillian (Mary Ann Brennan, c. 1892–April 17, 1955) San Francisco born Ziegfeld showgirl cast in his *Miss Innocents* in 1908, when she was 16 by her estimate. Her affair with her employer was a major catalyst in the gradual end of his marriage to Anna Held. Later in the *Midnight Frolics* Last married to Jack O'Brien, Lorraine died broke at 63 in 1955. First placed in a free grave in sec. 14, Calvary Cemetery, Woodside, Queens, she was moved May 18, 1955, to sec. 14, range 5, grave 109 (Dunn-Flynn monument), (Old) St. Raymond's Cemetery, The Bronx, N.Y.C.

5638. Lorre, Peter (Laszlo Lowenstein, June 26, 1904–March 23, 1964) Hungarian born actor raised in Vienna began his film career in Germany, famous as the child murderer in Fritz Lang's *M* (1931). He fled Germany with the coming of the Third Reich and filmed in England in 1934 and America by 1935, mastering the language and tempering his typing as a menacing horror figure with a sense of humor and light hearted flair that allowed him to fit into many roles outside the horror genre, including *The Maltese Falcon* (1941), *Casablanca* (1942) and several others with Bogart and Sidney Greenstreet at Warner Bros. In 1951 he wrote, produced, directed and starred in his pet project *Der Verlorene* in postwar Germany. He suffered increasingly from morphine addiction and high blood pressure; filming in Spain in 1959, he had to be bled by leeches. Married to actress Celia Lovsky (*q.v.*) in the 1930's and actress Kaaren Verne (*q.v.*) in the 1940's, he was to appear in court for a hearing on his third divorce, from his wife Ann Marie, when his housekeeper found him dead in his Hollywood apartment from a stroke at 59. A rabbi conducted his funeral at Pierce Brothers in Hollywood, with Vincent Price speaking the eulogy. Cremated at Hollywood Cemetery, the ashes of he and his last wife are together, on the same wall as his first wife Celia Lovsky. Right rear corridor (Alcove of Reverence), bottom tier on left, Cathedral Mausoleum, Hollywood Forever Cemetery, Hollywood (Los Angeles), CA.

5639. Lortel, Lucille (Lucille Wadler, Dec. 16, 1900–April 4, 1999) Manhattan born stage actress 1926 to 1939 (in *Caesar and Cleopatra, The Dove*), married to cigarette paper tycoon Louis Schweitzer from 1931 to his death in 1971, left the stage at his request. She subsequently became an innovative promoter of Off Broadway, in 1947 founded the White Barn Theater in Westport, Connecticut, bringing a long list of talent before the public, and was the namesake for both the Lucille Lortel Theater in Greenwich Village — given by her husband in 1955 — and a room named for her in the library at Lincoln Center. She died in Manhattan at 78. The tribute on her upright monument reads *Theatrical pioneer/ Patron of the Arts/ Loving Mentor to all who worked with her/ Her children were her theater*. Block G, N1498, beyond Lee Strasberg, Westchester Hills Cemetery, Hastings-on-Hudson, NY.

5640. Loud, Lance (June 26, 1951–Dec. 22, 2001) The eldest son of the Loud family, the subject of PBS television's 1971 expose *An American Family*, enormously popular and considered groundbreaking at the time; a forerunner by three decades of the onslaught of reality television. He died thirty years later at 50. Ashes to his mother in Los Angeles.

5641. Loudon, Dorothy (Sept. 17, 1933–Nov. 15, 2003) Actress-comedienne on Broadway from 1962 won a Tony in 1977 as Miss Hannigan in *Annie*, was in *West Side Waltz* opposite Katherine Hepburn (1981), *Noises off* (1983), and several well known flops. She was nominated for Tonys for both *Ballroom* (1979), which ran four months, and *The Fig Leaves Are Falling* (1969), which ran four days. Films include *Garbo Talks* (1984, as Sonya) and *Midnight in the Garden of Good and Evil* (1997, as Serena Dawes). Married to composer **Norman Paris**, who died in 1977. She died from cancer at 70 in a New York hospital. Frank E. Campbell mortuary. Buried with Paris. Iroquois plot, sec. 71, lot 12, Kensico Cemetery, Valhalla, NY.

5642. Louis XIV, King of France (Sept. 5, 1638–Sept. 1, 1715) "The Sun King" ruled France seventy-two years, longer than any other monarch in European history. Guided by the Machiavellian imperial tactics of Cardinal Richelieu, Louis XIV is associated with French grandeur both as a world power and at his palace in Versailles. He died from a gangrenous leg and was buried in the Bourbon vault of the Abbey of St. Denis Basilica. The tombs of the kings were desecrated by the mobs of the French Revolution in 1790. Louis XVIII attempted to restore the bones but the accuracy of those efforts is unknown. The Louis XIV tomb is there anyway, though the Palace at Versailles is considered his true memorial. St. Denis Basilica, Paris.

5643. Louis XVI, King of France (Aug. 23, 1754–Jan. 21, 1793) Declared enemies of the Republic, the French royal family were imprisoned for three years in the Tuileries Palace, then the Temple Tower in Paris. The king was taken by coach on the two hour ride to Place Louis XV (now Place de la Concorde) and beheaded at the guillotine. After the mobs clamored to dip their handkerchiefs in his blood, he was taken (as were most of the victims) to St. Madeleine Parish Churchyard, shoveled into a grave and covered with quicklime. **Marie Antoinette** (Nov. 2, 1755–Oct. 16, 1793), Vienna born wife of Louis XVI of France and daughter of Francis I of Austria, infuriated the masses with her reported frivolous lifestyle. She was taken to the guillotine in a rubbish cart nine months after her husband. With the restoration of the Bourbons in 1814, Louis XVIII, aided by a witness to many burials at St. Madeleine's Churchyard, managed to have recovered some chalk-like mud determined to be Louis XVI and Marie Antoinette and returned them to St. Denis where they, like the others, are commemorated by shining black marble slabs in the Royal Tombs, though the remains are buried beneath a circular stone without inscription, in St. Denis Basilica, Paris. At St. Madeleine's Parish Churchyard Louis XVIII had a neoclassical chapel erected with crypt and memorial garden "To beg pardon for France." Statues of Louis and Marie dominate the interior of La Chapelle Expiatore, the memorial to them and the many others who perished during the Reign of Terror.

The heart of **Louis XVII**, the Dauphin, long rumored to have escaped death, was identified by DNA from the House of Bourbon and taken from its urn for burial in the royal crypt at St. Denis Basilica on June 8, 2004, the anniversary of his death in 1795.

5644. Louis-Phillipe (Oct. 6, 1773–Aug. 26, 1850) The last King of France, a member of the Orleans family, a younger branch of the Bourbons, had fought in the French Revolution. Suspected of conspiring to restore the monarchy, he fled the country, returning in 1814. In 1830, when the restored Bourbon King Charles X was ousted, Louis Phillipe was made king by Orleanist supporters, but increasingly resisted representative rule and was ousted February 24, 1848 as the Second Republic began. He fled to England, where he died at Claremont, Surrey. Monument with statue among other Orleans in the Chapelle royale Saint-Louis at Dreux.

5645. Louis, Joe (Joe Louis Barrow, May 13, 1914–April 12, 1981) The second Black heavyweight boxing champion, considered by many to be the greatest of them all. A soft spoken gentleman, Louis held the title for twelve years (1937–1949), taking time out to serve in World War II. He retired undefeated, known for his "bum of the month" tour, but was later forced back into the ring due to governmental demands for back taxes, although he had given up considerable boxing purse income to enlist in World War II. In later years, the Brown Bomber was a greeter at Caesar's Palace, where he lay in state during his funeral service, the eulogies spoken from the boxing ring. His brown granite stone lists his full name and an image of him on the stone, next to Lee Marvin along the drive leading up to the Tomb of the Unknown Soldier. Sec. 7A, site 177, grid U-24, Arlington National Cemetery, Arlington, VA.

5646. Louise, Anita (Anita Louise Frenault, Jan. 9, 1915–April 25, 1970) Blonde actress began as a child star and appeared as an ingénue in many productions of the 1930's, from B's (*The Phantom of Crestwood* 1932, *The Firebird* 1934) to A's (*A Midsummer Night's Dream* 1935, *Anthony Adverse* 1936). In 1940 she married producer **Buddy Adler** (June 22, 1909–July 12, 1960), after his death marrying importer Henry Berger. In later years she appeared on TV's *My Friend Flicka* (1956) and was prominent in raising funds for various children's charities. She died from a stroke at 55 and was buried with Adler. A classical statue stands over their rectangular marker. His epitaph is *From here to eternity* (one of his more successful productions). Hers reads *Love surrounds her beauty.* Little Garden of Tranquility, left, Garden of Memory (private), Forest Lawn, Glendale, CA.

5647. Louise, Ruth Harriet (Ruth Goldstein, Jan. 13, 1903–Oct. 12, 1940) Portrait photographer, lured from New York to Hollywood with her brother Mark (later director Mark Sandrich) by her cousin Carmel Myers (*q.v.*) was hired by MGM in 1925 and pioneered the glamorous star photographs with various types of specific lighting that soon became the norm, though she was let go by Metro in 1932 and freelanced afterward, until her death at 37 from complications of childbirth. Buried as Ruth Jason. Half block, plot 12, row 6, grave 1, Home of Peace Memorial Park, east Los Angeles.

5648. Lourie, Eugene (April 8, 1903–May 26, 1991) Russian born French art director (*This Land is Mine, The River*), turned director, known for his dinosaur-runs-amok films: *The Beast from 20,000 Fathoms, The Colossus of New York, Gorgo*. He died in Woodland Hills, California, at 88. Cremated through Pierce Bros. Cunningham and O'Connor. Ashes scattered at sea.

5649. Love, Bessie (Sept. 10, 1898–April 26, 1986) Silent screen actress from Midland, Texas, introduced the Charleston to the screen in *The King of Main Street* (1925), and starred in *The Lost World* (1925) and *The*

Broadway Melody (1929), for which she received an Oscar nomination. She settled in London in 1935, working in smaller roles in primarily British films into the 1980's (*Sunday Bloody Sunday* 1971, *Lady Chatterly's Lover, Ragtime* 1981) until her death at 87 in Denville Hall, the Actors Trust retirement home at Middlesex. Cremated May 6, 1986 at Breakspear Crematorium, where a small tree marks the spot (30BB) where her ashes were buried, and a small memorial plaque near by under a cedar tree is inscribed *Bessie Love. At Rest. 1898–1986.* Breakspear Crematorium, Breakspear Road, Ruislip, Middlesex.

5650. Love, Montagu (Montague Love, March 15, 1877–May 17, 1943) Silent screen villain from Portsmouth, England, alternated with Noah Beery as the most frequent cad of the 1920's in *Don Juan, The Wind,* many others. With the 1930's he graduated to more pompous, officious characters (*The Last Warning, Outward Bound, The Adventures of Robin Hood, Gunga Din*). Cremated through Forest Lawn, Glendale, California. Ashes in vaultage, Pierce Brothers' Chapel of the Pines Crematory, Los Angeles.

5651. Lovecraft, H.P. (Howard Phillips Lovecraft, Aug. 20, 1890–March 15, 1937) Reclusive author of macabre stories (*The Dunwich Horror* and others), primarily published in *Weird Tales* magazine between 1916–1936. Born at Providence, Rhode Island, he lived most of his life there in the family home. He died from cancer at 46 and was buried in the family lot, where in 1977 his growing legion of posthumous admirers bought a separate headstone inscribed in fine cut letters with his name and dates and the epitaph *I am Providence.* Phillips lot (obelisk), sec. 281, Swan Point Cemetery, Providence, RI.

5652. Lovejoy, Elijah (Nov. 9, 1802–Nov. 7, 1837) Abolitionist newspaper editor from Maine wrote a scathing editorial indictment of slavery in his *Alton Observer* in Alton, Illinois, July 20, 1837. His press was repeatedly dumped into the river or otherwise destroyed, but he refused to temper his editorial views. Finally his office was burned and he was fatally shot five times with a rifle, becoming one of the first martyrs to the abolitionist cause. Long unmarked, he was exhumed and a large inscribed slab surrounded by an iron fence placed over his second grave in the Hunter's Addition, north of the flagpole. A towering monument to him, a column surmounted by a statue, was erected at the side entrance to the cemetery in 1897. Alton City Cemetery, Alton, IL.

5653. Lovejoy, Frank (March 28, 1912–Oct. 2, 1962) Character actor in authority parts in many films of the 1950's, as detectives (*In a Lonely Place* 1950, *House of Wax* 1953) or military commanders, as well as radio (Randy Stone in *Night Beat*). TV series *Meet McGraw* 1957–58. He was appearing in *The Best Man* at Paramus, New Jersey, when he died in his sleep at 50 from a heart attack at the Warwick Hotel in Manhattan. Mass at the Roman Catholic Church of St. Paul the Apostle on West 59th St. in New York, with later services in Los Angeles. His plaque bore the epitaph, from *Hamlet*: *Now cracks a noble heart* until replaced by a double one after the death of his wife **Joan Banks** in 1998. Sec. P, lot 306, grave 5, Holy Cross Cemetery, Culver City, CA.

5654. Lovejoy, Owen (Jan. 6, 1811–March 25, 1864) Abolitionist congressman from Illinois 1857–1864, brother of Elijah Lovejoy, gave the speech at the 1856 (first) Republican National Convention which caused the abolition of slavery to be added to the party's platform. Old part, lot 64, Oakland Cemetery, Princeton, IL.

5655. Lovelace, Linda (Linda Boreman, Jan. 10, 1949–April 22, 2002) Bronx born star of the 1972 adult film *Deep Throat* was forced at gunpoint, she later said, by her abusive first husband to make the film of her being raped. She remarried and raised a family, while speaking to women's groups and campaigning against pornography. Autobiography *Ordeal.* Injured April 3, 2002, when thrown from her car in an accident in Denver, Colorado, she was removed from life support after three weeks and died at 53. Private family cremation.

5656. Lovett, Josephine (Oct. 21, 1877–Sept. 17, 1958) San Francisco born screen writer 1916–1934 worked on several films directed by her husband John S. Robertson (*q.v.*), but her best known product was *Our Dancing Daughters* (1928). She died in Rancho Santa Fe, California. Buried with Robertson. Sec. C, lot 220, Mount Pleasant Cemetery, London, Ontario.

5657. Lovett, "Wild" Bill (William Lovett, 1892–Nov. 1, 1923) Leader of the Irish White Hand gang in Brooklyn in the early 1920's was pitted against Frank Yale's organized Sicilians for control of the waterfront. Reportedly so fond was Lovett of animals that he shot one man for pulling a cat's tail. Distinguished Service Cross for bravery in France during World War I. Known to always carry a .45, it was his stalking of Capone for the beating of Arthur Finnegan in a Brooklyn bar in early 1919 that caused Yale to send Capone to Johnny Torrio in Chicago for safety. Lovett was killed three years later while drunk on a battery bench, surprised, allegedly by one of Yale's men. Sec. 2, lot 9005, Cypress Hills Military Cemetery, Brooklyn, N.Y.C.

5658. Lovsky, Celia (Cecile Lovsky, Feb 21, 1897–Oct. 12, 1979) Vienna born actress in many Hollywood film roles from 1947, later appearing frequently in TV drama. Married in the 1930's to Peter Lorre, she remained his close friend. Her ashes are interred in the same wall as his. Niche 8, tier 12, Alcove of Reverence, Cathedral Mausoleum, Hollywood Forever Cemetery, Hollywood (Los Angeles), CA.

5659. Low, Juliette Gordon (Oct. 31, 1860–Jan. 18, 1927) Founder of the Girl Scouts of America, in Savannah, Georgia, in 1912. She served as the national director until 1920. Her home in Savannah is part of the restored downtown historic district. Stone cross monument. Lot 1283/1286, Laurel Grove Cemetery, Savannah, GA.

5660. Lowe, Edmund (March 3, 1890–April 20, 1971) Silent screen star in several films teamed with Victor McLaglen, beginning with *What Price Glory* (1926). In talkies he wore a mustache and sleek black hair in suave roles (*Dinner at Eight* 1932) and B's (*Chandu the Magician, The Great Impersonation*). Married to actress Lilyan Tashman until her death in 1934. At the time of his death in the Motion Picture Country Home in Woodland Hills, California, he had been divorced from his third wife for twenty years and had no children. Mass at St. Meis Catholic Church in Los Angeles. Unmarked. Sec. B, lot 1113, grave 7, San Fernando Mission Cemetery, Mission Hills, CA.

5661. Lowe, Edward T. (June 29, 1890–April 17 or 19, 1973) Screen-writer penned *The Vampire Bat, Charlie Chan in Paris, in Shanghai, at the Racetrack,* three *Bulldog Drummond* entries, *House of Frankenstein* (1944) and *House of Dracula* (1945), several others. Columbarium of Honor, niche G2201, Gardens of Honor, Forest Lawn, Glendale, CA.

5662. Lowell, Amy (Feb. 9, 1874–May 12, 1925) American poet from Brookline, Massachusetts, a free spirit who smoked cigars, influenced by Ezra Pound and the Imagists circle in Europe. She published her first volume of free verse, *Sword Blades and Poppy Seeds*, in 1914. She also published a biography of Keats (1922) and was a noted critic of poetry past and present. She died suddenly in Brookline at 51. Bellwert Path, lot 3401, above Walnut Ave., Mount Auburn Cemetery, Cambridge, MA.

5663. Lowell, Helen (June 2, 1865–June 28, 1937) New York born stage actress played mothers and generally kindly dowagers in films from 1919, most between 1934 and 1937 (*Midnight Alibi, Madame DuBarry, Doctor Socrates, Valiant is the Word for Carrie, High wide and Handsome*). She died in Los Angeles at 71, married name Robb. Cremated July 2, 1937 at Inglewood Park Cemetery. Ashes removed 1939 to Independence Cemetery, Independence, California, though they have no records before 1955.

5664. Lowell, James Russell (Feb. 22, 1819–Aug. 12, 1891) Cambridge, Massachusetts, born poet, editor (*The North American Review*), and professor of modern languages at Harvard after Longfellow's tenure in that office. Also a diplomat, he was appointed by President Hayes Minister to Spain (1877) and to Great Britain (1880). Lowell died from cancer at 72. Buried off Fountain Avenue below Catalpa Path, lot 323, Mount Auburn Cemetery, Cambridge, MA.

5665. Lowell, Percival (March 13, 1855–Nov. 12, 1916) Astronomer established the observatory in his name in Flagstaff in 1894. Because of the visible "canals" on Mars, Lowell promoted the theory that Mars had at one time been inhabited. Based on the abnormalities in the orbit of Uranus, he predicted the existence of a ninth planet, later identified in 1931 and named Pluto but demoted to a dwarf planet in 2006. Lowell Observatory, Mars Hill, Flagstaff, AZ.

5666. Lowell, Robert (March 1, 1917–Sept. 12, 1977) Pulitzer Prize winning poet was a New England bred non-conformist, at first a Catholic, also influenced by Calvinism. Pulitzer Prize for *Lord Weary's Castle* (1947). He lived alternately in Boston and New York, refusing most political groups who sought his support. In the early 70's he published *History, For Lizzie and Harriet* and *The Dolphin. Day By Day* appeared a month before his fatal heart attack at 60 in a taxi in Manhattan. Service at the Church of the Advent, Beacon Hill, Boston, with burial among his ancestors in the Stark Family Burial Ground, Dunbarton, NH.

5667. Lowery, Robert (Robert Lowery Hanks, Oct. 17, 1914/1916–Dec. 26, 1971) B film leading man (*The Mummy's Ghost* 1944, *House of Horrors* 1946) in the serial *Batman* (1949), appeared as Big Tim the ringmaster in TV's "*Circus Boy*" (1956–58). He died from a heart attack. New plaque in the 1980's. Graceland, 6500, lot 4, Valhalla Memorial Park, North Hollywood, CA.

5668. Lowndes, Marie Belloc (Marie Adelaide Belloc, 1868–Nov. 14, 1947) Novelist, sister of Hillaire Belloc, was born in France — a descendant of chemist Joseph Priestley — and spent most of her life between there and England. The best known of her early novels, *Barbara Rebell* (1905) was eclipsed by *The Lodger* (1913), her lasting claim to fame, filmed four or more times. Married from 1896 until his death to **F.S.A. Lowndes** (Jan. 1868–March 26, 1940), a *London Times* editor from 1893–1938, she died at the home of her daughter, Countess Iddesleigh, in Eversley Cross, Hampshire, at 79. Mass at Westminster Cathedral's Lady Chapel. Located by David Brown in September 2002, the grave of her and her husband is surrounded by a stone curbing border, but has no inscription. Their son is marked by an inscribed monument just diagonal to their location. No. OA146, Wimbledon Cemetery, Gap Road, Wimbledon, Surrey.

5669. Lowry, Judith (Judith Ives, July 27, 1890–Nov. 29, 1976) Diminutive actress from Oklahoma on Broadway from 1916 appeared in a few films (*The Trouble With Angels* as Sister Prudence, *Valley of the Dolls, The Night They Raided Minsky's, Husbands, The Anderson Tapes, The Effect of Gamma Rays on Man-in-the-Moon Marigolds*) before becoming Mother Dexter on the sitcom *Phyllis* in 1975. She died from a heart attack on a New York street the next year at 86, just before the airing of her marriage on *Phyllis* to Burt Mustin. Buried with Rudd Lowry. Sec. 2D, grave 3052, Long Island National Cemetery, Farmingdale, NY.

5670. Lowry, Morton (Feb. 13, 1916–Nov. 26, 1987) English character actor in Hollywood films of the 1930's and 40's, often in pompous, obnoxious or scheming roles, including Stapleton in the 1939 *The Hound of the Baskervilles*, the bullying schoolmaster in *How Green Was My Valley* (1941), *Pursuit to Algiers, The Picture of Dorian Gray* (1945), *The Verdict* (1946).

He died indigent in San Francisco. Cremated at Pleasant Hill Crematory, Sebastopol, California. Ashes held by College Chapel Mortuary for a year. Unclaimed, they were buried in Bodega Bay.

5671. Loy, Myrna (Myrna Williams, Aug. 2, 1905–Dec. 14, 1993) Urbane actress from Helena, Montana, adept at underplaying a wide variety of types, from sirens and oriental villainesses of silents and early talkies to her long career as the perfect wife with an ever present free spirit (*Topaze, Manhattan Melodrama, The Thin Man* and several sequels with William Powell, *Libeled Lady*, as Billie Burke in *The Great Ziegfeld, Test Pilot*). She left films during World War II to work with the Red Cross. Post war films include *The Best Years of Our Lives* and *Mr. Blandings Builds His Dream House*. Sporadic appearances in film and TV through the 1970's. In 1991 she received an Oscar for her lifetime body of work via satellite in her upper east side Manhattan apartment. She died at 88 in Lenox Hill Hospital. Cremated at Garden State Crematory through Frank E. Campbell mortuary, the ashes were sent for burial with her mother Della and father David Williams, a pro Wilson Montana state legislator who had inspired her lifelong liberal politics prior to his death in the 1918 influenza epidemic. The stone with her name and dates was placed in the Williams lot in July, and her ashes buried the week of her birthday in 1994. Valley View, lot 4, east ½, Forest Vale Cemetery, Helena, MT.

5672. Lubbe *see* **von der Lubbe.**

5673. Lubin, Arthur (July 25, 1898–May 12, 1995) Director from Los Angeles acted in a few silents before turning to directing in 1934. His wide variety of work included *The Phantom of the Opera* (1943), some *Abbott & Costello* comedies, *Ali Baba and the Forty Thieves* (1944), *The Spider Woman Strikes Back* (1946), *Impact* (1949). He later directed the *Francis the Talking Mule* series and the TV take-off *Mr. Ed*. Never married, he died in Glendale, California, at 96, his age reported as 94. Cremation through Westwood mortuary in west Los Angeles, his ashes were scattered May 19 at sea off the Newport Beach, California, shoreline.

5674. Lubin, Lou (Nov. 9, 1895–Jan. 30, 1973) Slight actor from Pittsburgh in many bit to supporting roles in films 1938–1954 (Rainbow Benny in *Shadow of The Thin Man,* Irving August in *The Seventh Victim; Scarlet Street, The People Against O'Hara,* etc.) He died in Sylmar, California, at 77. Block H, Garden of Rest, space 184, (Pierce Bros.) Valhalla Memorial Park, North Hollywood, CA.

5675. Lubitsch, Ernst (Jan. 28, 1892–Nov. 30, 1947) German born director came to America in 1922. His films were sophisticated and whimsical with light sexual innuendo, said to have the Lubitsch Touch, including Jeanette MacDonald musicals at Paramount 1929–32, Garbo in *Ninotchka* (1939) and Carole Lombard's last film, *To Be or Not to Be* (1942). Just before a planned Christmas vacation with his nine year old daughter, he suffered a heart attack at his Bel Air home at 55 and efforts of a fire department rescue squad to revive him failed. He was buried in a glass topped coffin, holding a cigar. Eventide sec., lot 2896, Forest Lawn, Glendale, CA.

5676. Lucas, Henry Lee (Aug. 13, 1936–March 12, 2001) Texas serial killer arrested in 1983 and sentenced to death for the slaying of an unidentified woman found in a ditch in 1979 was the only person whose death sentence was commuted to life by then Governor George W. Bush in 1998, just four days prior to the execution date. He claimed to have killed as many as 600 people, and had served fifteen years in Michigan for beating his mother to death. Lucas died at 64 from a heart attack while serving six life sentences plus 210 years at the state prison's Ellis Unit at Huntsville. Prison no. 830114. Sec. I, row J, grave 9, Captain Joe Byrd (aka Peckerwood Hill) Cemetery, Huntsville, TX.

5677. Luce, Clare Boothe (April 10, 1903–Oct. 9, 1987) American Renaissance woman, the wife of *Time-Life* publisher Henry Luce, edited *Vanity Fair* until 1934, was a Broadway playwright (*The Women* 1935, *Kiss the Boys Goodbye* 1938, *Margin For Error* 1939), reported for *Time* from Europe during World War II, and as representative from Connecticut 1943–46 was a frequent critic of Roosevelt. A strong anti-communist, she served as Ambassador to Italy under Eisenhower, and was later nominated as Ambassador to Brazil but resigned after insulting Wayne Morse, who opposed her appointment. She was considered too far right to run for the Republican senate seat in 1964. She died from cancer in Washington at 84. A Catholic since her daughter Ann's death in a car wreck at 19 on January 11, 1944, mass was said for her in both New York City and Washington, D.C. Buried with her husband and daughter, her name and dates are on the left side of a white marble tree of life in bas-relief on their monument. Along the base is inscribed *The sun shall be no more your light by day, nor for brightness shall the moon give light to you by night, but the Lord will be your everlasting light, and your God will be your glory—Isaiah 60;19*. Grounds of the Trappist monastery of Our Lady of Mepkin Abbey, Monck's Corner, SC.

5678. Luce, Henry R. (April 3, 1898–Feb. 28, 1967) Founder of *Time* (1923), *Life* (1936) and *Sports Illustrated* (1954) died from a heart attack at St. Joseph's Hospital in Phoenix, his winter home. He had contributed the grounds at the Trappist monastery of Our Lady of Mepkin Abbey, Monck's Corner, South Carolina, and was buried there in the family graveyard, now called the Nancy Bryan Luce garden, with a cross standing behind six graves. That of Henry and Clare Boothe Luce is a white marble stone with a sculpted tree of life; she is on the left (twenty years after him); on the right is inscribed *Here lies Henry R. Luce* and the dates. Mepkin Abbey, Monck's Corner, SC.

5679. Lucheni, Luigi (April 22, 1873–Oct. 19, 1910) Assassin of Elizabeth "Sissi," wife of Franz Josef, Archduke of Austria, on September 10, 1898, was an Italian anarchist who committed suicide in his cell. His body was given to an anatomy school, but his head was preserved. Switzerland handed it over to the Criminal Museum in Vienna with the pre-condition that it is never shown to the public. Cellar of the Pathologisch-Anatomisches Bundesmuseum (Pathological-Anatomic Federal Museum), Vienna.

5680. Luchese, Thomas "Three Finger Brown" (Thomas Luckese, Dec. 2, 1899–July 13, 1967) Sicilian born New York underworld figure involved in narcotics and gambling, closely associated with Lucky Luciano. Nicknamed "Three Finger Brown" (after the Cubs' ace pitcher) from the loss of two digits as a child; the name was not used to his face. Allegedly one of Luciano's top hit men in New York, he managed to stay clear of any arrest after 1923. When Luciano was deported in 1946 he became the effective head of one of New York's five Cosa Nostra families, and lived to die of natural causes (cancer) at his Lido Beach, Long Island, home. Sec. 69, plot 164, grave 13, (4th) Calvary, Woodside, Queens, N.Y.C.

5681. Luciano, Charles "Lucky" (Salvatore Lucania, Nov. 24, 1897–Jan. 26, 1962) One of a confederation of heads of the New York crime syndicate from 1931, closely allied with both Benjamin "Bugsy" Siegel and Meyer Lansky. For trafficking in narcotics and prostitution, New York State Attorney General Thomas E. Dewey had him indicted, tried and convicted in 1936. He served ten years in prison before he was deported to Sicily in 1946. At the Naples airport to greet a TV producer regarding his life story, he died from a sudden, massive heart attack at 64. Allowed back in the U.S. only in death, the coffin was taken in a horse drawn hearse through the streets of Naples, then transported to the family mausoleum (Lucania). His crypt lists his birth year as 1888. Corner of sec. 3, St. John's Cemetery, Middle Village, Queens, N.Y.C.

5682. Ludden, Allen (Oct. 5, 1917–June 9, 1981) TV game show host from Mineral Point, Wisconsin, hosted *Password* through three separate runs (1962–67, 1961–75 days and 1979–80 days). During the 1960's run, he married frequent guest, actress Betty White, who survived him. Ludden died from cancer at 63 in L.A. Burial through Forest Lawn Hollywood Hills June 11. Upright brown stone near road. Graceland Cemetery, Mineral Point, WI.

5683. Ludendorff, Erich Friedrich Wilhelm (April 9, 1865–Dec. 20, 1937) German general in World War I was Chief of Staff to Von Hindenburg after capturing the Belgian fortress city of Liege in 1914. Subsequent victories on the Eastern front made the two national heroes, and by 1916 they were given near total control of the war by Kaiser Wilhelm II. With a stalemate on the western front, their unleashing of submarine warfare brought the U.S. into the war in 1917. Ludendorff differed with his colleagues

over the 1918 armistice terms and resigned in protest. Though he participated in the Beer Hall Putsch of 1923 was a National Socialist member of the Reichstag 1924–28, he did not participate in the Third Reich. Neuer Friedhof, Tutzing, Bayern, Germany.

5684. Ludlam, Charles (April 12, 1943–May 28, 1987) Founder and star of New York's Ridiculous Theatrical Company, specializing in farcical interpretations of female characters, including Camille, Maria Callas in *Galas* and the princess in *Salambo*, winning six Obies. He also played a sleazy lawyer in the film *The Big Easy*. He died from pneumonia related to AIDS at 44. Sec. G, plot 30, grave 16, St. Patrick's Cemetery, Huntington, Long Island, NY.

5685. Ludlam, Robert (May 25, 1927–March 12, 2001) New York born author served in the South Pacific with the Marines in World War II, afterward had minor roles on Broadway and in films and TV before he began a series of best selling spy novels in 1971 centering usually on government cover-ups and corruption, including the *Bourne* series, *The Scarlatti Inheritance, The Chancellor Manuscript, The Holcroft Covenant, The Matarese Circle* and *The Aquitane Progression*. He died from an apparent heart attack at 73 in Naples, Florida. Cremated, with no services, through Hodges Funeral Chapel, Naples. Ashes taken out of state by family.

5686. Luft, Sid (Michael Sidney Luft, Nov. 2, 1915–Sept. 15, 2005) New York born producer credited with resurrecting the career of Judy Garland — his wife from 1952–65 — notably with the 1954 film *A Star is Born*. He died from a heart attack at 89. Ashes to family through Gates-Kingsley-Gates mortuary, Santa Monica, CA.

5687. Lugosi, Bela (Bela Blasko, Oct. 20, 1882– Aug. 16, 1956) Hungarian leading man and one time character essayed the role of *Dracula* on stage in London and New York in 1927 and in the 1931 Tod Browning film at Universal, and became indelibly typecast as leering vampires or various other monsters and menaces in increasingly low budget films for the next twenty five years. His bad run of luck in roles began when he turned down the non-speaking role of *Frankenstein* in 1931 and was soon eclipsed in the genre by Boris Karloff. So glued was Lugosi to the Dracula image that even in the Count in the PBS educational program *Sesame Street* mimics his thick accent. Other films of note include *White Zombie* (1932), *The Black Cat* (1934), *Mark of the Vampire, The Raven, The Invisible Ray* (all 1935), *Son of Frankenstein* and *Ninotchka* (1939) before his career began its slide into poverty row films. In March 1955 Lugosi made headlines by checking into the California Metropolitan State Hospital at Norwalk for treatment of long term dependency on morphine for leg pains, compounded by alcohol. Recently divorced and extremely emaciated, he elicited considerable public sympathy, completed his treatment program and remarried for the fifth time. He had made two low budget horror films in 1955–56 and shot some footage for director Ed Wood (which became *Plan 9 From Outer Space*) when he died from a heart attack in his apartment on Harold Way in Hollywood. Services were at Utter-McKinley mortuary with Lugosi, as he requested, buried in his Dracula outfit, including the cape. Grotto sec., lot 120, gravel, Holy Cross Cemetery, Culver City, California. Lugosi's wife of twenty years and the mother of his son, **Lillian Arch Lugosi Donlevy** (April 21, 1911–Oct. 9, 1981) was cremated and, like her last husband, actor Brian Donlevy, scattered at sea. Lugosi's fifth wife and his widow, **Hope Lininger Lugosi** (March 23, 1919–April 1, 1997) is buried with a headstone inscribed *Beloved Curmudgeon,* at St. Joseph's Church Cemetery, Kamalo, Maui, HI.

5688. Lukas, Karl (Karl Louis Lukasiak, Aug. 21, 1919–Jan. 15, 1995) Actor on Broadway as Lindstrom in *Mr. Roberts* and much television over forty-five years. Buried through Pierce Brothers Valley Oaks mortuary. Mausoleum D10, block 17, sec. E, San Fernando Mission Cemetery, Mission Hills, CA.

5689. Luke, Keye (June 18, 1904–Jan. 12, 1991) Actor from Canton, China, raised in Seattle, appeared in over 150 American films, including many as Charlie Chan's "number one son" in the 30's, as occasional Oriental villains (*Across the Pacific* 1942), and as Master Po in TV's *Kung Fu* (1972–75). Later films included *Gremlins* (1984) and his last, as the acupuncturist in Woody Allen's *Alice* (1990). He died in Whittier, California, from a stroke at 86. Memorial Chapel Garden, lot 434, grave 2, Rose Hills Memorial Park, Whittier, CA.

5690. Lunceford, Jimmie (June 6, 1902–July 12, 1947) Jazz and Big Band leader and musician of the 1930's and 40's recorded on Victor 1930–34; he later had several hits elsewhere, including *Margie*. Upright stone. South Grove 10, lot 437, Elmwood Cemetery, Memphis, TN.

5691. Lund, John (Feb. 6, 1911–May 10, 1992) Tall, blonde, blue eyed actor of Norwegian descent from Rochester, New York, on Broadway from 1941, wrote and performed for radio and films (*The Hasty Heart, To Each His Own* 1946, *The Night Has a Thousand Eyes* 1948, the *My Friend Irma* series). His memorial service was held at the Chapel of the Psalms in Hollywood Memorial Park Cemetery (now Hollywood Forever), Hollywood (Los Angeles). Ashes scattered at sea June 10 off Point Fermin, Los Angeles County.

5692. Lund, Lucille (Lucille Althea Lund, June 3, 1912–Feb. 16, 2002) Blonde actress from Buckley, Washington, in films 1933–39, including The Three Stooges' *Healthy, Wealthy and Dumb*, was best known as Karen, the young wife of Hjalmar Poelzig (and doubling for the dead character of her mother, suspended vertically in a glass case) in Edgar Ulmer's *The Black Cat* (1934). The widow of Kenneth Higgins, she died in Torrance, California, at 89 from pneumonia

complicated by debilitating osteoporosis and Parkinson's Disease. No funeral. Cremated through Green Hills mortuary, the ashes were kept by her daughter at Palos Verdes, CA.

5693. Lundgren, Carl (Carl Leonard Lundgren, Feb. 16, 1880–Aug. 21, 1934) Pitcher for the Chicago Cubs 1901–1909, including their 1908 controversial series win, overshadowed somewhat by his team-mate Mordecai "Three-Finger" Brown. Block 1, lot 45, grave 3, Marengo City Cemetery, Marengo, IL.

5694. Lundigan, William (June 12, 1914–Dec. 20, 1975) Deep voiced leading man in over 125 films through the 1940's and 50's (*The Fighting 69th, Follow Me Quietly, Love Nest*), TV series *Man into Space* (1959). Unmarked beside his father Michael. Sec. D, lot 269, grave 3, Holy Cross Cemetery, Culver City, CA.

5695. Lunt, Alfred (Aug. 19, 1892–Aug. 3, 1977) Milwaukee born stage great with his wife, actress Lynne Fontanne, were considered the First Couple of the American Theatre for decades. Their better known plays included *Pygmalion* (1926), *Design for Living* (1933, the first of several collaborations with Noel Coward), *Idiot's Delight* (1936), many more. Their only film was *The Guardsman* (1931). Lunt was buried in the family plot on a hillside, dominated by a large monument marked A.D. Lunt with the inscription *Alfred Lunt and Lynne Fontanne were universally regarded as the greatest acting team in the history of the English speaking theatre. They were married for 55 years and were inseparable both on and off the stage.* Sec. 33, lot 42, Forest Home Cemetery, Milwaukee, WI.

5696. Lupino, Ida (Feb. 4, 1918–Aug. 3, 1995) London born actress, the daughter of actors Stanley Lupino and Connie Emerald and the cousin of song-and-dance man Lupino Lane; she appeared in Hollywood films and TV in strong, hard edged performances in *The Light That Failed* (1939), *They Drive By Night* and *High Sierra* (1940), *The Sea Wolf* (1941), *Ladies in Retirement* (1941), *Women's Prison* (1955), *While the City Sleeps* (1956), and *Junior Bonner* (1972). She directed and helped write several low budget films in the 1950's and was a part of TV's Four Star Productions with Dick Powell, Charles Boyer, and her third husband (from 1951), Howard Duff. They were later divorced. Long in ill health, she died in her California home from cancer, bronchopneumonia and the effects of a stroke at 77. Cremation through Forest Lawn, Hollywood Hills, Los Angeles. Her will stipulated her ashes were to go into two brass urns. All or part were sprinkled over the grave of her mother **Constance "Connie" Lupino** (Aug. 20, 1892–Dec. 26, 1959), next to Errol Flynn, Garden of Everlasting Peace, lawn crypt 5415, Forest Lawn, Glendale, CA.

5697. Lupino, Stanley (May 15 1894–June 9, 1942) English actor and dancer on the stage and in sound films. Married to actress Connie Emerald, father of actress Ida Lupino. He died at Balham, England. Lambeth Cemetery, Blackshaw Road, Tooting, London.

5698. Lupo the Wolf (Ignazio or Ignatius Lupo aka Ignazio Saietta, March 19, 1877–Jan. 13, 1947) Notorious Black Hand extortionist in turn of the century New York's Little Harlem, was by the 1920's out of prison and back at it in New York. Sent back to prison at the federal penitentiary in Atlanta, he returned to Brooklyn-Queens after his term and lived out the rest of his life there. There are no Saiettas at Holy Cross or Calvary. There are three Ignazio Saiettas in St. John's Cemetery, Queens, but with the ages too young or old. Research by Bill Heneage, however, identifies him as Ignatius (Ignazio) Lupo, Saietta having been his mother Onorfia Saietta's maiden name. He came to the U.S. from Italy in 1897 or '98. The brother-in-law of gangster Ciro Terranova, he is in his lot. Though the office records list only an Ignazio Lupo there, 54, buried October 16, 1947 rather than in January, the stone lists *Ignatius Lupo 1877–1947.* Sec. 35, range 10, plot 5, grave 12, (3rd) Calvary, Woodside, Queens, N.Y.C.

5699. Lupton, John (John Rollin Lupton, Aug. 22, 1928–Nov. 3, 1993) Film and TV actor, starred as Tom Jeffords in the series *Broken Arrow* 1956–1960. Cremated through Westwood Memorial Park, west Los Angeles. Ashes to family.

5700. *Lusitania* (victims) Cunard Line steamship torpedoed by a German U-boat on her 102nd voyage, a sunny Friday afternoon, May 7, 1915, sailing from New York to Liverpool and in sight of the Irish coast, within eight to ten miles of the Old Head of Kinsale. It sank within twenty minutes, taking 1,198 people to their deaths. Responses to SOS calls rescued 764. Of those lost, over 100 of the recovered bodies were buried in a mass grave, now marked by a boulder with a plaque, on May 10 at The Old Church/ Cobh Cemetery, Cobh (Queenstown), Ireland. Many others were buried at Kinsale, closer to the site of the sinking. See also Charles Frohman, Elbert Hubbard, Margaret Makworth and David Thomas (Viscount and Viscountess Rhondda), Capt. William Thomas Turner, Alfred Gwynne Vanderbilt, George and Inez Jolivet Vernon.

5701. Luther, Martin (Nov. 10, 1483–Feb. 18, 1846) German theologian became the father of the Protestant Reformation, posting his ninety-five theses — containing both points for discussions and criticisms papal policy — on the door of the castle church at Wittenburg October 31, 1517. He continued to write, including hymns, notably *A Mighty Fortress is Our God,* until his death from the effects of traveling in icy winter weather to arbitrate a dispute at Eisleban. His white cask with a bronze plaque covers the general area of this tomb, center of the church, below the pulpit, Schloßirch (Schloss Kirch), (Castle Church), Wittenberg, Sachsen-Anhalt, Germany.

5702. Lyden, Pierce (Jan. 8, 1908–Oct. 10, 1998) Heavy in over 300 B westerns of the 30's, 40's and 50's. Later wrote reminiscences for Classic Images, etc. He died in Orange, California, at 90. Lawn AY, lot 6, space 1, Fairhaven Memorial Park, Santa Ana, CA.

5703. Lyman, Abe (Aug. 4, 1899–Oct. 23, 1957) Band leader of the 1930's; among his better known numbers was *Serenade in the Night.* Garden of Memory (private), lawn crypt 930, Forest Lawn, Glendale, CA.

5704. Lyman, Arthur (Feb. 2, 1932–Feb. 24, 2002) Hawaiian musician adept at four-mallet vibraphones had a huge hit with *Yellow Bird* in 1961. He died from throat cancer at 70. Handled by Hawaiian Memorial Park-mortuary, Kaneohe, Oahu, Hawaii. Ashes scattered.

5705. Lymon, Frankie (Sept. 30, 1942–Feb. 27, 1968) Harlem vocalist recorded *Why Do Fools Fall in Love* with the Teenagers in 1956 and was briefly famous with lesser hits (*I'm Not a Juvenile Delinquent, The ABC's of Love,* chiefly for Roulette records). He had supposedly kicked his drug habit when he was found dead from an overdose at 25 while on leave from the service, at 370 West 156th St. and Edgecombe in Harlem. St. Anthony, range 13, grave 70, St. Raymond's Cemetery (new section), the Bronx, N.Y.C.

5706. Lynch, David, Jr. (July 3, 1929–Jan. 2, 1981) Tenor with the Platters in the 1950's through their many hit ballads. Sec. K, lot 21, grave 8, Lincoln Memorial Park Cemetery, Carson (Compton), CA.

5707. Lynch, Joe (July 16, 1925–Aug. 1, 2001) Irish actor in various films (*The Siege of Sidney Street* 1960, *The Running Man* 1963, *Ulysses* 1967) and several UK television series including *Never Mind the Quality — Feel the Width, Rule Britannia, Coronation Street* and *Glenroe.* He died at Alicante, Spain, at 76. Ashes scattered near his home at Villajoyosa, Spain.

5708. Lynch, Ken (July 15, 1910–Feb. 3, 1990) Actor in films and numerous TV spots in the 1950's and 60's, often as tight lipped detectives or gangsters. Sec. BB, tier 19, grave 135, San Fernando Mission Cemetery, Mission Hills, CA.

5709. Lynde, Paul (June 13, 1926 — found Jan. 11, 1982) Witty, cynical comedian of stage and screen (*Bye Bye Birdie*) on TV from 1952, a semi-regular on *Bewitched* and a regular on *Hollywood Squares.* Found dead in his home at 509 North Palm Drive, Beverly Hills, from a heart attack at 55, he was cremated at Grandview Memorial Park through Westwood mortuary and the ashes buried next to his brother, their brown monument next to the identical one of their parents. Amity (formerly Ebenezer Baptist Church) Cemetery, Amity (three miles east of Mt. Vernon), OH.

5710. Lynn, Diana (Dolores Loehr Hall, Oct. 7, 1926–Dec. 18, 1971) Innocent faced actress, former child musical prodigy, in many films of the 40's and 50's (*The Miracle of Morgan's Creek, Our Hearts Were Young and Gay, The People Against O'Hara, Track of the Cat*) died from a stroke in Los Angeles at 45. Cremated by Pierce Brothers' Chapel of the Pines in L.A. Columbarium of the Church of the Heavenly Rest, East 90th St., Manhattan, N.Y.C.

5711. Lynn, Jeffrey (Ragnar Godfrey Lind, Feb. 16, 1909–Nov. 24, 1995) Actor from Auburn, Massachusetts, in forthright leads and second leads at Warner Brothers from 1937 (*Four Daughters, The Roaring Twenties* 1939, *The Fighting 69th, It All Came True* 1940, *All This and Heaven Too, The Body Disappears* 1941, *Butterfield 8* 1960). He served as a captain in Army Intelligence in World War II, appearing sporadically afterward (*Strange Bargain*) and working in various managerial jobs to support seven adopted children. Plaque notes *A man we truly loved, admired and respected.* Murmuring Trees, lot 6642, space 1, Forest Lawn Hollywood Hills, Los Angeles.

5712. Lynn, O.V. "Mooney" (Aug. 27, 1926– Aug. 22, 1996) Husband of country singer Loretta Lynn; they married when she was thirteen. He died at 69. Buried on their estate in Hammond Hill, TN.

5713. Lynn, Sharon (D'Auvergne Sharon Lindsay, April 9, 1908–May 26, 1963) Silent and talkies actress from Weatherford, Texas, in *Sunny Side Up* (1929) and many B films, particularly westerns, through the 1930's, sometimes billed as Sharon Lynne. Interred as Sharon Glaser Sershen. Chapel of the Chimes mausoleum, crypt 7, Inglewood Park Cemetery, Inglewood, CA.

5714. Lynn, William H. "Billy" (Feb. 27, 1890– Jan. 5, 1952) Stage actor from Providence, Rhode Island, with an eccentric nasal delivery, appeared in memorable film roles only in the last two years of his life (as Judge Gaffney in *Harvey*, Mr. Beebe in *Mr. Belvedere Rings the Bell*). He died in New York City at 63. Mass at St. Vincent Ferrer Church through The Abbey January 8. Although the cemetery lists the age as 44 rather than 63, the burial date and relatives match the funeral notice; his dates in the right hand column of names on the McManus stone indicate the death date of the actor and the age as 61. Sec. 33, plot 8, grave 1, Gate of Heaven Cemetery, Hawthorne, NY.

5715. Lynott, Phil (Aug. 20, 1949–Jan. 4, 1986) Lead vocalist, songwriter and bass player for the rock group Thin Lizzy 1969–1983. Their numbers include *Dancing in the Moonlight, Whiskey in the Jar, Rosalie, Jailbreak* and *The Boys Are Back in Town,* a hit in the U.S. in 1976. He died from heart failure and pneumonia in Wilts at 36 following eight days in a coma from a drug overdose. St. Fintan's Cemetery, Howth/Sutton, Ireland, overlooking Dublin Bay.

5716. Lyon, Ben (Feb. 6, 1901–March 22, 1979) Silent and sound actor memorable as the weaker, disillusioned brother Monte in *Hell's Angels* (1930). An accomplished flyer, he did many of his own scenes. He and his wife, actress Bebe Daniels, went to England in 1936 and were popular in radio while he worked there for Fox and later as a talent agent. After Daniels died in 1971, he married silent screen actress Marian Nixon. They were on a cruise in the Pacific when he died

aboard ship. Returned to Hollywood, his ashes were placed beside those of Daniels, hers in a box shaped urn, his in the shape of a book. Second floor, north wall, Chapel of the Psalms, Hollywood Forever Cemetery, Hollywood (Los Angeles), CA.

5717. Lyons, Leonard (Sept. 10, 1906–Oct. 7, 1976) Broadway columnist wrote his political column *The Lyons Den* 1934–1974. Formerly a practicing attorney, he served as special assistant to the New York Attorney General 1954–1968. Block 2, path R, Beth Moses Cemetery, Farmingdale, Long Island, NY.

5718. Lyons, Ruth (Oct. 4, 1907–Nov. 7, 1988) Cincinnati based radio personality on the air since 1929. Known for her *50–50 Club* on radio and television from the late 40's through the late 60's, as well as several musical compositions. Shortly after her daughter Candy died while at sea June 19 1966, she retired from the program but continued sponsoring charitable organizations, notably the Ruth Lyons Children's Christmas Fund. She died in Cincinnati at 81. Cremated by the Cincinnati Cremation Company, her ashes were briefly returned to her husband Herman Newman but after his death in 1990 were placed back with his and their daughter's urns in Hillside Chapel, Cincinnati, OH.

5719. Lyons, Ted (Ted Amar Lyons, Dec. 28, 1900–July 25, 1986) Pitcher from Louisiana won more games for a consistently losing team, the Chicago White Sox, than any other pitcher except Walter Johnson between 1923–1946. He pitched a no hitter in 1926 and a 21 inning game in 1929. Hall of Fame 1955. Big Woods Cemetery, Edgerly, LA.

5720. Lys, Lya (Natalia Lyecht, May 18, 1908– June 2, 1986) French actress in *The Andalusian Dog* (1936), in Hollywood from 1930 (*Confessions of a Nazi Spy* and *Return of Dr. X,* both 1939), she retired in 1943. The wife of George Feit, she died from a heart ailment in Newport Beach, California. Cremated through Pacific View Memorial Park, Newport Beach, the ashes were returned to the family.

5721. Lytell, Bert (Feb. 24, 1885–Sept. 28, 1954) New York born stage and silent screen actor, brother of radio star Wilfrid Lytell, played the *Lone Wolf* several times, returning primarily to the stage with sound. President of Actors Equity. He died in New York, was cremated at Ferncliff Crematory in Hartsdale, N.Y., and the ashes returned to his wife actress **Grace Menken** at their residence, the Meurice Hotel at 145 West 58th St. She died in August 1976, was cremated at Ferncliff through the Frank E. Campbell mortuary and her ashes also returned to the family.

5722. Mabley, Jackie "Moms" (March 19, 1899– May 23, 1975) Vaudeville, stage, film and television comedienne known for her underground records (*Knockers Up*); a frequent talk show guest in her later years. Knollwood Garden 1, row 14, grave 4, Ferncliff Cemetery, Hartsdale, NY.

5723. McAdoo, William (Oct. 25, 1853–June 7, 1930) Congressman, Assistant Secretary of the Navy and New York police commissioner. Sometimes confused with Woodrow Wilson's son-in-law. Alpine hillside, sec. 173, Woodlawn Cemetery, the Bronx, N.Y.C.

5724. McAdoo, William Gibbs (Oct. 31, 1863–Feb. 1, 1941) Secretary of the Treasury under Wilson and Democratic contender for the 1924 presidential nomination, later senator from Ca. He married Wilson's daughter Eleanor (*q.v.*); they were later divorced. Sec. 2, lot 4969, grid W-32/33, Arlington National Cemetery, Arlington, VA.

5725. McAlary, Michael (Dec. 15, 1957–Dec. 25, 1998) Journalist won the 1998 Pulitzer Prize for his coverage of the brutalization of a Haitian immigrant, Abner Louima, at a Brooklyn police station. He also authored three books, including *Good Cop, Bad Cop.* Lot 701, Woodland Cemetery, Bellport, NY.

5726. McAllister, Ward (Dec. 1827–Jan. 31, 1895) Southern born lawyer in New York's Gilded Age organized the acceptable four hundred persons of consequence for *The* Mrs. (Caroline) Astor in 1888. He died from the flu and, hated by many he had socially excluded, he was tucked deep for post mortem security into the catacombs at Locust and Vine in Greenwood Cemetery, Brooklyn, N.Y.C.

5727. MacAnnan, George Burr (Nov. 30, 1887–June 12, 1970) Actor in films 1932–42 (*White Zombie,* as Von Gelder; *Supernatural, The Black Room, Sherlock Holmes and the Secret Weapon*). Sec. B-23, lot 149, Desert Memorial Park, Cathedral City (Palm Springs), CA.

5728. MacArthur, Arthur (June 2, 1845–Sept. 5, 1912) U.S. General cited for bravery on Missionary Ridge at Chattanooga in 1863 also served in the Spanish American War and as Military Governor of the Philippines 1900–1901. Medal of Honor. Father of General Douglas MacArthur. He died suddenly while giving a speech. Buried in sec. 10 (near the Sholes monument) at Forest Home Cemetery, Milwaukee, Wisconsin, where his mother **Aurelia**'s small stone (1864) remains. He was moved in 1926 to sec. 2, Arlington National Cemetery, Arlington, VA.

5729. MacArthur, Charles (Nov. 5, 1895–April 21, 1956) Playwright long in collaboration with Ben Hecht; they wrote *The Front Page* (1928), *Twentieth Century* (1933) and a long string of other stage hits with hard edged humor and drama, many of them filmed. MacArthur was married to stage actress Helen Hayes, who survived him. They lived at Nyack, New York, where he was buried next to his daughter Mary, who had died from polio in 1949. Hayes was buried beside them in 1993. Their small, nearly flat off-white stones are slightly rounded on the surface. Just a few yards above them on the same hillside, Hecht was buried in 1964, joined by his daughter in 1971 and wife in 1978, their upright stones of the 18th century charcoal slate type. Lot 51, Grand View Lawn sec., Oak Hill Cemetery, Nyack, NY.

5730. MacArthur, Douglas (Jan. 26, 1880–April 5, 1964) Former chief of staff of the Army 1930–35 became a major figure of World War II. As U.S. Commander in the South Pacific, he was driven out of the Philippines but, as he predicted, triumphantly returned, a high point for Allied morale in 1944. He accepted the official Japanese surrender aboard the U.S.S. *Missouri* September 2, 1945, but later had a clash of wills with President Truman over strategy in Korea and was relieved of command in 1951. In his farewell speech to congress he delivered what became his signature line, "Old soldiers never die; they just fade away." In later years he lived at the Waldorf-Astoria in Manhattan, not far from his old commander-in-chief Herbert Hoover. After his death at 84 from acute liver and kidney failure in Walter Reed Army Hospital, Washington, D.C., he lay in state in the Capitol rotunda, with the funeral in New York at the Seventh Regiment Armory at 66th and Park Avenue. Buried in his faded suntan fatigues in a government issue steel coffin. MacArthur Memorial at the old court house, MacArthur Square, Norfolk, VA.

5731. McAuliffe, Christa (Sept. 2, 1948–Jan. 28, 1986) The Concord, New Hampshire, teacher chosen to be the first educator in space, with astronauts aboard the space shuttle Challenger, lost her life with the rest of the crew when the shuttle exploded in the sky on national television just after takeoff, in one of the medium's most shocking moments. The cabin and its occupants were not recovered from the sea until April, when she was returned to Concord for a private burial service on May 1. A large black granite stone has the symbol of NASA's Teacher in Space program, with the inscription written by her husband Stephen: *She helped people. She laughed. She loved and is loved. She appreciated the world's beauty. She was curious and sought to learn who we are and what the universe is about. She relied on her own judgment and moral courage to do right. She cared about the suffering of her fellow man. She tried to protect our spaceship earth. She taught her children to do the same.* Sec. M, lot 51 L, Calvary Cemetery, Concord, NH.

5732. McAvoy, May (Sept. 8, 1899–April 26, 1984) Silent screen actress in *Ben Hur* (1926), *The Jazz Singer* (1927), *The Terror* (1928), pioneer sound films. Unmarked (Cleary). Sec. W, tier 36, grave 83, Holy Cross Cemetery, Culver City, CA.

5733. McBain, Ed *see* **Evan Hunter.**

5734. MacBride, Donald (June 23, 1893–June 21, 1957) Actor played detectives, hotel managers, of the slow burn variety, in *Room Service* (1938, both stage and screen), *The Invisible Woman* (1941), *The Time of Their Lives* (1946), *The Seven Year Itch* (1957), etc. Sec N, lot 200, grave 5, Holy Cross Cemetery, Culver City, CA.

5735. McBride, Mary Margaret (Nov. 16, 1899–April 7, 1976) Radio personality from Paris, Missouri, was "the female Arthur Godfrey" of talk programs and author of *How Dear to My Heart* (1940) and *A Long Way From Missouri* (1959). Her ashes were placed in the rose garden of her home, where she died, in the Catskills at West Shokun, NY.

5736. McCabe, John (John Charles McCabe III, Nov. 14, 1920–Sept. 27, 2005) Film historian, author and biographer from Detroit did more than any other individual to promote and preserve an appreciation of the comedy of Stan Laurel and Oliver Hardy, with the book *Mr. Laurel and Mr. Hardy* in 1961 and the formation of *The Sons of The Desert* in 1965. He wrote subsequent books on the duo as well as two on James Cagney, one on George M. Cohan, and others. Long a professor at Lake Superior State University in Sault Saint Marie, Michigan, and a resident of Mackinac Island, he died in Petoskey, Michigan, at 84. Memorial mass. Cremated through Dodson mortuary, St. Ignace. Ashes to be buried later by his wife with other relatives at St. Ann's Catholic Cemetery, Mackinac Island, MI.

5737. McCabe, Patti (Patricia Ann Barnes, June 6, 1939–Jan. 17, 1989) Lyndhurst, Ohio, singer with the Poni-Tails (*Born Too Late* 1958), died from cancer at 49. Flush plaque. Ashes buried sec. S, lot 396-C, #3, near Memorial Drive, White Haven Cemetery, Mayfield (Cleveland), OH.

5738. McCall, Jack (dec. March 1, 1877) Primarily for notoriety, Broken Nose Jack McCall shot Wild Bill Hickok in the back, holding aces and eights with his back to the door, in Deadwood, Dakota Territory, on August 2, 1876. Hanged the following March, he was buried in the southwest corner of the Catholic Cemetery. All the bodies were moved in 1881 to Yankton to make way for the Territorial Insane Hospital. When his coffin was opened, the noose was still around the neck. Grave unmarked and the gravesite lost. Yankton Cemetery, Yankton, SD.

5739. McCalla, Irish (Dec. 25, 1928–Feb. 1, 2002) Actress from Pawnee City, Nebraska, in films and television, where she was best known, as *Sheena, Queen of the Jungle* in the 1950's. She resided from 1982 at Prescott, Arizona, until her death in Tucson from a brain tumor at 73. Cremated in Tucson. Private memorial service and burial — private property; not in the cemeteries — in Prescott, AZ.

5740. McCallion, James (Sept. 27, 1918–July 11, 1991) Irish born character actor in films from the late 1930's (*Illegal, Vera Cruz, North By Northwest, PT 109*) and numerous television appearances. Ashes scattered at sea, as were those of his wife.

5741. McCallister, Lon (Herbert Alonzo McCallister, April 17, 1923–June 11, 2005) Actor from Los Angeles in many bits from 1936 was featured in films as good hearted innocents 1942–53 (*Quiet Please Murder,* notably in *Stage Door Canteen* and *Home in Indiana,* also *Winged Victory, The Red House, The Big Cat, The Story of Seabiscuit, The Boy from Indiana, A Yank in Korea*). He left films at 30 and went into real estate. Preparing to move to Arizona, he died from a heart attack at 82 in the Lake Tahoe, California, area. Cremated through McFarlane mortuary, South Lake Tahoe. Ashes reportedly scattered at sea, or interred Inglewood Park Cemetery, Inglewood, CA.

5742. McCalman, Macon "Sonny" (Willis Macon McCalman, 1933–Nov. 29, 2005) Memphis stage actor in many television and film appearances from the 1970's through the 90's, usually as provincial officials (*Deliverance, Fried Green Tomatoes, Doc Hollywood, The Client, A Walk in the Clouds, Rosewood*). He died in Memphis at 72. Stephenson's Chapel Cemetery, Memphis, TN.

5743. McCambridge, Mercedes (Carlotta Mercedes Agnes McCambridge, March 16, 1916 [later given as March 17, 1918]–March 2, 2004) Versatile actress from Joliet, Illinois, on Broadway and radio prior to films, won an Oscar for *All the King's Men* (1949), appeared in *Johnny Guitar* (1954), *Giant* (AA nom., 1956), *Touch of Evil* (1958), as the demonic voice of Linda Blair in *The Exorcist* (1974), many others. Beset by alcoholism, her second marriage, to radio writer Fletcher Markle 1950–62, ended in divorce. In November 1987, her only child, Little Rock, Arkansas, broker John Lawrence Markle, fatally shot his wife, two daughters, 13 and 9, and himself. Their ashes were buried at Trinity Episcopal Cathedral Cemetery in Little Rock. McCambridge died at 87 in a care facility at La Jolla, California, where she had lived since the 1980's, with no services and leaving no survivors. Ashes scattered at sea through the Neptune Society March 8, 2004, off the coast of San Diego County.

5744. McCann, Donal (May 7, 1943–July 17, 1999) Dublin born Irish actor in some thirty films 1966–98, many released in America, including *Out of Africa* (1985, as the doctor), *The Dead* (1987, as Gabriel Conroy opposite Anjelica Huston) and *The Nephew* (1998, as Tony Egan), his last film. He died in Dublin at 56 from pancreatic cancer. St. Patrick's Church cemetery, Monaseed, Gorey, County Wexford.

5745. McCarey, Leo (Oct. 3, 1896–July 5, 1969) Acclaimed American director of Irish descent best known for *Duck Soup* (1933), *The Awful Truth* (Academy Award, 1937) and *Going My Way* (Academy Award, 1944). Sec. T, tier 134, grave 43/44, Holy Cross Cemetery, Culver City, CA.

5746. McCargo, Marian (Feb. 19, 1932–April 7, 2004) Actress and tennis champion from Pittsburgh in some films (*Dead Heat on a Merry Go Round* 1966, *Buona Sera Mrs. Campbell*) and television, sometimes credited as Marian Moses. Married to Richard Moses and for thirty four years to California Representative **Alphonzo Bell, Jr.** (Sept. 19, 1914–April 25, 2004), who survived her by eighteen days. She died from pancreatic cancer at 72 in Santa Monica. Whispering Pines, lot 1058, spaces 5 and 6, Forest Lawn, Glendale, CA.

5747. McCarthy, Eugene (Eugene Joseph McCarthy, March 29, 1916–Dec. 10, 2005) Democratic congressman (1949–59) and senator (1959–1971) from Watkins, Minnesota, known for his urbane wit, poetry and sometimes biting sarcasm, made his mark in 1968 with a groundswell of support, showcased with "Clean for Gene" students, behind his opposition to the Vietnam War, garnering 42 percent of the vote in New Hampshire's Democratic primary, but pushed aside by the subsequent entry of New York Senator Robert Kennedy into the race four days later. The combined events induced President Johnson to announce he would not seek re-nomination and split the party, which lost the close race in November. He died in Washington, D.C., at 89. St. Paul's Episcopal Churchyard, Woodville, VA.

5748. McCarthy, Joseph Raymond (Nov. 14, 1908–May 2, 1957) Republican Senator from Wisconsin from 1946, Tail Gunner Joe gained national fame and eventually infamy with a widespread smear campaign damaging and ruining the careers of writers, artists, actors, politicians and members of the U.S. military who he named, most often without foundation, as communists during senate hearings and speeches, feeding on a growing hysteria and eventually going so far as to claim General George C. Marshall was a communist sympathizer. When he labeled a young lawyer protégé of U.S. Army attorney Joseph Welch a communist sympathizer, Welch dressed him down in the senate on June 9, 1954, drawing applause. McCarthy was censured by his colleagues and thereafter lost his influence, descending into alcoholism. He died at 48 from liver failure in Bethesda Naval Hospital. St. Mary's Cemetery, Appleton, WI.

5749. McCarthy, Joseph Vincent (April 21, 1887–Jan. 13, 1978) "Marse Joe," manager of the Cubs 1926–30, the Yankees 1931–46 and the Red Sox 1948–50. The winningest manager in baseball; in twenty four years his teams took nine pennants, finished second seven times and won seven world series with the Yankees, four consecutively 1936–39. Hall of Fame 1957. Flush plaque. St. Anthony's Garden, lot 46, grave 1, Mt. Olivet Cemetery, Kenmore/Tonawanda (Buffalo area), NY.

5750. McCarthy, Tommy (Thomas Francis McCarthy, July 24, 1864–Aug. 5, 1922) Baseball player, one of Boston's Heavenly Twins of the 1890's, outstanding outfielder and base stealer, a legend in the outfield with Hugh Duffy. Though baseball records show 1864, his stone lists his birth year as 1863. Hall of Fame 1946. Sec. 9, range 26, grave 74, Mount (old) Calvary Cemetery, Boston, MA.

5751. McCartney, Linda Eastman (Sept. 24, 1941–April 17, 1998) Westchester County, New York, native, the daughter of an entertainment lawyer, was an accomplished photographer when she wed Beatle Paul McCartney in March 1969. Over their 29 year marriage, she increasingly devoted herself to animal rights and vegetarianism. Her death, not announced for two days, at 56 from breast cancer diagnosed in December 1995 which had spread to her liver, was reported as having occurred in Santa Barbara, California, causing a minor furor three days later when it was learned she had really died at the family's ranch east of Tucson, Arizona, and was cremated through Brings Crematorium in Tucson. The family returned to their farm near Rye in East Sussex, southern England, where her ashes were scattered Monday April 20, 1998. Part may also have been sprinkled on their Arizona property.

5752. McCay, Winsor (Sept. 26, 1869–July 26, 1934) The first successful animated feature cartoonist drew *Little Nemo in Slumberland* for animated movies beginning in 1909, released in 1911, *How a Mosquito Operates* (1912) and *Gertie the Trained Dinosaur* (1914), his most famous work. The Lawn 64, Cemetery of the Evergreens, Brooklyn, N.Y.C.

5753. McClellan, George B. (Dec. 3, 1826–Oct. 29, 1885) Lincoln tried his first promising commander of the Army of the Potomac twice but after the Peninsula Campaign in 1862 determined that "Old Mac" had a permanent case of "the slows." He ran unsuccessfully against Lincoln in 1864, later serving as Governor of New Jersey. His towering obelisk and column is topped by an American eagle. Sec. B, lot 637–704, Riverview Cemetery, Trenton, NJ.

5754. McClellan, Hurd Sam (Heard) (May 8, 1884–April 17, 1933) Actor-stuntman died in a shooting accident on the Universal lot. Sec. 53, row A, grave 4, Los Angeles/Sawtelle Natl. Cemetery, Westwood, west Los Angeles.

5755. McClellan, John Little (Feb. 25, 1896–Nov. 28, 1977) Senator from Arkansas 1943–1977. Hillcrest sec, lot 161, Roselawn Memorial Park, Little Rock, AR.

5756. McClendon, Rose (Aug. 27, 1884–July 12, 1936) Early African American actress dubbed "the Sepia Barrymore" of her day and compared to Eleonora Duse as well. Sec. 74, lot 101, plot 2, Mount Hope Cemetery, Hastings-on-Hudson, NY.

5757. McClendon, Sarah (July 8, 1910–Jan. 8, 2003) The longest serving White House reporter in the American press corps, spanning twelve presidents, from 1944–2001. Sec. 5-KK, row 23, site 4, Arlington National Cemetery, Arlington, VA.

5758. McClintock, Walter (April 25, 1870–March 24, 1949) Curator of the Yale University Library and an historian and ethnologist specializing in the study of the Blackfoot Indian tribe. A Victorian maiden tops the shaft above the monument. Sec. 19, lot 17, Allegheny Cemetery, Pittsburgh, PA.

5759. McCloskey, Frank (June 12, 1939–Nov. 2, 2003) Philadelphia born mayor of Bloomington, Indiana 1972–82, U.S. representative from Indiana's eight district 1983–1995, and later director of Kosovo programs for the National Democratic Institute of International Affairs. He died from bladder cancer at 64. Sec. 54, grave 5432, Arlington National Cemetery, Arlington, VA.

5760. McCloskey, Robert (Sept. 14, 1914–June 30, 2003) Ohio, native, wrote and illustrated books for children, primarily in his adopted state of Maine.

Works include *Make Way For Ducklings, Blueberries For Sale, Homer Price, Lentil, One Morning in Maine.* The recipient of two Caldecott Medals, he died at Deer Isle, Maine. Buried at Scott's Island, ME.

5761. McClure, Doug (May 11, 1935–Feb. 5, 1995) Blonde actor from Glendale, California, in TV series from the late 50's (*The Twilight Zone, The Overland Trail* 1960, *Checkmate* 1961, and as Trampas in *The Virginian* 1962–1971). He died from lung cancer at his Sherman Oaks home at 59. His flush black plaque has his picture in the corner. B-15-3M, Woodlawn Cemetery, Santa Monica, CA.

5762. McCluskey, Roger (Aug. 24, 1930–Aug. 29, 1993) Veteran racer in seventeen Indianapolis 500's finished in five and as high as third, won championships in three USAC divisions and was President of the U.S. Auto Club from 1979. Cremated through Flanner and Buchanan mortuary, Zionsville, Indiana. Ashes to family.

5763. McCool, William (William Cameron McCool, Sept. 23, 1961–Feb. 1, 2003) Navy Pilot Commander of the Space Shuttle Columbia, which exploded as it re-entered the earth's atmosphere, primarily over Texas. Funeral March 1 at the U.S. Naval Academy Chapel and private mass February 28 in St. Andrew's Chapel. Ashes interred North Prairie Cemetery, Huegely (Hoyleton Township), IL.

5764. McCord, David Thompson Watson (Nov. 15, 1897–April 13, 1997) Harvard poet and professor known for his sometimes whimsical verse and for his fund raising work. Upright rectangular charcoal-black stone with the lines *Blessed Lord, what it is to be young/ To be of, to be for, be among; Be enchanted, enthralled/ Be the caller, the called —/ The singer, the song, and the sung./ Blessed Lord, what is to be old/ Be the teller, and not the told/ Be serene in the wake, of a triumph, mistake/ Of life's rainbows with no pots of gold.* Chestnut Ave., lot 7012, Mt. Auburn Cemetery, Cambridge, MA.

5765. McCorkle, Sussanah (Jan. 1, 1946–May 19, 2001) Versatile jazz and cabaret singer born in Berkeley, California, released seventeen albums from 1976 to her death, including translations of Portuguese lyrics for Brazilian songs on *Sabia* (1990), and wrote both fiction and essays for periodicals as well. She left instructions regarding her estate and her cats, then jumped sixteen stories to her death at 55 from her apartment on West 86th St. in Manhattan. Per CK citing *The Daily News* or a jazz periodical, she was cremated and the ashes returned to her family. She had reportedly requested they be scattered in Central Park.

5766. McCormack, John (John Count McCormack, June 14, 1884–Sept. 16, 1945) Irish tenor in operatic concerts and popular recordings, a favorite in both America (he became a citizen in 1919) and Ireland for many years. He died in Dublin, where a bronze bust of him tops his monument and grave surrounded by a low stone curb. 119/120 E. St. Patrick sec., Deans Grange Burial Ground, County Dublin, Ireland.

5767. McCormack, John W. (Dec. 21, 1891–Nov. 22, 1980) Boston born Democrat in congress from 1928; Speaker of the House of Representatives 1962–71 following the death of Sam Rayburn. He died in Boston at 88. Field of Sacred Heart, lot 4, St. Joseph Cemetery, West Roxbury (Boston), MA.

5768. McCormick, Cyrus Hall (Feb. 15, 1809–May 13, 1884) Virginia born inventor of the reaper in 1831 renewed his patent in 1848, eventually moved to Chicago and died there. They have small stones in a large L shaped lot with his son **Cyrus Hall McCormick, Jr.** (May 16, 1859–June 2, 1936) behind the large lot of Marshall Field, Ridgeland sec., Graceland Cemetery, Chicago, IL.

5769. McCormick, Edith Rockefeller (Aug. 31, 1872–Aug. 25, 1932) Cleveland born daughter of John D. Rockefeller married Harold McCormick and became Chicago's social leader after Bertha Palmer's death in 1918. She fostered the zoological gardens and the opera but lost her fortune to the depression. Divorced from McCormick. Slab over grave at the edge of the Willomere lake, Graceland Cemetery, Chicago, IL.

5770. McCormick, Harold Fowler (May 2, 1872–Oct. 16, 1941) Socialite son of Cyrus Sr. was married first to Edith Rockefeller, then became infatuated with Polish opera singer Ganna Walska in 1920 and tirelessly but futilely promoted her "career," allegedly the actual basis of the relationship in *Citizen Kane*, until she left him for another tycoon and he remarried. Ridgeland sec., Graceland Cemetery, Chicago, IL.

5771. McCormick, Myron (Feb. 8, 1908–July 30, 1962) Actor from Albany, Indiana, on Broadway as Luther Billis in *South Pacific* and as Sgt. King in *No Time For Sergeants*, filmed in 1958; also *The Hustler* (1961). He died from cancer in New York. Ashes to Frank E. Campbell mortuary, Manhattan, N.Y.C.

5772. McCormick, Robert R. (July 30, 1880–April 1, 1955) Grandson of *Chicago Tribune* founder Joseph Medill inherited Medill's estate, Red Oaks Farm, at Wheaton in DuPage County, Illinois. A Colonel in the U.S. Army with the First Division, Field Artillery, in France during World War I and with the Officer's Reserve Corps until 1929, Col. McCormick re-christened the estate Cantigny, after the First Division's 1918 battle there, the first decisive American victory. He willed it to the state and in 1960 it became the War Memorial of the First Division. His tomb is guarded by a stone dog at the head of his slab, which notes *Buried with full military honors*. Gardens of the Cantigny Estate/First Division War Memorial, 1 South 151 Rd., Wheaton, IL.

5773. McCourt, Angela (Angela Sheehan, d. 1981) The once obscure Irish mother of teacher and author Frank McCourt, whose 1996 best-seller *Angela's Ashes* detailed his family's poverty in the slums of Limerick through the 1930's and 40s, having returned there in 1935 after living in Brooklyn, where he was born in 1930. A family of seven, brothers **Oliver** and **Eugene** died as children and were buried at St. Patrick's Burying Ground, Limerick. Frank's teenage affair, with the consumptive **Theresa Carmody**, ended soon in her premature death from tuberculosis. She was buried at (Mount) St. Lawrence Cemetery, Limerick. Returning to America in 1949, Frank became a teacher, his brother Malachy a bar owner. Upon their mother's death in New York, they unexpectedly had her cremated, at Garden State Crematory through Walter B. Cooke mortuary. Although actor Richard Harris and others subscribed to the rumor that her ashes were left in a pub and lost, or placed in baggage and lost at Kennedy Airport, or buried in an obscure area near the airport, Frank McCourt says they returned her to Limerick as she wished in August 1985, albeit ashes, and spread them three miles outside Limerick over the Sheehan grave(s) in historic Mungret graveyard, County Limerick.

5774. McCoy, Elijah (May 2, 1844–Oct. 10, 1929) Versatile railroad engineer and inventor of the drip cup automated lubrication process for machinery, he amassed fifty seven patents, including the steam cylinder lubricator, ironing table and lawn sprinkler. "The Real McCoy" is also said to have been coined to distinguish his works from imitators, though the phrase has other alleged sources as well. Sec. 2, grave 1516, Detroit Memorial Park, Warren (north of Detroit), MI.

5775. McCoy, Kid (Norman E. Selby aka Charles McCoy, Oct. 13, 1872/1873–April 18, 1940) Boxer from Rush County, Indiana, won the welterweight title from Tommy Ryan in 1896 with his corkscrew punch, and the middleweight title from Dan Creedon in 1898. In a fight with Joe Choynski in San Francisco in 1899 the term "the real McCoy" was (by some accounts) first used, to distinguish him from a local fighter, Pete McCoy. Married ten times, he was convicted in Los Angeles in August 1924 of the murder of Theresa Mors and did eight years at San Quentin. Paroled in 1932, he worked for the Ford Motor Co. in Detroit and was found dead in the Hotel Tuller there eight years later at 66, a suicide by sleeping pills or poison. Service at Grace Episcopal Church. Cremated April 20 at White Chapel Memorial Park in Troy (then Birmingham), through Wm. R. Hamilton Co. mortuary, Detroit. Garden of Prophets, sec. 193, space 2, White Chapel Memorial Cemetery, Troy, MI.

5776. McCoy, Randolph (Oct. 30, 1825–March 28, 1914) The head of half of the Hatfield and McCoy mountain feud participants. At least six of the participants are buried at Hardy, Pike County, Kentucky, and at Dils Cemetery near Pikeville. The Hatfields lived primarily on the other side of the Two Forks River. The feud allegedly began when Ellison Hatfield, younger brother of preacher Devil Anse Hatfield, was stabbed to death (and shot) on Election Day 1882. In retaliation, the Hatfields took three sons of Ranl (Randolph) McCoy, tied them to a paw-paw bush and executed them. Randolph, his wife **Sarah** (1829–189?) and their daughter **Roseanna** (1859–1889) are buried (all marked) at Dils Cemetery, Pikeville, KY. See also **Hatfield.**

5777. McCoy, Tim (April 10, 1891–Jan. 29, 1978) Colonel Tim McCoy was a favorite Saturday matinee hero in silent cowboy and firefighter pictures in the 1920's, going on to make many sound B westerns. He died in Nogales, Arizona. Buried with his parents and his wife Inga Arvad (*q.v.*). Sec. E, lot 3, se ½, Mount Olivet Cemetery, Saginaw, MI.

5778. McCoy, Van (Jan. 6, 1940–July 6, 1979) Washington, D.C. born singer-songwriter (*Baby I'm Yours,* a hit for Barbara Lewis, among others) and popularized and recorded *The Hustle* (1975). He died from cancer at 39 in Englewood, New Jersey. Upright stone. Sec. H, lot 105-4, Lincoln Memorial Cemetery, Capitol Heights, Suitland Rd., MD.

5779. McCracken, Branch (Emmet Branch McCracken, June 9, 1908–June 4, 1970) Indiana University basketball coaching great, The Sheriff of Monrovia led IU for 24 seasons 1940–1965 with a 364–174 record, taking two NCAA titles (1940, with the Pont A Minute Club, and 1953) and four Big Ten wins. He coached the game to a fiery pace that set new standards in its development as a spectator sport. Rose double stone facing road along west edge of cemetery, just beyond utility building. Mt. Pleasant Cemetery, ½ mile east of Monrovia at Hall, IN.

5780. McCrae, John (Nov. 30, 1872–Jan. 28, 1918) Canadian doctor from Guelph, Ontario, while a medical officer with the First Brigade Artillery at Ypres in 1915 wrote the poem *In Flanders Fields*, used as an incentive in recruiting and found in the pockets of dead soldiers through the duration of the war. He died from pneumonia and fever at Wimereux. Named on his parents' stone in Woodlawn Cemetery, Guelph, where his home is a shrine, he was buried at Wimereux Cemetery, Wimereux, near Bologne, France.

5781. McCrary, Billy Leon (Dec. 7, 1946–July 14, 1979) 747 pound circus performer with brother Benny rode tiny motorcycles under the big top. Crab Creek Baptist Church Cemetery, south of Hendersonville, NC.

5782. McCrea, Joel (Nov. 5, 1905–Oct. 20, 1990) Rugged actor from South Pasadena in strong, silent leads of the 1930's, later switched primarily to westerns. Films include *Bird of Paradise* and *The Most Dangerous Game* (both 1932), *These Three* (1936), *Dead End* (1937), *Sullivan's Travels* (1941), *Foreign Correspondent* (1941). Married to actress Frances Dee, they retired to their ranch at Camarillo, California. He died from a lung ailment at the Motion Picture Country Hospital at 84. As he requested, he was cremated and his ashes scattered at sea.

5783. McCullers, Carson (Feb. 19, 1917–Sept. 29,

1967) Author of *The Heart is A Lonely Hunter* (1940) and *Member of the Wedding* (1946), her work reflecting the trauma of outcasts and her own sensitivity to loneliness and rejection. After a stroke, she was in a coma nearly a month before her death in Nyack, New York, at 50. She is marked by a small rose stone, obscured for years appropriately by a bush as it looks across and down toward the Hecht and MacArthur lots. High View Lawn 54A, Oak Hill Cemetery, Nyack, NY.

5784. McCullough, Paul (1884–March 25, 1936) The straight half of vaudeville and Broadway comedy team Clark and McCullough; both from Springfield, Ohio, and friends since childhood. By the 1930's Clark lived in New York and McCullough in Brookline, Massachusetts. Suffering from nervous depression, he had spent some time in a sanitarium when he walked into a Medford barber shop on March 23 and, while seated in the chair, reached for a straight razor and slit his own throat, dying two days later in Lawrence Hospital. Clark said he guessed it was something his partner couldn't help and had carried around with him for a long time. Mass at St. Aldan's Church, Brookline. 6006 Celosia Path, Woodlawn Cemetery, Everett, MA.

5785. McCullough, Ruth (Dec. 13, 1919–June 15, 2001) Big Band vocalist sang with Isham Jones, Sonny Dunham and Tony Pastor. She married trumpeter **Richard Dyer** and retired from Pastor's band, giving way to Betty and Rosemary Clooney. Gate of Heaven Cemetery, Silver Spring, MD.

5786. McCurdy, Elmer (Jan. 1879 — Oct. 7, 1911) Oklahoma outlaw shot by a posse whose mummified body remained on exhibit at carnivals or as a prop, either known to be a corpse or believed to be a mannequin, for sixty six years. He was finally given a burial April 22, 1977 at Guthrie, Oklahoma, where by 1991 regular weekend pilgrimages were being made to his tombstone, arousing the ire of some locals who claimed (without proof) that the gatherings were satanic. Block 22, lot 353, Summit View Cemetery, Guthrie, OK.

5787. McCutcheon, George Barr (July 26, 1866– Oct. 23, 1928) Writer of novels from Tippecanoe County, Indiana, penned *Brewster's Millions* (1903), several others. Brother of cartoonist John T. McCutcheon. He died while at a luncheon in Manhattan. Sec 27, lot 11 (along road), Spring Vale Cemetery, Lafayette, IN.

5788. McCutcheon, John T. (May 6, 1870–June 10, 1949) Political cartoonist for the *Chicago Tribune* won a Pulitzer Prize in 1931. Best known for *Indian Summer*, showing the specter of Indians amid the corn shocks. Sec. D, east side near north end, lot 79, Graceland Cemetery, Chicago, IL.

5789. McCutcheon, Wallace (Dec. 23, 1894–Jan. 27, 1928) Silent screen director 1903–08, cinematographer, and actor 1915–20, married to Pearl White 1919–21, ended his life by gunshot. Buried unmarked in the family plot (bench) of Wallace Sr. Sec. 8, lot 49, grave 2, Glenwood Cemetery, Long Branch, NJ.

5790. McDaniel, Etta (Dec. 1, 1890–Jan. 13, 1946) Actress sister of Hattie and Sam. Many B films. Buried under her married name, Spaulding. Sec. R, lot 146, Calvary Cemetery, East Los Angeles.

5791. McDaniel, Hattie (June 10, 1895–Oct. 26, 1952) Heavy actress in saucy maid roles won the first Oscar awarded a black, as Mammy in *Gone With the Wind* (1939). She later played *Beulah* on radio, replaced by Louise Beavers when she became ill. She died from cancer at 57 in the Motion Picture Country Home. Sec D, across from the office, Rosedale Cemetery, Los Angeles. Since she had reportedly wanted to be buried at Hollywood Cemetery, which barred blacks in 1952, on October 26, 1999, the owners of the cemetery and a nephew dedicated a cenotaph to her, inscribed *To honor her final wish. Hattie McDaniel 1895–1952. Academy Award 1939, Gone With the Wind* and from her nephew Edgar Goff, *Aunt Hattie, you were a credit to your race and our family.* Sec. 8/Garden of Legends, Hollywood Memorial Park Cemetery (Hollywood Forever), Hollywood (Los Angeles), CA.

5792. McDaniel, Mildred (Nov. 3, 1933–Sept. 30, 2004) Atlanta born athlete at Tuskegee Institute in both track and field and basketball was the U.S. Women's High Jump champion in 1953, 1955 and 1956, won a gold medal in 1955 at the Pan-Am Games, and won the gold while setting a new record in the high jump with 5 feet, 7 inches, at the Olympics in Melbourne in 1956. A physical education teacher in Pasadena for thirty two years, Mildred McDaniel Singleton retired in 1993, eleven years before her death there at 70. Pasadena Mausoleum, row D1, crypt Y59, Mountain View Cemetery, Altadena, CA.

5793. McDaniel, Sam "Deacon" (Jan. 29, 1886– Sept. 24, 1962) Brother of Hattie and Etta played a variety of roles, many cooks, servants and field hands, a favorite supporting player through the 1930's and 40's (*Manhattan Melodrama* 1934, *The Prisoner of Shark Island* 1936, *Captains Courageous* 1937, *Son of Dracula* 1943). Block (Memorial) E, 4114, lot 3, Valhalla Memorial Park, North Hollywood, CA.

5794. McDermott, Marc (Marcus McDermott, July 24, 1881–Jan. 5, 1929) Actor from New South Wales, Australia, in silent films from 1909, including *He Who Gets Slapped, The Sea Hawk, Dorothy Vernon of Hadden Hall* (all 1924), and as the betrayed husband or paramour of Greta Garbo in both *The Temptress* and *Flesh and the Devil.* He died from cirrhosis in Hollywood at 47. Columbarium of Benevolence, niche 15092, Gardenia Terrace, Great Mausoleum, Forest Lawn, Glendale, CA.

5795. McDevitt, Ruth (Ruth Thane Shoecraft, Sept. 13, 1895–May 27, 1976) Actress from Coldwater, Michigan, played elderly ladies from sharp secretaries to befuddled spinsters, primarily on television 1950–1976 (*Kolchak, The Night Stalker* 1974–5), some films and TV movies. She died in Hollywood at 80. Ashes in rose garden, Westwood Memorial Park, west Los Angeles.

5796. MacDonald, Dave (David G. MacDonald, July 23, 1936–May 30, 1964) Rookie in the 1964 Indianapolis 500 died in Methodist Hospital there from inhaling blazing gasoline after his car hit a wall during the second lap and the Thompson Ford's gas filled rear engine exploded. Veteran Eddie Sachs, also in a rear engine car, died instantly when he ran into the fire. The explosion closed the track for nearly two hours, the first time the race was stopped because of a wreck. The worst accident in speedway history, it led to the banning of gasoline engines from the brickyard. The coffin adorned with a checkered flag from his two young children, he was buried June 3. The crossed checkered flags, as with many race drivers, appear on his flush plaque. Garden of Rest, lot 8034, Rose Hills Memorial Park, Whittier, CA.

5797. McDonald, Francis (Francis J. McDonald, Aug. 22, 1891–Sept. 16, 1968) Character actor in nearly three hundred silent and sound films from 1913 into the 1960's, in all variety of supporting to bit parts. Mausoleum L, sec. 1057, Valhalla Memorial Park, North Hollywood, CA.

5798. McDonald, Grace (June 15, 1918–Oct. 30, 1999) Boston born singer, dancer and actress, sister of Ray McDonald, made a handful of films (*It Ain't Hay, Follow the Boys, Murder in the Blue Room, Destiny*) but retired from the screen by 1945. Married name Green, she died at 81 in Scottsdale, Arizona. Shipped from Messinger Indian School mortuary, Scottsdale, for burial November 9th at (4th) Calvary Cemetery, sec. 59, lot 65/William McDonald lot, grave 13, Woodside, Queens, N.Y.C.

5799. MacDonald, J. Farrell (April 14, 1875–Aug. 2, 1952) Bald, bulbous nosed actor in small roles over forty years, originally a director and a star in early silents. Later many Irish cops, cranky old men, etc (*The Crosby Case, It's A Wonderful Life, Mr. Belvedere Rings the Bell*). Memory Hall (four to a drawer with small nameplates), sec. K, niche G2, Chapel of the Pines Crematory, Los Angeles.

5800. MacDonald, James (John James MacDonald, May 19, 1906–Feb. 1, 1991) The voice of Mickey Mouse in Walt Disney cartoons, features and TV's *Mickey Mouse Club*. Victory sec., lot 459, Forest Lawn, Glendale, CA.

5801. MacDonald, Jeanette (June 18, 1901–Jan. 14, 1965) Philadelphia born soprano followed her sister Blossom onto the stage and went on to musicals at Paramount 1929–1934, but was best known for operettas opposite Nelson Eddy at MGM 1935–42, including the duets *Ah, Sweet Mystery of Life* (from *Naughty Marietta* 1935), *Indian Love Call* (from *Rose Marie* 1936), *San Francisco* (1936) and *Will You Remember?* from *Maytime* (1937). She retired from the screen in 1949, but continued on radio and in concerts. At Methodist Hospital in Houston awaiting heart surgery, she died from a heart attack at 63 (reported as 57). Her funeral at Forest Lawn Glendale, was widely attended, with pallbearers including Barry Goldwater, Leon Ames and Meredith Willson. She was entombed holding the pink satin prayer book used at her wedding to actor Gene Raymond in June 1937, with her recordings of *Ah, Sweet Mystery of Life* and *Ave Maria* played at the service. Crypt below Nat Cole with her signature over the dates and her birth moved up to 1907. Raymond was interred beside her in March 1998. Right wall, second from top, Sanctuary of Heritage, Freedom Mausoleum, Forest Lawn, Glendale, CA.

5802. MacDonald, John D. (John Dann MacDonald, July 24, 1916–Dec. 28, 1986) Writer of mysteries, born at Sharon, Pennsylvania, most closely identified with his private eye Travis McGee. Among his books made into films was *The Executioners*. He died in Milwaukee after what was to have been a routine bypass operation. Cremated at Valhalla Memorial Park, Milwaukee, through Feerick Funeral Home. Ashes given to his son Maynard and reportedly (per his web site) buried where he grew up, in Utica, New York, though he has not been located there. He resided in Sarasota, FL.

5803. MacDonald, Katherine (Dec. 14, 1891–June 4, 1956) Silent screen actress known as the American Beauty, retired in 1928. Married name Holmes. Sunset sec., block A, lot 64, Santa Barbara Cemetery, Santa Barbara, CA.

5804. MacDonald, Kenneth (Kenneth Dollins, Sept. 8, 1901–May 5, 1972) Mustached actor from Portland, Indiana, in films of the 1930's and 40's (*The Last Mile, Before I Hang, The Devil Commands, The Caine Mutiny*, many B westerns). Sheltering Hills sec., lot 155, Forest Lawn Hollywood Hills, Los Angeles.

5805. McDonald, Marie (July 6, 1923–Oct. 21, 1965) Starlet of the early 1940's from Burgin, Kentucky, nicknamed "The Body" but her career failed to materialize. She died from an overdose of sleeping pills at 42. Crypt 203712, right wall, Sanctuary of Heritage, Freedom Mausoleum, Forest Lawn, Glendale, CA.

5806. McDonald, Maurice J. (Nov. 26, 1902–Dec. 11, 1971) Co-founder of McDonald's Hamburger stands in the late 40's, later sold to Ray Kroc. Sec. B-8, lot 43, Desert Memorial Park, Cathedral City (Palm Springs), CA.

5807. MacDonald, Ross (Kenneth Miller, Dec. 13, 1915–July 11, 1983) Writer of detective novels later wrote environmental articles. Ashes spread in the channel at Santa Barbara, CA.

5808. McDonough, Will (July 6, 1935–Jan. 9, 2003) Sports writer for *The Boston Globe* from 1959 to his death, five time Massachusetts Sportswriter of the Year, covered the NFL games and was a commentator on NBC's *NFL Live*. Ashes to family in Hingham, MA.

5809. McDougal, James (Aug. 25, 1940–March

8, 1998) Arkansas savings and loan operator whose dealings with Bill and Hillary Clinton prompted the Whitewater investigation in 1994, headed by independent counsel Kenneth Starr. Both McDougal and his wife Susan were convicted in 1996, but while she did not cooperate with the prosecution, he did. He died at 57 in a federal medical prison in Fort Worth, Texas. Buried in the plot of former Lt. Governor James Riley. Rest Haven Memorial Gardens, Arkadelphia, AR.

5810. McDowall, Roddy (Roderick McDowall, Sept. 17, 1928–Oct. 3, 1998) English child star left London for Hollywood in 1940, in *How Green Was My Valley, Lassie Come Home, The White Cliffs of Dover, My Friend Flicka* etc., and adult roles from 1960 (*Midnight Lace, Cleopatra* 1963, as Octavian, *Five Card Stud, The Legend of Hell House, Dead of Winter,* and as Cornelius in *Planet of the Apes* and its sequels, many others). He later did books of photos of stars, and took an interest in honoring cinematic names from the past. McDowall died from lung cancer at 70 in his Studio City, California, home. No services. Cremated by the Neptune Society, his ashes were scattered at sea October 7 off Los Angeles County.

5811. McDowell, Claire (Nov. 2, 1876–Oct. 23, 1966) New York born actress on stage, in films (*Human Wreckage, The Big Parade* 1925, as Jim's mother; *Ben Hur* 1926, *An American Tragedy* 1931) Married to actor Charles Hill Mailes (d. 1937). Block G, 6516-1, Valhalla Memorial Park, North Hollywood, CA.

5812. MacDowell, Edward Alexander (Dec. 18, 1861–Jan. 23, 1908) Composer and pianist penned sonatas and concertos, the piano piece *To A Wild Rose* (1896) and *Indian Suite* (1897) for orchestra. With his European educational background and "romantic lyricism," he was considered the foremost American composer of the 19th century and, with his wife **Marian Griswold Nevins MacDowell** (1857–1965), established the MacDowell Colony for composers, writers and artists at Peterborough, New Hampshire. Both were buried in the private MacDowell Colony Cemetery, Peterborough, NH.

5813. McDowell, Irvin (Oct. 15, 1818–May 4, 1885) Lincoln's first acting commander of the Army of the Potomac was defeated at First Manassas (Bull Run) in July 1861. He later commanded the Army of the Rappahannock and the Army of the Virginia, where he was defeated at Second Manassas (Bull Run) in 1862 and relieved of command. Sec. OS, plot 1, grave 1, Presidio National Cemetery, San Francisco, CA.

5814. McEnroe, Robert E. (July 1, 1916–Feb. 6, 1998) Author of *The Silver Bell* (1948), filmed in 1951 as *Mr. Belvedere Rings the Bell.* Fairview Cemetery, West Hartford, CT.

5815. McEnery, Red River Dave (Dec. 15, 1914–Jan. 15, 2002) Cowboy balladeer and singer, with his Swift Cowboys, credited with writing thousands of songs, ranging from *Amelia Earhart's Last Flight,* written in 1937 and later recorded by Kinky Friedman and the Texas Jewboys, to *Shame is the Middle Name of Exxon,* which eventually got $258 taken off a service repair bill he was not pleased with. He died at 87. Garden of the Good Shepherd (sec. 20), lot 35, Sunset Memorial Park, San Antonio, TX.

5816. McErlane, Frank (1894–Oct. 7, 1932) Vicious southside Chicago hoodlum of the 1920's, associated with Joe Saltis, reportedly introduced the Thompson sub-machine gun to the city, against Spike O'Donnell in September 1925 and killed several others, including five members of the O'Donnell gang. He later broke with his partner, John "Dingbat" Oberta, killing him in March 1930 after Oberta had made an attempt on his life. In 1931 he allegedly shot and killed his wife along with their two dogs and left them in the back seat of her car. Ironically, he did not die violently but from pneumonia at 38. Sec. 2, Holy Sepulchre Cemetery, Worth, IL.

5817. MacFadden, Bernarr (Aug. 16, 1868–Oct. 12, 1955) Physical culturist and publisher was an exponent of health foods and fasting as well as publishing pulp periodicals. Still demonstrating what he espoused, he parachuted into Paris on his 84th birthday. Bust on pedestal. Syringa plot off Canna Ave., Woodlawn Cemetery, the Bronx, N.Y.C.

5818. McFadden, Bob (Robert H. McFadden, Jan. 19, 1923–Jan. 7, 2000) Performer on the *First Family* albums spoofing the Kennedys 1961–63, known for his "ring around the collar" voiceovers. Memorial Park sec. 37B, grave 77, Madonna Cemetery, Fort Lee, NJ.

5819. McFadin, Sam (Samuel J. McFadin, March 3, 1952–Aug. 31, 2001) Colorado born vocalist fronted the group Herbie and the Heartbeats, singing at the high school dance in George Lucas's *American Graffiti* (1973). He also appeared in *Happy Days.* His death at 49 resulted from a heart attack. Ashes in Rose Garden #3, Shrine of Remembrance Mausoleum(s), Colorado Springs, CO.

5820. McFarland, Spanky (George Emmett McFarland, Oct. 2, 1928–June 30, 1993) Chubby child actor from Dallas replaced Joe Cobb in the Hal Roach *Our Gang* two reelers 1934–1944 as Spanky. He retired at sixteen and developed several businesses, returning to the Dallas metroplex area. He died from a heart attack in Grapevine, Texas, at 64. Cremated through Lucas mortuary, Hurst, Texas. Ashes to family.

5821. McGee, Frank (Sept. 12, 1921–April 17, 1974) NBC newscaster from 1957 won a Peabody Award in 1966 for Pope Paul VI's visit to New York, and a Brotherhood Award in 1967 from the National Conference of Christians and Jews for *Same Mud, Same Blood,* about blacks and whites fighting in Vietnam. He co-anchored the nightly news 1970–71 and appeared on the *Today* Show until his death in Manhattan at 52 from pneumonia related to multiple myeloma. *We know that autumn does not begin with the turning of the leaves, but earlier, on some forgotten afternoon, when a shadow passed over the fields and it was no longer summer. Don't go far.* St. Paul's Episcopal Cemetery, Hawlin Road (618), just off Rte. 522, Woodville, VA.

5822. McGee, Sam (May 1, 1894–Aug. 22, 1975) Guitarist at the Grand Ole Opry. Flush bronze plaque with guitar on it. Christus, lot 70C, grave 3, Williamson County Memorial Gardens, Franklin, TN.

5823. MacGibbon, Harriet (Oct. 5, 1905–Feb. 8, 1987) Stage, screen and television actress best known as Mrs. Drysdale on TV's *The Beverly Hillbillies* 1962–69. Columbarium of Remembrance, niche 61046, Forest Lawn Hollywood Hills, Los Angeles.

5824. McGill, Ralph (Ralph Emerson McGill, Feb. 5, 1898–Feb. 3, 1969) Newsman, publisher of the *Atlanta Constitution,* won the Pulitzer Prize (for editorials) in 1959. Flush bronze plaque. Sec 48, lot 488, Westview Cemetery, Atlanta, GA.

5825. McGinnity, Joe "Iron Man" (Joseph Jerome McGinnity, March 19, 1871–Nov. 14, 1929) Pitcher with over 400 innings two years and in 1903 had a N.L. record 434. At his peak with the pennant winning New York Giants in 1904. An offseason job in an iron factory, coupled with his mighty arm, brought about his moniker. Hall of Fame 1946. He died in Brooklyn. Masonic (Mann) sec., block 161, lot 12, Oak Hill Cemetery, McAlester, OK.

5826. McGiver, John (Nov. 5, 1913–Sept. 9, 1975) Actor with jowls in droll roles. Films *Breakfast at Tiffany's* (1961), *The Manchurian Candidate* (1962), *Twilight Zone* episode *Sounds and Silences,* TV series *Many Happy Returns* 1964. He died at West Fulton, New York. Cremated at Gardner-Earl Crematory in Troy. Ashes to family in West Fulton.

5827. McGlynn, Frank (Oct. 26, 1866–May 18, 1951) American character actor known for his numerous portrayals of Abraham Lincoln. He died in Newburgh, New York. Sec. 43, plot 40, lot 19, Resurrection Cemetery, Farmingdale, Long Island, New York. His son actor **Frank McGlynn Jr.** (July 9, 1904–March 29, 1939) is in the Murmuring Trees sec., lot 3672, Forest Lawn Hollywood Hills, Los Angeles.

5828. McGovern, Terry (Joseph Terence McGovern, March 9, 1880–Feb. 26, 1918) Featherweight boxing champion 1900–1901, Terrible Terry McGovern was defeated by Young Corbett II but boxed for several years afterward. He died at 37. St. Johns sec., range A, plot 55, Holy Cross Cemetery, Brooklyn, N.Y.C.

5829. McGowan, Bill (William A. McGowan, Jan. 18, 1896–Dec. 9, 1954) Colorful N.L. umpire worked for thirty years from the early 20's and went sixteen and a half years and 2,541 games without missing an inning. Hall of Fame 1992. He died at Silver Spring, Maryland. Sec. 3B, lot 124, Cathedral Cemetery, Wilmington, DE.

5830. McGrath, Frank (Feb. 2, 1903–May 13, 1967) Bearded sidekick in western films best known as Charlie Wooster, the cook with the worst coffee on the prairie, in TV's *Wagon Train* 1957–1965. He died from a heart attack at 64. Columbarium of Heavenly Peace, niche G-892, Forest Lawn, Glendale, CA.

5831. McGrath, Jack (John James McGrath, Oct. 8, 1919–Nov. 6, 1955) Race driver nicknamed The Thin Man of Racing drive in sixty eight AAA races, won nine pole positions and drove to four victories. He dueled with Bill Vukovich for first place through the first fifty four laps of the 1955 Indianapolis 500 until his engine failed some three laps before Vukovich's fatal crash. McGrath died driving in a dirt track race later that year when his car flipped several times after an axle broke. San Gabriel Mission Cemetery, San Gabriel, CA.

5832. McGraw, Charles (Charles Butters, May 10, 1914–July 30, 1980) Character actor in many films over forty years, played many police officers, detectives, marshals and sheriffs of varying effectiveness and integrity (*The Mad Ghoul* 1943, *The Killers* 1946, *His Kind of Woman, The Defiant Ones* 1958, *In Cold Blood* 1967, as Perry Smith's father, *Hang Em High* 1968, *The Night Stalker* 1972, many others). He died as the result of falling through his glass shower door in Studio City, California, at 66. Ashes scattered at sea.

5833. McGraw, John J. (John Joseph McGraw, April 7, 1873–Feb. 25, 1934) Pugnacious baseball legend played infield for the fabled Orioles and the New York Giants, taking over as their manager from 1902–1932. Generally considered the finest manager in baseball history, he took the Giants to ten pennants and five world championships in his twenty years at the helm on the Polo Grounds. Hall of Fame 1937. Family mausoleum built into hillside. Sec. L, lot 187, New Cathedral Cemetery, Baltimore, MD.

5834. McGraw, Tug (Frank Edwin McGraw, Aug. 30, 1944–Jan. 5, 2004) Exuberant, free spirited National League pitcher 1965–1984, a top reliever, with the New York Mets through 1974, known for his motto "You gotta believe" in the 1973 playoffs, and with the Philadelphia Phillies 1975 through 1984, where he helped them to the post-season in six of eight years, at his peak in 1980 with twenty saves, and two of three efforts in the world series, in the sixth game pulling them out of a bases loaded peril to give Philly its first world championship in thirty years. Diagnosed with brain cancer in early 2003, he participated in the closing ceremonies at Veterans' Stadium in September, four months before his death at 59 in the Nashville home of his son Tim. His ashes were reportedly scattered, in part at Veterans' Stadium before its implosion March 22, 2004.

5835. McGreevey, Michael T. "Nuff Ced" (c. 1870–May 6, 1939) Head of the Boston Red Sox's loyal Royal Rooters ran the Third Base Saloon at 940 Columbus Ave., near the Huntington Ave. Grounds, where the Americans began play in 1901. The Rooters' singing of *Tessie*, a song then popular, was credited with helping Boston A.L. win the first world championship, over Pittsburgh, in 1903. Their attendance and prime seats were unchallenged until sold out from under them in the 1912 series, resulting in their ejection and a riot, though harmony was later restored. Nuff Ced died at 69 and is buried as Michael McGreevy in the Catherine Rooney lot, Field of Nazareth, sec. 3, grave 152, St. Joseph's Cemetery, West Roxbury, Boston, MA.

5836. MacGregor, Clark (July 12, 1922–Feb. 10, 2003) Republican congressman from Minnesota's Third District in the 1960's, a moderate liked by both parties, went on to head CREEP (The Committee to Re-elect the President) from July to November 1972, during the unraveling story of the Watergate break-in, though he was not involved or indicted. He went on to head United Technologies, retiring in 1988. He died at 80 in Pompano Beach, Florida, the same day Nixon's press secretary Ron Ziegler died in San Diego. Cremated at Gold Coast Crematory, Fort Lauderdale, through Baird-Case-Jordan-Fannin mortuary there. Ashes sent to Gawlers mortuary, Washington, D.C., where he resided with his wife Barbara. Forest Hill Cemetery, Duluth, MN.

5837. McGrory, Mary (Aug. 22, 1918–April 21, 2004) Boston Irish born liberal reporter and political columnist from Roslindale known for elegance came to prominence covering the Army-McCarthy hearings in 1954. With the *Washington Star* from 1947 until it folded in 1981, she wrote her column from 1960, and in 1981 moved to *The Washington Post*. The recipient of many awards, notably the Pulitzer Prize in 1975, her last column appeared in March 2003. Never married, she died in Washington at 85. Mass at the Shrine of the Most Blessed Sacrament. Burial at Antrim, NH.

5838. McGrory, Matthew (May 17, 1973–Aug. 9, 2005) 7'6" actor from West Chester, Pennsylvania, in films and television during his last decade, including as Karl in *Big Fish* (2003), prior to his death at 32 in Los Angeles. Saints Peter and Paul Cemetery, Springfield, PA.

5839. McGuffey, William Holmes (Sept. 23, 1800–May 4, 1873) Editor and founder of the *McGuffey Reader*, the standard 19th century American elementary school textbook, beginning in Cincinnati in 1836 when he taught at Cincinnati College. Later professor at the University of Virginia. Buried in the University Cemetery on the edge of the campus, unmarked for many years until a stone was raised by public subscription. University of Virginia Cemetery, Charlottesville, Virginia. His brother **Alexander Hamilton McGuffey** (Aug. 13, 1816–June 3, 1896) worked on many of his books, compiled the *Eclectic Speller* in 1838 and authored the fifth Reader (1844). Sec. 77, lot 82, Spring Grove Cemetery, Cincinnati, OH.

5840. McGuire, Al (Alfred Emmanuel McGuire, Sept. 7, 1928–Jan. 26, 2001) Head coach at Belmont 1957–4 and at Marquette 1964–77, where he had a 295–80 record and won 20 or more games over eleven consecutive seasons, including the NCAA championship in 1977. Afterward he announced with Dick Enberg and Billy Packer, for NBC to 1992 and for CBS 1992–2000. Charismatic and colorful, McGuire once noted that a huge football player who had lost fifteen ponds was "like the Queen Mary losing a deck chair." He died from leukemia at 72. Mass at Gesu Church in downtown Milwaukee. Cremated at Wisconsin Memorial Park, Milwaukee, WI.

5841. McGuire, Dorothy (June 14, 1916–Sept. 13, 2001) Actress from Omaha in *Claudia* (1943), *The Enchanted Cottage, A Tree Grows in Brooklyn* (both 1945), *The Spiral Staircase* (1946), *Gentleman's Agreement* (1947), *Mr. 880* (1949), *Three Coins in the Fountain* (1954), *Friendly Persuasion* and *Old Yeller* (1957), *A Summer Place* and *The Dark at the Top of the Stairs* (1960). The widow of John Swope, airline founder and *Life* photographer, she died from heart failure at 85 in St. John's Hospital, Santa Monica, three weeks after breaking her leg. Cremated immediately at Live Oak Crematory, Monrovia, through Pierce Bros. Westwood. Scattered at sea off Los Angeles County.

5842. McGuire, Frank (Nov. 6, 1913–Oct. 11, 1994) Hall of Fame NCAA basketball coach had an unbeaten season at North Carolina in 1957. With South Carolina 1964–80. The only coach to top 100 wins at three major schools and to win Atlantic Coast Conference championships, with North Carolina in 1957 and South Carolina in 1971. St. Peter's Cemetery, Columbia, SC.

5843. McGuire, John (John J. McGuire, Oct. 22, 1910–Sept. 30, 1980) Actor in films from the late 1930's to the early 50's (*The Invisible Ghost* etc.), including the lead in *Stranger on the Third Floor* (1940), frequently recognized as the first example of pure film noir. A resident of Los Angeles and Stepside, Ireland, he died suddenly at 69 in St. Vincent's Hospital, Elm Park, Dublin. Mass at St. Mary's Church, Sandyford, Ireland. Sec. L, lot 248, grave 4, Holy Cross Cemetery, Culver City, CA.

5844. McGuire, Kathryn (Dec. 6, 1903–Oct. 10, 1978) Actress from Peoria, a 1922 Wampas Baby Star, primarily in silent films, best known opposite Buster Keaton in *Sherlock Jr.* (1924). Married to publicist George Landy, she died in Los Angeles from cancer at 74. Cremated at Pierce Bros. Chapel of the Pines Crematory. Sanctuary of Iona, 213, Inglewood Mausoleum, Inglewood Park Cemetery, Inglewood, CA.

5845. McGuire, Peter J. (July 6, 1852–Feb. 18, 1906) Father of Labor Day co-founded the United Brotherhood of Carpenters and Joiners and organized the first Labor Day parade in New York City in 1884. President Cleveland signed it into law in 1894. Along with his monument, there is a memorial with a marble statue of him at Arlington Cemetery, Pennsauken, NJ.

5846. McGurn, Machine Gun Jack (Vincent Gabaldi/Gebardi, July 2, 1902–Feb. 15, 1936) Italian born enforcer for Al Capone in Chicago in the 1920's, also a talented boxer and golfer. Long thought to have been one of the assassins in the St. Valentine's Day killings in 1929, his alibi was provided by his common-law wife, Louise Rolfe. Seven years later, after he had allegedly eliminated several assassins sent to Chicago to kill Capone (reputedly pressing coins into their hand afterward as a trademark), McGurn was surprised just after midnight in a Chicago bowling alley on the northwest side and executed by gunfire (life imitating art in a scene replayed from the 1932 film *Scarface*). The killers missed the St. Valentine's Day date by an hour, but did press a coin in his hand and left a comic valentine on the body. His younger brother **Anthony DeMora** was also killed shortly afterward, on March 2. McGurn's death certificate gives his birth as 1903 but his flat gray headstone, marked *Vincent Gebardi,* has 1902. Sec. O, block 31, grave 86, Mt. Carmel Cemetery, Hillside, IL.

5847. Machiavelli, Niccolo (May 3, 1469–June 22, 1527) Author of *The Prince,* considered the first model of political maneuvering how a nation or person might acquire and maintain power. Exiled from Florence, where he had been Secretary of the Ten. Tomb in the Church of Santa Croce, Florence, Italy.

5848. McHugh, Dorothy (Aug. 14, 1907–July 19, 1995) Former 5' Ziegfeld Follies dancer and model was paid $60 circa 1985 to fall from a chair and call out "I've fallen and I can't get up." The rest is TV commercial history. Long a colorful local character, she died in Philadelphia at 87. Ashes returned to the family.

5849. McHugh, Frank (Frank Curry McHugh, May 23, 1898–Sept. 11, 1981) Actor from Homestead, Pennsylvania, a staple at Warner Bros. in the 1930's and 40's as sidekicks to Cagney, Bogart, etc. (*One Way Passage, Mystery of the Wax Museum, Footlight Parade, A Midsummer Night's Dream, The Roaring Twenties, The Fighting 69th, All Through the Night, The Last Hurrah,* dozens more). From the early 50's he lived at Cos Cob, Connecticut. Buried with his wife and son, who died in a car wreck in 1955, in his wife's family lot; the two columned Spencer family monument is the tallest in the cemetery. Sec. 3, Fairview Cemetery, West Hartford, CT.

5850. McHugh, Jimmy (James Francis McHugh, Sr., July 10, 1894–May 23, 1969) Songwriter known for *I Can't Give You Anything But Love, The Sunny Side of the Street, I'm in the Mood For Love,* etc. He composed for both film and Broadway, beginning in 1928. Mausoleum block 33, crypt E9, Calvary Cemetery, East Los Angeles.

5851. McHugh, Matt (Jan. 22, 1894–Feb. 22, 1971) Elder brother of Frank McHugh, also in many films, generally in less endearing, more buffoonish roles. (*Street Scene, Freaks, Night of Terror, The Bells of St. Mary's, The Blue Dahlia*). Communal niche, name on master plaque, mausoleum #1, Oakwood Memorial Park, Chatsworth, CA.

5852. McInnis, Stuffy (John Phalen McInnis, Sept. 19, 1890–Feb. 16, 1960) First and third baseman from Gloucester, Massachusetts, in the majors from 1909, with the Philadelphia Athletics to 1918, the Boston Red Sox 1918–21, then Cleveland, the Boston Braves, Pittsburgh, and the Phillies. He set a first base record in 1921 with one error in 152 games, and with Boston and Cleveland 1921–22 handled 1700 chances with no errors. Rosedale Cemetery extension, Manchester-by-the-Sea, MA.

5853. McIntire, Carl (May 17, 1906–March 19, 2002) Fiery radio evangelist from the 1930's to 1970, once heard daily on over 600 stations, raged against the Catholic Church, which he labeled fascist, the Protestants, which he warned leaned toward Communism, and his fellow fundamentalists, including Billy Graham and other Southern Baptists, which he called "soggy compromisers." In 1948 he said the U.S. had a moral responsibility to strike the Soviet Union with nuclear weapons. McIntire died at Voorhees, New Jersey, at 95; he had lived in the same house at Collingswood since 1939. Overlook, lot 315 ½, grave 1, Harleigh Cemetery, Camden, NJ.

5854. McIntire, John (June 27, 1907–Jan. 30, 1991) Actor in over one hundred films from 1947–86 (*Call Northside 777, The Asphalt Jungle, Winchester 73, Psycho, Rooster Cogburn, Honkytonk Man*) played Chris Hale the wagonmaster on TV's *Wagon Train* 1961–65. His later years were spent between Laguna Beach, California, and a ranch in the Yaak region of remote northwestern Montana. He died at 83 in Los Angeles, survived by his wife, actress Jeanette Nolan. Burial through Armstrong mortuary in L.A., some thirty five miles east of their ranch. Tobacco Valley Cemetery (Eureka Cemetery), Eureka, MT.

5855. McIntire, Tim (July 19, 1944–April 15, 1986) Actor son of John McIntyre starred as Alan Freed in *American Hot Wax* (1978). He died from heart failure at 41 and was buried through Utter-McKinley Wilshire in L.A., on the John McIntyre farm, the family ranch in the remote Yaak River region of northwest Montana, Routel, Yaak, some 35 to 40 miles west of Eureka, MT.

5856. McIntosh, Burr (Aug. 21, 1862–April 28, 1942) Actor, the Cheerful Philosopher, on stage, screen and radio, played the intolerant elder who orders Lillian Gish out into the storm in Griffith's *Way Down East* (1920), dozens of other roles. Wee Kirk Churchyard, Forest Lawn, Glendale, CA.

5857. McIntyre, Christine (April 16, 1911–July 8, 1984) Actress in Three Stooges shorts 1944–1958, later a realtor. Married name Wilson. Sec Z, tier 6, grave 15, Holy Cross Cemetery, Culver City, CA.

5858. McIntyre, James (Aug. 8, 1857–Aug. 18, 1937) Half of the blackface vaudeville team McIntyre and Heath 1874–1924; they were also Long Island neighbors. McIntyre claimed to have originated "ragtime" from a buck and wing dance, though disputed. Catholic mass and burial in the Sacred Heart section at Southampton Cemetery, Long Island, NY.

5859. McIntyre, Leila *see* **Hyams.**

5860. Mack, Andrew (William McAloon, July 25, 1863–May 21, 1931) Musical comedy star through the late 19th century, appeared in a few silent films in his later years (*The Ragged Earl* 1914, *Bluebeard's Seven Wives* 1926). Thomas McAloon lot (not named on stone), sec. 16 (roadside), (2nd) Calvary Cemetery, Woodside, Queens, N.Y.C.

5861. Mack, Charles (Nov. 22, 1887–Jan. 11, 1934) Of Moran and Mack, comedy team on Oriole Records in the 20's and 30's as *Two Black Crows* not to be confused with Charles Emmett Mack. Mack was killed in an auto accident near Mesa, Arizona. Sanctuary of Refuge, crypt 6098, Memorial Terrace, Great Mausoleum, Forest Lawn, Glendale, CA.

5862. Mack, Connie (Cornelius McGillicuddy, Dec. 23, 1862–Feb. 8, 1956) Courtly gentleman of baseball wore a suit and starched collar throughout his record forty nine years managing the Philadelphia Athletics 1901–1950, winning nine pennants and five world series. Hall of Fame 1937. Granite slab with a cross on top and only *McGillicuddy* on the side. Underground vault. Sec. 27, range 1, lot 17–20, Holy Sepulchre Cemetery, Cheltenham, northwest edge of Philadelphia, PA.

5863. Mack, Helen (Helen McDougal, Nov. 13, 1913–Aug. 13, 1986) Actress in B films (*Son of Kong* 1933, *The Milky Way* 1934, *The Return of Peter Grimm, She* 1935, *The Mystery of the White Room* 1939). Later a successful radio writer and producer. No services. Married to Thomas McAvity. Cremated at Pierce Bros Chapel of the Pines in L.A. Lot 200, row 3 west, grave 3, Westwood Memorial Park, west Los Angeles.

5864. Mack, Joan (June 19, 1930–July 11, 1976) TV producer; her boulder with a plaque reads *I am not dead. I have just become inhuman.* Green River Cemetery, East Hampton, Long Island, NY.

5865. Mack, Nila (Oct. 24, 1891–Jan. 20, 1953) The original host of radio's *Let's Pretend* from 1934, sponsored after a few years by Cream of Wheat. Arkansas City, KS.

5866. Mack, Ted (William Edward Maguiness, Feb. 12, 1904–July 12, 1976) Greeley, Colorado, born host of the Original Amateur Hour, after Major Bowes, lived at Irvington, New York. He died in North Tarrytown from cancer at 72. Ashes to the widow.

5867. Mack, Willard (Charles McLaughlin, Sept. 17, 1877–Nov. 18, 1934) Playwright and screen-writer 1916–1934 from Morrisburg, Ontario, authored *The Monster* (1925), the play and script *the Dove* (1927), *His Glorious Night, Madame X* (1929), *A Free Soul* (play), *Night of Terror* (1933), many others, He died at home in Los Angeles at 57 from heart and kidney failure related to ALS. Taken to a holding crypt at Calvary Cemetery, and sent January 9, 1935, to Salt Lake City.

Mausoleum, Corridor of Memories, tier B, crypt 11, Larkin Sunset Lawn Cemetery, Salt Lake City, UT.

5868. Mackaill, Dorothy (March 4, 1903–Aug. 12, 1990) Actress from Hull, England, in Ziegfeld's *Midnight Frolics* and *Sally*. In films 1920–1938, when she retired to Hawaii. She appeared in a few episodes of *Hawaii Five-O* thirty years later. Found dead at 87 in her room in Honolulu, her ashes were scattered off Oahu by her boyfriend as she requested, from the area where they often sat and played cards.

5869. McKay, Claude (Sept. 15, 1889–May 22, 1948) Jamaica born writer (*Home to Harlem* 1928, *A Long Way From Home* 1937). Services were in Harlem but without his body, which arrived late from Chicago. Epitaph *Piece o' my rebel heart.* (2nd) Calvary Cemetery, sec. 42, Woodside, Queens, N.Y.C.

5870. MacKay, Fulton (Aug. 12, 1922–June 6, 1987) Scottish actor in British and American films and television from *The Brave Don't Cry* in 1952 (Ben in *Local Hero* 1983, The Captain on *Fraggle Rock*). O.B.E. Married to actress **Sheila Manahan** (Jan. 1, 1924–March 29, 1988) who appeared in *Seven Days to Noon, The Story of Esther Costello, Only Two Can Play.* Upright stone. Plot JC 187, East Sheen Cemetery, Surrey.

5871. McKay, Wanda (Dorothy McKay, June 22, 1915–April 11, 1996) Actress in films of the 40's (at Monogram in *Bowery at Midnight, Voodoo Man,* etc.) and 50's, married to Hoagy Carmichael. Columbarium of Courage, niche 1228, Garden of Honor, Forest Lawn, Glendale, CA.

5872. McKay, Gardner (George Cadogan Gardner McKay, June 10, 1932–Nov. 21, 2001) Actor and writer played freelance skipper Adam Troy on TV's *Adventures in Paradise* 1959–1962. He then left acting to travel before settling at Koko Head, five miles from Honolulu, as a playwright (*Sea Marks*) and novelist (*Toyers*), reading *Stories of the Wind* Sunday nights on Hawaiian public radio until shortly before his death at his home from prostate cancer at 69. Cremated the same day, his ashes were buried with his father, Hugh Dean McKay. The granite tablet lists his full and professional name, dates and is inscribed with a poem by him: *Now comes the end of the day/ Now comes the rush of night/ The luminous sea turns grey/ The faces of friends lose their light./ I have sailed toward a high steep island/ Where my dreams would all come to be./ Never wanting to be done with the ocean/ Till each wave was done with me.* Hebron Cemetery, Shepherdsville, KY.

5873. McKaye, Dorothy *see* **Ray Raymond.**

5874. McKean, Thomas (March 30, 1734–June 24, 1817) Signer of the Declaration of Independence from Delaware. Three term governor of Pennsylvania (1799–1808). Marble box-slab near tree. Sec. G, Laurel Hill Cemetery, Philadelphia, PA.

5875. McKechnie, Bill (William Boyd McKechnie, Aug. 7, 1886–Oct. 29, 1965) Manager with Pittsburgh 1922–26, Boston N.L. 1930–37, Cincinnati

1938–46, the only manager in the N.L. to win pennants with three different clubs (Pittsburgh 1925, St. Louis 1928, and Cincinnati 1939 and 1940). World series wins in 1925 and 1940. Hall of Fame 1962. Same section, near fellow hall member Paul Waner. Sec. L, lot 185, space 1, Manasota Memorial Park, Bradenton (Sarasota), FL.

5876. MacKenna, Kenneth (Leo Mielziner, Aug. 19, 1899–Jan. 15, 1962) Actor and director on stage returned to character parts in film and TV in later years. Married to actress Mary Phillips, following her divorce from Humphrey Bogart. Iris Columbarium, niche 27261, Iris Terrace, top level, Great Mausoleum, Forest Lawn, Glendale, CA.

5877. McKenna, Siobhan (Siobhan Nic Cionnait Aisteoir, May 24, 1923–Nov. 16, 1986) Belfast born actress with the Abbey Theatre in several films, including Mary in *King of Kings* (1961), Nora in *Of Human Bondage* (1964) and Anna in *Dr. Zhivago* (1965). She died in Dublin from cancer at 63. There is a plaque in her memory in the lobby of the Gramercy Park Hotel in Manhattan. Stone cross on a circular base. Rahoon Cemetery, Galway, Ireland.

5878. McKenzie, Alfred (Jan. 3, 1918–March 30, 1998) Black bomber pilot with the Tuskegee Airmen during World War II was among 100 who refused to accommodate the segregation policies of an officers' club at Seymour, Indiana, and were to be court-martialed, but the criminal charges were dropped and the reprimands removed in 1995. He later led a successful discrimination suit against his employer, the Government Printing Office, in 1972. An award for funding civil rights lawsuits was established in his name in 1994. Columbarium court 1, EE, stack 14, niche 1, Arlington National Cemetery, Arlington, VA.

5879. MacKenzie, Gisele (Marie Marguerite Louise Gisele LaFleche, Jan. 10, 1927–Sept. 5, 2003) Singer and violinist from Winnipeg, Manitoba, sang on CBC radio in *Meet Gisele* 1946–50, in Hollywood on *Club 15, The Mario Lanza Show,* and from 1953–57 starred on *Your Hit Parade* as well as recording albums for Capitol Records, touring with Jack Benny and appearing frequently on his TV show from 1955. She also acted, primarily in television guest spots, from *Kraft Television Theatre* to *Boy Meets World.* Divorced from bandleader Robert Shuttleworth and later businessman Robert Klein, she died in Burbank, California, from colon cancer at 76. Cremated through J.T. Oswald mortuary, North Hollywood. Ashes to family in North Hollywood, CA.

5880. McKernan, Ronald "Pigpen" (Sept. 8, 1945–March 8, 1973) Keyboard player with The Grateful Dead, the first of three of their keyboard players to die young, was found dead in his San Francisco apartment from cirrhosis at 27. Hillview sub sec. 16, lot 374, Alta Mesa Memorial Park, Palo Alto, CA.

5881. Mackey, Bill (William C. Gretsinger, Dec. 15, 1927–July 29, 1951) Formula One race driver killed in a mishap at Winchester Speedway; Cecil Green died there the same day, and Walt Brown in a wreck at the Williams Grove Speedway in Pennsylvania. Sec. 6, lot 11, grave 12, Dayton Memorial Park Cemetery, Dayton, OH.

5882. McKinley, Chuck (Jan. 5, 1941–Aug. 11, 1986) A top American amateur tennis star, won the Wimbledon Singles title. He died from a brain tumor in Dallas at 45. Buried with his parents. Sec E, lot 390, Mt. Lebanon Cemetery, St. Louis, MO.

5883. McKinley, Ray (June 8, 1910–May 7, 1995) Musician and bandleader of the 1930's and 40's led the Glenn Miller Orchestra in the 1950's and 60's. He died in Largo, Florida, at 84. National Cremation Society; ashes returned to the widow.

5884. McKinley, William (Jan. 29, 1843–Sept. 14, 1901) 25th President of the U.S., former Ohio governor, congressman and senator, conducted his 1896 front porch campaign from his Canton, Ohio, home (repeated by Harding in 1920), defeating William Jennings Bryan then and again in 1900. A popular president known for his amiability, conservative policies and devotion to his epileptic and reclusive wife **Ida Saxton McKinley** (June 8, 1847–May 26, 1907), he presided over the Spanish American War and subsequent annexations, leading the way for America's role as a 20th century world power. In the Temple of Music at the Pan-American Exposition in Buffalo, shaking hands, a man with a bandaged hand, anarchist immigrant Leon Czolgosz, pressed it against the president's stomach and fired. He was taken to the Milburn mansion, the home of the exposition's director on Delaware Avenue, and was thought to be recovering, but the bullet could not be extracted; his death after eight days was due to the destruction of the pancreas and to gangrene. Today the lives of both Garfield and McKinley would possibly have been saved. Funerals followed in Washington and in Canton, where the coffin was placed in a stone vault in Westlawn Cemetery until the massive McKinley Tomb was completed and dedicated by Theodore Roosevelt in 1907. It is a large, domed memorial adjacent Westlawn Cemetery and atop a long flight of steps at the end of a long sunken garden. A bronze statue of McKinley reading his last speech stands on a pedestal half way up the steps. Inside the circular interior on marble pedestals are the black polished sarcophagi of the president and his wife, who died in 1907, and their two baby daughters, interred in the inner wall of the rotunda. McKinley Tomb, Canton, OH.

5885. McKinney, Florine (Dec. 13, 1909/1912–July 28, 1975) Blonde actress from Mart, Texas, in supporting to roles in films 1932–37 (*The Miracle Man, Horse Feathers, Cynara, Beauty For Sale, David Copperfield* 1935 as Emily, *Night Life of the Gods*). In bits and uncredited parts until 1940–49. She died in Van Nuys at 63. Cremated (as Florine McKinney aka Florine Guest) at Roosevelt Memorial Park, Gardena, July 30. Inurned as Florine McKinney. Devotion (wall of niches), niche 9, row L, space 1, Valhalla Memorial Park, North Hollywood, CA.

5886. Mackworth, Margaret Haig Thomas, Viscountess Rhondda (June 12, 1883/86–July 20, 1958) Daughter of Welsh colliery magnate in the Rhondda Valley **David Thomas, Viscount Rhonda** (March 26, 1856–July 3, 1918). She was the wife of Sir Humphrey Mackworth and a strong supporter of the Women's Social and Political Union, including its arson campaign; sent to prison for trying to blow up a postal box with a chemical bomb, she was released after a hunger strike. Both were aboard the *Lusitania*'s last voyage in May 1915 and survived the sinking to be reunited at Queenstown. Upon his death three years later, she attempted to succeed to his seat in the House of Lords but was kept out. She went on to found and edit the literary magazine *Time and Tide*. Viscount Rhondda was cremated at Golders Green, London. His daughter was cremated forty years later at Putney Vale, London. Marked by a stone tabletop foundation supporting an obelisk, he is identified as *Viscount Rhondda of Llanwern, Privy Councillor, Member of Parliament for 22 years, President of the Local Government Board and Food Controller in the Great War... He counted not his life dear unto himself. Blessed Be the Pure in Heart.* His daughter's inscription ends *Proprietor and Editor of Time Tide for 31 years. Rest in Peace.* Both of their ashes were buried, as was his wife and her mother, Sybil Margaret Haig Thomas (1857–1941) in the churchyard at Llanwern, Monmouthshire, Wales.

5887. McLaglen, Victor (Dec. 10, 1886–Nov. 7, 1959) Burly English actor, once a boxer defeated by Jack Johnson, was teamed with Edmund Lowe as Quirt and Flag in *What Price Glory* (1926) and won an Oscar as Gippo Nolan in John Ford's *The Informer* (1935). He remained a favorite of Ford's, appearing in several of his other films (*The Lost Patrol, Wee Willie Winkie, Fort Apache, She Wore A Yellow Ribbon, The Quiet Man*) and other epics, often regarding the British in India (*Gunga Din*). Niche G641at far right, same wall as Humphrey Bogart, Columbarium of Eternal Light, Garden of Memory (pvt.), Forest Lawn, Glendale, CA.

5888. MacLane, Barton (Dec. 25, 1902–Jan. 1, 1969) Actor from Columbia, South Carolina, former football star at Wesleyan, in hard boiled roles through the 1930's and 40's, primarily at Warners (*G-Men, The Walking Dead, San Quentin, High Sierra, The Maltese Falcon, Dr. Jekyll & Mr. Hyde* [MGM 1941], *The Mummy's Ghost* [Universal], *Cry of the Werewolf* [Columbia], *The Treasure of the Sierra Madre*). Last seen in a recurring role on television's *I Dream of Jeannie*. He died from pneumonia in Santa Monica. Block (Memorial) F, sec. 5460, lot 5, Valhalla Memorial Park, North Hollywood, CA.

5889. MacLaren, Mary (Jan. 19, 1900–Nov. 9, 1985) Silent screen actress, once a beauty, made the news again in her old age when authorities in Los Angeles sought a conservatorship based on her poor liv-

ing conditions and questionable sanity. Interred as Mary MacLaren MacDonald. Crypt 6824, Dawn of Tomorrow, Forest Lawn, Glendale, CA.

5890. McLaren, Wayne *see* **The Marlboro Man.**

5891. McLaughlin, Emily (Dec. 1, 1928–April 26, 1991) Actress known as Nurse Jesse Brewer on the ABC soap opera *General Hospital* 1963–1991. The widow of actor Jeffrey Hunter, she died from cancer at 61 and was buried with him (Henry McKinnies). Olive sec., lot 141, Glen Haven Memorial Park, Sylmar, CA.

5892. MacLean, Alistair (Alistair Stuart MacLean, April 21, 1922–Feb. 2, 1987) Scottish writer, a POW of the Japanese during World War II, published his best-seller *H.M.S. Ulysses* in 1955, followed by *The Guns of Navarone, Force Ten From Navarone, Ice Station Zebra, Where Eagles Dare*—all made into popular films. Though his works were characterized by some as formulaic, with a band of men repeatedly led by a hero into a dangerous climate with a ruthless enemy and usually a treacherous character who upsets the mission, eighteen of his books selling over a million copies. On his boulder-monument is the epitaph *Come my friends/ Tis not too late/ To seek a newer world.* Protestant churchyard, Celigny, Switzerland.

5893. McLean, David *see* **The Marlboro Man.**

5894. MacLean, Donald Duart (May 25, 1913–March 6, 1983) Cambridge graduate with MI5, the British Security Service, passed information to the Communists, along with two others and Kim Philby, who warned him in time for his escape to Moscow in 1951. Ashes buried in secret at his parents' grave, with no mention on their monument. Church of the Holy Trinity Cemetery, Penn, Buckinghamshire, near Oxford.

5895. MacLean, Douglas (Jan. 10, 1890–July 9, 1967) Silent screen actor turned to producing and writing with the coming of sound. Vale of Memory sec., lot 1046, Forest Lawn, Glendale, CA.

5896. McLean, Evalyn Walsh (Aug. 1, 1886–April 26, 1947) The most famed owner and victim of the ominous Hope Diamond was a Washington socialite married to publisher Edward McLean. She acquired the diamond in 1923 and promptly lost two friends she had shown it to. Shortly after, the McLeans' friend President Harding died amidst mounting scandal, their nine year old son was killed by a car, they divorced and he died in a mental institution, she was seriously injured in a car wreck, and her daughter committed suicide by sleeping pills. The Hope Diamond is now in the Smithsonian Institution. Evalyn Walsh McLean died in Washington, D.C. at 60. Family mausoleum, sec. 1., lot 6, Rock Creek Cemetery, Washington, D.C.

5897. McLean, Wilmer (May 3, 1814–June 3, 1882) Virginian who had the distinction of having the Civil War begin and end on his property. He lived in 1861 at Bull Run, and after the battle there in July, removed west, away from the fray, to Appomattox Court House, where on April 9, 1865, Lee surrendered to Grant in his front parlor. St. Paul's Cemetery, Alexandria, VA.

5898. MacLeish, Archibald (May 7, 1892–April 20, 1982) American poet, advisor to and poet of the New Deal. His *Collected Works 1917–1952* won a Pulitzer Prize. He also served as Librarian of Congress during World War II. He died in Boston. Name and dates engraved on a large rock. Pine Grove Cemetery, Conway, MA.

5899. McLeland, Wayne (Wayne Gaffney McLeland, Aug. 29, 1924–May 9, 2004) Baseball player from Iowa dubbed Nubbin, voted Texas pitcher of the year in the minors in 1950, pitched for thirteen seasons in the majors, with the Detroit Tigers 1951–2 and St. Louis Cardinals. No marker. Sec. 11, lot 390, Forest Park Lawndale, Houston, TX.

5900. McLeod, Catherine (July 2, 1921–May 11, 1997) Actress in films from the mid 1940s, wife of Don Keefer, whose headache induced outburst "Mother please, I'd rather do it myself!" on a TV commercial became a national phrase in the 1960's. Block 13-S, lot 14, Woodlawn Cemetery, Santa Monica, CA.

5901. McLeod, Norman Z. (Sept. 20, 1895–Jan. 26, 1964) Director did the Marx Brothers' first two pictures made in Hollywood, *Monkey Business* (1931) and *Horse Feathers* (1932), as well as *Alice in Wonderland, Topper* and later several with Danny Kaye, Bob Hope, etc. Court of Freedom, space 2387, along the sidewalk, Forest Lawn, Glendale, CA.

5902. McLuhan, Marshall (Herbert M. McLuhan, July 21, 1911–Dec. 31, 1980) Communications theorist whose concept that the cumulative electronic transference of ideas to the masses became more significant than their content, condensed into the trademark phrase "The medium is the message." He authored several books and taught in Toronto until his first stroke in 1979 and died from a second one a year later. His flush marker reads *The truth shall make you free.* Holy Cross Cemetery, Toronto, Ontario.

5903. MacMahon, Aline (May 3, 1899–Oct. 12, 1991) Actress from McKeesport, Pennsylvania, in supporting roles on stage and in forty three films, including *Five Star Final* (1931), *Golddiggers of 1933, Ah, Wilderness, Kind Lady* (1935), *Dragon Seed* (AA nom, 1944), *The Search* (1948), *The Eddie Cantor Story* (1953), *All the Way Home* (1963). Widow of architect Clarence Stein. She died in Manhattan at 92. Cremated at Garden State Crematory through the Frank E. Campbell mortuary, her ashes were buried with her parents, marked by a boulder designed by her husband with her name and dates cut into it. Sec. 6, lot 124, Mount Pleasant Cemetery, Hawthorne, NY.

5904. McMahon, Horace (May 17, 1907–Aug. 17, 1971) Gangster or cop in many films (*Detective Story* 1951, *The Detective* 1968) played Lt. Parker in TV's *The Naked City* 1959–1963. He died from a heart ailment in a Norwalk, Connecticut, hospital. Buried with his family. John T. McMahon plot, with all names listed on the one large pink stone cross marking the plot. West side, lot 30, St. Mary's Cemetery, Norwalk, CT.

5905. McManus, George (Jan. 23, 1884–Oct. 22, 1954) Creator of the comic strip *Bringing Up Father* with Maggie and Jiggs from 1913–1954. Mausoleum on a wooded hillside, with his cartoon signature over the door. Interior of Parkview sec., in from Chestnut Ave., Woodlawn Cemetery, the Bronx, N.Y.C.

5906. McManus, Louis (May 31, 1898–April 17, 1968) Film artist did titles for Mack Sennett and worked long at Hal Roach Studios, but is noted for having designed the television awards' statue — a winged woman holding an atom — in the image of his wife, though she did not inspire its name. Originally called an Immy — the nickname for early image orthicon cameras — it was changed to Emmy. Sec. D, lot 384, grave 5, San Fernando Mission Cemetery, Mission Hills, CA.

5907. McMein, Neysa (Marjorie McMein, Jan. 24, 1888–May 12, 1949) Commercial artist, illustrator and colorful socialite, a member of the selected wits of the Algonquin Round Table in the New York of the 1920's and 30's. Married to John Gordon Baragwanath. Services at Holy Trinity Episcopal Church on East 88th St. Cremated May 14 at Fresh Pond Crematory, Middle Village, Queens, the ashes were returned to R.S. King mortuary at 251 West 80th, Manhattan (out of business and no records extant).

5908. MacMillan, Donald (Nov. 10, 1874–Sept. 7, 1970) Navy admiral known for his explorations of the Arctic. He led thirteen expeditions from 1924–1957, locating coal deposits, charting glaciers present and past. New sec. 1, lot 171, grave 1, Provincetown town Cemetery, Provincetown (tip of Cape Cod), MA.

5909. McMillan, Kenneth (Kenneth Harry McMillan, Sept. 12, 1932–Jan. 8, 1989) Stout character actor from Brooklyn often in coarse, abusive roles in films of the 1970's and 80's, appeared in *Serpico, The Taking of Pelham One Two Three, Salem's Lot* (as the constable), *Ragtime* (as fire chief Willie), *Dune, Cat's Eye, Runaway Train.* He died in greater Los Angeles at 56 from liver failure. Ashes to residence.

5910. McMillan, Roy (Roy David McMillan, July 17, 1929–Nov. 2, 1997) Shortstop with the Cincinnati Reds 1951–60, Braves and Mets 1961–66. Lifetime fielding average of .972. Sec. L, block 515, grave 1 northeast, Willow Wild Cemetery, Bonham, TX.

5911. McMullin, Fred (Oct. 13, 1891–Nov. 21, 1952) Pinch hitter with the Chicago White Sox, one of eight banned for life by Commissioner Landis in 1921 for having thrown the 1919 series to Cincinnati. He died in Los Angeles at 61. Dahlia plot, lot 290, div. A, Inglewood Park Cemetery, Inglewood, CA.

5912. MacMurray, Fred (Frederick Martin MacMurray, Aug. 30, 1908–Nov. 5, 1991) Saxophone player from Kankakee, Illinois, in amiable roles in films from the mid 1930's, some dark and somber (*Double Indemnity* 1944, *The Caine Mutiny* 1954, *The Apartment* 1960). The light, flippant persona came through in *The Egg and I*, *The Absent Minded Professor* and as Steve Douglas in TV's *My Three Sons* 1960–1972. He died at 83 from pulmonary edema and leukemia at St. John's Hospital, Santa Monica. Cremated through Gates-Kingsley-Gates. In 2002, a photo of him circa *Double Indemnity* was placed at the bottom corner of his crypt two tiers below John Candy. In 2005 his wife, actress June Haver, was interred in their crypt and his urn placed in her coffin. Block 84, room 7, crypt D1, Holy Cross Cemetery mausoleum, Culver City, CA.

5913. McNair, Ronald E. (Oct. 21, 1950–Jan. 28, 1986) Mission specialist aboard the space shuttle Challenger lost his life with six others in the explosion shortly after lift off. The capsule and bodies were recovered in the spring. Dr. McNair was buried May 17 in his home town. Rest Lawn Cemetery, Lake City, SC.

5914. McNally, Dave (Oct. 31, 1942–Dec. 1, 2002) Three time All-Star pitcher won twenty or more games in four consecutive seasons 1968–1971 but gained his greatest fame in 1975 when he retired, though the Montreal Expos offered him $125,000 to sign. He joined Andy Messersmith of the Los Angeles Dodgers in a grievance filed by the Major League Baseball Players Association, claiming teams could not renew their contracts in perpetuity. The decision in Messersmith and McNally's favor issued by arbitrator Peter Seitz on December 23, 1975, put an end to baseball's reserve clause and opened the door for free agency. McNally died from cancer at 60 in his hometown of Billings, Montana, where he was born. Yellowstone Valley Memorial Park, Billings, MT.

5915. McNally, Stephen (Horace Vincent McNally, July 29, 1911–June 4, 1994) New York born actor in films from the 1940's (*Thirty Seconds Over Tokyo* 1944, *Bewitched* 1945, *Criss Cross* 1949), best known as the heavy in *Johnny Belinda* (1948). Plaque with his real name. Sec. Y, tier 14, grave 35, Holy Cross Cemetery, Culver City, CA.

5916. McNamara, Edward (Aug. 13, 1884–Nov. 9, 1944) Vaudeville and stage actor known as the Singing Cop. Few films include *I Am A Fugitive From A Chain Gang*, *20,000 Years in Sing Sing*, *Strawberry Blonde*, *Arsenic and Old Lace*. Upright stone notes *A Player*. West Tisbury Cemetery, West Tisbury, Martha's Vineyard, MA.

5917. McNamara, Maggie (June 18, 1928–Feb. 18, 1978) Petite New York born actress in the stage and screen (1953) production of Otto Preminger's *The Moon is Blue*, also in *Three Coins in the Fountain* (1954) and *The Cardinal* (1963), some TV (*Twilight Zone* episode *Ring-a-Ding Girl* 1963) and other stage work. Away from performing for fifteen years, she took her life with sleeping pills at 49 in New York.

Divorced from David Swift. Buried as Marguerite McNamara February 22. Unmarked. Sec. 18, row MM, grave 165, St. Charles Cemetery, Farmingdale, Long Island, NY.

5918. McNamee, Graham (July 10, 1888–May 9, 1942) The dean of radio announcers through the 1920's and 30's did various programs and sports. Cathedral G sec., Mt. Calvary Cemetery, Columbus, OH.

5919. McNear, Howard (Jan. 27, 1905–Jan. 3, 1969) Doc Adams on radio's *Gunsmoke* was in several films (*Anatomy of A Murder*, *Voyage to the Bottom of the Sea*) but best known as Mayberry's Floyd the barber on *The Andy Griffith Show* 1960–68. Columbarium 323, row A, niche 12, Los Angeles/Sawtelle National Cemetery, Westwood, west Los Angeles.

5920. McNeil, Claudia (Aug. 13, 1917–Nov. 25, 1993) Baltimore born stage actress, singer and dancer, played Sidney Poitier's mother in Lorraine Hansberry's *A Raisin in the Sun*, filmed in 1961. She appeared primarily on the stage and made only a few other films. Died at the Actors Fund Home, Englewood, New Jersey. Actors Fund of America plot, lot 329, Kensico Cemetery, Valhalla, NY.

5921. McNeill, Don (Donald Thomas McNeill, Dec. 23, 1907–May 7, 1996) Orchestra leader and radio announcer hosted *Don McNeill's Breakfast Club* mornings from Chicago and to the armed forces for nearly 36 years, from June 23, 1933–December 27, 1968. He died at 88 in Evanston, Illinois. Sec. 34, block 13, lot 10, grave 6, All Saints Cemetery, Des Plaines, IL.

5922. Macon, Dave (Oct. 7, 1870–March 23, 1952) Comedic Tennessee born banjo player was a star at the Grand Ole Opry in Nashville on radio. His marker notes *The world's most outstanding banjoist*. Coleman Cemetery, near Woodbury, TN.

5923. McParland, James (March 22, 1844–May 18, 1919) Pinkerton detective worked against the Molly Maguires, Irish trade unionists active in the anthracite coal mines of western Pennsylvania 1862–78. As a result of his infiltration, eighteen men were hanged. Sec. 2, block 1A, grave 3, Mt. Olivet Cemetery, Denver, CO.

5924. McPartland, Jimmy (March 15, 1907–March 13, 1991) Chicago born cornet player replaced Bix Beiderbecke with the Wolverines at seventeen, later working with Benny Goodman and Gene Krupa in the distinctive Chicago Jazz style of the late 20's. He played with bands including Ben Pollack and Jack Teagarden during World War II. After serving with the Army in Europe he continued playing, frequently with English pianist Marian Page, whom he married. He died at Port Washington, Long Island, from lung cancer two days before his 84th birthday. Rev. John Garcia Gensel, the Jazz Pastor of St. Peter's Lutheran Church in Manhattan, conducted the service, with burial of the ashes in Chicago, or retained by his widow.

5925. McPhail. Addie (Addie Dukes, July 15, 1905–April 14, 2003) Silent screen actress from White Plains, Kentucky, formerly married to songwriter Lindsay McPhail, in various comedies (*Midnight Daddies, Three Sisters*) was directed by Roscoe "Fatty" Arbuckle in the short *Up A Tree* (1930) and others before becoming his third wife in Erie, Pennsylvania, in June 1932. He died in New York a year later. She retired by 1940, and for years was a volunteer nurse at the Motion Picture Country Home in Woodland Hills, California. Divorced from her last husband (Shelton), she died at 97 in Canoga Park. Cremated by Crawford mortuary. Ashes April 17 to her granddaughter, to be scattered.

5926. McPhail, Douglas (April 16, 1914–Dec. 6, 1944) Singer in films of the 1930's (*Born to Dance, Maytime, Sweethearts, Babes in Arms*) died at 30 from the effects of poison. Sec. 206, row B, site 13, Los Angeles National Cemetery, west Los Angeles.

5927. MacPhail, Larry (Leland Stanford MacPhail, Feb. 3, 1890–Oct. 1, 1975) Innovative baseball executive introduced the night game at Crosley Field while heading Cincinnati in 1935. President of the Dodgers (pennant winners in 1941) and the Yankees (series winners in 1947). He put lights in Ebbets Field and Yankee Stadium and began plane travel and pension plans. Hall of Fame 1978. Rose family obelisk on lot with flush bronze military marker. Block 5, lot 178, Elkland Township Cemetery, Cass City, MI.

5928. McPhatter, Clyde (Nov. 15, 1932–June 13, 1972) Lead singer with the Drifters in the late 1950's recorded also with Billy Ward's group and as a solo (*Lover Please, A Lover's Question*). Listed as 41 though the dates on his plaque make him 39, he died from an apparent heart attack while visiting friends in the Bronx. He resided at Teaneck, New Jersey. Buried through Nesbit mortuary. Flush bronze plaque. Sec. O, lot 121 near maple tree, D4, George Washington Memorial Park, Paramus, NJ.

5929. McPhee, Bid (John Alexander McPhee, Nov. 1, 1859–Jan. 3, 1943) 19th century infielder from Massequa, New York. He died in San Diego. Hall of Fame 2000. Bonham Bros. Mortuary Columbarium (now Cypress View Crematory and Mausoleum), North Building, Shepherd Lane, sec. (corridor) 4, niche 98, San Diego, CA.

5930. McPherson, Aimee Semple (Oct. 9, 1890–Sept. 27, 1944) Flamboyant evangelist of the 1920's founded her International Church of the Four Square Gospel in 1918. Her Angelus Temple in Los Angeles was funded by the public. She vanished in 1926 and was found living with a man, but that and other indiscretions were credited to a nervous breakdown. Her death from an overdose of barbiturates at 53 was ruled accidental. White sarcophagus with angels kneeling at either end. Sunrise Slope, Forest Lawn Glendale, CA.

5931. MacPherson, Christina Rutherford (June 19, 1864–March 27, 1936) Composer of *Waltzing Matilda*. The words were by A.B. "Banjo" Paterson (*q.v.* 1864–1941). St. Kilda Cemetery, Melbourne, Australia.

5932. McPherson, James Birdseye (Nov. 14, 1828–July 22, 1864) Union General fought at Forts Henry and Donelson, Shiloh and Vicksburg, with the Army of the Tennessee. At Atlanta, Sherman sent him east of the city to cut off railway links with Richmond. An amiable man and a favorite of Sherman's, when he encountered Confederate troops who ordered him to surrender, he doffed his hat and smiled politely before turning to ride away, and was shot in the back. Sherman covered the body with a flag and wept, shortly afterward routing John Bell Hood from the city by spurring on Union troops with the cry "McPherson and revenge, boys!" Fearing Confederate bombardment would ignite the building, he had the body removed to Marietta and on to Clyde, Ohio, where it was buried in the cemetery later named for him near his birthplace. A large monument and his statue was erected over him on a mound just inside the entrance. Out-of-the-way Clyde was later used as the model for Sherwood Anderson's *Winesburg, Ohio* and as the setting for the film *Welcome Home, Roxy Carmichael*. McPherson Cemetery, Clyde, OH.

5933. MacPherson, Jeannie (May 18, 1887–Aug 26 1946) Actress 1908–1915 turned writer for DeMille (*The Ten Commandments* 1923, *King of Kings* 1927, *The Buccaneer*). Chapel of the Psalms, (Sequoia) Colonnade columbarium, south wall, tier 2, niche 17, Hollywood Forever Cemetery, Hollywood (Los Angeles), CA.

5934. McQueen, Butterfly (Thelma McQueen, Jan. 8, 1911–Dec. 23, 1995) Actress from Tampa was given her nickname after dancing the Butterfly Ballet with a Harlem theatre group. On Broadway by 1937 in *Brown Sugar*, she was best known on film as Prissy, the timid, tearful slave with the squeaky voice in *Gone With the Wind* (1939). Later active in theatre, she received her bachelor's degree in political science from the City College of New York in 1975 at 64. She died from burns at 84 when a kerosene heater in her home outside Augusta, Georgia, caught fire. Donated to the Medical College of Georgia at Augusta. Ashes later buried in Emory sec., grave 9 (mass grave), City of Decatur Cemetery, Decatur, GA.

5935. McQueen, Steve (March 24, 1930–Nov. 7, 1980) Rugged actor from Indianapolis at his peak in the 1960's went from the juvenile lead in *The Blob* (1958) to tight lipped tough, heroic roles in *The Great Escape* 1963, *The Cincinnati Kid, The Thomas Crown Affair, Bullitt* (1968), *Grand Prix, The Getaway* (1972), *Papillon* (1974), *The Towering Inferno* (1975), *Tom Horn* (1979) and *The Hunter* (1980). Living on his Santa Paula ranch with a wealth of old cars, toys and planes, he received considerable publicity in his last year while seeking alternative treatments for cancer in Mexico, including laetrile. He died in Juarez from a heart attack following cancer surgery at 50. A memorial service was held at his Santa Paula, California, ranch, where a large white cross was later erected in his memory on a hilltop by a friend. Cremated in Ventura, California, his ashes were scattered by two friends from his yellow Stearman biplane over the Pacific on November 15. His mother **Julian McQueen** (1910–1965) is buried at Forest Lawn, Glendale, with the remembrance *Love from your son Steve*. His daughter **Terry** (June 5, 1959–March 19, 1998) died at 38 from respiratory ailments several months after a liver transplant and was buried with a vial of his ashes she had kept. Rose plaque. Westwood Memorial Park, west Los Angeles.

5936. McRae, Carmen (April 8, 1920–Nov. 10, 1994) Harlem born smoky voiced jazz singer began at the Apollo, sang with Earl Hines and Count Basie, adept at scat on a par with Vaughan and Fitzgerald. She died at 74 from a stroke in Beverly Hills, requesting no services or memorial but to be remembered for her music. Among her signature songs were *God Bless the Child* and *I've Got You Under My Skin*. Ashes scattered at sea through Armstrong mortuary three miles off Marina Del Ray on November 17.

5937. MacRae, Gordon (March 12, 1921–Jan. 24, 1986) Singer and actor known as Curly in *Oklahoma* (1955). He later became a spokesman for AA until his death from oral cancer at 64 in Bryan Hospital, Lincoln, Nebraska. His upright dark charcoal gray stone bears the lines *Nothing is lost in God's world* and the tribute from then President Reagan: *Gordon will always be remembered wherever beautiful music is heard*. Sec. 4, along the road, Wyuka Cemetery, Lincoln, NE.

5938. MacRae, Meredith (May 30, 1944–July 14, 2000) Actress daughter of Gordon and Sheila MacRae first appeared with her father in *By The Light of the Silvery Moon* (1953) and later played (the third incarnation of) Billie Jo on TV's *Petticoat Junction* 1966–70. She was also on *My Three Sons* and hosted *Mid-Morning L.A.* for eight years in the 1980's. The wife of Phil Neal, she died from brain cancer at 56 in Manhattan Beach, California, and, as her will specified, her ashes were buried at sea through the Neptune Society off Los Angeles County July 17.

5939. McRae, Norman (Sept. 26, 1947–July 25, 2003) Pitcher from Elizabeth, New Jersey, with the Detroit Tigers 1969–70 and the Washington Senators 1970–72, afterward joining the Mexican League, with the Los Dorados de Chihuahua to 1981. He retired to Garland, Texas. Garden of Serenity, lot 48, block B, Restland Memorial Park, Dallas, TX.

5940. MacReady, George (Aug. 29, 1899–July 2, 1973) Character actor from Rhode Island with whispery, conspiratorial delivery, usually cast as a villain. Films include *The Seventh Cross* (1944), *I Love a Mystery* (1945), *Gilda* (1946), *The Big Clock* (1948), *Paths of Glory* (1957). His last role was as recluse Martin Peyton on the prime time soap opera *Peyton Place* in the mid 1960's. Sources list his birth as 1909, but the death certificate shows it a decade earlier and lists his

age as 73. He donated his body to the UCLA School of Medicine.

5941. McReynolds, Jim (James Monroe McReynolds, Feb. 13, 1927–Dec. 31, 2002) Tenor from Carfax, Virginia, with the Grand Ole Opry for thirty-eight years, known for his bluegrass and gospel vocal harmonies with his brother Jesse. He died from cancer at 75 in Gallatin, Tennessee. Burial in the McReynolds family cemetery at Carfax, near Coeburn, Wise County, VA.

5942. McSherry, John (Sept. 11, 1944–April 1, 1996) National League umpire, a 25 year veteran, collapsed and died from sudden cardiac death walking away from home plate, seven pitches into the opening day game of the 1996 baseball season between the Cincinnati Reds and the Montreal Expos at Riverfront Stadium, Cincinnati. Liturgy at St. Nicholas of Tolentine Catholic Church in his native Bronx. Sec. 44-480-3, Gate of Heaven Cemetery, Hawthorne, NY.

5943. McSorley, John A. (c 1823–1910) Founder (1854) of McSorley's Old Ale House, Manhattan's oldest saloon, at 15 E. 7th St. off Cooper Square at the end of the Bowery. Well into the 1980's a portrait of old John still graced the bar, with only beer (and no females) served. Same section as Grover Whalen. Sec. 9, (1st) Calvary Cemetery, Woodside, Queens, N.Y.C.

5944. McSwiggin, William (dec. April 27, 1926) Chicago assistant state's attorney, assassinated outside the Pony Inn in Cicero by Capone and friends after a night of drinking with rival northsiders Klondike O'Donnell, his boyhood friend, and others. Until the McSwiggin murder the Chicago gangsters were said to only kill each other. Sec. K, Mt. Carmel Cemetery, Hillside, IL.

5945. McTigue, Mike (Michael Francis McTigue, Nov. 26, 1892–Aug. 12, 1996) Bold Mike, world light-heavyweight boxing champion 1923–25, boxed 1909–1930 and defeated Battling Siki in Dublin on March 17, 1923. McTigue died in New York at 103 and was buried there. Unmarked, directly in front of McCarthy stone. Calvary Cemetery, Woodside, Queens, N.Y.C.

5946. McVay, Charles B., 3rd (Aug. 30, 1898–Nov. 6, 1968) U.S. Navy Rear Admiral was the captain commanding the U.S.S. *Indianapolis*, the last American ship sunk in World War II. They sailed in July 1945 from San Francisco to Guam, delivering parts for the Atomic bomb that would soon be dropped on Hiroshima and Nagasaki. Returning across the Philippine Sea, it was torpedoed by a Japanese submarine July 30 and sank within twelve minutes. Of app. 880 that went into the water, sharks and exposure claimed all but 316 after four days, the ship never reported missing and the survivors only rescued after a plane spotted them. McVay survived and was court-martialed the following February, with points off his career for failing to zig-zag in the area where they were torpedoed. Though Secretary of the Navy Forrestal restored his rank, the stigma followed him until his retirement as rear admiral in 1949, and afterward. Residing in Morris, Connecticut, he shot himself in the had at 70 in front of his home on Alain White Road, and was pronounced dead in Charlotte Hungerford Hospital in Torrington. Private memorial service through Sepple (now Rowe) mortuary in Litchfield, Connecticut. Cremated at Mountain View Cemetery in Bridgeport, the ashes were sent November 27 to the U.S. Naval Air Station at Algiers, Louisiana, c/o Chaplain Robert E. Tatum, and buried at sea by air off Bayou Liberty. The U.S.S. *Indianapolis* memorial was dedicated in Indianapolis August 3 1995, the fiftieth anniversary of the end of the ordeal. McVay's sons, supported by a Florida schoolboy and the men who served under McVay, were then attempting to have the court martial, considered unjust by most, wiped off their father's record. Exoneration in congress finally came in a resolution passed in October 2000. He was formally exonerated by the Secretary of the Navy in July 2001, two weeks after the death of his last surviving son.

5947. McVea, Jack (Nov. 5, 1914–Dec. 27, 2000) Tenor saxophone player with Lionel Hampton and later Dixieland bands had a hit in 1947 with *Open the Door, Richard*. Angelus mortuary, Los Angeles. Garden of Faith, crypt 115, tier F, Inglewood Park Cemetery, Inglewood, CA.

5948. McVeigh, Timothy (April 23, 1968–June 11, 2001) Veteran of the Gulf War from Pendleton, New York, a sergeant who had earned a Bronze Star, became the nation's most infamous home-grown mass murderer when he parked a Ryder truck filled with explosives by the Alfred P. Murrah Federal Building in Oklahoma City April 19, 1995, ostensibly in a protest over the federal government's handling of Ruby Ridge and Waco, and in the ensuing explosion killed 168 people, including 19 children. He voluntarily stopped his appeals and opted for execution by lethal injection after six years in the federal penitentiary at Terre Haute, Indiana. He requested no service or burial. Cremated June 11 at Terre Haute Crematory through Mattox-Ryan mortuary, the ashes were turned over to his Tulsa based lawyer Robert Nigh.

5949. McVitie, Jack the Hat (dec. Oct. 28, 1967) London East End criminal worked for the Kray twins but failed to carry out a murder or to return the deposit he had been paid. Antagonism built until Reggie Kray fatally stabbed him in the face, chest and torso, and the body was disposed of by the Krays and their entourage, possibly by cremation, in cement, at sea, etc. The remains were never found.

5950. McWade, Margaret (Sept. 3, 1872–April 1, 1956) Actress in films from 1914 played Mrs. Adams in *Alice Adams* (1923), Mrs. Challenger in *The Lost World* (1925), and a series of prying or eccentric spinsters through the 1930's and 40's (*Postal Inspector, Theodora Goes Wild, The Remarkable Andrew, The Bishop's Wife*). Best known with Margaret Seddon

(*q.v.*) as the pixilated sisters in *Mr. Deeds Goes to Town* (1936). She died in Los Angeles at 83. Unmarked in Fish-Haggard-Rosenbach lot (no Edward McWade). Sec. 106, lot 47, Rosehill Cemetery, Chicago, IL.

5951. McWade, Robert (June 17, 1872–Jan. 19, 1938) Buffalo born actor son of Robert McWade (1913), in films of the 1930s often as corrupt executives, shady lawyers, etc. (*Cimarron, I Am A Fugitive From A Chain Gang, Back Street, Movie Crazy, The Phantom of Crestwood, Two Seconds, Big City Blues, 42nd Street, The Kennel Murder Case, Of Human Hearts*). He died at the MGM studios in Culver City, California, from heart disease at 65. Cremated January 21 at Rosedale Cemetery, the ashes were returned (through Edward Bros. mortuary) to his widow M(innie) L. McWade.

5952. Macy, Anne Sullivan *see* **Helen Keller.**

5953. Macy, John Albert (April 10, 1877–Aug. 26, 1932) Writer, literary critic (*The Spirit of American Literature, Edgar Allan Poe, Feminism and Femininity, Walter James Dodd*), divorced from Helen Keller's teacher Anne Sullivan, edited her autobiography *The Story of My Life*. Mount Hebron Cemetery, Montclair, NJ.

5954. Macy, Roland H. (Aug. 30, 1822–March 29, 1877) Founder of Macy's Department Store in Manhattan in 1858, for years in competition with Gimbel's, based in Philadelphia. Macy died in Paris and was returned to America. Crown Grove sec. 34, Woodlawn Cemetery, the Bronx, N.Y.C.

5955. Madden, Owney (Owen Vincent [or Victor] Madden, Dec. 25, 1891–April 24, 1965) Gangland figure from Liverpool, England, came to New York City as a child. By 1914 he was sent to Sing Sing on a manslaughter charge, but emerged in New York again in the 1920's as a powerful force among the beer barons, etc. Accused of six murders and dubbed the clay pigeon because he was shot numerous times but never fatally. After another term in Sing Sing for parole violation he retired in 1935 to Hot Springs, Arkansas, where he lived the next thirty years as a citizen without incident until his death there at 73 from emphysema. Sec. C, lot 141, space SE, Greenwood Cemetery, Hot Springs, AR.

5956. Maddox, Lester (Lester Garfield Maddox, Sept. 30, 1915–June 25, 2003) Colorful and controversial Georgia restaurateur ran the Pickrick Restaurant and espoused segregationist views with equal gusto, gaining national attention in 1964 when he met the attempted integration of the Pickrick with armed resistance. As a surprisingly mild governor 1967–1971, he oversaw the first hiring of black state troopers, appointed the first black to the board of pardons and, after four black escapees from a south Georgia work camp visited his office in Atlanta, took up a progressive stand on prison reform. Yet he never changed his views against integration or most liberal ideas. He died at 87 in an Atlanta hospice. Arlington Memorial Park, Sandy Springs, GA.

5957. Maddux, Holly (Helen Maddux, May 26,

1947–Sept. 1977) Former cheerleader from Tyler, Texas lived in Philadelphia with counter-culture figure Ira Einhorn from 1972 to July 1977, when she left him and took up with one Saul Lapidus near New York City. On September 9 Einhorn called her and demanded she return to Philadelphia to get her belongings; when she did, she never returned. Despite complaints of odors by neighbors, detectives did not search Einhorn's apartment and find the trunk in his closet containing Maddux's mummified body until March 28, 1979. Released on bail, Einhorn fled the country in January 1981, just before his trial, which took place anyway, convicting him in absentia. He defiantly lived a pleasant life in Europe, settling in France, until extradition was agreed upon by French authorities in 1998 and he was returned and jailed in Pennsylvania in 2001. Maddux was buried at Tyler, TX.

5958. Madison, Dolley (Dorothea Dandridge Payne, May 20, 1768–July 12, 1849) Dolley Payne Todd — familiarly but incorrectly called Dolly — was a well known Washington society figure before she married her second husband, James Madison, future fourth President of the United States. She served often as hostess for the widowed Jefferson 1801–09 and was a well versed and popular First Lady 1809–1817. During the British burning of the Executive Mansion in 1814, she is said to have rescued the Gilbert Stuart portrait of Washington and carried it out with her. In her later years, after Madison's death in Virginia in 1836, she resided on Lafayette Square in Washington, D.C. In the 1840's, with the development of the daguerreotype, she became the first (chronological) First Lady to be photographed. Upon her death she was interred in the brick receiving vault in Congressional Cemetery in Washington, D.C., where she remained until February 10, 1852. She was then removed to the private vault of her niece, and moved again on January 12, 1858, when she was taken back to the Madison family graveyard and buried behind her husband's monument, marked by a small white marble obelisk which incorrectly lists her death date as July 8. Madison graveyard, Montpelier estate, Orange County (near Orange), VA.

5959. Madison, Guy (Robert Ozell Moseley, Jan. 19, 1922–Feb. 6, 1996) Actor known in the title role in TV's *The Adventures of Wild Bill Hickok* 1951–58, also on radio 1951–56. In 85 films from the early 40's, he died from emphysema at 74 in Palm Springs. Sanctuary of the Good Shepherd North, crypt 7C, second level, with his picture on it, Palm Springs Mausoleum, Cathedral City (Palm Springs), CA.

5960. Madison, James (March 16, 1751–June 28, 1836) Slight and shy political wizard, co-author of the Federalist Papers, Father of the American Constitution and 4th President of the United States (1809–1817), married to the vivacious Dolley Payne Todd (*q.v.*). Having survived most of his contemporary Founding Fathers, he slipped quietly from life at his estate "Montpelier" in Orange County, Virginia, at 85.

When his niece asked him what was wrong he replied "Merely a change of mind, my dear," his reported last words. He was buried in the family graveyard on the estate, marked by a large stone obelisk with only *Madison* and his dates of birth and death on it. Surrounded by a brick wall with an iron gate marked *Madison*, it is accessible by a dirt road, isolated and little changed from when Madison and his wife were buried there. Madison family graveyard, Montpelier estate, Orange County (near Orange), VA.

5961. Madison, Noel (Nathaniel Moscovicz/Moscovitch, April 30, 1897–Jan. 6, 1975) Actor son of Yiddish Theater great Maurice Moscovitch (*q.v.*), on stage in dignified parts prior to and after a string of Hollywood roles 1930–1948, often as thugs (*Doorway to Hell, Little Caesar, Symphony of Six Million, The Last Mile, The House of Rothschild, Manhattan Melodrama* [as Manny Arnold], *G-Men, Charlie Chan in the City of Darkness, Footsteps in the Dark,* many others). He died in Fort Lauderdale, Florida, at 77. Cremated through Baird-Case, Tamarac. Ashes scattered at sea.

5962. Madox-Brown, Ford (April 16, 1821–Oct. 6, 1893) and his wife **Emma** (1835–Oct. 11, 1890) were pre-Raphaelite artists associated with William Morris. Chipped stone in Chapel Hill sec., St. Pancras and Islington Cemetery, North Circular and Finchley High Road, London.

5963. Magaddino, Stefano (Oct. 10, 1891–July 19, 1974) Head of the western New York crime family for decades, cousin of Joseph Bonnano. St. Joseph Cemetery, Niagara Falls, NY.

5964. MaGee, John Gillespie (June 9, 1922–Dec. 11, 1941) English poet wrote *The Last Flight* in August or September 1941. The beginning and end are on the bottom of his stone: *Oh I have slipped the surly bonds of Earth ... put out my hand, and touched the face of God.* He had been with the R.C.A.F. fourteen months when he died in a mid air training flight at 19. Scopwick village cemetery, Scopwick, Lincolnshire.

5965. Magellan, Ferdinand (c. 1480–April 27, 1521) Portuguese explorer tried to circumnavigate the world and sailed through the strait now named for him, calling the ocean the Pacific. In the Philippines he baptized natives and had them swear allegiance to the King of Spain but met violent resistance on the island of Mactan, where he was shot with poisoned arrows and spears and beaten to death. His body was not recovered. A monument to him was erected in 1869 at the tip of Mactan in what is now Magellan Bay.

5966. Maglie, Sal (Salvatore A. Maglie, April 26, 1917–Dec. 28, 1992) Pitcher for the New York Giants in the early 1950's, Sal the Barber was known for his high, hard curveball. He was the last player to have played for all three New York teams before the Giants and Dodgers went west, his record including 25 shutouts and three world series. Crypt in building 4. He also has a stone with his first wife. St. Joseph Cemetery, Niagara Falls, NY.

5967. Magnani, Anna (March 7, 1908–Sept. 26,

1973) Egyptian born actress raised in Rome, known for Roberto Rosselini's *Roma Citta Aperta* (*Open City* 1945), and for *The Rose Tattoo* (AA, 1955), afterward primarily working in Italy. She died from pancreatic cancer at 65; after a funeral service with throngs of admirers lining the streets, she was to be interred in the Rosselini tomb in the Cimitero del Verano in Rome. Interred at San Felice Circeo, the western seaport town where she lived. Cimitero Comunale di San Felice Circeo.

5968. Magnin, Edgar F. (July 1, 1890–July 17, 1984) Rabbi of Temple Israel in Los Angeles presided at the bar mitzvahs, weddings and funerals of the stars for many years from the 1920's and became as such a celebrity in his own right. Private mausoleum. Sec. C, Home of Peace Memorial Park, east Los Angeles.

5969. Magnuson, Keith (April 27, 1947–Dec. 15, 2003) Saskatchewan born Chicago Blackhawks defenseman 1969–1980 and coach 1980–82, known for his aggression and competitive nature, died in an auto accident in suburban Toronto at 56. Weben mortuary, Lake Forest (suburban Chicago). Lake Forest Cemetery, Lake Forest, IL.

5970. Maguire, Sean (Dec. 26, 1927–April 13, 2005) Irish fiddle master of traditional music from a musical family in Belfast, played with the Malachy Sweeny Célli Band from 1948 before forming his own Célli Band, with which he toured and recorded, appearing at Carnegie Hall, on *The Ed Sullivan Show*, and from the 1960's playing with the Gael-Inn Cabaret. He died at 77. Milltown Cemetery, Belfast.

5971. Mahan, Alfred Thayer (Sept. 27, 1840–Dec. 1, 1914) American naval officer, historian, and pres. of the Naval War College in Newport, was a major voice in jingoistic approaches to war and colonization, encouraging the Spanish-American War in 1898. Quogue Cemetery, Quogue, Long Island, NY.

5972. Mahin, John Lee (Aug. 23, 1902–April 18, 1984) Screenwriter from Evanston, Illinois, long at MGM, married for a time to actress Patsy Ruth Miller, wrote *Scarface, Red Dust, Bombshell, Naughty Marietta, Captains Courageous* (AA nom.), *Boom Town, Dr. Jekyll and Mr. Hyde* (1941), *Heaven Knows Mr. Allison* (1957, AA nom.), *Elephant Walk,* many others. Cremated by the Neptune Society, Los Angeles through Angeles Abbey. Ashes reportedly scattered at sea.

5973. Mahler, Gustave (July 7, 1860–May 18, 1911) Austrian composer noted particularly for his First, Second and Fourth Symphonies. He was director of the opera in Budapest 1888–1891, of the Vienna State opera 1897–1908 and at the New York Philharmonic 1908–1910. His wife **Alma Mahler Werfel** (Aug. 31, 1879–Dec. 11, 1964), composer and his biographer, is interred with him. His monument, designed by Josef Hoffman, bears only his name. Gruppe 6, reihe 7, nummer 1, Grinzig Friedhof (Cemetery), Vienna, Austria.

5974. Mahone, William (Dec. 1, 1826–Oct. 8, 1895) Confederate general at most of the battles of the Army of Northern Virginia received the surprising explosion from Ledlie's unsupervised Union troops advancing into the crater at Petersburg July 30, 1864. Mahone's men fired down on them, trapped in the crater. Confederate sec., Blandford Cemetery, Petersburg, VA.

5975. Mahoney, Jock (Jacques O'Mahoney, Feb. 7, 1919–Dec. 14, 1989) Chicago born actor in films from 1945, at first as a stuntman, then as heavies in westerns, was the screen's thirteenth Tarzan (1960–63) and starred in the TV series *Range Rider* and *Yancy Derringer.* He died at Memorial Hospital in Bremerton, Washington, two days after an auto accident. Ashes scattered off Washington State and reportedly off the coast of Malibu, CA.

5976. Main, Marjorie (Mary Tomlinson Krebs, Feb. 24, 1890–April 10, 1975) Actress from Elkhart, Indiana, did drama on stage and screen, notably as Bogart's mother in *Dead End* (1937), before being cast opposite Percy Kilbride in the *Ma and Pa Kettle* series in the late 1940's. An unassuming woman, she lived alone as a widow, continuing to do her own housekeeping into her last years. Like the stone with her husband, **Stanley LeFevre Krebs** (Jan. 14, 1864–Sept. 26, 1935) at Mount Carmel Cemetery, Littlestown, Pennsylvania, her own plaque lists both *Mrs. Mary Tomlinson Krebs* and *Marjorie Main.* Enduring Faith sec., lot 2083, Forest Lawn Hollywood Hills, Los Angeles.

5977. Maione, Happy (Harry Maione, 1908–Feb. 20, 1942) Hit man with Murder Inc. convicted on the testimony of Abe Reles, died in the electric chair at Sing Sing along with Frank "The Dasher" Abbandando for a 1937 ice pick murder. Sec. 37, range L, plot 1, St. John's Cemetery, Middle Village, Queens, N.Y.C.

5978. Malamud, Bernard (April 26, 1914–March 18, 1986) Brooklyn born writer began with *The Natural* (1952) but primarily chronicled Jewish life in America in a variety of environments: *The Assistant* (1957), *A New Life* (1961), *The Fixer* (1967, National Book Award and Pulitzer Prize), *Dubin's Lives* (1977). He lectured extensively until his death in Manhattan at 71. Cremated Garden State Crematory through Frank E. Campbell mortuary. His tablet is inscribed *Art celebrates life and gives us our measure.* Flush stone near pond. Azalea Path, lot 10652, grave 1, Mount Auburn Cemetery, Cambridge, MA.

5979. Malcolm X (Malcolm Little, May 19, 1925–Feb 21, 1965) Native of Omaha, one time hoodlum, became a black militant leader and a major force for violence in the civil rights movement of the 1950's and 60's. In 1964 he broke with the Muslims and formed the Organization of Afro-American Unity, his policies and theories more mellow after his visit to Mecca. With this alteration in his views and his break with Elijah Muhammid, his home in Queens was fire bombed and he began receiving increased death threats, culminating in his assassination while speaking in the Audubon Ballroom at 166th and Broadway in Harlem. He was buried in white Muslim garb, his marker inscribed with both *Malcolm X* and his Muslim name, *El-Haji Malik El-Shabazz*. His wife Betty Shabazz (*q.v.*) was buried beside him in 1997. Pinewood B, grave 150, Ferncliff Cemetery, Hartsdale, NY. See also **Shabazz.**

5980. Malle, Louis (Oct. 30, 1932–Nov. 23, 1995) Film director from Thumeries, France, made *The Silent World* (*Le Monde du Silence*, 1956), *The Lovers* (*Les Amants*, 1958), *Viva Maria* (1965), *The Thief of Paris* (*Le Volier*, 1967), *Black Moon* (1975), and his American debut *Pretty Baby* (1978). Other works include *Atlantic City, Au Revoir Les Enfants* and *My Dinner With Andre*. Married to actress Candace Bergen. He died from lymphoma in his Beverly Hills home at 63. Service at St. Sulpice Church with a eulogy by Wallace Shawn. Cremation at Pere Lachaise Cemetery, Paris. Ashes returned to family, reportedly scattered at his home in the Province of Lot (46).

5981. Mallon, Typhoid Mary (c. 1870–Nov. 11, 1938) Carrier of typhoid was herself immune to the deadly effects of the disease but continued to work as a cook and periodically started typhoid plagues in 1904, 1907 and 1914, when she was apprehended a last time and incarcerated at North Brother Island in New York City. Sec. 15, range 19, grave 55, St. Raymond's Cemetery (old section), the Bronx, N.Y.C.

5982. Mallory, Boots (Patricia Mallory, Oct. 22, 1913–Dec. 1, 1958) Actress in films of the 30's and 40's, last married to Herbert Marshall, died from a lung ailment at 45. Her ashes, like Marshall's, remain in vaultage at Pierce Brothers' Chapel of the Pines Crematory, Los Angeles.

5983. Malone, Vivian (July 15, 1942–Oct. 13, 2005) Black student from Alabama A&M whose transfer to the University of Alabama required the presence of Deputy Attorney General Nicholas Katzenbach and federal marshals to allow the admission through the front door of she and fellow African-American student James Hood, after Governor George Wallace read a statement and was forced to step aside from blocking their entry. A retired federal worker and the wife of Dr. Mack A. Jones, she died in Atlanta from a stroke at 63. Westview Cemetery, Atlanta, GA.

5984. Malraux, Andre (Nov. 3, 1901–Nov. 23, 1976) French novelist, art philosopher and political activist fought for the Resistance during World War II and exemplified France's postwar intellectual, serving as Minister of Culture under Charles de Gaulle 1959–1969. He died at Crzteil, France. In August 1996, President Jacques Chirac ordered his ashes transferred to (cell 6) the Pantheon, Paris.

5985. Malvern, Paul (Jan. 28, 1902–May 29, 1993) Former circus acrobat and stuntman (*The Beloved Rogue*, many others) produced westerns at Monogram in the 1930's and melodramas at Universal in the 1940's (*House of Frankenstein, House of Dracula*). Abbey of the Psalms/Hollywood Forever Mausoleum, Sanctuary of Memories, crypt 1301, Hollywood Forever Cemetery, Hollywood (Los Angeles), CA.

5986. Malyon, Eily (Eily Sophia Craston, Oct. 30, 1879–Sept. 26, 1961) English born actress with long, sorrowful features in supporting and bit parts in films of the 1930's and 40's played many a maid, nurse (*Dracula's Daughter* 1936) and occasional conniving shrew (*On Borrowed Time* 1939). She died from heart disease at Braewood Sanitarium, South Pasadena. Unmarked. Block L, sec. 999, lot 14, Valhalla Memorial Park, North Hollywood, CA.

5987. Mamoulian, Rouben (Oct. 8, 1897–Dec. 4, 1987) Innovative Russian born director of Armenian descent, in America from 1929 excelled with sophisticated scripts, creative camera and sound work in stylish and acclaimed films including *Applause* (1929), *City Streets* and *Dr. Jekyll & Mr. Hyde* (1931), *Love Me Tonight* (1932) and *Queen Christina* (1933) and the Technicolor milestone *Becky Sharp*. He died at 90 in Los Angeles. His plaque notes *A great director*. Garden of Ascension, lot 9329, Forest Lawn, Glendale, CA.

5988. Manahan, Sheila *see* **Fulton Mackay.**

5989. Manchester, William (April 1, 1922–June 1, 2004) Historian from Attleboro, Massachusetts, a Marines Corps sergeant in World War II with a purple heart, wrote noted biographies of Winston Churchill (*The Last Lion: Visions of Glory 1874–1932* in 1983 and *The Last Lion: Alone 1932–1940* in 1988), John Kennedy (*Portrait of A President* 1962, *Death of A President* 1967, *One Brief Shining Moment* 1983), and Douglas MacArthur (*American Caesar* 1978), as well as *The Glory and the Dream* (1973), a history of the United States 1933–1973, and *Goodbye Darkness* (1980), a memoir of his experiences in the South Pacific and their after affects. He died from cancer at 82 at his Connecticut home in Middletown. Buried with his wife Julia (1988). Indian Hill Cemetery, Middletown, CT.

5990. Mancini, Henry (April 16, 1924–June 14, 1994) Cleveland born composer raised at Aliquippa, Pennsylvania, won acclaim for his many film themes, including two Oscars, for *Moon River* from *Breakfast at Tiffany's* (1961) and the title theme from *The Days of Wine and Roses* (1963). Others include *Peter Gunn, Charade* and *The Pink Panther* (1965). He died at 70 from pancreatic cancer in his Beverly Hills home two months after a birthday tribute. There were no public services. Cremated at Forest Lawn, Glendale, the ashes were returned to his family in Los Angeles.

5991. Mancuso, Gus (August Rodney "Blackie" Mancuso, Dec. 5, 1905–Oct. 26, 1984) Catcher for the St. Louis Cardinals 1928–32, the New York Giants 1933–44, Chicago Cubs 1939 and the Brooklyn Dodgers 1940. Sec. 55, lot 100, Forest Park Lawndale, Houston, TX.

5992. Mander, Miles (Lionel or Luther Mander, May 14, 1888–Feb. 8, 1946) Actor, director and writer from Wolverhampton, England, in British films from 1918 and Hollywood from 1935 in roles ranging from detectives (*Return of the Vampire* 1943) to villains (*The Phantom of the Opera* 1943, and as Giles Conover in *The Pearl of Death* 1944) to various bystanders and victims (*Wuthering Heights, Tower of London* 1939, *Shadows on the Stairs* 1941, *The Scarlet Claw* 1944, *The Brighton Strangler* 1946). He died in Los Angeles from a heart attack at 57. Removed by Utter-McKinley mortuary for burial, according to the death certificate, at Forest Lawn Cemetery, Vancouver, British Columbia. Burial was instead in Imperial sec., lot 56, grave 3, Ocean View Burial Park, Burnaby (Vancouver area), B.C.

5993. Manet, Edouard (Jan. 23, 1832–April 30, 1883) French painter of ample women, both nudes and clothed, whose work was panned and largely unappreciated in his lifetime. He died at 51 after many years of philandering. Marble slab has at its head a pedestal with his bust on it. Div. 4, Passy Cemetery, Paris.

5994. Mangano, Philip (1898–April 19, 1951) Capo or underboss in the New York crime family (now the Gambino family) run by his older brother **Vincent Mangano** for twenty years, having succeeded Frank Scalise in 1931, who succeeded mustache Pete Salvatore D'Aquila in 1928. Philip was found shot three times in the head and left in a marsh at Bergen Beach near Jamaica Bay, Brooklyn. Vincent disappeared the same day; his body was never found. There was idle speculation that one or both Manganos wanted out of the mob life. Albert Anastasia took over the slot until his murder six years later, after which it was helmed by Carlo Gambino, whose name has stuck with the faction through the Gotti years. Philip is buried at Holy Cross Cemetery, Brooklyn, N.Y.C.

5995. Mangano, Silvana (April 21, 1930–Dec. 16, 1989) Roman born beauty married to director Dino De Laurentiis from 1949 until her death from cancer at 69 forty years later in Madrid. She appeared in many films, including *Ulysses* (1954), *The Tempest* (1958), *A Branded Woman* (1960), *Barabbas* (1962). Cremated at Almudena Cemetery there, her ashes were buried with a brother and her son, who had died in a plane crash. Three red granite slanted stones, behind boulder to John Worden, straight in from route 22. Pawling Cemetery, Pawling, NY.

5996. Mangelsdorff, Albert (Sept. 5, 1928–July 25, 2005) German jazz trombonist noted for his multiphonic approach first gained attention at the 1958 Newport Jazz Festival and led a quintet popular in West Germany through the 1960's. Recordings include *Animal Dance* (1962), LPs *Trombirds* (1972), *Wide Point* (1975), *Mood* (1990). Gewann (section) XV, lot 31, Hauptfriedhof, Frankfurt am Main, Germany.

5997. Mangrum, Lloyd E. (Aug. 1, 1914–Nov. 17, 1973) Golfer won the U.S. Open in 1946, was long a tournament fixture. Golf ball on a tee on his niche plaque. Sec. 4, niche 206, Victor Valley Memorial Park, Victorville, CA.

5998. Mankiewicz, Herman J. (Nov. 7, 1897–March 5, 1953) New York born writer, brother of Joe Mankiewicz, was a noted wit among several of Hollywood's inflated egos. Known today for his major contributions to *Citizen Kane* among others, for which he often received no credit, including three of the Marx Brothers films at Paramount. Mankiewicz died from uremia, Bright's Disease and congestive heart failure at 55 at Cedars of Lebanon Hospital in Los Angeles. Cremated at Hollywood Memorial Park Cemetery in Hollywood, his ashes remained at the cemetery until removed by Groman's mortuary April 14, 1956. While his wife **Sara S. Mankiewicz** (1897–Dec. 11, 1985) is buried at Mt. Sinai Memorial Park, Los Angeles, and his mother in N.Y.C., his ashes were buried unmarked with those of his father Peter on his property (no markers) in the Catskills at Mt. Tremper, NY.

5999. Mankiewicz, Joseph L. (Feb. 11, 1909–Feb. 5, 1993) Academy Award winning writer and director won in both categories for *A Letter to Three Wives* (1949) and *All About Eve* (1950), produced *The Philadelphia Story* (1940) and directed the controversial *Cleopatra* (1963). He died at his home in Bedford, New York. The epitaph on his stone reads *TIME is finite. It's your TIME now. No longer just God's TIME: Make it good to live in.—JLM.* Ashes buried at the rear of St. Matthew's Episcopal Church Cemetery, Bedford (village), eastern Westchester County, NY.

6000. Manley, Effa L. (March 27, 1900–April 16, 1981) Owner of the Newark Eagles, the first professional baseball team owned by a woman. Her 1946 Eagles won the Negro Leagues World Series. Though she protested the raiding of Negro Leagues talent without adequate compensation, the Eagles disbanded in 1948. She was the first woman elected to the Baseball Hall of Fame (2006). Sec. R, tier 35, grave 28, Holy Cross Cemetery, Culver City, CA.

6001. Mann, Anthony (Emil Anton Bundesmann, June 30, 1906–April 29, 1967) San Diego born assistant director for Preston Sturges (*Sullivan's Travels*), co-wrote *Follow Me Quietly,* directed most of *He Walked By Night* (uncredited), but made his mark with *Winchester 73* (1950) and a handful of other westerns (*Bend of the River, The Man from Laramie, The Tin Star*), focusing both on outdoor photography and the conflict within the protagonist. He died while making *A Dandy in Aspic* (completed by its star, Laurence Harvey). Ashes scattered at sec. 3-S, Golders Green Crematorium, north London.

6002. Mann, Erika (Nov. 9, 1905–Aug. 27, 1969) German actress who married W.H. Auden in order to obtain a British passport and remain out of Nazi Germany. She later wrote for the screen as well as several children's books. Friedhof Kilchberg, Zurich, Switzerland.

6003. Mann, Heinrich (March 27, 1871–March 12, 1950) Lubek born German writer, brother of Thomas Mann. His works focused on both political and social commentaries, best known among them was *Professor Unrat,* filmed in 1930 as *Der Blau Engel* (*The Blue Angel*), which made a star of Marlene Dietrich. He immigrated to France in 1933 and to America by 1940, where he died in Santa Monica a decade later. Evangelisher Friedhof Dorotheenstadt I, Chausseestr. 126 (Mitte), Berlin.

6004. Mann, Horace (May 4, 1796–Aug. 2, 1859) Famed educator known for his contributions to teaching. Briefly a congressman from Massachusetts following John Quincy Adams' death, he was president and administrator of Antioch College at Yellow Springs, Ohio, 1852–59. Rod Serling, an Antioch alumnus, used a statue of Mann and the quote *Be ashamed to die until you have won some victory for mankind* in the *Twilight Zone* episode *The Changing of the Guard.* Mann died at Yellow Springs. Buried beneath a stone shaft with marble inscriptions on all four sides. Linden Ave., North Burial Ground, Providence, RI.

6005. Mann, Kal (Kalman Cohen May 6, 1917–Nov. 28, 2001) Lyricist with Dave Appell wrote many late 1950's and early 1960's tunes, including *South Street, The Bristol Stomp, Let's Twist Again (Like We Did Last Summer), Wah-Watusi,* etc. He died at 84. Montefiore Cemetery, Philadelphia, PA.

6006. Mann, Louis (April 20, 1865–Feb. 15, 1931) New York born stage actor and comedian from age three had his biggest success with Sam Bernard in *Friendly Enemies* (1918) and wrote several plays including *The Cheater* (1910) in which he also acted, *The Laughing Girl, The Bubble, The Thieves' Paradise.* He opposed the Actors' Equity Strike in 1919 and formed the Actors Fidelity League, serving as its second vice president for ten years. His few films include *The Sins of the Children* (1930) a year before his death following surgery for an intestinal ailment in Mt. Sinai Hospital, Manhattan, survived by his wife, actress **Clara Lipman.** Service at Temple Emmanu-El through the Plaza funeral home February 18, followed by cremation. Niche 890, upper (second floor) columbarium, original building, Fresh Pond Crematory, Middle Village, Queens, N.Y.C.

6007. Mann, Ted (April 16, 1916–Jan. 15, 2001) Producer and theatre chain owner renamed Grauman's Chinese Theatre — with its footprints in cement dating to 1927 — after himself in 1973. It was still Mann's upon his death at 84, survived by his wife since 1977, actress Rhonda Fleming. Acacia Gardens, estate 8-1, Hillside Memorial Park, Los Angeles.

6008. Mann, Thomas (June 6, 1875–Aug. 12, 1955) German writer from Lubek was among the foremost novelists of the 20th century, awarded the Nobel Prize in literature in 1929 for works including his novella *Death in Venice* (1912) and *The Magic Mountain* (1924). He died at 80 near Zurich. Stone with his name, Katia Mann's, and their dates in Roman numerals. Church cemetery, Kilchburg, Switzerland.

6009. Mann, Woodrow Wilson (Nov. 13, 1916–Aug. 6, 2002) Mayor of Little Rock, Arkansas, in 1957, when Governor Orval Faubus defied President Eisenhower's order to allow black students into Little Rock High School and used the Arkansas National Guard to prevent their entry, which were then met by federal troops sent by Eisenhower. Mann opposed Faubus's stand, saying the Constitution should be followed, and that the move set back the industrialization of Arkansas by twenty five years. He moved to Houston by 1961, where he died at 85. Sec. 220, lot 11, grave 11, Memorial Oaks Cemetery, Houston, TX.

6010. Manners, David (Rauff de Ryther Duan Acklom, April 30, 1900–Dec. 23, 1998) Halifax born actor in Hollywood 1930–36 in *Journey's End, Dracula, The Miracle Woman, A Bill of Divorcement* (opposite Katherine Hepburn in her first film), *The Mummy, The Death Kiss* (lead role, 1933), *The Black Cat, The Mystery of Edwin Drood.* He left films by 1936, ran a ranch in the Mojave Desert c. 1937–58 and wrote several novels, declining through the years to partake of any interest in or reminiscing about the several classics he appeared in. He died at 98 in Valle Verde Health Center, Santa Barbara. No services at his request. Survived by a niece, he was cremated through McDermott-Crockett mortuary and his ashes spread near Yucca Loma, his long time home, in the Mojave Desert.

6011. Manners, Dorothy (July 30, 1903–Aug 25, 1998) Long time Hearst columnist died in Palm Springs at 95. Married name Haskell. No service, through Weifel and Sons mortuary. Columbarium of Victory, niche 32331, Freedom Mausoleum, Forest Lawn, Glendale, CA.

6012. Mannheim, Lucie (April 30, 1899–July 28, 1976) German actress in the Berlin Theatre left with the advent of the Nazis and made sporadic films in England — best known as the mysterious spy Annabella Smith in Hitchcock's *The 39 Steps* (1935). Returning to Germany after the war, she filmed there and in England and the U.S. (*The Man Who Watched Trains Go By* 1953, *Bunny Lake is Missing* 1965). Married to Marius Goring from 1941 until her death at 77 in Braunlage. He remarried after her death. Cremated at Wilmersdorf cemetery crematorium in Berlin, the urn was sent to London.

6013. Manning, Irene (Inez Harvout, July 17, 1912–May 28, 2004) Cincinnati born blonde actress and singer trained at the Eastman School of Music in Rochester, New York, appeared on Broadway, in films (*The Big Shot* with Humphrey Bogart, as Fay Templeton in *Yankee Doodle Dandy* opposite James Cagney, *Shine On Harvest Moon,* etc.). Married to rocket scientist **Maxwell Hunter** from 1964 until his death in San Mateo November 10, 2001, she died in San Bruno at 91. Cremated by the Neptune Society, Belmont, California. Ashes buried at sea June 4 off the coast of Marin County.

6014. Mannix, Eddie (Edgar Joseph Mannix, March 11, 1891–Aug. 30, 1963) Powerful MGM assistant to Louis B. Mayer made sure unseemly stories regarding the studio's stars and films were cleaned up and kept largely from the press. One of the popular theories, never substantiated, regarding actor George Reeves' death was that he was shot on the orders of Mannix's wife **Camille "Toni" Mannix** (Feb. 22, 1906–Sept. 1983). Block 71, crypt E-1, Mausoleum at Holy Cross Cemetery, Culver City, CA.

6015. Mannock, Mick (Edward Corringham Mannock, May 24, 1887–July 26, 1918) English World War I ace from Aldershot, originally interned in Turkey as an enemy, ill, and despite little to no vision in his left eye, flew with the Royal Air Force Flying Corps from April 1917, earning sixty-one victories, the Military Cross with bars and Distinguished Service Order with bars. Struck by anti-aircraft fire near Lestrem in the Pas-de-Calais area, his plane burst into flames. Later a body, possibly Mannock's, was recovered near Pacaut, France, though never positively identified. Marked as "A British Airman." Plot III, row F, grave 12, Laventie Military Cemetery, Lagorgue, Nord, Pas-de-Calais area. His name is on the Flying Services Memorial, Arras, Pas de Calais, France.

6016. Mansfield, Jayne (Vera Jayne Palmer, April 19, 1933–June 29, 1967) Blonde actress from Bryn Mar, Pennsylvania, known for her voluptuous image in a few films including *Will Success Spoil Rock Hunter?* (1957). Her stage name came from her first husband, Paul Mansfield. Later married to Mickey Hargitay, by whom she had three children. She and her companion Sam Brody died when a mosquito spraying vehicle blinded their chauffeur to a truck in their path on U.S. 90 near New Orleans, where she was to appear on TV following appearances at Biloxi, Mississippi. Her children, in the back seat, survived, but she was decapitated, or nearly; the death certificate lists "crushed skull with avulsion of cranium" rather than decapitation. She was buried beneath a large pink heart shaped stone with her name and dates below the heart and the sentiment *We live to love you more each day.* Fairview Cemetery, Pen Argyl, Pennsylvania. In 1987 a small cenotaph, a headstone with her picture, dates and the same epitaph as that over her grave, was placed in sec. 8/Garden of Legends, lot 218, Hollywood Forever Cemetery, Hollywood (Los Angeles). **Sam Brody**, also killed, was entombed in the Garden of Memory, Court of Honor B, crypt 359, outside the Garden Mausoleum, Hillside Memorial Park, Los Angeles.

6017. Mansfield, Katherine (Katherine Mansfield Beauchamp, Oct. 14. 1888–Jan. 9, 1923) Wellington, New Zealand, born writer revolutionized the English story in revealing character through a specific moment. Collections included *In a German Pension* (1911), *Prelude* (1918), *The Garden Party* (1922), and *The Dove's Nest* (1923). Her husband John Middleton Murry published editions of her journals and letters posthumously. She resided in London, Bavaria, and at Fontainebleau, France, where, ill with consumption, she died from a sudden hemorrhage at 34. Monument and stone slab. Cimetiere d'Avon, Avon (near Fontainebleau), France.

6018. Mansfield, Martha (Martha Erlich, July 14, 1899–Nov. 30, 1923) Actress born in New York grew up in Mansfield, Ohio, and took the name of her home town as a stage name. She had appeared on the stage for Ziegfeld and in films opposite John Barrymore in *Dr. Jekyll & Mr. Hyde* (1920). During a break while filming *The Warrens of Virginia* on location at Brackenridge Park in San Antonio, Texas, a match used to light a cigarette caught her hoop skirt on fire. She died in a San Antonio hospital the next day, listed as 23. Her stone lists her birth as 1900. Myosotis sec. along Walnut Ave. next to her mother Harriet (1958) and adjacent the James K. Hackett lot, Woodlawn Cemetery, the Bronx, N.Y.C.

6019. Mansfield, Mike (Michael Joseph Mansfield, March 16, 1903–Oct. 5, 2001) Montana Democrat in congress 34 years, known for his fairness and an opponent of escalation in Vietnam, was Senate majority leader from 1961 until his retirement in 1976. He served as Ambassador to Japan under Carter and Reagan 1977–1988. A New York City born Irish Catholic, he moved to Montana at age 3. From Japan he retired to Washington, D.C., where he died at 98 a year after his wife Maureen. Sec. 2, grave 4969, Arlington National Cemetery, Arlington, VA.

6020. Mansfield, Richard (May 24, 1854–Aug. 30, 1907) Stage great of the 19th century American and European stage, known for *Beau Brummel* and *Cyrano de Bergerac* made the play *Dr. Jekyll and Mr. Hyde* (1887) his own, but closed it down in London in the autumn of 1888 when it was deemed a possible influence on the Ripper then at work in Whitechapel. Mansfield died at New London, Connecticut, and was buried there. He and his wife are marked by a large boulder with two plaques. Mansfield's now green tablet reads *Richard Mansfield, passed on from this life Aug. 30, 1907. For God is love, and he that abideth in God and God in him. Thy leaf has perished in the green, and while we breathe beneath the sun, the world which credits that is done, is cold to all that might have been. So here shall silence guard thy fate, but somewhere out of human view, whate'er thy hands are set to do, is wrought with tumult of acclaim. Far off thou art but ever nigh. I have thee still and I rejoice. I prosper, circled with thy voice. I cannot lose thee, though I die.* A smaller black plaque simply notes *Beatrice 1868–1940.* On a second boulder are two elaborately inscribed plaques to their son Richard and his friend Jack Wright, both casualties of World War I. Extreme right rear corner, Gardner Cemetery, New London, CT.

6021. Manson, Alan (Feb. 6, 1919–March 5, 2002) Stage actor (*This is the Army, The Tenth Man and Gideon, Broadway Bound, Allegro* and *Funny Girl,* as Ziegfeld) in several films (*Bang the Drum Slowly,*

The Rain People, The Doors, The Devil's Advocate) and much TV in the 1970's and 80's. Service at Williams mortuary, East Hampton, Long Island. Green River Cemetery, East Hampton, NY.

6022. Mantell, Robert B. (Feb. 7, 1854–June 27, 1928) Acclaimed Irish Shakespearian stage actor on the American stage from 1878, a tragedian of the Old School. The flowers in his cortege were borne by the fire truck of the Mantell Hose Co., largely supported by him. Sec. B, lot 71/75, Bayview Cemetery, Atlantic Highlands, NJ.

6023. Mantle, Mickey (Mickey Charles Mantle, Oct. 20, 1931–Aug. 13, 1995) Country boy from Spavinaw, Oklahoma, named after Mickey Cochrane, succeeded Joe DiMaggio in the New York Yankees' center field in 1952, with them from 1951 to 1968, the most powerful switch hitter in the history of the game and among its biggest heroes. Despite an arrested case of osteomyelitis and numerous injuries that plagued him throughout his career, he was known for giving a maximum effort and coming back injury after injury, the most dramatic in 1964. He hit 536 home runs, won the Triple Crown in 1956, hit .300 or better for ten consecutive seasons, three time MVP (1956, '57 and '62), was on twenty A.L. All Star teams, often running on legs wrapped in rubberized bandages. As one of the M&M Boys, he and Roger Maris chased Ruth's home run record in 1961 but Mantle was sidelined by injuries. He retired in 1968, his number 7 retired the following June. Hall of Fame 1974. Coming from a family where a majority of the men had died in their forties with Hodgkin's Disease, he was known as a heavy drinker. In early 1994 he entered the Betty Ford Clinic for treatment of alcoholism; cancer was diagnosed in spring 1995 and he received a liver transplant at Baylor University Medical Center in Dallas in June but failed to recover as the cancer spread. Funeral at Lovers Lane United Methodist Church in Dallas with a eulogy delivered by sportscaster Bob Costas and the song *Yesterday When I Was Young* sung by Roy Clark, both by Mantle's prior request. Interred with his son **Billy**, who died at 36 from a heart attack. St. Mark, NE-N-C-13-A, bottom tier. His son **Mickey Jr.** died from cancer in 2000; Merlin Mantle had her husband and sons moved by January 2003 to couch crypts (long front rather than square). Mantle's new bronze plaque has his full name and dates, and *A magnificent New York Yankee, true teammate and Hall of Fame centerfielder with legendary courage! The most popular player of his era! A loving husband, father and friend for life.* Enclosure behind (waist high) gate, St. Matthew Extension between D-14 and D-15, Hillcrest Mausoleum, (Sparkman) Hillcrest Memorial Park, Dallas, TX.

6024. Mantovani (Annunzio Paolo Mantovani, Nov. 15, 1905–March 29, 1980) Composer-conductor recorded many collections through the 1940's, 50's and 60's. North Cemetery, Bournemouth, England.

6025. Manuel, Richard George (April 3, 1943–

March 4, 1986) Canadian born musician was a founding member of *The Band* in 1964, on vocals, piano and keyboard, until their finale in 1976, documented by Martin Scorsese. They had reformed a decade later when Manuel hanged himself in Winter Park, Florida, at 42. Sent for burial to Avondale Cemetery, Stratford, Ontario.

6026. Manush, Heinie (Henry E. Manush, July 20 1901–May 12 1971) Batting champion of the 1920's with six teams began with Detroit in 1923. In 1926 he eclipsed Babe Ruth with the American League batting championship at .378. Lifetime average .330. Hall of Fame 1964. Flush plaque near front of section. Garden of Devotion, block E, lot 18E, Sarasota Memorial Park, Sarasota, FL.

6027. Manville, Charles B. (Dec. 16, 1834–Nov. 24, 1927) Founder of Johns-Manville Insulation Co. in 1901. Family mausoleum, sec. 77, Kensico Cemetery, Valhalla, NY.

6028. Manville, Tommy (Thomas Franklyn Manville, April 9, 1894–Oct. 8, 1967) Notorious heir to the family fortune, known for his thirteen marriages. Family mausoleum, Pocantico plot, sec. 77, Kensico Cemetery, Valhalla, NY.

6029. Manzoni, Alessandro (March 7, 1785–May 22, 1873) Writer and patriot from Milan was the primary Italian figure of the Romantic period of poetry and literature and throughout the 19th century. Influenced by Walter Scott, his best known work was *The Betrothed* (*I Promessi Sposi,* translated 1827), a novel of 16th century Milan. He also wrote in defense of the Catholic church (1819) and on the unity of the Italian language (1868). Elevated marble sarcophagus. Cimitero Monumentale, Milan, Italy.

6030. Mao Zedong (Mao Tse-tung, Dec. 26, 1893–Sept. 9, 1976) Founder of the People's Republic of China (1949), long a staunch foe of the West, thawed in his later years, receiving U.S. President Nixon in a historic February 1972 visit. Chairman Mao is interred in his own mausoleum. Mao Tomb, Tiananmen Square, Beijing.

6031. Mapes, Jacques (June 14, 1913–May 4, 2002) Set decorator in films 1945-61 (*The Hunchback of Notre Dame* 1939, *Champagne For Caesar, The People Against O'Hara, Kind Lady, Singin in the Rain*) and co-producer with Ross Hunter of *Thoroughly Modern Millie, Airport,* several others. Crypt next to Ross Hunter. Westwood Memorial Park, west Los Angeles.

6032. Mapplethorp, Robert (Nov. 4, 1946–March 9, 1989) Controversial artist-photographer. Ashes buried without record with his mother Joan (1989). Sec. 48, range B, grave 131, St. John's Cemetery, Middle Village, Queens, N.Y.C.

6033. Mara, Wellington (Aug. 14, 1916–Oct. 25, 2005) Owner of the New York Giants, the son of original owner Tim Mara and brother of Jack Mara, with whom he co-owned the team until Jack's death in 1965, then with his nephew Tim, Jr., until Tim's death. Respected as a low key gentleman among sports executives, he died at 89 in Rye, New York. Mass at St. Patrick's Cathedral. Sec. 2, grave 370 ½, Gate of Heaven Cemetery, Hawthorne, NY.

6034. Marable, Fate (Clifford Marable, Dec. 2, 1890–Jan. 16, 1947) Dixieland musician, ragtime and stride piano player influenced several pioneer jazz musicians including Jelly Roll Morton. His headstone has a piano and musical notes on it, with the name and dates and *Musician and director from 1906 to 1940 on the Streckfus steamboats plying the Mississippi River during the era of Dixieland jazz.* Old sec. 13, lot 201, Oak Grove Cemetery, Paducah, KY.

6035. Marais, Jean (Jean Alfred Villain-Marais, Dec. 11, 1913–Nov. 8, 1998) Blonde French actor from Cherbourg promoted by Jean Cocteau to stardom in the late 1930's and showcased by him in *La Belle et la Bete* (*Beauty and the Beast* 1946), *L'Aigle a Deux Tetes* (1947), *Les Parents Terribles* (1948), *Orphee* (1950) and others through 1960. He died at 84 from chest problems in a hospital at Cannes. His tomb has two lions in front and a striking sculpted figure with antlers on top Village cemetery at Vallaurius, where he lived, near Antibes in the Cannes region.

6036. Maranville, Rabbit (Walter J. Maranville, Nov. 11, 1891–Jan. 5, 1954) Colorful 5'5" stocky N.L. baseball great known for his "basket catch." Beginning with the Boston Braves in 1912 and a member of the 1914 Miracle Braves, he played for twenty three years 1912–1933 in 2,670 games, exceeded only by Ty Cobb and Eddie Collins in his day. Hall of Fame 1954. Sec. Holy Family, B, lot 206, grave 5, St. Michael's Cemetery, Springfield, MA.

6037. Maranzano, Salvatore (1886 [most sources list 1868 but his stone says 1886]–Sept. 10, 1931) Sicilian immigrant to New York after World War I led the Mafia faction from Castellammarre. Though an old world "Mustache Pete" himself, he advocated the organization of structured Cosa Nostra in New York, resulting in the Castellammarese War by 1930 with Joe the Boss Masseria and their various armies. Masseria was killed in April 1931 and Maranzano, proclaimed himself the Boss of Bosses and labeled their business the Cosa Nostra ("our thing," roughly). He made peace with the top men, Luciano, Genovese, Lansky and Siegel, but was wary of them and eventually went outside Mafia ranks to hire Irish gunman Vincent "Mad Dog" Coll to kill them, but too late. Assassins with bogus police badges entered his Park Avenue real estate office and stabbed him to death, finishing him off with gunshots. The stone is partially covered by plantings (as are those of Frank Yale and Al Capone). Sec. 14, range C, plot 18, grave 2, St. John's Cemetery, Middle Village, Queens, N.Y.C.

6038. Marat, Jean Paul (May 24, 1743–July 13, 1793) Writer and agitator who led the French revolt against the monarchy became over-zealous and was stabbed in his bath by **Charlotte Corday** (1768–July 17, 1793), who held him responsible for the reign of terror that followed the revolution. She went to the guillotine in four days. Marat lay in state but putrefied quickly due to his skin disease (requiring those frequent baths). He was buried quickly and re-buried a year and a half later in the Pantheon. After a ruling that only those ten years dead could be interred there, he was removed across the street six months later to the Church of St. Etienne-du-Mont. He was first buried outside but when the churchyard was destroyed he was moved inside, beneath a statue of Mater Misericordie near the front. Church of St. Etienne-du-Mont, Paris. Corday (Charlotte de Corday d'Armont dite) went to the guillotine on July 17 and with at least 133 other known victims of the reign of terror, was interred at St. Madeleine's (Cimetiere de la Madeleine) in Paris.

6039. Maravich, Pete (Peter Press Maravich, June 22, 1947–Jan. 5, 1988) Leading career and single season scorer in college basketball history starred with Louisiana State 1967–70, totaling 3,667 points and an average of 44.2 over eighty three games. Son of Louisiana coach Pete Maravich. His ten seasons with the NBA never matched his days at LSU. Later involved in religious work, he had just finished playing a pickup game at a church in Pasadena, California, when he died from heart failure at 40, stemming from a heart defect that had gone undetected. Flush bronze plaque. Garden of Prayer, lot 88C, Resthaven Gardens of Memory, Baton Rouge, LA.

6040. March, Eve (Adalaide Doyle, Sept. 27, 1910–Sept. 19, 1974) California born actress on stage and in many films of the 1940's, sister of Maxine Doyle (the wife of Robert Wise), married first to Damien O'Flynn and later to Ian MacDonald, in small roles including *How Green Was My Valley, The Seventh Victim, Curse of the Cat People* (as the teacher), *They Were Expendable, Danny Boy, Adam's Rib, The Sun Shines Bright.* She died from cancer at home 63 in Los Angeles. Cremated September 23, 1974, at Oddfellows Crematory through Cunningham and O'Connor. Ashes buried at sea off Malibu. Married to Ian MacDonald, their daughter was the political writer **Katherine March MacDonald** (Nov. 12, 1949–Jan. 12, 1997) who died from cancer at 47 in Clarksville, California. Cremated through W.F. Gormley and Sons, her ashes were sent to her brother.

6041. March, Fredric (Fred Bickel, Aug. 31, 1897–April 14, 1975) Stage and screen star from Racine, Wisconsin, former banker, married to Florence Eldridge, came to Hollywood with sound as a matinee idol and later a character actor. He won two Oscars, for *Dr. Jekyll & Mr. Hyde* (1931) and *The Best Years of Our Lives* (1946). Stage triumphs included *Death of A Salesman, Long Day's Journey Into Night* (New York Drama Critics Award 1956) and *The Skin of Our Teeth* both on Broadway and on tour with his wife, who appeared in many of his films. By the 1940's they retired to Firefly Farm, north of New Milford, Connecticut, their home until 1974 when they returned to Los Angeles, where March died from cancer at 77. Cremated through Westwood Memorial Park, his ashes were returned to Firefly Farm and buried beneath a favorite tree of theirs dubbed "The Freddie Tree." When Eldridge died in Santa Barbara in 1988, her ashes were taken by her brother and buried beside March's. A small tombstone with a plaque marks the site, inscribed *Our Tree. Freddie 1897–1975. Florence 1901–1988.* Firefly Farm (private property), Merryall Road, New Milford, CT.

6042. March, Hal (April 22, 1920–Jan. 19, 1970) Host of the *$64,000 Question* 1955–58, revealed to be fraudulent, survived the scandal and did other TV, including *Burns and Allen* as Harry Morton, and *I Love Lucy.* He died from lung cancer at 49. Hillside slope, Mount Sholom, block 4, lot 144, space 6, Hillside Memorial Park, Los Angeles.

6043. Marchand, Nancy (June 19, 1928–June 18, 2000) Actress from Buffalo long on stage, known for her TV roles, as Mrs. Pynchon, Ed Asner's regal boss on *Lou Grant* 1979–1982, for which she won four consecutive Emmys, and as Livia, the scheming family matriarch on HBO's *The Sopranos* during the last two years of her life, which also brought her an Emmy nomination. She died from cancer at 71 in her Stratford, Connecticut, home. Cremated, with no services, through the William R. McDonald funeral home in Stratford. Ashes returned to family.

6044. Marciano, Rocky (Rocco Francis Marchegiano, Sept. 1, 1923–Aug. 31, 1969) Heavyweight boxing champion from Brockton, Massachusetts, took the title from Jersey Joe Walcott in 1952 and retired undefeated after five knockouts and one decision (over Ezzard Charles) in 1956. He died the night before his 46th birthday when his plane crashed in an Iowa cornfield. Among those at his funeral mass at St. Pius Catholic Church in Fort Lauderdale were Walcott and Cassius Clay (Muhammed Ali). Joe Louis, paying his respects, said "God has got himself a beautiful man." At Lauderdale Memorial Gardens, a 13 year old bugler from the Palm Beach Military Academy, where Marciano was on the board of advisors, played *Taps* for The Rock. Sec. AA, crypt 32–33, Forest Lawn (Central) Cemetery mausoleum, Fort Lauderdale, FL.

6045. Marconi, Guglielmo (April 25, 1874–July 20, 1937) Father of the wireless studied the work on electromagnetic waves done by Heinrich Hertz. His ireless telegraphy system, refused by Italy, was patented in London in 1896. It was demonstrated in a message from England to Newfoundland in 1901, and by its use in signaling from the *Titanic* in 1912. Marconi shared the Nobel Prize in physics in 1909 and represented Italy at the Paris Peace Conference in 1919. Ornate tomb at Villa Falcone, Sasso Marconi, Italy.

6046. Marcos, Ferdinand (Sept. 11, 1917–Sept. 28, 1989) Ousted dictator of the Philippines. The corrupt administration of he and his wife Imelda had long been news by the time of his death from heart failure in exile in Honolulu at 72. President Corazon Aquino denied his burial in the Philippines and he was placed in the Valley of the Temples Memorial Park in Kaneohe, Hawaii, while frozen. In September 1993 he was returned for interment and kept in a glass viewing case in an air conditioned mausoleum at Laoag/Batac, Province of Ilocos Norte in the Philippines. He was moved again in July 1998 and buried at Libingan ng mga, Bayani (a cemetery for the prominent), Manila.

6047. Marcus — Carrie and Herbert *see* **Neiman.**

6048. Marcus, Marie Doherty (Marie Eleanor Doherty, May 25, 1914–Oct. 10, 2003) Boston born Irish jazz pianist, a protégée of Fats Waller, dated to 52nd Street's Swing Club before World War II and to Harlem, but after the war was a fixture at the Coonamessett Club at Falmouth on Cape Cod, where she remained for forty years, the cape's first lady of jazz. Her funeral mass was intertwined with a traditional jazz funeral. Central Ave., lot 706, grave 4, Island Pond Cemetery, Harwich, Cape Cod, MA.

6049. Marcuse, Theodore (Theodore Carroll Marcuse aka Theo Marcuse, Aug. 2, 1920–Nov. 29, 1967) Actor usually with his head shaved in generally villainous or threatening roles as Russians or Germans in films from 1950 (*Jeanne Eagels, Operation Eichmann, Hitler, The Cincinnati Kid, The Glass Bottom Boat*) and many television appearances (*Twilight Zone* episodes *To Serve Man* and *The Trade Ins*, both 1962; as the commandant in both *The Wild Wild West* episode *The Night of the Bottomless Pit* and *The Time Tunnel* segment *Devil's Island*, both 1966; Korob in the *Star Trek* episode *Cat's Paw* 1967, several *Hogan's Heroes*, many others). He died in an auto accident in Hollywood at 47. Sec. 2-C, grave 1835, Golden Gate National Cemetery, San Bruno, CA.

6050. Marcy, William (Dec. 12, 1786–July 4, 1857) New York Democratic senator and governor in the 1830's, Secretary of War under Polk and Secretary of State under Pierce. Sec. 62, lot 94, Albany Rural Cemetery, Menands, Albany, NY.

6051. Margaret Rose, Countess of Snowden (HRH Princess Margaret, Aug. 21, 1930–Feb. 9, 2002) Younger sister of Britain's Queen Elizabeth II, well known for her troubled and sometimes scandalous private life, notably the romance with Group Capt. Peter Townsend of the Royal Air Force, which she publicly broke off because the Church of England forbid divorce, and marriage to the divorced Townsend would have lost the princess the title Her Royal Highness. She married Anthony Armstrong-Jones in 1960; they divorced in 1978. She suffered a nervous breakdown in 1974, two strokes in 1998 and was increasingly reclusive until her death at 71 in King Edward VII Hospital. Her coffin rested at Kensington Palace and then in the Queen's Chapel. After her funeral February 15, she was cremated at Slough Crematorium according to her wishes, only the eighth Royal cremation in British history and the first member of the sovereign's immediate family to be so disposed of. There were unconfirmed reports her ashes would be scattered over the island of Mustique in the Caribbean, but they were interred with her father George VI in St. George's Chapel, Frogmore, Windsor.

6052. Margo (Maria Marguerita Guadelupe Bolado y Castillo, May 10, 1917–July 17, 1985) Mexican actress in films (*Crime Without Passion* 1934, *Winterset* on both stage and screen 1936, *Lost Horizon* 1937, *The Leopard Man* 1943) married from 1945 to actor Eddie Albert (*q.v.*). Appointed Commissioner of Social Services for the city of Los Angeles in 1962. Sec. D, lot 61, Westwood Memorial Park, west Los Angeles.

6053. Margolin, Janet (July 25, 1943–Dec. 17, 1993) New York born actress on Broadway in *Daughter of Silence* (1961), the film *David and Lisa* (1962), many others, including Woody Allen's *Take the Money and Run* and *Annie Hall*. She died from ovarian cancer at 50. Married name Wass. Ashes buried above and left of Burt Lancaster. Urn garden, sec. D, Westwood Memorial Park, west Los Angeles.

6054. Maria Louise (Maria Louise Gemahlin Napoleon, Dec. 12, 1791–Dec. 17, 1847) Austrian archduchess, the daughter of the Holy Roman Emperor Franz II was Napoleon's second wife. She represented him in Paris while he was in Russia, but declined to join him in exile at Elba and became estranged from him after his threat to abduct her. Capuchin vaults (Neuegruft, Kaisergruft, Kapuzinerkirche), Vienna.

6055. Maria Theresa (May 13, 1717–Nov. 29, 1780) Hapsburg Archduchess of Austria and Queen of Bohemia and Hungary known for internal reforms. Among her nine adult children were Leopold II and Marie Antoinette. Ornate tomb, Kapuzinerkirche (Capuchin vaults), Vienna.

6056. Marion, Frances (Marion Benson Owens, Nov. 18, 1888 [often listed as 1890]–May 12, 1973) Screenwriter, former model, illustrator and actress, was one of the first female war correspondents to report from the front during World War I. She wrote several of Mary Pickford's best vehicles including *Poor Little Rich Girl* and *Little Lord Fauntleroy* as well as others including *Stella Dallas, The Winning of Barbara Worth* (1926), *The Wind* (1928), *The Big House* (1930, Academy Award), *The Champ* (1931, Academy Award), *Dinner at Eight* (1932), many others. Married to actor Fred Thomson (dec. 1928) and George Hill (a suicide, 1934). Cremated at Oddfellows crematory through Armstrong mortuary in L.A. (no records prior to 1976). According to Fred Thomson's biographer, her ashes were scattered in the Pacific. Her biography states she wanted her ashes spread in a rose garden but they were taken in a small Cessna to scatter over her father's property at Aetna Springs, California, part of them blowing back in the cabin.

6057. Marion, Francis (1732–Feb. 27, 1795) Colonial guerilla leader during the American Revolution, particularly in Georgia and the Carolinas, known as the Swamp Fox. Enclosed by an iron fence and brick posts, his monument (granite with bronze plaques, erected in 1893) and grave (the original marble top tomb inscribed over the grave of his wife) are on the family estate are accessible to the public down a long dirt road. Gabriel's (Belle Isle) Plantation, near St. Stephen, SC.

6058. Marion, George F. (July 16, 1860–Nov. 30, 1945) Stage and screen actor and stage director in films from 1914, in the talkies *Man to Man* and *The Big House* but best known as the father in the stage and 1930 screen version of *Anna Christie*. The lot, marked only *Marion* on the stone curbing, has an uninscribed stone slab with recumbent cross atop it. St. Dominick's Catholic Cemetery, Benicia, CA.

6059. Maris, Mona (Rosa Emma Mona Maria Marta Capdevielle, Nov. 7, 1906–March 23, 1991) South American actress in films in England from 1925 and in Hollywood from 1929–34 (*A Devil with Women, The Arizona Kid, The Death Kiss* (as Mrs. Avery, the cause of the murder), and again from 1940–46 *A Date with the Falcon, Berlin Correspondent, My Gal Sal, I Married An Angel, The Falcon in Mexico, Monsieur Beaucaire.* Panteon de Actores, 2S 3 #256, Cementerio de la Chacarita, Buenos Aires, Argentina.

6060. Maris, Roger (Roger Eugene Maras, Sept. 10, 1934–Dec. 14, 1985) New York Yankees power hitter with Mickey Mantle formed the slugging M&M Boys of 1960 and '61. Maris did not enjoy a good rapport with the press, but did manage to knock out 61 home runs in 1961, breaking Babe Ruth's record of runs in a season set in 1927. Commissioner Ford Frick, however, placed an asterisk in the record books, since the season had been extended from its number of games in 1927. Maris died from cancer at 51, unaware that the asterisk blemish would be removed in September 1991. At his memorial service in St. Patrick's Cathedral in Manhattan, Richard Nixon remarked, quoting from Sophocles, "Often one must wait until the evening to see how splendid the day has been." Maris's diamond shaped stone has a swinging batter engraved on it and the remembrance *Against all odds. 61 in 61.* Sec. 15, lot 232, Holy Cross Cemetery, Fargo, ND.

6061. Mark, Michael (Maurice Schulmann, March 15, 1886–Feb. 3, 1975) Russian born character actor, a staple in Universal horror films of the 1930's and 40's, beginning with *Frankenstein* (1931), as the father of the drowned girl, later turned up seemingly everywhere. He died at 88 in the Motion Picture Country Hospital. Cremated at Pierce Brothers' Chapel of the Pines in Los Angeles, his ashes were buried at sea.

6062. Markey, Enid (Feb. 22, 1896–Nov. 15, 1981) Silent screen actress from Dillon, Colorado, was the first Jane opposite Elmo Lincoln in *Tarzan of the Apes* (1918) and *The Romance of Tarzan*, reappearing in a few films (*The Naked City* 1948), and television (Aunt Violet on *Bringing Up Buddy*, Barney's landlady on *The Andy Griffith Show*). She died while visiting friends at Bayshore, Long Island. Cremated at Washington Memorial Park, Coram, Long Island, New York, the ashes were returned to her residence on East 71st St. in Manhattan.

6063. Markey, Gene (Dec. 11, 1895–May 1, 1980) Screen-writer (*Baby Face, Female*) and producer 1923–56, married to Joan Bennett 1932–38, Hedy Lamarr 1939–40, Myrna Loy 1946–50, and to Kentucky's Calumet Farms' head Lucille Parker Wright from 1952 to his death. Sec. 45, lot 754, Lexington Cemetery, Lexington, KY.

6064. Markham, Beryl (Oct. 26, 1902–Aug. 3, 1986) English born aviation pioneer from Melton Mowbray, gained fame in Kenya. First a bush pilot, she was the first female to fly westward across the Atlantic in her single engine Percival Gull monoplane in September 1936, landing in a bog in Nova Scotia after running low on fuel. Described as a pantherine beauty, she remained primarily in Kenya, where she was also active as a race horse trainer. A memoir, *West With the Night*, was published in 1942. She died in Nairobi at 83 after a leg operation following her tripping on her dog at home. Her ashes were scattered by her lawyer and a friend over Nairobi Racecourse, there being superstitions about the scattering of human ashes over N'Joro.

6065. Markham, Dewey "Pigmeat" (April 18, 1906–Dec. 13, 1981) Popular black stage comedian in Jazz revues and vaudeville as well as a few films. Van Cortland Mausoleum 3, Oak Court, bottom tier crypt (the sculpture *The Gift of Knowledge* is at the end of the hall), Woodlawn Cemetery, the Bronx, N.Y.C.

6066. Marks, Adrian (Feb. 18, 1917–March 7, 1998) U.S. Navy Lieutenant instrumental in the rescue of 315 sailors from the U.S.S. *Indianapolis* August 3, 1945. Ignoring regulations against an open sea landing, his PBY picked up 56 of the injured and radioed for help, bringing ships to pick up the rest. He died in Frankfort, Indiana, at 81. Cremated through Goodwins mortuary in Frankfort. Ashes to family for reported scattering.

6067. Marks, Gerald (Oct. 13, 1900–Jan. 27, 1997) Tin Pan Alley composer from Saginaw, Michigan, wrote *All of Me* with Seymour Simmons in 1931. He died in Manhattan at 96. Memorial service at Riverside Chapel, New York City. Cremated, his urn at his request was inscribed *All of Me*.

6068. Marks, Leo (Leopold Samuel Marks, Sept. 24, 1920–Jan. 15, 2001) Son of the owner of Marks and Co. Bookshop featured in *84 Charing Cross Road* used code poems as a cryptographer during World War II. head of code development and security for SOE (Special Operations Executive). Awarded the M.B.E. Plaque in Rose Garden, Golders Green Crematorium, north London.

6069. Markus, Winnie (Winifred Maria Markus, May 16, 1921–March 9, 2002) Prague born actress in

over one hundred postwar German films (*Bild am Sonntag, Innerlich Vertrocknet, Die Geierwally, Bruderlein fein, Kaisermanover, Teufel in Seide, Der Priester und das Madchen*. The widow of Carl Adolf Vogel, she died in Munich at 80. Buried at Friedhof Bogenhausen, Tegernsee, Bavaria.

6070. Marlatt, Earl B. (May 24, 1892–June 13, 1976) Composer of hymns (*Art Thou Willing* to *be Crucified with Me?*). Sec. 16, Fountain Park Cemetery, Winchester, IN.

6071. The Marlboro Man TV cowboy of 60's TV commercials for Marlboro cigarettes, played by both **Wayne McLaren** (Sept. 12, 1940–July 22, 1992) and **David McLean** (May 19, 1922–Oct. 12, 1995). Both died from lung cancer. McLaren was buried as L.E. McLaren at Highland Memorial Park, Lake Charles, Louisiana. McLean is in sec. BB, tier 69, grave 55, Holy Cross Cemetery, Culver City, CA.

6072. Marlen, Trude (Nov. 7, 1912–June 9, 2005) Austrian actress in films from 1933, including *Sherlock Holmes* (Austrian 1937), *Borderline* (1988). The second wife of Wolf Albach-Retty, father of Romy Schneider. She died days after Leon Askin; they had appeared together in *Ene mene muh ... und tot bist du*. Gruppe 32C, nummer 50, Zentralfriedhof, Vienna.

6073. Marley, Bob (Feb. 6, 1945–May 11, 1981) Jamaican born king of Reggae music who wrote and recorded standards with his Wailers, died in Miami from cancer at 36. Returned to Jamaica for burial, with his favorite guitar and a bible, to his marble and stone mausoleum at Nine Mile (two hours from Kingston). In January 2005, his widow Rita announced plans — widely protested in Jamaica — to remove his remains to Ethiopia, his "spiritual home," in part because of his Rastafarian faith, at Shashemene, 155 miles south of Addis Ababa. Nine Mile, Rhoden Hall, St. Ann Parish, Jamaica.

6074. Marley, John (Oct. 17, 1907–May 22, 1984) New York born actor with abundant white hair in films from the 1950's including *Cat Ballou* (1965), *Love Story* (1970, as Ali McGraw's father), *The Godfather* (1972, the recipient of the horse's head). He died in Los Angeles. Single upright stone. Tremont Benevolent Society, block 12, line 4, grave 35, Cedar Park Cemetery, Paramus, NJ.

6075. Marlowe, Christopher (Feb. 6, 1564–May 30, 1593) Forerunner of The Bard authored *Dr. Faustus*. He was living at Chiselhurst southeast of London during the plague and died in a barroom brawl at Deptford near Greenwich on the south bank of the Thames when a knife was plunged just over his eye. He was to appear in court as an atheist when he died and may have fled England. In a 1955 book Calvin Hoffman theorized Marlowe to have been Shakespeare. He was buried at Deptford Church in an unknown spot; a tablet in his memory was placed on the wall in 1919. St. Nicholas Church, Deptford, London.

6076. Marlowe, Hugh (Hugh Hipple, Jan. 30, 1911–May 2, 1982) Character actor on the stage and radio in many films and TV of the 1950's and 60's in sometimes stuffy or back-slapping roles (*Twelve O'Clock High, All About Eve, Mr. Belvedere Rings the Bell, The Day the Earth Stood Still*). He died from a heart attack at 71. Unit 10, alc. BB-CC, niche 9A, wall over stairs, main mausoleum, Ferncliff Cemetery, Hartsdale, NY.

6077. Marlowe, Julia (Sarah Francis Frost, Aug. 17, 1866–Nov. 12, 1950) English stage actress associated with her role as *Barbara Fritchie* (1900) and in several Shakespearian plays with her husband **Edward H. Sothern** (Dec. 6, 1859–Oct. 28, 1933). Slab beneath the Sothern monument along the brick wall. Brompton Cemetery, west London.

6078. Marlowe, June (Gisela Valaria Goetten, Nov. 3, 1903–March 10, 1984) Screen actress from St. Cloud in silent films from 1923 including *Pardon Us* (1931) played Miss Crabtree in the Hal Roach *Our Gang* (later called *The Little Rascals*) two reel comedies 1931–32. She died in Burbank, California, at 80 from Parkinson's' Disease. Buried as June Sprigg with her brother **Louis Goetten**. Sec. B, block 5, lot 845, San Fernando Mission Cemetery, Mission Hills, California. By May 2005 she and her brother had been moved; he to crypt 301A, she to crypt 301B, near the Resurrection Window, Our Lady of the Angels Cathedral, Los Angeles.

6079. Marly, Florence (Hana Smekalova, June 2, 1918–Nov. 9, 1978) Czech actress in the French films of Pierre Chenal, her husband 1937–55, in Hollywood from 1948 (*Sealed Verdict, Tokyo Joe*) and some television (*Twilight Zone* episode *Dead Man's Shoes*). She died from a heart attack at 60. Unmarked. Sec. F, tier 69, grave 59, Holy Cross Cemetery, Culver City, CA.

6080. Marquand, Christian (March 15, 1927–Nov. 22, 2000) French actor in *Beauty and the Beast* (1946), Henri Clouzot's *Quai des Offevres* (1947) and particularly known for *And God Created Woman* (1956). American appearances include *Apocalypse Now* (1978). Pere Lachaise Cemetery, Paris.

6081. Marquand, John P. (Nov. 10, 1893–July 16, 1960) American writer of the Mr. Moto series of mystery novels, also kept the respect of literary critics with his satirical works on the old and proper New England way of life, best exemplified in *The Late George Apley* (1937). Other works looked back on lost youth with sadness as well as satire. He died at Newburyport, Mass. Shunning his Sedgwick relatives buried in the "Sedgwick Pie" at Stockbridge, Massachusetts, he lies beneath a charcoal gray-black tombstone with the epitaph *Build me more stately mansions*. Sawyer Hill Burial Ground, Newburyport, MA.

6082. Marquard, "Rube" (Richard Marquard, Oct. 9, 1889–June 2, 1980) Cleveland born southpaw pitcher 1908–1925 with the Giants, Brooklyn and Cincinnati. At his peak with New York in 1912, after three seasons as the "$11,000 lemon," he blossomed and threw what would have been a record breaking

twenty straight, had present day rules been in effect. Married for a time to singer-actress Blossom Seeley; they were later divorced. Hall of Fame 1971. Hecht lot, division 8, sec. 13, lot 147, grave 1, (Baltimore or United) Hebrew Cemetery, Baltimore, MD.

6083. Marquet, Mary (April 14, 1895–Aug. 29, 1979) Stage, screen and TV actress, former cabaret star, divorced from Victor Francen. Films 1957–68 include *Maid of Paris*. Div. 23, Montmartre Cemetery, Paris.

6084. Marquette, Jacques (June 1, 1637–May 18, 1675) French missionary explored the Mississippi, died at the mouth of the Marquette and was buried at his mission. Re-buried 1877 at the Marquette monument, St. Ignace, Michigan. A cross marks the site and another alleged site at Frankfort, MI.

6085. Marriott, Steve (Stephen Peter Marriott, Jan. 30, 1947–April 20, 1991) London born former child actor founded The Small Faces in 1965, doing the vocals and playing guitar; their string of hits included *Watcha Gonna Do About It, I've Got Mine, Hey Girl, All or Nothing*, their album *Ogden's Nut Gone Flake* (1968), and their first U.S. hit, *Itchykoo Park* (1968). In March 1969 he left and formed Humble Pie, working with them until 1975. He died in a fire at his house in Arkesdon, near Saffron Walden, Essex, while full of drugs and alcohol. Ashes returned to friends.

6086. Marsh, Lucy Isabelle (Lucy Gordon, April 10, 1879–Jan. 20, 1956) Opera singer, soprano, recorded many 78's. Sec. 48, lot 6A, grave 2, Quidnessett Cemetery, North Kingston, RI.

6087. Marsh, Mae (Nov. 9, 1895–Feb. 13, 1968) Silent screen actress starred in Griffith's *Birth of a Nation* (1915) and *Intolerance* (1916, in the modern story). Later in John Ford films (*Three Godfathers* 1948), she retired to Hermosa Beach, California, with her husband Lee Arms. She died from a heart attack at 72. Sec. 5, Companion Memorial plot 10, lot 838, Pacific Crest Memorial Park, Redondo Beach, CA.

6088. Marshal, Alan (Alan Marshal Willey, Jan. 29, 1909–July 9, 1961) Australian actor in Hollywood from 1936 (*After the Thin Man* 1936, *Night Must Fall* 1937, *The Adventures of Sherlock Holmes, The Hunchback of Notre Dame* 1939, *Tom, Dick and Harry* 1941, *The White Cliffs of Dover* 1944, *House on Haunted Hill* 1958). He died at the Edgewater Hotel in Chicago from a heart attack at 52. Cremated at Graceland Cemetery, Chicago. Columbarium of Victory, niche 32434, Freedom Mausoleum, Forest Lawn, Glendale, CA.

6089. Marshall, Brenda (Ardis Anderson Gaines, Sept. 29, 1915–July 30, 1992) Philippines born actress at Warner Bros. in the 1940's (*The Sea Hawk, The Smiling Ghost, Footsteps in the Dark, Captains of the Clouds*), formerly married to William Holden. She died in Palm Springs, California. Ashes scattered at sea through the Neptune Society.

6090. Marshall, E.G. (Everett Gunnar Marshall, June 18, 1910/1914–Aug. 24, 1998) Actor of Norwegian descent from Owatonna, Minnesota, in curt, forceful roles on stage, radio, in films (*The Caine Mutiny* 1954, *Twelve Angry Men* 1957, *Compulsion* 1959, *Interiors* 1971, *Absolute Power* 1997, many others). TV series *The Defenders* 1961–65, for which he won two Emmys, *The Bold Ones* 1969–73, and *Chicago Hope* 1994–95. He died at 84 (or 88) at his home in Mount Kisco, New York. Cremated at Ferncliff Crematory, Hartsdale, New York, through Oellker and Cox mortuary in Mount Kisco. No services. Ashes interred c. 15–20 feet in from Curry Drive on the left. Stone marked *E.G. Marshall*. Middle Patent Rural Cemetery, Bedford Banksville Road, North Castle (near Bedford), NY.

6091. Marshall, Everett (Everett R. Marshall, Dec. 30, 1901–April 3, 1965) Singer from Lawrence, Massachusetts, plucked from the opera for two films, *Dixiana* (1930) and *I Live For Love* (1935), later toured in various musicals for the Shuberts. He died at 63 in Carmel, California. St. Luke sec., 30–31, row 13, grave 37, San Carlos Catholic Cemetery, Monterey, CA.

6092. Marshall, George Catlett (Dec. 31, 1880– Oct. 16, 1959) U.S. Army Five Star General, Chief of Staff during World War II, Secretary of State under Truman and the father of the Marshall Plan (1947) for European post war economic recovery. Nobel Peace Prize 1953. Sec. 7, site 8198, grid VW-24, Arlington National Cemetery, Arlington, VA.

6093. Marshall, George E. (Dec. 29, 1891–Feb. 17, 1975) Chicago born film director began at Universal in 1912 and worked through the 1960's, best known for comedies with Bob Hope or W.C. Fields and a handful of comedy dramas including *Destry Rides Again* (1939), *The Ghost Breakers* (1940), *Murder He Says* (1944), *Fancy Pants* (1950). Block 78, crypt F1, Holy Cross Cemetery mausoleum, Culver City, CA.

6094. Marshall, Gloria (Gloria Marshall Gamble, Aug. 27, 1931–Dec. 18, 1994) Actress in films and TV (*Love That Bob*) of the 1950's and 60's. Cremated through Palm Springs mortuary. Ashes to family, Bermuda Dunes, CA.

6095. Marshall, Herbert (May 23, 1890–Jan. 22, 1966) English actor with distinctive delivery exuded quiet dignity in many roles including *Murder* (1930), *The Letter*, *Foreign Correspondent* (both 1940), *The Little Foxes* (1941), *The Enchanted Cottage* (1945) and as Somerset Maugham in both *The Moon and Sixpence* (1942) and *The Razor's Edge* (1946). He died from a heart attack at 75. Ashes in vaultage below Pierce Brothers' Chapel of the Pines Crematory, Los Angeles.

6096. Marshall, John (Sept. 24, 1755–July 6, 1835) The fourth and most significant Chief Justice of the United States Supreme Court (1801–1835) until the term (1953–69) of Earl Warren, Marshall's court contained decisions establishing the long term power and scope of the court. He died after a carriage accident, and it was during the tolling of the bells for his funeral that the Liberty Bell in Philadelphia received its famous crack. His family plot is enclosed by an iron fence; his spot marked by a grave length marble tomb top with an eroded inscription on the surface. A historical sign was placed at the site in 1976. Shockoe Cemetery, Richmond, VA.

6097. Marshall, Laurence (May 18, 1889–Nov. 5, 1980) Inventor of the microwave oven, revolutionizing cooking. Flush plaque. Aratia Path, Mt. Auburn Cemetery, Cambridge, Mass. He was removed in October 1996 to Peterborough, NH.

6098. Marshall, Mike (Sept. 13, 1944–June 2, 2005) Los Angeles born actor son of William Marshall and French actress Michele Morgan appeared in over forty American and French films, including *A Little Romance* and *Moonraker* (both 1979). He died from cancer at 60 in Caen, Normandy. Funeral at the Normandy coastal town of Deauville (Calvados region), France.

6099. Marshall, Peter (May 27, 1902–Jan. 25, 1949) Scottish born Presbyterian clergyman pastored in Washington, D.C., before becoming Chaplain of the U.S. Senate 1947–49. Renowned for his sermons filled with common sense and earthly connections, he died from a heart attack at 46. The subject of his widow's memoir, *A Man Called Peter*, filmed with Richard Todd in 1955. Sec. C, lot 344, grave 11, Fort Lincoln Cemetery, Brentwood, MD.

6100. Marshall, Thomas Riley (March 14, 1854– June 1, 1925) Native of North Manchester, Indiana, served as Vice President under Woodrow Wilson 1913–1921. When Wilson suffered a debilitating stroke in September 1919, Marshall did not assume the power of the presidency, which by all accounts was taken over largely by the First Lady, who screened matters brought to Wilson's attention. Marshall is best known for having remarked during a particularly boring senate speech on what the country needed that "what this country needs is a good five cent cigar." Entombed first in a family mausoleum at the I.O.O.F. Cemetery, Marion, Indiana, but removed. Family mausoleum on an island, intersection of sections 12, 45, 46 and 23, Crown Hill Cemetery, Indianapolis, IN.

6101. Marshall, Thurgood (July 2, 1908–Jan. 24, 1993) Influential Supreme Court justice, the first black to sit on the court, was appointed by President Johnson October 2, 1967. Marshall, a Baltimore born lawyer and judge, was the primary force in working toward racial equality through legislation. Of his many court victories as a lawyer, Brown vs. the Board of Education, argued before the Supreme Court in 1954, was his most notable, bringing an end to "separate but equal" racial segregation in the schools of twenty one states. He was known on the Supreme Court for his liberal interpretations of the Constitution including the right to picket in a public forum, the right to read or view any materials in one's home, and staunch opposition to the death penalty. Vocal in later years in his criticism of the Reagan-Bush administration, upon his retirement in 1991 he was replaced, after a sensationalized senate hearing, by Clarence Thomas. Sec.

5, site 40-3, Arlington National Cemetery, Arlington, VA.

6102. Marshall, Trudy (Feb. 14, 1922–May 23, 2004) Brooklyn born actress in ingénue parts played the sister, Genevieve, in *The Fighting Sullivans* (1944), Elizabeth Van Borden in *Dragonwyck* (1946), *The Fuller Brush Girl,* several others into the 1970's. The widow of Philip Raffin; they were the parents of actress Deborah Raffin. Hillside Slope, plot 54, lot 2, space 2, Hillside Memorial Park, Los Angeles.

6103. Marshall, Tully (William Phillips, April 10, 1864–March 10, 1943) Gaunt character actor in silent and sound films (*The Cat and the Canary* 1927, *Queen Kelly* 1928, *Arsene Lupin* and *Red Dust* 1932, dozens more). He died in Encino. Service at St. Mary of the Angels. Unmarked for some forty years, his flush gray marker, placed by Larry Arthur in the 1980's, reads *Beloved actor Tully Marshall. God needed another angel. 1864–1943.* Sec. 8/Garden of Legends, lot 44/45, Hollywood Forever Cemetery, Hollywood (Los Angeles), CA.

6104. Marshall, William (G. William Marshall, Oct. 2, 1917–June 8, 1994) Chicago born singer (with Fred Waring), actor from 1940 to the early 50's, and director. Formerly married to Ginger Rogers and Michele Morgan. Not to be confused with black actor William Marshall. Buried at Richarville, France.

6105. Marshall, William (William Horace Marshall, Aug. 19, 1924–June 11, 2003) Black actor from Gary, Indiana, in films and television from the early 1950's, made his mark in and as *Blacula* (1972) and in *Scream Blacula Scream* (1973), though his work had a wide range, including the lead in the 1981 filming of *Othello.* He died from a heart ailment at 78 in North Hollywood. Cremated by the Neptune Society. Ashes given June to family or friends at Pacoima, CA.

6106. Marshman, Bobby (G. Robert Marshman, Sept. 24, 1936–Dec. 3, 1964) Race driver was Rookie of the Year in 1961 and qualified in three other Memorial Day classics before his death at 28 in a San Antonio burn center from injuries received a week before in the crash of his Lotus Ford at Phoenix International Speedway. Flush plaque with a racecar and the crossed checkered flags on it, area right of entrance. Garden of Time, lot 213, Limerick Garden of Memories, 44 Swamp Pike, Limerick (near Pottstown), PA.

6107. Marsillach, Adolfo (Jan. 25, 1928–Jan. 21, 2002) Spanish actor, writer and director, on stage and screen from 1947, theater director from 1956, and from 1965 director of the Teatro Espanol de Madrid, directing films from 1972. Cremated at Cementerio de la Almudena, Madrid. Ashes scattered at sea.

6108. Martin, Barney (Oct. 11, 1922–March 21, 2005) Beefy New York police detective from Queens got into acting and was seen often on television and in films from 1956 (*The Producers, Charly*—both 1968, *Arthur* 1981, TV pilot *Us* 1991), best known as Jerry's retired father Morty on TV's *Seinfeld.* He died from gallbladder cancer in Los Angeles at 82. Cremated by

the Nautilus Society. Ashes March 25 to his family at Studio City, CA.

6109. Martin, Ben (June 28, 1921–July 24, 2004) Coach of the Air Force Academy Falcons football team 1958–1977 (though a 1945 Navy graduate) had a 96–103–9 record, with trips to the 1959 Cotton Bowl, 1963 Gator Bowl and 1970 Sugar Bowl, afterwards broadcasting the games as an analyst for fifteen years. U.S. Naval Academy Cemetery, Annapolis, MD.

6110. Martin, Benny (May 8, 1928–March 13, 2001) Fiery fiddler played with Bill Monroe and Roy Acuff before becoming part of Flatt and Scruggs' Foggy Mountain Boys. Meditation 9D, grave 4, Forest Lawn Memorial Park/Gardens, Goodlettsville, TN.

6111. Martin, Billy (Alfred Martin, May 16, 1928–Dec. 25, 1989) New York Yankees player under Casey Stengal in the early 50's was later their manager, hired and fired by George Steinbrenner five times in the 1970's and 80's; their love-hate relationship (and Martin's with Reggie Jackson) was as much in evidence as Martin's temper and brawling on and off the field. He died on Christmas Day 1989 when the car in which he was riding skidded on an icy road and came to rest at the foot of his driveway near Fenton, New York. Mass at St. Patrick's Cathedral in Manhattan, with burial on the same hillside as Babe Ruth. The large brown granite monument bears the epitaph *I may not have been the greatest Yankee to put on a uniform but I was the proudest.* Sec. 25, near the top of the hill, Gate of Heaven Cemetery, Hawthorne, NY.

6112. Martin, Charles (Aug. 31, 1958–Jan. 23, 2005) NFL lineman from Canton, Georgia, dubbed "Too Mean" played 1983–88, with the Birmingham Stallions, Green Bay Packers 1984–87, Houston Oilers and Atlanta Falcons, as a defensive end with Green Bay slammed Bears quarterback Jim McMahon into the turf, ending his season in 1986; McMahon had been at the top of Martin's displayed "hit" list, and was ejected and suspended for two games. He died from kidney failure at 46 in Houston. Funeral at Canton. Enon Cemetery, Woodstock, GA.

6113. Martin, Chris-Pin (Nov. 19, 1893–June 27, 1953) Mexican-American actor played various sidekicks in films (*Three Godfathers*) and on television in *The Cisco kid* and *Zorro.* Ave. 25, lot 46, grave 12, Oddfellows Cemetery, Los Angeles.

6114. Martin, Dean (Dino Paul Crocetti, June 17, 1917–Dec. 25, 1995) Actor-comedian and crooner from Steubenville, Ohio, with Jerry Lewis in a nightclub act and on film until their split in 1956. Leaving the role of Lewis's straight man, he developed as a part time serious actor, often with "Rat Pack" cronies Frank Sinatra, Sammy Davis Jr. and Peter Lawford. Films 1958–1970 include *The Young Lions, Some Came Running, Rio Bravo, Bells Are Ringing, Four For Texas, Robin and the Seven Hoods, The Sons of Katie Elder, Five Card Stud, Airport,* and a series of *Matt Helm* detective films 1965–67. His recordings, led by his theme

Everybody Loves Somebody Sometime (1964), flourished on Reprise in the 1960's and, though largely just part of the act, he honed to perfection the image of the blasé, ever half soused TV host in *The Dean Martin Show* 1965–74 and a series of celebrity roasts afterward. A year after his son's death in 1987, he left his last tour with Sinatra and Davis, living afterward in seclusion. He died in Beverly Hills from respiratory arrest and lung cancer on Christmas Day at 78. Private service and interment near his parents (Guy and Angela Crocetti, Sanctuary of Peace). Below his name and dates on the crypt plaque is *Everybody Loves Somebody Sometime*. Sanctuary of Love, Westwood Memorial Park, west Los Angeles.

6115. Martin, Dean Paul (Nov. 17, 1951–March 21, 1987) Son of singer-actor Dean Martin was part of the 1960's band Dino, Desi and Billy, also featuring Desi Arnaz, Jr. USAF Capt. Martin died in the crash of his fighter plane in the San Bernardino Mountains while serving with the Air National Guard. Sec. 419, row P, grave 28, Los Angeles/Sawtelle National Cemetery, Westwood, west Los Angeles, CA.

6116. Martin, Freddy (Frederick A. Martin, Dec. 9, 1906–Sept. 30, 1983) Big Band leader of the 30's and 40's popularized *Tchaikovsky's Piano Concerto No. 1* as *Tonight We Love* (his theme) and introduced vocalist Merv Griffin as well. Mausoleum of the Pacific, Magnolia Court, crypt 884, bottom tier, Pacific View Memorial Park, Newport Beach, CA.

6117. Martin, Grady (Thomas Grady Martin, Jan. 17, 1929–Dec. 3, 2001) Country western guitarist did a lot of studio work, notably the considerable solo accompaniment to Marty Robbins' vocal on *El Paso* (1959). Hopper Cemetery, Laws Hill, TN.

6118. Martin, Harvey (Nov. 16, 1950–Dec. 24, 2001) Dallas cowboy defensive end, with a record 125 career sacks. Whispering Waters, area 1, 22A, Restland Memorial Park, Dallas, TX.

6119. Martin, Jimmy (James H. Martin, Aug. 10, 1927–May 14, 2005) Practitioner of the High Lonesome sound from the late 1940's recorded with Bill Monroe, with his own Sunny Mountain Boys and a variety of artists including the Nitty Gritty Dirt Band; the "king of Bluegrass music" in the 1970's, as described in several paragraphs, plus a photo — a replica of his Bluegrass Hall of Honor plaque — on his pre-erected 4' monument across from Roy Acuff. He died in Nashville from bladder cancer at 77. Spring Hill Cemetery, Gallatin Road near Madison, outside Nashville, TN.

6120. Martin, John (Giovanni Martini, d. Dec. 24, 1922) Immigrant from Italy landed in Brooklyn before he joined the U.S. Army and survived The Little Big Horn, a bugler who was reportedly the last man to carry General Custer's orders from the field, requesting reinforcements. By 1908 he had become a ticket chopper in the relatively new New York City subway system, at the 103rd St. station on the Upper West Side, and later worked at the Brooklyn Navy Yard before being run down by a beer truck and killed. In the 1990's historians placed a granite monument at his standard military marker. Sec. 2, grave 8865, Cypress Hills National Cemetery, Brooklyn, N.Y.C.

6121. Martin, Kiel (July 26, 1944–Dec. 28, 1990) Pittsburgh born actor was a regular on TV's *Hill Street Blues* 1981–86 as alcoholic, streetwise detective J.D. LaRue. He died from cancer at 46 in Rancho Mirage, California. No services. Ashes reportedly scattered in the desert.

6122. Martin, Len (1917–Sept. 2, 1963) Composer of many radio and TV jingles co-owned Calico Records and helped develop The Skyliners in the late 1950's. He died from cancer at 46. Mt. Carmel Cemetery, Pittsburgh, PA.

6123. Martin, Lock (Joseph Lockard Martin, Jr., Oct. 12, 1916–Jan. 19, 1959) Actor played Gort the robot in *The Day the Earth Stood Still* (1951). Klaatu barada nikto. Vale of Peace, lot 3954/55, Forest Lawn Hollywood Hills, Los Angeles.

6124. Martin, Marion (June 7, 1909–Aug. 13, 1985) Blonde actress in gold digger roles at MGM in the 40's. Married name Krzykowski. Block 143, crypt A2, mausoleum at Holy Cross Cemetery, Culver City, CA.

6125. Martin, Mary (Dec. 1, 1913–Nov. 3, 1990) Broadway singer-actress from Wetherford, Texas, mother of Larry Hagman, starred in Rodgers and Hammerstein's *South Pacific* (1949) for 1,925 performances. As *Peter Pan* (1954) she gave 152 performances and filmed the stage version for television. When her husband of thirty years, story editor Richard Halliday, died in Brazil in 1973, she had to take him to Miami to be cremated, after which she buried his ashes with her parents and brother at Wetherford and designed their flat bisque marker, with hands clasped and both names. Beneath Halliday's name and dates and under the space for her death date she had inscribed *whose heart belongs to him forever*, paraphrased from one of her trademark numbers *My Heart Belongs to Daddy*. Her ashes were buried there after her death at 76 from cancer in Rancho Mirage, California. Sec. B, surrounded by an iron fence, Greenwood Cemetery, Wetherford, TX.

6126. Martin, Pepper (John L. Martin, Feb 29 1904–March 5 1965) The Wild Horse of the Osage, part of the Gashouse Gang, played third base and outfield for the St. Louis Cardinals 1928–1940 and 1944. Sec. 25, 91–1, Memorial Park Cemetery, Oklahoma City, OK.

6127. Martin, Quinn (May 22, 1922–Sept. 5, 1987) TV producer of the 1960's and 70's; QM Productions did *Twelve O'Clock High, The F.B.I.*, others. Cremated through Westwood mortuary, west Los Angeles.

6128. Martin, Rose (Nov. 28, 1913–May 2, 1998) Tiverton, Rhode Island, resident wished to be buried in her white 1962 Corvair she had driven around town for 35 years, and was, by pre-arrangement. After she died at 84, the seats were removed and her casket was placed in the car and lowered by crane into the four plot grave. The stone was already inscribed with the image of she and the car. Pocasset Hill Cemetery, Tiverton, RI.

6129. Martin, Ross (Martin Rosenblatt, March 22, 1920–July 3, 1981) Polish born actor in film and TV, in *Experiment in Terror* (1962), and the Rod Serling TV scripts *Death Ship* (*Twilight Zone*, 1963) and *Camera Obscura* (*Night Gallery*, 1971), but was best known as Artemus in the series *Wild Wild West* 1965–69. He died from a heart attack at 61. Maimonides 30, lot 3628, space 2, Mt. Sinai Memorial Park, Los Angeles.

6130. Martin, Strother (March 26, 1919–Aug. 1, 1980) Character actor in films and TV as agitators in numerous westerns also played the sadistic straw boss in *Cool Hand Luke* (1967) with the trademark line "What we have here is a failure to communicate." Many other appearances (*The Man Who Shot Liberty Valance, True Grit, The Wild Bunch, Butch Cassidy and the Sundance Kid*). Columbarium of Radiant Dawn, niche G62420, Courts of Remembrance, Forest Lawn Hollywood Hills, Los Angeles.

6131. Martina, Joe (July 8, 1889–March 22, 1962) Oyster Joe, one of the Texas League and Southern Association's finest pitchers, had a long career in double A baseball. He made it to the majors for one season and managed to pitch a scoreless inning for the Washington Senators in the 1924 world series. In *The Bill James Historical Baseball Abstract* (1986), he was named the ugliest player of the 1920's. Jessamine 31, between Magnolia and Hawthorne, Greenwood Cemetery, New Orleans, LA.

6132. Martinez, Tony (Jan. 27, 1920–Sept. 16, 2002) San Juan born musician, singer and actor best known as Pepino in *The Real McCoys* 1957–1963. He later played Sancho Panza on Broadway and in the national company tour of *Man of La Mancha*, from 1967 into the 1990's. He died at Nathan Adelson Hospice in Las Vegas at 82. Ashes picked up from his wife from Nevada Cremation and Burial service, Las Vegas, September 26, possibly — but unconfirmed — to be taken eventually back to Puerto Rico.

6133. Martlew, Mary (Aug. 8, 1919–Oct. 27, 1989) British actress married to a Swiss (Escher) lived most of her life in Vienna. Her few films (1946–49) include *The Laughing Lady, Cry Havoc, Ghosts of Berkeley Square, Anna Karenina* (1948, as Princess Nathalia) and *Britannia Mews* (1949). She died in Vienna and was buried in a private cemetery, Hohe Promenade, in Zurich.

6134. Martwick, Bob (c.1925–Aug. 26, 2001) Owner and agent for Morris the Cat, the Chicago based animal that became a popular "talking" advertiser of cat foods in the 1970's. The cat was buried in his back yard. Martwick died at 75. Burial through Steuerle mortuary, Villa Park, Illinois. Lakeside Cemetery, Phillips, Price County, WI.

6135. Marvell, Andrew (March 31, 1621 [or 22]–Aug. 16/18, 1628) English poet from Yorkshire wrote on politics and satirical prose in his lifetime but is best known for his posthumously published lyric poems, including *To His Coy Mistress* and *The Garden*, often open to varying interpretation. Secretary to Cromwell's Latin Secretary Milton, he also wrote *Cromwell's Return to England*, and served in Parliament from Hull. Saint Giles Church in the Fields, London.

6136. Marvin, Johnny (John Senator Marvin, July 11, 1897–Dec. 20, 1944) Recording artist of the 1920's penned several songs for Gene Autry. Sec. 300, niche K12, Los Angeles/Sawtelle National Cemetery, west Los Angeles.

6137. Marvin, Lee (Feb. 19, 1924–Aug. 29, 1987) Tow headed character actor in tough guy roles, tight lipped and often sadistic, on either side of the law (*The Big Heat* 1953, *Bad Day at Black Rock* 1954, *The Man Who Shot Liberty Valance* 1962, *The Killers* 1964, *The Dirty Dozen* 1967) could also play comedy with relish, winning an Oscar for *Cat Ballou* (1965) and offering samples of his singing voice in *Paint Your Wagon* (1967). In a landmark legal case in 1979 his ex live-in girlfriend of six years sued for half his money and lost. He was re-married and living in Tucson when he died from a heart attack at 63 at Tucson Medical Center. A marine veteran of World War II, he was buried beneath a white military headstone beside boxing champion Joe Louis. Sec. 7A, site 176, Arlington National Cemetery, Arlington, VA.

6138. Marvin, Tony (Oct. 5, 1912–Oct. 10, 1998) The Voice of the 1939 New York World's Fair and announcer for Arthur Godfrey for fourteen years. Block 35, grave 303, Beth Moses Cemetery, Farmingdale, NY.

6139. Marx, Chico (Leonard Marx, March 22, 1887–Oct. 11, 1961) Eldest of the Marx Brothers comedy team from Manhattan's Yorkville section on East 93rd St.; they supposedly got their lifelong nicknames in a card game, Chico because he was a chicken (girl) chaser. On stage and screen he essayed the illogical Italian with Groucho and played straight man for Harpo, while managing to get a piano number or two into every picture (except *Duck Soup*). He had suffered at least two heart attacks prior to his death in his Hollywood home at 74. His funeral in the Wee Kirk o' the Heather Chapel at Forest Lawn, Glendale, was widely attended and generally considered a travesty by his brothers, none of whom had public funerals. Although his daughter had asked the minister to say that her father was the "least malicious" of men, the officiator misspoke and called him "the least mischievous," no greater error being possible. The service was further marred by two children dressed in Marx Brothers costumes who were rushed up to the open coffin by an adult who snapped their picture there. Crypt at top level, right side, Sanctuary of Worship, (rear lower level) Freedom Mausoleum, Forest Lawn, Glendale, California. Chico's widow, Mary Dee [de Vithas]

Marx (1928–Dec. 22, 2002), his wife from August 1958 until his death three years later, died at 74 the same day as Susan Marx, Harpo's widow. Magnolia Court, 939, space 5, Pacific View Memorial Park, Newport Beach, CA.

6140. Marx, Groucho (Julius Henry Marx, Oct. 2, 1890–Aug. 19, 1977) The best known of the Marx Brothers was the wise cracking, insulting, leering lothario with the painted eyebrows, mustache and long cigar. In real life, the third of five brothers was quiet and literate with little formal education but well versed in Gilbert & Sullivan, an avid reader and correspondent with some of the great wits and literary figures of his time. He enjoyed a second career as quizmaster on radio and TV's *You Bet Your Life* into the 1960's and, unlike Chico and Harpo, lived to see their old films, particularly *Duck Soup* and *A Night at the Opera* become cult favorites with a new generation in the 1970's. He gave a widely acclaimed (reminiscing) concert at Carnegie Hall in May 1972, but suffered a stroke that summer and grew increasingly feeble, although he accepted a special Oscar at the Academy Awards ceremonies in 1974. His last years were controversial due to the polarization of his friends and family over his young companion, Erin Fleming (*q.v.*), a long legal battle ensuing over his estate after his death. Hospitalized at Cedars Sinai in Los Angeles since June 22, 1977, he died from respiratory failure and complications from the series of strokes at 86. A private memorial gathering was held at his son Arthur's home. Cremated at Oddfellows Crematory through Groman mortuary, the ashes were inurned in the San Fernando Valley. In May 1982 the urn was stolen and found on the steps of Mt. Sinai Memorial Park in Los Angeles, after which it was returned to its niche. Only *Groucho Marx 1890–1977* and the Star of David are on the niche cover, at eye level in a side columbarium of the lower mausoleum, Eden Memorial Park, Mission Hills, CA His third wife Eden Hartford Marx (April 10, 1930–Dec. 15, 1983), who divorced him in 1969, died from cancer at 53. Her ashes are in an outdoor columbarium at Westwood Memorial Park, west Los Angeles.

6141. Marx, Gummo (Milton Marx, Oct. 21, 1893–April 21, 1977) The fourth Marx Brother, his birth listed — including his crypt plaque — as 1893, appeared in their vaudeville act but never made it to Broadway or films. He went to France in World War I and afterward worked as a dress manufacturer in New York and an agent in Hollywood, as did Zeppo. He died in Eisenhower Medical Center in Palm Springs where he, Zeppo and formerly Harpo had retired to play golf. Groucho survived him by only four months but was in frail health and was never told of Gummo's death from a heart attack at 83. Crypt at eye level, left side, a few yards from his brother Chico across the hall. Sanctuary of Brotherhood, rear lower level, Freedom Mausoleum, Forest Lawn, Glendale, CA.

6142. Marx, Harpo (Adolph Arthur Marx, Nov. 23, 1888–Sept. 28, 1964) The second of five Marx brothers became a mute in the act early on, added a horn, battered top hat and coat, girl chasing and a red wig (changed to blonde after it photographed too dark in their first film) to create the cherubic child-like member of the quartet turned trio, the favorite of children on screen and of many off screen. A serious harpist but not well read, he became the darling of the literati of the Algonquin Round Table from 1924 into the 30's and a perennial member of Alexander Woollcott's closest circle of friends because, he said, they needed someone who could just listen. Like Gummo, Harpo married once and permanently, to actress Susan Fleming. He retired to Palm Springs to play golf by the late 40's, and had suffered several heart attacks by the time he entered Mt. Sinai Hospital in Los Angeles for heart surgery, during which complications ended his life at 75. Groucho's son Arthur said that the only time he had seen his normally dry eyed and matter-of-fact father cry were when his (Groucho's) mother died and when Harpo died. He was the most widely loved of the Marx Brothers, not entirely unlike his character in films, adopting all the children he could fill his house with. There were no announced services. He was cremated at Hollywood (Memorial Park Cemetery) Crematory September 30, placed in a china urn and held at Groman mortuary until October 6, when it was taken with an October 5 burial permit to Desert Memorial Park, Palm Springs. The cemetery has no record of the interment, however, and the ashes are believed to have been returned to this widow at their home in Cathedral City, CA.

6143. Marx, Karl (May 5, 1818–March 14, 1883) German Jewish political philosopher whose writings became the basis of communism. Marx settled in London in 1849 and was supported by a series of loans, finally, and ironically, by Friedrich Engels, a retired capitalist. The first volume of *Das Kapital* appeared in 1867 but ill health prevented Marx from publishing the other two in his lifetime. His death came on the heels of that of his wife from liver cancer in December 1881, and of his daughter, who died in Paris in January 1883. He died intestate from tuberculosis in his row house at Maitland Park Road, south of Hampstead Heath. In 1956 a large marble block surmounted by a huge cast iron head of Marx was placed at his grave. The inscription lists he and his wife, a grandson, and his housekeeper Helena Demuth, who secretly bore his son in 1851. A slab marks the original grave. They were removed to the spot where the bust is in November 1954. East sec., Highgate Cemetery, London.

6144. Marx, Louis (Aug. 11, 1896–Feb. 5, 1982) Brooklyn born toy manufacturer with Abraham-Strauss, founded his own company in Manhattan in 1919, making toys of all kinds, from model trains to figures, with his brother David. He sold the company in 1976 for $52 million. Family mausoleum, Woodlawn Cemetery, the Bronx, N.Y.C.

6145. Marx, Minnie (Minnie Schoenberg, Nov. 1864 [some sources, including her headstone, list 1865]–Sept. 13, 1929) and **Samuel "Frenchy" Marx** (Oct. 1860 [headstone lists 1861]–May 11, 1933) The parents of the Marx Brothers became, largely through the reminiscences of Groucho and Harpo, familiar figures on their own. German born Minnie Schoenberg was the sister of vaudevillian Al Shean and pushed her sons into stage acts early on, with the eldest (Chico) already an accomplished piano player, and prompted them tirelessly. She lived to see them on Broadway in *I'll Say She Is* (1924), *The Cocoanuts* (1928) and the film version (their first) of the latter in 1929, just before her death from a stroke in New York on the way to her home in Great Neck. The burial was in Mt. Carmel, where Alexander Woollcott, seeing an apparent Irish name on a stone, remarked to Harpo "spy"; he wrote a glowing editorial tribute to her afterward. Frenchy, a not too successful tailor from Alsace-Lorraine, went to Hollywood after his sons did in 1931 and managed to appear, waving from both the boat and the pier, in *Monkey Business*. He died in Los Angeles and was returned for burial in New York beside his wife. Family stone inscribed *Marx* with two headstones in front of it reading *Devoted wife Minnie* and *Devoted husband Samuel*, and their years of birth and death. Block 10, walk 9, lot w ½ 373, New (#2) Mt. Carmel Cemetery, Glendale, Queens, N.Y.C. Minnie's mother, **Fanny Schoenberg** (died April 10, 1901) is buried beside her grandson, the first Marx brother, **Manfred Marx**, who died at seven months of "entero-colitis" and asthenia, July 17, 1886. Washington Cemetery, Brooklyn, N.Y.C.

6146. Marx, Samuel "Frenchy" *see* **Minnie Marx.**

6147. Marx, Samuel (Jan. 26, 1902–March 2, 1992) Story editor at MGM from the 1920's was a literary institution in Hollywood, securing the rights to such studio classics as *Grand Hotel, Tarzan the Ape Man, Mutiny on the Bounty* and *Goodbye Mr. Chips,* co-wrote and produced *Lassie Come Home,*" several others. He also oversaw the screenwriting careers of such luminaries as George S. Kaufmann, F. Scott Fitzgerald, Ben Hecht, William Faulkner and Dorothy Parker. In later years he wrote several histories of Hollywood, including *Mayer and Thalberg* and *Deadly Illusions* (about Jean Harlow and Paul Bern). He last appeared on the TNT history of MGM, *When the Lion Roars* (1992). His flat niche plaque lists his name, *Chronicler,* his dates, and *A Gaudy Spree.* Urn garden, Westwood Memorial Park, west Los Angeles.

6148. Marx, Susan Fleming (Susan Fleming, Feb. 19, 1908–Dec. 22, 2002) New York born Ziegfeld Follies beauty Susan Fleming appeared in films 1931–39, notably *Million Dollar Legs* (1932) with W.C. Fields, and in fact made more films at Paramount than the Marx Brothers, but it was as Mrs. Harpo Marx, from September 28, 1936 until his death on their 28th anniversary in 1964, that she maintained her notoriety.

As a force in civic affairs in the Palm Springs area from the early 1950's, she served on various boards and was instrumental in establishing the desert community as a residential area. In her last decades she was most famous as an honored figure among the large cult following the Marx Brothers had acquired by the 1970's. She died from a heart attack at 94 in Eisenhower Medical Center, Palm Springs. Ashes through Palm Springs mortuary to her family at Rancho Mirage, CA.

6149. Marx, Zeppo (Herbert Marx, Feb. 25, 1901–Nov. 30, 1979) Youngest of the Marx Brothers, on Broadway and film as Groucho's straight man and often the romantic interest in their five films for Paramount 1929–1933, afterward leaving the act and opening an office as an agent. He later worked as an inventor, both for the war department and independently. Like Harpo and Gummo, he lived in Palm Springs, where he died at Eisenhower Medical Center from lung cancer at 79. Cremated the same day at Montecito Memorial Park, San Bernardino, through Wiefels and Sons mortuary in Palm Springs. Ashes scattered at sea.

6150. Mary I (Feb. 18, 1516–Nov. 17, 1558) Bloody Mary Tudor, daughter of Henry VIII and Catherine of Aragon, ascended to the throne in 1553, attempting to return England to Catholicism. In 1556 she married King Philip of Spain; she erroneously believed she was pregnant shortly before her death; the cause may have been an ovarian tumor, influenza or congenital syphilis. She named her half-sister Elizabeth as heir to the throne. North side of the Chapel of Henry VII in Westminster Abbey, London.

6151. Mary, Queen of Scots (Dec. 8, 1542–Feb. 8, 1587) Mary Stuart, after having married the Earl of Bothwell who had murdered her husband Lord Darnley, was overthrown and forced to abdicate in favor of her four year old son James. She fled to England to Elizabeth, who had her imprisoned. Mary was accused of complicity in a 1585 assassination attempt and, although she defended herself and was innocent of the charge, was beheaded at the block, after which her pet terrier was found trembling beneath her petticoat. All connected with the execution was burned to prevent their becoming Catholic holy relics. Walled in a lead coffin at Frotheringhay Castle near Peterborough, where she had been imprisoned and executed, her heart and organs were secretly buried there. At her son's request, the body was taken to Peterborough in July and interred in the Cathedral. When James became king in 1603, he had his mother's remains moved to Westminster Abbey beneath a white marble tomb with her recumbent effigy atop it. Ironically it is near Elizabeth's tomb and a Catholic shrine. Chapel of Henry VII, Westminster Abbey, London. Her protégé, Italian singer **David Riccio or Rizzio** (1533–March 9, 1566), murdered by Darnley in Mary's presence, was buried in Canongate churchyard, Edinburgh. **Henry Stewart, Lord Darnley** (1546–Feb. 10, 1567) is at Holyrood Abbey, Edinburgh. **James Hep-**

burn, 4th Earl of Bothwell (1536–April 14, 1578) died insane in a Danish prison and was buried (his mummified corpse now on display under glass in the crypt) at Faarvejle, Copenhagen, Denmark.

6152. Masaryk, Jan (Sept. 14, 1886–March 10, 1948) The son of Czech leader Thomas Masaryk was foreign minister in the exiled Czech government in London during World War II, and afterward in the coalition government of Eduard Benes. After the communist coup of February 25, 1948, he asked the deposed Benes to release him from his office. On the night of March 9 he went to bed and took the usual two seconal to help him sleep. His body was found in the courtyard below the Czernin Palace in Prague the next morning and the death ruled a suicide (though paint and plaster were found under his fingernails). Interest resurfaced in 1968 with the liberalization under Dubcek. Though not proven, murder was the likely means of death. Although investigations halted with the Soviet takeover later in 1968, in December 1969 the suicide verdict was withdrawn but the government announced murder had been excluded as a possibility and that it must have been an accident. Buried in the village of Lany, near Prague.

6153. Mason, George (Dec. 11, 1725–Oct 7, 1792) Founding father wrote the Constitution for Virginia in 1776, including the Declaration of Human Right, the foundation for the later Bill of Rights amended to the U.S. Constitution. Mason opposed it because of its extension of slavery until 1808 and because of too much centralized government. Buried in the graveyard at Gunston Hall, his Lorton estate near Alexandria, VA.

6154. Mason, James (May 15, 1909–July 27, 1984) English actor from Huddersfield, educated at Cambridge, with smooth, precise delivery, three time Oscar nominee (for *A Star is Born* 1954, *Georgy Girl* 1966, and *The Verdict* 1982) continued filming in America and England throughout his forty year career, residing in Switzerland from 1962 at Corseaux, a village near Vevey, east of Lausanne. He suffered a massive heart attack there and died at Lausanne University Hospital at 75. His widow Clarissa Kaye, his wife since 1976, had him cremated and according to a 1991 news story on the ongoing battle in Vevey over his estate, never revealed to his children where his ashes were. She died in 1994, however an article in London at the end of December 1998 noted the legal battle was ongoing, with the ashes in a safe deposit box in the vaults of Darier Hantsch and Cie Bank in Geneva. Though the battle over the estate continued, Mason's daughter Morgan and son Portland finally gained possession of his ashes and sprinkled them into a grave near that of his friend Charles Chaplin in a ceremony November 24, 2000, marked by a slab and upright monument with the epitaph *Never say in grief you are sorry he's gone. Rather say in thankfulness you are grateful he was here.* Village cemetery, Corsier-sur-Vevey, Switzerland.

6155. Mason, Lowell (Jan. 8, 1792–Aug. 11, 1872) Hymn writer (*Nearer My God to Thee, My Faith Looks Up to Thee*) and arranger. Old Cemetery lot 871, Rosedale Cemetery, Orange, NJ.

6156. Mason, Pamela (Feb. 10, 1916–June 29, 1996) British actress, panelist and author from Kent, married to Roy Kellino and later to James Mason, appeared in numerous films (*Jew Suess* 1934, as Pamela Ostrer, *Caught*, as Pam Kellino, *Lady Possessed* [1952], *Charade* [1954, with James Mason]). Divorced from Mason, she died at 80. Ashes in the rose garden, name on a memorial tablet, and later with her daughter Portland Schuyler, with the remembrance *Beautiful, witty and loving.* Pierce Bros.' Westwood Memorial Park, west Los Angeles.

6157. Mason, Sully (Sully Poole Mason, Jan. 15, 1907–Nov. 27, 1970) Saxophone player and part time comic as called for with Kay Kyser's Orchestra and in his films 1939–44. Like Kyser a native of Durham, North Carolina, he died from a stroke at 63 in Los Angeles. Damascus Church Cemetery, 522 Damascus Road, Chapel Hill, NC.

6158. Masseria, Joe (Giuseppe Masseria, c. 1891–April 15, 1931) New York gang chieftain Joe the Boss was opposed by Salvatore Maranzano as Masseria began to escalate opposition to the Mafiosi from Castellammare in New York by 1930. In the ensuing Castellammarese War several men were gunned down before Masseria himself was executed in a Coney Island restaurant by Luciano's associates while he (Luciano) excused himself during a meeting, ostensibly to end the war and make peace with Maranzano (who was himself assassinated by the same confederation in September). The mass was at the Italian Church of Mary, Help of Christians, followed by the traditional long procession of cars. The papers erroneously reported the burial would be at Woodlawn. Family mausoleum facing the road, Sec. 49-138-116, (1st) Calvary, Woodside, Queens, N.Y.C.

6159. Massey, Curt (Dott Curtis Massey, May 3, 1910–Oct. 20, 1991) Emmy winning composer from Midland, Texas, received the Diamond Circle Award from the Pacific Pioneer Broadcasters in 1987. Best known for his TV themes co-written with Paul Henning (*The Beverly Hillbillies, Petticoat Junction, Green Acres*). Urn in south wall, Room of Prayer, Westwood Memorial Park, west Los Angeles.

6160. Massey, Edith (May 29, 1918–Oct. 24, 1984) Character actress known for her roles in John Waters' earlier films, including *Pink Flamingos, Female Trouble* and *Desperate Living.* Ashes scattered in rose garden, Westwood Memorial Park, west Los Angeles.

6161. Massey, Guy Stapleton (Oct. 2, 1898–Feb. 13, 1926) Author of *The Prisoners Song*, as noted on his upright monument (though he had never done time), recorded by Vernon Dalhart in 1924. Block 4, lot 58, space 8, Greenwood Cemetery, Dallas, TX.

6162. Massey, Ilona (June 16, 1910–Aug. 20,

1974) Hungarian actress grew up in poverty in Budapest; she came to America and worked in Hollywood, making eleven films from 1937–1950, often as Nazi spies, double agents, etc. (*Invisible Agent, Frankenstein Meets the Wolf-Man, Love Happy*). Married to retired Air Force Gen. Donald Dawson; their farm "Chatterton" was in King George County, Virginia, on the Potomac. She died in Bethesda Naval Hospital after a three month illness at 64. Her name and dates appear on the rear of Dawson's standard military stone. Sec. 5, grave 7056, Arlington National Cemetery, Arlington, VA.

6163. Massey, Raymond (Raymond Hart Massey, Aug. 30, 1896–July 29, 1983) Canadian actor became a distinguished star for over three decades on stage and screen. Among his best known roles was as John Brown in *Santa Fe Trail*, in the title role of *Abe Lincoln in Illinois* (both filmed in 1940), as the stern father in the 1954 version of John Steinbeck's *East of Eden*, and as Dr. Gillespie on the TV series *Dr. Kildare* in the early 1960's. He died from pneumonia and complications in Los Angeles at 86. Cremated at Pierce Brothers' Chapel of the Pines Crematory in L.A., his ashes were buried with his daughter and wife Dorothy. Ludington lot, near rear of sec. D, Beaverdale Memorial Park, New Haven (near the Hamden border), CT.

6164. Massi, Nick (Nicholas Macioci, Sept. 19, 1935–Dec. 24, 2000) Bass singer who Frankie Valli called his musical mentor was with The Four Seasons from 1961 and sang on all of their hits from *Sherry*, their first, in 1962, through 1965, when he left the group. Massi was especially fond of *Rag Doll*. He died from cancer at 63 (reported as 73) in Newark, New Jersey. Chapel Garden plot 61 #0, Graceland Memorial Park, Kenilworth, NJ.

6165. Massie, Robert F. (died Dec. 25, 1817) Second Lieutenant, Light Artillery, fought a duel at Fort Independence in Boston Harbor that was said to be the basis for Poe's *The Cask of Amontillado*. Sec. 3, site 62, Fort Devens Post Cemetery, Fort Devens, Ayer, MA.

6166. Masson, Paul (Feb. 14, 1859–Oct. 22, 1940) Vintner founded the wine company bearing his name which, as audiences were told for years, will sell no wine before its time. Fern Corridor west, mausoleum, Oak Hill Memorial Park, San Jose, CA.

6167. Masters, Edgar Lee (Aug. 23, 1869–March 5, 1950) American poet, student of history, folklore and cemeteries and the stories of their occupants, specialized in the Illinois of Abraham Lincoln, weaving Lincoln's Springfield in and out of *Spoon River Anthology* (1915), a collection of poems spoken by persons in a small town cemetery, including contemporaries of Lincoln such as Duff Green and Lincoln's supposed first love, Ann Rutledge. The two cemeteries and stones used as models were Oakdale Cemetery in Petersburg, Illinois, and Oak Hill Cemetery in Lewistown, Illinois. Upon its publication, *Spoon River* was scandalous, a milder precursor of Anderson's *Winesburg, Ohio* and Lewis's *Main Street*, dwelling on the gossip and reality beneath small town piety. Masters died in a convalescent home near Philadelphia, but was returned for burial to Petersburg, not far from Lincoln's New Salem village. Buried among the names who had spoken in *Spoon River*, his grave is marked by a boulder with a plaque on it, down the road from Ann Rutledge, inscribed: *Good friends, let us to the fields. After a little walk, and by your pardon, I think I'll sleep. There is no sweeter thing, nor fate more blessed than to sleep. I am a dream out of a blessed sleep. Let us walk and hear the lark.* Sec. 3, lot 490, Oakland Cemetery, Petersburg, IL.

6168. Masterson, Bat (William Barclay Masterson, Nov. 24, 1854–Oct. 25, 1921) Dodge City, Kansas, marshal and associate of Wyatt Earp in Tombstone, Arizona, participated in some gun fights and made a name for himself, popularized with derby and cane. By 1902 he had given it up and gone to New York to work as a sports writer. He had been off sick with a cold and was back at his desk in the *New York Morning Telegraph* when he died there suddenly. Services from the Campbell funeral church. Upright stone with the sentiment *Loved by everyone* in the interior of the Primrose section, lot 185, Woodlawn Cemetery, the Bronx, N.Y.C.

6169. Masterson, Ed (Edward J. Masterson, Sept. 23, 1852–April 9, 1878) Brother of Bat Masterson was marshal of Dodge City, Kansas, when he died at 25; shot in the stomach by a cowboy he was trying to arrest, he managed to fatally wound his assailant and stagger into a saloon before he died. Buried at Fort Dodge Military Cemetery, then moved for a time to Wichita, and finally to Maple Grove Cemetery, Dodge City, Kansas. An article in *The Dodge City Legend* in March 1994, however, notes that five unknown bodies removed from Fort Dodge without markers may have included Ed Masterson, thus skipping the brief interment (at an unnamed spot) in Wichita. The cowboy who killed him, **Jack Wagner**, lies beneath a stone originally inscribed *Killed Ed Masterson April 9, 1878. . . . He argued with the wrong man's brother.* Boot Hill Cemetery, Dodge City, KS.

6170. Masterson, Jim (James P. Masterson, Sept. 16, 1855–March 31, 1895) Lawman and brother of Bat and Ed, died from consumption at 39. Sec. 2, lot 70, space 6, Highland Cemetery, Wichita, KS.

6171. Mastin, Will (June 30, 1897–March 1, 1979) Uncle of Sammy Davis, Jr. was a vaudevillian who with Davis, Sr., introduced Sammy Jr. at age four in 1929. By the late 40's the act was billed as the Will Mastin Trio featuring Sammy Davis, Jr. All three are buried in the Davis plot, guarded by a classical statue, Mastin's plaque has only his name and *He was a vaudevillian.* Garden of Honor (private), Forest Lawn, Glendale, CA.

6172. Mastroianni, Marcello (Sept. 28, 1924–Dec. 19, 1996) Italian actor from Fontana Liri, near Rome, known for *La Dolce Vita* (1960), *Divorce*

Italian Style (1961), won two best actor awards at Cannes and three Oscar nominations. American films include *Used People* (1992). He died from cancer at 72 in his Paris home. Funeral at St. Sulpice Church. Rose slab, Cimitero di Campo Verano (Verano Cemetery), Rome.

6173. Mata Hari *see under* **H.**

6174. Matawn, NJ, 1916 Shark Attack victims *see* **New Jersey 1916 Shark Attack victims.**

6175. Matchabelli, "Prince" Georges (July 23, 1885–March 31, 1935) Russian born makeup magnate established the line of scents and cosmetics bearing his name. Sec. X Edgewood, lot 5903, Mt. Olivet Cemetery, Queens, N.Y.C.

6176. Mate, Rudolph (Jan. 21, 1898–Oct. 27, 1964) Polish born photographer in Hollywood from 1935. His previous work in Europe included Carl Dreyer's imaginative *Vampyr* (1932) with memorable lighting and cinematography by Mate. Oscar nominations for *Foreign Correspondent, That Hamilton Woman, Pride of the Yankees, Sahara,* and *Cover Girl.* Later a director (*D.O.A.* 1950, *All the Way Home* 1963), he died from a heart attack. Block 71, crypt D4, Holy Cross Cemetery mausoleum, Culver City, CA.

6177. Mather, Aubrey (Dec. 17, 1885–Jan. 16, 1958) English actor from Minchinhampton, the son of Frank Mather, a Prebendary of Wells Cathedral. On stage from 1905, he served in the First World War, returning to the English theatre, where he was known for *The Madras House* and *Brewster's Millions,* among others. In films from 1930, many as clerics, professors, civic officials (*Night Must Fall, Rage in Heaven, Ball of Fire, Random Harvest, The Song of Bernadette, Jane Eyre, The Lodger, The House of Fear*— as the naive, pixieish Alastair, *The Secret Garden, The Importance of Being Earnest* 1952). He suffered a stroke in 1957 and died the next year at 72 in Stanmore, Middlesex. Cremation January 22, with the ashes dispersed at sec. 1D of the dispersal lawn, Golders Green Crematorium, London.

6178. Mather, Cotton (Feb. 12, 1663–Feb. 13, 1728) and his father **Increase Mather** (June 21, 1639–Aug. 23, 1723) Puritan clergymen of Boston, famed leaders of their faith. They are buried in Copps Hill at Charter and Hull Streets in downtown Boston, on the city's Freedom Trail in sight of Bunker Hill and the U.S.S. Constitution. The Mather vault is covered by a red brick structure covered by a long stone slab. Copps Hill Burial Ground, Boston, MA.

6179. Mathews, Carmen (Carmen Sylva Mathews, May 8, 1914–Aug. 31, 1995) Actress from Philadelphia in numerous plays (*Road to Mecca, In Fashion, Holiday For Lovers, Dear World*), some films (*Butterfield 8, Sounder, Rage To Live*) and much television through the 1950s and 60s (several *Alfred Hitchcock Presents, Twilight zone* episode *Static,* as Col. Lillian Rayburn on *M.A.S.H.,* last seen in the TV movie *The Last Best Year of My Life* 1990). In 1968 she founded New Pond Farm at West Redding, Connecticut, a camp for underprivileged children as well as a wildlife and nature preserve. She died in West Redding at 81 and was buried near her home beneath a boulder, taken from her farm, with a plaque. Umpawaug Cemetery, Umpawaug Road, Redding, CT.

6180. Mathews, Dorothy (Feb. 13, 1903–May 18, 1977) Blonde actress from New York in some silent and early sound films (*Love Em and Leave Em, The Widow from Chicago, The Doorway to Hell,* 1930, opposite Lew Ayres and James Cagney). She died in Los Angeles from a stroke at 74. Married name Davis. Cremated at Rosedale Cemetery through Westwood mortuary. Ashes buried without record. Westwood Memorial Park, west Los Angeles.

6181. Mathews, Eddie (Edwin Lee Mathews, Oct. 13, 1931–Feb. 18, 2001) Outstanding N.L. third baseman from Texarkana, Texas, raised in Santa Barbara, was the only player with all three Braves teams, in Boston, Milwaukee and Atlanta, compiling 512 home runs, playing in nine All Star games and helping earn two pennants and the world championship with Milwaukee in 1957. Ty Cobb said Mathews had one of the three or four perfect swings he had ever seen. Hall of Fame 1978. He died at 69 in Scripps Memorial Hospital, La Jolla, near his home at Del Mar, California. Welch-Ryce-Haider mortuary, Santa Barbara. Ocean View Triangle, lot 151, Santa Barbara Cemetery, Santa Barbara, CA.

6182. Mathews, John (Feb. 1, 1835–Jan. 11, 1905) Actor in Laura Keene's Company of *Our American Cousin* at the time of Lincoln's assassination (confirmed by Ford's Theatre). A researcher in Arizona informed Kensico Cemetery in 2000 that the same Matthews was interred there (the only one there was buried January 13, 1905). Matthews is of interest because he 1) declined to participate in Booth's plot, so he later said, and 2) claimed he was given a letter by Booth hours before the assassination to give to a newspaper the next day, which he could quote the last part of, justifying his deed, with the names of Paine, Herold and Atzerodt attached. Matthews went to his room after Lincoln was shot, opened the letter, and was so alarmed he burned it, fleeing to Canada. Small stone, Mecca Temple sec., Kensico Cemetery, Valhalla, NY.

6183. Mathews, Joyce (Dec. 5, 1919–Jan. 17, 1999) New York born actress in films of the 1930's and 40's, often in bits, married seven times, twice to three of her four husbands, including Billy Rose and Milton Berle, who said he married her again because she reminded him of his first wife. The widow of actor Don Beddoe, she died in Laguna Hills, California, from liver failure at 79. Cremated through O'Connor Laguna Hills mortuary. Ashes to her daughter in Seattle, WA.

6184. Mathewson, Christy (Christopher Mathewson, Aug. 12, 1880–Oct. 7, 1925) Matty, Master of Them All, the Christian Gentleman was considered the greatest baseball pitcher in the first quarter of the 20th century, hurling for John J. McGraw's New York Giants 1900–1916. With his famed fadeaway pitch, he had three successive thirty victory seasons 1903–05 with three shutouts over the A's in the1905 world series, and set an N.L. record with thirty seven wins in 1908. A captain in the 128th Pa. Division during World War I, his lungs were seared by poison gas that gradually weakened them and caused his death at Saranac Lake, New York, at 45. An original inductee (1936) into the Hall of Fame, he was the only one inducted posthumously at the Cooperstown opening ceremonies in 1939. Family stone and military headstone, Lewisburg Cemetery, Lewisburg, PA.

6185. Mathewson, Wild Bill (William Mathewson, Jan. 1, 1829–March 21, 1916) The original Wild Bill was later police commissioner of Wichita. His monument is topped by a pillar and a statue of an Indian scout and the identification *Last of the Scouts*. Highland Cemetery, Wichita, KS.

6186. Mathis, June (June 30, 1892–July 26, 1927) Script writer and supervisor at Metro known for promoting Rudolph Valentino to stardom in Rex Ingram's *The Four Horsemen of the Apocalypse* (1921). When Valentino died, she offered her crypt in Hollywood Cemetery's Cathedral Mausoleum until his proposed memorial could be built. She was involved in the writing and production of *Ben Hur* in 1926. While attending a performance of *The Squall* at the 48th St. Theatre in New York with her mother the following summer, she called out from her seat, rose and collapsed, dying from heart failure at 35. Eleven months after Valentino, she was laid out in the gold room at the Frank E. Campbell Funeral Church and transported to Hollywood. Valentino was moved up one, out of her vault, where she was interred in the Balboni crypt. Valentino's brother later bought the crypt from Balboni. Her name on the crypt appears in a bronze unrolled scroll. Corridor A, Cathedral Mausoleum, Hollywood Forever Cemetery, Hollywood (Los Angeles), CA.

6187. Matisse, Henri (Dec. 31, 1869–Nov. 3, 1954) French artist of immense influence in the 20th century exhibited with the Fauve group from 1905, using bright and sweeping, clashing colors; he later worked in cubism influenced shapes and moved on to sculpture and to decoupes (cut shapes from paper and pasted on to a field of white). Tomb adjacent Cimitiere Cimiez, Nice, France.

6188. Matsui, Robert (Robert Takeo Matsui, Sept. 17, 1941–Jan. 1, 2005) Japanese-American Democratic congressman from Sacramento represented California's third and fifth districts 1979–2003, helping push through the approval of NAFTA on behalf of President Clinton, and working at permanent trading relations with China. The third ranking Democrat on the House Ways and Means Committee, he died in Bethesda Naval Hospital at 63 from pneumonia and a rare stem cell disorder. East Lawn Memorial Park, Sacramento, CA.

6189. Matthau, Walter (Walter Matthow, Oct. 1, 1920–July 1, 2000) New York born actor on Broadway, winning Tonys for *A Shot in the Dark* (1962) and *The Odd Couple* (1965), was best known for his several comedic teamings on film with Jack Lemmon, including *The Fortune Cookie* (1966), *The Odd Couple* (1968), *The Front Page* (1974), *Buddy Buddy* (1981), *Grumpy Old Men* (1993), its sequel, and the more mellow *The Grass Harp*. An actor of great versatility, he enlivened thrillers such as *A Face in the Crowd, King Creole, Charade, Fail Safe, Charlie Varrick, The Laughing Policeman* and *The Taking of Pelham One Two Three* (1974), but was increasingly known for sometimes complex if irascible characters ranging from Mr. Wilson in *Dennis the Menace* (1993) to *I'm Not Rappaport* (1996), many others over four decades. A once heavy smoker, he suffered his first heart attack in 1966. His last occurred in Santa Monica at 79. He was buried the next day in a lot enclosed by a hedge in front of the new Gardens of Serenity, joined by Lemmon two lots to his left a year later, along the south drive east of the office. Westwood Memorial Park, west Los Angeles.

6190. Matthews, Jessie (May 11, 1907–Aug. 19, 1981) London born musical stage and screen star from a Soho family of eleven was on stage from age ten. Immensely popular in light fare and a graceful dancer, in films including *The Good Companions* (1932), *Evergreen* (1934) and *tom thumb* (1958). A favorite in England and America, at her peak before World War II. Her plaque in the graveyard wall is inscribed *At peace. Jessie Margaret Matthews O.B.E.,* the dates, and *Ecclesiastes Chapter 3, verse 3 and 4.* St. Martin's Parish Cemetery, Ruislip, Middlesex.

6191. Matthews, John (1808–Jan. 12, 1870) New York soda king owned some 5,000 soda fountains and manufactured soda water. His elaborate monument over his grave in Brooklyn features his recumbent figure lying beneath a canopy supported by columns and complete with gargoyles. Sometimes called the Matthews monstrosity, it has drawn a fair amount of both admiration and derision. Sec. 61 at Valley and Walnut, Greenwood Cemetery, Brooklyn, N.Y.C.

6192. Matthews, Lester (Dec. 3, 1900–June 6, 1975) Mustached English leading man in largely ineffective boyfriend and husband roles in Hollywood including *Werewolf of London, The Raven* (both 1935), *The Prince and the Pauper* (1937), *The Adventures of Robin Hood* (1938), *The Invisible Man's Revenge* (1944), *I Love a Mystery* (1945), etc. He died from respiratory failure in Arleta, Los Angeles County, Ca., at 74. Cremated at Rosedale Cemetery in Los Angeles, his ashes were buried at sea by the Neptune Society.

6193. Matthews, Neal (Oct. 26, 1929–April 21, 2000) Second tenor with the Jordanaires from 1953 backed up not only Elvis Presley but Patsy Cline, Ricky Nelson, many others; their rhythmic harmony well known in the music world for over 40 years. Matthews developed a numbering system for chords that enabled quicker learning for session players. He died from a heart attack at 70. Fountain View, sec. A, lot 335, grave 4, Woodlawn Memorial Park, Nashville, TN.

6194. Mattox, Martha (Martha Jane Mattox, June 19, 1879–May 2, 1933) Natchez, Mississippi, born character actress of stage, silents from 1913 and later talkies as several dour, grim housekeepers (*Huckleberry Finn* 1920, as Miss Watson, *Penrod and Sam, Three Wise Fools*, both 1923, *The Cat and the Canary* 1927, as Mammy Pleasant, *The Little Shepherd of Kingdom Come* 1928, *The Fatal Warning* 1929, *Murder By the Clock* 1931, *The Monster Walks, The Bitter Tea of General Yen* 1932). She died of a heart ailment at 53 while staying at Sidney, New York. Cremated at (or ashes delivered to) Waterville (south of Utica), through C.H. Landers funeral home, 21 Main St., Sidney. Notation at the bottom of their card reads "Ashes to be thrown in Pacific Ocean."

6195. Mature, Victor (Jan. 29, 1913–Aug. 4, 1999) Brawny, curly haired actor from Louisville starred in films of the 1940's and 50's, including *One Million B.C.* (1940), *I Wake Up Screaming* (1941), *My Gal Sal* (1942, as Paul Dresser), *My Darling Clementine* (1946, as Doc Holliday), *Kiss of Death* (1947), *Samson and Delilah* (1949) and *The Robe* (1953), retiring by 1960 to play golf, appearing sporadically afterward to 1984. No Olivier, he was known for his sense of humor about his career, particularly the line "Hell, I'm no actor, and I've got 28 pictures to prove it...." He died in Rancho Santa Fe, San Diego County, California, at 86 after three years illness with cancer. Service and burial August 10 through Bosse mortuary, Louisville. The family monument was removed and a new one of Carerra marble with a statue of a weeping angel atop it ordered from Italy, set in June 2001. Sec. 7, lot 46, St. Michael's Cemetery, Louisville, KY.

6196. Mauchly, John William (Aug. 30, 1907–Jan. 8, 1980) Cincinnati born physicist, a major figure in the invention and integration into daily life of the computer, building the first, the ENIAC, by 1946, in partnership with John Eckert (1919–1995). Rose Hill Cemetery, Ambler, PA.

6197. Maugeri, Rudy (Rudolph V. Maugeri, Jan. 27, 1931–May 7, 2004) Baritone from Toronto with The Crew Cuts had hits for Mercury in 1954–55 with popular covers of *Sh-Boom* and *Earth Angel*. He later worked in radio as both announcer and programmer, and co-founded the Fully Alive Charity in Las Vegas prior to his death from pancreatic cancer at 73. Palm Memorial Park, Las Vegas, NV.

6198. Maugham, W. Somerset (Jan 25 1874–Dec 16 1965) English novelist and playwright, his best known works, *Of Human Bondage* (1915) and *Rain* (*Miss Sadie Thompson*, 1922) dealt with moral men's emotional slavery to fallen women. Other works include *The Moon and Sixpence* and *The Razor's Edge*. He died at 91 in his villa on the French Riviera. There is

a plaque close by where his ashes were buried December 22, 1965, near the Maugham Library at the King's School (where he had been unhappy as a boy), Canterbury.

6199. Mauldin, Bill (William Henry Mauldin, Oct. 29, 1921–Jan. 22, 2003) Cartoonist from Mountain Park, New Mexico, was a rifleman with the 180th Infantry from 1940, known for his characters Willie and Joe, first in the *Division News* for the 45th Division, and later in *Stars and Stripes* throughout the war; the two dog faced soldiers slogging their way through Europe endeared themselves to the countless servicemen they spoke for. Adept at puncturing the pompous no matter which way they leaned politically, he was twice awarded the Pulitzer Prize for editorial cartooning—for his series *Up Front* in 1945 and for his 1959 cartoon of Boris Pasternak imprisoned in a gulag, asking "I won the Nobel Prize for literature. What was your crime?" He co-starred in *The Red Badge of Courage* with Audie Murphy in 1951, drew for the *St. Louis Post Dispatch* 1958–62 and the *Chicago Sun Times* from 1962. Ill with Alzheimer's Disease, he died at 81 in a nursing home at Newport Beach, California. Sec. 64, grave 6874, Arlington National Cemetery, Arlington, VA.

6200. Maupassant, Guy de (Aug. 5, 1850–July 6, 1893) French writer of macabre stories such as *Was it a Dream?* and *The Horla*. His later, better known works (*The Necklace*) dealt with irony and injustice. Plagued by long years of debt and gradual insanity, he died in an asylum at 42. Asked to be buried without a coffin so as to mingle with nature, he was buried in a triple thick container, giving his death an irony akin to the themes of many of his tales. Div. 26, (Old) Montparnasse Cemetery, Paris.

6201. Maurer, Linda Collins (March 10, 1939–Oct. 13, 2004) Golfer from Turlock, California, was the first member of Medic Alert, the provider of medical information, started by her parents, Dr. and Mrs. Marion Collins, after she nearly died in 1956 from an allergic reaction to a tetanus antitoxin. She died from breast cancer at 65. Cremated through Allen mortuary there. Ashes to residence.

6202. Maury, Matthew Fontaine (Jan. 14, 1806–Feb. 1, 1873) American naval officer made charts of the Atlantic resulting in a naval conference in Brussels based on his calculations. Unfit for active duty because of lameness, he was in charge of southern harbors for the Confederacy during the Civil War. After some time in exile he returned to teach at the Virginia Military Institute in Lexington. Buried near Presidents Monroe and Tyler. Presidents Circle, lot 26, Hollywood Cemetery, Richmond, VA.

6203. Maxey, Paul (March 15, 1907–June 3, 1963) Ponderous hefty character actor as detectives or henchmen in films of the 1940's and 50's. Sec. C, tier 4, grave 170, Resurrection Cemetery, San Gabriel, CA.

6204. Maximillian, Ferdinand Joseph (July 6, 1832–June 19, 1867) Archduke of Austria and Emperor of Mexico, brother of Franz Joseph, emperor of Austria-Hungary. The crown of Mexico was given to Maximillian by Napoleon III in 1864 after he had conquered there. When the French left, his government fell apart and he was seized and assassinated by firing squad at Querataro. The remains were released in late November 1867 and transported on the Novara back to Trieste and thence by train to Vienna. His mother accompanied the coffin through ice and snow from the Hofburg to der Kapuzinekirche (the Church of the Capucines) and to the vaults beneath, where he was interred next to his father, the Duke of Reichstadt. His wife **Carlota** (**Charlotte, Empress of Mexico**, June 7, 1840–Jan. 19, 1927) had gone mad by her later years. She faded in and out of reality and did not accept his death, retiring to a moated castle at Bouchout, Belgium, where she would periodically act out leaving once more for Mexico with Maximillian. Completely insane, she died at 87 and was placed in the crypt with her family in the Church of Our Lady of Laeken in Brussels, with her father, the Emperor **Leopold** and her mother **Louise Marie**.

6205. Maxwell, Edwin (Feb. 9, 1886–Aug. 12, 1948) Stocky Irish born character actor in countless small roles of the 1930's, in parts varying from officious and pompous to crooked and sadistic (*Dinner at Eight, Night of Terror, Duck Soup, Mystery of the Wax Museum*). He died from a stroke while on tour in Falmouth, Massachusetts. Cremated August 17 at Forest Hills Cemetery, Jamaica Plain, Boston, the ashes were given to his brother-in-law Morris Bond to take to West New York, New Jersey, and from there "to California."

6206. Maxwell, Elsa (May 24, 1883–Nov. 1, 1963) Society columnist and radio host best known for her parties. She also authored books on the art of entertaining, primarily New York and Hollywood celebrities. She died in New York City at 80. Rosewood 2, grave 1132, along a hedge row, Ferncliff Cemetery, Hartsdale, N.Y.

6207. Maxwell, Frank (Nov. 17, 1916–Aug. 4, 2004) Actor for over sixty years and union activist, former president of the American Federation of Television and Radio Artists and vice president of Actors Equity, appeared in *Lonelyhearts, The Intruder, Rage to Live, Madame X,* as Dan Rooney on *General Hospital,* many others. He died in Santa Monica at 87. Sec. R, tier 22, grave 181, Holy Cross Cemetery, Culver City, CA.

6208. Maxwell, Marilyn (Aug. 3, 1921–March 20, 1972) Blonde actress from Clarinda, Iowa, in films from the 1940's introduced *Silver Bells* (with Bob Hope and William Frawley) in *The Lemon Drop Kid* (1951) and later starred in the 1961 TV series *Bus Stop.* She had been suffering from high blood pressure and pulmonary ailments when her son found her dead at 50 in their Beverly Hills home. Bob Hope delivered the eulogy at her funeral in the Beverly Hills Presbyterian Church. Cremated through Pierce Brothers

Chapel of the Pines in Los Angeles, her ashes were scattered at sea.

6209. Maxwell, Robert (June 10, 1923–Nov. 5, 1991) Billionaire head of the global and communications empire including several British tabloids, *The European* and *The New York Daily News*, which he acquired in March 1991 after a heated newspaper strike. Based in London, Maxwell Communications Corp. and its affiliate *Mirror Group Newspapers*, Inc., as well as *British Printing and Communications*, were heavily in debt at the time of his death. He had recently filed a libel suit against allegations that he was linked with the Israeli secret service Mossad when he was found dead off the Canary Islands, having fallen from his yacht after an apparent heart attack at 68. Buried in the Mount of Olives, Jerusalem.

6210. May, Joe (Joseph Mandel, Nov. 7, 1880–April 29, 1954) German film director of melodramas in his own country, often starring with his wife Mia launched the career of Fritz Lang and others. He came to America in 1933 and did mostly B films, among them the atmospheric *The Invisible Man Returns* and *The House of Seven Gables*, both at Universal in 1940. He was married to Austrian actress **Mia Pfleger** (Maria Pfleger, June 12, 1884–April 28, 1980). Flat plaque. Beth Olam Cemetery, sec. 14, row HHH, lot 44/45, Hollywood Forever Cemetery, Hollywood (Los Angeles), CA.

6211. May, John *see* **St. Valentine's Day Massacre.**

6212. Maybrick, James (Oct. 24, 1838–May 11, 1889) The victim of arsenic poisoning in his Liverpool home Battlecrease; the English cotton merchant was believed to have been poisoned by his wife, **Florence Chandler Maybrick** (Sept. 3, 1862–Oct. 23, 1941), a Mobile, Alabama, belle he married while in the U.S. in 1881. Her trial was sensational, followed by her imprisonment for fifteen years for poisoning him, despite evidence that he had long taken both arsenic and strychnine and likely died from the eventual effects of his drug habit. He was buried in Anfield Cemetery, Anfield, Liverpool. After her release, Florence Maybrick returned to America, living out her days as Florence Chandler in South Kent, Connecticut, where she was buried, marked by a white cross, in 1941. A strange postscript to the Maybrick story occurred in 1991 when a detailed diary was presented to a publisher by its so-called discoverer and published in 1993 as *The Diary of Jack the Ripper*, purporting to be Maybrick's secret journal, kept during his murders of five Whitechapel prostitutes in the autumn of 1888. Debate over its authenticity ensued, with the conclusion that the ink or paper did not predate c.1920, and the eventual admission of the "discoverer" that it had been a hoax. Rebuttals to the rebuttal have to some extent given life, however, to continuing debate over the authenticity, though most well known Ripper scholars discount it.

6213. Maye, Lee (Arthur Lee Maye, Dec. 11, 1934–

July 17, 2002) Tuscaloosa born singer and baseball outfielder recorded 78's and 45's in the 1950's as Arthur Lee Maye, with and without The Crowns, and voices such as Richard Berry and Jesse Belvin, including *Gloria, Oh Ruby Lee, A Fool's Prayer* (1956), *Halfway,* and covers of the hits of the day, as late as *He'll Have to Go* (1969). He played for the Milwaukee Braves 1959–65, the Houston Astros 1965–6, the Cleveland Indians 1967–9, the Washington Senators 1969–70, and the Chicago White Sox 1970–71, retiring with a lifetime batting average of .274, three .300 plus seasons, and forty four league leading doubles in 1964. Evergreen, lot 375, space B, Inglewood Park Cemetery, Inglewood, CA.

6214. Mayer, Carl (Nov. 20, 1894–July 1, 1944) Austrian born screenwriter from Graz penned film scripts in Germany from 1919, including *The Cabinet of Dr. Caligari, The Haunted Castle, The Last Laugh,* an adaptation of *Tartuffe, Sunrise* (for F.W. Murnau, filmed in Hollywood 1927), *Berlin, Symphony of A Great City* (1928), *Ariane* (1931). He wrote only three films through the 1930s, and died from cancer in London at 49. Raised (peaked) slab, east sec., Highgate Cemetery, London.

6215. Mayer, Frank H. (May 28, 1850–Feb. 12, 1954) New Orleans born buffalo hunter, the most famous in Colorado. Lived to 104. Rose granite stone, Fairview Cemetery, Fairplay, CO.

6216. Mayer, Louis B. (July 4, 1885–Oct. 29, 1957) Russian born junk dealer in Boston went on to Hollywood, where he merged with Metro and Samuel Goldfish (Goldwyn) to form Metro-Goldwyn-Mayer in 1924; Goldwyn soon sold out and Mayer ran the studio with an iron hand for twenty four years. The mogul of moguls, he alternated authority with Irvin Thalberg until his death in 1936, after which Mayer had sole control over the most polished and prestigious of film studios and its films and stars, bullying, cajoling, pleading and threatening as needed. He ruled at Culver City until 1948, when he was replaced by Loew's distribution head Nicholas Schenck, who put Dore Schary in the place of Mayer until the latter's resignation in 1951. He died from leukemia six years later at UCLA Medical Center. The eulogy was delivered by Spencer Tracy. Corridor of Immortality, crypt SW-405, right rear corridor of the mausoleum, Home of Peace Memorial Park, east Los Angeles.

6217. Mayer, Oscar F. (March 29, 1859–March 11, 1955) German immigrant with two brothers established the Oscar Mayer Sausage Store in 1883 Chicago, expanding to become the #1 hot dog producer in the U.S. and remaining in the family over one hundred years. Sec. 15, lot 44, Rosehill Cemetery, Chicago, IL.

6218. Mayfair, Mitzie (Juanita Emylyn Pique, June 6, 1914–May 1976) Broadway tap dancer from Tucson replaced Eleanor Powell in *At Home Abroad* (1936), appeared in *Four Jills in A Jeep,* a few others. Block 24–6D-10, East Lawn Cemetery, Tucson, AZ.

6219. Mayfield, Curtis (June 3, 1942–Dec. 26, 1999) Chicago born soul vocalist and songwriter sang with the Impressions from 1958 on *For Your Precious Love* and *Gypsy Woman* but gained his greatest fame with the 1964 *Keep On Pushing,* a Civil Rights anthem, the later *People Get Ready, Superfly,* and several works recorded by others (*A Change is Gonna Come, Say It Loud — I'm Black and I'm Proud*). Paralyzed when struck by a toppled rig while performing in Brooklyn in 1990, he died at 57 in Atlanta's North Regional Hospital in Roswell. A private memorial service was held, with cremation through Patterson Arlington Chapel, Atlanta, Georgia. The family took the ashes and according to the mortuary, no burial was planned.

6220. Mayfield, Percy (Aug. 12, 1920–Aug. 11, 1984) Singer-pianist from Minden, Louisiana, primarily wrote (*Hit the Road, Jack*) following a 1952 auto accident. El Portal plot, lot 74, Inglewood Park Cemetery, Inglewood, CA.

6221. Maynard, Ken (July 21, 1895–March 23, 1973) Cowboy film hero of the 1920's and 30's, credited as the first singing cowboy. After a series of low budget films, he retired in 1945. His last years were spent in poverty in the San Fernando Valley, where he lived in a trailer, suffering from alcoholism and finally malnutrition. Churchyard, lot 2840, Forest Lawn Memorial Park, Cypress, CA.

6222. Maynard, Kermit (Sept. 20, 1897–Jan. 16, 1971) Tex Maynard, brother of Ken, screen and circus performer and frequent double for his brother and many others. Ashes buried Garden of Rest, lot 408, Valhalla Memorial Park, North Hollywood, CA.

6223. Mayo, Archie (Jan. 29, 1891–Dec. 4, 1968) Film director at his best at Warner Brothers in the 1930's (*The Doorway to Hell, Svengali*) best remembered for his crime dramas with social commentary (*The Petrified Forest* 1936, *Black Legion* 1937). Beth Olam Mausoleum/Hall of Solomon, south corridor, crypt 317, Hollywood Forever Cemetery, Hollywood (Los Angeles), CA.

6224. Mayo, Virginia (Virginia Clara Jones, Nov. 30, 1920–Jan. 17, 2005) Hazel eyed blonde actress from St. Louis appeared in brassy roles in films from 1943, notably as Dana Andrews party-girl wife in *The Best Years of Our Lives* (1946), opposite Danny Kaye in *The Secret Life of Walter Mitty* (1947) and James Cagney in *White Heat* (1949), several others. Married from 1947 until his death in 1973 to actor Michael O'Shea, they lived from 1965 at Thousand Oaks, California. She died at a nursing home there at 84 and was buried beside him. Garden of Gethsemane, lot 313, Pierce Bros. Valley Oaks Memorial Park, Westlake Village, CA.

6225. Mayo, Whitman (Nov. 15. 1930–May 22, 2001) New York born actor best known as Grady on the TV series *Sanford and Son* 1973–75, later in various TV and films, including *Boyz N the Hood* and *Boycott.* He taught acting at Clark Atlanta University and lived at Fayetteville, Georgia, upon his death there at 70. Service at Elizabeth Baptist Church, Atlanta, through Willie Watkins mortuary. Garden of the Saints, lot 302B, grave 3, Forest Lawn Memorial Gardens, 5755 Mallory Road, College Park (Atlanta area), GA.

6226. Mayo, William (June 29, 1861–July 28, 1939) and his brother **Charles Mayo** (July 19, 1865–May 26, 1939) were physicians who founded the famed clinic bearing their name in Rochester, Minnesota. They were both surgeons at St. Mary's Hospital in Rochester when they donated money to establish a clinic in 1915. Sec. 3, lots 166–167, Oakwood Cemetery, Rochester, MN.

6227. Mays, Carl (Nov. 12, 1891–April 4, 1971) Pitcher 1915–29 with the Red Sox, Yankees, Reds and Giants, known for his aggressiveness, was on the mound for the Yankees at the Polo Grounds in August 1920 when he threw the pitch that killed Cleveland Indians batter Ray Chapman, the only fatality in the game's history. As a result, new white baseballs were continually issued throughout games to increase their visibility. Mays died in El Cajon, California. Flush military plaque. Sec. 13, lot 49, River View Cemetery, Portland, OR.

6228. Mays, Rex (March 10, 1913–Nov. 6, 1949) Auto racer of the 1940's finished second in the 1940 and 1941 Indianapolis 500's, two triple A victories, and finished fifth in the 1949 500. He died when his Wolfe Special hit a hole in the Del Mar, California, racetrack during a race. The track was closed the next month. Mays, not wearing a belt, was thrown from his car and run over. Everlasting Love sec., lot 677, space 4, Forest Lawn, Glendale, CA.

6229. Mazurki, Mike (Mikhail Mazurwski, Dec. 25, 1907–Dec. 9, 1990) Austrian born football star at Manhattan College and pro heavyweight wrestler, of Ukrainian descent, in the U.S. from age six. He turned to films in the 1940's, as tough dull witted thugs in *Murder My Sweet* (1944), *Nightmare Alley* (1947), *Night and the City* (1950). Late in life he was featured as the childlike adventurer in *Challenge To Be Free* (1976). Ukranian Catholic mass was said in Los Angeles. Columbarium of Victory, niche 32121, Freedom Mausoleum, Forest Lawn, Glendale, CA.

6230. Mead, Margaret (Dec. 16, 1901–Nov. 15, 1978) Noted anthropologist whose works studying the roles, values, standards and mores of various other societies as opposed to conventional ones began in the mid twenties. She taught at Columbia and worked with the American Museum of Natural History in New York. Her works are the established texts for much of the advanced anthropological studies of the twentieth century. Small upright headstone. Sec. B, lot 413, Trinity Episcopal Church Cemetery, Buckingham, PA.

6231. Meade, George Gordon (Dec. 31, 1815–Nov. 6, 1872) Union general appointed Commander of the Army of the Potomac by Lincoln in 1863 met Lee at Gettysburg in the first three days of July 1863, driving the Confederacy from its high water mark back into Maryland, but failing to pursue as Lincoln wanted. Meade continued to lead the Army of the Potomac, supporting Grant upon his appointment in 1864. Meade died in Philadelphia. Buried beneath a small white marker in the family plot, just above a bluff. Sec. L, lot 1-7, Laurel Hill Cemetery, Philadelphia, PA.

6232. Meader, Vaughn (Abbott Vaughn Meader, March 20, 1936–Oct. 29, 2004) Maine born impressionist whose imitation of then President John Kennedy's voice made him a favorite and sold 7.5 million copies of his 1962 album, *The First Family*, though his career faded after JFK's death. He died at 68 in Auburn, Maine. Cremated at Greenlawn Memorial Park through (Chuck Kincer) Funeral Alternatives, Auburn. Ashes buried November 3 at Pine Grove Cemetery, Waterville, ME.

6233. Meadows, Alberta (dec. July 6, 1922) Victim of a notorious Los Angeles murder was a young widow Mrs. Clara Phillips believed was involved with her husband. After meeting Meadows after work and having her drive to a remote area in Montecito Heights (now Mt. Washington), she accused Meadows, hit her, chased her out of the car and bashed in her face and head with a dimestore claw hammer, then disemboweled her with the claw. Tagged the Tiger Woman, Phillips fled the U.S. after a jail escape, went to prison and was paroled in 1935. Meadows is unmarked. Slumberland sec., lot 107, space 1, Forest Lawn, Glendale, CA.

6234. Meadows, Audrey (Feb. 8, 1926–Feb. 3, 1996) Actress born to missionary parents in Wu Chang, China, sister of Jayne Meadows, came to the U.S. in the 1930's, went on to Broadway and TV immortality as Alice, the spirited wife of Brooklyn bus driver Ralph Kramden (Jackie Gleason) in *The Honeymooners* on CBS (Oct. 1955–Sept. 1956). Her memoir *Love Alice* (1994) was staunchly loyal to Gleason after two unflattering biographies of him. The widow of Continental Airlines chairman Robert Six, she died from lung cancer in Cedar Sinai Medical Center at 71. Sec. F, tier 29, grave 58, Holy Cross Cemetery, Culver City, CA.

6235. Means, Gaston B. (July 11, 1879–Sept. 12, 1938) Infamous swindler acquitted of the murder of his wife in 1917. After President Harding's death he wrote a book sensationalizing it. Convicted of graft, he went to prison, but resurfaced in 1932 and falsely claimed he could locate the missing Lindbergh Baby. He absconded with the ransom money, provided by Evalyn Walsh McLean, and went back to prison, where he died from a heart attack in Leavenworth six years later. Oakwood cemetery, Concord, NC.

6236. Meany, George (Aug. 16, 1894–Jan. 10, 1980) Labor leader, head of the AFL at its rejoining with the CIO in 1955 and active in its leadership up into the 1970's. Sec. 7, lot 968, Gate of Heaven Cemetery, Silver Spring, MD.

6237. Medford, Kay (Sept. 14, 1920–April 10, 1980) New York born stage actress in films from 1942 including *A Face in the Crowd* and *Angel in My Pocket* won a Tony as the mother in *Bye Bye Birdie* and was nominated for both a Tony and an Oscar as the mother in both the Broadway and film versions of *Funny Girl*. She died in New York from cervical cancer at 59. Ashes scattered from a Manhattan building.

6238. Medill, Joseph (April 6, 1823–March 16, 1899) Owner and publisher of the *Chicago Tribune* 1854–1874. Mayor of Chicago 1871–75 and a founder of the Republican Party. He was the maternal grandfather (through his daughter Elinor "Nellie" [Mrs. Frank] Patterson) of Eleanor "Cissy" Medill Patterson, who was later editor and publisher of the *Washington Times Herald*. Both his daughter's and granddaughter's ashes are buried in the family plot with him. Ridgeland sec., Graceland Cemetery, Chicago, IL.

6239. Medwick, Joseph "Ducky" (Joseph M. Medwick, Nov. 24, 1911–March 21, 1975) Outfielder with the Cardinals' Gashouse Gang of the 1930's, known for hitting bad balls and for the waddle that earned him the nickname "Ducky Wucky." He hit over .300 fourteen times and won the Triple Crown in 1937. Hall of Fame 1968. Park Hill sec, block B, lot 27, St. Lucas Cemetery, St. Louis County, six miles south of St. Louis, MO.

6240. Meek, Donald (July 14, 1878–Nov. 18, 1946) Scottish born slight, bald actor in many supporting roles in films of the 1930's usually cast as timid character (*Mrs. Wiggs of the Cabbage Patch, Mark of the Vampire, Stagecoach,* dozens more). He died from leukemia in Los Angeles at 78. Mausoleum, main floor, sec. 392, tier BB, Fairmount Cemetery, Denver, CO.

6241. Meek, Joe (Robert George Meek, April 5, 1929–Feb. 3, 1967) English record producer had the first British Invasion hit with The Tornados' *Telstar* (1963), and the next year hit again with The Honeycombs' *Have I the Right*. A suicide at 37, he shot his landlady and himself. Monument, plot 99 near middle, Newent parish churchyard, Newent, Gloucestershire.

6242. Meeker, George (March 4, 1904–Aug. 19, 1984) Blonde, mustached actor from Brooklyn in numerous shady roles in films of the 1930's (*Night of Terror, Mr. Deeds Goes to Town*) with some sympathetic parts (*Back Street* 1932) and many brief appearances in films of the 40's, including *Casablanca*. He died from Alzheimer's Disease at his home in Capenteria, California. Cremated at Coastal Crematory in Pasadena through McDermott-Crockett mortuary in Santa Barbara, his ashes were spread in the Santa Barbara Channel by the physician who had attended him.

6243. Meeker, Ralph (Ralph Rathberger, Nov. 21, 1920–Aug. 5, 1988) Minneapolis born stage actor took over from Brando in *A Streetcar Named Desire* and through the 1950's and 60's specialized in beefy, cocky characters — in *Kiss Me Deadly* (1955, as Mike Hammer), *Paths of Glory* (1957), *The Detective* (1968). Columbarium of Vigilance, niche 62987, Courts of Remembrance, Forest Lawn Hollywood Hills, Los Angeles.

6244. Megna, John (Nov. 9, 1952–Sept. 4, 1995) New York born child actor, graduate of Cornell, played Dill in *To Kill a Mockingbird* (1962) and in the Broadway production of James Agee's *All the Way Home*. In films and TV into the mid 80's, he died at 42 from pneumonia complicated by AIDS in Midway Hospital, Los Angeles. Cremated through Forest Lawn, Glendale, Ca., the ashes were returned to the residence of a relative in Pasadena, CA.

6245. Megowan, Don (May 24, 1922–June 26, 1981) Actor in B films of the 1950's and 60's (*The Creature Walks Among Us, The Werewolf*) died from throat cancer. Rosehill plot, lot 58, Inglewood Park Cemetery, Inglewood, CA.

6246. Meighan, Thomas (April 9, 1879–July 8, 1936) Popular leading man of the silent screen in *The Miracle Man* with Lon Chaney, *Male and Female* with Gloria Swanson, many others. He died of cancer at 57 in his home at Great Neck, Long Island, New York. Mass at St. Patrick's in Manhattan with interment in the receiving vault at Calvary Cemetery, Queens, N.Y.C. A year later the body was removed and buried on a hillside with his parents and (later) his wife, actress **Frances Ring** (July 4, 1882–Jan. 15, 1951). Sec. H, lot 220, St. Mary's Cemetery, Pittsburgh, PA.

6247. Meigs, Montgomery (May 3, 1816–Jan. 2, 1892) General in the Union Army during the Civil War, bitter after his son was killed, conceived the idea of turning Robert E. Lee's residence (the Custis-Lee mansion) on an eminence in Arlington, Virginia, into a cemetery for the war dead so that Lee and his family could never live there again. The first sixty five burials there took place June 15, 1864. By the end of the Civil war there were sixteen thousand. Meigs' monument is next to the recumbent effigy of his son, Lieutenant **John Meigs**. Sec. 1, grave 1, grid N 32/33, Arlington National Cemetery, Arlington, VA.

6248. Meilhac, Henri (Feb. 23, 1832–July 6, 1897) Librettist for Offenbach and Bizet's *Carmen*. Hooded semi-nude. Div. 21, Montmartre Cemetery, Paris.

6249. Meir, Golda (Golda Mabovitch Myerson, May 3, 1898–Dec. 8, 1978) Prime Minister of Israel 1969–1974. Born in Kiev, Russia, she grew up in Milwaukee and taught there, moving to Israel with her husband Morris Myerson in the 1920's (Meir being the Hebrew version of Myerson) and increasingly active in the Zionist movement. She worked for the entrance of Jews into Palestine and for the creation of the state of Israel through both the raising of money and negotiations with other nations. She served in the

Israeli parliament 1949–1974, and as Minister of Labor 1949–1956. During her term as Prime Minister she sought to achieve peace with Israel's neighbors, though war broke out with Egypt and Syria in October 1973. After she left, the Labor Party, united under her influence, fell into factionalism and defeat. She died at 80 in a Jerusalem hospital from a variety of ailments related to leukemia, diagnosed in 1966. She was buried in a plain pine coffin in a driving rain on December 12, 1978, the services attended by delegations from many governments and tens of thousands of Israelis. Mount Herzl Cemetery on the southwestern outskirts of Jerusalem.

6250. Meisel, Kurt (Aug. 18, 1912–April 4, 1994) Viennese actor in films 1934–1989, primarily in Germany and Austria. American appearances include *The Longest Day* (1962) and *The Odessa File* (1974, as Alfred Oster). Flat plaque with his name. Gruppe 40, nummer 168, Zentralfriedhof, Vienna.

6251. Meisner, Sanford (Aug. 31, 1905–Feb. 2, 1997) Actor and teacher with the Group Theatre of New York also taught acting in Los Angeles. He died from cancer at 91 in Van Nuys. Ashes through Groman mortuary July 11 to his residence in Van Nuys, CA.

6252. Melcher, Martin (Aug. 1, 1915–April 20, 1968) Producer of many of the films of his wife, Doris Day, former agent and father of record producer Terry Melcher, died from coronary and cerebral ailments at 52. Columbarium of Remembrance, niche 61162, Courts of Remembrance, Forest Lawn Hollywood Hills, Los Angeles.

6253. Melcher, Terry (Feb. 8, 1942–Nov. 19, 2004) Record producer, son of Doris Day and Martin Melcher, oversaw the initial 1965 hits by The Byrds, among others at Columbia and — the former occupant of the house Sharon Tate later shared with Roman Polanski — was the alleged inspiration for the Tate murders in 1969, having turned Charles Manson down for a record deal. Melcher died at 62 from melanoma. Ashes through Pierce Bros. Westwood to his wife family in Beverly Hills.

6254. Melchior, Lauritz (March 20, 1890–March 18, 1973) Acclaimed Danish opera tenor performed at the New York Met, most often doing Wagner. A large, gregarious man, he appeared in several films of the 1940's in America and made numerous recordings. Assistens Cemetery, Copenhagen, Denmark.

6255. Melford, George (Feb. 19, 1877–April 25, 1961) Film director. Among his work was at Universal in 1930, filming both *The Cat Creeps* and *Dracula* in Spanish language versions at night on the same sets being used for the English versions during the day directed by Rupert Julian and Tod Browning, respectively. Block L-999-6, Valhalla Memorial Park, North Hollywood, CA.

6256. Melies, Georges (Dec. 8, 1861–Jan. 21, 1938) Pioneer French film director-producer was making movies by 1896, notably *Le Voyage dans la Lune* (*A Trip to the Moon* 1902). Awarded the Legion of Honor in 1932, he spent his later years in a rent free apartment in Paris. Div. 64, Pere Lachaise Cemetery, Paris.

6257. Mellinger, Frederick (Nov. 26, 1913–June 2, 1990) Founder of Frederick's of Hollywood, the fashion store chain specializing in alluring and erotic apparel. Courts of the Book, block 5, plot 600, space 2, Hillside Memorial Park, Los Angeles.

6258. Mellish, Fuller (Jan. 3, 1865–Dec. 7, 1936) London born stage star made a few silent films (*The Royal Family* 1916). Actors Fund of America Plot, Kensico Cemetery, Valhalla, NY.

6259. Mellish, Fuller, Jr. (Harold I. Fuller-Mellish, Jr., 1893–Feb. 8, 1930) Actor played the worthless boyfriend in *Applause* (1929). He died from a stroke at 36 shortly after making the film. Buried as Harold I. Fuller. South border, range 38, grave 5, Maple Grove Cemetery, Kew Gardens, Queens, N.Y.C.

6260. Mellix, Lefty (George Ralph Mellix, April 29, 1896–March 23, 1985) Black semi-pro pitcher in Pittsburgh in the 1910's and 20's was a left hander known for his exaggerated windmill windup and other antics such as faking throwing a spitball. He pitched part time in the Negro Leagues 1922–24 with the Cuban X Giants and the Homestead Grays. Sec. 33, div. 1, row 1, grave 1, Homewood Cemetery, Pittsburgh, PA.

6261. Mellon, Andrew (Andrew William Mellon, March 24, 1855–Aug. 26, 1937) Banking magnate, secretary of the Treasury under Harding, Coolidge and Hoover 1921–32. His outstanding art collection was donated to the government as the Mellon Collection and National Gallery of Art. Originally buried at Allegheny Cemetery in Pittsburgh, Pa., where he was born, he was removed in the late 1940's by Paul Mellon near his estate, Rokeby Farms. Stones along wall in family enclosure. Trinity Episcopal Church Cemetery, Upperville, VA.

6262. Melrose, Kitty (Agnes Butterfield, 1883–June 3, 1912) Stage actress popular in Edwardian London in *The Quaker Girl* (1910) and lesser efforts, a suicide by poison after a failed love affair. Epitaph *Peace perfect peace.* Kensal Green Cemetery, London.

6263. Melton, James (Jan. 2, 1904–April 21, 1961) Tenor from Moultrie, Georgia, with the Chicago and New York Metropolitan Opera companies appeared in a few films of the 1930's: *Stars over Broadway, Sing Me a Love Song, Melody for Two.* He died in New York from pneumonia at 55. Plot near entrance. Woodlawn Cemetery, Ocala, FL.

6264. Melville, Herman (Aug. 1, 1819–Sept. 28, 1891) American novelist of seafaring tales, including *Moby Dick* (1851), *Typee* (1846) and *Billy Budd* (1889). Largely unrecognized in his lifetime, he worked as a clerk in the New York customs house from 1866–1885, and his *New York Times* obituary listed *Typee* as his greatest work, rather than *Moby Dick.* He died in New

York from a heart ailment at 72. His stone has an unrolled granite scroll with his name and dates below it, along the sidewalk beneath a large oak tree. Catalpa sec., lot 24, Woodlawn Cemetery, the Bronx, N.Y.C.

6265. Melvin, Harold (June 25, 1939–March 24, 1997) Rhythm and Blues vocalist with the Blue Notes (*If You Don't Know Me By Now*) died of a stroke at 57 in Philadelphia. Sec. P, lot 101, Ivy Hill Cemetery, Philadelphia, PA.

6266. Memphis Minnie (Lizzie Douglas, June 3, 1897–Aug. 6, 1973) Louisiana born country Blues composer (*Bumble Bee, Hoodoo Lady*), singer, a guitarist, a pioneer in female musicians, "Kid" Douglas recorded with Kansas Joe McCoy from 1929, the year after they were married, switching to steel guitar in the 30's, using the smoother "Melrose sound" and recording in the 1940's with Little Son Joe (Ernest Lawlers, her then husband). She died from a series of strokes at 76. Her monument was dedicated in 1997 by the Mount Zion Fund, with contributors including Bonnie Raitt and John Fogerty. New Hope M.E. Church Cemetery, Walls, MS.

6267. Mencken, H.L. (Henry Louis Mencken, Sept. 12, 1880–Jan. 29, 1956) Irascible and witty editor of the *Baltimore Sun* thrived on satirical observations on the politics and figures of his time, from the turn of the century through the post-war era. He was married 1930–35 to Sarah Haardt until her death from tubercular meningitis, from which she was already suffering at the time of their marriage. Other than those five years, he spent most of his life in his row house at 1524 Hollins Street in Baltimore. He suffered a severe stroke while out to dinner on November 23, 1948, and never regained the full ability to speak or write for the remaining seven years of his life, cared for by his brother August. After listening to *Die Meistersinger* on the radio on the evening of January 28, 1956, he went to bed and died in his sleep from a coronary occlusion. In his memory, Mencken had for years advised his friends to "wink at a homely girl." He was cremated and his ashes buried next to Sarah. Sec. W, lot 224 south ½, Louden Park Cemetery, Baltimore, MD.

6268. Mendel, Gregor (Johann Mendel, July 22, 1822–Jan. 6, 1884) Austrian monk from Heizendorf, Austrian Silesia, considered the father of the principles of genetics and heredity. Based on his work with over 28,000 pea pod plants in a monastery garden from 1856, studying seven characteristics, he announced his findings in 1865, summarized by three laws: first, segregation (of the sex cells during formation), independent assortment, and dominance (the principle of dominant and recessive genes). His findings were not fully appreciated and enlarged upon until after 1900. Grave length family slab. Central Cemetery, Brno, Czech Republic.

6269. Mendelssohn, Felix (Felix Mendelssohn-Bartholdy, Feb. 3, 1809–Nov. 4, 1847) German composer famed for his *Spring Song* and other works. His oratorios *Elijah* and *St. Paul* were considered his two greatest works, ranking only behind the finest works of Handel. His *Hymn of Praise* and *Wedding March* remain popular. He died at his home in the Konigstrasse in Leipzig after a series of strokes. After a service in St. Paul's he was taken by train to Berlin and buried. Stone cross in family lot along iron fence. Dreifaltigkeitskirchof I, Blncherplatz/Baruther Str. (Kreuzberg), Berlin.

6270. Menendez, Jose (May 6, 1944–Aug. 20, 1989) and **Mary Louise "Kitty"** (Oct. 14, 1941–Aug. 20, 1989) Cuban born millionaire video distributor, 45, and his wife, 47, were brutally murdered in their Beverly Hills home, shot in the head by their sons for the money in a case garnering heavy media coverage. The sons got life. Cremated through Pierce Bros. Westwood mortuary. Ashes buried in the northeast corner area of Princeton Cemetery, Princeton, NJ.

6271. Mengele, Josef (March 16, 1911–Feb. 7, 1979) Infamous Nazi doctor at Auschwitz fled to Argentina in 1949, later removing to Paraguay and Brazil. Known as the Angel of Death, he was accused of sending some 400,000 people to the gas chamber and conducting sadistic experiments on the inmates. In 1985 it was reported he had drowned six years earlier and was buried in Brazil under the name Wolfgang Gerhard. The body was exhumed and declared to be Mengele but a report by Israeli police investigator Menachem Russack, unpublished until 1991, stated there were inconsistencies indicating the body was not Mengele. The Israeli branch of the Simon Weisenthal Center said the Russack report did not successfully undermine the forensic evidence, but the investigation continued into 1992. Embu Cemetery, Sao Paolo, Brazil.

6272. Menjou, Adolphe (Feb. 18, 1890–Oct. 29, 1963) Dapper, mustached actor from Pittsburgh known as Hollywood's best dressed man, in *The Front Page* (1931, AA nom), *A Farewell to Arms* (1932), *Little Miss Marker* (1934), *A Star is Born* (1937). An ardent conservative, he was an enthusiastic witness for the House Un American Activities Committee in the early 1950's. He died in Beverly Hills from hepatitis, survived by his wife, Verree Teasdale. Sec. 8/Garden of Legends, lot 11, Hollywood Forever Cemetery, Hollywood (Los Angeles), CA.

6273. Menken, Adah Isaacs (June 15, 1835–Aug. 10, 1868) New Orleans born actress known for *Mazeppa*, for being strapped largely undressed to a horse in her grand finale, and for her many affairs. A 10' stone monument at her grave inscribed *Thou Knowest* was gone by 1875. Montparnasse Cemetery, Paris.

6274. Menken, Helen (Dec. 12, 1901–March 27, 1966) New York born stage actress, married to Humphrey Bogart briefly in the 1920's, was president of the American Theatre Wing when she died from a heart attack at 65 while dining at the Lambs' Club with her third husband, broker George Richard. He remarried and was buried at Woodlawn in the Bronx upon his death, but there is no record of her there. Cremated at Ferncliff Cemetery, Hartsdale, N.Y., March 30, her ashes were returned to the Plaza mortuary at 40 West 58th St., now out of business. Both her sister, actress **Grace Menken** (dec. 1978) and Grace's husband Bert Lytell were cremated through the Frank E. Campbell mortuary and the ashes returned to the family.

6275. Menninger, Charles F. (July 11, 1862–Nov. 28, 1953) and his son, **William G. Menninger** (Oct. 15, 1899–Sept. 6, 1966) were psychiatrists who established a clinic at Topeka in 1920, adding and expanding into a research and educational center for psychiatry. Singing Tower, lots 144 and 372, Mount Hope Cemetery, Topeka, KS.

6276. Menuhin, Yehudi (April 22, 1916–March 12, 1999) New York born Russian-Jewish violinist was a prodigy from age 7, performed for the Allies in Europe during World War II and afterward in countries liberated from the USSR, raising funds for refugee relief. He died at 82 while on tour in Berlin. Buried in England according to his wishes, near a tree he had planted and marked by a tall flat shaft with the epitaph *He who makes music in this life makes music in the next.* Yehudi Menuhin School, Stoke D'Abernon, Surrey.

6277. Menzies, William Cameron (July 29, 1896–March 5, 1957) Film director and set designer from New Haven, Connecticut, best known for his art direction, winning Oscars for *The Dove, Tempest,* and *Gone With the Wind.* He also directed the futuristic *Things to Come* (1936). Columbarium of Benevolence, niche 15251, Gardenia Terrace, Great Mausoleum, Forest Lawn, Glendale, CA.

6278. Merande, Doro (Dora Matthews, March 31, 1892–Nov. 1, 1975) Delightful character actress from Columbia, Kansas, in whimsical roles with off the cuff asides that enlivened such films as *Mr. Belvedere Rings the Bell* (1951), *The Gazebo* (1959), many others. TV series *Bringing Up Buddy.* Long a resident of New York, she was in Miami taping a *Honeymooners* anniversary show when she died at 83. No services. Cremated at Van Orsdel Crematory, her ashes were scattered at sea off the Florida coast by Van Orsdel mortuary.

6279. Mercer, Beryl (Aug. 13, 1882–July 28, 1939) A child actress in London, she came to Hollywood in 1922 and with sound specialized in shy, timid, long suffering mothers (*Outward Bound* and *All Quiet on the Western Front* 1930, *The Public Enemy* 1931). Sunrise Slope, lot 337, Forest Lawn, Glendale, CA.

6280. Mercer, Hugh (Hugh Weedon Mercer, Nov. 27, 1808–June 9, 1877) Confederate Brigadier General built the ante-bellum mansion on Bull Street in restored Savannah later owned by Jim Williams and made famous in John Berendt's book *Midnight in the Garden of Good and Evil* over the shooting there of Danny Hansford in May 1981. Mercer died in Baden-Baden, Germany and was initially buried there but was reportedly returned home in 1879. Sec. F, lot 19, grave 7, Bonaventure Cemetery, Savannah, GA.

6281. Mercer, Johnny (John Herndon Mercer, Nov. 18, 1909–June 25, 1976) Prolific lyricist-composer from Savannah wrote or helped write some of the finest tunes of the 1930's and 40's, including *Blues in the Night, That Old Black Magic, Jeepers Creepers, Laura, One for the Road,* and *Accentuate the Positive,* which he also recorded (1944), *Summer Wind* (1966), many others. Awarded four Oscars, for *On the Atchison, Topeka and the Santa Fe* (from *The Harvey Girls* 1946), *In the Cool, Cool, Cool of the Evening* (from *Here Comes the Groom* 1951), the lyrics for *Moon River* (named for the river running through Savannah, and written with Henry Mancini, from *Breakfast at Tiffany's* 1962), and the lyrics for *The Days of Wine and Roses* (1962). President of Capitol Records in the late 1940's, he died in Los Angeles, was cremated and his ashes buried in Savannah with his family. On the grave length marble slab is his full name, nickname, dates of birth and death, and the line *And the Angels Sing,* the title of a song he wrote, allegedly with Bette Davis in mind. Sec. H, lot 48, Bonaventure Cemetery, Savannah, GA.

6282. Mercer, Mabel (Feb. 3, 1900–April 20, 1984) English born vocalist, a sophisticated stylist, in the U.S. from 1938, introduced *Fly Me to the Moon, Love For Sale,* many others. Presidential Medal of Freedom 1983. Red Rock Cemetery near Chatham, NY.

6283. Mercier, Louis Gabriel (March 7, 1901–March 25, 1993) Film and television actor 1926–77 in dozens of films. He died in Los Angeles at 92. Ashes to residence.

6284. Mercouri, Melina (Maria Amalia Mercouri or Merkouri, Oct. 18, 1925–March 6, 1994) Greek actress-politician known for her films with director-husband Jules Dasson, notably her signature role as the prostitute in *Never on Sunday* (1960, Cannes award and AA nom), reprised on Broadway in *Ilya Darling* (1967). In the Greek Parliament from 1977, she was fiercely anti-Fascist, living in exile until the Socialists gained control and serving as Minister of Culture 1981–89. She died in New York's Sloane-Kettering Cancer center at 68. State funeral. Spire with an angel engraved on the front and on the rounded top the symbolic engraved burning flame. In clear view above her is the temple of Heinrich Schliemann at the top of the necropolis. First Cemetery, Athens, Greece.

6285. Mercury, Freddie (Frederick Bulsara, Sept. 5, 1946–Nov. 24, 1991) Singer with Queen announced he was ill with AIDS only a day prior to his death at home in Kensington, west London. Memorial services were widely attended, with cremation at Kensal Green Crematorium, Harrow Road, west London. The ashes were returned to family and were reported for a time to have been placed in an unmarked grave at Brookwood Cemetery, Surrey, but were by most accounts scattered at Lake Geneva, Switzerland.

6286. Meredith, Burgess (Oliver Burgess Meredith, Nov. 16, 1907–Sept. 9, 1997) Actor from Lakewood, Ohio, starred in *Winterset* (1936), *Of Mice and Men, The Story of G.I. Joe,* appeared in *The Man on the Eiffel Tower* (also directed), *Advise and Consent,* played the Penguin in TV's *Batman, Day of the Locust* (AA nom., 1975) and *Rocky* (1976). He died at 89 in his Malibu home. Cremated through Pierce Bros.' Valley Oaks mortuary, Westlake Village. Ashes to his family at Malibu.

6287. Meredith, Cheerio (July 12, 1890–Dec. 25, 1964) Actress with a cherubic face in films and TV, played Emma Watson on the *Andy Griffith Show* 1960–63. Plaque inscribed *In memory of our beloved Cheerio/ E.L.H.M. Ely.* Homeward sec., lot 4522, Forest Lawn Hollywood Hills, Los Angeles.

6288. Meredyth, Bess (Helen MacGlashan, Feb. 12, 1889–July 13, 1969) Buffalo born silent actress turned screen writer (*Ben Hur, The Sea Beast, Don Juan,* all 1926, *Charlie Chan at the Opera* 1936). Married to Michael Curtiz from 1939. Buried as Beth Meredyth Curtiz. Resthaven sec., lot 286, space 5, Forest Lawn Glendale, CA.

6289. Merivale, Philip (Nov. 2, 1880–March 12, 1946) British actor in films from silents (*The Stranger* 1946), married to Viva Birkett (d. 1934), and to Gladys Cooper (*q.v.*) until his death in Los Angeles. Cremated by Pierce Bros. Ashes sent to London.

6290. Merkel, Una (Dec. 10, 1903–Jan. 2, 1986) Actress from Covington, Kentucky, in usually sweet or naive roles from 1930 in *The Bat Whispers, 42nd Street, Destry Rides Again* (featuring her saloon brawl with Marlene Dietrich), *On Borrowed Time, The Bank Dick.* She won a Tony for *The Ponder Heart* (1956) and was acclaimed as Geraldine Page's mother in *Summer and Smoke,* filmed in 1962. Buried beside her parents. Phares lot, sec. 14, lot 65, Highland Cemetery, Fort Mitchell (next to Covington), KY.

6291. Merkle, Fred (Dec. 20, 1888–March 2, 1956) Substitute for the New York Giants in the deciding game of the 1908 pennant race against the Chicago Cubs authored the fabled Merkle Boner when, while at first base, he was swarmed by fans pouring onto the field after Al Bridwell lined a single and drove in a run by Moose McCormick. When Merkle failed to touch second base and headed for the clubhouse, the Cubs' Johnny Evers sought the ball, eventually found and tossed by Tinker to Evers, who jumped up and down on the bag until he got the umpire's attention. The force out caused the game to be scrapped and replayed, when it was won by the Cubs, who went on to win the series from Detroit, their last world championship to date. Merkle played fourteen more years but never lived down the error, which lives on after him in baseball lore. Unmarked, sec. G, lot 14, grave 8, Cedar Hill Cemetery, Daytona Beach, FL.

6292. Merlo, Mike (Michele Merlo, Jan. 4, 1880–Nov. 9, 1924) Head of the Chicago Unione Sicilione kept peace among bootleggers until his death from cancer. The city's gang wars of the 20's soon followed. Dion O'Banion was preparing displays for Merlo's funeral in his State St. flower shop when he was killed. A wax flower effigy of Merlo accompanied his long funeral cortege. Mausoleum on island between sections D and E, across from sec. B, Mt. Carmel Cemetery, Hillside, IL.

6293. Merman, Ethel (Ethel Zimmerman, Jan. 16, 1908–Feb. 15, 1984) Broadway star with booming voice known for *I Got Rhythm* and *There's No Business Like Show Business.* Ill with a brain tumor for a year, she died in her home on 76th St. in N.Y. After services through Frank E. Campbell, her urn was driven slowly down Broadway, the theatre lights dimmed in tribute. She and her daughter **Ethel Levitt Geary** (1942–1967) have plaques in an alcove near the chapel, Shrine of Remembrance Mausoleum, Colorado Springs, Colorado. The ashes reportedly remain with her son, however, possibly to be interred there at a later date.

6294. Merrick, John ("The Elephant Man") (Joseph Carey Merrick, Aug. 5, 1862–April 11, 1890) Severely deformed man born at Leicester was cruelly exhibited at freak shows until he was rescued by a doctor and sheltered until his death at c. 28 in a London medical college, as depicted in the 1980 film *The Elephant Man.* Parts of his body and tissue were preserved until the bombing during the London blitz caused the disintegration of the preservation fluid, destroying the DNA. His illness was long labeled as neurofibromatosis, but is thought more likely to have been Proteus syndrome, or even a deformity within the skin rather than the bones, according to Dr. William Maples. The skeleton remains at the Royal London College of Medicine.

6295. Merrill, Frank (March 21, 1893–Feb. 12, 1966) Athletic actor was the fifth screen Tarzan, in the serials *Tarzan the Mighty* (1928) and *Tarzan the Tiger* (1929). Abbey of the Psalms/Hollywood Forever Mausoleum, Sanctuary of Peace, crypt 5342, Hollywood Forever Cemetery, Hollywood (Los Angeles), CA.

6296. Merrill, Gary (Aug. 2, 1915–March 5, 1990) Actor in films, notably *All About Eve* (1950) with Bette Davis, his wife from 1950–1960. A graduate of Bowdoin, he was a well known free spirit, wearing skirts in summer to keep cool because, he said, it was practical. He died from cancer in Portland, Maine, where he had lived many years. Ashes returned to his son and later buried. On his stone is *A self professed Mr. Do Nothing who did everything for everybody.* Falmouth-Foreside Cemetery, Falmouth, ME.

6297. Merrill, Robert (Moishe Milstein, June 4, 1917–Oct. 23, 2004) Baritone from Williamsburg, Brooklyn, with the New York Metropolitan Opera, in over five hundred performances there from 1945 to 1976, known for *Rigoletto,* Germont in *La Traviata,* Figaro in *Il Barbiere di Siviglia,* Escamillo in *Carmen,* Tonio in *Pagliacci.* A favorite at Yankee Stadium, he sang the national anthem before opening home games for many years, with his recording of it used in his absence, appearing in films (*Aaron Slick from Punkin Crick*) and nightclubs as well. He died at 87 in his New Rochelle, New York, home while watching the first game of the World Series. He was buried before his death was announced October 25. Sec. Temple Israel of New Rochelle, row F, lot 12A, grave 1, Sharon Gardens (adjacent Kensico Cemetery), Valhalla, NY.

6298. Merritt, A. (Abraham Merritt, Jan. 20, 1884–Aug. 21, 1943) Science fiction and fantasy author from Beverly, New Jersey, was also with *The American Weekly* for Hearst, as associate editor from 1911 and editor from 1937. His best known novels include *The Moon Pool, The Face in the Abyss, The Ship of Ishtar, Seven Footprints to Satan* (filmed in 1929), and *Burn Witch Burn* (filmed in 1936 as *The Devil Doll*). He lived at Hollis, Queens, New York City, when he died at 59 from a heart attack while at his vacation home and farm at Indian Rock Beach, near Clearwater, Florida, where he worked in sub-tropical horticulture. Handled through Alexander Funeral Home, Clearwater (now out of business), he was removed (per the death certificate) to St. Petersburg, where (according to the local newspapers), he was cremated. No crematories extant there in 1943 have a record of him.

6299. Merritt, Theresa (Theresa Hines, Sept. 24, 1922–June 12, 1998) Black actress in TV's *That's My Mama* and on Broadway in *Ma Rainey's Black Bottom*. Stone marked *Hines*. Sec. K, lot 242, unit A, grave 2, Maple Grove Cemetery, Kew Gardens, Queens, N.Y.C.

6300. Merton, Robert K. (Meyer Schkolnick, July 5, 1910–Feb. 23, 2003) Philadelphia born sociologist credited with establishing the field as legitimate and introducing such terms as "focus group," "self fulfilling prophecy" and "role model," on the staff at Columbia University from 1941 until his death and the author of several dozen books and articles, best known for *On the Shoulders of Giants* (1965). He died from cancer in Manhattan at 92. Cohasset, 1620, grave 2, Kensico Cemetery, Valhalla, NY.

6301. Mescall, John J. (John Joseph Mescall, Jan. 10, 1899–Feb. 10, 1962) Cinematographer from Litchfield, Illinois, in Hollywood from 1920 photographed *The Yankee Clipper* (1926), *The Black Cat* (1934), *One More River, Night Life of the Gods, Bride of Frankenstein* (1935), *Show Boat* (1936), but drifted into alcoholism and fewer works; his last was *Not of This Earth* (1957). He died in Los Angeles County General Hospital following surgery for colon cancer at 63. Cremated through Armstrong Family mortuary at Inglewood Park Cemetery, where he owned a niche, the urn of Rebecca Mescall is there, but his is not. Sanctuary of Iona, 174, Inglewood Mausoleum, Inglewood Park Cemetery, Inglewood, CA.

6302. Messick, Don (Sept. 7, 1926–Oct. 24, 1997) The voice of many Hanna-Barbera cartoon characters, including Dino the Dinosaur, Ranger Smith, Boo-Boo the bear. Ashes scattered at sea off Point Lobos, CA.

6303. Messmer, Otto (Aug. 16, 1892–Oct. 28, 1983) Cartoonist created *Felix the Cat*. Cem. 6, sec. 42, grave 106, Madonna Cemetery, Fort Lee, NJ.

6304. Mesta, Perle (Oct. 12, 1889–March 16, 1975) Washington socialite and hostess appointed Ambassador to Luxembourg 1949–53 was the basis for the Irving Berlin musical *Call Me Madam* (1950). George Mesta mausoleum, sec. 21, lot 21, Homewood Cemetery, Pittsburgh, PA.

6305. Metalious, Grace (Sept. 8, 1924–Feb. 26, 1964) The author of *Peyton Place* (1956) was largely resented by the residents of Gilmanton, New Hampshire, because of her controversial book about hidden small town passions and other secrets. She died at 39 from chronic liver disease at Beth Israel Hospital in Boston and wished her body donated to Dartmouth Medical School, but the family objected and the case went to the state supreme court. The family won over the will, and she was ordered buried. The TV series *Peyton Place* was at its peak at the time. Smith Meeting House Cemetery, Gilmanton, NH.

6306. Methot, Mayo (March 3, 1904–June 9, 1951) Actress (*Marked Woman* 1937), the third wife of Humphrey Bogart was his drinking companion and frequent opponent in verbal and physical battles, dubbed by their friends the "battling Bogarts." He divorced her in 1945 to marry Lauren Bacall. She died from cancer six years later. Interred with her parents. Washington south alcove AF, tier 3, no. 4, Portland Memorial Mausoleum, Portland, OR.

6307. Meurisse, Paul (Dec. 21, 1912–Jan. 19, 1979) French actor in several comedic roles (le serie du *Monocle*) also played the evil husband in Henri Georg Clouzot's *Les Diaboliques* (*Diabolique*, 1955), many other films. 5th division, Neuilly-sur-Seine (ancien) Cimetiere, Hauts-de-Seine region, Paris.

6308. Meusal, Bob (Robert Meusal, July 19, 1896–Nov. 28, 1977) Outfielder for the New York Yankees in the 1920's, a member of the Murderer's Row line-up of 1927. "Long Bob" died in Downey, California. Ashes buried December 5, 1977. Garden of Prayer sec., lot 5310, space 3, Rose Hills Memorial Park, Whittier, CA.

6309. Meusal, Irish (Emil Frederick Meusal, June 9, 1893–March 1, 1963) Older brother of Bob, right handed hitting great with the Giants in the 1920's, the best in the N.L. after Hornsby. Evergreen plot, lot 80, grave B, Inglewood Park Cemetery, Inglewood, CA.

6310. Mew, Charlotte (Nov. 15, 1869–March 24, 1928) English poet whose works reflected a fear and hint of madness, died by drinking Lysol shortly after her sister Ann's death from cancer. Hampstead Cemetery, London.

6311. Meyer, Emile (Aug. 18, 1910–March 19, 1987) Actor from New Orleans in tough roles in over fifty films (*The People Against O'Hara, Shane, The*

Blackboard Jungle, Paths of Glory) and much TV from c. 1950. Lot 26, Lemon-Hawthorne and Cedar, Greenwood Cemetery, New Orleans, LA.

6312. Meyer, Louis (July 21, 1904–Oct. 7, 1995) First three time winner of the Indianapolis 500, in 1928, 1933 and 1936, and the first to drink a bottle of milk in Victory Lane. He later bought Offenhauser, whose engines won every 500 from 1947–64. Died in Las Vegas at 91. Acacia, lot 11, grave C, Inglewood Park Cemetery, Inglewood, CA.

6313. Meyer, Russ "The Mad Monk" (Oct. 25, 1923–Nov. 16, 1997) Fiery pitcher from Peru, Illinois, with Philly's Whiz Kids of 1950 and the Brooklyn Dodgers of the 1950's (1955 series winners) known for outbursts, including a May 1953 eruption at Philadelphia where he threw a resin bag into the air, only to have it land on his own head. In 1981, returning to Brooklyn with Carl Erskine and Sandy Amoros to promote bringing the Dodgers back to Brooklyn from L.A., he was robbed in Manhattan and had both series rings stolen. He died in Oglesby, Illinois. at 74. Ashes buried block 7, lot 2, grave 8, Peru City Cemetery, Peru, IL.

6314. Meyer, Torben (Dec. 1, 1884–May 22, 1975) Bald Danish actor in the U.S. from 1927 in many films ranging from *The Black Room* (1935) to *Judgment at Nuremberg* (1961). Vaultage, Chapel of the Pines Crematory, Los Angeles.

6315. Micale, Paul J. (Jan. 2, 1916–Jan. 16, 1999) Character actor in many films, including *Pocketful of Miracles* (1961) and as Father Carmine in three of the *Rocky* films. Mausoleum block 39L, crypt D-7, San Fernando Mission Cemetery, Mission Hills, CA.

6316. Michael, Gertrude (Lillian Gertrude Michael, June 1, 1911–Dec. 31, 1964) Actress from Talladega, Alabama, with Stuart Walker's Cincinnati stock company in the 1920's, in films 1932–62, often as scheming, jealous women (*Night of Terror* 1933, *Murder at the Vanities, Murder on the Blackboard, Cleopatra* 1934, the *Sophie Lang* films, *Flamingo Road*). Ashes in vaultage, Chapel of the Pines Crematory, Los Angeles.

6317. Micheaux, Oscar (Jan. 2, 1884–March 25, 1951) Pioneer black film-maker from Metropolis, Illinois, had sold two novels by 1917 and from the profits formed the Micheaux Film and Book Company in Sioux City and Chicago and wrote, produced, directed and distributed his own pictures (*The Homesteader, Body and Soul, Dark Princess, Harlem After Midnight, Murder in Harlem*) 1918–1948, when African-Americans were ignored by the white film industry or reduced to servants or comedy relief. His grave had only a metal plaque until a monument was set in 1988. Great Bend Cemetery, Great Bend, KS.

6318. Michel, Louise (Clemence Louise Michel, May 29, 1830–Jan. 10, 1905) French communist involved in the 1871 Commune uprising and later riots, also called the Red Sister of Charity for her good works when not agitating the capitalists. Bronze bust atop three books. Left side of circular center, Levallois Cemetery at the edge of Paris.

6319. Michelangelo (Michelangelo Buonarriti, March 6, 1475–Feb. 18, 1564) Renaissance painter, sculptor and architect died in Rome and wished to be buried in Florence, Italy, but Pope Pius IV had his funeral at the Church of the Holy Apostles in Rome and intended the artist to be interred there. Michelangelo's nephew Lionardo arranged for the body to be stolen and taken to Florence to the gothic Church of Santa Croce, where his burial place is marked by a tomb designed by his friend Vasari. At Forest Lawn Memorial Park in Glendale, California, Hubert Eaton collected replicas of all the most famous works of Michelangelo, the only such accumulation in the world. Church of Santa Croce, Florence, Italy.

6320. Michelson, Rhode Lee (March 9, 1943–Feb. 15, 1961) Figure skater had placed third and then second in the 1959 and 1960 Junior Ladies Championships, was the senior bronze medalist and part of the eighteen member world figure skating team killed when their plane crashed over Belgium. Unmarked. Oceanview Lawn, plot 481, space K, Green Hills Memorial Park, Rancho Palos Verdes, CA.

6321. Michener, James A. (Feb. 3, 1907–Oct. 16, 1997) Author inspired by his tour with the U.S. Navy in World War II won the Pulitzer Prize for *Tales of the South Pacific* (1947), which inspired the musical. Later works include *The Bridges at Toko-Ri, Sayonara* and *Hawaii* (1959). He died at 90 in Austin from renal failure. Ashes buried beside his wife. Block 11, lot 1, Austin Memorial Park, Austin, TX. Cenotaph Republic Hill, sec. 1, row H, number 21, State Cemetery, Austin, TX.

6322. Middleton, Arthur (June 26, 1742–Jan. 1, 1787) Signer of the Declaration of Independence from South Carolina. Tomb at Middleton Place plantation, near Charleston, SC.

6323. Middleton, Charles (Oct. 7, 1874–April 22, 1949) Gaunt, deep voiced character actor with deep set eyes in many villainous roles in films of the 30's and 40's, from *Mrs. Wiggs of the Cabbage Patch* to *Strangler of the Swamp*, plus his stint as Ming the Merciless in the *Flash Gordon* serials opposite Buster Crabbe. He died in Torrance, California. Sec. 13 (Pineland) Garden of Exodus, lot 105, Hollywood Forever Cemetery, Hollywood (Los Angeles), CA.

6324. Middleton, Robert (Samuel G. Messer, May 13, 1911–June 14, 1977) Cincinnati born actor played many heavies (*The Desperate Hours* 1955), and lastly appeared as Stanton in *The Lincoln Conspiracy* (1977). Buried under his real name. Messer plot, sec. 8, lot 38, grave 1, Walnut Hills United Jewish Cemetery, Walnut Hills, Cincinnati, OH.

6325. *Midnight in The Garden of Good and Evil* (characters) *see* **Danny Hansford, Emma Kelley, Hugh Mercer, Joseph Odom, Jim Williams.**

6326. Migliori, Jay (Nov. 14, 1930–Sept. 2, 2001) Saxophone great, a Grammy winner member of Supersax and a studio musician who played on some 4,000 records, was with bands ranging from Woody Herman to Frank Zappa. He died at 70 from colon cancer. Garden of Valor, lot 79, space B, Pacific View Memorial Park, Newport Beach, CA.

6327. Mikan, George (George Lawrence Mikan, Jr., June 18, 1924–June 1, 2005) NBA star from Joliet, Illinois, at 6 feet 10 inches was the league's first and tallest star. Having forced the NCAA goal-tending rule as a center with Depaul, he kept the new National Basketball Association afloat in its first few seasons, and led the Minneapolis Lakers to five league championships over seven years, retiring after 1956 and later serving as commissioner of the ABA. A statue of him was erected outside the Target Center in Minneapolis. Lakewood Cemetery, Minneapolis, MN.

6328. Milanov, Zinka (Aug. 8, 1906–May 30, 1989) Croatian born immigrant was among the best sopranos of the twentieth century, with the New York Metropolitan Opera for twenty eight years, particularly acclaimed for *Aida*; she also appeared on the Texaco opera broadcasts from the Met 1938–41. Milanov died from a stroke in New York. She was cremated and her ashes sent to the Kunc plot, Mirogoj Cemetery, Zagreb, Croatia.

6329. Milberg, Irving (1903–Sept. 29, 1938) Brooklyn born member of Detroit's Purple Gang, acquitted of killing two Black men in a bar fight in Detroit's Paradise Valley in August 1927 but was sentenced to life for the September 1931 Collingwood Massacre, along with Ray Bernstein and Harry Keywell. He died from peritonitis following an operation for an intestinal obstruction. Buried two spaces from **Charles "The Professor" Auerbach**, advisor and arms supplier for the Purple Gang. Machpelah Cemetery, Ferndale, MI.

6330. Milburn, Amos (April 1, 1925–Jan. 3, 1980) Boogie piano master cranked out many numbers of the postwar and pre-rock era, turning out generally upbeat songs about the effects of booze, both pro and con. Sec. A, grave 1271, Houston National Cemetery, Houston, TX.

6331. Milburn, Rodney (March 18, 1950–Nov. 11, 1997) 1972 Olympic gold medalist in the 110 meter hurdles died at 47 working in a railroad car full of a bleach solution. Homeless and his medals given away, he was still ranked 5th in the world. Green Chapel Cemetery, St. Landry Parish, near Opelousas, LA.

6332. Miles, C(harles) Austin (Jan. 7, 1868–March 10, 1946) Composer of many hymns, including *In the Garden* (1912). Sec. 6, lot 7, grave 1 H-25, Hillcrest Memorial Park, Huffeville (Pitman), NJ.

6333. Milestone, Lewis (Sept. 30, 1895–Sept. 25, 1980) Russian born director in Hollywood won an Oscar for comedy in 1927 with *Two Arabian Knights* but was at his peak in the 1930's with *All Quiet on the Western Front* (AA, 1930), *The Front Page* (1931), *Of Mice and Men* (1939). Crypt, Sanctuary of Tenderness, Westwood Memorial Park, west Los Angeles.

6334. Miley, James "Bubber" (James Wesley Miley, April 3, 1903–May 20, 1932) Trumpeter with Duke Ellington's orchestra used a plunger mute to its best effectiveness, in *East St. Louis Toodle-oo, Black and TanFantasie, Diga Diga Doo*, many others. Ellington fired him in late 1928 for chronic substance abuse. Admitted to Welfare Island (listed on the death certificate as Metropolitan Hospital) with Tuberculosis April 18, 1932, he died there at 29, listed as 28, a month later. The certificate lists burial by Tho. W. Turner May 25 at "Elks S.C. South Carolina"— no town named.

6335. Miljan, John (Nov. 9, 1893–Jan. 24, 1960) Mustached character actor from Lead City, South Dakota, in many films 1923–1958, often in shady roles (*The Yankee Clipper, The Terror, The Unholy Night, The Sea Bat, The Unholy Three, The Secret Six, Susan Lenox, Her Fall and Rise; Emma, Arsene Lupin, Night Court, The Ghost Walks*, many others). He died from cancer in Hollywood. Cremated at Chapel of the Pines Crematory through Pierce Brothers Hollywood. Ashes released February 1, 1960 and "interred" (per card) at Vista, California (no cemetery there), where Victoria Miljan lived.

6336. Milk, Harvey (May 22, 1930–Nov. 27, 1978) San Francisco city supervisor was shot to death in the city building, along with Mayor George Moscone, by former city official Dan White, who was upset over political moves he felt Milk was largely responsible for which had cost White his position. Part of Milk's ashes were scattered in San Francisco Bay. Part were sent to Congressional Cemetery in Washington, D.C., where a group named "Never Forget" paid for a space for the ashes, but no order for burial had been given by 1993.

6337. Mill, John Stuart (May 20, 1806–May 8, 1873) British Victorian social and political philosopher espoused utilitarian reforms along the lines of Jeremy Bentham, but differed from him on the significance of physical or intellectual pleasure. He later collaborated with his wife Harriet Taylor (d 1858) on writings including *On Liberty* and *The Subjection of Women*. Cimetiere Saint-Veran, Avignon, France.

6338. Milland, Ray (Reginald Truscott-Jones, Jan. 3, 1905–March 10, 1986) Welsh born actor in U.S. films from 1929 in urbane, usually semi-reserved roles: *Payment Deferred* (1932), *Beau Geste* (1939), *The Major and the Minor* (1942), Ministry of Fear, *The Uninvited* (1944), *The Lost Weekend* (Academy Award, 1945), *Golden Earrings, The Big Clock, It Happens Every Spring, Night Into Morning* (1955), later in AIP horrors, *Love Story* (1970), etc. He died from cancer at 81. Cremated at Pacific Crest Memorial Park, Redondo Beach, California. Ashes scattered at sea.

6339. Millay, Edna St. Vincent (Feb. 22, 1892–Oct. 19, 1950) New England born poet, the first woman to receive the Pulitzer Prize for poetry (1923) for *The Harp Weaver' and Other Poems*. She died from a drunken fall down stairs and a broken neck at her estate at Austerlitz, New York, and was buried in her woods, marked by a boulder with her name and dates in the Azalea grove. Millay Colony for the Arts, Austerlitz, NY.

6340. Miller, Alice Duer (July 28, 1874–Aug. 23, 1942) Author of the poem *The White Cliffs* of *Dover*, set to music at the outbreak of World War II and penned near the end of her career. As a journalist she ghost wrote speeches for Woodrow Wilson, worked for women's suffrage, was an honored senior member of the Algonquin Round Table of the 1920's, managing to do several film scripts as well. She died from cancer just months before the death of Round Table co-founder Alexander Woollcott. Epitaph reads *Beauty itself doth of itself persuade without an orator.* Sec. 37, lot 58, Evergreen Cemetery, Morristown, NJ.

6341. Miller, Ann (Johnnie Lucille Collier, April 12, 1923–Jan. 22, 2004) Raven haired tap dancer and actress from Chireno, Texas, at RKO from 1937 in *Stage Door, Room Service*, as Essie in *You Can't Take It With You* (Columbia), *Too Many Girls, Reveille with Beverly,* and at MGM through the 1940's, at her peak 1948–53 in *Easter Parade, On the Town, Kiss Me Kate.* She left films in 1956, later starring on Broadway and touring with Mickey Rooney in *Sugar Babies.* Her last appearance was as Coco in David Lynch's *Mulholland Drive* (2001). She died at Cedars-Sinai Medical Center in Los Angeles from lung cancer at 80. Married three times, last to Arthur Cameron, she miscarried her only child, Mary, while married to her second husband, Reese Milner, in 1946. Buried beside her mother. Plaque with her baby. Sec. F, tier 57, grave 58, Holy Cross Cemetery, Culver City, CA.

6342. Miller, Arthur (Oct. 17, 1915–Feb. 10, 2005) New York born playwright first showcased in the 1930's by the Federal Theatre Project, was at his peak during the postwar era, focusing on internal struggles with moral compromises, in *All My Sons* (1947, filmed in 1948, Drama Critics Circle Award) and *Death of A Salesman* (1949, filmed in 1952); won both the Drama Critics Circle Award and the Pulitzer Prize. *The Crucible* (1953) implied a parallel between the Salem witch trials and congressional subversion hunts, and *A View From the Bridge* (1955) looked at immigration laws. His novel *Focus* (1945) was an ironic look at anti–Semitism, and several screen plays included *The Misfits* (1960), the last film of his second wife (1956–61) Marilyn Monroe. His third and last, from 1962, was photographer **Inge Morath**, who died in 2002. He died at 89 in his home at Roxbury, Connecticut. Cremated at Evergreen Crematory, New Haven, through Connecticut Cremation Service, New Haven. Ashes buried beside Morath. New Roxbury Center Cemetery, Roxbury, CT.

6343. Miller, Arthur C. (July 8, 1895–July 13, 1970) Cinematographer from Roslyn, New York, expert in black and white lighting, photographed *The Perils of Pauline* (1914), later working with George Fitzmaurice, DeMille, and at Fox 1932–51. He won three Oscars, for *How Green Was My Valley* (1941), *The Song of Bernadette* (1943) and *Anna and the King of Siam* (1946). Haven of Remembrance, tier 1, niche 3, Abbey of the Psalms/Hollywood Forever Mausoleum, Hollywood Forever Cemetery, Hollywood (Los Angeles), CA.

6344. Miller, Bing (Edmund John Miller, Aug. 30, 1894–May 7, 1966) Outfielder with the Philadelphia A's 1922–26 and 1928–1934, during their domination 1929–31. Calvary Cemetery, West Conshohocken, northwest of Philadelphia, PA.

6345. Miller, Don (March 30, 1902–July 28, 1979) Halfback from Defiance, Ohio, one of the original Four Horsemen in Notre Dame's famed backfield of the 1920's. Sec. 25, lot 69, grave 2, All Souls Cemetery, Chardon, OH.

6346. Miller, Elva ("Mrs. Miller") (Oct. 5, 1907–July 5, 1997) Impromptu pop celebrity of the 1960's was a talk show audience regular, later released off-key LPs (*Will Success Spoil Mrs. Miller?*) and had a few small parts in film and TV. Corridor C, crypt 14F, Pomona Cemetery Mausoleum, Pomona, CA.

6347. Miller, Glenn (Alton Glenn Miller, March 1, 1904–Dec 15, 1944) Yale educated trombone player led the most popular Big Band in America at the outbreak of World War II. His use of blended high range saxophones was and is known as the Glenn Miller Sound. A captain in the army and leader of a marching military band, he had been entertaining troops when his plane disappeared in the English Channel on a London to Paris flight. His body was never recovered. Cenotaphs, Memorial sec. H, grave 464-A, Arlington National Cemetery, Arlington, Virginia, one at the American Military Cemetery at Hamm, Luxembourg, Belgium, and by 2000 a black monument with his picture and a tribute was placed by Yale University in Grove Street Cemetery, New Haven, CT.

6348. Miller, Henry (John Pegge, Feb. 1, 1859–April 9, 1926) London born stage star and director in the U.S. from 1908. The Henry Miller Theater in New York was named for him. His Celtic cross is broken off at the base. The gravesite is visible from the circular Roosevelt lot across the road. Sec 51, lot 12655, Greenwood Cemetery, Brooklyn, N.Y.C.

6349. Miller, Henry (Dec. 26, 1891–June 7, 1980) New York born author wrote primarily biographical novels with frequent anarchistic undercurrents, included *The Tropic of Cancer* (1935) and *The Tropic of Capricorn* (1939). Because of their sexual content, his books were the subject of a 1964 Supreme Court obscenity ruling, in his favor. The film *Henry and June* was a study of Miller and Anais Nin. Miller was cremated and his ashes scattered in the Pacific from Big Sur.

6350. Miller, Jason (John Anthony Miller, April 22, 1939–May 13, 2001) Actor-playwright born in Long Island City, New York, and raised in Scranton, Pennsylvania, where he played basketball in the 1950's, the basis for his play *That Championship Season*, which won the Pulitzer Prize and a Tony Award in 1973, the same year he essayed his Oscar nominated portrayal of Father Damien Karras in *The Exorcist*. Other roles include Ara Parseghian in *Rudy* (1993). Married in the 1960's to Jackie Gleason's daughter Linda, the father of actors Jason Patric and Josh Miller, he returned to Scranton in the 1980's, where he organized and acted in local theatre. He died there at 62 from a heart attack. Mass at St. Patrick's Church, Scranton. Cremation through Albert P. O'Donnell mortuary, Dunmore. His ashes were to be spread from the courthouse in Scranton.

6351. Miller, J.B. (James B. Miller, AKA Killing Jim Miller, Oct. 25, 1861–April 19, 1909) Paid killer and bounty hunter killed over a dozen men, including (allegedly) Pat Garrett. When he ambushed and killed Gus Bobbitt in Ada, Oklahoma, he was arrested and hanged by a mob, many of them friends of Bobbitt. Block 100, lot 14, Oakwood Cemetery, Fort Worth, TX.

6352. Miller, Marilyn (Mary Ellen Reynolds, Sept. 1, 1898–April 7, 1936) Evansville, Indiana, born dancer and singer, a Broadway star of the 1920's known for Ziegfeld's *Sally* (1920), in which she introduced the song *Look For the Silver Lining*, the same year her husband, **Frank Carter** (March 22, 1892–May 9, 1920) was killed in a car crash. She married Jack Pickford in the 1920's but later divorced him and married a third time (Chester O'Brien). Following her other major theatrical success, in *Sunny* (1925), she made a few talkies, including *Sally* (1929). She died at 37 from toxemia related to a sinus infection in Doctors Hospital, Manhattan, and was interred with her first husband. Her name is over the outer section of his mausoleum; Carter's name in darker letters is over the inner roof, above the door, facing Whitewood Ave. Heather sec., Woodlawn Cemetery, the Bronx, N.Y.C.

6353. Miller, Marvin (July 18, 1913–Feb. 8, 1985) Actor from St. Louis, a frequent film villain of the 1940's (*Dead Reckoning*) and 50's, made his mark in TV's *The Millionaire* 1955–1960, where he, Michael Anthony, knocked on a different door each week to present the occupant with a check for a million dollars from his employer, John Beresford Tipton. He did many voices, including Robby the Robot in *Forbidden Planet* (1956) and *The Invisible Boy* (1957), and narrated the television series *The F.B.I.* from 1965. Sanctuary of Tenderness, Westwood Memorial Park, west Los Angeles.

6354. Miller, Merle (May 17, 1919–June 10, 1986) Historian from Monitor, Iowa, known for his oral histories of Harry S Truman and LBJ, the satirical *Only You, Dick Daring, or How to Write One Television Script and Make $50 Million*, and his 1971 essay in the *New York Times*: *What It Means To Be Gay*. He died at Danbury, Connecticut. Cremated at Cedar Hill Cemetery in Newburgh, New York, through Cornell funeral Home in Danbury. Ashes to his companion at Sherwood Hill, Brewster, NY.

6355. Miller, Nathan (May 26, 1927–Oct. 22, 2004) U.S. Historian from Baltimore authored *The U.S. Navy: A History* (1977), published as a textbook by the Naval Institute *FDR: An Intimate History* (1983) and *Theodore Roosevelt: A Life* (1992), as well as *Star Spangled Men* (1998) and *New World Coming: The 1920's and the Making of Modern America* (2003). He died in Washington at 77. Arlington-Chizuk Amuno Congregation Cemetery, Baltimore, MD.

6356. Miller, Patsy Ruth (Patricia Miller, Jan. 17, 1904–July 16, 1995) St. Louis born silent film actress who played Esmeralda in *The Hunchback of Notre Dame* (1923). She retired with the 1930's and switched to writing, winning three O. Henry Awards. Autobiography *My Hollywood* (1988). Her final marriage was to E.S. Deans (dec. 1986). She died in Palm Desert at 91. Cremated by Palm Springs mortuary. Ashes to her son.

6357. Miller, Roger (Jan. 2, 1936–Oct. 25, 1992) Folk singer-songwriter won eleven Grammys, best known for *King of the Road* (1965), also wrote for the Broadway show *Big River*. He died at 56 from cancer in Los Angeles. Ashes sent from Westwood mortuary there to his residence at Santa Fe, NM.

6358. Miller, Seton I. (Seton Ingersoll Miller, May 3, 1902–March 29, 1974) Silent film actor turned to writing and collaborating on screenplays through the 1930's (*The Dawn Patrol* 1930, *The Criminal Code*, *Scarface*, *The Crowd Roars*, *If I Had A Million*, *The Eagle and the Hawk*, *G-Men*, *The Adventures of Robin Hood*, *The Dawn Patrol* 1938, *The Sea Hawk*, *Here Comes Mr. Jordan* [Academy Award with Sidney Buchman, 1941]). In the 1940's and 50's he produced as well, including Fritz Lang's *Ministry of Fear* (1944). Ashes scattered at sea.

6359. Miller, Sidney (Oct. 22, 1916–Jan. 9, 2004) Actor from Shenandoah, Pennsylvania, in many films of the 1930's and 40's as practical joking juveniles (*Symphony of Six Million, Three on A Match, The Penguin Pool Murder, Our Daily Bread, Boys Town, Strike Up the Band, Andy Hardy Gets Spring Fever*) and later various parts and voices. He died in L.A. at 87 from Parkinson's Disease. Building M, row 8, crypt 3408, Beth Olam Cemetery adjacent Hollywood Forever Cemetery, Hollywood (Los Angeles), CA.

6360. Miller, Virgil (Virgil Emitt Miller, Dec. 20, 1886–Oct. 5, 1974) Cinematographer from Coffeen, Illinois, in Hollywood from the 1910's to 1956; his work included (parts of) *The Phantom of the Opera* (1925), *The Garden of Allah* (1936), *Mr. Moto* and *Charlie Chan* films at Fox 1939–40, *Dr. Renault's Secret* (1942), at Universal 1943–45 (*Calling Dr. Death, Weird Woman, The Pearl of Death, The Mummy's Curse, The House of Fear, The Woman in Green*), TV's *You Bet Your Life, Unchained* (1955). He died in North Hollywood at 87. Sec. 3, lot 153, grave 4, Oakwood Memorial Park, Chatsworth, CA.

6361. Miller, Walter C. (March 9, 1892–March 30, 1940) Character actor in serials, gangster films (from *Musketeers of Pig Alley* 1912) and westerns. Flush plaque, southwest corner area of sec. O, Calvary Cemetery, Evanston (north of Chicago), IL.

6362. Miller, William Christy (Aug. 10, 1843–Sept. 23, 1922) Stage actor in films 1909–1913, died on Staten Island. Ashes beneath a small marker in the Actors Fund plot, Prospect Hill sec., Cemetery of the Evergreens, Brooklyn, N.Y.C.

6363. Miller, William E. (March 22, 1914–June 24, 1983) New York Republican congressman 1951–1965 was the Vice Presidential candidate on the GOP ticket with Barry Goldwater in 1964. Black monument. Sec. 5, grave 93, Arlington National Cemetery, Arlington, VA.

6364. Millhauser, Bertram (March 25, 1892–Dec. 1, 1958) New York born screen-writer from early silents authored *Hot Leather*, the story of boxer Jimmy Dolan, Pearl White serials, many later crime and horror melodramas (*They Made Me A Criminal, The Big Shot, Sherlock Holmes in Washington, ...Faces Death, ...and the Spider Woman, The Pearl of Death, The Suspect, The Invisible Man's Revenge, Tokyo Joe*). He also directed a few films, including *Midnight Mystery* (1929). Sec. 8/Garden of Legends, lot 27, Hollywood Forever Cemetery, Hollywood (Los Angeles), CA.

6365. Millican, James Andrew (Feb. 17, 1910–Nov. 24, 1955) Actor in heavy roles and other leads, from *The Sign of the Cross* through many crime and western films. He died at 45 from bladder cancer. Court of Freedom, lot 4123, Forest Lawn, Glendale, CA.

6366. Milligan, Spike (Terence Alan Milligan, April 16, 1918–Feb. 27, 2002) India born son of an Irish Army captain was the backbone and last survivor of *The Goon Show* on British television in the 1950's, a precursor of Monty Python and others at whose core was the absurdity of much of life. The other three Goons had all preceded him in death: Peter Sellers in 1980, Michael Bentine in 1996, and Harry Secombe in 2001. Milligan died at Rye of kidney disease at 83. Covered by an Irish flag, his funeral was held March 8 at St. Anthony of Padua Catholic Church in Rye, East Sussex. Tributes included a wreath from the Prince of Wales, a lifelong fan and official patron of the Goon Show Preservation Society. Burial with bagpipes. A small temporary marker served until May 2004, when a black stone was set with his preferred epitaph *I told you I was ill*, but in Gaelic as specified by the Chichester Diocese: *Duirt me leat go raibh me breoite.* added in English is *Love, light, peace.* St. Thomas Church cemetery, Winchelsea, East Sussex.

6367. Millikan, Robert A. (March 22, 1868–Dec. 19, 1953) Physicist with the University of Chicago 1896–1921 and the California Institute of Technology 1921–1945 won the Nobel Prize for research and isolation of the electron and proton theory, founding the basis for theories on the structure of atoms. Memorial Court of Honor below the Last Supper Window,

Memorial Terrace, Great Mausoleum, Forest Lawn, Glendale, CA.

6368. Millman, Harry (1911–Nov. 25, 1937) Purple Gang younger member from the north end of Detroit; the Jewish Millman continually expressed his dislike of the Italian mafia and intentionally annoyed them. An attempt to kill him in an explosion failed in August 1937, but three months later he was shot to death at Boesky's restaurant and deli, allegedly by Harry "Pep" Strauss and Happy Maione of New York's Murder Inc. Workmens Circle Cemetery, Clinton Township, Macomb County, MI.

6369. Mills, Billy (William Randolph Mills, Sept. 6, 1894–Oct. 21, 1971) Orchestra leader, a mainstay on radio's *Fibber McGee and Molly* from 1938–1952, and more briefly on *The Great Gildersleeve* (1941–43) and *Amos n Andy* (1944–45). Handled by Forest Lawn, Glendale, California. Sec. G, lot 160, grave 2, Grace Lawn Community Cemetery, Flint, MI.

6370. Mills, Donald *see* **Mills Brothers.**

6371. Mills, Eleanor (1888–Sept. 16, 1922) Choir member and the alleged lover of the Rev. Dr. Edward Hall, with whom she was found murdered under a crabapple tree on the Phillips farm at New Brunswick, New Jersey. She was shot three times and her throat cut. He was also killed, with a gunshot to the head, allegedly by his wife and her brothers, who were indicted but acquitted in a sensationalized 1926 trial. Van Liew Cemetery, New Brunswick, NJ.

6372. Mills, Florence (Jan. 25, 1895–Nov. 1, 1927) Black stage star in musicals of the 1920's (*Dixie to Broadway* 1924, *Blackbirds* 1926). Among her best known numbers was *I'm a Little Blackbird Looking for a Bluebird, Too*. Frail and overworked, she died suddenly at 32 in New York upon her return from London. As the funeral cortege wound its way north through Harlem, an airplane overhead released a flock of bluebirds. Her monument has a cross on top. Arbutus sec., lot 181, above Myosotis Ave., Woodlawn Cemetery, the Bronx, N.Y.C.

6373. Mills, Harry *see* **Mills Brothers.**

6374. Mills, Herbert *see* **Mills Brothers.**

6375. Mills, John (Feb. 22, 1908–April 23, 2005) Acclaimed English actor of great range in over one hundred film parts from 1932, in World War II era efforts (*In Which We Serve, We Dive At Dawn, This Happy Breed, Waterloo Road*) and many character roles including *Great Expectations* (1946, as Pip the young man), *The Rocking Horse Winner, Hobson's Choice* (as Will Mossop), *War and Peace, Tiger Bay* and *The Swiss Family Robinson* (both with his daughter Hayley), *Ryan's Daughter* (1970, Academy award as the mute village idiot Michael), *The Big Sleep* (1978), *Gandhi, Murder With Mirrors, Who's That Girl*, and the 1996 *Hamlet*. CBE 1960. Knighted 1976. Married from 1941 to **Mary Hayley Bell**—the parents of Juliette, Hayley and Jonathan Mills—he died at their home Hills House at 97. Funeral at the church adjacent their home, where their marriage was blessed in 2001; he had been in the army at war in 1941 and was denied a church wedding at that time. Lady Mills died later in the year and was buried beside him. St. Mary the Virgin Church cemetery, Denham, Buckinghamshire.

6376. Mills, John, Jr. *see* **Mills Brothers.**

6377. Mills, John, Sr. *see* **Mills Brothers.**

6378. Mills, Roger Quarles (Nov. 30, 1832–Sept. 2, 1911) Democratic congressman from Texas 1873–1892, one of the "Confederate Brigadiers," was a friend of Grover Cleveland's and pictured in an 1888 political cartoon opening the tariff floodgates to drown U.S. industry. The election went to the Republicans, but Quarles remained in the House, and served as senator 1892–99. Sec. P, row 5, Oakwood Cemetery, Corsicana, TX.

6379. Mills, Wilbur (May 24, 1909–May 2, 1992) Arkansas congressman whose career was destroyed when he was found with a burlesque stripper as she jumped into the tidal basin near the Jefferson Memorial in October 1974. He was elected to a 19th term a month after the incident but retired in 1976, undergoing treatment for alcoholism. He died from a heart attack at 82 in Searcy, Arkansas. Kensett Cemetery, Kensett, AR.

6380. Mills Brothers Originally billed as "Four Boys and a Guitar," the four Mills brothers were a vocal quartet from Piqua and Bellefontaine, Ohio. **John Mills, Jr.** (Oct. 19, 1911–Jan. 23, 1936), the original fourth member and guitar player, died from tuberculosis at 24 and was buried in Bellefontaine Cemetery, Bellefontaine, Ohio. He was replaced by his father **John Mills, Sr.** (Feb. 11, 1882–Dec. 8, 1967), who sang with his three other sons, Harry, Herbert and Donald until 1956, when he retired and returned to Bellefontaine. He died there twelve years later and was buried in the family plot, without an individual flush stone as his son has, in Bellefontaine Cemetery. The other three continued to perform and record through the 1970's. The unofficial leader, baritone **Harry Mills** (Aug. 19, 1913–June 28, 1982) died in Hollywood at 68. Courts of Remembrance, wall crypt 3446, Forest Lawn Hollywood Hills, Los Angeles. **Herbert Mills** (April 2, 1912–April 12, 1989) died in Las Vegas. Cremated through Palm mortuary; his ashes were returned to the family. **Donald Mills** (April 29, 1915–Nov. 13, 1999), the last Mills Brother, died from pneumonia in L.A. at 84, a year after accepting a Lifetime Achievement Grammy for the group. Columbarium of Radiant Dawn, niche G2033, Courts of Remembrance, Forest Lawn Hollywood Hills, Los Angeles.

6381. Milne, A.A. (Alan Alexander Milne, Jan. 18, 1882–Jan. 31, 1956) English author best known for his stories featuring his son in the guise of Christopher Robin: *Winnie the Pooh* (1926) and *The House at Pooh Corner* (1928), with drawings by Ernest Shepard. Ashes scattered at Salisbury.

6382. Milstein, Nathan (Dec. 31, 1904–Dec. 21, 1992) Noted violinist. Epitaph reads *With his violin,*

Nathan has taken our hand and gently walked us through Heaven. Putney Vale Cemetery, London.

6383. Milton, John (Dec. 9, 1608–Nov. 8, 1674) English poet, author of *Paradise Lost*, was blind from 1652 and increasingly plagued with gout until his death in his cottage at Chalfont St. Giles, twenty miles northwest of London. Buried near his father in the Church of St. Giles, Cripplegate, London.

6384. Milton, Tommy (Thomas W. Milton, Nov. 14, 1893–July 10, 1962) Winner of the Indianapolis 500 in 1921 and 1923, at 89.62 and 90.95 miles per hour, respectively. Forest Lawn Memorial Park, St. Paul, MN.

6385. Mineo, Sal (Jan. 10, 1939–Feb. 12, 1976) Young actor from the Bronx first gained fame as Plato in *Rebel Without A Cause* (1954, AA nom.), later in *Giant* (1955) and *Exodus* (1961), graduating from troubled juveniles to producing plays and TV work in Hollywood. He was working in *P.S. Your Cat Is Dead* when he was stabbed to death in his Hollywood carport returning from play practice. The killer was later apprehended, tried and sentenced to 51 years in prison. Flush plaque with his brother. Sec. 2, near the rear of Gate of Heaven Cemetery, Hawthorne, NY.

6386. Miner, Jan (Janice Miner, Oct. 15, 1917–Feb. 15, 2004) Actress from Boston on stage from 1945 and in films and television, but best known as Madge in Palmolive commercials over twenty seven years. Married to actor-writer Richard Merrell, who died in 1988, she lived at Southbury, Connecticut, until her death in nearby Bethel at 86. Cremated at Charter Oak Crematory, Oxford, the ashes went temporarily to Munson-Lovetere mortuary, Southbury, Connecticut.

6387. Mingus, Charlie (April 22, 1922–Jan. 5, 1979) Jazz bass player from Nogales, Arizona, known for his explosive temperament as well as his innovations, improvised and experimented, teaching workshops through the 50's and 60's as well as leading his own group. He died at Cuernavaca, Mexico. Ashes scattered on the Ganges River in India.

6388. Minjir, Harold (Oct. 5, 1895–April 16, 1976) Colorado born actor in films 1931–1945, often as foppish assistants, whining characters, etc. (*Daughter of the Dragon, Monkey Business, The Death Kiss, Night Mayor, Fog Over Frisco, Blondie, Miracles For Sale*). He died in Los Angeles from a heart attack at 80. Lagunita Alcove, niche 327, Pacific View Memorial Park, Newport Beach, CA.

6389. Mink, Patsy (Patsy Matsu Takemoto, Dec. 6, 1927–Sept. 28, 2002) Democratic congresswoman from Hawaii served twelve terms, from 1965–77 and from 1990 until her death twelve years later at 74 from viral meningitis. She had served in several positions in state government and ran unsuccessfully in 1972 for president, in 1976 for the senate, in 1986 for governor and in 1988 for mayor of Honolulu. Sec. U, grave 1001-B, National Memorial Cemetery of the Pacific (The Punchbowl), Honolulu, HI.

6390. Minnelli, Vincente (Feb. 28, 1903–July 25, 1986) Film director with a flair for production design in his musicals: *Meet Me in St. Louis* (1944) with Judy Garland, his wife 1945–51, *An American in Paris* (Best Picture AA 1951) and *Gigi* (Best Picture and Director AA 1958). He and Garland were the parents of Liza Minnelli. Enclosure, Garden of Enduring Faith, Forest Lawn, Glendale, CA.

6391. Minnesota Fats (Rudolf Wanderone, Jr., Jan. 19, c. 1913–Jan. 18, 1996) Champion pool shark tagged New York Fats until portrayed by Jackie Gleason as Minnesota Fats in the 1961 film *The Hustler*. When he died in Nashville, his real age was unknown, ranging from 82 to 95, but his wife knew his epitaph: *Beat everybody living on Earth. Now, St. Peter, rack 'em up.* Garden of Peace, sec. C, lawn crypt 171, Hermitage Memorial Gardens, Hermitage (Old Hickory), TN.

6392. Minor, George A. (Dec. 7, 1845–Jan. 29, 1904) Composer of hymns, including the music for *Bringing in the Sheaves* (words by Knowles Shaw). Sec. 3, lot 55, Hollywood Cemetery, Richmond, VA.

6393. Minter, Mary Miles (Juliet Reilly, April 1, 1902–Aug. 5, 1984) Silent screen actress whose name may have met with obscurity if not for her link to the murder of her favorite director, William Desmond Taylor, on February 1, 1922. Lingerie and other romantic links to Taylor found in his bungalow effectively ended her career. Many studies of the case, including one done by director King Vidor in 1967, point to Minter's mother **Charlotte Shelby** (dec. 1957) as the killer, either avenging her daughter's deflowering or because of her own jealousy. There was never any proof, however, and various theories point to an employee of Taylor's, among others. Years after their deaths, Minter, living alone in Santa Monica, had the bodies of her mother and her sister **Margaret** (dec. 1939) disinterred from a private garden in the Gardens of Honor, cremated, and their ashes scattered at sea. Cremated August 17 at Pierce Brothers' Chapel of the Pines Crematory under the name Mary O'Hildebrandt, her ashes were also scattered, in Santa Monica Bay as she has requested.

6394. Minuit, Peter (c. 1580–June 1638) Dutch governor of New Amsterdam obtained it from the Indians for (supposedly) about $24 in trinkets. Manhattan Island and New Amsterdam later became New York when the British defeated the Dutch. Minuit was lost at sea on a trading expedition to the West Indies.

6395. Miranda, Carmen (Feb. 9, 1909–Aug. 5, 1955) Portuguese dancer-comedienne in several musicals of the 1940's and early 50's, known for her hats of high piled fruit. The Brazilian Bombshell died at 51 (or 46, or 40) from an apparent heart attack in Beverly Hills, California, the wife of David Sebastian. The birth date is variously given as 1904 and 1909, and on her death certificate is listed as 1915. Her red-brown granite tomb has a bench built into the front and statues of Catholic saints on either side. Sao Joao Baptista Cemetery, Rio de Janeiro, Brazil.

6396. Miranda, Ernesto (March 9, 1941–Jan. 31, 1976) The basis of *Miranda vs. Arizona* (1966) was a twenty-three year old indigent arrested for kidnapping and raping an eighteen year old girl. Interrogated for two hours, he admitted the crime and signed a confession which was used as evidence for his conviction. The Supreme Court, speaking through Earl Warren, ruled that evidence obtained during custodial interrogation is inadmissible when the subject is not informed of his right to remain silent, to have an attorney present, that anything said can and will be used against them in a court of law, etc., hence the routine recitation of Miranda rights with each arrest. Block 677, lot 1, space 2, City of Mesa Cemetery, Mesa, AZ.

6397. Mitchell, Billy (William Joseph Mitchell, Jan. 30, 1931–Nov. 15, 2002) Vocalist with the Washington, D.C., based Rhythm and Blues group The Clovers in the 1950's; their hits included *Devil or Angel, One Mint Julep* and *Love Potion No. 9*, written by Jerry Lieber and Mike Stoller in 1959, on which Mitchell sang lead. He died in a D.C. hospital from colon cancer at 71. Sec. Adams, lot 77, grave 5, Harmony Memorial Park, Landover, MD.

6398. Mitchell, Cameron (Cameron Mitzell, Nov. 4, 1918–July 6, 1994) Actor from Dallastown, Pennsylvania., gained fame as Happy in the stage and screen versions of *Death of A Salesman*. In over ninety films and much TV but best known as Buck Cannon on NBC's *High Chaparral* 1967–71. He died at 75 from cancer in his Pacific Palisades home. His plaque lists the date of death as July 7, while the death certificate lists July 6. Sec. A-23, lot 83, Desert Memorial Park, Cathedral City (Palm Springs), CA.

6399. Mitchell, Chuck (Charles Thomas Mitchell, Jr., Nov. 28, 1927–June 22, 1992) Portly actor in various TV roles and films of the 1970's and 80's, best known as Porky in Bob Clark's *Porky's* (1981) and its two sequels. Sec. 32, grave 839, Riverside National Cemetery, Riverside, CA.

6400. Mitchell, Geneva (Feb. 3, 1907–March 10, 1949) Ziegfeld girl from Medarysville, Indiana, appeared with Leon Errol in *Louie the 14th* before turning to films 1930–36 (*Millie, Night World, Morning Glory, Springtime For Henry, The Captain Hates the Sea*), including Three Stooges shorts (*Restless Knights, Hoi Polloi, Pop Goes the Easel*, all 1935). She made two later appearances in small roles prior to her death at 42 from pancreatitis complicated by alcoholism and cirrhosis of the liver. Cremated at Pacific Crest Memorial Park, Redondo Beach. Marker reads *Geneva Doris Mitchell Tuttle*. Memory Hall, sec. F, niche F-22, Pierce Bros.' Chapel of the Pines Crematory, Los Angeles.

6401. Mitchell, Grant (John Grant Mitchell, Jr., June 17, 1874–May 1, 1957) Short, stocky, balding character actor in a variety of roles, usually as sensible husbands or fathers (and a few judges and wardens): *Star Witness, Dinner at Eight* 1933, *The Grapes of Wrath* 1940, *The Man Who Came to Dinner* 1942, many others. Buried unmarked in the Platt-Mitchell plot of his grandmother, Fanny Hayes Platt, the sister of President Rutherford B. Hayes, next to his mother and father, John Grant Mitchell. By June 2001 a new marker matching his parents marked his grave. Sec. L, lot 3, Greenlawn Cemetery, Columbus, OH.

6402. Mitchell, Guy (Albert Cernik, Feb. 22, 1927–July 1, 1999) Yugoslavian born singer had hits with *My Heart Cries For You* (1950), appeared in a few films, and later the better known *Heartaches By the Number* and *Singing the Blues*. He died in Las Vegas at 72. Cremated through Palm mortuary (downtown). Memorial service July 6 at Prince of Peace Catholic Church. Ashes picked up by family.

6403. Mitchell, John (Sept. 5, 1913–Nov. 9, 1988) Attorney General under Richard Nixon, brought down in part by the gossiping of his wife Martha, was sentenced to prison for perjury and his part in the Watergate coverup. Sec. 7A, site 121, grid U-24, Arlington National Cemetery, Arlington, VA.

6404. Mitchell, John Grant (Nov. 6, 1838–Nov. 7, 1894) Piqua, Ohio, born Union Brigadier General, a colonel at Chickamauga under General Thomas, was later part of the Atlanta campaign and present at Joseph Johnston's surrender in North Carolina. He left the military to practice law in Columbus, where he died at 56. Father of stage and screen actor Grant Mitchell, buried next to him. Sec. L, lot 3, Platt-Mitchell plot, Greenlawn Cemetery, Columbus, OH.

6405. Mitchell, Joseph (Joseph Quincy Mitchell, July 27, 1908–May 24, 1996) North Carolina native wrote on New York from the 1920's, at the *New York Herald Tribune, The World-Telegram,* and *The New Yorker,* where he wrote articles on McSorley's Old Ale House, Bowery inhabitants, and particularly Joe Gould, the Greenwich Village character whose *Oral History of Our Times* turned out to have never existed. Among Mitchell's collections were *Up in the Old Hotel* and *My Ears Are Bent.* He died from cancer in Manhattan at 87. Floyd Memorial Cemetery, North Main St., Fairmont, NC.

6406. Mitchell, Margaret (Nov. 8, 1900–Aug. 16, 1949) Former reporter with the *Atlanta Journal,* the author of *Gone With the Wind* (1936) won the 1937 Pulitzer Prize for Literature and saw her book become the most anticipated film of the century in 1939. Crossing Peachtree Street in Atlanta with her husband John Marsh on August 11, 1949, she was struck by a speeding off duty taxi driver and died five days later. Marsh monument, near sidewalk, block 22, lot 1, Oakland Cemetery, Atlanta, GA.

6407. Mitchell, Martha (Sept. 2, 1918–May 31, 1976) The wife of Richard Nixon's Attorney General was, through 1972–74, a constant media source through her busy telephone and gossip about the goings on in the administration. She died from cancer at 57. A wreath at her graveside service was inscribed "Martha was right." Ferguson lot, block 14, lot 4, Bellwood Cemetery, Pine Bluff, AR.

6408. Mitchell, Millard (Aug. 14, 1903–Oct. 13, 1953) Lanky character actor in several tough, world weary roles 1940–1953, often as detectives (*Grand Central Murder, A Double Life, Kiss of Death, Mr. 880, Winchester 73*). Sec. L, lot 575, Holy Cross Cemetery, Culver City, CA.

6409. Mitchell, Rhea (Dec. 10, 1890/1893–Sept. 16, 1957) Actress from Portland, Oregon, in silent films (the aborted serial *Diamond from the Sky* 1916) and later bit parts in sound (*Mrs. Parkington,* many others) was running an apartment house when she was strangled by a disgruntled houseboy at 66 (or 63). Her will specified she have no final resting place, and she remains in vaultage at Hollywood Forever Cemetery, Hollywood (Los Angeles), CA.

6410. Mitchell, Thomas (July 11, 1892–Dec. 17, 1962) Actor from Elizabeth, New Jersey, in many roles including *Stagecoach* (Academy Award 1939), *Gone With the Wind* (as Gerald O'Hara), *Our Town* (1940, as Doc Gibbs), *The Five Sullivans* (1944) and several Frank Capra films (*Lost Horizon, Mr. Smith Goes to Washington, Meet John Doe,* and *It's A Wonderful Life*). He died from cancer in Los Angeles two days after Charles Laughton. Ashes in vaultage, Pierce Brothers' Chapel of the Pines Crematory, Los Angeles.

6411. Mitchell, William "Billy" (Dec. 29, 1879–Feb. 19, 1936) U.S. Army Air Corps general and aviation pioneer was court martialed in 1926 for criticizing inadequate U.S. air power. With the outbreak of World War II he became a hero posthumously for both his foresight and the unjust treatment he received from the military. Polished gray monument with pink granite columns at the corners. Sec. 32, block 19, Forest Home Cemetery, Milwaukee, WI.

6412. Mitchum, John (Sept. 6, 1919–Nov. 28, 2001) Younger brother of Robert Mitchum also appeared in (sixty) films, in smaller roles, including *Stalag 17, Chisum, Paint Your Wagon, High Plains Drifter, The Outlaw Josie Wales,* was Harry Callahan's partner Frank in *Dirty Harry, Magnum Force* and *The Enforcer,* and appeared with his brother in *The Lusty Men* (1952) and *Jake Spanner, Private Eye* (1989), in which they played brothers. A writer and poet, he was nominated for a Grammy for his patriotic poems on the LP *America, Why I Love Her,* which grew out of his *Why Are You Marching Son?,* recited by John Wayne. He died in Los Angeles at 82. Cremated by the Neptune Society of Burbank. Ashes scattered at sea December 5 off the coast of Santa Barbara County.

6413. Mitchum, Julie (Annette Mitchum, July 23, 1914–Feb. 21, 2003) Older sister of Robert and John Mitchum had been on stage and encouraged Robert to join the Pasadena Playhouse. Films include *The High and the Mighty* (1954), *Edge of Hell* (1956), *Hit and Run* (1957), and as Ruth Bridges in *House on Haunted Hill* (1958). She retired to Scottsdale, Arizona, with her husband, ad executive Elliott Sater

(March 1918–Jan. 1986), subscribed to the Baha'i faith, and died in Sun City from Alzheimer's Disease at 88. Her death was not announced until May 2004. Her flat plaque reads *Maid-servant of God*. Sec. 2, block 3, lot 3, space 1, (East) Resthaven Park Cemetery, 4310 E. Southern Ave., Phoenix, AZ.

6414. Mitchum, Robert (Aug. 6, 1917–July 1, 1997) Distinctive, sleepy eyed actor from Bridgeport, Connecticut, moved from an adventurous youth into acting in a variety of roles from the mid 1940's (*The Locket, Pursued, Out of the Past, His Kind of Woman, Night of the Hunter, Heaven Knows Mr. Allison, The Sundowners, Cape Fear* 1962, *The Longest Day, El Dorado, Ryan's Daughter, The Friends of Eddie Coyle, Farewell My Lovely,* many others). Oscar nomination for *The Story of G.I. Joe* (1945). In films into the 1990's. Ill with emphysema and lung cancer, he died in his sleep at 79 at home in Montecito, Santa Barbara County, California. Taken directly to the Neptune Society, his ashes were scattered at sea July 9 three miles off the Santa Barbara Channel.

6415. Mitford Sisters **Nancy Mitford** Rodd (Nov. 28, 1904–June 30, 1973) The eldest of five well known daughters of **David Bertram Freeman Mitford, Lord Redesdale** (1878–1958) and **Sidney Bowles Mitford** (1880–1963), upon whom she based a central character in her novels lampooning British nobility (her own background): *Don't Tell Alfred* (1960) and *Noblesse Oblige*. She also wrote biographies, residing for many years near St. Cloud in France, where she died from Hodgkin's Disease at 68. Cremated at Pere Lachaise, her ashes were taken by her sister Diana for burial — Marked by a stone with the heraldic device from her writing paper on it — beside her younger sister (the third of five), **Unity Mitford** (Aug. 8, 1914–May 28, 1948), a Nazi supporter and intimate of Hitler who attempted suicide at the outbreak of World War II and never recovered from the gunshot wound to the head. Her epitaph reads *Say not the struggle naught availeth* (from Arthur Hugh Clough). Their sister, socialite **Pamela Mitford** Jackson (1907–April 12, 1994), considerably less controversial, is also buried at Swinbrook with a marker, with an oak dedicated to her on the village green. She is some forty yards from Nancy, Unity, and Diana, who are together in St. Mary's Churchyard, Swinbrook, Oxfordshire. **Jessica Mitford** (Sept. 11, 1917–July 23, 1996) Witty writer and social critic, author of *The American Way of Death* and *The Trial of Dr. Spock*, died in Oakland, California, her home since 1943, the wife of Dr. Robt. Treuhaft. For her funeral, she said she wanted "six black horses with plumes and one of those marvelous jobs of embalming that take twenty years off ... streets to be blocked off, dignitaries to declaim sobbingly over the flower-smothered bier, proclamations to be issued — that sort of thing." Her service was held at Delancey St. Hall with kazoos playing and her books (but no body) in an Edwardian coffin. Her ashes were scattered at sea July 27 off

the coast of Marin County, California. **Diana Mitford, Lady Mosley** (June 17, 1910–Aug. 11, 2003), the third of the Mitford sisters, left her husband Bryan Guinness in 1932 for Sir Oswald Mosley, founder of the British Union of Fascists. Even more than her husband in later years, she remained fond of Hitler and refused to directly denounce Nazi policies against Jews. They were both imprisoned at Holloway from May 1940 until November 1943, when they were released on house arrest. Her pro-Axis politics were later forgiven by her Francophile sister Nancy, who denounced her during the war, but never by Jessica. Mosley died in 1980, and she followed in Paris twenty three years later at 93. Her ashes were buried with her sisters Nancy and Unity. They are some forty yards from Pamela and sixty-five yards from their parents. St. Mary's Churchyard, Swinbrook, Oxfordshire.

6416. Mitterand, Francois (Oct. 26, 1916–Jan. 8, 1996) President of France 1981–1995 was the first Socialist president of the Fifth French Republic, its most influential leader since DeGaulle. From his victory in 1981 he began a series of sweeping social reforms, much of them halted in 1982 with ensuing economic decline. Despite political victories on the right, he was re-elected in 1988. He died from prostate cancer at 79. Mass at Notre Dame Cathedral. Tomb in Mount Beuvray Cemetery (Cimetiere des Grands-Maisons), Jarnac, (southwestern) France.

6417. Mix, Tom (Jan. 6, 1880–Oct. 12, 1940) Silent screen cowboy hero — with trademark white hat — from Mix Run, Pennsylvania, succeeded William S. Hart as the most popular film cowboy of his day. In later years he was traveling as an advance man for a circus when he died in a car accident eighteen miles south of Florence, Arizona. A 7' stone riderless horse with bowed head atop a stone monument is at the site of his death, with a plaque inscribed *In Memory of Tom Mix, whose spirit left his body on this spot and whose characterizations and portrayals in life served to better fix memories of the old west in the minds of living men.* There is also a marker at his birthplace at Mix Run. His grave plaque has his signature and dates. Whispering Pines, lot 986, Forest Lawn, Glendale, CA.

6418. Mize, Johnny (John Robert Mize, Jan. 7, 1913–June 2, 1993) Powerful slugger and first baseman, The Big Cat began with St. Louis in 1936, led the NL in 1939 with a .349 batting average, and led in runs four times 1939–48, homered in every stadium in the country and ended his career as part of five straight world series winners with the Yankees. Hall of Fame 1981. Stats listed on his flush bronze plaque. Sunset Hill sec., Yonah Memorial Gardens, Demorest, GA.

6419. Mizell, Jason (Jan. 21, 1965–Oct. 30, 2002) Rapper Jam Master Jay with the group Run-DMC, pioneers in their format dating to 1983, was shot and killed in a Queens, New York, recording studio at 37; no history of violence or motive was connected with his murder. Hillcrest C, grave 1120, Ferncliff Cemetery, Hartsdale, NY.

6420. Mizner, Wilson (May 19, 1876–April 3, 1933) Son of California lawyer and statesman Lansing Mizner from Benicia, was a playwright, adventurer and bon vivant who went to the Klondike with the Gold Rush in 1897, later marrying a New York society matron for her fortune in January 1906 just a month after her husband's death. He published his first plays in 1907 (*The Deep Purple, The Greyhound* 1912) and later went into real estate development in Florida, selling land in Boca Raton. In the last years of his life he wrote for films. The Clark Gable character Blackie Norton in *San Francisco* (1906) was said to be based on Mizner. He died from a heart attack in Los Angeles. Cremated there, his ashes were placed in the family vault at Cypress Lawn Cemetery, Colma, California, but were later removed and scattered in San Francisco Bay.

6421. Moakley, Joe (April 27, 1927–May 28, 2001) Fifteen term Democratic representative from Massachusetts' 9th congressional district served from 1973 until his death at 74 from leukemia. He had announced hill illness in February. Moakley's funeral at St. Bridget's Church in South Boston drew to the front pew the opponents from the recent presidential contest, George W. Bush and Al Gore, as well as former President Clinton and Senator Edward Kennedy. Sec. 26-N, lot 931, Blue Hill Cemetery, Braintree, MA.

6422. Mockridge, Cyril (Aug. 6, 1896–Jan. 18, 1979) English composer in Hollywood at Fox from 1933 into the 1950's scored or wrote incidental music for numerous films (*Judge Priest, Poor Little Rich Girl, The Hound of the Baskervilles, The Adventures of Sherlock Holmes, The Gorilla, Johnny Apollo, I Wake Up screaming, The Undying Monster, The Ox-Bow Incident, My Darling Clementine, The Dark Corner, Cluny Brown, Nightmare Alley, I Was A Male War Bride, Mr. Belvedere Rings the Bell, Love Nest, River of No Return, How to Marry A Millionaire, The Man Who Shot Liberty Valance*) and TV series including *Wagon Train, Peyton Place* and *Lost in Space*. He died in Honolulu at 82. Columbarium of Radiant Dawn, bottom tier, niche G61692, Courts of Remembrance, Forest Lawn Hollywood Hills, Los Angeles, CA.

6423. Model, Walther (Jan. 24, 1891–April 21, 1945) German field marshal, chief of staff of Nazi forces in Poland and France. Surrounded by the Allies at the Ruhr in Russia near the war's end, he committed suicide. Knight's Cross with oak leaves, swords and diamonds. Military Cemetery at Hurtgen Forest, near Aachen, Hurtgenwald-Vossenack, Germany.

6424. Modjeska, Helena (Helena Moorzejewska Chlapowska, Oct. 12, 1840–April 8, 1909) Polish born stage star in America by 1876 in Shakespearian roles. She died at East Newport, California, and was shipped to Poland. Her stone vault has a profile of her on the front. Sec. 54, Rakowicka Cemetery, Krakow, Poland.

6425. Mohan, Earl (Earl John Mohan, Nov. 12, 1889–Oct. 15, 1928) Actor in silent films from 1915, a favorite drunk in Harold Lloyd films. Sec. K, tier 4, grave 92, Calvary Cemetery, east Los Angeles.

6426. Mohr, Gerald (June 11, 1914–Nov. 9, 1968) New York born actor first on radio as *The Whistler, The Lone Wolf, Philip Marlowe* (1948–51) alternated from gangsters to leads in films, including *The Monster and the Girl, Lady of Burlesque, The Notorious Lone Wolf, The Catman of Paris, Passkey to Danger, The Lone Wolf in Mexico, The Lone Wolf in London, Sirocco, Detective Story, The Eddie Cantor Story, The Angry Red Planet,* and *Funny Girl,* as well as over eighty appearances on television. He died from a heart attack at 54 while in Stockholm producing and starring in a television program. Wall plaque finely cut with his name and full dates. Lidingö Kyrkogård, Lidingo (Stockholms Lan), Sweden.

6227. Mohr, Hal (Aug. 2, 1894–May 10, 1974) San Francisco born cinematographer introduced complex crane shots (*Broadway* 1929) and heavily employed early use of dolly and boom shots. Academy Award for *A Midsummer Night's Dream* (1935), co-Oscar for *The Phantom of the Opera* (1943). Married to actress Evelyn Venable. Cremated at the Chapel of the Pacific, Woodlawn Cemetery, Santa Monica. Ashes scattered at sea in San Francisco Bay.

6428. Mohr, Josef (Dec. 11, 1792–Dec. 4, 1848) Writer of the lyrics to *Stille Nacht* (*Silent Night*), composed in 1818, the most popular of Christmas carols. Katholischer Friedhof, Wagrain, province of Salzburg, Austria.

6429. Moisant, John B. (April 25, 1868–Dec. 31, 1910) Designer and builder of the first all metal airplane was the first to fly the English Channel with a passenger (1910). Buried near Roy Knabenshue and Charles E. Taylor. Plaque with traditional eagle's wings. Portal of the Folded Wings, Valhalla Memorial Park, North Hollywood, CA

6430. Molchan, George (June 5, 1922–April 12, 2005) The Oscar Mayer wiener man played the company mascot, Little Oscar, for over thirty years. Accordingly, "I Wish I were an Oscar Mayer wiener" was sung at his funeral, and the Oscar Mayer Wienermobile was parked near the gravesite at his burial. Calumet Park Cemetery, Merrillville, IN

6431. Mole, Miff (Irving Milfred Mole, March 11, 1898–April 29, 1961) Jazz trombone player worked and recorded with Paul Whiteman, with Phil Napoleon and the Memphis Five, in partnership with Red Nichols, with Benny Goodman's Orchestra, and recorded with his Molers in the late 1920's. He died at the Central Apartments, 250 west 88th St., Manhattan, at 63. Family monument and headstone (marked *Miff*). Sec. 21, lot 80, grave 2, Greenfield Cemetery, Hempstead, NY.

6432. Moliere (Jean Louis Poquelin, Jan. 15, 1622–Feb. 17, 1673) France's earliest comic dramatist. In the Napoleonic period, when Nicholas Frochot was seeking esteemed residents to get Pere Lachaise Cemetery started in Paris, the bones of Moliere and Jean de La Fontaine were on deposit in Alexander Lenoir's Museum of French monuments. Moliere (or someone) had been exhumed by order of the National Assembly from St. Eustache/St. Joseph's Graveyard (and La Fontaine from the Cimetiere des Innocents) where he had been denied a Christian burial and interred during the night 144 years before. The body from St. Joseph's was reburied in 1817 beneath a stone canopy. Div. 25, Pere Lachaise Cemetery, Paris.

6433. Molnar, Ferenc (Jan. 12, 1878–April 1, 1952) Hungarian playwright from Budapest, in the U.S. from the 1930's, best known for "Liliom" (1909). Married to actress Lili Darvas. He died in New York. His upright stone reads (in Hungarian) *te esak most afudjal Liliom.* Non-sectarian sec., Linden Hills Cemetery, Maspeth/Ridgewood, Queens, N.Y.C.

6434. Molotov, Vyacheslav Mikhailovich (March 9, 1890–Nov. 8, 1986) Founder of the Soviet newspaper *Pravda* and a Bolshevik leader in the 1917 Revolution in Russia. Foreign minister before, during and after World War II. He was ousted by Khrushchev in 1957. The firebomb in a bottle (the Molotov Cocktail) was named for him. Novodevichy Cemetery, Moscow.

6435. Monaco, James V. (Jan. 13, 1885–Oct. 16, 1945) Songwriter whose works included *I'm Crying Just For You* and *You Made Me Love You,* which is inscribed on his marker with the bars of music from the first line of the song. Sec. D, lot 211, grave 1, Holy Cross Cemetery, Culver City, CA.

6436. Monahan, Jay (John Patrick Monahan, Jan. 9, 1956–Jan. 24, 1998) NBC legal analyst, husband of Katie Couric, died from colon cancer at 41. Holy Rood Cemetery, Westbury, Long Island, NY.

6437. Monarch Pass Crash On September 11, 1971, a bus carrying the Gunnison Junior Varsity football team and their coaches plunged off Monarch Pass, Colorado, killing eight players (Tim Dutton, Pat Graham, Mike Pasqua, Brad Hall, Billy Miles, Ted Maw, Mark Broadwater, Kent Cooper) and Coach L.D. Floyd. All have their photos on the 8' brown granite monument in their memory at Gunnison Cemetery, Gunnison, CO.

6438. Monet, Claude (Nov. 14, 1840–Dec. 5, 1926) Paris born painter, one of the founders of Impressionism with Renoir, developed the technique of drabs of color, or broken color, side by side to be interpreted by the viewer. Particularly in later paintings (*Water Lillies*), the subject and light merge as one. Monet lived in later years at Giverny, four miles from Vetheuil. He died there and was interred in the tomb marked Ernest Hoschede in Giverny churchyard, Giverny, France.

6439. Mong, William V. (June 25, 1875–Dec. 10, 1940) Character actor in silents (*Love's Prisoner* with Olive Thomas 1919) and talkies, often as villainous or miserly characters (*The Vampire Bat* 1933, Pew in the 1934 *Treasure Island* and the mercenary Cleon

in *The Last Days of Pompeii* 1935, many others). Unmarked. Sec M, tier 6 grave 54, Grandview Memorial Park, Glendale, CA.

6440. Monk, Thelonius (Oct. 10, 1917–Feb. 17, 1982) Jazz pianist who promoted "bop" in the post World War II era. He played with Coleman Hawkins and Dizzy Gillespie before forming his own quartet combo groups. Compositions include *Straight, No Chaser* and *Well, You Needn't.* He died in Englewood, New Jersey. Marker set c. April 2001. Hillcrest I, grave 405, Ferncliff Cemetery, Hartsdale, NY.

6441. Monks, John, Jr. (June 25, 1910–Dec. 10, 2004) Screenwriter co-wrote the play *Brother Rat* on Broadway (1936), filmed in 1938, and after service in World War II penned the documentary *We Are the Marines* and screenplays including *The House on 92nd Street, 13 Rue Madeleine, Knock on Any Door, The People Against O'Hara, The West Point Story,* and after nearly a decade made *No Man Is An Island* (1962) in England, which he co-wrote and directed. He died of prostate cancer in Los Angeles at 94. Cremated by Gates-Kingsley-Gates, Santa Monica. Ashes to Preshute Churchyard, Marlborough, Wiltshire, England.

6442. Monroe, Bill (William Smith Monroe, Sept. 13, 1911–Sept. 9, 1996) The father of bluegrass, with vocal known as "High Lonesome." Songs include *Blue Moon of Kentucky,* many others. He died at Springfield, Tennessee, at 84. Buried at his hometown, with a towering obelisk erected before his death. Rosine Cemetery, Rosine, KY.

6443. Monroe, James (April 28, 1758–July 4, 1831) 5th President of the United States 1817–1825 whose name was given to the 1823 Monroe Doctrine, warning against foreign intervention in the western hemisphere. A Democrat-Republican and friend of fellow Virginia presidents Jefferson and Madison, he lived for several years at Ash Lawn, near Jefferson at Charlottesville, before moving to his estate Oak Hill near Lynchburg in Loudon County, Virginia. In later years, like Jefferson, he was deeply in debt and was forced to sell Oak Hill. Shortly before, his wife **Elizabeth Kortright Monroe** (June 30, 1768–Sept. 23, 1830) died and was interred in a vault on the estate which the former president had had constructed for them both. His health and finances declined rapidly and he spent his last months at the home of his daughter, **Maria Hester Gouvernor** (1804–1850), at 66 Prince Street at the corner of Prince and Marion in the Bowery in Manhattan. He died there and was interred in the Gouvernor vault in the 1831 Marble Cemetery on East 2nd St. in Manhattan, New York City. It was then new, the first (1830) Marble Cemetery around the corner on 2nd Avenue having filled up. Most vaults in the early New York graveyards have doors just under the ground which open into the chambers below, housing the tombs of separate families. The names were most often inscribed in the walls surrounding the cemeteries, which were largely bare of upright stones. The 1831 Marble Cemetery remains on East 2nd St. in Manhattan, behind a black iron fence and locked gate. Monroe's body was removed on the centennial of his birth and returned to Virginia after much petitioning by his native state to secure the remains. The coffin was placed on a barge and taken south from the East River to Richmond, where upon its arrival along the James River to unload, an accident occurred and Alexander Hamilton's son was killed (this was particularly ironic, since Hamilton and Monroe had hated each other over the Reynolds affair and had nearly fought a duel). Monroe's tomb in Hollywood Cemetery, designed by Albert Lybrock, is a cage like structure of black cast iron, with a sarcophagus inside and Monroe buried 5' beneath it. On each end of the stone sarcophagus is a gold plate inscribed with his name, dates, title and the notation *By order of the General Assembly, his remains were removed to this cemetery 5th of July, 1858, as an evidence of the affection of Virginia for her good and honored son.* It sits in the center of President's Circle on a summit overlooking the James River. In the ground outside of the monument are flat, small bronze plaques noting his wife and daughter Maria Gouvernor (and her husband) are also buried there. His daughter eventually returned to Oak Hill in Loudon County, Virginia. She died in 1850 and was interred in the vault with her mother. In 1903 they were moved to Hollywood Cemetery and reburied just outside the president's tomb. In the only case of two un-related presidents buried in such close proximity to one another, John Tyler, the 10th President, lies just a few yards away in President's Circle, buried in 1862 after his death in Richmond. President's Circle, Hollywood Cemetery, Richmond, VA.

6444. Monroe, Marilyn (Norma Jean Baker, June 1, 1926–Aug. 5, 1962) Los Angeles born actress known for her breathy, sensual roles through the 1950's, including *How to Marry a Millionaire, The Seven Year Itch* and *The Misfits* (1960), the last completed film for both she and Clark Gable, written by her third and last husband, Arthur Miller (*q.v.*). She became one of a handful of Hollywood stars to attain ongoing legend status. Fired from Fox in June 1962 for repeated absences, a few months earlier she had bought her first house, at the end of a cul-de-sac on Helena Drive in Brentwood. In Latin at the entrance was inscribed "My Journey Ends Here." Reputedly depressed over the termination of a relationship with the attorney general, or the president, or both, depending on the source, she apparently committed suicide, though friends claimed otherwise. Her housekeeper became alarmed when she found the telephone cord still under the bedroom door well after midnight and called Monroe's psychiatrist, who broke into the bedroom and found her dead from an overdose of sleeping pills at 36. Her second husband, Yankee slugger Joe DiMaggio (*q.v.*), handled the services, including only a few friends and pointedly excluding the Kennedys, Sinatra, Lawford, etc. The eulogy was spoken by her former acting coach Lee Strasberg. Interred

in a wall crypt at Westwood, for twenty years roses were sent there by DiMaggio but were discontinued in 1982. In the early 1980's evidence was published appearing to implicate both Robert Kennedy and his brother-in-law, actor Peter Lawford, as having been present the day of her death, and possibly having later had the body moved and arranged, etc., as policemen on the scene described its appearance. The 4.5 mg. of barbiturates found in the blood was a large quantity, equal to approximately forty seven pills, to have been taken without water, and no glass was found near the body, so that an injection has been suspected and the ruling of Coroner Nogucji considered questionable by some. No conclusive evidence pointed to foul play either, so the case remains a conversation piece. An exhumation was overruled in the early 80's, and the ruling remains an overdose of sleeping pills, possibly accidental, but listed as a probable suicide. Corridor of Memories, sec. A, wall crypt 24, Westwood Memorial Park, west Los Angeles.

Monroe's first husband, **James Dougherty**, from 1942–46, before she changed her name, died at 84 in the San Francisco area Aug. 15, 2005. Burial at Lewiston, Maine.

6445. Monroe, Rose Will *see* **Rosie the Riveter.**

6446. Monroe, Vaughn (Oct. 7, 1911–May 21, 1973) Baritone vocalist of the 1940's known for *Ghost Riders in the Sky, Seems Like Old Times, Racing With the Moon.* He died from cancer at 61 in Stuart, Florida. Plaque by bench along the road. Sec. 2–1, Fernhill Memorial Cemetery, Stuart, FL.

6447. Montague, Monte (Walter H. Montague, April 23, 1891–April 6, 1969) Actor and stuntman from Somerset, Kentucky, in dozens of films from 1920–1952, many westerns and crime films, and occasional horrors (*The Invisible Man*, as the dim witted bobby who utters the line "Oh I see — pretty good"). Grandview Memorial Park, Glendale, CA.

6448. Montalban, Manuel Vázquez (July 27, 1939–Oct. 18, 2003) Spanish author, creator of the Barcelona based detective Pepe Carvalho, over forty years produced many works, including *Galindez* (1990), which won two awards, and was filmed as *The Galindez Mystery* (2003). He died at 64 during a stopover at Bangkok airport while returning from lecturing in Sydney, Australia. Cementerio de Coliserola, Barcelona.

6449. Montana, Bull (Lewis Montagna, May 16, 1887–Jan. 24, 1950) Stunt man and actor played several bestial characters in silent films, including *The Lost World* (1925), *Son of the Sheik* (1926), *Tiger Rose, Show of Shows* (1929).Unmarked. Sec. R, lot 478, grave 6, Calvary Cemetery, east Los Angeles.

6450. Montana, Patsy (Rubye Blevins, Oct. 30, 1914–May 3, 1996) Singer and yodeler from Arkansas best known for *I Want to Be a Cowboy's Sweetheart.* The first female country-western singer to sell over a million records, she also appeared in two reelers, and *Colorado Sunset* (1935) with Gene Autry. Married name Rose. Columbarium A, Court C, niche F-29, Riverside National Cemetery, Riverside, CA.

6451. Montand, Yves (Ivo Livi, Oct. 13, 1921–Nov. 9, 1991) Italian born actor-singer raised in Marseille, France, sang at the Moulin Rouge with Edith Piaf, who promoted him and later starred with him in the film *La Salaire de la Peur/Star Without Light* (1946). He later appeared with Marilyn Monroe in *Let's Make Love* (1960) and several films with his wife, actress Simone Signoret, who died in 1984. He died from a heart attack at 70 in Senlis, twenty eight miles northeast of Paris. Buried with Signoret. Div. 44, Pere Lachaise Cemetery, Paris.

6452. Montcalm, Louis Joseph, Marquis de (Feb. 28, 1712–Sept. 14, 1759) French general opposing English General Wolfe on the Plain of Abraham during the climactic battle over Quebec in the Seven Years/French and Indian War. Both were fatally wounded as Quebec City fell to the British. Montcalm was buried in a grave partially formed by a bomb outside the Ursuline Convent on the edge of the city and was later buried beneath the convent chapel. Records are in the Church of Notre Dame de Quebec. In September 2001, the remains, consisting of the skull and a leg bone, were removed in a ceremony and re-buried with over 1,000 of his soldiers (formerly unmarked), with markers and a monument to be erected, in the (closed) Cemetery of Hospital General de Quebec, Lower Town area, Quebec.

6453. Montenegro, Hugo (Sept. 2, 1925–Feb. 6, 1981) Composer and conductor known for haunting scores to several films, including *The Good, the Bad and the Ugly*. Sec. 11–3, lot G, Wellwood Murray Cemetery, Palm Springs, CA.

6454. Montessori, Maria (Aug. 31, 1870–May 6, 1952) Pioneer innovative educator from Chiaraville, Italy, "La Dottoressa" came to the United States in 1913. The first Italian woman to become a physician, she promoted the development of the child through freedom of expression, spiritual renewal, and the process of humanity through the child, leading to enhanced coordination and sense perception, the basis for Montessori Schools flourishing decades after her death. There is a memorial tablet to her with tributes in her family plot in Rome. Burial in the Catholic Cemetery (van den Mortelstraat), Noordwijk, Holland.

6455. Montez, Lola (Marie Dolores Eliza Rosanna Gilbert, Feb. 17, c. 1818–Jan. 17, 1861) Native of Limerick, Ireland, made the rounds in her day, numbering among her lovers Liszt, Dumas and the King of Bavaria, whom she infected with the syphilis that eventually killed them both. She came to America posing as a Bavarian countess and soon became famous for her spider dance, a stage sensation for a time, but ended her days preaching to prostitutes about the error of their ways. Her eroded, illegible stone inscribed *Eliza Gilbert* was replaced by early 1999 with a new, legible one inscribed on the front *Mrs. Eliza Gilbert, Died Jan. 17, 1861 AE. 42* and on the back *Born at Grange County Sligo February 17, 1821/ Known as Lola Montez/ Countess of Landsfield*. Sec. 8, 12730, in from Summit Ave., Greenwood Cemetery, Brooklyn, N.Y.C.

6456. Montez, Maria (Maria de Santo Silas, June 6, 1918–Sept. 7, 1951) Actress from the Dominican Republic in exotic roles in films of the 1940's, many at Universal in south sea epics opposite Jon Hall. The wife of Jean-Pierre Aumont, she lived at Suresnes, a suburb of Paris. Her sister found her dead in her over heated reducing bath with only her face above water. The cause was listed as a heart attack at 33. Name and dates on a light plaque atop the beige family sarcophagus. Div. 24, Montparnasse Cemetery, Paris.

6457. Montgomery, Bernard Law (Nov. 17, 1887–March 24, 1976) First Viscount, Montgomery of Alamein, Field Marshal Montgomery commanded the English troops in Africa and in Europe during World War II, including the campaign against Rommel in North Africa. Gray grave length slab, Holy Cross Churchyard, Binsted, Hampshire.

6458. Montgomery, Douglass (Robert Douglass Montgomery or Kent Douglas(s), Oct. 29, 1907–July 23, 1966) Canadian actor in films of the 1930's (*Waterloo Bridge* 1931, *Little Women* 1933, *The Mystery of Edwin Drood* 1935, *The Cat and the Canary* 1939). From 1951 he lived at Eagle Rock, his home at Norwalk, Connecticut. He died from cancer in Norwalk Hospital at 58. Cremated at Mountain Grove Cemetery in Bridgeport, his ashes were returned to his wife Kathleen at Eagle Rock in August 1966.

6459. Montgomery, Elizabeth (April 15, 1933–May 18, 1995) Actress daughter of Robert Montgomery and Elizabeth Allen (not the British actress), in films and TV from the mid 50's, best known as Samantha on *Bewitched* 1964–72. Afterward she did several made for TV movies. Married to Gig Young, *Bewitched* producer William Asher, and to actor Robert Foxworth, who survived her. She died at 62, reported as 57, from colon cancer a month after surgery to remove a tumor. Cremated through Pierce Bros. Westwood mortuary in west Los Angeles. Ashes to her family in Benedict Canyon, Beverly Hills, CA.

6460. Montgomery, George (George Montgomery Letz, Aug. 29, 1916–Dec. 12, 2000) Montana born actor in horse operas, musicals and romantic comedies including *The Cisco Kid and The Lady* (1940), *The Last of the Duanes* and *Riders of the Purple Sage* (1941), *Orchestra Wives* (1942) and the television series *Cimarron City*. Married to Dinah Shore 1943–1962 he died in Rancho Mirage, California, at 84. Most of his ashes were buried in part on June 23, 2001, in the Letz plot, beneath a statue he sculpted of himself, along the road in sec. 12, Highland Cemetery, Great Falls, Montana. His daughter retained part of his ashes, interred at Palm Springs, and part of Dinah Shore's ashes were placed near him. Mission San Luis Rey foyer; Mission Santa Rosa, south wall, niche

SE34D, Palm Springs Mausoleum, Cathedral City, CA.

6461. Montgomery, Jack (Jack Cleveland Montgomery, July 23, 1917–June 11, 2002) Oklahoma born part Cherokee served with the integrated Company I, 180th Infantry of the 45th Division of the Oklahoma National Guard, re-enlisted after Pearl Harbor, and at Anzio on February 22, 1944, left his platoon armed with an M1 rifle and hand grenades, and in three attempts on as many German positions accounted for 11 enemy dead and 32 prisoners. He was awarded the Medal of Honor, one of eight earned by his division. Sec. 20, grave 963, Fort Gibson National Cemetery, Fort Gibson, OK.

6462. Montgomery, Lucy Maud (Nov. 30, 1874–April 24, 1942) Authoress who spent summers at her grandmother's house on Prince Edward Island in the Atlantic Provinces north of Nova Scotia based her book *Anne of Green Gables* (1906) there, at the house in Cavendish on the north shore of the island, as well as several sequels. Buried with her husband, Rev. Ewan MacDonald, in Cavendish village churchyard, Cavendish, Prince Edward Island, Atlantic Provinces, Canada.

6463. Montgomery, Richard (Dec. 2, 1738–Dec. 31, 1775) American general in the Revolutionary War killed during the siege of Quebec had captured Montreal and was attempting to take Quebec City with Benedict Arnold during a snowstorm when he was killed. St. Paul's Churchyard, Broadway and Fulton Streets, downtown Manhattan, N.Y.C.

6464. Montgomery, Robert (Henry Montgomery, Jr., May 21, 1904–Sept. 27, 1981) Actor from Beacon, New York, in films from talkies (*The Big House, The Mystery of Mr. X, Trouble For Two*); his baby face used to best advantage in *Night Must Fall* (1937) which earned him an Oscar nomination, as did *Here Comes Mr. Jordan* (1941). A Lieutenant Commander in the Navy during World War II, he was awarded both the Bronze Star and the French Legion of Honor. In the 1950's he turned to directing, with TV's *Robert Montgomery Presents* (1950–57) and was also active in Republican politics. Father of Elizabeth Montgomery. He resided on a farm at Canaan, Connecticut, until his death in Columbia Presbyterian Medical Center in Manhattan from cancer at 77. Ashes scattered on his Connecticut farm.

6465. Montgomery, Smokey (Marvin D. Wetter, March 7, 1913–June 6, 2001) Iowa born banjo great and three time Grammy nominee joined the western swing band The Light Crust Doughboys in 1935, as Bob Wills left to form the Texas Playboys; in their heyday, the Doughboys were heard on 170 radio stations. The stage name came from his favorite actor, Robert Montgomery. He died from leukemia at 88. Block A Memories, lot 69, space 1 and 2, Restland Memorial Park, Dallas, TX.

6466. Montgomery, Wes (March 6, 1925–June 15, 1968) Indianapolis born jazz guitarist, self taught and unable to read music, played in Lionel Hampton's band in the late 40's but toured and recorded with his own group, including his brothers, winning a Grammy in 1966. He died from a heart attack at 43 in Indianapolis. His headstone has a guitar engraved on it. Sec. 20, row 29, grave 99, New Crown Cemetery, Indianapolis, IN.

6467. Monti, Carlotta *see* **W.C. Fields.**

6468. Montoya, Alex (Oct. 19, 1907–Sept. 25, 1970) Actor from El Paso in films 1938–68 (*The Ghost of Zorro, Streets of Laredo, Crisis, Macao, Back From Eternity, The Flight of the Phoenix*) and in numerous television roles in westerns. He died in Los Angeles from congestive heart failure at 62. Sec. M, lot 376, grave 10, Calvary Cemetery, Los Angeles.

6469. Montoya, Joseph M. (Sept. 24, 1915–June 5, 1978) Congressman from New Mexico 1957–65 and senator 1965–76 was a member of the 1973 Watergate investigative committee. E East, space 10, Rosario Cemetery, Santa Fe, NM.

6470. Montsalvatge, Xavier (March 11, 1912–May 7, 2002) Spanish composer and critic known for his Neo-Romantic works of the 1940's and 50's, ballet, piano, chamber and vocal works, and the use of Cuban and West Indian music, including *Canciones Negras, Cuarteto Indiano, Concierto Breve*. He died in Barcelona at 90. Cementerio de Sant Gervasi, Barcelona.

6471. Monty, Harry (Hymie Lichenstein, March 14, 1902 [listed as April 14, 1904]–Dec. 28, 1999) Stunt man from Dallas in several films, best known as both a Munchkin and flying monkey in *The Wizard of Oz* (1939). He died in Los Angeles at 95 (97). Epitaph *A giant of a man.* Sec. L, row 8, lot 16, Shearith Israel Cemetery, Dallas, TX.

6472. Moody, Dwight (Feb. 5, 1837–Dec. 22, 1899) New England evangelist founded Northfield (Massachusetts) Seminary for Girls in 1879 and Mount Herman School for Boys there in 1881, as well as the Chicago (Moody) Bible Institute. Buried at Round Top, the Northfield School For Girls, Northfield, MA.

6473. Moody, Helen Wills *see* **Helen Wills.**

6474. Moody, Ralph (Nov. 5, 1886–Sept. 16, 1971) Stage, radio, film and television actor, in pictures from 1948 as various elderly characters. Garden of Peace 242, Valhalla Memorial Park, North Hollywood, CA.

6475. Moog, Robert (May 23, 1934–Aug. 21, 2005) Engineer and physicist from Flushing, New York, developed the first voltage controlled synthesizer in 1964, showcased four years later by Walter Collins with *Switched-on-Bach*, followed several LPs taking the new toy in various other directions, picked up by various musical groups including The Beatles, Rolling Stones, Byrds, Doors, and Emerson, Lake and Palmer, and used in the score for *A Clockwork Orange* (1971). His 1970 Minimoog was used extensively in disco music, but as digital synthesizers replaced analog through the 1970's, he was forced from his company, and moved to North Carolina to teach and develop further innovations until his death at 71 from a brain tumor. Lou Pollack Cemetery, Asheville, NC.

6476. Moon, Keith (Aug. 23, 1947–Sept. 8, 1978) Drummer with The Who on their recordings from 1964 and tours through the 1960's and 70's died from an overdose of Heminevrin, prescribed to combat alcoholism, at 31 in the same London flat where Cass Elliott died four years earlier. Cremated at Golders Green, his name is in their Book of Remembrance. Ashes spread in section 3P, Golders Green Crematorium, north London.

6477. Mooney, Tom (Thomas J. Mooney, Dec. 8, 1882–March 6, 1942) Labor agitator imprisoned for twenty two years for a Preparedness Day bombing in 1916. He was originally sentenced to death, later commuted to life in prison. Released in 1939, after he had been proven innocent. His funeral at the San Francisco Civic Auditorium was attended by some four thousand people. Palm Mound, Cypress Lawn Cemetery, Colma, CA.

6478. Moore, Alvy (Jack A. Moore, Dec. 5, 1921–May 4, 1997) Actor from Vincennes, Indiana, played county extension agent Hank Kimball on TV's *Green Acres* 1965–71. He died in Rancho Mirage, California. Columbarium of Remembrance, niche 61142, Courts of Remembrance, Forest Lawn Hollywood Hills, Los Angeles.

6479. Moore, Archie (Archibald Lee Wright, Dec. 13, 1913–Dec. 9, 1998) Boxer from Benoit, Mississippi. fought from 1936, won the light heavyweight title in 1952 from Joey Maxim and defended it nine times, losing along the way to heavyweight champions Rocky Marciano, Floyd Patterson and Muhammad Ali; he was the only man to fight both Marciano and Ali, and with 141 knockouts in 228 bouts, was known as the Knockout King. He retired in 1963 and died at 84 in a San Diego hospice. Apostle Gallery, East columbarium, niche 401, Cypress View Mausoleum, San Diego, CA.

6480. Moore, Brian (Breeon Moore, Aug. 25, 1921–Jan. 11, 1999) Belfast born author of a wide variety of novels, often focusing on the loneliness of an individual within narrow social or religious confines, beginning with *The Lonely Passion of Judith Hearne* (1956) and including *The Mangan Inheritance* (1978), *The Black Robe* (1985), *The Statement* (1996) and *The Magician's Wife* (1998), as well as screenplays, among them Hitchcock's *Torn Curtain* (1966). He resided in Canada from 1948, but later lived in Malibu, California, though he kept a summer home at Lunenburg, Nova Scotia. He died in Ventura County, California (reported in his obituaries as at home in Malibu), of pulmonary fibrosis at 77. Cremated by the Neptune Society of Santa Barbara, his ashes were returned January 14 to his wife Jean Denney in Malibu. According to an article in *The London Daily Mail*, when recently asked, Moore had said he wished to be returned

to Ireland, yet at least part of his ashes were reportedly released into the Atlantic off Nova Scotia near his cabin at Lunenburg.

6481. Moore, Clayton (Jack Carlson Moore, Sept. 14, 1914–Dec. 28, 1999) Chicago born actor in B films and serials from 1938 became *The Lone Ranger* on CBS TV 1949–52 and 1954–57, righting wrongs with his Indian friend Tonto, played by Jay Silverheels. Moore embraced the character and adopted it as his own for the rest of his life, appearing as The Lone Ranger and giving talks to children on doing the right thing. A 1979 court injunction prevented him from wearing the trademark black mask in light of an upcoming film. Moore sued, backed by popular support, and the ban on the mask was lifted in 1984. "When I go," he said, "I want them to say 'Who was that masked man?'" He died from a heart attack at 85 in West Hills Hospital, northwest of Los Angeles. Burial December 31. Along the sidewalk, Garden of Everlasting Peace, lot 5294/5, Forest Lawn, Glendale, CA.

6482. Moore, Clement Clark (July 15, 1779–July 10, 1863) Minister whose farm once encompassed what is now the Chelsea section of Manhattan was immortalized as the author of *A Visit From St. Nicholas* (1822), made up to amuse his children and later known as *The Night Before Christmas*. On Christmas Eve, carolers visit the grave, at the bottom of the hill and north of the office in the western section of Trinity Cemetery, 155th and Riverside in Harlem, N.Y.C.

6483. Moore, Colleen (Kathleen Morrison, Aug. 19, 1902–Jan. 25, 1988) Silent screen star from Port Huron, Michigan, in impish roles, known for her bobbed hair, in *Flaming Youth* (1923), *So Big* (1925), *Ella Cinders* (1926), *Lilac Time* (1928). She retired from films in the early 30's and went into business in Chicago, working later for Merrill-Lynch. Five years after her last marriage, to Paul Maginot, she died from cancer at her ranch near Paso Robles, Ca., where she had lived since 1971. Service at St. James Episcopal Church in Paso Robles. Cremated at Los Osos Crematory through Kuehl-Nicolay mortuary, her ashes were scattered at sea from Cayucos, CA.

6484. Moore, Constance (Mary Constance Moore, Jan. 18, 1920–Sept. 16, 2005) Blonde actress and singer from Dallas in films from 1937 at Universal (*The Crime of Dr. Hallet, The Missing Guest*), best known as Victoria Whipsnade in *You Can't Cheat An Honest Man* with W.C. Fields, as Wilma Deering in *Buck Rogers*, and in a series of Republic musicals through the 1940's (*Show Business, Atlantic City*). She made sporadic appearances after 1947, including the TV series *Window on Main Street* (1961) with Robert Young. The wife of agent John Maschio from 1939 to his death in 1998, she died in Woodland Hills, California, at 84. Cremated at Live Oak by Pierce Bros. Westwood Memorial Park, west Los Angeles.

6485. Moore, Del (May 14, 1917–Aug. 30, 1970) Actor on radio and in several Jerry Lewis films and

TV. Columbarium of Dawn, niche 30566, bottom tier, Holly Terrace, Great Mausoleum, Forest Lawn, Glendale, CA.

6486. Moore, Dennis (Jan. 26, 1908–March 1, 1964) Actor in films from the early 1930's through the late 50's, in many westerns, several as "Smoky" Moore, and melodramas (*The Mummy's Curse, The Frozen Ghost*) died at 56 from circulatory collapse caused by rheumatic heart disease at his home at Big Bear Lake. Lawn R, lot 364, grave 1, Mountain View Cemetery, San Bernardino, CA.

6487. Moore, Dudley (Dudley Stuart John Moore, April 19, 1935–March 27, 2002) Diminutive English musician, actor and comedian from Dagenham was originally a jazz pianist until joining Peter Cook and the Beyond The Fringe comedy revue in 1960. Over the years he and Cook received a New York Drama Critics Special Citation, a special Tony (1963) and another for "Good Evening" (1974), as well as a Grammy the same year. Moore gained his real fame in Blake Edwards' film *10* (1979) and *Arthur* (1981), for which he received an Oscar nomination. He continued in films and musical appearances until his announcement in 1999 that he suffered from a terminal brain disorder, progressive supranuclear palsy, or PSP. Named a CBE in November 2001. Divorced four times, he died at the home of friends Rena Fruchter and Brian Dallow in Plainfield, New Jersey, at 66. Funeral April 2 at Higgins Home for Funerals in Watchung. Sec. D-3, Hillside Cemetery, Scotch Plains, Plainfield, NJ.

6488. Moore, Eva (Feb 9, 1870–April 27 1955) Actress from Brighton known for her beauty as a young actress on the British stage in *Old Heidelberg* was married to playwright and actor Henry V. Esmond from 1891 to his death in Paris in 1922, and was rumored to have been among the lovers of Edward VII. They were the parents of actress Jill Esmond, the wife of Laurence Olivier 1930–40. Her best known film role was as Rebecca Femm in James Whale's *The Old Dark House* (1932). She died at her home near Maidenhead at 85. Her ashes (and those of Jill Esmond, in 1990) were scattered on the 17th fairway of the Temple Golf Course, from which their home (now the Apple Hill Nursing Home at Maidenhead, Berkshire) afforded a view.

6489. Moore, Florence (1886–March 23, 1935) Vaudeville and stage actress known for *Parlor, Bedroom and Bath* 1917–19 also did films. She died from cancer at 49 in her native Philadelphia. Her last married name was Kerner. Family monument on lot, no individual marker. Sec. E annex, lot 40, grave 3, Mount Peace Cemetery, Philadelphia, PA.

6490. Moore, Garry (Thomas Garrison Morfit, Jan. 31, 1915–Nov. 28, 1993) Baltimore born radio announcer and sidekick to Jimmy Durante in the 1940's hosted *The Garry Moore Show* on TV 1950–67 off and on, introducing many future stars, *I've Got a Secret* on CBS 1952–1966 and *To Tell the Truth* 1969–1976. He left TV in 1977 after developing cancer, and for his last seven years battled emphysema. He died at 78 at home in Hilton Head, South Carolina. Cremated by the Island mortuary, the ashes were returned north by the family and eventually buried, under his real name, with his first wife. Forest Hill Cemetery, Northeast Harbor, ME.

6491. Moore, Grace (Dec. 5, 1901–Jan. 26, 1947) Operatic soprano from Jellico, Tennessee, sang on Broadway and with the New York Metropolitan Opera. She appeared in a few films (*New Moon* 1931, *One Night of Love* 1934) but was primarily a concert singer. She had been entertaining troops overseas when she died in a plane crash near Copenhagen. Married to Valentin Parera. Moore family plot, sec. K, Forest Hills Cemetery, Chattanooga, TN.

6492. Moore, Hal The wife of U.S. Army General Harold "Hal" Moore, **Julia Compton Moore** (Feb. 10, 1929–April 18, 2004) gained notoriety in her husband's book, co-written with combat photographer Joe Galloway, *We Were Soldiers Once, And Young,* and the subsequent film *We Were Soldiers* (2002). Living at Columbus, Georgia, outside Fort Benning in November 1965, while her husband commanded the 1st Battalion's 7th Cavalry in the Ia Drang Valley of Vietnam — with heavy losses, she was horrified at taxis pulling up to deliver telegrams notifying Army wives of their husbands' deaths, began accompanying the taxis and petitioned the Army to change the practice, now done with a service branch representative and chaplain. She died from cancer at 75 outside Auburn, Alabama. In his tribute to her in his syndicated *Chicago Tribune* column, Joe Galloway wrote: "...we are burying Julie Moore ... near her mother and father, and in the middle of the 7th Cavalry troopers whose wives she comforted and whose funerals she attended in 1965. Her grave is beside that of Sgt. Jack E. Gell of Alpha Company.... She will rest in the arms of the Army she loved so long and served so well. Garry Owen, Miss Julie. Godspeed." Sec. C, site 259, Fort Benning Post Cemetery, Fort Benning, GA.

6493. Moore, Howard (Feb. 8, 1889–June 6, 1993) The first official conscientious objector was drafted into World War I in 1917 but objected to fighting and was sentenced to two years in Leavenworth Federal Penitentiary. He was the only recorded c.o. in World War I. A lifelong political leftist and an agnostic, he lived to 104 in Cherry Valley, New York. Body donated to science.

6494. Moore, Ida (March 1, 1882–Sept. 26, 1964) Actress in a few silents showed up in the 1940's and 50's as sweet natured, often confused, elderly ladies (*The Egg and I, Johnny Belinda, The Sun Comes Up, Ma and Pa Kettle, Fancy Pants, Harvey, The Lemon Drop Kid, Comin' Round the Mountain, Desk Set*). Sec. F, lot 4, space 3, Oakwood Memorial Park, Chatsworth, CA.

6495. Moore, Jo-Jo (Joseph Gregg Moore, Dec. 25, 1908–April 1, 2001) The Gause Ghost, All-Star outfielder who helped the New York Giants to three pennants and the 1933 World Series, manning left field at the Polo Grounds 1932–1941. He died in Bryan, Texas at 92. Gause Cemetery, Gause, TX.

6496. Moore, Joanna (Joanna Cook Moore, Nov. 10, 1934–Nov. 22, 1997) Blonde actress from Americus, Georgia, in films and television of the 1950's and 60's (Marcia Linneker in *Touch of Evil* 1958, Peggy McMillan on *The Andy Griffith Show* October–December 1962) left at the peak of her career to marry actor Ryan O'Neal in 1963. Divorced in 1967, the parents of actress Tatum O'Neal. In sporadic films from the 1970's, she was involved in Palm Springs area theater prior to her death at 65 from lung cancer in Indian Wells, California. Fitzhenry mortuary, Palm Desert. Ashes scattered at sea.

6497. Moore, Johnny (John Darrel Moore, Dec. 15, 1934–Dec. 30, 1998) Selma born lead singer with The Drifters from 1963 best known for anchoring *Under the Boardwalk* and *Save the Last Dance For Me*. He moved to Great Britain with the group, resided there from 1982, and died in London at 64 en route to Mayday Hospital from what was ruled pneumonia. Funeral at St. Luke's Church, Croydon, followed by cremation.

6498. Moore, Marianne (Nov. 15, 1887–Feb. 5, 1972) St. Louis born poet known for *No Swan So Fine* and *Peter*, among others. Collections included *What Are Years?* (1941), *Nevertheless* (1944) and her *Collected Poems* (1952), which won the Pulitzer Prize. Sec. G, Evergreen Cemetery, Gettysburg, PA.

6499. Moore, Matt (Jan. 8, 1888–Jan. 21, 1960) Actor brother of Owen Moore, in silents (*The Unholy Three* 1925) and talkies (*The Front Page* 1931). Buried with Owen, both unmarked. Sec. F, lot 1625, Calvary Cemetery, east Los Angeles.

6500. Moore, Owen (Dec. 12, 1886–June 9, 1939) Irish born silent screen star in films 1908–37, originally with D.W. Griffith at Biograph. Married to Mary Pickford 1910–1920. Films include *The Road to Mandalay, The Blackbird, She Done Him Wrong, A Star is Born*. He died from a heart attack at 52. Unmarked next to his brother Matt. Sec. F, lot 1625, Calvary Cemetery, east Los Angeles.

6501. Moore, Rosie Lee (June 22, 1899–Feb. 12, 1967) The last Aunt Jemima for the Quaker Oats Company. Hammond Colony Cemetery, northwest of Hearne, TX.

6502. Moore, Terry (Terry Bluford Moore, May 27, 1912–March 29, 1995) Outfielder with the St. Louis Cardinals 1935–1948. The rear of his double stone with his wife Patty has a ball player in uniform, glove ready for the catch. Cardinals and ball bats grace the front of the stone, and a World War II military marker is on his grave. Holy Cross Lutheran Cemetery, Collinsville, IL.

6503. Moore, Tim (Harry R. Moore, Dec. 9, 1887–Dec. 13, 1958) Actor remembered for his portrayal of "Kingfish" in the television series *Amos 'n'*

Andy 1951–53. A marker was placed by January 1990, following the death of his wife. Sec. O, lot 120, grave 1NW, Rosedale Cemetery, Los Angeles.

6504. Moore, Victor (Feb. 24, 1876–July 23, 1962) Broadway and film star usually cast as bumbling, timid, confused or helpless little characters. His favorite and best known stage role was as Alexander Throttlebottom in Gershwin's *Of Thee I Sing* (1931). Films include *Make Way For Tomorrow* (1937). He died at East Islip, Long Island. Crypt on second floor, aisle NN, Cypress Hills Abbey, Cypress Hills Cemetery, Brooklyn, N.Y.C.

6505. Moorehead, Agnes (Agnes Robertson Moorehead, Dec. 6, 1900 [often given as 1906]–April 30, 1974) Actress born at Clinton, Massachusetts, often in acid tongued roles, came to films from radio — where she continued to act — as part of Orson Welles' Mercury Players, in *Citizen Kane* (1942) and *The Magnificent Ambersons* (1942). Others include *Our Vines Have Tender Grapes* (1945), *Dark Passage* (1947), *The Left Hand of God* (1955) and *The Bat* (1959), and stage productions including Shaw's *Don Juan in Hell*, but best known as Endora on TV's *Bewitched* 1964–72. One of several cast and crew members exposed to radiation while filming *The Conqueror* in Nevada in 1955, she died from cancer at Methodist Hospital in Rochester, Minnesota, under the care of physicians from the Mayo Clinic. Her father had been an Ohio minister and she was returned for entombment with her family. First corridor on left, crypt on left half way down, Abbey Mausoleum, Dayton Memorial Park Cemetery, Dayton, OH.

6506. Moorhead, Natalie (Nathalia Messner, July 27, 1901–Oct. 6, 1992) Pittsburgh born actress went from the New York stage to films in 1929, characterized by a distinctive short blonde hairdo similar to Lilyan Tashman. Married to director Alan Crosland, later to soccer champion and actor Juan Torena. They retired to Montecito, California. Sec. A2, lot 22, grave 6, Calvary Cemetery, Santa Barbara, CA.

6507. Moran, "Bugs" (George Moran, Aug. 21, 1891–Feb. 25, 1957) Chicago bootlegger was Al Capone's main rival for control 1927–29 until successfully put out of power with the execution of six of his men on St. Valentine's Day 1929. Moran himself narrowly missed being among them. He was eventually reduced to petty crime and spent his later years in the federal penitentiary at Leavenworth, Kansas, where he died from lung cancer and was buried in a $35 coffin. Leavenworth Prison Cemetery, Leavenworth, KS.

6508. Moran, Dolores (Dolores Moran Bogeaus, Jan. 27, 1926–Feb. 5, 1982) Blonde actress of the 1940's in various sultry roles (*Old Acquaintance* 1942, the wife of the wounded resistance soldier in *To Have and Have Not* 1944). Married name Bogeaus. Urn garden, Westwood Memorial Park, west Los Angeles.

6509. Moran, George (George Searcy, Oct. 3, 1881–Aug. 1, 1949) Elwood, Kansas, born half of the vaudeville and radio team of Moran and Mack, stars from *Over the Top* in 1917 at their zenith in the mid 20's with their recorded comedy routines as Two Black Crows. Mack died in a car wreck in Mesa, Arizona, in 1934. Moran appeared in several films including *The Bank Dick*. He died in an Oakland, California, hospital. Buried at St. Joseph, Missouri, supposedly at Mt. Mora Cemetery. No record.

6510. Moran, Lois (Lois Darlington Dowling, March 1, 1908–July 13, 1990) Pittsburgh born actress in silents and talkies, former dancer 1922–24 with the Paris National Opera. Best known as Laurel in *Stella Dallas* (1925) and a few sound films (*Behind That Curtain* 1929 and *Mammy* 1930). She retired from films in 1931 and appeared briefly on Broadway and TV. She died in Sedona, Arizona, cremated through Westcott mortuary and the ashes scattered in the mountains around the Red Rock country there by her family.

6511. Moran, Pat (Patrick Joseph Moran, Feb. 7, 1876–March 7, 1924) Catcher with the Braves, Cards and Phillies 1901–14, managed the Phillies and the Reds 1915–23, including the 1919 team that had the series thrown to them by the Blacksox. He died of Bright's Disease at 58. A bronze plaque with his career summary and profile is on a memorial in town. Family monument, St. John, range 5, lot 3, St. Bernard's Cemetery, Fitchburg, MA.

6512. Moran, Peggy (Marie Jeanette Moran, Oct. 23, 1918–Oct. 24, 2002) Actress from Clinton, Iowa, raised in Los Angeles, in films for four years, 1938–42 (*Girls' School, Rhythm of the Saddle, Ninotchka* [as the cigarette girl], *One Night in the Tropics*) whose lasting fame came as the feisty heroine opposite Dick Foran in Universal's *The Mummy's Hand* (1940) and *Horror Island* (1941). She retired in 1942 at 24 to marry Henry Koster, who had directed her in *First Love.* They resided in later years at Camarillo, California, where Koster died in 1988. Moran died in St. John's Pleasant Valley, Camarillo, at 84 as the result of injuries sustained in an auto accident August 26. Cremated through Pierce Bros. Griffin, Camarillo, her ashes were returned October 27 to her family. A private funeral was held November 2 and a Christian Science memorial service November 16 in Camarillo. Ashes buried in the Pacific.

6513. Moran, Polly (Pauline Theresa Moran, June 28, 1883–Jan. 24, 1952) Chicago born comedienne in raucous parts in vaudeville, silents and several comedies with Marie Dressler. Married to Martin T. Malone. Mass at Immaculate Heart of Mary Church in Los Angeles. Whispering Pines, lot 874, Forest Lawn, Glendale, CA.

6514. Moran, Thomas (Jan. 12, 1837–Aug. 26, 1926) English born painter of murals whose *Grand Canyon of Yellowstone* influenced congressional creation of the area as a national park. It and another of his works hang in the capital rotunda. Coming to the Hamptons on Long Island in 1884, he and his wife **Mary Nimmo Moran** (1842–1899) began the influx

of artists there. Most are in Green River Cemetery, but the Morans have a large gothic stone monument in the South End Burying Ground, East Hampton, Long Island, NY.

6515. Morant, Breaker (Harry Harbord Morant or Edwin Henry Murrant, Dec. 9, 1864–Feb. 27, 1902) English adventurer from Bridgewater landed in Australia in 1883 and gained a reputation as a colorful drinker, fighter, liar, daredevil and above all a master at breaking wild horses, which gave him his nickname. Over the period 1883–1897 he worked off and on around Queensland and New South Wales, writing and publishing ballads and verse as well. In 1897, likely to avoid many he had cheated as much as for patriotism, he enlisted in the service to fight in the Boer War. In August 1901 with the Bushvelt Carbineers, he was charged with executing Boer prisoners and a German missionary to avenge the murder of his captain and, with **Peter Joseph Handcock**, was executed by firing squad at the old Pretoria gaol, refusing to be blindfolded. As Morant had executed Boers wearing English uniforms, just as Lord Kitchener had ordered, that Kitchener signed his death warrant came to make Morant and Handcock martyrs, as popularized in *Scapegoats of the Empire* (1907) by George R. Witton, who had been with them and served a prison sentence until his conviction was overturned. The case gained further notice with the 1980 film *Breaker Morant*. Although there have been plans discussed to return them to Australia, Handcock's family reportedly want them left where they are. Church Street Cemetery, Pretoria, South Africa.

6516. More, Kenneth (Kenneth Gilbert Moore, Sept. 20, 1914–July 12, 1982) English actor from Gerrards Cross in films from 1946, notably as Second Officer Charles Lightoller in *A Night to Remember* (1958). He also appeared in the all-star *The Longest Day* (1962) and on British television in *The Forsythe Saga* (1967) and *Father Brown* (1974). He died from Parkinson's Disease at 67. Cremated at Putney Vale Cemetery, London. Ashes removed.

6517. More, Thomas (Feb. 6, 1477 or 1478–July 6, 1535) English statesman and intellect supported the Parliamentary privilege for free speech as speaker of the House of Commons in 1523. Lord Chancellor from 1529, he stood by the Roman Catholic faith, resigned in 1532, refused to site Henry VIII as head of the Church of England, and was beheaded for treason. Canonized 1935. He was the subject of Robert Bolt's play *A Man For All Seasons*, filmed in 1966 and 1988. Buried at St. Peter-ad-Vincula in the Tower of London, his head was buried by his daughter Margaret Roper in the Roper vault at St. Dunstan's Church, Canterbury, Kent.

6518. Morehouse, Johnny (1855–1860) Five year old son of a Dayton cobbler. His grave is marked by a detailed marble statue of the boy and his dog. Sec. 82/3 along the road, the most famous statue in Woodland Cemetery, Dayton, OH.

6519. Moreland, Mantan (Sept. 3, 1902–Sept. 28, 1973) Black actor primarily in comedic roles, often as Charlie Chan's wide eyed, confused or frightened chauffeur Birmingham Brown, with frequent asides, and many other melodramas at Universal (*The Strange Case of Dr. RX*) and Monogram. He reprised the character briefly in *Spider Baby* (1964). Block G (Graceland), lot 6868, lot 1, Valhalla Memorial Park, North Hollywood, CA.

6520. Moreno, Antonio (Sept. 26, 1887–Feb. 15, 1967) Spanish born silent screen matinee idol of the 1920's (*The Temptress* 1926, *It* 1927) moved on to character roles (*Creature From the Black Lagoon* 1954, *The Searchers* 1956). He died from a heart attack in Hollywood. Sanctuary of Valor, crypt 13358, Holly Terrace, Great Mausoleum, Forest Lawn, Glendale, CA.

6521. Moreno, Paco (Francisco Viñolas, Sept. 26, 1882–Oct. 15, 1941) Spanish actor and painter in some thirty films (*The Devil is A Woman*). Father of Rita Moreno. Sec. 13, lot 1520, Hollywood Forever Cemetery, Hollywood (Los Angeles), CA.

6522. Moret, Neil (Charles N. Daniels, April 12, 1878–Jan. 23, 1943) Prolific songwriter from St. Joseph and Kansas City, Missouri, used a variety of pen names, most often Neil Moret, but also Jules Lemare, L'Albert, Paul Bertrand, LaMonte C. Jones, Julian Strauss and as a lyricist Sidney Carter. Works include *Margery* (1898), *You Tell Me Your Dream, I'll Tell You Mine* (1899) and *Mickey* (1918) for the Mabel Normand film, the first association of a song with a film. Later numbers he co-wrote include *She's Funny That Way* and *Sweet and Lovely*. He died in L.A. Cremated through Westwood Memorial Park, west Los Angeles.

6523. Morgan, Daniel (July 6, 1736–July 6, 1802) Revolutionary War general captured at Quebec in 1775 was exchanged the next year and went on to serve in the Carolina campaign and to defeat the British at the Battle of Cowpens in 1781. A marble monument with his image stands beside his cracked and eroded grave slab. Mount Hebron Cemetery, Winchester, VA.

6524. Morgan, David (1862–1937) Pioneer in the development of the X-Ray and *reformer of medical services at sea*, as noted on the faded copper plaque on his monument. Hampstead Cemetery, Fortune Green Road, London.

6525. Morgan, Dennis (Stanley Morner, Dec. 20, 1908–Sept. 7, 1994) Former Milwaukee radio announcer and singer from Prentice, Wisconsin, worked in films from 1936 as Stanley Morner (*The Great Ziegfeld* 1936) or Richard Stanley, and as Dennis Morgan from 1939, chiefly at Warner Brothers (*Return of Dr. X, The Fighting 69th, Kitty Foyle, Captains of the Clouds, Christmas in Connecticut, My Wild Irish Rose*). Retired 1956. He died at 85 in Fresno, Ca., adjacent Madera County, where he lived. Buried as Stanley Morner, his red flush marker has both his names, his birthplace, and across the top (from *The Desert Song*) "*My des-ert is wait-ing*" with musical notes. Block A,

Oak Hill District Cemetery, Oakhurst, Madera County, CA.

6526. Morgan, Frank (Frank Wupperman, June 1, 1890–Sept. 18, 1949) MGM staple character actor of the 1930's and 40's, with long stage experience, in many roles as loveable but hopelessly crooked or irresponsible fathers or grandfathers. Best known as Professor Marvel and the title character in *The Wizard of Oz* (1939). A native of New York, he died in Beverly Hills and was returned for burial with his parents. The upright white stone reads *Wupperman. Frank Morgan 1890–1949*. His brother Ralph was later buried there also. Sec. 168/4 along Grape Ave., Greenwood Cemetery, Brooklyn, N.Y.C.

6527. Morgan, Gene (Eugene Morgan, March 12, 1893–Aug. 15, 1940) Actor and orchestra leader in Pathé *Folly* comedies, Hal Roach silents, later showed up in the films of Frank Capra (*Mr. Deeds Goes To Town, Mr. Smith Goes to Washington, Meet John Doe*) and Leo McCarey (*Make Way For Tomorrow*). He died from a heart attack at 47. Block 13 N ½, lot 267, grave C, Woodlawn Cemetery, Santa Monica, CA.

6528. Morgan, Helen (Aug. 2, 1900–Oct. 8, 1941) Actress and torch singer of the 1920's known for her numbers *Bill* from *Showboat* (1927, filmed in 1936) and *What Wouldn't I Do For That Man?* from *Applause*, filmed in 1929. With Ruth Etting, she was the first white woman to sing in the style of the Blues, perched atop the piano. In later years she suffered financial reverses. She died at 41 in Henrotin Hospital in Chicago from a chronic liver ailment and the effects of alcohol. Her large brown granite cross is inscribed *Our Helen Morgan*. Sec. 14, block 2, lot 10, grave 2, near the cemetery's right front corner area, Holy Sepulchre Cemetery, Worth (western Chicago suburb), IL.

6529. Morgan, Jane (Dec. 6, 1880–Jan. 1, 1972) Actress from North Platte, Nebraska, best known as Mrs. Margaret Davis on radio's *Our Miss Brooks* from 1948, transferred to CBS television 1952–56 made into a 1956 film. The widow of Leo C. Bryant (1955), she died from a heart attack at 91 in Burbank, California, Community Hospital. Service at the Church of the Hills, Forest Lawn Hollywood Hills, Los Angeles. Ashes scattered at sea January 10, 1972.

6530. Morgan, John Hunt (June 1, 1825–Sept. 4, 1864) Confederate commander of Morgan's Raiders led a cavalry group during the Civil War raiding Union supplies and destroying property. He was fatally wounded at Greeneville, Tennessee. Section C (across the road from John C. Breckenridge), lot 17, Lexington Cemetery, Lexington, KY.

6531. Morgan, J.P. (John Pierpont Morgan, April 17, 1837–March 31, 1913) Powerful banking tycoon, founder of Wall Street's House of Morgan, which by the early 1890's was the biggest banking institution in the country. Morgan helped avert a panic in 1895 and aided President Theodore Roosevelt in relieving a recession in 1907. A native of Hartford, Connecticut, his ashes are buried there, as is his son **J. P. Morgan,**

Jr. (Sept. 7, 1867–March 13, 1943) and daughter **Anne Tracy Morgan** (1873–1964), known for her humanitarian works particularly on behalf of France in both World War I and II. Their family monument is a large pink-brown block of polished granite with a sloping top and inserts like windows, each inscribed with a name and dates. Section 11, Cedar Hill Cemetery, Hartford, CT.

6532. Morgan, Kate (Lottie Bernard, c. 1868–Nov. 29, 1892) Legendary ghost of the Del Coronado Hotel in San Diego, where she was murdered (or a suicide) in room 3312 at 24. A new marker was placed on her grave by a descendant supposedly motivated by a dream to investigate and research what was listed for over ninety years as a suicide. Div. 5, sec. 1, block 6, grave 28, Mt. Hope Cemetery, San Diego, CA.

6533. Morgan, Ralph (Ralph Kuhner Wupperman, July 6, 1882–June 11, 1956) Older brother of Frank Morgan was somewhat less known and more anemic looking but in several prestigious films (*Strange Interlude, Rasputin and the Empress*, both 1932) and effective as a villain (*Star of Midnight* 1935, *Night Monster* 1942). He survived Frank by seven years, died in New York, and was buried with his brother and parents in the Wupperman lot. His white stone, a replica of Frank's, bears his real name and dates and that of his wife Georgianna. Sec. 168/4 along Grape Ave., Greenwood Cemetery, Brooklyn, N.Y.C.

6534. Morgan, Robert (Robert Knight Morgan, July 31, 1918–May 15, 2004) B-17 pilot from Asheville, North Carolina, a captain in the Army Air Corps, flew the *Memphis Belle* safely through World War II. The first to complete twenty-five safe missions, in 1943, the crew were hailed as heroes, and their last flight, with Hollywood fiction added, became the basis for the 1990 film *Memphis Belle*. The plane was named for Margaret Polk, Morgan's Tennessee sweetheart in 1942. Back in action in 1944, he flew the new B-20 bomber over Tokyo and in the South Pacific until April 1945. He retired a full colonel twenty years later and settled back in Asheville, where he died at 85. Ashes buried May 22. Sec. 2D, grave 21, Western Carolina State Veterans Cemetery, Black Mountain, NC.

6535. Morgan, Russ (April 29, 1904–Aug. 7, 1969) Bandleader from Scranton, Pennsylvania, known for slower rhythms (*Cruising Down the River*) used the slogan "Music in the Morgan Manner." Devotion Lawn (urn garden), 9017B, (Old) Palm Valley Memorial Park, Las Vegas, NV.

6536. Morgan, Vicki (Aug. 9, 1952–July 7, 1983) Former mistress of Alfred Bloomingdale, fallen from wealth after his death in 1982, was beaten to death in her sleep the next year in a Los Angeles apartment she shared with her killer. Funeral at the Old North Church, Forest Lawn Hollywood Hills, Los Angeles, with cremation through there and the ashes scattered at sea.

6537. Morgan, William George (1870–Dec. 27, 1942) Inventor of volleyball, as noted on his stone. Sec. 2, lot 60, Glenwood Cemetery, Lockport, NY.

6538. Morgenthau, Henry (May 11, 1891–Feb. 6, 1967) Secretary of the Treasury under Franklin Roosevelt 1933–1945 worked out much of the financing of the New Deal. He later proposed a harsh economic plan for postwar Germany which was not adopted. Sec. 6, lot 56, Mt. Pleasant Cemetery, Hawthorne, NY.

6539. Morin, Alberto (Nov. 26, 1902–April 7, 1989) Actor of Spanish ancestry in American films 1928–1993, including *Suez, Gone With the Wind, Charlie Chan in Panama, Casablanca, Key Largo, The Asphalt Jungle, King of the Khyber Rifles, To Catch A Thief, An Affair to Remember, The Milagro Beanfield War*, and as Armando Sidoni on the television series *Dallas*. Sec. 32, grave 725, Riverside National Cemetery, Riverside, CA.

6540. Morison, Samuel Eliot (July 9, 1887–May 15, 1976) Boston born U.S. historian with a special affection for and knowledge of naval history. Born at his grandfather's house at 44 Brimmer Street in Boston, he lived there much of his life. He was Professor of History at Harvard periodically from World War I into the 1950's, won Pulitzer Prizes in History for his biographies of Columbus (1943) and John Paul Jones (1959). His *Oxford History of the American People* (1927, updated through 1965), was long used as a standard text. He died in Boston but was buried near his summer home in Maine, with the epitaph *Dream dreams then write them/ Aye but live them first*. Forest Hill Cemetery, Northeast Harbor, ME.

6541. Morita, Pat (Noriyuki Morita, June 28, 1932–Nov. 24, 2005) Japanese-American actor-comedian born in Northern California, sent to an internment camp in Arizona during World War II, developed characters in television and films relying on both wit and wisdom with a good nature, from Arnold in *Happy Days* (1974) to Mr. Miyagi in *The Karate Kid* (1984, AA nom.) and its three sequels. He died from liver failure at 73 in his Las Vegas home. Palm Green Valley mortuary and Cemetery, Las Vegas, NV.

6542. Morley, Christopher (May 5, 1890–March 28, 1957) Essayist, founder of the *Saturday Review of Literature*, novelist (*The Haunted Bookshop* 1919) and renowned member of the Baker Street Irregulars, a literary group devoted to the study and analysis of the Sherlock Holmes stories by Sir Arthur Conan Doyle. He and his wife have small rounded tombstones by a large Yew tree, half way up the left side of Roslyn Cemetery, Roslyn, Long Island, NY.

6543. Morley, Karen (Mildred Linton, Dec. 12 [or 9], 1909–March 8, 2003) Blonde actress from Ottumwa, Iowa, in films 1929–37 (*The Sin of Madelon Claudet, Mata Hari, Arsene Lupin, Scarface* 1932, as Poppy, *The Phantom of Crestwood, The Mask of Fu Manchu, Dinner at Eight, Gabriel over the White*

House, Our Daily Bread, Black Fury, Outcast). Seen only sporadically afterward, her affiliations with far left causes resulted in her being blacklisted after she was called before the House Un-American Activities Committee in 1952, when she invoked the Fifth Amendment. Married to Charles Vidor through the 1930s and from 1943 to actor Lloyd Gough, who was also blacklisted. They lived in New York for many years. Gough died in 1984. Morley died at 93 from pneumonia at the Motion Picture Country Hospital, Woodland Hills, California. Her death was not reported until April 20. Cremated by Pierce Bros. Valhalla in North Hollywood, her ashes were scattered March 21, 2003, at sea off the coast of Los Angeles County.

6544. Morley, Robert (May 25, 1908–June 3, 1992) Rotund English actor from Semley, Wiltshire, adept at a variety of film roles (*The African Queen, The Loved One, Who is Killing the Great Chefs of Europe?*) from light comedy to satire. He received an Oscar nomination for his role as Louis XVII opposite Norma Shearer in *Marie Antoinette* (1938). Several stage productions include *Oscar Wilde* (1936) and *Pygmalion* (1937). He also co-wrote several plays including *Edward, My Son* with Noel Langley. Son-in-law of Dame Gladys Cooper and father of theater critic Sheridan Morley. Reportedly asking to have his credit cards buried with him just in case, his funeral was held at St. Mary's Church in Wargrave. His ashes were buried in the churchyard July 18 near a gray stone plaque to him in the red brick wall. St. Mary's Churchyard, Wargrave, Berkshire.

6545. Morrill, John (Feb. 19, 1855–April 2, 1932) Outfielder, infielder, pitcher and manager in early major league baseball for twenty-three years, with the Boston Red Caps 1876–82, the Boston Beaneaters 1883–88, the Senators 1889 and the Red Stockings 1890. Field of Bethel, lot 2053, grave 3, Holyhood Cemetery, Brookline, MA.

6546. Morrill, Priscilla (June 4, 1927–Nov. 9, 1994) Actress, best known as Lou Grant's wife Edie on *The Mary Tyler Moore Show* 1973–74. TV movies include *Right of Way* (1983). Married name Bryson. She died from cancer at 67. Ashes scattered at sea.

6547. Morris, Adrian (Jan. 12, 1907–Nov. 30, 1941) Portly actor from Mount Vernon, New York; son of **William** and brother of Chester Morris (*q.v.*), in films at Warners, then at Fox, until his death at 34 from edema and congestion of the brain and lungs related to excess sedation with barbiturates. Films include *The Mayor of Hell, Wild Boys of the Road, G-Men, Doctor Socrates, The Petrified Forest*, as Ruby; *Angels With Dirty Faces, Gone With the Wind, The Grapes of Wrath, Blood and Sand*. Buried with his parents. Sec. 5/Garden of Eternal Love, Hollywood Forever Cemetery, Hollywood (Los Angeles), CA.

6548. Morris, Anita (March 14, 1943–March 2, 1994) Actress from Durham, North Carolina, won the 1982 Tony Award for her role in the musical *Nine*. She was also on Broadway in *Sugar Babies* and *The*

Best Little Whorehouse in Texas. Films include *Ruthless People, Maria's Lovers* and *A Sinful Life*. She died from cancer at 50 in Los Angeles, the wife of director Grover Dale. Cremation Society of South Bay. Ashes to residence in Beverly Hills.

6549. Morris, Barboura (Oct. 22, 1932–Oct. 23, 1975) Actress in several Roger Corman films (*The Man With the X-Ray Eyes, The Haunted Palace, The Dunwich Horror*). Epitaph reads *After the winter comes the fine weather*. Married name Freed. E-471-17, Woodlawn Cemetery, Santa Monica, CA.

6550. Morris, Chester (Feb. 16, 1901–Sept. 11, 1970) New York born square jawed star of the talkies (*The Divorcee, The Big House* 1930, *The Bat Whispers* 1931, *Red Headed Woman* 1932, *Three Godfathers* 1936, *Five Came Back* 1939) later played *Boston Blackie*. He was appearing as Captain Queeg in *The Caine Mutiny* at the Bucks County Playhouse when he took his own life with an overdose of barbiturates in his room at the Holiday Inn in New Hope, Pennsylvania. He was ill with stomach cancer at the time. A memorial service was held at St. Bartholomew's Church in Manhattan on September 14. Cremated at Sunset Memorial Park in Somerton, Bucks County, Pennsylvania, his ashes were scattered by the mortuary as instructed at Buckingham, PA.

6551. Morris, Clara (March 17, 1848–Nov. 20, 1925) Stage actress born in Canada and raised in Cleveland appeared with Augustin Daly's company in New York, first acclaimed as the governess in *Man and Wife* in 1870. She retired in 1895, later suffering publicized financial woes, a nervous breakdown and the loss of her sight, becoming known as "The Woman of Sorrow." The widow of Frederick C. Harriot, she died from heart disease at 79 in New Canaan, Connecticut. Sec. 168, Kensico Cemetery, Valhalla, NY.

6552. Morris, Elida (Nov. 12, 1886–Dec. 25, 1977) Stage singer and actress from Philadelphia was an early recording artist and introduced *Pretty Baby* in J.J. Shubert's *World of Pleasure* at the Palace Theater in Chicago in 1916. Married to aviation pioneer **Ray Cooper** from 1923 to his death in 1947, she was a pilot as well. Touring in *Teahouse of the August Moon* and other works until her later years, she died in Santa Barbara at 91. Cremated at Santa Barbara Cemetery through Welch-Ryce mortuary. Ashes buried unmarked with her mother (marked) January 10, 1978. Forest sec., lot 531, grave 3, Northwood Cemetery, Philadelphia, PA.

6553. Morris, Glenn (June 18, 1912–Jan. 31, 1974) Colorado State football and track star won a gold medal in the decathlon at the 1936 Olympics and starred as Tarzan in *Tarzan's Revenge* (1938) before playing pro football for the Detroit Lions and serving in the Navy, where he was wounded in the Pacific during World War II. He resided in later years at Menlo Park, California, and died at Palo Alto at 61, listed as 62, after a long illness. Garden of Inspiration, lot 2315, space 3, Skylawn Memorial Park, San Mateo, CA.

6554. Morris, Gouverneur (Jan. 31, 1752–Nov. 6, 1816) Revolutionary financier and diplomat planned a decimal system of financial coinage, chaired the committee that finalized the writing of the Constitution and served as minister to France under Washington and senator from New York 1800–1803. He was buried at Morrisania, the family estate in what is now the South Bronx. An oval topped tomb built into the hillside marks the entrance to the vault. In 1841 **Gouverneur Morris, Jr.** built St. Anne's Church adjacent the graveyard in memory of his mother **Ann Randolph Morris**. A monument to Gouverneur Morris sits just behind the iron fence surrounding the churchyard. Troubled by a deteriorating area, it is a New York Historic site. St. Ann's Church of Morrisania, 140th at St. Ann's Ave., south Bronx, N.Y.C.

6555. Morris, Greg (Francis Morris, Sept. 27, 1934–Aug. 27, 1996) Actor from Cleveland played electronics expert Barney Collier on TV's *Mission Impossible* 1966–73, one of the first black TV stars. He died at 61 in his Las Vegas home after being ill with brain cancer. Ashes to family through Palm Mortuary, Las Vegas, NV.

6556. Morris, Howard (Sept. 4, 1919–May 21, 2005) Diminutive actor, comedian, writer and director from New York City worked in early television with Sid Caesar and Mel Brooks, appeared in films (*Boys' Night Out, The Nutty Professor, High Anxiety, Life Stinks*), television (including the *Twilight Zone* episode *I Dream of Genie*), directed pictures (*With Six You Get Eggroll, Don't Drink the Water*) and TV (*Dick Van Dyke, Bewitched, Get Smart*), but was best known as drawling hillbilly Ernest T. Bass on *The Andy Griffith Show* in the early 1960's. He died in Hollywood at 85 from heart failure. His plaque bears his Mayberry character's greeting: *It's me, it's me, it's Ernest T.* Laurel Gardens, crypt E-450, Hillside Memorial Park, Los Angeles.

6557. Morris, Lelia Naylor (April 15, 1862–July 23, 1929) Prolific hymn writer composed both the words and music to some 1300 hymns, beginning with *Refining Fire* in 1892 and including *Nearer Still Nearer, Sweeter As the Years Go By, Let Jesus Come Into Your Heart, Wounded By Our Transgressions, Sweet Will of God* and *We Will Talk It Over Together By and By*. She spent most of her life at McConnelsville, Morgan County, Ohio, with the Methodist Episcopal Church there, the wife of C.H. Morris. Blind in her last years, she died at the home of her daughter in Auburn, New York. McConnelsville Cemetery, McConnelsville, OH.

6558. Morris, Lewis (April 8, 1726–Jan. 22, 1798) Signer of the Declaration of Independence from New York, half brother of Gouvernor Morris. Family graveyard adjacent St. Anne's Church of Morrisania, 140th and St. Ann's Ave., south Bronx, N.Y.C.

6559. Morris, Mary (June 24, 1895–Jan. 16, 1970) Actress on stage, known for two films: *The Double Door* (1934) and *Victoria the Great* (1937). Not to be confused with the actress Mary Morris born in 1915. She died at 74 in East Islip, Long Island, New York. Body donated to science.

6560. Morris, Robert (Jan. 31, 1734–May 8, 1806) Signer of the Declaration of Independence did much to personally finance the Revolutionary War effort, yet upon losing his own fortune was placed for three years (1798–1801) in a debtors' prison. Marble box tomb along the side of the church, near another signer, James Wilson. Churchyard of Christ Church, 2nd St. between Market and Arch, Philadelphia, PA.

6561. Morris, Wayne (Bert DeWayne Morris, Feb. 17, 1914–Sept. 14, 1959) Actor in amiable roles at Warners in the late 1930's (*Kid Galahad* 1937, *Return of Dr. X* 1939, *The Smiling Ghost* 1941), later in some darker parts, including Stanley Kubrik's *Paths of Glory* (1957). A flyer in the U.S. Navy during World War II, he was Hollywood's top air ace, with seven planes to his credit, awarded the Distinguished Flying Cross. Watching an air show with his father-in-law, he died from a heart attack at 45. Sec. H, grave 5941 LH, Arlington National Cemetery, Arlington, VA.

6562. Morris, William (March 24, 1834–Oct. 3, 1896) English artist whose work included much acclaimed stained glass, as well as working with pre-Raphaelite artist Ford Madox-Brown. St. George's, or Kelmscott Churchyard (village cemetery) near Lechlade, eleven miles north of Swindon.

6563. Morris, Willie (William Weaks Morris, Nov. 29, 1934–Aug. 2, 1999) Rhodes scholar from Yazoo City, Mississippi, was the youngest editor-in-chief of *Harper's* 1967–71, bringing many insights on the southern viewpoint to the New York literary world, and promoting revolutionary changes, devoting an entire issue to anti-war protests in March 1968. He returned to Mississippi in 1980. Books include *My Dog Skip, North Toward Home, New York Days* and *The Ghosts of Medgar Evers*. He died from heart failure in Jackson at 64. Split gray monument and plaque. Epitaph, *Even across the divide of death/ Friendship remains an echo/ Forever in the heart.* Glenwood Cemetery, Yazoo City, MS.

6564. Morrison, Adrienne *see* **Richard Bennett**.

6565. Morrison, Bret (May 5, 1912–Sept. 25, 1978) Radio actor did the voice of Lamont Cranston, *The Shadow*, with the familiar introduction through a filter, followed by the sinister laugh, during its last decade 1944–54, most shows done live at the Longacre Theater in New York City. He went on to appear in films 1955–70. Ashes scattered at sea.

6566. Morrison, Florence (Lela Strait LeNoir, Oct. 1, 1886–June 15, 1942) Screen, stage and radio actress, married to actor Pass LeNoir. Block 3 lot 4, Fairview Cemetery, Dennison, TX.

6567. Morrison, Herbert (May 14, 1905–Jan. 10, 1989) News announcer for WLS in Chicago known for his emotional live coverage of the Hindenburg disaster ("Oh, the humanity!") at Lakehurst, New Jersey, May 8, 1937. He died in a Morgantown, West Virginia, nursing home. Scottdale Cemetery, Scottdale, PA.

6568. Morrison, Jim (Dec. 8, 1943–July 3, 1971) Lead singer with the Doors 1967–1971, the son of a conservative naval officer, had by 1970 reportedly grown tired of his fame. He liked Paris and the anonymity it brought, but was plagued by alcoholism and excess weight when he died, supposedly from a heart attack while taking a bath at 27. Arriving in Paris, the Doors' manager was shown only a sealed coffin and a death certificate before the burial. The only witness, Morrison's wife Pamela, died in a car crash in Africa in 1974. The singer had expressed fantasies of a fake death and starting a new life, eventually contacting his friends as "Mr. Mojo Risin'," but (as with Houdini) no such message ever came. Soon after Morrison's death, the stone block over his sealed concrete grave became covered with graffiti (extending to surrounding monuments), bottles of wine and flowers, and a bust of him with a wig on it. The site has been cleaned up several times. The lease expired in 2001, but Morrison and the decorations remain. Div. 6, Pere Lachaise Cemetery, Paris. **Pamela Sue Morrison** (Dec. 22, 1946–April 25, 1974) is in the mausoleum's Rose Alcove, niche 164, Fairhaven Memorial Park, Santa Ana, CA.

6569. Morrison, Sunshine Sammy (Ernest Fredric Morrison, Dec. 20, 1912–July 24, 1989) Child star with Hal Roach from 1919 in Harold Lloyd and Snub Pollard comedies and an original *Our Gang* member 1922–24. In vaudeville 1924–40, later returning to comedy films, 145 in all. Capistrano Gardens, memorial panel 49, sec. 14, row 3, Inglewood Park Cemetery, Inglewood, CA.

6570. Morrow, Dwight Whitney and family *see* **Lindbergh.**

6571. Morrow, Honore (1880–April 12, 1940) Author of several sentimental and historical novels, including *Still Jim, On to Oregon, The Splendor of God,* and *Benefits Forgot* (filmed as *Of Human Hearts* 1938). Exeter Cemetery, Exeter, NH.

6572. Morrow, Jeff (Jan. 13, 1907–Dec. 26, 1993) Actor from the 1950's and 60's in several adventure and science fiction films (*This Island Earth, The Creature Walks Among Us*), *Twilight Zone* episode *Elegy,* much on radio and TV as well. Ashes scattered at sea January 10, 1994, three miles off Santa Monica, CA.

6573. Morrow, Susan (Jacqueline Anne Attix, May 25, 1932–May 8, 1985) Actress in low budget films and television of the 1950's and 60's (*Gasoline Alley, Problem Girls, Cat Women of the Moon, Missile Base at Taniak*). Sister of Judith Campbell Exner. Peacehaven, block 171, lot 5, Eternal Hills Memorial Park, Oceanside, CA.

6574. Morrow, Vic (Feb. 14, 1929–July 23, 1982) Actor cast as the most surly of the delinquents in *The Blackboard Jungle* (1954), later known as Sgt. Saunders

in TV's *Combat* 1962–66. He was killed by a helicopter blade, along with two children he was carrying when the chopper lowered itself too close, in the (deleted) Vietnam sequence of the first episode of *Twilight Zone, The Movie* (1983). Director John Landis was tried and acquitted in the case. Mount of Olives, block 5, 80–1, Hillside Memorial Park, Los Angeles.

6575. Morse, Carlton E. (July 4, 1901–May 24, 1993) Creator of radio's *One Man's Family*, the saga of the Barbours of San Francisco, "dedicated to the mothers and fathers of the younger generation and their bewildering offspring," running from April 29, 1932 to May 8, 1959. Azalea urn garden, row 3, 15E, grave 15, East Lawn Mem. Park, Sacramento, CA.

6576. Morse, Lee (Lee Taylor, Nov. 30, 1897–Dec. 16, 1954) Vocalist of the 1920's starred in *Artists and Models* and *Hitchy Coo* on the New York stage, wrote *Don't Even Change A Picture on the Wall, Shadows on the Wall,* recorded *Old Man Sunshine* (*Little Boy Bluebird*), *Moanin' Low,* etc. with her Blue Grass Boys, featuring the Dorsey Brothers, Glenn Miller, Benny Goodman, various others. Her brother Glen Taylor had been the Democratic senator from Idaho. The wife of the city's fire and police communications officer Ray Farese, she died in Rochester, New York. Riverside Cemetery, Rochester, NY.

6577. Morse, Samuel Finley Breese (April 27, 1791–April 2, 1872) Artist who was better known for his invention of the telegraph and sending of the first message (1844) "What hath God wrought?" from Washington, D.C. to Baltimore. He died in New York and was buried in Brooklyn; a plaque honoring him by the Morse Telegraph Co. was attached to his large rose granite monument in 1968, on a shaded hill. Interior of sec. 25/32, lot 5761/9, Greenwood Cemetery, Brooklyn, N.Y.C.

6578. Morse, Wayne L. (Oct. 20, 1900–July 22, 1974) Republican senator from Oregon 1944–1952, changing politics and serving as a Democrat 1952–1969. A liberal, he was one of the first to speak out against American involvement in Vietnam. Block 9, sec. 14, Rest Haven Memorial Park, Eugene, OR.

6579. Morton, Gary *see* **Lucille Ball.**

6580. Morton, Jelly Roll (Ferdinand Joseph La Menthe Morton, Sept. 20, 1885–July 10, 1941) New Orleans born musician credited as a primary developer of jazz, best known for *King Porter Stomp*. His work is considered unclassifiable, combining elements of several kinds of music, including ragtime, blues, opera, Spanish and folk. He died in Los Angeles. Though all references list his birth year as 1885, his grave marker lists 1890. Sec. N, lot 347, grave 9, Calvary Cemetery, east Los Angeles.

6581. Morton, John (1724–April 1777) Signer of the Declaration of Independence from Pennsylvania cast a decisive vote for its passage. Old St. Paul's Churchyard, Chester, PA.

6582. Morton, Levi Parsons (May 16, 1824–May 16, 1920) Minister to France under Arthur served as

Vice President of the United States under Benjamin Harrison 1889–1893 and as Republican governor of New York in the 1890's. He died on his 96th birthday at Rhinebeck, New York, along the Hudson in Duchess County, and was buried there, the family lot surrounded by a low iron railing and a large stone sarcophagus in the center listing all the interments. Rhinebeck Cemetery, Route 9, Rhinebeck, NY.

6583. Morton, Oliver Perry (Aug. 4, 1823–Nov. 1, 1877) Republican governor of Indiana during the Civil War served 1861–67, exercising dictatorial pro Union powers. Afterward as a senator he voted with the Radicals for the impeachment of President Andrew Johnson. His monument, with the graves of Union soldiers, is topped by a white marble bust of him and the inscription *He loved his country's good with a respect more tender, more holy and profound, than his own life.* Sec. 9, along main road (marked with a guide line), Crown Hill Cemetery, Indianapolis, IN.

6584. Morton, Samuel J. "Nails" (July 8, 1893–May 13, 1923) A member of Dean O'Banion's northside faction in Chicago's ongoing bootlegging wars of the 1920's was a decorated veteran of the World War and served as the fence in whose garage O'Banion deposited his hijacked whiskey. Riding a horse with O'Banion and his wife Viola in Lincoln Park, Morton was thrown by the nag and his skull crushed. In a scene later worked into the 1931 film *The Public Enemy*, with Leslie Fenton as Nails Nathan, the horse was executed, shot to death by Louis "Two Gun" Alterie and or O'Banion and or Hymie Weiss, depending on the version. He has a stele in the style of O'Banion's. A plaque on the cemetery gate in his memory, as well as a bench inscribed *S.J. Morton,* have been removed. Independent Progress Society, gate 93, lot 502, row 2, just off Greenburg Road, Jewish Waldheim Cemetery group, Forest Park, IL.

6585. Morton, William Thomas Green (Aug. 9, 1819–July 15, 1868) Dentist from Charlton, Massachusetts, experimented with the use of ether by 1846 and applied for a patent on it as Letheon. Though debated as its discoverer, his monument states *Inventor and revealer of anesthetic inhalation by whom pain in surgery was averted and annulled. Before whom in all time, surgery was agony. Since whom, science had control of pain.* Spruce Ave., lot 3940, Mt. Auburn Cemetery, Cambridge, MA.

6586. Mosby, John Singleton (Dec. 6, 1833–May 30, 1916) Confederate raider during the Civil War, primarily at Union bases in Virginia. The raiding parties of Mosby or John Hunt Morgan, though famous and feared, did not have the same reputations for viciousness as Quantrill or Bloody Bill Anderson. Mosby later served as the consulate to Hong Kong under Hayes, Garfield and Arthur. He was buried in what was a family cemetery on land that their estate was on. Now near the Confederate memorial, Warrenton City Cemetery, Warrenton, VA.

6587. Moscone, George (Nov. 24, 1929–Nov. 27, 1978) Mayor of San Francisco for two years was assassinated in the city building, along with Supervisor Harvey Milk, by former Supervisor Dan White. White had resigned on November 10 and was turned down in his request for reinstatement, as well as being treated in what he described as a cavalier manner by both Moscone and Milk. On November 27 he shot Moscone in his inner office four times (twice in the head), while talking with him. St. Michael sec, row 22, grave 42, Holy Cross Cemetery, Colma, CA.

6588. Mosconi, Willie (William Joseph Mosconi, June 27, 1913–Sept. 16, 1993) Philadelphia born pocket billiards champion regarded as the best ever, taking over the spot held for decades by Willie Hoppe. He won fourteen world championships 1941–1957, and once pocketed 526 consecutive balls without a miss, a record later broken. Garden Mausoleum, St. Mary's Cemetery, Bellmawr, NJ.

6589. Moscovitch, Maurice (Nov. 23, 1871–June 18, 1940) Noted Russian born actor with the Yiddish Theater in New York, in a few films (*Winterset* 1936 as Esdras; *Make Way For Tomorrow* 1937, as Max Rubens; *The Great Dictator* 1940, as Mr. Jaeckel). Father of actor Noel Madison (*q.v.*). Sec. 18, grave 509, Beth Olam Cemetery, adjacent Hollywood Forever Cemetery, Hollywood (Los Angeles) CA.

6590. Moscowitz, Stacy (Stacy Robin Moscowitz, June 6, 1957–Aug. 1, 1977) Twenty year old secretary was fatally shot by New York City's .44-caliber killer, dubbed the Son of Sam, as she sat in a parked car in the Bath Beach section of Brooklyn in the early morning hours of Sunday, July 31. Her date, Robert Violante, was blinded in one eye and most of the other but survived. She was the last victim of the phantom that had terrorized the city for over a year. Within the month David Berkowitz was arrested in Yonkers, traced from a traffic ticket acquired while in Bath Beach. King Solomon Cemetery, Clifton, NJ.

6591. Moses, "Grandma" (Anna Mary Robertson, Sept. 7, 1860–Dec. 13, 1961) Primitive American painter of the rural settings of her youth began painting and exhibiting at age 76 only because she could no longer embroider. A stone at the foot of her grave in upstate New York just west of the Vermont line, in addition to the headstone, reads *Her primitive painting captured the spirit and preserved the scene of a vanishing countryside.* Maple Grove Cemetery, Hoosick Falls, NY.

6592. Moses, Robert (Dec. 18, 1888–July 29, 1981) New York political mainstay for forty years headed the state park commission 1924–1963, the Triborough Bridge and Tunnel Authority 1946–1968 and was concurrently New York City's park commissioner 1934–1960, heading several massive and often controversial projects; his work included Jones Beach, the Robert Moses state parks, Shea Stadium situated in Queens, and the Triborough and Verrazano-Narrows Bridges. He died at 92. Crypt, Magnolia sec. 9, Woodlawn Cemetery, the Bronx, N.Y.C.

6593. Mosley, Diana *see* **Mitford Sisters.**

6594. Mosquini, Marie (Dec. 3, 1899–Feb. 21, 1983) Actress 1917–38 in many silent comedies with Harold Lloyd, Charley Chase, Snub Pollard, dramas including *Seventh Heaven* (1927), married inventor Lee de Forest in 1930 and retired later in the decade. She remarried briefly after his death in 1961, but is buried with him as Marie de Forest, though no dates are under her name. Sec. C, lot 416, grave 2, San Fernando Mission Cemetery, Mission Hills, CA.

6595. Moss, Frank E. "Ted" (Sept. 23, 1911–Jan. 29, 2003) Senator from Utah 1959–1977 served as secretary of the Democratic Caucus and sponsored legislation to protect the environment as well as banning cigarette ads from television. He died in Salt Lake City at 91. Salt Lake City Cemetery, Salt Lake City, UT.

6596. Mostel, Zero (Samuel Joel Mostel, Feb. 28, 1915–Sept. 8, 1977) Large actor from Brooklyn best known for the lead role in *Fiddler on the Roof* on Broadway in 1964. He also appeared in films from 1950, including *Panic in the Streets* (1950), *The Enforcer* (1951) and *The Producers* (1968) and *The Front* (1976). He died from a heart attack at Jefferson University Hospital in Philadelphia at 62. At his specific request, there were no services, with cremation "just like Einstein" and no known burial place.

6597. Moten, Bennie (Nov. 13, 1894–April 2, 1935) Kansas City born pianist, composer and bandleader (*The Moten Stomp*). The Missourians and the Count Basie orchestra were outgrowths of his influence (Basie was his second piano player). He died at 38 from a heart attack after a tonsillectomy. Unmarked. Block 4, lot 87, grave 7, #8131, Highland Cemetery (office at Blue Ridge Lawn), Kansas City, MO.

6598. Mott, Lucretia (Jan. 3, 1793–Nov. 11, 1880) Pioneer in women's rights joined with Elizabeth Cady Stanton and Susan B. Anthony at the Seneca Falls Convention in 1848. A Hicksite Quaker, she also preached in favor of abolition. Buried in the Friends Fair Hill Burial Ground in Philadelphia, by the late 1980's it was owned by another church; situated in a run down area, overgrown and permanently locked. By 1995 a historical site sign had been erected in memory of Mott and abolitionist **Robert Purvis**, also buried there. The stones are small and identical in the Quaker tradition. Old Friends Fair Hill Burial Ground, Cabria and Germantown St., Philadelphia, PA.

6599. Mottola, Tony (Anthony C. Mottola, April 18, 1918–Aug. 9, 2004) Jazz and pop guitarist from 1936, recorded in the 1940's with Frank Sinatra, played on *The Tonight Show* with Skitch Henderson's orchestra 1958–72, and toured with Sinatra 1980–88, performing at Carnegie Hall and The White House. Gate of Heaven Cemetery, East Hanover, NJ.

6600. Moulin, Jean (June 20, 1899–July 8, 1943) French prefect known for leftist sympathies supported the republicans in Spain in 1936, was twice arrested by the Gestapo after Vichy took over occupied France and was removed from his post, after which he met with De Gaulle and others organizing the French resistance. Placed at its head in early 1942, he parachuted back into the country to set up the underground press, uniting various groups to form the Conseil National de la Resistance in Paris by May 1943. Arrested by the Gestapo under Klaus Barbie at Lyon on June 21, he died weeks later en route to (or after arrival in) Paris from the results of torture. His supposed ashes — reportedly in urn 3857 of the columbarium (division 87) at Pere Lachaise Cemetery, according to German records — were removed in 1964 and enshrined in crypt VI, The Pantheon, Paris.

6601. Mountbatten of Burma, Louis Francis Albert Victor Nicholas, First Earl (June 25, 1900–Aug. 27, 1979) Great grandson of Queen Victoria was originally a Battenburg but changed his name during World War I. In World War II he was in command of the combined operations of the British Navy, and was later the last Viceroy of India, transferring power to the Indian government in 1947. First Sea Lord 1955–59 and Chief of the Defense Staff 1959–65. His nephew Philip married Princess Elizabeth, later Elizabeth II, in 1947. Mountbatten was assassinated when a bomb planted by the Irish Republican Army exploded in his fishing boat off the northwest coast of Ireland. Memorial in Westminster Abbey, London. Buried beneath the south transept, Romsey Abbey Church, Romsey, Hampshire.

6602. Mowbray, Alan (Aug. 18, 1896–March 25, 1969) Portly English character actor in films of the 1930's and 40's, often in stuffy or devious roles, frequently a villain (*House of Rothschild, My Man Godfrey, Terror By Night* 1946, *Abbott & Costello meet The Killer, Boris Karloff* 1949). He died from a heart attack in Hollywood Presbyterian Hospital. Sec. N, lot 390, Holy Cross Cemetery, Culver City, CA.

6603. Moxley, Martha (Martha Elizabeth Moxley, Aug. 16, 1960–Oct 30 1975) Teenage girl murdered in Greenwich, Connecticut, with a golf club, allegedly by Michael Skakal, a nephew of Ethel Kennedy, according to *Murder in Greenwich* (1998) by former Los Angeles homicide detective Mark Fuhrman. The accused killer was arrested and charged with the murder by 2000, tried, convicted, and sent to prison, based largely on the attention Fuhrman's book re-focused on the case. Flush plaque. Sec. L1, farther down on the right from Victor Borge's lot and in the same approximate row. Putnam Cemetery, Greenwich, CT.

6604. Moylan, Catherine (1904–Sept. 9, 1969) Miss Universe of 1926 became a silent film actress and star of the *Ziegfeld Follies*. Married name Singleton. Garden of Our Lady of Peace, D-126-B, Mount Olivet Cemetery, Fort Worth, TX.

6605. Moynihan, Daniel Patrick (March 16, 1927–March 26, 2003) New York politician and scholar born in Tulsa but raised in New York City. A Fulbright scholar and colorful Irishman, his views on social justice often defied partisan politics. He went to work in President Kennedy's Department of Labor in 1961, remained there under Johnson to 1965, directed the Harvard–MIT Center for Urban Studies 1965–9, served as urban affairs advisor to Nixon 1969–70, Ambassador to India under Nixon and Ford, Ambassador to the United Nations 1975–76, and four term Democratic Senator from New York 1977–2000, and in later years was a professor at Syracuse University, near the cabin where he spent much time writing. He died at 76 in Washington Hospital Center from complications stemming from a ruptured appendix. Mass at St. Patrick's Church, Washington, D.C. Sec. 36, grave 2261, Arlington National Cemetery, Arlington, VA.

6606. Mozart, Wolfgang Amadeus (Jan. 27, 1756–Dec. 5, 1791) Austrian child musical prodigy had written his first opera and seen it performed by age ten. With maturity came adversity in finding patrons. Only in his last years did he achieve success, with his operas *The Marriage of Figaro, Don Giovanni, The Magic Flute*, symphonies, piano concertos, and his *Requiem*. Poverty returned to plague he and his wife Constanze; his last days were spent in a second floor apartment of the Klein-Kaiserstein House in the Rauhensteingasse in Vienna, now the Mozarthof. Suffering from fever and a swelling of the extremities, he foresaw his death and sang portions of his *Requiem* for visiting friends. Theories that he was poisoned by rival musician and composer Salieri have abounded and were promoted in the film *Amadeus* (1984). The recorded symptoms also suggest uremic poisoning or heart failure resulting from rheumatic heart disease. Mozart's remains were taken by cart to St. Stephen's Cathedral in Vienna. With Constanze at home prostrated by grief, only a dog reportedly followed the cart with the coffin to St. Marx's Cemetery outside the city wall, where he was buried in a common grave with others. The exact site could not be located later, and a monument to him was erected in St. Marx's in 1859. In 1888, with the removal of the great composers to Vienna's Central Cemetery, the area in St. Marx's was again scoured but Mozart was not located. A large obelisk to him with a bronze cameo on it was erected near the graves of Beethoven and Schubert in gruppe 32 A, nummer 55, Der Zentralfriedhof (the Central Cemetery), but the actual grave is at Der St. Marxer Friedhof (St. Marx's Cemetery), Vienna. Mozart's wife **Constanze** (**Constantia**, Jan. 6, 1763–March 6, 1842) and his father **Leopold** (Nov. 14, 1719–May 28, 1778), Salzburg Kappelmeister, though at odds over the composer in life, lie side by side; her monument is in the center, his smaller stone to her left. St. Sebastian Cemetery, Salzburg, Austria. Mozart's mother **Anna Maria Pertl Mozart**, and his sister, are at St. Peter's Church cemetery, Salzburg. A skull rescued by a gravedigger at St. Marx's and alleged to have been Mozart's was to be compared through DNA testing with Mozart's father Leopold, his maternal grandmother, and his sixteen year old

niece Jeanette in October 2004, when the three graves were exhumed in Salzburg.

6607. Mr. Ed *see* **Ed.**

6608. Mudd, Samuel (Dec. 20, 1833–Jan. 10, 1883) Physician near Bryantown, Maryland, who treated (probably unknown to Mudd) Lincoln's assassin, John Wilkes Booth. The president's murderer was fleeing from Washington with a leg injury suffered when he jumped onto the stage at Ford's Theatre. Mudd, despite his ignorance of his patient having shot the president, was sentenced to Dry Tortugas until his pardon by President Johnson March 9, 1869, in part for saving lives during an epidemic there. He returned to his home in Maryland. His stone, not over one hundred yards from where he first met Booth in church there, was inscribed simply *Samuel A. Mudd. Died January 10 1883*. Another family stone later replaced it, at the front of St. Mary's Church Cemetery, Bryantown, MD.

6609. Mudie, Leonard (Leonard Mudie Cheetham, April 11, 1883–April 14, 1965) English character actor, thin with nasal delivery, in small roles in Hollywood through the 1930's and 40's (*The Mummy, The Mystery of Mr. X, Cleopatra, The House of Rothschild*). Deodora Hall South, sec. O, niche 68, Pierce Brothers' Chapel of the Pines Crematory, Los Angeles.

6610. Mueller, Karl (Karl H. Mueller, July 27, 1962–June 17, 2005) Bass guitarist, founding member of Soul Asylum (1984) had hits over the next decade with *Grave Dancers Union* and *Runaway Train*. He died from throat cancer at 42. Lakewood Cemetery, Minneapolis, MN.

6611. Muhammad (The Prophet Muhammad) (c.570–June 8, 632) Native of Mecca in western Arabia had a vision c. 610 to spread the word of God, founding the religion of Islam, as written in the text of the Koran. His ornate tomb in Medina was photographed only once, by an unknown source in the 19th century. The picture was auctioned at Sotheby's in 2001. Mosque of the Prophet, Medina (north of Mecca), Saudi Arabia.

6612. Muhammad, Elijah (Elijah Poole, Oct. 10, 1897–Feb. 25, 1975) Black Muslim leader established Muhammed's Temple of Islam number 2 in Chicago in 1934, leading the growing number of Black Muslims in America. Muhammad and the Muslims promoted separation of the races; he inspired and worked with Malcolm X until their division over ideas in the 1960's. Mount Glenwood Cemetery, Glenwood, IL.

6613. Muir, Esther (March 11, 1903–Aug. 1, 1995) Actress in *Earl Carroll's Vanities* and *My Girl Friday* (1929), best known in the stage run and the film version of the Marx Brothers' *A Day at the Races* (1937). She later worked as a realtor in southern California. Married to Busby Berkeley until 1931 and to Sam Coslow until 1948. She died at Mt. Kisco, near her home in Somers (northeastern Westchester County), New York. Cremated at Ferncliff Cemetery, Hartsdale. Ashes returned to Clark and Associates mortuary at Somers, NY.

6614. Muir, Gavin (Sept. 8, 1900–May 24, 1972) Chicago born actor, English educated with a pronounced British accent and velvet delivery often used in suave villainy *Hitler's Children* and *Nightmare* 1942, *Sherlock Holmes Faces Death* 1943, *The House of Fear* 1945, etc. He resided at Palm Springs, California, but died at Fort Lauderdale, Florida. Cremated at Royal Palm Crematory, Pompano Beach, the ashes were returned to family in La Jolla, CA.

6615. Muir, John (April 21, 1838–Dec. 24, 1914) Scottish born naturalist promoted conservation tirelessly. He lived amid nature as well, walking all over Canada and making a hike from Indianapolis to the Gulf of Mexico. His writings led to the establishment of the National Parks and gave birth to the conservation program established under Theodore Roosevelt and promoted and administered under Gifford Pinchot. He was buried next to his wife, marked by a tombstone, on his ranch at Martinez, CA.

6616. Muldoon, William A. (May 25, 1852–June 3, 1933) World wrestling champion known as the Iron Duke. Mausoleum in the Iroquois plot, sec. 58 (near those of May Irwin and E.F. Albee), Kensico Cemetery, Valhalla, NY.

6617. Mulhall, Jack (John Joseph Francis Mulhall, Oct. 7, 1887–June 1, 1979) Prolific leading man in silent films played comedy and later character parts through the 1950's in hundreds of films. He died from heart failure at 91. Sec. T, tier 59, grave 135, Holy Cross Cemetery, Culver City, CA.

6618. Mulhare, Edward (April 8, 1923–May 24, 1997) Irish actor in the theatre, films and much TV (*The Ghost and Mrs. Muir* 1968–70), last seen in *Out to Sea* (1997), died in Van Nuys, California. Sent through Praisewater, Myer and Mitchell, Van Nuys, to St. Joseph Cemetery, Cork, Ireland.

6619. Mulholland, William (Sept. 11, 1855–July 22, 1935) Chief engineer of the Los Angeles water department planned and built the $24.5 million viaduct system to bring water to L.A. from the Sierras 250 miles away. Crypt 6395 (across from Lon Chaney and up), Sanctuary of Meditation, Great Mausoleum, Forest Lawn Glendale, CA.

6620. Mullaney, Jack (Sept. 18, 1929–June 27, 1982) Character actor from Pittsburgh in television dramas from the 1950's through the 70's; many roles as happy drunks, playboys, psychopaths (several *Alfred Hitchcock Presents* episodes), in films including *Seven Days in May* (1964), *Dr. Goldfoot and the Bikini Machine* (1965), etc. He died at 52. Cremated at Chapel of the Pines. Ashes to residence.

6621. Mullen, Michael Eugene (Sept. 11, 1944–Feb. 18, 1970) Sgt. E-5 killed in Vietnam by artillery fire from friendly forces. His mother's search for the facts regarding his death led to C.D.B. Bryan's book *Friendly Fire* (1976) and a subsequent TV movie. The stone reads *killed Feb 18 1970* and bears the epitaph *He*

dared to ripple my pond. Mt. Carmel Church of St. Mary Cemetery, Eagle Centre, IA.

6622. Müller, Renate (April 26, 1906–Oct. 7, 1937) Munich born stage actress in German films 1929–1937, also appeared in the English speaking *Sunshine Susie* (1931) and *Marry Me* (1932). An intimate of Adolf Hitler, she fell out of favor when it was learned in his absence she was involved with a Jewish man. Confined to a clinic, she jumped from an upper story window to her death at the approach of SS officers. It was reported as an accident and attributed to epilepsy. Hitler did not attend the cremation at Wilmersdorf; Goebbels sent a wreath. Div. 107, Parkfriedhof Lichterfelde, Thuner Platz 2–4 (Steglitz), Berlin.

6623. Mulligan, Gerry (April 6, 1927–Jan. 20, 1996) Baritone sax jazz great in the postwar era helped identify California as the area for the Cool School of jazz, recording with Thelonius Monk, Stan Getz and Ben Webster. He died at 68 in his Darien, Connecticut, home from complications following surgery. Cremated through Lawrence-Edward mortuary, the ashes were reportedly buried privately January 23. A March 1 AP story stated his wife Franca Rota planned to have the ashes blessed and made into little Buddhas to put in a shrine in her spare bedroom, to the dismay of his son, who pointed out Mulligan was Catholic, not Buddhist.

6624. Mulligan, Richard (November 13, 1932–Sept. 26, 2000) New York born actor in films from the 1960's best known for his roles on TV's *Soap* 1977–81 and *Empty Nest* 1988–1995. He died from cancer at 67 in Los Angeles. Cremated through Forest Lawn Hollywood Hills. Ashes to family.

6625. Mullins, "Moon" (Larry Mullins, June 13, 1908–Aug. 10, 1968) Pasadena born star fullback at Notre Dame 1928–1930. National champions 1929 and '30 later coached at several schools. Headstone along road on left, left of chapel. Cedar Grove Cemetery on the Notre Dame campus, South Bend, IN.

6626. Mullins, Rich (Richard Wayne Mullins. Oct. 21, 1955–Sept 19, 1997) Country-gospel singer and songwriter from the Richmond, Indiana, area, died in a highway crash while touring in Kansas. Black monument with a piano along the south (left) drive, Hollansburg Cemetery, Hollansburg, OH.

6627. Mumma, Robert E. (July 28, 1905–Jan. 31, 2003) National Cash Register engineer at Dayton, Ohio, took over the secret bomb project to develop high speed deciphering machines to crack Nazi codes for the U.S. Navy National Computing Laboratory during World War II. He died in Lebanon, Ohio, at 97. Roselawn Cemetery, Lewisburg, OH.

6628. Munch, Edvard (Dec. 23, 1863–Jan. 23, 1944) Norwegian painter, a major figure in the development of modern expressionism, best known for *The Scream* (1893). Pedestal with his bust in bronze, Var Frelsers Gravlund, Oslo, Norway.

6629. Münch, Richard (Richard Munch or

Muench, Jan. 10, 1916–June 6, 1987) German actor in Peter Lorre's *Der Verlorene* (1951, as the criminal inspector), *The Longest Day, The Train* (1964), *Patton* (as General Jodl). He died in Malaga, Spain, at 71. Friedhof Küsnacht Hinterriet, Zurich, Switzerland.

6630. Münchhausen, Karl Friedrich Hieronymous, Freiherr von (Baron) (May 11, 1790–Feb. 22, 1797) German teller of tales whose sagas of his life as an adventurer, sportsman, soldier, and hunter gained fame throughout Hanover, later collected, added to and subtracted from, published, and filmed. Der Klosterkirche, Kemnade, Kr. Holzminden, Niedersachsen, Germany.

6631. Muncrief, Bob (Robert Muncrief Jr., Jan. 28, 1916–Feb. 6, 1996) Pitcher with a career record of 80 and 82 threw in two world series games, in 1944 with St. Louis A.L. and for the 1948 Cleveland Indians, pitching 27 scoreless innings in relief to help them to the series title. Sec B (Good Shepherd), lot 216, Cedar Lawn Memorial Park, Sherman, TX.

6632. Mundin, Herbert (Aug. 21, 1897–March 4, 1939) Lancashire born actor dubbed the Twinkling Little Cockney appeared in many films of the 30's including *Cavalcade, Mutiny on the Bounty*, Barcus in *David Copperfield*, usually in timid roles. He died at 41 from injuries suffered in a car wreck at Bell, California. Charter Oak plot, lot 117, Inglewood Park Cemetery, Inglewood, CA.

6633. Mungo, Van Lingle (June 8, 1911–Feb. 12, 1985) Member of Leo Durocher's Brooklyn Dodgers of the early 1940's. First Baptist Church Cemetery, Pageland, SC.

6634. Muni, Paul (Muni Weisenfreund, Sept. 22, 1895–Aug. 25, 1967) Star of the Yiddish Theater graced films of the 1930's with memorable performances in *Scarface* (1932), *I Am a Fugitive From a Chain Gang* (1932, without the heavy make-up and accent used in other roles), *The Life of Emile Zola* (1937), *The Good Earth* (1937) and *The Story of Louis Pasteur* (1939, Academy Award). He chose his roles carefully and in later years appeared mainly on the stage, as he had in the 1920's. After a tumor was removed from his eye in the 1950's, he retired from the theatre and a successful run as Clarence Darrow. He and his wife **Bella** avoided publicity, living out their later years at Santa Barbara. Confined to bed with heart disease, his last known words were "Papa, I'm hungry," which he had said as a youth in relation to improving his craft. Sec. 14, row OO, grave 57, Hollywood Forever Cemetery, Hollywood (Los Angeles), CA.

6635. Muni, Scott (Donald Allen Munoz, May 10, 1930–Sept. 28, 2004) New Orleans raised radio disc jockey replaced Alan Freed in Akron, Ohio, before moving to New York City in 1959, with WNEW from the 1970's, and Q-104.3 FM from 1998 until his stroke in January 2004, eight months before his death at 74. St. Gertrude's Cemetery, Colonia, NJ.

6636. Munn, Frank (Feb. 27, 1894–Oct. 1, 1953) Tenor dubbed the Golden Voice of Radio, in the 1920s prior to baritone crooners, credited with 350 plus recordings. Oakwood sec. 107, Woodlawn Cemetery, the Bronx, N.Y.C.

6637. Munro, H.H. (Saki) (Hector Hugh Munro, Dec. 18, 1870–Nov. 13, 1916) Scottish writer born in Burma, India, was raised by strict aunts at Pilton near Barnstable, Devonshire, after his mother was kicked to death by a mule. His first book of short stories appeared in 1904, the pen name supposedly taken from Omar Kayyam. Among the best known of his tales was *The Open Window*. He was killed in the German assault at Beaumont-Hamel, France, while a corporal with the 22nd Royal Fusiliers. Wrote Christopher Morley "The empty glass we turn down for him is the fragile, hollow stemmed goblet meant for driest champagne. It is one of the finest." Buried near where he fell, at Beaumont-Humel, France. Memorial at Thiepval, Pas-de-Calais.

6638. Munro, Janet (Janet Neilson Horsburgh, Sept. 28, 1934–Dec. 6, 1972) Actress from Blackpool, Lancashire, in Disney films from 1959, best known in *Darby O'Gill and the Little People* and *Swiss Family Robinson*; she later appeared in *The Day the Earth Caught Fire, Life for Ruth* and *Bitter Harvest*, considered her best performance. Married to Tony Wright and later to actor Ian Hendry from 1963–1971. Her death in London at 38 was from a heart attack caused by chronic ischemic heart disease en route to the hospital, the result of choking while drinking tea. Ashes scattered at sec. 1-C, Golders Green Crematorium, north London.

6639. Munroe, Ebenezer (c.1748–May 25, 1825) Colonial combatant who claimed to have fired the first shot in defense of the Colonies against British redcoats at Lexington, Massachusetts, April 19, 1775. No other claims refuted his. The cemetery at Cambridge is named for he and his family. Obelisk, Old Cemetery, Ashburnham, MA.

6640. Munshin, Jules (Feb. 22, 1915–Feb. 19, 1970) New York born vaudeville and Broadway performer in a few Hollywood musicals, notably *Easter Parade, Take Me Out to the Ball Game*, and *On the Town* (1949), with Frank Sinatra and Gene Kelly. He died from a heart attack in New York just before his 55th birthday. Sec. 2R, grave 2635, Long Island National Cemetery, Farmingdale, Long Island, NY.

6641. Munson, Ona (June 16, 1903–Feb. 11, 1955) Stage and screen actress from Portland, Oregon, introduced *You're the Cream in My Coffee* on Broadway in *Hold Everything* (1927). Films include *Five Star Final* (1931, as Kitty Carmody), *Gone With the Wind* (1939, as Belle Watling), *The Shanghai Gesture* (1941, as Mother Gin-Sling), *The Red House*, many others. The wife of Professor Eugene Berman, she died from an overdose of sleeping pills in New York at 47. Her plaque gives her birth year as 1910; other sources list 1906. Ashes interred in Unit 8, col. G, tier Y, niche 5 (lower level), main mausoleum, Ferncliff Cemetery, Hartsdale, NY.

6642. Munson, Thurman (June 7, 1947–Aug. 2, 1979) Catcher with the New York Yankees and their captain since 1969 helped win back to back World Series championships in 1977 and '78. He died in the crash of a small plane at Canton, Ohio, at 32. His services, attended by the Yankees, were held in Canton. As with the most honored of ball players, his number 15 was retired. Atop his polished brown granite sarcophagus is his engraved image in full Yankee uniform, with the number 15 of the back of the shaft. Left of circle at bottom of hill. Sec. 1, Sunset Hills Burial Park, Canton, OH.

6643. Murdoch, Iris (Jean Iris Murdoch, July 15, 1919–Feb. 8, 1999) Irish born writer and novelist taught philosophy at Oxford 1948–1963. Her varied works include *With Sartre: Romantic Rationalist* (1953), *The Sea The Sea* (1978), *Metaphysics as a Guide to Morals* (1992) and twenty-six novels as well as plays and a volume of poetry. Made a Dame of the British Empire in 1987, she was diagnosed with Alzheimer's Disease in the 1990's, the subject of her husband John Bayley's tribute *Elegy For Iris* and the 2002 film *Iris*. Her body was donated to science at Oxford, Oxfordshire.

6644. Murger, Henri (March 27, 1822–Jan. 28, 1861) Writer whose autobiographical *Scenes de la vie de Boheme* (1845) was the basis for Puccini's *La Boheme*. He also wrote *The Latin Country* and much poetry. A marble draped maiden stands over his grave. Div. 5, Montmartre Cemetery, Paris.

6645. Murnau, F.W. (Friedrich Wilhelm Murnau, Dec. 28, 1888–March 11, 1931) Innovative German film director from Bielefeld made *Nosferatu* (1922), *The Last Laugh* (1924), *Faust* (1926) and (in Hollywood) *Sunrise* (1927) and *Tabu* (1931). He was killed in an auto accident at 42 near Santa Barbara returning to Los Angeles from Monterey. After services in Hollywood, he was returned to Germany. Monument with a bronze bust of him. Block Schöneberg, Feld 3A, Erdbergräbnis 5, Südwestfriedhof Stahnsdorf, Bahnhofstr./Rudolf Brietscheidplatz (Stahnsdorf), Berlin.

6646. Murphy, Audie (June 20, 1924–May 28, 1971) The most decorated American hero of World War II grew up in Kingston, Texas, and lied about his age to join the Army. At Holtzwihr, France, on January 26, 1945, he jumped into a burning tank destroyer and killed fifty Nazi soldiers, fighting off an attack on three sides and later forcing their retreat from the town. He was decorated by three countries and returned to the U.S. to a film career (*The Red Badge of Courage* 1951, *To Hell and Back* as himself, 1955, *No Name on the Bullet* 1959). Modest to a fault, he gave some of his medals away to children. Killed at 46 in the crash of his plane while on a business trip in the mountains of Virginia. Standard military marker, near the Amphitheatre, sec. 46, site 366–11, grid O/P – 22/23, Arlington National Cemetery, Arlington, VA

A monument to Murphy and to all who have served was dedicated May 28, 1973 in his home town, with the lines from St. John 15;13: *Greater love hath no man than that he lay down his life for his friends.* City Square, Farmersville, TX.

6647. Murphy, Charles Francis (June 20, 1858–April 25, 1924) Leader of New York's powerful Tammany Hall machine from 1902 until his death from a heart attack in 1924 was a national convention delegate in 1904, 1912, 1916 and 1920, promoted state senator and later Mayor James J. Walker, and oversaw Tammany's gradual embracing of unions during the 1909 shirtwaist workers strike, the 1911 Triangle Fire, and the gradual shift of the party to the left and the legislative reforms of the New Deal. Calvary Cemetery, Woodside, Queens, N.Y.C.

6648. Murphy, George (George Lloyd Murphy, July 4, 1902–May 3, 1992) New Haven, Connecticut, born singer, dancer and actor turned politician appeared in several musicals including *For Me and My Gal* (1942), Shirley Temple vehicles and *This is the Army* with Ronald Reagan. A head of the Screen Actors Guild, like Reagan, he switched to the Republican Party by 1949. Senator from California 1964–70. He died at 89 from leukemia in his Palm Beach, Florida, home. Mass at St. Edward's Church. Cremated by Quattlebaum mortuary in West Palm Beach, the ashes given to his widow. They were reportedly to be scattered at Bohemian Grove on the Russian River in Sonoma County, CA.

6649. Murphy, Jack (John Raymond Murphy or John Patrick Murphy, Feb. 5, 1923–Sept. 24, 1980) Sports editor and columnist for thirty years with the *San Diego Union* campaigned to bring major league ball to San Diego. The San Diego Stadium housing the Padres was subsequently named for him. Cremated September 27 at Cypress View Crematory, San Diego. Ashes scattered at sea.

6650. Murphy, Lambert (April 15, 1885–July 24, 1954) Irish tenor from Springfield, Massachusetts, recorded extensively 1911–1931 and sang four years with the Metropolitan Opera. He lost his voice to cancer many years before his death at Hancock, New Hampshire, his home for many years. Paucatuck Cemetery, West Springfield, MA.

6651. Murphy, Big Tim (Timothy D. Murphy, 1885–June 26, 1926) Chicago political figure involved in bootlegging and racketeering during the liquor wars of the 1920's, was gunned down and is buried next to his wife's other husband, "Dingbat" Oberta, who, unlike Murphy, does not have a monument. Sec. 6, Holy Sepulchre Cemetery, Worth, IL.

6652. Murphy, Turk (Melvin Edward Elton Murphy, Dec. 16, 1915–May 30, 1987) San Francisco trombone player and jazz great. A trombone is on his dark brown upright marker, and the remembrance *Little Enough*. Sec. D, div. 6, lot 488, Cypress Lawn Cemetery, Colma, CA.

6653. Murray, Arthur (Arthur Murray Teichman, April 4, 1895–March 3, 1991) Renowned dance teacher from New York City built a chain of over two hundred studios beginning during the World War I era, with many elite clients. Married from 1925 to Kathryn Kohnfeider, they resided in retirement at Rye, New York, and at Honolulu, where he died at 95. Borthwick mortuary to Hawaii Crematory. Ashes scattered at sea before the San Souci apartments off Honolulu. **Kathryn Murray** died at 92 August 6, 1999, and was also cremated and scattered at sea.

6654. Murray, Billy (May 25, 1877–Aug. 17, 1954) Popular tenor of early recordings, c. 1910–1925. He, like Henry Burr, recorded hundreds of popular tunes of the period for Columbia, Victor and other labels. He died from a heart attack suffered while on an outing at Jones Beach. Small marker inscribed only *Murray*. Sec. 19, range HH, plot 51, Holy Rood Cemetery, Old Country Road, Westbury, Long Island, NY.

6655. Murray, Charlie (June 22, 1872–July 29, 1941) Silent and talking screen comic from Laurel, Indiana, was at Biograph and Keystone with Mack Sennett, later known as Patrick Kelly in the *Cohens and the Kellys* film series 1925–1933. He died from pneumonia. Old mausoleum, crypt 2230, Inglewood Park Cemetery, Inglewood, CA.

6656. Murray, James (Feb. 9, 1901–July 10, 1936) Bronx born film actor known for the lead role in King Vidor's *The Crowd* (1928). There was irony in the role's mimicking of his real life. Afterward, due partially to alcoholism, his career declined rapidly. Walking along Pier 86 in New York City, he either jumped or fell into the Hudson River and was drowned at 35 despite rescue efforts. His name was never inscribed on his parents' monument. Christopher Murray stone, sec. 21, range 1, plot R, grave 21, (3rd) Calvary Cemetery, Woodside, Queens, N.Y.C.

6657. Murray, Jim (Dec. 29, 1919–Aug. 16, 1998) Renowned sports writer for the *Los Angeles Times* from 1961 won the Pulitzer Prize for commentary in 1990, with his insightful, sometimes warm, sometimes biting, writing in the fashion of Red Smith. Baseball Hall of Fame 1987. He was still doing three syndicated columns a week when he died at 78 from a heart attack in Brentwood, California. Sec. R, tier 30, grave 150, Holy Cross Cemetery, Culver City, CA.

6658. Murray, Ken (Don Court, July 14, 1903–Oct. 12, 1988) New York born vaudeville star later known for his 16mm home movies shown and marketed as *Ken Murray's Hollywood*. He received a special Oscar in 1947. Cremated by a Los Angeles cremation society, his ashes were scattered at sea.

6659. Murray, Mae (Marie Adrienne Koening, May 10, 1889–March 23, 1965) Blonde silent screen actress with "bee sting" lips had her finest moment in Von Stroheim's *The Merry Widow* (1925). Known at the height of her fame for her tremendous ego, her career nosedived when she left MGM in a contract dispute in 1926. She was found wondering the streets without shelter or money in St. Louis in February 1964. Returned to the Motion Picture Country Home

in Woodland Hills, California, she suffered a stroke in August and died the following spring, with the *Merry Widow Waltz* played on the organ as her coffin was borne from the church. Block G, 6328–6, Valhalla Memorial Park, North Hollywood, CA.

6660. Murray the K (Murray Kaufman, 1922–Feb. 21, 1982) WNEW New York City disc jockey tagged the Fifth Beatle after their February 1964 visit. Unmarked. Green-Kaufman lot, Westchester Hills Cemetery, Hastings-on-Hudson, NY.

6661. Murrow, Edward R. (April 25, 1908–April 27, 1965) The dean of American broadcast journalism was a World War II news correspondent who broadcast from Britain during the Blitz and flew over Germany during bombing runs. He pioneered the television news interview and developed the programs *See It Now* and *Person to Person*. He also publicly and at great risk to his career opposed the unfounded accusations leveled against government officials by grandstanding Senator Joseph McCarthy, and later narrated a series of *I Can Here It Now* historical recordings. Murrow died from cancer at 57. Cremated at Greenwood Cemetery, Brooklyn, his ashes were scattered at his home at Pawling, NY.

6662. Murtaugh, Danny (Daniel E. Murtaugh, Oct. 8, 1917–Dec. 2, 1976) Baseball player and manager from Chester, Pennsylvania, played infield for the Phillies, Braves and Pirates 1941–51 and managed the Pirates for fifteen years, taking them to the 1971 world championship. He died at Chester. Sec. 9, range 67, lot 137, SS. Peter and Paul Cemetery, Marple Township, Springfield, PA.

6663. Muse, Charlie (Charles Richard Muse, Aug. 19, 1917–May 5, 2005) Pirates executive created the modern batting helmet with inventor Ralph Davia and designer Ralph Crick, first used in 1952. Sec. 405, grave 1222, Florida National Cemetery, Bushnell, FL.

6664. Muse, Clarence (Oct. 7, 1889–Oct. 13, 1979) Black stage and screen actor from Baltimore held a law degree from Dickerson University and was a founder of Harlem's Lafayette Players prior to entering films with the advent of sound. He played many submissive blacks (*Huckleberry Finn* 1931, as Jim, *White Zombie* 1931, *The Invisible Ghost* 1941) but occasionally broke out of the typecasting. Elected to the Black Filmmakers Hall of Fame in 1973. He resided on a ranch at Perris in southeastern California until his death from a stroke just after his 90th birthday. Cremated at Harbor Lawn Memorial Park, Costa Mesa, California. The ashes were returned to a Perris mortuary for reported scattering at his ranch or at sea.

6665. Music, Lorenzo (Gerald David Music, May 2, 1937–Aug. 4, 2001) Comedy writer from Duluth, Minnesota, worked on *The Smothers Brothers Comedy Hour,* co-wrote *The Bob Newhart Show* and wrote its theme with his wife, wrote for *The Mary Tyler Moore Show* and began his audio role as Carlton the Doorman, heard weekly through the intercom, on *Rhoda* in 1974–78, with the flat, dry delivery that later became the voice of Garfield, the cartoon cat. He died from lung cancer at 64 in Los Angeles. Ashes scattered at sea August 9 through the Cremation Society of America 3 miles off Los Angeles County.

6666. Muskie, Edmund Sixtus (March 28, 1914–March 26, 1996) Democratic senator from Maine 1959–1980, resigning to become President Carter's secretary of state through January 1981. He ran unsuccessfully in the vice presidential slot on the Democratic ticket with Hubert Humphrey in 1968 and briefly in the presidential primaries in 1972, the campaign destroyed after an emotional speech in defense of his wife in Manchester, New Hampshire. He died in Washington, D.C. from a heart attack at 81. Sec. 6, site 8724-ALH, Arlington National Cemetery, Arlington, VA.

6667. Mussolini, Benito (July 29, 1883–April 28, 1945) Italian Fascist dictator in power from 1922, Il Duce later allied with Hitler and Japan to form the Axis powers opposing the Allies in World War II. With the downfall of Italy in 1943, Mussolini was arrested and imprisoned but Hitler arranged his escape and he fled to North Italy, finally to Milan. He and his mistress, Clara Petacci (b. Feb. 28, 1912), were arrested while trying to escape to Dongo. Tried by Italian partisans, they were riddled with bullets by a firing squad, their bodies beaten and urinated on, then hung upside down by their ankles on public display in a gas station lot in the Piazzale Loreto in Milan. Buried in unmarked graves in Musocco Cemetery in Milan, they were removed in 1946 by pro Fascists and interred beneath the altar of the Franciscan Monastery of the Angelicum in Padua, but the government found them and hid them in a Capuchin monastery at Cerro Maggiore, fifteen miles north of Milan. The remains were not released to his wife Donna Rachele until 1957; she placed the square zinc box the government gave her in a stone sarcophagus, a bust of him in a niche over the vault and separate from the rest of the family, at the rear of the Cemetery of San Cassiano at Predappio. Petacci was moved from Maggiore in 1956 to Cimitero Monumentale al Verano, Rome.

6668. Mussorgsky, Modest Petrovich (March 21, 1839–March 28, 1881) Russian composer whose works include the opera *Boris Godunov* (1874) and the piano suite *Pictures from An Exhibition* the same year. His death at 42 was due in part to alcoholism. Alexander Nevsky Larva, Alexander Nevsky Monastery complex, St. Petersburg.

6669. Mustin, Burt (Burton Hill Mustin, Feb. 8, 1882–Jan. 28, 1977) Endearing elderly television actor began his career at 67 after retiring from business. Among his roles was Gus the fireman on *Leave it to Beaver* in the early 60's, many other spots including *Twilight Zone* episodes (*Night of the Meek, Kick the Can*). His last regular appearance was in *Phyllis* (1976–77) before his death at 94. Loving Kindness sec., lot 7843/44, Forest Lawn Hollywood Hills, Los Angeles.

6670. Musuraca, Nicholas (Oct. 25, 1892–Sept.

3, 1975) Italian born cinematographer at RKO from the late 1920's was a pioneer and chief practitioner of *film noir* lighting and angles, notably with *Stranger on the Third Floor* (1940), *Cat People* (1942), *The Seventh Victim* (1943), *Curse of the Cat People* (1944), *The Spiral Staircase, The Locket, Bedlam* (1946), *Out of the Past* (1947), *Blue Gardenia*, many others. Mausoleum, block 37, crypt G-1, Holy Cross Cemetery, Culver City, CA.

6671. Müthel, Lothar (Lothar Lütke, Feb. 18, 1896–April 9, 1964) German actor appeared in both *Der Golem* (1920, as Florian) and Murnau's *Faust* (1926, Friar). Gruppe 33E, reihe 3, nummer 22, Zentralfriedhof (Central Cemetery), Vienna.

6672. Mutrie, James J. (June 13, 1851–Jan. 24, 1938) Smilin Jeems, manager of the New York Giants and the Metropolitans (American Association) 1883–91, though Buck Ewing led them on the field. Legend attributes to Mutrie the change in the team's nickname when he hailed them as "My big fellows! My giants!" Sec. XVII, sub B, lot 16, Moravian Cemetery, Staten Island, N.Y.C.

6673. Myers, Carmel (April 4, 1900/1901–Nov. 9, 1980) Silent screen actress in *Intolerance* (1916), *Beau Brummel* (1924), *Ben Hur* (1926), *Tell it to the Marines* (1926). Talkies include *Svengali* and *The Mad Genius*, both 1931, with John Barrymore. She died at 80 from a heart attack. She had requested her ashes be strewn through the rose garden at Pickfair in Beverly Hills but was buried beneath a plaque inscribed *L'chaim*. Half block plot 3, row 3, grave 3, Home of Peace Memorial Park, east Los Angeles.

6674. Myers, James (James E. Myers, Oct. 26, 1919–May 9, 2001) Bit actor in over forty films co-wrote with Max Freedman, the song *Rock Around the Clock* (1954), recorded by Bill Haley and the Comets and used in the film *The Blackboard Jungle*, bringing rock and roll to mainstream white audiences with long lasting results. Sec. K, range 4, lot 47, Holy Sepulchre Cemetery, Philadelphia, PA.

6675. Nachman, Jerry (Jerome Nachman, 1946–Jan. 19, 2004) Newsman from Red Hook, Brooklyn, raised in Pittsburgh, known for his anecdotes and old style "Walter Burns" persona, edited the *New York Post*, reported for and later helmed WCBS there, was GM at WRC radio in Washington, and eventually editor-in-chief at MSNBC, last seen reporting on the Michael Jackson case in Santa Barbara. He died at home in Hoboken, New Jersey, at 57, a year after cancer was found during a gall bladder operation. Service January 29 at the Riverside Chapel, Manhattan. Sent to Pittsburgh, PA.

6676. Nader, George (Oct. 19, 1921–Feb. 4, 2002) Pasadena born actor in leads through the 1950's including *Robot Monster, Six Bridges to Cross, Lady Godiva, Sins of Jezebel*. He later appeared on TV and authored the novel *Chrome* in 1978. A close friend of Rock Hudson and one of few privy to Hudson's last illness, Nader died from pneumonia at 80 in the Motion Picture Country Home in Woodland Hills. Ashes scattered at sea.

6677. Nagel, Anne (Anne Dolan, Sept. 29, 1915–July 6, 1966) Boston born actress (several sources list her birth as Sept. 30, 1912) married briefly to actor Ross Alexander until his suicide in 1937 was featured in B films of the late 1930's and early 1940's at Universal including *Black Friday, Man Made Monster, The Secret Code* and as Madame Gorgeous in *Never Give a Sucker an Even Break* (1941). Her last marriage (1941–1957) was to James H. Keenan. She died following surgery for cancer of the liver at 50 (or 53), survived by a brother in Fresno. Unmarked, along road behind Clara Angel (marked). Sec. T, tier 31, grave 183, Holy Cross Cemetery, Culver City, CA.

6678. Nagel, Conrad (March 16, 1897–Feb. 24, 1970) Leading man from Keokuk, Iowa, in usually forthright roles in films of the 1920's and 30's. He was found dead in his home in the Park Vendome at 340 West 57th in Manhattan. Cremated at Garden State Crematory in North Bergen, New Jersey. Ashes to family.

6679. Nagurski, Bronko (Bronislau Nagurski, Nov. 4, 1908–Jan. 7, 1990) Fullback and tackle at the University of Minnesota 1927–29, fullback and linebacker for the Chicago Bears 1930–37. College and Pro Football Hall of Fame 1963. St. Thomas Cemetery, International Falls, MN.

6680. Naish, J. Carrol (Joseph Patrick Carrol Naish, Jan. 21, 1896–Jan. 24, 1973) New York born character actor of Irish ancestry specialized in playing Indians, Mexicans, Italians, East Indians, and all variety of ethnic types (except Irish) in over two hundred films 1930–1971 (*The Hatchet Man, Two Seconds, Tiger Shark, The Lives of A Bengal Lancer, Captain Blood, Charlie Chan at the Circus, The Return of Jimmy Valentine, The Charge of the Light Brigade, Night Club Scandal, Beau Geste, Jackass Mail, Dr. Renault's Secret, Sahara, Calling Dr. Death, The Whistler, The Monster Maker, Jungle Woman, Dragon Seed, House of Frankenstein, Strange Confession, Bad Bascomb, Humoresque, The Beast With Five Fingers, The Fugitive, Joan of Arc, Black Hand, New York Confidential*). He was nominated for an Oscar as the father in *A Medal for Benny* (1945). TV series *Life With Luigi* (1952), *Guestward Ho* (160). In ill health for some time, he died from a heart attack at 77 (or 76) in Scripps Memorial Hospital, La Jolla, California. Lot marked after his wife's death in 1987. Corner of sec. G, lot 1098, grave 22, Calvary Cemetery, east Los Angeles.

6681. Naismith, James (Nov. 6, 1861–Nov. 28, 1939) The inventor of the game of basketball, first devised in 1891 at the YMCA in Springfield, Massachusetts, was later athletic director of the University of Kansas. He died in Lawrence and was buried there. In 1993–4 a 10' statue of him and memorial was erected near the cemetery entrance. Flush red plaque. Acacia A, Masonic Gardens, Lawrence Memorial Park Cemetery, Lawrence, KS.

6682. Nalder, Reggie (Alfred Reginald Natzler, Sept. 4, 1922–Nov. 19, 1991) Actor played, among other things, the assassin in *The Man Who Knew Too Much* (1956), a Chinese communist in *The Manchurian Candidate* (1962) and the vampire Barlow in the 1979 TV movie version of Stephen King's *Salem's Lot*. He died in Santa Monica from cancer, listed as 80, making his birth year 1911. The cemetery records give the 1922 date. Unmarked with his mother Ida Natzler (marked), sec. D, lot 113, grave 9, Holy Cross Cemetery, Culver City, CA.

6683. Naldi, Nita (Anita Donna Dooley, April 1, 1897–Feb. 17, 1961) New York dancer-actress spotted by John Barrymore at the Winter Garden became Nita Naldi, the name borrowed from a friend named Rinaldi, and was publicized as of royal Italian blood. Films include *Dr. Jekyll and Mr. Hyde* (1920, with Barrymore) and *Blood and Sand* (1922, with Valentino). In later years she lived at the Wentworth Hotel at 59 West 46th St., Manhattan. Her death in her room was ruled the result of a heart attack, listed as 61. Buried in the Dooley plot, the family stone topped by a relief of Christ. On October 23, 1970, a relative had her real name on the stone replaced by her screen name. Sec. 1W-5AA-13/14, (1st) Calvary Cemetery, Woodside, Queens, N.Y.C.

6684. Nalon, Duke (Dennis Nalon, March 2, 1913–Feb. 26, 2001) Sixteen time Indianapolis 500 veteran won the pole position in 1949 and 1951. His best finish was third in 1948; the next year he survived a fiery crash from a broken rear axle while he led early in the race, and placed in the top ten in 1951. Court of the Living Bible Mausoleum, exterior — west side, Washington Park North Cemetery, Indianapolis, IN.

6685. Nance, Jack (Marvin John Nance, Dec. 21, 1943–Dec. 30, 1996) Star of David Lynch's *Eraserhead* (1978) also appeared in *Blue Velvet, The Hot Spot, Wild At Heart*, TV's *Twin Peaks*, etc. He died in South Pasadena at 53 from a blow to the head after an argument at a doughnut shop. Ashes scattered at sea through the Neptune Society of Orange County January 16, 1997 off Newport Beach, CA.

6686. Napier, Alan (Alan Napier-Calvering, Jan. 7, 1903–Aug. 8, 1988) Tall, mustached English character actor in many films in England and America from the late 30's (*The Invisible Man Returns* 1940, *The Uninvited* 1944, *House of Horrors* 1946, *Julius Caesar* 1953, etc.), and later as Alfred the butler on the TV's *Batman* 1965–67. With a wealth of knowledge on old Hollywood, he lived to 85 in the Pacific Palisades overlooking the ocean. Services through Pierce Bros. Westwood mortuary, west Los Angeles. Ashes returned to family.

6687. Napoleon (Napoleon Bonaparte, Aug. 15, 1769–May 5, 1821) Emperor of France 1805–1814. One of history's great conquerors, the 5'2" Corsican was defeated at Waterloo and exiled to the island of St. Helena in the south Atlantic. He had been ill with tuberculosis and may have contracted hepatitis on the island. Though there was evidence he was given poison in the various measures used to treat him, the cause of his death was most likely a cancerous perforated stomach ulcer with amebic dysentery. The body was placed in four coffins (tin, mahogany, lead and another of mahogany) and buried in a favorite spot beside a stream on the island of Elba. Exhumed in 1840, the coffin was brought to Paris and placed in Les Invalides in a polished wooden sarcophagus, 43' × 21' × 48' high, designed by Louis Visconti. On the lintel is the inscription *Let me be buried on the banks of the Seine, near the people whom I loved so much.* Near by are his brothers **Joseph** and **Jerome** and his only legitimate son **Napoleon II.** (Francis Charles Bonaparte, March 20, 1811–July 22, 1832) The son was taken to Austria by his mother Maria Louise after Napoleon's exile. He died at 21 and was buried in Austria. The Germans returned the body to Les Invalides in 1940 and placed it at the foot of the emperor's tomb. **Josephine** (June 23, 1763–May 29, 1814), formerly Viscountess Alexandre Beauharnais, whose husband was guillotined after the fall of Robespierre, married Napoleon in a civil ceremony in 1796 and a church ceremony in 1808 at the insistence of the Pope. She had two children by Alexandre but was unable to bear more, leading to Napoleon's divorcing her in 1809 to sire an heir of his own. She died of a gangrenous sore throat and pneumonia. Her tomb is in the church at Rueil Malmaison, Paris. *See also* **Bonaparte.**

6688. Napoleon III (Louis Napoleon) (April 20, 1808–Jan. 9, 1873) Son of Josephine and Alexandre's daughter Hortense and Louis Bonaparte, King of Holland, returned to France in 1848 upon the abdication of Louis Phillipe and restored the Republic to an Empire. He fought several wars, including the overthrow of Maximilian in Mexico, but met defeat after the Franco-Prussian War in 1870 and left France. He died at Chiselhurst, England, in exile. Buried in the Abbey Church of St. Michael, Farnborough, Hampshire.

6689. Napoli, James "Jimmy Nap" (Nov. 4, 1911–Dec. 29, 1992) Chieftain in the Genovese crime family controlled the gambling industry. Monument topped by a statue of the Virgin Mary. St. John's Cemetery, Middle Village, Queens, N.Y.C.

6690. Nash, Charles Williams (Jan. 28, 1864–June 6, 1948) Automobile executive and designer headed Nash and Nash-Kelvinator as well as Buick and General Motors for a time. Sarcophagus, Sanctuary of Courage, Holly Terrace, Great Mausoleum, Forest Lawn Glendale, CA.

6691. Nash, Clarence "Ducky" (Dec. 7, 1904–Feb. 20, 1985) The voice of Donald Duck from his creation at Disney in 1934. His marker has Donald and Daisy, encircled by a heart. Sec. F, tier 47, grave 25, San Fernando Mission Cemetery, Mission Hills, CA.

6692. Nash, Frank (Feb. 6, 1887–June 17, 1933) Twice pardoned, once for murder and once for burglary, Nash was serving a twenty five year sentence for assaulting a U.S. mail custodian when he escaped from Leavenworth October 19, 1930 and stayed free until captured in Hot Springs, Arkansas, June 16, 1933. Taken by train to Kansas City, he had been transferred to a car when gunfire erupted and killed FBI Agent Raymond Caffrey, McAlester, Oklahoma, police chief Otto Reed, Kansas City detectives William Grooms and Frank Hermanson, and Nash. Known as the Kansas City Massacre, it was blamed on Vernon C. Miller — found mutilated in a ditch near Detroit November 29, Pretty Boy Floyd — killed in Ohio in October, and Adam Richetti, executed in the Missouri gas chamber October 7, 1938. Nash was buried at Linwood Cemetery, Paragould, AR.

6693. Nash, Mary (Mary Ryan, Aug. 15, 1885–Dec. 3, 1976) Character actress from Troy, New York, in many films (the evil governess in *Heidi* 1937, also in *Come and Get It, The Little Princess, The Human Comedy*). Divorced from Jose Rubin. Private mausoleum section, St. Agnes Cemetery, Cohoes (north of Albany), NY.

6694. Nash, Ogden (Frederic Ogden Nash, Aug. 19, 1902–May 19, 1971) Master of humorous poetry, often using animal and human behavior and its ironies as his theme. Little River Cemetery, North Hampton, NH.

6695. Nasiff, Hank, Jr. (April 20, 1962–Sept. 4, 2001) Hank The Angry Drunken Dwarf, popular from the late 1990's through the Howard Stern program and with selected appearances and writings. He died, apparently related to alcohol abuse, at 39. Buried with a can of Budweiser in a child size coffin. Des Jardins lot, sec. 5-B, Notre Dame Cemetery, Fall River, MA.

6696. Nassar, William K. (1933–Sept. 2, 2005) Cardiologist son of a Syrian father and graduate of Indiana University Medical School, himself a heart patient from 1961, in 1973 began a cardiology program — Nassar, Pinkerton and Smith — at St. Vincent's Hospital, Indianapolis, that pioneered a networking system for advanced heart research and care in the state of Indiana and beyond. He died from heart failure at 72 in his Carmel, Indiana, home. Roselawn Memorial Park, Terre Haute, IN.

6697. Nasser, Gamal Abdel (Jan. 15, 1918–Sept. 28, 1970) Egyptian president from 1952 drove European colonialism out of the country; seen as an aggressive nationalist by many, he nationalized the Suez Canal and precipitated the 1956 crisis, united for a time with Syria, relied heavily on alliances with Soviet Russia, and went to war with Israel in 1967. He died from a heart attack at 52. His tomb was designed and built by Hassan Fathy. Nassar mausoleum, Cairo, Egypt.

6698. Nast, Conde (March 26, 1873–Sept. 19, 1942) New York born publisher of *Vanity Fair* and *Vogue*, founded in 1909, several others. Monument and plaque right of Billy Martin, facing the road behind. Sec. 25, lot 23, Gate of Heaven Cemetery, Hawthorne, NY.

6699. Nast, Thomas (Sept. 27, 1840–Dec. 7, 1902) Victorian era illustrator known for his Santa Claus (the lasting image) and political cartoons for both *Frank Leslie's Illustrated* and *Harper's Weekly*. He died at Guayaquil, Ecuador, and was buried there until his reinterment in New York January 30, 1906. Epitaph reads *He who practices his teaching is crucified*. Birch Hill sec. 77/78, lot 11322, along path, Woodlawn Cemetery, the Bronx, N.Y.C.

6700. Nathan, George Jean (Feb. 14, 1882–April 8, 1958) Journalist, theatre critic and historian co-founded the *American Mercury* with H.L. Mencken in 1914. Monument with Julie Haydon, with a tall cross and a bench on either side. Sec. 14, lot 58, Gate of Heaven Cemetery, Hawthorne, NY.

6701. Nathan, Robert (Jan. 2, 1894–May 25, 1985) New York born poet and novelist, author of *Portrait of Jennie* (1939, filmed in 1948). Married to actress Anna Lee, his seventh wife, he died at 91 in Los Angeles. Epitaph *Beauty is only altered, never lost*. After Lee's death in 2004, her ashes were buried at sea, and Nathan's plaque was replaced by a base joining their twin plaques, without his epitaph, but with their names, dates, and *Forever together* at the bottom. Sec. D, urn garden (sw), Westwood Memorial Park, west Los Angeles.

6702. Nathan, Syd (April 27, 1904–March 5, 1968) Founder of King Records in the 1940's recorded many country and rhythm and blues artists for twenty years. Twenty yards inside circle from half way around the drive on the right. Judah Touro Cemetery, 1675 Sunset, Price Hill area, Cincinnati, OH.

6703. Nation, Carrie (Nov. 25, 1846–June 9, 1911) Temperance leader from 1890–1911, the former wife of an alcoholic took to roaming dry Kansas busting up saloons with her hatchet. Her stone, erected in 1923, has the epitaph *Faithful to her cause, she hath done what she could*. Belton Cemetery, Belton, MO.

6704. Natwick, Mildred (June 19, 1905–Oct. 25, 1994) Baltimore born actress in whimsical, eccentric and perky characters on stage and in many films including *The Enchanted Cottage* (1945), *The Late George Apley* (1947), *Three Godfathers, She Wore a Yellow Ribbon* (1949), *The Quiet Man* (1952), *The Trouble With Harry, Barefoot in the Park* (AA nom., 1967). She died in her Manhattan home at 89. Service through Frank E. Campbell. Exterior crypt, Lorraine Park Cemetery, Woodlawn (western Baltimore), MD.

6705. Natwick, Myron (Aug. 16, 1890–Oct. 7, 1990) Cartoonist behind *Betty Boop* and several other works, died on his 100th birthday. Block 91, lot 4, space 5, Forest Hill Cemetery, Wisconsin Rapids, WI.

6706. Navarro, David, Jr. (June 22, 1861–March 7, 1882) Illinois Giant Boy traveled with P.T. Barnum until his death at twenty. Sec. S, div. 1, lot 26, range 8, Uniondale Cemetery, Pittsburgh, PA.

6707. Navin, Frank (April 22, 1871–Nov. 13, 1935) Founder of the organization and Navin Field that became Briggs and finally Tiger Stadium in Detroit. Two bronze tigers guard his mausoleum. Sec. 22, lot 1, Holy Sepulchre Cemetery, Southfield, MI.

6708. Nazimova, Alla (May 22 or June 4, 1879–July 13, 1945) Yalta born actress of the Russian and American stage and silent films. She was in America from 1905 on stage, in films 1916–1925 and again in character roles in the early 40's (*Escape, Since You Went Away*). Known for her intense portrayals, she had a large following, particularly with female actresses, and was also the aunt of RKO producer Val Lewton. Upon her death from a heart attack at 66, she was cremated and her ashes buried beneath a plaque inscribed *Voice of the world's conscience — Immaculate beyond our concept — Christ is Thy name. Teach us to shun the ways of greed and prejudice and strife; to earn our bread, to share our bread, to heed, to follow Thee forever. Amen. A.N.* Whispering Pines, lot 1689, Forest Lawn, Glendale, CA.

6709. Neagle, Anna (Marjorie Robertson, Oct. 20, 1904–June 3, 1986) Leading London born stage actress at her peak in the 1930's, married to producer-director **Herbert Wilcox** (April 19, 1892–May 15, 1977). She made many films 1930–60 while continuing her stage career. Named Dame Commander of the British Empire 1969. Buried with her husband and parents. City of London Cemetery, London.

6710. Neal, Charlie (Jan. 30, 1931–Nov. 16, 1996) Baseball player of the 1950's and 60's, with the Mets, etc. Black monument with gold lettering. Grace Hill Cemetery, Longview, TX.

6711. Neal, Tom (Jan. 28, 1914–Aug. 7, 1972) Former athlete, actor and sometime lead in B films of the 1940's and 50's (*Another Thin Man, Bowery at Midnight*, particularly *Detour* 1945), made headlines for injuring actor Franchot Tone in a 1951 fist fight over actress Barbara Payton. He faded from films afterward, and in 1965 was convicted of involuntary manslaughter in the death of his third wife Gail, served six years of a one-to-fifteen year sentence, and died from a heart ailment less than a year after he left prison. Cremated by Pierce Bros. Chapel of the Pines Crematory, Los Angeles. Ashes scattered at sea.

6712. Neff, Hildegarde—*see* **Hildegard Kneff.**

6713. Negri, Pola (Apolonia Chalupec, Dec. 31, 1894–Aug. 1, 1987) Polish born star of the German cinema, promoted by director Ernst Lubitsch, came to Hollywood in 1923 as a vamp of the Theda Bara, Nita Naldi variety. Her histrionics at Valentino's funeral caused much amusement and by some accounts exceeded most of her screen performances. She returned to Germany in the 1930's but came back to America with the outbreak of World War II. Married to Prince David Mdvhani, who died in 1984, she retired to San Antonio, Texas, where she died in Northeast Baptist Hospital of a brain tumor complicated by pneumonia at 92 (or 87, as her crypt lists her birth as 1899). Block

56, crypt E-19, Calvary Cemetery mausoleum, east Los Angeles.

6714. Negulesco, Jean (Feb. 26, 1900–July 18, 1993) Rumanian born film director came to New York in 1927 and began directing in the early 30's. Best known for his melodramas at Warner Brothers in the 1940's (*The Mask of Dimitrios, The Conspirators, Three Strangers, Humoresque*), he also directed *Johnny Belinda* (1948), *How to Marry a Millionaire* (1953), *Three Coins in the Fountain* (1954). He died at 93 in Marbella, Spain, where he had lived since the late 60's. Town cemetery, Marbella, Spain.

6715. Nehru, Jawaharial (Nov. 14, 1889–May 27, 1964) The first prime minister of an independent India had suffered several strokes prior to his death from a ruptured aorta. His body was taken from the palace in Delhi to the bank of the River Yamuna, near where Gandhi had been cremated. Nehru's grandson lit the funeral pyre while Hindu and Buddhist priests chanted. On June 9, as he had requested, a portion of his ashes were scattered into the River Ganges and the rest over the fields of India.

6716. Neilan, Mickey (Marshall Ambrose Neilan, April 11, 1891–Oct. 26, 1958) Actor-director of Irish ancestry began as an actor in 1911, appeared in several films with Mary Pickford at Selig 1915–16, then turned to directing, including many Pickford vehicles such as *Daddy Long Legs*. His career faded with the 1930's and increased alcoholism. He last worked as an actor in Elia Kazan's *A Face in the Crowd* (1957). Neilan kept in touch with Pickford as well as a regular array of cronies; she made a rare appearance at his funeral in 1958. Marker inscribed only with his initials. Sec. K, lot 35 3SW, Rosedale Cemetery, Los Angeles.

6717. Neiman, Carrie Marcus (May 5, 1883–March 6, 1953) and **A. L. Neiman** with **Herbert Marcus** (Sept. 6, 1878–Dec. 11, 1950) founded the Neiman-Marcus retail stores. Neiman is buried in plot 108, Emmanuel Hebrew Cemetery, Dallas, Texas. Marcus's crypt is in Kings SW D-22-A, Sparkman-Hillcrest Memorial Park mausoleum, Dallas, TX.

6718. Nelson, Baby Face *see* **George "Baby Face" Nelson.**

6719. Nelson, Frank (May 6, 1911–Sept. 12, 1986) Comedic actor on Jack Benny's radio and television shows whose trademark response was a deep, extended "yessssssss" was also a frequent face in a variety of characters (Freddy Fillmore, etc.) on *I Love Lucy*. As President of the American Federation of TV and Radio Artists 1954–57, he established a pension and welfare plan for freelance performers. He died in Hollywood at 75. Columbarium of Heavenly Peace, niche G762, off the Garden of Honor at the end of the Court of Freedom, Forest Lawn, Glendale, CA.

6720. Nelson, Gaylord (June 4, 1916–June 3, 2005) Democratic governor (1959–63) and senator (1963–71) from Wisconsin, a staunch conservationist, started Earth Day in 1970, still observed each April 22. Medal of Freedom 1995. He died in Kensington,

Maryland, at 89. Ashes buried with his parents at a stone he purchased years before his death. Clear Lake Cemetery, Clear Lake, WI.

6721. Nelson, George "Baby Face" (Lester Gillis, Dec. 6, 1908–Nov. 27, 1934) Chicago born bank robber worked with the John Dillinger gang, known for his 5'4" stature and his quick temper. He survived both Dillinger and Homer Van Meter by only months. Having robbed and shot his way across Illinois, Indiana, Iowa, and Wisconsin, he killed two FBI agents and was shot and killed in a gun battle with them at Fox River Grove, Illinois. Buried under his real name Dec. 1, 1934. Sec. C, lot 18, block 8, St. Joseph Cemetery, River Grove (Chicago suburb), IL.

6722. Nelson, Ham (Harmon Oscar Nelson, July 5, 1907–Sept. 28, 1975) Musician, later talent agent, was the high school sweetheart and first husband, in the 1930's, of Bette Davis. He died at 68 from pneumonia and traumatic encephalopathy after a fall from a ladder July 4, 1971. Cremated at Rosedale Cemetery through Pierce Bros. Westwood, Los Angeles. Ashes released to Westwood and to his wife to be spread at Bald Mountain near Palm Desert, CA.

6723. Nelson, Harriet (Harriet Snyder, July 18, 1909–Oct. 2, 1994) Des Moines born vocalist Harriet Hilliard married her bandleader Ozzie Nelson in 1935. After appearing on Red Skelton's radio show in the early 40's, they began *The Adventures of Ozzie and Harriet* on radio in 1944, soon joined by their sons David and Ricky, mainstays of the program by the time they moved to TV 1952–1966. Like *Leave it to Beaver, Father Knows Best* and *The Donna Reed Show*, the Nelsons came to symbolize the laid back, problem free families of early TV. Harriet Nelson died at 85 from congestive heart failure in her Laguna Beach, California, home. Ashes buried next to Ozzie and near Rick. Revelation sec., lot 3540, Forest Lawn Hollywood Hills, Los Angeles.

6724. Nelson, Horatio (Sept. 29, 1758–Oct. 21, 1805) British admiral shot at the Battle of Trafalgar asked that his hair be removed and given to his wife, Lady Hamilton, and that he not be thrown overboard. His body was placed in a cask filled with brandy and preserved until his ship *The Victory* reached England in December. It was interred in a black marble sarcophagus surrounded by a viscount coronet and his name and dates beneath the cupola of St. Paul's Cathedral, London.

6725. Nelson, Lindsey (May 25, 1919–June 10, 1995) Hall of Fame baseball and football sportscaster from Columbia, Tenn. With NBC 1952–62, college football on CBS 1962–66 and the NFL there from 1966, as well as the voice of Notre Dame football and the New York Mets 1962–1979. Baseball Hall of Fame 1986. He resided at Knoxville, Tennessee but died in Atlanta at 76. Everlasting Life 83D, Polk Memorial Gardens, Columbia, TN.

6726. Nelson, Nathaniel (April 10, 1932–June 1, 1984) Lead singer with the Flamingos, late 50's vocal group best known for their improbable arrangement of *I Only Have Eyes For You*. Flush military plaque. Southborough Cemetery, Southborough, MA.

6727. Nelson, Ozzie (Oswald George Nelson, March 20, 1906–June 3, 1975) Bandleader and former Rutgers All American married his vocalist Harriet Hilliard in 1935. With their sons David and Ricky, they starred on radio in *The Adventures of Ozzie and Harriet*, moving to TV from 1952–66. Easily TV's most laid back husband and father, Ozzie's job in the show, though unofficially a bandleader, was never specified. He died from colon cancer at 69. Typically mellow, he had commented that that was odd for a non drinker or smoker. Cremated at Forest Lawn. Ashes buried Revelation, lot 3540, Forest Lawn Hollywood Hills, Los Angeles.

6728. Nelson, Richard H. (April 26, 1925–Feb. 1, 2003) Youngest member of the twelve man crew of the B-29 *Enola Gay* crew that dropped the bomb on Hiroshima. His brief report back "Results excellent" was radioed to Allied Headquarters. Cenotaph at sec. MA, grave 172-A, Riverside National Cemetery, Riverside, California. Ashes scattered at sea.

6729. Nelson, Rick (Eric Hilliard Nelson, May 8, 1940–Dec. 31, 1985) Younger son of Ozzie and Harriet had a second career as a rock 'n' roll singer 1958–1964, with soft voiced renditions of *Hello Mary Lou, Travelin' Man* (both 1961), many others. He made a successful comeback in 1972 with *Garden Party* and subsequent touring with his folk-country-rock Stone Canyon Band. He, his fiancée and members of the band died on New Year's Eve 1985 when their plane crashed near DeKalb, Texas. Cremated January 4 at Martin Oaks Crematory in Lewisville, Texas, his ashes — initially missent — were buried near his parents. Revelation sec., lot 3538, Forest Lawn Hollywood Hills, Los Angeles.

6730. Nelson, Thomas, Jr. (Dec. 16, 1738–Jan. 2, 1789) Revolutionary War leader, signer of the Declaration of Independence and military commander in Virginia. The slab over his grave is inscribed *Patriot. Soldier. Christian Gentleman. Mover of the Resolution of May 15 1776 in the Virginia Convention instructing her delegates in congress to declare the colonies free and independent states. Signer of the Declaration of Independence. War Governor of Virginia. Commander of Virginia's forces. He gave all for liberty.* Grace Churchyard, Yorktown, VA.

6731. Nero (Dec. 15, 37 A.D.–c. June 9, 68 A.D.) Roman emperor known for fiddling while Rome burned and feeding Christians to the lions in the arena for sport. The Romans rebelled and were coming to torture and kill him, so he had his own grave dug and (with help) stabbed himself in the throat. His ashes were put in an urn and placed in the Domitian burial chamber beneath the Pincian Hall, where the Church of Santa Maria del Popolo now stands in Rome.

6732. "Nervous Norvus" (James William Drake, May 13, 1912–July 24, 1968) Truck driver from Oakland had a hit in 1956 with the novelty evergreen *Transfusion*. Slip the blood to me, Bud. He died at 56 from a liver ailment in Fairmont Hospital, San Leandro, Alameda County, California. Body donated to the Anatomy Dept. of the University of California.

6733. Nesbit, Evelyn (Dec. 25, 1884–Jan. 17, 1967) Beauty of the 1900–1910 era known as The Girl in the Red Velvet Swing because of architect Stanford White's fondness for having her swing across his suite; she later appeared in a nightclub act with the same prop. Her jealous husband Harry K. Thaw, a Pittsburgh socialite, shot and killed White during a rooftop dinner above Madison Square Garden in June 1906. Her story was loosely told in several films, including *The Girl in the Red Velvet Swing* and *Ragtime* (1981). She died at 82 in Santa Monica. Sec. M, lot 232, grave 2, Holy Cross Cemetery, Culver City, CA.

6734. Nesmith, Ottola (Ottola D'Usseau, Dec. 12, 1889–Feb. 7, 1972) Actress from Washington, D.C. in many bit, often uncredited roles, sometimes billed as Tola Nesmith, in films 1915–1965, including *Becky Sharp* (Lady Jane Crawley), *Anthony Adverse* (Sister Ursula), *Fools for Scandal* (Agnes), *Lillian Russell* (Miss Smyth), *Blossoms in the Dust* (governess), *The Wolf-man* (Mrs. Balley), *The Invisible Ghost* (Mrs. Mason), *The Seventh Victim, The Leopard Man* (Mrs. Lowood), *Return of the Vampire* (governess), *The Uninvited* (Mrs. Carlton), *The Notorious Landlady* (flower lady), many others. Later a Los Angeles area TV horror film host, she was sued by Mae Clarke for impersonating her during a showing of *Frankenstein*. Ashes buried without record/unidentifiable space, Westwood Memorial Park, Los Angeles.

6735. Ness, Eliot (April 19, 1903–May 16, 1957) Federal agent headed the so-called Untouchables in Chicago 1929–1932 that brought about Al Capone's conviction on income tax evasion. Their work was the basis for the Desilu TV series and the 1987 film *The Untouchables*. From Chicago Ness went to Cleveland as the director of public safety but was unsuccessful in solving the torso killings there. He had lived in Coudersport, Pennsylvania, only a year when he died from a heart attack at 54. A memorial service was held at the Presbyterian Church of the Covenant in Cleveland, where his wife returned to live. Cremated at Forest Lawn Cemetery, Buffalo, New York, the ashes were sent to his lawyer's office in Cleveland. Along with those of his (third) wife and son, they were dispersed September 10, 1997 over the lagoon beside Wade Chapel and a cenotaph, a boulder with a plaque, dedicated there to all three in sec. 5. By June 2001 it had been moved up and across the road to sec. 7 along the road, facing the intersection of Lake and Edgehill Roads, Lakeview Cemetery, Cleveland, OH.

6736. Neumann, Dorothy (Jan. 26, 1914–May 20, 1994) Gaunt New York born actress with pinched features played numerous spinsters, busybodies, maids, in films (*The Snake Pit, The Blackboard Jungle,*

The Ghost of Dragstrip Hollow, The Terror) as well as Mrs. Otis Campbell on *The Andy Griffith Show*. Never married. She died from pneumonia at 80 in Santa Monica, California. Cremated by Pierce Bros. Westwood, Los Angeles. Ashes June 1 to her niece in Encinitas, CA.

6737. Neumann, Kurt (April 5, 1898–Aug. 21, 1958) Director from Nuremburg, Germany, in Hollywood from the early 30's did several atmospheric, above average B films (*Secret of the Blue Room, The Unknown Guest, The Fly* and several other science fiction and Tarzan films). He died suddenly at 60. Crypt in Corridor of Eternal Life, E115A, Home of Peace Memorial Park mausoleum, east Los Angeles.

6738. Nevins, Allan (May 20, 1890–March 5, 1971) Pulitzer Prize winning historian was awarded the honor for his 1932 biography of Grover Cleveland (*A Study in Courage*) and of Hamilton Fish (1936). He also wrote the multi volume *Ordeal of the Union* 1947–1960, and edited the diaries of John Quincy Adams (1928) and James Knox Polk (1929). For many years he was professor of history at Columbia University. Garden of the Apostles, lot 124, grave 2, Kensico Cemetery, Valhalla, NY.

6739. New Jersey 1916 Shark Attack (victims) A severe and outstanding case of a rogue shark seeking out bathers and swimmers and killing them, such as depicted in the 1975 film *Jaws*, actually occurred only once in recorded U.S. history: along the eastern coast of New Jersey and up Matawan Creek in July 1916. On July 1, **Charles Vansant** (born 1892) was bitten to death at Beach Haven, about twenty miles north of Atlantic City. Burial was listed at South Laurel Hill Cemetery, 3822 Ridge Ave., Philadelphia (actually sec. 10, lot 151, Laurel Hill Cemetery). On July 6, **Charles Bruder**, with both legs bitten off, was killed by a shark a short distance in front of the Essex and Sussex Hotel at Spring Lake. Atlantic View Cemetery, Manasquan (south of Spring Lake), New Jersey. The third and most infamous attack came on July 12; a shark, believed to be a tiger, had moved inland up Matawan Creek to the Matawan, where it attacked and killed 12 year old **Lester Stillwell**. In a heroic attempt to retrieve the boys' body, **Stanley Fisher**, 24, was also attacked, badly bitten and died from his injuries that day. Stillwell's remains were recovered July 14, and both he and Fisher were buried the same day: Stillwell in sec. L, lots 25 & 26, stone 3; Fisher in sec. H, lot 54, Rose Hill Cemetery, Matawan, NJ.

6740. Newbury, Mickey (Milton S. Newbury, May 19, 1940–Sept. 29, 2002) Houston born singer and songwriter blended country, r&b, pop and rock, with numbers recorded across the spectrum of type. In 1966–67 he had a top selling hit in four categories: *Sweet Memories* (Andy Williams, easy listening), *Here Comes the Rain* (Eddy Arnold, country-western), *Time is A Thief* (Solomon Burke, rhythm and blues), and *Just Dropped In* (Kenny Rogers and the First Edition,

pop-rock). Others include *Funny Familiar Forgotten Feelings* (Tom Jones), *American Trilogy* (1971), *You've Always Got the Blues, San Francisco Mabel Joy*, many more. Greenwood Cemetery, Leaburg, OR.

6741. Newell, Marjorie *see* **Titanic.**

6742. Newhouser, Hal (Harold Newhouser, May, 20, 1921–Nov. 10, 1998) Prince Hal, pitcher with the Detroit Tigers 1939–53, won the AL MVP in 1944 and 1945, when he led their World Series win over the Cubs. Hall of Fame 1992; the only Detroit born Tiger elected. The Tigers retired his number, 16, in 1997. Masonic Garden, lot 195A, grave 3, Oakland Hills Memorial Gardens, West 12 Mile Road, Novi (north of Detroit), MI.

6743. Newley, Anthony (Sept. 24, 1931–April 14, 1999) London born singer-composer-actor in films from *Oliver Twist* (1947, as the Artful Dodger), wrote, composed and directed *Stop the World—I Want to Get Off* (featuring *What Kind of Fool Am I?*) for the London stage and Broadway, co-wrote the title song for *Goldfinger* (1965), scored *Willy Wonka and the Chocolate Factory* (featuring *The Candy Man* 1971), appeared in films (*Doctor Doolittle* 1967, *Sweet November* 1968) and made numerous recordings. Married for a time to Joan Collins. He was diagnosed with renal cell cancer in 1985 but was free of recurrence until 1997. He moved from London to Florida in December 1998 and died from cancer at 67 in Stuart. Forest Hills Memorial Park, Palm City, FL.

6744. Newman, Alfred (March 17, 1901–Feb. 17, 1970) Composer of film scores including *Wuthering Heights, Foreign Correspondent* and *The Grapes of Wrath* won nine Oscars including *Alexander's Ragtime Band, With A Song in My Heart*, and *Love is A Many Splendored Thing*. Uncle of composer Randy Newman. Crypt inscribed *He will take him in his arms/ He will lift him up on high/ He will show him all his charms of his mansions in the sky/ He will let him hear the songs that the angel voices sing. He will be where he belongs, in the chorus of the King.* Sanctuary of Eternal Prayer, crypt 14033, Holly Terrace, Great Mausoleum, Forest Lawn, Glendale, CA.

6745. Newman, Sid (Sidney Newman, Jan. 18, 1920–April 10, 2001) Actor appeared in *The Wedding Singer*, many TV appearances including *The Larry Sanders Show*, etc. Plaque at the foot of the steps. Garden of Ramah 12, lot 2058, lawn crypt 3, Mt. Sinai Memorial Park, Los Angeles.

6746. Newsom, Bobo (Louis Norman Newsom, Aug 11 1907–Dec 7 1962) Pitcher with the 1940 Tigers traded sixteen times (five to the Senators) in a twenty year career in which he threw to both Ruth and Mantle. Magnolia Cemetery, Hartsville, SC.

6747. Newton, Huey (Huey Percy Newton, Feb. 17, 1942–Aug. 22, 1989) Co-founder with Bobby Seale and Eldridge Cleaver of the Black Panthers in the 1960's. Their defense minister Newton symbolized black anger. Convicted in the 1967 death of an Oakland police officer, the conviction was overturned in

1970. There were no suspects in his assassination on an Oakland street at 47. Cremated at Evergreen Cemetery, Oakland, California, the ashes were returned to the family.

6748. Newton, Isaac (Dec. 25, 1642–March 20, 1727) English mathematician known for his discovery and explanation of the laws of gravity. Ornate tomb designed by John Ryrsback in 1731. The floor plaque over his crypt reads *Hic dpositum est Quod Mortale fuit Isaaci Newtoni.* Center aisle, Westminster Abbey, London.

6749. Newton, John (July 24, 1725–Dec. 21, 1807) Former slave trader who had an awakening, finding it wrong and contrary to Christian teachings. He halted the practice, became an Anglican minister and wrote the words to *Amazing Grace,* as well as inspiring William Wilberforce, who brought about the abolition of slavery in Britain. His remains were removed in 1893 from St. Mary Woolnoth Church in London. Along with a wall plaque in the church, a granite sarcophagus marks the grave of he and his wife Mary and notes his life and work. St. Peter and Paul Churchyard, Olney, Buckinghamshire.

6750. Newton, Robert (June 1, 1905–March 25, 1956) English actor from Shaftesbury, Dorset, renowned for his drinking. Films include *Gaslight* (*Angel Street* 1940), *Oliver Twist* (1946, as Bill Sykes), *Treasure Island* (1950, as Long John Silver), *Blackbeard the Pirate* (1952) and other costume drama villains played with a relish. He died from a heart attack in Beverly Hills at 50. Cremated by Pierce Brothers' Chapel of the Pines in L.A., the ashes were sent to Lamorna Cove near Cornwall, England. They were not placed in a cemetery but were taken by his ex wife or by friends there; one story has the ashes stored in the wine cellar of a friend; another relates that the ashes were flushed down the toilet in fond farewell by his friends while drunk, while a third account has them scattered near Cornwall. A cenotaph to him was placed beside the marker for his wife **Vera** (1924–2000) when she died. While her ashes are there, office records show only a marker for him. Southwest urn garden near tree by office, Westwood Memorial Park, west Los Angeles.

6751. Ney, Richard (Nov. 12, 1916–July 18, 2004) Actor from the Bronx played Vin Miniver in the 1942 film *Mrs. Miniver,* then married (until 1947) his on-screen mother, Greer Garson, only two years his senior. He appeared in *The Late George Apley, Ivy, Joan of Arc, Midnight Lace, Premature Burial,* but left acting to become an investment adviser, published *The Wall Street Jungle* in 1960,and became a well known stock market "muckraker" on *The Ney Report,* advocating early on computerized buy and sell orders and regulating the market as a public utility. He died in Pasadena at 87, survived only by his third wife, Mei-Lee Ney. Cremated by Cabot and Sons, Pasadena. Ashes to the widow at their residence there.

6752. Ngor, Haing S. (March 22, 1940–Feb. 25, 1996) Cambodian doctor won an Oscar for his role as *New York Times* correspondent's aide Dith Pran, imprisoned by the Khmer Rouge in *The Killing Fields* (1984), the first non actor winner since Harold Russell in 1946. He learned his role from life as a prisoner of the Khmer Rouge for four years, emigrating to the U.S. in 1980. Later roles included the healer in *My Life* (1993). He was found shot to death beside his car in L.A.'s Chinatown. Flush plaque has his picture on it. Alpine Terrace, lot 2274, grave 2, Rose Hills Memorial Park, Whittier, CA.

6753. Niblo, Fred (Frederico Nobile, Jan. 6, 1874–Nov. 11, 1948) Director of silent costume epics including *The Mark of Zorro* 1920, *The Three Musketeers* 1921, *Blood and Sand* 1922, and the chariot race in *Ben Hur* (1926). He died in New Orleans. Inurned with his wife, actress Enid Bennett (*q.v.*). Her sister, actress Marjorie Bennett (*q.v.*), is also in the niche, unmarked. Columbarium of Dawn, niche 30247, Great Mausoleum, Forest Lawn, Glendale, CA.

6754. Niblo, Fred, Jr. (Jan. 23, 1903–Feb. 18, 1973) Son of the director, was a Hollywood screenwriter, primarily of action films. Sec. D, lot 73, grave 11, San Fernando Mission Cemetery, Mission Hills, CA.

6755. Nicholas II, Emperor of Russia (Nikolai Alexandrovich, May 18, 1868–July 17, 1918) The last Czar of Russia abdicated after the government resigned. He and the royal family, consisting of his wife the Empress **Alexandra Feodorovna** (Alix, Princess of Hesse-Darmstadt, born June 6, 1872) and their children, the Grand Duchesses **Olga** (born November 1895), **Tatiana** (June 1897), **Marie** (May 1899), **Anastasia** (June 1901), and the Tsarevich **Alexis** (August 1904) were moved to Tobolsk, a river town in western Siberia, by the Bolsheviks. He was ordered back to Moscow in April 1918 but the family was stopped at Ekaterinburg (now Sverdlovsk) in the Urals and kept in five upper rooms of a private house. As anti–Bolshevik forces were preparing to advance, they were awakened at midnight, taken downstairs, shot and bayoneted to death. The bodies were allegedly taken to an unused mine near Koptyaki, partially cremated, dismembered, covered with sulfuric acid and tipped into a mine shaft, so history read for over seventy years. There was from the beginning much speculation as to whether the Czarina Alexandra and all four daughters died this way or were, as reported, alive in Perm at the end of 1918. An **Anna Anderson** surfaced in Berlin in 1920 and claimed to have been the Princess Anastasia, who — if true — would alone have escaped alive, though there was never an explanation of how. She moved to America, married John Manahan, and died in Martha Jefferson Hospital in Charlottesville, Virginia, February 12, 1984. On June 18, which would have been her 83rd birthday, her ashes were interred according to her wish in the churchyard of Castle Seeon, at the edge of a secluded lake in upper Bavaria. In October 1994, DNA tests done on hair samples of Anna Anderson Manahan showed that she and Anastasia were not the same person. With the demise of the U.S.S.R., Russian scientists revealed that the bones of all but Anastasia and the boy Alexis were found in a grave at Ekaterinburg in February 1982. Exhumed in 1991, it was revealed in August 1992 that by the previous February they were at the Department of Criminal Pathology in Yekaterinburg for identification and study by forensics experts, including Americans. In August 1994, the son of Bolshevik secret police commandant Yakov Yurovsky said his father's reports stated unequivocally that all seven of the Romanov family and four retainers died in the fusillade of gunfire in July 1918. They were at first placed in the mineshaft, but because the spot became quickly known, were disinterred. Attempts to cremate them destroyed only the Princess Anastasia and the Tsarevich Alexis. Their ashes were then dispersed, according to Yurovsky, accounting for the absence of their bones in the 1991 exhumation at Ekaterinburg where the others had been reburied at a crossroads. The bones of the Romanovs and three daughters (less Anastasia or Olga or Marie — which was missing was never a certainty) were to be interred at St. Petersburg by 1995 but due to shifting political influences the funeral and interment did not take place until July 15–17, 1998, when the small coffins were flown to St. Petersburg and, in a ceremony attended by Russian President Boris Yeltsin, entombed in St. Catherine's Chapel at St. Peter's Cathedral on the 80th anniversary of their murders.

6756. Nicholas, Harold (Harold Lloyd Nicholas, March 27, 1921–July 3, 2000) With his elder brother Fayard appeared as the dancing Nicholas Brothers, acrobatic phenoms, on film from 1932, the same year they made their debut at the Cotton Club. Their performances uplifted *Kid Millions, Sun Valley Serenade, Orchestra wives, Stormy Weather, The Pirate.* Harold appeared without Fayad in *The Emperor Jones,* introduced *Come Rain or Come Shine* in *St. Louis Woman* (1944) and later showed up in *Uptown Saturday Night (1974), Tap* (1989), and toured in *Sophisticated Ladies* in 1982. He died in New York at 79. Unmarked. Alpine plot, center sec. along Heather Ave., Woodlawn Cemetery, the Bronx, N.Y.C.

6757. Saint Nicholas (died c. 345–350) Patron saint of giving, church bishop born in Asia Minor, now Turkey, in the third century A.D., was the son of wealthy parents who renounced his wealth to help the poor, said to have thrown bags of gold through an open window three times to help a poor farmer without dowries for his daughters, the bags landing in stockings drying by a fire. The remains were interred in the ancient Turkish town of Myra but were stolen in 1087 by Italian sailors and smuggled across the Mediterranean Sea to the Adriatic coast of Italy where they remain, marked *Tomba del Santo* behind an iron grill, in the crypt of the Basilica di San Nicola, Bari, Italy.

6758. Nichols, Barbara (Barbara Marie Nickerauer, Dec. 10, 1928–Oct. 5, 1976) Former stripper turned actress from Jamaica, Queens, N.Y.C., appeared as dumb blondes, usually easy, in *Pal Joey* (1957), *The Naked and the Dead* (1958), *The Loved One* (1965). *Twilight Zone* Episode *Twenty-Two.* She died from a liver ailment in Los Angeles at 47. Returned through Jacobsen mortuary to Garden of Sanctuary, row 3, plot 34, Pinelawn Memorial Park, Farmingdale, Long Island, NY.

6759. Nichols, Charles A. "Kid" (Sept. 14, 1869–April 11, 1953) Pitcher won thirty or more games seven consecutive seasons 1891–97 with Boston. In his first nine seasons he led them to five championships. Later with Kansas City and St. Louis. Hall of Fame 1949. Block 16 (Last Supper), lot 237, space 8, Mt. Moriah Cemetery, Kansas City, MO.

6760. Nichols, Dudley (April 6, 1895–Jan. 4, 1960) Acclaimed screen-writer from Wapakoneta, Ohio, wrote several scripts for John Ford films, including *The Lost Patrol, Stagecoach*, won Oscars for *The Informer* (1935), *The Long Voyage Home* (1940), *Air Force* (1943) and *The Tin Star* (1957), and directed several pictures, including *Sister Kenny* and *Mourning Becomes Electra.* Sec. 13 (Pineland)/Garden of Exodus, lot 520, Hollywood Forever Cemetery, Hollywood (Los Angeles), CA.

6761. Nichols, "Red" (Ernest L. Nichols, May 8, 1905–June 28, 1965) Trumpet and cornet jazz bandleader at his peak in the late 1920's and 30's with his band, the Five Pennies. Columbarium of Remembrance, niche 60780, Courts of Remembrance, Forest Lawn Hollywood Hills, Los Angeles.

6762. Nichols, Roy (Roy Ernest Nichols, Oct. 21, 1932–July 3, 2001) Musician born in Chandler, Arizona, lead guitarist with Merle Haggard for 22 years, died at 68 in Bakersfield, California. Greenlawn mortuary and Memorial Park, Bakersfield, CA.

6763. Nicholson, Harold (Nov. 21, 1886–May 1, 1968) Knighted English diplomat, critic and writer, author of *Diplomacy*, was married to Vera Sackville-West; they were known for their gardens at Sissinghurst Castle. Sissinghurst churchyard, Sissinghurst, Kent.

6764. Nicholson, James H. (Sept. 14, 1916–Dec. 10, 1972) Co-founder with Samuel Z. Arkoff of American International Pictures (AIP), known for low budget horror films from the late 1950's upgraded through the mid 60's, many starring Vincent Price, both straightforward and tongue-in-cheek. Avalon plot, lot 5036, Inglewood Park Cemetery, Inglewood, CA.

6765. Nicholson, Pauline (April 16, 1929–July 13, 2005) Elvis Presley's housekeeper and cook, noted for fixing his sometimes peculiar dishes, worked for him from the mid 1960's, often conversing with him in the kitchen, and for the family after his death, remaining loyal to his memory and playing herself in *This is Elvis.* She died from cancer in Memphis at 76.

Mount Pisgah Baptist Church Cemetery, Weaver Road, Memphis, TN.

6766. Nick the Greek (Nicholas Andreas Dandolos, April 27, 1884–Dec. 25, 1966) Famed gambler, king of the oddsmakers. Plaque reads *Gambler and sage*. Sec. K, lot 217, sw ¼, Woodlawn Cemetery, Las Vegas, NV.

6767. Nicol, Alex (Jan. 20, 1916–July 29, 2001) Character actor from Ossining, New York, on Broadway in *South Pacific, Mr. Roberts* and *Cat on A Hot Tin Roof*; in about 40 films, primarily in the 1950's and 60's, ranging from *Strategic Air Command* to *the Screaming Skull* (also directed), and on TV in *The Twilight Zone* (*Young Man's Fancy*), *The Outer Limits* (*Moonstone*), etc. He died at 85 in Santa Barbara, California. Cremated through Welch-Ryce-Hader mortuary. Ashes scattered at sea.

6768. Nicolay, John G. (Feb. 26, 1832–Sept. 26, 1901) German-American secretary, with John Hay, to President Lincoln. They were later his biographers. Lot 273 East, Oak Hill Cemetery, Georgetown, Washington, D.C.

6769. Nietzsche, Friedrich Wilhelm (Oct. 15, 1844–Aug. 25, 1900) German philosopher suffered from various ailments and spent many years in a mental institution. His fame rests largely on his writings theorizing an existence without an omnipresent power figure, based on the morality of the strong, some of which was later adopted by Hitler. The ideas brought about the inevitable (paraphrased) line "'God is dead — Nietzsche.' 'Nietzsche is dead — God.'" Grave length slab, churchyard at Röcken, Thuringen.

6770. Nigh, William (Emil William Kreuske, Oct. 12, 1881–Nov. 27, 1955) Director of generally polished silent films, many melodramas (*Mr. Wu* 1927) did primarily B's with sound (*The Ape* 1940, etc.). Columbarium of Patience, niche 21259, Great Mausoleum, Forest Lawn, Glendale, CA.

6771. Night of the Living Dead site The setting for the opening scene of George Romero's cult classic *Night of the Living Dead*, was filmed in fall 1967 at Evans City Cemetery, Peters Road, just south of Evans City, Pennsylvania, north of Pittsburgh and just west of Renfrew, PA.

6772. Nightingale, Florence (May 12, 1820–Aug. 13, 1910) English nurse whose heroics during the Crimean War in the 1850's made nursing the noble profession it has since become, particularly in war time. In 1907, aged and blind, she received the Order of Merit of the British Empire. She died in her sleep at 90 and was buried beside her parents, marked by a four sided stone with a peaked top and small cross on top, inscribed *F.N. Born 1820. Died 1910*. St. Margaret's Churchyard, East Wellow, west of Romsey, Hampshire.

6773. Nijinsky, Vaslav (March 12, 1888–April 8, 1950) Russian ballet great from Kiev performed with the *Ballets Russes* for Serge Diaghilev from 1909–13 and 1916–17. Diagnosed a schizophrenic in 1919, he was in and out of mental institutions until his death in London at 62. Buried first at St. Marylebone Cemetery there, he was reburied in 1953. Div. 22, Montmartre Cemetery, Paris.

6774. Nikel, Johannes (Johannes Maria Bernhard Nikel, April 13, 1931–Sept. 26, 2001) German film editor 1963–1997 (*Sonderurlaub* 1963, *Jack of Diamonds* 1967, *Enemy Mine* 1985, *Stalingrad* 1993, *Last Chance Love* 1997), nominated for an Oscar for *Das Boot* (1981). Feld 132, reihe 3, nummer 130, Waldfriedhof Alter Teil, Munich, Bayern.

6775. Nikulin, Yury (Dec. 18, 1921–Aug. 21, 1997) Well known Russian "everyman" actor known for the Soviet era films *Brillyantovaya Ruke* (*The Diamond Arm*) and *Kavkaskaya Plennitsa* (*Prisoner of the Caucasus*), as well as the more somber *They Fought For the Motherland* and *Twenty Days Without War*. A collector of some 10,000 jokes from 1936, he published several collections and rebuilt and directed a circus. He died at a Moscow clinic at 75. Novodevichy Cemetery, Moscow.

6776. Niland, Robert (1919–June 6, 1944) and **Preston T. Niland** (1915–June 7, 1944) were two brothers killed during and just after the Allied invasion of Normandy. The third brother, Fritz, was the object of a search ordered until he was located and sent home, the basis for Steven Spielberg's film *Saving Private Ryan* forty-five years later. Plot F, row 15, graves 11 and 12. Normandy American Cemetery, Colleville-sur-mer, France.

6777. Niles, Ken (Dec. 9, 1906–Oct. 31, 1988) Radio announcer from the 1920's on the Don Lee network began his *Theatre of the Mind* in 1928 on the west coast, a pioneer in presenting radio drama rather than music and comedy. He died at 81 in Los Angeles. Cremated by Pierce Bros. Chapel of the Pines. Ashes to his wife, Los Angeles.

6778. Nilsson, Anna Q. (Anna Querentia Nilsson, March 30, 1888–Feb. 11, 1974) Swedish born silent screen actress in films from 1910. Her career was ended with a riding accident and the advent of sound but she returned in smaller roles (joining Buster Keaton, Gloria Swanson and H.B. Warner playing cards in *Sunset Boulevard* 1950). She died in a nursing home at Hemet, California. Cremated through the McWayne mortuary in Hemet, her ashes were scattered in the Pacific off Huntington Beach, CA.

6779. Nilsson, Birgit (Marta Birgit Svensson, May 17, 1918–Dec. 25, 2005) Swedish soprano with the Stockholm Royal Opera from 1946, known for her mastery of Wagnerian opera, particularly in *Tristan and Isolde*, from her debut at the New York Metropolitan Opera in 1959. Buried with her parents in her home town. Village kyrkogård, Vastra Karup, Sweden.

6780. Nilsson, Harry (Harry Edward Nilsson, June 15, 1941–Jan. 15, 1994) Brooklyn born songwriter and singer won Grammys for *Everybody's Talkin'* (from *The Midnight Cowboy* 1969), *Without You* and composed several whimsical numbers including *Me and My Arrow* from his 1971 animated film *The Point*. Platinum album *Nilsson Schmilsson* (1971). He died in his sleep from a heart attack at 52 in his Agoura Hills, California, home. His plaque has his picture, with the epitaph from his song, *Remember...* Gethsemane 830H, Valley Oaks Memorial Park, Westlake Village, CA.

6781. Nimitz, Chester W. (Feb. 24, 1885–Feb. 20, 1966) U.S. Admiral in command of the Pacific Fleet during World War II rebuilt U.S. Naval power, at a low ebb when Pearl Harbor was bombed. He was aboard the U.S.S. *Missouri* to accept the Japanese surrender in 1945. Standard military headstone, one row in front of Congressman Leo Ryan. Sec. C-1, grave 1, Golden Gate National Cemetery, San Bruno, CA.

6782. Nin, Anais (Feb. 21, 1903–Jan. 14, 1977) French born writer of diaries and short stories. Her diaries, not published until 1966, were widely acclaimed, while she had published her frequently erotic novels and short stories for many years with less notice. Her relationship with Henry Miller was the subject of the film *Henry and June*. Ashes scattered by plane in Mermaid Cove, Santa Monica Bay, CA.

6783. Nippert, Jimmy (James Gamble Nippert, March 6, 1900–Dec. 25, 1923) Grandson of James Gamble, co-founder of Procter and Gamble, was a center on the University of Cincinnati football team who sustained injuries when kicked in the leg and spiked in the Thanksgiving Day 1923 game against Miami University. He continued to play, but was hospitalized and died on Christmas Day of blood poisoning, his last words "Five more yards to go, then drop."—the yardage left to go at the time of his injury a month earlier. Nippert Stadium at UC was named for him the next year. Burial January 1, 1924. Family bench. Sec. 18, lot 47, space 1, Spring Grove Cemetery, Cincinnati, OH.

6784. Nissen, Greta (Grethe Rutz-Nissen, Jan. 30, 1905–May 17, 1988) Norwegian born silent screen actress in U.S. films, later in low budget British sound pictures. She died at Montecito, Santa Barbara County, California. Arroyo Valley Crematory, Arroyo Grande, Ca. Ashes to the Neptune Society.

6785. Nitti, Frank (Frank Nitto, 1888–March 19, 1943) Capone organization figure known as the Enforcer became the Chicago syndicate leader in the 1930's. He had already done time for tax evasion and was about to be indicted a third time when he shot himself in the head. His monument, with a large cross on it, has beneath it *Nitto* and on the sides the epitaph *There is no life except by death. There is no vision but by faith*. Across the road and on the other side of the Roosevelt Road gate from the Capone plot. Sec. 32, Mt. Carmel Cemetery, Hillside, IL.

6786. Nitze, Paul (Jan. 16, 1907–Oct. 19, 2004) Influential U.S. government advisor and architect of the policy of containment of the Soviet Union, though he held no cabinet posts or elective offices, from Hiroshima through Glasnost. He was associated with two Walk in the Woods talks which brought about the 1972 Anti-Ballistic Missile treaty and in 1982 on reducing intermediate nuclear weapons deployed in Europe, which came to fruition in the 1987 INF treaty. He died in Washington at 97. Burial on his estate overlooking the Potomac in Charles County, MD.

6787. Nitzsche, Jack (Bernard Alfred Nitzsche, April 22, 1937–Aug. 25, 2000) Chicago born musician worked on records with The Rolling Stones, Phil Spector, co-wrote *Needles and Pins* with Sonny Bono, and scored many films including *The Exorcist, One Flew Over the Cuckoo's Nest* (AA nomination), *Heroes, Hard Core, An Officer and A Gentleman* (AA for co-writing *Up Where We Belong*), *Next of Kin, Mermaids, The Hot Spot, Blue Sky, The Crossing Guard*. He died of a heart attack in L.A at 63. Hollywood Forever Cemetery, Hollywood (Los Angeles), CA.

6788. Niven, David (March 1, 1910–July 29, 1983) Suave, mustached English actor in Hollywood from the late 30's with a light hearted approach that spanned three decades and a wide variety of films (*The Dawn Patrol* 1938, *Wuthering Heights* 1939, *The Bishop's Wife, The Guns of Navarone*). He authored three volumes of witty reminiscences and aged little until stricken with the neuro-muscular disease which proved fatal but failed to crush his spirit; his last gesture was reportedly a thumbs up sign. Marked by a stone cross in the cemetery of the town where he had lived for thirty years. Village cemetery, Chateau d'Oex, Switzerland.

6789. Niven, Primmie (Primula Susan Rollo Niven, Feb. 18, 1918–May 21, 1946) Young British wife of David Niven took a fatal fall down Tyrone Power's cellar steps during a game of sardines (hide and seek). Cremated at Chapel of the Pines Crematory in Los Angeles, her ashes were sent to England for burial with her parents, marked by a long lichen covered stone cross in the churchyard at Huish, Wiltshire.

6790. Nix, Orville O., Sr. (April 16, 1911–Jan. 17, 1972) Dallas air conditioning maintenance man whose home movie of the JFK assassination was taken from the opposite direction than the Zapruder film, showing the so-called grassy knoll. Nix shunned publicity and largely because of that his film was not as well known as Zapruder's. In the fall of 2000, a first generation print was donated to the Sixth Floor Museum at what was the Texas School Book Depository in Dallas. Sec. A., lot 108, space 7, Edgewood Cemetery, Lancaster, TX.

6791. Nixon, Joan Lowery (Feb. 3, 1927–June 28, 2003) Mystery writer geared toward young adults wrote over 140 books, including *The Kidnapping of Christine Lattimore, The Seance* and *The Other Side of Dark*, which was filmed. The recipient of four Edgar Awards, she died at 76 in Houston. Sec. 18, space 820S, Memorial Oaks Cemetery, Houston, TX.

6792. Nixon, Marian (Oct. 20, 1904–Feb. 13,

1983) Actress in silents and talkies retired in 1936 to marry director William Seiter, who died in 1964. In 1972 she married actor Ben Lyon, who died while they were on a cruise at sea in 1979. She died after heart surgery three years later. Ashes with Seiter; their plaque was updated to include a daughter (1980) and son (2003). Columbarium of Honor, niche 2349, Gardens of Honor (private), Forest Lawn, Glendale, CA.

6793. Nixon, Richard Milhous (Jan. 9, 1913– April 22, 1994) 37th President of the United States, born in Yorba Linda, California, and raised by Quaker parents in nearby Whittier, went to Congress after navy service in World War II, became a Republican congressman in 1946 and senator in 1950 as a staunch anti-Communist. After allegations of financial wrongdoing forced him to answer his accusers on live TV (the first such political cleansing) in the 1952 Checkers Speech (so named for his reference to the political gift of a puppy for his daughters), his spot on the ticket was salvaged. As Eisenhower's vice president 1953–61, he stepped in during the president's 1955 heart attack and made memorable a belligerent discussion over modern technology with Soviet Premier Khrushchev in 1959 dubbed the "Kitchen Debate." Suffering by contrast with John Kennedy in the first televised presidential debates, he lost the close 1960 presidential election and sealed a tenuous relationship with the press in 1962 when, after losing the California gubernatorial election to Edmund "Pat" Brown, he erroneously told reporters "You won't have Nixon to kick around anymore." However five years later, after a period as a New York corporate attorney, he won the Republican nomination and defeated Hubert Humphrey for the presidency in 1968. During his five years in office 1969–1974, improvements in foreign relations resulted from his meetings with Soviet Premier Brezhnev and with his opening relations with Communist China. The peace treaty ending American military involvement in Vietnam was signed in January 1973, but by then he was already mired in the unraveling saga of the June 1972 break in at the Democratic headquarters in the Watergate complex. Soon known as Watergate, the ongoing cover-up by his closest aides and the president himself led to nearly two years of congressional investigations, stand-offs and finally pressure from his own party. Nixon resigned August 9, 1974, the first U.S. President to do so. He retired to his former Western White House at San Clemente, California, moving to New York City, then to Saddle River and Park Ridge, New Jersey, where he spent the final decade of his life. He made numerous diplomatic trips and missions overseas from 1981–1994, rising once again and finally as a respected elder statesman and acknowledged expert in foreign affairs, consulted by all five presidents who followed him. His wife **Pat Nixon** (Thelma Catherine Patricia Ryan, March 16, 1912–June 22, 1993) was known for her quiet demeanor and penchant for privacy through her husband's long and turbulent career. In ill health

after a stroke in later years, she died at their Park Ridge, New Jersey, home from lung cancer at 81. Services were conducted by Rev. Billy Graham at the Nixon Birthplace and Library/Museum at Yorba Linda, Ca., opened in 1991. She was buried adjacent the small house where her husband was born in what is called the First Lady's Garden, marked at first by a flush rose colored plaque. Ten months later, and only weeks after a trip to Russia, Nixon suffered a stroke while sitting on the deck of his Park Ridge home in the early evening of April 18. Left with paralysis and unable to speak, he was taken to New York Hospital-Cornell University Medical Center in Manhattan, where he lapsed into a coma. A living will prohibited any extraordinary means of prolonging or preserving life artificially. He died at 81 on Friday evening, four days after suffering the stroke. No services in Washington were held. From a Wykoff, New Jersey, mortuary, the body arrived at Stewart Air Force Base in Newburgh, New York, for a brief ceremony and was placed aboard the same 747 that had taken him back to California in 1974. From El Toro Air Force Base near Los Angeles, the Rose Hills hearse moved to the Nixon Library and Birthplace some thirty miles away, where it lay in state in the library lobby April 26 and 27, some 42,000 passing the bier. The funeral was held outdoors on Wednesday, April 27, conducted by Rev. Billy Graham (who had conducted the last presidential funeral, that of Lyndon Johnson, twenty one years before). Eulogies were delivered by former Secretary of State Henry Kissinger, Kansas Senator and majority leader Bob Dole, California Governor Pete Wilson, and President Clinton. All four living ex-presidents as well as Clinton were seated with their wives in the front row; a first in American history. Though not known at the time, it was the last public appearance of former President Reagan. The interment, with the playing of *America the Beautiful* and *The Navy Hymn* as the flag was folded (just as it had been done at the burial of his long ago colleague John Kennedy) followed in the First Lady's Garden area behind the birthplace, attended only by the family, the presidents and their wives, and the eulogists and their wives. Nixon's stone was placed immediately. Designed by Gil Arnet, Jr., it is of polished black granite imported from India, the same material used in the Vietnam Veterans Memorial in Washington, D.C. Pat Nixon's flat rose colored marker bearing just her name and dates was replaced with one to match his. Only his name and dates appear in gold leaf lettering, with the epitaph, from his first inaugural, *The greatest honor history can bestow is the title of peacemaker.* Nixon Birthplace-Museum, Yorba Linda, California. Richard Nixon's parents, **Francis (Frank) Nixon** (Dec. 3, 1878–Sept. 4, 1956) and **Hannah Milhous Nixon** (March 7, 1885–Sept. 30, 1967) operated a lemon ranch at Yorba Linda, California, before moving to Whittier, where Frank ran a grocery and gas station and where his sons grew up. Services for both were held at the Friends Church in Whittier. **Arthur** (May 26, 1918–Aug. 10, 1925), who died from meningitis and **Harold** (June 1, 1909–March 7, 1933), who died from TB, are both buried with their parents and with Hannah Nixon's parents, the Milhouses, who migrated west from Jennings County, Indiana. In the same area is the president's brother, lawyer **Donald** (Francis Donald Nixon, Nov. 23, 1914–June 27, 1987). Milhous upright monument and flush plaques, Sunset Lawn sec., lot 47, near south side of mausoleum (gate 14), Rose Hills Memorial Park, Whittier, California. The family dog **Checkers** (1952–1964), immortalized in the 1952 TV speech of the same name, was buried in the Bide-a-Wee Pet Cemetery at Wantagh, Long Island, New York, until late 1997 when he was removed and reburied near the Nixons at the Nixon Birthplace-Museum complex Yorba Linda, CA.

6794. Nixon, Willard (June 17, 1928–Dec. 10, 2000) Boston Red Sox pitcher 1950–58 known as The Yankee Killer, beating them six games in a row in the 1954–55 season. East View Cemetery, Rome, GA.

6795. Nizer, Louis (Feb. 6, 1902–Nov. 10, 1994) Noted lawyer, founder of the firm Phillips, Nizer, Benjamin, Crim and Ballon in 1926. Among his many celebrated cases was his defense of CBS radio personality John Henry Faulk against AWARE, an anticommunist "clearing" group, in 1956, against whom Nizer won Faulk $725,000 in damages. His autobiography *My Life in Court* (1962) rose to the top of the *New York Times* Bestseller list and stayed there for seventy two weeks. Family mausoleum, range 356, Washington Cemetery, Brooklyn, N.Y.C.

6796. Nobel, Alfred (Oct. 21, 1933–Dec. 10, 1896) Founder of the Nobel Prize was a scientist and inventor, who devised dynamite from nitroglycerin, calling it ballisite. In poor health, he lived out his days at San Remo, Italy. The destructive use of his invention led him to leave his fortune to those whose works most benefited science, literature, and peace. The first Nobel Peace Prize was awarded in 1901. Sec. KV 4A, grave 170, Norra Begravningsplatsen (Northern Cemetery), Stockholm, Sweden.

6797. Nolan, Doris (July 14, 1916–July 29, 1998) Blonde New York born stage actress in a few films 1936–43 (*Top of the Town, Irene, Moon Over Burma*), best known as Katherine Hepburn's sister Julia in *Holiday* (1938), and on stage in *Doughgirls*. Married to actor Alexander Knox from 1943, they moved to England in the 1950's after his blacklisting by the House Un-American Activities Committee, settling in Berwick-upon-Tweed, Northumberland, where he died in April 1995. She kept his urn until her own death three years later at 82, and planned a grandson would inter both of their ashes at his home in the Channel Islands.

6798. Nolan, Jeanette (Nov. 30, 1911–June 5, 1998) Los Angeles born actress played Lady Macbeth in Orson Welles' *Macbeth* (1948), with many other roles in films (*the Big Heat*) and television (*The Twilight Zone* episodes *The Hunt* and *Jess-Belle*; a regular on *The Virginian*). Married to actor John McIntyre and the mother of Tim McIntyre. Last seen in *The Horse Whisperer* (1998), she died from the effects of a stroke in Los Angeles at 86. Ashes sent to Eureka/Tobacco Valley Cemetery, Eureka, MT.

6799. Nolan, Lloyd (Lloyd Benedict Nolan, Aug. 11, 1902–Sept. 27, 1985) Steady character actor from the 1930's whose parts ran the gamut from gangsters (*Johnny Apollo* 1940), and jaded detectives (*Somewhere in the Night, The Lady in the Lake,* both 1946) to shy Irish cops (*A Tree Grows in Brooklyn* 1945). He played Dr. Chegley on TV's *Julia* in the 1960's, last appearing in Woody Allen's *Hannah and Her Sisters* (1985). He had for many years been a spokesman for the American Cancer Society, having survived it in the 1960's. He died from lung cancer at 83. Cremated at Grandview Memorial Park. Sec. D, lot 84, Westwood Memorial Park, west Los Angeles.

6800. Nolan, Mary (Mary Robertson, Dec. 18, 1905–Oct. 31, 1948) Blonde silent film actress, former Ziegfeld girl, began her career in Germany before returning to America in late silents and talkies (*West of Zanzibar* 1928). Suffering emotional breakdowns, she retired from the screen in 1932. Abbey of the Psalms/Hollywood Forever Mausoleum, Hope, crypt 594, Hollywood Forever Cemetery, Hollywood (Los Angeles), CA.

6801. Nolde, William Benedict (Aug. 8, 1929–Jan. 27, 1973) Forty three year old colonel was an advisor to the South Vietnam Army when an artillery shell exploded near An Loc and took his life just eleven hours before the truce began, making him the last name officially Killed In Action in Vietnam. Sec. 3, grave 1775-B, Arlington National Cemetery, Arlington, VA.

6802. Noone, Jimmy (James Noone, April 23, 1896–April 19, 1944) Clarinetist at his peak in the 1920's, considered smoother and more romantic than his New Orleans contemporaries, Johnny Dodds and Sidney Bechet. He was credited with inspiring Maurice Ravel to compose *Bolero*. In Chicago he played with King Oliver 1918–20, Doc Cooke's Dreamland Orchestra 1920–26, led his own band at the Apex Club from 1927 and recorded with Vocalion. Later with Kid Ory in California, he died from a heart attack in Hollywood at 47. Sec. J, lot 2112 (two graves), Evergreen Cemetery, Los Angeles.

6803. Nordica, Lillian (Lillian Norton, May 12, 1857–May 14, 1914) Opera soprano from Farmington, Maine, sang all over the world, including the New York Academy of Music, at the Met, and Carnegie Hall. Best known for Wagner. She died from pneumonia after the grounding of her ship at Batavia, Java, now Indonesia. Buried unmarked in the plot of her second husband George Young at New York Bay Cemetery, Jersey City, NJ.

6804. Norman, Maidie (Oct. 16, 1912–May 2,

1998) Black actress in films and TV was born on a Georgia plantation and grew up in Lima, Ohio. Refusing to play maids, etc. in the traditional "Yes'm" fashion, she brought intelligence and dignity to her characters, best known for *Whatever Happened to Baby Jane?* (1962). She also taught drama at Texas State University–Tyler, UCLA and Stanford. She died from lung cancer in San Jose, California, at 85. A memorial service was held at the Alum Rock United Methodist Church there, with cremation by the Neptune Society, San Jose. Ashes scattered at sea May 21, 1998.

6805. Norman, Merle (Jan. 15, 1887–Feb. 1, 1972) Founder of the cosmetics empire bearing her name. Mausoleum, sec. Q, unit 3, crypt 76, Woodlawn Cemetery, Santa Monica, CA.

6806. Normand, Mabel (Nov. 10, 1894–Feb 23, 1930) Silent screen comedian from Staten Island starred for Mack Sennett from 1914, in *Tillie's Punctured Romance* (1914), several comedies with Roscoe "Fatty" Arbuckle, and her starring feature *Mickey* (released in 1918), produced by Sennett. Her career faded after the William Desmond Taylor murder in 1922 when she was linked with the case as the last visitor he had. In 1923 there followed the shooting of millionaire and drug addict Courtland Dines, with her gun, by her chauffeur. She returned to two reelers but without her former popularity. Married to actor Lew Cody, supposedly on a lark, in 1926. Along with a drug habit, she was ill with tuberculosis as far back as 1917. Her death at Pottenger's Sanitarium in Monrovia, California, at 35 was due to TB. Entombed as Mabel Normand-Cody just below her mother (1932), with the 1895 birth date she had used. The actor John Hodiak (no connection) was entombed on her left twenty five years later. Block 303 D-7, Calvary Cemetery mausoleum, east Los Angeles.

6807. Noro, Line (Feb. 22, 1900–Nov. 4, 1985) French stage and screen actress, appeared in *Pépe Le Moko* (1937), *J'Accuse!* (1938, as Edith), many others. Case n. 18383, Pere Lachaise Cemetery, Paris.

6808. Norris, Edward (S.E. Norris, March 10, 1911–Dec. 18, 2002) Former newspaper reporter from Philadelphia in films from 1933 (*They Won't Forget* 1937, as the accused Professor Hale, *Boys Town* 1938, as Joe Marsh, *The Gorilla* 1939, *Scandal Sheet* 1940, *Dr. Ehrlich's Magic Bullet* 1940, *The Mystery of Marie Roget* 1942, as Marcel Vigneaux, *The Man With Two Lives* 1942, *I Was a Communist for the F.B.I.* 1951, *The Kentuckian* 1955, many others). Retired from films in 1956, he died at 92 in Fort Bragg, California. Ashes released to his family through Chapel By the Sea, Fort Bragg, to scatter at sea.

6809. Norris, Frank (Benjamin Franklin Norris, March 5, 1870–Oct. 25, 1902) Chicago born newspaper correspondent and author of *McTeague*, filmed as *Greed* (1923) and *The Octopus* (1901), lived in San Francisco. Sec. 12, Mountain View Cemetery, Oakland, CA.

6810. Norris, George W. (July 11, 1861–Sept. 22,

1944) Influential Nebraska congressman 1901–1913 and Senator 1913–1942. As a congressman he led Republican insurgents toward the Progressive reform implemented in part in Wilson's first term 1913–1917, and led the fight which successfully reduced the power of Speaker Joseph Gurney Cannon. Norris supported the New Deal and was a major force in creating the Tennessee Valley Authority. McCook Memorial Park, McCook, NE.

6811. North, Alex (Dec. 4, 1910–Sept. 8, 1991) Composer penned *Unchained Melody* among others and scored many films, including *A Streetcar Named Desire, Death of A Salesman, Viva Zapata, The Rose Tattoo, The Bad Seed, The Rainmaker, Spartacus, The Misfits, The Children's Hour, Cleopatra, Who's Afraid of Virginia Woolf?, Willard, Prizzi's Honor, The Dead, Good Morning Vietnam.* Ashes scattered at sea.

6812. North, Sheree (Dawn Bethel, Jan. 17, 1932–Nov. 4, 2005) Actress from Los Angeles, originally a dancer, replaced Marilyn Monroe at Fox in *How To Be Very Very Popular* (1955), later in *The Best Things in Life Are Free*, dramas *The Outfit, The Shootist, Defenseless*, many television roles through the 1960's and 70's, memorable as Charlene Maguire on the 100th episode of *The Mary Tyler Moore Show* (1974), with Emmy nominations for *Marcus Welby M.D.* and *Archie Bunker's Place*. The wife of Philip Norman, Pacific Palisades, she died from renal failure and cervical cancer at Cedar-Sinai Medical Center, Los Angeles, following surgery at 73. Cremated by Gates-Kingsley-Gates, Santa Monica. Ashes November 11 to family in Santa Monica.

6813. Norton, Edgar (Edgar Harry Mills Norton, AKA Harry Mills, Aug. 11, 1868–Feb. 6, 1953) Fauning butler in numerous films of the 1930's with a wrinkled face full of character, in *Dr. Jekyll & Mr. Hyde* (1931), *Dracula's Daughter* (1936), *Son of Frankenstein* (1939), many others. Norton had played the butler Poole in *Jekyll & Hyde* on stage to Richard Mansfield forty years before. He died at the Motion Picture Country Home in Woodland Hills. Unmarked. Block G, sec. 7718, lot 1, Valhalla Memorial Park, North Hollywood, CA.

6814. Norton, Jack (Mortimer John Naughton, Sept. 2, 1889–Oct. 15, 1958) Actor often cast as incoherent drunks, etc. Died at Will Rogers Hospital in Saranac Lake, New York. Sacred Heart (Catholic) section, Southampton Cemetery, Southampton, Long Island, NY.

6815. Norton, Joshua A. "Emperor" (1819–Jan. 8, 1880) Once wealthy rice merchant, Joshua Norton lost his fortune and declared himself Emperor of the United States, collecting 50 cents a month from San Francisco merchants as he patrolled the city on his bicycle, wearing a uniform and plumed hat. Among his proclamations over the years was that Queen Victoria should marry President Lincoln, that Maximillian of Mexico should be put to death, and that a bridge be constructed across San Francisco Bay (where a plaque on the Golden Gate Bridge was erected to his memory). He dropped dead at the corner of Market and Dupont and was buried in Lone Mountain Cemetery until its destruction in 1934. Plain granite marker inscribed *Norton I, Emperor of the United States and Protector of Mexico* followed by his real name and dates. Sec. H, lot 240, grave 1, Woodlawn Memorial Park, Colma, CA.

6816. Norton, W. Elliot (May 17, 1903–July 20, 2003) Boston theater critic for forty-eight years influenced the doctoring of plays before they moved to Broadway. Tony Award 1971 for distinguished commentary. Azalea Path, lot 9455, Mount Auburn Cemetery, Cambridge, MA.

6817. Norvo, Red (Kenneth Norville, March 31, 1908–April 6, 1999) Innovative jazz xylophonist and pianist from Beardstown, Illinois, was with Paul Whiteman 1932–35 and formed his own sextet in 1935, switching to the vibraphone in 1943. Married to singer Mildred Bailey in the 1930's, with whom he recorded Hoagy Carmichael's *Rockin Chair, Please Be Kind* and others. Though divorced, he and her brother Al Rinker scattered her ashes at her farm in 1951. He later married Eve Rogers, who died in 1992. Norvo died at 91 in Santa Monica. Mausoleum 121 L-E Wisdom Addition 7, Woodlawn Cemetery, Santa Monica, CA.

6818. Norworth, Jack (Jan. 5, 1879–Sept. 1, 1959) Philadelphia born songwriter in association with Albert Von Tilzer wrote *Take Me Out to the Ball Game, Shine on Harvest Moon*, many others. Also a former blackface comedian, he appeared 1907–1913 with wife Nora Bayes. Later married to Louise Dresser. He died in Laguna Beach, California, at 80. Carnation, lot 638, grave 1, Melrose Abbey Memorial Park, Anaheim, CA.

6819. Nostradamus (Michael de Nostredame, Dec. 14, 1503–July 2, 1566) French physician and astrologer whose predictions, over 900 in *Centuries* (1558), may in part be interpreted as having been accurate, have fascinated people for over four hundred years. Tomb in Eglise Saint-Laurent at Salon-de-Provence, France.

6820. Notorious B.I.G. aka **Biggie Smalls** (Christopher Wallace, May 21, 1972–March 9, 1997) 6'3," 300 plus pound east coast rapper from Bedford-Stuyvesant was shot to death in 9 mm. gunfire as he sat in a car on Fairfax in Los Angeles six months after his west coast rival, Tupac Shakur. The hearse driven through his native Brooklyn, he was cremated at Fresh Pond Crematory, Middle Village, Queens, through Frank E. Campbell mortuary, Manhattan. The ashes were reportedly split between his estranged wife and his girlfriend, though according to his biography they were given to his mother.

6821. Nova, Hedda (May 15, 1895–Jan. 16, 1981) Russian born brunette silent screen actress from Odessa in American films 1917–1926. Full burial as Hedda Roberts through Chapel of the Roses. Sec. N, lot 37, grave 2, third row from the street, Atascadero District Cemetery, Atascadero, CA.

6822. Novak, Eva (April 11, 1898–April 17, 1988) and **Jane Novak** (Jan. 12, 1896–Feb 6, 1990) were sisters who left St. Louis together in 1914 and went to Hollywood. Eva appeared as the chaste heroine in several Tom Mix pictures, while Jane was cast in William S. Hart westerns and other films with Chester Bennett, including *Thelma* (1922). They are buried together, Eva as Eva Reed. Sec. EE, row 1, grave 7 (one plaque), San Fernando Mission Cemetery, Mission Hills, CA.

6823. Novak, Paul (Chester Ribonsky AKA Charles Krauser, Feb. 24, 1923–July 14 1999) Baltimore born body builder and a member of Mae West's so-called beef trust was reportedly "the love of her life," thirty years her junior and with her from the 1950's until her death in 1980, her husband in all but name. He died during treatment for advanced prostate cancer in Santa Monica at 76. Ashes scattered at sea.

6824. Novarro, Ramon (Ramon Samaniago, Feb. 6, 1899–Oct. 31, 1968) Mexican born silent screen actor best known as the star of *Ben Hur* (1926) and *Pagan Love Song* (1928) and a few talkies, including *Mata Hari* with Garbo (1931). He was murdered at 69 in his Hollywood apartment, bludgeoned to death by two male hustlers who came away with $5,000 in cash after tearing his home apart. Sec. C, lot 586, grave 5, Calvary Cemetery, east Los Angeles.

6825. Novello, Ivor (Ivor Novello Davies, Jan. 15, 1893–March 6, 1951) Welsh actor, writer, director and composer. Film roles included the lead in Alfred Hitchcock's *The Lodger*, both 1926 and 1932. He also composed the World War I song *Keep the Home Fires Burning* (1915) and directed several plays as well. He died from a heart attack in London at 58. A stone bust of him sits atop a plaque in the memorial brick columbarium at Golders Green. His ashes are commemorated by a large lilac bush with a small sign inscribed *Ivor Novello. 6th March 1951. Till you are home once more*. Golders Green Crematorium, north London.

6826. Novello, Jay (Aug. 22, 1904–Sept. 2, 1982) Slight Italian-American actor usually typecast in crooked, cowardly, or confused roles in films of the 1950's and 60's (*The Mad Magician, The Lost World* 1960) and much TV (*I Love Lucy, Andy Griffith*, etc.) Near the mission. Sec. H, tier 8, grave 6, San Fernando Mission Cemetery, Mission Hills, CA.

6827. Nozaki, Albert (Jan. 1, 1912–Nov. 16, 2003) Japanese-American Hollywood art director 1934–69, placed in Manzanar internment camp during World War II, had a productive period afterward, with *The Big Clock, When Worlds Collide, War of the Worlds*— his best known work — and *The Ten Commandments* (AA nom.). In 1963 he began to lose his sight, and retired as supervising art director six years later. He died at 91. God's Acre, lot 625, space 3, Forest Lawn Hollywood Hills, Los Angeles.

6828. Nugent, Elliott (Sept. 20, 1896–Aug. 9, 1980) Film director, former actor (*The Unholy Three*

1930) wrote the successful play *The Male Animal* (1940) in collaboration with James Thurber. By the 1950's his career faded from the effects of alcoholism and mental problems, but he continued to direct until 1957, and later authored a novel and an autobiography. Buried with the ashes of his wife, actress **Norma Lee** (1899–1980). Near water tower, sec. 50, lot 351, Gate of Heaven Cemetery, Hawthorne, NY.

6829. Nungesser, Charles Eugene Jules Marie (March 15, 1892–May 8, 1927) A leading French air ace in World War I, with 43 aerial combat victories. He and his co-pilot, **Francis Coil**, left Paris in an attempt to fly non-stop to New York — the reverse of what Lindbergh was doing — but were lost over the Atlantic and never seen again.

6830. Nunn, Bobby (Ulysses B. Nunn, Sept. 20, 1925–Nov. 5, 1986) Bass singer with the original Coasters, specializing in clever novelty tunes by Jerry Leibert and Mike Stoller. Nunn sang with the Robins on *Smokey Joe's Cafe* (1955), with the Coasters 1956–58 on *Down in Mexico, Young Blood,* etc. He also worked with the Johnny Otis Band and had a hit with *Double Crossin' Blues.* Shortly after performing with the Coasters, he died in Los Angeles from a heart attack at 61. Buried under his full name. Sec. L, lot 392-B, Evergreen Cemetery, Los Angeles.

6831. Nureyev, Rudolf (March 17, 1938–Jan. 6, 1993) Flamboyant, charismatic Russian born ballet star, called the greatest male dancer of his time. He defected from the Soviet Union in 1961 and for nearly thirty years dominated his art with performances including *Sleeping Beauty* and a long running teaming with ballerina Margot Fonteyn at London's Royal Ballet, beginning in 1962, including the classics as well as contemporary works. He also performed, choreographed and conducted with the Paris Opera, which he directed from 1983–89. He and Fonteyn appeared often with the Martha Graham Dance Company. Nureyev also starred in the films *Valentino* and *Exposed.* His last public appearance, though ill with AIDS, was in Paris at the premiere of his production of "La Bayadere" in October 1992. He died at 54 in a Paris hospital three months later. His funeral was held at the Paris Opera, with burial in the place once chosen for many Russian exiles, St. Genevieve-des-Bois Cemetery, outside Paris.

6832. Nurmi, Paavo (July 13, 1897–Oct. 2, 1973) The Flying Finn, among the greatest of runners, won nine gold and three silver medals in three Olympic contests, 1920, '24 and '28. Later a successful businessman, he died from heart disease in Helsinki at 76, was given a state funeral there and buried at his hometown on the southwestern coast. Old Cemetery, Turku, Finland.

6833. Nurse, Rebecca (c 1620–June 19, 1692) Martyr of the Salem Witch Trials in what is now Danvers, but was in 1691–92 Salem Village, five miles northwest of the present town of Salem. Hysterical girls, after naming the town women Tituba, Sarah Good and Sarah Osborn as witches also accused, on March 19, 1692, the frail, elderly Rebecca Nurse. She was taken from her bed on March 23 and hanged on June 19 despite the frantic efforts of her family to save her. After the execution, her family secretly removed her body and buried it behind her home, a red saltbox house still standing at what is now 149 Pine Street in Danvers. The exact location of the grave is lost, but the family graveyard is reached by a footpath leading from the rear of the house through a cornfield. There in 1891 the Nurse family erected a monument to her with the lines from John Greenleaf Whittier: *O Christian martyr, who for truth could die, When all about thee owned the hideous lie! The world, redeemed from superstition's sway, is breathing freer for thy sake today!* Forty of her neighbors had signed a petition vouching for her exemplary character in an effort to prevent her death, and a monument to them stands nearby in the quiet and secluded graveyard. Rebecca Nurse homestead, family graveyard, Danvers, MA.

6834. Nyby, Christian (Sept. 1, 1913–Sept. 17 1993) Film editor on *To Have and Have Not* and *The Big Sleep* for Howard Hawks later directed, including *The Thing* (1951, produced by Hawks). He died at 80 in Temecula, California. Ashes scattered at sea.

6835. Nye, Carroll (Robert Carroll Nye, Oct. 4, 1901–March 17, 1974) Character actor from Canton, Ohio, also a radio commentator and columnist. He played Scarlett O'Hara's second husband, Frank Kennedy, in *Gone With the Wind* (1939). Loving Kindness, lot 8739, Forest Lawn Hollywood Hills, Los Angeles.

6836. Nye, Gerald P. (Dec. 19, 1892–July 17, 1971) Isolationist Senator from North Dakota 1925–1945. Sec. I, lot 218, #5, Fort Lincoln Cemetery, Bladensburg Road, Brentwood, MD.

6837. Nye, Louis (May 1, 1913–Oct. 9, 2005) Actor-comedian from Hartford, Connecticut, active on radio and in clubs played snobbish, effete Gordon Hathaway on *The Steve Allen Show* 1956–61, with the greeting "Hi Ho Steverino!," reprised in part as Banker Drysdale's foppish heir Sonny in the 1962 season of *The Beverly Hillbillies.* Last seen in HBO's *Curb Your Enthusiasm* 2000–2002. He died in Los Angeles from lung cancer at 92. Acacia Gardens, cr/wall, space TT-643, Hillside Memorial Park, Los Angeles.

6838. Nyro, Laura (Laura Nigro Bianchini, Oct. 18, 1947–April 8, 1997) Bronx born songwriter of the late 60's and 70's penned *Stoned Soul Picnic, Sweet Blindness, Wedding Bell Blues,* all recorded by the Fifth Dimension, *And When I Die* (Blood, Sweat and Tears), *Eli's Coming* (Three Dog Night), and *Stoney End* and *Time and Love,* recorded by Barbra Streisand. Her own recordings included several albums 1968–71, notably *Eli and the Thirteenth Confession* (1968). She died at 49 from ovarian cancer in her home at Danbury, Connecticut. Cremated at Pine Grove Crematory in Waterbury through the Tomlinson mortuary in Danbury, her ashes were returned to her companion Maria Desiderio at their residence near Danbury and were buried, along with those of her Belgian Tervuran Ember, at the foot of a Japanese maple tree outside her window. Desiderio also died of ovarian cancer, on November 26, 1999, at 45, and her ashes were buried there too.

6839. Oakie, Jack (Lewis Delaney Offield, Nov. 12, 1903–Jan. 23, 1978) Stocky comedic actor in genial roles in over a hundred films in the 1930's and 40's. Retired since 1962, he died from an aneurysm in Northridge, California, survived by his wife **Victoria Horne** (*q.v.*). His first wife, Venita Varden, died in a plane crash in 1948. His tablet is inscribed with both his real and stage names, dates of birth and death, and the epitaph, from Shakespeare, *In a simple double take thou hast more than voice e'er spake* and *When you hear laughter, that wonderful sound, you know that Jack Oakie's around.* Whispering Pines, lot 1066, Forest Lawn, Glendale, CA.

6840. Oakland, Simon (Aug. 28, 1915–Aug. 29, 1983) New York born character actor of great versatility; his film roles include *I Want to Live* (1958), *Murder Inc., Psycho* (1960, as the psychiatrist), *Bullitt* (1968), *The Night Stalker, The Night Strangler,* many others. Frequent guest shots on numerous TV shows through the 1960's and 70's (*Twilight Zone* episode *The Thirty Fathom Grave* 1963), and a regular on *Kolchak: The Night Stalker* (1974–5). He died in Palm Springs. Cremated by Wiefels and Sons mortuary. Ashes buried at sea.

6841. Oakley, Annie (Phoebe Ann Oakley Mozee, Aug. 13, 1860–Nov. 3, 1926) Wild west show sharpshooter from Darke County, Ohio, known as Little Sure Shot won a shooting match at age fifteen against Frank Butler, who she later married. She traveled with Buffalo Bill's Wild West Show for several years until she was partially paralyzed in a Chicago train wreck in 1901. She died in Greenville, Ohio, of pernicious anemia at 66. As specified beforehand, she had a female embalmer and a private funeral, held quietly on November 5 at the home of Mr. and Mrs. Fred Grote in Greenville, one day earlier than the press was told it would be. She was cremated in Cincinnati and returned to Greenville, with the ashes placed in a silver cup inscribed *To Annie Oakley from the people of France. Exposition Universal 1889.* The cup with her ashes was put into an oak box and held until November 23, when it was buried on Thanksgiving Day in the coffin of **Frank Butler**, who was dying at the time of his wife's death. A red granite stone with her name and dates on it was erected in line with that of Butler's, though there is actually nothing under her stone. Brock Cemetery, Brock, Darke County, OH.

6842. Oakley, Barry (April 4, 1948–Nov 11, 1972) Chicago born member of the Allman Brothers Band, killed in a motorcycle wreck just over a year after a similar wreck at the same location killed fellow band member Duane Allman. They are buried beside one another with white marble headstones and grave length slabs. Oakley's stone reads *Set free Nov. 11, 1972, And the road goes on forever* and, at the base of his slab *Help thy brother's boat across and lo! Thine own has reached the shore.* Valley below Carnation Ridge, Rose Hill Cemetery, Macon, GA.

6843. Oakman, Wheeler (Wheeler Eichelberger, Feb. 21, 1890–March 19, 1949) B melodrama and western actor of the 1920's and 30's, often a villain (*Lights of New York, The Western Code*), died at Van Nuys, California, at 59. Unmarked. Block I, sec. 11201, lot 2, Valhalla Memorial Park, North Hollywood, CA.

6844. Oates, Johnny (Johnny Lane Oates, Jan. 21, 1946–Dec. 24, 2004) Baseball catcher and manager from Silva, North Carolina, with the Orioles 1970–72, Atlanta Braves 1973–5, Phillies 1975–6, Dodgers 1977–79, and Yankees 1980–81, then coached before managing Baltimore 1991–94 and the Texas Rangers from 1996–2001, where he won the division, taking them to postseason play again in 1998 and '99, but eliminated all three times by the Yankees. He died from brain cancer at 58. Sunset Memorial Park, Chester, VA.

6845. Oates, Warren (July 5, 1928–April 3, 1982) Actor from Depoy, Kentucky, often cast in redneck roles of either humorous, tough, or sadistic nature (*Ride the High Country, In the Heat of the Night, The Wild Bunch, Two Lane Blacktop, Tribes, Bring Me the Head of Alfredo Garcia, Stripes*). He died from a heart attack at 53. Unsubstantiated, per *Find-A-Grave*, his ashes were scattered in Montana. Cremated at Forest Lawn, Glendale, through Forest Lawn Hollywood Hills, Los Angeles. Ashes returned to family.

6846. O'Banion, Dean aka **Dion O'Banion** (Charles Dean [death certificate] or Dean C. [gravestone] O'Banion, July 8, 1892–Nov. 10, 1924) Maroa, Illinois, born former altar boy at Chicago's Holy Name Cathedral grew up in the city's Little Hell section. The name "Dion" often given him was likely a reporter's invention or mistake. He became the head of the northside bootlegging operations allied with Johnny Torrio, as well as running a flower shop across State Street from Holy Name. Having offended the Genna brothers and other members within the Torrio configuration, as well as setting up Torrio himself for an arrest, O'Banion was arranging a floral tribute for Mike Merlo, the late head of the Unione Sicilione in Chicago, when he was approached in his flower shop by three men. One, long believed to be Frank Yale in town for Merlo's funeral, shook his hand and held it firmly while the other two, believed to be John Sacalise and Albert Anselmi, shot him six times at close range. Like Big Jim Colosimo four years before, O'Banion had a colossal "send off" from his "pals"; his funeral cost upwards of $100,000, with elaborate wreaths from several enemies. He was denied Catholic rites but the Rev. Patrick Malloy, who had known him as an altar boy, went to the grave without his vestments to say three Hail Marys and the Lord's Prayer. O'Banion lay only 40' from where a bishop and two archbishops were entombed, so when his wife Viola built a towering spire over the grave, Cardinal Mundelin asked her to take it down in favor of a less conspicuous monument. An obelisk still marks the grave in section L, across from the Bishop's mausoleum, Mount Carmel Cemetery, Hillside, Illinois. O'Banion's mother **Emma O'Banion** died in 1901 of tuberculosis when he was nine, causing the move to Chicago. He bought her red granite headstone with the wrong date (1868–1898) in the cemetery at Maroa, Illinois. An older brother, **Floyd,** nicknamed Jock, died at 25 February 25, 1913, from lobar pneumonia and was buried (never marked) in Mt. Carmel Cemetery, Hillside, IL.

6847. O'Bannon, Frank (Frank Lewis O'Bannon, Jan. 30, 1930–Sept. 13, 2003) Democratic governor of Indiana from Corydon, elected in 1996 and 2000, had just over a year left in his second term was he was found unconscious from a massive stroke in his Chicago hotel room, and died five days later at 73 in Northwestern Memorial Hospital there. Service and cremation through Crown Hill Funeral Home, Indianapolis. Ashes buried Cedar Hill Cemetery, Corydon, IN.

6848. O'Bannon, Presley (1776–Sept. 12, 1850) The first U.S. serviceman to plant an American flag on foreign soil was Marine Lt. O'Bannon, at Tripoli in 1805. Marble slab, other end of central section from Richard Mentor Johnson. Frankfort (State) Cemetery, Frankfort, KY.

6849. Ober, Philip (March 23, 1902–Sept. 13, 1982) Character actor in officious parts, ranging from Deborah Kerr's husband in *From Here to Eternity* and the V.I.P. Cary Grant is accused of stabbing in *North By Northwest* to Dore Schary in the *I Love Lucy* episodes set in Hollywood. He was married at the time to actress Vivian Vance. Cremated by Chapel of the Pines Crematory in Los Angeles, his ashes were returned to the residence in Puerto Vallarta, Mexico.

6850. Oberholtzer, Madge *see* **D.C. Stephenson.**

6851. Oberon, Merle (Estelle Merle O'Brien Thompson, Feb. 19, 1911–Nov. 23, 1979) Actress born in Bombay and educated in both India and England was promoted by British film producer Alexander Korda, who married her. Among her best known films were *The Scarlet Pimpernel, These Three, Till We Meet Again, Lydia,* and particularly as Kathy, opposite Olivier as Heathcliff in *Wuthering Heights* (1939). She and Korda were divorced in 1945. Her fourth husband was Robert Wolders, who survived her. Long in fragile health, she suffered a stroke at her Malibu home. Services at All Saints Episcopal Church in Beverly Hills. Her plaque as well as her death certificate lists her birth date as 1917. Garden of Remembrance sec., Forest Lawn, Glendale, CA.

6852. O'Berta, "Dingbat" (John Oberta, 1903–March 5, 1930) Southside Chicago hoodlum during the city's bootlegging heyday of the 1920's, associated with Joe Saltis and Frank McErlane. The name was given Oberta as a child, based on a comic strip. When Saltis absented himself from operations, a feud developed, and six weeks after McErlane was wounded by gunfire, Oberta was found shot to death in his Lincoln, along with his driver (whose gun had winged McErlane in the hospital). Buried unmarked in the plot of racketeer Big Tim Murphy, whose wife he married after Murphy was killed in June 1928. Sec. 6, Holy Sepulchre Cemetery, Worth, IL.

6853. Obici, Amadeo (July 15, 1877–May 21, 1942) Italian immigrant co-founded with Mario Reruzzi Planter's Nut Co. (Planter's Peanuts) in 1907. His ashes are behind his portrait in Obici Hospital, Suffolk, VA.

6854. Oboler, Arch (Dec. 7, 1907–March 19, 1987) Radio and film producer, writer and announcer made the first 3D film *Bwana Devil* (1953) but is better known for the radio program *Lights Out.* Cremated at Angeles Abbey, Compton, California (Los Angeles), through Aftercare Funeral Service.

6855. O'Brien, Darcy (Darcy George O'Brien, July 16, 1939–March 2, 1998) Author of true crime sagas including *Two of A Kind,* the story of The Hillside Strangler(s). Among his later works was *The Hidden Pope,* related to the Vatican's recognition of Israel; the work received the honor of being blessed by the Pope. The son of actors George O'Brien and Marguerite Churchill, he died from a heart ailment at 58 in Tulsa, Oklahoma. Cremated through Ninde mortuary and crematory, the ashes were returned to his family.

6856. O'Brien, Dave (David Barclay, May 31, 1912–Nov. 8, 1969) Tex O'Brien, character actor in many B films, best known as the luckless subject of the *Pete Smith Specialty* shorts of the 1940's. He died from a heart attack at 57. Ashes scattered at sea.

6857. O'Brien, Edmond (Edmond Joseph O'Brien, Sept. 10, 1915–May 9, 1985) Actor in films from 1939 (*The Hunchback of Notre Dame* 1939, *The Killers* 1946, *A Double Life* 1947, *D.O.A.* and *White Heat,* both 1949) won an Oscar as the press agent in *The Barefoot Contessa* (1954) and was nominated again for his role in *Seven Days in May* (1964). He died in Inglewood, California, from Alzheimer's Disease at 69. Military stone, sec. F (St. Joseph), tier 54, grave 50, Holy Cross Cemetery, Culver City, CA.

6858. O'Brien, George (April 19, 1899–Sept. 4, 1985) Silent and sound rugged screen star, son of a San Francisco chief of police, was the heavyweight boxing champion of the Pacific Fleet during World War I. Starring roles include F.W. Murnau's *Sunrise* (1927), *Noah's Ark* (1929) and *Daniel Boone* (1936). Many supporting roles, including *Fort Apache* (1948) and *She Wore A Yellow Ribbon* (1949). Married to actress Marguerite Churchill 1933–48; they were the parents of writer Darcy O'Brien. He died in a Broken Arrow, Oklahoma, convalescent home, six years after a debilitating stroke. Full burial at sea by the U.S. Navy.

6859. O'Brien, Lawrence (July 7, 1917–Sept. 27, 1990) Two time chairman of the Democratic National Committee helped engineer the election of John Kennedy to the senate from Massachusetts in 1952 and 1958 and to the presidency in 1960. He continued as a strategist for Johnson in 1964, serving as postmaster general 1965–68 and in the campaigns of Robert Kennedy and Hubert Humphrey in 1968. Democratic National Chairman 1970–72 and Commissioner of the National Basketball Association 1975–1984. He was credited with instituting a comprehensive drug and alcohol policy as well as introducing the three point shot and approving free agent status after two years. He died at Cornell Medical Center in Manhattan at 73. St. Catherine sec., lot 163, grave 2, St. Michael's Cemetery, Springfield, MA.

6860. O'Brien, Pat (Nov. 11, 1899–Oct. 15, 1983) Actor from Milwaukee, a childhood friend of Spencer Tracy. Both Irish Catholics, they attended the same school and joined the Navy together in World War I. O'Brien became a star as the fast talking reporter in *The Front Page* (1931), and later as a favorite priest at Warner Brothers trying to save Cagney's soul (*Angels With Dirty Faces, The Fighting 69th*), or as *Knute Rockne, All American* (1940), wringing the most out of the Gipper speech, and in later years in occasional Tracy films (*The People Against O'Hara* and *The Last Hurrah*). He also turned up in Cagney's last film, *Ragtime* (1981). The Irishman's Irishman, he was a perennial St. Patrick's Day celebrity. He died at 84 from cardiac arrest following prostate surgery in St. John's Hospital, Santa Monica, where The Gipper (then President Ronald Reagan) had phoned him regularly. Buried near Jackie Coogan, Jimmy Durante and Edmond O'Brien. Sec. F (St. Joseph), tier 56, grave 62, Holy Cross Cemetery, Culver City, CA.

6861. O'Brien, "Philadelphia Jack" (John or Joseph Francis Hagen, Jan. 17, 1878–Nov. 12, 1942) Light heavyweight boxing champion 1905–1912. Sec. 4, lot 2, grave 6, Holy Cross Cemetery, Yeadon, Philadelphia, PA.

6862. O'Brien, Tom (Thomas O'Brien, July 25, 1891–June 9, 1947) Silent and sound character actor in burly serio-comic roles (Bull in *The Big Parade* 1925). Masonic sec., lot 377, Forest Lawn, Glendale, CA.

6863. O'Brien, Virginia (April 8, 1919–Jan. 16, 2001) Deadpan singer-comedienne in primarily musicals 1940–47 (*Sky Murder, The Big Store, Ringside Maisie, Lady Be Good, Ship Ahoy, Panama Hattie, Thousands Cheer, DuBarry Was A Lady, Ziegfeld Follies, The Harvey Girls, Till the Clouds Roll By, Merton of the Movies*). Married to Kirk Alyn 1943–55, her last appearance was in *Gus* (1976). She died at the Motion Picture Country Hospital at 81. Buried as Virginia O'Brien. Resurrection Slope, lot 2486, space 2, Forest Lawn, Glendale, CA.

6864. O'Brien, Willis H. (March 2, 1886–Nov. 8, 1962) Master animator of models in films, particularly lauded for his superior work in *The Lost World* (1925) and *King Kong* (1933). He received an Oscar for *Mighty Joe Young* (1949). Deodora Hall South, sec W, niche 15, Pierce Brothers Chapel of the Pines Crematory, Los Angeles.

6865. O'Brien-Moore, Erin (May 2, 1902–May 3, 1979) Los Angeles born actress in films of the 1930's, also on radio. Her better films included *Seven Keys to Baldpate* (1935), *The Ex–Mrs. Bradford* (1936), *Black Legion* (1937) and others at Warner Brothers. Ashes scattered in the rose garden at Westwood Memorial Park, west Los Angeles.

6866. O'Callaghan, Mike (Donal O'Callaghan, Sept. 10, 1929–March 5, 2004) Chairman of the *Las Vegas Sun* and Democratic Governor of Nevada 1971–79. A decorated Korean War veteran. Sec. Q, grave 1079, Southern Nevada Veterans Memorial Cemetery, Boulder City, NV.

6867. O'Carolan, Turlough (1670–March 25, 1738) Blind Irish harpist and composer of over 200 melodies, including baroque, jigs and laments, he was given the title Chief Musician of Ireland. Kilronan Churchyard outside of Keadue, Kilronan, Roscommon.

6868. O'Casey, Sean (John Casey, March 30, 1880–Sept. 18, 1964) Irish playwright whose gritty, realistic portrayals of Dublin slum areas and tragedy during times of violence yet mixed with humor interlaced his best known works, *Shadow of A Gunman, Juno and the Paycock,* and *The Plough and the Stars.* Cremated at Golders Green Crematorium, north London.

6869. Ochs, Adolph (March 12, 1858–April 8, 1935) Publisher of the *New York Times* from 1896 until his death made the *Times* the most respected American newspaper and raised its circulation to five times the readership he began with at the turn of the century. Family mausoleum, on right at turn up hill. Temple Israel Cemetery, Hastings-on-Hudson, NY.

6870. Ochs, Phil (Dec. 19, 1940–April 9, 1976) Folk singer, guitarist and lyricist considered second only to Bob Dylan in his output of protest songs 1963–68, though he considered himself a topical and not a folk singer. His theme *I Ain't Marching Anymore* (1963) was among the first anti–Vietnam songs. Others include *Nobody Buys from the Flower Lady, A Toast to Those Who Are Gone, I'll Be There* and *Outside of a Small Circle of Friends.* His output declined soon after 1968; he lost his singing voice and descended into depression and alcoholism before hanging himself in his sister's home in Far Rockaway, Queens, N.Y.C., at 35. He was cremated the next day and the ashes taken to Scotland by a friend, who scattered them from Edinburgh Castle as the Pipe Band of the Queen's Own Highlanders played *Flowers of the Forest.*

6871. O'Connell, Arthur (March 29, 1908–May 19, 1981) New York born stage and screen actor of Irish descent usually portrayed bewildered, mild mannered

583 6872–6881 • O'Connor

characters. He was nominated for an Oscar for both *Picnic* (1955) and *Anatomy of a Murder* (1959). TV series *The Second Hundred Years* 1967–8. He died from Alzheimer's Disease at 73. Sec. 34, (3rd) Calvary Cemetery, Woodside, Queens, N.Y.C.

6872. O'Connell, Helen (May 23, 1920–Sept. 9, 1993) Popular blonde vocalist with Jimmy Dorsey in the 1940's known for duets with Bob Eberly including *Amapola, Tangerine, Green Eyes*. She also co-hosted TV's *Here's Hollywood* in the early 1960's, continuing to perform into the 1990's. She died in San Diego from cancer. Sec. CC, tier 56, grave 55, Holy Cross Cemetery, Culver City, CA.

6873. O'Connell, Richard (Sept. 19, 1914–Aug. 18, 2002) Boston Red Sox executive who revived the sinking franchise and helped assemble the pennant winning teams of 1967 and 1975. Willow Court garden crypts, Birch Avenue, Mt. Auburn Cemetery, Cambridge, MA.

6874. O'Connor, Basil (Jan. 8, 1892–March 9, 1972) Friend of FDR organized the March of Dimes in 1946. Polished black cylinder has a granite base with *Only as he lives in both the private and the public world can a man today take hold of his own destiny.* Westhampton Cemetery, Westhampton, Long Island, NY.

6875. O'Connor, Carroll (John Carroll O'Connor, Aug. 2, 1924–June 21, 2001) New York born stage and screen actor had appeared in films of the 1960's (*Lonely Are the Brave, Cleopatra, In Harm's Way, What Did You Do in the War Daddy?, Marlowe*) before being cast as blustery bigot Archie Bunker in the CBS television series that opened sitcoms up to reality, *All in the Family*, from January 1971 to 1979, winning him four Emmys. It was followed by the more bland *Archie Bunker's Place* 1979–83, but in 1988 he re-emerged with a second hit series *In the Heat of the Night*, which ran for six years and featured his adopted son Hugh. Following the younger O'Connor's suicide in 1995, O'Connor successfully fought a slander suit from the drug supplier he blamed for his son's death. Last seen in *Return to Me* (1999), he died from a heart attack at Brotman Medical Center in Culver City, California, at 76. Mass at St. Paul the Apostle Church in Westwood through Gates-Kingsley-Gates/Moeller-Murphy, followed by cremation. The ashes were kept in a safe at the mortuary until completion of a new area at Westwood. O'Connor's enclosed lot and gray upright monument is between those of Jack Lemmon and Billy Wilder, just east of the chapel. Inscribed by January 2003. Westwood Memorial Park, west Los Angeles.

6876. O'Connor, Donald (Donald David O'Connor, Aug. 28, 1925–Sept. 27, 2003) Rubber limbed song and dance comedian, a child actor in Hollywood (*Tom Sawyer Detective, Beau Geste* 1939), best known for the number *Make Em Laugh* in the 1952 film *Singin' in the Rain* as well as six *Francis the Talking Mule* pictures. In his later years he lived at Sedona, Arizona,

with his wife Gloria but in his final illness stayed at the Motion Picture Country Home and Hospital, Woodland Hills, California, where he died from heart failure at 78. Ashes buried October 3 through Forest Lawn Hollywood Hills, at sea off Los Angeles County.

6877. O'Connor, Flannery (Mary Flannery O'Connor, March 25, 1925–Aug. 3, 1964) Savannah born novelist wrote on themes toward the south but applicable to life anywhere, with a slant toward wry or black humor, including *A Good Man is Hard to Find and other short stories* (1953). Novels include *Wise Blood* (1952) and *The Violent Bear It Away* (1960). She died at 39 after ten years illness with lupus. Buried beneath a grave length slab near the front fence, Memory Hill Cemetery, Milledgeville, GA.

6878. O'Connor, Frances (Frances Bell O'Connor, Sept. 9, 1914–Jan. 30, 1982) Minnesota born girl with no arms, adept at using her feet for any and all tasks usually done with hands, appeared in Tod Browning's film *Freaks* (1932). She died from heart disease at 67 in her home at Long Beach, California. Buried February 5. Marked. Sec. L, lot 381-B, Evergreen Cemetery (Memorial Park), Los Angeles.

6879. O'Connor, Hugh (April 7, 1962–March 28, 1995) Actor son of actor Carroll O'Connor appeared with his father as a deputy in the TV series *In the Heat of the Night* 1988–1994. His death, a suicide by gunshot at 32, his father tried in vain to prevent over the phone. The elder O'Connor blamed his son's death squarely on an individual who had fostered and perpetuated his son's drug habit. The ashes were returned to the family in Pacific Palisades. By January 2003 when Carroll O'Connor's stone was inscribed, his son's ashes had been buried with his and Hugh's name and dates also placed on the stone. Garden enclosure between Billy Wilder and Jack Lemmon, east of the office and facing the road. Westwood Memorial Park, West Los Angeles.

6880. O'Connor, John, Cardinal (Jan. 15, 1920–May 3, 2000) Philadelphia native served as a chaplain with the U.S. Navy in Korea and Vietnam and retired a rear admiral. The Bishop of Scranton, he became cardinal in New York in January 1984 and was elevated to Cardinal of New York's archdiocese in 1985. As a conservative Catholic, he took stands against gay-lesbian protection by mayoral order, and against any support of abortion rights. He died at 80, nine months after having a brain tumor removed. Mass and entombment (below, no admittance) St. Patrick's Cathedral, Manhattan, N.Y.C.

6881. O'Connor, Pat (Oct. 9, 1928–May 30, 1958) Race driver at the Indianapolis 500 from 1953, a test driver for Firestone. In the first lap of the 1958 memorial day race his Sumar Special ran into a wreck (eventually involving thirteen cars) on the first lap of the race and burst into flames, ending his life at 29. His grave, like Wilbur Shaw's a short distance away, is usually marked by crossed checkered flags on Memorial Day. They are also engraved on the monument above his name plate. Vernon Cemetery, North Vernon, IN.

6882. O'Connor, Robert Emmet (March 18, 1885–Sept. 4, 1962) Chubby Irish character actor from Milwaukee specialized in tough gang bosses (*The Public Enemy* 1931), wardens (*Up the River* 1930), cops (*Mystery of the Wax Museum* (1933), detectives (*A Night at the Opera* (1935) with many stints as the proverbial Irish cop. He died from burns suffered in a fire. Garden of Meditation, lot 45, Valhalla Memorial Park, North Hollywood, CA.

6883. O'Connor, Una (Agnes Teresa McGlade, Oct. 23, 1880–Feb. 4, 1959) Actress from Belfast, Northern Ireland, began with the Abbey Players in 1911. By the early 1930's in Hollywood she had appeared as wailing, acid tongued women, often maids, in James Whale's *The Invisible Man* (1933) and *Bride of Frankenstein* (1935) as well as *Cavalcade* (1933), *The Barretts of Wimpole Street* (1934), *The Informer* (1935, as Mrs. McPhillip), *David Copperfield* (as Mrs. Gummage), many others. Her roles varied from whiny caricatures to devoted, pixieish maids with sharp features and delivery, last used in *Witness for the Prosecution* (1957). From January 1957 she lived at the Mary Manning Walsh home in Manhattan, where she died. Mass at Holy Family Chapel. Her small marker has both her real and stage names on it. Sec 70, lot 46, grave 16, (4th) Calvary Cemetery, Woodside, Queens, N.Y.C.

6884. O'Daniel, Wilbert Lee "Pappy" (March 11, 1890–May 11, 1969) Governor of Texas 1939–1941 and Senator 1941–49, defeating Lyndon Johnson for the office (which LBJ later won). A flour mill executive, earning him the sobriquet "Pass the Biscuits Pappy," who spoke segregation and promoted country music with his Hillbilly Boys. His persona was lampooned in the Cohen Brothers' 2000 film *O Brother Where Art Thou?* Historical marker near grave. Monument Garden near Maureen Connolly, Sparkman Hillcrest Memorial Park, Dallas, TX.

6885. O'Day, Molly (Suzanne Noonan, Oct. 16, 1911–Oct. 15, 1998) Actress from Bayonne, New Jersey, sister of actress Sally O'Neil, in films from 1927 (*The Patent Leather Kid*), left c. 1935 during a rapid weight gain. Married name Kenaston. Mass at St. Patrick's Catholic Church, Arroyo Grande, California. Cremated, her ashes were not buried in area cemeteries. Reportedly scattered at sea.

6886. O'Day, Nell (Nell Oday, Sept. 22, 1909–Jan. 5, 1989) Texas born actress in films from *The King of Jazz* (1930) and on stage through the 1930s was also known as the leading lady in many Johnny Mack Brown westerns, as well as the second lead in *The Mystery of Marie Roget* (1942). By the 1950s she left films for writing, including the play *The Bride of Denmark Hill*, written in Europe and produced on television and the BBC. She died at Temple Hospital, Los Angeles, at 79. Cremated January 13 at the Los Angeles County Crematory through the L.A. County Medical Center Mortuary. Ashes released to friend March 22, 1989.

6887. O'Dea, Jimmy (April 26, 1899–Jan. 7, 1965) Irish music hall star, a favorite with Gaelic audiences, teamed with Maureen Potter often from 1939 until his death. Films include some silents, *Jimmy Boy* (1935), *Ireland's Border Line* (1939), *The Rising of the Moon* (1957), and *Darby O'Gill and the Little People* (as King Brian, 1959). He died in Dublin at 65 and was given a large state funeral. Glasnevin Cemetery, Dublin.

6888. Odets, Clifford (July 18, 1906–Aug. 14, 1963) Top rated author and playwright from the Group Theatre penned *Golden Boy* and wrote the 1939 screenplay. Directorial works include *None But the Lonely Heart* (1944) and *The Story on Page One* (1959). Odets died from cancer at 57. Niche G2079, Columbarium of Honor, Gardens of Honor (private), Forest Lawn, Glendale, CA.

6889. Odom, Andrew (Dec. 15, 1936–Dec. 23, 1991) Chicago Blues singer, with limited recordings, died from a heart attack while driving from Buddy Guy's Legends to the Checkerboard Lounge. Unmarked. Good Shepherd, lot 196B, space 2, Washington Memorial Cemetery, Homewood, IL.

6890. Odom, Joe (Joseph Algerine Odom, March 22, 1948–Nov. 2, 1991) Attorney in Savannah was a colorful character in John Berendt's book *Midnight in the Garden of Good and Evil*, portrayed in the story as the love interest of Mandy, based on Nancy Hillis. The relationship was fictional. Odom died from complications related to AIDS in Savannah's Hamilton-Turner House at 43. Family lot behind the church, inside chain link fence. Bull Creek Cemetery, Claxton, GA.

6891. O'Donnell, Cathy (Ann Steely, July 6, 1923–April 11, 1970) Alabama born screen actress in sweet and gentle roles including Harold Russell's fiancée Wilma in *The Best Years of Our Lives* (1946). Also *The Miniver Story* (1951). Sister-in-law of William Wyler. Wyler lot, Eventide sec., lot 3023, Forest Lawn, Glendale, CA.

6892. O'Donnell, Kenny (Kenneth P. O'Donnell, March 3, 1924–Sept. 9, 1977) Close friend and secretary to Congressman, Senator and President John Kennedy 1951–63 was later an unsuccessful candidate for Governor of Massachusetts. He also worked on the Robert Kennedy campaign in 1968. Co-authored (with Dave Powers) *Johnny, We Hardly Knew Ye* (1973). He died in Boston at 53. Cushing Knoll, lot 15, Holyhood Cemetery, Brookline, MA.

6893. O'Donnell, Klondike (William Aloy[s]ius O'Donnell, May 12, 1894–Dec. 12, 1976) The leader of the Westside O'Donnells during Chicago's murderous prohibition wars of the 1920's, allied himself off and on with the Torrio-Capone factions, though a dispute with Capone over Cicero operations led to the accidental killing of attorney William McSwiggin (*q.v.*), while in Klondike's company. His brothers

Bernard and Myles (*q.v.*) are both with their parents in Mt. Carmel Cemetery, Hillside, west of Chicago, but Klondike is not. A veteran of the U.S. Army Sept. 22, 1917 to April 10, 1919, he died (as found by Mari Abba in June 2004) in the Veterans Administration Hines Hospital, Proviso Township, Cook County, at 82, two years after Bernard. Entombed with his wife Rae Kohn. Alcove of Love, level D, Chapel floor, Tower of Memory Mausoleum, Oakwoods Cemetery, Chicago, IL.

6894. O'Donnell, Myles (1903–Feb. 22, 1932) Youngest of the Westside O'Donnells, with brothers Bernard and Klondike (William), were enforcers for Capone in the early to mid 1920's. Myles was shot in a bar while forcing Capone alcohol on the establishment. He later escaped injury in the murder of William McSwiggin by Capone and others. By the late 1920's Klondike went to prison, later returning to Chicago to work again for the Capone organization they had opposed for a time. Myles died in bed from heart disease and pneumonia at 28. Family lot with his parents, **Bernard** (1896–April 10, 1974) and other brothers (though not William "Klondike"). Sec. N, block 10, lot 9, Mt. Carmel Cemetery, Hillside, IL.

6895. O'Donnell, Spike (James Edward O'Donnell, Nov. 29, 1889–Aug. 26, 1962) Leader of the southside O'Donnell brothers, bootleggers and gunmen in Chicago in the early 1920's. Released from Joliet in 1923, he engaged in a two year war with the Torrio-Capone and Saltis-McErlane factions on the southside. After his brother Walter was killed with Harry Hasmiller in January 1925, he boasted that he could "lick this bird Capone" in a fist fight any day. In September 1925, having been shot or shot at several times, he was the first Chicago target of a machine gun, used by Frank McErlane. Spike survived, faded from the scene, and sought other pursuits, dying from a second heart attack at 72 in his Chicago home. **Walter** and **Tommy** (dec. 1958), are in the P.J. O'Donnell lot, block 40, s 1/2 lot 8, Mt. Olivet Cemetery, Chicago, Ill. Spike O'Donnell was buried in sec. N, St. Mary's Cemetery, Evergreen Park, IL.

6896. O'Donnell, Tim (Timothy G. O'Donnell, July 28, 1943–Dec. 13, 2000) ABC news radio anchor from 1968, doing hourly coverage of the world's top stories. Maryrest Cemetery, Mahwah, NJ.

6897. O'Donnell, Walter "Spec" (April 9, 1911–Oct. 14, 1986) Red haired, freckled juvenile actor of the 1920's and 30's. Block 6, row 20, plot P, Arbor Vista Memorial Park, Madera, CA.

6898. O'Donoghue, Deirdre (July 16, 1946–Jan. 21, 2001) New York City born radio host, first in Boston in 1974 and in Los Angeles at KCRW FM by 1980 with her program *Snap* (Saturday Night Avant Pop) and in the mid 1980's began her *Breakfast With the Beatles* show, first at KMET, then at KNX and KLSX until 1991, with a wide following, known for her devotion to talent and emotion over popularity. She

was found dead in her home in Santa Monica at 54. Half her ashes were scattered and half sent to Ireland.

6899. O'Donoghue, Michael (Jan. 5, 1940–Nov. 8, 1994) Comedy writer from Sauquoit, New York, co-created *National Lampoon* magazine in 1969 and NBC's *Saturday Night Live* in the Fall of 1975, appearing in the first opening sketch with John Belushi as a language instructor. He won two Emmys for writing on the show, as well as a Grammy for *Single Bars, Single Women*, recorded by Dolly Parton. He died in Manhattan from a cerebral hemorrhage at 54. Ashes scattered in Ireland.

6900. O'Doul, Lefty (Francis Joseph O'Doul, March 4, 1897–Dec. 7, 1969) Former pitcher switched to the outfield and made his reputation as a slugger with a record 254 hits with the Philadelphia Phillies in 1929, winning the N.L. batting championship that year and in 1932 when he hit .368 with the Brooklyn Dodgers. Retired in 1933 with the Giants. Equally popular in the minors and as a coach, he initiated Kids' Day, distributing bags of baseballs. His green marble monument, quarried from the Brazilian Andes, bears a white Carrara marble ball and bat and inscriptions of affection to *The Man in the Green Suit. He was here at a good time and had a good time while he was here,* along with his accomplishments, titles and averages. Sec. I, Cypress Lawn Cemetery, Colma, CA.

6901. O'Driscoll, Martha (March 4, 1922–Nov. 3, 1998) Blonde actress from Tulsa in over 30 films 1938–47, including *Lil Abner* (1940, as Daisy Mae), *Ghost Catchers* (1944), *Here Come the Co-Eds* and *House of Dracula* (1945). Married to Arthur Appleton, they resided for thirty years at Northbrook, Illinois, outside Chicago. She died at 76 in Indian Creek Village (Miami), Florida. Service through Walsh and Wood mortuary at the Church-by-the-Sea, Bal Harbor, Florida, November 7, 1998. Cremated, her ashes were placed in the Appleton family room, south end of Aster Hall, Rosehill Mausoleum, Rosehill Cemetery, Chicago, IL.

6902. O'Dwyer, William (July 11, 1890–Nov. 24, 1964) Popular Irish born New York City mayor, Bill-O gained fame as the gang busting district attorney for Kings County 1939–1941, exposing Murder, Inc., and resulting in the eventual execution of Lepke Buchalter and six henchmen. Mayor of New York 1946–50; he resigned in 1950 and was appointed Ambassador to Mexico by President Truman, returning in 1960 to practice law. At his death from a heart attack at 74, over 1700 attended his mass at St. Patrick's Cathedral in Manhattan. Sec. 2, grave 889, Arlington National Cemetery, Arlington, VA.

6903. Offenbach, Jacques (June 20, 1819–Oct. 5, 1880) German born composer of the *Can Can* wrote many light operettas but is best known for his *Tales of Hoffman*, produced posthumously. Rose colored slab and monument surmounted by a bronze bust. Div. 9, Montmartre Cemetery, Paris.

6904. Ogdon, Ina Mae Duley (April 3, 1872–

May 18, 1964) Ohio housewife and lyricist wrote the words to *Brighten the Corner Where You Are* in 1913. Set to music in Wilkes-Barre, Pennsylvania, it caught on to such an extent that Theodore Roosevelt used it at his political rallies by 1916. Sec. 26, lot 69, grave 2, Woodlawn Cemetery, Toledo, OH.

6905. Ogle, Charles (June 5, 1865–Oct. 11, 1940) Silent screen actor from Steubenville, Ohio, created his own makeup as the monster in the Edison *Frankenstein* (1910), the first screen version of the story. Also in *Treasure Island* (1920) and *The Covered Wagon* (1923), he retired with the advent of sound. Sunrise Slope, lot 5961, Forest Lawn, Glendale, CA.

6906. Oglethorpe, James Edward (Dec. 22, 1696–June 30, 1785) English explorer and member of the House of Commons landed at Yamacaw Bluff along the Savannah River in 1733, naming that part of North America Georgia in honor of King George, and created a plan for squares comprising a town, Savannah, still in existence and the first planned city in the United States. He remained there for several years, defending the colony against Spain in 1742, before returning to England the next year. Parish Church of All Saints, Cranham Hall, Essex.

6907. O'Grady, Lani (Lanita Rose Agrati, Oct. 2, 1954–Sept. 25, 2001) Actress played Mary, the eldest daughter on TV's *Eight is Enough* 1977–1981. Because of panic attacks, she later said, she came to abuse prescription drugs, including Valium, as well as alcohol. Though she had overcome the addictions by the mid 1990's, in 1998 she checked herself into another detox center; she was found dead three years later at 46 in her Valencia mobile home. Her ashes were scattered over Maui.

6908. O'Hair, Madelyn Murray (April 13, 1919–c. Sept. 29, 1995) The force behind the 1963 banning of prayer and Bible reading in the public schools disappeared at 76 from San Antonio, Texas, in September 1995, along with her son John Garth Murray, 40, and a granddaughter Robin Murray O'Hair, 30. Apparently robbed of $500,000 in gold coins and killed by four people including O'Hair's office manager, an estate auction of their possessions was held in Plugerville, Texas, in 1999. Their bones were unearthed at Camp Wood, about 125 miles from San Antonio, in January 2001, when David Roland Waters led them there to arrange a plea bargain. They were positively identified March 14, based in part on the elder O'Hair's hip replacement. The bodies had been dismembered and the legs laid atop one another. Though O'Hair's American Atheists wanted the bones, her son, San Antonio evangelist William Murray, the child over whom the court case was originally filed, said he would take charge of the remains and bury them but without prayer. "You cannot pray them out of hell," Murray said. Their ashes were buried beside another son, without markers, in a cemetery at Austin, TX.

6909. O'Hanlon, George (Nov. 23, 1912–Feb. 11, 1989) Voice of George Jetson on *The Jetsons* 1962–63

and in endless reruns. Ashes unmarked in the rose garden, Valley Oaks Memorial Park, Westlake Village, CA.

6910. O'Hanlon, Virginia (Laura Virginia O'Hanlon, July 20, 1889–May 13, 1971) As she recalled it in later years, as an eight year old in New York City, confused by differing stories from her friends, she asked her father if there was really a Santa Claus and he told her to write and ask the *New York Sun*, which she did. An editorial response was anonymously penned by assistant editor Francis P. Church and printed in the *Sun* September 21, 1897, with the excerpted line "Yes, Virginia, there is a Santa Claus," becoming part of Christmas lore and making Virginia O'Hanlon (later Mrs. Virginia Douglas) famous for the remainder of her eighty one years. A retired New York school teacher, she died at Volatie in upstate New York, near Kinderhook. North Chatham Cemetery, North Chatham, NY.

6911. O'Hara, Frank (Nov. 27, 1926–July 25, 1966) Playwright and poet (*A City Winter*), art curator, wrote *Invitation to the Theatre* (1951). Hit and killed by a car on Fire Island at 39. His flat stone has the epitaph *Grace to be born and live as variously as possible.* Green River Cemetery, East Hampton, Long Island, NY.

6912. O'Hara, John (Jan. 31, 1905–April 11, 1970) Writer from Pottsville, Pennsylvania, whose novels and short stories focused primarily on the upper or upper middle economic strata of society. Among his works adapted for the screen were *Butterfield 8* and *From the Terrace.* His upright tombstone, shaped and decorated in 17th century Colonial style, is inscribed *Better than anyone else he told the truth about his time. He was a professional. He wrote honestly and well.* Facing the Grover Cleveland lot, Princeton Cemetery, Princeton, NJ.

6913. O'Hare, Edward J. (Nov. 5, 1893–Nov. 8, 1939) Chicago sportsman worked undercover to help federal agents bring Al Capone to trial for tax evasion in 1931. In 1939 he was fingered for death by Chicago gang leaders for refusing to contribute money for Capone as well as his part in the conviction. In his last days he began carrying a gun, but was machine gunned in his car while fleeing from assassins. His son Butch was an outstanding World War II air ace, killed in action, for whom Chicago's O'Hare Airport was named. Mass for O'Hare, Sr., was at St. Patrick's Cathedral in St. Louis. Family monument, sec. 6, lot 801, grave 4, Memorial Park Cemetery, St. Louis, Missouri. **Butch O'Hare** (Edward Henry O'Hare, March 13, 1914–Nov. 27, 1943) is commemorated on the Wall of the Missing at the National Cemetery of the Pacific (The Punchbowl), Honolulu, HI.

6914. O. Henry (William Sidney Porter, Sept. 11, 1862–June 5, 1910) American writer best known for his short stories with ironic endings, penned as O. Henry. He was from Greensboro, North Carolina, and lived in Texas 1882–86 until he was convicted of embezzling while a teller in an Austin bank. He served three years (1898–1901) in the Ohio State Penitentiary at Columbus, which accounted for his aversion to giving out photographs or information about his life, particularly to his daughter. In 1910 he entered a New York hospital as Will S. Parker, suffering from cirrhosis of the liver, diabetes and a dilated heart. His last words, to a nurse, were to turn up the lights and that he didn't want to go home in the dark. His funeral was held at the Little Church Around the Corner (the Church of the Transfiguration) in Manhattan, where the solemnities had to compete with a happy wedding party. His headstone has on it only his real name and the dates, with no mention of his pen name or work. Thomas Wolfe was buried in the same cemetery in 1937. Sec. K, Riverside Cemetery, Asheville, NC.

6915. O'Herlihy, Daniel (May 1, 1919–Feb. 17, 2005) Irish actor from Wexford in over seventy plays at the Abbey and Gate theaters came to Hollywood after appearing in Carol Reed's *Odd Man Out* (1947), playing McDuff in Orson Welles' version of *Macbeth* (1948), and Oscar nominated for the lead in Luis Bunuel's *The Adventures of Robinson Crusoe* (1954). Later appearances include *Imitation of Life* (1959), *The Cabinet of Dr. Caligari* (1962), *Fail Safe*, TV's *The Travels of Jamie McPheeters*, *MacArthur* (as FDR, 1977), *The Dead* (1987, John Huston's last film, made in Dublin) and in the TV series *Twin Peaks* (1990–91). He died in Malibu at 85. Cremated by Gates-Kingsley-Gates, Santa Monica. Ashes to his wife for burial at Prospect graveyard, Gorey, County Wexford, Ireland.

6916. O'Keefe, Dennis (Edward Flanagan, March 28, 1908–Aug. 31, 1968) Leading man in films from the 1930's to the 60's, much at RKO in the 1940's (*You'll Find Out* 1940, *Topper Returns* 1941, *The Leopard Man* 1943). He died at 60 from lung cancer, survived by his widow, Steffi Duna. Ashes scattered at sea.

6917. O'Keeffe, Georgia (Nov. 15, 1887–March 6, 1986) Leading 20th century American artist, a former advertising illustrator, worked from 1918 under the sponsorship of photographer Alfred Stieglitz, her husband. Her paintings were primarily simplistic, colorful images of flowers, desert scenes, etc. She died at 98 in Santa Fe, New Mexico. No funeral or memorial services. Ashes scattered in the desert in New Mexico.

6918. Oland, Warner (Johan Warner Olund, Oct. 3, 1880–Aug. 6, 1938) Actor from Umea, Sweden, associated with his roles as Oriental villains in Pearl White serials and later silent and sound films (*Before Dawn* 1933, *Werewolf of London* 1935) and as Chinese detective *Charlie Chan* at Fox 1931–37. He came to Connecticut at 13, was educated in Boston and had a home near there as well as in Los Angeles and off the west coast of Mexico. Divorced in 1937 from his wife Edith Shearer, his health had deteriorated from alcoholism and a nervous breakdown when he sailed for Sweden to recuperate but died from bronchial pneumonia in a Stockholm hospital at 57. He was cremated and part of his ashes reportedly buried in his native Umea. All or part of the ashes, however, were returned to the U.S. and buried beneath a large rounded pink flagstone from his nearby home. Along the front, Southborough Cemetery, Southborough, MA.

6919. O'Laughlen, Michael (June 1840–Sept. 23, 1867) Conspirator with John Wilkes Booth and others in the murder of President Lincoln in April 1865 was sentenced to Dry Tortugas off Florida, as were Arnold and Dr. Mudd, but died two years later in a yellow fever epidemic. White obelisk. Sec. AA, lot 43, Green Mount Cemetery, Baltimore, MD.

6920. Olcott, Chauncey (Chancellor Olcott, July 21, 1858/1859–March 18, 1932) Irish tenor and Broadway musical comedy star from Buffalo, New York, composer of *My Wild Irish Rose* and *Mother Machree*. A favorite personality of turn of the century New York. He died in Monte Carlo. He and his wife have a bench and flat plaques. Hickory Knoll sec. 125, in from Chestnut Ave., Woodlawn Cemetery, the Bronx, N.Y.C.

6921. Olcott, Sidney (John Sidney Allcott, Sept. 20, 1873–Dec. 16, 1949) Early actor began managing Biograph Studios in New York c. 1906 and directing from 1907–1927 many films about Ireland and *From the Manger to the Cross* (1913), several early westerns and Mary Pickford films. He died from a heart attack in Hollywood. Buried in his mother's grave at Park Lawn Cemetery, Toronto, Ontario.

6922. Oldfield, Barney (Jan. 29, 1878–Oct. 4, 1946) Speed racing driver set a record in 1910 (131 mph) and in a 1914 three day run from L.A. to Phoenix. Like many flamboyant sports figures. he appeared in the movies (*Barney Oldfield's Race for Life* 1916). He died from a stroke in Los Angeles. Sec D, lot 290, grave 11, Holy Cross Cemetery, Culver City, CA.

6923. Olds, Ransom Eli (June 3, 1864–Aug. 26, 1950) Auto manufacturing pioneer built the first gasoline powered four wheeler in 1893. His "Merry Oldsmobile" was first built in 1899. The song *In My Merry Oldsmobile* in 1904 was inspired by a cross country trip taken in one. In early 1992 the family mausoleum was broken into and several urns, nameplates and a baby's coffin were stolen, though R.E. Olds' crypt was not disturbed. Sec. F, lot 157, Mount Hope Cemetery, Lansing, MI.

6924. O'Leary, Catherine (Mrs. Patrick) (Mrs. James P. O'Leary, c.1827–July 3, 1895) A firmly imbedded segment of Chicago historical lore, *The Mrs. O'Leary* lived with her husband and children at 137 DeKoven Street, where on October 8, 1871, she or her infamous cow allegedly knocked over a lantern in her barn, beginning the devastating Great Chicago Fire. Sec. 13, corner, Mt. Olivet Cemetery, Chicago, IL.

6925. Olin, Steve *see* **Tim Crews.**

6926. Oliver (William Oliver Swofford, Feb. 22, 1945–Feb. 12, 2000) Vocalist had hits in 1969 with *Good Morning Starshine* (from the Broadway musical *Hair*) and *Jean* (from the film *The Prime of Miss Jean Brodie*). He left the business and became a sales representative for a pharmaceutical company, moving to Shreveport, Louisiana, where he was a vestryman at St. Paul's Episcopal Church until his death from cancer at 54 in LSU Hospital. Marked by August 2004. Sec. 69, lot 11, space 9, Laurel Land Memorial Park, Dallas, TX.

6927. Oliver, Edna May (Edna May Cox Nutter, Nov. 9, 1883–Nov. 9, 1942) Actress from Malden, Massachusetts, played eccentric spinsters, aunts or maids with elongated features and crisp diction, always mixed with biting and condescending sarcasm tempered with a warm heart. Roles include the Hildegarde mysteries with James Gleason, *Little Women* (1933), *David Copperfield* (as Aunt Betsy) and *A Tale of Two Cities* (both 1935), *Romeo and Juliet* (1936). She was ill from August 1941 with an intestinal infection prior to her death on her 59th birthday at Cedars of Lebanon Hospital in Los Angeles. Her friend Virginia Hammond was with her when she died. She had planned to be buried in Malden but was not. At her service at Forest Lawn, playwright Lynn Starling read from Kahlil Gibran's *The Prophet*: *And let today embrace the past with remembrance and the future with longing*. Ornamental black urn, near comedian Franklin Pangborn. Columbarium of Security, niche 16879, Gardenia Terrace, Great Mausoleum, Forest Lawn, Glendale, CA.

6928. Oliver, Gordon (April 27, 1910–Jan. 26, 1995) Los Angeles born actor in thirty seven films, primarily in the 1930's through the 50's, including *Jezebel, Brother Rat, Since You Went Away,* and *The Spiral Staircase* (1946, as Steven). Sec 6, lot 661, Hollywood Forever Cemetery, Hollywood (Los Angeles), CA.

6929. Oliver, Joseph "King" (May 11, 1885–April 8, 1938) New Orleans jazz cornet player began his Creole Jazz Band in 1920, featuring Louis Armstrong, Lil Hardin, Kid Ory, etc. He was a major influence on Armstrong's career and the premier black jazz band prior to Fletcher Henderson. Many of his recordings have been preserved and re-issued, but in his own lifetime he was less appreciated. His career declined with the 30's and he was forgotten, working as a janitor in the years prior to his death at 52. Unmarked until the 1990's, when an upright marker with his name, dates, and *Jazz pioneer* was erected. Near the fence at 211th St., Salvia sec., range 16, 18 spaces left of the two trunk tree, Woodlawn Cemetery, the Bronx, N.Y.C.

6930. Oliver, Susan (Susan/Charlotte Gercke, Feb. 13, 1932–May 10, 1990) Blonde TV actress of the 1950's, 60's and 70's (*Twilight Zone* episode *People Are Alike All Over* 1959, *Andy Griffith* episode *Prisoner of Love* 1964, *Peyton Place* as Ann Howard, *Star Trek* as Vina) in a few films (*Butterfield 8*). A licensed pilot, she attempted to become the first woman to fly a single engine plane from New York to Moscow but was refused use of Soviet air space and deterred in Denmark. She died from cancer at 58. Ashes scattered at sea off the coast of Long Beach, CA.

6931. Olivier, Laurence (Lord Olivier) (May 22, 1907–July 11, 1989) British thespian, knighted, the most highly acclaimed actor of his day and the only member of his profession elected to the House of Lords. He was widely hailed for his Shakespearian work, as director and actor in the filmed *Henry V* (1944), which brought him a special Oscar, and for *Hamlet* (1948), for which he won an Oscar as best actor. He was subsequently nominated for Oscars nine times and awarded a special one in 1979 for the full body of his work. Among his other noted films were *Wuthering Heights* (1939, as Heathcliff) and *Rebecca* (1940). Married to actresses Jill Esmond in the 1930's, Vivien Leigh 1940–1960, and lastly to Joan Plowright. He died from cancer at 82 in his sleep at his London home. Theatre lights were dimmed in London's west end and for a moment on Broadway at curtain time. Flags were lowered to half staff at the National Theater (which he had founded) and the Royal Shakespearian Theater in Stratford-on-Avon. Though his tablet in the floor was not unveiled until September 1991, by Sir John Geilgud, he was cremated and in 1990 was honored by being only the fifth actor to have his ashes interred (near Shakespeare's statue in the Poets Corner) in Westminster Abbey, London.

6932. Olmstead, Gertrude (Nov. 13, 1904–Jan. 18, 1975) Chicago born silent screen actress at Universal from 1920, in *Trilby, Babbitt, George Washington Jr., The Girl of the Limberlost, The Monster, Ben Hur, Mr. Wu,* retiring in 1929 with sound, though she appeared in a few talkies (*Show of Shows, Sonny Boy* 1929). Married to director Robert Z. Leonard (*q.v.*). Sanctuary of Vespers, crypt 5231, Memorial Terrace, Great Mausoleum, Forest Lawn, Glendale, CA.

6933. Olmsted, Frederick Law (April 27, 1822–Aug. 28, 1903) Architect who planned and landscaped Central Park in Manhattan worked on many other well known projects but is best known as the father of the green oasis in the center of America's melting pot. Old North Cemetery, Hartford, CT.

6934. Olsen, Johnny (Johnny Olson, May 22, 1910–Oct. 17, 1985) Longtime radio and TV announcer. Wall niche, Rosewood Cemetery, Lewisburg, WV.

6935. Olsen, Moroni (June 27, 1889–Nov. 22, 1954) Character actor from Ogden, Utah, in a wide range of roles in many films from 1935 until his death, including John Knox in *Mary of Scotland* (1936) and Robert E. Lee in *Santa Fe Trail* (1940). E-4-25, Ogden City Cemetery, Ogden, UT.

6936. Olsen, Ole (John Sigvard Olsen, Nov. 6, 1892–Jan. 26, 1963) Comedian teamed with Chic Johnson in films of the 1930's, early at Fox and later Universal. Best known for *Hellzapoppin* on stage and screen. He died from a kidney ailment and is buried with Johnson (the only comedy team except Smith and Dale buried together). Garden of Devotion (upper), space 101B, Palm Memorial Park, Las Vegas, NV.

6937. Olson, Barbara (Dec. 27, 1955–Sept. 11, 2001) Former U.S. federal prosecutor, attorney, author, frequent conservative political commentator and the wife of U.S. Solicitor General Ted Olson. A passenger aboard American Airlines flight 77 that was hijacked and crashed into the Pentagon September 11, 2001. Funeral at the Cathedral of St. Thomas More, Arlington, and through Shepherd of the Bay near Ellison Bay, forty miles north of Sturgeon Bay, Wisconsin. Sent from Delaware for burial at Ellison Bay Cemetery, Ellison Bay, Door County, Wisconsin. Her name is also on a memorial at Arlington National Cemetery, along with the 183 other victims of the flight. Unidentifiable remains were buried there September 12, 2002. For five of the victims it is their only grave.

6938. Olson, Carl "Bobo" (July 11, 1928–Jan. 16, 2002) Hawaii's middleweight boxing champion fought from age 16 in 1944, won the middleweight title over Randy Turpin in October 1953 and lost it to Sugar Ray Robinson in 1955; he continued boxing, retiring in 1966. Mass at Our Lady of Peace Cathedral in Honolulu January 23. Ashes scattered afterward fronting the Honolulu Elks Lodge.

6939. Olson, Charles (Dec. 27, 1910–Jan. 10, 1970) Massachusetts born poet and critic known for his *Maximus Poems* 1953–1968, and as a theoretician of the post World War II open form, using canto in the tradition of Ezra Pound. Seventeenth century style upright tombstone, with a death's head at the top. Beech Brook Cemetery, Gloucester, MA.

6940. Olson, Christina (May 3, 1893–Jan. 27, 1968) The subject of Andrew Wyeth's 1948 painting *Christina's World* was a resident of Cushing, Maine, who — because of a probable degenerative disease never officially diagnosed — had began having trouble walking as a child. A romance from 1912 ended in 1917 when the boy met a girl he described as athletic. She soon lost the ability to walk but more often crawled than used a wheelchair. The painting by Wyeth, a family friend, showed her crawling down the hill from her house to visit her parents' graves. She never left her residence until November 1967, when she and her brother were forced into facilities due to ill health. She died weeks later at 74. Pleasant Point Road Cemetery, Cushing, ME.

6941. Olson, Frank R. (d. Nov. 28, 1953) Germ warfare researcher whose leap from a New York City window was ruled a suicide. Forty years later, on June 2, 1994, he was exhumed on orders from his sons from Linden Hills Cemetery, Frederick, Maryland. Their contention that he was murdered after being given doses of LSD was supported in part in that there were no glass cuts or bruises on the head of the well preserved body, though no definite conclusion was drawn. He was reburied with his wife at Mt. Olivet Cemetery, Frederick, Maryland. Removed 2002.

6942. Olson, Lyndon (Lyndon Lowell Olson, Sr., Jan. 22, 1925–Dec. 20, 2005) Lawyer successfully argued *Avery vs. Midland County* before the U.S. Supreme Court in 1968, extending the "one man, one vote" principle to local governments, stating their makeup must reflect the population represented, as in state and U.S. congressional districts. Oakwood Cemetery, Waco, TX.

6943. O'Malley, J. Pat (James Patrick O'Malley, March 15, 1904–Feb. 27, 1985) Jowl faced Irish born English revue performer landed in Hollywood as a character actor, from *Lassie Come Home* (1943) through voices in several Disney cartoon features (*Alice in Wonderland, One Hundred and One Dalmatians, The Jungle Book*) and literally hundreds of television roles from the 1950's, often as crafty characters, including the *Spin and Marty* series, *The Swamp Fox,* several *Twilight Zone* episodes, notably *The Fugitive,* many others up to 1981. A resident of San Juan, Capistrano, California he died at 80 from a lung ailment at Orange County Hospital, Mission Viejo. Cremated through Armstrong Family mortuary, Los Angeles, at Coastal Cremation Inc., Pasadena. Ashes reportedly scattered at sea.

6944. O'Malley, Patrick (Sept. 3, 1890–May 21, 1966) Leading man of silents later in character roles in films into the 60's. Sec. F, tier 8, grave 13, San Fernando Mission Cemetery, Mission Hills, CA.

6945. O'Malley, Walter F. (Oct. 9, 1903–Aug. 9, 1979) Baseball executive gained his greatest fame and animosity when he broke Brooklyn's heart by moving the Dodgers to Los Angeles after the 1957 season. He bought the team with Branch Rickey in the 1940's and was sole owner by the time he made the move. O'Malley, like the Dodgers, remained in L.A. Sec. P, lot 526 (across from the front of the mausoleum), Holy Cross Cemetery, Culver City, CA.

6946. Omarr, Sydney (Sydney Kimmelman, Aug. 5, 1926–Jan. 2, 2003) Philadelphia born astrologer to the stars; he authored thirteen books as well as writing horoscopes in *The Chicago Sun Times* and over 200 other newspapers. Sec. 57A, grave 1904, Riverside National Cemetery, Riverside, CA.

6947. Onassis, Aristotle (Jan. 20, 1906–March 15, 1975) Greek shipping and airline tycoon drew his greatest fame in 1968 with his marriage to former U.S. First Lady Jacqueline Kennedy. Amid rumors of impending divorce and with his Olympic Airlines bankrupt, he was hospitalized in France, accompanied by his wife, at the American Hospital in Neuilly. Despite some friction between his wife and his family, she returned to the hospital after his death and escorted his body to his private Greek Island, Skorpios, accompanied by her former brother-in-law, Senator Edward Kennedy. Onassis was buried on Skorpios next to his son **Alexander**, who died in a plane crash in 1973.

His daughter **Christina Onassis** (Dec 11 1950–Nov 19 1988) died unexpectedly at 37 and was also interred with her family on Skorpios.

6948. Onassis, Jacqueline Lee Bouvier Kennedy (July 28, 1929–May 19, 1994) Southampton, Long Island, born debutante, educated at Vassar and fluent in several languages, was the daughter of Janet Norton, descended from the Virginia Lees, later (1942) Mrs. Hugh Auchincloss, and John "Black Jack" Bouvier. A photographer with the *Washington Times-Herald* prior to 1953, when she married Massachusetts Senator John Kennedy, as First Lady 1961–63 she brought an emphasis on cultural events to the White House, emphasizing its art and history, showcased in her televised 1962 tour. Widely admired for her poise during the trauma of her husband's assassination and funeral in 1963, she retired to an increasingly private life while interest in her never waned. Remarried to Greek shipping tycoon Aristotle Onassis in 1968, she was for three decades the object of intense curiosity and pursuit by tabloids and much of the general public, familiarly known as Jackie O. From the late 1970's she worked in New York publishing, bringing out several books and remaining active in funding for the arts as well as historic preservation. Diagnosed with non–Hodgkin's lymphoma in December 1993, she died five months later in the Fifth Avenue suite where she had lived since 1964. The Frank E. Campbell mortuary brought the casket, through the pressing crowds outside, to her apartment, where her wake was held privately from Friday May 20 through Sunday May 22. Only on Monday did the casket leave her suite, for the funeral mass at St. Loyola Church on 84th and Park Avenue, two blocks away. The service was broadcast over a public address system, with readings by her companion Maurice Templesman, her children, and the eulogy delivered by her former brother-in-law Sen. Edward Kennedy. Flown by air force jet to Washington, D.C., she was placed to the left of President Kennedy at Arlington, where crowds also lined the route. Her committal service was simpler and briefer than the funeral she planned for her husband thirty years before, with readings again by her children and brief remarks by President Clinton, the burial service was conducted by retired New Orleans Archbishop Philip Hannan, who delivered the eulogy for John Kennedy at his service in St. Matthew's in Washington in 1963. On October 5, 1994, the president's black granite plaque was moved to the left approximately 30" to maintain symmetry, as her similar one bearing her name and dates was installed. Their two infant children have smaller plaques at either end of the terraced area. Sec. 45, grid U-35, Arlington National Cemetery, Arlington, VA.

6949. O'Neal, Patrick (Sept. 26, 1927–Sept. 9, 1994) Actor from Ocala, Florida, grew up in Cleveland. Various film (from *The Mad Magician, The Kremlin Letter, In Harms' Way, The Way We Were, The Stepford Wives*) and TV (*Twilight Zone* episode *A Short Drink From A Certain Fountain*), from leads to cads. He was also a New York restaurateur, he co-owned O'Neals with his wife and his brother Michael. He died from cancer in Manhattan. A memorial service was held at his restaurant. Reportedly cremated and ashes to family.

6950. O'Neal, Ron (Calvin Ron O'Neal, Sept. 1, 1937–Jan. 14, 2004) African-American actor born in New York, raised in Cleveland, in thirty five films 1970–2002, indelibly identified for his title role in *Superfly* (1972) and its sequel the next year. Others include *When A Stranger Calls* (1979). He died in Los Angeles from pancreatic cancer at 66. Cremated through Forest Lawn, Hollywood Hills. Ashes to his family in Los Angeles.

6951. O'Neil, Barbara (July 17, 1910–Sept. 3, 1980) New England born actress in *Stella Dallas* (1937), *Tower of London* (1939), as Mrs. O'Hara in *Gone With the Wind* (also 1939), *I Remember Mama* (1948, as Uncle Chris's wife) and nominated for an Oscar for her role in *All This and Heaven Too* (1940). Never married, she died at Cos Cob, Connecticut. Cremated at Ferncliff Cemetery, Hartsdale, New York. Small blue flush metal plaque. Blackman lot, sec. G, block 1, site 2, lot 2, El Carmela Cemetery, Pacific Grove, CA.

6952. O'Neil, Nance (Gertrude Lamson, Oct. 8, 1874–Feb. 7, 1965) Stage and silent screen actress from Oakland, California, essayed the roles of Lady Macbeth, *Camille, Hedda Gabler*, many others, but was best known as the close friend — and rumored lover (though unsubstantiated) — of reputed murderess Lizzie Borden, in the years after Borden's acquittal of the 1892 axe murder of her father and step-mother in Fall River, Massachusetts, when she moved to her own house, dubbed *Maplecroft*. O'Neil appeared in silents for Fox 1915–17, but acted primarily on the stage through the 1920s, and returned to films with talkies, including the disastrous *His Glorious Night* (1929) with John Gilbert. Married to actor Alfred Hickman until his death in 1931. She died at 90 in the Actors Fund Home, Englewood, New Jersey. Cremated at Ferncliff Cemetery, Hartsdale, New York, her ashes were interred (unmarked, as Gertrude Hickman aka Nance O'Neil) with Hickman's on March 10, 1965. Niche 10022, Columbarium of the Sanctuaries, Memorial Terrace, Great Mausoleum, Forest Lawn, Glendale, CA.

6953. O'Neil, Sally (Virginia Louise Noonan, Oct. 23, 1908/1910–June 18, 1968) Actress from Bayonne, New Jersey, in films 1925–1938 (*Sally Irene and Mary* 1925, *The Battle of the Sexes* 1928, *Kathleen Mavourneen* UK 1930 and U.S. 1937, *The Brat, Murder By the Clock* 1931, many others). Buried as Sally O. Battles, her married name. She died from pneumonia in Galesburg, Illinois. Block 3, lot 10, space 6, Galesburg Memorial Park, Galesburg, IL.

6954. O'Neill, Dick (Richard Francis O'Neill,

Aug. 29, 1928–Nov. 17, 1998) TV actor in hard nosed urban parts (Charlie Cagney in *Cagney and Lacey*, Detective Kelly in *Barney Miller*) died from a heart attack in Santa Monica at 70. Cremated December 3 by Cremation Society South Bay. Ashes returned December 8 to family in Beverly Hills.

6955. O'Neill, Eugene (Oct. 16, 1888–Nov. 27, 1953) Dramatist, author of *Beyond the Horizon, Anna Christie* (1922), *Strange Interlude* (1928), *The Iceman Cometh* (1946) and *Long Day's Journey Into Night* (produced three years after his death), all Pulitzer Prize winners. Among his other works was *Ah, Wilderness* and *Morning Becomes Electra*. He had lived among waterfront bums until 1913, when he began writing in a sanitarium. In 1950 his son had committed suicide by slitting both his wrist and his ankle. O'Neill wrote no more after that. Suffering from palsy, he resided at Marblehead, twenty miles northeast of Boston. After much fighting, separations and reunions, he and his wife Carlotta lived in adjoining rooms in a suite at the Shelton Hotel in Boston. His last words were reported to have been "I knew it! I knew it! Born in a hotel room, goddamn it, and dying in a hotel room!" Carlotta attempted to keep the burial a secret but was unsuccessful. She died in 1970; their daughter Oona was the last wife of Charles Chaplin. A half boulder with a flat face inscribed with their names and dates marks O'Neill and his wife. Sec. 8, off Chestnut Ave., Forest Hills Cemetery, Jamaica Plain, Boston, MA.

6956. O'Neill, Henry (Aug. 10, 1891–May 18, 1961) Versatile character actor from Orange, New Jersey, in over two hundred films, generally as benevolent lawyers, doctors, judges, officers (*Midnight Alibi, Fog Over Frisco, Midnight, The Florentine Dagger, Doctor Socrates, Bullets or Ballots, Anthony Adverse, Marked Woman, Jezebel, Juarez, The Fighting 69th, They Drive By Night, Shadow of the Thin Man, Three Wise Fools, The Return of October, The People Against O'Hara*, dozens more). Military marker. Sec. C, lot 124, grave 7, San Fernando Mission Cemetery, Mission Hills, CA.

6957. O'Neill, Tip (Thomas Philip O'Neill Jr., Dec. 9, 1912–Jan. 5, 1994) Democratic congressman from Cambridge, Massachusetts, known for the slogan "All politics is local" took John Kennedy's House seat in 1952 when Kennedy moved to the Senate, becoming assistant majority leader in 1971, majority leader in 1973, and Speaker of the House 1977–1986, at his most visible as leader of the opposition during the Reagan years 1981–86, when he retired. Ill with cancer for several years, he died from a heart attack in a Boston hospital. Funeral at St. John the Evangelist Church in Cambridge. Marked by a polished charcoal plaque and bench; on the top rear of the bench is inscribed *I'll Be With You in Apple Blossom Time*. Mt. Pleasant Cemetery, Harwich Port, Cape Cod, MA. He also has a cenotaph at range 53, site 124, Congressional Cemetery, Washington, D.C.

6958. Onizuka, Ellison (June 24, 1946–Jan. 28, 1986) Mission specialist aboard the space shuttle Challenger was killed along with six others when it exploded shortly after lift-off. The Hawaiian born Onizuka was buried with Buddhist ceremonies June 3, the last of the seven funerals. Sec. D, grave 1, National Memorial Cemetery of the Pacific (The Punchbowl), Honolulu, HI.

6959. Opatoshu, David (Jan. 30, 1918–April 29, 1996) New York born character actor from the Yiddish Theater on Broadway from 1938 and in films from 1948 (*The Naked City, Torn Curtain*), notably as the resistance leader in *Exodus* (1960). Much TV (*Twilight Zone* episode *Valley of the Shadow* 1963) including an Emmy for *Gideon's Trumpet* (1991). He died in Los Angeles at 78. Garden Mausoleum Court of Dedication, block 1, plot 40, space 6B, Hillside Memorial Park, Los Angeles.

6960. Ophuls, Max (May 6, 1902–March 26, 1957) German director married to **Hilde Wall** went to France in 1932 and remained until the Nazi occupation in 1940, moving to Switzerland and to Hollywood 1941–49, directing under the name **Max Opuls** (*Letter From An Unknown Woman, Caught, The Reckless Moment*). His films gained fame for their form, the *mise-en-scene*—a particularly fluid camera movement. He returned to Europe and died of a rheumatic heart condition in Hamburg at 54. Div. 86, columbarium, Pere Lachaise Cemetery, Paris.

6961. Oppenheim, E. Phillips (Edward Phillips Oppenheim, Oct. 22, 1866–Feb. 3, 1946) London born novelist known for his espionage thrillers, over 150 from 1884 until his death, including *The Mysterious Mr. Sabin, The Great Secret*—which anticipated the war in 1914, and *The Great Impersonation*, his best known work, filmed several times. He also predicted the second world war as early as 1928; caught at their villa on the French Riviera when Germany swept over France, he and his wife fled to Lisbon and to England. He died at 79 at La Vaquiedor, his home at St. Peter Port on Guernsey. Funeral and burial February 5 at St. Martin's Church cemetery, Guernsey, Channel Islands.

6962. Oppenheimer, J. Robert (April 22, 1904–Feb. 18, 1967) University of California physicist developed the atomic bomb, tested at Los Alamos, New Mexico, 1942–45. He later declined to work on the hydrogen bomb on moral grounds. At Princeton University 1947–1966. Ashes scattered off the Virgin Islands.

6963. Opuls *see* **Ophuls.**

6964. Orbach, Jerry (Jerome Bernard Orbach, Oct. 20, 1935–Dec. 28, 2004) Bronx born Broadway singer and actor introduced *Try to Remember* in *The Fantastiks* in 1960 and won a Tony in 1969 for *Promises, Promises,* but after appearing in a few films through the 1980's—*Prince of the City, Crimes and Misdemeanors, Dirty Dancing, Mr. Saturday Night*—widened his image and came to personify the street wise, world weary, quintessential New Yorker, personified as detective Lennie Briscoe in the television series *Law and Order* from 1992 until his death at 69 from prostate cancer in Sloane-Kettering Hospital, Manhattan. Service at The Riverside Memorial Chapel on the upper west side. Garden State Crematory, North Bergen, New Jersey. Ashes to family. Interred in a niche, north end of Riverside Terrace Mausoleum, left of Riverside Drive entrance, western sec., Trinity Cemetery, 155th St., upper Manhattan, N.Y.C.

6965. Orbison, Roy (April 23, 1936–Dec. 6, 1988) Star singer from rockabilly origins topped the charts 1960–64 with *Only the Lonely, Crying, Blue Angel, Blue Bayou, Running Scared, Oh, Pretty Woman* and others, his jet black hair matched by the ever present sun glasses. He had returned to the charts and had just finished an album as one of the Traveling Wilburys when he died from a heart attack at 52 in Hendersonville, Tennessee. Though his family (wife **Claudette**, killed in a motorcycle crash at 25 in June 1966, and two sons, **Roy Dewayne**, 10, and **Anthony King**, 6, killed in an explosion and fire in 1968) are buried in the Sermon on the Mount section at Woodlawn Memorial Park in Nashville, Tennessee. He was buried in a still unmarked grave, just above that of Frank Tuttle. Sec. D, lot 97, Westwood Memorial Park, west Los Angeles.

6966. Orchard, Harry (Albert E. Horsley, March 18, 1866–April 13, 1954) Alleged killer of former Idaho Governor Frank Steunenberg was the hit man, adept at explosives, for Big Bill Haywood and other union organizers. Sec. C, block 8, grave 1, Morris Hill Cemetery, Boise, ID.

6967. Orellana, Sandra Lorena (Nov. 12, 1969–Nov. 3, 1996) An *Unsolved Mysteries* case, while allegedly engaged in sex on the balcony of a Los Angeles high rise, she went over the railing. Forest Park Westheimer, Houston, TX.

6968. Orgen, Little Augie (Jacob Orgen, 1901–Oct 16, 1927) New York gangster affiliated with Lepke Buchalter in the garment industry rackets employed Legs Diamond as a gunman from the early 20's. He was walking with Diamond when a machine gun cut him down on New York's lower east side. Block 3, Krashnoshetz, range 10, Mt. Judah Cemetery, Bushwick-Ridgewood, Queens, N.Y.C.

6969. Orion (Jimmy Bell Ellis, real name Jimmy H. Ellis, Sr., Feb. 26, 1945–Dec. 12, 1998) Rockabilly and country-rock, crossover singer and dead-on Elvis Presley impersonator worked with the Oak Ridge Boys, Jerry Lee Lewis, and recorded *Ebony Eyes* as a single on Sun in 1979. He was shot during a robbery of his pawn shop at 53. Div. 10, lot 62E, space 5, Live Oak Cemetery, Selma, AL.

6970. Ormandy, Eugene (Nov. 18, 1891–March 12, 1985) Conductor of the Philadelphia Symphony Orchestra recorded several collections. Pine Street Presbyterian Cemetery, Philadelphia, PA.

6971. O'Rourke, Heather (Dec. 27, 1975–Feb. 1, 1988) Child actress played Carol Ann in *Poltergeist* (1982) and its two sequels, repeatedly the object of the malevolent spirit's attentions. She died from a congenital intestinal obstruction and suspected septic shock at twelve during surgery at Children's Hospital in San Diego. Wall crypt, northwest corner area, with her plaque identifying her as *Carol Ann, Poltergeist I, II, III.* Westwood Memorial Park, west Los Angeles.

6972. O'Rourke, James H. (Aug. 24, 1852–Jan. 8, 1919) Baseball great known as The Orator for his extensive vocabulary was a power slugger with Boston, Providence and Buffalo in the 1870's and 80's. He won the N.L. batting title in 1884, managed at Buffalo and later umpired briefly in the 1890's after hitting .306 for Washington at forty one in 1893. Hall of Fame 1945. Sec. 2, lot 10, St. Michael's Cemetery, Stratford, CT.

6973. Orr, Robert D. (Robert Dunkerson Orr, Nov. 17, 1917–March 10, 2004) Ann Arbor, Michigan born governor of Indiana, with the Army in the Pacific during World War II before returning to his family's iron business in Evansville, served as Republican state senator, lieutenant governor 1973–81 and governor 1981–89, known for his 1987 educational reform package. He died in Indianapolis at 86. Sec. 24, lot 63, Crown Hill Cemetery, Indianapolis, IN.

6974. Orry-Kelly (Orry George Kelley, Dec. 31, 1896–Feb. 26, 1964) Australian designer at Warner Brothers and Fox. Academy Awards for *An American in Paris* and *Some Like It Hot.* Columbarium of Remembrance, niche 60282, Courts of Remembrance, Forest Lawn Hollywood Hills, Los Angeles.

6975. Orth, Frank (Feb. 21, 1880–March 17, 1962) Actor, former vaudevillian with his wife Ann Codee, in many films 1929–1953 in supporting roles (*The Ox Bow Incident, The Big Clock*) played Mike Sullivan (turned into Mike Ryan) in the *Dr. Kildare* films, and bumbling Inspector Tweedy in the Bonita Granville *Nancy Drew* films 1938–9. Devotion, lot 8863, Forest Lawn Hollywood Hills, Los Angeles.

6976. Orwell, George (Eric Blair, June 25, 1903–Jan. 23, 1950) English author of *Animal Farm* (1946) and *1984* (1949), futuristic predictions of gradual takeover by totalitarian governments and allegorical satires on the evolution of Soviet Russia. After the unexpected death of his wife in 1946 he went to live in the wilds of Jura off the west coast of Scotland. There, ill and without proper medical care, he wrote *1984* from August 1946 to November 1948. He had married editor Sonia Brownell in his room at University College Hospital in London, shortly before his death there from a massive hemorrhage of the lungs, caused by a tubercular condition he had neglected. Funeral at Christ Church, Albany Street. The burial was arranged by the Astor family. His upright tombstone is marked *Here lies Eric Arthur Blair* with his dates on it, All Saints Church Cemetery, Sutton Courtenay, near Abingdon, Berkshire.

6977. Ory, "Kid" (Edward Ory, Dec. 25, 1886–Jan. 23, 1973) Jazz trombone great led his own band in the 1910's but recorded and played later in the bands of King Oliver and Louis Armstrong, accompanied Ma Rainey and composed and recorded on his own. He died in Hawaii. Plans were being discussed in early 2000 to move him from the Los Angeles area to New Orleans. His plaque reads *Father of Dixieland Jazz.* Grotto, lot 59, Holy Cross Cemetery, Culver City, CA.

6978. Osborne, Jimmy (James Osborne, Jr., April 8, 1923–Dec. 26, 1957) Country-western vocalist known for his recordings *My Heart Echoes* (1947) and *The Death of Kathy Fiscus* (1949), which sold over a million copies. A suicide at 34. Sec. F, lot 241, Winchester Cemetery, Winchester, KY.

6979. Osborne, Vivienne (Dec. 10, 1896–June 10, 1961) Character actress in jaded roles, including the shrewish wife of Edward G. Robinson in *Two Seconds* (1932) and the executed murderess Ruth Rogen in Victor Halperin's *Supernatural* (1933). She was also Vincent Price's first wife in *Dragonwyck* (1946). Block L, lot 9, sec. 999, Valhalla Memorial Park, North Hollywood, CA.

6980. O'Shea, Michael (Edward Francis Michael O'Shea, March 17, 1906–Dec. 4, 1973) Amiable leading man in B films of the 1940's and 50's and the TV series *It's A Great Life* (1954–56) later worked as an undercover agent in Ventura County, California. Residing in Thousand Oaks from 1965 with his wife, actress Virginia Mayo, he died in Dallas from a heart attack at 67. Garden of Gethsemane, 313-C, Valley Oaks Memorial Park, Westlake Village, CA.

6981. O'Shea, Oscar (Oct. 8, 1881–April 5, 1960) Actor from Peterboro, Canada, played irascible old men in numerous films 1937–1953 (*Captains Courageous* 1937, as Cushman, *Of Mice and Men* 1939, *Riders of the Purple Sage* 1941, *The Mummy's Ghost* 1944, as the security guard, *My Wild Irish Rose* 1947, etc.). He died at the Motion Picture Country Hospital in Los Angeles from emphysema at 78. Sec. D, lot 361, grave 1, Holy Cross Cemetery, Culver City, CA.

6982. Osterloh, Robert (May 31, 1918–April 16, 2001) Actor in varied film and television roles 1948–1972, usually quiet and often sinister, including *Criss Cross* (as Mr. Nelson), *White Heat, The Well, The Wild One, Riot in Cell Block 11, Invasion of the Body Snatchers* (ambulance driver), *I Bury the Living, Inherit the Wind.* He died at Los Osos, California, at 82. Cremated April 19 at Benedict-Retter in San Luis Obispo, for Coast Family Cremation Service there. Ashes to family at Los Osos, CA.

6983. Ostriche, Muriel (March 24, 1896–May 3, 1989) New York born silent screen actress with Biograph and Thanhouser, where the Princess Film Department was formed for her pictures, over sixty through 1915. From 1915–1920 she was known as the Moxie Girl. She later worked at IMP and Vitagraph, divorced Frank Brady and married Charles Copp (for a time the mayor of Manorhaven, Long Island), remaining in the New York area and out of films after the mid 1920's. After her husband's death in 1957, she

lived in Virginia and Florida with a daughter. She died in St. Petersburg, Florida, at 93. Southeastern Crematory, Clearwater, Fla. through the National Cremation Society. Ashes buried within the month in the Copp plot. Sec. 13, division A, plot 12, grave 5, Flushing Cemetery, Flushing, Queens, N.Y.C.

6984. O'Sullivan, Maureen (Maureen Paula O'Sullivan, May 17, 1911–June 22, 1998) Actress from Boyle, Ireland, in films from Frank Borzage's *Song O' My Heart* (1930). Famed as Jane to Johnny Weissmuller's Tarzan for a decade beginning with *Tarzan the Ape Man* (1932), as well as *Payment Deferred* (1932), *Tarzan and His Mate, The Barretts of Wimpole Street, The Thin Man* (all 1934), *David Copperfield* (1935), *Tarzan Escapes, The Devil Doll* (1936), *A Day at the Races* (1937), *Tarzan Finds a Son* (1939), *Tarzan's Secret Treasure* (1941) and *Tarzan's New York Adventure* (1942). Married to John Farrow, who directed her in *The Big Clock* (1948), from 1936 until his death in 1963. They were the parents of seven children, including actress Mia Farrow. Their son Michael died in an airplane collision at 18 in 1958. Her sporadic later appearances in films include *Never Too Late* (1965), *Hannah and Her Sisters* (with her daughter, 1985) and *Peggy Sue Got Married* (1986). Remarried in 1983 to James Cushing. A lifelong Catholic, she died at 87 in Scottsdale, Arizona, from a heart attack. Sent by Messengers mortuary in Phoenix to Gleason mortuary, Schenectady, New York (where she also had a home). Burial June 30 in Most Holy Redeemer Cemetery, Niskayuna, Schenectady County, NY.

6985. Oswald, Lee Harvey (Oct. 18, 1939–Nov. 24, 1963) The assassin of President Kennedy and Dallas policeman J.D. Tippit was himself assassinated on national television by Dallas nightclub owner Jack Ruby as he was being led from jail on Sunday morning, November 24. Rose Hill Memorial Park in Fort Worth had to accept the body for burial under Texas law since Oswald's mother had purchased a four grave plot there, but they were not pleased. Newsmen assigned to the burial served as pallbearers, and when the family's minister failed to appear, the committal service was performed by a clergyman who had been there by coincidence. He offered the words "We are not here to judge. We are here to lay him away before an understanding God." After endless theories that it was someone else buried in the grave, the body was exhumed October 4, 1981, was determined to be Oswald, and was reburied. The flat rose marker reads only *Oswald.* Sec. 17, near last set of steps on left, Rose Hill (Shannon-Rose Hill) Memorial Park, Fort Worth, TX.

6986. Otis, Harrison Gray (Feb. 10, 1837–July 30, 1917) Journalist and publisher, the Union Army veteran, took over the *Los Angeles Times* in 1886 and controlled it until 1914. His son-in-law **Harry Chandler** (1864–1944) took over the *Times* in 1914. Both men and their wives are in the Otis lot, marked by a large obelisk. Corner of sec. 12, Hollywood Forever Cemetery, Hollywood (Los Angeles), CA.

6987. Otis, James (Feb. 5, 1725–May 23, 1783) Colonial patriot resigned as Advocate General in 1760 when English revenue officers attempted to gain blanket search warrants for smuggled goods. He published *The Rights of the British Colonies Asserted and Proved* in 1764. Otis was killed by lightning. His grave is marked by a boulder with a plaque, like Sam Adams near by. Old Granary Burial Ground in historic downtown Boston, MA.

6988. Ott, Mel (Melvyn T. Ott, March 2, 1909–Nov. 21, 1958) "Master Melvyn," the Boy Wonder from Gretna, Louisiana, was among baseball's top sluggers during twenty two years with the New York Giants 1926–1948. Catcher, later a third baseman and outfielder, lauded for his RBI's. Hall of Fame 1951. Family mausoleum. Sec. 146, Metairie (Lake Lawn-Metairie) Cemetery, New Orleans, LA.

6989. Otterson, Jack (John E. Otterson, Aug. 25, 1905–Dec. 22, 1991) Art director primarily at Universal Pictures in the 1930's and 40's constructed many gothic and other settings, for 281 films 1934–1947 (*Three Smart Girls, Night Key, The Crime of Dr. Hallet, Son of Frankenstein, You Can't Cheat an Honest Man, The Mystery of the White Room, East Side of Heaven, The House of Fear, The Sun Never Sets, The Witness Vanishes, Tower of London, Charlie McCarthy Detective, Destry Rides Again, The Invisible Man Returns, Green Hell, My Little Chickadee, The House of the Seven Gables, Black Friday, Argentine Nights, The Mummy's Hand, Seven Sinners, One Night in the Tropics, The Bank Dick, The Invisible Woman, Buck Privates, Man Made Monster, Horror Island, In the Navy, Hold That Ghost, Badlands of Dakota, Never Give a Sucker an Even Break, Keep Em Flying, The Wolf-Man, The Mad Doctor of Market Street, Ride Em Cowboy, Ghost of Frankenstein, The Strange Case of Dr. RX, Saboteur, The Mystery of Marie Roget, Invisible Agent, Pardon My Sarong, Sherlock Holmes and the Voice of Terror, Night Monster, The Mummy's Tomb, Who Done It?, Sherlock Holmes and the Secret Weapon, Sherlock Holmes in Washington, She-Wolf of London, The Cat Creeps, Dressed to Kill, The Black Angel, The Time of Their Lives, The Killers*). He received seven Academy Award nominations 1936–42 (*The Magnificent Brute, You're A Sweetheart, Mad About Music, First Love, The Flame of New Orleans, Arabian Knights, The Spoilers*), though none for the horror genre for which he is best remembered. He died in Fireside Nursing Home, Santa Monica, at 86. Stored at Los Angeles County mortuary and cremated and buried at the county crematory April 3. Ashes reburied May 21, 1992. Sec. 36, grave 7, Riverside National Cemetery, Riverside, CA.

6990. Ottiano, Rafaela (March 4, 1888–Aug. 14, 1942) Italian born stage and screen actress made several films in the 1930's (*Grand Hotel* 1932, *Great Expectations* 1934, *Remember Last Night, The Florentine Dagger* 1935, *Anthony Adverse, The Devil Doll* 1936, *Marie Antoinette* 1938), usually in eccentric parts. She died from intestinal cancer at 54 in her family home at East Boston. Buried with her parents, their plot is marked by a pillar surmounted by a draped urn. Sec. 41, St. Michael's Cemetery, Roslindale (Boston), MA.

6991. Big Otto *see* **Briekbentz.**

6992. Ouimet, Francis D. (May 8, 1893–Sept. 2, 1967) Golfing great took the game out of the hands of the very rich, according to Herbert Warren Wind, and gave it to the whole people. A former caddy in Brookline, Massachusetts, he took the U.S. Open from the pros when it was held in Brookline in 1913, the first amateur to do so. He played from 1922–1949 but never turned pro, and played in or captained every Walker Cup team. He also set up a scholarship fund for caddies. Field of Hebron, Holyhood Cemetery, Brookline, MA.

6993. Ouray (Chief Uray) (c1833–Aug. 27, 1880) Son of Apaches, Chief of the Uncompahgre Utes in Colorado, was recognized by the U.S. as spokesman for the Utes; he signed four treaties between 1863–1880, and died a Methodist Christian. His stone pyramid obelisk is beside that of his successor **Buckskin Charley,** chief of the Southern Utes in Colorado, who lived until May 9, 1936. Grave near the center of Ouray Memorial Cemetery, Ignacio, CO.

6994. Ouspenskaya, Maria (July 29, 1876 or 1887–Dec. 3, 1949) Actress and acting coach from Tula, Russia, small in stature, taught Stanislavsky's methods learned from the Moscow Art Theatre, beginning in 1929, when she founded her School of Dramatic Art in the U.S. Her pronounced accent and imposing demeanor were used to advantage in memorable roles from her first film *Dodsworth* (1936, AA nom.), *Love Affair* (AA nom.), and *King's Row* (1941) to her best known part as Maleva the gypsy in *The Wolfman* (1941) and *Frankenstein meets the Wolfman* (1943). Contemporaries said her role as the dictatorial ballet teacher in *Waterloo Bridge* (1940) was closest to the real Madame Ouspenskaya. She died from burns suffered in a fire caused by her falling asleep in bed with a lit cigarette. Cremated at Pierce Bros.' Chapel of the Pines Crematory, Los Angeles. Plaque inscribed *Our Beloved Madam*; the birth date 1887 on it is wrong by all written accounts. Eventide sec., lot 3741, space 6, Forest Lawn, Glendale, CA.

6995. Overman, Jack (Jack Benjamin Oberman, March 26, 1917–Dec. 24, 1949) Actor in burly parts in many films 1944–49 (*Johnny Angel, The Naughty Nineties, Jungle Captive, The Secret Life of Walter Mitty, Unconquered*) died from a heart attack at 32 in Los Angeles. New Montefiore Cemetery, West Babylon, Long Island, NY.

6996. Overman, Lynne (Sept. 19, 1887–Feb. 19, 1943) Character actor in generally light, congenial roles of the 1930's (*Midnight* 1934, *Night Club Scandal* 1937, many others) was a part of the unofficial "Irish Mafia" social group in Hollywood that included Cagney, Tracy, Pat O'Brien and Frank Morgan, among others. He died from a heart attack at 55. Crypt in Mausoleum, 4-L-2, Woodlawn Cemetery, Santa Monica, CA.

6997. Overton, Frank (March 12, 1918–April 23, 1967) Character actor from Babylon, New York, with a bass voice in quiet, dignified roles in films (*The Dark at the Top of the Stairs, To Kill a Mockingbird, Fail Safe*) and television (*Twelve O'Clock High, Twilight Zone* episodes *Walking Distance* and *Mute; Star Trek* episode *This Side of Paradise*). He died from a heart attack at 48. Sec. 6, lot 44, Hollywood Forever Cemetery, Hollywood (Los Angeles), CA.

6998. Owen, Maribel Vinson (Oct. 12, 1911–Feb. 15, 1961) Bronze medalist in figure skating at the 1932 Lake Placid Olympics coached her two daughters, **Laurence Rachon Owen** (born May 9, 1944) and **Maribel Yerxa Owen** (born April 25, 1940), to championship placings. All three died when the Sabena Airline flight carrying the eighteen member U.S.A. skating team to the 1961 world championships at Prague crashed in Belgium. Story Columbarium, Mt. Auburn Cemetery, Cambridge, MA.

6999. Owen, Mickey (Arnold Malcolm Owen, April 4, 1916–July 13, 2005) Catcher from Nixa, Missouri, in the majors 1937–1954, known for his error behind the plate as the Brooklyn Dodgers catcher, one strike away from a 4–3 victory at Ebbets Field that would have evened the 1941 world series with the New York Yankees. Hugh Casey threw a curveball, Tommy Henrich swung and missed, but the ball got away from Owen, putting Henrich on base, and allowing the Yankees to rally, take the game, and the series. Like Fred Merkle and Fred Snodgrass, he lived with the muffed ball all his life, but gracefully, serving as sheriff of Greene County, Missouri 1965–80 and founder of Mickey Owen's Baseball Camp. He died in Mount Vernon, Missouri, at 89. Patterson Cemetery, near Nixa in Greene County, southwest of Springfield, MO.

7000. Owen, Reginald (Aug. 5, 1887–Nov. 5, 1972) British character actor often in pompous roles in many films from the 1930's, forever weaving his head from side to side as he spoke (*Platinum Blonde, Of Human Bondage* 1934, *A Tale of Two Cities* 1935, *Trouble For Two*, as Scrooge in MGM's 1938 version of *A Christmas Carol*). He retired to Boise, Idaho, where he died from a heart attack at 85. Flush plaque. Q-46-3, Morris Hill Cemetery, Boise, ID.

7001. Owen, Robert (May 14, 1771–Nov. 17, 1858) Welsh industrialist and social reformer founded cooperative communities in New Harmony, Indiana 1825–27, and at Lancashire, England 1839–45, though both experiments failed due to dissension among the members. He spent his later years working for the establishment of trade unions. St. Mary's Churchyard, Newton, Powys, Wales.

7002. Owen, Robert Dale (Nov. 9, 1801–June 24, 1877) Scottish son of the Welsh founder of the Utopian commune at New Harmony, Indiana, 1825–

1829. He later served in congress from Indiana 1844–47, drafted the bill founding the Smithsonian Institution, and was a strong voice against slavery. Ambassador to Naples 1853–58. Owen died at Caldwell, New York, where he had lived with his second wife. Originally buried there, he was (partially) reburied in 1937 at Maple Hill Cemetery in New Harmony. Also there are his siblings **William Owen** (1842), **David Dale Owen** (1850), **Jane Dale Owen Fauntleroy** (1861) and **Richard Owen** (1890). Maple Hill Cemetery, New Harmony, IN.

7003. Owen, Seena (Signe Auen, Nov. 14, 1894–Aug. 15, 1966) Spokane born silent screen actress 1914–29 and screenwriter, divorced from George Walsh. Abbey of the Psalms/Hollywood Forever Mausoleum, Sanctuary of Refuge, crypt 2130, Hollywood Forever Cemetery, Hollywood (Los Angeles), CA.

7004. Owen, Tudor (Jan. 20, 1898–March 13, 1979) Welsh actor in films from the 1940's through the 60's, adept as stern elder Scotsmen, in *Lorna Doone, The Black Castle, How to Marry A Millionaire, Brigadoon, 101 Dalmatians* (voice of Towser), *How the West Was Won, The Twilight Zone* episode *No Time Like the Past,* many others. Columbarium of Sunlight, niche 270, Garden of Memory, Forest Lawn, Glendale, CA.

7005. Owen, Wilfred (Wilfred Edward Salter Owen, March 18, 1893–Nov. 4, 1918) Celebrated English poet from Shrewsbury. Injured in March 1917 in World War I, he returned to duty in France in August 1918. A letter he wrote his parents days before the armistice assured them he was safe and the end of the war was near, but as Shrewsbury celebrated the armistice on November 11, the Owens received word their son had died in an attack of German machine gun fire a week earlier. Communal Cemetery, Ors, France.

7006. Owens, Commodore Perry (July 29, 1852–May 10, 1919) Arizona lawman became a legend from a gunfight in Holbrook, Arizona, wherein he killed three men (Andy Cooper, Mose Roberts and Sam Blevins) and wounded one (John Blevins) while firing only five shots. He died from paresis of the brain at 66. Grave surrounded cy a chain link fence. Tract J, block A, lot 13, space 2, Citizens Cemetery, Flagstaff, AZ.

7007. Owens, Harry (April 18, 1902–Dec. 11, 1986) Nebraska born bandleader and songwriter, musical director at The Royal Hawaiian Hotel in Waikiki 1934–1941 promoted Hawaiian jazz, tagged hapahaole. Among his three hundred compositions was *Sweet Leilani,* which Bing Crosby sang in *Waikiki Wedding* (1937) and earned Owens an Oscar. Block 9, sec. B, lot 95, Rest Haven Memorial Park, Eugene, OR.

7008. Owens, Jesse (Sept. 12, 1913–March 31, 1980) Olympic track star won four gold medals at the 1936 Olympics in Berlin, humiliating Hitler and the "master race." Rather than honor a black American, Hitler not only refused to stand for the American National Anthem but left the stadium incensed, refusing to present the medals to Owens. Later a successful businessman and a heavy smoker, Owens died from lung cancer at 66. His polished brown monument alongside a lake bears the inscription *Athlete and humanitarian, a master of the spirit as well as the mechanics of sports. A winner who knew that winning was not everything, he showed extraordinary love for his family and friends. His achievements have shown us all the promise of America. His faith in America inspired countless others to do their best for themselves and their country.* Sec. C-1-32 (lakeside), Oakwoods Cemetery, Chicago, IL.

7009. Owens, John E. (John Edward Owens, 1823–Dec. 7, 1886) Liverpool born stage comic, actor and manager, in the U.S. from age three and on stage from 1840, best known as Solon Shingle in J.S. Jones' *The People's Lawyer* and as Caleb Plummer; his fame was eclipsed by the rise of Joseph Jefferson. Owens resided in the south, at Charleston and at his home Algburth Vale, ten miles north of Baltimore, where he died from stomach cancer at 63. Spruce, lot 50, Green Mount Cemetery, Baltimore, MD.

7010. Owens, Patricia (Patricia Molly Owens, Jan. 17, 1925–Aug. 31, 2000) English born actress in films of the 1950's, notably *Sayonara, No Down Payment* (both 1957) and *The Fly* (1958). Divorced, she died from respiratory failure at 75 in her Lancaster, California, home. Cremated through Joshua Mortuary. Ashes to her family in Palmdale, CA.

7011. Owens, Priscilla Jane (July 21, 1829–Dec. 5, 1907) Lifelong Baltimore resident taught school, composed hymns for the Union Square Church Sunday School, and wrote poetry for *The Methodist Protestant* and *The Christian Standard.* Her lyrics include *Jesus Saves, We Have an Anchor, Give Me the Bible,* and *Victorious.* She died from a pulmonary thrombosis at 78. Sec. AAA, lots 21–24, Green Mount Cemetery, Baltimore, MD.

7012. Owens, Tex (Doie Hensley Owens, June 15, 1892–Sept. 9, 1962) Country-western singer and songwriter penned over one hundred numbers, notably *Cattle Call,* a million seller for Eddy Arnold in 1955 and recorded by numerous others. Behind Woods lot at front entrance, Franklin City Cemetery, Franklin, TX.

7013. Owens, William J. "Bill" (Nov. 14, 1901–May 5, 1999) Negro Leagues shortstop with the Indianapolis ABCs for eight years in the 1920's and 30's, lived to 97. Unmarked at bend in road. Sec. 6G, row 14, grave 476, Holy Cross Cemetery, Indianapolis, IN.

7014. Owsley, Monroe (Monroe Righter Owsley, Aug. 11, 1900–June 7, 1937) Actor from Atlanta, son of stage actress Gertrude Owsley in films 1928–37, often as inebriated socialites (*Holiday* 1930, *Ten Cents A Dance, Remember Last Night?*), died from a heart attack at 36, triggered by an auto accident the same day as Jean Harlow. Whispering Pines section, lot 1115, Forest Lawn, Glendale, CA.

7015. Paar, Jack (Jack Harold Paar, May 1, 1918–Jan. 27, 2004) Soft spoken, urbane, sophisticated, and often emotional host of *The Tonight Show* 1957–1962, born in Canton, Ohio, and raised in Jackson, Michigan, and Detroit. A veteran of a few films (*Love Nest* 1951), he pioneered the couch-by-the-desk format of late night television, known for his signature phrase "I kid you not." When a joke involving the term "water closet" was edited out by NBC in 1960, he left the show, but returned a few weeks later. In the late 1960's, he bought a television station in Poland Springs, Maine, and retired at 50, settling in New Canaan, Connecticut, and later in Greenwich, where he died at 85. Cremated at Garden State Crematory, North Bergen, New Jersey. Ashes returned to Leo P. Gallagher and Son, Greenwich.

7016. Pabst, Fred (March 28, 1836–Jan. 1, 1904) Founder of the Pabst Brewing Company of Milwaukee in 1892, long the world's largest, taken over by his son Gustave (1866–1943). A marble maiden, half kneeling atop a flight of steps, with her head leaning against the short shaft on the large Victorian monument overlooking the lot. Facing both Schlitz and Blatz across the intersection. Sec. 40, lot 16, Forest Home Cemetery, Milwaukee, WI.

7017. Pabst, G.W. (Georg Wilhelm Pabst, Aug. 27, 1885–May 29, 1967) Director of the German Weimar cinema of the 1920's. Raised in Vienna. His films, made in Berlin, include *Die Freudlose Gasse/The Street of Sorrow* (1925), *Secrets of a Soul* (1926), moving from expressionism to pessimistic reality. Among his best known works were *Pandora's Box* and *Diary of a Lost Girl*, both made in 1929 with American actress Louise Brooks. He worked later in France and back in Hollywood during the Nazi era and later, retiring after suffering a stroke in 1956. Gruppe 32C, nummer 31, Der Zentral Friedhof (Central Cemetery), Vienna.

7018. Paca, William (Oct. 31, 1740–Oct. 13, 1799) Signer of the Declaration of Independence and Governor of Maryland 1782–1785. His stone has a sculpted scroll partially unrolled, on his estate at Abingdon, MD.

7019. Packard, James Ward (Nov. 5, 1863–March 20, 1928) Founder of the Packard Auto Co. 1902. along with **William D. Packard** (Nov. 3, 1861–Nov. 11, 1923). James has a two columned monument in sec. 2, lot 119; William has the car's logo on his family monument in the Old Part, lot E, 1/2 106, Oakwood Cemetery, Warren, OH.

7020. Packer, Alferd (or Alfred) (Jan. 21, 1842–April 23, 1907) America's most famed cannibal of the 19th century was said to have devoured five of his six companions after their deaths in a winter storm in 1874 in order to stay alive, though he denied it. In 1883 Judge M.B. Gerry accused him of only eating Dimmycrats, and he went to prison. The victims, **Israel Swan, George Noon, Frank Miller, James Humphreys** and **Wilson Bell** are buried at Cannibal Plateau, marked by a boulder with a plaque erected in

1928, near Lake City, Colorado. Packer, paroled in January 1901, is in sec. 3, southeast corner lot 65, Littleton Cemetery, Littleton, CO.

7021. Packer, Doris (May 30, 1904–March 20, 1979) Actress from Menominee, Michigan, on stage, in films and television, played the principal Mrs. Rayburn on TV's *Leave It to Beaver* 1957–63. Married name Edwards. She died in Glendale, California, at 74 from a stroke. Wee Kirk Churchyard, lot 2649, space 4, Forest Lawn, Glendale, CA.

7022. Padden, Sarah (Oct. 16, 1881–Dec. 4, 1967) Actress in films 1926–1955. Mausoleum crypt Block 71, crypt D-6 (Sackett), Holy Cross Cemetery, Culver City, CA.

7023. Paderewski, Ignace Jan (Nov. 6, 1860–June 29, 1941) Polish pianist and composer was the exiled head of the government in 1941 when he died in New York. He was buried in Arlington National Cemetery near the Maine Memorial, with the understanding that it was the wish of both he and President Roosevelt that his body was to be returned to Poland when it was again free. His heart was removed upon his death and was kept in a glass niche at the Abbey in Cypress Hills Cemetery, Brooklyn, until 1982, when it was removed to Our Lady of Czestochowa Shrine in Doylestown, Pennsylvania. His body was removed from Arlington at the end of June 1992 and sent to Poland for burial at St. John the Baptist Cathedral, Warsaw.

7024. Paganini, Niccolo (Oct. 27, 1782–May 27, 1840) Italian violinist died in an apartment in Nice, and from there began extensive posthumous traveling over the years. Offended by his ignoring the Church both in his life and in his will, church officials refused him burial in consecrated ground. His body was reportedly kept in the apartment for two months before health officials in Nice had it moved to the basement. From there it went to a leper house in Villefranche, then into a vat in an olive oil factory, then to an estate at the water's end of Cape Ferrati. In April 1844 it was buried in the Villa Paganini in Polcevera. In 1845 it was reburied at the Villa Gainone in Parma, but in 1876, when the bishop's provisions were revoked, Paganini was buried in consecrated ground in Parma. The body was exhumed and inspected in 1893 out of curiosity and again in 1896 upon the opening of a new burial ground. Since then it has remained in place. If accurate, he was moved seven times and inspected twice after his death, a record number of disturbances of the dead. Four columned monument with a bust above the tomb. Cemetery Della Villetta, Parma, Italy.

7025. Page, Dorothy (Dorothy Lillian Stoffett, March 4, 1904–March 26, 1961) Actress from Northampton, Pennsylvania, in a handful of films 1935, from *Manhattan Moon* to *Ride Em Cowgirl* and *The Singing Cowgirl* (1939) — the first one, it was claimed, in a failed attempt to save Grand National Pictures. She retired, last married name McCormick, and died from cancer in Florida at 56. Allen Union Cemetery, Northampton, PA.

7026. Page, Gale (Sally Perkins, July 23, 1910–Jan. 8, 1983) Actress from Spokane sang with Ted Weems' orchestra prior to wholesome second leads in films at Warner Bros 1938–1942 (*Crime School, Four Daughters, Daughters Courageous, They Drive By Night, Four Mothers*). Cremated under the name Sally Rutter Solito Desolis at Chapel of the Pines Crematory, Los Angeles. Ashes to residence.

7027. Page, Geraldine (Geraldine Sue Page, Nov. 22, 1924–June 13, 1987) Stage and film actress from Kirksville, Missouri, raised in Chicago, often in eccentric or neurotic roles, was acclaimed on Broadway from 1952, in *Summer and Smoke, Midsummer, Sweet Bird of Youth,* won Emmys for *A Christmas Memory* (1966) and *The Thanksgiving Visitor* (1967). In films regularly from 1961 (*Summer and Smoke, Sweet Bird of Youth, Whatever Happened to Aunt Alice?, The Beguiled, Interiors*) was nominated for an Oscar nine times and won for *The Trip to Bountiful* (1985). Married to actor Rip Torn. While appearing on Broadway in *Blithe Spirit,* a resident of the Chelsea section of Manhattan, she died from a heart attack at 62. Cremated June 16 at Long Island Crematory, West Babylon, New York, through Gramercy Chapel, 152 2nd Ave., Manhattan. Ashes to the family in Chelsea.

7028. Page, LaWanda (Alberta Pearl/Page, Oct. 19, 1920–Sept. 14, 2002) Actress best known as Aunt Esther on *Sanford and Son,* appeared in films of the 1980's and 90's as well (*Shakes the Clown, My Blue Heaven, Mausoleum, Goodbye Cruel World*). She died from complications of diabetes at 83. Capistrano Garden crypt 1952 (*non-visitation, underground crypts?), Mausoleum of the Golden West, Inglewood Park Cemetery, Inglewood, CA.

7029. Page, Leopold "Paul" (Leopold Pfefferberg, March 20, 1913–March 9, 2001) Worker no. 173 on Oskar Schindler's later famed list worked at the Nazi party member's enamelware works for Krakow and from 1944 at his munitions plant in Brinnitz, surviving the war as he and the other workers were promised. The story of his protector's heroism was pitched by Page, particularly after 1950 when he migrated to Los Angeles from New York, but not until 1980 did he interest Australian writer Thomas Keneally in writing a book based on the story, and gradually in getting the attention of Steven Spielberg, who made the award winning *Schindler's List* in 1993. Without Page, the remarkable actions of Oskar Schindler might have been lost to history. Crypt along bottom tier, Courts of the Book, Jacob G-144-B, Hillside Memorial Park, Los Angeles.

7030. Page, Oran "Hot Lips" (Jan. 27, 1908–Nov. 5, 1954) Trumpeter and vocalist ala Louis Armstrong, worked with Benny Moten on *Mihlenberg Joys* and later with Count Basie, Artie Shaw 1941, and on his own. Block 18, lot 86, grave 8, Lincoln Memorial Cemetery, Dallas, TX.

7031. Page, Ruth (March 22, 1899–April 7, 1991) Noted dancer. Her black polished stone has a dancer leaping upward on it, and an exclamation mark. Willowmere, 19-20, Graceland Cemetery, Chicago, IL.

7032. Paige, Mabel (Dec. 19, 1880–Feb. 8, 1954) American character actress in films (*Lucky Jordan, Someone to Remember*, lead role 1943). Married name Ritchie. Block A, sec. 405, lot 1, Valhalla Memorial Park, North Hollywood, CA.

7033. Paige, Mitchell (Aug. 31, 1918–Nov. 15, 2003) U.S. Marine colonel from Charleroi, Pennsylvania, at Guadalcanal with his machine gun platoon of thirty three men repelled an estimated 27,000 Japanese in their assault on Henderson Field there, October 26, 1942. With his men killed or wounded, he fought alone, moving from one machine gun to another until reinforcements arrived and he formed a counter-attack. About half of the Japanese were killed, ensuring victory at Guadalcanal, which turned the tide in the Pacific war. Awarded the Medal of Honor and promoted to second lieutenant, he served in Korea, as an advisor in Vietnam, and from the 1950s tracked down and confronted hundreds who falsely presented themselves as Medal of Honor recipients, and into the medal's illegal false reproductions and sales. Paige was also a model for the action figure G.I. Joe. He died at 85 from congestive heart failure in his La Quinta, California, home. Sec. 20A, grave 533, Riverside National Cemetery, Riverside, CA.

7034. Paige, Robert (John Arthur Paige, Dec. 2, 1911–Dec. 21, 1987) B lead of the1940's in light films with Louise Allbritton; both effective in the grim *Son of Dracula* (1943). He later hosted quiz shows and was a Los Angeles newscaster. Flush unrolled black scroll. Sec M, lot 115, Holy Cross Cemetery, Culver City, CA.

7035. Paige, Satchel (Robert Leroy Paige, July 7, 1906–June 8, 1982) Star pitcher of the Negro Leagues, considered the fastest of them all, threw twenty seven years, lastly with the Kansas City Monarchs, and entered the majors with Cleveland in 1948 when he was 42 to pitch a 5–0 shutout against Chicago. He hurled until age 59, mostly for Bill Veeck, playing at the end of his career with the Kansas City Athletics. The nickname came from his handling of satchels as a redcap when he worked for the railroad. Hall of Fame 1971. He and his wife (1986) were removed to "Paige Island" in 1989 when his elaborate monument was erected with advice on How to Stay Young including: *1. Avoid fried meats which angry up the blood. 3. Go very light on the vices, such as carrying on in society. The social ramble ain't restful. 6. Don't look back. Something might be following you.* Paige Island between sections 38, 51, 20 and 21, Forest Hills Cemetery, Kansas City, MO.

7036. Pain, Elizabeth (1652–Nov. 26, 1704) 17th century Boston Puritan who bore the child of her minister and was made to wear an A on her dress for adulteress, the basis for Hester Prinne in Hawthorne's *The Scarlet Letter*. King's Chapel Burying Ground, Boston, MA.

7037. Paine, Lewis aka **Lewis Thornton Powell** (April 22, 1844–July 7, 1865) Accomplice of Lincoln's assassin John Wilkes Booth, the former Confederate private with Mosby's Rangers broke into Secretary of State Seward's house and beat and stabbed him just as Booth was fleeing Washington after having shot Lincoln. Seward was badly injured but survived. Paine was hanged with George Atzerodt, David Herold and Mrs. Mary Surratt in the Washington Prison Yard on July 7, 1865. The bodies were at first buried at the D.C. prison and arsenal. Surratt, Herold and Atzerodt were removed by their families in 1869, but Paine was unclaimed. In 1991 the Smithsonian Institution found Paine's skull among thousands of bones kept in storage. One hundred and twenty-nine years after his death, it was released to his closest relative and buried as Lewis Thornton Powell, under the direction of Helen Alderman, November 12, 1994. His flush marker notes his CSA Civil War service. Geneva Cemetery, Geneva, FL.

7038. Paine, Robert Treat (March 11, 1731–May 12, 1814) Signer of the Declaration of Independence from Massachusetts. Old Granary Burial Ground, Boston, MA.

7039. Paine, Thomas (Jan. 29, 1737–June 8, 1809) English born agitator, author of the inflammatory *Common Sense* (1776) which argued for revolution against England. After the American Revolution he went to France promoting the same thing and narrowly escaped the guillotine. He returned to New York and from 1807 was an invalid, swollen with dropsy. He requested a Quaker burial, naming other sects as arrogant and hypocritical. His housekeeper and her son took the body from New York to New Rochelle for burial at what was once his farm. A 12' wall was erected around the grave with a marker inscribed *Thomas Paine, author of "Common Sense," died on the 8th of June 1809, aged 72 years.* In 1819 William Cobbett unearthed the bones to return them to England for a proposed monument to Paine, but they were kept by Cobbett until his death in 1835 and subsequently lost. The grave marker has since disintegrated, but photographs of major portions of it do exist. There is a marker to him at the Thomas Paine Museum, New Rochelle, NY.

7040. Paiva, Nestor (June 30, 1905–Sept. 9, 1966) Bald character actor in over 150 films in roles with any number of accents and dialects. Eternal Love sec., lot 4950, Forest Lawn Hollywood Hills, Los Angeles.

7041. Pakula, Alan (April 7, 1928–Nov. 19, 1998) New York born director (*Klute, All the President's Men, Sophie's Choice, The Pelican Brief*) and producer (*To Kill A Mockingbird*) died when a metal pipe crashed through the windshield of his 1995 Volvo on the Long Island Expressway some thirty-five miles east of New York City. Green River Cemetery, East Hampton, Long Island, NY.

7042. Pal, George (Feb. 1, 1908–May 2, 1980) Innovative Hungarian puppeteer developed claymation films in America. He also made several feature fantasies, including *Destination Moon* (1950), *War of the Worlds* (1953), *tom thumb* (1958), *The Time Machine* (1960) and *The Wonderful World of the Brothers Grimm* (1962). Several Academy Awards. Sec. H, lot 691, Holy Cross Cemetery, Culver City, CA.

7043. Paley, William S. (Sept. 28, 1901–Oct. 26, 1990) Head of CBS 1928–1990, with first rate broadcasting from Europe during World War II, TV programs including the news anchored by Walter Cronkite, and prime time favorites such as *I Love Lucy*. He died from a heart attack related to pneumonia in his Manhattan home at 89. Buried with his wife **Barbara Cushing Paley** (1915–July 6, 1978). St. John's Memorial Cemetery, Cold Spring Harbor, Long Island, NY.

7044. Pallette, Eugene (July 8, 1889–Sept. 3, 1954) Rotund actor with a deep, gravel voice in films of the 30's and 40's, always feisty, in *The Ghost Goes West, My Man Godfrey* (1936), *The Adventures of Robin Hood* (1938, as Friar Tuck), *Mr. Smith Goes to Washington* (1939), etc. He died in Los Angeles from oral cancer. Cremated through Armstrong mortuary at Restland Cemetery, now part of Valhalla Memorial Park in North Hollywood. The ashes were buried unmarked behind the stone of his parents, William and Ella Pallette, Greenfield Cemetery, Grenola (35 miles east of Winfield), KS.

7045. Palme, Olof (Jan. 30, 1927–Feb. 28, 1986) Swedish Social Democratic prime minister 1969–76 and 1982–86 was assassinated on a Stockholm street, where a gold tablet marks the site. His grave is marked by a boulder with a signature and a large black tablet. Alfred Fredriks Kyrkogarden, Stockholm.

7046. Palmer, A. Mitchell (Alexander Mitchell Palmer, May 4, 1872–May 11, 1936) Attorney General under Wilson 1919–1921 organized and promoted the Red Scare of immediate postwar America, hunting Bolsheviks at every turn, thirty years ahead of Sen. Joe McCarthy. Palmer died in Washington and was returned for burial with his wife. Their lot, with a bench and flush bronze plaques, is in a wooded enclosure reached by steps from the road. Sec. 13 (Ridge), lot 3, Laurelwood Cemetery, Stroudsburg, PA.

7047. Palmer, Alice Freeman (Feb. 21, 1855–Dec. 6, 1902) and **George Herbert Palmer** (March 19, 1842–May 7, 1933) She was president of Wellesley College 1882–88, founding the American Association of University Women in 1885, and Dean of Women at the University of Chicago. He taught at Harvard 1872–1913. Crypt with two classical Greeks in bas-relief. Chapel at Wellesley College, Wellesley, MA.

7048. Palmer, Joe (June 1789–Oct. 30, 1873) Sporting a beard in the 1820's, forty years ahead of fashion, he was the target of goods bought at his own vegetable stand and was also stoned. When he retaliated, he was jailed; the civil rights case went to court. Later glorified as an individualist, both Palmer and

his beard are sculpted in relief on the side of his monument in Evergreen Cemetery, Leominster, MA.

7049. Palmer, Lilli (Lillie Marie Peiser, May 24, 1914–Jan. 27, 1986) German leading lady of international films married to Rex Harrison 1943–1958, and later to Carlos Thompson, appeared in U.S. films 1945–1954 and sporadically afterward (*Body and Soul,* 1947, *Anastasia* 1957, *But Not For Me* 1959, *The Amorous Adventures of Moll Flanders* 1965, *Murders in the Rue Morgue* 1971, *The Boys from Brazil* 1978). Her actual grave is marked by a long tablet heavily inscribed, ending with the line *To die is but to pass from one room to another.* Commemoration sec., Forest Lawn, Glendale, California. A black cenotaph in her memory is in the lot of her family (Peiser) at West Hampstead Cemetery, Fortune Green Road, London.

7050. Palmer, Potter (May 20, 1826–May 4, 1902) Chicago business leader began as a dry goods merchant with Marshall Field, later owned and operated the Palmer House hotel and other interests, rebuilt after the 1871 fire. His wife, **Bertha Honore Palmer** (May 22, 1849–May 15, 1918), was the equivalent of New York's Mrs. Astor in her day. Their monument, Greek Doric columns surrounding sarcophagi with ornate carvings, indicates that they did to some extent take it with them. Willowmere sec., Graceland Cemetery, Chicago, IL.

7051. Palmer, Robert (Alan Robert Palmer, Jan. 19, 1949–Sept. 26, 2003) British singer from Batley, Yorkshire, with the blues rock band Vinegar Joe in the 1970's recorded *Every Kinda People* (1978), but had his biggest hit with the 1986 song and video *Addicted to Love*, which went to number one in the United States and earned him a Grammy, and *Simply Irresistible* the next year. He died at 54 from a heart attack in Paris. Funeral and burial, where he had lived since 1987, at Lugano, Switzerland.

7052. Palmer, Stuart (June 21, 1905–Feb. 4, 1968) Writer from Wisconsin penned several B film mysteries of the 1930's and 40's, including those deciphered by Hildegarde Withers (*The Penguin Pool Murder, Murder on the Blackboard, Murder on a Honeymoon, Murder on the Bridle Path*), *One Frightened Night,* three *Bulldog Drummond* entries 1938–9, *The Smiling Ghost, Secrets of the Lone Wolf, The Falcon's Brother, The Falcon Strikes Back, X Marks the Spot, Murder in Times Square.* He died at home in Glendora, California, at 62 from an overdose of barbiturates. Donated February 6 as a medical specimen to Loma Linda University.

7053. Palmerston, Henry John Temple, 3rd Viscount (Lord) (Oct. 20, 1784–Oct. 18, 1865) Influential British Whig foreign secretary 1830–34, 1835–41, 1846–51, home secretary 1852–55, and prime minister 1855–58 and 1859–65. He supported liberal national movements around the world — in Belgium, Switzerland, and Sicily — and used belligerent force in attaining British interests, including against Egypt in the Ottoman Empire, the seizing of Greek ships over a debt, and advancing colonial interests in China. He became prime minister in the wake of the Crimean War, which many felt he may have prevented. Always controversial, he repeatedly regained his popularity until defeated by Bismarck over Schleswig-Holstein in 1864. Buried with his wife, his statue stands in the center aisle off the north transept, Westminster Abbey, London.

7054. Pan, Hermes (Dec. 10, 1909–Sept. 19, 1990) Hollywood choreographer known for his work with Fred Astaire and Ginger Rogers and later with Betty Grable. Oscar for *Damsel in Distress* (1937). Mausoleum block 127, crypt D-5, Holy Cross Cemetery, Culver City, CA.

7055. Panama, Norman (April 21, 1914–Jan. 13, 2003) Screenwriter, often with Melvin Frank, and director did *The Road to Utopia* (1945), *Mr. Blandings Builds His Dream House* (1948), *White Christmas* (1954). Faith, second floor, crypt 1020, mausoleum, Hillside Memorial Park, Los Angeles.

7056. Pangborn, Franklin (Jan. 23, 1893–July 20, 1958) Newark born stage actor, once acclaimed as Messala in *Ben Hur*, became typecast in films of the 1930's and 40's as haughty, effeminate, flustered characters. A foil for W.C. Fields in *International House* (1933) and *The Bank Dick* (1940). Niche below that of Edna May Oliver, his close friend. 17062, Columbarium of Security, Gardenia Terrace, Great Mausoleum, Forest Lawn, Glendale, CA.

7057. Pantages, Alexander (1867–Feb. 17, 1936) Greek immigrant operated Pantages Variety Theatre at 7th and Hill St. in Los Angeles. Imprisoned in 1930 for rape, the sentence was overturned in a new trial when his lawyer, Jerry Giesler, presented evidence of the victim's past history, the first case of past behavior being admissible in a U.S. court. Sanctuary of Benediction, Memorial Terrace, Great Mausoleum, Forest Lawn, Glendale, CA.

7058. Panzer, Paul (Paul Wolfgang Panzerbeiter, Nov. 3, 1872–Aug. 16, 1958) German born early silent screen actor entered films with Vitagraph in 1904 and by 1914 was menacing Pearl White in *The Perils of Pauline* and several others. Vale of Peace sec., lot 5515, space 3, Forest Lawn, Hollywood Hills, Los Angeles.

7059. Pape, (Edward) Lionel (April 17, 1877–Oct. 21, 1944) English actor (*Raffles* 1940) died at Woodland Hills. Memorial niche (cenotaph), Alcove I, Chapel of the Pines Crematory, Los Angeles, where he was cremated. Ashes buried at Bruxton, Derbyshire, England.

7060. Papen, Franz von (Oct. 29, 1879–May 2, 1969) Once military attaché to the Imperial German Embassy in Washington during World War I and later right wing member of the Prussian Diet of the 1920's served as chancellor from June to December 1932, backing the National Socialists. His plan to control the Nazis with himself as Vice-Chancellor under Hitler was short lived. He served as Ambassador to

Austria 1934–8, Turkey 1939–44, and was one of three acquitted of war crimes at Nuremburg in 1946 and set free. He died at 90 in Obersabach, Baden-Wurtemburg. Wallerfangen town cemetery, province of Saarland, Germany.

7061. "Papillon" (Henri Charriére, Nov. 16, 1906–July 29, 1973) French prisoner known for his escapes from various penal colonies including Devil's Island. The persistence and tenacity was chronicled in the 1974 film *Papillon* with Steve McQueen. He died in Madrid from throat cancer. Buried at Lanas, Ardeche, southwest of Privas, France.

7062. Papp, Joseph (Joseph Papirofsky, June 22, 1921–Oct. 31, 1991) New York theatrical giant created the outdoor New York Shakespeare festival and was behind *Hair, That Championship Season* and *A Chorus Line*. He died from prostate cancer at 70 in New York. Flush plaque. 1st Independent Pilover Association, Baron Hirsch Cemetery, Staten Island, N.Y.C.

7063. Paret, Benny "Kid" (March 14, 1937–April 3, 1962) Cuban born boxer died ten days after being knocked out by Emile Griffith in the twelfth round of their third fight, a championship bout, hit with several two handed punches and ten consecutive uppercuts, pinned to the post, unable to fall. St. Luke, range 4, grave 13, (New) St. Raymond's Cemetery, the Bronx, N.Y.C.

7064. Paris, Albert R. (April 15, 1926–Feb. 7, 2002) Reading, Pennsylvania, traffic cop who plied his craft with an animated dance routine, featured in 1962 as one of *Candid Camera's* best known offerings. He died at 75. Gethsemane Cemetery, Laureldale, PA.

7065. Paris, Jerry (July 25, 1925–March 31, 1986) Actor in films of the 1950's (*The Caine Mutiny, Marty*), later on TV as Dick Van Dyke's neighbor Jerry in *The Dick Van Dyke Show*, which he directed, as well as *Happy Days* in the 1970's and films including *Police Academy*. He died from cancer of the brain at 60. Cremation at Grandview Memorial Park through Westwood mortuary, west Los Angeles. Ashes returned to residence.

7066. Paris, Manuel (Manuel Conesa Redó, July 27, 1894–Nov. 19, 1959) Spanish actor from Valencia in films including *For Whom the Bell Tolls, Madame Bovary, Macao, To Catch A Thief*. He died of congestive heart failure in Woodland Hills, California, at 65. Buried as Manuel Conesa Redo. Commemoration sec., lot 3896, Forest Lawn, Glendale, CA.

7067. Parish, Mitchell (July 10, 1900–March 31, 1993) Lithuanian born lyricist in the U.S. from age seven. Best known for putting words to Hoagy Carmichael's *Stardust* in 1929. By the time of his death it numbered over 1300 renditions. Other works include *Deep Purple, Moonlight Serenade* and *Sophisticated Lady*. He died in New York at 92. Services at Riverside Chapel in Manhattan included a floral tribute from the Grateful Dead, of whom Parish was reportedly a fan. On his monument is the first line from the introduction to *Stardust: And now the purple dusk*

of twilight time, steals across the meadows of my heart.
Sec. F8 First Grodeker, Ladies A&B Society, Beth
David Cemetery, Elmont, NY.

7068. Parker, Alton B. (May 14, 1852–May. 10,
1926) New York Court of Appeals judge ran unsuccessfully for the presidency against Theodore Roosevelt
in 1904. After his poor showing the Democrats tried
Bryan again in 1908. Judge Parker was preparing to
return to his country home at Kingston, New York,
when he died from a heart attack while riding in Manhattan's Central Park. Wiltwyck Cemetery, Kingston,
NY.

7069. Parker, Bonnie (Oct. 1, 1910–May 23, 1934)
With Clyde Barrow embarked on a robbery spree
across the southwest including several murders in 1933
and '34. They were ambushed and riddled with bullets while in their car on a remote country road in Bi-
enville Parish, Louisiana. The death scene drew a
crowd of six thousand souvenir hunters. Despite her
wish to be buried with Barrow, she was claimed by
her mother and buried first in Fish Trap Cemetery,
and later moved to Dallas, across town from Clyde.
The tablet at her grave includes lines from one of her
many poetic efforts: *As the flowers are all made sweeter
by the sunshine and the dew, so this old world is made
brighter by the lives of folks like you.* Behind cypress
trees on left. Crown Hill Memorial Park, Dallas, TX.

7070. Parker, Cecil (Cecil Schwabe, Sept. 3,
1897–April 20, 1971) Actor from Hastings, Sussex,
known on the British stage for *Blithe Spirit* (1941) and
various roles mixing stuffiness with obtuseness. In
films from 1933, including *The Man Who Changed
His Mind* (1936), *Dark Journey* (1937), *The Lady Van-
ishes* (1938), *She Couldn't Say No* (1940), *The Saint's
Vacation, Dangerous Moonlight* (1941), *Ships with
Wings* (1942), *Caesar and Cleopatra* (1946), *Hungry
Hill* (1947), *The First Gentleman* (1948), *Father Brown
The Detective* (1954), *23 Paces to Baker Street* (1956),
The Night We Dropped a Clanger (1959), many others.
A resident of Brighton, where he died at 73. Handled
by Hannington's, 4/6 Montefiore Road, Hove, Sus-
sex. Burial at Milford Cemetery, Haslemere Road,
Milford (near Godalming), Surrey.

7071. Parker, Cecilia (April 26, 1914–July 23,
1993) Actress of the 1930's and 40's played Andy
Hardy's sister in the *Andy Hardy* series as well as the
juvenile lead in *Ah, Wilderness* (1935), many others.
Married name Baldwin. Enduring Faith, lot 1137,
grave 4, Forest Lawn Hollywood Hills, Los Angeles.

7072. Parker, Charlie "Bird" (Aug. 29, 1920–
March 12, 1955) Alto sax great, a major figure in the
evolution of jazz and promotion of bop music in the
postwar era. The story of his life and struggle with
drug addiction, *Bird*, was filmed in 1988. He died in
New York at 34. Grave length slab with a saxophone
and *Bird* on it, on left half way along center drive. In
October 1998 plans were announced to remove Parker
and his wife from Lincoln Cemetery to a tomb and
statue to be dedicated in March 1999 at the American

Jazz Museum at 18th and Vine in downtown Kansas
City, but the plans were abandoned by February 1999
after the family voiced objections. Renewed efforts by
the museum in fall 2004, which were also stopped by
the family, pointed out that his slab depicts a tenor
sax rather than his trademark alto sax. Lincoln Cemetery, Kansas City, MO.

7073. Parker, Dorothy (Dorothy Rothschild,
Aug. 22, 1893–June 7, 1967) Playwright, screenwriter,
columnist and a favorite caustic wit of the Algonquin
Round Table of the 1920's married briefly, she said,
to change her name. Among her sarcastic prose and
verses were *Men seldom make passes At girls who wear
glasses, Resume* (1925), *Tombstones By Starlight* (1929)
and *You Might as Well Live,* penned after more than one
botched suicide attempt. At her death from a heart
attack in Manhattan's Volney apartments on East 74th
St., she was cremated at Ferncliff Cemetery, Hartsdale, New York, but her executrix, playwright Lillian
Hellman, refused to pay a funeral bill or determine a
disposition. The ashes remained at Ferncliff or at
Frank E. Campbell mortuary until Hellman was notified they would be disposed of. They were mailed to
her lawyers O'Dwyer and Bernstein July 16, 1973 and
went into a file drawer there for fifteen years, until
four years after Hellman's own death. Negotiations to
place them in the Algonquin Hotel failed and they
were claimed by the NAACP, Parker having been a
strong exponent of civil rights legislation and left her
literary estate to Rev. Martin Luther King, Jr., though
she had never met him. Dr. Benjamin Hooks buried
the urn outside their national headquarters in Baltimore in a ceremony officially dedicating the Dorothy
Parker Memorial Garden behind the main building
there. On the circular plaque is inscribed a typical
Parkerism *Excuse My Dust.* NAACP Headquarters,
4805 Mt. Hope Drive, Baltimore, MD.

7074. Parker, Eddie (Edwin L. Parker, Dec. 12,
1900–Jan. 20, 1960) Hollywood stunt man from 1925
in many films, usually unbilled, frequently a monster
in action shots at Universal horror and B films of
the 1940's and 50's. He did some scenes in the Lon
Chaney, Jr. *Mummy* films, doubled along with Gil
Perkins for Bela Lugosi and Chaney in *Frankenstein
Meets the Wolfman* (1943), *Abbott and Costello Meet
Dr. Jekyll and Mr. Hyde* (for Boris Karloff as Mr.
Hyde, 1953), *Abbott and Costello meet the Mummy*
(1955, as Klaris), many others. He died from a heart
attack at 59. Sec. L, lot 12, grave 17, Calvary Cemetery, east Los Angeles.

7075. Parker, "Fast Eddie" (Edward Parker, June
2, 1931–Feb. 2, 2001) Born in Springfield, Missouri,
the inspiration for Paul Newman's character in *The
Hustler* and *The Color of Money* had retired from the
road and was giving exhibitions when he suffered a
heart attack during a Billiards Eight Ball Showdown
on South Padre Island, Texas. Services were to be at his
home town of fifteen years. Sec. 12, lot 10, space 1,
Holy Cross Cemetery, San Antonio, TX.

7076. Parker, Ellis H. (Sept. 12, 1871–Feb. 4, 1940) New Jersey detective once dubbed The Sherlock Holmes of America investigated an estimated 1,000 or more cases a year, based in Mount Holly and Burlington County for nearly forty years 1898–1937, credited with solving 304 of 310 murder cases. Working on the Lindbergh case, he produced the Wendel confession which delayed Hauptmann's execution in 1936. It was deemed a hoax, and Parker and his son went to prison, where the detective died from a brain tumor before a presidential pardon, all but completed, could send him home. Mount Holly Cemetery, Mount Holly, NJ.

7077. Parker, Jean (Lois Mae Green, Aug. 11, 1915–Nov. 30, 2005) Actress born in Deer Lodge, Montana, former gymnast, in films 1932–46 and sporadically 1950–66, often as innocent to wholesome leads (*Rasputin and the Empress, Gabriel Over the White House, Lady For A Day, Little Women* 1933, as Beth; *Operator 13, Sequoia, The Ghost Goes West, Zenobia, Beyond Tomorrow, The Pittsburgh Kid, Tomorrow We Live, One Body Too Many, Dead Man's Eyes, Bluebeard*). Married four times, the last (1951–7) to actor Robert Lowery (*q.v.*), she died from a stroke at 90 in the Motion Picture Country Hospital, Woodland Hills, California. Ashes interred December 9. Columbarium of Providence, niche 65039, Courts of Remembrance, Forest Lawn Hollywood Hills, Los Angeles.

7078. Parker, Marian (1915 – c. Dec. 15, 1927) The victim of a sensationalized murder case, twelve year old twin daughter of Los Angeles businessman Perry Parker was lured from her school by **William Edward Hickman.** When the ransom money was given him, he dumped her mutilated body on a roadside, strangled and the legs severed. Arrested in Oregon, he was hanged at San Quentin October 19, 1928, aged 20, and buried immediately (unmarked), sec. G, row 16, area 21, grave 5, Holy Cross Cemetery, Colma, California. Marian Parker's ashes are in an urn alone, the family having moved away. Columbarium of Peace, niche 7920, Dahlia Terrace, Great Mausoleum, Forest Lawn, Glendale, CA.

7079. Parker, Suzy (Cecilia Ann Renee Parker, Oct. 28, 1932–May 3, 2003) Red headed model from San Antonio epitomized beauty in the 1950's through photographer Richard Avedon, appearing in films including *Funny Face*— the actual inspiration for Audrey Hepburn's character, *Save One For Me* (both 1957), *Ten North Frederick* (1958) and in six roles in the 1963 *Twilight Zone* episode *Number Twelve Looks Just Like You.* Married from 1963 to actor Bradford Dillman, she died from renal failure at their Santa Barbara home at 70. No services, through Welch-Rycc-Hader mortuary. Ashes buried May 7. Island sec., addition C, grave 186, Santa Barbara Cemetery, Santa Barbara, CA.

7080. Parker, "Colonel" Tom (Thomas A. Parker, June 26, 1909–Jan. 21, 1997) Former carnival barker managed Elvis Presley's career from start to finish. He died in Las Vegas from a stroke at 87. Cremated through Palm Mortuary East, Las Vegas. Ashes to family.

7081. Parkman, Francis (Sept. 16, 1823–Nov. 8, 1893) Boston born Harvard graduate in law traveled west and described his adventures in articles consolidated into *The Oregon Trail* (1849). He later was hampered by failing nerves and eyesight, until a publication on roses in 1866 and a professorship of horticulture at Harvard in 1871. A foremost historian of his day, among his contributions was his extensive use of documentation. Indian Ridge Path, lot 2919, above Fountain Ave. below Lilac Path, Mt. Auburn Cemetery, Cambridge, MA.

7082. Parks, Bert (Dec. 30, 1914–Feb. 2, 1992) Atlanta born host and annual serenader of Miss America 1954–1980, his firing in 1980 generated an extensive campaign of written protests. He also worked on radio and hosted TV game shows (*Yours for a Song*). Last seen lampooning his own image in the film *The Freshman* (1990), he died from lung cancer in Scripps Hospital, La Jolla, California, at 77. Cremated by the Telophase Society in San Marcos. Ashes to his widow and residence in Greenwich, CT.

7083. Parks, Gordon, Jr. (Dec. 7, 1934–April 3, 1979) Son of the composer, author and director had directed a few films, including *Super-Fly* (1972) when he and three others died when their small plane crashed on takeoff at Wilson Airport in Nairobi, Kenya, where they were on location for his film *Revenge.* The explosion and fire reduced the body to ashes, which his father, because of his son's love of the mountain, asked to have spread over Kilimanjaro but **Gordon Parks** died in March 2006 and was buried with at least part of his son's ashes; both names are on the plaque. Evergreen Cemetery, Fort Scott, KS.

7084. Parks, Larry (Dec. 13, 1914–April 13, 1975) Second lead at Columbia known for his starring role in *The Jolson Story* (1946) and *Jolson Sings Again* (1949) was ruined in 1951 when he admitted past membership in a communistic organization before the House Un American Activities Committee. Though he begged the HUAC not to force him to name other members, they did, and he was blacklisted by all. His last film was *Freud* (1963) for his friend John Huston. He died from a heart attack in his Studio City, California, home at 60. Cremated at Rosedale Cemetery in Los Angeles, his ashes were returned to his widow, actress Betty Garrett, and buried in the rose garden of their home.

7085. Parks, Rosa (Rosa Louise McCauley, Feb. 4, 1913–Oct. 24, 2005) Pioneer in the civil rights movement of the 1950's and 60's was a seamstress and secretary of the NAACP who on December 1, 1955, refused to give up her seat to a white man on a bus in Montgomery, Alabama, was subsequently arrested and fined $14, bringing about a boycott of city transportation, a Supreme Court ruling and a federal injunction ending segregation on the buses by December 1956. She moved to Detroit the next year, where she died at 92. Flush plaque with her husband Raymond (1977) and mother Leona McCauley (1979). Woodlawn Cemetery, Detroit, MI.

7086. Parkyakarkus (Harry Einstein, 1904–Nov. 24, 1958) Popular comedian on the *Eddie Cantor* radio show appeared in several light films, also under the name Harry Parke. Rear corridor, near Louis B. Mayer, Corridor of Eternal Life 248, Home of Peace Memorial Park mausoleum, east Los Angeles.

7087. Parlo, Dita (Grethe Gerda Kornstadt, Sept. 4, 1906–Dec. 13, 1971) Actress from Stettin, Germany, now Szeczin, Poland, in films from the 1920's to 1965, including *Homecoming* (1928), *Melody of the Heart* (1930), *L'Atlante* (1934), *Mademoiselle Docteur* (title role, 1936), and *La Grande Illusion* (1937, as Elsie, the German widow). She died in Paris at 65. Tombe, au sud de Montbeliard, in the village cemetery at Montecheroux, France.

7088. Parnell, Charles Stewart (June 27, 1846–Oct. 6, 1891) Irish nationalist leader whose career faded when he was named co-respondent in a divorce action by the husband of Kitty O'Shea. He was portrayed in a biopic by Clark Gable in what was generally considered the worst casting of his career. Buried in a shaded grove beneath a large boulder with *Parnell* cut into it. Glasnevin Cemetery, Dublin.

7089. Parrino, Roario (Sasa) (1890–May 31, 1930) Member of the Schiro (now Bonanno) crime family in Brooklyn had moved to Detroit where, allied with the Milazzo family and the Maranzano side in the Castellammarese War, he and Gaspare Milazzo were shot to death in a Detroit fish market. His brother **Giuseppe**, with the same faction in the same war, was shot and killed in a Manhattan restaurant January 19, 1931. Both names are on the family monument. Sec. 2, range H, plot 15, grave 2, St. John's Cemetery, Middle Village, Queens, N.Y.C.

7090. Parrish, Helen (March 12, 1923–Feb. 22, 1959) Former child actress from Columbus, Georgia (*The Public Enemy, Bride of Frankenstein*), later in light roles (*Three Smart Girls, You'll Find Out* 1940, *Stage Door Canteen* 1943) last played Fred Rutherford's wife in one 1957 appearance on *Leave it To Beaver*. The wife of TV producer John Guedel, she died from cancer at 35. Cathedral Mausoleum, Alcove of Devotion, tier1, niche 4, Hollywood Memorial Park Cemetery (Hollywood Forever), Hollywood (Los Angeles), CA.

7091. Parry, Harvey (April 23, 1900–Sept. 18, 1985) Hollywood stunt man for decades dating back to silent films, including John Barrymore's catapult over the roofs of Paris through Marceline Day's window in *The Beloved Rogue* (1926). Mausoleum, sec. H, block 29, crypt F7, San Fernando Mission Cemetery, Mission Hills, CA.

7092. Parsons, Gram (Nov. 5, 1946–Sept. 19, 1973) Country rock pioneer and former Byrd became a cult figure after his death from an overdose of drugs.

His road manager and valet stole the body from the LAX en route to his family in New Orleans and drove it 300 miles east to Joshua Tree National Monument in the Mojave Desert, where they cremated it in a grotto at Cap Rock as they said had been his wishes. Burnt into the rock is the line *Gram Safe at Home.* They were fined $300 each and the cost of the coffin. The ashes were reportedly left to scatter from the site. What remained was buried beneath a small circular bronze marker with his name and *God's own singer.* Sec. R-12-11-2, Garden of Memories Cemetery, New Orleans, LA.

7093. Parsons, Johnny (July 4, 1918–Sept. 8, 1984) Race driver won the Indianapolis 500 in 1950 and was a fixture there before and after. La Ramada sec., lot 747, Inglewood Park Cemetery, Inglewood, CA.

7094. Parsons, Louella (August 6, 1881–Dec. 9, 1972) Hollywood gossip columnist for decades competed with Hedda Hopper for news regarding anyone in the film colony. She died from a stroke at 91. Buried with her husband "Dockie" Martin. Sec. D, lot 235, grave 8, Holy Cross Cemetery, Culver City, CA.

7095. Parsons, Milton (Ernest Milton Parsons, May 19, 1904–May 15, 1980) Gaunt, bald character actor in many small roles with a droll flair, from butlers to undertakers in films (*The Hidden Hand, Fingers at the Window, Cry of the Werewolf,* three *Dick Tracy* films, *The Secret Life of Walter Mitty, The Haunted Palace*) and TV (*I Love Lucy, Twilight Zone* episode *The New Exhibit*). Cremated through Westwood mortuary in west Los Angeles. Ashes scattered at sea.

7096. Parsons, Nancy (Jan. 17, 1942–Jan. 5, 2001) Burly actress from Minnesota known for her role as the sexually repressed gym teacher Beulah Ballbricker in three *Porky's* films, but had appeared in numerous fare, from *I Never Promised You a Rose Garden* (1977) to TV movies (*Mary Jane Harper Cried Last Night*) and several other TV and film roles (*Pennies from Heaven, Sudden Impact, The Lady in Red, The Doctor, Ladybugs*). She died from the effects of diabetes in La-Crosse, Wisconsin, at 56. Mass at St. Mary's in Viroqua. Viroqua Cemetery, Viroqua, WI.

7097. Parsons, William Barclay (April 15, 1859–May 9, 1932) New York born engineer directed, among other things, the 1900–1904 construction of New York's IRT (Interurban rapid transit) subway line, first opened October 27, 1904 and consisting of 9 miles of line from city hall in Manhattan. The system now connects the outer boroughs and totals 238 miles. A Brigadier General in the National Guard. He died in New York at 73. Funeral at Trinity Church. All Saints Church cemetery, Navesink, NJ.

7098. Pass, Joe (Joseph Anthony Jacobi Passalaqua, Jan. 13, 1929–May 23, 1994) Jazz guitar great. Sec. 8, block 10, lot 14, grave 12, Resurrection Cemetery, Piscataway, NJ.

7099. Passe, Loel (May 29, 1917–July 14, 1997) Voice of the Houston Colts/Astros 1962–75. Sec. 410, lot 112, space 3, Forest Park Westheimer, Houston, TX.

7100. Pasternak, Boris (Feb. 10, 1890–May 30, 1960) Moscow born novelist won the Nobel Prize in Literature for *Dr. Zhivago* (1957), but "chose" to refuse it, as the epic novel portrayed many aspects of the Russian Revolution in a bad light. He died in his sleep and was buried near his home at Peredelkino, Russia, a writers' colony approximately twenty miles from Moscow. **Olga Ivinskaya** (June 16, 1912–Sept. 8, 1995) The model for Lara in *Dr. Zhivago* was an editor who had an affair with Pasternak from 1946 until his death. Imprisoned in Soviet Moscow (while pregnant by Pasternak) because of her closeness to the writer in an attempt to persuade him to abandon his anti–Soviet themes, she lost their baby while in the prison camp for five years, until after Stalin's death in 1953. She died from cancer at 83 and was buried in a religious ceremony in a church in Moscow.

7101. Pasternak, Joseph (Sept. 19, 1901–Sept. 13, 1991) Hungarian producer in the U.S. and Europe from the 1920's, best known for lighter films at Universal in the late 30's including the money making Deanna Durbin musicals and *Destry Rides Again* (1939). Laurel Gardens, block 12, Hillside Memorial Park, Los Angeles.

7102. Pasteur, Louis (Dec. 27, 1822–Sept. 28, 1895) French chemist and bacteriologist researched fermentation of organisms in dairy products from 1854–57 and developed the purifying process called Pasteurization. Regarded as the father of the modern science of bacteriology. Interred in an ornate chapel adjacent where he worked and taught, at the Pasteur Institute in Paris.

7103. Pastor, Tony (Antonio Pastor, May 28, 1837–Aug. 20, 1908) New York theatrical producer opened the first variety theatre in 1865 and expanded to vaudeville in the late 1880's. A marble maiden with a cross on a pedestal stands guard over his lot. Shadowy Way sec., point facing intersection, Cemetery of the Evergreens, Brooklyn, N.Y.C.

7104. Pastor, Tony (Antonio Pestritto, Oct. 26, 1909–Oct. 31, 1969) Tenor saxophonist, vocalist (*Jeepers Creepers*) and bandleader (*Bell Bottom Trousers, What a Dolly*) introduced Cincinnati area vocalists Betty and Rosemary Clooney. He died in New London, Connecticut, his age listed as 62, though his headstone gives his birth year as 1909. St. Sebastian Cemetery, Middlefield, CT.

7105. Pastorelli, Robert (June 21, 1954–March 8, 2004) Actor from New Brunswick, New Jersey, best known as Eldin Bernecky, the free spirited painter on CBS's *Murphy Brown* 1988–94. Film roles include *Beverly Hills Cop II, Dances With Wolves, Striking Distance, Michael*. His girlfriend Charemon Jonovich, 25, by whom he had a daughter, died from an accidental gunshot wound to the head March 15, 1999. He was found dead at 49 of a suspected drug overdose in the bathroom of his Hollywood Hills home. Wall

crypt, St. Catherine's (Catholic) Cemetery, Sea Girt, NJ.

7106. Patch, Alexander McCarrell (Nov. 23, 1889–Nov. 21, 1945) U.S. Army general commanded forces at Guadalcanal and led the 7th Army into southern France in 1944. Standard upright military stone. Sec. 1, site 33, Post Cemetery, West Point Military Academy, West Point, NY.

7107. Patch, Sam (1807–Nov. 13, 1829) Stunt diver made numerous harrowing dives prior to his fatal plunge into the Gennessee River in Rochester, New York. His body was not recovered from the ice until the following March 17, and buried in Charlotte Cemetery, Rochester, NY.

7108. Patchen, Edward, Joe and **Sam** Early professional baseball playing brothers at shortstop, right field, and the infield, respectively. All three fought in the Civil War. H. Patchen mausoleum, hillside, Tulip Hill, Greenwood Cemetery, Brooklyn, NY.

7109. Pater, Walter (Walter Horatio Pater, Aug. 4, 1839–July 30, 1894) Late Victorian British writer whose themes espoused an abandoning of the absolute and rigid morality that ruled much of 19th century English thought and print. Works, influential to both Wilde and Yeats, include *Studies and History of the Renaissance* (1873) and *Marius the Epicurean* (1885). A bachelor, he was a fellow at Brasenose College from 1864. Holywell (St. Cross) Churchyard, St. Cross Road, Oxford, Oxfordshire.

7110. Paterson, Andrew Barton "Banjo" (Feb. 17, 1864–Feb. 5, 1941) Australian poet and journalist who co-wrote *Waltzing Matilda* with Christina Rutherford MacPherson (June 19, 1804–March 27, 1936). Reportedly drawn from the death of Samuel "Frenchy" Hoffmeister during the 1894 Australian sheep shearer's strike, Paterson wrote the words to MacPherson's tune, based on the Scottish march *Crairielee*, when he encountered her playing it on a zither at Dagworth Station. MacPherson (*q.v.*) is at Saint Kilda Cemetery, Melbourne, Australia. Paterson was taken to Northern Suburbs Crematorium, Sydney.

7111. Paterson, Jennifer (April 3, 1928–Aug. 10, 1999) Co-star, with Clarissa Dickson Wright, of the popular and quirky *Two Fat Ladies* cooking show on the BBC and Food Network in America from 1996. Described as unashamedly corpulent and opinionated, their many fans included Prince Charles. Paterson died in London from lung cancer at 71. Block B5, grave 587, Putney Vale Cemetery, London.

7112. Pathé, Charles (Dec. 25, 1863–Dec. 24, 1957) French cinema pioneer began importing and marketing phonographs in France in 1894 and with his brother Emile was selling projectors and directing films as the Pathé Freres Co. by 1896. In 1901 he went exclusively into film production, by 1903 turning out short films at Vincennes and in London, Moscow and New York; by 1908 Pathé was the largest film production company in the world and in a few years experimented with color and began the first weekly newsreel, operating from the U.S. 1914–17 He returned to France in 1917, sold his empire over the next decade, and retired to the Riviera, where he died at Monte Carlo just before his 94th birthday. Ancien (Old) Cimetiere, 7th division, Vincennes, France.

7113. Patkin, Max (Jan. 10, 1920–Oct. 30, 1999) The Clown Prince of Baseball for over fifty years in both the majors and the minors, appeared in films as well, including *Bull Durham*. Sec. H, lot 2827, grave 1, Mt. Lebanon Cemetery, Collingdale, PA.

7114. Saint Patrick (c. 369–461) British bishop raised in slavery escaped and returned to Britain at 22 to convert the Irish to Christianity. By 431 he was ordained and appointed first bishop of the Irish, converting many including some royals and fostering monasticism and dioceses. Grave marked by a boulder in the cemetery at Downpatrick, County Down, Northern Ireland.

7115. Patrick, Dennis (March 14, 1918–Oct. 13, 2002) Philadelphia born actor in many TV series guest spots from the mid 1950's played Jason McGuire (1967) and Paul Staddard #2 (1969) in the television horror soap opera *Dark Shadows*, as well as appearances in many features (*Chances Are, The Air Up There*), particularly TV movies of the 1970's and 80's. He died in a house fire in Hollywood at 84. Ashes scattered at sea along with those of his dog, who also died in the fire.

7116. Patrick, Gail (Margaret Fitzpatrick, June 20, 1911–July 6, 1980) Actress from Birmingham, Alabama, in films of the 1930's and 40's (*If I Had a Million, Murders in the Zoo, My Man Godfrey*), often as cold, aloof "other" women. She retired in 1948 as the wife of literary agent Thomas Jackson and finally of John Velde. Later executive producer of TV's *Perry Mason*, she died from leukemia at 69. Cremated at Grandview Memorial Park by Westwood mortuary in west Los Angeles. Scattered at sea by the family off the Santa Monica shoreline.

7117. Patrick, Lee (Nov. 22, 1901–Nov. 21, 1982) Blonde actress ranged from Sam Spade's secretary in the 1941 *The Maltese Falcon* to Blondie White in *Footsteps in the Dark* and later the wife in TV's *Topper* 1953–55. Among her last roles was in *The Black Bird*, a 1975 send-up of the *Falcon*. Married name Wood. Top tier, Room of Prayer, Westwood Memorial Park, west Los Angeles.

7118. Patricola, Tom (Jan. 22, 1891–Jan. 1, 1950) New Orleans born vaudeville and theatrical song and dance man, in films from 1929. Last appearance as himself in *Rhapsody in Blue* (1945). He died following brain surgery. Sec. M, Grand View Memorial Park, Glendale, CA.

7119. Patten, Luana (July 6, 1938–May 1, 1996) Child star at age eight opposite Bobby Driscoll in Disney's *Song of the South* as well as *So Dear To My Heart*; later in *Home From the Hill, Follow Me Boys, The Little Shepherd of Kingdom Come*. She died from respira-

tory failure at 57. Hibiscus, lot 702, Forest Lawn Sunnyside (Forest Lawn, Long Beach), Long Beach, CA.

7120. Patterson, Eleanor Medill "Cissy" (Elinor Medill Patterson, Nov. 7, 1884–July 24, 1948) Granddaughter of Joseph Medill and a sister of **Joseph Medill Patterson** (Jan. 6, 1879–May 26, 1946) was a socialite until 1930 when she took over the *Washington Herald* as an eccentric (anti–New Deal) editor-in-chief, sometimes arriving in a riding outfit. The paper declined by the 1950's. Joseph Patterson, who founded *The New York Daily News* in 1919, is in sec. 6, grave 5681-A, Arlington National Cemetery, Arlington, Virginia. Their father is also at Arlington. She died in bed reading at her Washington, D.C. home. Ashes with her mother and grandfather Medill in the Ridgeland sec., Graceland Cemetery, Chicago, Ill.

7121. Patterson, Elizabeth (Mary Elizabeth Patterson, Nov. 22, 1874–Jan. 31, 1966) Actress played timid spinsters in films (*Secret of the Blue Room* 1933, *The Cat and the Canary* 1939, *Remember the Night* 1940) and Mrs. Trumbull on *I Love Lucy* 1953–7. Cremated at Chapel of the Pines Crematory in Los Angeles. Ashes buried in her home town beneath a 19th century style obelisk with her full name, dates and epitaph *She walked with kings, nor lost the common touch*. Savannah Cemetery, Savannah, TN.

7122. Patterson, Frank (Oct. 5, 1938–June 10, 2000) Ireland's Golden Tenor, the heir to the legacy of John McCormack, sang before Pope John Paul II in Dublin in 1979 and was the first Irish artist to sell out Radio City Music Hall, among other honors. He appeared in the films *The Dead* (1987) and *Michael Collins* (1993). Residing in Bronxville, New York, he died at 61 from a brain tumor at Sloane-Kettering Hospital in Manhattan. Mass at St. Patrick's Cathedral in Manhattan and at Pro Cathedral, Dublin. Burial in his native Tipperary. On the ornate black and gold Celtic cross is the final stanza from *Danny Boy*, which he said he never tired of singing: *You'll come and find the place where I am lying/ And kneel and say an Ave there for me/ And I shall hear, though soft you tread above me/ And all my grave will warmer sweeter be/ For you will bend and tell me that you love me/ And I shall sleep in peace until you come to me.* Below that, on the base, is *St. Therese of the child Jesus. Little Flower, Pray for us.* St. Patrick's Cemetery, Clonmel, Tipperary County, Ireland.

7123. Patterson, Hank (Elmer Calvin Patterson, Oct. 9, 1888–Aug. 23, 1975) Alabama born actor from vaudeville days in film and television, usually in westerns or as sour tempered rubes (including Fred Ziffel on *Green Acres*). Murmuring Trees, lot 4345, Forest Lawn Hollywood Hills, Los Angeles.

7124. Patton, George S. (George Smith Patton, Jr., Nov. 11, 1885–Dec. 21, 1945) World War II General of the Third Army, known for his tough, demanding measures, died from injuries suffered in an auto accident on the road near Heidelberg in occupied Germany where he was going bird hunting. His wife could have had his body returned to the U.S. but chose instead to have him interred beneath a standard white military cross in the place where the majority of Third Army casualties were interred. Top of sec. B, Luxembourg American Cemetery, Hamm, near Luxembourg, Belgium. His wife **Beatrice Banning Ayer Patton** (Jan. 12, 1886–Sept. 30, 1953), suffered an aneurysm she had known she had in her aorta while riding in a hunt at Green Meadows, Hamilton, Massachusetts, and fell from her horse, already dead. She was buried beneath an elm at Green Meadows, but in 1957 her wish was granted when her children took her ashes to General Patton's grave at Hamm and sprinkled them there, where military regulations had forbidden her burial. Patton has a flush cenotaph in the lot of his parents, **George** and **Ruth Patton**. Block G, lot 22, San Gabriel District Cemetery, San Gabriel, CA.

7125. Paul, Alice (Jan. 11, 1885–July 9, 1977) Founder of the National Woman's Party and the militant wing of the suffrage movement. In 1923 she helped draft the Equal Rights Amendment and worked for its passage the rest of her life. Westfield Friends Burial Ground, Cinnaminson, north of Pennsauken, NJ.

7126. Paul VI (Giovanni Montini, Sept. 26, 1897–Aug. 6, 1978) Italian priest from Brescia continued the reforms of Pope John XXIII when he was crowned in 1963, reconvened the Second Vatican Council and continued reforming the vernacular of the Catholic liturgy. The first pope in over a century to leave Italy, he made a pilgrimage to the Holy Land in 1964, and addressed the United Nations in 1965. St. Peter's Basilica, Vatican City (Rome).

7127. Pauling, Linus Carl (Feb. 28, 1901–Aug. 19, 1994) Renaissance man of science was a proponent of Vitamin C and health, the only two time non-co Nobel laureate. He won in chemistry in 1954 for his research on the bonding of molecules in the structure of complex compounds, authored *No More War* in 1958 and presented a plea for a nuclear test ban to the United Nations, signed by 11,000 scientists worldwide. He won the Nobel Peace Prize in 1963 as the Nuclear Test Ban Treaty took effect. Pauling died of prostate cancer at Big Sur, California. Ashes buried at Lake Oswego Cemetery, Lake Oswego, OR.

7128. Pavlova, Anna (Jan. 31, 1885–Jan. 23, 1931) Russian born ballerina excelled in classical roles such as *Giselle* and in *Swan Lake*, popularizing ballet around the world to the extent that "Pavlova" became a synonym for "ballerina." She collapsed and died at the beginning of a performance from what was attributed to the effects of pleurisy. Inurned at Golders Green, she was to be removed and re-interred, according to her wishes, at Novo-Devichy Cemetery, Moscow, on September 14, 2000, but the move did not take place as her niece, who had agreed to the Russian government's requests for her ashes, changed her mind, preferring they remain in London. White urn,

Ernest George Columbarium, east wing, ground floor. Golders Green Crematorium, London.

7129. Pawle, Lennox (John Lennox Pawle, April 27, 1872–Feb. 22, 1936) Stout London born actor (*The Sin of Madelon Claudet* 1931, and *David Copperfield* 1935, as Mr. Dick) died at 63 from cirrhosis of the liver at Good Samaritan Hospital in L.A. Informant Montagu Love. Cremated February 25 at Pierce Bros.' Chapel of the Pines Crematory. Ashes sent March 12 to "Miss. M. Poole, Sussex, England."

7130. Pawley, Edward (March 16, 1901–Jan. 27, 1988) Dark haired actor in films 1930–1943, often as villains, including *Thirteen Women*, 1932, as Burns the chauffeur, *Treasure Island* 1934, as William, *Mississippi, G-Men, Angels With Dirty Faces* (1938, as Edwards the sadistic guard), *Each Dawn I Die* (1939, as Dale), *Castle on the Hudson* (1940), *Hold That Ghost* (1941). After 1943, married to actress **Helen Shipman** (*q.v.*), he left films to farm at Rock Mills, Rappahannock County, Virginia. He had survived his wife by under four years upon his death at University Hospital in Charlottesville. Cremated January 28 — authorized by a relative at Highland, Maryland — at Metropolitan Funeral Service and Crematory, Alexandria, Virginia, through Clore (now Clore-English) mortuary, Culpeper. Ashes sent back to Clore's; no burial or other disposition indicated in their records.

7131. Pawnee Bill *see* **Lillie.**

7132. Paxinou, Katina (Katina Constantopoulos, Dec. 17, 1900–Feb. 22, 1973) Greek actress from Piraeus, port of Athens, earned an Oscar as Pilar in *For Whom the Bell Tolls* (1943), and subsequently appeared in *Confidential Agent, Mourning Becomes Electra, Prince of Foxes*, several others before returning to Europe by 1960. She died from cancer in Athens at 72, where there is a Katina Paxinou Museum. At the head of her elevated beige slab is a bronze bust of her on a pedestal. First Cemetery, Athens, Greece.

7133. Paycheck, Johnny (Donald Eugene Lytle, May 31, 1938–Feb. 18, 2003) Country singer from Greenfield, Ohio, best known for his dark humored numbers *Take This Job and Shove It* (1977), *Don't Take Her She's All I've Got, I'm the Only Hell My Mama Ever Raised*, etc. He served two years in prison 1989–91 at Chillicothe for shooting a man in the head in an Ohio bar in 1985, and resumed his career for a decade before his death in Nashville from emphysema and asthma at 64. Singer George Jones donated a plot next to his own for the burial. Dogwood Garden, Woodlawn Memorial Park, Nashville, TN.

7134. Payne, Glen Weldon (Oct. 20, 1926–Oct. 15, 1999) Lead vocalist with the Cathedrals Quartet also sang with the Frank Stamps and Stamps-Ozark Quartets, as well as the Weatherfords, dubbed the smoothest group in southern Gospel history. Good Shepherd sec., lot 81-D, grave 1, Williamson Memorial Gardens, Franklin, TN.

7135. Payne, John (John Howard Payne, May 28, 1912–Dec. 6, 1989) Actor from Roanoke, Virginia, in musicals at Fox with Alice Faye and Betty Grable in the 40's and early 50's, and dramatic parts including *Miracle on 34th Street* (1947). He died in Malibu, California. Ashes returned to family there through Gates-Kingsley-Gates mortuary.

7136. Payne, John Howard (June 9, 1791–April 9, 1852) The first American *Hamlet* also wrote the words to the song *Home, Sweet Home* (in Paris in 1822 for *Clari, the Maid of Milan*). After his involvement with the widowed Mary Shelly, he returned to the U.S., was appointed consul to Tunisia, died and was buried there. In 1883 he was returned to Washington in a ceremony attended by President Arthur. A bearded bust was made for the monument but no one remembered the beard, so it was carefully chipped from the face. The second embarrassment occurred when a picture showed that he had indeed had a beard, though the bust at his grave had to remain without one. Ellipse, Oak Hill Cemetery, Georgetown, Washington, D.C.

7137. Payne, Sally (Sally Payne Kelly, Sept. 5, 1912–May 8, 1999) Character actress of the 1930's and 40's, died in Bel Air, California. Cremated through Gates-Kingsley-Gates and returned to the residence.

7138. Payne, Virginia (June 19, 1908–Feb. 9, 1977) Radio actress from Cincinnati played *Ma Perkins*, "America's mother of the air," in fictional Rushville Center from August 1933 (when she was twenty-five), on NBC and CBS, at times simultaneously, until 1960. She remained in Cincinnati, where she died at 67. John L. Payne lot, sec. 12, lot 12, range 5, St. Joseph New Cemetery, Cincinnati, OH.

7139. Payson, Joan Whitney (Feb. 5, 1903–Oct. 4, 1975) Colorful owner of the New York Mets and co-founder of the New York Museum of Modern Art. Falmouth-Foreside Cemetery, Falmouth, ME.

7140. Payton, Barbara (Barbara Redfield, Nov. 16, 1927–May 8, 1967) Actress in *Kiss Tomorrow Goodbye* (1950) whose career and personal life nosedived with alcoholism, an arrest on morals charges, etc. She died from liver failure at 39 while staying with her parents in San Diego. Ashes interred under her last married name Rawley. Chapel of Promise, niche 28, top tier, Cypress View Mausoleum, San Diego, CA.

7141. Payton, Lawrence (March 2, 1938–June 20, 1997) One of the Four Tops sang harmony on their many hits. Unique among rock and soul groups, the same four, mainstays with Motown, were together 43 years until his death at 59 from liver cancer. Sec. 40, lot 114, grave 13, Woodlawn Cemetery, Detroit, MI.

7142. Payton, Walter (July 25, 1954–Nov. 1, 1999) NFL great from Columbia, Mississippi, a star running back with the Chicago Bears 1975–88, setting the all time rushing record with 16,726 yards. Known as "Sweetness"—a reference to his personality. Announcing in Feb 1999 that he had primary sclerosing cholangitis and would need a liver transplant. Subse-

quently diagnosed with liver cancer, it spread rapidly and prevented the transplant. He died in his suburban Chicago home at 45. A Service was held at Life Changers International Church, South Barrington, Illinois, on November 5, with his urn present before the alter. A second public service was held the next day at Soldier Field.

7143. Peabody, Endicott (May 30, 1857–Nov. 17, 1944) Founder of Groton Prep. School for boys in Groton, Massachusetts, and headmaster 1884–1940. **Mary Parkman Peabody** (July 24, 1891–Feb. 6, 1981) participated in civil rights demonstrations in the south in her 70's and was briefly jailed, though mother of the governor of Massachusetts. Upright stones side by side. Groton Town Cemetery, Groton, MA.

7144. Peabody, Endicott H. "Chub" (Feb. 15, 1920–Dec. 2, 1997) The Baby Faced Assassin went from Groton, founded by his family, to Harvard, becoming a crimson gridiron great 1937–1941 and All American. Governor of Massachusetts 1963–65. His flat stone is in the lot in front of his mother and the founder of Groton. Groton Town Cemetery, Groton, MA.

7145. Peabody, George (Feb. 18, 1795–Nov. 4, 1869) Banker, financier and philanthropist was the first well known tycoon to fund institutions, notably the Peabody Institutes. He operated for many years from London, where he was honored by a bust in Westminster Abbey. Locust Path, Harmony Grove Cemetery, Salem, MA.

7146. Peale, Charles Willson (April 15, 1741–Feb. 22, 1827) Portrait painter of the Colonial American period and the early years of the Republic captured the likenesses of several signers of the Declaration of Independence. St. Peter's Churchyard in historic downtown Philadelphia, PA.

7147. Peale, Norman Vincent (May 31, 1898–Dec. 24, 1993) Dutch Reformed minister from Ohio known for *The Power of Positive Thinking* (1952), which sold over twenty million copies. He also published the magazine *Guideposts* with his wife Ruth Stafford, and ministered at Marble Collegiate Church in Manhattan 1932–84, where he founded the Peale Center for Christian Living in 1938, starting with one psychiatrist. He died at his Pawling farm. Christ Church of Quaker Hill/Quaker Redemption Cemetery, Pawling, NY.

7148. Peale, Rembrandt (Feb. 22, 1778–Oct 3, 1860) Painter, eldest son of Charles Willson Peale, did portraits of prominent colonial figures, including Washington, Jefferson, and others. His *Roman Dragon* hangs in the Boston Museum, and *The Court of Death* in the Detroit Art Gallery. Sec. F, Woodlands Cemetery, Philadelphia, PA.

7149. Peale, Titian (Nov. 17, 1799–March 13, 1887) Younger brother of Rembrandt Peale, also an artist and historian, Titian was a science illustrator who drew nature specimens on expeditions into Florida and to the South Pacific and the Antarctic.

Franklin Peale plot, Laurel Hill Cemetery, Philadelphia, PA.

7150. Pearce, Al (July 25, 1898–June 2, 1961) Radio comedian popular as a nervous salesman in his long running routine. Repose E-22, niche 5, tier 8, Abbey of the Psalms/Hollywood Forever Mausoleum, Hollywood Forever Cemetery, Hollywood (Los Angeles), CA.

7151. Pearce, Alice (Oct. 16, 1917–March 3, 1966) New York born actress-comedienne known as Lucy the sneezer in *On the Town* (1949) and as nosy neighbor Gladys Cravits on TV's *Bewitched* 1964–66. Married to Paul R. Davis. She died from cancer at 48 in Cedars of Lebanon Hospital, Los Angeles. Cremated at Chapel of the Pines Crematory in L.A., her ashes were to be scattered at sea by her family.

7152. Pearl, Daniel (Oct. 10, 1963–Feb. 22, 2002) *Wall Street Journal* South Asian bureau chief based in Bombay since December 2000, was kidnapped January 23, 2002, and murdered — confirmed on a videotape in February 2002 — while in Pakistan working on a story about the so-called shoe bomber, Richard Reid, and his links to Islamic extremists. The four militants responsible were tried, three given life sentences, and the leader, British born Ahmed Omar Saced Sheikh, sentenced to death. Pearl's body was found in May in a shallow grave in Karachi and identified through DNA. His funeral was held in Encino, California, the following August 10. Zion 5, lot 126, Mt. Sinai Memorial Park, Los Angeles.

7153. Pearl, Minnie (Sarah Ophelia Cannon, Oct. 25, 1912–March 4, 1996) Comedian with the Grand Ole Opry fifty years and on TV's *Hee Haw* known for her straw hat with price tag and shrill, extended salutation "Howdee." She died from a stroke at a Columbia, Tennessee, hospital, at 83. Sec. K, lot 131, Mount Hope Cemetery, Franklin, TN.

7154. Pearson, Drew (Dec. 13, 1897–Sept. 1, 1969) Political columnist authored *Washington Merry Go Round*, later continued by Jack Anderson, with a gossip and rumor slant to it, aimed at embarrassing and exposing corrupt politicians. Books include *Drew Pearson's Diary*. His ashes were placed in a bronze urn in a hole drilled in a high rock, with a plaque, on his Merry-Go-Round farm in Montgomery County, Maryland, overlooking the Potomac.

7155. Pearson, Virginia (Virginia Belle Pearson, March 7, 1888–June 6, 1958) Silent film actress from Louisville, Kentucky, specialized in vamp roles, known as the Screen's Heretic. She had played the lead in *A Fool There Was* on stage in 1909 which went to Theda Bara in the film six years later, but was popular in similar roles at Fox 1916–19. She played Carlotta in the 1925 *Phantom of the Opera*, but in the 1929 reissue was given the newly created role of Carlotta's mother, appeared again opposite Lon Chaney in *The Big City* and opposite Oliver Hardy in *Hog Wild*. Married to actor Sheldon Lewis, she died at the Motion Picture Country Home a month after her husband.

Unmarked next to Lewis. Block L, sec. 942, lot 26, Valhalla Memorial Park, North Hollywood, CA.

7156. Peary, Harold "Hal" (July 25, 1908–March 30, 1985) Heavy, mustached actor and singer with a unique deep voice, laugh, and delivery, played *The Great Gildersleeve*, originally a part of *Fibber McGee and Molly*, then Summerfield's water commissioner, on radio in the 1940's to the early 50's and in a few films. He also appeared as Herb Woodley on TV's *Blondie* (1957) and the mayor on *Fibber McGee and Molly* (1959–60), 1970's Red Pop commercials, etc. Cremated by the Neptune Society in Los Angeles, his ashes were scattered at sea.

7157. Peary, Robert (May 6, 1856–Feb. 20, 1920) Explorer with Matthew Henson reached the North Pole in 1908. Frederick Cook claimed to have reached it in 1907, but most credit Peary as the true pioneer (or Henson). A large stone Earth, with a bronze star marking the pole, was erected by the National Geographic Society at his grave April 6, 1922. Sec. 8, grave S-15, Arlington National Cemetery, Arlington, VA.

7158. Peattie, Donald Culross (June 21, 1898–Nov. 16, 1964) Writer of studies of nature and biographer of Audubon also dabbled in short stories, such as *The Mystery in Four and a Half Street*, written in 1931 with wife **Louise**. Central sec., block D, lot 168, Santa Barbara Cemetery, Santa Barbara, CA.

7159. Peck, Bob (Aug. 23, 1945–April 4, 1999) English actor from Leeds in the 1985 TV series *Edge of Darkness*, and films *Jurassic Park* (1993, as the game keeper) and *Fairie Tale* (1998) died from cancer at 53. Service at St. John's Church, Spencer Hill, Wimbledon. Ashes to family, tentatively to be sprinkled on Wimbledon Common and a bench placed there in his memory.

7160. Peck, George W. (Sept. 28, 1841–April 16, 1916) Governor of Wisconsin, newspaper editor and creator of *Peck's Bad Boy*, which ran on Broadway in the late 19th century. Sec. 6, block 1, lot 7, Forest Home Cemetery, Milwaukee, WI.

7161. Peck, Gregory (Eldred Gregory Peck, April 5, 1916–June 12, 2003) Actor from California in films from 1944–1991 exuded morality and a stern dignity in most of his roles (excepting *Duel in the Sun* 1946, *The Boys from Brazil* 1978), particularly as Atticus Finch in *To Kill A Mockingbird* (Best Actor AA, 1962). Other signature films include *The Keys of the Kingdom* (AA nom., 1945), *Spellbound, The Yearling* (AA nom., 1946), the landmark *Gentlemen's Agreement* (AA nom., 1947), *The Paradine Case, Twelve O'Clock High* (AA nom., 1950), *The Gunfighter, Captain Horatio Hornblower, David and Bathsheba, Roman Holiday, The Man in the Gray Flannel Suit, Moby Dick* (as Captain Ahab), *The Guns of Navarone, Cape Fear* (1962), *MacArthur, The Omen, Old Gringo* (1989). Presidential Medal of Freedom 1968. A cameo as the villain's lawyer in the 1991 remake of *Cape Fear* was his last film appearance. Married to Veronique Passani for forty-eight years until his death in his Los Angeles home at 87. Mass June 16, with a eulogy by Brock Peters. Entombment, crypt 112, tier B, Cathedral of Our Lady of the Angels, Los Angeles.

7162. Peckinpah, Sam (Feb. 21, 1925–Dec. 28, 1984) Screen writer and director from Fresno associated with action and western films in wide open spaces, particularly known for frequent graphic violence presented as a necessary and natural force worked into his plots, including *The Wild Bunch* (1969) and *Straw Dogs* (1972). Ashes buried at sea from a rowboat off Paradise Cove, CA.

7163. Pedi, Tom (Sept. 14, 1913–Dec. 29, 1996) Portly New York born Runyonesque actor in numerous tough, serio-comic supporting roles: several films 1948–50, including *The Naked City, Up in Central Park, Criss Cross, Sorrowful Jones, Cry Murder,* various TV series through the 1950's, and again in films of the 1970's, including *The Iceman Cometh* and *The Taking of Pelham One Two Three.* He died from a heart attack in Burbank, California, at 83. Cremated through White and Day mortuary. Ashes buried January 8. Unmarked. Enduring Faith sec., lot 532, grave 2, Loma Vista Memorial Park, Fullerton, CA.

7164. Peerce, Jan (June 3, 1904–Dec. 15, 1984) New York born tenor with the Metropolitan Opera made his debut in 1941, singing 205 performances in eleven operas, last appearing in *Faust* in 1968. Among his many popular recordings was *The Bluebird of Happiness* (1940). He died from pneumonia in New York City at 80. Service at the Riverside Chapel in Manhattan. Beth El sec. (N.R.), plot 403, grave 1, Mt. Eden Cemetery, Valhalla, NY.

7165. Peet, Bill (William Bartlett Peet, Jan. 29, 1915–May 11, 2002) Disney artist and writer drew *Dumbo,* wrote *101 Dalmatians,* thirty five children's books and contributed to *Fantasia, Song of the South, Cinderella* and *Alice in Wonderland.* Murmuring Trees, lot 9882, space 4, Forest Lawn Hollywood Hills, Los Angeles.

7166. Pegler, Westbrook (Aug. 2, 1894–June 24, 1969) Syndicated columnist with the *New York World Telegram* won the Pulitzer Prize in 1941 for his expose on labor unions. Increasingly known for his conservatism and name calling, with accelerated opposition to both the Roosevelt and Truman administrations. He cherished, it was said, the enemies he had made. He faced several libel suits and later wrote for the John Birch Society. Above O'Rourke and next to Carroll, five rows up from sec. 40 sign, near intersection of secs. 40, 41 and 46. Sec. 40, lot 859, Gate of Heaven Cemetery, Hawthorne, NY.

7167. Peller, Clara (Aug. 4, 1902–Aug. 11, 1987) Chicago manicurist-beautician became a celebrity in 1984 with her "Where's the Beef?" commercials for Wendy's. She died from heart failure in Chicago at 85. Gate 55, Waldheim Jewish Cemeteries, Forest Park, IL.

7168. Pemberton, Brock (Dec. 14, 1885–March 11, 1950) New York theatrical producer was a critic

until 1917 and produced 1917–1920, including *Miss Lulu Bett* (Pulitzer Prize 1920). Associated from 1929 with Antoinette Perry, their collaborations included *Strictly Dishonorable* (1931). He produced Claire Booth's *Kiss the Boys Goodbye* (1938) but had his biggest success with *Harvey,* which won the Pulitzer Prize in 1944, sometimes playing the lead himself. He died from a heart attack at 64 in his Manhattan home. Receiving vault at Woodlawn Cemetery, the Bronx. Removed April 3, 1950 to Orange, New Jersey. Epitaph *He is not dead, for souls can never die. He is not gone, his presence still is nigh. And lives within our hearts with holiest prayer. May we not mourn — we that loved him so? His hopes were ours. his triumphs were our pride.* McCoy lot, along road, sec. 42, lot 5, grave 11, Rosedale Cemetery, Orange, NJ.

7169. Pemberton, John C. (Aug. 10, 1814–July 13, 1881) Lt. Gen. CSA in the Civil War commanded the Department of the Mississippi, the Tennessee and Louisiana 1862–63, surrendering to Grant at Vicksburg July 4, 1863. Exchanged, he resigned in May 1864. Sec. 9, lot 53; the only Confederate general in Laurel Hill Cemetery, Philadelphia, PA.

7170. Pemberton, John S. (July 8, 1831–Aug. 16, 1888) Doctor and chemist from Columbus, Georgia, devised the formula which became the soft drink Coca Cola, derived from wine of coca, which was sold into the 1880's as an all purpose cure for various illnesses and malfunctions, first mixed together in his backyard at 107 Marietta Street, Atlanta, in 1885. Three years later, just prior to his death, he sold the formula for $1,750 to Asa Candler, who went on to found the Coca-Cola Company in 1892. Family monument and slabs; his notes *Originator of Coca-Cola.* Linwood Cemetery, Columbus, GA.

7171. Pender, Paul (June 20, 1930–Jan. 12, 2003) Two time middleweight boxing champion twice defeated Sugar Ray Robinson in 1960. He died from Alzheimer's Disease in Medford, Massachusetts. Holyhood Cemetery, Brookline, MA.

7172. Pendergast, Thomas (July 22, 1872–Jan. 26, 1945) Kansas City political boss, once Harry Truman's mentor and long time friend, eventually went to prison. Block 9, lot 249, space 1, Calvary Cemetery, Kansas City, MO.

7173. Pendleton, George H. (George Hunt Pendleton, July 28, 1825–Nov. 24, 1889) Cincinnati born Democratic representative to congress from Ohio 1857–65 and senator 1879–85 on the Ways and Means Committee authored The Pendleton Act (1883), which began civil service reform through merit qualifications and examinations. Appointed Minister to Germany in 1885, he died in Brussels in 1889. Grave length slab. Sec. 36, lot 7, Spring Grove Cemetery, Cincinnati, OH.

7174. Pendleton, Nat (Nathaniel Greene Pendleton, Aug. 9, 1895–Oct. 11, 1967) Former Olympic wrestler turned to acting and appeared in scores of films in the 1930's and 40's as dumb cops (*The Thin*

Man series), gangster henchmen (*Star Witness, Manhattan Melodrama*), athletes (*Horse Feathers, The Mad Doctor of Market Street*). He died from a heart attack in San Diego. Inurned in March 1968. Corridor A, Court of the Apostles, nw 9, Cypress View Mausoleum, San Diego, CA.

7175. Penn, John (May 17, 1741–Sept. 14, 1788) Signer of the Declaration of Independence from North Carolina, buried with fellow signer William Hooper at Guilford Courthouse Battlefield, Greensboro, NC.

7176. Penn, Lemuel (Sept. 19, 1915–July 11, 1964) Teacher and civil rights worker, World War II Army veteran — a Lt. Colonel in the Infantry — was returning to Washington from Georgia nine days after President Johnson signed the Civil Rights Bill, when he was ambushed by three Ku Klux Klan members near Athens, Georgia, who pulled up beside his moving car and fired into the left side of his head. Initially acquitted in Georgia, they were re-tried on federal charges in 1966 and convicted. Sec. 3, grave 1377, Arlington National Cemetery, Arlington, VA.

7177. Penn, Leo (Leo Z. Penn, Aug. 27, 1921–Sept. 5, 1998) Actor, director and writer blacklisted in the 1940's and 50's later directed in film and considerable television work. He died in Los Angeles at 77. Father of actor-director Sean Penn and actor Christopher Penn, who died at 40 January 24, 2006, and is buried in the same lot. Sec CC, tier 54, grave 20, Holy Cross Cemetery, Culver City, CA.

7178. Penn, William (Oct. 14 [N.S.], 1644–July 30 [N.S.], 1718) London born religious reformer and founder of Pennsylvania in 1682, the charter granted him by the king and named after his father, Admiral Sir William Penn. He later returned to England, but left established in the New World his commonwealth of toleration for Quakers and other dissenters. He suffered a crippling stroke in 1712 and died six years later at Ruscombe. Burial in the family plot of simple Quaker stones at Jordans, near Chalfont St. Giles, Buckinghamshire.

7179. Penner, Joe (Josef Pinter, Nov. 11, 1904–Jan. 10, 1941) Hungarian born comedian in light films and on radio, known for his line "Wanna buy a duck?" died from a heart attack at 36. Sarcophagus with his signature on a landing. Crypt C, Sarcophagus LL, Fuchsia Terrace, Great Mausoleum, Forest Lawn Glendale, CA.

7180. Penney, James Cash (Sept. 16, 1875–Feb. 12, 1971) Founder of the chain of J.C. Penney's 5 & 10 cent (dime) stores used cost cutting measures, like having his traveling salesmen sleep three to a bed. He had 500 stores across America by the early 1920's, and over 1600 by his death. A bronze Greek maiden in bas-relief on the bronze door guards his small mausoleum, across the road from the much larger Egyptian style mausoleum of F.W. Woolworth, along Chestnut Ave., Pine sec., Woodlawn Cemetery, the Bronx, N.Y.C.

7181. Pennick, Jack (Dec. 7, 1895–Aug. 16, 1964) Character actor in many small parts as rugged characters including several John Ford films, from *Air Mail* (1932) to *The Man Who Shot Liberty Valance* (1962). He was also a horse trainer. Concordia plot 262 div. D center grave, Inglewood Park Cemetery, Inglewood, CA.

7182. Pennington, Ann (Dec. 23, 1893–Nov. 4, 1971) Camden, New Jersey born *Ziegfeld Follies* dancer from 1913 known as Tiny (at 4'11" in heels), in several later *Follies, Midnight Frolics, Miss 1917*, etc. With *George White's Scandals* 1918–26, she popularized the Black Bottom in the 1926 edition. In three films 1916–31, she last appeared stage in 1946. Actors Fund of America plot, Kensico Cemetery, Valhalla, NY.

7183. Pennock, Herb (Herbert J. Pennock, Feb. 10, 1894–Jan. 30, 1948) The Squire of Kennett Square, tall, willowy left handed pitcher in the A.L., with the Yankees 1923–1934. He pitched eleven years with them, never losing a world series game and winning five. Hall of Fame 1948. Sec. CC, Union Hill Cemetery, Kennett Square, PA.

7184. Penrose, Boies (Nov. 1, 1860–Dec. 31, 1921) Republican senator from Pa. 1897–1922 was among the major voices against the League of Nations in 1919–20. Sec. 7, lot 380, Laurel Hill Cemetery, Philadelphia, PA.

7185. Peppard, George (Oct. 1, 1928–May 8, 1994) Detroit born blond leading man of the 1950's and 60's in *Breakfast at Tiffany's, Pork Chop Hill, How the West Was Won* and *The Carpetbaggers* later played Col. Hannibal Smith in TV's *The A Team* in the 1980's. He died in Los Angeles from pneumonia at 65. Sent by Forest Lawn Hollywood Hills, for burial with his parents. Upright rose family stone. North View Cemetery, Dearborn, MI.

7186. Pepper, Art (Arthur Edward Pepper, Sept. 1, 1925–June 15, 1982) Jazz alto sax player. Abbey of the Psalms/Hollywood Forever Mausoleum, Sanctuary of Trust, tier D2, crypt 1171, Hollywood Forever Cemetery, Hollywood (Los Angeles), CA.

7187. Pepper, Barbara (May 31, 1915–July 18, 1969) Former Goldwyn girl in B films, later a semi-regular on *I Love Lucy* and a regular on *Green Acres* (as Doris Ziffel, Arnold's mother). Married name Enfield. Sec. 2, lot 12, Hollywood Forever Cemetery, Hollywood (Los Angeles), CA.

7188. Pepper, Claude (Sept. 8, 1900–May 30, 1989) Congressman from Florida known for his work on behalf of the aged. His upright headstone reads *He loved God and the people and sought to serve both.* Block G, lot 5, grave 5, Oakland Cemetery, Tallahassee, FL.

7189. Pepper, Jack (June 14, 1902–April 1, 1979) Slight vaudeville and radio singer and comedian from the 1920's later appeared in several Hope and Crosby *Road* pictures. U.S. Army sergeant in World War II. Tribute, lot 1306, grave 1, Forest Lawn Hollywood Hills, Los Angeles.

7190. Pepys, Samuel (Feb. 23, 1633–May 26,

1703) English diarist and administrator was secretary of affairs for the Navy 1660–1668, during the reign of both Charles II and James II. His diary, written 1660–69, is considered one of the most insightful books of the era, with vivid descriptions of day to day court life during the Restoration period. He was buried in front of the altar, beside the communion table. St. Olave's Church, Clapham, London.

7191. Peraino, Giuseppe (1889–1930) Capo of the Profaci crime family and **Carmine Peraino** (1909–1930), a soldier with the same organization, killed in the Castellammarese War in 1930. Sec. 4, range A, grave 26, St. John's Cemetery, Middle Village, Queens, N.Y.C.

7192. Percy, Walker (May 28, 1916–May 10, 1990) Alabama born writer with existentialist philosophies reflected in *The Moviegoer* (National Book Award 1961). He also wrote *Love Among the Ruins* (1971). St. Joseph Abbey Cemetery, Covington, LA.

7193. Perelman, S. J. (Sidney Joseph Perelman, Feb. 1, 1904–Oct. 17, 1979) American humorist and screen writer was identified with the Marx Brothers at Paramount in the early 1930's, much to his disgust as it detracted in later years from any attention to his other work, to the extent that one of his books was titled *Don't Mention the Marx Brothers*. He had lived for forty years at Erwinna in Bucks County, Pennsylvania, when his wife died in 1970, after which he lived in London for a time and later at the Gramercy Park Hotel in Manhattan. His ashes were buried beneath a tree approximately a mile from his daughter Abby's home at West Hurley, NY.

7194. Perier, Francois (Francois Pilu, Nov. 10, 1919–June 28, 2002) French actor in films from 1938 into the 1990's, including works by Rene Clair (*Le Silence Est D'or* 1947), Federico Fellini (*Nights of Cabiria*), and Roman Polanski (*Amadeus in Paris*), but best known as Heurtebise, the angel of death in Jean Cocteau's *Orphee* (1950). Div. 8, Passy Cemetery, Paris.

7195. Perkins, Anthony (April 4, 1932–Sept. 12, 1992) Actor son of Osgood Perkins in films from 1953 (*Friendly Persuasion*, AA nomination 1956), forever known as Norman Bates in Alfred Hitchcock's *Psycho* (1960). He reprised the role three times, the last slant (*Psycho IV, The Beginning*) shortly before his death at 60 from pneumonia complicated by AIDS in his Los Angeles home. His wife actress Berry Berenson (*q.v.*), later died when her plane was flown into the World Trade Center in Manhattan September 11, 2001. Private service by Pierce Brothers-Cunningham & O'Connor-Utter-McKinley, Santa Monica. His ashes were returned September 17 in two halves — part or all tentatively to be scattered — to the residence in Los Angeles.

7196. Perkins, Carl (April 9, 1932–Jan. 19, 1998) Rockabilly pioneer known for *Blue Suede Shoes*, which in January 1956 topped the rock, country and R&B charts. He wrote songs later recorded by Elvis Presley, Patsy Cline and the Beatles, among others. He died at 65 in Jackson, Tennessee, his birthplace, after several strokes. His funeral was attended by many renowned names, including George Harrison. Exterior crypt, Ridge Crest Memorial Mausoleum, Jackson, TN.

7197. Perkins, Frances (April 10, 1882–May 14, 1965) Secretary of Labor in the administration of Franklin Roosevelt 1933–45. She was the first female to hold a major cabinet post, jokingly known as having been in labor for twelve years. Glidden Cemetery, New Castle, ME.

7198. Perkins, Gil (Gilbert Perkins, Aug. 24, 1907–March 28, 1999) Stuntman and actor (*Journey's End* 1930, as Sgt. Cox) in films from 1929 for over fifty years. He doubled for Spencer Tracy in *Dr. Jekyll and Mr. Hyde* (1941), also appeared in *Captains Courageous* (1937), *Frankenstein meets the Wolf-Man* (1943, reportedly doubling both monsters), *The Three Musketeers* (1948), *Abbott & Costello Meet Dr. Jekyll & Mr. Hyde* (1953, double), *How the West Was Won* (1962), many others. He died in Los Angeles at 91. Ashes scattered at sea.

7199. Perkins, Jean (Jean Edward Perkins, Feb. 22, 1893–Dec. 25, 1922) Stunt man filming the serial *Around the World in Eighteen Days* for Universal at March Field near Riverside, California, grabbed the bottom rung of a ladder hanging from a swooping plane and could not hang on, falling to his death (the next day at Riverside Community Hospital). The death certificate gives the cause as "acute pneumonia following and as a result of injuries sustained by falling from an airplane." Flinn undertakers, Riverside (now out of business). Certificate lists disposition as "removal, Los Angeles, Ca., Dec. 27" Buried December 28. Sec. E, lot 1174, Calvary (Catholic) Cemetery, east Los Angeles.

7200. Perkins, Luther (Jan. 8, 1928–Aug. 5, 1968) Guitarist with Marshall Grant formed the Tennessee Two (later Three, with W.S. Holland) and played lead for Johnny Cash from 1955 until his death in a house fire caused by a lit cigarette. Brother of Thomas Wayne (*q.v.*). Sermon on the Mount sec., 64A, space 1, Woodlawn East Memorial Park, Hendersonville, TN.

7201. Perkins, Marlin (March 28, 1905–June 14, 1986) Host of TV's *Wild Kingdom* died from cancer at home in St. Louis. Cremated through Knell mortuary, Carthage, Missouri, where his family is buried and a statue of him stands in the park. His ashes were scattered in Africa.

7202. Perkins, Maxwell (Sept. 20, 1854–June 17, 1947) Editor at *Scribner's* from 1910 promoted Wolfe, Fitzgerald, Hemingway. Sec. K, lot 23, Lakeview Cemetery, New Canaan, CT.

7203. Perkins, Osgood (May 16, 1892–Sept. 21, 1937) Mustached character actor from Newton, Massachusetts, a Harvard graduate, appeared in many films including *The Front Page* (both on stage in 1928 and film, 1931), *Scarface* (1932), many others. He was the first vice president of Actors Equity, an office he held at the time of his death from a heart attack at 45 while on tour in Washington, D.C. Father of actor Anthony Perkins. Cremated at Cedar Hill Cemetery in Prince George County, Maryland, the ashes were returned in a bronze urn to the widow in New York City, who scattered them in Long Island Sound.

7204. Perla, Mario (dec. Oct. 18, 1938) Mob figure had his head blown off by a shotgun. L'Unione Italiana Cemetery, 25th Ave. and 25th St., Tampa, FL.

7205. Perlberg, William (Oct. 22, 1899–Oct. 31, 1968) Producer of films at Fox, Paramount and MGM, often with George Seaton. Mausoleum, Columbarium of Hope, niche 215-BHillside Memorial Park, Los Angeles.

7206. Peron, Eva (Maria Eva Duarte, May 7, 1919–July 26, 1952) Actress and political leader from the Buenos Aires area performed on radio and in a few films before her marriage to **Juan Peron** (Oct. 8, 1895–July 1, 1974) in 1945, the year before he became president of Argentina. Evita (Little Eva) was considered a major power behind the throne. Diagnosed with cancer at 29, she died at 33 and her body was exhibited for three days at the Ministry of Labor in Buenos Aires. Peron had her preserved by a Spanish pathologist for intended permanent exhibition, but when he was overthrown in 1955, her body disappeared, buried under another name in Milan, Italy, by the new administration — who did not want the grave to become a shrine — for fourteen years. In 1971 when Peron returned to power, the Argentine government returned the body, traded for a stolen corpse the Italians wanted back, and found it perfectly preserved by the embalming work of 1952–55. "The Altar of the Fatherland," a 110' pantheon, was built in Buenos Aires in 1974 and she was returned and briefly interred there with her husband. In October 1976 the new president refused to occupy the palace until they were removed and returned to the family. On October 22, Eva Peron was placed in a chamber two levels below a mausoleum, a small tomb, and her husband placed below ground level in the same tomb. There was for a time no marking on the structure to indicate who is in the lower chambers, and only the sister of Evita was given a key. Later, memorial plaques to the Duartes and Eva Peron were attached to their small tomb — one with *Don't cry for me, Argentina* in Spanish — west of the main entrance to Recoletta Cemetery, Buenos Aires, Argentina. Juan Peron was later reinterred, also with a plaque on the tomb, at Chacarita Cemetery, Buenos Aires. He was reburied again Oct. 17, 2006, at San Vicente, Argentina.

7207. Perrin, Nat (March 15, 1905–May 9, 1998) Writer and producer worked on several Marx Bros. films among others, a long time friend of Groucho and briefly his executor. He died in Los Angeles at 93. T Building/Hall of David, T-7-1, crypt 1445, Beth Olam Cemetery adjacent Hollywood Forever Cemetery, Hollywood (Los Angeles), CA.

7208. Perrot, Kim (Jan. 18, 1967–Aug. 19, 1999) Star with the Ragin' Cajuns of Southwestern Louisiana set an NCAA record with 58 points scored against Southeastern Louisiana on February 5, 1990. After playing overseas, she returned to lead the WNBA's Houston Comets to back to back championships in 1997 and 1998. Diagnosed with cancer early the next year, she died at 32 in a Houston hospital. Assumption Cemetery, Carenco, LA.

7209. Perry, Antoinette (June 27, 1888–June 28, 1946) New York theatrical director and president of the Dramatists Guild designed to discover new talent. A former stage actress, she retired from acting as the wife of businessman Frank Frueauff. He died in 1922 and she returned to the theatre in 1924. Besides acting and directing, she was instrumental in organizing and operating stage door canteens during World War II. The annual Tony Award in theatre is named for her. She died from a heart ailment in her Manhattan home and was buried with her husband in a large circular lot beneath an Evergreen tree shading their two small stones, Hickory Knoll sec. 126, Woodlawn Cemetery, the Bronx, N.Y.C.

7210. Perry, Matthew Galbraith (April 10, 1794–March 4, 1858) Naval commodore who opened U.S. trade with Japan 1852–54. He died at his home on 32nd St. in Manhattan. Most biographies list his burial place as the Island Cemetery at Newport, Rhode Island. A biography, *The Great Commodore*, stated that his wife only had a monument to him erected there and that he remained in his original burial place, the Slidell vault in St. Mark's Church-in-the Bowery churchyard on E. 10th St. in Manhattan. A Japanese delegation had visited New York previously and decorated the Slidell vault in St. Mark's, however on the 100th anniversary of the trade agreement in 1954, the Slidell vault was opened and searched and the coffins of the commodore and his daughter were not there. An order dated March 21, 1866 was also found, which gave authorization by the New York health department to remove them to Newport. His name remains on the Slidell slab but the ornate monument in the center of the circular August Belmont lot marks his actual burial site in the Island Cemetery, Newport, RI.

7211. Perry, Oliver Hazard (Aug. 23, 1785–Aug. 23, 1819) Colonial admiral, victor at the Battle of Lake Erie in September 1813 and elder brother of Commodore Matthew Perry whose fame came forty years after that of his brother. He died at sea in 1819 and was brought in 1826 to the family lot, dominated by an obelisk to him with inscribed marble tablets on all four sides. Island Cemetery, Newport, RI.

7212. Pershing, John J. (Sept. 13, 1860–July 15, 1948) Commander of American Expeditionary Forces in France during World War I, "Black Jack" was the only general since Washington to hold the rank of General of the Armies. He was the exception to the rule in that a military leader from each war between the Revolution and World War II was elected president in the decade after the war. From 1941 he lived in a special wing of Walter Reed Army Hospital, where he charted the progress of World War II through maps on the wall. He was buried in a plot he had chosen, so that "when the last bugle is sounded," he would be with his soldiers. Sec. 34, grave S-19, Arlington National Cemetery, Arlington, VA.

7213. Petain, Henri Philippe (April 24, 1856– July 23, 1951) World War I French military leader became Marshall of Vichy controlled France during the Nazi occupation 1940–44. He was afterward tried for collaboration with the Nazis, sentenced to military degradation and death, which was commuted to life. He died six years after the war at 95. Cimetiére de Port-Joinville, Port-Joinville, Vendee (85), France.

7214. Peter the Great (Peter I, Emperor of Russia) (June 9 [N.S.], 1672–Feb. 8 [N.S.], 1725) Czar Peter I, founder of the Russian empire. On the 10th of February 1725, his body was taken from the palace at St. Petersburg to the Cathedral of St. Peter and Paul. In June 1931 it was placed in a vault below the church floor. Sarcophagi above mark his tomb, that of Catherine the Great, and others. Cathedral of Saints Peter and Paul, St. Petersburg, Russia.

7215. Peters, Andrew J. (April 3, 1872–June 26, 1938) Boston mayor 1918–1922, during the 1919 police strike. His cousin, Starr (Wyman) Faithfull, was the subject of a notorious New York murder case in 1931. Sec. 6, 1511, Althea Path, Forest Hills Cemetery, Jamaica Plain, Boston, MA.

7216. Peters, Ben (Benjamin Peters, June 20, 1933–May 25, 2005) Grammy winning country songwriter penned several hits, fourteen going to number one on the charts, including *Kiss An Angel Good Morning, Daytime Friends,* and *Before the Next Teardrop Falls.* Field of Honor, lot 143C, grave 3, Woodlawn Memorial Park, Nashville, TN.

7217. Peters, Brock (George Fisher, July 2, 1927– Aug. 23, 2005) New York born black actor with bass delivery exuded dignity on stage and screen in *Carmen Jones* (1954), *Porgy and Bess* (1959), as Tom Robinson in *To Kill A Mockingbird* (1962) — his best known role, *The Pawnbroker, Soylent Green,* and two *Star Trek* features, among others. Tony nomination for *Lost in the Stars.* he died at home in Los Angeles at 78 from pancreatic cancer. Buried next to his wife DiDi. Revelation, lot 3529, Forest Lawn Hollywood Hills, Los Angeles.

7218. Peters, Frederick (Frederick Peter Tuite, June 30, 1884–April 23, 1963) Burly actor from Waltham, Massachusetts, in silent films (*Tarzan and the Golden Lion*) and a handful of talkies, notably as Chauvin, the former executioner and most prominent zombie in *White Zombie* (1932). He died in L.A. at 78. Enduring Faith, lot 4474, space 2, Forest Lawn Hollywood Hills, Los Angeles.

7219. Peters, House (March 12, 1880–Dec. 7, 1967) British born silent screen actor 1913–1928, later in a few character parts (*O. Henry's Full House* 1952). Cremated through Forest Lawn, Glendale, California. Ashes scattered in the Pacific.

7220. Peters, Jean (Elizabeth Jean Peters, Oct. 15, 1926–Oct. 13, 2000) Actress from Canton, Ohio, in films 1947–1955, including *Captain from Castille, It Happens Every Spring, Viva Zapata!, O. Henry's Full House, Pickup on South Street, Wait Till the Sun Shines Nellie, Blueprint For Murder, Niagara* and *Three Coins in the Fountain.* She retired in 1955 and virtually vanished while married to reclusive oil tycoon Howard Hughes 1957–1971. Afterward she wed writer-producer Stanley Hough until his death in 1990, and appeared in TV movies. She died from leukemia at 73 in La Jolla, California. Sec. AA, tier 22, grave 39, Holy Cross Cemetery, Culver City, CA.

7221. Peters, Susan (Susan Carnahan, July 3, 1921–Oct. 23, 1952) Actress in films of the early 40's (*Santa Fe Trail* 1940, *The Big Shot, Tish, Random Harvest,* AA nom, 1942) received a spinal injury in a hunting accident on New Year's Day 1945. She attempted acting from a wheelchair on radio but refused the MGM film parts offered her because she felt they were Pollyanna roles trading on her disability. She continued performing on stage but by fall 1952 was ill with depression and an eating disorder that left her frail. She died from a chronic kidney disorder and bronchial pneumonia at 31. Whispering Pines, near the *Finding of Moses* statue and pond, Forest Lawn Glendale, CA.

7222. Peterson, Laci (May 4, 1975–December 24, 2002) Modesto California woman, eight months pregnant, disappeared at Christmas time 2002 and became a national news obsession. Her body and that of her unborn infant, named **Conner,** washed up in San Francisco Bay in April 2003, after which her husband Scott was arrested for murder and later convicted. Forensics teams completed their work and burial took place August 29, 2003. Burwood Cemetery, Escalon, San Joaquin County (near Modesto), CA.

7223. Peterson, Ray (April 23, 1939–Jan. 25, 2005) Singer from Denton, Texas, stricken with polio as a child, recovered and moved to Los Angeles at 18, where he had a hit in 1960 with *Tell Laura I Love Her* on RCA, his signature song, and *Corrina, Corrina* three years later on his own Dunes Records with producer Phil Spector. He later moved to the Nashville area, where he died at 65 from cancer in his Smyrna home. Roselawn Memorial Gardens, Murfreesboro, TN.

7224. Peterson, Robert (Robert Clark Peterson, Jan. 13, 1932–Dec. 1, 2003) Broadway singer and actor filled in for Robert Goulet as Lancelot in *Camelot* over seventy times before taking over the part for eight months of the play's New York run and its national tour. He later returned to Utah, where he died while playing handball at 71. Tonaquint Cemetery, St. George, UT.

7225. Peterson, Roger (May 24, 1937–Feb. 3, 1959) Pilot of the small plane that crashed in a field near Clear Lake, Iowa, killing Buddy Holly, Ritchie

Valens and J.P. "The Big Bopper" Richardson. Its status in rock and roll folklore was multiplied with Don McLean's 1971 record *American Pie*. Peterson encountered sudden snow, and may or may not have had his direction reversed, thinking he was climbing. Buena Vista Memorial Park Cemetery, Storm Lake, IA.

7226. Peterson, Roger Tory (Aug. 28, 1908–July 28, 1996) Ornithologist, artist and writer on the study of birds, wrote *A Field Guide to Birds*. His stone has sculpted birds in an oval inset above the name and notes *Birds to me are the most vivid expression of life*. Duck River Cemetery, Old Lyme, CT.

7227. Petit, Ira S. (May 12, 1841–Oct. 18, 1864) Union soldier from Wilson, New York, a private with the 11th Regiment, 5th Army Corps. His diaries and letters, written home from 1862–64, were compiled and published by Jean P. Ray as *Diary of a Dead Man*. Captured at Gaines Mill near Mechanicsburg, Virginia, in June 1864, he died at 23 in the infamous stockade at Andersonville Prison in Georgia a few months later from scorbutus. Buried with 13,000 others. Sec. H, gr. 11170, formerly Camp Sumter Military Cemetery, now Andersonville National Cemetery, Andersonville National Historic Site, Andersonville, GA.

7228. Petrillo, James (March 16, 1892–Oct. 23, 1984) Influential and colorful head of the American Federation of Musicians was among the best known and most combative of labor leaders. During World War II he defied President Roosevelt by calling a strike to protest a lack of royalty payments. He died from a stroke in Chicago at 92. Mausoleum crypt, Queen of Heaven Cemetery, Hillside, IL.

7229. Petrosino, Joseph (Aug. 30, 1860–March 12, 1909) New York City police lieutenant organized the Italian Squad in the first decade of the twentieth century to combat the Black Hand's extortionists, terrorists and murderers in Little Italy. His work was effective, and his zeal took him to Sicily where he began mailing warrants back to New York which enabled police to begin deporting members of the Black Hand. Their membership contacted Sicily's mafia chieftain Vito Cascio Ferro, who allegedly shot Petrosino as he waited in the Gardini Garibaldi, a garden with a fountain, in Palermo. The American consul reported later that two hired gunmen fired the shots; he was hit three times, a fourth bullet lodging in his coat. Don Vito was questioned and released. The lieutenant's life was the subject of the 1960 film *Pay or Die*. The body was returned to New York a month later and buried from Old St. Patrick's Cathedral on Mott Street. The monument over his grave is surmounted by a marble bust of him. Sec. 22-9-K-17, (3rd) Calvary Cemetery, Woodside, Queens, N.Y.C.

7230. Petrova, Olga (Muriel Harding, May 10, 1886–Nov. 30, 1977) English born star of silent films in vamp roles, billed as a Russian noblewoman from Warsaw; she was actually from Liverpool. Films include *The Vamp* and *The Tigress* (1915), *The Soul Market* (1916) and *Panther Woman* (1918). She retired from the screen in 1918, later returned to the stage and authored three of the plays in which she starred. She spent her later years as Mme. Olga Willoughby in Clearwater, Florida, where she died at 91. Cremated through Moss-Duneden mortuary, her ashes were mixed with those of her husband and returned to friends to be scattered at sea.

7231. Petrovic(h), Drazen (Oct. 22, 1964–June 7, 1993) Croatian basketball star with the New Jersey Nets, killed in an auto accident on a rain slick autobahn in Germany. Known in his homeland as the Mozart of Basketball, he was the premier hero of the war torn region. Mirogoj Cemetery, Zagreb, Croatia.

7232. Petrovich, Ivan (Petrovits-Szevetiszlar, Jan. 1, 1894–Oct. 18, 1962) Actor in over eighty films 1918–1962, primarily in Europe (*The Garden of Allah* 1927, *Monika* 1937, *The Journey* 1957). Feld 139, Anlagengrab nummer 18, Nordfriedhof, Munich.

7233. Pettigrew, Johnson (James Johnson Pettigrew, July 4, 1828–July 17, 1863) Military theorist and strategist had penned a book on field tactics prior to his service in the Civil War, including command of a brigade in Pickett's charge up Cemetery Ridge at Gettysburg, which he survived. He was shot and fatally wounded just two weeks later. Buried in the family cemetery at his home Bonarva, now Pettigrew State Park, Tyrell County, NC.

7234. Pettingell, Frank (Frank Edmund George Pettingell, Jan. 1, 1891–Feb. 17, 1966) Stout English character actor and playwright from Liverpool, on stage from 1910 and in films from 1931 (*Jealousy* 1931, *My Old Dutch* 1935, *Busman's Honeymoon, Angel Street /Gaslight* 1940, *Kipps* 1941, *Becket* 1964). He died suddenly in London at 75. Service February 22 at St. Paul's, The Ridgeway, Mill Hill. Golders Green Crematorium, north London. Ashes taken by John Nodes mortuary.

7235. Pettit, Tom (William Thomas Pettit, April 23, 1931–Dec. 22, 1995) TV reporter was the only news man on the scene when Lee Harvey Oswald was assassinated in Dallas November 24, 1963, and alone provided the live commentary, captured for history. Later executive vice president of *NBC News* 1982–85. Sec. 43, lot 259, St. Columbia Catholic Cemetery, Middletown, RI.

7236. Petty, Adam (July 10, 1980–May 12, 2000) Nascar driver, grandson of champion Richard Petty, was killed at 19 during practice for the Busch 200 at New Hampshire International Speedway, at virtually the same spot where Kenny Irwin died two months later. Ashes to family, Level Cross, NC.

7237. Peyton, Patrick (Jan. 9, 1909–June 4, 1992) Irish priest founded the *Family Theatre* on radio in 1947. It ran for twenty two years, promoting family values. Holy Cross Cemetery, North Easton, MA.

7238. Pforzheimer, Walter (Aug. 15, 1914–Feb. 10, 2003) Founding father of the Central Intelligence Agency helped write the National Security Act of 1947 which formed the outfit. He was the agency's first liaison to congress and its first historical curator. Sec, 66, grave 7427, Arlington National Cemetery, Arlington, VA.

7239. Phagan, Mary (June 1, 1900–April 26, 1913) Thirteen year old employee of the Atlanta Pencil Factory was found there, molested and strangled. Her employer Leo Frank, a Jew from the north and unpopular in the area, was accused of the murder and convicted. When Governor Slaton commuted his death sentence to life in prison, a mob took him from the jail to Marietta, intending to hang him at her grave but lynching him before they got that far. The 1937 film *They Won't Forget* and the 1988 TV movie *The Murder of Little Mary Phagan* recounted the case. Little Mary's headstone was provided by the United Confederate Veterans in 1915. Covering the grave is a flush white slab with a lengthy sentimental inscription by Tom Watson, placed in 1933. The second paragraph reads *Sleep little girl, sleep in your humble grave, but if the angels are good to you in the realms beyond the trouble, sunset and the clouded stars, they will let you know that many an aching heart in Georgia beats for you, and many a tear, from eyes unused to weep, has paid you a tribute too sacred for words.* Leo Frank was posthumously pardoned over seventy years later when a man thirteen years old at the time testified that he knew another man had committed the crime and Frank was innocent. A historical marker on the road indicates the gravesite. Citizens Cemetery, Marietta, GA.

7240. Pham Van Dong (March 1, 1906–April 29, 2000) Communist prime minister of North Vietnam 1955–76 and the Socialist Republic of Vietnam 1976–86. Mai Dich Cemetery, on the outskirts of Hanoi, Vietnam.

7241. Phelps, Lee (May 15, 1893–March 19, 1953) Character actor from Pennsylvania in over 550 films 1917–1953, most often as world weary, no nonsense detectives, guards, court bailiffs, bartenders, boxing announcers, umpires (*Anna Christie*—bartender, *The Criminal Code, The Public Enemy*— intimidated bartender, *A Free Soul, The Champ, Manhattan Melodrama, Midnight Alibi, The Spanish Cape Mystery, Laughing Irish Eyes, The Walking Dead, Postal Inspector, Cain and Mabel, Black Legion, A Star is Born, Think Fast Mr. Moto, San Quentin, The Saint in New York, Angels With Dirty Faces*—arresting detective, *Each Dawn I Die, Golden Boy, The Roaring Twenties*— bailiff, *Gone With the Wind, The Saint's Double Trouble, Castle on the Hudson, It All Came True, Brother Orchid, City For Conquest, Knute Rockne All-American, Murder Over New York, The Face Behind the Mask, High Sierra, Ball of Fire, All Through the Night, Fingers at the Window, Flesh and Fantasy, Whistling in Brooklyn, Arsenic and Old Lace*—umpire, *Scarlet Street, Dark Corner, Blonde Alibi, The Web, Knock on Any Door, The Window*). Sec. C, lot 556, grave 4, Holy Cross Cemetery, Culver City, CA.

7242. Philbin, Mary (Mary Loretta Philbin, July 16, 1902–May 7, 1993) Silent screen actress played Christine in the Lon Chaney version of *The Phantom of the Opera* (1925), and had the lead in *The Merry Go Round* (1923) and *The Man Who Laughs* (1928). She retired with sound and died at Huntington Beach, California, at 90. Birth dates vary; her Social Security Death Index listing gives August 25, 1902, while the California Death Index and her death certificate list July 16, 1902. Never married, she was interred with her parents in the mausoleum, block 35, crypt D-4, Calvary Cemetery, east Los Angeles.

7243. Philbrick, Herbert (May 11, 1915–Aug. 16, 1993) U.S. counterspy through the 1940's in 1949 testified and helped convict eleven communist leaders. His cover blown, he authored *I Led Three Lives* in 1952. Central Cemetery, Rye, NH.

7244. Philby, Kim (Harold Adrian Russell Philby, Jan. 11, 1912–May 11, 1988) Member of British Intelligence along with Guy Burgess, Donald MacLean and Anthony Blum passed vital information from the top levels of government to the Soviet Union from 1944. In Washington from 1949 working with the FBI and CIA he passed information along that assured the defeat of anti–Communist groups in Albania in 1950. A journalist from 1956, he was interrogated a second time in 1962 and sought political asylum in the U.S.S.R. in 1963, where he remained. Troekurovo Cemetery, St. Petersburg, Russia.

7245. Philipp, Gunther (June 8, 1918–Oct. 2, 2003) Actor-writer from Toplitza (now Romania), Austria-Hungary, former champion swimmer 1937–38 and race car driver from 1943, team owner from 1960, in many films from the 1940's up to his death at 85 in Bonn-Bad Godesberg, Germany. Sector D, no. 383, Melatenfriedhof, Köln/Cologne, Germany.

7246. Philips, Lee (Jan. 10, 1927–March 3, 1999) New York born actor in *Peyton Place* (1957) and much on TV (*Twilight Zone* episode *Passage on the Lady Anne*) died in Brentwood, California, of Parkinson's Disease at 72. Cremated through Pierce Bros. Westwood, the ashes were divided among relatives in the Los Angeles area.

7247. Philips, Mary (Jan. 23, 1901–April 22, 1975) B film actress, the second wife of Humphrey Bogart, appeared with him in *Broadway's Like That* (1931). She re-married actor playwright Kenneth MacKenna (dec 1962) and survived him by thirteen years until her death from cancer at 75 in Santa Monica. Iris Columbarium, niche 27261, Iris Terrace (top level), Great Mausoleum, Forest Lawn, Glendale, CA.

7248. Phillips, Barney (Bernard Ofner Phillips, Oct. 20, 1913–Aug. 17, 1982) Actor in blue collar and detective roles (*I Was A Teenage Werewolf, Twilight Zone* episodes *Will the Real Martian Please Stand Up?* and *A Thing About Machines*). Cremated at Grandview Crematory, Glendale, through Westwood mortuary in west Los Angeles. Ashes scattered at sea.

7249. Phillips, Carrie Fulton (Sept. 22, 1875–Feb 3, 1960) The mistress of Ohio Senator Warren G.

Harding from circa 1905–1914 was the wife of his Marion, Ohio, friend Jim Phillips. By 1914 Harding had drifted toward the teenage Nan Britton. Their letters, disclosed in 1964 by historian Francis Russell, were deleted by the Harding family from his book *The Shadow of Blooming Grove.* Phillips later lived in dilapidated surroundings with her dogs, was taken over by the county welfare department in 1956 and died in a nursing home. Sec. 56, lot 27, Marion Cemetery, Marion, OH.

7250. Phillips, David Graham (Oct. 31, 1867–Jan. 24, 1911) Novelist and political editorialist from Madison, Indiana, an associate of Senator Albert Beveridge, authored *The Second Generation* (1907) and *The Treason of the Senate.* Labeled a muckraker by Theodore Roosevelt. He was shot six times outside the Princeton Club on the south side of Gramercy Park by Fitzhugh Goldsborough, a crazed violinist who thought he had stolen his ideas. The assassin killed himself on the spot. Phillips, commenting that he might have survived two shots but not six, died during the night. Removed October 30, 1913 from the New York City Marble Cemetery on 2nd St. His Celtic cross has the words *Father forgive them for they know not what they do.* Carolyn Frevert lot, sec. 20/21, lot 4093, Kensico Cemetery, Valhalla, NY.

7251. Phillips, Dorothy (Dorothy Gwendolyn Strible, Oct. 30, 1889–March 1, 1980) Silent screen actress from Baltimore married to director **Alan Holubar** (Aug. 3, 1889–Nov. 20, 1923). Among his work was directing and starring as Capt. Nemo in the 1916 *Twenty Thousand Leagues Under the Sea.* She was known as the Kid Nazimova in films from 1911 through the 20's. With Holubar, near director George Loane Tucker, her name is on the side of the base of Holubar's monument. Sec. 19/Secret Gardens, 369, Hollywood Forever Cemetery, Hollywood (Los Angeles), CA.

7252. Phillips, Esther (Dec. 23, 1935–Aug. 7, 1984) Rhythm and Blues great, influential vocalist with English rock and roll of the early 60's as much as in America. She performed with Johnny Otis and later recorded several hits including *Release Me.* Appeared at several Newport Jazz Festivals. Plaque inscribed *Legendary vocalist, style original, unique teen superstar Little Esther. Her career spanned four decades. Grammy award and NAACP Image award. "In my father's house are many mansions."—John;14.* Morning Light sec., lot 2591, space 2, Forest Lawn Hollywood Hills, Los Angeles.

7253. Phillips, Flip (Joseph Filippelli, Feb. 26, 1915–Aug. 17, 2001) Tenor saxophonist played from the Swing era, best known at the epic jazz concerts at the New York Philharmonic in the 1940's and 50's. St. John's Cemetery, Middle Village, Queens, N.Y.C.

7254. Phillips, John (John Edmund Andrew Phillips, Aug. 30, 1935–March 18, 2001) Singersongwriter born at Parris Island, South Carolina, was the founder of the Mamas and The Papas, first signed in L.A. in 1965 and featuring the voices of Phillips and his wife Michelle along with Denny Doherty and "Mama" Cass Elliot. From early 1966 through 1967 they had hits with *California Dreamin, Monday Monday,* which won a Grammy, *I Saw Her Again Last Night* and *Creque Alley,* the latter two partially personal histories of the group. A major influence in organizing the Monterey Pop Festival in 1967, they disbanded the next year. Phillips also wrote for others, including the Beach Boys, the Grateful Dead, and Scott MacKenzie's *San Francisco.* The father of actress MacKenzie Phillips (originally Laura, by his first wife) and singer Chynna Phillips, by his third wife, Farnaz. He received a liver transplant after decades of substance abuse in 1992 and died at 65 from heart failure nine years later at UCLA Medical Center in Los Angeles. Roman Catholic service March 24 at Palm Springs mortuary. Between his name and dates is *Papa John Phillips. "California Dreamin." Beloved husband, father and friend.* Sanctuary of Faith and Hope, lower level, core 3, int. wall 12E, crypt 1, Palm Springs Mausoleum, Cathedral City (Palm Springs), CA.

7255. Phillips, Julia (Julia Miller, April 7, 1944–Jan. 1, 2002) New York born film producer was the first female executive in the business to win an Oscar, for *The Sting* (1974). Nearly two decades later her scandalous autobiography, *You'll Never Eat Lunch in This Town Again* (1991) was published. She died from cancer at 57. Acacia SS, crypt 433, Hillside Memorial Park, Los Angeles.

7256. Phillips, Peg (Margaret M. Linton, Sept. 20, 1918–Nov. 7, 2002) Late blooming actress from Everett, Washington, known as the straight shooting if warm hearted storekeeper Ruth Ann on television's *Northern Exposure* 1990–95. She founded the Woodinville Repertory Theatre at Woodinville, Washington, where she lived during her last seven years and died at 84 from COPD (lung disease) in Bothell. A service was held at East Shore Unitarian Church in Bellevue, and at the Unitarian Universalist Fellowship Church of her daughter, Rev. Elizabeth Greene, Garden City (Boise), Idaho. Cremated November 20 at Seattle Service Group Crematory, Seattle, through Bleitz mortuary, Seattle.

7257. Phillips, Sam (Samuel Cornelius Phillips, Jan. 5, 1923–July 30, 2003) Florence, Alabama, born record producer at Sun Records in Memphis from 1951, when Ike Turner's Kings of Rhythm recorded what Phillips deemed the first rock 'n' roll record, *Rocket 88.* He welcomed black artists such as Howlin' Wolf, Rufus Thomas, Roscoe Gordon and B.B. King at his label from 1951, saving them the trips to Chess or Duke, and promoting what had previously been pigeon-holed as "race music," rhythm and blues. After Elvis Presley cut his first record at Sun, Phillips found the voice and face through which he could showcase rock and roll; in 1954–55 Presley recorded *That's All Right (Mama), Good Rockin' Tonight, Milkcow Blues Boogie, Baby Let's Play House* and *Mystery Train* at Sun before his contract was sold to RCA in 1956 and Phillips went on to promote Jerry Lee Lewis, Carl Perkins, Johnny Cash, Roy Orbison and others before he invested in Holiday Inns and sold his entire Sun catalogue in 1969. An icon in the birth of rock and roll, he died in Memphis at 80. Exterior crypt, Memphis Memorial Park mausoleum, Memphis, TN.

7258. Phillips, Wendell (Nov. 29, 1811–Feb. 2, 1884) Boston born Harvard educated lawyer left his practice to enlist in the cause of abolition. With William Lloyd Garrison, Phillips became the most noted and inspiring orator of his era, promoting women's suffrage, penal reform, labor unions, regulations on monopolies, fair treatment of Indians and prohibition. He died in Boston. Buried beneath a stone pyramid. Laurel Ave., lot 349, Milton Cemetery, Milton (west of Quincy), MA.

7259. Phoenix, River (Aug. 23, 1970–Oct. 31, 1993) Young actor named for the River of Life in Herman Hesse's *Siddhartha* achieved stardom at 16 in *Stand By Me* (1986). Oscar nomination for *Running on Empty* (1988). Other films *Little Nikita* (1988), *The Mosquito Coast* (1986), *My Own Private Idaho* (1991) and *Sneakers* (1992). He collapsed and died at 23 outside the Viper Club on the Sunset Strip from a drug overdose consisting of a cold medication, marijuana, cocaine and heroin. The body was sent to Gainesville City Cemetery, Gainesville, Florida, was cremated at Gainesville and the ashes spread at a tree on the family's property at Micanopy, near Gainesville, FL.

7260. Phyfe, Duncan (c. 1768–Aug. 16, 1854) Scottish born cabinet maker whose excellence set the style for later craftsmen came to New York in the 1790's and opened a business patronized by the wealthy. He was among the earlier noted residents of the new "rural" cemetery in Brooklyn. Red sandstone vault built into the hillside, inner sec. 77, back from Dell Ave., Greenwood Cemetery, Brooklyn, N.Y.C.

7261. Physick, Philip Syng (July 7, 1768–Dec. 15, 1837) Doctor at Pennsylvania Hospital 1794–1816. The Father of American Surgery; his name is the origin of the word "physician." He developed the use of ligatures for sutures and invented surgical tools. Eroded marble tomb. Christ Church Burial Ground, Philadelphia, PA.

7262. Piaf, Edith (Edith Giovanna Gassion, Dec. 19, 1915–Oct. 10, 1963) French singer known for her intense rendition of songs (*La Vie en Rose, Mon Legionnaire*) and for her long series of lovers. Increasingly depressed by the death of two of them and by her declining health through rheumatism and dependence on alcohol and pain killers, she suffered two hematic comas the summer prior to her death in Paris at 47. A favorite of the working class, a crowd of thousands gathered during her burial. Polished black slab marked Gassion, bearing a crucifix bearing Christ. Div. 97, Pere Lachaise Cemetery, Paris.

7263. Piatigorsky, Gregor (April 17, 1903–Aug. 6, 1976) Russian born cello virtuoso reportedly escaped Russia by swimming with his cello held over his head, hence his entrance at concerts holding it aloft. He performed with Rachmaninoff, Horowitz and Heifetz, finally settling in Los Angeles where he taught at U.S.C. Sec. D, lot 154, Westwood Memorial Park, west Los Angeles.

7264. Picasso, Pablo (Oct. 25, 1881–April 8, 1973) Spanish painter and sculptor founded Cubism, creating abstract language of form separated from visual appearance. Leader of the post–Impressionist school. He died at Vendrell, Spain, and was buried April 10 at the foot of the stairway at the main entrance to his home he had bought in 1958 but had not visited in ten years, in the park, marked by his 1933 sculpture *Woman With the Vase* at his Chateau at Vauvenargues, near Aix-en-Provence, France.

7265. Piccolo, Brian (Oct. 21, 1943–June 16, 1970) Football player, half back with the Chicago Bears from 1966–69 continued playing until felled by testicular cancer at 36. His fellow player, roommate and friend Gale Sayers gave his award as most outstanding player to Piccolo in the hospital. Their friendship and Piccolo's illness was the basis of the 1971 film *Brian's Song*. Flush brown plaque with the inscription surrounded by the shape of a football. Sec. A-M, lot 222, grave ne, St. Mary's Cemetery, Evergreen Park (Chicago), IL.

7266. Pichel, Irving (June 24, 1891–July 13, 1954) Pittsburgh born actor in villainous ogre roles of the 1930's (*Murder by the Clock, Oliver Twist* 1933, as Fagin, *Dracula's Daughter*) provided the narrative for pictures including *How Green Was My Valley* and *None But the Lonely Heart* and turned to directing, including *A Medal for Benny* (1945), *Tomorrow is Forever* (1945) and *Destination Moon* (1950). He died from a heart attack at 63 in his La Canada, California, home. Cremated at Pasadena Crematory through Lamb mortuary, the ashes were returned to his widow Violette Wilson Pichel. There is no record of his later burial with her in 1964 in the Wilson plot (all unmarked) in Mountain View Cemetery, Oakland, CA.

7267. Pickens, Slim (Louis Bert Lindley, June 29, 1919–Dec. 8, 1983) Hefty cowboy character actor with a thick twang parlayed the foxy or thick headed caricature into many a scene stealing part, including riding The Bomb into infinity in *Dr. Strangelove* (1965), the straw boss in *Blazing Saddles* (1974), many others. He died from pneumonia in Modesto, California. Service at the Presbyterian Church of the Forty Niners, Columbia, California. Ashes scattered over a favorite trail or area.

7268. Pickett, Bill (Dec. 5, 1879–March 23, 1932) Black cowhand known for introducing steer wrestling into rodeos. White Eagle Monument, five miles north of Marland on route 156, south of Ponca City, OK.

7269. Pickett, George (Jan. 25, 1825–July 30, 1875) Confederate general commanded a division at Gettysburg. Under Lee's orders he charged up Cemetery Ridge on the third day, July 3, 1863, and lost most of his men as Union troops fired from behind a stone wall at the top. He was later in several other engagements and was present for the Union surrender at Appomattox, but never forgave Lee for the devastating loss at Gettysburg. He died at 50. Buried near many of his division, marked by an octagonal monument of stone with inscribed tablets in the center. Along Idlewood Ave., Hollywood Cemetery, Richmond, Virginia. His widow **LaSalle Corbell Pickett** lived until 1931. As she could not then be buried with her husband and his men at Hollywood, her ashes were inurned in the Abbey Mausoleum, Arlington, Virginia. Vandalized and soon to be condemned and razed by 2001, her urn was removed from a top tier niche in the Abbey on January 8, 1998. Sent to Hollywood, it was stored in an unmarked niche until burial in General Pickett's grave March 21, 1998. Hollywood Cemetery, Richmond, VA.

7270. Pickett, Ingram B. (May 12, 1898–Feb. 14, 1963) Actor, one of the Keystone Kops. Plaque reads *He blessed and graced this world with his presence between 1898 and 1963.* Sec. 2, lot 371, space 4, Memorial Gardens Cemetery, Santa Fe, NM.

7271. Pickford, Jack (Jack Smith, Aug. 18, 1896–Jan. 3, 1933) Younger brother of silent screen star Mary Pickford began at Biograph under his sister's sponsorship in 1910 in juvenile, boy next door types. He later did some directing. Though generally politely ignored by the press of the day, his personal life was complicated by drug addiction and by syphilis, one or both allegedly responsible in part for the death and possible suicide of his wife, Selznick star Olive Thomas, in Paris in 1920. Two later marriages, the first to Broadway star Marilyn Miller, ended in divorce. He died from the effects of venereal disease and multiple neuritis in Paris at 36. Originally in crypt 2259, Dahlia Corridor, the Great Mausoleum, Forest Lawn, Glendale, he (with his mother and sister Lottie) was moved March 2, 1948 into the Pickford lot, marked by the marble sculpture *Motherhood*. Little Garden of Eternal Love (private) Garden of Memory, Forest Lawn, Glendale, CA.

7272. Pickford, Lottie (Charlotte Smith/Pickford Rupp Gillard Lock, June 9, 1895–Dec. 9, 1936) Younger sister of Mary and older sister of Jack made a few films, the least known of the three. Her last of four husbands was John William Lock. She died (standing up, and sank to the floor) from heart disease at 41, brought on in part by alcoholism. Crypt beside her brother Jack and mother Charlotte in the Dahlia Corridor, Great Mausoleum, Forest Lawn, Glendale. With them, she was moved March 2, 1948 into a lawn crypt in the family plot marked by the sculpture *Motherhood*. Little Garden of Eternal Love, (private) Garden of Memory, Forest Lawn, Glendale, CA.

7273. Pickford, Mary (Gladys Smith, April 8, 1892–May 29, 1979) Canadian actress became the American silent screen's first movie star. America's Sweetheart remained adorned in girlish curls up to age 30 and into her second marriage. Born in Toronto, the Smiths came to New York where she began films in 1909. Her screen name came from David Belasco or from her maternal grandfather Hennessey's middle name (Pickford). Of her many silent films, standouts include *Rebecca of Sunnybrook Farm* and *Poor Little Rich Girl* (1917), *Daddy Longlegs* (1919), *Pollyanna* (1920), *Little Lord Fauntleroy* (1921) *Tess of the Storm Country* (1922), the darker melodrama *Sparrows* (1926), and *My Best Girl* (1927, with Buddy Rogers) and *The Taming of the Shrew* (1929) with her husband Douglas Fairbanks, a talkie (it was this film that inspired howls with the credit "by William Shakespeare. Additional dialogue by Sam Taylor"). She won an Academy Award for her talkie *Coquette* (1929), retiring from the screen in 1933. With Fairbanks, Charles Chaplin and D.W. Griffith, she co-founded United Artists in 1919. Married in 1914 to actor Owen Moore and in 1920 to Fairbanks. With him she built "Pickfair" on Summit Drive in Beverly Hills, the showcase for entertaining Hollywood in the 1920's. They divorced in the mid 30's and in 1937 she married actor and bandleader Buddy Rogers, who survived her. She became increasingly a recluse, never leaving Pickfair in later years and protected from the public and the press by Rogers, other than her acceptance from her home by satellite feed of a special Oscar in 1976. She died from a stroke at 87 (not 86; her birth certificate shows she was born in 1892). Cremated at Live Oak Memorial Park, Monrovia, California, her ashes were interred with her mother, brother and sister in the family plot where she had them reburied in March 1948, marked by the sculpture *Motherhood*. Little Garden of Eternal Love, Garden of Memory (private), Forest Lawn, Glendale, California. *Motherhood* was selected as a memorial to her mother **Charlotte Hennessey Smith** (Charlotte Smith Pickford, 1872–March 21, 1928), who died from cancer at 55 and was originally interred in crypt E, Dahlia Corridor, Great Mausoleum, Forest Lawn, Glendale, Ca. She was moved March 2, 1948 with Jack and Lottie Pickford into the new plot beneath the sculpture, Little Garden of Eternal Love, (private) Garden of Memory, Forest Lawn, Glendale, Ca. Mary Pickford's father **John C. Smith** (1867–Feb 1, 1898) had died at 30 in an accident, and is buried at Mt. Pleasant Cemetery, Toronto, Ontario.

7274. Pickles, Wilfred (Oct. 13, 1904–March 27, 1978) British actor from Yorkshire, read the news over the BBC during World War II, appeared in some films (*Billy Liar* 1963, *For the Love of Ada* 1972, from the British television series he starred in), and was the presenter on the program *Have a Go* 1946–1967. OBE 1950, with his wife Mabel. Plot 1 1012, Southern Cemetery, Manchester.

7275. Picon, Molly (Feb. 28, 1898–April 5, 1992) New York born comedic star of the Yiddish Theatre, radio and Broadway, best known for *Milk and Honey* on Broadway (1961) and Yiddish operas written by her husband **Joseph Kalich** (Yankel Kalich, Nov. 18, 1891–March 16, 1975). Films included *Come Blow Your Horn* and *For Pete's Sake*. She died at 93 in Lancaster, Pennsylvania. Yiddish Theatre Alliance, block 67, Mt. Hebron Cemetery, Flushing, Queens, N.Y.C.

7276. Pidgeon, Walter (Sept. 23, 1897–Sept. 25, 1984) Canadian born actor in films as common sense leaders with a dignified air, including *How Green Was My Valley* (1941) and *Blossoms in the Dust* (1941), *Mrs. Miniver* (1942) and others with Greer Garson, later playing commanders in *Forbidden Planet* (1956) and *Voyage to the Bottom of the Sea* (1961). He died after several years illness in Santa Monica at 87. Donated to the U.C.L.A. School of Medicine.

7277. Pierce, Benjamin (Dec. 25, 1757–April 1, 1839) General in the American Revolution, Governor of New Hampshire and father of Franklin Pierce, 14th President of the United States. Born at Chelmsford, Massachusetts, he died at his mansion in Hillsborough (now Hillsboro), New Hampshire. Buried with both his first and second wives, **Elizabeth Andrews** (Aug. 17, 1767–Aug. 13, 1788) and **Anna Kendrick** (Oct. 30, 1768–Dec. 7, 1838), the mother of the president. All names are on one obelisk. Pine Hill Cemetery, Hillsboro, NH.

7278. Pierce, Charles (July 14, 1926–May 31, 1999) Female impersonator from Watertown, New York, long popular on stage and TV. Niche 64953, with his picture on it, beneath the statue facing the entrance to the Columbarium of Providence, Courts of Remembrance, Forest Lawn Hollywood Hills, Los Angeles.

7279. Pierce, Franklin (Nov. 23, 1804–Oct. 8, 1869) 14th President of the United States 1853–57. Born in Hillsborough, New Hampshire, the son of General and Governor Benjamin Pierce, his career before and after his term in the White House was undistinguished. As president he failed to take a pro northern stand in the face of Bleeding Kansas' wars over the extension of slavery, and was subsequently labeled a doughface (a northerner with southern sympathies). When his friend Nathaniel Hawthorne dedicated a book to him and gave a copy to Emerson, the sage of Concord tore the dedication page from his copy. Pierce's personal life was particularly melancholy. He and his wife **Jane Means Appleton** (March 12, 1806–Dec. 2, 1863) had lost two sons when their third, **Benjamin Pierce**, 11, was killed in a railroad accident January 6, 1853, near Andover, Massachusetts, on their way to Washington to begin Pierce's term as president. She had long been a recluse and shied away from politics and Washington, but from the death of her son was overcome with melancholia and seldom left her room, writing letters to the boy while in the White House. When she died in Concord, New Hampshire, she was buried in the lot of their friend Josiah Minot, a large area enclosed by an iron fence adjoining the Old North Cemetery in Concord, with Benny and **Frank** (who died at 4 of typhus on November 14, 1843). Their first son, infant **Franklin**, who had died at four days in 1836, is not mentioned on the monument and his burial site, likely at Hillsborough or Amherst, has been lost, along with any records of it. Pierce attended her funeral leaning on his friend, Nathaniel Hawthorne. The following spring, while on a trip with Pierce to the White Mountains, he died from cancer in an adjoining room. Pierce lived out his days at 52 South Main St. in Concord, increasingly alcoholic, until his death there from stomach inflammation and probable cirrhosis of the liver at 64. He lay in state in Doric Hall in Concord and was buried in the Minot lot with his wife and children. The lot originally had a marble shaft to Pierce (inscribed *Francis Pierce*). His wife's smaller spire bore the epitaph *Other refuge I have none* over a Heaven pointing hand. In 1946 these deteriorating markers were replaced by a single granite one with a spire in the center replicating the original monument to the president, and all the names inscribed on the base and attached sides. None of the epitaphs from the originals were transferred. The house at 52 South Main St. where Pierce died was destroyed by fire in 1981. Minot enclosure, half way down along the left fence, adjoining Old North Cemetery, Concord, NH.

7280. Pierce, George (Jan. 9, 1846–March 23, 1910) Automobile manufacturer of the Pierce-Arrow 1903–1908. Family mausoleum, sec. 3, Forest Lawn Cemetery, Buffalo, NY.

7281. Pierce, Jack P. (May 5 1889–July 19 1968) Greek immigrant Hollywood make-up artist had been a short stop with the Logan Square team in Chicago. Beginning with *The Monkey Talks* at Universal in 1926, he headed the studio make up department for twenty years, creating all of their familiar monster images through painstaking experimentation, including the flat head and bolted neck of the Frankenstein monster, first applied to Boris Karloff in 1931, the mummy, the wolf-man, etc. Dropped by Universal in 1947, he continued to freelance, working in films and TV into the 1960's. He died from uremia at St. John's Hospital in Burbank. Whispering Pines, lot 2499, near the *Finding of Moses* fountain, Forest Lawn, Glendale, CA.

7282. Pierce, James H. (Aug. 8, 1900–Nov. 12, 1983) Hoosier born star of *Tarzan and the Golden Lion* (1927, the screen's fourth) appeared in several other films including *Horse Feathers* (1932). He married Edgar Rice Burroughs' daughter **Joan Burroughs** (Jan. 12, 1908–Dec. 30, 1972) in 1928. She was Jane to his Tarzan on radio in 1933. They retired to Apple Valley, California. Identified as *Tarzan* and *Jane* on their stones, facing the road. Sec 19, lot 23, Forest Hill Cemetery, Shelbyville, IN.

7283. Pierce, Larry (Dallas L. Pierce, 1936–Feb. 15, 1961) Champion pairs skater in dancing, with his partner Diane Sherbloom and the rest of the U.S.

figure skating team, was headed to the Olympics where their plane crashed near Brussels, Belgium, killing all aboard. Pierce, along with coach **Daniel C. "Danny" Ryan**, 32, was from Indianapolis. Pierce is in Obelisk Court, sec. N, crypt 55, exterior crypt on road facing the lake, Washington Park East, Indianapolis. Ryan is in sec. 17, lot 649, Calvary Cemetery, Indianapolis, IN.

7284. Pierce, Webb (Aug. 8, 1926–Feb. 24, 1991) Country music star known for *Wondering*. Grave length tablet with his image and tributes. Gethsemane, lot 1D, grave 1, Woodlawn Memorial Park, Nashville, TN.

7285. Pierlot, Francis (Jan. 15, 1875–May 11, 1955) Short, balding actor in timid or kindly parts in films of the 30's and 40's, often as doctors (*Night Monster* 1942) or ministers (*A Tree Grows in Brooklyn* 1945). Iris Columbarium, niche 26603, Iris Terrace (top level), Great Mausoleum Forest Lawn, Glendale, CA.

7286. Pierpont, Harry (Oct. 13, 1902–Oct. 17, 1934) Bank robber "Handsome Harry" became a close associate of John Dillinger during their incarceration at Pendleton Reformatory and at the Indiana State Prison in Michigan City between 1925 and 1933. Dillinger aided in his escape from Michigan City in September 1933, after which Pierpont was second in the chain of command. When Dillinger was jailed briefly in Lima, Ohio, in October 1933, Pierpont led the rescue that broke him out of jail and killed Sheriff Sarber. After their arrest in Tucson, Arizona, in January 1934, he and **Charles "Fat Charley" Mackley** were returned to Ohio to stand trial for the Lima murder and imprisoned in the Ohio State Penitentiary at Columbus. In an escape attempt September 21, 1934, their guns allegedly carved from soap, Mackley was fatally shot, buried unmarked at Sugar Ridge Cemetery, Leipsic, Ohio (near Findlay). Pierpont was also shot but was saved for the electric chair and executed for Sarber's murder the following month. After services at Lakeville, Indiana, he was buried with his family. Sec. 3G, lot 252, Holy Cross Cemetery, Indianapolis, IN.

7287. Pierpont, James (April 25, 1822–Aug. 5, 1893) Composer from Medford, Massachusetts, had been a whaler and gold prospector by the time he wrote one of the world's best known songs, *Jingle Bells*, published and copyrighted in 1857, while he was living in Savannah and working as an organist at the Unitarian church of his clergyman brother. During the Civil War, the brothers were loyal to the south where they lived, in opposition to their abolitionist father. James died impoverished and was buried in his brother's lot, surrounded by an iron fence, with the family obelisk in the center. Lot 342–344, Laurel Grove Cemetery, Savannah, GA.

7288. Piggott, Tempe (Feb. 2, 1884–Oct. 13, 1962) English actress cast as many an old hag or shrew, used by Rouben Mamoulian in both *Dr. Jekyll & Mr.*

Hyde (1931) and *Becky Sharp* (1935). Unmarked under the name Wilton. Block E, sec. 4113, lot 4, Valhalla Memorial Park, North Hollywood, CA.

7289. Pike, Zebulon (Jan. 5, 1779–April 27, 1813) Explorer and soldier never made the summit of the Colorado mountain peak named for him. He died in battle in the War of 1812 while leading a victorious assault on York, now Toronto, Ontario. He was buried outside of Fort Tompkins, preserved supposedly in a hogshead of whiskey. After a 1909 flood it was removed and, when the barrel was opened, the body disintegrated. A marker with an upturned cannon barrel is over what is believed to be his grave. Madison Barracks military cemetery, Sackets Harbor (southwest of Watertown), NY.

7290. Pilatus, Rob (Robert Pilatus, June 8, 1965–April 2, 1998) Half of the rock duo Milli Vanilli, with Fabrice Marvan, won the 1989 Grammy for best new artist, but later had it taken away when it was revealed they did not sing on their records. Pilatus died of a cocaine and alcohol overdose at 32 in Munich, Germany. Uninscribed on their flat family stone. Feld 254, waldgrab (forest grave, perimeter of section) nummer 15, Waldfriedhof Alter Teil, Verwaltung, Furstenrieder Strasse, München (Munich).

7291. Pillsbury, John (July 29, 1828–Oct. 18, 1901) Partner in the Pillsbury Co, Governor of Minnesota 1876–82, and benefactor to the University of Minnesota. Uncle of **Charles Pillsbury** (Dec. 3, 1842–Sept. 17, 1899), who established the Pillsbury Co. in 1872, the largest flour milling company by 1889. Both in sec. 2, Lakewood Cemetery, Minneapolis, MN.

7292. Pinard, Lancelot *see* **Sir Lancelot.**

7293. Pinchback, P.B.S. (Pinckney Benton Stewart Pinchback, May 10, 1837–Dec. 21, 1921) African American Union officer in the Civil War was a leader in the founding of the Louisiana Republican party and the first black governor of a state, Louisiana, from December 1872 to January 1873, until Douglas Wilder became governor of Virginia in 1989. Sec. 16 along Metairie Ave., (Lake-Lawn) Metairie Cemetery, New Orleans, LA.

7294. Pinchot, Gifford (Aug. 11, 1865–Oct 4, 1946) Creator of national reserves was head of the forestry service in the Department of Agriculture under Presidents McKinley and Theodore Roosevelt and Professor of Forestry at Yale 1903–1936. His dismissal as head of the Forest Service by Taft in 1910 brought about the irreparable rift between Taft and Roosevelt. Pinchot was also Governor of Pennsylvania for two non-consecutive terms in the 1920's and 30's. Mausoleum on large wooded lot along upper drive. Milford Cemetery, Milford, PA.

7295. Pinckney, Charles (Oct. 26, 1757–Oct. 29, 1824) Governor, senator and constitutional convention representative from South Carolina, credited with up to thirty provisions included in the U.S. Constitution. He later served as governor of South Carolina, minister to Spain under Jefferson and in congress. St. Philip's Churchyard, Charleston, SC.

7296. Pinckney, Charles Cotesworth (Feb. 25, 1746–Aug. 16, 1825) Revolutionary War officer in the Colonial army, delegate to the Constitutional Convention and minister to France under John Adams. It was Pinckney who rebuffed the bribe of the French in the X,Y,Z Affair with the statement "Millions for defense but not one cent for tribute" (1798). He later ran unsuccessfully as a Federalist for the presidency in 1804 and 1808. St. Michael's Churchyard, Charleston, SC.

7297. Pinckney, Thomas (Oct. 23, 1750–Nov. 2, 1828) Colonial soldier and diplomat, like his brother Charles Cotesworth Pinckney and their cousin Charles, was from Charleston, South Carolina. Governor 1787–88, Minister to England 1791–95 and envoy to Spain, where he organized Pinckney's Treaty (1795), settling boundary disputes over Florida and Louisiana and gaining navigation rights on the Mississippi and a port of entry at New Orleans. St. Philip's Churchyard, Charleston, SC.

7298. Pingitore, Mike (Michael Pingitore or Pingatore, Oct. 14, 1888–Oct. 30, 1952) Diminutive banjo player joined the Oakland Symphony while still in high school and became a mainstay with Paul Whiteman's orchestra(s) from 1920 through the 1940's, as well endless sessions with other musicians. Brother of **Eugene Pingitore**. He died at home in North Hollywood from stomach and liver cancer at 64. Cremated at Grandview and interred there. Chapel sec., unit F, niche 70, West Mausoleum, Grand View Memorial Park, Glendale, CA.

7299. Pink, Sidney (March 6, 1916–Oct. 12, 2002) Producer famed for introducing 3-D movies in the early 1950's, beginning as associate producer with *Bwana Devil* (1952). Later gimmicks included pink printing of Mars scenes in *The Angry Red Planet* (1961). His *Finger on the Trigger* was an early spaghetti western, and among his discoveries was Dustin Hoffman, who he cast in *Madigan's Millions*. In later years he was based in Puerto Rico and Florida, where he died in Pompano Beach at 86. Star of David Memorial Chapel and Cemetery, North Lauderdale, FL.

7300. Pinkard, Fred (Jan. 25, 1920–Aug. 2, 2004) Actor on radio in Chicago after World War II appeared extensively on stage in New York and elsewhere prior to turning to television and films from 1969 until the year before his death in Los Angeles at 84. Among the one man plays he wrote and performed in were *Thurgood Marshall, Justice; Lift Every Voice* and *Rehearsal for the Gods*. Homewood Memorial Gardens/Cemetery, Homewood, IL.

7301. Pinkerton, Allan (Aug. 25, 1819–July 1, 1884) Scottish born detective, sheriff of Cook County, Illinois, opened a national detective agency in 1850 and solved several railroad robberies. He discovered a plot to assassinate Lincoln in 1861 and continued undercover work during the Civil War, later operating the detective agency bearing his surname. Obelisk, northwest area of sec. C, Graceland Cemetery, Chicago, IL.

7302. Pinkham, Lydia (Feb. 9, 1819–May 17, 1883) Patent medicine manufacturer born in Lynn, Massachusetts, where she lived all her life. She concocted an herb combination for "women's weakness" and gave it away until financial reverses brought about the sales idea in 1875. Any actual medicinal value was never proven. Sec. 46, lot 1343, grave 8, Oak Grove Cemetery, Lynn, MA.

7303. Pinson, Vada (Aug. 11, 1938–Oct. 21, 1995) Star center fielder with the Cincinnati Reds was a master of the tricky incline at Crosley Field in the 1960's through eleven of his eighteen seasons with the team. One of only six players to hit 250 runs and steal 300 bases. He died from a stroke at 57 in Oakland, California. Garden of Faith, lot 108, Rolling Hills Memorial Park, Richmond, CA.

7304. Pinza, Ezio (May 8, 1892–May 9, 1957) Italian operatic basso, star of Milan's La Scala, the New York Metropolitan Opera, and Broadway, where he starred with Mary Martin in *South Pacific*. The monument at his grave features a bas-relief of Christ. Sec. L-1, lot 23, Putnam Cemetery, Greenwich, CT.

7305. Pious, Minerva (March 5, 1903–March 16, 1979) Radio actress of the 1930's and 40's, played Mrs. Nussbaum on *Allen's Alley*. Her stone lists her birth as 1908. Adath Israel Cemetery, Fairfield, CT.

7306. Pipp, Wally (Walter Clement Pipp, Feb. 17, 1893–Jan. 11, 1965) Chicago born first baseman with the New York Yankees from 1915 was replaced by Lou Gehrig in 1925, beginning Gehrig's famed record of consecutive games played that stood for seventy years. Pipp played for Cincinnati for three more seasons. Block B, lot 131, grave 4, Woodlawn Cemetery, Grand Rapids, MI.

7307. Pissarro, Camille (July 10, 1830–Nov. 13, 1903) Impressionist painter who encouraged and helped many other independent artists but had less success on his own until later years. There is no definitive work left by him. Two of his most successful protégés were Cezanne and Gauguin. Pissarro died from blood poisoning at 73, leaving behind a large family, many of them painters. Div. 7, Pere Lachaise Cemetery, Paris.

7308. Pitcher, Molly (Mary Ludwig Hays McCauley, Oct. 13, 1754–Jan. 22, 1832) American Revolution heroine of the Battle of Monmouth, New Jersey, where her husband John Hays was fighting. She braved enemy fire by bringing the colonials water in a pitcher, hence the name. When Hays collapsed from the heat she took his rifle and began firing. Pennsylvania later gave her a pension of $40 a year. Old Graveyard at Carlisle, PA.

7309. Pitt, William (May 28, 1759–Jan. 23, 1806) Prime Minister of Great Britain just after the American colonies broke free with the defeat of Cornwallis at Yorktown in 1781. Formerly the Chancellor of the

Exchequer, he served for seventeen years, until 1801, and again 1804–1806, when he died from exhaustion. Interred in the tomb of **William Pitt the Elder, First Earl of Chatham** (Nov. 15, 1708–May 11, 1778), in the west end of the nave, North Transept, central aisle, Westminster Abbey, London.

7310. Pittman, Tom (March 16, 1932–Oct. 31, 1958) Young actor in B films of the 1950's (*Bernadine, The True Story of Jesse James, Apache Territory, High School Big Shot*) died in a car crash at 26. Interred as Tom Pittman-Allen in the Room of Prayer, Westwood Memorial Park, west Los Angeles.

7311. Pitts, ZaSu (Jan. 3, 1898/1900–June 7, 1963) Actress from Parsons, Kansas, named after two aunts (Eliza and Susan) had virtually two separate careers in film. A favorite of director Erich Von Stroheim in dramatic roles (*Greed* 1923, as Trina), with sound she was relegated to hapless maidens in comedic roles, whining and wringing her hands through two reelers with Thelma Todd and in many features. She and her first husband, Thomas Gallery, adopted the son of actress Barbara LaMarr at her death in 1926. She remarried, to realtor John Woodall, residing in Pasadena. Among her last work was as a sidekick to Gale Storm on TV's *Oh, Susanna*. She died from cancer at Good Samaritan Hospital at 63 the day after she checked in. Her plaque lists her birth year as 1900. St. Anne's Garden, rear of Grotto, lot 195, grave 1, Holy Cross Cemetery, Culver City, CA.

7312. Pivar, Ben (March 23, 1901–March 28, 1963) Producer from Manchester, England, had been a film editor in Hollywood 1927–29 and over the years wrote or contributed to a few scripts (*Air Hawks, Mutiny on the Blackhawk, The Mummy's Hand, The Leech Woman*), but primarily produced, steadily from 1936 (*The Man Who Lived Twice*), a string of Universal horrors 1940–46 (*The Mummy's Hand, Horror Island, The Mummy's Tomb, The Mad Ghoul, Calling Dr. Death, The Mummy's Ghost, Weird Woman, The Mummy's Curse, Strange Confession, Pillow of Death, House of Horrors, She-Wolf of London, The Brute Man*) and *Hakuja den* (1958), which he also wrote. Canaan 6, lot 2843, space 1, Mt. Sinai Memorial Park, Los Angeles.

7313. Pivar, Maurice (Aug. 11, 1894–June 14, 1982) Manchester, England, born film editor in Hollywood from 1921–1936. At Universal from 1921, he worked on *The Merry-Go-Round, The Hunchback of Notre Dame, The Phantom of the Opera, The Man Who Laughs, Scandal* (with Ben), *The Cat Creeps* and supervised the editing of *The King of Jazz, All Quiet on the Western Front, Dracula, Strictly Dishonorable, Frankenstein, Murders in the Rue Morgue, Night World, Imitation of Life, Werewolf of London, The Raven* and *Dracula's Daughter*. He retired when Carl Laemmle lost the studio in 1936. Courts of the Book, Jacob G257B, Hillside Memorial Park, Los Angeles.

7314. Pizzaro, Francisco (1475–June 26, 1541) Spanish conquistador secured Peru for Spain and set-tled there, founding Lima in 1535. Assassinated. Dark semi-glass coffin in the Chapel of the Kings, Lima Cathedral, Lima, Peru.

7315. Plank, Eddie (Edward Stewart Plank, Aug. 31, 1875–Feb. 24, 1926) Among the top ten pitchers in major league baseball history, Gettysburg Eddie, known for delaying on the mound, threw more victories by a southpaw than anyone until Warren Spahn. With Philadelphia A.L. 1901–1914, St. Louis 1915–16. Hall of Fame 1946. Sec. X, lot 219, Evergreen Cemetery, Gettysburg, PA.

7316. Plath, Sylvia (Oct. 27, 1932–Feb. 11, 1963) Boston born poet known for *The Bell Jar*, her autobiographical novel published under a pseudonym in early 1963. With her husband Ted Hughes she had removed to England by the mid 1950's. Though she wrote of her children as being a reason for living in a poem penned in the late 50's, a breakdown and intermittent suicidal depression plagued the last several years of her life. Her final act was to place her head in her gas oven at her home in England. Three volumes of her poems were published posthumously by Hughes and added to her reputation. Her stone bears the epitaph *Even amidst pierce flames the golden lotus can be planted*. Heptonstall Churchyard, Hebden Bridge, West Yorkshire, England.

7317. Plato, Dana (Nov. 7, 1964–May 8, 1999) Juvenile actress on TV's *Different Strokes* 1978–84 later made headlines for robbing a Las Vegas video store in 1991 and forging Valium prescriptions the following year. While visiting her fiancé's parents in Moore, Oklahoma, she died at 34 from an overdose of a painkiller and Valium, ruled a suicide. She wished her ashes scattered in the Pacific, but at last report her fiancé still had them.

7318. Platt, Ed (Edward Platt, Feb. 14, 1916–March 20, 1974) Actor in many films (*Rebel Without a Cause* 1954, as Ray the detective) and as the chief in TV's *Get Smart* 1965–1970. He died in Santa Monica from a heart attack. Ashes scattered at sea.

7319. Platt, Louise (Aug. 3, 1915–Sept. 6, 2003) Broadway actress born at Stamford, Connecticut, appeared in a few films 1938–42, notably as Lucy Mallory in John Ford's *Stagecoach* (1939). She later appeared in several television programs, including a role on *The Guiding Light* 1958–9. She died at Greenport, Long Island, New York, at 88, married name Gould. Cremated by DeFriest-Gratten mortuary in nearby Southold. Ashes to be buried in Connecticut, likely at Guilford, where she had a home.

7320. Platt, Thomas Collier (July 15, 1833–March 6, 1910) Three term senator from Oswego, New York, Boss Platt ruled Republican state politics in the 1890's. He boosted Theodore Roosevelt for governor in 1898, but in 1900 helped push the independent minded governor into the vice presidential slot to get him out of the way. Out of power with Roosevelt's ascension to the presidency in 1901, he was described as a king in exile until his death from a stroke in his fifth floor apartment at 133 West 11th St. in Manhattan. Sec. 4, lot 114, Evergreen Cemetery, Owego, NY.

7321. Pleasence, Donald (Oct. 5, 1919–Feb. 2, 1995) Balding, wild eyed English actor from Worksop and Sheffield noted on stage for *The Caretaker* (1960), filmed in 1963. In the U.S. in *The Great Escape, The Eagle Has Landed*, a poignant performance in the *Twilight Zone* episode *The Changing of the Guard*, and as the tirelesss doctor in John Carpenter's *Halloween* (1978) and five of six sequels, one released posthumously. He died unexpectedly at 75 in his home at St. Paul de Vence in the south of France. As he wished to be buried in English soil, he was returned to London for services and cremation at Putney Vale Crematorium, London, with the ashes returned to the widow.

7322. Plenty Coups (1848–May 3, 1932) Chief of the Crow Indian tribe. Marked by a large boulder with a plaque and an irregular shaped stone over the grave. Plenty Coups State Park, Pryor, MT.

7323. Plessis, Alphonsine (Jan. 15, 1824–Feb. 3, 1847) Actually a courtesan engaged to a count at the time of her death at 23 from tuberculosis in Alexandre Dumas fils' arms, she inspired his *La Dame aux Camelias* and became Marguerite Gautier, the patron saint of unrequited love, with its closing line "Sleep in peace, Marguerite. Much will be forgiven you because you were greatly loved." Verdi's *La Traviati* was also based on her. Her sarcophagus is regularly decorated with flowers. Div. 15, Montmartre Cemetery, Paris.

7324. Plunkitt, George Washington (Nov. 1842– Nov. 19, 1924) Colorful Irish-American New York politician, ward healer and state senator. Ward boss of the 15th Assembly District, his *Very Plain Talks on Very Practical Politics*, delivered from his rostrum, the bootblack stand in the New York county courthouse, was published in 1905, recorded by William A. Riordan, and later republished as *Plunkitt of Tammany Hall*. It detailed the daily workings of a New York City politician from the 1870's to the turn of the century, when Tammany and the Democratic party were synonymous. Plunkitt's narrative, with honesty and wit, stressed "honest graft" with the catch line "I seen my opportunities and I took 'em." He died in his Manhattan home at 82. Funeral at Sacred Heart Church. Unmarked. Sec 5, range 30, plot E, grave 14/15, (1st) Calvary Cemetery, Woodside, Queens, N.Y.C.

7325. Plunkitt, T. Hugh *see* **Doheny.**

7326. Pocahontas (c 1595 — early 1617) Indian "princess" given the title because she was the daughter of the head of the Powhatan Confederacy in Virginia, married English settler John Rolfe in 1614 and took the name Rebecca with her marriage and Christianity. They went to London and she became ill, probably with tuberculosis and pneumonia, as they were returning. They docked at Gravesand, where she died at about 22 years of age and was buried there in St. George's Churchyard. It became a garden in 1957

and though a search was made, her bones were not located. In 1994–95, under the financing of entertainer Wayne Newton, further searches were made with the intent to rebury her bones at Jamestown. A replica of the statue of her at Jamestown was erected in the general area of her grave in the garden at Gravesand, England.

7327. Poe, Edgar Allan (Jan. 19, 1809–Oct. 7, 1849) The dean of American mystery writers penned both stories and poems of the macabre and melancholy. Born in Boston and raised by a stern uncle in Richmond, Virginia, he had lived a mostly impoverished life as a literary critic for several papers, residing in cramped houses in Richmond, Philadelphia, New York City (then consisting only of Manhattan), the Bronx and Baltimore. He suffered from melancholia and from chronic alcoholism when he left his mother-in-law Maria Clemm July 30, 1849, at their home in the Bronx, embarking on a lecture tour to Richmond through Philadelphia. In Richmond he renewed his relationship with an old flame, Sarah Elmira Royster Shelton, and was supposedly planning marriage at the time he left the city on September 27. What happened to him afterward is unclear. He was found outside a polling station in Baltimore on East Lombard Street, wearing someone else's clothes, and in a state of delirium. Taken to Washington College Hospital, now Church Home Hospital, he died two days later at 40 after suffering fits of delirium tremens. His grandfather **David Poe** (1743–1816) had a plot in Westminster Churchyard in Baltimore, so he was buried there. A marker was ordered but was destroyed in a train accident, and the grave remained unmarked until 1875, when Baltimore school teachers financed a white marble monument with his bronze image on it, erected at the entrance to the churchyard, just right of the gate. When Poe and his mother in law **Maria Clemm** were exhumed and buried beneath it, his coffin was split and the skeleton was visible, the brow still recognizable, with hair clinging to the skull and the teeth gleaming white, according to witnesses. At the dedication in November 1875 only Walt Whitman, of all the living men of letters of the day, attended the ceremony. In 1885 a box with all that remained of Poe's young wife **Virginia Clemm Poe** (his cousin) was interred with he and her mother. She had died from tuberculosis January 30, 1847) at Fordham in the Bronx and was buried in the Valentine family vault in the Dutch Reformed Churchyard there for thirty eight years. Hervey Allen in *Israfel* states that the church cemetery was destroyed and by 1875 Virginia's bones had been rescued by Gill, an earlier biographer, and kept under his bed until re-interred in Baltimore. Poe's grandfather is still in the rear of Westminster Churchyard, in the lot with four stones marked "P" at the corners, along with a marker later placed over the grave Poe had been in. It has a sculpted raven on it, noting Poe was buried there 1849–1875. Each year on Poe's birthday, in the middle of the January night, a visitor, never identified and to date never bothered, leaves a flower and a bottle of wine at his grave. Westminster Presbyterian Churchyard, Fayette and Green St., Baltimore, Maryland. Poe's mother **Elizabeth Poe**, a stage actress, died December 8, 1811 and was buried in an unmarked grave along the east wall of St. John's Churchyard, Richmond, Virginia, the church where Patrick Henry made his Liberty or Death speech. A marker to her is in the cemetery. Poe was adopted by his uncle **John Allan** (d. March 27, 1834), with whom he seldom got along. The Allans are buried in Shockoe Cemetery, Richmond, Virginia, not far from the subject of Poe's *To Helen*, **Jane Smith Stannard**, who died April 28, 1824. She was the mother of a school friend and reputed to have been the first idealistic love of Poe's life. Then fourteen, he supposedly haunted Shockoe Cemetery after her death, going there at night by himself. A small marker at the foot of her grave has some lines from *To Helen*. **Sarah Helen Whitman** (1803–1878) Poetess and the object of Poe's later affections, was believed to have broken off their engagement in 1848 due to his drinking. Their meetings in Providence included, according to legend, at least one in a churchyard. North Burial Ground, Providence, RI.

7328. Poelzig, Hans (April 30, 1869–June 14, 1936) German architect headed the Academy of Arts and Crafts in Breslau 1903–1916. Associated with the Progressive movement, he worked as an Expressionist, famed for the Grosses Schauspielhaus (Great Theatre) in Berlin (1919) and the Bauhaus. Edgar Ulmer used both his name and the avant garde Bauhaus as the basis for the architect Poelzig and the modernistic house in the film *The Black Cat* (1934). Dismissed by the Nazis, he died in Berlin at 66. Feld 008, nummer 31/33, Friedhof Wannsee, Friedenstraße 8, (Zehlendorf) Berlin.

7329. Poincare, Raymond (Raymond Nicolas Landry Poincare, Aug. 20, 1860–Oct. 15, 1934) French prime minister 1912–13 and president (Third Republic) 1913–1920, serving again as prime minister 1922–24 and 1926–29. Nubécourt, Meuse (55), France.

7330. Pol Pot (Salath Sar, May 19, 1925–April 15, 1998) Notorious leader of the Khmer Rouge in Cambodia in the 1970's responsible for the deaths of up to two million. He died, in captivity, before he could be brought to trial for genocide. Cremated on a pile of refuse in the jungle near Thailand.

7331. Poles, Spottswood (Dec. 9, 1887–Sept. 12, 1962) Noted 5'7" switch hitting outfielder in the Negro Leagues dubbed "The Black Ty Cobb" played from 1909 to 1923, with the Philadelphia Giants, New York Lincoln Giants from 1911, hitting from .398 to .487 in four consecutive seasons, and scored eleven runs in the ten game 1915 black championship series. Credited with a .610 batting average, partly while playing in Cuba. Serving in France during World War I, he earned five battle stars and a purple heart. Sec.

42, grave 2324, Arlington National Cemetery, Arlington, VA.

7332. Polglase, Van Nest (Aug. 25, 1898–Dec. 20, 1968) Brooklyn born art director at RKO 1933–45, then at Columbia. Oscar nominations for *The Gay Divorcee* (1934), *Top Hat* (1935), *Carefree* (1938), *Love Affair* (1939) and *Citizen Kane* (1941). Among his many other works were *Of Human Bondage, Mary of Scotland, Gunga Din, The Hunchback of Notre Dame, Stranger on the Third Floor, The Devil and Daniel Webster.* He died from burns in a house fire at 80. Sec. B, tier 17, grave 62, San Fernando Mission Cemetery, Mission Hills, CA.

7333. Polk, James Knox (Nov. 2, 1795–June 15, 1849) Eleventh President of the United States 1845–49, born in Mecklenburg County, North Carolina, was a Democratic protégé of Jackson and the only Speaker of the House to become president. The first dark horse candidate for the presidency, he defeated Henry Clay in 1844. A driven and intense man who took on many of the responsibilities of underlings, he accomplished in four years his major goals, which included acquiring more land in the west (through the Mexican War) than with any other treaty since the Louisiana Purchase. At the close of his term he took a trip south and was stricken with cholera in a plague. Returning home to Nashville, he died shortly after taking up residence in the Felix Grundy mansion he had renamed Polk Place. He was 53 and only three months out of office. Because of the fear of cholera, he was buried immediately in the City Cemetery at Nashville. Removed in 1850 or 1851, he was re-buried in the front lawn of Polk Place. The four columned monument over his grave was designed by William Strickland from limestone and bears inscriptions on all four sides of the stone in the center of the monument. It details Polk's career and notes *The mortal remains of James Knox Polk are resting in the vault beneath.* His wife, **Sarah Childress Polk** (Sept. 14, 1803–Aug. 14, 1891) wore black widow's weeds for over forty years until her death. In 1892 Polk Place was demolished and the tomb and bodies moved to an eminence on the state capitol grounds a few blocks away, overlooking downtown Nashville. This was done in direct opposition to Sarah Polk's wishes, which were to remain buried at Polk Place and put the property in the hands of the state of Tennessee or a relative who would care for the house and grounds. They had no children. Tennessee State Capitol Grounds, Nashville, Tennessee. Polk's parents, **Samuel Polk** (July 5, 1772–Nov. 5, 1827) and **Jane Knox Polk** (Nov. 13, 1776–Jan. 11, 1852) were married in December 1794 in Mecklenburg, North Carolina. The president's mother survived him by over two years. They both have tabletop monuments — hers with a DAR plaque — in Greenwood Cemetery, Columbia, TN.

7334. Polk, Leonidas (April 10, 1806–June 14, 1864) Confederate general, former Episcopal Bishop of Louisiana, became commander in the western department in Tennessee and Mississippi. He was killed at Pine Mountain, Georgia, during Sherman's approach to Atlanta. Tomb beneath floor right of the altar, Christ Church Cathedral, New Orleans, LA.

7335. Polk, Leonidas (Leonidas Lafayette Polk, April 24, 1837–June 11, 1892) President of the Farmers Alliance, associated with the Populist Party in the 1890's. He died suddenly at the height of his influence, just a month before their nominating convention, where he would have been a likely candidate. The Populists carried 22 electoral votes in 1892, the only time between 1860 and 1912 that a third party carried any states in a presidential election. Oakwood Cemetery, Raleigh, NC.

7336. Polk, Oscar (April 16, 1899–Jan. 4, 1949) Black actor from Marianna, Arkansas, on stage and screen (*The Green Pastures, It's A Great Life,* Pork in *Gone With the Wind, Cabin in the Sky*) died in New York at 49. Unmarked. Sec. C (St. Peter), lot 4723, Mt. Olivet Cemetery, Maspeth, Queens, N.Y.C.

7337. Pollack, Ben (June 22, 1903–June 7, 1971) Jazz bandleader from the 1920's and 30's appeared in a few films and brought out such greats as Glenn Miller and Benny Goodman. His death in Palm Springs was a suicide by hanging. New Beth Olam Mausoleum/Hall of David, T-J-1, crypt 7639/7369, Beth Olam Cemetery adjacent Hollywood Forever Cemetery, Hollywood (Los Angeles), CA.

7338. Pollard, Al (Alfred L. Pollard, Sept. 7, 1928–March 3, 2002) Fullback for the Philadelphia Eagles 1951–53 went on to become their broadcaster and commentator through the 1970's. Sec. 2, range 44, lot 69, St. Peter and Paul Cemetery, Broomall, PA.

7339. Pollard, Art (May 5, 1927–May 12, 1973) Five time Indianapolis 500 veteran died at 46 after his Eagle-Offy hit the wall at 191 m.p.h. It swerved into the infield and caught fire during qualifying for his sixth start at the speedway. Sec. L, west ½ lot 122, grave 2, Evergreen Cemetery, McMinnville, OR.

7340. Pollard, Daphne (Oct. 19, 1891/1892–Feb. 22, 1978) Australian actress in Laurel and Hardy's *Our Relations* (1936), among others. Married name Bunch. Churchyard, lot 1997, grave 4, Forest Lawn Hollywood Hills, Los Angeles.

7341. Pollard, Harry (Harry A. Pollard, Jan. 23, 1879–July 6, 1934) Prolific director in silent films and talkies acted at Selig 1912–16 before remaining behind the camera for *The Reckless Age, Show Boat* (1929), many others, several (*Uncle Tom's Cabin* 1927) with his wife Margarita Fischer (*q.v.*). He died from cancer in Pasadena at 54. Sanctuary of Praise, crypt 5350, Memorial Terrace, Great Mausoleum, Forest Lawn, Glendale, CA.

7342. Pollard, John "Red" (Oct. 27, 1909–March 7, 1981) Jockey known for riding Seabiscuit through most of his career, winning the Santa Anita Handicap in 1940, a comeback for both horse and jockey, recovering from injuries the two previous years. Seabiscuit retired at 7 after his win; Pollard con-tinued riding until 1955. Sec. 8, grave 953, Notre Dame Cemetery, Pawtucket, RI.

7343. Pollard, Snub (Harry Frazer, Nov. 9, 1889–Jan 19, 1962) Australian born comedian, one of Sennett's Keystone Kops, with walrus mustache. Sheltering Hills, lot 545, Forest Lawn Hollywood Hills, Los Angeles.

7344. Pollock, Jackson (Jan. 28, 1912–Aug. 11, 1956) American artist reacted against realism prevalent in the painting of the 1940's, delving into abstract works involving the splashing and weaving of lines and colors, known as Abstract Expressionism. He died in an auto crash at East Hampton, Long Island. Marked by a boulder with his signature on a plaque attached to it, Green River Cemetery, East Hampton, Long Island. His wife, artist **Lee Krasner** (Oct. 27, 1908–June 19, 1984) has a smaller stone in front of his which she had originally chosen for *his* grave, later choosing a larger boulder. Green River Cemetery, East Hampton, Long Island, NY.

Many other noted artists lie in Green River, East Hampton having long been an artists' colony. Among them are **Fred Lake** (1904–1974), artist and conservationist, with an abstract bird atop a block of stone; **Osvaldo Guglielmi** (April 9, 1906–Sept. 3, 1956), abstract painter known for *Terror in Brooklyn*, also with boulder and plaque; **John Ferren** (Oct. 17, 1905–July 24, 1972); **John Little** (March 18, 1907–July 1984) with boulder and plaque; **Jimmy Ernst** (June 24, 1920–Feb. 6, 1984), German born linear artist and son of Max Ernst, also marked with a boulder and plaque, as is **Jan Yoors** (1922–1977), with the epitaph *The problem is still one of interpretation, and the response of man is the meaning of his life.* Many others in the arts lie in Green River among the boulders, unusual epitaphs and abstract forms. It is now closed to burials other than those already owning lots. See also **Stuart Davis, de Kooning, O'Hara, Stafford, Pakula, Rattner, Stafford.**

7345. Polonsky, Abraham (Abraham Lincoln Polonsky, Dec. 5, 1910–Oct. 26, 1999) New York born director and screenwriter was nominated for an Oscar for writing *Body and Soul* (1947) and directed *Force of Evil* (1948). When he refused to testify about his Communist Party affiliations he was blacklisted for two decades, working under pseudonyms or using fronts; he co-wrote *Odds Against Tomorrow* (1959) as John O. Killens, returning to direct *Tell Them Willie Boy is Here* (1969) and others. He was found dead by his housekeeper at 88 from a heart attack in his Beverly Hills home. Cremated through Pierce Bros. Westwood mortuary, his ashes were scattered at sea November 3 off the coast of Los Angeles County, CA.

7346. Pommer, Eric(h) (July 20, 1889–May 8, 1966) German born film producer whose extensive credits include *The Cabinet of Dr. Caligari* (1919), *The Last Laugh* (1924), *Faust, Metropolis* (1926) and *The Blue Angel* (1930). Briefly in Paris and in Hollywood, he was a partner with Charles Laughton in Mayflower

Films in England 1937–1940. In Germany after World War II. He died in Hollywood. Ashes in Maimonides 6, lot 8717, space 3, Mt. Sinai Memorial Park, Los Angeles, CA.

7347. Pompez, Alex (Alejandro Pompez, May 14, 1890–March 14, 1974) Owner and executive of the Negro Leagues from 1916 oversaw the international-ization of the organization, and in his later years scouted black players for the New York Giants. Hall of Fame 2006. Woodlawn Cemetery, the Bronx, N.Y.C.

7348. Pompidou, Georges (July 5, 1911–April 2, 1974) Advisor to and protégé of DeGaulle was French premier (1962–68) and president (1969–74) of France's Fifth Republic He died in office at 62. Buried at Orvilliers, France.

7349. Pompilli, Rudy (April 16, 1924–Feb 5, 1976) Sax player with Bill Haley and his Comets can be heard on *Rock Around the Clock, Shake Rattle and Roll*, etc. He died from cancer at 51. Sec. 16, range 24, lot 56, St. Peter and Paul Cemetery, Sproul Road north of Springfield (south of Broomall), PA.

7350. Pomus, Doc (Jerome Solon Felder, June 27, 1925–March 14, 1991) Brooklyn born song-writer, crippled by polio as a child, known as one of the best white blues singers/shouters in the 1940's, penned some of the most popular music of the pre-Beatles rock and roll era, many with Mort Shuman, includ-ing *Save the Last Dance for Me, This Magic Moment, Sweets for My Sweet, Little Sister, (Marie's the Name) His Latest Flame, Viva Las Vegas, Suspicion, Can't Get Used to Losing You*. After a decade out with a gambling problem, he returned to writing, and was the first white person to be awarded the Rhythm and Blues Foundation's Pioneer Award, in 1991, shortly before his death from lung cancer in New York at 64. Service at The Riverside. Sec. His elaborately inscribed foot-stone has, below both of his names and dates, a three line quotation from him, *Save the Last Dance For Me*, two tributes along the front, and below them *A man among men*. Sec. A, block 8, plot 33–5, Beth-El Ave. around the corner from his parents, Beth David Cemetery, Elmont, NY.

7351. Ponce de Leon, Juan (c 1460–Feb 1521) Spanish explorer searching for the Fountain of Youth found Florida and named it "Easter Time" (Pascua Florida) on Easter Sunday 1513. Returning with set-tlers seven years later, he was attacked by Indians and died from his wounds in Havana. Metropolitan Cathedral, San Juan, Puerto Rico.

7352. Pons, Lily (April 12, 1898–Feb. 13, 1976) French born coloratura soprano came to America, singing at the New York Metropolitan Opera from 1931 through the 1950's. She divorced conductor Andre Kostelanetz in 1958 and retired four years later. A town in Maryland was named in her honor. She died from pancreatic cancer in Dallas at 77. Cimetiere du Grand-Jas, Cannes, France.

7353. Ponselle, Rosa (Rosa Melba Ponzillo, Jan.

22, 1897–May 25, 1981) Operatic soprano with the New York Metropolitan Opera 1918–1936, known as "Caruso in Petticoats." She later directed the Balti-more Opera Company. Mausoleum crypt 1898 W-4-F-3, Druid Ridge Cemetery, Baltimore, MD.

7354. Poole, Kent (Dec. 9, 1963–Sept. 11, 2003) Actor who played Merle Webb in the 1986 film *Hoosiers*, was found hanged from a tree at his home on Lake Holiday, Crawfordsville, Indiana, at 37. He also appeared in *Fresh Horses* (1988) before returning to Indiana to farm. He had been a basketball star before *Hoosiers* as a member of the 1982 Frankfort Western Boone regional champs. Old Union Cemetery, Mid-dle Jamestown Rd., south of Lebanon, Boone County, IN.

7355. Poole, William "Bill the Butcher" (July 1821–March 8, 1855) Early 19th century New York City gang leader, a butcher by trade, opposed the rival Irish gangs under John Morrisey, who he beat badly in the Stanwix Hall at 579 Broadway on February 24, 1855. Poole was shot through the heart later that night but lived two weeks, uttering his fabled last words "I think I'm a goner. If I die, I die a true American." His funeral boasted 155 carriages. With his renewed no-toriety from the 2002 film *Gangs of New York*, a new stone was erected on his grave. Sec. 34, lot 9165, Greenwood Cemetery, Brooklyn, N.Y.C.

7356. Pope, Alexander (May 21, 1688–May 30, 1744) Pre-eminent poet of the Augustin Age, the most accomplished satirist in verse in the English language. Crippled from birth by a deformity of the spine, he de-scribed life from birth as "this long disease." His *Essay on Criticism* (1711) contains the line "To err is human, to forgive, divine" and "A little learning is a dang'rous thing." He translated Homer's *Iliad* 1715–20, thirteen years before the first of his miscellaneous satires was published. A monument was erected at his tomb in 1761. Since the exhumation of his skull for phreno-logical study, he is reported at intervals to "haunt" the church. St. Mary's Church, Twickenham, London.

7357. Pope, John (March 16, 1822–Sept. 23, 1892) Union major general in the Civil War com-manded the Army of the Mississippi before taking over the Army of Virginia. At Second Manassas, he thought he was victorious and was pursuing the Con-federates when his army was crushed by the combined forces of Lee, Longstreet and Jackson. He later com-manded the Department of the Northwest. Block 86, lot 197, Bellefontaine Cemetery, St. Louis, MO.

7358. Pope, Theodate (Feb. 2, 1867–Aug. 30, 1946) Assertive architect and educator refused to an-swer to her given name of Effie. After touring Europe she restored a cottage at Farmington, Connecticut, designed a home there (now the Hill-Stead Museum), reconstructed Theodore Roosevelt's birthplace in Manhattan, designed the Westover School in Mid-dlebury, the Hop Brook School in Naugatuck, and managed to survive the sinking of the *Lusitania* in 1915. In 1920 she built Avon Old Farms School, progressive in design, which occupied the rest of her life. In 1916 at 49 she married diplomat **John Wallace Riddle** (1864–Dec. 8, 1941), formerly (1905–06) Ambassador to Romania, Serbia and Russia, he served as Ambassador to Argentina 1921–25. Riverside Cemetery, Farmington, CT.

7359. Pope, Tony (March 22, 1947–Feb. 11, 2004) Cleveland born voice in many animated films, including Goofy in *Who Framed Roger Rabbit?*, Detective Ban in *Metropolis*, the interactive toy Furby, etc. Lincoln Terrace, lot 5003, space 1A, Forest Lawn Hollywood Hills, Los Angeles.

7360. Popeye characters *see* **Elzie Segar.**

7361. Popwell, Albert "Poppy" (July 15, 1926–April 9, 1999) Black character actor on Broadway and in films, including *Dirty Harry* (1971) and three sequels: *Magnum Force* (1973, as a pimp), *The Enforcer* (1976, as a black militant leader) and *Sudden Impact* (1983, as Harry's partner). Eternal Love, lot 4181, space 4, Forest Lawn Hollywood Hills, Los Angeles.

7362. Porcaro, Jeff (April 1, 1954–Aug. 5, 1992) Drummer with the rock group Toto, winner of several Grammys through the 70's and 80's, died at 38 from a heart attack after exposure to pesticides in his garden at Hidden Hills, California. A later ruling listed cocaine induced arteriosclerosis, which was in turn disputed. Lincoln Terrace, lot 120, Forest Lawn Hollywood Hills, Los Angeles.

7363. Porcasi, Paul (Jan. 1, 1879–Aug. 8, 1946) Round faced actor from Sicily with white hair and clipped black mustache in ethnic roles in many films, particularly through the 1930s, including *Svengali, Smart Money, King Kong* (apple vendor), *Imitation of Life, Charlie Chan in Egypt, The Florentine Dagger, Maytime* (Trentini), *Crime School, Casablanca,* etc. Sec. A, lot 346, grave 2, Holy Cross Cemetery, Culver City, CA.

7364. Porter, Cole (June 9, 1891–Oct. 15, 1964) Composer from Peru, Indiana, known for sophisticated popular numbers and show tunes of the 1920's and 30's, including *Night and Day, Let's Do It, You're the Top*. His leg was crushed in a fall from his horse in 1937 and he was in frequent pain for the rest of his life. His wife Linda died in 1954 and left him her fortune, though he continued to work, increasingly beset by various ailments. He died from pneumonia and a bladder infection at St. John's Hospital in Santa Monica, California. Buried with his wife and his relatives, the pink rounded stones lined up on either side of the cone shaped monument at the head of the Cole lot. Mount Hope Cemetery, Peru, IN.

7365. Porter, Darrell (Jan. 17, 1952–Aug. 6, 2002) Major league all star catcher from Joplin, Missouri, played seventeen years with Milwaukee, St. Louis, Kansas City and Texas. He hit .291 with 112 RBIs in 1979, his best season, with Kansas City. He dropped out in 1980 and entered a drug rehab clinic, but returned as the World Series MVP with the Cardinals in 1982, and played in his third series, against

the Royals, in 1985. Retired in 1987, his 1984 book *Snap Me Perfect* recounted his struggle with addiction. Porter was found dead at 50, lying beside his car, apparently hung up on a stump in La Benite Park at Sugar Creek, a Kansas City suburb. Service through D.H. Newcomer's Longview mortuary. Longview Memorial Gardens, Raytown Road, Kansas City, MO.

7366. Porter, David Dixon (June 8, 1813–Feb. 13, 1891) Union admiral commanded naval forces at Vicksburg that broke the blockade. Later led the fleet of sixty vessels in the blockade of the Confederate Atlantic coast. Adopted brother of David Farragut. Sec. 2, grave S-5, Arlington National Cemetery, Arlington, VA.

7367. Porter, Don (Sept. 24, 1912–Feb. 11, 1997) Actor from Miami, Oklahoma, in films from 1939 (*Night Monster, She-Wolf of London, Youngblood Hawke, The Candidate*) appeared on TV with Ann Sothern in both *Private Secretary* 1953–57 and *The Ann Sothern Show* 1959–61. Cremated through Westwood mortuary in west Los Angeles. Ashes to his son in Kensington, CA.

7368. Porter, Edwin S. (April 21, 1869–April 30, 1941) Director and producer of the first feature film, *The Great Train Robbery*, made in New Jersey in 1903, stopped directing during World War I. He died at the Taft Hotel in Manhattan and was placed in the receiving vault at Kensico Cemetery, Valhalla, New York, until December 11, 1943 when his wife had him removed to the family mausoleum. Husband Cemetery, Somerset, PA.

7369. Porter, Eleanor Hodgman (Dec 19 1868–May 21, 1920) Author from Littleton, New Hampshire, best known for the sentimental *Pollyanna* (1913). Cuphea Path, lot 6809, Mt. Auburn Cemetery, Cambridge, MA.

7370. Porter, Gene Stratton (Aug. 17, 1863 Dec. 6, 1924) Writer from Hopewell Farm, Indiana, near Wabash, best known for *The Girl of the Limberlost* (1907) and other related stories written while living at Limberlost Cabin at Geneva, Indiana, from the 1890's–1913 when, because the swamp was being drained, she removed to "Wildflower Woods" and Limberlost North, the log home she built on Sylvan Lake near Rome City, Indiana. From 1920 she wintered in California, where she died at 61 from injuries suffered when her auto was struck by a streetcar in Bel-Air. In a receiving vault at Hollywood Cemetery for ten years, she was placed in 1934 in a crypt next to that of actress Renee Adoree — with a plaque in the shape of a scroll with a quill pen — in the main foyer (named for her), Abbey of the Psalms, Hollywood Memorial Park Cemetery (now Hollywood Forever), Hollywood (Los Angeles), California. In Spring 1999 her two grandsons had she and her daughter **Jeanette Porter Meehan** (1887–1977) removed and reinterred May 1 at the large oak tree where she had wanted to be buried, marked by a new double sarcophagus with an (old) marble angel atop it, on the right along the path leading from the parking lot to the house. Wildflower Woods, the Gene Stratton Porter State Historic Site, near Rome City, Noble County, IN.

7371. Porter, Katherine Anne (Calle Russell Porter, May 15, 1890–Sept. 18, 1980) Author whose 1962 novel *Ship of Fools* was filmed in 1965, the same year her *Collected Stories* won the Pulitzer Prize. Ashes buried beside her mother; her stone is inscribed *In my end is my beginning*. Indian Creek Cemetery, Indian Creek, TX.

7372. Porter, William Sidney *see* **O. Henry, under O.**

7373. Portman, Eric (July 13, 1903–Dec. 7, 1969) British actor from Yorkshire began with leads as often cynical aristocrats, moving to character parts (*A Canterbury Tale* 1944), frequently heavies; among his last roles was as Edith Evans' estranged ne'er do-well husband in *The Whisperers* (1966). He died in England at 66. Service through Chapels of Repose, West End. Penmount Crematorium, Truro, England.

7374. Posey, Cum (Cumberland Posey, Jr., June 20, 1880–March 28, 1946) Owner of the Homestead Grays, a dominant force in Negro Leagues baseball from 1912 through the 1940's. Hall of Fame 2006. Homestead Cemetery, Homestead, PA.

7375. Post, Emily (Oct. 3, 1873–Sept. 25, 1960) Author of *Etiquette, the Blue Book of Social Usage* (1922), updated many times until her name became synonymous with correct behavior, table manners, etc. She died in New York at 86. Grave length slab, St. Mary's Cemetery, Tuxedo Park, NY.

7376. Post, Guy Bates (Sept. 22, 1875–Jan. 16, 1968) Silent screen actor, married to Lillian Kemble Cooper, appeared in a few notable later films (*Camille* 1935, *A Double Life* 1947). Interred with his wife. Abbey of the Psalms/Hollywood Forever Mausoleum, Corridor E-2 (Sanctuary of Trust), crypt 4084, Hollywood Forever Cemetery, Hollywood (Los Angeles), CA.

7377. Post, Wiley (Nov. 22, 1898–Aug. 15, 1935) Texas born flyer stunt pilot was killed with Will Rogers when their plane crashed at Point Barrow, Alaska. Eskimos were able to remove Rogers but Post was pinned in the wreckage and had to be extricated later. He was returned to Oklahoma for burial, planes flying low and dropping wreaths and streamers. Sec. 48, Memorial Park Cemetery, Oklahoma City, OK.

7378. Potok, Chaim (Feb. 17, 1929–July 23, 2002) New York born rabbi turned author whose Orthodox and Hasidic Jewish background inspired the best sellers *The Chosen* (1967), *The Promise* (1969) and *My Name is Asher Lev* (1972). He died at 73 from brain cancer at his home in Merion, Pennsylvania. Shalom Memorial Park, Huntingdon Valley, Philadelphia, PA.

7379. Potter, Beatrix (Helen Beatrix Potter Heelis, July 28, 1866–Dec. 22, 1943) English author and illustrator of 28 children's books featuring animals as characters. Best known for her first stories, which were based on letters she had written to children, including *The Tale of Peter Rabbit* (1901). Many were set at Hill Top Farm. Cremated at Blackpool, her ashes were scattered in secret by Tom Storey on her fells, as she specified, at Sawrey (Near Sawrey), in the Lake District, Cumbria.

7380. Potter, Henry "Hank" (Sept. 22, 1918–May 27, 2002) Navigator for Jimmy Doolittle on the United States' raid over Tokyo April 18, 1942, the first decisive retaliatory strike of World War II. A retired Air Force colonel, he died on Memorial Day sixty years later in Austin, Texas, at 83. Capital Memorial Park, Pflugerville, TX.

7381. Potter, Luz (Luz Villalobo, Dec. 5, 1914–Nov. 21, 2005) Mexican born actress, a munchkin in *The Wizard of Oz* (1939), and a science fiction mainstay for her roles in *Invaders from Mars* (as the gold head in the bubble dubbed Martian Intelligence) and as Violet opposite Grant Williams in *The Incredible Shrinking Man* (1957). The widow (2004) of Edwin "Midge" Potter, she died in Rancho Mirage at 90. Mass at Forest Lawn Cathedral City, Cathedral City/Palm Springs, CA.

7382. Potter, Maureen (1925–April 7, 2004) Dublin born Irish comedienne and actress from the music and variety hall days through films and television appeared often at the Gaiety Theater, frequently with Jimmy O'Dea from 1939 until his death in 1965, then for fifteen years from 1965 in the annual Gaels of Laughter revue, on television in dance routines with Danny Cummins, in films from 1957 (*The Rising of the Moon* 1957, *Ulysses* 1967, *A Portrait of the Artist As A Young Man* 1977) and a one woman stage show *The Queen of Irish Comedy* in the 1990's. Married to Jack O'Leary, she worked always in the Dublin area, where she died at her home in Clontarf at 79. Mass at St. Brigid's Church, Killester. Clontarf Cemetery, Clontarf, Dublin.

7383. Pound, Ezra (Oct. 30, 1885–Nov. 1, 1972) American poet and critic published *Personae* and *Exultations* (1909), *Ripostes* (1912) and *Hugh Selwyn Moberly* (1920). He was also an editor and translator. His lifelong work *The Cantos* acquired 109 cantos on historical themes, written 1917–1959. Long an intermittent resident of Italy, he was arrested there in 1945 by U.S. forces for treason, pro–Fascist and anti–Semitic writings and broadcasts. Confined to a mental institution, he was later released and returned. Reparto Evangelico (Foreigners' section), Cimitero di San Michele (accessible by boat), Venice, Italy.

7384. Povah, Phyllis (July 21, 1893–Aug. 7, 1975) Detroit born actress, made only a few films, notably *The Women* (1939, as Edith Potter) and *Pat and Mike* (1952, as Mrs. Berringer). She retired to Port Washington, Long Island, the wife of Henry Drayton, where she died at 82. Cremated through Austin F. Knowles mortuary there. Ashes buried Dogwood Lane, grave 5, Nassau Knolls Cemetery, Port Washington, Long Island, NY.

7385. Povich, Shirley (July 15, 1905–June 4,

1998) Sports columnist from Bar Harbor (and later Bath), Maine, once mistakenly included in the *Who's Who of American Women*, began his columns at the *Washington Post* in 1924, a wordsmith second only to Red Barber. Though he officially retired in 1974, his semi-regular column (the last comparing baseball slugger Babe Ruth to Mark McGwire) appeared in the *Post* the morning after his death from a heart attack at 92. Father of TV personality Maury Povich. Elesavetgrad Cemetery (D.C. Lodge or Congress Heights Cemeteries), Congress Place, Washington, D.C.

7386. Powell, Abner Charles (Dec. 15, 1860– Aug. 7, 1953) Baseball executive, former player in the American Association League, first manager of N.O.'s Southern League 1887, introduced both Ladies Day and the rain check ticket. Hope Mausoleum, first floor, C72 C-D, New Orleans, Louisiana.

7387. Powell, Adam Clayton, Jr. (Nov. 29, 1908–April 4, 1972) Black congressman and minister. In his 11th term in the House of Representatives in 1966 he was barred from his seat and accused of misusing some $45,000 in public funds. Subject to subpoena in New York, he spent much of his time in the Bahamas, though he was re-elected in 1968 and the Supreme Court the next year denied the House's ability to deprive him of his seat. Defeated in the 1970 primary, he retired to Bimini in the Bahamas and died in Miami, Florida, of cancer two years later at 63. Ashes spread over Bimini. His father, **Adam Clayton Powell, Sr.** (May 5, 1865–June 12, 1953) was a noted minister, pastor of the Abyssinian Baptist Church in Harlem, turning the pastorship over to his son, who ministered there from 1936 and through his political career until 1971. Sec 9, div. M, plot 8, Flushing Cemetery, Flushing, Queens, N.Y.C.

7388. Powell, Bud (Earl Rudolph Powell, Sept. 27, 1924–July 31, 1966) Innovative jazz pianist used his left hand to state chords in an irregular manner rather than the striding the left had primarily been used for. He was said to have essentially transformed Charlie Parker's saxophone vocabulary to the piano. His younger brother **Richie Powell** (Sept. 5, 1931–June 26, 1956) had a budding career and had played with Johnny Hodges, then the Clifford Brown — Max Roach Quintet, when he died in a car wreck at 24. They are buried beside one another. Jenkintown II, lot 48-A, graves 1 and 2, Fairview Cemetery, Willow Grove, PA.

7389. Powell, Dick (Richard Ewing Powell, Nov. 14, 1904–Jan. 2, 1963) Crooning tenor in early Warner Brothers musicals including *42nd Street* (1933) and *Golddiggers of 1933* was re-invented in 1944 as hard boiled detective Philip Marlowe in *Murder, My Sweet*. Also a pioneer TV producer-director, he formed Four Star Productions with Ida Lupino, Charles Boyer and David Niven. While producing the film *The Conqueror* in Utah in 1954 he may have been exposed, along with the rest of the cast and crew, to atomic radiation; a majority of those on the site developed cancer before old age. Powell resigned as head of Four Star in October 1962 and became chairman of the board. He died from cancer in his Hollywood home at 58 the same day actor Jack Carson also died from cancer. Married first to Joan Blondell, he was survived by his second wife, actress June Allyson. It was she who placed his cremation urn in the niche, with the plaque bearing the epitaph *God is Love.* Top corner, Columbarium of Honor, Gardens of Honor (private), Forest Lawn, Glendale, CA.

7390. Powell, Eleanor (Nov. 21, 1912–Feb. 11, 1982) Tap dancer, singer and actress made several films (*Born to Dance* 1936) and sang and tapped with the Tommy Dorsey Orchestra (1935). Her last appearance was in April 1981 at the American Film Institute salute to Fred Astaire. Ill with cancer from July 1981, she died the following February in her Beverly Hills home. Book shaped urn, Cathedral Mausoleum, east wall of foyer, tier 3, niche 432, Hollywood Forever Cemetery, Hollywood (Los Angeles), CA.

7391. Powell, Jake (Alvin Jacob Powell, July 15, 1908–Nov. 4, 1948) Baseball player born at Silver Spring, Maryland, with the Yankees and the Senators 1929–1945. He got into trouble for a racist remark he made about cracking blacks on the head while working as a police officer during the off season. In 1948 he was arrested on a bad check charge and shot himself in the head while in custody, age 40. St. John the Evangelist Cemetery, Forest Glen, MD.

7392. Powell, John Wesley (March 24, 1834– Sept. 23, 1902) Union major who lost part of his right arm at Shiloh returned to teach geology at Illinois Wesleyan University in Bloomington, Illinois, where he planned his exploration of the Colorado River and its canyons, made from May 24 through August 30, 1869, beginning at the Green River in Wyoming and ending at the junction of the Colorado, remarkable for the simple boats his crew used, and their lack of supplies early in the journey. Powell sketched and mapped the Grand Canyon, paving the way for the wilderness region as a tourist attraction. A founding member of the National Geographic Society and director of the U.S. Geological Survey 1881–1892. He died in Haven, Maine, at 68. Sec. 1, site 408, grid L-35, Arlington National Cemetery, Arlington, VA.

7393. Powell, Lee B. (Lee Berrien Powell, May 15, 1908–July 30, 1944) B film actor was the first *Lone Ranger*, in the 1938 serial. He died while serving with the Marines in the South Pacific during World War II. Buried March 14, 1949. F-1246, National Memorial Cemetery of the Pacific (the Punchbowl), Honolulu, HI.

7394. Powell, Lewis *see* **Lewis Paine.**

7395. Powell, Lewis F. (Sept. 19, 1907–Aug. 25, 1998) Slight, bespectacled Supreme Court justice appointed by Nixon served from 1972–1987, best known for the 1978 Bakke racial discrimination case upholding affirmative action while limiting its scope. He also voted with the majority opinions in upholding presidential immunity from monetary suits if misconduct is within their official duties, and in 1982 that there were no constitutional rights to homosexual relationships. He died at 90 in Richmond, Virginia. Services September 1 at Grace Covenant Presbyterian Church in Richmond were attended by all nine Supreme Court justices. Upright stone in the shade of a dogwood tree. Sec. 35, Hollywood Cemetery, Richmond, VA.

7396. Powell, Michael (Sept. 30, 1905–Feb. 19, 1990) British producer-director from Canterbury. Known for prestigious films in collaboration with Emeric Pressburger, dubbed The Archers (*The Life and Death of Colonel Blimp* 1943, *Black Narcissus* 1947, *The Red Shoes* 1948). He died at his home in Avening. Holy Cross Churchyard, Avening, Gloucestershire.

7397. Powell, William (William Horatio Powell, July 29, 1892–March 5, 1984) Pittsburgh born actor in silents became a star in light hearted, debonair roles of the 1930's, best known for *The Thin Man* series with Myrna Loy, beginning in 1934. Dramatic highlights include *One Way Passage* (1932), *Manhattan Melodrama* (1934) and *The Great Ziegfeld* (1936), the latter two also with Loy, *My Man Godfrey* (1936) with his ex-wife Carole Lombard, and *Libeled Lady* (1936) with both Loy and his rumored fiancée Jean Harlow, who died in 1937. He went on to mature, wise sage roles in *Life With Father* (1947) and *Mr. Roberts* (1955), his last film. He successfully recovered from cancer several decades before his death at 91 in a Palm Springs nursing home. Ashes buried beside his son, who died in 1968. Sec. B-10, lot 20, Desert Memorial Park, Cathedral City (Palm Springs), CA.

7398. Power, Frederick Tyrone (May 2, 1869–Dec. 30, 1931) Stage and screen actor, grandson of famed Irish thespian Tyrone Power (1797–1841) and father of the matinee idol of the same name. He made only one talkie, *The Big Trail* (1930), before his death from a heart attack at 62. Cremated at the Los Angeles Crematory, the ashes were sent to his widow Patia in Aisle-Aux-Noix, Quebec, Canada. In early 1932 she and his son Tyrone scattered the ashes up the Richelieu River in Canada, near his home Two Pines.

7399. Power, Tyrone (May 5, 1913–Nov. 15, 1958) Dark, handsome leading man in films, a native of Cincinnati and the son of actor Frederick Tyrone Power, made his first appearances in *Lloyds of London* (1936) and *Marie Antoinette* (1938) At Fox he repeatedly won Alice Faye from Don Ameche (*In Old Chicago* 1938, and others) or was swashbuckling his way through costume dramas (*The Mark of Zorro* 1940, *Blood and Sand* 1941) and darker works, (*Johnny Apollo* 1940 and notably *Nightmare Alley* 1947). His last completed film was *Witness for the Prosecution* (1957). While filming a sword fight with George Sanders on the set of *Solomon and Sheba* in Madrid, he suffered a heart attack, having complained of pain in his left arm

earlier in the day. Begging off the set, he retired to his dressing room and was rushed to a hospital but died at 45 (or 44; many sources list his birth year as 1914). A marble bench a few yards from the tomb of Marion Davies marks his grave. On the bench is inscribed the line from Hamlet, Act V, Scene II, concluding *Good Night, Sweet Prince, and Flights of Angels Sing Thee to Thy Rest.* Near the pond in sec. 8/Garden of Legends, Hollywood Forever Cemetery, Hollywood (Los Angeles), CA.

7400. Powers, Dave (April 25, 1912–March 27, 1998) Boston Irishman known as John F. Kennedy's "coat holder" and "Sancho Panza" helped managed Kennedy's political campaigns from 1946, served as special assistant in the Kennedy White House and afterward was curator of the JFK Library 1979–1994. With Kenneth O'Donnell he co-authored *Johnny, We Hardly Knew Ye* (1973). Sec. VV, lot 859, Mount Pleasant Cemetery, Arlington, MA.

7401. Powers, Francis Gary (Aug. 17, 1929–Aug. 1, 1977) Pilot of the U-2 spy plane downed behind Communist lines in Russia in 1960. Though President Eisenhower denied knowledge of the plane at first, the news that the pilot was alive gave Soviet Premier Khrushchev an edge. He was returned safely to the U.S., where he later died in a helicopter crash in California at 47. Sec. 11, site 685-2, Grid O-P 15/16, Arlington National Cemetery, Arlington, VA.

7402. Powers, Tom (July 7, 1890–Nov. 9, 1955) Stage and screen actor since silent films from Owensboro, Kentucky. Among his roles was the ill fated husband of Barbara Stanwyck in *Double Indemnity* (1944). He died from a heart ailment at 65. Garden of Light, ground niche, Valhalla Memorial Park, North Hollywood, CA.

7403. Prater, Dave (May 9, 1937–April 9, 1988) Blues and soul singer of Sam and Dave fame with Sam Moore, in the 1960's (*Soul Man, Hold On [I'm Comin']*). Sec. 14, row 34, grave 9, Holy Sepulchre Cemetery, Totowa, west of Paterson, NJ.

7404. Pratt, Anthony E. (Aug. 10, 1903–April 9, 1994) Creator of the game *Clue (Cluedo)* in 1948 vanished without a clue until his burial was reported two years later. Sec. B-861, Bromsgrove Municipal Cemetery, 12 miles from Birmingham, England.

7405. Prefontaine, Steve (Jan. 25, 1951–May 30, 1975) Champion runner dubbed "Pre" helped promote and popularize the exercise, helped by his competitive and sometimes audacious nature. He was killed by an automobile. There is a memorial, always decorated, at the site of the fatality. Running shoes are frequently placed near his grave plaque, which bears the remembrance *Our beloved son & brother who raced through life now rests in peace.* Rosemont sec., lot 6, block 42, Sunset Memorial Park, Coos Bay, OR.

7406. Preisser, June (June 28, 1923–Sept. 19, 1984) Musical comedy actress, singer and dancer began at MGM in 1939 with *Strike Up the Band, Babes in Arms, Sweater Girl,* two *Andy Hardy* entries — as

Phrasie Daisy Clark, then appeared in a *Henry Aldrich* part, *Murder in the Blue Room* at Universal in 1944 (as one of the Three Jazzy-Belles, with Betty Kean and Grace McDonald), and in the later 1940s as Dodie Rogers in a series of Monogram campus films with Freddie Stewart. She died at 61 in a car accident at Boca Raton, Florida, in which her only child, J. Moss Terry IV, was also killed. Sec. 3, lot 29, plot 14, Memorial Cemetery, Deerfield Beach, FL.

7407. Preminger, Otto (Dec. 5, 1906–April 23, 1986) Vienna born director and actor studied with and worked for Max Reinhardt before coming to the U.S. in 1935. As director, his better known works include *Laura* (1944), *The Moon is Blue* (1953) and *The Man With the Golden Arm* (1955). He appeared with shaved head as Nazi officers in *The Pied Piper* (1942) and *Stalag 17* (1953). He died from cancer in his Manhattan home at 79. Cremated at Woodlawn; ashes interred just a few feet from Ricardo Cortez. Chapel Mausoleum B, Azalea Room, niche NDA2, Woodlawn Cemetery, the Bronx, N.Y.C.

7408. Prentiss, Clifton (d. June 24, 1865) and **William** (d. Aug. 18, 1865) A classic, though far from singular, case of brother against brother in the Civil War, Clifton joined the Union Army in 1862, the same year his brother William joined the Confederates. Near the war's end, by then a brevet colonel, Clifton led an assault on the rebel line at Petersburg, April 2, 1865, in which both were mortally wounded, eventually reconciling in the field hospital in Washington, their story catching the attention of Walt Whitman. Marked by rounded, eroded twin stones, side by side at Greenwood Cemetery, Brooklyn, N.Y.C.

7409. Presley, Elvis (Elvis Aron [Aaron] Presley, Jan. 8, 1935–Aug. 16, 1977) One time truck driver from Tupelo, Mississippi, attained as much larger-than-life status as any celebrity of the 20th century. From his days at Sun Records in Memphis in the mid 1950's and popularizing mainstream rock and roll on RCA by 1956, to his film career through the 1960's and his final run as a concert draw from 1968 until his death, he remained a star. He had gained considerable weight and a dependency on combined prescription drugs which contributed to his death from heart failure at 42 on the floor of the bathroom at his Memphis mansion Graceland. His physician was later tried for malpractice but Presley also suffered from the clogged arteries usually seen in a much older man. A private service was held at Graceland, with hysterical mobs outside not seen since the death of Valentino. He was taken in a white hearse followed by sixteen white Cadillacs to Forest Hill Cemetery in Memphis and placed in a vault for burial with his mother **Gladys**, who died in 1958, but within a month attempts at grave robbing forced a change of plans and both he and his mother were buried on the grounds of Graceland, followed a few years later by his father **Vernon**. The family monument is a sculpture of Christ with arms outstretched beneath a cross and angels kneeling on either side. Over his grave is a long bronze tablet elaborately inscribed with tributes. The epitaph reads *Legend in his own time*, while at the bottom of the tablet is a lightning bolt with the insignia *TCB* ("Taking care of business"). There are lines of visitors most days of the year, with ceremonies and vigils held on the anniversary of his birth and death. Graceland (Elvis Presley estate), Memphis, TN.

7410. Pressburger, Arnold (Aug. 27, 1885–Feb. 17, 1951) Hungarian born producer of over 200 films in Europe and the U.S., including *The Shanghai Gesture* and *Der Verlolene*. He died from a stroke at 65. Garden of Moses/urn garden, sec. 18, Hollywood Forever Cemetery, Hollywood (Los Angeles), CA.

7411. Pressburger, Emeric (Imre József Emmerich Pressburger, Dec. 5, 1902–Feb. 5, 1988) Hungarian journalist and film writer at Ufa in Berlin and Paris 1930–34, authored the novel *The Miracle of St. Anthony's Lane*. In England by World War II, he is best known for his association with Michael Powell; together as The Archers they wrote, produced and directed several landmark works, including *The Life and Death of Colonel Blimp* (1943), *A Matter of Life and Death* (*Stairway to Heaven* 1946), *Black Narcissus* (1947) and *The Red Shoes* (1948). Grave length slab, Aspall church cemetery, Aspall, Stowmarket, Suffolk.

7412. Presser, Jackie (Aug. 6, 1926–July 9, 1998) President of the Teamsters 1983–88, indicted on racketeering charges in 1986. He died in Lakewood, Ohio, from brain cancer. Sec. 51, row W, grave 63, Mount Olive Cemetery, Solon, OH.

7413. Preston, Robert (Robert Preston Meservey, June 8, 1918–March 21, 1987) Actor from Newton, Massachusetts, in many forthright, rugged roles on stage and in films, from *Beau Geste* (1939) and *This Gun For Hire* (1942) to the engaging vitality he brought to *The Music Man* (Tony Award for the Broadway production, filmed in 1962) as well as the sensitive plots of *The Dark at the Top of the Stairs* (1960) and *All the Way Home* (1963). Among his last leads was *Victor/Victoria* (1981). He died from cancer at Santa Barbara Hospital at 68. Cremated by Santa Barbara Cemetery, his ashes were buried at sea.

7414. Pretty, Arline (Sept. 5, 1885–April 15, 1978) Silent screen actress (under her real name) from Washington, D.C. appeared in serials at Vitagraph and Pathé during her film career 1913–1928. She invested well and retired, dying in Hollywood fifty years later at 92. Ashes scattered at sea.

7415. Previn, Charles (Jan. 11, 1888–Sept. 22, 1973) Musical director at Universal Pictures developed, with H.J. Salter and Frank Skinner, the themes that continued to run through the studio's horror cycle and melodramas 1938–45. Maimonides 19, lot 5495, space 3, Mt. Sinai Memorial Park, Los Angeles.

7416. Prevost, Marie (Marie Bickford Dunn, Nov. 6, 1899–Jan. 20, 1937) Canadian born silent screen actress, a Mack Sennett bathing beauty, reached her zenith in the Ernst Lubitsch films *The Marriage Circle*, *Three Women* (both 1924) and *Kiss Me Again* (1925). After a few talkies including *The Sin of Madelon Claudet* (1931), a weight problem and alcoholism finished her career by the mid 1930's. She was found in her Hollywood apartment, malnourished, bitten by her dogs, and one to two days dead from alcohol poisoning, age 37. Whether suicide or accident was not determined. Her only survivor was her sister, actress Marjorie Prevost March, then living in San Francisco. She was cremated at Forest Lawn, Glendale, along with her mother, killed in a car wreck in 1926 and exhumed from her crypt in the Azalea Corridor of the Great Mausoleum. The ashes of both were given to a Charlotte Young on February 5, 1937 for return to the family. Charles Foster in *Stardust and Shadows* states that Prevost's surviving sister related to him that Joan Crawford paid for a graveside service at Hollywood Memorial Park Cemetery, although there is no record of Prevost's ashes there under any of her possible names or potential lot owners.

7417. Price, Dennis (Dennistoun Franklyn John Rose-Price, June 23, 1915–Oct. 6, 1973) English actor born at Twyford, Berkshire, adept at displaying emotion stifled by refinement, particularly in Robert Hamer's *Kind Hearts and Coronets* (1949) and later on British television as the Wooster manservant Jeeves. He died from cirrhosis of the liver at Princess Elizabeth Hospital on Guernsey in the Channel Islands, where he had lived since 1966 on Sark. After a funeral October 9, his ashes were buried October 11, 1973 in St. Peter's Church cemetery on Sark, Channel Islands.

7418. Price, Kenny (May 27, 1931–Aug. 4, 1987) Rotund Cincinnati area entertainer, the Round Mound of Sound was originally a musician with Horace Heidt's orchestra while serving in Korea, later a guitarist, singer and comedian on radio and TV's *Midwestern Hayride* and *Hee Haw*. In the 1980's he hosted a TV travel program *Wish You Were Here* until his death from a heart attack at 56. Flush military marker, sec. A, behind the chapel, Forest Lawn Memorial Park, Erlanger, KY.

7419. Price, Sterling (Sept. 14, 1809–Sept. 29, 1867) Confederate general from Missouri during the Civil War, notably at Wilson's Creek in Missouri in August 1861, and in the last major CSA trans-Mississippi offensive when he attempted an invasion into Missouri in 1864. A former governor and congressman, he went to Mexico after the war and died from cholera shortly after his return. He was posthumously honored as the name of John Wayne's unofficial tiger cat in the 1969 film *True Grit*. Towering obelisk. Block 96, lot 1734, Balm Ave., Bellefontaine Cemetery, St. Louis, MO.

7420. Price, Vincent (Vincent Leonard Price, May 27, 1911–Oct. 25, 1993) St. Louis born actor attended Yale and studied in England for his masters in art history. On stage opposite Helen Hayes in *Victoria Regina* (1935). In films from 1938, he essayed a variety of character and villain parts at Universal and Fox through the 1940's (*Tower of London*, *House of the Seven Gables*, *The Invisible Man Returns*, *Laura*, *Dragonwyck*). His gradual type casting as scene chewing horror film villains began with the 3D *House of Wax* (1953) and continued with a string of films for William Castle and series based on stories by Edgar Allan Poe at AIP from 1960 into the 1970's, with his tongue often planted firmly in his cheek. He founded the Art Gallery at East Los Angeles College, was for several years the art consultant for Sears, Roebuck and Co., wrote a syndicated art column and served as chairman of the U.S. Department of the Interior's Arts and Crafts Board. He authored several books on art as well as gourmet cooking, last appearing in *The Whales of August* (1987) and as the inventor in *Edward Scissorhands* (1990). He died in his Sunset Hills, California, home from lung cancer at 82 after five years illness. His third wife, Coral Browne, died in 1991. He was cremated through Gold Cross mortuary with a small service at Hollywood Cemetery. The ashes were scattered at sea as he wished, but specifically not in Santa Monica Bay, which he deemed too polluted. They were taken October 29, 1993 three miles out by private boat to a spot off Point Dune, according to his daughter Victoria. The ashes, mixed with long stemmed red roses, were followed by his ever present wide brimmed straw hat bearing an African necklace.

7421. Prickett, Maudie (Maude Cooper, Oct. 25, 1914–April 14, 1976) Film and TV actress, often played snoops or sour characters; a regular on *Hazel* 1961–66. She died from uremic poisoning at 61. Niche PE 27 map 26, Pasadena Mausoleum, Mountain View Cemetery, Altadena, CA.

7422. Priest, Ivy Baker (Sept. 7, 1905–June 23, 1975) Utah born treasurer of the United States during the Eisenhower administration 1953–1960. Her signature graced U.S. currency for decades. Arlington Park, lot 86, grave 1W, Wesatch Lawn Cemetery, Salt Lake City, UT.

7423. Priestley, J.B. (John Boynton Priestley, Sept. 13, 1894–Aug. 14, 1984) Yorkshire born playwright and novelist known for sharp characterizations of Brits. Plays include *Laburnum Grove* (1930), stories including *The Benighted* (filmed in the U.S. as *The Old Dark House* 1932), novels *The Good Companion* and a variety of Salt detective stories, all generally with a droll and biting wit. He died at his home, the Kissin Tree House, at Alveston near Stratford-on-Avon. Service at Stratford-on-Avon with cremation at Oakley Wood. The ashes were buried at St. Michael's Church in Hubberholme, where in April 1986 a plaque was unveiled within the church inscribed *Remember J.B. Priestley, O.M. 1894–1934. Author and dramatist whose ashes are buried nearby. He loved the Dales and found Hubberholme, one of the smallest and pleasantest places in the world.* St. Michael and All Angels Church, Hubberholme, Yorkshire.

7424. Priestley, Joseph (March 13, 1733–Feb. 6,

1804) English scientist and minister. Radical theologian isolated and identified gaseous compounds including hydrogen and oxygen. Founder of chemistry and of English Unitarianism, he was driven from England because of sympathy with the French Revolution and radical religious theories. Riverview Cemetery, Northumberland, PA.

7425. Prima, Louis (Dec. 7, 1910–Aug. 24, 1978) New Orleans born trumpet player and band leader known for his manic antics as his wife (1953–61) Keeley Smith sang deadpan into the microphone. He died in New Orleans at 65 after being in a coma for three years following surgery for a benign tumor on the brain stem. The Louis Prima (1906–1979) at Greenwood Cemetery in New Orleans is not the musician. He is interred in the family tomb in Metairie with a line from his theme inscribed on the front: *A legend. When the end comes I know/ They'll say "Just a Gigolo"/ As life goes on without me.* Sec. 88, Metairie (Lake Lawn-Metairie) Cemetery, New Orleans, LA.

7426. Primrose, Dorothy (Mamie L. Griffith, Feb. 23, 1879–July 13, 1960) Stock and vaudeville actress appeared as Dorothy Primrose and in the 1952 film *Come Back Peter.* Buried under her real name, Joseph Griffith lot, Orange 554, Mount Holly Cemetery, Little Rock, AR.

7427. Prince, Jack (John Upchurch, Jan. 19, 1920–Jan. 8, 1994) Stout vocalist from Shreveport, Louisiana, appeared on *The Andy Griffith Show* 1961–63 first as Ben Sewell, then Luke Rainier, and finally three times as Rafe Hollister, all incantations of the hill dwelling moonshiner with golden pipes. He died in Las Vegas at 73. Cremated through Bunker mortuary, Las Vegas. Ashes picked up by his daughter, Las Vegas, NV.

7428. Princip, Gavrilo (July 25 [July 13 O.S.] 1894–April 28, 1918) Serbian anarchist from Bosnia-Herzegovina, assassinated Austrian Archduke Franz Ferdinand and his wife in 1914, and was given a twenty year sentence, but died from tuberculosis after four years. The bridge at the murder scene was renamed the Princip Bridge, and his footprints are pressed in the cement at the spot where he fired, with a black plaque commemorating the event. Serbian Orthodox Cemetery (stone is a possible cenotaph), Sarajevo, Bosnia-Herzegovina.

7429. Pringle, Aileen (Aileen Bisbee, July 23, 1895–Dec. 16, 1989) Actress from San Francisco, daughter of George Bisbee, the president of the Pioneer Fruit Co. She appeared in over sixty films, mostly silents, including Elinor Glyn's *Three Weeks, His Hour* and *Souls For Sale* (1923 and '24) and in diminishing roles in sound films, retiring in 1939. Married and divorced from Charles Pringle and James M. Cain, she died in Manhattan at 94. Cremated at Garden State Crematory through the Frank E. Campbell mortuary. Ashes to her godson in London.

7430. Prinze, Freddie (June 22, 1954–Jan. 29, 1977) Spanish stand-up comic specialized in Chicano humor and starred with Jack Albertson in the TV series *Chico and the Man* 1974–77. Drug or alcohol use and impending divorce allegedly contributed to his shooting himself in the head during a period of depression, although accident was not ruled out. He had mentioned having someone over to witness it, hence the speculation. Sanctuary of Light, crypt 2355, near George Raft, Courts of Remembrance, Forest Lawn, Hollywood Hills, Los Angeles.

7431. Prival, Lucien (July 14, 1901–June 3, 1994) German born actor in Teutonic parts, as the commandant in *Hells' Angels* (1930); later in *The Sphinx* (1933), *Bride of Frankenstein* (1935, as the butler), *Mr. Wong, Detective* 1938) etc., died in Daly City, San Mateo County, California, at 92. Unmarked, at his own request. Sec. K, lot 65, grave 2, Atascadero District Cemetery, Atascadero, CA.

7432. Profaci, Joseph (Oct. 2, 1897–June 6, 1962) A reputed boss of the New York underworld allegedly headed one of the five families, though he supposedly ran only an olive oil business. Dome topped mausoleum, across the road from Genovese and near the cloister, facing the road. Sec. 11, St. John's Cemetery, Middle Village, Queens, N.Y.C.

7433. Prokofiev, Sergei (April 15 (O.S.) or 23 (N.S.), 1891–March 5, 1953) Russian composer from the Ukraine whose style was distinguished by emotional restraint. He left Russia in 1918, associated with Diaghilev's Ballets Russes. Among his works are the ballet *Peter and the Wolf* (1936), operas, symphonies and film scores. He died the same day as Stalin. Novodevichy Cemetery, Moscow.

7434. Proudhon, Pierre Joseph (Jan. 15, 1809–Jan. 19, 1865) French social philosopher, author of *What is Property?* (1840), with the lines "property is theft," and *Philosophy of Poverty* (1846) contributed to the French Syndicalism movement. Div. 2, Montparnasse Cemetery, Paris.

7435. Proust, Marcel (July 10, 1871–Nov. 18, 1922) French author of *Remembrance of Things Past* lived in Paris with his parents, writing his mammoth work after their deaths. He gave intensity to all aspects of his observations. Accordingly, a friend seeing Proust after his death remarked that he looked more dead than other dead people. He was attended by a housekeeper and his brother until his death from pneumonia. Buried at the grave of his father, a doctor, there is far more mention of the father on the tablet than of the son. Div. 85, Pere Lachaise Cemetery, Paris.

7436. Prouty, Jed (April 6, 1879–May 10, 1956) Boston born actor played stuttering Uncle Jed in *The Broadway Melody* (1929), later the father in the *Jones Family* films at Fox in the late 1930's. Actors Fund of America plot, Kensico Cemetery, Valhalla, NY.

7437. Provost, Gary (Nov. 14, 1944–May 10, 1995) Author of real life crime dramas. His grave is marked by a stone in the shape of an open book set on closed books, with the epitaph *Dream the dream on.*

A few feet away is a pair of mushrooms with sleeping gnomes at their bases and a mailbox marked *Gary* with the flag up. Eastwood Cemetery, South Lancaster, MA.

7438. Prowse, Juliet (Sept. 25, 1936–Sept. 14, 1996) Dancer-actress raised in South Africa, in Hollywood from *Can Can* (1960). She died in Holmby Hills, California, from pancreatic cancer at 59. Cremated by Pierce Bros. Chapel of the Pines in Los Angeles. Ashes to father at Vanderbijl Park, Transvaal, South Africa.

7439. Proxmire, William (Nov. 11, 1915–Dec. 15, 2005) Wisconsin Democrat, born at Lake Forest, Illinois, who took Sen. Joseph McCarthy's senate seat in 1957 and made a career through five terms of tightening the federal budget with his Golden Fleece Awards given for conspicuous waste of tax dollars in his estimation. Repeatedly winning re-election without accepting campaign donations, he also worked on an anti-genocide treaty, approved two years before his 1988 retirement. He died from Alzheimer's Disease in Sykesville, Maryland, at 90. Lake Forest Cemetery, Lake Forest, IL.

7440. Pryor, Arthur (Sept. 22, 1870–June 18, 1942) Sousa band leader played trombone and later led his own orchestra, recording on early Victor labels. Greenwood Cemetery, West Long Branch, NJ.

7441. Pryor, Richard (Dec. 1, 1940–Dec. 10, 2005) Groundbreaking black stand-up comic from Peoria whose insights into the realities of urban life and race relations, laced with profanity, paved the way for many later versions of his act with dozens of successors and imitators. A natural comedian who could draw laughs with only the expression on his face, he hit his stride in the 1970's with concerts and films, appearing in *Lady Sings the Blues,* co-scripted *Blazing Saddles,* starred in *Silver Streak* and *Stir Crazy* (both with Gene Wilder), *Which Way is Up?, Richard Pryor Live in Concert, The Toy,* and the semi-autobiographical *Jo Jo Dancer Your Life is Calling.* He won an Emmy for writing a Lily Tomlin special and was nominated again for a 1995 performance on *Chicago Hope.* He made the news several times, notably when seriously burned while freebasing cocaine in 1980. He recovered but his health deteriorated with multiple sclerosis diagnosed in 1986 and a heart attack in 1990. He died at 65 from a second coronary suffered at his home in the San Fernando Valley. Service December 17 at Forest Lawn Hollywood Hills, Los Angeles. Ashes returned to the family.

7442. Puccini, Giacomo (Dec. 23, 1858–Nov. 29, 1924) Italian composer. His most famed works were *La Boheme* (1896) and the libretto *Madame Butterfly* (1904), first performed at the New York Metropolitan Opera. He died from throat cancer at 65. His coffin rests in a small chapel especially constructed between his study and his bedroom at his home at Torre del Lago, just below Viareggio, Italy.

7443. Puente, Tito (Ernest Anthony Puente, Jr., April 20, 1923–May 31, 2000) Puerto Rican-American from Harlem was a pioneer in popularizing Latin music in America; a contemporary of Desi Arnaz. He played drums, forming his own orchestra in 1948, recorded over 100 albums and won five Grammys. He died in New York City from a heart ailment at 77. Rose brown monument with a set of drums and musical notes. St. Anthony's Church Cemetery, 36 East Rte. 59A, Nanuet, Rockland County, NY.

7444. Puglia, Frank (March 9, 1892–Oct. 25, 1975) Sicilian born character actor, often as impresarios, maestros, etc. He died in South Pasadena, California. Abbey of the Psalms, Faith—1250, Hollywood Forever Cemetery, Hollywood (Los Angeles), CA.

7445. Puleo, Johnny (Oct. 7, 1907–May 3, 1983) Harmonica playing musician-comedian with the Harmonicats. He was the center of the act, the midget repeatedly crowded out of front and center and swept from view by the others. Sec. 1, lot 390, grave 3, Gate of Heaven Cemetery, Silver Spring, MD.

7446. Pulitzer, Joseph (April 10, 1847–Oct. 29, 1911) Influential publisher bought and combined two St. Louis papers, then came to N.Y. and bought the *New York World* in 1883, making it the paper with the highest national circulation for years. Bequeathing prizes in literature, journalism and music, he lay in state holding a copy of the World on his chest. Near him is his son **Ralph Pulitzer** (June 11, 1879–June 14, 1939) who continued publishing the World, which later went out of business. Monument with a bench dominated by a classical Bronze seated figure. Evergreen sec. 48/49, lot 4977-4982, Woodlawn Cemetery, the Bronx, N.Y.C. See also **Margaret Leech.**

7447. Puller, Lewis "Chesty" (June 26, 1898–Oct. 11, 1971) Lieutenant General in the United States Marine Corps, the most decorated marine in U.S. history with five Navy Crosses, Distinguished Service Cross, Silver Star, two Legions of Merit, a Bronze Star, and Purple Heart. The inscription on the stone slab at his grave closes with *Semper Fidelis* and, on a raised tablet, the Marine Corps insignia. Christ Episcopal Churchyard, Saluda, VA.

7448. Puller, Lewis B. Jr. (Aug. 18, 1945–May 11, 1994) Disabled Vietnam veteran stepped on a mine in 1968, losing both legs and part of his hands. Awarded the Silver Star, two Purple Hearts, the Navy Commendation Medal and the Vietnam Cross of Gallantry. His book *Fortunate Son, the Healing of a Vietnam Vet,* won the Pulitzer Prize in 1992. He died 49, a suicide by gunshot. Epitaph reads *Fortunate Son. Semper Fidelis.* Ashes buried with full honors. Sec. 3, grave 2229B, Arlington National Cemetery, Arlington, VA.

7449. Pullman, George (March 3, 1831–Oct. 19, 1897) Inventor of the railroad car for sleeping, which bore his name beginning in 1865. In 1894 the Pullman Strike in Chicago brought violent rioting and saw the national emergence of organizer and socialist

Eugene V. Debs. Federal intervention was used to mediate the strike. So hated was Pullman and the family so fearful of body snatching after his death that he was buried in a coffin wrapped in tar paper, bolted with steel bolts and embedded in a concrete chamber topped with bolted steel rails. Over it looms a Corinthian column on a large base with benches. Northeast corner area, Fairlawn sec., Graceland Cemetery, Chicago, IL.

7450. Punsly, Bernard (July 11, 1923–Jan. 20, 2004) New York born juvenile actor, the last of the Dead End Kids, later the Bowery Boys, in films from *Dead End* (1937), played Milton, the last to join. He left after nineteen films and became a doctor, serving as chief of staff at South Bay Hospital in Redondo Beach and in private practice until his retirement in 2002. He died from cancer at 80 in Little Company of Mary Hospital, Torrance, California. Ashes scattered at sea through the Neptune Society January 27, 2004, off the coast of Los Angeles County.

7451. Pupin, Michael I. (Oct. 4, 1858–March 12, 1935) Hungarian born physicist and inventor with Columbia University 1889–1931, responsible for the long distance telephone call through its improvement by induction coils, and for X Ray photography (1896). He also worked with AC current and radio transmission. Pulitzer Prize winning autobiography *Immigrant to Inventor* (1923). Marked by a stone bench, Hickory section near Park, Woodlawn Cemetery, the Bronx, N.Y.C.

7452. Purcell, Dick (Richard Purcell, Aug. 6, 1905–April 10, 1944) Fordham educated actor in B films from 1935 (*Bullets or Ballots, The Bank Dick*) died from a heart attack at 36. Sec. E, lot 174, grave 6, Holy Cross Cemetery, Culver City, CA.

7453. Purcell, Irene (Aug. 7, 1901–July 9, 1972) Screen actress from Hammond, Indiana, the wife of Herbert Fisk Johnson, Jr. (1899–1978), president of Johnson Wax 1928–65. Johnson family mausoleum, sec. 34, Mound Cemetery, Racine, WI.

7454. Purcell, Noel (Patrick Joseph Noel Purcell, Dec. 23, 1900–March 3, 1985) Dublin born Irish actor in supporting to bit roles in films from the 1940's (*Odd Man Out, Moby Dick* 1956, as the ship's carpenter); *The Rising of the Moon, The Millionairess, Mutiny on the Bounty* 1962, as Seaman McCoy; *Lord Jim, The Mackintosh Man*). His stone, with his wife Mary, reads *Noel Purcell/ Actor/Freeman of Dublin City*. St. Oliver's sec. (northern part of cemetery), Deans' Grange Burial Ground, Booterstown, County Dublin.

7455. Purdue, John (Oct. 31, 1802–Sept. 12, 1876) New York stockbroker and merchant founded Purdue University, donating $100,000 to its establishment along with public subscription, at Lafayette in Tippecanoe County, Indiana, where he lived. Interred on the campus at Purdue University, Lafayette, IN.

7456. Purviance, Edna (Oct. 21, 1894–Jan. 13, 1958) Charlie Chaplin's leading lady in several of his best silents including *Easy Street* (1917), *A Dog's Life* (1918), *The Kid* (1920) and six others from 1915–1925. Married name Squire. Her plaque lists her birth as 1896. West Mausoleum, left columbarium, east wall, Grandview Memorial Park, Glendale, CA.

7457. Purvis, Melvyn (Melvyn Horace Purvis, Jr., Oct. 24, 1903–Feb. 29, 1960) The FBI agent who in the early 1930's led the successful, sometimes lengthy hunts for the #1 public enemies, notably John Dillinger, who he cornered in Chicago in 1934, tracking down several members of the gang the same year. He died from a gunshot by his own hand at 56. Mt. Hope Cemetery, Florence, SC.

7458. Push Ma Ta Ha (c. 1765–Dec. 24, 1824) Indian Choctaw chief ceded land in Alabama and Mississippi and supported Andrew Jackson in the Creek War 1813–1814. He became a flamboyant Washington figure during ensuing land negotiations with Indian tribes. Buried near Elbridge Gerry. Range 31, site 41, Congressional Cemetery, Washington, D.C.

7459. Pushkin, Alexander (June 6 [N.S] 1799–Jan. 29 [Feb. 10 N.S.] 1837) Russian poet used the vernacular as the language of poetry, making inroads in style for other Russian writers and novelists. Works include *Eugene Onegin* 1823–31, a verse novel which succeeded in making him as a literary radical; *Wasteland Sower of True Freedom* (1823), *Boris Godunov* (1831), *Poltava* (1829), *The Captain's Daughter* (1834), *The Queen of Spades* (1834) and *The Bronze Horseman* (1837). Sviatogorski Monastery Cemetery, Sviatye Gory, Pskov region, Russia.

7460. Pusser, Buford (Dec. 12, 1937–Aug. 21, 1974) Sheriff of McNairy County, Tennessee 1964–70 whose life story was the basis for the 1973 film *Walking Tall*. He was killed in a car wreck the following summer at Selma, Tennessee. Buried with his wife Pauline. Tall polished charcoal gray monument on lot. War Memorial Park, Adamsville, TN.

7461. Putnam, G.P. (George Palmer Putnam, Sept. 7, 1887–Jan. 4, 1950) Heir to the publishing house G.P. Putnam & Sons 1918–1930, Vice President of Brewster & Warren Pub. 1930–32 and Chairman of the Editorial Board of Paramount Pictures 1932–35. In 1926 he covered 8,5000 miles in an expedition to the Arctic, later going to Baffin Island and Africa. His second marriage was to Amelia Earhart (1929) until her disappearance over the Pacific eight years later. From 1939 he lived at Lone Pine, California and operated the Stovepipe Wells Hotel in Death Valley at Trona. Sources list his birth in 1887, though his niche reads 1886. Deodora Hall South, section V, niche 60, Chapel of the Pines Crematory, Los Angeles.

7462. Putnam, Israel (Jan. 17, 1718–May 29, 1790) Colonial general in the American Revolution with experience in the French and Indian War and a hero at Bunker Hill, having more distinction as a scout in earlier warfare than later in the Revolution. Washington blamed him for losses in Long Island and for responding too late to orders in subsequent battles. He suffered a paralytic stroke in 1779 which ended his military service. Interred at the Israel Putnam Monument, Brooklyn, CT.

7463. Putnam, Rufus (April 9, 1738–May 4, 1824) Lieutenant colonel in the Continental Army oversaw the defensive works at Roxbury and Dorchester Heights around Boston 1775–76, moving the next year to Manhattan fortifications, when he was appointed chief engineer, promoted to colonel, later brigadier general, and after hostilities was a frontiersman at the beginnings of westward expansion, founding the Ohio Company, settling Marietta, and serving as U.S. Surveyor General 1796–1803. Mound Cemetery, Marietta, OH.

7464. Puzo, Mario (Oct. 15, 1920–July 2, 1999) Novelist from New York's Hells Kitchen had been writing novels for twenty years before he penned *The Godfather* in 1969. It sold 21 million worldwide and was made into two films, *The Godfather* (1972) and *The Godfather II* (1974). Puzo co-wrote both Oscar winning screenplays with Francis Ford Coppola. He continued writing with *Fools Die, The Sicilian, The Fourth K* and *The Last Don* (1996). He died from heart failure at 78 at his home in Bay Shore, Long Island. Funeral at the Boyd mortuary in nearby Babylon, his pink-red upright headstone already in place. Sec. H, block 14 southwest, three rows behind the Mastro mausoleum, North Babylon Cemetery, Livingston St., North Babylon, Long Island, NY.

7465. Pyle, Denver (May 11, 1920–Dec. 25, 1997) Actor from Bethune, Colorado, in many film and TV roles as provincial, rural patriarchs; best known as Briscoe Darling on *The Andy Griffith Show* 1960–68 and as Uncle Jesse on *The Dukes of Hazzard* 1979–85. He died from lung cancer in Providence St. Joseph Hospital, Burbank, California, at 77, two weeks after attending the unveiling of his star on the Hollywood Walk of Fame. Sent through Forest Lawn Hollywood Hills, for burial. Unmarked. Forreston Cemetery, Forreston, TX.

7466. Pyle, Ernie (Aug. 3, 1900–April 18, 1945) Popular Pulitzer Prize–winning World War II correspondent from Dana, Indiana, chronicled the daily life of the enlisted man with touches of poignancy (the Captain Waskow column) and humor. He befriended island children and enlisted men by the score. The 1945 film *The Story of G.I. Joe* was based on his life. Remaining at the front, he was killed by a stray bullet on Ie Shima in the South Pacific near the end of the war. Servicemen buried him there with a marker inscribed *At this spot the 77th Infantry Division lost a buddy, Ernie Pyle, 18 April 1945.* He was later reburied in the National Memorial Cemetery of the Pacific (the Punchbowl), Honolulu, Hawaii. Pyle and his wife Jerry planned to retire to their house at 900 Girard Blvd. Southeast in Albuquerque, New Mexico. When Jerry died a few months after Pyle was killed, their Shetland sheepdog **Cheetah** was taken in by a neighbor. When the dog died, it was buried on the Pyles' former property, now a branch library, with a tombstone.

7467. Pyne, Joe (Joseph Edward Pyne, Dec. 22, 1924–March 23, 1970) Radio and TV actor known for his pioneer TV talk show. He died from a heart attack at 45 resulting from a tumor crushing the heart. Cremated at Mountain View Mausoleum Crematory through Cabot and Sons, Pasadena, California. Ashes to family.

7468. Qualen, John (John Oleson, Dec 8 1899–Sept 12 1987) Norwegian-Canadian actor with a Nordic accent, a John Ford regular, in over 100 films, among them *Street Scene* (1931), *Our Daily Bread* and *Chasing Yesterday* (1934), *The Grapes of Wrath* (1940, as Muley), *The Devil and Daniel Webster* (as Miser Stevens) and *Out of the Fog* (1941), *The Long Voyage Home, Casablanca* (1942), *The Searchers* (1956), *The Man Who Shot Liberty Valance* (1962), *The Sons of Katie Elder* (1965). He died in Los Angeles at 87. Sanctuary of Reliance, crypt 9632, bottom tier corner, Gardenia Terrace, Great Mausoleum, Forest Lawn Glendale, CA.

7469. Quantrill, William Clarke (July 31, 1837–June 6, 1865) Guerilla leader in the Midwest during the Civil War rode under the guise of a Confederate officer but had little apparent interest in the cause. At Lawrence, Kansas, in August 1863, he and his men rounded up over 150 civilian men and boys and killed them in front of the town's women. He rode into Kentucky after the war's end, intending to surrender as a Confederate, but was shot from the saddle by Union troops. He died either on the field or in the prison hospital and was buried in the prison cemetery at Louisville, Kentucky, later St. John's Cemetery. His family claimed to have gone there later, unearthed the body and returned it to the Fourth Street Cemetery in Canal Dover (now Dover), Ohio. A flush military marker is in the lot, but the exact site of the grave there is unknown. What is in the grave is unknown as well, since the skull, sold by a "friend" of the family, was placed in the Dover historical museum. Half to three fourths of the way back along the right edge. Fourth Street Cemetery, Dover, Ohio. Still other bones regarded as his were buried in fall 1992, marked by a standard white military headstone, in the Confederate Cemetery, Higginsville, MO.

7470. Quarles, Benjamin A. (Jan. 23, 1904–Nov. 16, 1996) Historian of the Blacks' role in U.S. history, notably with *The Negro in the Making of America* (1964) and *The Negro in the American Revolution* (1961) updated and reprinted through 1996. He died in Cheverly, Maryland, at 92. Donated to science at the Maryland Anatomy Board in Baltimore. Ashes buried there later in communal area.

7471. Quarry, Jerry (May 15, 1945–Jan. 3, 1999) Heavyweight contender from Bakersfield defeated Floyd Patterson in 1967 but had less success against Muhammad Ali (in October 1970 and 1972) and Joe

Frazier. Brain damaged, he was cared for in later years by his brother. He died at 53 in Templeton, California. Shafter Memorial Cemetery, Shafter, CA.

7472. Quayle, Anthony (Sept. 7, 1913–Oct. 20, 1989) Stage and screen actor, knighted in 1984, associated with Stratford-on-Avon, died in London. According to the Stratford town council, he had a private funeral at Golders Green Crematorium, London, though there is no record of his cremation there.

7473. Questel, Mae (Sept. 13, 1908–Jan. 4, 1998) The voice of cartoon characters Betty Boop and Olive Oyl; Helen Kane might have done the voice of the former, a takeoff on her, had she not sued cartoonist Max Fleischer, and lost. Questel later turned up in TV commercials and several films, including *New York Days* (1989), as Woody Allen's mother. Zwicker lot, sec. 1, block 2, grave 7, New Montefiore Cemetery, West Babylon, Long Island, NY.

7474. Quillan, Eddie (Edward Quillan, March 31, 1907–July 19, 1990) Slight actor best known for wholesome if timid roles in the 1930's and 40's, in *Mutiny on the Bounty* (1935), *The Grapes of Wrath* (1940). In TV's *Julia* (1968–71), as apartment supt. Eddie Edson. Sec. M, tier 20, grave 102, San Fernando Mission Cemetery, Mission Hills, CA.

7475. Quimby, Fred (Fredrick C. Quimby, July 30, 1886–Sept. 16, 1965) MGM's head of short features 1926–1956 oversaw the development of several animation favorites, including *Tom and Jerry*, and received eight Academy Awards. Court of Freedom, lot 4265, space 1, Forest Lawn, Glendale, CA.

7476. Quimby, Harriet (May 1, 1884–July 1, 1912) Journalist was the first American woman to receive a pilot's license and the first to fly over the English Channel. She fell from her dipping plane en route to Boston. Monument with a plane on the plaque. Katonah plot, in from Katonah Ave. at second circle, Kensico Cemetery, Valhalla, NY.

7477. Quincy, Josiah (Feb. 23, 1744–April 26, 1775) Prominent colonial lawyer from Braintree (now Quincy), Massachusetts, with John Adams defended the British soldiers who fired the fatal shots in the Boston Massacre in 1770. Buried, along with many Quincys, Boylstons and Adamses, in Hancock Cemetery (1666), Quincy, MA.

7478. Quincy, Josiah (Feb. 4, 1772–July 1, 1864) Son of lawyer Josiah Quincy was an historian and Federalist representative from Massachusetts opposed to the Louisiana Purchase, the spread of slavery and the War of 1812. Though drummed out of the party, he maintained he was a Federalist until he died, returning to the Boston area as mayor and president of Harvard. Sweetbriar Path, lot 396, Mount Auburn Cemetery, Cambridge, MA.

7479. Quine, Richard (Richard Harding Quine, Nov. 12, 1920–June 10, 1989) Actor through the 1940's (*For Me and My Gal, Tish*) married to Susan Peters 1943–48, directed from the late 40's (*My Sister Eileen, The Solid Gold Cadillac, Paris When It Sizzles, Sex and the Single Girl*). A suicide by gunshot at 68. Ashes to residence, Los Angeles.

7480. Quinlan, Karen Ann (March 29, 1954–June 11, 1985) Twenty-one year old comatose patient became a national name and the center of the right-to-die controversy in 1975 when her parents sought to turn off her life support system. The legal system allowed the disconnection, but she remained comatose and breathing on her own for ten years. Gate of Heaven Cemetery, East Hanover, NJ.

7481. Quinn, Anthony (April 21, 1915–June 3, 2001) Actor of Spanish and Irish descent born in Chihuahua, Mexico and raised in East Los Angeles played a variety of exuberant characters of various ethnicity in over 100 films, including Indians and Italians, from 1936, winning two Oscars, for *Viva Zapata* (1952) and *Lust For Life* (1956). Among his many other pictures were *The Plainsman* (1936), *The Ghost Breakers* (1940), *The Road to Morocco* (1942), *The Ox Bow Incident* (1943), *The Hunchback of Notre Dame* (1956), *The Guns of Navarone* (1961), *Lawrence of Arabia* (1962), *Zorba the Greek* (1964, and the role he was most closely identified with), *The Secret of Santa Vittoria* (1969), *Only the Lonely* (1990) and *A Walk in the Clouds* (1995). Also a sculptor, painter and author, his several wives included actress Katherine DeMille. When their son **Christopher** (1938–1941) drowned in W.C. Fields' swimming pool, Fields had the pool cemented over. Sec. 8/Garden of Legends, southeast of C.B. DeMille, Hollywood Forever Cemetery, Hollywood (Los Angeles). Quinn had lived at Bristol, Rhode Island, on an eastern peninsula, since 1995 when he died at 86 from respiratory failure at a Boston hospital, having earlier expressed a wish to have his ashes spread at his birthplace in Mexico. A memorial service was to be held at the First Unitarian Church in Providence but was moved to the larger First Baptist Church in America June 9, the day after his private burial, through Nardolillo mortuary in Cranston, beneath his favorite tree on his nineteen acre estate overlooking Narragansett Bay. His widow had to request a zoning board grant her property distinction as a cemetery. At the end of August 2002, she announced she was selling much of the estate, including the land containing the family cemetery. Quinn's grave is in a garden at approximately 2 o'clock on the property, covered by small, flat stones, with a rough hewn 10' stone at the head, about 3' thick, topped by a small bust of the actor. Quinn estate "cemetery" (private property), Poppasquash Road, Bristol, RI.

7482. Quinn, Don (Nov. 18, 1900–Dec. 30, 1967) Creator and writer of radio's *Fibber McGee and Molly* 1935–1950— and their handful of films in the early 40's. He also wrote *The Halls of Ivy* 1950–52. Urn with his wife Edythe. Alcove of Devotion, tier 6, niche 1, Cathedral Mausoleum, Hollywood Forever Cemetery, Hollywood (Los Angeles), CA.

7483. Quinn, Glenn (May 28, 1970–Dec. 3, 2002) Dublin born Irish actor in several films of the

1990's (*Call Me Anna, Dr. Giggles, Live Nude Girls, Campfire Tales, Outlaw, R.S.V.P.*, best known as Becky's boyfriend and husband Mark on TV's *Roseanne* 1988–1995. He died from a drug overdose at 32 in North Hollywood. Luyben Family-Dilday-Mottell mortuary, Laguna Beach. Grave right of entrance area. Garden of Protection, lot 7324, grave 2A, Forest Lawn, Cypress, CA.

7484. Quinn, Mary Alice (Dec. 28, 1920–Nov. 8, 1935) Chicago girl with supposed healing powers. Her stone has become a shrine and is said to give off a scent of roses. Reilly stone, sec. 7, Holy Sepulchre Cemetery, Worth, IL.

7485. Quirk, James T. (March 13, 1911–Jan. 18, 1969) Publisher of *TV Guide*, the nation's most read weekly magazine, from 1953 until his death. Sec. 20, range 5, lot 15, grave 4 front, Holy Cross Cemetery, Yeadon, Philadelphia, PA.

7486. Quisenberry, Dan (Daniel R. Quisenberry, Feb. 7, 1953–Sept. 30, 1998) Popular and colorful relief pitcher with the Kansas City Royals 1979–1988 made three trips to the All Star game and appeared in the 1980 and '85 world series. Known not only for his side-armed submarine delivery but for his poetry and optimistic spiritual outlook, he was inducted into the Royals Hall of Fame in May 1998, four months after being diagnosed with the brain cancer that claimed his life at 45. Block 19, lot 37, space 8, Mt. Moriah (Mt. Moriah-Freeman) Cemetery, Holmes Rd., Kansas City, MO.

7487. Quisling, Vidkun (Vidkun Abraham Lauritz Jonsson Quisling, July 18, 1887–Oct. 24, 1945) Norwegian fascist was the minister of defense 1931–33, founding the National Union Party, modeled on the Nazis, aiding in their conquest of Norway and serving as their puppet ruler during World War II. His name subsequently became a synonym for traitor, an updating of the similar use of Benedict Arnold, with a more vicious connotation. Arthur Seyss-Inquart, who was hanged at Nuremburg in 1946, was called "the Austrian Quisling." At the end of the war he was convicted of treason and executed by firing squad. Gjerpen Cemetery, Skien, Norway.

7488. Raab, Kurt (July 20, 1941–June 28, 1988) Actor from the Sudetenland (now the Czech Republic), in German films from the 1960's, died from AIDS in Hamburg at 46. Urnengrab, unmarked under bushes. Bq 63, 371-372, Ohlsdorfer Friedhof, Hamburg.

7489. Rabbitt, Eddie (Edward Thomas Rabbitt, Nov. 27, 1941–May 7, 1998) Brooklyn born country-western singer-songwriter, raised in East Orange, New Jersey, wrote *Kentucky Rain* recorded by Elvis Presley in 1969, and had hits in the late 70's and 80's with *Drivin My Life Away, Every Which Way But Loose, I Love a Rainy Night*, etc. He died in Nashville at 56 from lung cancer. His stone reads *In loving memory of my dearest Irish American husband.* Sec. 15, lot 235, Calvary Cemetery, Lebanon Road, Nashville, TN.

7490. Rabelais, Francois (c. 1494–April 9, 1553) Humanistic cleric and scholar of the French Renaissance known for his satirical *Gargantua and Pantagruel* (1532–64), translated into English 1653–94, from which came the adjectives *gargantuan and Rabelaisian.* Originally buried in the Cimetiere Saint-Paul (Saint Paul — Saint Louis Churchyard) in Paris, like Moliere's mother-in-law Madeleine Bejart and countless others, he was removed into the Catacombs (consecrated for burials in 1786) in 1791.

7491. Rabin, Yitzhak (March 1, 1922–Nov. 4, 1995) Israeli prime minister had served in the office 1974–77 and then as defense minister. Co-winner with Yassar Arafat of the 1994 Nobel Peace Prize, he had just finished a speech at a peace rally in Tel Aviv when he was assassinated by a 27 year old right wing gunman, the first murder of a Jewish statesman by a Jew since the founding of the state of Israel. Buried just over 36 hours later in Mount Herzl Cemetery, reserved for state and other Israeli leaders, named after the state's founder Theodre Herzl, Mount Herzl Cemetery, Jerusalem.

7492. Rabinowitz, Solomon *see* **Sholom Aleichem.**

7493. Rachel (Mademoiselle Rachel, born Elisa Felix, Feb. 28, 1820–Jan. 3, 1858) Tragedienne of the *Theatre Francaise*, acclaimed for her *Phaedre* and various other works of Corneille and Racine. Broken down by a long series of love affairs, her death at 38 resulted from tuberculosis. Tomb in div. 7, Pere Lachaise Cemetery, Paris.

7494. Rachell, Yank (James Rachell, March 16, 1910–April 9, 1997) Blues pioneer did vocals and mandolin, recording in later years with John Sebastian. Burial April 19. His flush bronze plaque has his picture and a lengthy tribute. Sec. 42, row 8, grave 28, New Crown Cemetery, Indianapolis, IN.

7495. Rachmaninoff, Sergei (April 1 [plaque lists April 2], 1873–March 28, 1943) Russian composer protégé of Tchaikovsky's family left Russia with the Revolution and came to New York, where he remained as composer and conductor. He is more highly regarded today as a pianist, his compositions often considered sentimental and heavy, reflecting a melancholy air not unlike Tchaikovsky. He spent his last year in Beverly Hills, California, where he died from lung cancer at 69. His plot is marked by a Russian Orthodox cross surrounded by a hedge. Sec. 187, across from the Actors Fund of America plot, Kensico Cemetery, Valhalla, NY.

7496. Rachmil, Lewis J. (July 3, 1908–Feb. 19, 1984) Hollywood art director (1934–40) turned producer (1941–1984), nominated for an Oscar for his sets on *Our Town* (1940). Among his other set designs through the 1930s were *Murder By Television* and *Tarzan's Revenge.* Garden Mausoleum (of Love), J-469, Hillside Memorial Park, Los Angeles.

7497. Radatz, Dick (Richard R. Radatz, April 2, 1937–March 16, 2005) Powerful relief pitcher with a

95 mile-an-hour fastball dubbed The Monster after he repeatedly threw out Mickey Mantle at Yankee Stadium, stood 6 foot 6 inches and weighed 230 pounds. With the Red Sox 1962–66, he twice led the league in saves and was a two time All Star, holding the record for strikeouts in a season as a reliever, with 181 in 79 games, totaling 157 innings in 1964. He died at 67 from a probable heart attack following a fall down stairs Sec. 27, lot 122, grave 1, Holy Sepulchre Cemetery, Southfield, MI.

7498. Radbourne, Charles G. "Old Hoss" (Dec. 11, 1854–Feb. 5, 1897) King of 19th century hurlers, with Providence, Boston and Cincinnati N.L. 1881–91. Hall of Fame 1939. A tablet with his image and stats was placed is on the back of his rose stone in 1944. Sec. 17, Evergreen Memorial Cemetery, Bloomington, IL.

7499. Radcliffe, Ann (July 9, 1764–Feb. 7, 1823) English gothic-horror writer known for her influential masterpiece *The Mysteries of Udolpho* (1794). Her exact gravesite is lost. St. George's burial ground, Bayswater Road, near Hyde Park Nursery School, (west end) London.

7500. Radcliffe, Ted "Double Duty" (Theodore Roosevelt Radcliffe, July 7, 1902–Aug. 11, 2005) Versatile Negro Leagues great from Mobile, Alabama, played with various teams from 1928, given his nickname by Damon Runyon in the 1932 Negro League world series at Yankee Stadium when he caught a Satchel Paige shutout for the Pittsburgh Crawfords, then threw one of his own. He played for or coached an estimated thirty teams, had 4,000 hits, 400 home runs, won 500 games with 4,000 strikeouts, and appeared in six East-West All Star games, pitching in three and catching in three. He lived near U.S. Cellular Field in Chicago, where he threw out the first pitch on his birthday from 1999 until 2005, his 103rd, a month before his death. Linden Hill sec., Oakwoods Cemetery, Chicago, IL.

7501. Radner, Gilda (June 28, 1946–May 20, 1989) Detroit born comedienne, a member of the original Not Ready For Prime Time Players on TV's *Saturday Night Live* 1975–1980, made several films in the 1980's with Gene Wilder, who she married in 1984. Diagnosed with ovarian cancer in October 1986, her two and a half year struggle was chronicled in her memoir *It's Always Something* (1989). Her last appearance, displaying humor and openness about the illness, was on *The Gary Shandling Show* in late 1988. Wilder later organized Gilda's Club(s) for those living with ovarian and other cancers. She died at 42 in Cedars Sinai Hospital in Los Angeles. A low bench and flush, rippled stone marker inscribed *Comedienne and ballerina* between her name and years mark her grave, near their Connecticut home. Long Ridge Union Cemetery, Erskine Road, Stamford, CT.

7502. Raffensberger, Ken (Kenneth David Raffensberger, Aug. 8, 1917–Nov. 10, 2002) N.L. pitcher threw for fifteen seasons (1939–41, 1943–54) with the Cardinals (one inning), Cubs, and Phillies (their lone representative and the first to pitch in an All Star Game (1944), who traded him to the Reds in 1947, allegedly in part because he refused Ben Chapman's orders to throw at Jackie Robinson. With Cincinnati for seven and a half seasons, he led the league in shutouts in 1949 and 1952, won eighteen games in 1949 and 17 in 1952 and retired in 1954. Stan Musial claimed Raffensberger was the toughest pitcher he ever faced. Mount Rose Cemetery, York, PA.

7503. Rafferty, Frances (June 16, 1922–April 18, 2004) Actress from Sioux City, Iowa, in films of the 1940's (*Eyes in the Night, Hitler's Madman, Dragon Seed, Abbott & Costello in Hollywood, Bad Bascomb*), best known as Ruth Henshaw on TV's *December Bride* 1954–1961. The wife of Thomas R. Baker, she died in her sleep at 81 in her home at Paso Robles, California. Memorial April 24 service in the gazebo at the rose garden, where her ashes are to be interred eventually. Paso Robles District Cemetery, Paso Robles, CA.

7504. Rafferty, Max (May 7, 1917–June 13, 1982) Syndicated columnist focused on education. Dean of the School of Education at Troy State University in Alabama. He died when his car plunged off an earthen dam into a pond. Sec.2, lot 17, Green Hills Memorial Park, Troy, AL.

7505. Raft, George (Sept. 26, 1895–Nov. 24, 1980) New York actor from the real gangster world of the 20's was a dancer and protégé of Texas Guinan. His dancing ability was put to use in films like *Bolero* (1934) but he was better known for his air of quiet menace, as the coin flipping henchman Guino Rinaldo in *Scarface* (1932) and many later tough guy roles. He fell out of favor over income tax evasion in 1965 and was banned in England as an undesirable in 1967. He died from leukemia at 85 in Los Angeles. Sanctuary of Light, crypt 2356, Courts of Remembrance, Forest Lawn Hollywood Hills, Los Angeles.

7506. Ragland, Rags (John Lee Morgan Beauregard Ragland, Aug. 28, 1906–Aug. 20, 1946) Actor-dancer-comedian on stage and screen in light films of the 1940's: *Whistling in the Dark, Whistling in Brooklyn, Girl Crazy, The Canterville Ghost, Panama Hattie, Anchors Aweigh* (1945), and in amiable parts in many other MGM vehicles of the 1940's. He died in Los Angeles of uremia at 39. Unmarked. Sec. 10, lot 219, grave 3, Evergreen Cemetery, Louisville, KY.

7507. Raines, Ella (Aug. 6, 1920–May 30, 1988) Brunette actress from Snoqualmie Falls, Washington, in several film noir pictures at Universal in the 1940's, notably Preston Sturges's *Hail the Conquering Hero*, and *Phantom Lady* and *The Suspect*, both directed by Robert Siodmak in 1944. She died at 67 from throat cancer in Los Angeles. Cremated through Grandview Memorial Park in Glendale. Poplar sec., lot 162, grave A, Glen Haven Memorial Park, Sylmar, CA.

7508. Rainey, Joseph Hayne (June 21, 1832–Aug. 2, 1887) Former slave, the first black to serve in the

U.S. House of Representatives, was the son of a white barber who had bought his freedom. He fled to the West Indies during the Civil War, returning to serve as a congressman from South Carolina 1871–79 and was re-elected four times, the longest a seat was held by any black during Reconstruction. Baptist Cemetery, Georgetown, SC.

7509. Rainey, Ma (Gertrude Malissa Nix Pridgett Rainey, April 26, 1886–Dec. 22, 1939) Pioneer blues singer from Columbus, Georgia, recorded primarily in the 1920's and toured on the black vaudeville circuit. A slab with her real name and dates, the original grave marker, was joined by a headstone c. 1990 identifying her as *Ma Rainey, Mother of the Blues*. Porterdale Cemetery, Columbus, GA.

7510. Rainger, Ralph (Oct. 7, 1901–Oct. 23, 1942) Composer wrote the music for the future theme songs of both Bob Hope and Jack Benny. He won an Oscar for *Thanks for the Memory* (1938) and was nominated for *Love in Bloom* (1935), as well as *Faithful Forever* (1940). Sanctuary of Trust, crypt 5783 (opposite Gable and Lombard), Memorial Terrace, Great Mausoleum, Forest Lawn, Glendale, CA.

7511. Rains, Claude (Nov. 10, 1889–May 30, 1967) London born actor, short in stature, with a powerful, commanding presence, on stage from 1901, taught theatre in England before his first screen role, in and as *The Invisible Man* (1933), but his versatility kept him from being typed as raving madmen. He took on murderous parts for over a decade at Warners with the same ease as his sympathetic characters in *Now Voyager, Mr. Skeffington*, or the roguish police prefect Louis Renault in *Casablanca* (1942). Married six times, the last to Rosemary McGroerry, who died in 1964 at 47. He had a home at Bucks County, Pennsylvania, and later near Sandwich, New Hampshire, where the he died at 77 in Lakes Region Hospital and was buried beside his last wife, their polished black marble tombstones rising to a point, surrounded by shrubbery. Her epitaph reads *When I am gone, my dearest, sing no sad songs for me. Father in Thy gracious keeping leave me now Thy servant sleeping*. His is inscribed *All things once are things forever. Soul, once living, lives forever*. Red Hill Cemetery, Bean Road, near Multonborough (or Center Harbor), NH.

7512. Raisch, Bill (Carl William Raisch, April 5, 1905–July 31, 1984) Actor played the elusive one armed man on TV's *The Fugitive* 1963–67. Cremated at Grandview Memorial Park, Glendale, California. Ashes scattered at sea.

7513. Raitt, John (John Emmett Raitt, Jan. 29, 1917–Feb. 20, 2005) Baritone from Santa Ana, California, known as Billy Bigelow in *Carousel* on Broadway from 1945 and *The Pajama Game* in 1954, filmed with him opposite Doris Day in 1957, his only starring film, though he remained busy on the musical stage and gained a second claim to fame as the father of singer Bonnie Raitt. He died from pneumonia at 88 in his Pacific Palisades home. Cremated through

Gates-Kingsley-Gates, Santa Monica, after the funeral February 25. Ashes buried Anaheim Cemetery, 1400 E. Sycamore St., Anaheim, CA.

7514. Rajo Jack (Dewey Gatson aka Roger Jack DeSoto, July 28, 1905–Feb. 27, 1956) Pioneer black race car mechanic and driver endorsed the Rajo cylinder, which earned him his nickname. Popular on the west coast, he won in a V8 at Silvergate Speedway in San Diego in 1934, in 1936 was the first to lower the 28 second mark on the half mile track at Southern Speedway, and won the Pacific Coast championship at South Gate Speedway in 1939. He died from a heart attack in Los Angeles. Lincoln Cemetery, Carson, CA.

7515. Raksin, David (Aug. 4, 1912–Aug. 9, 2004) Composer from Philadelphia worked on films from 1936, long at Fox, best known for the score and title song *Laura* (1944) and nominated for Oscars for *Forever Amber* (1947) and *Separate Tables* (1958). He also worked on or scored *The Hound of the Baskervilles, The Adventures of Sherlock Holmes, The Secret Life of Walter Mitty, Force of Evil, The Man With A Cloak, The Bad and the Beautiful*. He died at his home in Van Nuys, California, at 92. National Cremation Service. Ashes to family in Studio City, CA.

7516. Raleigh, Walter (1554–Oct. 29, 1618) A favorite of Elizabeth I, Raleigh fell from favor under the rule of James I in 1603. Accused of treason for favoring peace with Spain and leaning toward Catholicism, he was imprisoned in the Tower of London until 1617, when he was released and sent to steal gold from Guiana. When he failed, James had him condemned to death on the old charges. Raleigh was beheaded and his body buried south of the altar in St. Margaret's Church. His wife Bess had the head embalmed and kept on view. It was intended to be buried with Raleigh's son Carew but by the time he died the head had disappeared. White marble monument, St. Margaret's Church, Westminster, London.

7517. Ralph, Jesse (Jesse Ralph Chambers, Nov. 5, 1870–May 30, 1944) Stage and screen character actress at MGM in the 30's as loving maids, spinsters, etc. in *David Copperfield* (1935, as Peggoty), *Little Lord Fauntleroy, San Francisco* (1936), and as W.C. Fields' merciless mother-in-law in *The Bank Dick* (1940). She was the daughter of Captain James Chambers, a Gloucester, Massachusetts, fisherman. For the last three years of her life, following the amputation of a leg in California, she lived in West Gloucester at the home of her nephew's wife, where she died at 79, according to her obituaries, putting her birth at 1864, although the monument lists her birth as 1870. Cremated at Harmony Grove Cemetery in Salem, her ashes were buried with her parents, her name listed on the back of the rose-brown monument with the notation *Hollywood Actress*. Mount Pleasant Cemetery, Gloucester, MA.

7518. Ralston, Esther (Sept. 17, 1902–Jan. 14, 1994) The American Venus of silent films, a blonde beauty from Bar Harbor, Maine, in films from 1916, including *Peter Pan* (1925, as Mrs. Darling), *Old Iron-sides* (1926), *A Kiss For Cinderella*. Known as Paramount's clotheshorse of the day, she also had a limo and chauffeur dressed to match her outfits. In later years she worked in an upstate New York utility company, retiring to Ventura, California, where she died at 91. Cremated through Ted Mayer mortuary there. Ashes sent to a relative in Glendale, Arizona. No record in any cemetery there.

7519. Ralston, Jobyna (Nov. 21, 1899/1900–Jan. 22, 1967) Actress from Pittsburg, Tennessee, in silent films from 1921–31 including several Harold Lloyd comedies (*Hot Water, The Freshman, The Kid Brother*) after he married his leading lady Mildred Davis. Married to Richard Arlen 1927–45, with whom she appeared in *Wings* (1927). She retired with sound, allegedly due to a lisp. Sec. B, lot 70, grave 27, San Fernando Mission Cemetery, Mission Hills, CA.

7520. Ralston, Vera Hruba (Vera Helena Hruba, July 12, 1920/1923 [plaque lists 1923]–Feb. 9, 2003) Prague born Czech skating star raised in a convent won the silver (to Sonja Henie's gold) at the 1936 winter Olympics. Fleeing Prague in 1939, she was cast by Herbert Yates in *Ice Capades* at Republic Pictures in 1941, taking the name Ralston from the cereal company. She starred with John Wayne in *Dakota* and with Erich Von Stroheim in *The Lady and the Monster*, among others, but her wooden delivery and poor English hindered her popularity, though not with Yates, who left his family for her in 1947. They were married from 1952 until his death in February 1966. In June 1973, she married Charles De Alva, and resided with him in Santa Barbara until her death there nearly thirty years later from cancer at 82, reported as 79. Mass February 15 at San Roque Catholic Church through Welch-Ryce-Hader mortuary. Ashes buried the day before. Sunrise Urn Garden, #73, Santa Barbara Cemetery, Santa Barbara, CA.

7521. Rambeau, Marjorie (July 15, 1889–July 7, 1970) Stage and screen star in silents went on to character parts as world wise women in *Min and Bill* (1930) and was nominated for an Oscar for *Primrose Path* (1940). Married name Gudger. Sec. B-10, lot 26, Desert Memorial Park, Cathedral City (Palm Springs), CA.

7522. Rambo, Dack (Norman Jay Rambo, Nov. 13, 1941–March 21, 1994) TV actor in several series, twin brother of actor **Dirk Rambo** (Orman Ray Rambo, Nov. 13, 1941–Feb. 5, 1967). Buried near each other. Block 29, lots I and J, west side 2, Delano Cemetery, Delano, CA.

7523. Rambova, Natacha (Winifred Shaugnessy Hudnut, Jan. 19, 1897–June 5, 1966) Dancer-actress disciple of Nazimova adopted a Russian name in the style of other sirens of the day. Rambova is best known as the aloof wife of Rudolph Valentino for whom he built his home Falcon Lair in Beverly Hills. She made one film *When Love Grows Cold* (1925). Her adopted family (Hudnut) were buried in Woodlawn Cemetery, the Bronx, where she wanted Valentino buried but was overruled. She died forty years later in Pasadena from dietary complications. Cremated at Pasadena Crematory, her ashes were given to Kay Patterson in Monrovia and later to her cousin Ann Wollen, who scattered them, according to Rambova's wishes, in the forests of northern Arizona.

7524. Ramey, James "Baby Huey" (1944–Oct. 28, 1970) Front man for The Babysitters in Chicago from 1963, considered a soul legend and precursor of hip-hop and rap, known for working the stage "like a young James Brown" despite his size, which gave him the moniker after the *Harvey Comics* cartoon character Baby Huey. He died from a heart attack at 26 in a Chicago motel, the probable result of both his weight and heroin addiction, and was returned to his home town for burial. Sec. 4, lot 19D, space 1 (east — rear — edge of section, near road, just right of cart drive), Glen Haven Memorial Gardens, Richmond, IN.

7525. Ramon, Ilan (June 20, 1954–Feb. 1, 2003) The first Israeli to fly with fellow U.S. astronauts in space was lost with his six companions when the Space Shuttle Columbia exploded as it re-entered the earth's atmosphere during the final fifteen minutes of its mission after two weeks in space. Debris was recovered from Arizona, Texas and into Louisiana. Ramon's remains were recovered, enough for burial as soon as possible according to Orthodox Judaism. Interred February 11 in the hilltop cemetery at Moshav Nahalal, northern Israel.

7526. Ramone, Dee Dee (Douglas Glenn Colvin, Sept. 18, 1952–June 5, 2002) Fleenortown, Virginia, born bass player for The Ramones, died in Santa Monica from a drug overdose at 49. His black monument bears, in a circle around the American eagle, the line *I feel so safe flying on a ray/ on the highest trails above,* and at the bottom, below his real and stage name and dates, the exit line *O.K ... I gotta go now.* Sec. 8/Garden of Legends, lot 2003, space 4, Hollywood Forever Cemetery, Hollywood (Los Angeles), CA.

7527. Ramone, Joey (Jeffrey Hyman, May 19, 1951–April 15, 2001) Punk rock icon in leather and torn jeans led the Ramones and their three chord thrash from 1974 from Queens, N.Y.C. Later punk groups such as Clash and the Sex Pistols were influenced by the Ramones' English tour in 1976; they also formed the musical scene that produced Patti Smith, Blondie and others. They appeared in *Rock 'n' Roll High School* (1979) and did the soundtrack for *Pet Sematary*. Their 1980 Phil Spector collaboration *End of the Century* was their biggest hit at number 44 on the charts. Ramone died from lymphoma at 49 in a Manhattan hospital. Mt. Zion Cemetery, Lyndhurst, NJ.

7528. Ramone, Johnny (John Cummings, Oct. 8, 1948–Sep. 15, 2004) Guitarist and co-founder of the premier punk band The Ramones, known for *I Want To Be Sedated, Blitzkrieg Bop*, etc., died from prostate cancer at home in Los Angeles at 55. A statue of him, a cenotaph, was erected near the grave of Dee Dee Ramone (Douglas Colvin) in sec. 8/Garden of Legends, Hollywood Forever Cemetery. Cremated in a private ceremony through Hollywood mortuary, the ashes were kept by his wife Linda Cummings.

7529. Ramsey, Anne (Anne Mobley, March 27, 1929–Aug. 11, 1988) Actress played Mama in *Throw Mama From the Train* (AA nom., 1987). The loss of part of her tongue during cancer surgery in 1985 produced the speech impediment so effective in the film. She died from cancer in an L.A. hospital at 59 the next year. Burial unmarked next to her mother, Eleanor Mobley. Monroe E. Smith lot, sec. 21, lot 97, grave 10, Forest Lawn Cemetery, Omaha, NE.

7530. Ramsey, JonBenet (Aug. 6, 1990–Dec. 25, 1996) Six year old girl found murdered in the basement of her Boulder, Colorado, home. The case received endless media attention over her entry in beauty contests at such a young age, her wealthy parents refusal to talk with police, and the lack of an arrest or anyone being charged. Buried next to her half sister Elizabeth, who died in a 1992 car crash and her mother Patsy, who died from cancer in 2006. In the rear and next to the road. St. James Episcopal Cemetery, Marietta, GA.

7531. Rand, Ayn (Feb. 2, 1905–March 6, 1982) Russian born playwright and novelist immigrated to the U.S. in the 1920's, producing most of her better works in the 1940's and 50's, primarily *The Fountainhead* (1943). Her writing was identified with themes of objectivism, self indulgent theories stressing the importance of the individual as opposed to democratic or socialistic works for the common good. She died in New York from lung cancer. At the calling, her favorite tunes were played, including *C'mon Get Happy*, Chopin's *Minute Waltz* and *It's a Long Way to Tipperary*. Buried with her husband Frank O'Connor, a few yards from Tommy Dorsey. Sec. 41, Uncas plot off Cherokee Ave., Kensico Cemetery, Valhalla, NY.

7532. Rand, Sally (Jan. 2, 1904–Aug. 31, 1979) Circus and silent screen dancer boosted her career with her nude Fan Dance and Lady Godiva impersonation at the 1933 Chicago World's Fair. She made a few films and continued her exotic dancing over several decades. Elm lot 34, space 10, Oakdale Memorial Park, Glendora, CA.

7533. Randall, Addison "Jack" (Addison Owen Randall, May 12, 1906–July 16, 1945) B western cowboy actor, sometimes singing, died when he fell from his horse while filming at Canoga Park, California. Married to actress Barbara Bennett. Lawn crypt 104, Garden of Memory (private), Forest Lawn, Glendale, CA.

7534. Randall, J. G. (James Garfield Randall, June 24, 1881–Feb. 20, 1953) U.S. historian, professor of History at the University of Illinois, focused on Lincoln and the Civil War, including *Mr. Lincoln* (1945), *The Civil War and Reconstruction* (with David Donald, reprinted in 1969), numerous other works. He

died at Champaign, Illinois, at 71. East Lawn, block 3, lot 115, Mt. Hope Cemetery, Champaign, IL.

7535. Randall, Sue (Susan Randall McSparron, Oct. 8, 1935–Oct. 26, 1984) Philadelphia born actress best known as Beaver Cleaver's school teacher Miss Landers on *Leave it to Beaver* 1957–1961. She returned to Philadelphia in 1969 and worked as an agent and with various charities until her death at 49 from cancer of the lungs and larynx in Pennsylvania Hospital, Philadelphia; the same hospital where she was born. She donated her body to science through Heritage Gifts Registry in Philadelphia. Ashes buried June 18, 1986 in a communal area, #86, Mt. Peace Cemetery, Philadelphia, PA.

7536. Randall, Tony (Leonard Rosenberg, Feb. 26, 1920–May 17, 2004) Actor from Tulsa in many comedic and amiable parts on stage, screen and television, appeared in *Will Success Spoil Rock Hunter?, Pillow Talk, Lover Come Back, The Seven Faces of Doctor Lao, The King of Comedy,* but was best known as fastidious, obsessively neat photographer Felix Unger opposite Jack Klugman's Oscar Madison on television's *The Odd Couple* 1970–75, for which he won an Emmy after the show was cancelled. Florence, his wife of fifty-four years, died from cancer in New York April 18, 1992, with no services. In 1995 he married Heather Harlan, by whom he had two children, his first at age 77. He died in New York University Medical Center at 84. Garden State Crematory through The Riverside, Manhattan. Westchester Hills Cemetery, Hastings-on-Hudson, NY.

7537. Randion, "Prince" (c.1871–Dec. 19, 1934) British Guiana native, brought to the United States by P.T. Barnum in 1889, was known as The Human Torso; he had no arms or legs, yet was married and had a family in Paterson, New Jersey. He appeared in Tod Browning's 1932 film *Freaks,* lighting a cigarette on his own with a match despite no limbs or digits. After appearing at a show in Times Square in Manhattan, he died suddenly at 63. Buried facing east, as a Muslim, according to the Paterson paper. The cemetery records do not locate his burial site. Laurel Grove Cemetery, Totowa, NJ.

7538. Randolph, A. Philip (Asa Philip Randolph, April 15, 1889–May 16, 1979) Black labor leader organized the Brotherhood of Sleeping Car Porters in 1917 and published the monthly *Messenger,* helping to bring black Americans into organized labor. He worked with FDR on the Fair Employment Practices Committee, Vice President of the newly merged AFL-CIO 1955; he led the march on Washington for Jobs and Freedom in 1963. A. Philip Randolph Memorial Library, Manhattan, N.Y.C.

7539. Randolph, Amanda (Sept 21, 1896–Aug. 23, 1967) African-American actress from Louisville, Kentucky, on radio made several films as well and played both Sapphire's mama Ramona Smith in TV's *Amos 'n' Andy* (1951–53) and the Williams' maid Louise in *Make Room For Daddy* (1953–64). She died from a stroke at 70. Married name Hansberry. Elaborately inscribed tablet beside her younger sister Lillian. Gentleness sec, lot 1054, space 1, Forest Lawn Hollywood Hills, Los Angeles.

7540. Randolph, Edmund (Aug. 10, 1753–Sept. 12, 1813) Former aide-de-camp to Washington, Attorney General of Virginia and member of the Continental Congress who introduced the Virginia Plan to the Constitutional Convention on May 29 1787, the first formal presentation of the new concept of government, consisting of three branches and representation based on population. He was disgusted with the amended document but signed in 1788. Attorney General 1789–95 and Secretary of State 1794–95, he resigned after being accused of taking bribes from the French ambassador. Old Chapel Cemetery, Milwood, VA.

7541. Randolph, Jennings (March 8, 1902–May 8, 1998) Democratic congressman (for seven terms, 1933–47) and senator (for four terms, 1958–85) from West Virginia authored the 26th Amendment, ratified in 1972, giving 18 year olds the right to vote, introducing it eleven times before it was finally approved. He died in a St. Louis nursing home at 96. Seventh Day Baptist Church Cemetery, Salem, WV.

7542. Randolph, John (June 2, 1773–May 24, 1833) John Randolph of Roanoke was an early and powerful advocate of states' rights and a fiery opponent of too much power within the federal government of the young United States. In the House of Representatives from Virginia 1799–1829, with a term in the senate and another term out of office in the interim. He remained a tertium quid, a political maverick who stood on principle, sometimes opposing the acts of his own party, then called Democrat-Republicans. The "of Roanoke" was tagged onto his name in 1810 to distinguish him from a relative of the same name who he hated. He declined mentally and physically in the years before his death in Philadelphia at 59. He was buried at Roanoke, his Charlotte County, Virginia, plantation, facing west as he wished, so he could "keep an eye on Henry Clay," with whom he had once fought an uneventful duel. Like James Monroe and Jefferson Davis, Virginia later sought to have him moved to Richmond. Reburied in December 1879 beneath a granite slab at an intersection atop a hillside. Southwest corner of sec. 16, Randolph Ave., Hollywood Cemetery, Richmond, VA.

7543. Randolph, John (Emanuel Cohen, June 1, 1915–Feb. 24, 2004) New York born actor with the Federal Theatre project in the 1930's and the Actors Studio after service in World War II was blacklisted in 1955 along with his wife, actress **Sarah Cunningham**, for championing leftist causes, but re-appeared in John Frankenheimer's *Seconds* (1966) and worked steadily afterward in films (*Serpico, Earthquake, Frances,* as Jack Nicholson's father in *Prizzi's Honor,* as Chevy Chase's father in *National Lampoon's Christmas Vacation,* Tom Hanks' grandfather in *You've Got Mail*) and on Broadway, winning a Tony as the communist, left-wing grandfather in Neil Simon's *Broadway Bound* (1987). His wife died from an asthma attack at the 1986 Oscar ceremonies. He retired by 2000, and died in Hollywood four years later at 88 from multi-infarct dementia. Cremated March 5 through Stricklin-Snively mortuary, his ashes were buried in the Theatricum Botanicum, Topanga Canyon, Los Angeles.

7544. Randolph, Lillian (Dec. 14, 1914–Sept. 11, 1980) African-American actress from Louisville, younger sister of Amanda Randolph, was a staple on radio as Birdie on *The Great Gildersleeve* 1941–1954, in films (*It's a Wonderful Life*) and on TV in *Amos 'n' Andy, The Great Gildersleeve*. She later played Sister Sarah in the 1977 TV miniseries *Roots* and turned up in *The Onion Field* (1979). Married name McKee. Plaque beside Amanda Randolph (Hansberry). Gentleness sec., lot 1054, Forest Lawn Hollywood Hills, Los Angeles.

7545. Randolph, Mary (Aug. 9, 1762–Jan. 28, 1828) Early American author of *The Virginia Housewife*, a cousin of the Virginia Custis, Randolph and Lee families and sister to Jefferson's son-in-law. When she died in 1828, George Washington Parke Custis allowed her burial on his estate at Arlington, Virginia. Her son, who she had nursed from near death, erected an elaborate stone surrounded by a brick wall, the first burial (sec. 45, special lot near Custis Walk, T-36) in what would become Arlington National Cemetery, Arlington, VA.

7546. Randolph, Wallace Fitz (June 11, 1841–Dec. 9, 1910) Brevet captain in the Civil War and brigadier general in the Spanish American War, retired a Major General. His grave is remarkable in that, having spent his career behind artillery pieces (cannons), he is marked by one, his bronze plaque atop the rear carriage of a 19th century cannon. Sec. 1, grave 132, Arlington National Cemetery, Arlington, VA.

7547. Rankin, Jeanette (June 11, 1880–May 18, 1973) Feminist, suffragette and pacifist, the first woman elected to the U.S. House of Representatives 1917–19, three years before the 19th Amendment giving women the vote. She served again 1941–43, the only member of congress to vote against U.S. entry into war, both in 1917 and 1941. In 1968, at 87, she led a march on Washington protesting U.S. involvement in Vietnam. She died in Carmel, California. at 92. Ashes scattered.

7548. Raphael (Raffaello Sanzio, April 6, 1483–April 6, 1520) Painter and architect of the Italian Renaissance period, best known for his Madonnas and his figures in The Vatican, bespeaking the Neoplatonic ideal of the human form. The Pantheon, Rome.

7549. Rapp, Barney (March 25, 1900–Oct. 12, 1970) Orchestra leader from the 1920's with Barney Rapp's New Englanders married his vocalist, Ruby Wright (*q.v.*), in 1936. They opened the Sign of the Drum nightclub in Cincinnati, where Doris Day, then

Kappelhoff, replaced Wright when she became pregnant. He later ran the Barney Rapp Agency there. Memorial Mausoleum, sec. E-28, D-2, Spring Grove Cemetery, Cincinnati, OH.

7550. Rapp, Danny (May 10, 1941–April 4, 1983) Lead singer with Danny and the Juniors; their hits were *At the Hop* and *Rock and Roll is Here to Stay* (1958). He was performing with the band on a reunion tour at the time of his death from a self inflicted gunshot wound at the Yacht Club Motel in Quartzite, Arizona. Parker mortuary in Parker, Arizona, shipped him to Earl mortuary in Blackwood, Pennsylvania., for burial. Unmarked. Sec. N, lot 38, path1, grave 2, New St. Mary's Cemetery, Bellmawr, NJ.

7551. Rappaport, David (Nov. 23, 1951–May 2, 1990) 3'11" actor from Hackney, London, shot himself in the chest in Laurel Canyon Park in the San Fernando Valley, California. Returned for burial to Waltham Abbey Cemetery, Essex, England.

7552. Rappe, Virginia (July 7, 1891/1895 [1895 on plaque]–Sept. 9, 1921) Starlet little known until she died from a ruptured bladder, allegedly raped by a drunken Roscoe "Fatty" Arbuckle with a bottle at the St. Francis Hotel in San Francisco during a Labor Day weekend party. Her reputation as a long time party girl, already suffering from disease, gradually came out and Arbuckle, who maintained his innocence until his death, was acquitted after three trials. Character references including Viola Dana and Buster Keaton believed Arbuckle entirely, and in later years the role of a Babina Maude Delmont in promoting the story to ruin Arbuckle became evident. Sec. 8/Garden of Legends, lot 257, near the pond, Hollywood Forever Cemetery, Hollywood (Los Angeles), CA.

7553. Rapper, Irving (Jan. 1, 1897–Dec. 20, 1999) Polish born film director in America first with the New York stage, as second director at Warners in the late 1930's, and on his own there in the 1940's, where he made such theatrical but memorable A films as *Now Voyager, The Corn is Green, Rhapsody in Blue* and *The Glass Menagerie.* He died at 102 in the Motion Picture Country Hospital, Woodland Hills, California. Cremated by Gardenside Funeral Service. Flush plaque with name and dates. Sec. B (Linden), lot 10, unit B, Maple Grove Cemetery, Kew Gardens, Queens, N.Y.C.

7554. Rasberry, Ted (Theodore Roosevelt Rasberry, Oct. 8, 1913–April 17, 2001) Negro Leagues player and owner played for the Grand Rapids Athletics from 1935, founded the Grand Rapids Black Sox in 1946, and bought the Kansas City Monarchs and the Detroit Stars in the 1950's, during the last few years of the Negro Leagues. Garden of the Apostles, lot 200C, grave 4, Chapel Hill Memorial Gardens, Grand Rapids, MI.

7555. Rasputin, Gregory (c.1865–Dec. 30, 1916) The Mad Monk from Siberia gained favor with Czarina Alexandra of Russia by relieving her son's hemophilia. Through his influence and, through her, his

hold on the Royal Family, he increased the growing public unrest that was then building toward revolution. Prince Felix Yussupov, husband of the czar's niece, attempted to kill him by luring him to the cellar at a party where the phonograph was playing loudly upstairs. He fed Rasputin poisoned cakes and wine, but the intended victim only became more lively; finally Yussupov shot him in the back, but he rose up and chased the prince outside, where he was shot twice more, once in the head. With help, Yussupov then wrapped and bound the body and dropped it in a hole in the ice in the River Neva, where (according to the story as it has been passed down) an inexplicably free hand rose out of the water as it disappeared. The body was found three days later, with drowning ruled as the cause of death. It was buried secretly in the Imperial Park at Tsarskoye Selo, now Pushkin, fourteen miles south of St. Petersburg. After midnight on March 22, 1917, revolutionary bands stole the body, cremated it and scattered the ashes.

7556. Rasputin, Maria (Maria G. Bern, March 27, 1899–Sept. 27, 1977) Daughter of the mad monk became a touring lion tamer through the 1930's and moved to L.A. Sec. H, lot 189, grave 1, North Walk Way. Rosedale Cemetery, Los Angeles.

7557. Rastelli, Philip "Rusty" (Jan. 31, 1918– June 24, 1991) Boss of the New York based Bonanno crime family. Bottom tier crypt. St. John's Cemetery, Middle Village, Queens, N.Y.C.

7558. Rath, Morrie (Morris Charles Rath, Dec. 25, 1886–Nov. 18, 1945) Second and third baseman with the Athletics, Indians, White Sox and Reds over six seasons from 1912 to 1920. As second baseman for the pennant winning Cincinnati Reds in 1919, he led the league in double plays and hit .264 with 29 RBI's. and was the lead off batter hit by White Sox pitcher Eddie Cicotte, his signal that the fix was on. He retired after 1920 and settled in Philadelphia, a suicide by gunshot at 58. Lawnview sec., lot 946, grave 3, Arlington Cemetery, Drexel Hill, PA.

7559. Rathbone, Basil (Philip St. John Basil Rathbone, June 13, 1892–July 21, 1967) British actor with crisp delivery, born at Johannesburg, South Africa. In films from the late 1920's, his villains include Mr. Murdstone in *David Copperfield,* the marquis in *A Tale of Two Cities* (1935) and Richard III in *Tower of London* (1939), as well as the over-the-top Baron in *Son of Frankenstein* (1939) and several swashbuckling devils destined for death, dispatched by Errol Flynn in *Captain Blood* (1935) and *The Adventures of Robin Hood* (1938), by Leslie Howard in *Romeo and Juliet* (1936), and by Tyrone Power in *The Mark of Zorro* (1940), though he was an expert swordsman in real life. Through the 30's and 40's he and his wife **Ouida Bergere** (Dec. 14, 1896–Nov. 29, 1974) were known for throwing some of Hollywood's more lavish parties. But it is as Sherlock Holmes, aided by Nigel Bruce's befuddled Dr. Watson, that he is best remembered, beginning with the period pieces *The*

Hound of the Baskervilles and *The Adventures of Sherlock Holmes* at Fox in 1939, and in twelve mysteries at Universal 1942–46, updated to the modern era. Rathbone had just returned from buying a recording when he died from a heart attack in the study of his apartment at 135 Central Park West in Manhattan. Services were held at St. James Episcopal Church in New York, where Cornelia Otis Skinner read Elizabeth Barrett Browning's *How Do I Love Thee* (from his wife), and the lines from Rupert Brooke: *If I should die, think only this of me, that there is some corner of a foreign field that is forever England.* As he wished, he was placed next to where his wife would later be, above ground, as he felt death was an ascension. Top tier, left side, Unit 1, tier K, crypt 117, Shrine of Memories Mausoleum, Ferncliff Cemetery, Hartsdale, NY.

7560. Rathbone, Clara Harris (1844/45–Dec. 24, 1883) and **Henry Reed Rathbone** (July 1, 1837–Aug. 14, 1911) accompanied the Lincolns to *Our American Cousin* the night Lincoln was shot. Eighteen years later, having lost his mind, Rathbone shot and stabbed his wife to death in Hanover, Germany. She was the daughter of New York Senator **Ira Harris** (May 31, 1802–Dec. 2, 1875). He was buried, with her family and the Rathbones, in Albany Rural Cemetery, Albany, New York. She however, (and he beside her some 30 years later, having been confined to an institution) went to the village cemetery near Hildesheim (south of Hanover), Germany. According to *The Haunted Major* by Gene Smith in *American History Magazine* (February–March 1994), they were disinterred in 1952 and their remains disposed of by the cemetery.

7561. Rathebe, Dolly (Josephine Kedibone, April 2, 1928–Sept. 16, 2004) The first acknowledged black South African singer, star of *Jim Comes to Johannesburg* (1949), the first film to portray urban Africans in a positive light, later appeared with James Earl Jones in *Cry, The Beloved Country.* For years the lover of a Sophiatown gang leader, she continued under apartheid to sing African, Jazz and popular music, moving to Capetown where she ran a shebeen, and in 1994, with South Africa's return to the commonwealth, sang at Westminster Abbey. She died in Mabopane from a stroke at 76. Roodepoort Cemetery, Soweto, South Africa.

7562. Rathmann, Dick (Jan. 6, 1924–Feb. 1, 2000) Race driver appeared in several Indianapolis 500's in the late 1950's and early 1960's. Brother of winner Jim Rathmann. It was Dick Rathmann's crash into the turn 3 wall at the beginning of the 1958 race which caused the wreck that killed Pat O'Connor. Rathmann died at 76. Block 71, sec. A, space 34, Melbourne Cemetery, Melbourne, FL.

7563. Ratoff, Gregory (April 20, 1897–Dec. 14, 1960) Russian director and actor from the Moscow Art Theatre and the Yiddish Theatre in New York, in Hollywood from the early 30's, playing foreign characters from villains (*Secrets of the French Police*) to sympathetic immigrants *Symphony of Six Million* 1932, *The Last Leaf* segment of *O. Henry's Full House* 1952). Directorial works include *Intermezzo* (1939). He died from a form of leukemia at a clinic in Solothern, Switzerland. Cremated there, his ashes were returned to the Universal Chapel in Manhattan. Semel Society, block 103, path 6, lot 102, grave 5, Mt. Hebron Cemetery, Flushing, Queens, N.Y.C.

7564. Rattenbury, Alma (Alma Victoria Clark, c. 1898–June 4, 1935) Native of Kenloop, British Columbia, a violinist and pianist who wrote music under a pseudonym, caused a stir when she took up with the older architect, **Francis Mawson Rattenbury**, who became her third husband and removed to the Villa Madeira near Bournemouth, England. In March 1934, at 36 having taken up with her 17 year old driver and mechanic George Stoner, she or Stoner (the latter by both their testimonies) bludgeoned her 67 year old husband to death. Both stood trial; she was acquitted, he was convicted and given a death sentence, though public opinion was heavily against her. She stabbed herself in the chest three times and fell dead into the River Stour at Christchurch near Bournemouth, never knowing Stoner's death sentence was soon commuted. The case was the subject of the 1987 film *Cause Célébre.* Her funeral brought out some 3,000 sightseers, climbing over tombstones despite police efforts to control them. She is unmarked, as is her husband (beneath a hydrangea bush) at Wimbourne Road Cemetery, Bournemouth, England.

7565. Rattner, Abraham (June 8, 1893–Feb. 14, 1978) Painter did several religious based works, notably *Victory — Jerusalem, the Golden,* commemorating the Six Day War. His black polished cylinder stone has his illegible scrawl across it in white. Green River Cemetery, East Hampton, Long Island, NY.

7566. Raubal, Geli (Angela Maria Raubal, June 4, 1908–Sept. 18, 1931) Adolf Hitler's niece and alleged mistress. After Hitler refused her permission to return to Vienna and resume voice lessons, she was found shot in the heart in her room. Though he was plunged into grief, rumors abounded that either Hitler had killed her or Himmler had done it for him. She originally had a headstone in the Central Cemetery in Vienna at Arkadengruft no. 9, opposite the entrance to the Lueger-Kirche, inscribed *Here sleeps our beloved child Geli. She was our ray of sunshine. Born 4 June 1908 Died 18 September 1931. The Raubal family.* The lease only ran to 1938, but it remained undisturbed until March 11, 1946, when the zinc coffin was exhumed and moved to area 23E, position no. 73 in the second row of small graves. In the 1960's the burial mounds were leveled, trees and bushes planted, and the old graves only identified through a diagram, with later plans to transfer all unmarked burials to a mass burial pit. Zentralfriedhof (Central Cemetery), Vienna.

7567. Raudnitz, Illa aka **Illa Roden** (Aug. 10, 1911–Nov. 30, 1996) Austrian actress (*Ein Sonntag im*

Sommer in Wien, 1934) married to actor John Banner for ten years. In the U.S. from 1936, she appeared on Broadway, and later taught dance in Los Angeles. Courts of Remembrance, wall crypt 6683, Forest Lawn Hollywood Hills, Los Angeles.

7568. Ravel, Maurice (Joseph-Maurice Ravel, March 7, 1875–Dec. 28, 1937) French composer (*Boléro*) never fully recovered from an auto accident in Paris in 1932. Buried beside his parents, off the main road to right of entrance, Levallois-Paret Community Cemetery, Levallois, Paris.

7569. Ravenscroft, Thurl (Thurl Arthur Ravenscroft, Feb. 6, 1914–May 22, 2005) Deep bass vocal performer from Norfolk, Nebraska, sang with quartets and did voices in Disney films but found fame as the voice of Tony the Tiger, the spokesman for Kellogg's Frosted Flakes from 1952 until his death. Among his many other mainstays was the song *You're A Mean One Mr. Grinch* in the 1966 Christmas perennial *How the Grinch Stole Christmas.* A resident of Fullerton, California, he recorded The Book of Psalms for the blind, and annually narrated *The Glory of Christmas* at The Crystal Cathedral, where he was interred after his death from prostate cancer at 91. Memorial Garden, Crystal Cathedral, Garden Grove, CA.

7570. Rawlings, Marjorie Kinnan (Aug. 8, 1896–Dec. 15, 1953) Novelist whose story *The Yearling* won the Pulitzer Prize in 1938. She lived at a farmhouse at Cross Creek, Florida, and was researching a biography of Ellen Glasgow when she died from a coronary thrombosis at 57 in St. Augustine, Florida. Grave marked by a granite slab. Antioch Cemetery, nine miles from her house, outside Cross Creek, FL.

7571. Rawlinson, Herbert (Nov. 15, 1885–July 12, 1953) Actor from Brighton, England, a lead in silents, did character parts with middle age. He died from lung cancer. Ashes in vaultage. Chapel of the Pines Crematory, Los Angeles.

7572. Ray, Aldo (Aldo Dare, Sept. 25, 1926–March 27, 1991) World War II navy frogman from Pen Argyl, Pennsylvania, in films of the 50's and 60's as bull necked toughs, in *We're No Angels, The Naked and the Dead,* many others. He died in Marinez, California, at 64. Mass at St. Rose Catholic Church in Crockett. His mother is buried at St, Joseph Cemetery in San Pablo, but he was cremated and scattered by the Neptune Society; his wishes were to have his ashes scattered at sea.

7573. Ray, Charles (Charles Edgar Alfred Ray, March 15, 1891–Nov. 23, 1943) Silent screen star played innocent heroes, brought from the stage by director Thomas Ince. His career faded with sound. He died from a jaw infection at 52. Unmarked. Whispering Pines lot 672, space 3, Forest Lawn, Glendale, CA.

7574. Ray, James Earl (March 10, 1928–April 23, 1998) Convicted assassin of Rev. Martin Luther King, arrested in London weeks after the murder in Memphis April 4 1968, recanted his confession and in later years was believed by many, including the King family, to have been the pawn of a larger conspiracy to have King killed. There was continuing pressure for a new trial when he died, still serving a life sentence, from liver disease in a Nashville hospital at 70. He reportedly wanted his ashes scattered on the FBI Building in D.C. but, according to his brother Jerry, resentful of the U.S. at the last, wished them scattered or buried near the grave of a great great grandmother (Fitzsimmons), the location undetermined, in Ireland.

7575. Ray, Johnnie (Jan. 10, 1927–Feb. 24, 1990) Emoting ballad singer of the 1950's with tear filled voice had hits with *Please Mr. Sun, Cry,* etc. He died in Los Angeles. Service and cremation through Forest Lawn. Ashes buried at Hopewell Cemetery, ten miles northwest of Salem in Yamhill County, OR.

7576. Ray, Man (Aug. 27, 1890–Nov. 18, 1976) Philadelphia born innovative painter and photographer in the Dada, abstract and surrealist movements of the 1920's and 30's. In Paris as an expatriate from 1921, he produced a few films but is best known for his striking photographs and experimentation with rayographs and various techniques including solarization techniques and negative prints. His unusual monument has the upright oval headstone at an angle at the head of the slab, with the epitaph *Unconcerned, but not indifferent.* Div. 7, Montparnasse Cemetery, Paris.

7577. Ray, Margaret Mary (1952–Oct. 5, 1998) Stalker made headlines several times from 1988–93 for repeatedly breaking into David Letterman's New Canaan, Connecticut. home, once taking his Porsche and identifying her child in the passenger seat as David Jr. Confined several times, though not vigorously prosecuted by Letterman, by 1994 she had transferred her obsession to astronaut Story Musgrave. On October 5, 1998, she walked onto the railroad tracks in her hometown of Hotchkiss, Colorado, and knelt in front of an oncoming train. She was 46. Cremated, her ashes were scattered in Colorado near Hotchkiss.

7578. Ray, Nicholas (Raymond Nicholas Kienzle, Aug. 7, 1911–June 16, 1979) Director from Galesville, Wisc., considered the consummate auteur (*They Live By Night* 1948, *In a Lonely Place* 1950, *Rebel Without a Cause* 1954), his protagonists often anguished misfits. He was the subject of *I'm a Stranger Here Myself.* Ashes sent from Westwood Memorial Park in west Los Angeles to the grave of his mother Lena Kienzle. She he is marked, he is not. Sec. 53, lot 248, Oak Grove Cemetery, LaCrosse, WI.

7579. Rayburn, Gene (Gene Rubessa, Dec. 22, 1917–Nov. 29, 1999) Game show host from Christopher, Illinois, son of Croatian immigrants, known for *The Match Game* during the 1960's and 70's, completing sentences with laughs from Nipsey Russell, Charles Nelson Reilly, etc. Rayburn had also done TV acting and summer stock. He died at 81 at the home of his daughter in Lynne in Gloucester, Massachusetts. A radio report stated he wanted no funeral and his ashes spread in the garden of his home at Beverly, MA.

7580. Rayburn, Sam (Jan. 6, 1882–Nov. 16, 1961) Mr. Sam, powerful Democratic Speaker of the House of Representatives 1940–47, 1949–53 and 1955–61. A congressman from Texas since 1912, he helped push through much New Deal legislation and was the confidante of presidents from FDR through (then Vice President) Johnson. He died from cancer at 79, the Speaker's chair in congress draped in black and his desk covered by a bouquet. Though quite possibly apocryphal, his last words were reported to have been "This is the damnedest thing that ever happened to me." At his funeral service, Truman, Eisenhower, Kennedy (then president) and Johnson sat side by side in the front pew of the First Baptist Church at Bonham, the last such gathering of chief executives until the Richard Nixon obsequies in 1994. Willow Wild Cemetery, Bonham, TX.

7581. Raye, Don (Donald MacRae Wilhoite, Jr., March 16, 1909–Jan. 29, 1985) Film composer and arranger wrote for many pictures, including *I'll Remember April* in *Ride Em Cowboy* (1942), *Alice in Wonderland* (1951), *Thunder Road,* many others. Cremated at Pierce Bros.' Chapel of the Pines Crematory, Los Angeles. Ashes to residence.

7582. Raye, Martha (Margaret Teresa Yvonne Reed, Aug. 27, 1916–Oct. 19, 1994) Singer, dancer, actress and comedienne, in films (*The Big Broadcast of 1938, Hellzapoppin, Keep 'Em Flying, Four Jills in a Jeep* and as the indestructible wife in Chaplin's *Monsieur Verdoux* 1947) and known for entertaining troops in World War II, Korea and Vietnam. Awarded the Jean Hersholt Humanitarian Award at the Oscars in 1969, and the Presidential Medal of Freedom in 1993. Ill with diabetes, she had lost a leg prior to her death at 78 in Cedars-Sinai Medical Center, Los Angeles. Buried October 22 by the Green Berets, who knew her as Colonel Maggie. Row 28, grave 780-B, Post Cemetery, Fort Bragg, Fayetteville, NC.

7583. Raymond, Gene (Raymond Guion, Aug. 13, 1908–May 3, 1998) New York born actor in second leads of the 30's and 40's, married to Jeanette MacDonald from 1937 until her death in 1965. Films include *Red Dust, If I Had a Million, Sadie McKee, Smilin Through* (1941, with McDonald), *The Locket, The Best Man* (1964), doing only TV after 1964. He died at Cedars-Sinai Med. Center in L.A. from pneumonia at 90 (listed as 89). Interred with MacDonald, right wall, Sanctuary of Heritage, Freedom Mausoleum, Forest Lawn, Glendale, CA.

7584. Raymond, Paula (Paula Ramona Wright, Nov. 23, 1924–Dec. 31, 2003) Actress from San Francisco in films from 1938 (*The Beast from 20,000 Fathoms, The Flight that Disappeared, Blood of Dracula's Castle*) and many television appearances 1949–1964 (*Perry Mason, M Squad, Hawaiian Eye, 77 Sunset Strip*). She died in Los Angeles at 79. Mausoleum, block 282, E-2, Holy Cross Cemetery, Culver City, CA.

7585. Raymond, Ray (c. 1893–April 19, 1927) *Ziegfeld Follies* and Broadway song and dance man married to **Dorothy MacKaye** (May 8, 1896/1899–Jan. 5, 1940) died after a brawl with her boyfriend, actor Paul Kelly. Kelly did two years in San Quentin, as did MacKaye for concealing evidence. Freed by the early 1930's, Kelly resumed his career, having married MacKaye. She was killed in a car wreck in 1940 in the San Fernando Valley. Cremated at Oakwood Memorial Park, Chatsworth, California, her ashes are in undisclosed or unidentifiable space there. Raymond is buried in the Masonic section, tier 2, space 116, Forest Lawn, Glendale, CA.

7586. Razaf, Andy (Andreamenentania Razafinkeriefo, Dec. 16, 1895–Feb. 3, 1973) Black lyricist and nephew of the Queen of Madagascar wrote the words for some 1,000 songs including *Ain't Misbehavin,' Honeysuckle Rose* and *In the Mood*. Near Tim Moore. Sec. V, lot 109, Rosedale Cemetery, Los Angeles.

7587. Read, Barbara (Barbara French Read, Dec. 29, 1917–Dec. 11, 1963) Brunette actress from Port Arthur, Canada, in films 1937–1942 (*Three Smart Girls, Make Way For Tomorrow, The Road Back, The Man Who Cried Wolf, The Crime of Dr. Hallett*), and from 1946–48 as Barbara Reed. Married to actor William Talman (*q.v.*) 1953–59, she was a suicide by gas at 45 in her home at 860 Fenway, Laguna Beach, California. Cremated at Melrose Abbey through Laguna Beach mortuary. Sanctuary of Devotion, niche 120, Melrose Abbey Memorial Park, Anaheim, CA.

7588. Read, George (Sept. 18, 1733–Sept. 21, 1798) Signer of the Declaration of Independence from Delaware, later President of the Continental Congress, senator and Chief Justice of Delaware 1793–98. Immanuel Churchyard, New Castle, DE.

7589. Reagan, Ronald (Ronald Wilson Reagan, Feb. 6, 1911–June 5, 2004) and **Nancy Davis Reagan** (born July 6, 1921) 40th President of the United States (1981–89), born in Tampico, Illinois, and raised in nearby Dixon, was a lifeguard and sports announcer before going to Hollywood. Married to actress Jane Wyman in the 1940's, he was divorced and married the future first lady in 1952. Both were in films, he from the late 1930's (*Dark Victory, Santa Fe Trail,* as George Gipp in *Knute Rockne All American, King's Row, The Hasty Heart, Bedtime for Bonzo, The Winning Team, The Killers,* his last, in 1964) and she from the late 40's (*The Next Voice You Hear, Night Into Morning, Donovan's Brain*). They co-starred in *Hellcats of the Navy* (1957). Nicknamed Dutch from his youth and The Gipper from the *Knute Rockne* film, he was a New Deal Democrat and Screen Actors' Guild head, became a Republican with the 1960's, campaigning for Barry Goldwater in 1964, and served as Governor of California 1967–1975. His defeat of Jimmy Carter in 1980 and subsequent term as president saw the revival of a tough anti-communist stance by Washington, leading indirectly, under the partial cooperation of Soviet Premier Gorbachev, to the tearing down of the Berlin Wall in 1989 and the dissolving of the U.S.S.R. with the 1990's. Affable and seldom showing his age, Reagan survived gunshot wounds in a March 1981 assassination attempt and colon cancer surgery in summer 1985. His last public appearance was at Richard Nixon's funeral in April 1994. The following October he announced he was suffering from Alzheimer's Disease and remained in increased seclusion until his death a decade later in his Bel-Air (Los Angeles) home at 93 years and 4 months, the longest lived of American presidents at the time. Gerald Ford passed him at 93 years and 5 months. Tributes with flags and his trademark jars of jelly beans were piled high outside Gates-Kingsley-Gates mortuary, Santa Monica, before he was taken to his library in Simi Valley, then to Washington for lying in state in the Capitol rotunda and funeral at the National Cathedral — attended, significantly, by former Soviet premier Gorbachev — with eulogies by former British prime minister Margaret Thatcher, former Canadian prime minister Brian Mulroney, and former and current President(s) Bush. Flown back to his library for interment at sunset Friday, June 11, he was buried in the middle of the night. The monument is constructed of Georgian gray granite, with a semi-circular wall behind it bearing Reagan's words: *I know in my heart that man is good, that what is right will always eventually triumph, and that there is purpose and worth to each and every life.* The gravesite is on the grounds of the Ronald Reagan Library, dedicated in 1991 at Simi Valley, California. Reagan's parents, **John Edward "Jack" Reagan** (July 13, 1883–May 18, 1941) and **Nelle Reagan** (July 24, 1883–July 25, 1962) were both from Fulton, Illinois. His parents eventually followed him to California, where both lived out their days. They saw him become a film star but neither saw his political rise to the top. Though his mother did not share his father's adherence to the Catholic faith, she is buried with him in a Catholic cemetery. New stones put down in 1991. Sec. R, lot 306, Calvary Cemetery, east Los Angeles. **Maureen Reagan Revill** (Jan. 4, 1941–Aug. 8, 2001) The only biological child of Reagan and Jane Wyman — another daughter died after birth and her brother Michael was adopted — served as a semi-spokesperson for Reagan and a buffer between his administration and liberal causes, supporting both abortion and the Equal Rights Amendment, though he did not. She made two unsuccessful bids for public office in California, and after her father was diagnosed with Alzheimer's Disease crusaded for its awareness and funding, even as she battled through her last five years the malignant melanoma from which she died at 60 in her Granite Bay, California, home near Sacramento. Calvary Catholic Cemetery, Citrus Heights, Sacramento, CA. *See also* **Loyal Davis.**

7590. Ream, Vinnie (Sept. 25, 1847–Nov. 20, 1914) Sculptor of Lincoln; he sat for her in the White House several times just before his death, although she was poor and an unknown. Her statue of him, commissioned in 1866 and completed in 1870, stands in the U.S. Capitol rotunda. Buried as Mrs. Lt. Richard Hoxie, her grave bears a bronze reproduction of her work Sappho, the poetess, atop the monument. Sec. 3, site 1876, grid T-16, Arlington National Cemetery, Arlington, VA.

7591. Reardon, Beans (John Edward Reardon, Nov. 23, 1897–July 31, 1984) Taunton, Massachusetts, born major league umpire for decades. When Casey Stengel, incredulous over calls, would pretend to faint, it was Reardon who fainted along with him. He died in Long Beach, California, at 86. Sec. G, lot 1048, grave 3, Calvary Cemetery, East Los Angeles.

7592. Reasoner, Harry (April 17, 1923–Aug. 6, 1991) Silver haired TV newsman, winner of three Emmys, best known for his fifteen years with *60 Minutes* 1968–1970 and 1978–1991, in the interim co-anchoring the *ABC Evening News* 1970–75. He retired from the program three months prior to his death from a blood clot to the brain complicated by pneumonia. He died at Westport, Connecticut, near his home at Norwalk. Returned to the town of his birth. White grave length slab with tilted bronze plaque at one end, near corner of section, right of center cemetery area. Union Cemetery, Humboldt, IA.

7593. Rebozo, Charles "Bebe" (Nov. 17, 1912–May 8, 1998) Close friend of Richard Nixon from 1950, the Tampa born son of Cuban parents headed Key Biscayne Bank. It was while vacationing with Rebozo in 1972 that Nixon learned of the break-in at the Democratic headquarters in the Watergate building. Rebozo died in Baptist Hospital, Miami, at 85. Burial at Woodlawn Park North Cemetery, Miami, FL.

7594. Red Jacket (c. 1755–Jan. 20, 1830) Chief of the Seneca Indian tribe in what became upstate New York. His name came from red coats given him by the British when he joined them against encroaching colonists during the American Revolution. He made peace with the settlers after the war and remained on their side during the War of 1812. The most powerful chief among the Seneca, his weakness for drink coupled with growing Christianity among the Indians had him deposed by 1827. He was buried on the Seneca reservation in what became part of Buffalo until 1884 when he was reburied in Forest Lawn. A tall pedestal supports a statue of him, arms upraised. On the pedestal are his words: *When I am gone and my warnings are no longer heeded, the craft and avarice of the white man will prevail. My heart fails me when I think of my people, so soon to be scattered and forgotten.* Island at front of sec. 12, Forest Lawn Cemetery, Buffalo, NY.

7595. Redden, Don (Levy Donald Redden II, Oct. 10, 1963–March 8, 1988) Louisiana State basketball great. Garden of Prayer, lot 88-A, near Pete Maravich, Rest Haven Gardens of Memory, Baton Rouge, LA.

7596. Redding, Otis (Sept. 9, 1941–Dec. 10, 1967) Soul singer died in the crash of his plane into Lake Minona at Madison, Wisconsin. His recording *(Sitting on the) Dock of the Bay* became his only #1 hit, released several weeks after his death. Services were held in the city auditorium at Macon, Georgia. He was interred in a marble sarcophagus in the front yard of his 500 acre estate, with a plaque later placed beside it inscribed *Ten thousand miles I roamed just to make this dock my home.* The Big O Ranch (private), thirty miles east of Macon at Round Oak, GA.

7597. Redenbacher, Orville (July 16, 1907–Sept. 19, 1995) Ebullient popcorn king from Brazil, Indiana, with a gleeful attitude about his whiter, fluffier popcorn in TV commercials during the last fifteen years of his life. He drowned in a whirlpool in his Coronado, California, condominium after suffering a heart attack at 88. He requested no services. Telophase Cremation Society. Ashes scattered at sea off the coast of San Diego September 21, 1995.

7598. Redgrave, Michael (March 20, 1908– March 2, 1985) Distinguished British stage and screen actor, knighted 1959. Films include *The Lady Vanishes* (1938), *Dead of Night* (1946), *Morning Becomes Electra* (1947, Oscar nomination). He also directed several plays and authored three books. Father of Lynn and Vanessa Redgrave. He died from Parkinson's Disease at 77. Services at Mortlake Crematorium in Richmond, West London. A wooden plaque was erected in St. Paul's, Covent Garden, near Ellen Terry, Edith Evans and May Whitty. The ashes were held at Mortlake until 1993, were then in the possession of his son Corin and were eventually sprinkled, on behalf of his widow and at the urging of his daughter Lynn, in the garden of St. Paul's, Covent Garden (The Actors' Church), London.

7599. Redmond, Liam (July 27, 1913–Oct. 28, 1989) Stout, balding Irish actor from Limerick in films in the U.K. and U.S. 1945–1975, including *23 Paces to Baker Street* (1956), *Curse of the Demon* (1958), *The Ghost and Mr. Chicken* (1966), *Moll Flanders* (1970), *Barry Lyndon* (1975). He died in Dublin at 76. Removed from Flanajan's funeral home, Dundrum, to mass at Church of the Sacred Heart, Donnybrook, and to Glasnevin Crematorium, Dublin. His daughter Muriel McAuley took the ashes home for disposition to Black Rock, County Dublin.

7600. Reed, Alan (Edward Bergman, Aug. 20, 1907–June 14, 1977) Burly character actor in films (*The Postman Always Rings Twice* 1946) and much radio, where he was the voice of poet Falstaff Openshaw, among others. Later the voice of Fred Flintstone in the original prime time cartoon series *The Flintstones* 1960–66. Body donated to Loma Linda Medical School, Loma Linda, CA.

7601. Reed, Bill (William Reed, Jan. 11, 1936– Oct. 22, 2004) Toronto born bass singer with the doo-wop quartet The Diamonds, who had hits with *Little Darlin'* (1957) and *The Stroll* (1958); the former, originally done by Maurice Williams and the Gladiolas, was given new life with Reed's talking bridge. He became a record promoter in Florida, where he died in Port St. Lucie at 68. Ashes picked up by his widow through All County Funeral Home and Crematory, Stuart, FL.

7602. Reed, Carol (Dec. 30, 1906–April 25, 1976) English director, knighted 1952. Films include *The Stars Look Down* (1939), *Odd Man Out* (1947), *The Fallen Idol* (1948), *The Third Man* (1949), *The Key* (1958), *Our Man in Havana* (1959), and *Oliver!* (1968), bringing him an Oscar and featuring his nephew, Oliver Reed. His stone is carved on top with daisies, a reference to his mother's house Daisyfield. Gunnersbury Cemetery, Kensington, west London.

7603. Reed, Donna (Donna Mullenger, Jan. 27, 1921–Jan. 14, 1986) Actress from Denison, Iowa, known for Frank Capra's *It's A Wonderful Life* (1946, as Mary Bailey), as Alma the prostitute in *From Here to Eternity* (AA, 1953), and as Donna Stone on TV's *The Donna Reed Show* 1958–66. She was briefly in the prime time soap opera *Dallas* before her death from pancreatic cancer at 64, survived by her husband Grover Asmus. Buried near Natalie Wood. Sec. D, lot 142, Westwood Memorial Park, west Los Angeles.

7604. Reed, Florence (Jan. 10, 1876–Nov. 21, 1967) Stage star from the turn of the century through the 1920's. Films include the 1934 *Great Expectations* (as Miss Haversham). She shares a plaque (listing 1880) with Blanche Yurka in the Actors Fund of America plot, Kensico Cemetery, Valhalla, NY.

7605. Reed, Jimmy (Sept. 6, 1925–Aug. 29, 1976) The Bossman of the Blues flourished in Chicago 1953–66 with 22 chart topping guitar and vocal numbers, influential in later rock groups. He died from alcoholism at 50. Flush stone with guitar. Sec N, lot 335, Lincoln Cemetery, Chicago, IL.

7606. Reed, John (Oct. 22, 1887–Oct. 17, 1920) Radical journalist who championed revolutionary causes joined the staff of the magazine *The Masses* and was first arrested in 1914 for helping to organize strikes. More arrests followed and he went to Russia to work for the Bolsheviks, dying there from kidney disease. The subject of Warren Beatty's 1981 film *Reds.* He was buried October 20 with the honored at the Kremlin Wall, Moscow.

7607. Reed, Jonathan (1827–Sept. 1905) One of the legends of the Cemetery of the Evergreens in Brooklyn is the Reed mausoleum, where Jonathan Reed kept a twelve year vigil by his wife's crypt, supposedly spending most waking hours there from her death in 1893 until his death in 1905. He arrived at 8 a.m. most days, placing his wife's belongings in the mausoleum, and frequently greeting visitors who stopped by. Gibron sec., Cemetery of the Evergreens, Brooklyn, N.Y.C.

7608. Reed, Oliver (Feb. 13, 1938–May 2, 1999)

Roguish actor from south London, nephew of director Sir Carol Reed, in exuberant, earthy or brutal roles in films for forty years, including the lead in *Curse of the Werewolf* (1961), as Bill Sikes in *Oliver!* (1968, directed by Carol Reed)), Ken Russell's *Women in Love* (1969), *The Devils* (1971), Richard Lester's *The Three Musketeers* (as Athos, 1973), Russell's *Tommy* (1975) and numerous others from *Burnt Offerings* (1976) to *Fanny Hill*. He was in Villetta, Malta, making his one hundredth film *The Gladiator*, produced by Steven Spielberg, when he fell ill in a pub, accompanied by his wife Josephine, and was pronounced dead from a heart attack at 61 before reaching the hospital. Burial May 8 in the churchyard across from O'Brien's, his favorite bar. Epitaph *He made the air move*. Bruhenny Churchyard, Churchtown (formerly Bruhenny), in the north of County Cork, Republic of Ireland.

7609. Reed, Philip (March 25, 1908–Dec. 7, 1996) Actor in films from the 1930's to the mid 60's, often as suave but shady characters (*Old Acquaintance, Song of the Thin Man,* several *Alfred Hitchcock Presents*). Garden of Honor, lot 7227, space 1, Forest Lawn, Glendale, CA.

7610. Reed, Robert (John Robert Rietz, Oct. 19, 1932–May 12, 1992) Actor from Illinois trained with the Royal Shakespeare Company had extensive stage and television experience but was best known, often to his regret, as the patriarch of TV's *The Brady Bunch* 1969–74. He died at 59 in Pasadena from intestinal cancer complicated by the HIV virus. Cremated at Mountain View Cemetery in Altadena, California, the ashes were returned to his daughter through Cabot and Sons mortuary in Pasadena. His stone next to his father and grandparents reads *Robert Reed 1932–1992. Good Night Sweet Prince,* with the masks of comedy and tragedy. Sec. 6 extension, lot 21, grave 4, Memorial Park Cemetery, Skokie (north Chicago), IL.

7611. Reed, Thomas Brackett (Oct. 18, 1839–Dec. 7, 1902) Republican congressman and senator from Maine, Speaker of the House from 1889. A powerful leader, he helped define new rules on voting, the speaker's power to silence dilatory motions, and pushed through considerable GOP legislation including the McKinley Tariff in 1890, earning him the title Czar Reed. He resigned in 1899 and died three years later in Washington, D.C. Large, squat monument with wreath, Elks sec., Evergreen Cemetery, Portland, ME.

7612. Reed, Walter (Sept. 13, 1851–Nov. 22, 1902) Bacteriologist with the U.S. Army Medical Corps isolated and found a remedy for yellow fever in Havana in 1898 during the Spanish-American War. He died from an appendicitis attack at 51. Sec. 3, site 1864, grid TU-16/17, Arlington National Cemetery, Arlington, VA.

7613. Reese, Jimmie (James H. Reese, Oct. 1, 1901–July 13, 1994) Member of the New York Yankees of the 1920's including the 1927 team, considered by many the greatest ever. Niche on north wall, Room of Prayer, Westwood Memorial Park, west Los Angeles.

7614. Reese, John Manifold (May 18, 1904–Feb. 1, 1990) He of the Cups and Pieces developed various chocolate products. Hershey Cemetery, Hershey, PA.

7615. Reese, Pee Wee (Harold Henry Reese, July 23, 1918–Aug. 14, 1999) Louisville native played shortstop with the Brooklyn Dodgers 1940–1957 and in L.A. 1958. The captain of the Boys of Summer, he became a hero of the civil rights movement when the Little Colonel put his arm over Jackie Robinson's shoulder as a show of friendship during a game at Crosley Field in Cincinnati in 1947, a gesture long remembered. He broadcast games with Dizzy Dean and later Vin Scully in the 1960's, then worked for Hillerich & Bradsby in Louisville. Hall of Fame 1984. He died from cancer at 81 in his home there. A 7' black monument shows both him and his wife. Sec. 11, lot 1182, Resthaven Memorial Park, Bardstown Rd., Louisville, KY.

7616. Reeve, Christopher (Sept. 25, 1952–Oct. 10, 2004) New York born actor raised in Princeton, New Jersey, had a role on the soap opera *Love of Life* from 1974 and appeared on Broadway before his physique and chiseled features won him the lead in the 1978 film *Superman*. Though a star, he eschewed blockbuster roles for thoughtful films including *Somewhere in Time, Deathtrap, The Bostonians* and *Remains of the Day,* but his career came to a halt in May 1995 when he landed on his head in a horseback riding accident at Culpeper, Virginia, which left him paralyzed from the neck down. Considered nearly hopeless at first, he learned to function in a wheelchair, to speak again, and eventually to direct films. Reeve's determination to make the best of his situation, to walk again, and to push tirelessly for increased research to fight spinal cord injuries brought him worldwide recognition and admiration. His death at 52 in Northern Westchester Hospital near his Pound Ridge, New York, home resulted from systemic infection caused by a pressure wound. A commemorative service was held October 12 on his property with words from Unitarian Universalist minister Frank Hall as well as actor-comedian Robin Williams. According to Hall in an October 14 *New York Post* article, the actor-activist was cremated and his wife Dana planned to scatter the ashes in the wind. She survived her husband less than a year; though a non-smoker, she died from lung cancer at 43 in March 2006.

7617. Reeves, George (George Besselo, Jan. 6, 1914–June 16, 1959) Actor, born at Woodstock, Iowa, and raised at Ashland, Kentucky, in films from 1939 (*Gone With the Wind*— as one of the Tarleton Twins in the first reel, *So Proudly We Hail* 1943, *From Here to Eternity* 1953) was famous in and as Superman and his alter ego, mild mannered reporter Clark Kent, on TV's *The Adventures of Superman* 1951–57. He was in his Benedict Canyon home with his fiancée and some house guests when he went upstairs without explanation and apparently shot himself at 45. The only possible cause mentioned at the time by his fiancée was lack of work. Speculation and rumor abounded that the wife of MGM executive Eddie Mannix had him killed in a jealous rage, but no conclusive evidence was produced to substantiate the story. His mother had his body sent to Spring Grove Cemetery in Cincinnati, Ohio, where some of her family were buried, and kept in a vault there pending another autopsy to prove the death was not a suicide; money was missing from his home and she did not accept the suicide verdict, but with no proof of murder, the body was removed from the vault at Spring Grove and cremated through Hillside Chapel in Cincinnati in February 1960. The ashes were sent to California, where his urn is next to that of his mother, Helen Besselo. Sunshine Corridor, Pasadena Mausoleum, Mountain View Cemetery, Altadena, CA.

7618. Reeves, Jim (Travis James Reeves, Aug. 20, 1924–July 31, 1964) Soft voiced Texas born country singer turned to music after he suffered an injury during spring training with the St. Louis Cardinals. A star of the Grand Ole Opry, he had many hits including *Mexican Joe, Bimbo, He'll Have to Go* and *Distant Drums.* He died in the crash of his small plane in a wooded area south of Nashville, Tennessee. Search parties took three days before finding the wreckage. He was returned to Texas and buried near his birthplace in Panola County, at a spot where he had often played while growing up. His statue stands atop a pedestal over the grave, inscribed *If I, a lonely singer, dry one tear, or soothe one humble heart in pain/ Then my homely verse to God is dear, and not one stanza has been in vain.* Jim Reeves Memorial Park, U.S. 79 three miles east of Carthage, TX.

7619. Reeves, Richard "Dick" (Richard Jourdan Reeves, Aug. 10, 1912–March 17, 1967) Burly character actor, former opera singer from New York, appeared, often as bullies, in *This is the Army* (stage and screen 1943), *Come Fill the Cup* (1951), *Target Earth* (1954), dozens of others and TV. He died from a liver ailment (cirrhosis) at 54. Veterans marker, Elm, lot 209, grave 4, Oakwood Memorial Park, Chatsworth, CA.

7620. Reeves, Steve (Jan. 21, 1926–May 1, 2000) Bodybuilder from Glasgow, Montana, won the Mr. America title in 1947, Mr. World in 1948 and Mr. Universe in both 1948 and 1950. His real fame came as *Hercules* and in a series of "sword and sandal" films made in Italy and distributed with dubbing in the U.S. He died from lymphoma at 74 in Escondido, California. Ashes scattered in Montana.

7621. Regan, Donald T. (Dec. 21, 1918–June 10, 2003) Wall Street financier served as Ronald Reagan's Treasury Secretary 1981–85 and Chief of Staff from 1985 until his ouster in February 1987 following a feud with the First Lady in which he charged that executive decisions were not un-related to Nancy Reagan's advice from her astrologer. While the presiden-

tial board of inquiry headed by John Tower reported that Regan was largely responsible for the Iran-Contra arms for hostages debacle, Regan claimed he had been made the scapegoat. He died from cancer at 84 in Williamsburg, Virginia. Ashes buried July 15. Sec. 35, grave 4953, Arlington National Cemetery, Arlington, VA.

7622. Regan, Phil (Philip Joseph Regan, May 28, 1906–Feb. 11, 1996) Irish tenor from Brooklyn in films of the 1930's and 40's known for singing *Happy Days Are Here Again.* Later involved in politics and a bribery conviction in 1973. Mausoleum 2, columbarium, block 5, row D, niche 2, Calvary Cemetery, Santa Barbara, CA.

7623. Reggiani, Serge (May 2, 1922–July 22, 2004) Italian born singer and actor in France from age eight was a mainstay in films from 1943 (*Le Carrefour Des Enfants Perdus, Les Portes De La Nuit, Manon, La Ronde, Casque d'Or, Napoleon, Act of Love, Paris Blues*) before becoming an acclaimed chanson singer in 1965, with *Sarah, Les loups sont entres dans Paris, La femme qui est dans mon lit.* Montparnasse Cemetery, Paris.

7624. Rehan, Ada (April 22, 1857–Jan. 8, 1916) Irish born actress associated with Augustin Daly's theatrical company in America, played often opposite John Drew. Best known for *The Taming of the Shrew* (1887). A large rectangular monument bears her name and death date. Sec. 145, lot 26963, along Border Ave., Greenwood Cemetery, Brooklyn, N.Y.C.

7625. Rehnquist, William (William Hubbs Rehnquist, Oct. 1, 1924–Sept. 3, 2005) The sixteenth Chief Justice of the Supreme Court, Milwaukee born, appointed associate justice by President Nixon in 1972 and moved to the top spot by President Reagan in 1986, guided the court in a conservative direction just as Earl Warren had moved it the other way. He focused on states' rights over federal adjudication, presided over the impeachment trial of President Clinton in 1999, and led the majority decision in *Bush v. Gore,* deciding the contested 2000 presidential election. Diagnosed with thyroid cancer in October 2004, he died eleven months later. Sec. 5, grave 7049-LH, Arlington National Cemetery, Arlington, VA.

7626. Reicher, Frank (Dec. 2, 1875–Jan. 19, 1965) German born director and actor in Munich until the turn of the century. He directed silent films for a few years, then returned to the stage before coming to Hollywood as a frequently seen character actor in supporting to bit parts in many films of the 1930's and 40's, including *King Kong* and *Son of Kong* (1933, as Captain Englehorn, with an uncharacteristic walrus mustache), *The Great Impersonation, Kind Lady, The Invisible Ray, Night Key Night Monster, The Mummy's Tomb, The Mummy's Ghost,* dozens of others as doctors, professors, etc. Sanctuary of Devotion, crypt N364, Golden West Mausoleum, Inglewood Park Cemetery, Inglewood, CA.

7627. Reid, Carl Benton (Aug. 14, 1893–March

15, 1973) Character actor in both stage and screen versions of *The Little Foxes* (1941) as Oscar Hubbard. He often played officials (*In A Lonely Place* 1950) and was a regular in the TV series *Burke's Law* in the early 1960's. Enduring Faith sec., lot 3722, Forest Lawn Hollywood Hills, Los Angeles.

7628. Reid, Daniel Gray (Aug. 1, 1858–Jan. 17, 1925) The Tin Plate King, international financier and owner of the American Tin Plate Co. started as a $12.50 a month messenger boy in Richmond, Indiana, where his philanthropy later built a church and hospital. He died in his 5th Avenue apartment in Manhattan. Service at St. Thomas Episcopal Church, attended by a throng of business associates including Bernard Baruch. Family mausoleum, sec. 7, Earlham Cemetery, Richmond, IN.

7629. Reid, Dorothy Davenport (March 13, 1895–Oct. 12, 1977) Actress, writer and producer, daughter of Harry Davenport and wife of Wallace Reid. After his death from drugs she made the film *Human Wreckage* (1923) and afterward was billed as "Mrs. Wallace Reid" or Dorothy Reid, producing films into the 1950's. Ashes mixed with Reid's. Black urn on pedestal, Azalea Corridor, Alcove B, Azalea Terrace (lowest level, near exit), Great Mausoleum, Forest Lawn, Glendale, CA.

7630. Reid, Sarah Addington (April 6, 1891–Nov. 7, 1940) Newspaper reporter wrote for the *Ladies Home Journal*, which published her *Pudding Lane* juvenile stories in the 1920's. She died in her Manhattan home at 49. Buried with her parents, northwest corner sec. 6, along the road, Earlham Cemetery, Richmond, IN.

7631. Reid, Wallace (April 15, 1892–Jan. 18, 1923) Silent screen matinee idol in wholesome roles from 1910. Following a head injury in a 1919 train wreck he became gradually addicted to morphine, first used as a pain killer. He collapsed in tears on a Hollywood set in 1922 and spent the rest of his days in a sanitarium until his death at 31. His death rocked the film industry, coming on the heels of the murder of William Desmond Taylor and the rape/manslaughter trial of Roscoe "Fatty" Arbuckle. The first film star at Forest Lawn, then only six years in existence, he was cremated and his ashes placed in a black urn on a pedestal in the Azalea Corridor, Alcove B, the Great Mausoleum, Forest Lawn, Glendale, CA.

7632. Reid, Whitelaw (Oct. 27, 1837–Dec. 15, 1912) Newspaper editor from Xenia, Ohio, was a correspondent with Horace Greeley's *New York Tribune* and managing editor from 1869. The *Tribune* maintained objective and factual news reporting, but in 1880 Reid supported the Stalwart wing of the Republican party and alienated President elect James Garfield. He was later Minister to France under Benjamin Harrison and Harrison's running mate on the losing 1892 ticket. Appointed Ambassador to Britain by Theodore Roosevelt in 1905, he died in London seven years later, as his son Ogden took over as editor of the

Tribune. Family mausoleum, Highland Ridge, Sleepy Hollow Cemetery, Tarrytown (Sleepy Hollow), NY.

7633. Reilly, Hugh (Hugh V. Reilly, Oct. 30, 1915–July 17, 1998) New Jersey born actor on stage, in films and TV best known as Paul Martin, Timmy's dad, in TV's second *Lassie* family (1958–64). He died in Burbank, California, from emphysema at 83. Ashes buried Sheltering Hills, lot 5176, space 4, Forest Lawn Hollywood Hills, Los Angeles.

7634. Reina, Gaetano (1889–Feb. 26, 1930) Boss of the New York crime family that evolved into the Luchese family ran operations in the 1920's until hit with a shotgun blast (allegedly by Vito Genovese) on a Bronx street, part of the beginning of the Castellammarese War. Both his boss, Joe Masseria, and his replacement, Joseph Pinzola, were murdered by the next year. Reina was the father-in-law of Joe Valachi. Woodlawn Cemetery, The Bronx, N.Y.C.

7635. Reinhardt, Django (Jean Reinhardt, Jan. 24, 1910–May 16, 1953) Belgian musician born to gypsies at Liberchien was a master of the jazz guitar, his dexterity complicated but unhindered after a fire in 1928 left only two fingers on his left hand with full mobility, from which he evolved a new fingering system. He was featured on the periphery of Woody Allen's film *Sweet and Lowdown*. At his peak in France in 1934, where he made many records with his Quintet, he later toured in England and with Duke Ellington, but retired in 1951 to the village of Samois sur Seine, France, where he died from a brain hemorrhage two years later. Black stone and grave length slab. Village cemetery, Samois sur Seine, France.

7636. Reinhardt, Max (Max Goldman, Sept. 8, 1873–Oct. 31, 1943) Austrian theatrical producer in Europe and New York brought out many talents in the German theatre and cinema of the 1920's. His only American film was *A Midsummer Night's Dream* (1935). He died in New York at 70. Community mausoleum of the Stephen Wise Free Synagogue (no inscription), Westchester Hills Cemetery, Hastings-on-Hudson, NY.

7637. Reis, Irving (Irving G. Reis, May 7, 1906–July 3, 1953) New York born director, writer and cinematographer, founder in the 1930's of CBS Radio's Columbia Workshop. Films as director include *One Crowded Night* (1940), *Footlight Fever* (1941), *The Gay Falcon, A Date with the Falcon, The Falcon Takes Over* (1942), *Hitler's Children* (1943), *The Bachelor and the Bobby Soxer* (1947), *All My Sons* (1948), *Dancing in the Dark* (1949). He died of cancer in Woodland Hills, California, at 47. Valley of Remembrance, Hillside Memorial Park, Los Angeles.

7638. Reiser, Pete (Harold Patrick Reiser, March 17, 1919–Oct. 25, 1981) Outfielder with the Brooklyn Dodgers 1940–48, the first rookie (1941) to win the NL batting title. Sec. C-12, lot 219, Desert Memorial Park, Cathedral City (Palm Springs), CA.

7639. Reisman, Leo (Leo Frank Reisman, Oct. 11, 1897–Dec. 18, 1961) Band leader of the 1920's through the 40's with the theme *What is This Thing*

Called Love?, recorded *Happy Days Are Here Again*, many others, and was credited with discovering both Eddy Duchin and Dinah Shore. He died in New York at 64. Handled through Riverside Chapel, his obituary noted he was to be cremated and had "whimsically suggested" that his ashes be scattered over Carnegie Hall.

7640. Reit, Seymour (Nov. 11, 1918–Nov. 21, 2001) Author and illustrator began *Casper the Friendly Ghost* in the early 1940's, the first drawings done by Joe Oriolo. Books include *The Day They Stole the Mona Lisa* (1981). Fairview Cemetery, Westfield, NJ.

7641. Rejane, Gabriella (June 6 1857–June 14 1920) Stage and screen actress Mme. Rejane appeared in France, England and in the U.S. in silent films. Div. 8, Passy Cemetery, Paris.

7642. Reles, Abe (1906–Nov 12, 1941) Killer with New York's Murder Inc., nicknamed Kid Twist, testified through 1940 and 1941 about the inner workings of the organization following an arrest in 1940. The terms "contract," "hit," "mark," etc. were first revealed to the world through his extensive accounts of numerous murders. Heavily guarded by detectives, he was held in a sixth floor room in the Half Moon Hotel at Coney Island, Brooklyn. Bed sheets tied together indicated an escape attempt when his body was found on the kitchen roof below his window, however the distance he was found lying out from the window and the improbability that he had a safe place to go pointed to murder and gave birth to the tag "the canary that could sing but couldn't fly." His testimony implicated many and sent Lepke Buchalter and six henchmen to the electric chair at Sing-Sing between 1941 and 1944. Sec. 1, line 12, grave 23, (Old) Mt. Carmel Cemetery #1, Glendale-Ridgewood, Queens, N.Y.C.

7643. Relf, Keith (William Keith Relf, March 22, 1943–May 14, 1976) Richmond, Surrey, born cofounder of The Yardbirds in 1963, which included at times Eric Clapton and Jimmy Page, had mainstream hits with *For Your Love* and *Heart Full of Soul*, *I'm A Man* (1965), *Shapes of Things*, *Over Under Sideways Down* and *Happenings Ten Years Time Ago* (1966), all fronted by Relf on vocals and harmonica. He went on to play with Medicine Head and Armageddon, but was electrocuted in his London home at 33 while playing or tuning his guitar. No water, drugs or alcohol were involved. Grave marked only by rose bushes and a flower pot. Block 21, grave 301A, along the road, Richmond Cemetery, Richmond, Surrey, at the southwest edge of London.

7644. Remarque, Erich Maria (June 22, 1898–Sept. 25, 1970) German author of *All Quiet on the Western Front* (1929) and *The Road Back* (1931). A naturalized American citizen, he divided his time between Hollywood, New York and Switzerland, where he died from heart failure at the St. Agnese Clinic in Locarno, survived by his wife, actress Paulette Goddard. Buried from the Catholic church in Ronco in the village cemetery overlooking Lake Maggiore. They have plaques in a stone wall perpendicular to one another. Village cemetery, Porto Ronco, Switzerland.

7645. Rembrandt (Rembrandt Harmenszoon Van Rijn, July 15, 1606–Oct. 4, 1669) Dutch painter lived in Amsterdam from age 23 until his death. Works include *The Anatomist Nicholas Tulp and His Pupils* (1632), *Christ at Emmaus* (1648) and *The Cloth Syndics* (1661), the landscape *The Mill* and over forty portraits of himself. The leading name among the Dutch masters. Buried in a church grave, efforts to locate his exact burial site as recently as Fall 1989 did not produce results. A carved oval plaque in the wall commemorates his burial somewhere beneath Der Westerkirk, Amsterdam.

7646. Remick, Lee (Dec. 14, 1935–July 2, 1991) Blonde actress from Quincy, Massachusetts, called "the thinking man's sex symbol" graced *A Face in the Crowd* (1957), *Anatomy of a Murder* (1959), *Experiment in Terror* (1962), *The Days of Wine and Roses* (1962, AA nomination), *Baby the Rain Must Fall* (1965), *No Way to Treat a Lady* (1968), *Tribute* (1981). Married to producer Kip Gowans. While filming a TV movie in 1989 she was diagnosed with lung and kidney cancer. Her last public appearance was April 29, 1991, at the unveiling of her star on the Hollywood Walk of Fame. She died two months later in her Brentwood home at 55. Private service and cremation through Westwood mortuary, Los Angeles. Her ashes were returned to the family in Brentwood.

7647. Remington, Frederic (Oct. 4, 1861–Dec. 26, 1909) Foremost painter and sculptor of the American west, notably of horses, which he also sculpted, with dedication to minute accuracy. His paintings and illustrations numbered in the thousands. He died at his home in Ridgefield, Connecticut. Sec. B, lot 115, Evergreen Cemetery, Canton, NY.

7648. Remsen, Bert (Herbert Birchell Remsen, Feb. 25, 1925–April 22, 1999) Actor from Glen Cove, New York, on stage, TV and in endless supporting roles in films, often as Irish cops or bartenders (*Brewster McCloud*, *Thieves Like Us*, *Jack the Bear*, *Only the Lonely*, *Independence Day*), TV movies *Crime of the Century* and *Lansky* etc. He died from a heart attack at 74 at home in Van Nuys, California. Ascending Dawn sec., block 5477, lawn crypt 4-A, Forest Lawn Hollywood Hills, Los Angeles.

7649. Renaldo, Duncan (April 23, 1904–Sept. 3, 1980) Actor in Latin hero roles from early talkies, including *Trader Horn* (1931). On TV as *The Cisco Kid* 1950–56. He died from lung cancer at Goleta, Ca. Sec. J, tier 6, grave 82, Calvary Cemetery, Santa Barbara, CA.

7650. Renaud, Madeleine *see* **Barrault.**

7651. Renault, Louis (Jan. 12, 1877–Oct. 24, 1944) French manufacturer of military equipment during the world wars also co-founded (1899) with his older brother **Marcel** (1872–May 24, 1903) the sports and small cars bearing his name. Marcel, killed in the first leg of a Paris to Madrid race, is in a polished black tomb, div. 3, Passy Cemetery, Paris. Louis is buried at Herqueville, France.

7652. Renavent, George (Georges de Cheux, April 23, 1894–Jan. 2, 1969) French actor in many films 1929–1952, often bits as spies, etc. (*Rio Rita, East of Borneo, Queen Christina, The Last Outpost, The Invisible Ray, Our Hearts were Young and Gay, Casablanca, The Catman of Paris*). Married to stage actress Selena Royle. He died in Guadalajara at 74. Zapopan Cemetery, Guadalajara, Mexico.

7653. Rennie, Michael (Aug. 29, 1909–June 10, 1971) Tall English actor played the visitor from outer space in *The Day the Earth Stood Still* (1951), warning world powers against further armed aggression, later starred other films (*The Lost World* 1960, *Ride Beyond Vengeance* 1966) and in the TV series *The Third Man*. He died while visiting his mother in Yorkshire, England. Buried beneath the family's large white cross. Harlow Hill Cemetery, Otley Road, Harrogate, Yorkshire.

7654. Reno Brothers   Frank (June 27, 1837–Dec. 12, 1868), **Simeon** (Aug. 2, 1843–Dec. 12, 1868) and **William Reno** (May 15, 1848–Dec. 12, 1868), along with their brothers Clinton and John, were Union veterans of the Civil War from Indiana who became a band of robbers and killers, staging the first U.S. train robbery of note at Seymour, Indiana, in October 1866. John was caught and sent to prison in 1867. The others were lynched by vigilantes in the jail at New Albany, Indiana, December 12, 1868. The bodies, less Clinton and John, have new veterans' markers in the lot, enclosed by an iron fence. The original military marker for William is now there also. Old City Cemetery, 9th and Ewing Streets, Seymour, IN.

7655. Reno, Marcus A. (Nov. 15, 1834–April 1, 1889) Major in the 7th Cavalry at the Little Big Horn led one of the Custer's two flanks prior to the attack by the Sioux. For not going swiftly to Custer's aid he was court-martialed in 1877, dying of cancer in 1889. In 1967 a review board reversed the discharge. He was removed after 1967 from Glenwood Cemetery in Washington, D.C. and reinterred in the Custer Battlefield National Cemetery. A Brevet Brigadier General, he is the highest ranking officer buried there. Sec. C, grave 1459, Little Bighorn/Custer Battlefield National Monument and Cemetery, Crow Agency, near Garryowen, MT.

7656. Renoir, Jean (Sept. 15, 1894–Feb. 12, 1979) French film director considered among the most creative cinema artists of the century, the son of painter Auguste Renoir, was born in Paris. He was best known for his 1937 film *Grand Illusion* and *The Rules of the Game* (1939, in which he also co-wrote the screenplay and directed). Renoir's work was a major influence on the so-called New Wave of French directors in the 1950's. He lived in Hollywood in the 1940's and in later years divided his time between Los Angeles and a Paris apartment. He died from a heart attack in Los Angeles and was given a state funeral in France, with burial beside his parents and brother, a circular plaque bearing a profile of him affixed to his father's monument at Essoyes in the Aube region southeast of Troyes and south of Paris.

7657. Renoir, Pierre-Auguste (Feb. 25, 1841–Dec. 3, 1919) French post–Impressionist painter spent his later years in a wheelchair painting at Cagnes on the Mediterranean. There, home and wounded from the war, his son Jean spent much time with him, and later (1962) wrote a memoir of his father. Renoir died at Cagnes and was buried in Essoyes beneath a monument with his bust atop it. On the front are plaques with profiles of both sons Jean and **Pierre Renoir** (March 21, 1885–March 11, 1952), an actor. Essoyes village cemetery in the Aube region, southeast of Troyes and south of Paris.

7658. Renwick, James, Jr. (Nov. 1, 1818–June 23, 1895) Architect of the original Smithsonian Institution (the castle), the Corcoran Art Gallery in Washington, and the massive St. Patrick's Cathedral in New York. Stone sarcophagus, Sassafras sec., Vine Ave., Greenwood Cemetery, Brooklyn, N.Y.C.

7659. Repp, Stafford (April 26, 1918–Nov. 6, 1974) Film actor in many cop roles best known as Chief O'Hara on TV's *Batman* 1965–67. Garden of Remembrance, sec. 279, space 1, Westminster Memorial Park, Westminster, CA.

7660. Resnick, Judith (April 5, 1949–Jan. 28, 1986) Mission specialist on the ill fated space shuttle Challenger had previously flown with shuttle flight 41D in 1984. A Ph.D. in electrical engineering from the University of Maryland, she was formerly with Xerox Corp., and a classical pianist from Akron, Ohio. After her death in the Challenger explosion, a service was held at Temple Israel, 133 Merriman Road, Akron. NASA (or the family) reportedly retained the remains. There is a plaque in memory of the entire Challenger crew, in her honor, with John Gillespie MaGee's poem *High Flight*, in the chapel at Rose Hills Burial Park, Akron, Ohio. She is also commemorated where unidentifiable remains were interred, at the Challenger cenotaph. Sec. 46, grid O-23/24, Arlington National Cemetery, Arlington, VA.

7661. Resnover, Gregory (Aug. 12, 1951–Dec. 8, 1994) The last person to die in the electric chair in Indiana, before the death house at Michigan City changed to lethal injection, was executed for the 1980 murder of an Indianapolis policeman. Sec. 95A, lot 635, Crown Hill Cemetery, Indianapolis, IN.

7662. Reston, James B. (Nov. 3, 1909–Dec. 7, 1995) Scottish born journalist with the AP joined the *New York Times'* Washington bureau in 1941, remaining for 46 years, as bureau chief from 1953, executive editor in 1968 and associate editor 1968–1987. Two time Pulitzer Prize winner, for a 1944 expose on the conference planning the UN and for a 1956 series on America's lack of national purpose. Noted for his clarity of prose in reporting and his editorials. He died in

Washington, D.C. of cancer at 86. Service at St. Albans Episcopal Church in Washington. Private burial or scattering in a family area in the Rappahannock region of Virginia.

7663. "Resurrection Mary" The most famous of a wide variety of national cemetery specters has given dubious fame to Resurrection Cemetery in Justice, Illinois, a southwestern Chicago suburb in the Back of the Yards area. In life she was allegedly Mary Bregovy, 21, killed in an auto accident on Wacker Drive in Chicago March 11, 1934. The ghost reportedly walks along Archer Road by the cemetery or gets rides to the gates, where she disappears. She was first seen in 1939 and with increasing frequency since the cemetery renovation in the 1970's. The connection of the alleged specter to Bregovy may have been made in error decades ago, since she is said to be coming from a southwestside ballroom and is usually seen in December, whereas Bregovy was killed downtown and in March, yet the story has been attached to her for over sixty years. She is said to be in a term grave, an area later renovated and re-used. Unmarked. Sec. MM, grave 9819, Resurrection Cemetery, Justice, Illinois. Similar tales abound, with many variations on the story, including the 1965 Dickie Lee record *Laurie (Strange Things Happen)*, based in part on the "**Lavender**" story at Ramapo Cemetery, Ramapo, New York, and in several other locations.

7664. Rettig, Tommy (Thomas Noel Rettig, Dec. 10, 1941–Feb. 15, 1996) Juvenile actor in films from age nine including *The 5,000 Fingers of Dr. T* (1953) and *River of No Return* (1955), best known as Jeff Miller on TV's *Lassie* 1954–58. He later ran a computer software company. Found dead in his Marina Del Rey, California, home at 54 from an aortic aneurysm, he was cremated through Inglewood Park mortuary. Ashes scattered at sea 3 miles off Marina Del Rey February 26, along with the ashes of Rusty Hamer.

7665. Reuter, Paul Julius, Baron de (Israel Beer Josaphat, July 21, 1816–Feb. 25, 1899) Cassel born German pioneer in rapid news transportation fled Germany in 1848, settled in London in 1851 and began a cross channel telegraph the same year, supplying London newspapers by 1858 and thereafter setting numerous speed records in exporting news across the seas at a rapid rate, establishing Reuters news wire service, still operating over a century after his death, in his villa at Nice. Obelisk with draped urn, sec. 36, (west) Norwood Cemetery, London.

7666. Reuther, Walter (Sept. 1, 1907–May 10, 1970) President of the United Auto Workers from 1946, took over the CIO in 1952 and the two merged under his leadership, though he later led the 1968 split from the AFL-CIO by the UAW. He died in a plane crash. The ashes of he and his wife, marked by Japanese lanterns, were buried at the United Auto Workers Camp, Black Lake, near Onaway, MI.

7667. Revels, Hiram R. (Sept. 1, 1822–Jan. 16, 1901) A.M.E. minister, educator and Union soldier was the first black in the senate, appointed from Mississippi in 1870. 5' obelisk on lot, Hillcrest Cemetery, Holly Springs, MS.

7668. Revere, Anne (June 25, 1903–Dec. 18, 1990) New York born actress in *The Double Door* (1934) had a brief film career 1941–50, in *The Devil Commands, National Velvet* (AA,1944), *The Song of Bernadette* and *Gentleman's Agreement* (both AA nominations), *Dragonwyck, A Place in the Sun*. Blacklisted by the House Un-American Activities Committee in 1951 for taking the fifth amendment. Married to producer-director Samuel Rosen, she returned to films by the 1970's and lived at Oyster Bay, Long Island. Donated to medical research upon her death. Her ashes were later placed with her sister and brother-in-law. Stone wall of inscriptions facing the pond, Willow Pond sec., Mt. Auburn Cemetery, Cambridge, MA.

7669. Revere, Paul (Jan. 1, 1735–May 10, 1818) Boston blacksmith and silversmith might have been just a historical footnote but for Longfellow's poem immortalizing him and his midnight ride through Lexington and Concord, Massachusetts, on April 18, 1775, warning that the British were coming. Revere was not the only riding crier, and he was captured. After the war he returned to his craft and regularly wore Colonial uniforms until his death. A white monument to him is across the sidewalk from his original, weathered small stone, at the rear of Old Granary Burial Ground, downtown Boston, MA.

7670. Revier, Dorothy (Dorothy Velegra, April 18, 1904–Nov. 18, 1993) Silent and talkies vamp from San Francisco took her screen name from husband Harry Revier, in films from *The Broadway Madonna* (1922), *The Iron Mask* (1929), *The Black Camel* (1931), *Night World* (1932). Retired 1936. She died in West Hollywood at 89. Her plaque gives her birth as 1906. Guardian sec., lot 5004, space 1, Forest Lawn, Hollywood Hills, Los Angeles.

7671. Revson, Peter (Feb. 27, 1939–March 22, 1974) Son of cosmetics magnate **Charles Revson** (Oct. 11, 1906–Aug. 24, 1975), Peter Revson was a champion race driver, winner of the Grand Prix in both the U.S. and Canada in 1973. He was killed in a race the next year at Johannesburg, South Africa. Unit 9, alcove F, crypt near his father, main mausoleum, Ferncliff Cemetery, Hartsdale, NY.

7672. Revy, Richard *see* **Richard Ryen.**

7673. Rey, Alejandro (Feb. 8, 1930–May 21, 1987) Character actor in film and TV also directed. He appeared as Carlos Ramirez in *The Flying Nun* and had recently worked in *Moscow on the Hudson*. A native of Buenos Aires. He died from respiratory failure and pneumonia at 57. Sec. L, lot 403, grave 1, Holy Cross Cemetery, Culver City, CA.

7674. Rey, Alvino (Alvin McBurney, July 1, 1908–Feb. 24, 2004) Oakland, California, born musician and orchestra leader popularized the steel guitar, his specialty, from the early 1930's with Horace Heidt's Orchestra and his own bands from 1940, with many recordings (*Deep in the Heart of Texas, Cement Mixer*) and film music (including the soundtrack for *The Bat,* 1959). Married for sixty years to singer **Luise King** (Dec. 21, 1913–Aug. 4, 1997) of the singing King Sisters, he appeared with the King Family on their ABC television show for several seasons from 1965. He died in Sandy, Utah, at 95. King was buried at sec. D, s ½, lot 362, Cypress Lawn Cemetery, Colma, CA.

7675. Rey, Fernando (Fernando Arambillet, Sept. 20, 1915/1917–March 9, 1994) Spain's most prominent actor played the French drug king in *The French Connection* (1971) and was named best actor at Cannes in 1977 for *Elisa Vida mia.* He died from bladder cancer in Madrid. State funeral and burial there. Cementerio de la Almudena, Madrid.

7676. Reynolds, Adeline DeWalt (Sept. 19, 1862–Aug. 13, 1961) The oldest member of the Screen Actors Guild did not become a film actress until she was 78, in 1940. She came to films through the sponsorship of Blanche Yurka and had brief but colorful roles in *The Tuttles of Tahiti* (1942), *Son of Dracula* (1943), *Going My Way* (1944) and *A Tree Grows in Brooklyn* (1945) etc. She died in L.A. at 98. Cremated at Evergreen Cemetery, Los Angeles, through Armstrong mortuary. Ashes buried in unrecorded and unidentifiable space October 10, 1961 at Westwood Memorial Park, west Los Angeles.

7677. Reynolds, Allie (Feb. 10, 1917–Dec. 27, 1994) Yankee pitcher on six series winning teams 1947–54, the first A.L. pitcher to throw two no-hitters in a season, 1951. Sec. 2, lot 18, space 6, Memorial Park Cemetery, Oklahoma City, OK.

7678. Reynolds, Carl Nettles (Feb. 1, 1903–May 29, 1978) Baseball player in the Texas Leagues and the majors. Wharton City Cemetery, Wharton, TX.

7679. Reynolds, Frank (Nov. 29, 1923–July 20, 1983) Reporter from East Chicago was ABC White House correspondent from 1965, co-anchor and later *ABC News* anchor from 1978 until his death at 59 from bone cancer. Epitaph reads *A man who cared.* Sec. 7A, grave 180, Arlington National Cemetery, Arlington, VA.

7680. Reynolds, John F. (Jan. 20, 1820–July 1, 1863) Major General with the Union Army at Gettysburg on the first day, in command of Meade's left wing of three corps. Exposed to enemy fire, he was shot from his horse on the edge of McPherson's woods. Plot 590, Lancaster Cemetery, Lancaster, PA.

7681. Reynolds, Joshua (July 16, 1723–Feb. 23, 1792) English portrait painter of the 18th century captured many gentry of his day including his friend and intellectual inspiration, Samuel Johnson. First President of the Royal Academy of Art 1768. Knighted 1769. He lost his sight before his death. St. Paul's Cathedral, London.

7682. Reynolds, Marjorie (Marjorie Goodspeed, Aug. 12, 1917–Feb. 1, 1997) Actress in *Holiday Inn* (1942), *Ministry of Fear* (1944), *The Time of Our Lives* (1946) etc., co-starred in TV's *The Life of Riley* in the 1950's. The widow of Jon M. Haffen, she died in Manhattan Beach, California, at 79. Cremated through White-Day mortuary. Ashes returned to her daughter in Playa del Rey, CA.

7683. Reynolds, Quentin (April 11, 1902–March 17, 1965) World War II news correspondent noted for his reports from Berlin. He won a 1954 libel suit against Westbrook Pegler, who had accused him of anti–American sentiments. Marker with family name. St. Peter's., range E, grave 16, Holy Cross Cemetery, Brooklyn, N.Y.C.

7684. Reynolds, R.J. (Richard Joshua Reynolds, July 20, 1850–July 29, 1918) Founder of the R.J. Reynolds Tobacco Company in 1874 began the manufacture of chewing tobacco and was a pioneer in the marketing and promotion of cigarettes, from which he amassed a fortune. He died only months after moving into a newly built mansion, Reynolda House, at Winston-Salem, North Carolina. His son, **Smith Reynolds** (Zachary Smith Reynolds, 1911-July 5 1932), heir to the family fortune and the husband of torch singer Libby Holman, was fatally shot in the head during a party at Reynolda. An inquest failed to indict Holman, who was suspected. Whether suicide or murder was never determined. A large four columned monument marks the plot and the founder, with Smith among the slabs in front of the monument. Salem Cemetery, Winston-Salem, NC.

7685. Reynolds, Vera (Nov. 25, 1899/1905–April 22, 1962) Actress in films from Christie Comedies in 1920, retired in 1932, shortly after *The Monster Walks.* Married to actor Robert Ellis. Unmarked. Mausoleum L, sec. 999, lot 26, (Pierce Bros.) Valhalla Memorial Park, North Hollywood, CA.

7686. Rhoads, Randy (Dec. 6, 1956–March 19, 1982) Guitarist with Ozzy Osbourne from 1979, known for his innovative fusing of classical with heavy metal, died in the crash of a small plane in Florida. Mausoleum near entrance, crypt, upper tier, Mountain View Cemetery, San Bernardino, CA.

7687. Rhodes, Billie (Levita Axelrod Collins, Aug. 15, 1894–March 12, 1988) San Francisco born early silent screen comedienne from 1913 at Kalem and in Al Christie comedies 1915–17. She returned to the stage and nightclubs after 1924 after a second marriage, to William H. Jobelman. Canaan 10, Mt. Sinai Memorial Park, Los Angeles.

7688. Rhodes, Cecil John (July 5, 1853–March 26, 1902) British imperialist in Africa from 1870 helped establish English rule there. He made a fortune from diamond mining by 1888 and in 1890 became prime minister of Cape Colony, extending the British empire and reducing Afrikaner influence in South Africa while promoting equality under the British flag. His British South Africa Co., set up in 1889, defeated the Ndebele and by 1893 controlled Southern and Northern Rhodesia, now Zimbabwe and Zambia, respectively. He bequeathed a part of his fortune for scholarships at Oxford but remained in Africa. Upon his death from a heart ailment at 48 he was placed in a granite tomb with a plaque inscribed *Here lie the remains of Cecil John Rhodes.* Though a 1970 attempt to remove him failed, political debate continues over removing him, a symbol to many of British oppression, for a shrine to indigenous religions. World's View, Matopos National Park, Matopos Hills near Bulawayo, Zimbabwe.

7689. Rhodes, Elisha Hunt (March 21, 1842–Jan. 14, 1917) Union soldier from Cranston, Rhode Island, served in the Civil War from First Bull Run through Appomattox, rising eventually to general. With Company D, 2nd R.I. Volunteers, he wrote vivid letters home and kept a diary, which were combined and published by his descendant Robert Hunt Rhodes as *All For the Union,* providing a first hand picture of the daily life of a Union soldier in and out of battle for the entire length of the war. He was active in government and the G.A.R. until his death. Sec. 416, lot 94, Swan Point Cemetery, Providence, RI.

7690. Rhodes, Erik (Earnest Sharpe, Feb. 10, 1906–Feb. 17, 1990) Small, mustached character actor played the naive co-respondent in *The Gay Divorcee* (1934), was equally confused in *Top Hat,* several others. He died in an Oklahoma City nursing home. Block 14, lot 24, grave A, El Reno Cemetery, El Reno, OK.

7691. Rhodes, James (Sept. 13, 1909–March 4, 2001) Ohio's only four term governor brought industry, highways and expanded education to the state but was remembered for his support of the National Guard in the killing of four students on the campus of Kent State University May 4, 1970. He was re-elected in 1974 and 1980 but defeated in 1986. Rhodes died in Columbus at 91. Chapel Mausoleum, right end hallway at eye level, Greenlawn Cemetery, Columbus, OH.

7692. Riano, Renie (Aug. 7, 1899–July 3, 1971) Character actress in comedic roles in films (*Tovarich, Nancy Drew and the Hidden Staircase, Bachelor Mother, Whispering Ghost*) and much TV. Sanctuary of Remembrance, Westwood Memorial Park, west Los Angeles.

7693. Ribicoff, Abe (Abraham A. Ribicoff, April 9, 1910–Feb. 22, 1998) Democratic congressman from Connecticut., the first Secretary of Health, Education and Welfare 1961–63, resigned to serve in the senate after the retirement of Prescott Bush. Protesting policy in Vietnam at the 1968 convention, Mayor Daley attempted to shout him down. Ill with Alzheimer's disease, he died at 87 in the Bronx. Marked by a curved bench at Cornwall Cemetery, Cornwall, CT.

7694. Ricca, Paul (Felice DeLucia, 1897–Oct. 11, 1972) Naples born Chicago based gang leader known as The Waiter — he had managed the Bella Napoli Cafe for Diamond Joe Esposito — gained his primary notoriety with the Hollywood extortion cases of the 1940's; he briefly followed Frank Nitti in overseeing the windy city's underworld before doing ten years in Leavenworth and again in 1959 for tax evasion. He was replaced by Tony Accardo. Mausoleum crypt, Queen of Heaven Cemetery, Hillside, IL.

7695. Rice, Alice Caldwell Hegan (Jan. 11, 1870–Feb. 10, 1942) Author of children's books, notably *Mrs. Wiggs of the Cabbage Patch* (1901), based on a poor neighborhood near her home in Louisville, Kentucky. She founded the Cabbage Patch Improvement League to help feed and clothe the needy. The book was a particular favorite of Eleanor Roosevelt's. Filmed in 1934. Sec. Q, lot 107, overlooking the lake, Cave Hill Cemetery, Louisville, KY.

7696. Rice, Dan (Daniel McLaren, Jan. 23, 1823–Feb. 22, 1900) Pioneer circus clown, the first one well known by the public, bought his own traveling show, both on wagons and a riverboat. Campaigning for Zachary Taylor in 1848, the candidate would ride with him, allegedly the basis for "jumping on the bandwagon." A friend of both Abraham Lincoln and Jefferson Davis, he financed the first Civil War veteran statue in his hometown of Girard, Pennsylvania. Sec. Z, row A, grave 32, West Long Branch Cemetery, West Long Branch, NJ.

7697. Rice, Edmund (Dec. 2, 1842–July 20, 1906) Weapons inventor of several bayonets was awarded the Medal of Honor for conspicuous bravery on the third day of the Battle of Gettysburg in a counter-charge against Pickett's troops in which he was wounded and taken prisoner. His grave in the southwest section of Arlington is a conspicuous boulder with a bronze facsimile of his Medal of Honor and his name and dates hand written on a star next to the medal. The star reads *The Congress to Lieut. Col. Edmund Rice 19th Mass. Volunteers for conspicuous bravery on the field during the Battle of Gettysburg.* Sec. 3, site 1875, grid T-16, Arlington National Cemetery, Arlington, VA.

7698. Rice, Florence (Feb. 14/15, 1907–Feb. 23, 1974) Actress from Cleveland, daughter of Grantland Rice, in films 1932–1943 (*The Marx Brothers At the Circus, Miracles For Sale*). Divorced from Robert Wilcox and remarried to Fred Butler, she died from lung cancer at 63 in Kaneohe, Hawaii. Cremated at Windward Crematory, Honolulu, through Williams mortuary, her ashes were scattered off the beach there, per her wishes.

7699. Rice, Grantland (Nov. 1, 1880–July 13, 1954) Sportswriter from Tennessee joined the *New York Herald Tribune* in 1914 and stayed until 1930, covering the many sports legends of the 1920's with flowing verse, bringing to his commentary a color and romanticism that included tagging the Notre Dame team the South Bend Cyclone and dubbing their backfield of 1924 The Four Horsemen of the Apocalypse. He succeeded Walter Camp at *Colliers* in selecting the All American football team and serving on the selection board until his death. His column *The*

Sportlight ran from 1930. He died shortly after the publication of his memoirs *The Tumult and the Shouting*. Family monument and headstone a short distance from the lot of Fiorello LaGuardia. Oakwood sec. along Alpine Ave., Woodlawn Cemetery, the Bronx, N.Y.C.

7700. Rice, Jack (Jack Clifford Rice, May 14, 1893–Dec. 14, 1968) Character actor in films 1933–63, including obnoxious Ollie in the *Blondie* films. Block (Memorial) C, sec. 2294, lot 6, Valhalla Memorial Park, North Hollywood, CA.

7701. Rice, John C. (John C. Hilburg, 1857–June 5, 1915) Comedian and actor born in Sullivan County, New York, on the stage and in early silent films, best known for *The Kiss* (1896) with May Irwin, the first titled and popular piece of filmed movement. He died at 57 (or 58) from Bright's Disease "after an illness of only two days" at the Hotel Majestic in Philadelphia while there to film a *Tillie* comedy with Marie Dressler. A resident of Mt. Vernon, New York, his funeral was held from the chapel of the Stephen Merritt Burial and Cremation Co. at 8th Ave. and 19th St., Manhattan, N.Y.C. Now out of business.

7702. Rice, Sam (Edgar Charles Rice, Feb. 20, 1890–Oct. 13, 1974) Washington Senators hitter from Morocco, Indiana, set a league record with 182 singles in 1925 and led the A.L. in hits with 216 in 1924 and 1926. Batted .350 his best year, 1925, with twelve hits in the World Series. Hall of Fame 1963. Cremated at Silver Spring, Maryland, the ashes went to lot 96, Woodside Cemetery, Haviland Mill Rd., Brinklow, MD.

7703. Rice, Stan (Nov. 7, 1942–Dec. 9, 2002) Dallas born poet and artist, married to gothic author Anne Rice, the former Anne O'Brien, with whom he had attended school. After teaching, he retired and opened Stan Rice's Gallery in New Orleans, where he died from cancer at 60. Funeral at Bultman mortuary. Holy Redeemer Corridor, crypt 5, tier B, Phase 1, All Saints Mausoleum, New Orleans.

7704. Rich, Buddy (June 30 or Sept. 30, 1917–April 2, 1987) Jazz drummer, a child prodigy, played from the 1930's with various big bands, leaving Harry James to go solo in 1966. He toured with his own band until the mid 70's and was still giving concerts until a few months before his death from a brain tumor which doctors had originally diagnosed as a stroke. Known for his hot temper and many fist fights, he later mellowed with his interest in the discipline of karate. He died at UCLA Medical Center at 69. The epitaph on his crypt is *One of A Kind*. Lower right, Sanctuary of Tranquility, Westwood Memorial Park, west Los Angeles.

7705. Rich, Charlie (Charles Henry Rich, 1859–July 7, 1929) Dealer who dealt aces and eights, since known as a Dead Man's Hand, to Wild Bill Hickok on Aug. 2, 1876 in Deadwood, South Dakota, just before Hickok was killed. A polished black monument with colored playing cards engraved on it was erected over the grave in 1989. Evergreen Cemetery, Miamiville (east of Cincinnati), OH.

7706. Rich, Charlie (Charles Allan Rich, Dec. 14, 1932–July 25, 1995) Colt, Arkansas, born vocalist, the Silver Fox bridged blues, country and western and pop music with hits *Behind Closed Doors* and *The Most Beautiful Girl* (1973). He died unexpectedly from a blood clot in the lung during his sleep at a Holiday Inn in Hammond, Louisiana, while traveling. He and his wife are pictured on their flush bronze plaque. Fairlawn, lot 810, grave 12, Memorial Park Cemetery, Poplar Ave., Memphis, TN.

7707. Rich, Irene (Irene Luther, Oct. 13, 1891–April 22, 1988) Buffalo born Broadway and screen actress in mature woman-of-the-world parts, in *Beau Brummel* (1924), *Craig's Wife* (1928), *The Champ* (1931). Radio program *Dear John* 1932–1942. Later in *The Mortal Storm* (1940), *Fort Apache* and *Joan of Arc* (1948). Married name Clifford. Cremated by Santa Barbara Cemetery through McDermott-Crockett mortuary, Santa Barbara, California. Ashes buried at sea.

7708. Rich, Lillian (Jan. 1, 1900–Jan. 5, 1954) English actress in silent films in America, frequently in B westerns and opposite Tom Mix, etc. She made a few appearances in sound films of the 1930's. Died in Woodland Hills, California. Burial filed under Lillian Rick. Block G, sec. 6856, lot 5, Valhalla Memorial Park, North Hollywood, CA.

7709. Richard, Louis (1869–July 12, 1940) Sculptor, credited with the lions guarding the New York Public Library, though they were finished in 1911 by Edward Clark Potter. St. Anthony's Church Cemetery, Nanuet, NY.

7710. Richard III (Oct. 2, 1452–Aug. 22, 1485) Last of the Plantagenet kings of England was made a villain largely through the writings of Shakespeare and Thomas More. The extent of his hunched back and the murder of the two princes in the Tower of London may also be all or partly fictional. Clubbed to death at the Battle of Bosworth Field by forces under Henry Tudor, the body was then taken naked to Leicester and buried at Grey Friars. When the monasteries were destroyed, his remains were thrown into the River Soar.

7711. Richards, Addison (Oct. 20, 1902–March 22, 1964) Character actor from Zanesville, Ohio, and the Pasadena Playhouse essayed many stern, often gruff roles in films 1933–64 (*The Walking Dead, Anthony Adverse, The Black Doll, Boys Town, Mystery of the White Room, The Mummy's Curse*). His flush marker, California Death Records, and the Social Security Death Index, list his birth year as 1902 but other sources say 1887. Listed as 61, he was taken initially to Forest Lawn, Glendale, California. Sec. 56, lot 1, space 7, Oak Park Cemetery, Clairmont, CA.

7712. Richards, Beah (July 1, 1920–Sept. 14, 2000) Vicksburg, Mississippi, born black actress in kind, dignified and insightful roles in *Guess Who's*

Coming To Dinner, Hurry Sundown, The Great White Hope, Beloved and others, plus TV appearances including *Roots: The Next Generation* and *E.R.* Suffering from emphysema, she was presented with an Emmy by actress Lisa Gay Hamilton for her last appearance, on ABC's *The Practice*, at her (niece's) Vicksburg home, days prior to her death there at 80. Initially to be buried at Tate Cemetery, Frontage Road, by her request, her ashes were scattered by Hamilton over Soldiers Rest, the Confederate soldiers' section at Cedar Hill Cemetery, Vicksburg, MS.

7713. Richards, Dudley (Feb. 4, 1932–Feb. 15, 1961) Figure skater partnered with Maribel Y. Owen; both were part of the 1960 Olympic team and the World Figure Skating team lost in the crash of their plane near Brussels, Belgium. Swan Point Cemetery, Providence, RI.

7714. Richards, Paul (Nov. 21, 1908–May 4, 1986) Baseball player, catcher and manager with the Braves, the Orioles and the White Sox. Sec. 4, lot 78A, Hillcrest Cemetery, Waxahachie, TX.

7715. Richardson, Elliot (July 20, 1920–Dec. 31, 1999) Secretary of health, education and welfare (1970–72), of defense (1972–73), and attorney general (1973) under Richard Nixon resigned the third post in October 1973 when he refused to fire special prosecutor Archibald Cox as ordered. He later served as ambassador to Great Britain and as secretary of commerce under Gerald Ford. Ill with Parkinson's Disease, he died at 79 from head trauma after a fall down stairs at his Wellesley, Massachusetts, home. Cremated through J.S. Waterman & Sons, Wellesley, at Mt. Auburn Cemetery, Cambridge, the ashes were picked up, reportedly to be scattered.

7716. Richardson, Henry Hobson (Sept. 29, 1838–April 27, 1886) Architect from Saint James Parish, Louisiana, considered the most innovative and influential designer of structures in the late 19th century. Among his noted works were Grace Church in Medford, Massachusetts, based on English Victorian models with pyramidal massing and rough faced granite, his house on Staten Island (1868), and the State Asylum at Buffalo, New York (1871–81). Later Romanesque works, with which he is particularly associated, include Trinity Church, Boston (1877) and Sever Hall at Harvard (1878), and among his last works Marshall Field's in Chicago (1885–87). Walnut Hills Cemetery, Brookline, MA.

7717. Richardson, J. P. "The Big Bopper" (Jiles Perry Richardson, Jr., Oct. 24, 1930–Feb. 3, 1959) Radio disc jockey rose to fame in 1958 with the record *Chantilly Lace*. He was killed in the crash of the small plane also carrying Buddy Holly and Ritchie Valens in an Iowa field en route to a concert date in North Dakota. Lily Pool Garden, block C, lot 31, space 3, Forest Lawn Cemetery, Beaumont, TX.

7718. Richardson, Lucy O'Donnell (c. 1957–June 1, 2005) The alleged inspiration for The Beatles' *Lucy in the Sky With Diamonds* was a girl John Len-

non's son Julian knew both through her family's jewelry and antique shop and an older school-mate at the Heath House School in Weybridge, Surrey. Julian's drawing of her, in the sky with diamonds, became one of the mainstays of the *Sgt. Pepper's Lonely Hearts Club Band* album in 1967. She became an art director for films until her death from breast cancer at 47. Her family sprinkled crystals on her grave at Weybridge, Surrey.

7719. Richardson, Ralph (Dec. 19, 1902–Oct. 10, 1983) Knighted English actor, prominent at the Old Vic in the 1930's and 40's, made many films starting with *The Ghoul* in 1933, *The Heiress* (AA nom, 1949), *Richard III* (1956, as Buckingham), *Long Day's Journey Into Night* (1962). Cast in well bred, upper crust roles, his film work was secondary to his theatrical eminence. A light beige slab over his grave is inscribed with his name and dates and *In treasured and tender memory.* East section, Highgate Cemetery, London.

7720. Richelieu, Armand Jean du Plessis, Cardinal et Duc de (Sept. 9, 1585–Dec. 4, 1642) Powerful cardinal ruled behind the throne of France during the reign of Louis XIII. He in many respects personified the theories of manipulative statecraft in Machiavelli's *The Prince.* His ornate tomb in the Chapelle de la Sorbonne bears a detailed sculpture of him surrounded by angels. The body was torn from the crypt during the French Revolution, but parts of it were gradually reinterred, the skull reportedly as recently as 1972. By other accounts, the Armez family held the face of the skull until it was reinterred December 15, 1866.

7721. Richler, Mordecai (Jan. 27, 1931–July 3, 2001) Canadian author chronicled Jewish life often with a wry and sarcastic bent, in *The Apprenticeship of Duddy Kravitz, Barney's Version*, several other works. Mount Royal Cemetery, Montreal, Quebec.

7722. Richman, Harry (Aug. 10, 1895–Nov. 3, 1972) Song and dance man in vaudeville, on Broadway and in films, with straw hat and cane. Alcove of Love B, Hillside Memorial Park, Los Angeles.

7723. Richmond, J. Lee (May 5, 1857–Oct. 1, 1929) Pitcher with Worcester, Massachusetts, was the National League's first left handed professional; he threw the first perfect game ever, against Cleveland in Worcester on June 12, 1880. Retired to Toledo, he was a doctor and teacher for forty years. A monument with his achievement and his stats was erected behind his simple brown headstone decades after his death. Sec. G, above Rose Garden, Forest Cemetery, Toledo, OH.

7724. Richmond, Kane (Frederick W. Bowditch, Dec. 23, 1906–March 22, 1973) Actor in films from the *Leather Pusher* series in 1930 through the early 50's. Sec. R, tier 31, Holy Cross Cemetery, Culver City, CA.

7725. Richmond, Warner (Jan. 11, 1895–June 19, 1948) Silent screen and B talkies actor from Culpepper, Virginia. (Pap in the 1931 *Huckleberry Finn* etc.) Chapel of the Pines Crematory, Los Angeles. Ashes to family.

7726. Richter, Charles F. (April 26, 1900–Sept. 30, 1985) Developer of the Richter Scale for measuring earthquakes. His unmarked grave has been marked by a monument company from Paducah, Kentucky, after visitors in 1996 found no stone there. Lot 3852, Mountain View Cemetery, Altadena, CA.

7727. Richter, Elizabeth (1840–April 12, 1923) Operator of a noted brothel made an additional fortune in real estate. A downcast marble maiden dominates her lot, where at least three of her girls reportedly also buried, though her stone, her parents and family are all that is grouped around the statue, which dates to a parent's death in the 1890's. It is said to have been an inspiration for the title of Thomas Wolfe's *Look Homeward Angel*, though biographies show he took the line from Milton. Sec. 103, lot 27–63, Woodland Cemetery, Dayton, OH.

7728. Richtofen, Manfred, Freiherr von (May 2, 1892–April 21, 1918) The Red Baron, Germany's terror of the skies during World War I with his Flying Circus, was credited with shooting down eighty enemy planes. Fatally shot behind French lines near Vaux-sur-Somme as his red Fokker DR-1 Triplane flew alone low along the Somme, pursuing Canadian Second Lt. Wilfrid R. May, Richtofen was shot either by Australian ground fire or — as most often claimed — by Canadian (Arthur) Roy Brown on his tail in a Sopwith Camel biplane. Both Brown and the Australians were firing the same type of bullets; only one pierced Von Richtofen's right side and exited his left side, tearing through his vital organs and causing loss of consciousness within sixty seconds. The nature of the wound and modern forensics and computerized timing and trajectory testing have tended to indicate that it was likely not Brown, who after firing from behind saw the Baron veer off to the right and head over the ground fire, but the Australians he then re-encountered in a u-turn who would have fired the unlikely but valid fatal shot, the likeliest candidate being "Snowy" Evans. Von Richtofen crashed near the Somme. Taken out of his plane, the Australians (according to their last survivor) heard only one word, "kaput," before he expired. He was buried first by Australian troops with military honors at Bertangles near Amiens, then at the German military cemetery at Fricourt, but was transferred in a state funeral in 1925 to Invaliden Cemetery (later in East), Berlin. Evidence later indicated that only the skull was transferred there. The rest of the skeleton from Bertangles was handed over to the military air attaché representing Germany in Paris in 1969 for return to Invalidenfriedhof. In 1976, East German plans to consolidate the border near the Berlin Wall necessitated the grave be vacated (the cemetery was subsequently abandoned, trashed, and the markers piled against a wall. Richtofen's stone was donated by his nephew Manfred to the Geschwader in Wittmund, where it was given a place of honor). At the family's request he was reburied in a plot with his mother (1962), brother and sister, reportedly at Mainz, western Germany, but actually near there at Wiesbaden, where his mother had fled in 1945 to live with her daughter. Family monument and headstones in a hedge surrounded lot, west of the main entrance, Westhain sec. Sudfriedhof, Wiesbaden. His brother, Oberleutenant **Lothar Freiherr von Richtofen** (Sept. 27, 1894–July 4, 1922), also a war ace, had forty downed planes to his credit. He was killed four years after the war while piloting an airliner. He was buried at Schweidnitz, Silesia, with their father (1920), but when the Soviets came through in 1945, the Red Army ploughed over the cemetery there. Both were later buried, with the mother (1962) at Wiesbaden along with Manfred. A cousin, **Wolfram Freiherr von Richtofen** (Oct. 10, 1895–July 12, 1945) served in the Red Baron's squadron, with eight downed planes by 1918. He survived the First World War, was chief of staff of the Condor Legion aiding the Nationalists in the Spanish Civil War in 1936, and commanded Air Fleet Four in Italy in 1945. Recipient of the Knights Cross and a generalfeldmarschall, he died at 49, following brain surgery in 1944. Buried first at Soldatenfriedhof in Bad Ischl, he was removed with others and reburied — with a plaque listing the names — near the middle of the local cemetery/ortsfriedhof, Bad Ischl, Austria.

7729. Rickard, Tex (George Lewis Rickard, Jan. 2, 1870–Jan. 6, 1929) Kansas City born sports promoter was the consummate showman of the 1910's and 20's, notably in his promotion of Jack Dempsey from 1919. In 1921 he staged the first million dollar gate with Dempsey and Carpentier. Subsequent title fights grossed over $10 million. He built and served as president of Madison Square Garden, the showcase for his fights. After his death in a Miami hospital following surgery for appendicitis, his $15,000 solid bronze coffin lay in the Garden, where 15,000 filed past. Juniper sec. on corner at Prospect Ave., Woodlawn Cemetery, the Bronx, N.Y.C.

7730. Rickenbacker, Eddie (Oct. 8, 1890–July 23, 1973) Counterpart of Richtofen; the leading American air ace in World War I, with twenty six planes to his credit. He later served in World War II, where he was forced down over the Pacific in 1942 and with seven others spent twenty days on a raft. He later owned a controlling interest in the Indianapolis Motor Speedway. He died in Switzerland at 82 and was cremated. The ashes are buried in the family lot, where a white marble monument bears a bronze plaque with his image and a record of his career engraved on it. Sec. 58, lot 31, Greenlawn Cemetery, Columbus, OH.

7731. Rickey, Branch (Wesley Branch Rickey, Dec. 20, 1881–Dec. 9, 1965) Founder of the baseball farm system, which he developed for the St. Louis Cardinals as business manager 1925–42 and with the

Brooklyn Dodgers as general manager 1943–50. He further revolutionized the game by signing Jackie Robinson as the first black player in the major leagues, with the Dodgers in 1947. Hall of Fame 1967. Buried not far from his birthplace, Stockdale, Ohio. Rush Township Cemetery, near both Rushtown and McDermott, OH.

7732. Rickover, Hyman (Jan. 27, 1900–July 8, 1986) Admiral called The Father of the Nuclear Navy commanded during and after World War II. Sec. 5, grave 7000, Arlington National Cemetery, Arlington, VA.

7733. Ricksen, Lucille (Lucille Ericksen, Aug. 22, 1909–March 13, 1925) Chicago born child and juvenile actress in silent films 1921–25 played Ginger in *Human Wreckage* (1923), Dorothy Davenport's ode to her husband Wallace Reid's death from drug addiction. Ricksen died at 15, the cause listed as pulmonary tuberculosis. Another version, related by Pauline Curley in her later years, attributed her death to a botched abortion, the result of her alleged pregnancy by Sidney Chaplin. The story has not been substantiated. Cremated at Rosedale Cemetery, Los Angeles, March 16, her ashes were interred December 27, 1929, in the Columbarium of Hope, niche 6707, Dahlia Terrace, Great Mausoleum, Forest Lawn, Glendale, CA.

7734. Riddle, Nelson (June 1, 1921–Oct. 6, 1985) Composer, conductor, arranger and orchestra leader appeared in many TV variety programs and recorded many top selling albums for Capitol Records with Frank Sinatra and Nat King Cole. Just prior to his death he made two LPs of standard Tin Pan Alley ballads with Linda Ronstadt. Corridor T-1 (New Beth Olam Mausoleum)/Hall of David, east wall, tier 7, 702, New Beth Olam Mausoleum, Hollywood Forever Cemetery, Hollywood (Los Angeles), CA.

7735. Ridgely, John (John Huntington Rea, Sept. 6, 1909–Jan. 18, 1968) Actor from Chicago in usually amiable roles, generally at Warners and most memorably for Howard Hawks, in the lead in *Air Force* (1943) and as Eddie Mars in *The Big Sleep* (1946). He died from a heart ailment in New York at 58. Columbarium of Independence, niche 34269, Freedom Mausoleum, Forest Lawn, Glendale, CA.

7736. Ridgely, Robert (Dec. 24, 1931–Feb. 8, 1997) New Jersey born actor with deep, resonant delivery first in TV's *The Gallant Men* (1962) did numerous cartoon voices and appeared in many film roles from the 1970's through the 90's, including *Blazing Saddles* (as Boris the hangman), *High Anxiety* (as the airport flasher), *Melvin and Howard, Something Wild, Beverly Hills Cop II, Life Stinks, Robin Hood: Men in Tights* (again as the hangman), *Philadelphia* and *Boogie Nights*, many others. He died from lung cancer at home in North Hollywood at 65. Cremated through Aftercare California Cremation and Burial Society, North Hollywood. Ashes to his family North Hollywood.

7737. Ridges, Stanley (July 17, 1891–April 22, 1951) Supporting actor of great versatility, long on stage and in films, including *Black Friday* (1940), *To Be or Not to Be* (1942), and in Robert Siodmak's *The Suspect* (1944) and *The File on Thelma Jordan* (1949). He died from a heart attack in Westbrook, Connecticut, at 59. Cremated at Springfield, Massachusetts, the ashes were returned to his wife in Westbrook, who left town some time later.

7738. Ridgway, Matthew B. (Matthew Bunker Ridgway, March 3, 1895–July 26, 1993) U.S. Commander led the 82nd Airborne and 18th Airborne Corps in Europe in World War II. His air strike on Sicily in 1943 was considered among the most crucial up to that time. In December 1950 he took command of the 8th Army in Korea and forced the halt of Chinese aggression, replacing MacArthur in 1951 as U.N. Commander. Promoted to four star general by Truman and to Supreme Commander of NATO 1952, Army Chief of Staff 1953 to 1955, when he retired. Presidential Medal of Freedom 1988. He died at 98 at his home in Pittsburgh. Sec. 7, grave 8196-1, Arlington National Cemetery, Arlington, VA.

7739. Riefenstahl, Leni (Helene Bertha Amalie Riefenstahl, Aug. 22, 1902–Sept. 8, 2003) Berlin born German film-maker, an actress in the 1920's, appeared in *Mountain of Destiny* (1926) and others before she added directing to starring, in *The Blue Light*. An admirer of Hitler, her films *Triumph of the Will* (1934), glorifying the Nazi rallies at Nuremburg, and *Olympia* (1936), a chronicle of the 1936 Berlin Olympics, were deemed then and later as masterful film compositions, but her affiliation with the Nazis was not forgiven after the war. Her one three year marriage to Major Peter Jacob ended in 1947; they had no children, and her only sibling died on the Eastern front. Under arrest for three years after the war, she lived with her mother and drifted into poverty. Her career resumed in the 1960s when she lived with and photographed the Nuba, then began scuba diving at 72 and photographing undersea life, releasing the film *Impressions Under Water* at 100. She died at 101 in the lakeside town of Poecking, Bavaria. Urn buried feld 509, Wald grab nummer 4, Waldfriedhof Neuer Tiel, Munich.

7740. Rigby, Eleanor (c. 1895–Oct. 1939) Wife of John Woods, age 44, and granddaughter of John Rigby. The family stone bearing her name is in the Liverpool cemetery adjoining the church where John Lennon met Paul McCartney at a rock and roll show July 6, 1957, so the story goes. Other reports on their meeting do not support this. Her stone was reportedly, in another likely apocryphal tale, the source of the Beatles' 1966 recording *Eleanor Rigby* (or a coincidence). St. Peter's Church Cemetery, Liverpool.

7741. Riggs, Bobby (Robert Larimore Riggs, Feb. 25, 1918–Oct. 25, 1995) Tennis player and impresario, the twenty one year old 1939 Wimbledon champion was known in later years for giving women's tennis its biggest boost after his defeat of Margaret Court by goading Billie Jean King into a Battle of the Sexes match in September 1973, which she won. He died from prostate cancer at 77 in Leucadia, California, a San Diego suburb. Private service and cremation through Encinitas mortuary. Ashes sent to Nassau Knolls Cemetery, Port Washington, Long Island, NY.

7742. Riis, Jacob (May 3, 1849–May 26, 1914) New York reporter whose photography and written exposes in *How the Other Half Lives* (1890) gave rise to an increasing cry for reform of slum conditions in large cities. His photographs remain startling in their depiction of filth and crowding. A cenotaph commemorates Riis near the entrance to the cemetery where an uninscribed boulder marks his grave. Riverside Cemetery, Barre, MA.

7743. Riles, Rosie (March 1, 1901–Dec. 1969) A model for the character "Aunt Jemima," for many decades gracing the front of pancake boxes, spent her last years in Cincinnati. A sign over her rose headstone and a gray granite monument with her laminated picture note her as *Aunt Jemima*. Redoak Presbyterian Church Cemetery, Redoak, Brown County, OH.

7744. Riley, James Whitcomb (Oct. 7, 1849–July 22, 1916) The Hoosier poet, born in Greenfield, Indiana, penned thousands of poems, most in rhyming sing-song style, including *Little Orphan Annie, The Raggedy Man, The Old Swimming Hole, Knee Deep in June*, etc. He spent his later years in a large house on Lockerbie Street in Indianapolis. Riley's tomb, with ten columns supporting an open rectangular roof, is at the crown, looking down over the hillside across the graves of Benjamin Harrison, Booth Tarkington, Eli Lilly and others, from the highest spot, top of sec. 61, Crown Hill Cemetery, Indianapolis, IN.

7745. Rimsky-Korsakov, Nikolai Andreyevich (March 18, 1844–June 21, 1908) Russian composer from Tikhvin, Novgorod province, one of the mighty five taught by Stasov, his nationalistic music was exemplified in his symphonic sketch *Sadko* (1867). Best known for his fifteen operas, including *The Snow Maiden* (1882) and his symphonic suite *Scheherazade* (1888). Tikhvin Cemetery, Alexandro-Nevskaya Lavra (Alexander Nevsky) monastery complex, St. Petersburg.

7746. Rinaldo, Frederic I. (Frederic Irwin Rinaldo, Sept. 27, 1913–June 22, 1992) Screen-writer, often in collaboration with Robert Lees (*q.v.*), at Universal 1936–1952, including *The Invisible Woman, The Black Cat, Hold That Ghost, Crazy House, Hit the Ice, Buck Privates Come Home, The Wistful Widow of Wagon Gap, Abbott and Costello meet Frankenstein, Abbott and Costello meet the Invisible Man, Comin' Round the Mountain*. Both he and Lees were blacklisted during the House Un-American Activities hearings. Rinaldo never wrote for films after 1952. His death certificate lists him as a paper supplyman. He died in Good Samaritan Hospital, Los Angeles, from shock after suffering a pulmonary embolism. Cremated through Pierce Bros. Westwood mortuary. Ashes buried in the ossuary (rose garden), Portal of the Folded Wings, Valhalla Memorial Park, North Hollywood, CA.

7747. Rinehart, Mary Roberts (Aug. 12, 1876–Sept. 22, 1958) American writer of mystery stories of the old dark house variety, from Allegheny, Pennsylvania, lived many years in Pittsburgh. Novels include *The Circular Staircase* (1908), *The Man in Lower Ten* (1909) and *The Bat* (1926), which was filmed at least three times. Her husband Stanley Rinehart was a U.S. Army doctor in Washington, D.C., where she lived until his death in 1932. She died 26 years later in New York City. Sec. 3, site 4269, grid X-17/18, Arlington National Cemetery, Arlington, VA.

7748. Ring, Blanche (April 24, 1876–Jan. 13, 1961) Turn of the century musical comedy star made a few silent films. Divorced from actor Charles Winninger. Unmarked. Sec. D, lot 28, Holy Cross Cemetery, Culver City, CA.

7749. Ring, Cyril (Dec. 5, 1892–July 17, 1967) Stage and screen actor in dozens of films (*The Cocoanuts* 1929). Brother of Blanche Ring. Sec. D, lot 10, Holy Cross Cemetery, Culver City, CA.

7750. Ring, Frances *see* **Thomas Meighan.**

7751. Ringling Brothers Founders of the second most famous traveling circus in America began in the 1880's, and later merged with Barnum and Bailey. The original founders were **Charles** (Dec. 2, 1863–Dec. 3, 1926) and his brother John. Charles was buried in a large octagonal beige mausoleum in sec. G, Manasota Memorial Park, Bradenton, Florida. **John** (May 31, 1866–Dec. 3, 1936) was buried in a mausoleum at Hackensack, New Jersey, until 1991, when he and his wife Mabel were moved to the garden behind an iron gate on his estate—which he had willed to the state of Florida—Ca' d'Zan, Sarasota, FL.

7752. Ringo, Johnny (John Peter Ringgold, May 3, 1850–July 13, 1882) Western outlaw, born in Greensfork, Indiana, and raised in Gallatin, Missouri, and San Jose, California, in dust-ups with the Earps and Doc Holliday in Tombstone, likely enlarged in posthumous legend. Wyatt Earp, Holliday, or Buckskin Frank Leslie may have put a bullet in his right temple where his body was found, sitting in the fork of an oak tree beside Turkey Creek, where he was buried, but a coroner's jury reported it a suicide. An unsubstantiated addendum states his sister had his bones removed from there and sent to an undetermined cemetery in or near San Jose, California. The accepted gravesite has an Arizona historical marker nearby. Along Turkey Creek near the Sanders Ranch, West Turkey Creek Road off 181, Cochise County in southeast AZ.

7753. Rinker, Al (Alton Rinker, Dec. 20, 1907–June 11, 1982) Vocalist brother of singer Mildred Bailey, with Harry Barris and Bing Crosby formed Paul Whiteman's Rhythm Boys 1927–30. Cremated at Grandview Memorial Park, Glendale, California, through Westwood mortuary, west Los Angeles. Ashes scattered in the mountains.

7754. Rinser, Luise (April 30, 1911–March 19, 2002) German political and social writer whose first novel *The Glass Rings* (1941) was suppressed as she was imprisoned in Traunstein by the Nazis; her diaries from her incarceration were published as *A Woman's Prison Journal*. Later works include her acclaimed *Jan Lobel From Warsaw* (1948), as well as various writings on Christianity and on the unnaturalness of celibacy, espousing the co-existence of spirituality and sexuality. She married and divorced composer Carl Orff prior to her death at 90. Burial at Wessobrunn in Upper Bavaria, Weilheim-Schongau, Germany.

7755. Rin-Tin-Tin (1916–Aug. 8, 1932) The original German Shepherd who became a hero of numerous silent screen adventures was found on a battlefield in France during World War I by his future trainer Lee Duncan. At his death he was buried beneath an onyx stone inscribed *Greatest Cinema Star* in the city's pet cemetery, now closed to further burials. Cimitiere du Chiens, Paris. The later Rin-Tin-Tin of the 1950's was returned to the owner at his home. A later one (1970–1986) is at the Los Angeles Pet Cemetery, Calabasas, CA.

7756. Rio, Frank (Frank Kline, June 30, 1895–Feb. 23, 1935) Capone gunman and bodyguard, an alleged assassin in the 1926 drive-by McSwiggan murder. He covered Capone in a Cicero restaurant later that year when it was sprayed with machine gun fire. He died at 39 in his Oak Park home from a heart attack, listed at the time as running a gas station, three years after his boss went to prison. Sec. 26, Mt. Carmel Cemetery, Hillside, IL.

7757. Riordan, Marjorie (Marjorie Jane Riordan, Jan. 24, 1920–March 8, 1984) Brunette actress from Washington, D.C., in films from the 1940's (*Stage Door Canteen, Mr. Skeffington* 1944, *Pursuit to Algiers* 1945, *Three Strangers* 1946). Buried with her husband Allan Schlaff. Sec. D, lot 1, Westwood Memorial Park, west Los Angeles.

7758. Riperton, Minnie (Nov. 8, 1947–July 12, 1979) Singer from Chicago with a five octave range, married to songwriter-producer Richard Rudolph, was known for her recording *Lovin You* in the spring of 1975. After a mastectomy in 1976, she was a spokesperson for the American Cancer Society. She died from cancer at 31. Her plaque is inscribed with the first line of her song and the tribute *Hers was a gift of love, a miracle of life, for all the world to see and hear forever.* Sec. D, lot 173, Westwood Memorial Park, west Los Angeles.

7759. Ripken, Cal, Sr. (Calvin Ripken, Dec. 17, 1935–March 25, 1999) Longtime Baltimore Oriole spent 36 years with the organization as a player, scout, coach and manager, helming the team in 1987–88 with 68–101. Father of Bill and Cal Jr. He died from cancer at 63. Service through Tarring-Cargo mortu-

ary at Grace United Methodist Church, Aberdeen, Maryland. Bakers Cemetery, Aberdeen, MD.

7760. Ripley, Robert L. (Dec. 25, 1893–May 27, 1949) Creator of *Ripley's Believe it or Not* in 1918 was originally a cartoon with facts sent in by his readers, it was later a feature on radio and TV. Several museums. Old section, Santa Rosa Memorial Park Cemetery, Santa Rosa, CA.

7761. Risberg, Swede (Charles Risberg, Oct. 13, 1894–Oct. 13, 1975) San Francisco born shortstop with the 1919 Chicago White Sox, one of the eight who agreed to drop the series to Cincinnati for $10,000 apiece. Risberg allegedly threatened to kill Joe Jackson if he talked, but Eddie Cicotte and others had already confessed. All eight were acquitted but were banned from major league baseball for life by Commissioner Kenesaw Mountain Landis. The last of the "eight men out," he died at Red Bluff, California, on his 81st birthday. Mount Shasta Memorial Park, Mount Shasta, CA.

7762. Risdon, Elisabeth (Aug. 26, 1887–Dec. 20, 1958) English born stage and screen actress, widow of silent screen director George Loane Tucker (dec. 1921), was in many kindly to snippy grandmother and aunt roles through films of the 30's and 40's (*Theodora Goes Wild, Five Came Back, The Roaring Twenties, Weird Woman,* many others). At her death, she was the widow of stage actor **Brandon Evans** (June 12, 1873–April 3, 1958). His ashes were placed in community vaultage at Inglewood Park Cemetery, Inglewood, California. She died from a stroke eight months later in Santa Monica. Donated to science at UCLA Medical School.

7763. Riskin, Robert (March 30, 1897–Sept. 20, 1955) New York born screenwriter penned many of Frank Capra's better films including *It Happened One Night* (1934, Academy Award), *Mr. Deeds Goes to Town* (1936), *Lost Horizon* (1937), *You Can't Take It With You* (1938) and *Meet John Doe* (1941). He worked for the Office of War Information during World War II and afterward formed his own company, making films (*The Thin Man Goes Home, Mr. 880*) which had a Capraesque flair for the whimsical. He suffered a clot to the brain in 1950 and was ill five years before his death at 57 in the Motion Picture Country Home in Woodland Hills, California. Married from 1942 until his death to actress Fay Wray. Sanctuary of Eternity, crypt L133, Mausoleum of the Golden West, Inglewood Park Cemetery, Inglewood, CA.

7764. Ritch, Steven (Dec. 26, 1921–July 20, 1995) Actor from Providence, Rhode Island, served five years with the 1st Marine Division in the South Pacific before beginning acting and later writing and directing. Best known as Duncan Marsh, the title role in *The Werewolf* (1956). He moved from L.A. to Oregon c 1989, where he lived at Rogue River until his death at Three Fountains Nursing Center in Medford at 73. A memorial service was held at Christ Unity Church in Medford. Cremated by Rogue Valley Funeral Alternatives in Grants Pass, Oregon, the ashes were picked up on July 24 by Mary Ritch.

7765. Ritchard, Cyril (Cyril Trimnell Ritchard, Dec. 1, 1897–Dec. 18, 1977) Australian born stage, screen and TV actor best known as Captain Hook to Mary Martin's *Peter Pan* on Broadway, televised in the 1950's. He died from a heart attack in Chicago. Under his name and dates on his monument is *Captain Hook.* St. Mary's Cemetery, Ridgefield, CT.

7766. Ritter, Dorothy see **Dorothy Fay.**

7767. Ritter, John (Johnathan Southworth Ritter, Sept. 17, 1948–Sept. 11, 2003) Actor son of Tex Ritter and Dorothy Fay, usually in likeable parts, best known as Jack Tripper on the sitcom *Three's Company* 1977–84, and in a long list of TV guest spots and recurring roles (*The Waltons* as Rev. Matthew Fordwick 1972–7, the minister in tennis attire who marries Ted and Georgette on *Mary Tyler Moore, Hooperman* 1987, *Anything But Love* 1989, *Hearts Afire* 1992, *Felicity* 2000–02), theatrical films (*The Stone Killer, Nickelodeon, The Comeback Kid, Problem Child* and its sequel, *Sling Blade, Tadpole, Manhood*) and many TV movies (*Letting Go, Unnatural Causes, It, The Dreamer of Oz, Holy Joe*) over a thirty year period. On the set of his series *8 Simple Rules for Dating My Teenage Daughter*, beginning its second season, he became ill and died that night at 54 in Providence St. Joseph Medical Center, Burbank, from what was identified as a dissected aorta. Marked March 2004, his epitaph is by the Beatles: *And in the end, the love you take is equal to the love you make...* Court of Liberty, lot 1622, near the wall, Forest Lawn Hollywood Hills, Los Angeles.

7768. Ritter, Tex (Woodward Maurice Ritter, Jan. 12, 1907–Jan. 2, 1974) Cowboy actor and singer in B westerns from the 1930's through the 60's, best known for his vocal *High Noon* in the 1952 film. Father of actor John Ritter. He died from a heart attack in Nashville, Tennessee. A Texas historical marker is near his flush bronze plaque, with a cowboy boot and hat on either side of his name. Sec. 8, Oak Bluff Memorial Park, Port Neches, TX.

7769. Ritter, Thelma (Feb. 14, 1905–Feb. 5, 1969) Actress on stage and screen for twenty years, in colorful performances ranging from comedy to drama. Nominated six times for an Oscar for best supporting actress (*All About Eve* 1950, *The Mating Season* 1951, *With a Song in My Heart* 1952, *Pickup on South Street* 1953, *Pillow Talk* 1959, and *The Birdman of Alcatraz* 1962). Also memorable in *Rear Window* (1954), and as Marilyn Monroe's partying companion in *The Misfits* (1960). She died from a heart attack in St. John's Hospital, Queens, N.Y.C. Services through Fox Funeral Home at the Congregationalist Church in the Garden. Cremated at Fresh Pond Crematory, Middle Village, Queens, the ashes were sent to her husband Joseph Moran in Forest Hills, Queens, N.Y.C.

7770. Ritz Brothers Al (Al Joachim, Aug. 27, 1901–Dec. 22, 1965), **Harry** (the leader, Harry Joa-chim, May 22, 1906–March 29, 1986) and **Jimmy** (Oct. 22, 1904–Nov. 17, 1985), a trio of brothers from Newark, worked their act through vaudeville and several films of the 1930's and 40's at Fox. The nightclub act ceased after Al's death from a heart attack in New Orleans. The other two appeared sporadically afterward, using a silhouette of Al on stage in his memory, until Jimmy's death from cancer twenty years later, followed four months later by Harry's death from heart failure. All three are interred in the T Building (New Beth Olam Mausoleum)/Hall of David, at the south end of the Abbey of the Psalms. Al is in T-4-1 (bottom row, crypt 1152); Harry in T-J-1-3 (3rd floor, 5th tier, crypt 7776), and Jimmy in T-J-1-1, 5th tier. Hall of David, Beth Olam Cemetery adjacent Hollywood Forever Cemetery, Hollywood (Los Angeles), CA.

7771. Rivera, Diego (Dec. 8, 1886–Nov. 24, 1957) Leading painter of the Mexican mural movement of the 1920's did contemporary scenes; his 1933 work in Rockefeller Center was destroyed because it contained a portrait of Lenin. He died of heart failure in his San Angel studio. Rotunda de los Hombres Ilustres in Panteon Dolores Cemetery, Mexico City, Mexico.

7772. Rixey, Eppa (May 3, 1891–Feb. 28, 1963) Eppa Jeptha, N.L. left handed pitcher with the Philadelphia Phillies 1912–1921 and the Cincinnati Reds 1921–1933. He led the league in victories in 1922, pitching until age 42. Hall of Fame 1963. Stone along road. Sec. 22, lot 7, Greenlawn Cemetery, Milford (east of Cincinnati), OH.

7773. Rizzo, Frank (Oct. 23, 1920–July 16, 1991) Philadelphia policeman, police commissioner and mayor through the 1970's. The controversial Rizzo was the best known city figure of his day. He was planning to regain the mayoralty when he collapsed in his office and died at Thomas Jefferson University Hospital. Holy Sepulchre Cemetery, Cheltenham, Cheltenham Township, northwest Philadelphia, PA.

7774. Rizzo, Jilly (May 6, 1917–May 6, 1992) New York restaurateur and close friend of Frank Sinatra's, a regular at his west side nightclub, Jilly's, which was worked into several Sinatra films. Rizzo died on his 75th birthday when his car was engulfed in flames after being broadsided by a hit-and-run driver in front of the Mission Hills Country Club in Rancho Mirage, California. The driver later returned and was charged. Same row, a few graves to Sinatra's left. Sec. B-8, Desert Memorial Park, Cathedral City (Palm Springs), CA.

7775. Roach, Bert (Egbert Roach, Aug. 21, 1891–Feb. 16, 1971) Chubby character actor in usually comedic roles in films from 1914 steadily through the 1940's (*The Crowd, The Last Warning, Murders in the Rue Morgue, The Thin Man, San Francisco*). Vaultage, Pierce Bros. Chapel of the Pines Crematory, Los Angeles.

7776. Roach, Hal (Jan. 14, 1892–Nov. 2, 1992) Pioneer comedy film producer from Elmira, New York, in films from 1912 created the Harold Lloyd films, *Our Gang* shorts and first put Laurel and Hardy together in two reelers in 1927. Unlike Mack Sennett, he stressed plot over slapstick. Among the serious features Roach later produced were *Of Mice and Men* (1939) and *Our Town* (1940). He died nine months after his 100th birthday in Los Angeles. Services at Westwood Memorial Park in west Los Angeles. Burial with his parents, where his stone reads *After leaving Elmira he found success in Hollywood and motion pictures, but always loved his hometown and has returned.* Sec. DD, lot 16, Woodlawn Cemetery, Elmira, NY.

7777. Roach, Hal, Jr. (June 15, 1918–March 29, 1972) Producer worked with his father on United Artists' *Of Mice and Men* (1939), *One Million B.C.* (1940). Our Lady's Garden Crypts, block 14, crypt 11A, Calvary Cemetery, east Los Angeles.

7778. Roach, Margaret (March 15, 1921–Nov. 22, 1964) Actress daughter of Hal Roach appeared in several films (*Swiss Miss, Fast and Furious* 1939, *Turnabout, Road Show* 1940, *Niagara Falls* 1941), sometimes billed as **Diane Rochelle**. She died after a long illness at 43. Married name Brady. Mausoleum, block 57, crypt F1, Calvary Cemetery, Los Angeles.

7779. Robards, Jason (Dec. 31, 1892–April 4, 1963) American stage star played many heroes in silents and character parts in sound films (Val Lewton's *Isle of the Dead* 1945, and *Bedlam* 1946). Father of actor Jason Robards. He died from a heart attack at 70. Remembrance sec., lot 975, Forest Lawn Hollywood Hills, Los Angeles.

7780. Robards, Jason (Jason Nelson Robards, Jr., July 26, 1922–Dec. 26, 2000) Actor son of the actor of the same name gained acclaim on Broadway in the 1950's in Eugene O'Neill's *The Iceman Cometh, Long Day's Journey Into Night* (filmed in 1962), *A Moon For the Misbegotten* and *The Disenchanted,* for which he won a Tony. In 170 films from 1959, including *A Thousand Clowns, Act One, Once Upon A Time in the West, Johnny Got His Gun, Comes A Horseman, Melvin and Howard, Reunion, Parenthood, Philadelphia, A Thousand Acres* and *Magnolia.* He won Oscars for *All the President's Men* (1976, as Ben Bradlee) and *Julia* (1977). Married to Lauren Bacall in the 1960's, he and his last wife Lois had lived "a quiet life on the water" for more than thirty years in the town of Fairfield, Connecticut, prior to his death from cancer in a Bridgeport hospital at 78. Cremated at Mountain Grove Cemetery, Bridgeport, through Shaughnessey mortuary in Southport. Ashes to his widow Lois at their residence in Southport, Connecticut, near Long Island Sound.

7781. Robbie, Joe (Joseph Robbie, July 7, 1916–Jan. 7, 1990) Owner of the Miami Dolphins, for whom the stadium in Miami, also used by the Marlins, was named. Sec. V (rear), Our Lady of Mercy Cemetery, Miami, FL.

7782. Robbins, Harold (May 21, 1916–Oct. 14, 1997) Best selling author known for his steamy novels *The Carpetbaggers, The Betsy,* etc. also penned *Never Love A Stranger* and *A Stone For Danny Fisher.* Mission San Luis Rey, niche 3 (book urn, below Phil Harris and Alice Faye), Palm Springs Mausoleum (now Forest Lawn), Cathedral City, CA.

7783. Robbins, Jerome (Jerome Rabinowitz, Oct. 11, 1918–July 29, 1998) Renowned New York born choreographer of over fifty ballets at the New York City Ballet in Manhattan also choreographed and or directed *On the Town, High Button Shoes, The King and I, The Pajama Game, Peter Pan, Gypsy, West Side Story* and *Fiddler on the Roof.* He won five Tony Awards, and an Oscar for the film *West Side Story,* which he co-directed with Robert Wise. He died from a stroke at his Manhattan home. Ashes scattered from his beach house on Fire Island.

7784. Robbins, Marty (Martin David Robinson, Sept. 26, 1925–Dec. 8, 1982) Country and pop crossover vocalist, star of the Grand Ole Opry. His hits included *A White Sport Coat and a Pink Carnation* and *El Paso* (1959). He died from a heart ailment in Nashville at 57. Bronze grave length tablet elaborately inscribed with his signature, tributes and quotations. Gethsemane, lot 15B, grave 3, Woodlawn Memorial Park, Nashville, TN.

7785. Rober, Richard (Richard Steven Rauber, May 14, 1906–May 26, 1952) Actor in films 1947–52 (*Call Northside 777, The File on Thelma Jordan, The Well, O. Henry's Full House*), died in a traffic accident at 46. Sec. 18, lot 87, Holy Sepulchre Cemetery, Rochester, NY.

7786. Robert, Yves (June 19, 1920–May 10, 2002) French director, writer and producer from Saumur appeared in many small roles prior to directing popular comedies and light hearted films, including *La Guerre des Boutons (War of the Buttons)* 1962, *Le Grand Blond Avec Une Chaussure Noire (The Tall Blond Man With One Black Shoe)* 1972, *La Gloire de Mon Pere (My Father's Glory)* and *Le Chateau de Ma Mere (My Mother's Castle),* both (from Marcel Pagnol's novels) 1990. Married to actress **Daniele Delorme**. He died in Paris at 81. Montparnasse Cemetery, Paris.

7787. Roberti, Lyda (May 20, 1912–March 12, 1938) Blonde Polish actress from Warsaw, former circus trapeze artist, veteran of vaudeville and Broadway. In Hollywood 1932–38 (*Million Dollar Legs, The Kid From Spain, College Rhythm, The Big Broadcast of 1936*). She died from a heart attack, reportedly at 26 while bending over to tie her shoe. Some sources list her birth as 1906, making her 31. Married name Ernst. Graceland sec., lot 1628, Forest Lawn, Glendale, CA.

7788. Roberts, Clete (Feb. 1, 1912–Sept. 30, 1984) Newscaster and war correspondent, appeared in a few films (*The Last Hurrah*). Oak Vale sec., lot 73B, Valley Oaks Memorial Park, Westlake Village, CA.

7789. Roberts, Floyd (Floyd Marion Roberts, Feb. 12, 1900–May 30, 1939) Winner of the 1938 Indianapolis 500 was killed in the 1939 event when he swerved to avoid driver Bob Swanson lying on the track; his car shot over a wall and caught fire. Sec. E, lot 227, grave 3, Oakwood Memorial Park, Chatsworth, CA.

7790. Roberts, Glenn "Fireball" (Jan. 20, 1929–July 2, 1964) Top stock car race driver had thirty two late model stock wins behind him when he died in a crash at Charlotte, North Carolina. His monument has his profile in bronze, with crossed checkered flags. Sec. B-7, lot D-2, Bellevue Memorial Park, Daytona Beach, FL.

7791. Roberts, Jim(my) (James R. Heltsley, April 6, 1929–Feb. 6, 1999) Vocalist from Madisonville, Kentucky, sang with Lawrence Welk's orchestra for twenty-six years, retiring in 1985 to Clearwater, Florida. He died at Largo Medical Center at 69. Hubbell mortuary and Crematory, Belleair Bluffs, Florida. Veteran Honor, Honor B, space 37, Royal Palm North Cemetery, St. Petersburg, FL.

7792. Roberts, Leona (Leona Doty, July 26, 1879–Jan. 29, 1954) Stage actress from Ohio in films 1937–1949 (*Of Human Hearts, Bringing Up Baby, Kentucky, Gone with the Wind* as Mrs. Meade, *The Blue Bird, Abe Lincoln in Illinois, Blondie Plays Cupid, Chicago Deadline*). She died in Santa Monica at 74. A widow, her last married name was Beck. Cremated February 1. Memory Hall, sec. L, niche P-18, Pierce Bros.' Chapel of the Pines Crematory, Los Angeles.

7793. Roberts, Lynne aka **Mary Hart** (Theda Mae Roberts, Nov. 22, 1922–April 1, 1978) El Paso born actress in films from 1938 at Republic, RKO, Fox (*Quiet Please, Murder*)—in many westerns as Mary Hart, retiring in 1953 after her third marriage. She was separated from her fourth husband, Don Sebastian, when she died after four months in a coma following a fall in her home December 16, 1977. Buried next to her mother. Sheltering Hills, lot 3203, space 4, Forest Lawn Hollywood Hills, Los Angeles.

7794. Roberts, Marguerite *see* **John Sanford.**

7795. Roberts, Rachel (Sept. 20, 1927–Nov. 26, 1980) Welsh actress on stage and screen (*This Sporting Life* 1963, AA nom.; *Picnic at Hanging Rock* 1975, *Murder on the Orient Express* 1976) died from an overdose of pills, a suicide at 53, found on a hillside behind her Los Angeles home. in her back yard. Cremated at Chapel of the Pines there, the ashes were given to Lindsay Anderson and kept in his London apartment until October 10, 1992, when they were spread in the Thames in London along with those of actress **Jill Bennett** (who had suggested it before her own suicide) from the ship *Connaught.*

7796. Roberts, Roy (March 19, 1906–May 28, 1975) Stout Florida born film (*My Darling Clementine, Gentleman's Agreement, Force of Evil, He Walked By Night, The Enforcer, House of Wax,* many others) and TV actor of the 1940's, 50's and 60's in blustery or bullying executive types in reportedly 1,000 films as mayors, sheriffs, back slapping and corrupt officials

and other unseemly characters. He died in Los Angeles at 69 from an aortic aneurysm. Sent from Callanan mortuary in Los Angeles. Flat plaque. Sec. 42, lot 314, Greenwood Memorial Park, Fort Worth, TX.

7797. Roberts, Theodore (Oct. 8, 1861–Dec. 14, 1928) Grand Old Man of the silent screen best known as Moses in DeMille's epic *The Ten Commandments* (1923). Rose-brown monument with the top in the shape of an open book or tablets. Sec. 13, lot 124, Hollywood Forever Cemetery, Hollywood (Los Angeles), CA.

7798. Robertson, John S. (John Stuart Robertson, June 14, 1878–Nov. 5, 1964) Film director from London, Ontario, turned out many films 1917–1935, notably *Dr. Jekyll and Mr. Hyde* (1920) with John Barrymore. Others include *Tess of the Storm Country* (1922), *The Enchanted Cottage* (1924), *Annie Laurie* (1927), *Beyond Victory* and *The Phantom of Paris* (1931), *Our Little Girl* (1935, his last). Married to Josephine Lovett (*q.v.*), he lived at Rancho Santa Fe, California, until his death in San Diego at 86. The Byrds' 1967 song *John Robertson,* which mentions his wife Jo, was reportedly inspired by bassist Chris Hillman's interest as a child in pictures of the director and his handle bar mustache. He was sent back to Canada through La Jolla Mortuary. Family obelisk. Sec. C, lot 220, Mount Pleasant Cemetery, London, Ontario.

7799. Robertson, Willard (Jan. 1, 1886–April 5, 1948) Character actor in many films 1930–1948, a stage actor, writer, director and attorney from Runnels, Texas, appeared often as detectives or lawyers (*Murder By the Clock, Behind the Mask, Dr. X, If I Had A Million, I Am a Fugitive From A Chain Gang, Tugboat Annie, Lady Killer, Supernatural, The Man Who Lived Twice, Winterset, Each Dawn I Die, Remember the Night, The Monster and the Girl,* many more). Robertson died from pancreatic cancer at 62 in Hollywood Presbyterian Hospital. Cremated April 8 at Rosedale Cemetery, Los Angeles, the ashes remained there until May 10, 1963, when they were mailed to "Memorial Hill Park, 503 San Jacinto, Austin, Texas." Not at Austin Memorial Park. The San Jacinto address was then the Memorial Hill office, according to Cook-Walden mortuary, which operates Memorial Hill Cemetery, off 35 north, Austin, Texas. No record.

7800. Robeson, Paul (April 9, 1898–Jan. 23, 1976) The son of a former slave was a graduate of Columbia Law School before gaining fame with his baritone singing voice, displayed with *Old Man River* in the 1936 film version of *Showboat.* Because of his left wing politics, the U.S. State Department withdrew his passport while he was out of the country in the 1950's. They later restored it. He died from a cerebral vascular disorder at Presbyterian Hospital in Philadelphia. On his plaque is an excerpt from a 1937 speech he made in support of the Loyalists in Spain: *The artist must elect to fight for freedom or slavery. I have made my* *choice. I had no alternative.* Hillcrest A, grave 1511, along walk, Ferncliff Cemetery, Hartsdale, NY.

7801. Robespierre, Maximilien (May 6, 1758–July 28, 1794) French reformer in the National Assembly from 1789, opposed to capital punishment, became a voice of the Revolution, justified the execution of imprisoned nobles and by September 1793 was a principle voice in the Reign of Terror. In the light of his subsequent laws and repression despite French military victories, he was arrested on July 27, 1794 and attempted suicide but was guillotined the next day. Buried at the Cimetiere des Errancis, in the 8th arrondisement, his remains with the many other executed persons there were removed into the Catacombes in the 14th arrondissement.

7802. Robi, Paul (Aug. 20, 1931–Feb. 1, 1989) Member of the 1950's vocal group The Platters, as noted on his marker. Enduring Faith, lot 4856, Forest Lawn Hollywood Hills, Los Angeles.

7803. Robin, Leo (April 6, 1895–Dec. 29, 1984) American lyricist wrote many standards including *Louise* (introduced by Maurice Chevalier in *Innocents of Paris* 1929), *Beyond the Blue Horizon* (Jeanette MacDonald in *Monte Carlo* 1930), *One Hour With You* (with Richard Whiting), *June in January*, a Bing Crosby standard, and won an Oscar for *Thanks For the Memory*, sung by Bob Hope and Shirley Ross in *The Big Broadcast of 1938* and Hope's theme from then on. Valley of Remembrance, crypt A-19-B, Hillside Memorial Park, Los Angeles.

7804. Robinson, Bill "Bojangles" (May 25, 1877–Nov. 25, 1949) Black tap dancer on Broadway and in films best known today for the staircase number with Shirley Temple in *The Little Colonel* (1935). He died from a heart ailment at 71 in Columbia Presbyterian Medical Center in New York. Services at the Abyssinian Baptist Church on west 138th St. in Harlem, with eulogies by Ed Sullivan and Adam Clayton Powell, Jr. Fans lined the streets as the church held only 300 of the 32,000 who turned out to say goodbye. A banner read "So Long Bill Robinson," "His feet brought joy to the world" was on the marquee at the Palace Theatre, and in Duffy Square a 30 piece band played *Give My Regards to Broadway* as the cortege moved through Manhattan to Brooklyn. His monument has a plaque with his face in bas-relief, and *Danced his way into the hearts of millions* as well as the line from Lincoln's second inaugural *With malice toward none. With charity for all.* Redemption sec., lot 1, Cemetery of the Evergreens, Brooklyn, N.Y.C.

7805. Robinson, Dar Allen (March 26, 1947–Nov. 21, 1986) Outstanding Hollywood stunt man known for 900 foot falls in spectacular death scenes. He died in a motorcycle accident in Arizona. Murmuring Trees, lot 8944, Forest Lawn Hollywood Hills, Los Angeles.

7806. Robinson, Edwin Arlington (Dec. 22, 1869–April 6, 1935) New England naturalist poet from Gardiner, Maine, met no success until his years at the McDowell Colony in Peterborough, New Hampshire, where he spent summers beginning in 1911. Much of his verse concerned Tilbury Town, modeled on Gardiner, his works noted for realism and some pessimism. Pulitzer Prize for *Collected Poems* (1921), *The Man Who Died Twice* (1924), and *Tristam* (1927). He died in New York City. Oak Grove Cemetery, Gardiner, ME.

7807. Robinson, Edward G. (Emmanuel Goldenburg, Dec. 12, 1893–Jan. 26, 1973) Rumanian born actor grew up in the Bronx and rose to fame in the theatre and then as tough cigar chewing gangsters in films from *Little Caesar* (1930) to *Key Largo* (1948), with many in between. Effective in many sympathetic and complex roles, including *Five Star Final* (1931), *Two Seconds* (1932), *Double Indemnity* (1944), *Scarlet Street* (1945), *Our Vines Have Tender Grapes* (1945), *The Stranger* (1946), *All My Sons* (1948), many others. Also a noted art collector and connoisseur. His last roles were as the dying grandfather in the *Night Gallery* episode *The Messiah on Mott Street* (1971) and as Sol in *Soylent Green* (1972). Dying of cancer in Mount Sinai Hospital in Los Angeles, he received a special Oscar for his lifetime of work shortly before his death. Goodman family mausoleum, three quarters around the first circle on the right and left of the sidewalk on right. Beth El Cemetery, Glendale, Queens, N.Y.C.

7808. Robinson, Edward G. Jr. (Nov. 15, 1933–Feb. 26, 1974) Son of Edward G. Robinson, appeared in *Screaming Eagles, Some Like it Hot*, etc. He died from natural causes in West Hollywood at 39. Corridor E-4, Abbey of the Psalms, Hollywood Forever Cemetery, Hollywood (Los Angeles), CA.

7809. Robinson, George H. (George Hiram Robinson, April 2, 1890–Aug. 30, 1958) Cinematographer did his best known work in Universal horror films and melodramas in the 1930's and 40's (*Dracula* [1931 Spanish version], *The Mystery of Edwin Drood, The Invisible Ray, Dracula's Daughter, Night Key, Son of Frankenstein, Tower of London, The Mummy's Tomb, Frankenstein Meets the Wolf-Man, Destiny, Son of Dracula, The Scarlet Claw, House of Frankenstein, House of Dracula, Abbott & Costello meet Dr. Jekyll & Mr. Hyde*). Mausoleum room E, crypt C-5, Pomona Cemetery, Pomona, CA.

7810. Robinson, Jackie (Jack Roosevelt Robinson, Jan. 31, 1919–Oct. 24, 1972) Landmark figure in the history of major league baseball was the first black player in the majors, hired by Branch Rickey to start the 1947 season with the Brooklyn Dodgers and bound by an agreement with Rickey to ignore the slurs, insults and name calling hurled at him for a three year period. First and second baseman and taunting base stealer, he was a slugger as well, leading the N.L. in 1949 with .342. He stayed until 1956 (leaving rather than be traded to the Giants) shortly before the fabled Boys of Summer were moved to Los Angeles. Hall of Fame 1962. Plagued in later years by ill health including diabetes, he died from a heart attack in Stamford, Connecticut. Buried with services conducted by Jesse Jackson not far from the site of Ebbets Field. In 1990 the flush marker over he and his son was replaced by individual stones in a landscaped enclosure and a monument with his signature inscribed *A life is not important except in the impact it has on other lives*. Sec. 6, across from the mausoleum, Cypress Hills Cemetery, Brooklyn, N.Y.C.

7811. Robinson, Mack (July 18, 1914–March 12, 2000) Older brother of Jackie Robinson, born in Cairo, Georgia, grew up in Pasadena and starred in the 1936 Olympics in Berlin, coming in second with the silver in the 200-meter dash, just behind Jesse Owens, humiliating Adolf Hitler, who left the stadium rather than present them with their medals. Robinson suffered a heart attack in 1990 and a stroke afterward, leaving him in ill health for the last decade of his life. Crypt in Vista Del Monte, Mountain View Cemetery, Altadena, CA.

7812. Robinson, Sugar Ray (May 3, 1921–April 12, 1989) Middleweight boxing champion of the 1950's, considered by many the best all around boxer ever. He died in Los Angeles at 67 from heart disease complicated by diabetes and Alzheimer's disease. Services conducted by Jesse Jackson with burial in Evergreen Cemetery, Los Angeles, but removed to Inglewood. A brown granite monument bears his picture and the title *Our Champion*. Pinecrest Addition, Inglewood Park Cemetery, Inglewood, CA.

7813. Robinson, Vicki Sue (May 31, 1954–April 27, 2000) Harlem born singer appeared in *Hair* and *Jesus Christ Superstar*, best known for her disco standard *Turn the Beat Around* (1976). She died from cancer at 45 in her home at Wilton, Connecticut, survived by her husband, William W. Good. Memorial service at the Unitarian Church in Westport. Cremated May 4 at Lakeview Crematory in Bridgeport through County Cremation Service, Fairfield. Ashes returned to her family in Wilton, CT.

7814. Robinson, Wilbert "Uncle Robbie" (June 29, 1863–Aug. 8, 1934) A .300 hitter and catcher with the feared Baltimore Orioles of the 1890's took over the team in 1902. He later coached for McGraw's New York Giants and managed the Brooklyn Dodgers from the time Ebbets Field was built (1913–14) until 1932, winning pennants in 1916 and 1920. Hall of Fame 1945. His monument gives his birth year as 1864. Sec. YY, lot 70, New Cathedral Cemetery, Baltimore, MD.

7815. Robison, Carson J. (Aug. 4, 1890–March 24, 1957) Singer, guitarist and whistler made many recordings over several decades. St. Joseph Cemetery, Millbrook, NY.

7816. Robson, Flora (Flora McKenzie, March 28, 1902–July 7, 1984) Acclaimed English actress from Durham in some sixty films and over 100 plays. Dame Commander of the English Empire 1960. Roles include as Elizabeth I in the film *Fire Over England* (1936), in *Wuthering Heights* (1939), the 1942 play *The Damask Cheek* by John Van Druten and in Leslie

Storm's *Black Chiffon* (1949). She never married. Plaque in St. Paul's Covent Garden, London. Cremated July 12, 1984 at Downs Crematorium, Bear Road in Brighton. Ashes buried in Saint Nicholas' Churchyard, Dyke Road, Brighton.

7817. Robson, Mark (Mark Rabinowitch, Dec. 4, 1913–June 20, 1978) Editor and director at RKO worked with Robert Wise editing *Citizen Kane* (1941); he also worked on *The Magnificent Ambersons* and edited *Cat People* (both 1942), before directing Val Lewton suspense films at RKO 1943–46 including *The Ghost Ship, The Seventh Victim, Isle of the Dead* and *Bedlam*. He later directed a wide variety of films including *The Bridges at Toko-Ri* (1955), *The Harder They Fall* (1956), *Peyton Place* (1957), *From the Terrace* (1960) and *Valley of the Dolls* (1967). In later years he was in partnership with Wise and Bernard Donnefeld. Robson suffered a heart attack while filming in Italy and died in a London hospital. Moses 27, lot 3812, Mt. Sinai Memorial Park, Los Angeles.

7818. Robson, May (Mary Jeanette Robison, April 19, 1858–Oct. 20, 1942) Actress from Melbourne, Australia, long on the stage, was memorable in many films of the 1930's as wise, feisty older ladies: *Lady For A Day* (1932, Oscar nomination), *If I Had a Million* (1932), as Granny in *A Star is Born* (1937) and in several B starring vehicles (*Grand Old Girl* 1935, *Granny Get Your Gun* 1940). She died in Los Angeles and was returned to New York for burial with her husband, Augustus Homer Brown. The stone, marked *Brown*, has their names and dates at the bottom. Sec 9, div. F, plot 9, Flushing Cemetery, Flushing, Queens, N.Y.C.

7819. Roche, Eugene (Sept. 22, 1928–July 28, 2004) Boston born actor known for his Ajax commercials in the 1970's, scrubbing away at pans, was a versatile character actor adept at comedy, drama, and villainy, on much television from 1958 and films from 1970 (*Cotton Comes to Harlem, Slaughterhouse Five, The Late Show* 1977, *Foul Play,* Pinky Peterson on TV's *All in the Family,* the landlord on *Webster,* Luther Gillis on *Magnum P.I.*). He died from a heart attack in an Encino, California, hospital, at 75. Service at St. Cyril of Jerusalem, Encino. Cremated at Valhalla Memorial Park, North Hollywood, through Praisewater mortuary. Ashes to his home.

7820. Rochefort, Joseph John (May 12, 1900–July 20, 1976) Chief code breaker for Admiral Nimitz at Pearl Harbor, broke the Japanese naval code JN-25, intercepting information regarding the upcoming Japanese attack on Midway, enabling Allied forces to prevail there and break the back of the Japanese navy, ensuring their eventual defeat. La Ramada plot, lot 742, Inglewood Park Cemetery, Inglewood, CA.

7821. Rock, Blossom (Blossom MacDonald, aka Marie Blake, Aug. 21, 1896–Jan. 14, 1978) Sister of singer-actress Jeanette MacDonald was a stage beauty who her sister followed into show business. She gave up acting early on except sporadically over the years as

Marie Blake until she resurfaced as Blossom Rock playing Grandmama on TV's *The Addams Family* 1964–66. Memory Slope, lot 1183, Forest Lawn, Glendale, CA.

7822. Rockefeller, John D. (July 8, 1839–May 23, 1937) Founder of the Standard Oil empire and of one of America's wealthiest families became the richest man in the country from his beginnings in Cleveland. The Supreme Court broke up the Standard Oil monopoly in 1911 but by then he was devoting much of his energy to philanthropy, giving some $500 million to various endowments and foundations. He died in Florida at 97. A towering obelisk marks the family lot and small individual markers. Sec. 10, Lakeview Cemetery, Cleveland, OH.

7823. Rockefeller, John D., Jr. (Jan. 29, 1874–May 11, 1960) Known primarily for his philanthropic support on various projects, he was the force behind the restoration of Colonial Williamsburg, Virginia, as well as Rockefeller Center in Manhattan, the USO during World War II and donation of the site for the United Nations after the war. His ashes were buried in the (private) Rockefeller Cemetery, Pocantico Hills, adjacent Sleepy Hollow Cemetery, Tarrytown, NY.

7824. Rockefeller, Nelson Aldrich (July 8 1908–Jan 26 1979) New York governor from 1958–1973 tried unsuccessfully for the Republican nomination for the presidency in 1960, 1964 and 1968. In 1974 he was chosen by President Ford to fill the remainder of the term as Vice President until January 1977. He died from a heart attack at 70 while in his office in Manhattan. Cremated at Ferncliff Cemetery, Hartsdale, New York. Ashes interred with his parents, John D. Rockefeller, Jr. and Abby Aldrich, in the (private) Rockefeller Cemetery, Pocantico Hills, adjacent Sleepy Hollow Cemetery, Tarrytown, NY.

7825. Rockefeller, William (May 31, 1841–June 24, 1922) Brother of John D. I, head of Standard Oil in New York City. Four columned mausoleum with a Greek frieze depicting the instruction of youth. Carmel sec. off Central Ave., Sleepy Hollow Cemetery, Tarrytown, NY.

7826. Rockefeller, Winthrop (May 1, 1912–Feb. 22, 1973) Son of John D. Jr. and brother of Nelson was two term Governor of Arkansas in the 1960's. Ashes on Petit Jean Mountain, Morrilton, AR.

7827. Rockne, Knute (March 4, 1888–March 31, 1931) Norwegian football coach at Notre Dame became an American sports legend as the football coach of the Fighting Irish 1918–30, losing only twelve games and with no losing years in thirteen seasons. He was on his way to California to make a film when his plane crashed in a field in Chase County, Kansas. A stone memorial was later erected at the crash site. Will Rogers and he were to appear together that night and Rogers went ahead with the show, telling jokes about Rockne with tears streaming down his face. Notre Dame team members were pallbearers in the first funeral covered on national radio. A monument

with a bronze plaque bearing his likeness, a replica of the monument at his birthplace in Norway, stands on an island by the section with his grave marker in the family plot. Highland Cemetery, South Bend, IN.

7828. Rockwell, Norman (Feb. 3, 1894–Nov. 8, 1978) The most popular American illustrator of the 20th century did most of his work as covers for the Saturday Evening Post, beginning in 1916. Among the more celebrated were *The Four Freedoms* done during World War II, many others. His specialty was capturing the spirit of America in a positive light, whether humorous, sentimental or poignant. His thin frame riding bicycles with his wife and the ever present pipe were familiar sights in Stockbridge, Massachusetts, his home town. Stockbridge Cemetery, Stockbridge, MA.

7829. Rockwell, Orrin Porter (June 28, 1813–June 9, 1878) Frontier lawman and gunman credited with over 100 killings, deputy marshal (1849) for the state of Deseret, was part of the attempted assassination of Governor Lilburn Boggs, issued extermination orders against early Mormons, and was later a bodyguard for Joseph Smith, Jr., and Brigham Young. C-77, Salt Lake City Cemetery, Salt Lake City, UT.

7830. Rockwell, Robert (Robert G. Rockwell, Oct. 15, 1916–Jan. 25, 2003) Actor best known as football coach Philip Boynton on radio's *Our Miss Brooks,* continued in the 1952 TV series and the 1956 film. He made numerous film appearances 1948–1995 and on television 1950–93. He died at 86 in Los Angeles. Cremated through Pierce Bros. Westwood. Ashes to family in Malibu, CA.

7831. Roddenberry, Gene (Eugene Wesley Roddenberry, Aug. 19, 1921–Oct. 24, 1991) Former pilot from El Paso created the TV series *Star Trek* (1966–69) from which sprang a massive and increasing cult following. He died at 70 in a Santa Monica Hospital after suffering a heart attack. Services were held at Forest Lawn Hollywood Hills' Hall of Liberty on November 1. The ashes were tentatively to be scattered in part at sea and in part over his home in Los Angeles, but were returned to his wife. According to an April 1994 news story, she had the ashes carried aboard the space shuttle into space. In January 1996 a report quoted her as saying his ashes had been scattered in deep space from the space shuttle Columbia in 1992.

7832. Rodeheaver, Homer (Oct. 4, 1880–Dec. 18, 1955) Religious recording artist and musical director for evangelist Billy Sunday. Rodeheaver and his trombone ("which has never played jazz music") traveled the Chautauqua circuits c. 1910–1930. He recorded many favorite hymns of the period as well. He died at Winona Lake, Indiana. The grave overlooks the lake. Block 16, lot 18, rear of Oakwood Cemetery, Warsaw, IN.

7833. Rodgers, Jimmie (Sept. 8, 1897–May 26, 1933) Country singer from Meridian, Mississippi, The Singing Brakeman was a pioneer in his field, a combination of folk and deep south. The largest legend in country music prior to Hank Williams, he died from tuberculosis at 35. Center area, two rows from road. Oak Grove Cemetery, Meridian, MS.

7834. Rodgers, John (July 11, 1772–Aug. 1, 1838) U.S. Naval hero of the War of 1812, as a Second Lieutenant helped capture the French frigate *L'Insurgente in 1799,* transported the French-American Peace Treaty back in 1801, commanded at Tripoli and in 1805 was appointed Commodore of the Mediterranean Squadron. In 1811 he twice defeated British ships off the Atlantic coast and assisted in the defense of Fort McHenry. Range 56, site 152, Congressional Cemetery, Washington, D.C.

7835. Rodgers, John (Jan. 15, 1881–Aug. 27, 1926) Great great grandson of Commodore John Rodgers commanded the Submarine Base in Connecticut during World War I, afterward led mine sweepers in the North Sea, for which he received the Distinguished Service Medal. He also commanded air squadrons. flew seaplanes and served as Assistant Chief of the Bureau of Aeronautics until his death in a plane crash at 45. Sec. 1, grave 130, Arlington National Cemetery, Arlington, VA.

7836. Rodgers, Richard (June 28, 1902–Dec. 30, 1979) Broadway composer of many hit musicals collaborated with Lorenz Hart on *The Boys from Syracuse, Pal Joey* and others. With Oscar Hammerstein II he wrote the music for his better known works, including *Oklahoma* (1943), *South Pacific* (1949), *The King and I* (1951) and *The Sound of Music* (1959). He also wrote *Victory at Sea* and numerous individual compositions including *Slaughter on Tenth Avenue* (from *On Your Toes*). He died in New York City. Cremated at Ferncliff and the ashes buried in unidentifiable communal space, an open area with no markers. Ferncliff Cemetery, Hartsdale, NY.

7837. Rodham, Hugh (April 2, 1911–April 7, 1993) Father of U.S. First Lady Hillary Rodham Clinton was a Chicago textile merchant who retired to Little Rock in 1987. He died there from a stroke at 82. The burial drew attention to the poor maintenance at the cemetery at the time due to a theft of funds by the (jailed) owner. Washburn Street Cemetery, Scranton, PA.

7838. Rodin, Auguste (Nov. 12, 1840–Nov. 17, 1917) French sculptor influenced by the Greek and Italian masters and by the writings of Dante. Many of his better known works were from studies for an unfinished decoration for bronze doors titled *The Gates of Hell.* These included his most famous sculpture *The Thinker.* Buried beside his wife in the garden of the Villa des Brillants, Meudon.

7839. Rodino, Peter (Peter Rodino, Jr., June 7, 1909–May 7, 2005) Newark born Democratic congressman from New Jersey served for four decades 1948–1988, chairing the House Judiciary Committee during the 1973–74 Watergate hearings that led to the resignation of President Nixon. He died at home in West Orange at 95. Lot with monument. Sec. 35, plot O, grave 19, Gate of Heaven Cemetery, East Hanover, NJ.

7840. Rodney, Caesar (Oct. 7, 1728–June 29, 1784) Signer of the Declaration of Independence from Delaware rode from Dover to cast the deciding vote for independence. The Broadway and film musical *1776* portrayed him as dying from cancer while in Philadelphia, although he returned to Dover and lived another eight years. Christ Church Cemetery, Dover, DE.

7841. Rodney, Red (Robert R. Chudnick/Rodney, Sept. 27, 1927–May 27, 1994) Philadelphia born red head played flugelhorn and trumpet, with Charlie Parker, Gene Krupa, Woody Herman and others. He died in Boynton Beach, Palm Beach County, Florida, at 66. Cremated at Gulf Cremation Services, Lantana, through Joseph Rubin Memorial Chapel, Delray Beach/Boca Raton, Florida. Ashes delivered in a light oak mica urn to Helene Rodney. Now deceased, Rubin's later gave her ashes to her sister.

7842. Roebling, John Augustus (June 2, 1806–July 22, 1869) German born architect completed the Suspension Bridge over the Ohio River at Cincinnati and had started work on the Brooklyn Bridge over the East River in New York City when he died in Brooklyn. Sec. D, lot 304, Riverview Cemetery, Trenton, NJ.

7843. Roebling, Washington Augustus (May 26, 1837–July 21, 1926) Son of John A. Roebling took over the construction of the suspension bridge from Manhattan to Brooklyn over the East River after his father's death in 1869 and saw it through to its completion in 1883. His health was destroyed by an attack of the "bends" in 1872, after which he supervised and watched the rest of the construction from his home in Brooklyn Heights. He died in Trenton at 89. Lot with two large crosses. Cold Spring Cemetery, Cold Spring-on-the-Hudson, NY.

7844. Roebuck, Alva Curtis (Jan. 9, 1864–June 18, 1948) Established the Sears and Roebuck mail order business in Chicago in 1893 with Richard Sears. Sec. 7, corridor west, crypt B-6, third floor, Acacia Park Cemetery mausoleum, Chicago, IL.

7845. Roehm, Ernst (Ernst Röhm, Nov. 28, 1887–June 30, 1934) German army officer who had part of his nose shot off in World War I pre-dated Adolf Hitler as a member of the National Socialist (Nazi) party, led the SA (brown shirts) from 1921 and had aided Hitler with the Beer Hall Putsch in 1923. In conflict with Hitler's inner echelon, he left Germany for Bolivia from 1925–30, but returned in 1933 when Hitler assumed power. Hitler was persuaded to rid the party of Roehm, a corpulent homosexual believed to have too much power, and he became the primary victim of the 1934 blood purge, after which the SA was disbanded and replaced by Himmler's SS. Arrested and shot in Munich, Roehm was presumably cremated like the others killed (including Gregor Strasser) and returned to the family in numbered urns to destroy any evidence of murder, while he became the party's necessary martyr. Tall monument with five names beginning *Dem Andenken an*; Rohm's is the third name down, with his name, *hauptmann 1.6*, and dates. Sec. 59, row 3, grave 1, Westfriedhof, Munich.

7846. Roerick, William (Dec. 17, 1911–Nov. 30, 1995) Stage, screen and television actor on stage in *Hamlet* (1936), *Our Town* (1938), in numerous films including *The Harder They Fall* (1956), *Not of This Earth* (1957), *A Lovely Way to Die* (1968), *A Separate Peace* (1972), *The Day of the Dolphin* (1973), *92 in the Shade, The Other Side of the Mountain* (1975), *The Betsy* (1978), and as Henry Chamberlain in the CBS soap opera *The Guiding Light* from 1980 to his death in an auto accident fifteen years later. Union Church Cemetery, Tyringham, MA

7847. Roemheld, Heinz (May 1, 1901–Feb. 11, 1985) German born musical director in Hollywood at Universal in the 1930's and Warner Bros. in the 40's. Scores include *The Invisible Man* (1933), *The Black Cat* (1934, with interspersing of bits of Tchaikovsky, Beethoven and others throughout), *Imitation of Life* (1934), *The Raven* (1935), *Dracula's Daughter* (1936), Academy Award for *Yankee Doodle Dandy* (1942) and a nomination for *The Strawberry Blonde* (1941). Ashes scattered at sea.

7848. Roethke, Theodore (May 25, 1908–Aug. 1, 1963) Pulitzer Prize winning poet (1953) for *The Waking Poems 1933–1953*. Sec. 86, lot 394, Oakwood Cemetery, Saginaw, MI.

7849. Rogan, "Bullet" Joe (Wilbur Joe Rogan, July 28, 1889–March 4, 1967) Oklahoma City born Negro Leagues pitcher with the Kansas City Monarchs from 1920. Known for his blazing fastball, he was also a slugger, hitting .416 and .412 in 1923–24, respectively. He managed the Monarchs 1926–1938. Umpired 1938–46. Hall of Fame 1998. Flush military marker. Sec. 4, grave 7674, Blue Ridge Lawn Cemetery, Kansas City, MO.

7850. Rogell, Albert S. (Aug. 21, 1901–April 7, 1988) Oklahoma City born director in films from 1923 (*Red Hot Leather,* also wrote); many western and action films (*In Old Oklahoma* 1943), as well as *The Black Cat* (1941), and *Song of India* (1949), which he also produced. He directed the television series *Broken Arrow* and *My Friend Flicka* in the mid 1950's before retiring. Brother of Sid Rogell. Courts of the Book, Joshua, wall H, crypt 563, Hillside Memorial Park, Los Angeles.

7851. Rogell, Sid (Jan. 16, 1900–Nov. 15, 1973) Film producer, at RKO and elsewhere, 1932–1952, Academy Award for *Design for Death* (1947). Brother of Al Rogell. Garden of Memories, Alcove of Love, Wall D, crypt 246, Hillside Memorial Park, Los Angeles.

7852. Rogers, Charles "Buddy" (Aug. 13, 1904–April 21, 1999) Actor from Olathe, Kansas, in amiable lead roles 1926–1957, notably in *Wings* and *My Best Girl* (both 1927). The latter co-starred Mary Pickford, to whom he was married from 1936 until her death in 1979. He remarried to realtor Beverly Ricono

in 1980 and moved to Rancho Mirage, California, where he died at his home at 94. Service at Palm Springs Mortuary and entombment. A picture of he and his last wife is on the crypt, with the label *America's Boyfriend*. Mission Santa Rosa, crypt C-1, Palm Springs Mausoleum (now Forest Lawn Cathedral City), Cathedral City (Palm Springs), CA.

7853. Rogers, Fred (Fred McFeely Rogers, March 20, 1928–Feb. 27, 2003) Ordained Presbyterian minister from Latrobe, Pennsylvania, began creating friendly, gentle television programs for children in the early 1950's, briefly in New York and Canada, but in Pittsburgh well before the inception of *Mr. Rogers' Neighborhood* at WQED there, first broadcast February 19, 1968 and filmed through December 2000. For over thirty two years, Mr. Rogers was familiar to children the world over on a daily basis, exchanging his sport coat and dress shoes for a cardigan and sneakers, offering to his impressionable viewers not only lessons and songs but acceptance, warmth, and the message that each was special. He died at Squirrel Hill outside Pittsburgh at 74 from stomach cancer diagnosed only eight weeks before. Interred in the mausoleum of his mother's family, from which not only his middle name but Mr. McFeely the mailman on his program was derived. McFeely mausoleum, Unity Chapel Cemetery, Latrobe, PA.

7854. Rogers, Ginger (Virginia Katherine McMath, July 16, 1911–April 25, 1995) Dancer, actress and singer from Independence, Missouri. After a variety of films including *The 13th Guest, 42nd Street* and *Golddiggers of 1933*, she first danced with Fred Astaire in *Flying Down to Rio* (1933) and in a series of lushly choreographed (by Hermes Pan) teamings (*The Gay Divorcee, Top Hat, Swing Time, Shall We Dance*). Dramatic parts include *Stage Door* (1938) and *Kitty Foyle* (1940, AA). Divorced five times, she had no children. A devout Christian Science practitioner, she died in her home at Rancho, Mirage, California, at 83. Her ashes were buried, through Palm Springs mortuary, with those of her mother **Lela Rogers** (Dec. 25, 1891–May 25, 1977), former silent screen writer who appeared with her (as her mother) in *The Major and the Minor* (1942). Sec. E, lot 303, Oakwood Memorial Park, Chatsworth, CA.

7855. Rogers, Jean (Eleanor Lovegreen Winkler, March 25, 1916–Feb. 24, 1991) Actress from Belmont, Massachusetts, in two *Flash Gordon* serials and many B's of the 30's and 40's (*Night Key, Whistling in Brooklyn*). Ashes through Praisewater mortuary to residence, Sherman Oaks, CA.

7856. Rogers, Mary Cecilia (c. 1820–July 25, 1841) Twenty year old girl, missing three days from her lower Manhattan home and boarding house on Nassau Street near City Hall, was found by two men on July 28, floating in the Hudson at Sybil's Cave near Hoboken. She had been beaten, sexually assaulted, and strangled. The murder case held the city's attention for a time, with suspicion falling on her suitor

672

and boarder, Donald Payne. Her clothing and some belongings were found in the woods at Weehawken a month later, the burgeoning "Penny Press" kept after the case, and Payne committed suicide with poison outside Sybil's Cave in October. By year's end an innkeeper at Weehawken, Frederika Loss, stated Rogers and a man had come there to "procure ... a premature delivery" which resulted in her death, and she was dumped in the river to give the appearance of murder. The story remains a matter of dispute. The case was the basis for Edgar Allan Poe's *The Mystery of Marie Roget*, moving the murder to Paris. According to Amy Gilman Srebnick's *The Mysterious Death of Mary Rogers*, she "was finally buried at the cemetery of West Presbyterian Church," at the north end of Varick Street in lower Manhattan, N.Y.C.

7857. Rogers, Roy (Leonard Franklin Slye, Nov. 5, 1911–July 6, 1998) The King of the Cowboys was reportedly born near second base at Riverfront Stadium in Cincinnati (but actually nearby at the site of the Crown) and grew up near Portsmouth, Ohio and in Cincinnati before going to California to stay in 1931. By 1937, singing with the Sons of the Pioneers and having taken his surname from Will Rogers, he began making westerns at Republic with his Palomino horse Trigger, three years old when purchased in 1936. Rogers flourished after the war, his horse operas always wholesome, with violence decidedly de-emphasized and the gun generally shot out of the villain's hand without harming him. His first wife **(Grace) Arlene Wilkins Rogers** (Dec. 14, 1914–Nov. 3, 1946), who he married in 1936, died from an embolism at 31 after the birth of their third child, son Roy Jr. "Dusty." She was buried in the Cathedral Slope at Forest Lawn, Glendale, Ca. He married **Dale Evans** (Frances Octavia Smith, Oct. 31, 1912–Feb. 7, 2001) in 1947; they had one daughter Robin, who died at two in 1951, and adopted three children, two of whom also pre-deceased him; Korean born Debbie died in a church bus accident in 1964 and John David "Sandy" choked to death while in the army in Germany in 1965. The three children are in the Great Mausoleum at Forest Lawn, Glendale. Breaking with Republic in 1951, Rogers and Evans starred in their TV series through 1957, co-starring their horses **Trigger** and Buttermilk, their dog Bullet, and Pat Brady replacing Gabby Hayes (in the films) as the comical sidekick. They remained favorites through their connection with Christian programs and the Roy Rogers Museum in Victorville, California, where Trigger was mounted after his death at 33 in 1965. Buttermilk and Bullet are there as well. Rogers died at 86 from congestive heart failure in his home at Apple Valley, near Victorville. Family and fans packed the Church of the Valley there on July 11 for his public memorial service, *Happy Trails* played along with two hymns by the Sons of the Pioneers, after which the white hearse twice circled his museum at Victorville, a frontier Army tradition he had requested. Accompanied by eight local members of the Single Action Shooters Society in 1880's outfits, a glass enclosed 1898 hearse drawn by a single Clydesdale bore the coffin, at sunset, into the cemetery. Their original names are on the two dark pinkish brown slabs in a landscaped garden enclosure at a pond, with *The Cowboy's Prayer* in the brick wall and a sculpted eagle, or falcon, rising from the water. A bench nearby marks the future gravesite of Evans' stunt double, **Alice Van Springsteen**, inscribed *Dearest Friend*. In October 2004, the cemetery announced plans to replace grass with astro-turf, which they did, a first in the burial industry. Sunset Hills Memorial Park, 24000 Waalew Road, Apple Valley, CA.

7858. Rogers, Tiana *see* **Sam Houston.**

7859. Rogers, Will (Nov. 4, 1879–Aug. 15, 1935) American humorist from Oolagah in Indian Territory that became Oklahoma, called Claremore his home. He became a star in the Ziegfeld Follies with homespun commentary on events of the day, starred in several silent and sound films, kidding presidents from Wilson to Franklin Roosevelt in speeches as well as his syndicated column. On a ten minute leg of a flight bound for Moscow, he and pilot Wiley Post were killed in the crash of their plane in the tundra several miles from Point Barrow, Alaska. Eskimos reached the scene and carried Rogers' body out, but Post had to be extricated from the wreckage later. Charles Lindbergh went to Point Barrow to fly the bodies back for their funerals. Radios were silent for a half hour, flags were lowered and theatres darkened. Rogers was interred in a holding vault at Forest Lawn, Glendale, Ca. On what would have been his 59th birthday, November 4, 1938, a twenty acre park in his memory at Claremore, Oklahoma, was donated by his widow Betty. His daughter unveiled a statue of him there with the epitaph *I never met a man I didn't like*. On May 22, 1944, his body was transferred from Forest Lawn to a subscription built crypt in the Claremore park. His wife died the next month and, with their infant son Freddie who died of diphtheria in 1920, was buried in the crypt also. It is topped by a sarcophagus shaped block of polished rose colored marble with their names and dates on it, the sarcophagus surrounded by an iron fence. Behind it, on the wall surrounding the garden, is an equestrian statue of Rogers above a tablet encapsulating his life, with the quotation *If you live right, death is a joke as far as fear is concerned*. Will Rogers Memorial, Claremore, Oklahoma. At the site of the plane crash near Point Barrow is a tablet inscribed *Will Rogers and Wiley Post, America's ambassadors of good will, ended life's flight here August 15, 1935. This stone was taken from the same quarry as that used in building Oklahoma's memorial to Will Rogers at Claremore, Oklahoma.*

7860. Rogers, Will, Jr. (William Vann Rogers, Oct. 20, 1911–July 9, 1993) Son of the humorist was decorated for heroism with the U.S. Army at the Battle of the Bulge in World War II. Active in Democratic politics and owner of the Beverly Hills Citizen

1935–1953, starred in the 1952 biopic of his father *The Story of Will Rogers,* and served as Assistant Commissioner of Indian Affairs 1967–69. He retired to Tubac, Arizona, where he was found dead in his car at 81 from a self inflicted gunshot wound. Stone reads *Bill* Rogers. Southwest area of Tubac Cemetery, Tubac, AZ.

7861. Rogers, William (William Pierce Rogers, June 23, 1913–Jan. 2, 2001) Noted lawyer born in Norfolk, New York, Attorney General in Eisenhower's second administration from January 1958 to January 1961 and Secretary of State in Nixon's first from 1969; he resigned September 3, 1973, and was replaced by Henry Kissinger. A resident of Bethesda, Maryland, until his death at 87. Sec. 30, grave 817 LH, Arlington National Cemetery, Arlington, VA.

7862. Rohmer, Sax (Arthur Henry Ward, Feb. 15, 1883–June 1, 1959) English author best known for his Oriental arch villain introduced in *Dr. Fu Manchu* (1913), lived for years at Old Mamaroneck Road, White Plains, New York, where much of his writing was done. He died at University College Hospital, London. Buried through Frank Leverton, Ltd. Black *Ward* stone with gold lettering inscribed *Their son Arthur Henry 1883–1959. British author best known to his countless readers as Sax Rohmer, and his beloved wife Rose Elizabeth Knox 1886–1979. Together in Eternity.* Grave 1780C, St. Mary's Catholic Cemetery, Kensal Green, London.

7863. Roker, Roxie (Aug. 29, 1929–Dec. 2, 1995) Black actress trained in Shakespeare played Helen Willis on TV's *The Jeffersons* 1975–85. Mother of guitarist Lenny Kravitz. She died in Los Angeles at 66. Sent from Inglewood Park Cemetery, Inglewood, Ca. East Court 2, lot 19, grave 2B, Southern Memorial Park, Miami, FL.

7864. Roland, Gilbert (Luis Antonio Damaso de Alonso, Dec. 11, 1905–May 15, 1994) Actor from Chichau, Mexico, in suave roles from 1927. After World War II his career was revitalized and he essayed his signature roles, in *The Bullfighter and the Lady* (1951) and eleven films as the *Cisco Kid.* He died at 88 from cancer in Beverly Hills. Ashes spread at sea May 18, 1994.

7865. Roland, Ruth (Aug. 26, 1892–Sept. 22, 1937) Child stage star Baby Ruth later specialized in silent film cliffhangers, particularly westerns, as well as several features. Married to actor Ben Bard (dec. 1974). She died in Los Angeles from cancer at 44. Interred in a family room, her signature is on her crypt and her name over the door. Azalea Corridor, lower level, private mausoleum 7, crypt B, Azalea Terrace, Great Mausoleum, Forest Lawn, Glendale, CA.

7866. Rolfe, Red (Robert A. Rolfe, Oct. 17, 1908–July 8, 1969) Third baseman and shortstop for the Yankees 1934–1942, later managed the Detroit Tigers 1949–51. Woodlawn Cemetery, Penacook, NH.

7867. Rolle, Esther (Nov. 8, 1920–Nov. 17, 1998) Stout black actress from Pompano Beach, Florida, played several TV characters including the maid on *Maude* and the lead in *Good Times* 1974–79, later winning an Emmy for *The Summer of My German Soldier.* Films include *Driving Miss Daisy, Down in the Delta* and *Rosewood* (1997). She died of complications from diabetes in Culver City, California, at 78. Burial November 28. Upright stone visible from the road. Westview Community Cemetery, Pompano Beach, FL.

7868. Rollins, Howard (Oct. 17, 1950–Dec. 8, 1996) Baltimore born black actor starred in *Ragtime* (1981, AA nom.), *A Soldier's Story* (1984) and on TV's *In the Heat of the Night* 1988–92. He died in Manhattan from lymphoma at 46. Funeral and cremation from March–West mortuary, 4300 Wabash Ave., Baltimore. Chapel Mausoleum 36A, Woodlawn Cemetery, Baltimore.

7869. Rollins, Walter E. "Jack" (Sept. 15, 1906–Jan. 1, 1973) Songwriter penned the perennial *Frosty the Snowman,* used in the 1969 TV special, among others. Queens Point Cemetery, Keyser, WV.

7870. Rolls, Charles S. (Aug. 27, 1877–July 12, 1910) with Henry Royce founded in 1903 the manufacture of fine automobiles and aircraft, powering the British spitfire in World War I. Marked by a Celtic cross. St. Cadoc's, Llangattock-Vibon-Avel, near Monmouth, Wales.

7871. Rolvaag, O. E. (Ole Edvart Rolvaag, April 22, 1876–Nov. 5, 1931) Norwegian born author-historian known for *Giants in the Earth* (1927), a saga of immigration and pioneer life in the Midwest of the 19th century. Written in Norwegian, it was translated by Rolvaag and Lincoln Colcord. Rolvaag taught Norwegian at Olaf College, Northfield, Minnesota. Oaklawn Cemetery, Northfield, MN.

7872. Roman, Ruth (Dec. 22, 1924–Sept. 9, 1999) Boston born actress in films of the 40's and 50's, notably *Champion* (1949), *The Window, Strangers on a Train* (1951), *The Far Country, Dallas,* appeared with Bette Davis in her last Warner Bros. film, *Beyond the Forest,* and was herself the last contract player at Warners. With her son Richard Roman Hall, she survived the sinking of the Andrea Doria in 1956. She later appeared frequently on TV. Divorced from Mortimer Hall and later from Bud Burton Moss, she died in her sleep at her Laguna Beach, California, home at 74 (reported as 75). Cremated through McCormick and Son mortuary, Laguna Beach, with a private service. Ashes scattered at sea.

7873. Romanoff, Michael (Harry Gerguson, Feb. 21, 1890–Sept. 1, 1971) "Prince Mike" ran the popular restaurant Romanoff's in Hollywood through the late 40's and 50's, with a parade of regulars including Bogart, who had his own booth and played chess there. Romanoff claimed to be a Russian prince related to the murdered Czar Nicholas. Whether he believed it himself or it was a lifelong joke, no one seemed sure. Cremated by Chapel of the Pines Crematory in Los Angeles. Ashes were buried at sea.

7874. Romanov *see* **Nicholas II.**

7875. Romberg, Sigmund (July 29, 1887–Nov. 9, 1951) Hungarian born composer wrote for the American stage from 1914. His many popular shows and operettas, many later filmed, include *Maytime* and *Naughty Marietta*. Crypt at top right just entering the right hallway inside the entrance. Unit 1, sec. BD-1, crypt 5, main mausoleum, Ferncliff Cemetery, Hartsdale, NY.

7876. Rome, Esther R. (Sept. 8, 1945–June 24, 1995) Author of *Our Bodies, Ourselves*. B'Nai B'rith Cemetery, Peabody, MA.

7877. Rome, Harold Jacob (May 27, 1908–Oct. 26, 1993) Broadway composer (*Wish You Were Here, Call Me Mister, Destry Rides Again*). Westchester Hills Cemetery, Hastings-on-Hudson, NY.

7878. Romero, Cesar (Feb. 15, 1907–Jan. 1, 1994) New York born Cuban-American actor in Latin roles from *The Thin Man* (1934) to evil rajahs, later the Joker in TV's *Batman*. He died in Santa Monica at 86. Sanctuary of Dreams, Alcove of Music (harp shaped urn), Mausoleum of the Golden West, Inglewood Park Cemetery, Inglewood, CA.

7879. Rommel, Eddie (Edwin A. Rommel, Sr., Sept. 13, 1897–Aug. 26, 1970) Star knuckleball pitcher with Connie Mack's Athletics 1920–1932 won 100 games over five years. Best year 1922 with 27–13. Sec MM, lot 183, New Cathedral Cemetery, Baltimore, MD.

7880. Rommel, Erwin (Nov. 15, 1891–Oct. 14, 1944) German field marshal in Africa during World War II, the Desert Fox fell from Hitler's favor when he was pushed back by British Field Marshal Montgomery. Daring to criticize Hitler's strategy, he was further doomed when his name was linked with the 1944 assassination attempt on his life, although he was not in fact involved. Hitler sent Gen. Burgdof and aides to Rommel's house at Herrlingen, offering him the choice of poison or being brought before a court. Rommel chose the former, declining to be "hanged by that man Hitler." Last seen sobbing in a car being driven away, he was later said to have died from a brain hemorrhage. Given a state funeral at Ulm, the coffin covered by a Nazi flag, he was cremated and the ashes buried in the churchyard at Herrlingen.

7881. Romney, George (July 8, 1907–July 26, 1995) Chairman of American Motors until 1962, 3 term governor of Michigan, GOP presidential candidate in 1968 up to the New Hampshire primary, and Secretary of HUD under Nixon 1969–72. A liberal Republican, he supported social programs and opposed the war in Vietnam. Romney collapsed on a treadmill at his home in Bloomfield Hills, a Detroit suburb, at 88. Service at the Church of Jesus Christ of Latter Day Saints. Sec. 7, lot 642, Fairview Cemetery, Flint Rd and Williamson, Brighton, MI.

7882. Rooney, Art (Arthur Rooney, Sr., Jan. 27, 1901–Aug. 25, 1988) Longtime owner of the Pittsburgh Steelers saw his team take the Super Bowl in 1975, 1976, 1979 and 1980, as well as NFL titles in 1974 and 1978. Sec. M, lot 155, Northside Catholic Cemetery, Ross Township, Pittsburgh, PA.

7883. Rooney, Barbara Ann (Barbara Ann Thomason, Jan. 25, 1937–Jan. 31, 1966) Actress wife of Mickey Rooney appeared in films as **Carolyn Mitchell** (*Dragstrip Riot, Cry Baby Killer* 1958), she was shot and killed by her companion Milos Milosevics during an impending custody battle with Rooney. Sanctuary of Liberty, crypt 20765, Freedom Mausoleum, Forest Lawn, Glendale, CA.

7884. Rooney, Pat (1844–March 31, 1892) Vaudeville star and father of vaudevillian **Pat Rooney** (July 4, 1880–Sept. 12, 1962), who was known for his clog dancing in *The Daughter of Rosie O'Grady* and on Broadway in *Guys and Dolls*. Rooney Jr. appeared often with his wife **Marion Bent** (Dec. 23, 1879–July 31, 1941). All are buried in the family lot, marked by a single monument with names and death dates. Mount Seir sec., Cemetery of the Evergreens, Brooklyn, N.Y.C.

7885. Rooney, Wallace (Dec. 29, 1910–Oct. 10, 1996) Actor on Broadway from the 1930's, in films and television from the 1950's, in roles ranging from good natured businessmen (*Twilight Zone* episode *Young Man's Fancy* 1962) to Bishop Michael in *The Exorcist* (1973). Plaque with Frank Belcher. Actors Fund of America plot, Kensico Cemetery, Valhalla, NY.

7886. Roosa, Stuart Allen (Aug. 16, 1933–Dec. 12, 1994) Command module pilot on the Apollo 14 moon mission. His charcoal-black monument has a spaceship lifting from the launch pad beside his name, rank, and dates. Sec. 7A, grave 73, Arlington National Cemetery, Arlington, VA.

7887. Roosevelt, Alice Hathaway Lee (July 29, 1861–Feb. 14, 1884) The first wife of then New York State Assemblyman Theodore Roosevelt was from Chestnut Hill, Massachusetts, where they met while he was at Harvard in the late 1870's. She died from Bright's Disease two days after giving birth to their daughter Alice in the Roosevelt family home at 6 West 57th St. in Manhattan. Her mother-in-law Martha Bulloch Roosevelt died from typhoid fever the same night. After the funeral, Theodore Roosevelt gave the baby to his sister's care for a time, going to the Dakota badlands and living as a cowboy for a period, returning and remarrying in 1886. The house he had begun planning on Long Island, originally called Leeholm, was renamed Sagamore Hill. According to all who knew him as well as in his writings, he never spoke of his first wife again. There was a double funeral with burial in the Roosevelt plot in Brooklyn, a circular lot of white marble stones, most eroded and no longer legible, including that of Alice. Sec. 51 on the corner of Locust and Grape Avenues, Greenwood Cemetery, Brooklyn, N.Y.C.

7888. Roosevelt, Eleanor (Anna Eleanor Roosevelt, Oct. 11, 1884–Nov. 7, 1962) The most prominent and influential First Lady in American history, the daughter of **Anna Hall** (dec. Dec. 7, 1892) and **Elliott Roosevelt** (Feb. 28, 1860–Aug. 14, 1894), brother of Theodore Roosevelt. Her mother died from diphtheria when Eleanor was eight, and was buried in the Hall family mausoleum in St. Paul's Churchyard at Tivoli-on-Hudson, New York. When her father Elliott died from alcoholism two years later at 34, Theodore insisted that he not be buried with the Halls but with his parents in the circular plot in section 51, Greenwood Cemetery, Brooklyn, N.Y.C., as a symbol of their happier days. Eleanor was raised primarily by the Halls. She married her distant cousin Franklin Roosevelt and went on to become the First Lady of New York 1929–1933 and of the United States 1933–1945. Living often at Val-Kil, her cottage on the estate at Hyde Park, New York, she spoke out for many causes, championed the poor and civil rights, visited the troops overseas, and penned a daily column *My Day*, serving after her husband's death as a delegate to the United Nations. She died at 78 in her home at 55 East 74th St., Manhattan, from tuberculosis in the bone marrow caused by steroids (prescribed to reduce internal bleeding caused by aplastic anemia) which reactivated a lesion dating to 1919. As she requested, she was not embalmed but her veins were cut to insure against premature burial. Her coffin was made of wood and covered with pine boughs taken from the woods around Val Kil. She was buried beside her husband in the rose garden of the Roosevelt estate at Hyde Park, Duchess County, NY.

7889. Roosevelt, Franklin Delano (Jan. 30, 1882–April 12, 1945) 32nd President of the United States (1933–1945), former Democratic governor of New York, crippled by polio in 1921, served twelve years, longer than any other president, guiding the nation through its worst financial depression and its greatest world war. His term was revolutionary in its creation of new social and economic recovery agencies, the repeal of prohibition, and the unprecedented four terms, which were outlawed after his death, limiting to two the amount of times a candidate may be elected to the White House. Like Lincoln, the president and the war he had presided over ended at nearly the same time. He had spent a lot of time at Warm Springs, Georgia, where the waters had helped him since stricken with polio. There in the Little White House, he was having his portrait painted when he remarked that he had "a terrific headache" and slumped in his chair from a cerebral hemorrhage; carried in to the bed, he died a short time later at 63, only three weeks before the end of the war in Europe. His funeral was the largest outpouring of emotion since that of Lincoln; most adolescents could not remember when FDR had not been president. After lying in state in Washington, the flag covered coffin was drawn through the streets on an army caisson, just as it would be eighteen years hence in the Kennedy funeral. He was embalmed, contrary to his requests, and taken by train to the family estate for burial in the manicured rose garden. The grave and that of his wife (1962) are covered by ivy and marked by a rectangular white marble block with their full names and years of birth and death. FDR's dog **Chief** (1918–33) and his famed pet terrier **Fala** (1940–52) are buried behind the president and first lady, marked by circular plaques in the open lawn near a birdbath. Franklin D. Roosevelt National Historic Site, Hyde Park, NY.

7890. Roosevelt, James (July 16, 1828–Dec. 8, 1900) and **Sara Delano** (Sept. 21, 1854–Sept. 7, 1941), parents of FDR. James was a wealthy lawyer, railroad financier and country squire who purchased the estate Springwood at Hyde Park in 1867. By the time of FDR's presidency it was called simply Hyde Park. Upon James' death he was buried in St. James Episcopal Churchyard, Hyde Park, New York, behind the church where all the family funerals had been held. According to his wishes he was buried beside his first wife (**Rebecca Howland**, Jan. 15, 1831–Aug. 21, 1876). Sara ordered a slab of pink Scotch granite placed over their grave. An identical one marks her grave next to them. Sara Delano Roosevelt's parents, **Warren Delano II** (July 13, 1809– Jan. 17, 1898) and **Catherine Delano** (Jan. 12, 1825–Feb. 10, 1896) survived five of their children. One daughter, **Laura Delano**, died from burns in July 1884 when a curling iron caught her dress on fire. The Delanos are buried in Riverside Cemetery in the coastal village of Fairhaven, MA.

7891. Roosevelt, James (Dec. 23, 1907–Aug. 13, 1991) Eldest son of Franklin Delano and Eleanor Roosevelt and six term Democratic congressman from Los Angeles was at the far right of his party, often aligning himself with Republican candidates. He resided at Newport Beach, California, from 1972. Oceanview 815B, Pacific View Memorial Park, Newport Beach, California. His siblings, **Anna Roosevelt Halsted** (May 3, 1906–Dec. 1, 1975) and **Franklin D. Roosevelt, Jr.** (Aug. 17, 1914–March 17, 1988) and **John A. Roosevelt** (March 13, 1916–April 27, 1981) are buried at St. James' Episcopal Church Cemetery, Hyde Park, NY.

7892. Roosevelt, Theodore (Oct. 27, 1858–Jan. 6, 1919) 26th President of the United States (1901–1909) rose from an asthmatic child to wrestle at Harvard, to box, work as a rancher and cowboy, lead a charge in the Spanish American War and continue to champion the strenuous life until his last year, taking his "bully pulpit," the presidency, upon the assassination of McKinley in Buffalo in 1901. It was while hunting bear during his presidency that he refused to shoot a cub and earned for baby bears his own nickname "Teddy." His father **Theodore Roosevelt** (Sept. 22, 1821–Feb. 9, 1878) died from stomach cancer at 56. His mother **Martha Bulloch Roosevelt** (July 8, 1834–Feb. 14, 1884) died from typhoid at 49 the same night his wife Alice Hathaway Lee Roosevelt died from Bright's Disease, two days after the birth of their daughter Alice, in the family home at 6 West 57th St.

All, along with Theodore's brother Elliott in 1894 (father of future first lady Eleanor Roosevelt) and others were buried in the circular family plot of eroded white marble stones in section 51 at the intersection of Locust and Grape Avenues in Greenwood Cemetery, Brooklyn, N.Y.C. Theodore remarried to **Edith Kermit Carow** (Aug. 6, 1861–Sept. 30, 1948) in 1886 and moved into his estate Sagamore Hill at Oyster Bay, Long Island, where they raised five children in addition to his daughter Alice (see Longworth). He was shot in 1912 (see John Schrank) and in 1914 was weakened by fever incurred on a jungle expedition. He retired to Sagamore Hill, beset by arthritis and a host of other ailments and crushed by the death of his youngest son Quentin in World War I. On the night of January 5, 1919, he told a housekeeper to "please put out the light" and died during his sleep from an embolism at 60. Burial was in the 250 year old cemetery at the foot of Cove Neck Road near Sagamore Hill. After the coffin was borne under the arch and up the steep hill in the snow to the grave and the burial service completed, former President William Howard Taft, his protégé and former friend, remained at the grave in silence, their broken friendship having never been repaired. Young's Memorial Cemetery, Cove Neck Road, Oyster Bay, Long Island, New York. Two of TR and Edith's five children, **Ethel Roosevelt Derby** (Aug. 13, 1891–Dec. 10, 1977) and **Archibald Bulloch "Archie" Roosevelt** (April 9, 1893–Oct. 13, 1979), the only one of his sons to reach old age, are buried in Young's Memorial Cemetery at Oyster Bay, atop the hill and behind the fence enclosed grave of their parents. Archie's epitaph reads *The old fighting man home from the wars.* On Ethel Derby's stone is inscribed *The heavens filled with stars, chanced he upon the way* under her husband's name, and under hers *and all the trumpets sounded on the other side.* The youngest son **Quentin Roosevelt** (Nov. 19, 1897–July 14, 1918) was shot down in an aerial dogfight over German lines in 1918 and was buried near Chamery, where he fell, at Oisne-Aisne American Cemetery until 1955, when he was removed to the Normandy American Cemetery at Colleville-sur-mer, France, and buried next to his brother, Theodore III, in plot D-28-46. The stone from his original grave, with the epitaph *He has outsoared the shadow of our night* was removed to the sloping lawn in front of Sagamore Hill after 1955. **Theodore Roosevelt III** (Sept. 13, 1887–July 12, 1944), a brigadier general who died from a heart attack at the time of the ongoing invasion of France in World War II, was buried at plot D-28-45 in the Normandy American Cemetery at Colleville-sur-mer, his brother Quentin placed beside him in 1955. Cenotaph at Young's. **Kermit Roosevelt** (Oct. 10, 1889–June 4, 1943), beset by alcoholism and illness, shot himself in the head at Anchorage, Alaska, during World War II and was buried at sec. A, site 22, Fort Richardson, Alaska. His name and dates are on a stone at Youngs' Memorial Cemetery, Oyster

Bay, New York, where his wife Bella (1892–1968) is buried.

7893. Root, Charlie (Charles H. Root, March 17, 1899–Nov. 5, 1970) Pitcher from Middletown, Ohio, with the Cubs 1923–1941, who pitched Babe Ruth's "called shot" at Wrigley Field in 1932, slammed into far center in the stands. Root claimed that if Ruth had really pointed, he would have "knocked him on his ass." His ashes were at Garden of Memories, Salinas, California, until picked up June 27, 1974 and taken to Hollister, San Benito County, California, to be buried in a family grave or scattered on his ranch.

7894. Root, Elihu (Feb. 15, 1845–Feb. 7, 1937) Secretary of War under Presidents McKinley and Theodore Roosevelt 1899–1903, and Secretary of State under Roosevelt 1905–1909. He won the 1912 Nobel Peace Prize and was a major force in moving America into international relations and involvement in promoting democracy and gaining trading rights around the world. Later senator from New York. Born at Clinton, New York, he is buried there, his family marked by long slabs in the left front area of the cemetery at his alma mater. Hamilton College Cemetery, Clinton, NY.

7895. Rorke, Hayden (Oct. 23, 1910–Aug. 19, 1987) Character actor in films (the blind husband in *The Night Walker* 1964) and TV (Dr. Alfred Bellows on *I Dream of Jeannie* 1965–70). Sec. P, lot 318, Holy Cross Cemetery, Culver City, CA.

7896. Rose, Billy (Sept. 6, 1899–Feb. 10, 1966) Producer, nightclub owner and song writer, married to Fannie Brice and later to swimmer Eleanor Holm. The family's disagreements over his estate and the disposition of his remains kept him in a vault until his sister, mindful of his saying "I gotta have space," finally bought a plot so large it had gone unsold for 35 years due to its $125,000 price. Beneath the stained glass in the crypt is inscribed *The fabulous legend who is really real. The man who is many men, who regards the crowning act of his life, the handing over to the people of Israel the fruits of his collection and knowledge, and creating the Billy Rose Art Garden.* Mausoleum across the drive from the Gershwin mausoleum and near the entrance to Westchester Hills Cemetery, Hastings-on-Hudson, NY.

7897. Rose, Bob (Feb. 4, 1902–March 8, 1993) Stunt man in films for decades, in *The Trail of '98, King Kong,* dozens of others. Ashes buried unmarked in his mother's grave, third row from fence and right of stone fountain, Cory Cemetery, Cory, near Delta, CO.

7898. Rose, David (June 24, 1910–Aug. 23, 1990) TV orchestra leader, composer and conductor (*The Stripper*), long with Jackie Gleason, Red Skelton etc. Gardens of Heritage 4, wall crypt 37J, second level, Mt. Sinai Memorial Park, Los Angeles.

7899. Rose, Mauri (Dec. 13, 1918–Jan. 1, 1981) Two time winner of the Indianapolis 500, in 1947 and 1948. Cremation plaque with a pipe engraved beside the name and dates. Garden of Prayer C-275, White Chapel Memorial Park Cemetery, Troy (north Detroit), MI.

7900. Rose, Robert L. (April 21, 1924–Aug. 13, 2001) Journalist won the Pulitzer Prize in 1963 for his stories on both organized crime and on the birth control controversy. Sec. 5-M2, row 15, site 2, Arlington National Cemetery, Arlington, VA.

7901. Roseboro, John (May 13, 1933–Aug. 16, 2002) All star catcher from Ashland, Ohio, dubbed Gabby for his quiet demeanor, played in the majors 1957–70, succeeding Roy Campanella as the Dodgers' catcher and over the years caught two of Sandy Koufax's no hitters, but was best known for his part in one of the game's most infamous brawls. On August 22, 1965 when, after the Giants' pitcher Juan Marichal, having knocked down two Dodgers in a row, came to bat against Koufax, Roseboro fired the ball out just past his nose, a confrontation ensued, and Marichal swung the bat at his head, inflicting a gash that took fourteen stitches. Though he filed suit against Marichal, who was suspended and fined, after seventeen years of silence he spoke up for Marichal's election to the Hall of Fame in 1982. Both Marichal and Koufax attended Roseboro's funeral at Forest Lawn's Hall of Liberty and delivered eulogies. Peaceful Memory sec., lot 5808, space 3, Forest Lawn Hollywood Hills, Los Angeles.

7902. Rosecrans, William Starke (Sept. 6, 1819–March 11, 1898) Union Army general in charge of the expulsion of Confederate forces from western Virginia and the creation of the state of West Virginia. As Commander of the Army of the Cumberland in the west, he suffered one of the worst defeats of the war at the hands of Braxton Bragg at Chickamauga on Sept 19 and 20, 1863, after which he was replaced by Ulysses S. Grant. After the war, he served as Minister to Mexico and as a representative from California. Sec. 3, site 1862, grid T-16/17, Arlington National Cemetery, Arlington, VA.

7903. Rosen, Phil (Philip E. Rosen, May 8, 1888–Oct. 22, 1951) Russian born cinematographer in silents from 1912 at Edison, later at Paramount to 1920, photographed *Two Orphans* (1915), *Romeo and Juliet* (1916), *The Light Within* (1918), *The Miracle Man* (1919), before turning only to directing (143 films from 1915–1949), including many B westerns and thrillers at Monogram (*The Sphinx, Beggars in Ermine, Little Men* 1935, *Bridge of Sighs* both 1925 and 1936, *It Could Happen to You* 1937, *Phantom of Chinatown* 1940, *The Mystery of Marie Roget* [at Universal], *Charlie Chan and the Secret Service, The Chinese Cat, Return of the Ape Man, Charlie Chan in Black Magic, The Jade Mask,* etc.). Sec. 14, row GG, grave 33, Hollywood Forever Cemetery, Hollywood (Los Angeles), CA.

7904. Rosenberg, Ethel (Sept. 28, 1915–June 19, 1953) and **Julius** (May 12, 1918–June 19, 1953) The first civilians to be executed for treason in peacetime America died in the electric chair at Sing Sing for passing secrets relating to atomic weaponry to the Soviet Union. Their guilt has periodically been called into question, but documents declassified by the CIA and National Security Agency in 1995 reportedly confirmed the prosecution's case. Block 5, plot ½ of G-12, half way down on right between F and G, just after Stein. Wellwood Cemetery, Farmingdale, Long Island, NY.

7905. Rosenbloom, Maxie (Nov. 1, 1907–March 6, 1976) Light heavyweight champion in the early 1930's dubbed "Slapsie Maxie" by Damon Runyon, in films later as punch drunk fighters, henchmen, etc., spent his last days in a nursing home, reportedly brain damaged by the blows to the head he had suffered decades earlier. He died from Paget's Disease. Block J, sec. 9820, lot 3, Valhalla Memorial Park, North Hollywood, CA.

7906. Rosenthal, Herman "Beansie" (Sept. 3, 1874–July 16, 1912) New York gambler who ran the Hesper in Manhattan ran afoul of police Lt. Charles Becker when he refused to increase his kickback. Becker closed and trashed the Hesper and put a man at Rosenthal's apartment. In retaliation, Rosenthal went to D.A. Charles Whitman and was shot outside the Cafe Metropole on W. 43rd shortly afterward, most of his skull blown away. Becker was executed at Sing Sing in 1915. Sec. 108, row A, grave 22, Washington Cemetery, Brooklyn, N.Y.C.

7907. "Rosie the Riveter" (Rose Will Monroe, March 12, 1920–May 31, 1997) Worker at Willow Run Aircraft Factory in Ypsilanti, Michigan, during World War II, noticed by Walter Pidgeon during the making of a war bond promotional film was the model for the J. Howard Miller poster. She died at 77 in Clarksville, Indiana. She has a flush bronze headstone with her husband, and a military footstone inscribed *Rosie the Riveter. WW II* and her dates of birth and death. Area right of circle, Abundant Life Cemetery, Kamer-Miller Road, New Albany, IN.

7908. Rosqui, Tom (Tom F. Rosqui, June 12, 1928–April 12, 1991) Oakland, California, born actor on Broadway in *Sticks and Bones, The Price,* as well as several television parts, but best known as bodyguard and assassin Rocco Lampone in *The Godfather* (1972) and *The Godfather II* (1974, where he met his end in killing Lee Strasberg's character at the airport). He died from cancer in Los Angeles at 62. Ashes buried April 24 by the Neptune Society at sea off Point Fermin, Los Angeles.

7909. Ross, Barney (Dec. 23, 1909–Jan. 18, 1967) Middleweight champion 1934–38 died from cancer in his native Chicago at 57. Veterans' marker. Sec. N, lot 19, Rosemont Park Cemetery, Chicago, IL.

7910. Ross, Betsy (Elizabeth Griscom Ross Ashburn Claypoole, Jan. 1, 1752–Jan. 30, 1836) American patriot known for having sewn the first American flag was first buried in the Free Quaker Cemetery at 5th and Locust St. in Philadelphia. When it was abandoned in 1857, she and her third husband were moved to Mount Moriah Cemetery at 62nd and Kingsessing Ave. On the eve of the American Bicentennial in 1975, her descendants got a court order to have her disinterred and reburied in the garden of her home on Arch St. Although an anthropologist stated that the high acid content of the soil would have left little to dig up, a coffin believed to contain the correct bones was buried beneath a marble slab in Atwater Kent Park, a brick court area outside the Betsy Ross house, 239 Arch St. in Philadelphia, PA.

7911. Ross, Betty (C.) *see* **Betsy Ross Clarke.**

7912. Ross, Bob (Oct. 29, 1942–July 4, 1995) Host of PBS's *The Joy of Painting* in Muncie, Indiana, from 1983, introduced painting to millions with gentle instructions on creating "happy little trees." He died in Florida from cancer at 52. His picture is on his flush marker. Sec. O, lot 588, space 2, Woodlawn Memorial Park, Windermere, Orlando, FL.

7913. Ross, Earl(e) (March 29, 1888–May 21, 1961) Actor in radio and some films best known as the Judge in *The Great Gildersleeve*. Community vaultage. Unmarked. Grandview Memorial Park, Glendale, CA.

7914. Ross, Edmund Gibson (Dec. 7, 1826–May 8, 1907) Senator from Kansas 1866–1871; in 1868 he cast the "not guilty" vote in the Senate which prevented the two thirds majority needed to impeach President Andrew Johnson. Ross's decision effectively finished his career. Fairview Memorial Park, Albuquerque, NM.

7915. Ross, George (May 10, 1730–July 14, 1779) Signer of the Declaration of Independence from Pennsylvania, one of five signers buried in Christ Church Burial Ground in historic downtown Philadelphia, PA.

7916. Ross, Harold (Nov. 6, 1892–Dec. 7, 1951) Editor and founder (1925) of *The New Yorker* and member of the Algonquin Round Table died in Boston. Cremated and placed at Ferncliff Cemetery, Hartsdale, New York, until December 6, 1956, when the ashes were removed by the Frank E. Campbell mortuary for return to the family.

7917. Ross, Jerry (Jerold Rosenberg, March 9, 1926–Nov. 11, 1955) Songwriter with Richard Adler co-wrote the songs for *Damn Yankees* and *The Pajama Game* prior to his death at 29 from bronchiectasis, a lung disease. St. James 519-C, Ferncliff Cemetery, Hartsdale, NY.

7918. Ross, Joe E. (March 15, 1914–Aug. 13, 1982) Short, squat comic actor from New York played Officer Gunther Toody in TV's *Car 54, Where Are You?* (1961–63). He died from a heart attack at 68. His plaque lists his name and dates and the notation *This Man Had a Ball.* Summerland sec., lot 149, Forest Lawn Hollywood Hills, Los Angeles.

7919. Ross, Lanny (Lancelot Patrick Ross, Jan. 19, 1906–April 25, 1988) Native of Kirkland and Seattle, Washington, the son of Shakespearian actor Douglas Ross, lived in New York from 1920 and attended Yale before his radio and recording career began in 1928. Noted songs include *The Last Time I Saw Paris, We Musn't Say Goodbye* (from *Stage Door Canteen* 1943), and his theme, *Moonlight and Roses.* Married to his manger Olive White from 1935 to her death in 1984, he died in Lenox Hill Hospital, Manhattan. Memorial service at St. Bartholomew's Episcopal Church. Cremated.

7920. Ross, Shirley (Bernice Gaunt, Jan. 7, 1909/ 1913 [on stone]–March 9, 1975) Singer-actress introduced *Blue Moon* (as *The Bad in Every Man*) in *Manhattan Melodrama* (1934), and *Thanks for the Memory* and *Two Sleepy People* with Bob Hope in *The Big Broadcast of 1938*. She died in Menlo Park, California, of cancer at 66 (or 62). Her flat plaque lists her as Bernice Dolan Blum. Sub div. 8, Wildwood lot 95, Alta Mesa Memorial Park, Palo Alto, CA.

7921. Ross, Ted (Theodore Ross Roberts, Jan. 30, 1935–Sept. 3, 2002) Zanesville born, Dayton, Ohio, raised actor won a Tony as the cowardly lion in *The Wiz* on Broadway in 1975 and appeared in several films (as Bitterman in *Arthur* and the sequel, *Ragtime, Police Academy, Stealing Home* and *The Fisher King*, as well as several TV appearances). He returned to Dayton in 1997 and opened a jazz club, but his health declined after a stroke in 1998. He died four years later at 68. Memorial service and cremation through Thomas Funeral Home chapel, 3701 west 3rd St., Dayton, Ohio. No burial. Ashes to family.

7922. Rossellini, Roberto (May 8, 1906–June 3, 1977) Italian director symbolized the neo-realist movement in Italian cinema in the post war years. Married to Ingrid Bergman in the 1950's; divorced in 1957, they were the parents of actress Isabella Rossellini. He died from a heart attack at 71 in Rome and was buried, with a major outpouring of tributes, in the family tomb. Cimitero Monumentale al Verano, Rome.

7923. Rossi, Marie Therese (Jan. 3, 1959–March 1, 1991) The first female combat commander to fly into battle, in Operation Desert Storm, as noted on her monument, along with a tribute from her husband, and on the base *Father bring us home.* Sec. 8, grave 9872, Arlington National Cemetery, Arlington, VA.

7924. Rossi, Pietro Carlo (Oct. 10, 1855–Oct. 8, 1911) Founder of Italian Swiss Colony Wineries. Mausoleum, sec. D, Holy Cross Cemetery, Colma, CA.

7925. Rossini, Gioacchino (Feb. 29, 1792–Nov. 13, 1868) Italian composer of *The Barber of Seville* (1816) and many other operas, was ranked as the greatest Italian composer of the bel canto school of opera. He died at Passy, France, and was buried in division 4, Pere Lachaise Cemetery, Paris. In May 1887, the body was removed to the north side of the Church of Santa Croce in Florence, Italy.

7926. Rossitto, Angelo (Angelo Salvatore Rossitto, Feb. 18, 1908–Sept. 21, 1991) Nebraska born dwarf actor of Italian descent in many films from 1926 into the 1980's (*The Beloved Rogue, Freaks, Spooks Run*

Wild, The Corpse Vanishes, Scared to Death, The Baron of Arizona, Pocketful of Miracles, The Magic Sword, Dracula vs. Frankenstein). He ran a newsstand and worked at a skating rink in Los Angeles prior to his death at 83 from a heart ailment. Donated October 31 to UCLA School of Medicine.

7927. Rossiter, Clinton (Clinton L. Rossiter III, Sept. 18, 1917–July 11, 1970) Historian from Bronxville, New York, wrote *The First American Revolution, Seedtime of the Republic* (1953), *Conservatism in America* (1955) and *The American Presidency* (1956). A moderate Republican, he taught at Cornell from 1946. Found dead in his Ithaca, New York, basement at 52, the cause was ruled a heart attack. Cremated at Traub Crematory, Central Square, New York, through Wagner mortuary, Ithaca. Ashes to wife.

7928. Rosson, Harold "Hal" (Aug. 24, 1895–Sept. 6, 1988) Cinematographer in Hollywood from 1915–1967. Married to Jean Harlow 1933–35. Oscar nominations for *Boom Town, Thirty Seconds Over Tokyo, The Asphalt Jungle* and *The Bad Seed*. Honorary Oscar for pioneering Technicolor in *The Garden of Allah* Sec. 8, lot 43, Hollywood Forever Cemetery, Hollywood (Los Angeles), CA.

7929. Rostow, Walt (Walt Whitman Rostow, Oct. 7, 1916–Feb. 13, 2003) New York born deputy special assistant for national security affairs to President Kennedy and again under Lyndon Johnson was a fervent supporter of the war in Vietnam. In 1969 he followed Johnson to Texas, teaching at the University of Texas at Austin, where he died at 86. Weed-Corley-Fish mortuary, Austin. Balsam plot, sec. 179–194, lot 16230, north middle, grave 3, Woodlawn Cemetery, the Bronx, N.Y.C.

7930. Rostron, Capt. Sir Arthur *see* **Titanic.**

7931. Roth, Ed "Big Daddy" (Edward Roth, March 4, 1932–April 4, 2001) Creator of fantastic cars and the anti-hero Rat Fink in the California hotrod cultural revolution of the 1950's and 60's was considered a pioneer in his use of fiberglass. In 1974 he converted to the Mormon Church and abandoned the rebel lifestyle while continuing to design cars. He died at his studio in Manti, Utah, at 69. Burial with military honors. Plat A, block 12, lot 33, grave 1, Manti City Cemetery, Manti, UT.

7932. Roth, Jules (July 23, 1900–Jan. 4, 1998) The manager of Hollywood Memorial Park Cemetery from 1937 was a former con man who, as Jack Roth, had done time at San Quentin for stock fraud. By the 1990's it was revealed that Roth had long mishandled the endowment funds and driven the cemetery into bankruptcy, forcing it to close until rescued by a new owner c. 1997. The 97 year old Roth died before he could be indicted. Entombed with his parents; despite his practices, his plaque has the respectful *General manager and president emeritus of Hollywood Cemetery.* Cathedral Mausoleum, Hollywood Forever Cemetery, Hollywood, Los Angeles.

7933. Roth, Lillian (Lillian Rutstein, Dec. 13, 1910–May 12, 1980) Actress-singer at Paramount in the early 1930's (*Madam Satan, Animal Crackers*) whose career was destroyed by alcoholism, detailed in her autobiography *I'll Cry Tomorrow* (1954), predating by thirty years tell-all stories of chemical dependency. In later years she worked at a series of odd jobs in New York. Her flat plaque, near the office, bears the epitaph *As bad as it was, it was good.* Sec. 26, single graves, Mt. Pleasant Cemetery, Hawthorne, NY.

7934. Rothafel, Samuel L. "Roxy" (July 9, 1882–Jan. 13, 1936) New York stage manager of the Capitol Theatre, the Roxy and Radio City Music Hall. The Rockettes are derived from his nickname, inscribed on his family monument. Gate to circle and left, then left, stop at path on right by Adler and Ames crypts. Monument down path on right. Linden Hills Cemetery, Maspeth, now Ridgewood, Queens, N.Y.C.

7935. Rothschild, Mayer Amschel (Feb. 23, 1744–Sept. 19, 1812) Founder of the Jewish banking family with branches of his empire throughout Europe. He started the firm after being an antique dealer. Jewish Cemetery, Frankfurt, Germany. His sons were stationed in various cities. **Nathan Mayer Rothschild** (Sept. 16, 1777–July 28, 1836) is buried in Willesden Cemetery, London. Many of the other English based Rothschilds are in Ferdinand Rothschild's wife's mausoleum in West Ham, Buckingham Road. The French branch of the family are in the Jewish section of Pere Lachaise Cemetery in Paris. The names are inscribed within a large, deep mausoleum, but not on the exterior.

7936. Rothstein, Arnold (Jan. 17, 1882–Nov. 6, 1928) New York gambler infamous for fixing the 1919 world series, though he was never indicted. After he reportedly welshed on a bet, he was shot in the stomach in a room at the Park Central Hotel in Manhattan and died at Polyclinic Hospital. He is buried beside his brother, the front of the stones in Hebrew and the backs in English. Path M, sec. 52, Union Field Cemetery (of Rodeph Sholom), Ridgewood, Queens, N.Y.C.

7937. Roush, Edd (May 8, 1893–March 21, 1988) N.L. star center fielder and slugger with Chicago A.L. 1913, and the Cincinnati Reds 1916–1926. Next to Tris Speaker, he was considered the best in his position in the 1920's, frequently a salary holdout (until late July 1922 and the entire 1930 season). Hall of Fame 1962. Montgomery Cemetery, Oakland City, IN.

7938. Rousseau, Jean Jacques (June 28, 1712–July 2, 1778) Geneva born writer and philosopher of the Age of Enlightenment, popular amid the salons of Paris from 1761 with *Julie ou la Nouvelle Heloise* and *The Social Contract.* He made a wide variety of enemies and upon his death was buried in the moonlight July 4, 1778 at The Poplars, an island in a small lake at Ermenonville Park, but soon became a posthumous genius and at the insistence of Robespierre in 1789 was removed to a tomb, ironically near his former rival Voltaire, in the Pantheon, Paris.

7939. Rousseau, Theodore (April 15, 1812–Dec. 22, 1867) French landscape painter, the leading figure of the Barbizon school, as opposed to the idealism of neo-classicists. Chailly-en-Biere, France.

7940. Roussimoff, Andre (the Giant) (May 19, 1946–Jan. 27, 1993) 7'4", 520 pound wrestler known as Andre the Giant played Fezzick in *The Princess Bride* (1987). He was in his native France for his father's funeral when he died from an apparent heart attack in his room at 46. He had suffered from acromegaly, an excessive accelerated growth of the head and limbs. Cremated in France, the ashes were returned to his ranch at Ellerbe, NC.

7941. Roventini, Johnny (Aug. 15, 1910–Nov. 30, 1998) Pint sized actor known for shouting "Call for Philip Moor-rees" (in Philip Morris cigarette commercials) on the radio later did several other bits. He died in White Plains, New York, at 88, listed as 86. Family name only on stone. Sec. 14, range C, 223-227, St. Charles Cemetery, Farmingdale, Long Island, N.Y.

7942. Rowan, Dan (Daniel H. Rowan, July 22 [SSDI lists 2], 1922–Sept. 22, 1987) Co-host of Rowan and Martin's *Laugh-In* 1968–1973, died in Florida from cancer at 65. Ashes to family through Farley mortuary, Venice, FL.

7943. Rowe, Lynwood "Schoolboy" (Jan. 11, 1910–Jan. 8, 1961) Pitching great with the Detroit Tigers in the 1930's, later with the Phillies. Sec. D, lot 213, Arlington Cemetery, El Dorado, AR.

7944. Rowlands, Addie *see* **Albanesi.**

7945. Royce, Frederick Henry (March 27, 1863–April 22, 1933) Knighted co-founder with Charles Rolls of the ultimate in luxurious automobiles, the Rolls-Royce. Cremated at Golders Green Crematorium, London. North wall of nave, St. Andrews Parish Church, Alwalton, Cambridgeshire.

7946. Royko, Mike (Sept. 19, 1932–April 29, 1997) Chicago native was, like Studs Terkel, one of the city's originals. At the *Chicago Daily News* from 1959–78, the *Sun Times* 1978–84 and the *Tribune* for his last 13 years, he wrote five columns a week, resplendent with working class no-nonsense observations on any and all topics, peppered with liberal doses of wry humor and cynicism. He died at 64 from heart failure in a northside hospital. He was cremated and half his ashes buried with his father in Acacia Park Cemetery, and the other half interred with his wife Carol, whose death in 1979 was the source of one of his best loved columns. Carnation, block 8, lot 16, grave 1, and New (rear) section of the mausoleum, Acacia Park Cemetery, Chicago, IL.

7947. Royle, Selena (Nov. 6, 1904–April 23, 1983) New York City born stage actress co-founded the Actors Free Diner Club in Union Church on West 48th Street. Her films, later in her career, include *Thirty Seconds Over Tokyo, Stage Door Canteen, The Fighting Sullivans, Mrs. Parkington, Courage of Lassie, Cass Timberlane, A Date With Judy, The Heiress, Come Fill the Cup*. The widow of actor George Renavent (*q.v.*), she died in Guadalajara at 78. Zapopan Cemetery, Guadalajara, Mexico.

7948. Rozelle, Pete (Alvin Ray Rozelle, March 1, 1926–Dec. 6, 1996) NFL commissioner from 1960–1989 shaped his post and the age of football on television, beginning the Super Bowl in 1967 and *Monday Night Football* in the 1970's. He died from brain cancer in Rancho Santa Fe, California, at 70. Lakeview Columbarium room 1, bay 2, niche 16 tier C, El Camino Memorial Park, La Jolla, CA.

7949. Rozsa, Miklos (April 18, 1907–July 27, 1995) Film composer whose works include *The Thief of Baghdad* (1940) and *Julius Caesar* (1953), received Oscars for *Spellbound* (1945), *A Double Life* (1947) and *Ben Hur* (1959). He was known for meticulous research into the recreation of ancient music. Blessed Assurance, lot 1656, space 1, Forest Lawn Hollywood Hills, Los Angeles.

7950. Rub, Christian (April 13, 1886/1887–April 14, 1956) Austrian actor in Hollywood in the 1930's and 40's, often as Swedes: *Secrets of the French Police, The Kiss Before the Mirror, Peter Ibbetson, Mr. Deeds Goes to Town, Pinocchio* (as the voice of Geppeto), *Tales of Manhattan, Rhapsody in Blue, Strange Confession*, etc. Cremated at Santa Barbara Cemetery through Welch-Ryce-Haider mortuary. Ashes sent May 11, 1956 for burial in Thomasberg Cemetery, Edlitz, Niederosterreich Province, Austria.

7951. Rubell, Steve (Dec. 2, 1943–July 25, 1989) Owner with his partner Ian Schrager of New York's Studio 54 in the 1970's, the city's mecca for social visibility, mixed liberally with drugs and sex. It faded by 1979 and both owners did thirteen months for tax evasion, afterward moving into the hotel business until Rubell died from AIDS at 45. Block 21, Sanders Association, grave 2, plot 15, Beth Moses Cemetery, Farmingdale, Long Island, NY.

7952. Rubens, Alma (Alma Smith, Feb. 19, 1897–Jan. 21, 1931) Silent screen actress from San Francisco, divorced from Franklin Farnum and separated from Ricardo Cortez at the time her career was destroyed by drug addiction, beginning with a public display of hysteria on Hollywood Boulevard in January 1929. She was twice hospitalized and claimed to be free of her habit when she was arrested a last time for smuggling morphine back from Agua Caliente. She died from pneumonia at 33 in the presence of her sister and brother-in-law Stanley Cortez. After a Christian Science funeral in Hollywood, Gates mortuary shipped the body to Stephens and Bean mortuary in Fresno for interment in what is the first of three Ararat Cemeteries on Hughes Ave. north of Nielson Ave. Sec. F, tier 2, row 1, Ararat Mausoleum, Fresno, CA.

7953. Rubens, Peter Paul (June 28, 1577–May 30, 1640) Flemish painter born in Prussia studied in Italy but returned to Antwerp, where he spent the rest of his life. Known for his *Adoration of the Magi* and *Descent from the Cross* (1612) and for his paintings of ample women. Rubens based many of them on his second wife, Helena Fourment, who he never tired of painting. He was buried first in the Fourment vault but was removed to St. James Church in Antwerp, where a memorial chapel was built with a marble Madonna and the painting *Madonna With Saints*, as he had requested. St. Jacobskerk (St. James Church), Antwerp, Belgium.

7954. Rubin, Benny (Feb. 2, 1899–July 15, 1986) Comedian of stage and screen and a staple on radio and TV with *The Jack Benny Show* and others. Veteran of vaudeville and burlesque, his green crypt plaque along the inside front of the cemetery is inscribed *The Palace—now Heaven*. Garden Mausoleum, Alcove of Dedication, wall C, crypt 518, Hillside Memorial Park, Los Angeles.

7955. Rubin, Irv (April 12, 1945–Nov. 13, 2002) Canadian born head of the Jewish Defense League from 1985 had immigrated with his family to the U.S. in 1961. Arrested over forty times and famed for brawling with members of the American Nazi Party or the KKK, his last arrest was in December 2001 in an FBI investigation of his alleged plans to bomb a Culver City mosque. He died at 57 a week after slitting his own throat and falling eighteen feet over a railing at the federal Metropolitan Detention Center in Los Angeles. Sholom Memorial Park, Sylmar, CA.

7956. Rubin, Jerry (July 14, 1938–Nov. 28, 1994) Cincinnati born anti-war activist was, with Abbie Hoffman, the most vocal of the Chicago Seven demonstrating outside the Democratic national convention there. Charged with conspiracy to incite violence and crossing state lines with intent to riot, their trial ran from September 1969 to January 1970, with the convictions later overturned by the Seventh U.S. Circuit Court of Appeals. The "one time Yippie turned Yuppie" evolved into a Wall Street banker. He died as a result of being hit while jaywalking in Los Angeles November 14. Mount of Olives, block 14, lot 466, space 3, Hillside Memorial Park, Los Angeles.

7957. Rubinstein, Arthur (Jan. 28, 1887–Dec. 20, 1982) Polish born concert pianist began as a teenage prodigy doing popular and classical interpretations until later years, when he devoted most of his work to Chopin. Special plot — ashes reportedly scattered or buried — at a forest on the edge of Jerusalem.

7958. Rubinstein, Helena (Dec. 25, 1870–April 1, 1965) Founder, developer and promoter of Helena Rubinstein Cosmetics. She died at 94. Sec. X, lot 7870, Mount Olivet Cemetery, Maspeth, Queens, N.Y.C.

7959. Rubinstein, Serge (May 18, 1908–Jan. 27, 1955) Russian born financier in America was flamboyant, controversial and widely hated. He was found dead with his face and throat taped and his throat crushed, in his apartment at 816 5th Avenue in Manhattan. One detective, remarking on persons with a motive, said that limited it to 10,000. The murder was never solved. Oakwood section, Woodlawn Cemetery, the Bronx, N.Y.C.

7960. Ruby, Harry (Jan. 27, 1895–Feb. 23, 1974) New York born songwriter collaborated mostly with Bert Kalmer and wrote songs for the Marx Brothers and others as well as *Three Little Words, Who's Sorry Now?*, many others. He later appeared in *Make Room For Daddy* in the 1950's. Ashes in vaultage below Pierce Brothers Chapel of the Pines Crematory, Los Angeles.

7961. Ruby, Jack (Jacob Rubenstein, April 25, 1911–Jan. 3, 1967) Chicago born owner of the Carousel Club in Dallas, Texas, became a household name on Sunday morning, November 24, 1963, when he stepped out of a crowd and fired a fatal shot into Lee Harvey Oswald, the alleged assassin of President Kennedy two days before. Theories abound that he was part of a plot to silence Oswald in light of some of Ruby's friends in the mob, despite the Warren Commission findings that Oswald acted alone. His explanation, never disproved, was that he was both infuriated by the murder of the president and wanted to spare the widow further anguish with a public murder trial. He was convicted of murder and sent to prison, where he died three years later from cancer. Rubinstein plot, Violet sec., plot 2, lot 9, Westlawn Memorial Park, Norridge (Chicago), IL.

7962. Rudd, Hughes (Sept. 12, 1921–Oct. 13, 1992) CBS newsman and host of *CBS This Morning* in the 1970's. Silver Star and Purple Heart. Columbarium court 3, sec. T, stack 24, niche 5, Arlington National Cemetery, Arlington, VA.

7963. Rudder, James (James Earl Rudder, May 6, 1910–March 23, 1970) Commander of the Second Ranger Battalion led the assault up the 100' cliffs at Pointe du Hoc during the Normandy invasion of June 6 to 8, 1944, losing 130 of 225 men in the eventually successful ascent to silence the German guns. He was president of Texas A&M University 1959–1970. College Station Cemetery, College Station, TX.

7964. Rudolf (Kron Prinz Rudolf, August 21, 1858–Jan. 29, 1889) Liberal minded Kronprinz of Austria, son of Franz Joseph and heir to the throne, carried out a murder-suicide pact with his mistress, **Baroness Marie Vetsera** (March 19, 1871–Jan. 29, 1889) at Mayerling, his country retreat. He shot her through the head as she lay clutching a rose, then shot himself the same way. His coffin was placed beneath the altar of St. Stephen's Cathedral in Vienna, with his heart placed in St. Augustin's, the court parish church. The body was later put into a metal sarcophagus in the crypt of the Capuchins, between Maria Theresa and Maximillian. Kapuzinerkirche (Kaisergruft), Vienna. Marie Vetsera was taken by coach at night — permission gained from the abbot at Heiligenkreuz Monastery in the Vienna Woods, and buried in consecrated ground through the requests of the royal family. The special permission was needed because she was declared a suicide rather than a homicide, to avoid the legal filing of a report with the police. She may have been buried at the secluded monastery churchyard at first, as described in Frederic Morton's *A Nervous Splendor*, but her grave is near the center of the city cemetery at Heiligenkreuz, the monument toward the wall, inscribed *Mary Frehn Vetsera* and her dates. Her coffin was opened by invading Soviets in 1945, was exhumed again in 1959 to make certain the skull was there, and to settle debates over a bullet hole in the skull or lack thereof. This could not be resolved, as part of the skull was missing. The entire coffin was stolen July 8, 1991, by one Helmut Flatzelsteiner and accomplices. He took the (unidentified) remains to Linz to a forensic specialist, though the purpose wasn't clarified. The empty grave was not discovered until December 22, 1992, when a newspaper was tipped off that the grave was empty. The bones were retrieved and taken to the Legal Medical Institute in Vienna until their reburial October 28, 1993 in the City Cemetery at Heiligenkreuz. **Mitzi Caspar** (Mizzi Caspar, Sept. 28, 1864–Jan. 29, 1907), one of Rudolf's other mistresses, of whom he was particularly fond, declined his invitation to die with him. Gruppe N, nummer 639, Gemeindefriedhof Maria Enzersdorf, Maria Enzersdorf, Austria. **Josef Bratfisch** (Aug. 26, 1847–Dec. 16, 1892) Rudolf's coachman, who drove him to Mayerling, and who discovered the bodies, is buried in gruppe K, nummer 130, Friedhof Hernals, Vienna.

7965. Rudolph, Wilma (Wilma Glodean Rudolph, June 23, 1940–Nov. 12, 1994) Track and field star from Clarksville, Tennessee, overcame polio as a child to win the 100-m and 200-m dashes and place first in the 4 × 100-m relay team in the 1960 Olympics in Rome, setting a 200-m dash world record and again in the 100-m dash in 1961. She later taught and coached near Nashville, and headed the Wilma Rudolph Foundation in Indianapolis 1982–92. She died near Nashville from a brain tumor at 54. Her polished black monument has her picture, the Olympic symbols, torch and flame, and the epitaph *citius, altius, fortius* (faster, higher, braver). Foston Memorial Gardens, Clarksville, TN.

7966. Ruffin, David (Davis Eli Ruffin, Jan. 18, 1941–June 1, 1991) Singer from Meridian, Mississippi, sang lead with the Temptations 1964–68 at Motown, his soulful, raspy voice alternating with the falsetto of Eddie Kendricks. Ruffin's leads included *My Girl, All I Need, (I Wish it Would) Rain*. He died from a drug overdose in Philadelphia at 50. Services in the New Bethel Baptist Church in Detroit. Grave length rose granite slab with his picture etched on it. Sec. 3, Woodlawn Cemetery, Detroit, MI.

7967. Ruffin, Edmund (Jan. 5, 1794–June 18, 1865) Southern U.S. agricultural expert was a staunch advocate of secession. It was he who fired the first shot at Fort Sumter to open the Civil War. Despondent over the defeat of the Confederacy four years later, he shot himself at Radmoor, Virginia. Buried on his estate Marlbourne, Hanover County, VA.

7968. Ruffing, Red (Charles H. Ruffing, May 3, 1905–Feb. 17, 1986) Major league pitcher, minus four toes on his left foot from a mining accident. With the Yankees 1930–1946, Rufus the Red threw four twenty victory seasons in a row 1936–39, as well as being a top flight hitter. Hall of Fame 1967. Corridor of Devotion, tier B (or D), crypt 1 (right of altar), Hillcrest Cemetery mausoleum, Bedford Heights, OH.

7969. Ruffo, Titta (Ruffo Cafiero Titta, June 9, 1877–July 5, 1953) Operatic baritone from Pisa debuted in *Lohengrin* in Rome 1898, and performed — often as Amleto — across Europe and in Philadelphia and New York, remaining with the Metropolitan Opera there 1922–29. His voice weakened in the 1930's and he retired. Arrested in Italy for opposing the Fascist regime in 1937, he survived the war and died from lung cancer in Florence at 76. Polished black monument with a musical motif above his name. Cimitero Monumentale, Milan, Italy.

7970. Rugg, Hal (Harald Rugg, July 21, 1936–Aug. 9, 2005) Steel guitar player from Tucson recorded in Nashville from 1963 and performed at The Grand Ole Opry as well as on various television variety programs. Among those he recorded with were Loretta Lynn, Porter Wagoner, Sammi Smith, Ray Stevens, Ronnie Milsap, Ray Price, Barbara Mandrell, Eddie Rabbit, Johnny Russell, and Joan Baez, among others. He died in Tucson at 69. Hermitage Memorial Gardens, Hermitage, TN.

7971. Ruggles, Charles (Feb. 8, 1886–Dec. 23, 1970) Character actor in perennially timid, henpecked roles including several pairings with Mary Boland. At Paramount in the 1930's in *If I Had a Million, Murders in the Zoo, Ruggles of Red Gap* and several hapless butlers, etc. He went on to varied roles in TV through the 1960's until his death from cancer at 84 in Santa Monica. Garden of Memory (private), lawn crypt 1007, Forest Lawn, Glendale, CA.

7972. Ruggles, Wesley (June 11, 1889–Jan. 8, 1972) Brother of Charles Ruggles was a minstrel and silent screen actor turned director 1918–1946 (*Silk Stockings* 1927, *Cimarron* 1931, *I'm No Angel* 1933). Buried near his brother. Garden of Memory (private), lawn crypt 1115, Forest Lawn, Glendale, CA.

7973. Ruick, Barbara (Dec. 23, 1932–March 2, 1974) Actress in films of the 1950's, wife of conductor John Williams. Columbarium of Blessedness, niche 37461, Freedom Mausoleum, Forest Lawn, Glendale, CA.

7974. Ruman, Sig (Siegfried Rumann, Oct. 11, 1884–Feb. 14, 1967) German born actor from Hamburg familiar as bumbling Teutonic or Russian characters in many films of the 1930's and 40's including *A Night at the Opera* (1935), *Ninotchka* (1939), *To Be or Not to Be* (1942), *House of Frankenstein* (1944), *A Night in Casablanca* (1946), and as Sgt. Schultz in *Stalag 17* (1953). He died at 82 outside his home in Julian, California, as he was returning from a camping trip. Flat plaque, Julian Cemetery, Julian, CA.

7975. Runnels, Pete (James Edward Runnells, Jan. 28, 1928–May 20, 1991) Senators and Red Sox infielder from Lufkin, Texas, played first and second base 1957–64. He won the league batting championship in 1960 and 1962. His career lasted from the early 50's until 1964. Sec. 210, lot 219, Forest Park East Cemetery, Webster, TX.

7976. Runyon, Damon (Oct. 4, 1884–Dec. 10, 1946) New York journalist, sportswriter and night owl who specialized in stories about New York City's sporting low lifes and big hearts among the gamblers and gangsters, the most famous of which became the musical *Guys and Dolls* (1931), films *Little Miss Marker, The Lemon Drop Kid*, etc. His wife Ellen is buried (1931) in his plot in the Alpine sec. 177 (top of the hill, along the road), Woodlawn Cemetery, the Bronx, N.Y.C. At his request, his son scattered his ashes over Times Square from a plane flown by Eddie Rickenbacker.

7977. Runyon, Marvin (Marvin Travis Runyon, Sept. 16, 1924–May 3, 2004) Dallas born Ford executive, Nissan president and CEO, chairman of the Tennessee Valley Authority and postmaster general 1992–98, during which he trimmed 23,000 management jobs while adding letter carriers to improve service. He died from lung disease in Nashville at 79. Service at St. George Episcopal Church, Nashville. Donated to Vanderbilt University School of Medicine.

7978. Rupp, Adolph (Sept. 2, 1901–Dec. 10, 1977) University of Kentucky basketball coach 1930–1972 won four NCAA championships. His monument has a basketball engraved on it. Sec. 45, lot 677, Lexington Cemetery, Lexington, KY.

7979. Ruppert, Jacob (Aug. 5, 1867–Jan. 13, 1939) Manager of the Ruppert Brewery in New York was owner of the New York Yankees for twenty five years (1914–1939), buying Babe Ruth from Boston owner Harry Frazee in 1919. Buried in the four columned mausoleum of his father, who founded the brewery. Family mausoleum, sec. 53, Cherokee Ave., Kensico Cemetery, Valhalla, NY.

7980. Rush, Benjamin (Dec. 24, 1746–April 19, 1813) Signer of the Declaration of Independence from Pennsylvania, Treasurer of the U.S. Mint in Philadelphia 1797–1813, was also a physician who worked during the 1793 Yellow Fever epidemic and developed several techniques improving the science, but with a dogmatic approach that slowed their progress in some areas. He also wrote the first American study of diseases of the mind (1812). Rush is buried, as are four other signers of the Declaration, in historic Christ Church Burial Ground, Philadelphia. His son **Richard Rush** (Aug. 29, 1780–July 30, 1859), statesman and diplomat, is at Laurel Hill Cemetery, Philadelphia, PA.

7981. Rushing, Jimmy (James Andrew Rushing, Aug. 26, 1903–June 8, 1972) Blues singer with Count Basie noted for his shouting style vocal approach. Led his own group 1950–1952. Sec. F, lot 267-D, Maple Grove Cemetery, Kew Gardens, Queens, N.Y.C.

7982. Rusie, Amos (May 30, 1871–Dec. 6, 1942) The Hoosier Thunderbolt from Mooresville, Indiana, was the fireball king of 19th century baseball pitchers, with thirty victories four years in a row with the N.Y. Giants 1891–1894. He was traded to Cincinnati in 1901 for Christy Mathewson. Hall of Fame 1977. Flush rose marker, G-5-165-C-2, Acacia Memorial Park, Seattle, WA.

7983. Rusk, Dean (David Dean Rusk, Feb. 9, 1909–Dec. 20, 1994) Georgia born U.S. Secretary of State under Kennedy and Johnson 1961–69 presided over the Vietnam War and its escalation as well as the Bay of Pigs fiasco in 1961, the Cuban Missile Crisis in 1962 and the signing of the 1963 Nuclear Test Ban Treaty with the Soviet Union. Though a prime target of anti-war demonstrators, he did receive credit with LBJ for the unconditional halt to bombing in the north in 1968. He taught at the University of Georgia at Athens, where he died at 85. Rounded light rose stone facing the road. Sec. J, lot se ¼ 13, Oconee Hill Cemetery, Athens, GA.

7984. Russell, Andy (Andres Rabago, Sept. 16, 1919–April 16, 1992) Singer from East L.A. replaced Frank Sinatra on *Your Hit Parade* in 1947 and had hits with *Besame Mucho, Magic is the Moon*, and million sellers with *Laughing on the Outside* and *Amor* (which is engraved on his plaque). In the 1950's and 60's he appeared in Spanish speaking films and TV in Mexico City and Buenos Aires, returning to the U.S. in the late 1960's. He died from a stroke at 72 in Phoenix. West Lawn 1, lot 24, Loma Vista Memorial Park, Fullerton, CA.

7985. Russell, Bertrand (May 18. 1872–Feb. 2, 1970) Welsh philosopher and mathematician from Trelleck, Wales, espoused pacifist views during World War I. He was removed as a lecturer at Cambridge and imprisoned for six months. His philosophy, logical atomism, stressed the significance of the individual and criticized social institutions. He died at Plas Penryndeudraeth, Merioneth, Wales. Colwyn Bay Crematorium, Clwyd, Wales. He wished his ashes scattered.

7986. Russell, Bobby (Robert Russell, April 19, 1940–Nov. 19, 1992) 1968 Grammy winning songwriter (for *Little Green Apples*) also wrote *Honey, The Night the Lights Went Out in Georgia*, recorded *Saturday Morning Confusion*, etc. He died at 52 from coronary artery disease at Nicholasville, Kentucky. Mausoleum crypt, Woodlawn Memorial Park, Nashville, TN.

7987. Russell, Charles (March 19, 1864–Oct. 24, 1926) Artist and sculptor who lived in the west, the subject of his work. Resided for a time with the Blood Indians, a division of the Blackfoot. A hole in the boulder over his grave was hollowed out so birds could nest inside. Town cemetery, Great Falls, MT.

7988. Russell, Elizabeth (Elizabeth Conve[r]y,

Aug. 12, 1906–May 4, 2002) Actress and model from Philadelphia with striking features, married in the 1930's to the elder brother of Rosalind Russell, made few but memorable appearances in films during the 1940's: *The Corpse Vanishes, Hitler's Madman, Weird Woman, The Uninvited* (the model for the painting and ghost of Mary Meredith), *Our Vines Have Tender Grapes,* and particularly in Val Lewton's string of thrillers at RKO (*Cat People, The Seventh Victim, Curse of the Cat People, Bedlam*). She died at Nazareth House, Cheviot Hills, Los Angeles, at 95, her death unreported until August 2005. Sec. K, tier LP, grave 8, Holy Cross Cemetery, Culver City, CA.

7989. Russell, Gail (Sept. 21, 1925–Aug. 27, 1961) Actress in young and innocent early parts made her debut in 1943; best known for *Our Hearts Were Young and Gay, The Uninvited* (1944) and *Wake of the Red Witch* (1948). Her career and health fell apart with her substance abuse. Divorced from actor Guy Madison, her last married name was Mosely when she was found dead in her Los Angeles apartment at 35, surrounded by empty liquor bottles. The cause was listed as severe fatty liver, acute and chronic alcoholism. Block E (Evergreen), sec. 4887, lot 2, Valhalla Memorial Park, North Hollywood, CA.

7990. Russell, Harold (Jan. 14, 1914–Jan. 29, 2002) Nova Scotia born and raised in the Cambridge, Massachusetts area, he joined the U.S. Army the day after Pearl Harbor was bombed. An explosives expert and instructor, he lost his hands to a defective fuse in an explosion at Camp Mackaill, North Carolina, in 1944. Upbeat and optimistic, he was used in an army film, *Diary of A Sergeant,* but gained fame as Homer Parrish in William Wyler's *The Best Years of Our Lives* (1946), displaying not only his healthy outlook but his dexterity with the hooks that had replaced his hands. He won an Oscar as best supporting actor and a special Oscar as well. Returning to Massachusetts and becoming an American citizen, he ran an advertising and public relations business, an insurance agency, served as commander of AMVETS, was on the Committee for Disabled Veterans under President Truman, President Kennedy's Committee on Employment of the Handicapped, and chaired it under Johnson, Nixon and Carter. In 1992 he sold his Oscar to help pay his wife's medical expenses, despite criticism from the academy over the sale. Long a resident of Cape Cod, he died at 88 in a nursing home at Needham, Massachusetts. Mass at St. Ann's Church in Wayland. Sec. L, lot 61, Lakeview Cemetery, Wayland, MA.

7991. Russell, John (Jan. 3, 1921–Jan. 19, 1991) Tall actor with piercing eyes from Los Angeles, in films (*Undertow, Rio Bravo, The Outlaw Josie Wales, Pale Rider*) from the 1940's. In many westerns, he starred in the TV series *Lawman* 1958–1962. Sec. 425, row D, grave 8, Los Angeles/Sawtelle National Cemetery, Westwood, west Los Angeles.

7992. Russell, Johnny (Johnny Bright Russell, Jan. 23, 1940–July 3, 2001) Country-western musician, a star of the Grand Ole Opry, wrote *Act Naturally* for Buck Owens in 1963. Pall-bearers included Jim Ed Brown, Porter Waggoner, Garth Brooks and Little Jimmy Dickens. Mausoleum chapel, tier C, crypt 4, Woodlawn East Memorial Park Hendersonville, TN.

7993. Russell, Lillian (Helen Louise Leonard, Dec. 4, 1861–June 6, 1922) Pittsburgh born actress adopted her stage name while appearing in Tony Pastor's New York Variety Theatre in 1880. A star of the stage for over thirty years, known for both her beauty and clear soprano singing voice. For decades she was the ideal of Diamond Jim Brady, her frequent companion. She lectured on beauty and on "How to live a hundred years" but died in Pittsburgh at sixty. Because of her fund raising Red Cross work in Europe during World War I, President Harding ordered that she be interred with full military honors. Small mausoleum facing the road, inscribed *Lillian Russell Moore* and *The world is better for her having lived.* Sec. 40, lot 5, Allegheny Cemetery, Pittsburgh, PA.

7994. Russell, Pee Wee (Charles Ellsworth Russell, March 27, 1907–Feb. 15, 1969) Jazz clarinetist from the late 1920's, with many bands including Red Nichols, Bix Beiderbecke, Frankie Trumbauer and Louis Prima. Jacob block F, row 8, B'Nai Abraham Memorial Park, Union, NJ.

7995. Russell, Richard (Richard Brevard Russell, Nov. 2, 1897–Jan. 21, 1971) Georgia legislator, governor 1933–33 and Democratic senator 1933–1971, chairing the Armed Services and Appropriations Committee and instrumental in pushing through Lyndon Johnson's requests for increased spending and involvement in Vietnam. President Pro Tempore 1969–1971. Russell Cemetery, behind his home, Highway 8 and Russell Cemetery Road, Winder, GA.

7996. Russell, Rosalind (June 4, 1907–Nov. 28, 1976) Versatile Hollywood actress from Waterbury, Connecticut, in sophisticated comedies and dramas from the mid 1930's at MGM, including *China Seas, Trouble For Two, Night Must Fall* (1937), *The Citadel, The Women, His Girl Friday* (1940), *My Sister Eileen* (1942, AA nom.), *Sister Kenny* (1946, AA nom.), *Mourning Becomes Electra* (1947, AA nom.) and *Picnic* (1956). She starred on Broadway in *Auntie Mame* and won an Oscar for the 1958 film version. In 1972 she received the Jean Hersholt Humanitarian Award for her charity work. Ill for some time with cancer originating in her breast, she died in her Beverly Hills home. After a requiem mass at the Church of the Good Shepherd in Beverly Hills on December 2, she was buried, joined by her husband Frederick Brisson in 1984, at the foot of the cross in section M, lot 536. Holy Cross Cemetery, Culver City, CA.

7997. Russell, William (April 12, 1886–Feb. 18, 1929) Silent screen actor from 1918, originally with Griffith. Formerly a vaudevillian. Married to actress Helen Ferguson (d. 1977). He died from pneumonia at 42. Sanctuary of Love, crypt 3495 (with signature), Great Mausoleum, Forest Lawn, Glendale, CA.

7998. Russo, Paul (April 10, 1914–June 23, 1976) Indianapolis 500 race driver, known for his association with Novi. Sec. 78, lot 106–107, Crown Hill Cemetery, Indianapolis, IN.

7999. Rutgers, Henry (Oct. 7, 1745–Feb. 17, 1830) Revolutionary era New York patriot, a captain in the 1st New York Militia at the Battle of White Plains, later a Colonel, and benefactor and trustee of Queens College in New Brunswick, New Jersey, renamed after him in 1825. Thought to be buried in the overgrown and neglected plot, marked by an obelisk marked *Rutgers,* at Belleville Reformed Church, Rutgers and Main Streets, Belleville, New Jersey, where 67 Revolutionary veterans lie. In 2001 a committee from Rutgers University researched the validity of the burial, and found it incorrect; he was first buried at the Old Middle Church Cemetery, Nassau and Cedar Streets, Manhattan. On March 5, 1858, he was removed to the Old Middle Church Lafayette St. Cemetery, and as that, like the earlier graveyard, was sold off by the church, he was removed finally on October 10, 1865, to Greenwood in Brooklyn. Marked by a concrete slab and a small concrete marker inscribed *D.R.C.–N.Y.* (Dutch Reformed Church of New York). Sec. 28, lot 10776, Greenwood Cemetery, Brooklyn, N.Y.C.

8000. Ruth, Babe (George Herman Ruth, Feb. 6, 1895–Aug. 16, 1948) The most recognized name in baseball was born in Baltimore and sent early on to a boys' industrial school there, where he took up the national pastime. By 1919, pitching for the Boston Red Sox and the best left handed pitcher in the American League, he was sold to the New York Yankees, and during the next decade became the country's best known sports hero, credited with bringing the public back to the ballparks after the disgust over the 1919 Blacksox scandal. Yankee Stadium in the Bronx, opened in 1923 and dubbed The House That Ruth Built, housed in the 1920's the best team to date, including the 1927 Murderers Row line-up, the same season Ruth hit a record 60 home runs, which stood until broken by Hank Aaron in 1974. His prowess at the plate endured in legend long after the Babe's ability had faded. Babe Ruth Day was held at Yankee Stadium April 7, 1947. By then his stout frame was shrunken, his hair white and his voice a raspy whisper from cancer which had originated in his nasopharynx in 1946. He established, and left much of his money to, the Babe Ruth Foundation for underprivileged children. He was one of the original group elected to the Hall of Fame (1936). After his death from cancer at 53 at Memorial Hospital in Manhattan, seventy five thousand filed through Yankee Stadium where he lay in state. Following mass at St. Patrick's Cathedral, the coffin was taken to a receiving vault at Gate of Heaven Catholic Cemetery, where it was buried in October. The monument features a bas-relief of Christ and a young boy; on one side of the base are the names of Ruth and his wife Clare (1900–1976). On the left side are the words of Cardinal Spellman: *May the divine spirit that animated Babe Ruth to win the critical game of life inspire the youth of America.* Sec. 25, near the top of the hillside, below the monument to Billy Martin, Gate of Heaven Cemetery, Hawthorne, New York. Ruth's first wife, **Helen Woodford "Kinder" Ruth** (1897–Jan. 11, 1929) died in a fire in Watertown, Massachusetts, at 31. Sec 10 west side, row 7, grave 7, Mt. Calvary Cemetery, Roslindale, Boston, MA.

8001. Rutherford, Alison (1713–Nov. 22, 1794) Scottish poet wrote the lament *Flowers of the Forest.* A plaque on the cemetery wall gives her married name (Cockburn). Buccleuch Cemetery, Edinburgh.

8002. Rutherford, Margaret (May 11, 1892–May 22, 1972) English actress and comedienne, Dame Commander of the British Empire, long on stage and in films from 1936, often as eccentric, whimsical characters, as Madame Arcati in *Blithe Spirit* (1945), later as Agatha Christie's Miss Marple in several mysteries in the 1960's, and won an Oscar for *The V.I.P.'s* (1963). She died at 80 in her home in Chalfont, St. Peter, Buckinghamshire, and was buried with her husband, actor **Stringer Davis** (James Buckley Stringer Davis, June 4, 1899–Aug. 29, 1973), who appeared in her Miss Marple films as Mr. Stringer. On the front of the curb enclosing the plot in front of their rose-brown stone is the remembrance *Blithe Spirit.* St. James Churchyard, Gerrards Cross, Buckinghamshire.

8003. Rutherford, Maude Russell (Jan. 30, 1897–March 8, 2001) High kicking singer and dancer of the 1920's. Born in Texas to a black mother and white father, she became a soubrette known as the Slim Princess, popular at the Cotton Club and on stage in *Dixie to Broadway* (1924), *Chocolate Scandals* (1927) and *Keep Shufflin'* (1928). The Charleston, though identified with *Runnin' Wild* in 1923, she actually introduced in *Liza* a year earlier. With her birth date carved into her headstone as 1902, which she admitted was a five year fudge, she died at 104 in Atlantic City. Greenwood Cemetery, Pleasantville, NJ.

8004. Rutledge, Ann (Jan. 7, 1813–Aug. 25, 1835) When Abraham Lincoln lived at New Salem, Illinois, in the 1830's he formed a friendship with Ann Rutledge, which may or may not have been platonic on one or both parts. The romantic aspects of their friendship were likely fictionalized and built into legend over the years, but when she died at 22 in 1835, Lincoln, who was prone to extreme melancholy anyway, suffered a severe and lingering depression. She was buried in Oakland Cemetery at Petersburg, twenty miles northwest of New Salem. The grave was marked by a small stone until it gained new attention through Edgar Lee Masters' *Spoon River Anthology* in 1915. Masters had wandered and studied the cemetery and its occupants, ascribing to many short poems about their lives, several connected to Lincoln. A large granite stone was later placed in the lot, with Masters' poem on it, painting her as a haunting memory in Lincoln's life: *Out of me unworthy and unknown the vibrations of deathless music, "With malice toward none; with charity for all." Out of me the forgiveness of millions toward millions, and the beneficent face of a nation shining with justice and truth. I am Ann Rutledge who sleep beneath these weeds, Beloved in life of Abraham Lincoln, Wedded to him, not through union, but through separation. Bloom forever, O Republic, from the dust of my bosom!* Sec. 4, lot 752, Oakland Cemetery, Petersburg, IL.

8005. Rutledge, Edward (Nov. 23, 1749–Jan. 23, 1800) Signer of the Declaration of Independence from South Carolina forced a debate over slavery before he would sign. The result, as dramatized in the play and film *1776* (1972) was the striking out of a clause Jefferson had in the document which would have emancipated the slaves. It was removed, and Rutledge signed. He was later Governor of South Carolina. St. Philip's Churchyard, Charleston, SC.

8006. Rutledge, John (Sept. 1739–July 18, 1800) President of South Carolina, governor 1778–1782 and a justice on the Supreme Court. St. Michael's Churchyard, Charleston, SC.

8007. Ruttman, Troy (March 11, 1930–May 19, 1997) Indianapolis 500 winner in 1952 was the youngest victor ever at 22. He raced at the Brickyard from 1949–1964. Died from a lung ailment in Lake Havasu City, Arizona. Mooreland Cemetery, Mooreland, OK.

8008. Ruysdael, Basil (July 24, 1888–Oct. 10, 1960) Radio announcer for *Your Hit Parade* was a voice coach for Lawrence Tibbitt and had toured with the Savage Grand Opera Company. He also sang with the New York Metropolitan Opera in the World War I era, and later appeared as an actor in films including *The Cocoanuts* (1929), *Pinky* (1949), *The Blackboard Jungle* (1954) *The Last Hurrah* (1958). Restland (Valhalla) Memorial Park, North Hollywood, California, to Forest Lawn Cemetery, Omaha, Nebraska. No record.

8009. Ryan, Blondy (John Collins Ryan, Jan. 4, 1906–Nov. 28, 1959) Rookie with the New York Giants slated to replace the injured Travis Jackson at shortstop in 1932 who sent a famed telegram to manger Bill Terry, "We can't lose now. Am en route!" It was prophetic, as the Giants went on to take the pennant and the series. Sec. 8, range F, lot 4, grave 1, St. Joseph's Cemetery, Lynn, MA.

8010. Ryan, Fran (Nov. 26, 1926–Jan. 16, 2000) Actress from Oakland appeared in films and TV from the 1960's through the 90's, including *The Doris Day Show* and *Barney Miller* (as the recurring bag lady), and films *The Apple Dumpling Gang, Pale Rider, Stripes, Shoot the Moon, Chances Are,* etc. Service and cremation through Forest Lawn Hollywood Hills. Ashes sent to Holy Sepulchre Cemetery, Hayward, CA.

8011. Ryan, Irene (Oct. 17, 1902–April 26, 1973) Veteran of vaudeville from El Paso toured with her husband Tim Ryan and appeared in numerous B movies of the 1940's and 50's, usually as a wise cracking comedic character, but was best known for her TV role as Granny Clampett in *The Beverly Hillbillies* 1962–1971. She died from a stroke in Santa Monica at 70, having become ill while appearing in *Pippin* in New York. Mausoleum, C-1, crypt 109, Woodlawn Cemetery, Santa Monica, CA.

8012. Ryan, Joseph Patrick (May 11, 1884–June 26, 1963) Leader of the International Longshoreman's Union 1927–1953. Sec. 41, range 31, plot O, grave 7, (2nd) Calvary Cemetery, Woodside, Queens, N.Y.C.

8013. Ryan, Kathleen (Sept. 8, 1922–Dec. 11, 1985) Dublin born Irish actress in the UK and Hollywood 1947–57, best known for Carol Reed's *Odd Man Out* (1947); others include *Christopher Columbus* (1949). Her marriage to Dermod Devane 1944–58 was annulled. The *Irish Times* on 12 December 1985 incorrectly lists Eileen M. Ryan, deeply regretted by her sister Kathleen; it was the reverse. Mass at St. Mary's Church, Haddington Road. Plot TD 18, South New Chapel, Glasnevin Cemetery, Dublin.

8014. Ryan, Leo (May 5, 1925–Nov. 18, 1978) California congressman was in Guyana investigating the Rev. Jim Jones and the People's Temple when he and his entourage were gunned down on the air strip as they prepared to leave the island. This was the beginning of the mass murder-suicide there, as the murders at the air strip finished any hope of privacy or cover for Jones. Posthumously awarded the Congressional Gold Medal, as noted on his standard military marker, in the row behind Admiral Nimitz. Sec. C-1, grave 15-A, Golden Gate National Cemetery, San Bruno, CA.

8015. Ryan, Peggy (Margaret O'Rene Ryan, Aug. 28, 1924–Oct. 30, 2004) Lanky dancer and actress from Long Beach, California, in USO shows and several musicals with Donald O'Connor during World War II (*Private Buckaroo, Mister Big, Chip Off the Old Block, The Merry Monahans, Bowery to Broadway, Here Come the Co-eds*) later turned up as Steve McGarrett's secretary Jenny on *Hawaii Five-O* in 1969. She died in Las Vegas at 80. Mass there at Christ the King Catholic Community. Cremation through Davis mortuary. Ashes spread beneath the Hollywood sign overlooking Hollywood, CA.

8016. Ryan, Robert (Nov. 11, 1909–July 11, 1973) Chicago born actor in rugged parts, both heroes and villains with equal aplomb, at his peak in the late 40's and early 50's, in Jean Renoir's *The Woman on the Beach* (1947), as the anti–Semite in *Crossfire* (1947), the washed up boxer in *The Set-Up* (1949) and memorable roles in *Clash By Night* (1952), *About Mrs. Leslie* (1954), *Bad Day at Black Rock* (1955), *The Wild Bunch* (1969), *Executive Action* (1973), many others. Ryan was a political liberal who said he thought his professional survival during the McCarthy witch hunts may have been due to his Irish Catholic and ex-marine background, in common with the Wisconsin senator. He and his wife lived in Manhattan's Dakota apartments until her death in 1972, when he moved to 135 Central Park West. He died from cancer at New York Hospital and was to be sent for burial with family in Queen of Heaven Cemetery in Hillside, Illinois. He was instead cremated at Garden State Crematory in North Bergen, New Jersey and the ashes sent for burial, according to his biographer, with those of his wife beneath a pear tree on the property of their friend Millard Lampell, across the river from New Hope, Pennsylvania, near Lambertville and Flemington, NJ.

8017. Ryan, Tommie (Thomas F. Ryan, April 15, 1902,–July 26, 1998) Irish born Chicago mainstay was as a young man a member of the IRA, imprisoned for sixteen months in County Kildare for his participation in blowing up bridges to halt British forces. Released with the creation of the Irish Free State in 1922, he came to Chicago, worked as a streetcar conductor, bus driver, tavern operator and snowplow driver, but earned his fame with the Shannon Rovers, which he co-founded in the 1920's, playing *Danny Boy* on his fiddle at Irish funerals, and the bagpipes in the annual St. Patrick's Day Parade in Chicago, which he organized in 1952 with Mayor Daley's support, there having been no "proper" observances of the day since 1898. His son and grandson played *Danny Boy* for him at St. Juliana Catholic Church after his death at 97, and the Shannon Rovers piped him to his rest. Sec. 32, block 16, grave 65, Queen of Heaven Cemetery, Hillside, IL.

8018. Ryan, Tommy (Thomas Joseph Ryan or Joseph Young, March 30, 1870–Aug. 3, 1948) World middleweight boxing champion in the 1890's, the only man to win two world titles and not lose either in the ring defeated in an upset by Kid McCoy and his corkscrew punch in 1896. Sanctuary of Reverence, Golden West Mausoleum, Inglewood Park Cemetery, Inglewood, CA.

8019. Ryen, Richard (Richard Revy, Sept. 13, 1885–Dec. 22, 1965) Hungarian actor and stage director in Germany with the Münchener Kammerspiele (Munich Chamber Theater), expelled by the Nazis, eventually landed in Hollywood 1942–48, where he specialized in Germans and Nazi officers (*Desperate Journey, Casablanca,* as Col. Heinze, Strasser's aide; *The Constant Nymph, The Strange Death of Adolf Hitler, Paris Underground, A Foreign Affair*). He died in Los Angeles at 80. Buried as Richard Revy. Sec. D, row 5, lot 202, space 5C, Westwood Memorial Park, west Los Angeles.

8020. Rymal, Reggie (May 9, 1921–Dec. 25, 2002) Paddle-ball expert featured in the 1953 showcase 3-D film *House of Wax*, batting the ball seemingly into the audience. He also made many television appearances and did stand-up comedy. He died from a heart attack at 81 in La Habra, California. Sec. 57A, grave 1894, Riverside National Cemetery, Riverside, CA.

8021. Sabin, Albert (Aug. 26, 1906–March 3, 1993) Polish immigrant developed the Sabin Polio vaccine, an oral medicine replacing the Salk injection, at Cincinnati Children's Hospital and put into widespread use in 1962, some 100 million Americans taking the cubes within a two year period. Awarded the National Medal of Science and the Presidential Medal of Freedom, he also developed vaccines for other viral diseases including encephalitis. Sec. 3, grave 1885RH, Arlington National Cemetery, Arlington, VA.

8022. Sabich, Spider (Wladimir Peter Sabich, Jan. 9, 1945–March 21, 1976) Ski racing champion, veteran of the 1968 U.S. Olympic team, was fatally shot by his girlfriend Claudine Longet, former wife of Andy Williams, in her Aspen, Colorado, home. (Despite scenarios on *Saturday Night Live*, it did not begin a series of athletes being Accidentally Shot by Claudine Longet.) She did thirty days and afterward married her defense attorney. Westwood Hills Memorial Park, Placerville, CA.

8023. Sabu (Sabu Dastigar, Jan. 27, 1924–Dec. 2, 1963) East Indian born actor cast in *The Elephant Boy* at 13 (1937), *The Thief of Baghdad* (1942), *Arabian Nights* (1943) *Black Narcissus* (1947). He died at 39 of a heart attack in his home in Chatsworth, California. Sheltering Hills, lot 482, Forest Lawn, Hollywood Hills, Los Angeles.

8024. Sacajawea (c 1787–Dec. 30, 1812 or April 9, 1884) Indian guide from the Montana area and Idaho was a member of the Snake tribe of the Shoshone. She was captured at a young age and sold to the French Canadian trapper Toussaint Charbonneau, who she married in 1804. The next year they went as guides with Lewis and Clark. Through her intervention the party was spared both being lost and trouble with the Shoshone and other tribes. On the return, Sacajawea and Charbonneau remained in North Dakota, later taking their son to be educated through Clark in St. Louis. She died, according to contemporary sources, on December 20, 1812, near Fort Manuel, South Dakota, or Fort Lisa, in present day Omaha, Nebraska, and was buried in an unmarked grave. A brick monument in Omaha marks the site of Fort Lisa (1807). Yet in 1875 an aged Indian claiming to be Sacajawea was found among the Wind River Shoshone in Wyoming. She was buried on the Wind River Reservation in what would have been her 97th year, her monument next to Baptiste Charbonneau, believed to have been her son. Wind River Reservation Cemetery near Fort Washakie, WY.

8025. Sacco, Nicola (April 22, 1891–Aug. 23, 1927) and **Bartolomeo Vanzetti** (June 11, 1888–Aug. 23, 1927) Anarchist immigrants from Italy arrested for the murder and murder of a paymaster and guard at a shoe manufacturing firm in South Braintree, Massachusetts, on May 5, 1920. The killers were described as "dark, Italian looking" and many believed Sacco and Vanzetti, known anarchists, were arrested on the basis of the Red Scare hysteria of 1920. Strong anti–Italian sentiment in Massachusetts helped convict them, and despite the confession of a man already sentenced for murder to the crime in South Braintree, their death sentences stood through several appeals and massive protests. Electrocuted in Charleston Prison August 23, 1927, they were cremated at Forest Hills Cemetery, Jamaica Plain, Boston, and the ashes divided. One half of the mixed cremains, bound for Italy, went to France aboard the Mauritania, where they were intercepted by police October 4 to prevent a riot in Paris, and sent by rail to Mondane, Italy, for burial near Turin. The other halves, originally given to the Sacco and Vanzetti Committee in America, were stored at the Boston Public Library, Boston, MA.

8026. Sachs, Eddie (Edward J. Sachs, Jr., May 28, 1927–May 30, 1964) Colorful Indianapolis 500 veteran dubbed the Clown Prince of Auto Racing, a favorite and a front runner, died in his car on the second lap of the 1964 Memorial Day classic when his American Red Ball Special, fueled by gasoline, ran into a conflagration caused by the crash of 500 rookie Dave MacDonald, who died later in an Indianapolis hospital. Sachs had a habit of holding a slice of orange or lemon in his mouth, and in an eerie footnote, the unscorched piece of fruit was found in the burnt debris afterward. The worst fire and explosion in speedway history, the track was shut down for two hours, and gasoline was henceforth banned from the Brickyard. Flush veterans' marker. Sec. 2, range 9, lot 12, grave 3, Holy Saviour Cemetery, Bethlehem, PA.

8027. Sackville-West, Victoria Mary "Vita" (March 9, 1892–June 2, 1962) Wife of diplomat Sir Harold Nicholson, known for her scandalous behavior, and daughter of **Lady Victoria Sackville** (Sept. 23, 1862–Jan. 29, 1936), also a shocking figure in Victorian England. At the latter's death, her ashes, as she specified, were flung into the sea. Vita, the model for Virginia Woolf's *Orlando* as well as her companion, wrote horticultural works as well as novels (*The Edwardians, All Passion Spent*), the memoir *Pepita* and several biographies. Family crypt within the church at Withyham, eastern Sussex.

8028. Sadat, Anwar-Al (Dec. 25, 1918–Oct. 6, 1981) President of Egypt from 1972 expelled Soviet influence, initiated negotiations with Israel in 1977 and signed the historic Camp David Accord peace treaty with Israel's Menachem Begin in 1979. Sadat was assassinated by militant Muslim fundamentalists while reviewing a parade in Cairo at 62. Buried in Egypt's Tomb of the Unknown Soldier in Cairo, across from the reviewing stand where he was assassinated. The service was attended by former U.S. Presidents Nixon, Ford and Carter on behalf of President Reagan. A marble mausoleum was later constructed 200 yards away from the temporary site at the Tomb of the Unknown Soldier, Cairo.

8029. Sadler, Barry (Nov. 1, 1940–Nov. 15, 1989) Amateur musician served in the U.S. Air Force 1958–60 and with the Army a few years later, earning his silver wings as a paratrooper and serving in Vietnam. While recovering from wounds to his leg, he gave away the rights to the song he had written, which became *The Ballad of the Green Berets*, recorded December 18, 1965, and released as a single January 11, 1966. He later wrote *CASCA, The Eternal Mercenary*, and moved to Nashville and to Guatemala. He was shot and fatally wounded in September 1988 and returned to Nashville, where he died fourteen months later at 49. Sec. NN, grave 64, Nashville National Cemetery, 1420 Gallatin Road South, Madison, TN.

8030. Sagal, Boris (Oct. 18, 1923–May 22, 1981) Russian born film director from 1963 (*Twilight of Honor, The Omega Man*) worked primarily in TV. Father of actress Katy Sagal. He died when hit by a helicopter blade while filming in Portland, Oregon. Sheltering Hills, lot 860, space 2, Forest Lawn Hollywood Hills, Los Angeles.

8031. Sagan, Carl (Nov. 9, 1934–Dec. 20, 1996) Astronomer and Pulitzer Prize winner whose 1980 PBS series *Cosmos* brought renewed interest in the stars. A professor at Cornell, he died in Seattle from pneumonia at 62 complicated by myelodisplasia, a bone marrow disease. Lakeview Cemetery, Ithaca, NY.

8032. Sagan, Francoise (June 21, 1935–Sept. 24, 2004) French writer of rebellious works penned *Bonjour Tristesse*, published in 1954 when she was nineteen; later works include *A Certain Smile*, both filmed with her screenplays. She directed the 1977 film *Les Fougéres* and continued to write though plagued by injuries from an auto accident, drug arrests, and tax fraud charges until her death at in Honfleur in northern France from a blood clot in her lung. Souza village cemetery near Cajarc in southeast France.

8033. Sahm, Doug (Nov. 6, 1941–Nov. 18, 1999) Singer and steel guitar player led the Sir Douglas Quintet on *She's About A Mover* (1965) and *Mendocino* (1969), and with the Grammy winning Texas Tornadoes. He died in Taos, New Mexico. at 58. Sec. 20, lot 201, space 3, Sunset Memorial Park, San Antonio, TX.

8034. Saietta, Ignazio a.k.a. "Lupo the Wolf" (c.1877–c.1945) Notorious Black Hand extortionist in turn of the century New York's Little Harlem, was by the 20's out of prison and back at it in N.Y. Sent back to the federal penitentiary in Atlanta, he returned to Brooklyn after his term and lived out his final years there. No Saiettas at Holy Cross or Calvary. One Ignazio Saietta, 56, in sec. 17 at St. John's Cemetery in Queens Sept 5 1945, would be too young. Another, 88, in 1946 at sec. 25 also in St. John's, would have likely been too old. Researcher Bill Heneage, in information shared with Jim Tipton's *Find-A-Grave* website, however, identifies him as **Ignatius (Ignazio) Lupo** (March 19, 1877–Jan. 13, 1947), Saietta having been his mother's maiden name, and buried in the lot of his brother-in-law, gangster **Ciro Terranova.** Although the cemetery records show the Lupo there was buried in October 1947 and was 54 rather than 69, the stone does list his dates as 1877–1947. Sec. 35, plot 5, range 10, plot V, grave 12, (3rd) Calvary Cemetery, Woodside, Queens, N.Y.C.

8035. St. Angelo, Robert (Cosmo F. Santangelo, May 7, 1901–July 21, 1992) Italian born actor in Hollywood 1922–57, often uncredited (as a Roman soldier), stabbed Christ in the 1927 *King of Kings*. He died at 91 in San Diego. Sec. 10, site 55, Massachusetts National Cemetery, Bourne, MA.

8036. St. Clair, Malcolm (May 17, 1897–June 1, 1952) Film director at his peak in the mid to late 1920's with highbrow social comedies such as *Are Parents People?* (1925). His talking films were less successful. Ashes unmarked. 19-SJ-28-B, Pasadena Mausoleum, Mountain View Cemetery, Altadena, CA.

8037. St. Cyr, Lili (Willis Marie Van Schaak or Vanschaack, June 3, 1918–Jan. 29, 1999) Striptease artist of the 1940's and 50's known for her onstage bubble baths was in some films (*Lili's Wedding Night* 1952, *The Miami Story* 1954, *The Naked and the Dead* 1958). Tried in 1951 for lewd and lascivious performances, she was acquitted and her work declared art. Ashes given to her daughter.

8038. St. Denis, Ruth (Jan. 20, 1879–July 21, 1968) Dancer and actress, married to her dance partner Ted Shawn, developed and taught exotic dances derived from Egypt and the far East. Plaque on her crypt inscribed *The Gods have meant that I should dance, and in some mystic hour I shall move to unheard of rhythms of the cosmic orchestra of Heaven. And you will know the language of my wordless poems and will come to me, for that is why I dance.* Courts of Remembrance, wall crypt 3116 Forest Lawn Hollywood Hills, Los Angeles.

8039. Saint-Gaudens, Augustus (March 1, 1848–Aug. 3, 1907) Dublin born sculptor in America from childhood known for *Adoration of the Cross by Angels* in St. Thomas Episcopal Church, Manhattan, the standing Lincoln in Lincoln Park, Chicago, the Miriam Hooper Adams memorial *Grief* in Rock Creek Cemetery, Washington, D.C., the statue of Admiral Farragut in Madison Square, *Diana* in Madison Square Garden and the statue of General Sherman at 5th Avenue and 59th St., all in Manhattan. He was buried beneath a four columned monument on his estate "Aspet" near Cornish, NH.

8040. St. Jacques, Raymond (James Arthur Johnston, March 1, 1930–Aug. 27, 1990) Hartford born, Yale educated actor with the Actors Studio had a successful stage career through the 1950's before turning to film in *Black Like Me* (1964), *The Pawnbroker* (1964), *The Green Berets* (1966), *Cotton Comes to Harlem* (1970), *Book of Numbers* (1973, his directing debut). Eternal Love, lot 4002, Forest Lawn Hollywood Hills, Los Angeles.

8041. St. John, Al "Fuzzy" ("Fuzzy Q. Jones," Sept. 10, 1892–Jan. 21, 1963) Keystone Kop and nephew of "Fatty" Arbuckle, died at Vidalia, Georgia, at 69. Ashes to family, later reportedly to be sent to a museum or showman's hall of fame in Hollywood,

California, instead went to the Double F Ranch, Homosassa Springs, FL.

8042. St. John, Dick (Richard St. John Gosting, 1940–Dec. 27, 2003) Santa Monica born vocalist teamed with Mary Sperling as Dick and Dee-Dee to record *The Mountain's High* (1961), followed by *Young and In Love, Tell Me, Thou Shalt Not Steal*, all using a unique blend of high harmonies. Sperling retired with the 1970's and St. John dubbed his wife Sandy a second Dee-Dee in the 1970's. He died in UCLA Medical Center after a fall from a ladder at 63. Cremated through Gates-Kingsley-Gates, Santa Monica. Ashes returned to family.

8043. St. John, John Patrick (Feb. 9, 1918–May 3, 1995) Los Angeles police detective handled a thousand cases or more, including the Black Dahlia murder, and solved two thirds of them or more, without ever firing his gun. He served for fifty-one years, carried badge number one, and was the subject of a book and the (15 episode) NBC series *Jigsaw John*. Valley View Lawn, lot 2124, grave 4, gate 17, Rose Hills Memorial Park, Whittier, CA.

8044. St. Johns, Adela Rogers (May 20, 1894–Aug. 10, 1988) Hollywood playwright and Hearst newspaper columnist was a confidante of film stars from the World War I era. Autobiography *The Honeycomb*. She died at 94 in Arroyo Grande, California. Ashes unmarked. Columbarium of Memory, niche 19873, Memorial Terrace, Great Mausoleum, Forest Lawn, Glendale, California. Her father, attorney **Earl Rogers**, is in sec. H, lot 4996, Evergreen Cemetery, Los Angeles.

8045. Saint-Saens, Charles (Oct. 9, 1835–Dec. 16, 1921) Composer and pianist wrote *Danse Macabre, Sampson and Delilah, Organ Symphony* and (the tongue-in-cheek) *Carnival of the Animals*. Mausoleum, div. 13, Montparnasse Cemetery, Paris.

8046. St. Valentine's Day Massacre (Victims) Seven men associated with Chicago northside gang chief Bugs Moran were in a garage at 2122 North Clark St. on the morning of February 14, 1929, when they were lined up facing the wall by men dressed in police uniforms and machine gunned to death from behind. The murderers were never positively identified. Speculation has included Fred "Killer" Burke, "Machine Gun" Jack McGurn, and Capone hit men John Scalise and Albert Anselmi, as well as a few other theories. One of the seven victims, Frank Gusenberg, lived a few hours but refused to name his killers other than to say they were cops, which may or may not have been what he believed. The site of the murders is now a parking lot. Best known among the group were the Gusenberg brothers, Frank and Pete, buried at Rose Hill Cemetery and removed to Irving Park Cemetery, Chicago (see separate entry under Gusenberg.) **Dr. Reinhart Schwimmer** (born 1900), a hapless optometrist who gravitated toward gangland figures, was buried in sec. 92, Rose Hill Cemetery, Chicago. **John Snyder, A.K.A. Adam Hyer,** Moran's accountant, was buried in sec. R (family stone marked *Heyer*), Forest Park Cemetery, Forest Park, Illinois. **Albert Weinshank** (Albert R. Weinshenker, born Dec. 23, 1893), proprietor of a speakeasy and point man for Moran, was buried in gate 24, Daughters of Job Cemetery, Jewish Waldheim Cemeteries, Forest Park. **James Clark, A.K.A. Albert Kallachek** (born 1887), Moran's brother-in-law, is in the Kallachek lot, Irving Park Cemetery, Chicago. **John May** (born Sept. 28, 1893), the mechanic working on a car in the garage, is unmarked, with his wife Hattie, who has a flush marker. Sec. 22, Mt. Carmel Cemetery, Hillside, IL.

8047. Sainte-Beuve, Charles Augustin (Dec. 23, 1804–Oct. 13, 1869) Pre-eminent French critic and poet of the 19th century whose credo was truth above all else. Accordingly, the bust of him on a pedestal over his grave features him scowling and wrinkled. Div. 17, Montparnasse Cemetery, Paris.

8048. Sakall, S. Z. (Szoke Szakall, Feb. 2, 1883–Feb. 12, 1955) Heavy, bespectacled comic Hungarian actor nicknamed "Cuddles" in films of the 1940's including *Ball of Fire, Yankee Doodle Dandy* and *Casablanca*, displaying a thick accent, fractured English (when called for), and a mania for scene stealing. He died from a heart attack at 72. Lawn crypt, (Private) Garden of Memory, Forest Lawn, Glendale, CA.

8049. Sakamoto, Kyu (Kyu "Kyu-chan" Sakamoto, Nov. 10, 1941–Aug. 12, 1985) Japanese vocalist recorded *Ue o Muite Aruko* (*I Look Up When I Walk*), a hit in Japan in 1961. The song, written by Hachidai Nakamura, with lyrics by Rokusuke Ei, who allegedly wrote it over a broken heart from actress Meiko Nakamura, had such a good melody that, despite the indecipherable Japanese words, it ousted Leslie Gore's *It's My Party* in the U.S. in June 1963 under the title *Sukiyaki*. Sakamoto died with 519 others when JAL Flight 123, a 747 bound from Tokyo to Osaka, lost pieces of its tail section and wound downward for thirty minutes, giving some of the doomed passengers time to scribble farewells. Black-gray exterior monument. Chokoku Temple (cemetery), Minato Ward, Tokyo.

8050. Sakata, Harold (Harold Toshiyuki Sakata, July 1, 1920–July 29, 1982) Large Polynesian actor best known as Oddjob in *Goldfinger* (1964), with the deadly flying derby. He died from cancer at 62 in St. Francis Hospital, Honolulu. Cremated at Oahu Crematory through Hosoi Garden mortuary, Honolulu. Ashes buried sec. III, grave 317, National Memorial Cemetery of the Pacific (The Punchbowl), Honolulu, HI.

8051. Sakharoff, Alexander (May 13, 1886–Sept. 25, 1963) Innovative solo Russian dancer, teacher and choreographer from Mariupol in the Ukraine, married to German dancer **Clothilde von der Planitz** (1893–1974), authored *Reflections on the Dance and Music*. He died in Siena, Italy. Grave 1-0-1-34, Cimitero Acattolico del Testaccio, Rome.

8052. Sakharov, Andrei (Andrei Demitriyevich Sakharov, May 21, 1921–Dec. 14, 1989) Russian scientist, writer and social critic awarded the Nobel Peace Prize in 1975 for his work toward disarmament and democracy in the USSR. A nuclear physicist, he incurred Soviet disapproval for denouncing steps toward violating the 1963 Nuclear Test Ban Treaty. Exiled in Gorky 1980–86, he was restored to freedom by Gorbachev and lived to see the collapse of the USSR in 1989, dying from a heart attack two months later. At the graveside Gorbachev noted the peace prize was deserved. Vostryako Cemetery, southwest Moscow.

8053. Salazar, Ruben (March 3, 1928–Aug. 29, 1970) Mexican born reporter for the Los Angeles Times had served as their bureau chief in Mexico City before returning. He was killed by police during a Chicano Vietnam War Moratorium March when they fired a random tear gas missile into the Silver Dollar Bar on Whittier Boulevard in East L.A. Niche, Pacific View Memorial Park, Newport Beach, CA.

8054. Sale, Chic (Charles Sale, Aug. 25, 1885–Nov. 7, 1936) Vaudeville comedian specialized in off color humor, and appeared in several shorts (*Old Shep*) and features 1922–36 as cantankerous old characters, including *The Star Witness* (1932) and *Treasure Island* (1934, as Ben Gun). He died from pneumonia. Niche in the Columbarium of Unity, niche 12009, Corridor of Unity, Holly Terrace, Great Mausoleum, Forest Lawn, Glendale, CA.

8055. Sale, Virginia (Virginia Sale Wren, May 20, 1899–Aug. 23, 1992) Sister of Chic Sale in films from 1927 later starred in TV's *Wren's Nest* with her husband in 1949 and was in over 200 films. She died at the Motion Picture Country Hospital at 92. Sec. 37, grave 1353, Arlington National Cemetery, Arlington, VA.

8056. Salerno, Anthony "Fat Tony" (Aug. 15, 1911–July 27, 1992) New York crime figure was the alleged boss of the Genovese family after the death in 1981 of Funzi Tieri long held sway over the numbers rackets in Harlem. Feared by many who refused to identify him, he went to prison on RICO charges following the Mafia Commission trials and died five years later. Family mausoleum, (Old) St. Raymond's Cemetery, the Bronx, N.Y.C.

8057. Salieri, Antonio (Aug. 18, 1750–May 7, 1825) Italian composer (*Falstaff*, among others), conductor and teacher known for his intrigues against Mozart — exaggerated into the story and belief by some that he poisoned the child prodigy. Gruppe O, reihe 1, nummer 54, Zentralfriedhof, Vienna.

8058. Salinger, Pierre (Pierre Emil George Salinger, June 14, 1925–Oct. 16, 2004) French-American journalist from San Francisco was press Secretary for U.S. President John Kennedy 1961–3 — the most visible up to that time, accentuated by television and becoming a celebrity in his own right. He remained with Lyndon Johnson through 1964, when he was appointed to fill a senate seat from California. Defeated for election on his own, Paris correspondent for ABC 1976–1993 and a consultant afterward, he died in Le Thor, France, at 79. Eulogized by Edward Kennedy at Holy Trinity Catholic Church in Georgetown. Columbarium Court 6, sec. PP, stack 7, niche 3, Arlington National Cemetery, Arlington, VA.

8059. Salisbury, Harrison (Nov. 14, 1908–July 5, 1993) Journalist for UPI and the *New York Times.* Pulitzer Prize for international reporting in 1955 and for his reports from Hanoi in 1966. Books, include *Behind the Lines — Hanoi* (1967), *Without Fear or Favor,* a *History of the New York Times* (1980) and a 1983 autobiography *Journey Into Our Times.* Ashes in the woods on his property at Salisbury, CT.

8060. Salisbury, Robert Cecil, 3rd Marquess of (Feb. 3, 1830–Aug. 22, 1903) British conservative served as Prime Minister 1886–1892, 1895–1900 and 1900–02. Buried in the churchyard at Hatfield, Hertfordshire.

8061. Salk, Jonas (Oct. 28, 1914–June 23, 1995) New York City born microbiologist developed the first polio vaccine in 1954, put into widespread use in 1955. He died in La Jolla, California, from heart failure at 80 and was cremated. Mt. Shalom, lot 386 space A, El Camino Memorial Park, La Jolla, CA.

8062. Sallman, Warner E. (April 30, 1892–May 25, 1968) Chicago born commercial artist drew and painted both religious and non-secular works, but was known for his *Head of Christ,* the brown tinted portrait first done in 1940 and mass produced in wallet size copies some 500 million times. He died in Chicago at 76. Mausoleum annex, block 38, lot 6, grave 6, Memorial Park Cemetery, Skokie, IL.

8063. Salmi, Albert (March 11, 1928–April 22, 1990) Beefy New York born character actor in many surly roles in films and TV in the 1960's, including three *Twilight Zones,* shot himself and his wife through the heart in their home at 815 Rockwood Boulevard, Spokane, Washington. Serenity, niche 243, Greenwood Memorial Terrace, Spokane, WA. Ashes to his daughter.

8064. Salomon, Ben (Benjamin Lewis Salomon, Sept. 1, 1919–July 7, 1944) Beverly Hills dentist was a surgeon with the 27th Infantry on Saipan in the Marianas when his medical unit was overrun with Japanese. Ordering the tent evacuated, he — with a machine gun, held off the enemy, killing 98; he was shot 24 times before he fell and 50 or more times afterward, still at his machine gun. When dentist Dr. Robert West discovered the Geneva Convention did not prevent medics from receiving the Medal of Honor for duty in combat, he campaigned on behalf of Dr. Salomon from 1997. In spring 2002 President Bush awarded Salomon the Medal of Honor. Accepted by West, there were no relatives to attend. Columbarium of Guidance, niche 21994, Iris Terrace, Great Mausoleum, Forest Lawn, Glendale, CA.

8065. Salomon, Haym (1740?–Jan. 6, 1785) Polish Jew in Philadelphia contributed much of his fortune to the Colonies during the Revolution, sometimes called the Financier of the Revolution. Unmarked in small Mikveh Israel Cemetery in downtown Philadelphia, PA.

8066. Salten, Felix (Sept. 6, 1869–Oct. 8, 1945) Austrian novelist and journalist born in Budapest wrote the sensitive children's story and adult allegory *Bambi* (1923). 2487, Friedof Unterer Friesenberg, Zurich, Switzerland.

8067. Salter, Hans J. (Jan. 14, 1896–July 23, 1994) Viennese born composer in the U.S. from 1937. His prolific scores were used repeatedly in Universal horror films and melodramas 1939–1946, the signature themes first used in *Son of Frankenstein* and *Tower of London* (1939), *The Invisible Man Returns, The Mummy's Hand* and *Man Made Monster* (1940), *The Wolfman* (1941), *Ghost of Frankenstein* (1942) and sequels to these and others. He died in Los Angeles at 98. Beth Olam Cemetery sec. 16, lot 66B, grave 3, Hollywood Forever Cemetery, Hollywood (Los Angeles), CA.

8068. Salter, Harry (Harry L. Solter, 1874–March 2, 1920) Early silent film actor in many of the Florence Lawrence–John Compson Mr. and Mrs. Jones ("Jonesy") pictures at Biograph. He married Lawrence, moved with her from Biograph to IMP and directed several of her later efforts as her popularity faded. They were divorced and Salter later died from a stroke in El Paso at 45. Solter obelisk and headstone. Sec. L, area 121-132, Baltimore Cemetery, Baltimore, MD.

8069. Saltis, Joe (Joseph F. Soltis, c. 1894–Aug. 2, 1947) Noted Chicago gang leader during the alcohol wars of 1923–30, "Polack" Joe Saltis, with Frank McErlane, controlled an area of southwest Chicago and environs, squeezed in between the Southside O'Donnell and Ralph Sheldon territories. Saltis built a lodge for himself in northern Wisconsin and prospered for a time. In late 1925 he was wounded by the Spike O'Donnell gang, causing the killing of Dynamite Joe Brooks and Edward Harmening, probably by McErlane. Tried and acquitted in 1926 for the murder of Ralph Sheldon associate Mitters Foley, his long-time association with Capone fell apart after his alliance with Hymie Weiss became known. His gunmen and alliances were gradually killed off, and McErlane's drinking sent him out of the city into a forced retirement after 1930. Saltis died in a northside rooming house at 52. Sec. EE, lot 130, Resurrection Cemetery, Justice, Chicago, IL.

8070. Saltonstall, Leverett (Sept. 1, 1892–June 17, 1979) Governor of Massachusetts 1939–1944, Senator 1944–1967, served with both John and Edward Kennedy. His family were from Chestnut Hill, Massachusetts, where they (Rose Saltonstall) had been close friends with the Lees before and during the marriage of Alice Lee and Theodore Roosevelt. 724/1293 Aspen, Ivy and Lupine Paths, Harmony Grove Cemetery, Salem, MA.

8071. Sample, Johnny (June 15, 1937–April 26, 2005) Defensive block started with the 1958 Baltimore Colts, playing in the fabled championship game against the New York Jets, where he finished his career in 1969 with an interception that helped them win the Super Bowl and established the old AFL as equal to the NFL after the leagues had merged. He died in Philadelphia at 67. Sec. 83, lot 13, west side, Fernwood Cemetery, Philadelphia, PA.

8072. Samples, "Junior" (Alvin Samples, Aug. 10, 1926–Nov. 13, 1983) Large country bumpkin comedian in television's "Hee Haw" from 1969 until his death from a heart ailment at 57. A bench marks the lot along with a bronze flush marker. Garden of Devotion, Sawnee Memorial Gardens, Cumming, GA.

8073. Sampson, Will (Sept. 27, 1933–May 27, 1987) 6'7" Creek Indian actor and noted western artist known for his portrayal of Chief Bromden in *One Flew Over the Cuckoo's Nest* (1975). Other films include *The Outlaw Josie Wales* (1976) and *Poltergeist II* (1986). He had undergone a heart-lung transplant forty three days prior to his death at 53 in Methodist Hospital, Houston, Texas. Grave Creek Indian Cemetery, Hitchita (east of Henryetta), OK.

8074. Sand, George (Amandine Lucie Aurore Dupin Dudevant, July 1, 1804–June 8, 1876) Paris born novelist, long the mistress of Chopin, lived at Nohant near La Chartre in Berry. Among her best known works were *Indiana, Valentine, Rose et Blanche, Consuelo,* and *Jean de La Roche,* most espousing rebellion against social conventions. She died from an intestinal obstruction, her last words reported as "Leave the grass," interpreted as her wish to lie beneath earth and not a slab. Buried in a private graveyard near her parents, grandmother and granddaughter, behind the chapel at Nohant.

8075. Sandburg, Carl (Jan. 6, 1878–July 22, 1967) Chicago journalist from Galesburg, Illinois, blended folklore, history and poetry as a brand of 20th century Walt Whitman. His three volume biography *Abraham Lincoln* won a Pulitzer Prize in 1940. Other works included volumes of poetry, the epic historical *Remembrance Rock,* his writing (and singing) of folk songs, and espousing social causes. He died from a heart attack and had a thirteen minute funeral service near his home at Flat Rock, North Carolina. A line from his poem *Finish* was read: *Death comes but once, let it be easy.* His ashes, and later his wife's, were placed at "Remembrance Rock," a boulder in the backyard of his birthplace, inscribed (from the book) *For it could be a place to come to and remember.* Carl Sandburg Birthplace, Galesburg, IL.

8076. Sanders, George (July 3, 1906–April 25. 1972) English actor frequently cast as opportunistic, self centered cads, always a cool sophisticate, played a virtuous character in *The Saint* series, but was more typically cold blooded in *The House of Seven Gables* and *Rebecca* (1940) and as Lord Henry in *The Picture of Dorian Gray* (1945). Other films include *All About Eve* (1950, Academy Award), and *Village of the Damned* (again virtuous, 1960). Though he had remarried briefly to Magda Gabor, sister of his ex-wife Zsa Zsa Gabor, friends felt he never found contentment after the death of his wife Benita Hume in 1967. He moved around California and Europe afterward until taking his own life with an overdose of Nembutal at the seaside Hotel Rey Don Jaime at Casteldefels near Barcelona, Spain. He wrote a note saying he was bored and that he was leaving "...you with your worries in this sweet cesspool. Good Luck." The body was sent to London to be met by his sister. After a funeral service he was cremated May 4. The ashes were reportedly scattered in the English Channel as he had requested, or at Charing Crematorium, as Benita Hume's had been.

8077. Sanders, Harland (Sept. 9, 1890–Dec. 16, 1980) Founder of Kentucky Fried Chicken, first opened in 1955 using his special recipe, became familiar on TV and as the company's logo, with trademark white suit and beard. He died at Louisville from leukemia at 90. Four columned monument with a bronze bust above the grave length slab. Sec. 33, lot F, Cave Hill Cemetery, Louisville, KY.

8078. Sanders, Hugh (March 13, 1911–Jan. 10, 1966) Actor in films and TV in a variety of roles. Died en route to New York City. Crypt 45A, Mountain View Mausoleum, Altadena, CA.

8079. Sanders, Joe L. (Oct. 15, 1896–May 15, 1965) With Carl A. Coon, Sr., formed the Coon-Sanders Orchestra in Kansas City in 1919, broadcasting jazz at midnight as the Coon-Sanders Nighthawks over WDAF there from 1922 and continued, with extensive touring sponsored and promoted by Jules Stein, until Coon's death in 1932. Block 23, lot 20, Mt. Moriah Cemetery (south), Kansas City, MO.

8080. Sanders, Ray (Raymond Floyd Sanders, Dec. 4, 1916–Oct. 28, 1983) First baseman for the St. Louis Cardinals replaced Johnny Mize, who they traded in 1941, helped them to National League flags in 1942, 1943, and 1944, before he was traded to the Boston Braves in 1946 and Musial took his place at first base. Injured in 1947, he retired the next year and scouted briefly for the Cleveland Indians. Mount Hope Cemetery of Lemay, St. Louis County, MO.

8081. Sanderson, Julia (Julia Sackett, Aug. 27, 1887–Jan. 27, 1975) Springfield, Mass. born daughter of stage actor Albert Sackett began on the New York stage in 1903 and was starring in Charles Frohman's *The Sunshine Girl* 1913–15. She married radio actor Frank Crumit in 1927. They lived at Longmeadow near Springfield. Interred together in Hillcrest Park Cemetery mausoleum, Springfield, MA.

8082. Sandow, Eugen (Friederich Wilhelm Mueller, April 2, 1867–Oct. 14, 1925) Pioneer body-builder gave exhibitions and "muscle displays" from the 1880's, at the 1893 Chicago World's Fair, and on tours and programs with the aid of Florenz Ziegfeld. He built a series of gyms and advocated both free school lunch programs and pre-natal care to foster proper nutrition. The award for Mr. Olympia bears a statue of him. His unmarked slab his wife requested was given a plaque in May 2002 by his biographer Tom Manly, inscribed *The great Eugene Sandow 1867–1925/ The father of bodybuilding.* Putney Vale Cemetery, London.

8083. Sands, Bobby (Robert Gerard Sands, March 9, 1954–May 5, 1981) Twenty seven year old Irish Republican Army political prisoner and hunger striker whose self imposed starvation death to protest Britain's refusal to recognize IRA prison inmates as political prisoners gained more publicity than any other Northern Ireland martyrs in recent years. Sands' death symbolized the long struggle and animosity between England and Northern Ireland. Buried with full IRA military honors in the section reserved for those associated with the outlawed Irish Republican Army. His name is on a polished black stone with other names under *Volunteers*. Milltown Cemetery, Belfast, Northern Ireland.

8084. Sands, Diana (Aug. 22, 1934–Sept. 21, 1973) Black actress on Broadway in *A Raisin in the Sun*, her best known of several plays, repeated the role in the 1961 film version. She died from cancer at 39. Ashwood 545, Ferncliff Cemetery, Hartsdale, NY.

8085. Sanford, Erskine (Nov. 19, 1885–July 7, 1969) Actor known for his work in Orson Welles' Mercury Theatre, including the films *Citizen Kane* (1941) and *The Magnificent Ambersons* (1942). Died in Hollywood. Bennie Dudley mortuary. Donated as a medical specimen to UCLA School of Medicine.

8086. Sanford, Isabel (Aug. 17, 1917–July 9, 2004) New York born actress in films from 1967 — as the opinionated cook in *Guess Who's Coming to Dinner* (1967) — best known as level headed Louise Jefferson opposite the excitable George (Sherman Hemsley) on CBS's *The Jeffersons* 1975–1985, and the first black woman to receive an Emmy (1981) as best actress in a television series. She from cardiopulmonary arrest died in Cedars-Sinai Medical Center, Los Angeles at 86 ten months after surgery on a neck artery. Burial July 21. Courts of Remembrance, wall crypt 2633, Forest Lawn Hollywood Hills, Los Angeles.

8087. Sanford, John (Julian Lawrence Shapiro, May 31, 1904–March 6, 2003) Prolific writer long associated with the Communist party and blacklisted for ten years remained unapologetic and steadfast in his political beliefs. His works include *The Water Wheel* (1933), *Every Island Fled Away* (1964), *A more Goodly Country* (1967) and *A Palace of Silver*, centering on his marriage to MGM screen-writer **Marguerite Roberts** (Sept. 21, 1905–Feb. 17, 1979) from 1938 until her death. Her screenplays include *Escape, Honky Tonk, Dragon Seed, Undercurrent, Sea of Grass, Five Card Stud, True Grit*, many others, whereas Sanford's only film credit was *Honky Tonk* (1941). He died at 98 in Montecito, California, and was buried next to his wife. Ocean View, row F, lot 70, Santa Barbara Cemetery, Santa Barbara, CA.

8088. Sanger, Margaret (Sept. 14, 1883–Sept. 6, 1966) Social reformer gave up nursing on the lower east side in 1912 to devote herself to birth control after coming in contact with many self-induced abortions among the impoverished. She later promoted legislation granting doctors the right to prescribe birth control and founded Planned Parenthood. She died in Tucson at 82. Cenotaph, sec. 170, Cypress and Grape Ave., Greenwood Cemetery, Brooklyn. Buried with her husband (Slee), sec. N, grave 1, Rural Cemetery, 2296 Rte. 9, Fishkill, NY.

8089. Santa Anna, Antonio López de (Feb. 21, 1794–June 21, 1876) Mexican general and dictator dominated the nation for three decades, defeating Texas at The Alamo in 1836 but in turn defeated by them at San Jacinto and captured. He lost a leg at Veracruz fighting a French naval raid in 1838, regained his popularity and was re-elected president in 1846, leading the resistance to U.S. invasion in the Mexican War. Deposed in 1855, in the 1860s, Santa Anna reportedly introduced chicle to inventor Thomas Adams, providing the basis for chewing gum. Tepeyac Cemetery, Guadalupe Hidalgo, Mexico.

8090. Santamaria, Mongo (Ramon Santamaria, April 7, 1922–Feb. 1, 2003) Cuban percussionist and bandleader blended Cuban music with jazz and soul, in a career long career in which he also worked with Perez Prado and Tito Puente, but was best known for recording Herbie Hancock's composition *Watermelon Man*, which became a top ten hit in the U.S. in 1963. He died in Miami at 80. Sec. 30, Woodlawn Park South Cemetery, Miami, FL.

8091. Santana, Merlin (March 17, 1976–Nov. 9, 2002) Dominican actor played Stanley on *The Cosby Show*, Romeo Santana on *The Steve Harvey Show* and had been in several films (*In the Line of Duty: Street War*, 1992; *Showtime*, 2002). He was fatally shot in the head at 26 while sitting in a parked car on a Los Angeles street. Sent through Malinow and Silverman to Riverside Chapel, Manhattan. Holy Cross, range 19, grave 48, New St. Raymond's Cemetery, the Bronx, N.Y.C.

8092. Santop, Louis (Lewis Santop Loftin, Jan. 17, 1890–Jan. 22, 1942) Negro Leagues slugger from Tyler, Texas, 1909–1926 and starting catcher for several clubs, teamed with both Smokey Joe Williams (*q.v.*) and Cannonball Dick Redding. Buried as Lewis Santop Loftin. Sec. N, site 259, Philadelphia National Cemetery, Philadelphia, PA.

8093. Santschi, Tom (Oct. 14, 1878/80–April 9, 1931) Swiss born actor from Luzerne — sometimes listed as born at Kokomo, Indiana, in films from 1907 until his death from hypertension and cardiac arrest at 50. He also wrote and directed several films. Sanctuary of Hope, crypt 472 near Henry B. Walthall, Abbey of the Psalms/Hollywood Forever Mausoleum, Hollywood Forever Cemetery, Hollywood (Los Angeles), CA.

8094. Saperstein, Abe (July 4, 1901–March 15,

1966) English born founder (1927) of the all black Harlem Globetrotters basketball team. Memorial sec., block 1, lot 4, grave 11, Westlawn Cemetery, Chicago, IL.

8095. Sarazen, Gene (May 27, 1901–May 13, 1999) Golfing great, one of only four to win all four pro championships: the PGA, Masters, U.S. Open and British Open. Marco Island Cemetery, Marco Island, FL.

8096. Sarber, Jess (June 28, 1886–Oct. 12, 1933) Allen County, Ohio, sheriff shot in the stomach by Harry Pierpont and repeatedly bashed over the head by Charlie Makley at the Lima, Ohio, jail, where they went to free John Dillinger, who was surprised and upset at the shooting; Sarber died the same night. Makley died in a jailbreak attempt the following year, but Pierpont was executed at Columbus for Sarber's murder in October 1934. Walnut Grove Cemetery, Delphos, OH.

8097. Sardi, Vincent (Dec. 23, 1885–Nov. 19, 1969) Founder of Sardi's restaurant on West 44th St. in Manhattan, long a gathering place for Broadway stars and other celebrities whose faces line the main dining room. Sec. 12, Flushing Cemetery, Flushing, Queens, N.Y.C.

8098. Sargent, Dick (Richard Cox, April 19, 1930–July 8, 1994) Actor from Carmel, California, son of actress Ruth McNaughton, played the second Darren on TV's *Bewitched* 1969–72. In 1991 he announced he was gay, and in March 1994 that he had prostate cancer, prompting the headline (Dick York, the original Darren, having died in 1992) "Samantha to lose another husband." Cremated by Forest Lawn Hollywood Hills, Los Angeles. Ashes to residence.

8099. Sargent, John Singer (Jan. 12, 1856–April 15, 1925) Painter born and raised in Europe of American parentage, best known for his portraits of many leading figures of the day, including several American presidents. He died in London at 69. Brookwood Cemetery, Woking, Surrey.

8100. Sarnoff, David (Feb. 27, 1891–Dec. 12, 1971) Former telegraph operator who received the initial news of the sinking of the *Titanic* later became manager of RCA, which spun off the National Broadcasting Corporation. Mausoleum, sec. 40, Powhatan plot, Kensico Cemetery, Valhalla, NY.

8101. Saroyan, William (Aug. 31, 1908–May 18, 1981) Writer from Fresno, first noted for the story *The Daring Young Man on the Flying Trapeze* (1934) later won the Pulitzer Prize and the New York Drama Critics Award 1940 for *The Time of Your Life,* a study of the patrons and owner of a saloon, and an Oscar for his play *The Human Comedy,* filmed in 1943. Many other short stories. His ashes were sent partly to Armenia, and other half in an urn at the columbarium of the Chapel of the Light, Fresno, California. On March 3, 2002, the urn was removed from the Chapel of the Light and buried near the railroad tracks on the outskirts of town at Ararat, the cemetery where

"he used to wander in the rain, talking to the headstones," according to his son Aram. His black granite headstone bears the epitaph he had composed: *In the time of your life, live — so that in that wondrous time you shall not add to the misery and sorrow of the world but shall smile at the infinite delight and mystery of it.* Ararat Cemetery, Fresno, CA.

8102. Sarton, May (May 3, 1912–July 16, 1995) Poet (*Encounter in April* 1937) and novelist (*The Fur Person*), her stories were first set in Europe and later New England. Personal works *The Hours By the Sea* (1977) and *After the Stroke* (1988). Her monument is a metal sculpted bird, likely a gull or swan, poised upward. Nelson Cemetery, Nelson, NH.

8103. Sartre, Jean Paul (June 21, 1905–April 15, 1980) French author and philosopher espoused an Existential view of choices, the worst possible existence being one of repetition. Living to seek new roads, he refused the Nobel Prize and the French Legion of Honor because it would, he felt, "turn him into an institution." Works include *The Troubled Sleep* (1940), a memoir of the Nazi takeover of Paris. Later a POW, he was again arrested for his left wing politics in 1970. Grave length marble slab, joined there in 1986 by his life-long companion, writer **Simone de Beauvoir** (Jan. 9, 1908–April 14, 1986). Div. 20, Montparnasse Cemetery, Paris.

8104. Sassoon, Siegfried (Sept. 8, 1886–Sept. 1, 1967) English poet of the miseries of World War I, edited the work of his friend Wilfrid Owen, killed at the end of the war. St. Dominic's churchyard, Mells, Somerset.

8105. Sauckel, Ernst (Fritz) *see* **Goering.**

8106. Sauer, Hank (Henry John Sauer, March 17, 1917–Aug. 24, 2001) National League outfielder and slugger with the Cubs 1949–1956, dubbed The Mayor of Wrigley Field. MVP 1952. He twice hit three runs in a game against the same pitcher, both against the Phillies' Curt Simmons at Wrigley Field in 1950 and '52. He died in Burlingame, California, after suffering a heart attack while playing golf. Sec. G2, lot 19, grave 18, Holy Cross Cemetery, Colma, CA.

8107. Saunders, John Monk (Nov. 22, 1897–March 10, 1940) Screenwriter married to actress Fay Wray 1928–39. A Rhodes scholar and aviator in World War I, his scripts often dealt with the strain of war and particularly aerial combat (*Wings* 1927, *The Dawn Patrol* both 1930 and 1938, *The Eagle and the Hawk* 1933). Related to the Jefferson, Dabney and Carr families at Charlottesville, Virginia, he had been researching a book there when he was found hanged, a suicide, in a Fort Myers, Florida, cottage after long depression. His ex wife Fay Wray had favorite stones he had liked as a boy placed in the coffin. Church of the Good Shepard Cemetery, east side of route 696 and just south of route 24, Cary's Wood, east of Evinton, Campbell County, VA.

8108. Saunders, John P. (Sept. 9, 1924–Nov. 15,

2003) Toledo pioneer television newsman and writer of the syndicated comic strips *Mary Worth* and *Steve Roper*. His father Allen Saunders had changed the strip from *Apple Mary* in the 1930's to *Mary Worth's Family;* John Saunders worked on it from the 1950's, but took over completely in 1979. Wakeman Cemetery, Waterville, OH.

8109. Saunders, Russell (May 21, 1919–May 29, 2001) Canadian gymnast, stunt man and actor in many films (*Saboteur, This Gun For Hire*). Sec. 6, family plot DD, lot 63, Hollywood Forever Cemetery, Hollywood, Los Angeles.

8110. Savage, Swede (David Earl Savage, Aug. 26, 1946–July 2, 1973) Race driver whose car disintegrated on the 57th lap of a second try for the Indianapolis 500 at the year's rain drenched event. He died a month later. Lawn S, lot 469, Mountain View Cemetery, San Bernardino, CA.

8111. Savalas, George (Dec. 5, 1924–Oct. 2, 1985) Bushy haired actor was Detective Stavros in his brother Telly's TV series *Kojak* 1973–78. Lincoln Terrace, lot 4596, Forest Lawn Hollywood Hills, Los Angeles.

8112. Savalas, Telly (Aristotle Savalas, Jan. 21, 1922–Jan. 22, 1994) Actor from Garden City, New York, of Greek descent in films from the late 50's in brute roles. As Pontius Pilate in *The Greatest Story Ever Told* (1965), director George Stevens ordered his head shaved and he left it, a trademark of his TV character, cynical detective *Kojak* 1973–78. He died from prostate cancer a day after his 70th birthday. Epitaph from Aristotle: *The hour of departure has arrived and we go our ways, I to die and You to live. Which is better God only knows.* Garden of Heritage, second level, plot 1281, Forest Lawn Hollywood Hills, Los Angeles.

8113. Saville, Frances (Fanny Martina Simonsen, Jan. 6, 1863–Nov. 8, 1935) Opera singer, the principal soprano with the Vienna Hofoper, later at the New York Metropolitan Opera. Sec. G, tier 5, niche 5, Woodlawn Memorial Park, Colma, CA.

8114. Savio, Mario (Dec. 8, 1942–Nov. 6, 1996) New York born leader of the Free Speech Movement at the University of California at Berkeley in the 1960's, beginning on December 2, 1964, with his speech in Sproul Plaza and the subsequent sit-in that closed the college and led to 800 arrests, protesting the school's limiting of the activities of civil rights and political groups on the campus. He later taught physics at Modesto Junior College and Sonoma State University. Savio died at 53 in Sebastopol, California, hospital from heart failure suffered while moving furniture; he had a history of coronary problems. Cremated November 7 at Pleasant Hills Memorial Park, Sebastopol, the ashes were returned the next day to family in Sebastopol.

8115. Savitch, Jessica (Feb. 1, 1947–Oct. 23, 1983) TV newscaster of the *NBC Weekend News* 1977–1983 and on *Prime Time Sunday* 1979–80. After a troubled period beset by drug use and her episode of slurred words on a live report in 1983, she was regrouping her life when her companion turned down a no outlet street in New Hope, Pennsylvania, during a blinding thunderstorm and drove into a canal, killing both of them and her dog Chewy, with whom she was cremated and the ashes cast by her sister from the beach into the Atlantic.

8116. Sawtell, Paul (Feb. 3, 1906–Aug. 1, 1971) Musical director at Universal did *The Inner Sanctum* music, *The Mummy's Curse,* later *The Whistler* at Columbia, etc. Fidelity sec., lot 2357, space 4, Forest Lawn Glendale, CA.

8117. Sawyer, Joe (Joseph Sauers, Aug. 29, 1906–April 21, 1982) A favorite menace and bully in crime films of the 1930's (*The Informer, The Petrified Forest, The Walking Dead, Black Legion, The Roaring Twenties*) played the detective in *A Double Life* (1947), and appeared as benevolent Sgt. Biff O'Hara in TV's *Rin-Tin-Tin* 1954–59. He died at Ashland, Oregon, from liver cancer at 75, having gone there to live with his son. Cremated at Mountain View Cemetery in Ashland, and the ashes returned to his son Riley.

8118. Sax, Adolphe (Antoine-Joseph Sax, Nov. 6, 1814–Feb. 7, 1894) Musician and teacher invented and patented the saxophone in 1845. Gold plaque with a sax on it on the side of the vault. Div. 5, Montmartre Cemetery, Paris.

8119. Saxe, Templar (Templar William Edward Edevein, Aug. 22, 1869–April 17, 1935) English actor from Redhill, Surrey, in American silent films 1913–1928. Urn, Chapel of Memory, Hillside Chapel, Cincinnati, OH.

8120. Saylor, Syd (May 24, 1895–Dec. 21, 1962) B western comic relief, in *The Outcasts of Poker Flat* (1935), many others. Block (mausoleum) L, sec. 998, lot 25, Valhalla Memorial Park, North Hollywood, CA.

8121. Scala, Gia (Giovanna Scoglio, March 3, 1935–April 30, 1972) Actress born in Liverpool to an Irish mother and Italian father came to the U.S. from Rome in 1951. Films include *The Guns of Navarone.* She died at 38 from an alcohol-drug overdose, ruled accidental. Sec. M, lot 542, Holy Cross Cemetery, Culver City, CA.

8122. Scali, John (April 27, 1918–Oct. 8, 1995) ABC news correspondent in 1962 was approached by the Soviets to act as an intermediary between the U.S.S.R. and the White House during the Cuban Missile Crisis. He was reportedly asked by President Kennedy not to disclose any role he may have had in the negotiations. Appointed Ambassador to the United Nations in 1973, he served two years and returned to ABC in 1975, retiring in 1993. Sec. 8, grave 10322, Arlington National Cemetery, Arlington, VA.

8123. Scalise, Frank (Frank Scalice, 1893–June 17, 1957) Reputed Bronx drug crime lord, associate of Albert Anastasia, ran drugs to and from Luciano in Italy. He reportedly refused to reimburse others for a lifted drug shipment and sold Mafia memberships, subsequently "Don Cheech," as dramatized in *The Godfather*, was shot at his favorite vegetable stand in the Bronx. Wild Rose sec. 167, Woodlawn Cemetery, the Bronx, N.Y.C.

8124. Scalise, John (John Scalisi alias John Costa, January 1903 – found May 9, 1929) and **Albert Anselmi** (June 1882 – found May 9, 1929) Sicilians from the same area of Sicily as the Gennas, were their triggermen in Chicago in the early to mid 1920's and after 1925 the trusted assassins of choice allegedly used by Al Capone. They often tipped their bullets, so legend says, in garlic, thought to cause gangrene if the wound was not fatal. They were linked to several Chicago murders, including Dean O'Banion in 1924 and the St. Valentine's Day Massacre. In early 1929, their disloyalty was revealed to Capone by his bodyguard Frank Rio. Scalise, Anselmi and the new Unione Sicilione president **Giuseppe "Hop Toad" Giunta**, were at a banquet on May 8 hosted by Capone at the Hawthorne Inn in Cicero, Illinois, when they were beaten nearly to death with a baseball bat, reportedly by Capone, the job finished by the guns of his underlings. Their bodies were found in and beside a car at an isolated spot at 139th and Baltimore in Hammond, Indiana, Scalise with multiple gunshot wounds to the brain, right arm and leg, and Anselmi with multiple gunshot wounds of the chest, abdomen, arms and neck with hemorrhage. Giunta was buried in sec. 26, Mt. Carmel Cemetery, Hillside, Ill. Scalise was claimed by his mother's sister, Mrs. Antonio Mangiolordo, and sent in a $6,000 coffin to his father for burial at Castelvertrano, Sicily. Anselmi was claimed by his brother Sam and sent, also in a $6,000 coffin, for burial at Marsala, Sicily.

8125. Scammell, Alexander (1747–Oct. 6, 1781) Colonial soldier killed at Yorktown. His exact burial site is unknown, but a boulder with a bronze plaque bears his image, *teacher. soldier, patriot* and the distinction *the only man who could make George Washington laugh.* Old Burial Hill, Plymouth, MA.

8126. Scarborough, George Adolphus (Oct. 2, 1859–April 6, 1900) Deputy U.S. Marshal killed John Selman April 6, 1896, after Selman had killed John Wesley Hardin the year before. Scarborough and lawman Walt Birchfield were ambushed while trailing outlaws in the Chiricahua Mountains. Wounded in the thigh, he was taken to Deming, New Mexico, where the leg was amputated but he died shortly afterward from the effects of the injury. Obelisk, IOOF sec., row J, space 14, Mountain View Cemetery, Deming, NM.

8127. Scarlett, Robert (c.1496–July 2, 1594) Noted English gravedigger dubbed The King of Spades buried two queens at Peterborough Castle (dating to 1118), Catherine of Aragon (in 1536) and Mary, Queen of Scots (in 1587). The latter was eventually reburied at Westminster Abbey. Supposedly he may have been the inspiration for the gravedigger in *Hamlet* (who utters the lines "Alas Poor Yorick. I knew him, Horatio; a fellow of infinite jest, of most excellent fancy.") Scarlett's epitaph appears on the wall in Peterborough Cathedral beside a mural of him above his tomb: *Yov see old Scarletts pictvre stand on hie/ Bvt at tovr feete there doth his body lye/ His gravestone doth his age and death time show/ His office by theis tokens yov may know/ Second to none for strength and stvrdye limm/ A scarebabe mighty voice with vintage grim/ He had interd two qveenes within this place/ And this townes hovse holders in his lives space Twice over/ Bvt at length his own tvrn came/ What he for others did for him the same was done/ No doubt his sovle doth live for Aye in Heaven: Tho here his body clad in clay.* The actual grave itself is just inside the west doorway (main entrance), a floor stone inscribed only *R.S. July 2nd 1594 Aetatis 98.* Peterborough Cathedral, Cambridgeshire.

8128. Schacht, Al (Alexander Schacht, Nov. 11, 1892–July 14, 1984) Vaudeville clown familiar on TV and primarily on the ball field as the Clown Prince of baseball. New North Cemetery, Woodbury, CT.

8129. Schacht, Hjalmar (Hjalmar Horace Greeley Schacht, Jan. 22, 1877–June 4, 1970) German banker and Nazi party member was president of the Reichsbank under Hitler 1933–39 and oversaw the financing of German rearmament. Suspected of plotting against Hitler in 1944, he was placed in a concentration camp until liberated, then tried at Nuremburg as a war criminal in 1946 and acquitted, then imprisoned for three years by Germany for crimes against the state. By 1953 he had resumed banking. He died at 93 in Munich. 55-19-7, Ostfriedhof, St. Martins-Platz 1, Munich.

8130. Schaeffer, Francis August (Jan. 30, 1912–May 15, 1984) Presbyterian minister, theologian and author of twenty four books translated into over twenty languages, espoused the all-importance of God's word in meeting daily problems and struggles. Sec. 1, lot 120, Oakwood Cemetery, Rochester, MN.

8131. Schaeffer, Rebecca (Nov. 6, 1967–July 18, 1989) Actress in *Radio Days, Scenes from the Class Struggle in Beverly Hills* had just reached the limelight with TV's *My Sister Sam* (1986–88) when a demented "fan" tracked her address through a government agency and fatally shot her in the chest when she answered the doorbell. Her epitaph is in her own words: *I am so wise/ To think love will prevail./ I am so wise.'* — *R.L.S. 1989.* Rectangular brown marble slab, new sec., Ahavai Sholom Cemetery, Portland, OR.

8132. Schafer, Natalie (Nov. 5, 1900–April 10, 1991) New York born stage actress in many films from the mid 1940's as upper crust matrons, known for her role as Mrs. Howell on TV's *Gilligan's Island* 1964–67. She died in Los Angeles from cancer at 90. Ashes scattered at sea.

8133. Schaffner, Franklin J. (May 30, 1920–July 2, 1989) Director of *The March of Time* and Edward R. Murrow's *Person to Person* switched to TV drama, winning three Emmys in the 1950's and another in 1962 for Jacqueline Kennedy's tour of the White

House. Acclaimed films include *The Best Man* (1964) and *Patton* (1970, AA for best director). Lot 236, near Hammer mausoleum, Westwood Memorial Park, west Los Angeles.

8134. Schalk, Louis W. (Louis Wellington Schalk, Jr., May 29, 1926–Aug. 16, 2002) Lockheed test pilot in 1962 first tested the A-12 Blackbird reconnaissance spy plane, reaching a top speed of 2,287 mph and an altitude of over 90,000 feet. Sec. 26, site A-21, West Point Academy, Post Cemetery, West Point, NY.

8135. Schalk, Ray (Raymond William Schalk, Aug. 12, 1892–May 19, 1970) Catcher with the White Sox 1912–1929 held several records. The only man to catch four no hitters. Hall of Fame 1955. Oakland sec., lot 124, part 1, grave 3/5, Evergreen Cemetery, Chicago, IL.

8136. Scharf, Walter (Leonard Scharf, Aug. 1, 1910–Feb. 24, 2003) Film and television composer, conductor and arranger received ten Oscar nominations. Works include the films *Brazil, Hans Christian Andersen, White Christmas, Funny Girl, Ben, Willie Wonka and the Chocolate Factory*, and TV's *Mission Impossible* and *The Man From U.N.C.L.E.* Court of Proverbs 19, wall crypt 43707A, Mt. Sinai Memorial Park, Los Angeles.

8137. Schary, Dore (Isadore Schary, Aug. 31, 1905–July 7, 1980) Newark born screenwriter and producer at MGM won an Oscar for best screenplay (*Boys' Town*) in 1938. At RKO in 1947 he produced *Crossfire*, which pre-dated *Gentleman's Agreement* in dealing with anti-Semitism. He replaced Louis B. Mayer as head of the studio 1948–1956 and was known for stressing more American realism in films, including *The Blackboard Jungle* (1954), *Bad Day at Black Rock* (1954) and *Executive Suite* (1955). An outspoken critic of McCarthy era blacklisting, after his dismissal from MGM in 1956 he produced on Broadway, including *The Unsinkable Molly Brown*, was New York's first Commissioner of Cultural Affairs (1970), and a leader of the Anti Defamation League. He died in Manhattan. Services at Riverside Chapel. Hebrew Cemetery (Hebrew Burial Ground of Monmouth Fields), West Long Branch, NJ.

8138. Scheff, Fritzi (Aug. 30, 1879–April 8, 1954) Vienna born opera soprano who graced vaudeville, "The Little Devil of Grand Opera" made her debut at the Met in 1900 in *Fidelio*, best known as Fifi in Victor Herbert's *Mlle. Modiste* and later known for her temperament. She died in her New York apartment at 74. Service at Santa Monica Catholic Church. Actors Fund of America plot, Kensico Cemetery, Valhalla, NY.

8139. Schell, Maria (Jan. 15, 1926–April 26, 2005) Austrian actress, sister of Maximilian Schell, fled the Nazis in 1938 and worked in the U.S. and elsewhere, in *The Magic Box* (1951), *Die Letze Brücke* (*The Last Bridge,* Cannes Best Actress Award 1954), *The Brothers Karamazov* (1958), *Cimarron* (1960), *Voyage of the Damned* (1976), and the subject of her brother's *Meine Schwester Maria* (2002). She died in Graz, Austria, from pneumonia at 79. Pfarrfriedhof (parish cemetery), Preitenegg, Karnten (region), Austria.

8140. Schenck, Joseph M. (Dec. 25, 1878–Oct. 22, 1961) With his brother Nick operated an amusement park before going into business with Marcus Loew in New York as film distributors. Nick stayed with Loew, controlling MGM, while Joe worked as an independent, producing films starring his wife Norma Talmadge. Chairman of United Artists 1924, he founded 20th Century Fox in 1934–35, returning there after serving four months in jail in 1941 for tax irregularities and union payoffs. He died in Beverly Hills. A service was held at the Wilshire Boulevard Temple in Los Angeles and at Frank E. Campbell mortuary in Manhattan. Family mausoleum, sec. 8, Maimonides Cemetery, Brooklyn, N.Y.C.

8141. Schenck, Joseph T. (1891–June 28, 1930) Piano playing vaudevillian with Gus Van. Van and Schenck specialized in ethnic songs done in Yiddish and Italian dialect, appearing several seasons with the *Ziegfeld Follies* and as regulars in early radio variety programs. Schenck died from a heart attack at the Book Cadillac Hotel in Detroit while on tour. His funeral notice said he was buried in Ridgewood, Queens, which the cemetery does extend north into, though located in Bushwick, Brooklyn. Monument with his wife Lillian (1895–1946). Main sec., lot 691, Cemetery of the Evergreens, Brooklyn, N.Y.C.

8142. Schenck, Nicholas (Nov. 14, 1881–March 3, 1969) MGM film distribution executive, brother of Joseph, took over after Marcus Loew's death in 1927. Head of the controlling office of Hollywood's most prestigious studio, the often asked question on the west coast was "What does Nick think?" He died of a stroke in Miami, Florida at 87. Family mausoleum, section 8, Maimonides Cemetery, Brooklyn, N.Y.C.

8143. Schenkel, Chris (Christopher Schenkel, Aug. 21, 1923–Sept. 11, 2005) Sports announcer from Bippus, Indiana, on radio and television in a sixty plus year career was the first to cover the Masters on TV (1956), the voice of the New York Giants from 1952–65, he announced their fabled contest with the Colts in 1958 (considered by many the greatest NFL game ever played), was the first to call a college football game coast to coast (1966, on ABC), and the first live sports anchor at the Olympics (Mexico City, 1968), one of ten he broadcast. Later the voice of the Pro Bowlers Association, he resided at Leesburg, Indiana, until his death at 82 from emphysema in Fort Wayne. St. John's United Church of Christ Cemetery, Bippus (northwest of Huntington), IN.

8144. Scherer, Ray (Raymond L. Scherer, June 7, 1919–July 1, 2000) NBC White House news chief from the early 1950's to the late 1960's, then their London correspondent to 1975. St. Paul's Episcopal Churchyard, Woodville, VA.

8145. Schiavelli, Vincent (Nov. 10, 1948–Dec.

26, 2005) New York born actor, balding with unruly hair and sleepy large eyes, a familiar face in television and films for thirty years, including *Fast Times at Ridgemont High, Amadeus,* the subway specter in *Ghost, Awakenings, Batman Returns, Waiting for the Light.* He also authored three cook-books, and lived in the Sicilian village where his grandparents had been born until his death there from lung cancer at 57 and where his funeral was held. Polizzi Generosa, Sicily.

8146. Schiavo, Terri (Theresa Marie Schindler, Dec. 3, 1963–March 31, 2005) The center of a right to life case which became an international story suffered a heart attack and permanent brain damage at 26 in February 1990, reportedly from a chemical imbalance related to bulimia. Her husband Michael had her feeding tube disconnected, for the third time, on March 18, 2005, after several appeals and court rulings since 1998, prompting demonstrations outside the Pinellas Park, Florida, hospice, where she was confined. Though doctors declared her in a vegetative state, her parents petitioned repeatedly to have the feeding tube left in, but were denied by state and federal courts. She died thirteen days after all food and liquid intake were removed. Although the Schindlers wanted a Catholic burial in Florida, her husband wished her cremated following an autopsy. A bronze tablet placed in June listed her death as the day she collapsed, February 25, 1990, and notes *I kept my promise.* Sylvan Abbey Memorial Park, Clearwater, FL.

8147. Schiff, Steve (March 18, 1947–March 25, 1998) Congressman from New Mexico 1988–1998 died from cancer at 51. Sec. 5, plot 13, space 2, Congregation Albert Cemetery at Fairview Memorial Park, Albuquerque, NM.

8148. Schiffer, Bob (Robert John Schiffer, Sept. 4, 1916–April 26, 2005) Make-up artist from Seattle active in Hollywood for decades helped popularize the women's look of the 1940's, with darkened lips and arched eyebrows, and later gained increased acclaim for his aging of Burt Lancaster in *The Birdman of Alcatraz.* He died in Los Angeles at 88. Cremated by the Neptune Society. Ashes to residence.

8149. Schiffman, Suzanne (Sept. 27, 1929–June 6, 2001) Film maker with the New Wave school of French cinema that included Francois Truffaut, Jean-Luc Godard and Jacques Rivette, with whom cumulatively she made thirty films began her association with the group in 1949 as a script girl, and by Truffaut's death in 1984 was involved in the entire creative construction of the screenplays; she received Oscar nominations for *La Nuit Americane* (*Day For Night*) in 1974, and was acclaimed, among others, for *Le Dernier Metro* (*The Last Metro*) in 1981. She died in Paris of cancer at 71. Pere Lachaise Cemetery, Paris.

8150. Schildkraut, Joseph (March 22 1896–Jan 21 1964) Vienna born actor, son of Rudolf, on stage from 1908. Films include *Orphans of the Storm* (1921), *King of Kings* (1927), *The Life of Emile Zola* (as Dreyfus, AA 1937), *Marie Antoinette, The Shop Around the Corner* (1939), *The Diary of Anne Frank* (1959, as Otto Frank). Television appearances include *Twilight Zone* episodes *Death's Head Revisited* and *The Trade-Ins.* He died in New York City from a heart attack. Beth Olam Mausoleum/Hall of Solomon, urn in foyer R, west wall, tier 4, niche 212, Beth Olam Cemetery adjoining Hollywood Forever Cemetery, Hollywood (Los Angeles), CA.

8151. Schildkraut, Rudolf (April 27, 1862–July 15, 1930) Actor with the Yiddish Theatre in silent films (as Caiaphas in *King of Kings* 1927) died in Los Angeles from heart disease. Father of Joseph Schildkraut. Beth Olam Mausoleum/Hall of Solomon, sec. R, crypt 214, Beth Olam Cemetery adjacent Hollywood Forever Cemetery, Hollywood (Los Angeles), CA.

8152. Schiller, Fred (Jan. 6, 1904–Feb. 8, 2003) Writer from Vienna in the UK and Hollywood from 1939, wrote several B films (*The Flying Deuces, Le Grand élan, Boston Blackie's Rendezvous*) and television episodes. Cremated through Armstrong Family Malloy-Mitten. Ashes scattered at sea.

8153. Schiller, Friedrich (Johann Christoph Friedrich von Schiller, Nov. 10, 1759–May 9, 1805) German poet, dramatist, philosopher and historian known for his tragedies (*The Bride of Messina, William Tell* 1804) which, with Goethe's works, marked the flowering of the classics in 18th century Germany. Entombed, along with Goethe, in the Prince's vaults, Friedhof von dem Frauentor, Weimar, Germany.

8154. Schindler, Oskar (April 28, 1908–Oct. 9, 1974) German businessman bought a bankrupt enamel warehouse-factory in Krakow in 1939. Protective of his Jewish workers, he kept as many as possible from the Plaszow camp nearby, convincing the Nazis of his crucial need for his employees. He saved many from death and from being sent on to Auschwitz, moving them to a munitions factory in Czechoslovakia after the enamel works was closed, and in many cases paying and otherwise bribing Nazi officers to allow him to retain the workers he had kept from death. From 1949–1958 he lived in Argentina, then left his wife and returned to Frankfurt, where he died at 66. Nineteen years after his death, his memory was resurrected by director Steven Spielberg in the Academy Award winning *Schindler's List.* The number of Jews alive in the 1990's because of Schindler's activities is estimated at 6,000 or more. As he wished, he was buried beneath a grave length slab in the Catholic Cemetery on Mount Zion in Jerusalem. His wife **Emilie Schindler** died at 93 in Strausberg, Germany, October 6, 2001. Lauded at her service for her own efforts, which saved over 1,200 Jews from the death camps, she was buried in 17, reihe 015, Waldfriedhof, Waldkraiburg, Bavaria, outside Munich.

8155. Schlegel, Friedrich (March 10, 1772–Jan. 12, 1829) German writer of the romantic movement, critic and philosopher, contemporary of Goethe and Schiller, was a pioneer in Indo-European linguistics and in the use of the term romanticism regarding literature. Alter Katholischer Friedhof, Dresden.

8156. Schlesinger, John (Feb. 16, 1926–July 25, 2003) English director won an Oscar for his then X rated *The Midnight Cowboy* (1969), the only X certificate film to be so honored. Other works include *Darling* (AA nom.), *Sunday Bloody Sunday, Marathon Man, Yanks, The Falcon and the Snowman and Pacific Heights*. He died in Palm Springs at 77. Ashes sent through Palm Spring Mortuary to London.

8157. Schlesinger, Leon (July 20, 1885–Dec. 25, 1949) Executive at Warners produced the ever popular *Looney Toons/Merry Melodies* of the 1930's and 40's. Beth Olam Mausoleum/Hall of Solomon, corridor M4, crypt 1193, Beth Olam Cemetery adjoining Hollywood Forever Cemetery, Hollywood (Los Angeles), CA.

8158. Schliemann, Heinrich (Jan. 8, 1822–Dec. 26, 1890) German pioneer field archaeologist, motivated by Homer and Virgil, excavated at Troy in 1870 and at Mycenae, revealing background on preclassical Greece 6000–1000 B.C, not previously known with certainty to have existed. His Greek temple tomb towers over Athens' premier necropolis from its highest point. First Cemetery, Athens, Greece.

8159. Schlitz, Joseph (May 15, 1831–May 7, 1875) Milwaukee brewer was lost at sea, as shown by the sculpted bas-relief ship and waves on his family monument beneath the statue, across the intersection from both Blatz and Pabst. Sec. 36, Forest Home Cemetery, Milwaukee, WI.

8160. Schmeling, Max (Sept. 28, 1905–Feb. 2, 2005) German world heavyweight champion famed for his two bouts with Joe Louis gained the title over Jack Sharkey — disqualified for a low punch — in 1930, lost it to Sharkey in 1932, and regained it when he knocked out the undefeated Joe Louis in New York on June 9, 1936. The return bout at Yankee Stadium June 22, 1938, with Schmeling touted as the representative of Hitler's super race, saw Schmeling felled by Louis after 124 seconds in the first round. In reality, he was not a Nazi, had a Jewish trainer and a Czech wife, film actress **Anny Ondra**, from 1932 to her death in 1987, and used his influence to protect or hide Jews when he could. He retired from the ring in 1948, bought the license to the Coca-Cola franchise in Germany and became wealthy, maintaining a friendship with Louis that included financial help and paying for his funeral in 1981. He died at 99. Friedhof der evangelischen Kirchengemeinde St. Andras, Hollenstedt, southwest of Hamburg in (the federal state of) Niedersachsen, Germany.

8161. Schmirler, Sandra (Sandra Marie Schmirler, June 11, 1963–March 2, 2000) Canadian Queen of Curling won three Canadian and world titles, taking the gold at the Olympics in Nagano, Japan, in 1988. She died from cancer at 36. Riverside Memorial Park Cemetery, Regina, Saskatchewan.

8162. Schmitz, Sybille (Dec. 2, 1909–April 13, 1955) German actress from Duran in films 1928–1953, notably as Leone in *Vampyr* (*Der Traum des Allan Grey/The Strange Adventure of David Gray*) and as Claire in *F.P.1 Antwortet Nicht* (*F.P.1 Does Not Answer*), both 1932, *Fahrman Maria* (1936), and *Tanz auf dem Vulkan* (1938). A suicide by overdose under what was described as mysterious circumstances in Munich at 43. Cremated at Ostfriedhof des Krematorium. Burial at location 166-U-32 (re-used), Ostfriedhof, Munich.

8163. Schneckenburger, Max (Feb. 17, 1819–May 3, 1849) German merchant wrote the patriotic poem *Die Wacht am Rhein* (*The Watch on the Rhine*) in 1840 during a war scare with France. Set to music in 1854 by Karl Wilhelm, with the refrain "Lieb' Vaterland, magst ruhig sein, Fein steht und treu die Wacht am Rhein," it became a national favorite, used to effect in films competing with the French *La Marseillaise* in both *La Grande Illusion* and *Casablanca,* the title became that of the pre world War II Lillian Hellman play, and the music used for *Tomorrow Belongs to Me* in the play and film *Cabaret.* Cemetery at Talheim, Baden-Württemburg, Germany.

8164. Schneerson, Menachem Mandel (April 18, 1902–June 12, 1994) Ukrainian born rebbe led his small but devoted Lubavitch Hasidic Jewish movement from his headquarters in Crown Heights, Brooklyn, thought by some of his following to be the messiah. His death at 92 left no successor. His wooden coffin was mobbed before its burial the day after his death. Mausoleum, block 94, Old Montefiore Cemetery, St. Albans, Queens, N.Y.C.

8165. Schneider, Louis (Dec. 19, 1901–Nov. 14, 1942) Indianapolis 500 winner in 1931 with a speed of 96.629 mph. Sec. 42, lot 124, Crown Hill Cemetery, Indianapolis, IN.

8166. Schneider, Magda (May 17, 1909–July 30, 1996) Bavarian born actress in German films and television 1930–1969. Mother of actress Romy Schneider (*q.v.*). A rough cut boulder marks her grave. Bergfriedhof, Berchtesgaden, Germany.

8167. Schneider, Romy (Rosemarie Albach-Retty, Sept. 23, 1938–May 29, 1982) Actress from German films in English speaking roles in *The Victors* (1963), *Good Neighbor Sam* (1964), *What's New Pussycat* (1965). Her last was *La Passante du San Souci*, made shortly after the death of her fourteen year old son, impaled on an iron fence in July 1981. She was found dead in her Paris apartment the next May, either from a heart attack or suicide. Buried outside Paris in the Boissy-Sans Avoir village cemetery.

8168. Schoedsack, Ernest B. (June 8, 1893–Dec 23, 1979) Director of the 1920's, 30's and 40's in partnership with Merian C. Cooper. Their best of several ambitious jungle epics was *King Kong* (1933). *The Most Dangerous Game, Son of Kong* and others were filmed on the same RKO jungle sets. His wife **Ruth Rose** (Jan. 16, 1896–June 8, 1978) co-wrote *Kong*'s screenplay with James Creelman. It is Cooper and Schoedsack who play the fliers that fire the last fatal shots at Kong in the 1933 film; "We brought him here" they observed, "we might as well finish the s.o.b. off." Ground niche markers. Sec. D, urn garden southwest, Westwood Memorial Park, west Los Angeles.

8169. Schofield, John McAllister (Sept. 29, 1831–March 4, 1906) Physics professor entered the army with the Civil War and stayed there, finally attaining the highest position, General in Chief of the Army, succeeding to the position after Phil Sheridan's death in 1888, retiring in 1895. Among his acts was to place the office under the authority of the Secretary of War, keeping it under civilian control. During the Spanish American War he was military advisor to President McKinley, and after Hawaii was annexed the barracks at Honolulu — which gained fame in 1941 when they were bombed — were named for him. Sec. 2, site 1108, grid T-31, Arlington National Cemetery, Arlington, VA.

8170. Schopenhauer, Arthur (Feb. 22, 1788–Sept. 21, 1860) German philosopher espoused the pessimistic view of human will over intellect, detailed in his major work, *The World as Will and Representation* (1818). Based in part on Kant, he took the focus on will further, elevating it to the all consuming inner force, extinguishable in the end only by turning in upon itself. His theories were in direct opposition to those of Hegel, whose work and views overshadowed the embittered Schopenhauer. Gewann A 24, Hauptfriedhof, Frankfurt-on-Main.

8171. Schott, Marge (Margaret Unnewehr, Aug. 18, 1928–March 2, 2004) Colorful, controversial owner of the Cincinnati Reds from July 1985, the daughter of a city lumber baron and widow (1968) of industrialist Charles Schott, she spent money for top talent and saw the team win the World Series in the 1990 wire to wire season, but was suspended and fined by the commissioner's office in 1993 for remarks deemed racially insensitive, and was forced to sell her controlling interest in the team in 1998. Known for her brash manner, political incorrectness, chain smoking and St. Bernards Schottzie and his sequel, she was also, until her death there at 73, one of the Queen City's major boosters and contributors to charity. Sec. 1, lot 49, graves 31–32, across from Priests' Circle, Gate of Heaven Catholic Cemetery, Montgomery, Cincinnati, OH.

8172. Schramm, Tex (Texas E. Schramm, June 2, 1920–July 15, 2003) NFL executive transformed the Dallas Cowboys into "America's Team," heading the organization for twenty nine years. Chapel Gardens Mausoleum, S-403, crypt 1, Restland Memorial Park, Dallas, TX.

8173. Schrank, John F. (John Flammang Schrank, March 5, 1876–Sept. 15, 1943) Bavarian born would-be assassin of third term presidential candidate Theodore Roosevelt. Running on the Bull Moose ticket, TR was giving a speech in Milwaukee on October 14, 1912, when a thick speech and spectacle case

in his breast pocket slowed and deflected Schrank's bullet. Roosevelt finished his speech before going to the hospital. Schrank, who opposed Roosevelt's serving a third term, spent two years at Northern State Hospital and from 1914 until his death at Central State Hospital, Waupin, Wisconsin. He left no survivors and was buried by Kohl's Community mortuary in a $25 coffin. Cattauragus Cemetery, Waupin, WI.

8174. Schratt, Katharina (Maria Katharina Kiss von Ittebe, Sept. 11, 1853–April 17, 1940) Austrian actress, rumored to have had a long standing affair with Emperor Franz Josef, but at the least his good friend. Gruppe 19, grab 108, Friedhof Hietzing, Vienna.

8175. Schreck, Max (Sept. 6, 1879–Feb. 20, 1936) Berlin born stage and screen actor known for his portrayal of Count Orlock in F.W. Murnau's *Nosferatu* (1922). Married to actress Fanny Norman. He died in Munich of a heart attack at 56. Cremated at Waldfriedhof, Munchen (Munich), the urn was sent to Wilmersdorfer Waldfriedhof Guterfelde, Potsdamer Damm, and installed March 14, 1936, in location U-670, the usefruct ending in 1956, and no care for the grave. Further help from former Munich cemeteries head and historian-author Erich Scheibmayr specified that the gravesite is today (at times) marked only by a red peg. Urnengrab Nr. 670, Wilmersdorfer Waldfriedhof Güterfelde, Potsdamer Damm 11 (Wilmersdorf), Berlin.

8176. Schreiber, Avery (April 9, 1935–Jan. 7, 2002) Curly haired, mustached comedian long teamed with Jack Burns, later did Doritos commercials. He died from a heart attack in Los Angeles at 66. Ashes to residence, Van Nuys, CA.

8177. Schubert, Bernard (Bernard Schupper, Jan. 1, 1895–Aug. 4, 1988) New York born screen-writer in Hollywood from 1931 (*The Public Defender, Symphony of Six Million, Mark of the Vampire, Kind Lady, Jungle Woman, The Mummy's Curse, The Frozen Ghost*), later produced television shows (*Topper*, several others). He died from pneumonia at 93 in Los Angeles. Buried August 7. Laurel Gardens, 9–183–8B, Hillside Memorial Park, Los Angeles.

8178. Schubert, Franz (Jan. 31, 1797–Nov. 19, 1928) Austrian composer had been treated with mercury for syphilis for some time. His death may have been due to a burst cerebral artery resulting from it, though it was attributed at the time to typhoid. He was buried near Beethoven in der Wahringstrasse Cemetery (Wahringer-Orts Friedhof) in Vienna, now Franz Schubert Park, separated by four graves. Their two monuments and part of the brick wall remain. Schubert's has a bust of him by Joseph Dialer in an enclosure and is inscribed *In the year 1828 Franz Schubert was buried at this site and on 22 September 1888 his remains were exhumed and transferred to the Centralfriedhof.* Below that is the original inscription *The art of music buried here a rich treasure, but even finer hopes. Franz Schubert lies here,* followed by his dates and age

(31). In 1888 when both were re-buried they were honored with large white monuments. Schubert's shows an angel placing a wreath over the bust of the composer. Gruppe 32A, nr. 28 Zentralfriedhof (Central Cemetery), Vienna.

8179. Schuck, Aurora (July 14, 1927–Nov. 7, 1989) Cuban immigrant settled in Aurora, Indiana, in 1947 and adopted the town. When she died from cancer at 62, her wish to be buried in her car was faithfully carried out. She was buried in an Aurora casket in her red 1976 Eldorado Cadillac convertible, surrounded by bricks stamped Aurora and an old license plate marked "Unique Aurora," in a 30' by 20' plot at Aurora Cemetery, Aurora, IN.

8180. Schulberg, B.P. (Benjamin Percival Schulberg, Jan. 19, 1892–Feb. 26, 1957) Producer and film mogul born in Bridgeport grew up on New York's lower east side. With Zukor's Famous Players from 1912 he discovered Clara Bow, etc. In charge of Paramount's west coast productions 1928–1932, he was later an independent. After a stroke in 1950 he retired to Key Biscayne, Florida, where he died of a stroke at 65. Cremated at Flagler Crematory by Gordon mortuary in Coral Gables, Miami. Ashes sent to lawyer N.S. Beanstock in New York City. His wife, agent Adeline Jaffe Schulberg died in New York July 15, 1977. Service at Frank E. Campbell, Manhattan.

8181. Schuller, Robert (born Sept. 16, 1926) TV evangelist began at a drive-in in Orange, County, California, in the 1950's, by the 1970's building the showcase cathedral where his polished rose-brown sarcophagus rests. Crystal Cathedral, Garden Grove, CA.

8182. Schultz, Dutch (Arthur Flegenheimer, Aug. 6, 1901–Oct. 23, 1935) New York gangster of the 1920's and 1930's controlled bootlegging and numbers in the Bronx, adopting his name from an infamous Bronx thug of the 19th century. The Dutchman ordered the deaths of both Legs Diamond and Vincent "Mad Dog" Coll, and at the time of his death was insisting on having special New York prosecutor Thomas E. Dewey killed, when his associates decided he had to be stopped. Assassins found him at the urinal in the men's room of the Palace Chop House in Newark, New Jersey. He staggered out to a table and collapsed, his henchmen, including AbbaDabba Berman, lying dead. Taken to a hospital, he babbled incoherently for hours before his death. Because a priest said he had been baptized in the Catholic faith, he was not buried as a Jew as his mother wanted, but as a Catholic at his wife's insistence. Curved stone bench inscribed *Flegenheimer*. Sec. 42, lot 96, Gate of Heaven Cemetery, Hawthorne, NY.

8183. Schultze, Norbert (Jan. 26, 1911–Oct. 14, 2002) German composer from Braunschweig known for writing the tune to what was arguably the most widely sung (or hummed) song of World War II, *Lili Marleen*, in 1938, setting to music a poem by Hans Leip, *The Song of a Young Sentry*. It became popular with the German troops first in North Africa, was set to wartime martial music, later recorded in forty eight languages including English, but eventually and primarily associated with Marlene Dietrich in its original form as a melancholy lament. He died at 91 in Bad Tolz, near Munich. Service at Nordfriedhof, Munich. Ashes to be interred at his birthplace, Braunschweig.

8184. Schulz, Charles (Nov. 26, 1922–Feb. 12, 2000) Minneapolis born cartoonist began drawing *Peanuts* in Oct. 1950, his characters Charlie Brown, Snoopy, Lucy, Linus and friends endearing themselves to readers and becoming embedded in American pop culture by the time of the original *Charlie Brown Christmas* telecast in 1965. Ill with colon cancer, his last strip after forty nine years appeared in January 2000. His farewell note to readers with the characters drawn around it appeared by chance the morning after his death at 77 in Santa Rosa, Ca, his adopted home town. A fitting memorial skate was held two days after his death at the skating rink "Sparky" built there in 1969. Marble bench at foot of grave, right rear of cemetery. Pleasant Hills Cemetery, Sebastopol, CA.

8185. Schumann, Conrad (c. 1942–June 20, 1998) The subject of a famous AP photo by Peter Leibing, Schumann, a 19 year old East German soldier, was frozen in time on August 15, 1961 as he leapt over a barbed wire barricade at the Bernauer Street sector into West Berlin. A suicide by hanging thirty six years later. Friedhof der Alten Wehrkirche, Irfendorf (near Ingolstadt), Bavaria.

8186. Schumann, Robert (June 8, 1810–July 29, 1856) German composer was manic depressive, in later days wandering Dusseldorf, his eyes turned upward, hearing music that was not there and on one occasion jumping into the Rhine. He was sent to a sanitarium at Edenich near Bonn, where he died. An autopsy showed tiny bone spicules lacerating the membrane of his small brain. The monument depicts his wife **Clara Wieck**, who was buried there forty years later, gazing at his image. Old Cemetery (Alter Friedhof), Bonn, Germany.

8187. Schumann-Heink, Ernestine (June 15, 1861–Nov 17, 1936) Austrian born contralto with the New York Metropolitan Opera, lauded for her Wagnerian roles, was considered the finest contralto of her time, varying from the Met to light opera and films of the 1930's. During World War I she remained in the U.S, though she had sons fighting on both sides in France. She was cheered in her last illness by admirers of many decades sending well wishes. Crypt, Corridor of Sunshine, mausoleum, Greenwood Memorial Park, San Diego, CA.

8188. Schumann-Heink, Ferdinand (Aug. 9, 1893–Sept. 15, 1958) Actor, son of opera great Ernestine Schumann-Heink, in over sixty films, generally in bit parts, including *Hell's Angels* (1930, Zeppelin's first officer), *Condemned to Live* (1935, as Franz), *The Florentine Dagger, British Intelligence, Invisible Agent*. Sec. T, grave 550, Fort Rosecrans National Cemetery, San Diego, CA.

8189. Schurz, Carl (March 2, 1829–May 14, 1906) German born statesman in the U.S. from the 1850's, correspondent and editor, senator from Missouri and proponent of civil service reform. As Hayes' Secretary of the Interior 1877–1881, he worked for better Indian relations and reform in government hiring and appointments, resulting in the 1883 Pendleton Act. He turned away from the Republican party over the war with Spain in 1898, and published both a biography of Henry Clay and an autobiography of his own. He died in New York at 77. Sec. 71 (Horeb) along Fairmont Ave., Sleepy Hollow Cemetery, Tarrytown, NY.

8190. Schuster, Arnold (c. 1928–March 8, 1952) Twenty four year old Brooklyn resident had notified police when he spotted bank robber Willie Sutton on a New York subway February 16, 1952. Interviewed on television as a hero, he infuriated a viewer, mob boss Albert Anastasia, who ordered the informer to be hit. Schuster, 24, was shot and killed by a lone gunman as he walked home along a dark Brooklyn street just over two weeks later. Not until Joseph Valachi testified on organized crime was the cause of Schuster's unsolved murder known. By then both Anastasia and the gunman were also dead. The traditional sign of a life cut short, a severed tree trunk, is engraved on the left of his monument. Block 76, Pirafiner Society, Old Montefiore Cemetery, Queens, N.Y.C.

8191. Schuster, George N. (Feb. 4, 1873–July 4, 1972) Race driver pre-dating the Indianapolis 500 made it from New York to Paris, heading westward, in 169 days in 1908. Maplewood Cemetery, Springville, NY.

8192. Schuyler, Philip (Nov. 20, 1733–Nov. 18, 1804) Upstate New York squire, soldier and diplomat. As a general in charge of upstate New York under Washington, he was blamed for the fall of Fort Ticonderoga and replaced by Gates, but was later exonerated. He served in the Continental Congress, worked to ratify the Constitution, and was briefly senator. Father-in-law of Alexander Hamilton, who was killed in a duel four months before Schuyler's death. Column atop a large base. Sec. 29, lot 2, Albany Rural Cemetery, Menands, Albany, NY.

8193. Schwab, Jacob (Oct. 6, 1904–March 17, 1980) and **Leon Schwab** (April 23, 1911–Jan. 4, 1996) Founders and proprietors of the fabled Hollywood drugstore. Wall crypts, Garden of Shemot 10 (62224) and 7 (64188), respectively. Mt. Sinai Memorial Park, Los Angeles.

8194. Schwann, William (May 13, 1913–June 7, 1998) Record seller founded Schwann's Catalogue, the "bible" of recorded music. Boulder with the epitaph *How lovely is thy dwelling place.* Lincoln Cemetery, Lincoln, MA.

8195. Schwartz, Delmore (Dec. 8, 1913–July 17, 1966) New York City critic, poet and writer primarily of short stories. Block 36, path 6, Beth El Cemetery (adjacent Cedar Park Cemetery), Paramus, NJ.

8196. Schwartz, Julie (Julius Schwartz, June 19, 1915–Feb. 8, 2004) Influential Bronx born editor of *DC Comics,* co-creator of the first science-fiction fanzine, *The Time Traveler,* with Mort Wesinger and Forrest J Ackerman in 1932, took over *All American Comics* in 1944, shortly before they merged with *DC,* and is credited with beginning the Silver Age of Comics with the publication of *DC's* "Showcase" #4 in 1956, reviving The Flash. He died at 88 in New York City. Block 17, path 6, sec. F-G, grave 8, Mt. Hebron Cemetery, Queens, N.Y.C.

8197. Schwartz, Maurice (June 18, 1890–May 10, 1960) Russian born founder of the Yiddish Art Theatre in New York, Schwartz was known as the John Barrymore of the Yiddish Theatre, particularly acclaimed for his King Lear. He appeared in several films as well, up into the 1950's including *Salome* (1953, as Ezra) and *Slaves of Babylon* (also 1953, as Nebuchadnezzar). He died from a heart attack in Tel Aviv, Israel. Yiddish Theater Alliance, block 67, Mt. Hebron Cemetery, Flushing, Queens, N.Y.C.

8198. Schwartz, Morrie (Morris S. Schwartz, Dec. 20, 1916–Nov. 4, 1995) Mitch Albom's old professor at Brandeis University provided the basis, in his declining months prior to his death, for Albom's best seller *Tuesdays With Morrie,* published in 1997. Flat plaque with name and full dates. Newton Cemetery, Newton, MA.

8199. Schwarzenegger, Aurelia (Sept. 28, 1922–Aug. 2, 1998) Mother of bodybuilder turned actor turned politician Arnold Schwarzenegger appeared with him often and on many Austrian and German television talk programs. She died at the place where she is buried, while visiting the grave of her husband (1972), the former chief of police. Feld 14, town cemetery, Weiz, Steiermark, Austria.

8200. Schwarzkopf, H. Norman (Sr.) (Herbert Norman Schwarzkopf, Aug. 28, 1895–Nov. 25, 1958) Superintendent of the New Jersey State Police 1921–1936 headed the investigation into the kidnapping and murder of the Lindbergh baby 1932–34. He afterward served with the New Jersey National Guard and was assigned to Iran by FDR and later to Germany and Italy, training the national police. Promoted to Brigadier General by his retirement. In the 1950's, as director of Law and Public Safety, he wound up investigating his old nemesis, Governor Harold Hoffman. Father of General H. Norman Schwarzkopf. Schwarzkopf, Sr. died at his home in West Orange, New Jersey, from a heart attack at 63. His son stayed with the body through cremation; the ashes buried with military honors. Sec. 10, row 1, grave 160, Post Cemetery, West Point Military Academy, West Point, NY.

8201. Schweitzer, Albert (Jan. 14, 1875–Sept. 4, 1965) World renown doctor from Alsace-Lorraine, humanitarian, Christian missionary, and anti-nuclear spokesman from the beginning of the age of atomic power. Still working in the field at 90, Dr. Schweitzer died in the African jungle and was buried beneath a white cross along the bank of the Ogowee River at what is now Albert Schweitzer Hospital, Lambaréné, Gabon, formerly part of French Equatorial Africa.

8202. Schwerner, Michael (dec. June 21, 1964) One of three civil rights workers killed near Philadelphia, Mississippi, could not be buried with his friend and fellow victim James Chaney in the Negro cemetery near Meridian and was returned to New York City and cremated.

8203. Schwieger, Walther (April 7, 1885–Sept. 5/17, 1917) German commander of the U-20 who torpedoed the British liner *Lusitania* in the Irish Sea May 7, 1915. He later commanded the U-88 and died when sunk by the Q-boat Stoncrop in the North Atlantic.

8204. Schwimmer, Reinhart *see* **St. Valentine's Day Massacre.**

8205. Scobee, Francis R. "Dick" (May 19, 1939–Jan. 28, 1986) Astronaut aboard the ill fated space shuttle Challenger died with six other crew members when Challenger exploded shortly after take-off, live on national television, the worst disaster in the history of the U.S. space program. After the remains were released to the families April 29, Commander Scobee was buried May 19 1986, on what would have been his 47th birthday. Sec. 46 (behind the amphitheatre), grave 1129-4, Arlington National Cemetery, Arlington, VA.

8206. Scopes. John T. (Aug. 3, 1900–Oct. 21, 1970) Biology teacher broke state law teaching Darwin's Theory of Evolution, prompting the Scopes "Monkey" Trial at Dayton, Tenn. in the summer of 1925, with defense lawyer Clarence Darrow facing down the once great orator and fundamentalist William Jennings Bryan. Scopes was found guilty, and fined $100; he later appealed and was acquitted. The trial was the basis of the play and film *Inherit the Wind.* Over his name is inscribed *A man of courage.* Old sec. 7, lot 104, Oak Grove Cemetery, Paducah, KY.

8207. Scorsese, Catherine (Catherine Cappa, April 16, 1912–Jan. 6, 1997) Native of New York's Little Italy, the mother of director Martin Scorsese appeared in several of his films, including *Mean Streets, New York, New York, Goodfellas, Cape Fear* and *Casino,* as well as *The Godfather II* and *Desperately Seeking Susan.* A central figure in her son's documentary *Italianamerican,* she also had a family cookbook published by Random House. She died in N.Y. University Medical Center at 84. Service at Colonial mortuary, Staten Island. Interred with her husband **Charles Scorsese** (May 1913–Aug. 29, 1993) in the family mausoleum. Moravian Cemetery, New Dorp, Staten Island, N.Y.C.

8208. Scott, Blanche Stuart "Betty" (Blanche Stuart Hennings, April 8, 1889–Jan. 12, 1970) Rochester, New York, motor and aviation pioneer was the first woman to drive an automobile cross-country, from New York to San Francisco in 1910, with only 218 of the miles paved. Through flying instructor Glenn Curtiss, she became the first woman to fly solo, in August or September 1910, although it remains in dispute, as Bessica Raiche is also said to have been the first female to solo. Scott was the first professional of her gender; billed as The Tomboy of the Air, she made the first long distance flight at 60 miles in 1911, and was the first female test pilot, for Martin prototypes 1912-13. She retired from flying in 1916. She worked in radio through the 1930's and 40's, and in 1948 rode with Chuck Yeager, the first woman to fly in a jet. She died at 80 and was cremated at Mt. Hope Cemetery, Rochester. Ashes buried through Hedges Memorial Chapel September 22, 1970. Sec. T, lot 524, grave 2, Riverside Cemetery, Rochester, NY.

8209. Scott, Debralee (April 2, 1953–April 6, 2005) Actress from Elizabeth, New Jersey, in TV and films of the 1970's and 80's, starting as the abducted (deceased) girl in *Dirty Harry* 1971, Bob Falfa's girlfriend in *American Graffiti,* and more substantial parts on *Welcome Back Kotter* (as Rosalie "Hotsy Totsy") and *Mary Hartman, Mary Hartman,* as Mary's younger sister Cathy Shumway, reprised on *Forever Fernwood.* She died four days past her 52nd birthday at her home in Fernandina Beach, Amelia Island, Florida. Cremated at I.C.S. Crematory, Lake City, through Oxley-Heard mortuary, Fernandina Beach. Ashes to family.

8210. Scott, Dred (c. 1799–Sept. 17, 1858) Slave who journeyed north with his master, who died. As slaves were free in the north, Scott sued for his freedom but in a long deplored decision, United States Supreme Court Chief Justice Roger Brooke Taney ruled in 1857 that a negro was property and not a person, thus negating the 1820 Missouri Compromise as unconstitutional. Scott was sold and freed, went to work in St. Louis and died there the next year. Small grave marker and a newer commemorative stone. Sec. 1 off Way of Nicodemus, Calvary Cemetery, St. Louis, MO.

8211. Scott, George C. (George Campbell Scott, Oct. 18, 1927–Sept. 22, 1999) Distinguished actor from Wise, Virginia, with a noted disinterest in Academy Awards was from 1945–49 part of the burial detail at Arlington National Cemetery while in the service. On stage through the 1950's, he began in films in 1957. Though he thanked the Academy but told them he was not interested in accepting popularity awards, he nevertheless received Oscar nominations for his supporting roles in *Anatomy of A Murder* (1959) and *The Hustler* (1961), and made headlines in 1970 when he refused the Oscar he won as *Patton.* His last nomination was for *The Hospital* (1971). Twice married to Colleen Dewhurst and to Tish Van Devere from 1972, he continued in films until his death from an abdominal aneurysm at 71 in his Westlake Village, California, home. Buried October 1, 1999. Gray monument, unmarked. Enclosed lot to Walter Matthau's right, along southern drive, fronting the Garden of Serenity, Westwood Memorial Park, west Los Angeles.

8212. Scott, Hazel (June 11, 1920–Oct. 2, 1981) Black actress from Trinidad in light films of the 1940's and 50's, died from cancer in New York City at 61. Divorced from Adam Clayton Powell, Jr., she was buried with his parents. Sec 9, plot 8, div. M, Flushing Cemetery, Flushing, Queens, N.Y.C.

8213. Scott, Homer A. (Homer Almerian Scott, Oct. 1, 1880–Dec. 23, 1956) Co-founder of the American Society of Cinematographers (A.S.C.) January 8, 1919, and its president 1925–26, shot films from 1914 with the Carlyle Blackwell Famous Players, merged with Jesse Lasky, later several Mack Sennett (*Molly-O* with Mabel Normand) and Warner Bros. (*The Little Church Around the Corner*) efforts until 1923. He died from heart failure in Sacramento at 76. Magnolia West (outdoor) Mausoleum, tier 1, crypt 32, East Lawn Memorial Park, Sacramento, CA.

8214. Scott, Hugh (Nov. 11, 1900–July 21, 1994) GOP Congressman from 1940 and Senator from Pennsylvania 1959–1977, minority leader from 1969, after Everett Dirksen. A staunch supporter of Vietnam until 1968, he moved for a cease-fire under Nixon. One of the last holdouts against Nixon's resignation, he and Goldwater urged the president to resign in a personal trip to the White House just prior to his decision. Born in Fredericksburg, he died in Falls Church, Virginia. Sec. 7A, site 139, Arlington National Cemetery, Arlington, VA.

8215. Scott, Julian (Feb. 15, 1846–July 4, 1901) First recipient of the Medal of Honor (February 1865) for bravery in bringing back wounded men under fire, April 1862. Sec A, div. 4, row 14, lot 75, Hillside Cemetery, Plainfield, NJ.

8216. Scott, Martha (Sept. 22, 1912–May 28, 2003) Actress from Jamesport, Missouri, gained fame on the stage as the original Emily in Thornton Wilder's *Our Town*, which she reprised in the 1940 film (her first) and was nominated for an Oscar. Her twenty plus films include *The Howards of Virginia, One Foot in Heaven* and *The Desperate Hours*—both opposite Fredric March, *Sayonara*, and twice as Charlton Heston's mother, in *The Ten Commandments* and *Ben Hur*. She also narrated *Charlotte's Web*, co-founded the Plumstead Theatre Company in 1968, which produced *First Monday in October*. She produced the 1979 film version as well. Her last stage appearance was as Goody Nurse in *The Crucible* (1991). Her husband of fifty two years, Pulitzer Prize winning composer and musician **Mel Powell**, died in 1998. She died in Van Nuys at 90. Funeral and burial at the cemetery where she found her inspiration for her *Our Town* soliloquy, full of her Scott and McKinley relatives. Masonic Cemetery, old 6 Highway north of Jamesport, MO.

8217. Scott, Randolph (George Randolph Scott, Jan. 23, 1898 March 2, 1987) Tall, rugged film hero from Orange County, Virginia, with weathered face and eternally honest, upright character. Though he appeared in non western films such as *Murders in the Zoo* (1933), *Supernatural* (1933), *She* (1935) and *Pitts-*

burgh (1942), it was as a forthright cowboy in westerns over thirty years that he was best known. Retired from the screen nearly twenty five years before the time of his death, he was buried in North Carolina, where the family moved as a boy. Grave length slab with full name and dates. Sec. R, Elmwood Cemetery, Charlotte, NC.

8218. Scott, Raymond (Harry Warnow, Sept. 10, 1908–Feb. 8, 1994) Jazz pianist, composer and bandleader experimented with electronic musical sounds, producing his quirky music in Warners' *Looney Toons* and *Merrie Melodies*, beginning in 1943. Ashes through Pierce Bros. Van Nuys to his residence in Van Nuys, CA.

8219. Scott, Shirley (March 14, 1934–March 10, 2002) Jazz organist from Philadelphia, popular from the 1950's with smooth jazz numbers, recorded with Eddie Davis and her later husband Stanley Turrentine, including *In the Kitchen, Soul Shoutin, Blue Flames* and *Hip Soul*. She died in Philadelphia from heart disease brought on by fen-phen, over which she sued and won $8 million in 2000. Fairview Cemetery, Willow Grove, PA.

8220. Scott, Walter (Aug. 15, 1771–Sept. 21, 1832) Knighted Scottish novelist authored *Ivanhoe, The Lady in the Lake*, and was a major figure in the Romantic period of literature. He suffered from dysgraphia, resulting from a childhood fever and causing a shortage of blood to the brain and tissue necrosis. He died at Abbotsford, his small estate in Scotland, and was interred nearby in a red stone sarcophagus along the wall in Dryburgh Abbey near Melrose, Scotland.

8221. Scott, Walter (Walter Notheis, Jr., Feb. 7, 1943–Dec. 27, 1983) Lead vocalist with the St. Louis based group Bob Kuban and the In-Men had one hit with *The Cheater* in early 1966. He left home in St. Louis two days after Christmas 1983 on an errand and was never seen again. Three and a half years later, in April 1987, his body was found in a St. Louis cistern, having been bound and shot in the back of the head execution style. His widow and her lover Jim Williams were tried, convicted; Williams was imprisoned for the murder and that of his (Williams') wife. Memorial mass in Seven Holy Founders Catholic Church, Affton, Missouri. Crypt 230, row 5, Hillcrest Abbey, St. Louis, MO.

8222. Scott, Winfield (June 13, 1786–May 29, 1866) U.S. army general, Old Fuss 'n' Feathers, in command from 1841, earned his fame during the Mexican War 1846–48. The unsuccessful Whig candidate for the presidency in 1852, he was still Commander of the Army in 1861 when the Civil War began but was beset with gout and weight. His advice was largely ignored, and he retired. His plan, an "anaconda" division of the Confederacy, however, was eventually adopted. He died at West Point at 79 and was buried there, near (later) Custer and Robert Anderson. Rectangular stone monument, surrounded by an iron fence with gate, inscribed *History records his unlim-*

ited services as a General in Chief of the Armies of the United States. Medals and an equestrian statue ordered by the congress in the capitol of his country are his public monuments. This stone is a mark of the love and veneration of his daughters. Recquiescat in Pace. Sec. 27, row A, grave 16, Post Cemetery, West Point Military Academy, West Point, NY.

8223. Scott, Zachary (Feb. 24, 1914–Oct. 3, 1965) Actor from Austin, Texas, in smooth, often detestable roles as heels (*The Mask of Dimitrios* 1944, *Mildred Pierce* 1945). He died from a brain tumor in Austin at 51. Buried next to his mother and father **Zachary Sr.** (Dec. 25, 1880–Jan. 19, 1964), a leader in the treatment of TB, beneath identical pink marble tombstones. On the actor's are inscribed the lines *Eternity* by William Blake: *He who binds himself a joy does the winged life destroy/ But he who kisses the joy as it flies/ Lives in Eternity's sunrise.* Block 4, lot 187A, spaces 11–12, Austin Memorial Park, Austin, TX.

8224. Scotti, Vito (Jan. 26, 1918–June 5, 1996) San Francisco born son of performers acted in some 70 films, including *Criss Cross* (1949), *Master of the World* (1961), *Von Ryan's Express* (1965) and *Get Shorty* (1996), as well as many TV appearances. Abbey of the Psalms/Hollywood Forever Mausoleum, Sanctuary of Light, crypt 1253, Hollywood Forever Cemetery, Hollywood (Los Angeles), CA.

8225. Scribner, Charles (Feb. 21, 1821–Aug. 26, 1900) Founder of Scribner's Publishing House (1846) established *Scribners' Magazine* in 1870, *Scribners & Sons* Publishers from 1875, run successively by his sons John Blair, **Charles, Jr.** (Oct. 18, 1854–April 19, 1930), and **Arthur Hawley Scribner** (March 15, 1859–July 3, 1932). Arthur is in sec. 160, Greenwood Cemetery, Brooklyn. Charles Sr. and Jr. are in Catalpa plot, lot 1117–1118, Woodlawn Cemetery, the Bronx, N.Y.C.

8226. Scripps, Edward Wyllis (June 18, 1854–March 12, 1926) Founder of the chain of Scripps newspapers in Cleveland in 1878 and the United Press Association in 1907, but his passion was the sea and he funded the museum of oceanography bearing his name in La Jolla, California. He died on his yacht off the coast of Liberia and was buried at sea. **Ellen Browning Scripps** (Oct. 18, 1836–Aug. 3, 1932), his older half-sister and the younger sister of James, worked in publishing as well and co-founded the Institute at La Jolla and Scripps College at Claremont, California. Her ashes were also buried at sea. **James Edmund Scripps** (March 19, 1835–May 29, 1906) preceded his brother Edward into the publishing business in Detroit in 1873 with the *Detroit Evening News*. He later helped Edward with his several mid-western papers, but they split in 1889, Edward a liberal and James a conservative. Family vault, no markers. Sec. A5, Woodmere Cemetery, Detroit, Michigan. Edward (E.W.) transferred his business interests in 1922 to his son **Robert Paine Scripps** (Oct. 27, 1895–March 2, 1938), who joined with Roy Howard to form Scripps-

Howard News Service. He was interred on his father's Miramar estate, San Diego, CA.

8227. Seales, Franklyn (July 15, 1952–May 14, 1990) New York theatrical actor memorable as Jimmy Smith in *The Onion Field* (1979), later appeared in *Southern Comfort, The Taming of the Shrew* and some television roles before his death from AIDS at 37. He died at his parents' home in Brooklyn. Cremated May 17, 1990, at Greenwood Cemetery and the ashes returned to Frank J. Barone mortuary (records only kept five years).

8228. Seaman, Phil (Aug. 28, 1924–Oct. 13, 1972) British jazz drummer, resident at Ronnie Scott's Jazz Club in London, performed with Scott, Tubby Hayes, Stan Getz, various others, and on recordings including Cilla Black's *Anyone Who Had A Heart* as well as with Ginger Baker and his Air Force. He died from drug and alcohol abuse at 48. Ashes sprinkled plot 4-G, Golders Green Crematorium, north London.

8229. Searl, Jackie (John Elnathon Searl, Jr., July 7, 1921–April 29, 1991) Child actor in films of the early to mid 1930's, as Sid in *Tom Sawyer* (1930) and *Huckleberry Finn* (1931), as well as *Topaze* (1933), *Great Expectations* (1934), *Little Lord Fauntleroy* (1936), many others. As an adult he was a manufacturing engineer, residing in Tujunga, Los Angeles County. He died from heart disease at 69. Cremated through Hade mortuary, Tujunga, the ashes were returned to his family.

8230. Sears, Richard Warren (Dec. 7, 1863–Sept. 28, 1914) Established the Sears-Roebuck mail order catalogue business with Alva Roebuck in 1893. The founder served until 1909 but the name now graces thousands of retail stores, the headquarters in Chicago's Sears Tower. Private room at the front of Rosehill mausoleum, Rosehill Cemetery, Chicago, IL.

8231. Seastrom, Victor (Victor Sjöström, Sept. 21, 1879–Jan. 3, 1960) Swedish stage and screen actor and innovative, stylish director in Hollywood from 1923. Noted works include *He Who Gets Slapped* and *The Tower of Lies, The Divine Woman* with Garbo, *The Scarlet Letter* and *The Wind* (1928) with Lillian Gish, the latter considered his masterpiece. He returned to Sweden with sound films and a prolific output, appearing as an actor in Bergman's *Wild Strawberries* (1957). Sec. KV 7A, grave 113–120, Norra begravningsplatsen (Northern Cemetery), Stockholm.

8232. Seaton, George (April 17, 1911–July 28, 1979) Film writer and director from South Bend, Indiana, wrote for MGM from 1933, later worked independently with William Perlberg from 1952. Scripts include *A Day at the Races* (1937), *Song of Bernadette* (1943), *Miracle on 34th Street* (Academy Award, 1947) and *The Country Girl* (Academy Award, 1954). Cremated at Chapel of the Pines Crematory in Los Angeles. Ashes buried at sea.

8233. Sebastian, Dorothy (April 26, 1906/1907–April 8, 1957) Birmingham born actress from George White's Scandals in many silents and talkies including *Our Dancing Daughters* (1928), *The Unholy Night* (1929). Married name Shapiro. Sec. Q, lot 138, grave 31, along the wall, Holy Cross Cemetery, Culver City, CA.

8234. Seberg, Jean (Nov. 13, 1938–Aug. 30, 1979) Iowa co-ed chosen by Otto Preminger to play *Saint Joan* in 1957, a role she never equaled afterward, though she made several films (*Paint Your Wagon*, etc.). She became a controversial figure through her association with the Black Panthers. At the time of her death she had been suffering from mental stress after a miscarriage. She was found dead September 8, 1979 from an overdose of barbiturates, wrapped in a blanket in the trunk of her white Renault in Paris. A suicide note stated that she could live no longer with her nerves. Grave length beige slab. Div. 13, Montparnasse Cemetery, Paris.

8235. Sebring, Jay *see* **Sharon Tate.**

8236. Secombe, Harry (Sept. 8, 1921–April 12, 2001) Welsh comedic performer, the most Dickensian of Britain's four members of *The Goon Show*, short, rotund and bespectacled, also sang at the London Palladium and acted, appearing as Mr. Bumble in *Oliver!* (1968). Among his charities was the golf classic bearing his name from 1967. Knighted in 1981, he died at 79 from prostate cancer in Guildford, Surrey. His service April 20 was officiated by his brother. Ashes buried beneath a flat charcoal plaque with the epitaph *To know him was to love him.* Shamley Green churchyard, Shamley Green, between Cranleigh and Guildford, Surrey.

8237. Sedan, Rolfe (Jan. 20, 1896–Sept. 15, 1982) Small, very proper store or hotel clerk or manager in many films and television. New Beth Olam Mausoleum/Hall of David, corridor T-5-2, crypt 1275, Beth Olam Cemetery adjacent Hollywood Forever Cemetery, Hollywood (Los Angeles), CA.

8238. Seddon, Margaret (Marguerite Hungerford Whiteley, Nov. 18, 1872–April 17, 1968) Washington, D.C, born actress in vaudeville and films from 1915 (*Quality Street, Smilin' Through, If I Had A Million, Raffles, Roxie Hart, The Remarkable Andrew, Sherlock Holmes in Washington*), best known with Margaret McWade as the "pixilated sisters" in *Mr. Deeds Goes to Town* (1936). Her scene as the Tarleton Twins' grandmother in *Gone With the Wind* was cut. She died in Philadelphia at 95. Monument with a maiden in relief inscribed *Sloan—Frank Howard 1866–1919/ City surveyor 1895–1899/ Buried in Santa Marta, Colombia/ Beloved husband of Marguerite Hungerford Whiteley/ Margaret Seddon of stage and screen 1872–1968.* Summit Annex, lot 32, Green Mount Cemetery, Baltimore, MD.

8239. Sedgwick, Edith (April 20, 1943–Nov. 16, 1971) Andy Warhol's queen of the underground art and film world of the 1960's, model, socialite, actress. She was a descendant of Judge and Speaker of the House Theodore Sedgwick of Stockbridge, Massachusetts, but like her fellow Sedgwick descendant, writer John P. Marquand, she chose to live and die far away from the Stockbridge aristocracy. Her husband Michael Post found her dead from what was ruled accidental barbiturate intoxication in their Santa Monica home. Small pink granite stone, behind office, Oak Hill Cemetery, Ballard, CA.

8240. Sedgwick, Edward (Nov. 7, 1892–May 7, 1953) Vaudeville star, one of five Sedgwicks from Galveston, Texas, later turned to screen acting and after 1919 to directing. His peak was considered the late 20's and early 30's with a string of Buster Keaton films, and the chase scene-finale of the 1925 *The Phantom of the Opera* (Rupert Julian had had the Phantom dying from a heart attack after being redeemed with a kiss). Buried near his wife **Ebba** (July 31, 1899–June 1, 1982) and sisters **Rosa** (1889–1962), silent screen actresses Eileen, Josie, and parents **Edward** (1868–1931) and **Josephine Walker Sedgwick** (1872–1964). Sec. D, lots 379, 380, 383, Holy Cross Cemetery, Culver City, CA.

8241. Sedgwick, Eileen (Oct. 17, 1898–March 15, 1991) Last survivor of the Five Sedgwicks in vaudeville, sister of Edward and Josie. Eileen was in films 1915–1928, when she retired, the wife of Fox executive Clarence Hutson. She died at 92. Sec. D, lot 379, grave 6, Holy Cross Cemetery, Culver City, CA.

8242. Sedgwick, John (Sept. 13, 1813–May 9, 1864) Union major general commanded a division in McClellan's Second Bull Run campaign and at Antietam. At Spotsylvania Court House in 1864, he was berating his aides for fearing they would be hit by sharpshooters ("They couldn't hit an elephant at this distance") just as he was shot below the left eye and killed. Cornwall Hollow Cemetery, Cornwall, CT.

8243. Sedgwick, Josie (March 13, 1899–April 30, 1973) Silent screen actress in westerns with Hoot Gibson, Buck Jones, etc. died from a stroke in Santa Monica. Sec. D, lot 379, Holy Cross Cemetery, Culver City, CA.

8244. Sedgwick, Theodore (May 9, 1746–Jan. 24, 1813) Massachusetts representative served as Speaker when the government was in Philadelphia and moving to Washington City 1799–1801. The Judge was the patriarch of a large line of descendants and his grave in Stockbridge forms the center of the Sedgwick Pie, with the judge in the center and descendants buried in a circular pattern, prepared to rise up and face him, or some side of him, on judgment day, one and all. Stockbridge Cemetery, Stockbridge, MA.

8245. Sedway, Moe (Morris Sidwirtz, July 1894–Jan. 3, 1952) Underworld figure associated with Bugsy Siegel operated in Las Vegas and Los Angeles. He testified before the Kefauver Committee before his death in Florida. Beth Olam Mausoleum/Hall of Solomon, Memory Hall/foyer H-22, Beth Olam Cemetery, adjacent Hollywood Forever Cemetery, Hollywood (Los Angeles), CA.

8246. Seedlock, Robert Francis (Feb. 6, 1913–

May 5, 2004) U.S. Army general oversaw the building of the Burma Road over the Himalayas in four months, from Kunming, China, to Myitkyina, Burma, opened January 20, 1945, and ending the Japanese blockade of China. Sec. 8, grave 505-B, Arlington National Cemetery, Arlington, VA.

8247. Seeger, Alan (June 22, 1888–July 4, 1916) American poet, alumnus of Harvard and Greenwich Village, joined the French Foreign Legion in 1914 and was killed two years later at Belloy-en-Santerre. His Poems, including *I Have A Rendezvous With Death* were published posthumously in 1917. Buried on the battlefield at hill 76, south of Belloy-en-Santerre, France.

8248. Seeley, Blossom (July 16, 1891–April 17, 1974) Vaudeville and Broadway singer from San Francisco was first married to baseball player Rube Marquard and then to Benny Fields, her vaudeville partner. When Fields died in 1959, he was buried in Milwaukee. She died in New York at 82 fifteen years later. Several sources list her birth as 1892. After a Catholic mass at St. Malachy's Church in Manhattan, she was cremated and her ashes buried near where her son (by Marquard) lived, north of Detroit. Unmarked, unspecified space, Utica Cemetery, Utica, MI.

8249. Segal, Vivienne (April 19, 1897–Dec. 29, 1992) Star of Broadway and operettas from age 16, in *Desert Song* (1926) and a handful of early sound films as well as the original cast of *Pal Joey* (1940). Ashes scattered in the rose garden, Westwood Memorial Park, Los Angeles.

8250. Segar, Elzie (Dec. 8, 1894–Oct. 13, 1938) Cartoonist from Chester, Illinois, creator of the comic strip *Thimble Theatre* (1919) featuring Olive Oyl and family, adding *Popeye the Sailor* in 1929, soon a national favorite. His plaque has *Pop Eye* under his name. 13 N ½ of B-319, Woodlawn Cemetery, Santa Monica, California. The characters were based on figures in Segar's home town, Chester, Illinois. Popeye was **Frank "Rocky" Fiegel** (Jan. 27, 1868–March 24, 1947), a local rounder; Olive Oyl was store keeper **Dora Schrader Paskel** (Nov. 13, 1872–May 6, 1953) and Wimpy was Segar's old boss **J. William Schuchert** (March 8, 1857–Feb. 20, 1941). A monument to Fiegel was placed in Evergreen Cemetery in 1997, though he is buried at St. Mary's Catholic Cemetery in Chester, according to his great niece. Paskel was unmarked until a ceremony Sept. 5, 2003. Both she and Schuchert are in Evergreen Cemetery, Chester, IL.

8251. Segovia, Andrés (Feb. 18, 1893–June 3, 1987) Spanish guitarist from Granada, father of the 20th century renaissance of the guitar, was giving concerts before age twenty, playing classical numbers by Tárrega and Bach. He appeared in New York in 1928, Europe and Asia, popularizing the acoustic guitar with the classics and modern numbers decades before it evolved, through Django Reinhardt, Charlie Christian and others, into the signature instrument of rock

and roll. He died in his home in Madrid at 94. San Isidro Cemetery, Madrid.

8252. Seidner, Irene (Irene Pollak, Dec. 10, 1880–Nov. 17, 1959) Austrian actress in Hollywood from 1940–58, often as indiscreet busybodies or friendly neighbor ladies, put-upon mothers, etc. Films include *All Through the Night* (Mrs. Miller), *The Seventh Cross, The Daughter of Rosie O'Grady, Miracle in the Rain* (Mrs. Hamer), *Wink of An Eye*. She died from a stroke in Los Angeles at 78. Buried by Malinow and Silverman. Sec. 18, lot 54, Beth Olam Cemetery, adjacent Hollywood Forever Cemetery, Hollywood (Los Angeles), CA.

8253. Seiler, Lewis (Sept. 30, 1890–Jan. 8, 1964) Director of American films specialized in action pictures, particularly westerns and crime films. Sec. 8/ Garden of Legends, lot 104, grave 5, Hollywood Forever Cemetery, Hollywood (Los Angeles), CA.

8254. Seiter, William (June 10, 1892–July 26, 1964) Hollywood director of many films in all genres was most at ease in sentimental plots. Married to actresses Laura LaPlante and to Marian Nixon, his widow. After his death she remarried actor Ben Lyon. Ashes interred with Seiter, Columbarium of Honor, niche 2349, Garden of Honor (private), Forest Lawn, Glendale, CA.

8255. Seitz, George B. (Jan. 3, 1888–July 8, 1944) Boston born actor, writer and director known as the serial king directed *The Perils of Pauline* (1914), later turning out features rapid fire from 1927 including the Andy Hardy series. Sec. 26, Coleus Path lot 6299, Forest Hills Cemetery, Jamaica Plain, Boston, MA.

8256. Seitz, John F. (June 23, 1892–Feb. 27, 1979) Cinematographer brother of George developed the matte shot for *The Four Horsemen of the Apocalypse* (1921) and low key lighting in films of the early 1920's. He later photographed Billy Wilder's *Double Indemnity* and *The Lost Weekend*, among others. Sec. F, tier 65, grave 24, Holy Cross Cemetery, Culver City, CA.

8257. Selander, Lesley (May 26, 1900–Dec. 5, 1979) Director of many B westerns and programmers of the 1930's and 40's. Columbarium of Sunlight, niche G218, Garden of Memory (private), Forest Lawn, Glendale, CA.

8258. Selassie *see* **Haile Selassie.**

8259. Selby, Sarah (Aug. 30, 1905–Jan. 7, 1980) Actress in small parts as busybodies at RKO in the 1940's (*The Seventh Victim, Curse of the Cat People*) played Miss Thomas on TV's *Father Knows Best* 1954–63. Under her married name Sarah Harteurn, her body was donated to the UCLA School of Medicine Dept. of Anatomy.

8260. Selee, Frank (Frank Gibson Selee, Oct. 26, 1859 [stone says 1857]–July 5, 1909) Amherst, New Hampshire, born manager with Boston and Chicago N.L. 1890–1905 had a winning percentage of .598. He died from TB at 51 in Denver, Colorado. Hall of Fame 1999. Pine Banks sec., lot 200, Poplar Ave., Wyoming Cemetery, Melrose, MA.

8261. Selena (Selena Quintanilla Perez, April 16, 1971–March 31, 1995) Twenty three year old Texas born Tejano singer, immensely popular in the Latin community in south Texas, was fatally shot by the founder of her fan club (later convicted and imprisoned) in a confrontation at a Days Inn motel room in Corpus Christi over the assassin's misuse of fan club funds. She had nearly completed her breakthrough album in English, *Dreaming of You,* released later that year. Black bench with signature and a bas-relief sculpture of her face looking upward added later. Sec. LL, Seaside Memorial Park, Corpus Christi, TX.

8262. Selig, William Nicholas (March 14, 1864–July 16, 1948) Pioneer film producer developed the Selig Polyscope projector in Chicago in 1896 and began making films there. Known for his innovative recreation of Theodore Roosevelt's trip to Africa in 1909 *Hunting Big Game in Africa* and the 1908 short *Dr. Jekyll & Mr. Hyde.* He was the first producer to set up a studio in Hollywood in 1909, turning out many two reelers and early features (*The Spoilers* 1914), and the first serial *The Adventures of Kathlyn* (1914). With Hearst he introduced the Hearst-Selig newsreel in 1912, later Metrotone News, and began Tom Mix westerns. The Selig Polyscope folded in 1918 and he retired in 1922. He died in Los Angeles. Hall of Memory (four to a drawer) H-L-6, Pierce Brothers Chapel of the Pines Crematory, Los Angeles.

8263. Sellers, Peter (Sept. 8, 1925–July 24, 1980) English actor and comedian in offbeat, eccentric roles, in *Lolita* (1962), *Dr. Strangelove, or How I Learned to Stop Worrying and Love the Bomb* (1964), The Inspector Clousseau series (*The Pink Panther*) through the 1960's and 70's, and *Being There* (1979, Oscar nomination). Named a Commander of the Order of the British Empire 1966. He had suffered recurring heart trouble from the mid to late 1960's prior to his death from a heart attack at 55. At his request Glenn Miller's *In the Mood* was played at his memorial service as he was being cremated. A black plaque on the left side of the arch, Cloister Bay 8, bears the epitaph (from *Being There*) *Life is a State of Mind.* His ashes are marked by a rosebush near by with a plaque listing his name, dates and a tribute from his wife. Cloister Garden, Golders Green Crematorium, London.

8264. Selman, John Henry (Nov. 16, 1839–April 6, 1896) The man who killed John Wesley Hardin, buried south and west of the Hardin gravesite. His grave was recently discovered, with the marker buried, and a new larger one ordered. Concordia Cemetery, El Paso, TX.

8265. Selvin, Ben (Benjamin B. Selvin, March 5, 1898–July 15, 1980) Bandleader from 1917 recorded *Dardanella* in 1919, the first to sell over a million copies, and over the next decade made "more recordings than anyone, anywhere." His side men included future greats Benny Goodman, Glenn Miller, both Dorsey Brothers and violinist Eugene Ormandy. He later headed Majestic Records and was musical direc-tor at Columbia. A resident of Manhasset, Long Island, he died at 82. Block 112, path 4 1/2 east, lot 328, grave 4, Mt. Hebron Cemetery, Flushing, Queens, N.Y.C.

8266. Selwyn, Edgar (Oct. 20, 1875–Feb. 13, 1944) Broadway producer, playwright and actor from Cincinnati owned a chain of theatres and wrote and directed for MGM. In partnership for a time with Sam Goldfish, (later Goldwyn). Among his directorial works were *The Sin of Madelon Claudet* (1931) and *Turn Back the Clock* (1933). Spiegelberg-Goldsmith mausoleum, lot 1909, Salem Fields Cemetery, Brooklyn, N.Y.C.

8267. Selznick, David O. (May 10, 1902–June 22, 1965) Son of film magnate Lewis Selznick and brother of Myron was the definitive film producer, maintaining tight control over his pet projects while at RKO (*King Kong, Little Women* 1933) and at MGM (*Dinner at Eight* 1933, *David Copperfield* and *A Tale of Two Cities* 1935) before beginning Selznick International in 1936, at which he produced his masterpiece *Gone With the Wind,* released in 1939 and a long string of quality films. He was married to Irene Mayer Selznick, Louis B. Mayer's daughter, through the 30's and part of the 40's, re-marrying to actress Jennifer Jones in 1949. He suffered a heart attack while in his lawyer's office in Beverly Hills and died at Mt. Sinai Hospital at 63. Entombed in private mausoleum 53, a marble family room, with his parents, brother, and daughter **Mary Jennifer Selznick** (1954–1976); she is above a white vase of flowers in the chamber with her father. Private mausoleum 53, Sanctuary of Trust, Memorial Terrace, Great Mausoleum, Forest Lawn, Glendale, CA.

8268. Selznick, Irene Mayer (April 2, 1907–Oct. 10, 1990) Daughter of MGM mogul Louis B. Mayer and wife of producer David Selznick 1930–1945. After their separation she left Hollywood for Broadway, where she staged *A Streetcar Named Desire* and others. She died at 83 in the Pierre Hotel in Manhattan. Cremated at Garden State Crematory through the Frank E. Campbell mortuary. Ashes interred with her mother Margaret. Sanctuary of Graciousness, FF-218, Hillside Memorial Park mausoleum, Los Angeles.

8269. Selznick, Lewis (Lewis Zeleznik, May 2, 1870–Jan. 25, 1933) Father of David and Myron immigrated from Russia and had operated a nickelodeon in Pittsburgh, assisted by his sons, before moving west as a distributor through Universal and the Clara Kimball Young Film Co. until he went bankrupt in 1923. Family room — private mausoleum 53, Sanctuary of Trust, Memorial Terrace, Great Mausoleum, Forest Lawn, Glendale, CA.

8270. Selznick, Myron (Oct. 5, 1899–March 23, 1944) Brother of David and son of Lewis produced in Hollywood in the teens and 1920's, becoming an agent after his father's bankruptcy in 1923. He was credited with bringing to his brother the English actress Vivien Leigh for the part of Scarlett in *Gone With the Wind* during the filming of the burning of Atlanta.

Removed from Hollywood Cemetery Sept. 15, 1944. Family room — private mausoleum 53, Sanctuary of Trust, Memorial Terrace, Great Mausoleum, Forest Lawn, Glendale, CA.

8271. Semon, Larry (July 6, 1889–Oct. 8, 1928) Hollywood silent screen comedian of the 1920's, usually as a hapless character with foolish grin and oversized pants. Bankrupt, he suffered a nervous breakdown and died from pneumonia and tuberculosis at 39 in a sanitarium at Victorville, California. Cremated at Mountain View Cemetery, San Bernardino (burial permit 737 per their records), the ashes were reported buried in a family plot in Philadelphia. His father Zera Semon (April 9, 1901), *his* father, and other relatives were buried in Beth El Emeth Cemetery (now closed), Philadelphia. The cemetery was razed and the graves moved to Philadelphia Memorial Park, Frazer, PA.

8272. Seneca, Joe (Jan. 14, 1919–Aug. 15, 1996) Bearded Black actor appeared in *Ma Rainey's Black Bottom* on Broadway in 1984, and films including *The Verdict* and *The Saint of Fort Washington*. He died at his home on Roosevelt Island, New York City. Service through Riverside Chapel. His polished black-charcoal headstone, set in 2000, features his picture, across the top *His last appearance on this stage*, and across the bottom *Everything is going to work out fine*. Sec. 22, lot 1897, sub lot 3, Highland Park Cemetery, Warrensville (Cleveland), OH.

8273. Sennett, Mack (Michael Sinnot, Jan. 17, 1880–Nov. 5, 1960) Pioneer comedy producer founded the Keystone Kops and launched the careers of Charlie Chaplin, Mabel Normand, Fatty Arbuckle, many others. Once engaged to Normand until she caught him with the ever popular Mae Busch in 1915, he later produced her showcase feature *Mickey*, released in 1918. Like D.W. Griffith, in later years he was given the cold shoulder by the Hollywood he had helped develop. He died at the Motion Picture Country Home in Woodland Hills. His marker, with name, dates and *Beloved King of Comedy*, was placed over the grave years after his death. Sec. N, lot 490, grave 1, Holy Cross Cemetery, Culver City, CA.

8274. Sen Yung, Victor (Victor Sen Young, Oct. 18, 1915–Nov. 9, 1980) Chinese American actor played Number One Son in Sidney Toler *Charlie Chan* films 1938–48, various Japanese spies during World War II (*Across the Pacific*) and later was Hop Sing, the cook on *Bonanza* in the 1960's. He was accidentally asphyxiated by a wood stove in his home. Burial with his parents. Sec. D, tier 7, grave 99, Greenlawn Cemetery, Colma, CA.

8275. Serling, Phil (Phillip Serling, May 21, 1931–Jan. 6, 2002) Syracuse director of the Landmark and Little Theatre also trained and managed boxers for over fifty years and headed the internationally known Cinefest annually, promoting and helping to preserve films from the silent era, the 1930's and 40's. On January 5, 2001, the night a re-run of him on *David Let-*

terman from only weeks before was shown, he blacked out while driving and died two days later at 69. Frumah Packard Cemetery, Syracuse, NY.

8276. Serling, Rod (Rodman E. Serling, Dec. 25, 1924–June 28, 1975) Playwright from Binghampton, New York, authored scores of sensitive and insightful teleplays through the 1950's (*Patterns* 1955, *Requiem for a Heavyweight* 1956) before he became a household name and face with *The Twilight Zone* 1959–64, the cigarette and vocal inflections familiar as he opened and closed each episode. A graduate of Antioch College at Yellow Springs, Ohio, he taught at Ithaca College from the mid 1960's. Though he hosted *Night Gallery* 1969–72, he had less influence in its content. Following a mild heart attack and no modification of his heavy smoking in the spring of 1975, he underwent open heart surgery at Strong Memorial Hospital in Rochester, New York, and died on the operating table at 50 when he suffered another attack. A memorial service was held July 7 at Sage Chapel on the Cornell campus in Ithaca. He was cremated July 1 at White Haven Memorial Park, Pittsford, outside Rochester. Ashes buried near his home, beneath a veterans' marker. Turn right inside gate, follow down to the last bend to the left. Grave in area on right. Lakeview Cemetery, Interlaken, NY.

8277. Serrano Suñer, Ramón (Sept. 12, 1901–Sept. 1, 2003) The last major political figure of World War II was second to Generalissimo Franco in Spain, head of the Falange, architect of the 1938 Law of Censorship, Minister of the Interior and the Press, and Minister of External Affairs. The brother-in-law of Franco, Serrano Suñer delayed Spain's entry into the conflict, weakened by the 1936 civil war, and kept the Germans from Gibraltar, but raised a Spanish Blue Division to fight the Communists on the Eastern front. Dismissed from office in September 1942, despised by both pro–Axis and pro–Franco factions, he became an international lawyer, and never mended his differences with Franco. He died in Madrid at 101. Del cementerio madrileño de Aravaca, Madrid.

8278. Sessions, Almira (Sept. 16, 1888–Aug. 3, 1974) Washington, D.C. born actress from a socially prominent family appeared in some 111 films (Phoebe in *Monsieur Verdoux*) plus theatre, radio and TV. Abbey of the Psalms/Hollywood Forever Mausoleum, Haven of Worship, tier 15 niche 5, Hollywood Forever Cemetery, Hollywood (Los Angeles), CA.

8279. Seton, Anya (Jan. 23, 1906–Nov. 8, 1990) American novelist, author of *Dragonwyk* and *My Theodosia*. Married name Chase. Sec. B, Putnam Cemetery, Greenwich, CT.

8280. Seton, Elizabeth Ann (Aug. 28, 1774–Jan. 4, 1821) The first American born Catholic saint attained sainthood in 1975. She lived in lower Manhattan and in Baltimore in earlier years before going to Emmittsburg, Maryland, upon becoming a nun in 1809. Two daughters had died of TB prior to her death from it at 47. Buried on the Daughters of Charity property, she was later moved to a vault below the chapel in the graveyard, where a marble slab in the stone wall still notes her entombment there. In the 1960's she was removed into the basilica, right of the altar, of the Seton Shrine, Emmittsburg, MD.

8281. Seton, Ernest Thompson (Ernest Seton Thompson, Aug. 14, 1860–Oct. 23, 1946) Author of nature books and a founder of the Boy Scouts of America. Ashes scattered near Seton Village, Santa Fe, NM.

8282. Seton, Grace Thompson (Jan. 28, 1872–March 19, 1959) Writer and feminist organized the Girl Volunteers, wrote several books, poetry and travelogues. Married 1896–1935 to Ernest Thompson Seton. Sec. B, Putnam Cemetery, Greenwich, CT.

8283. Settles, Ron (June 12, 1959–June 2, 1981) Long Beach State College football player, arrested in Signal Hill, was found beaten and hanged in his cell the next morning, with no adequate explanation. Facing charges from the L.A. prosecutor, the officers involved took the fifth amendment. There were no convictions, and the city of Signal Hill paid an out of court settlement to the family. The Settles case was one of several that resulted in videotaping and written reports of any physical contact with a citizen or prisoner. Galilee Memorial Gardens, Shelby County, TN.

8284. Seuss, Dr. (Theodor Seuss Geisel, March 2, 1904–Sept. 24, 1991) Springfield, Massachusetts, born author of children's books including *The Cat in the Hat* (1957), *Green Eggs and Ham, How the Grinch Stole Christmas* and others that helped get rid of Dick and Jane, which he claimed as his proudest achievement. He died in La Jolla, Ca. Though he owned a plot at El Camino Memorial Park, he was cremated through Humphrey mortuary with no services, at his request. Ashes reportedly scattered.

8285. Sevareid, Eric (Nov. 26, 1912–July 9, 1992) News commentator with CBS 1939–77, known for his impassioned oratory during Vietnam and Watergate. With the *CBS Evening News* he delivered two minute commentaries from 1964 until his retirement in 1977. He died at 79 from stomach cancer in his Washington home. Through Pumphrey mortuary his ashes were reportedly buried partly in Washington at an unspecified location or scattered at his cabin in Virginia. Part were sprinkled over Norway.

8286. Seville, David *see* **Ross Bagdasarian.**

8287. Seward, William Henry (May 16, 1801–Oct. 15, 1872) Leader in the Whig and Republican party from New York named Secretary of State by Lincoln. Near fatally stabbed by Lewis Paine the night of Lincoln's murder, he recovered, returned to his post and purchased Alaska ("Seward's Folly") before retiring in 1869 to his home in Auburn, New York, where he died on his horsehair sofa three years later. The graves of he, his wife and daughter Fanny are marked by slabs with draped urns. Glen Haven sec., lot 4, Fort Hill Cemetery, Auburn, NY.

8288. Sewell, Anna (March 30, 1820–April 25, 1878) English author of *Black Beauty* (1877) from Norwich, was an invalid most of her life. Quaker Burial Ground at Buxton Lamas, Norfolk, England.

8289. Sewell, Joe (Oct. 9, 1898–March 6, 1990) Shortstop hit over .300 in ten of fourteen seasons 1920–1933 with Cleveland and New York A.L. Hall of Fame 1977. Sec. 2, block 9, lot 6, Tuscaloosa Memorial Park, Tuscaloosa, AL.

8290. Seymour, Anne (Anne Eckert, Sept. 11, 1909–Dec. 8, 1988) Stage actress from New York in films from the 1940's, including *All the King's Men* (1949, as Willie Stark's wife), *Sunrise at Campobello,* and on television as Beatrice Hewitt on *General Hospital* 1963–1984. Her last appearance was as the newspaper writer in Chisholm, Minnesota (filmed in Galena, Illinois) who tells of the real life character Doc Graham and reads the tribute to him in *Field of Dreams* (1989). She died six months later from respiratory failure. Never married. Cremated at Chapel of the Pines December 16 through Pierce Bros. Westwood mortuary. Ashes released to her executor in Los Angeles.

8291. Seymour, Clarine (Dec. 9, 1898–April 25, 1920) Silent screen actress in D.W. Griffith films 1918–1920, including *The Girl Who Stayed Home, Scarlet Days* and *The Idol Dancer.* She died from complications after an intestinal operation in Misericordia Hospital. Service at her home, 12 Thomas Place, New Rochelle, New York, where she lived with her parents. Placed in a receiving vault at Woodlawn Cemetery, the Bronx, until October 22, 1921, when she was buried in the Hedgemont Acre, W ½ lot 106, grave 4 (unmarked behind her mother, Florence, 1959). Greenwood Union Cemetery, Rye, NY.

8292. Seymour, Dan (Feb. 22, 1915–May 25, 1993) Heavy character actor from Chicago best known for his continental villains of the 1940's, in *To Have and Have Not* (as Capt. Renard), also appeared in *Casablanca, Key Largo.* Mount of Olives, block 7, plot 175, Hillside Memorial Park, Los Angeles.

8293. Seymour, Horatio (May 31, 1810–Feb. 12, 1886) Anti-corruption Democratic governor of New York ran unsuccessfully for the Presidency in 1868, fought the Tammany Hall machine associated with his own party and seldom budged from what he felt were the guidelines set by the Bill of Rights. The Grant administration voted in over him was ironically the most corrupt the nation had yet known. He died in Utica at the home of his sister, the wife of Roscoe Conkling. After services at Trinity Church, prior to interment a death mask was made at the Chapel of the Roses in Forest Hill. His slab with large block lettering is not far from Conkling's monument. Sec 7, lot 47, Forest Hill Cemetery, Utica, NY.

8294. Seyrig, Delphine (April 10, 1932–Oct. 15, 1990) Actress in films (*Day of the Jackal, Last Year in Marienbad*). Div. 15, Montparnasse Cemetery, Paris.

8295. Seyss-Inquart, Arthur *see* **Goering.**

8296. Shaara, Michael J. (June 23, 1928–May 5, 1988) Author and historian whose book *The Killer Angels* (1974) focused on the personalities and emotions of several of the commanding officers at Gettysburg, winning the Pulitzer Prize for fiction in 1975. Associate Professor of English at Florida State University until his death from a heart attack at 58. Epitaph reads *From too much love of living, From hope and fear set free.* Whispering Pines Garden, 204-A-4, Meadowwood Memorial Park, Timberlane Road, Tallahassee, FL.

8297. Shabazz, Betty (May 28, 1936–June 23, 1997) Civil rights activist and widow of Malcolm X died at 61 from burns suffered in a fire set June 1, allegedly by her twelve year old grandson. Muslim services and burial beside her husband. Pinewood B-150, Ferncliff Cemetery, Hartsdale, NY.

8298. Shakespeare, William (April c. 23, 1564–April 23 1616) The greatest poet and dramatist in the English language retired in his last years to enjoy peace and quiet at New Place, his new home in his native town of Stratford-Upon-Avon, England. He died suddenly on or near his 52nd birthday while "merry making" with Ben Jonson and Michael Drayton, though Shakespeare seldom drank to excess. His warning epitaph reads *Good friend for Jesus sake forbare/ To dig the dust enclosed heare./ Blest be ye man yt spares thes stones/ And curst be he yt moves my bones.* The warning guarded against the frequent moving of bones to make room for others, has been strictly obeyed and accordingly deprived Westminster Abbey of its most prized literary figure, although his statue dominates Poets Corner there. It also prevented his wife **Anne Hathaway** (1556–1623) from being placed in the same grave. She lies nearby, to Shakespeare's left in the chancel. Their children are at various spots near by, including their daughter Susanna, with the inscription *Here lyeth ye body of Susanna, wife to John Hall, gent: ye daughter of William Shakespeare, gent: she deceased ye 11th of July A.D. 1699, aged 66 (?). Witty above her sexe, but that's not all, Wise to salvations was good Mistress Hall, Something of Shakespeare was in that, but this Wholy of him with whom she's now in blisse./ Then Passenger, hast nere a teare/ To weepe with her that wept with all?/ That wept yet set her selfe to chere/ Them up with comforts cordiall. Her love shall live, her mercy spread/ When thou hast nere a teare to shed.* Holy Trinity Church, Stratford-Upon-Avon.

8299. Shakur, Tupac Amaru (June 16, 1971–Sept. 13, 1996) Rap artist with Death Row Records died from wounds received September 7 while riding near the Las Vegas strip. Cremated the day after his death, his mother Afeni Shakur took the ashes home to Stone Mountain, Georgia, keeping part there and spreading part of them there in a garden and part reportedly on a "green hill" in Los Angeles.

8300. Shamroy, Leon (July 16, 1901–July 6, 1974) Acclaimed Hollywood cinematographer was for thirty years the dominant photographer at Fox in black and white as well as color. Winner of four Oscars for best cinematography (*The Black Swan* 1942, *Wilson* 1944, *Leave Her to Heaven* 1945, and *Cleopatra* 1963). Homeward, lot 4493, space 4, Courts of Remembrance at Forest Lawn, Hollywood Hills, Los Angeles.

8301. Shannon, Del (Charles Westover, Dec. 30, 1934–Feb. 8, 1990) Rock legend from Coopersville, Michigan, recorded his evergreen *Runaway* in 1961 and a couple of follow-ups. He had been touring on the oldies circuit at the time of his suicide by gunshot in his home at Canyon Country, California. Several close to him disputed it was intentional. Memorial services in both Coopersville and in California. Cremated by the Neptune Society, he requested his ashes be scattered in the California desert.

8302. Shannon, Frank (Patrick Connolly, July 27, 1874–Feb. 1, 1959) Character actor, played Dr. Zarkov in the *Flash Gordon* adventures of the 1930's. Sec. L, lot 330, grave 2, Holy Cross Cemetery, Culver City, CA.

8303. Shannon, Harry (June 13, 1890–July 27, 1964) Actor in films from 1940 in small roles as upright, dependable types, including Kane's father in *Citizen Kane* (1941), sheriffs (*The Mummy's Tomb,* etc.). Considerable previous work on the stage. Abbey of the Psalms/Hollywood Forever Mausoleum, corridor E-2, Sanctuary of Trust, tier 1, niche 2, Hollywood Forever Cemetery, Hollywood (Los Angeles), CA.

8304. Shannon, Peggy (Jan. 10, 1910–May 11, 1941) "The next Clara Bow" appeared in films of the 1930's, but her career declined with alcohol. Husband actor-cameraman Albert Roberts found her dead at their kitchen table from alcohol poisoning at 32. Epitaph *That Red Headed Girl.* Sec. 5, lot 31, grave 4, Hollywood Forever Cemetery, Hollywood (Los Angeles), CA.

8305. Shapey, Ralph (March 12, 1921–June 13, 2002) Philadelphia born controversial avant garde composer of over 200 pieces, including solos for piano, voice, chamber music, opera, and complex orchestrations. His acclaimed *Concerto Fantastique* was considered for the Pulitzer Prize in music in 1992. He died in Chicago at 81. Oakwoods Cemetery, Chicago, IL.

8306. Shapiro, Irving (1906–July 27, 1929) Notorious member of Detroit's Purple Gang, acquitted of extortion in the Cleaners and Dyers War of 1928, afterward branched out on his own, was taken for a ride over the proceeds of a kidnapping he had masterminded, and his body dumped at 2463 Taylor Street in Detroit, age twenty five. Machpelah Cemetery, Ferndale, MI.

8307. Shapiro, Jacob "Gurrah" (May 5, 1897 or 1900–June 9, 1947) The head of the strong arm end of extortion and racketeering in New York City's garment industry in the 1930's, with his partner Lepke Buchalter, joined the Luciano headed crime syndicate as leaders, with Albert Anastasia, of Murder Inc.

The nickname Gurrah came either from his slurring of "Get outta here" or from others slurring the same to him, depending on the story teller. Shapiro, like Dutch Schultz, was in favor of racket buster Thomas E. Dewey being eliminated but was restrained by Lepke (who, with six of his lieutenants, was executed). He died from a heart attack at 47 (or 50) while serving a term for extortion at Sing Sing. Block 20, row 11 left, grave 3, Society Uzlianer/Young Men's Benevolent Society, Old Montefiore Cemetery, Queens, N.Y.C.

8308. Shapiro Brothers   Meyer Shapiro headed the gang that controlled slot and vending machines in the Brownsville section of Brooklyn in the 1920's and early 30's; they had used Abe Reles and his men, soon dubbed Murder Inc, in eliminating the Ambergs as competition, but abandoned Reles to jail time without legal help, had he and Happy Maione set up to be shot, raped Reles's girlfriend, and soon found himself and his brothers to be hunted men. **Irving Shapiro**, 27, was shot by Reles in the doorway of his house at 691 Blake Avenue, Brooklyn, July 11, 1931, allegedly mistaken for Meyer, 23, who — after eighteen failed attempts — was found in a cellar on the lower east side of Manhattan two months later, September 18, shot behind his left ear the night before, and taken to the Bellevue morgue, where he was identified by his brother Willie. **Willie Shapiro** in turn was found at 23 three years later on July 20, 1934, buried alive in a hole in Canarsie by Harry "Pittsburgh Phil" Strauss and Reles, where he died. All three are near one another, Irving four rows in from the arch at the road, and Meyer and Willie in the same row. Lyssianker Society, sec. K, Mt. Lebanon Cemetery, Glendale, Queens, N.Y.C.

8309. Shapp, Milton (June 25, 1912–Nov. 24, 1994) Pennsylvania Democrat credited with suggesting the Peace Corps to JFK. As Governor of Pennsylvania 1971–79 he brought income tax and the lottery to the state, known for innovative programs for the elderly and handicapped. The first Jewish candidate for President (1976), he died at 82 from Alzheimer's in Philadelphia. Roosevelt Cemetery, Trevose, Bucks County (Philadelphia area), PA.

8310. Sharkey, Jack (Josef Paul Cuckoschay, Oct. 25, 1902–Aug. 17, 1994) Binghampton, New York, born heavyweight champ took his name from Jack Dempsey and Tom Sharkey. He lost to Dempsey in 1927, won the title from Max Schmelling in June 1932 and lost it a year later to Primo Carnera. He retired in 1936 to run his restaurant in Boston until 1952, when he retired to Epping, New Hampshire. He died in Beverly, Massachusetts, at 91, the oldest lived pro boxer. Mass and burial at Prospect Cemetery, Epping, NH.

8311. Sharkey, Ray (Nov. 14, 1952–June 12, 1993) Brooklyn born actor won a Golden Globe Award for *The Idolmaker* (1980), best known as Atlantic City mob boss Sonny Steelgrave in the CBS series *Wiseguy*

1987–90. A history of chemical dependency and intravenous drug use led to his contracting AIDS. Last seen in *Cop and a Half* (1993), he returned to his mother's home in Brooklyn and died at Lutheran Hospital there at 40. Mass from St. Stephen's Church in the Red Hook section where he grew up. Formisano lot, sec. 25, row V, grave 87, St. Charles Cemetery, Farmingdale, Long Island, NY.

8312. Sharkey, Tom (Jan. 1, 1871–April 17, 1953) Heavyweight boxer of the 1890's known as Sailor Tom, the moniker based on the battleship tattooed on his chest. Sec. R, grave 454, Golden Gate National Cemetery, San Bruno, CA.

8313. Sharpe, Lester (Lester Sharff, March 21, 1895–Nov. 30, 1962) New York born character actor in small and bit roles in films, including the bearded professor at the Scripps Museum in *The Mummy's Ghost* (1944). Cremated at Pierce Bros. Chapel of the Pines, Los Angeles. Ashes sent to Mount Sinai Cemetery (town unspecified), VA.

8314. Shaver, Eddy (John Edwin Shaver, June 20, 1962–Dec. 31, 2000) Guitar playing son of country star Billy Joe Shaver co-produced several albums with his father and toured with him. He died in Waco, Texas, at 38. A history of drug problems may or may not have contributed to his death. Waco Memorial Park, Waco, TX.

8315. Shaw, Artie (Arthur Jacob Arshawsky, May 23, 1910–Dec. 30, 2004) New York City born clarinet master and big band leader shot to fame with *Begin the Beguine* in the fall of 1938 and followed with a series of hits, including *Frenesi* (1940), *Stardust, I Cover the Waterfront, Dancing in the Dark, Nightmare*, his own compositions (*Concerto for Clarinet*), numbers with his Gramercy Five, and utilizing talents such as Buddy Rich, Mel Torme, and Billie Holiday on vocals (*Any Old Time*, 1938), the first big band other than Benny Goodman (with Ella Fitzgerald in 1935) to feature a black singer. An outspoken intellectual, Shaw referred to jitterbuggers at times as "morons," saying he made the music good enough to listen to. He left in 1942 to serve in World War II, and performed only sporadically afterward, retiring his clarinet in 1954 to write fiction (*I Love You, I Hate You, Drop Dead*) and paint. His eight marriages included Lana Turner, Jerome Kern's daughter Elizabeth, Ava Gardner, novelist Kathleen Winsor, and Evelyn Keyes (the longest, from 1957–85). All ended in divorce. He died at 94 in Newbury Park, near Thousand Oaks, California. Garden of Tranquility, plot 7, Pierce Bros. Valley Oaks Memorial Park, Westlake Village, CA.

8316. Shaw, Clay (March 17, 1913–Aug. 15, 1974) New Orleans businessman who, on charges and theories formulated by prosecutor Jim Garrison, was brought to trial for the murder of President Kennedy and acquitted in 1969, the subject of the 1991 film *JFK*. Fourth lot from center road near rear. Woodland Cemetery, Kentwood, LA.

8317. Shaw, George Bernard (July 26, 1856–

Nov. 2, 1950) Irish dramatist and renowned wit forbid his plays from being filmed until late in his life. His wife died in 1943 and he lived out his years at his home Shaw's Corner in England. He died from a kidney ailment following a fall at his home at the age of 94. At his request he was cremated without religious ceremony and his ashes mingled with those of his wife Charlotte, which had been kept in a crematory pending his death. The mixed ashes were then scattered in the garden at Shaw's Corner, Ayot St. Lawrence, Hertfordshire.

8318. Shaw, Janet (Ellen Martha Clancy, Jan. 23, 1919–Oct. 15, 2001) Blonde actress with deadpan delivery from Beatrice, Nebraska, moved to Los Angeles as a teenager and appeared in sixty films 1934–1950, usually in walk-ons to small roles, including *Jezebel* (1938, as Molly Allen), *Torchy Blane in Chinatown* (1939), *Waterloo Bridge* and *Escape* (1940), *Hold That Ghost* (1941, Alderman's girl), *Night Monster* (1942, Milly Carson), *The Mummy's Tomb* (1942, girl in the car who'd been listening to Jan Garber), *Shadow of A Doubt* (1943, Louise the waitress), *Arizona Trail* (1943), *Follow the Boys* (1944) and *House of Horrors* (1946, cab driver). She returned to Beatrice in 1994, where she died seven years later of complications from Alzheimer's Disease at 82, her last married name Ellen Clancy Stuart. Burial through Griffiths-Hovendick Chapel. Block 22, N ½ lot 58, Evergreen Home Cemetery, Beatrice, NE.

8319. Shaw, Oscar (Oct. 11, 1887–March 6, 1967) Stage and screen song and dance lead of the 1920's in *Music Box Revue*, *Oh, Kay*, and *The Cocoanuts* (filmed in 1929). In dramatic roles 1935–41. He died at Little Neck Hospital near his home at Great Neck, Long Island, New York. Cremated at Fresh Pond Crematory, Middle Village, Queens, N.Y.C. Sec. A (186A2), Evergreen Cemetery, Gettysburg, PA.

8320. Shaw, Reta (Sept. 13, 1912–Jan. 8, 1982) Heavy, bass voiced actress in comedic roles through the 1950's and 60's (*The Pajama Game*), usually bullying one male or another (*The Ghost and Mr. Chicken*). Columbarium of Remembrance (left), niche 60402, Courts of Remembrance, Forest Lawn Hollywood Hills, Los Angeles.

8321. Shaw, Robert (Aug. 9, 1927–Aug. 28, 1978) English actor raised in Scotland and Cornwall, on stage and screen from the early 1950's. He received an Oscar nomination as Henry VIII in *A Man for All Seasons* (1966) but gained his greatest fame as the target of *The Sting* (1973) and as the shark hunter Quint in *Jaws* (1975). His home was a large estate in County Mayo, Ireland, at Lough Mask in the Connemara region. He died from a heart attack while driving near Tourmakeady at 51. A wake was held at his house, Drimbawn, then a chartered plane flew him to Belfast for cremation, with the ashes — he had specified — to be scattered in England.

8322. Shaw, Robert (April 30, 1916–Jan. 25, 1999) Conductor of the Atlanta Symphony for 21 years and creator of the Robert Shaw Chorale won 14 Grammys. Sec. C, lot 303, Westview Cemetery, Atlanta, GA.

8323. Shaw, Robert Gould (Oct. 10, 1837–July 10, 1863) Massachusetts born Union officer led the 54th Massachusetts "all colored" regiment in an assault on Fort Wagner at Charleston, South Carolina. He and most of his landmark regiment lost their lives proving that blacks would and could fight valiantly for the Union cause. Battery Wagner was not taken; all were buried in trenches where they fell. The valor of the 54th led to the training of more black regiments which served with distinction. Shaw and his regiment were the subject of the 1990 film *Glory*. As an insult, the Confederates threw the bodies of some twenty five dead black soldiers atop Shaw's in the trench outside the fort. His father said he was proud to have him buried that way, the family requesting his body be left alone as a mark of honor. The bones were later washed to sea with the erosion of Morris Island in Charleston Harbor. A monument with a bronze bas-relief of Shaw and the 54th stands on Boston Common. There is a memorial to him at Moravian Cemetery, Staten Island, N.Y.C., and at his family plot in Mt. Auburn Cemetery, Cambridge, MA.

8324. Shaw, Wilbur (Oct. 31, 1902–Oct. 30, 1954) Indianapolis 500 race driver was the second to win three times, in 1937, '39, and '40. Later president of the Indianapolis Motor Speedway organization. Between Shaw and A.J. Foyt, only Bill Vukovich came close to taking three victories there. Shaw died in a plane crash in Decatur, Indiana, at 51. He is buried a short distance from driver Pat O'Connor; crossed checkered flags are placed at both stones each Memorial Day. Vernon Cemetery, Vernon (south of North Vernon), IN.

8325. Shaw, Wini (Winifred Lei Momi, Feb. 25, 1910–May 2, 1982) Singer-actress from San Francisco (or Hawaii) introduced *The Lady in Red* in *In Caliente* (1934) and *Lullaby of Broadway* in *Golddiggers of 1935*. She died in New York at 72. Both songs are noted on her monument with husband William O'Malley ("And Bill too"). Sec. 33, range 1F, grave 34, (3rd) Calvary Cemetery, Woodside, Queens, N.Y.C.

8326. Shawlee, Joan (March 5, 1926–March 22, 1987) Blonde actress from Forest Hills, Queens, in films from the mid 1940's, originally billed as **Joan Fulton** (Stella the model in *House of Horrors* 1946); she changed her name with the 1950's, appeared on *The Abbott and Costello Show*, and in a long list of films (*Some Like it Hot*, *Critics Choice*, *Irma la Douce*, *the St. Valentine's Day Massacre*, *Tony Rome*, *Something For A Lonely Man*) as well as playing Buddy Sorrell's wife Pickles on *The Dick Van Dyke Show* 1961–63. She died from cancer at 61. Ashes scattered at sea.

8327. Shawn, Dick (Richard Schulefand, Dec. 1, 1923–April 17, 1987) Nightclub and TV comedian with a broad range. Films include *It's a Mad, Mad, Mad, Mad World* (1963) and *The Producers* (1968, as Hitler in the *Springtime For Hitler* musical). He collapsed on stage and died from an apparent heart attack at 63. Main mausoleum, Memorial Court, crypt 734, Hillside Memorial Park, Los Angeles.

8328. Shawn, Ted (Edwin Meyers, Oct. 21, 1891–Jan. 9, 1972) Innovative modern dancer and instructor with his wife Ruth St. Denis developed their "Denishawn" method of exotic dancing. Later divorced from St. Denis, he founded the Jacob's Pillow Dance Theater and Festival at Lee, near Becket, Massachusetts, in the Berkshires. He died in Orlando, Florida, was cremated and his ashes spread around a boulder with a plaque inscribed *Ted Shawn 1891–1972. Founder, Jacob's Pillow Dance Festival.* Jacob's Pillow Theater grounds, Lee, MA.

8329. Shay, Larry (Aug. 10, 1897–Feb. 22, 1988) Songwriter known for *When You're Smiling.* Court of Liberty, lot 819, Forest Lawn Hollywood Hills, Los Angeles.

8330. Shays, Daniel (1747–Sept. 29, 1825) Revolutionary War veteran from New York state led a rebellious group of farmers in western Massachusetts 1786–87 protesting foreclosures. The squelching of the rebellion by the federal government helped establish the practice and principle of an assertive strong central government of united states. The exact grave site has been lost. Union Cemetery, Conesus, NY.

8331. Shea, Frank "Spec" (Francis Joseph Shea, Oct. 2, 1920–July 19, 2002) Pitcher from Naugatuck, Connecticut, with the New York Yankees 1947–1951, an All Star his first year; he faced the Dodgers in two games of the World Series that fall. With the Senators 1952–55, he retired with a 3.80 ERA. The Naugatuck Nugget died in his home town at 81. Sec. M, St. James Cemetery, Naugatuck, CT.

8332. Shea, Jack (John Shea, Sept. 7, 1910–Jan. 22, 2002) Native of Lake Placid, New York, and a member of one of its oldest families won the Gold in speed skating in 500 and 1500 meters in the 1932 Olympics. His son James was a 1964 Olympian in Nordic Combined and Cross Country skiing, and he was anticipating watching his grandson Jim Jr. in the 2002 Winter Olympics in Salt Lake City when he was killed by a drunk driver in an auto accident at Lake Placid. St. Agnes Cemetery, Lake Placid, NY.

8333. Shea, Michael (d. May 16, 1934) Buffalo theatrical producer for over thirty years, a prominent member of the Keith-Albee Circuit. Mt. Calvary Cemetery, Cheektowaga, NY.

8334. Shean, Al (Alfred or Albert Schoenberg, May 12, 1868–Aug. 12, 1949) German born vaudeville comedian long teamed in vaudeville with Ed Gallagher until their act, known for its *Mr. Gallagher—Mr. Shean* tune bookending their jokes, broke up over a quarrel in the 1920's. The brother of Minnie Schoenberg Marx, it was Shean who inspired her to put her sons, the Marx Brothers, on stage as boys circa 1905. Shean appeared later in several films, including *San Francisco* (1936). He died at 81 in New York City. The plaque on his marker bears his name and dates, and the parting line *I could've lived longer but now it's too late. Absolutely, Mr. Gallagher— Positively, Mr. Shean.* Southwest corner, Sec. 8, lot 48, Mt. Pleasant Cemetery, Hawthorne, NY.

8335. Shearer, Athole (Nov. 20, 1900–March 17, 1985) Elder sister of Norma, in small unbilled parts in *The Flapper, Way Down East* and *The Restless Sex* (all 1920). Divorced from director Howard Hawks, she spent many years in a mental institution. Garden crypt 124, Garden of Memory, Forest Lawn, Glendale, CA.

8336. Shearer, Douglas (Nov. 17, 1899–Jan. 5, 1971) Canadian born sound technician contributed more than any other single innovator to the development of sound film. The brother of actress Norma Shearer, he was with MGM for many years, winning twelve Academy Awards. Donated to the UCLA School of Medicine.

8337. Shearer, Norma (Aug. 10, 1900–June 12, 1983) Actress from Westmont, Montreal, at MGM from their first feature *He Who Gets Slapped* (1924) to 1942, was reportedly the most pampered star on the Metro lot, the wife of production head Irving Thalberg from 1927 until his death in 1936. Starring roles included *The Divorcee* (1930, Academy Award), *A Free Soul* (1931), *Strange Interlude* and *Smiling Through* (1932), *The Barretts of Wimpole Street* (1934) and *Romeo and Juliet* (1936). After Thalberg's death she made a few films including *Marie Antoinette* (1938), *The Women* (1939), and *Escape* (1940) before retiring in 1942 and re-marrying, to ski instructor Martin Arrouge. She died from bronchopneumonia at 82 in the Motion Picture Country Home, at Woodland Hills, having lost her sight some years before. Entombed in a crypt inscribed only *Norma Arrouge*, above Thalberg's sarcophagus in their marble family room. Left side, all the way down, Sanctuary of Benediction, Memorial Terrace, Great Mausoleum, Forest Lawn, Glendale, CA.

8338. Shearn, Edith (May 12, 1870–May 14, 1968) Actress and painter married to Warner Oland in the 1930s, though estranged from him at the time of his death. Cremated at Grandview Memorial Park, Glendale, California, May 20, 1968. Columbine sec. 81/82, lot 81, Woodlawn Cemetery, the Bronx, N.Y.C.

8339. Sheehan, Winfield (Sept. 24, 1883–July 25, 1945) Production executive, vice president and general manager of Fox films 1916–1935, when it merged with 20th century. Afterward he worked as an independent. Sec. D, lot 392, Holy Cross Cemetery, Culver City, CA.

8340. Sheekman, Arthur (Feb. 5, 1901–Jan. 12, 1978) Chicago born screenwriter from the early 30's to the 1960's, including the Marx Brothers' *Monkey Business* and *Duck Soup,* Eddie Cantor musical-comedies, many others. Married to actress Gloria Stuart, whom he met on the set of *Roman Scandals* (1933). His last years were spent in a Santa Monica nursing home. Cremated at Roosevelt Memorial Park in Gardena, California, the ashes were returned to Stuart at their home in Brentwood, Los Angeles, and buried at a plum tree there.

8341. Sheen, Fulton J. (May 8, 1895–Dec. 9, 1979) Bishop and Archbishop in New York, Bishop Sheen began a radio program *Life is Worth Living* in 1930 and from 1952–65 on TV. His approach was restrained, calm and positive as opposed to many televangelists before and after him. Tomb (area closed to the public) below the altar of St. Patrick's Cathedral, 50th St. and 5th Avenue, Manhattan, N.Y.C.

8342. Sheffield, Reginald (Reginald Sheffield Cassan, Feb. 18, 1901–Dec. 8, 1957) London born actor in films from 1923 (*Of Human Bondage* 1934). He died in Pacific Palisades, California. Cremated at Chapel of the Pines. Parkview sec., lot 174, between grave 445 and marked area, Oak Grove Cemetery, St. Louis, MO.

8343. Shelby, Charlotte *see* **Mary Miles Minter.**

8344. Sheldon, Ralph (Oct. 17, 1900–July 2, 1944) Ohio born Chicago gangster controlled bootlegging in the southside Irish belt, adjoining the territory of the westside O'Donnells to the north and east of the Saltis-McErlane gang. Other than a challenge from Spike O'Donnell to the westside combination, most gangs stayed in their areas until the murder of Dean O'Banion in November 1924 and the long list of vengeance killings that followed to 1930. Sheldon ended up imprisoned at San Quentin, where he died from heart failure at 43. Vale of Memory, lot 2744, space 1, Forest Lawn, Glendale, CA.

8345. Shelley, Mary Wollstonecraft (Mary Wollstonecraft Godwin, Aug. 30, 1797–Feb. 1, 1851) London born writer married to poet Percy Bysshe Shelley was still Mary Godwin when her fame came with *Frankenstein*, published in 1818, which she created while on a holiday near Geneva with Shelley, Lord Byron and a Dr. Polidori. After her husband's death in a boating accident four years later, she remained a widow, keeping Shelley's heart in her desk. She died in her London home from a stroke, having told her son that she did not care if she were buried in London, Field Place, or with Shelley in Rome, saying she would join him soon anyway. Burial was with her parents at Bournemouth, where the Anglican minister read as the service an excerpt from her journal dated June 1, 1840, in which she expounded on the hereafter, writing in part "...Surely this world ... is peopled in its intellectual life by myriads of loving spirits that mold our thoughts to good, influence beneficially the course of events and minister to the destiny of man. Whether the beloved dead make a portion of this company I cannot guess, but that such exist I FEEL — far off when we are worldly, selfish, evil; drawing near and imparting sympathy when we rise to noble thoughts and disinterested action. Such surely gather round one on such an evening, and make part of that atmosphere of love, so hushed, so soft, on which the soul reposes and is blest." Her grave is marked by a long, low stone slab with inscriptions for herself, her father and

mother **Mary Wollstonecraft Godwin** (April 27, 1759–Sept. 10, 1797), author of *A Vindication of the Rights of Women*, who died from complications eleven days after her daughter's birth. She and her husband **William Godwin** (March 3, 1756–April 7, 1836), author of *Political Justice*, were removed to Bournemouth from St. Pancras' Churchyard in London upon their daughter's burial. St. Peter's Churchyard, Bournemouth, Dorset.

8346. Shelley, Percy Bysshe (Aug. 4, 1792–July 8, 1822) Leading English poet of the early 19th century Romantic period, married to Mary Wollstonecraft Godwin. He and Edward Williams took their schooner *Don Juan* fifty miles across the Gulf of Spezia on the northwest coast of Italy, from their house to Liverno, and were drowned in a storm on the return trip. They were washed ashore between Massa and Viareggio ten days after their deaths, with Shelley identifiable only by his pants, still with a copy of Keats' poems in his pockets, as all the skin had been eaten away. He was buried in the sand in quicklime until August 15, when the remains were cremated on the beach in a portable iron furnace. Edward Trelawney snatched the heart from the fire with tongs and it was kept by Shelley's wife thereafter, finally buried at Bournemouth with their son in 1889. Shelley's ashes were eventually buried in the cemetery in Rome where Keats was buried. On the slab are Shelley's name in English, the dates in Roman numerals, and the epitaph *Nothing of him that doth fade, but doth suffer a sea change into something rich and strange*. Protestant Cemetery (Cimitero Acattolico), Rome.

8347. Shelton, Anne (Nov. 10, 1923–July 31, 1994) British singer popular during World War II and afterward. Camberwell New Cemetery, Brenchley Gardens, London.

8348. Shelton, Charles (April 29 1932 – c. April 29, 1965) USAF Colonel, the last MIA in Laos, was shot down there on his 33rd birthday in 1965 and parachuted onto a ridge. He radioed he was safe but helicopters were unable to reach him because of bad weather. Never found, a memorial service for him was held on the fourth anniversary of his wife's suicide, October 2, 1994. His name is inscribed on the stone at her grave. Sec. 36, grave 123, Arlington National Cemetery, Arlington, VA.

8349. Shelton, Joy (June 3, 1922–Jan. 28, 2000) London born actress in films from 1943, best known for *Waterloo Road* (1944) opposite John Mills and Stewart Granger, and as the wife on BBC Radio's *P.C. 49* 1947–1953. She married actor Sydney Tafler (*q.v.*) in 1944, retired with the 1950's and reappeared on stage and film in her later years, last seen on television in *Darling Buds of May*. Their stone is inscribed *Loved and missed by their children, grandchildren, and all of their family*. Rear of cemetery, row 83, Golders Green Jewish Cemetery, north London.

8350. Shepard, Alan (Alan Bartlett Shepard, Nov. 18, 1923–July 21, 1998) Astronaut from Derry, New

Hampshire, one of NASA's original seven, was America's first man into space, piloting the tiny Freedom 7 capsule in the historic fifteen minute suborbital flight May 5, 1961. Grounded until 1968 with an inner ear problem, he commanded the Apollo 14 nine day flight from January 31 to February 9, 1971, during which he hit golf balls on the moon's surface with a hand fashioned 6 iron, sending them an enormous distance. Medal of Honor 1979. He died at 74 from leukemia in a Monterey, California, hospital. Cremated July 24 through Paul Mortuary, the ashes were returned to his widow Louise at their residence in Pebble Beach. She died from a heart attack a month later, August 26, on a plane while returning from a visit with her daughter. The ashes of both Shepard and his wife were reportedly scattered over Pebble Beach.

8351. Shepherd, Arthur (Feb. 19, 1880–Jan. 12, 1958) Music teacher at the New England Conservatory and Western Reserve composed *Triptych* (1925) and *Choreographic Suite* (1930) as well as three string quartets. Family monument and flush stone, Salt Lake City Cemetery, Salt Lake City, UT.

8352. Shepherd, Jean (Jean Parker Shepherd, July 26, 1921–Oct. 16, 1999) Radio storyteller famed on New York's WOR for 21 years, was an original in using comical asides during his narrations, often about his childhood in Hammond, Indiana. Books include *In God We Trust, All Others Pay Cash* (1966), part of the basis for the 1983 film *A Christmas Story*, which he narrated. He died at 78 in Sanibel Island, Florida, a year after the death of Leigh, his wife of 21 years. Cremated at Lee Memorial Park Crematory in Lehigh Acres and the ashes kept at Phil Kiser Funeral Home, Fort Myers, Florida, pending disposition, likely with the ashes of his wife.

8353. Sheppard, James (April 7, 1935–January 24, 1970) Lead singer with Shep and the Limelites, a 1950's ballad group known for *A Thousand Miles Away* and *Daddy's Home*. He was murdered in his car on the Long Island Expressway. Path 100 (left), Rockville Cemetery, Lynbrook, Long Island, NY.

8354. Sheppard, Marilyn Reese *see* **Sam Sheppard.**

8355. Sheppard, Sam (Samuel Sheppard, Dec. 29, 1923–April 6, 1970) Cleveland osteopath accused and convicted of murdering his wife, **Marilyn Reese Sheppard** (1923–July 4, 1954) found bludgeoned to death in their suburban Cleveland home on the 4th of July 1954. She was entombed in the North Wing Extension, crypt 744-E, Knollwood Park Cemetery mausoleum, Mayfield Heights (Cleveland), Ohio. His conviction was overturned and he was released in 1966 after serving ten years, his defense conducted by F. Lee Bailey. The case was allegedly the basis for the TV program (1963–67) and later film *The Fugitive*. He practiced afterward briefly as well as a stint as a professional wrestler. Remarried and living in Columbus, he died from an overdose of alcohol and prescription drugs; friends said Sheppard believed he was ill with terminal cancer. For twenty seven years a flush bronze plaque with the physician's symbol of healing marked his grave in the Good Shepherd section, Forest Lawn Memorial Gardens (East), Columbus, Ohio. His son Sam Reese Sheppard had him exhumed September 17, 1997 for DNA testing in Cleveland. The body was cremated that night and the urn interred the next day in the vault of Marilyn Reese Sheppard. On October 5, 1999, in the wake of Sam Reese Sheppard's suit against the state of Ohio for damages and to declare his father innocent, Marilyn Reese Sheppard was exhumed (and returned the next day) on the orders of prosecutors for the state, to have her DNA tested. Also tested was the DNA of the fetus she was carrying, buried with her, which was shown to have been autopsied at her death 45 years before. From 1954 to 1997 her plaque in Knollwood read *Marilyn Reese Sheppard 1923–1954*. After her husband's ashes were interred with her in September 1997, a new plaque was placed over the crypt headed *Sheppard*, listing both their names and dates, and at the bottom *unborn son*. The primary suspect in the suit was **Richard Eberling**, who had been washing windows at the residence a few days before the murder. Incarcerated for many years for another murder charge, Eberling died in prison at 68 July 24, 1998 and was buried at the Orient Correctional Institution Cemetery, Orient, OH.

8356. Sherbloom, Diane (Sept. 21, 1942–Feb. 15, 1961) Ice dancer won the 1961 championships with partner Larry Pierce. The U.S. world figure skating team was killed in the crash of their plane near Brussels, Belgium. Sec. M, lot 764, grave 6, Holy Cross Cemetery, Culver City, CA.

8357. Sheridan, Ann (Clara Lou Sheridan, Feb. 21, 1915–Jan. 21, 1967) Perky red headed Warner Brothers star of the late 30's and 40's from Denton, Texas, tagged the Oomph Girl for no apparent reason. Frequently in contract disputes with Warners, she managed fine performances in usually saucy roles in films from 1935 including *Black Legion, San Quentin, Angels With Dirty Faces, They Drive By Night, It All Came True, City For Conquest, King's Row* (1941, as Randy Monaghan), *The Man Who Came to Dinner, Nora Prentiss, I Was A Male War Bride*. She had started a TV series, *Pistols and Petticoats*, shortly before her death from cancer of the esophagus and liver at 51, survived by her third husband, actor Scott McKay. McKay died in 1987. Her ashes were in vaultage below Pierce Brothers Chapel of the Pines Crematory, Los Angeles, for 38 years. In February 2005, through the efforts of her biographer Karen McHale and with the help of relatives, a glass niche containing her urn, photos of her and other items was dedicated in the Cathedral Mausoleum, Hollywood Forever Cemetery, Hollywood (Los Angeles), CA.

8358. Sheridan, Philip (March 6, 1831–Aug. 5, 1888) Union general during the Civil War fought in the western sector before coming into Virginia in the last year of the war, winning battles through the Shenandoah Valley and cutting off Lee's retreat at Appomattox in April 1865. He died at Nonquitt, Massachusetts, at 57. His stone monument bears only *Sheridan* with a weathered bronze medallion of him surrounded by an unfurling flag. Southeast of Arlington House. Sec. 2, site S-1, Arlington National Cemetery, Arlington, VA.

8359. Sherman, Allan (Nov. 30, 1924–Nov. 20, 1973) Hefty comedian from Chicago known for parodies of well known tunes, best known for *Camp Grenada* and the LP *My Son, the Folksinger*. He died from emphysema in Hollywood at 48. Columbarium of Hope, niche 513, mausoleum at Hillside Memorial Park, Los Angeles.

8360. Sherman, James Schoolcraft (Oct. 24, 1855–Oct. 30, 1912) Republican congressman from New York and Vice President of the United States under Taft 1909–1912. Although Sherman was renominated to run with Taft again in 1912 (and was in fact not speaking to Taft through 1912), he died just before the election. Family mausoleum, top of hill. Sec. 64, Forest Hill Cemetery, Utica, NY.

8361. Sherman, John (May 10, 1823–Oct. 22, 1900) Ohio Republican congressman and statesman from Lancaster, Ohio, brother of General William Tecumseh Sherman, was a cabinet member in the administrations of Hayes and McKinley. During his second term as senator, he authored the Sherman Anti-Trust Law, which gradually led to the break up of many monopolies. Large monument atop hill above the stone bleachers, lot 1101, Mansfield Cemetery, Mansfield, OH.

8362. Sherman, Lowell (Oct. 11, 1885–Dec. 28, 1934) Stage and screen actor played many sleek charmers and crafty villains, in *Way Down East* (1920), *A Lady of Chance* (1928), *Midnight Mystery* (1929), many others. He was the original fading star in *What Price Hollywood?* (1932), the prototype for the 1937 *A Star is Born*. Sherman died from pneumonia at 49. Sanctuary of Trust, crypt 5793, Memorial Terrace, Great Mausoleum, Forest Lawn, Glendale, CA.

8363. Sherman, Roger (April 19, 1721–July 23, 1793) Formulator of the Connecticut Compromise at the Constitutional Convention in 1787 which provided for representation by state and by population, creating two houses of congress, and preventing an impasse between large and small states which would have stopped ratification. He also signed the Declaration of Independence and the Articles of Confederation and those of Association, the only name on all four documents. He later served as mayor of New Haven and was believed buried on the common burying ground beneath and behind what is now Center Church on the Green. When Grove Street Cemetery was established in 1796, his remains were sought (whether they were located is unclear), and the table monument on four legs was removed there. The original monument became so eroded that a new upright

monument was dedicated behind it with the inscription re-written on it, though the original monument remains there. Sherman is the oldest major figure in America's oldest noted incorporated cemetery with grid layout and named roads. In 1845 the massive sandstone Egyptian Revival entrance gate arch was dedicated, with the inscription *The Dead Shall Be Raised*. Left side of Maple Ave., Grove Street Cemetery, New Haven, CT.

8364. Sherman, William Tecumseh (Feb. 8, 1820–Feb. 14, 1891) Tough, grizzled Union general in the Civil War engaged in many battles, famed for his march through Georgia to the sea, burning much in the path of his army, including large portions of Atlanta as well as Columbia, S.C. His remark "War is Hell" became a part of Americana. Brother of Senator John Sherman. At his funeral in New York City, his old nemesis, Joseph Johnston, standing outside with his hat off in Sherman's honor, caught cold and died a short time later. His monument has carved crossed flags in relief above his name and dates. Sec. 17 along the road, Calvary Cemetery, St. Louis, MO.

8365. Sherriff, R.C. (Robert Cedric Sheriff, June 6, 1896–Nov. 13, 1975) English playwright, novelist and screenwriter from Kingston-on-Thames, best known for the World War I play *Journey's End*, based on his three years service in the war. Like the works of Hemingway, Remarque, and screenwriter John Monk Saunders, it stressed the de-glamorization of war. First produced in England in 1928, it ran for 594 performances and was filmed in Hollywood by director James Whale in 1930. Other screenplays include *The Invisible Man* (1933), *Goodbye Mr. Chips* (1939), *Odd Man Out* (co-wrote, 1947). He died in England at 79. Service and cremation at Randalls Park Crematorium, Letherhead, Surrey. The ashes were taken to Selsey, West Sussex, on the coast, for likely scattering at sea.

8366. Sherrill, Patrick (Nov. 13, 1941–Aug. 20, 1986) The first of a seemingly endless series of postal workers who broke under the pressure of supervisors, and mental illness. Sherrill took a gun into the post office in the small Oklahoma town where he worked and killed and injured several, including himself. Veterans' marker, Watonga Cemetery, Watonga, OK.

8367. Sherwin, Manning (Jan. 4, 1898–July 26, 1974) Song-writer, co-wrote, with Eric Maschwitz, *A Nightingale Sang in Berkeley Square*. Garden of Devotion, Grandview Memorial Park, Glendale, CA.

8368. Sherwood, Corel (May 5, 1905–Feb. 23, 1925) Air instructor near Ellis, Nebraska, died when his plane crashed, killing he and his passenger. His grave is marked by a propeller from his plane, a picture of him and a letter to him from Charles Lindbergh. The family makes regular pilgrimages to the gravesite to re-shellac the propeller. Wyuka Cemetery, Lincoln, NE.

8369. Sherwood, Robert (Robert Emmet Sherwood, April 4, 1896–Nov. 14, 1955) Witty speech writer for FDR, Algonquin Round Table regular and acclaimed playwright. Works include *Waterloo Bridge, The Petrified Forest, Abe Lincoln in Illinois, There Shall Be No Light* and *Idiot's Delight*, the latter three winning Pulitzer Prizes. He was also awarded a Pulitzer Prize for his book *Roosevelt and Hopkins* (1949). He died in New York. Services at St. George's Episcopal Church in Stuyvesant Square. Cremated at Fresh Pond Crematory, Middle Village, Queens, N.Y.C. Ashes disposed of or returned to the family.

8370. Sherwood, Roberta (July 1, 1913–July 5, 1999) Torch singer (*Up A Lazy River, You're Nobody Til Somebody Loves You*), appeared in a few films. Frequent guest on the Jackie Gleason and the Ed Sullivan Shows. She died at 86 in Los Angeles. Court of Liberty, lot 1363, space 3, Forest Lawn Hollywood Hills, Los Angeles.

8371. Shields, Arthur (Feb, 15, 1896–April 27, 1970) Dublin born member of the Abbey Theatre and brother of Barry Fitzgerald. They strongly resembled each other, Shields wearing glasses and having darker hair and a deeper voice. Appearances together include *The Long Voyage Home* (1940), *How Green Was My Valley* (1941) and *The Quiet Man* (1952), all for director John Ford. Many other appearances, often as priests or evil busybodies. Buried beside his brother, their graves covered with periwinkle. St. Nessan section 58/59, Dean's Grange Burial Ground, County Dublin, Ireland.

8372. Shilkret, Jack (Oct. 13, 1896–June 16, 1964) Composer, younger brother of Nat Shilkret, wrote "April Showers Bring May Flowers," his best known of many songs, as well as scoring shorts, government films, leading a dance band in the 1930's and playing piano on the radio shows of Frank Crumit and Julia Sanderson. He died of a heart attack at 67 in his home, 302 East 88th St, Manhattan. Block 74, sec. E, lot 14, grave 1, Mt. Hebron Cemetery, Flushing, Queens, N.Y.C.

8373. Shilkret, Nat (Nathaniel Shilkret, *nee* Naftule Schuldkraut, Dec. 25, 1889–Feb. 18, 1982) Musician born and raised in Queens, New York, with RCA Victor from 1923, first playing and directing classical recordings, but recording popular and jazz numbers at his peak from 1925–29, including *Diane, Dancing With Tears in My Eyes* and *I'm Gonna Charleston Back to (My Old Shack in) Charleston* (1927), and co-wrote *The Lonesome Road* with Gene Austen, also in 1927. At the same time there was a growing rivalry at Victor with Paul Whiteman, who left angry during the recording (with Gershwin) of *Rhapsody in Blue* in April 1927; though Whiteman is credited as conducting, it was Shilkret who took over and finished leading the orchestra. Whiteman left Victor for Columbia in part because of Shilkret, who remained, also working as General Music Director for RKO Radio pictures from 1935, scoring *Swiss Miss, The Bohemian Girl, Mary of Scotland, Winterset* and both *Swing Time*

and *Shall We Dance* with Fred Astaire and Ginger Rogers, and many others, often uncredited. In the early 1950's, he became musical director at Columbia and worked into his 70's. With no mention in the papers, he died at 92 in Franklin Square, Nassau County, Long Island, New York. Cremated, his ashes (which he wished spread in the back yard there) are retained by family.

8374. Shipman, Helen (Feb. 5, 1901–April 13, 1984) Actress of the talkies through the 1930s (played Louise in *The Double Door* 1934). Married to Robert Keith in the 1920s, she was the mother of actor Brian Keith. She left films along with her last husband, actor Edward Pawley (*q.v.*) to farm at Rock Mills, Rappahannock County, Virginia. She died at nearby Castleton at 83. Sent through Clore (now Clore-English) mortuary in Culpeper for cremation April 14 at Metropolitan Funeral Service and Crematory, Alexandria, Virginia, and returned to Clore mortuary, Culpeper, VA.

8375. Shirer, William L. (Feb. 23, 1904–Dec. 28, 1993) Chicago born journalist and foreign correspondent broadcast from Europe including the 1936 Olympics and CBS radio coverage with Edward R. Murrow 1937–1941 until German occupation. Blacklisted in the 1950's, he left CBS and penned his best known work *The Rise and Fall of the Third Reich* (1960). Other works include *Berlin Diary, The Journal of a Foreign Correspondent* (1934–1941). He died in Boston at 89. Mountain View Cemetery, Lenox, MA.

8376. Shirley, Anne (Dawn Paris, April 17, 1919–July 4, 1993) Actress went from Dawn O'Day to Anne Shirley, the name of her character in the film *Anne of Green Gables* (1934). Others include *Chasing Yesterday* (1934), *Stella Dallas* (1937, AA nom.) *The Devil and Daniel Webster* (1941), *Murder My Sweet* (1944). Retired 1944. Last married to Charles Lederer. She died from lung cancer at 74. Cremated through Pierce Bros.–Utter McKinley–Cunningham and O'Connor. Ashes returned to the family in Malibu, CA.

8377. Shirley, William "Bill" (July 6, 1921–Aug. 27, 1989) The voice of Prince Phillip in Disney's *Sleeping Beauty* (1959) also dubbed Jeremy Brett's *The Street Where You Live* in *My Fair Lady* (1964) and starred in the Stephen Foster biopic *I Dream of Jeannie*. Second floor, half way down on the left, B-C-18, Community Mausoleum, Crown Hill Cemetery, Indianapolis, IN.

8378. Shoemaker, Ann *see* **Henry Stephenson.**

8379. Shoemaker, Edwin (June 2, 1907–March 15, 1998) Inventor from Monroe, Michigan, invented the La-Z-Boy recliner in 1928, updating it for the TV age in 1961. He died in his recliner at 90 during a nap at his Arizona home. Gethsemane Cemetery, Monroe, MI.

8380. Shoemaker, Bill "Willie" (William Lee Shoemaker, Aug. 19, 1931–Oct. 12, 2003) The Shoe, noted jockey over a forty year period, competed in 40,350 races with 8,833 victories, including two

Preaknesses, five Belmont Stakes, and four Kentucky Derby wins, the last, in 1986, making him the oldest victor in the Run For the Roses at 54. A quadriplegic for several years after an accident, he died at home in San Marino, Los Angeles County, California, at 72. Cremated through Cabot and Sons mortuary. Ashes returned to family in San Marino.

8381. Sholes, Christopher Latham (Feb. 14, 1819–Feb. 17, 1890) Journalist and inventor (with two colleagues) of the typewriter, issued the first patent in 1868, which was sold to Remington in 1873. The monument at his grave, with a bronze profile of him on it, was erected in appreciation by the Secretaries of America. Near the MacArthur lot, sec. 10, block 18, lot 3, Forest Home Cemetery, Milwaukee, WI.

8382. Sholom Aleichem (Solomon Rabinowitz, Feb 18 1859–May 13 1916) Ukrainian Jewish writer in the U.S. in 1914. His plays for the Yiddish Theatre were combined into the Broadway hit *Fiddler on the Roof* nearly fifty years after his death. The name translates roughly into *Peace Be Unto You*. Grave and large monument (originally in Mt. Neboh), Mt. Carmel (Old) Cemetery, Glendale, Queens, N.Y.C.

8383. Shor, Toots (Bernard Shor, May 6, 1903– Jan. 23, 1977) Manhattan restaurateur known for his many and varied opinions, friend to the sports, entertainment, journalistic and literary world for decades, insulting many of his regulars and reserving for selected targets his special term "crum bums." Next to author James Baldwin. Hillcrest A-1204, Ferncliff Cemetery, Hartsdale, NY.

8384. Shore, Dinah (Frances Rose Shore, March 1, 1916–Feb. 24, 1994) Honey blonde from Winchester, Tennessee, began her career as a vocalist in the 1940's, performing at the Hollywood Canteen and for Columbia, both solo and in several duets with Buddy Clark. She began *The Dinah Shore Show* on television in 1951, the musical variety format of the 50's and 60's, turning to talk shows 1970–1984. Her association with the LPGA and women's golf from 1972 brought greater recognition and advancement of women's sports. She died from cancer in Beverly Hills at 77. Part of her ashes are marked by a plaque inscribed *Loved by all who knew her and millions who never did.* Courts of the Book, Isaiah V, crypt 147, Hillside Memorial Park, Los Angeles. A part of her ashes were also placed near George Montgomery, in Faith and Hope, Corridor 1, wall 1, niche 10-D, Palm Springs Mausoleum, Cathedral City, CA.

8385. Shores, C.W. "Doc" (Cyrus Wells Shores, Nov. 11, 1844–Oct. 12, 1934) Western Colorado's most noted frontiersman, pioneer and lawman, as noted (verbatim) on his stone. Sec. 43, Gunnison Cemetery, Gunnison, CO.

8386. Short, Elizabeth ("The Black Dahlia") (July 29, 1924–Jan. 15, 1947) Twenty-two year old frequenter of Hollywood night spots known for her black jewelry and clothing, which earned her the sobriquet The Black Dahlia. Her body was found in an empty lot at 39th and South Norton in the Crenshaw district of southwest Los Angeles, completely cut in half, drained of blood, mutilated and the black hair dyed red. Among the most bizarre of all murder cases, it remains unsolved; nor was the means of killing or the motive ever explained. She was not buried in Berkeley, California, as listed on the death certificate. Sec. 66, grave 913, Mountain View Cemetery, Oakland, CA.

8387. Short, Walter (March 30, 1880–Sept. 3, 1949) General in command of ground forces at Pearl Harbor did not receive signals in time to avert or prepare for the Japanese attack on December 7, 1941. The target was anticipated as the Philippines. After congressional investigations, both he and Admiral Husband Kimmel resigned. Not until May 1999 did the U.S. Senate relieve them of responsibility and restore their ranks. Sec. 30, grave 1091, Arlington National Cemetery, Arlington, VA.

8388. Shostakovich, Dmitry (Sept. 25, 1906– Aug. 9, 1975) One of the foremost 20th century Soviet composers, his work was often reflective of his unofficial role as representative of Soviet music. Of his fifteen symphonies, four were topical themes, *To October* (2nd, 1927), *May First* (3rd, 1929), *The Year 1905* (11th, 1957) and *The Year 1917* (12th, 1961). Other works, including his opera *The Nose* (1930) and his *13th Symphony* (1962), which criticized Stalin and unstated Russian anti–Semitism, were widely denounced. Novodevichy Cemetery, Moscow.

8389. Show, Eric (May 19, 1956–March 16, 1994) Pitcher for the Padres 1981–1990 won the 1984 pennant and threw Pete Rose his record breaking hit number 4,192 in September 1985. He died at his home outside San Diego from cocaine and heroin while at a drug rehab center at Dulruza. W3, lot 113, grave 4, Olivewood Cemetery, Riverside, CA.

8390. Showalter, Max aka **Casey Adams** (June 2, 1917–July 30, 2000) Actor from Caldwell, Kansas, billed in the 1950's as Casey Adams, played mild mannered, back-slapping, sometimes opportunistic, second leads in films and TV 1954–84, including the original Ward Cleaver in *It's A Small World*, the 1957 pilot for *Leave It to Beaver*. He died from prostate cancer at Middletown, Connecticut, at 83. A resident of nearby Chester, he never married. Cremated at Charter Crematory, Waterford, Connecticut, through Robinson-Wright-Weymer mortuary in Centerbrook. Ashes taken by his sister, Fresno, CA.

8391. Showman's Rest(s) *see* **Circus Performers.**

8392. Shreve, Bob (July 16, 1912–Feb. 20, 1990) Pioneer Cincinnati TV comedian hosted many shows from the late 1950's to his all night movie festivals Saturday nights 1966–1985. In vaudeville style, he used one liners for all occasions between and during films, with such mainstays as Gororo the head and his rubber chicken, Chickee. Popular for three generations, he died from cancer at 77 in Cincinnati's Jewish Hospital. Outdoor crypt, eye level, Redbud sec., Garden Mausoleum, Spring Grove Cemetery, Cincinnati, OH.

8393. Shriner, Herb (May 29, 1918–April 23, 1970) Nightclub and TV comic, killed with his wife in an auto accident. Sec. C, block F10, grave 15, Queen of Heaven Cemetery, Pompano Beach, FL.

8394. Shubert, Lee (March 15, 1875–Dec. 25, 1953) and **Jacob Shubert** (Aug. 15, 1880–Nov. 17, 1962) Major New York theatrical producers, owned many of the theatres in New York from the turn of the century on, producing hundreds of plays and musicals between them, including the Ziegfeld Follies. Family mausoleum, lot 1938, Salem Fields Cemetery, Brooklyn, N.Y.C.

8395. Shull, Richard B. (Feb. 24, 1929–Oct. 14, 1999) Actor in films and TV parts over thirty years co-starred with John Schuck in the short lived sitcom *Holmes and Yoyo* on ABC in the fall of 1976. He died from a heart attack at 70. Actors Fund of America plot, Kensico Cemetery, Valhalla, NY.

8396. Shulman, Irving (May 21, 1913–March 23, 1995) Hollywood biographer with a sensational bent in the 1960's chronicled both *Harlow* and *Valentino*. Mt. Tabor sec., lot 608, space A, Eden Memorial Park, Mission Hills, CA.

8397. Shulman, Max (March 14, 1919–Aug. 28, 1988) Novelist, playwright and screen-writer penned *Barefoot Boy With Cheek* and later *The Many Loves of Dobie Gillis* (1953), *The Tender Trap* (1955), *Rally Round the Flag Boys* (1958) and *House Calls* (1978), several others. Eternal Rest urn garden, block 4, plot 31, Hillside Memorial Park, Los Angeles.

8398. Shuster, Frank (Sept. 5, 1916–Jan. 13, 2002) Half of the team of Wayne and Shuster, dubbed the "kings of Canadian comedy"; they appeared on *The Ed Sullivan Show* sixty-seven times. Johnny Wayne died in 1990. Shuster died of pneumonia at 85 in a Toronto hospital. Holy Blossom Memorial Park/Cemetery, Toronto, Ontario.

8399. Shuster, Joe (July 10, 1914–July 30, 1992) Artist and co-creator with writer Jerry Siegel of "Superman" in 1938, when the superhero was introduced through DC comics, a format then only five years old. Born in Toronto, he and Siegel grew up in Cleveland. Shuster died at 78 in his west Los Angeles home. Cremated through Pierce Bros. Westwood mortuary, the ashes were returned to his sister of Albuquerque, NM.

8400. Shute, Nevil (Nevil Shute Norway, Jan. 17, 1899–Jan. 12, 1960) English born novelist worked as an aeronautical engineer and aircraft factory manager while writing fiction, moving to Melbourne, Australia, in 1948. Best known for the anti-nuclear novel *On The Beach* (1957), filmed two years later. Cremated at Victoria, Australia, his ashes were scattered.

8401. Sickert, Walter Richard (May 31, 1860–Jan. 22, 1942) English painter, also resided in France, known for interiors, music hall scenes, several nudes

with clothed males, including *The Camden Town Murder*. A royal academician 1934–5, his writings were published as *A Free House* posthumously in 1947. In 1973, Joseph Sickert, claiming to be the illegitimate son of Walter Sickert, theorized in a BBC series on Jack the Ripper that his father had hinted to him and through his paintings that he knew of the conspiracy of murders in 1888 that was called Jack the Ripper, the prime mover being Sir William Withey Gull. Writer Stephen Knight, in *The Final Solution* (1978) decided Sickert was a third participant in the killings. Though Joseph Sickert recounted his story as a hoax, and it was dismissed by most Ripperologists anyway, author Patricia Cromwell in December 2001 embarked on revising the theory, proposing that Sickert alone was the Ripper. A respected artist, he died at 81 in St. George's Hill, Bathampton, Bath. Funeral at Bristol Crematorium, Arnos Vale, Bristol, Avon. Ashes buried St. Nicholas/Churchyard, Bathampton, Somerset.

8402. Sickles, Daniel (Oct. 20, 1819–May 3, 1914) Major General in the Union Army was a congressman from New York 1857–1861 before commanding a brigade of the Army of the Potomac in the Peninsula campaign, a division at Fredericksburg and a corps at Chancellorsville and Gettysburg where, his leg wounded and requiring amputation, he was carried from the field gamely smoking a cigar, to survive another fifty years. Sec. 3, grave 1906, Arlington National Cemetery, Arlington, VA.

8403. Siddal, Elizabeth (Elizabeth Eleanor Siddal, July 25, 1829–Feb. 11, 1862) Millinery clerk in Piccadilly plucked by Pre Raphaelite artist Walter Deverall as a perfect model for the works of he and his contemporaries, including John Everett Millais — becoming his *Ophelia*, lying in a bath of water heated by candles and oil lamps Holman Hunt and Dante Gabriel Rossetti, who she finally married in 1860. She died of an overdose of laudanum, possibly accidental, two years later at 32. A book of unpublished poems Rossetti had had buried with her were later extracted from the coffin with an exhumation, but did not sell. Rossetti plot, near the front, Highgate Cemetery (West), London.

8404. Siddons, Sarah Kemble (July 5, 1755–June 8, 1831) English actress, considered the greatest of her day, inspiration for the Tragic Muse. She has a memorial statue on Paddington Green and is buried nearby, within a railing and under a canopy, in the north end of the emparked extension of St. Mary Churchyard, Paddington Green, London.

8405. Sidney, George (Oct. 4, 1916–May 5, 2002) New York born director and producer of dozens of Hollywood musicals. His films included *Ziegfeld Follies* (1945), *Annie Get Your Gun* (1950), *Show Boat* (1951), *Kiss Me Kate* (1953) and *Bye Bye Birdie* (1963). He died from lymphoma in Las Vegas at 85. Sidney said he wanted no funeral; "We're in show business" he noted, "We know how the script ends." Sanctuary of Benevolence, second floor, family room FF, mausoleum, Hillside Memorial Park, Los Angeles.

8406. Sidney, Margaret (Harriet Mulford Stone Lothrop, June 22, 1844–Aug. 2, 1924) Author of children's books, notably "The Five Little Peppers and How They Grew," the series beginning in 1881. She was associated with the Wayside Inn at Concord, along with the Alcotts and Hawthorne, where she lived as a widow. Between Ridge and Birch Path, northeast of Hillside Ave., Sleepy Hollow Cemetery, Concord, MA.

8407. Sidney, Sylvia (Sophia Kosow, Aug. 8, 1910–July 1, 1999) Bronx born stage actress who took the surname of her stepfather was a favorite forthright working girl in films of the 1930's, including *City Streets, An American Tragedy, Street Scene, The Miracle Man, Madame Butterfly, Fury* and *Dead End*. She appeared on Broadway and TV through the 1950's and 60's and authored two books on needlepoint, returning to films and TV movies by the 70's, including *Do Not Fold, Spindle or Mutilate* (1971), *Summer Wishes, Winter Dreams* (AA nom, 1973), *I Never Promised You a Rose Garden* (1977), *An Early Frost* (Golden Globe and Emmy nom.), *Finnegan Begin Again* (1985), *Beetlejuice* (1988), *Used People* (1992) and *Mars Attacks!* (1996). Divorced from Bennett Cerf, Luther Adler, and Carlton Alsop, she died from throat cancer at 88 in Lennox Hill Hospital, Manhattan, listed as having no survivors. Cremated at Garden State Crematory July 2, her ashes were returned to her executor through the Riverside Chapel.

8408. Sieber, Rudi *see* **Marlene Dietrich.**

8409. Siedow, Jim (June 12, 1920–Nov. 20, 2003) Cheyenne, Wyoming, born stage director, actor, and carpet salesman in Houston played Cook in both *The Texas Chainsaw Massacre* (1974) and its sequel, earning him a cult following for what he saw as fun but a "grade B drive-in movie." He died in Houston at 83. Body donated to Baylor College School of Medicine, Houston.

8410. Siegel, Benjamin "Bugsy" (Feb. 28, 1906–June 20, 1947) New York racketeer and gangster moved west at the close of World War II, where his investments and casinos in Las Vegas built the city into the most popular gambling resort in the U.S. Living in Hollywood among friends in the film colony, he was pressed for debts he owed in New York, straining to the limit his relationship with his longtime partners Meyer Lansky and the exiled Lucky Luciano. While sitting on the couch in the home of his girlfriend Virginia Hill on Linden Drive in Beverly Hills, he was shot from a window three times with a rifle, the bullet entering the back of his head and blowing an eye across the room. Five people, his family, attended the service and interment. The plaque on his crypt is in the form of an open book with his real name beneath a Star of David. Beth Olam Mausoleum/Hall of Solomon, corridor M-2, crypt 3087, Beth Olam Cemetery adjacent Hollywood Memorial Park Cemetery (Hollywood Forever), Hollywood (Los Angeles), CA.

8411. Siegel, Don (Oct. 26, 1912–April 20, 1991) Chicago born film director known for such evergreens as *Invasion of the Body Snatchers* (1956), *Dirty Harry* (1971) and John Wayne's poignant swan song *The Shootist* (1976), also won two Oscars for shorts *Star in the Night* and *Hitler Lives* (1945). He died from lymphoma at 78 in his Nipomo, California, home. Ashes buried at Cayucos Morrow Bay Cemetery, Highway 1, Cayucos, CA.

8412. Siegel, Sol C. (March 30, 1903–Dec. 29, 1982) Producer of films from 1929 including *Blue Skies, High Society, Home From the Hill, Alvarez Kelly, No Way to Treat a Lady*, etc. Sunset Slope, block 4, lot 277, Hillside Memorial Park, Los Angeles, CA.

8413. Siegmann, George (Feb. 8, 1882–June 22, 1928) Burly actor in silent films (*Birth of A Nation*, as Silas Lynch, *Intolerance*, as Cyrus, *Hearts of the World, The Three Musketeers, Oliver Twist* 1922, as Bill Sikes, *Anna Christie* 1923, *King of Kings*, as Barabbas, *The Cat and the Canary, The Man Who Laughs*). He died at 46 from pernicious anemia. Sec. F, lot 1672, grave 8, Calvary Cemetery, Los Angeles.

8414. Sierra, Margarita (Jan. 5 [CA Death Index lists Dec. 31], 1936–Sept. 6, 1963) Spanish born actress played Cha-Cha O'Brien on TV's *Surfside 6* (1961). She died following heart surgery at 27. Sec. D, lot 172, Holy Cross Cemetery, Culver City, CA.

8415. Sigel, Franz (Nov. 18, 1824–Aug. 21, 1902) Prussian military officer fled to the United States following the failed 1848 insurrection there, became a major general of volunteers and a politician, losing in the 1862 Valley Campaign, the Battle of New Market in March 1864, several others, but had more success in politics. Boulder with plaque. Sec. 100/113, Holly plot, lot 10563 NW, Woodlawn Cemetery, the Bronx, N.Y.C.

8416. Signoret, Simone (March 25, 1921–Sept. 30, 1985) French actress (German born) in films, in Paris from 1946 as saucy, loose women or romantic leads, later moving to matronly roles. Notable films include *Les Diaboliques* (*Diabolique*, 1955, as Nicole, the role essayed by Sharon Stone in the 1996 American version), *Room at the Top* (British, 1958, Academy Award), *Ship of Fools* (U.S. 1965) and *La Vie devant soi/Madame Rosa* (French, 1977). She died from pancreatic cancer at 64, survived by her husband Yves Montand (later buried with her), and daughter, actress Catherine Allegret. Beige slab with her name and Montand's in gold at the head. Div. 44, Pere Lachaise Cemetery, Paris.

8417. Siki (Battling Siki) (Louis Fall, Sept. 22, 1897–Dec. 15, 1925) Boxing's first African world champion, born in Senegal, turned pro in 1916. Decorated four times fighting for France in World War I. In 1922 he was assigned to take a dive in his light heavyweight title bout with Georges Carpentier at Buffalo but changed his mind and knocked his opponent out, winning the light heavyweight and European championship, losing to Mike McTeague in Dublin on March 17, 1923. He came to the U.S. that year and continued to fight but never regained his title. Shot twice in the back with a .38 near his apartment in Hells Kitchen in Manhattan at 28, he was buried in section R, lot 1112, Flushing Cemetery, Flushing, Queens, N.Y.C. Disinterred March 5, 1993 for reburial in a Muslim tomb in St. Louis, Senegal on the west coast of Africa, long a goal of the head of the African boxing commission. The marker at Flushing was also removed.

8418. Sikorsky, Igor I. (May 25, 1889–Oct. 26, 1972) Russian born aeronautical engineer developed the first multi-motor plane, trans-oceanic amphibian clippers and built and flew the first successful helicopter (1939). Monument with tribute. St. John's Greek Cemetery, Stratford, CT.

8419. Silkwood, Karen (Feb. 19, 1946–Nov. 13, 1974) The subject of the 1983 film *Silkwood* was employed by a nuclear power plant. While on her way to meet a *New York Times* reporter she was killed in an auto accident, thought by many to have been arranged. The amount of dangerous plutonium she had taken into her system while working at the plant became a public issue and Silkwood a martyr to the cause of regulation of nuclear power. Buried at her birthplace. Danville Cemetery, Kilgore, TX.

8420. Sills, Milton (Jan. 12, 1882–Sept. 15, 1930) Silent screen lead from Chicago in many films 1915–1930. He died from a heart attack in Santa Monica, California, at 48. Family monument and headstone. Sec. 111, lot 38, Rosehill Cemetery, Chicago, IL.

8421. Silva, Trinidad, Jr. (Jan. 30, 1950–July 31, 1988) Puerto-Rican American actor known as Jesus the street smart go-between gang leader on TV's *Hill Street Blues* 1981–86, also appeared in *Colors* (1988). He was killed in a traffic accident while driving with his family in Whittier, California. Unmarked. Sec. BB, lot 16, grave 196, San Fernando Mission Cemetery, Mission Hills, CA.

8422. Silver, Joe (Joseph Silver, Sept. 28, 1922–Feb. 27, 1989) Gruff voiced actor-comedian in films from the 1940's through the 80's (*You Light Up My Life, Deathtrap, Almost You, The Gig, Magic Sticks, Switching Channels*). He died from liver cancer at 66. Mausoleum, Lakeview VI (Rose Hill side, not King David), Rose Hill Memorial Park, Putnam Valley, NY.

8423. Silver, Steve (Feb. 6, 1944–June 12, 1995) San Francisco impresario produced *Beach Blanket Babylon*, the biggest hit in the city's theatrical history. A cartoon likeness of him is on his monument. Sec F, lot 11, Cypress Lawn Cemetery, Colma, CA.

8424. Silverheels, Jay (Harold J. Smith, May 26, 1912–March 5, 1980) Canadian-Indian actor played Tonto on TV's *The Lone Ranger* in the 1950's, as well as various Indians (*Key Largo*) in westerns from the 1940's through the 70's. He died of complications from pneumonia and heart disease at the Motion Pic-

ture and TV Hospital at 67. Cremated at Pierce Brothers Chapel of the Pines Crematory in Los Angeles, the ashes were sent to Six Nations Indian Reservation, Brandford, Ontario.

8425. Silverman, Sime (May 18, 1873–Sept. 22, 1933) Founder of the show business weekly *Variety* (1905), died in Hollywood. Returned to Riverside Chapel in Manhattan, with eulogies by George M. Cohan and George Jessel. Family mausoleum, lot 1833, Salem Fields Cemetery, Brooklyn, N.Y.C.

8426. Silvers, Louis F. (Sept. 6, 1889–March 26, 1954) Composer-conductor scored many films from the 1920's, including *The Jazz Singer* (1927), *It Happened One Night* (1934), *Crime and Punishment* (1935), *Mr. Deeds Goes to Town* (1936). Whispering Pines, lot 1896, grave 7, Forest Lawn, Glendale, CA.

8427. Silvers, Phil (May 11, 1911–Nov. 1, 1985) Bald comedian with glasses invariably cast as fast talking con men starred as Sgt. Bilko in the TV comedy *You'll Never Get Rich* 1955–58. He died in his sleep at 73. Garden of Traditions, grave 1004, Mount Sinai Memorial Park, Los Angeles.

8428. Silverstein, Abe (Sept. 15, 1908–June 1, 2001) NASA's first director of space flight, credited with using the name Apollo for the series of flights through the 1960s which culminated with a man on the moon in 1969. He died at 92. Ridge Road Cemetery, Cleveland, OH.

8429. Silverstein, Shel (Sheldon or Shelby Silverstein, Sept. 25, 1932–May 10, 1999) Author, artist and songwriter from Chicago whose work ranged from children's books (*Where the Sidewalk Ends, A Light in the Attic, The Giving Tree*) to cartoons for *Playboy*, nine plays for adults, and songs including *The Unicorn, A Boy Named Sue* for Johnny Cash, *Sylvia's Mother,* and (collaborated on) *Cover of the Rolling Stone.* He died from a heart attack at 66 while writing in bed at his home in Key West, Florida. Returned to Chicago for burial May 13. Sec. B, block 9, lot 3, grave 1, Westlawn Cemetery, Norridge (Chicago), IL.

8430. Sim, Alastair (Oct. 9, 1900–Aug. 19, 1976) Actor born at Edinburgh played sly, witty, eccentrics, memorably in *Green For Danger* (1946), Hitchcock's *Stage Fright* (1949), *The Bells of St. Trinians* and in *Scrooge/A Christmas Carol* (1951), the best version of Dickens' perennial, due in large part to Sim's facial and vocal inflections. He died from cancer in London at 75. According to the vicar at Nettlebed near Highmoor, where Sim lived at Witheridge Hill, the body was donated to science.

8431. Simenon, Georges (Feb. 13, 1903–Sept. 4, 1989) Belgian writer of eighty novels featuring the pipe smoking French inspector Jules Maigret. The most widely published author since the invention of the printing press, in fifty five languages in forty countries, with 132 novels of people in crisis and some 300 adventures, westerns and romances under over twenty pseudonyms. He claimed his prolific output was due to ongoing sex with some 10,000 women (by his count). He died at 86 at his home in Lausanne, Switzerland. His ashes were placed with those of his daughter, Marie-Georges, a suicide in 1978 at 25, beneath a 250 year old Cedar tree outside of his home.

8432. Simien, Sydney (April 9, 1938–Feb. 25, 1998) Recording artist from Lebeau, Louisiana, dubbed Rockin Sydney Simien, active from the late 1950's with rhythm and blues, later incorporated the accordion and zydeco into the act, producing the LP *My Zydeco Shoes Got the Zydeco Blues* in 1984, with its subsequent hit *Don't Mess With My Toot Toot* the following year, which earned him a Grammy. Immaculate Conception Church Cemetery, Lebeau, LA.

8433. Simmons, Al (Aloyisius Harry Szymanski, May 22, 1903–May 26, 1956) Star hitter with the Philadelphia A's 1924–1934 had a lifetime average of .334, hitting three runs July 15, 1932, known as Bucketfoot Al because of his unorthodox batting stance. A part of Connie Mack's dynasty 1929–31 with Grove, Cochrane and Foxx, the Duke of Milwaukee won batting titles in 1930 and '31. Hall of Fame 1953. Large rose granite monument with his picture and record on it. Sec. 17, block 7, lot 1, along the road, St. Adalbart's Cemetery, Milwaukee, WI.

8434. Simmons, Dick (Richard Simmons, Aug. 19, 1913–Jan. 11, 2003) Minnesota born actor, sometimes billed as Richard Simmons, in small roles in films from 1940, starred as *Sergeant Preston of the Yukon* on television from 1955. He died from Alzheimer's Disease in Oceanside, California, at 89. Alcove of Hope, sec. D, niche 40, Eternal Hills Memorial Park, Oceanside, CA.

8435. Simms, Ginny (Virginia Simms Eastvold, May 25, 1912–April 4, 1994) Vocalist with Kay Kyser's orchestra 1938–1941 appeared with the band in films including *That's Right, You're Wrong* (1939), *You'll Find Out* (1940), etc. She was later on radio and in several musical comedies with Abbott & Costello, Edgar Bergen, and others. By the 1960's she was involved in real estate dealings with her husband Don Eastvold. She died in Palm Springs at 81. Lutheran services and burial. Sec. B-33, lot 15. Desert Memorial Park, Cathedral City (Palm Springs), CA.

8436. Simms, Hilda (April 15, 1918–Feb. 6, 1994) New York stage actress from Minneapolis known for the title role in *Anna Lucasta*. In later years a social worker and drug counselor in Manhattan, she died in Buffalo at 75. Resurrection Cemetery, Mendota Heights (St. Paul), MN.

8437. Simon, Charlie May (Aug. 17, 1897–March 21, 1977) Children's author of twenty seven books, won the Albert Schweitzer Book Prize in 1958 for her study *A Seed Shall Serve*. Married to Pulitzer Prize winning poet John Gould Fletcher. Juniper 715/716, Mount Holly Cemetery, Little Rock, AR.

8438. Simon, Paul (Paul Martin Simon, Nov. 29, 1928–Dec. 9, 2003) Former newspaper owner at Troy, Illinois, Democratic representative from Illinois' 22nd and 24th Districts 1975–85 and Senator 1985–1997, unsuccessfully sought his party's nomination as President in 1987–88. Known for his trademark bow tie as well as his integrity, he died after heart surgery at 75 in Springfield, Illinois. Buried with his wife Jeanne Hurley Simon (1922–2000). Rowan Cemetery, Makanda, IL.

8439. Simon, Robert F. (Dec. 2, 1908–Nov. 29, 1992) Actor in films and TV of the 1950's–70's, in *Twilight Zone, Bewitched, Quincy* and *M.A.S.H.* (as General Mitchell). Sec. G, lot 10, grave 1, Oakwood Memorial Park, Chatsworth, CA.

8440. Simon, S. Sylvan (Samuel Sylvan Simon, March 9, 1910–May 17, 1951) Hollywood director at Universal and MGM (*Tish, Abbott and Costello in Hollywood, Bad Bascomb, The Fuller Brush Man*, AA nom. for *Born Yesterday* 1950), later a producer. Columbarium of Memory, niche 20174, Memorial Terrace, Great Mausoleum, Forest Lawn, Glendale, CA.

8441. Simon, Simone (April 23, 1910–Feb. 23, 2005) French actress born at Béthune and raised in Marseille, in films from 1931, showcased in Europe in Marc Allegret's *Lac aux Dames* (1934), as Severine in *La Bête Humaine* (1938), in Hollywood in *Seventh Heaven* (1937), *All That Money Can Buy* (*The Devil and Daniel Webster*, 1941), but best known as Irena Dubrovna in Val Lewton's *Cat People* (1942) and a benign version of the character's ghost in the sequel, *The Curse of the Cat People* (1944). After a few more films in America (*Mademoiselle Fifi* 1944) and Europe (in Max Ophuls' *La Ronde* 1950, and *Le Plaisir* 1952), she retired in 1956. Never married and blind in her last years, she died in Paris at 94. Square E, grave 8, (Cimétiere) Chateau Gombert, near Marseille, Bouches du Rhone.

8442. Simone, Nina (Eunice Kathleen Waymon, Feb. 21, 1933–April 21, 2003) Singer and pianist from Tyron, North Carolina, studied at Juilliard before turning to non academic performing in 1954. She recorded soul, jazz and standard ballads (*My Baby Just Cares For Me, I Put A Spell on You, Forbidden Fruit*), Broadway numbers (*I Loves You Porgy*, 1959), gospel, African folk, and her own songs of the struggle of Blacks in America, including *To Be Young, Gifted and Black* and *Mississippi Goddam*. Resentful of American racism, she moved to France before her final decade, increasingly known for her contempt, often for her own audiences. She died at Carry-le-Rouet in southern France, between Marseille and Aix-en-Provence. Funeral followed by cremation at Cimetiere Saint-Pierre, Marseille. Ashes scattered in Africa.

8443. Simpkins, Andy (April 29, 1932–June 2, 1999) Richmond, Indiana, native co-founded the jazz trio The Three Sounds and played bass with George Shearing, Sarah Vaughn and others, working on some 75 albums and his own, *Summer Strut* (1994). He died in Los Angeles at 67 of complications from stomach cancer. Ashes to his wife in Simi Valley, California, through Aftercare Cremation and Burial Society.

8444. Simpson, Ivan (Ivan Freebody Simpson, Feb. 4, 1875–Oct. 12, 1951) Lithe character actor long on stage and screen in supporting roles as butlers etc (*Disraeli, The Green Goddess, The Man Who Played God, The Phantom of Crestwood, The Mystery of Mr. X, Mark of the Vampire, Trouble For Two, Random Harvest,* dozens of others). He died at Lenox Hill Hospital in Manhattan. Service at the Little Church Around the Corner (Church of the Transfiguration). Actors Fund of America plot, Kensico Cemetery, Valhalla, NY.

8445. Simpson, Napoleon (Napoleon Bonaparte Simpson, May 11, 1902–June 27, 1967) Illinois born black actor in films of the 1930's and 40's (*One Hour to Live, The Great Lie, Drums of the Congo, The Mummy's Curse, The Red Menace*). Vista Del Monte Garden Mausoleum, column 55, crypt MA, Mountain View Cemetery, Altadena, CA.

8446. Simpson, Nicole Brown (May 19, 1959–June 12, 1994) Thirty five year old wife of O.J. Simpson, Heisman Trophy winner with the Buffalo Bills, NBC sports commentator and occasional actor. She was brutally murdered, her throat slit, outside her condominium on South Bundy Drive in the Brentwood section of Los Angeles on Sunday night June 12, 1994, along with twenty five year old **Ronald Lyle Goldman** (July 2, 1968–June 12, 1994), an aspiring actor and waiter. Reportedly there returning glasses she had left at a restaurant during dinner, his throat was also slit. From the beginning, the investigation focused on her husband as the killer. After attending her funeral mass with their two young children, he failed to turn himself in and led police on a slow speed chase prior to his arrest that began endless coverage by the national media, from the arraignment to his acquittal October 3, 1995. Nicole Brown Simpson was buried at Ascension Cemetery, Lake Forest (near El Toro), California, and Ronald Goldman in the Beth Olam section of Valley Oaks Memorial Park, Westlake Village, CA.

8447. Simpson, Russell (Russell McCaskell Simpson, Jan. 17, 1880–Dec. 12, 1959) Character actor in films most often as stubborn, stern or crafty country bumpkins, including *The Grapes of Wrath* (1940, as Pa Joad), *My Darling Clementine, Bad Bascomb* (1946), *Friendly Persuasion* (1956). Inspiration Slope, lot 246, grave 6A, Forest Lawn, Glendale, CA.

8448. Sinatra, Frank (Francis Albert Sinatra, Dec. 12, 1915–May 14, 1998) America's acknowledged master song interpreter and among the greatest all around entertainers, Old Blue Eyes, The Chairman of the Board, hailed from Hoboken, New Jersey, and gained fame with Tommy Dorsey's orchestra by 1939. The idol of bobby soxers during the war, his popularity waned with the 1940's and a throat hemorrhage in 1950 threatened to end his career, but the role of Maggio in *From Here to Eternity* (1953) earned him an Oscar and revitalized his career, as an actor. At the same time his association with Nelson Riddle, Capitol Records and the long playing album produced arguably his best work, with a more sophisticated vocal style in the tradition of Billie Holiday or Mabel Mercer. Evergreens include *One For the Road, In the Wee Small Hours of the Morning, Come Fly With Me, My Kind of Town, Love and Marriage, Young at Heart, High Hopes* and later on Reprise *Strangers in the Night, That's Life,* and his last signature numbers *New York, New York* and *My Way.* His film career flourished as well, in over fifty pictures through 1980, including *The Man With the Golden Arm* (1955), *Guys and Dolls, High Society* (1956), *Pal Joey* (1957), *Some Came Running* (1959), *The Manchurian Candidate* (1962), *Von Ryan's Express* (1965) and *The Detective* (1968). Added color was provided by his alleged mob ties and his so called Rat Pack — a term borrowed from Humphrey Bogart's earlier social circle — of drinking and carousing friends, primarily Dean Martin, Sammy Davis, Jr., Peter Lawford and Joey Bishop, the group featured in *Oceans Eleven* (1960), *Sergeants Three* (1961) and *Robin and the Seven Hoods* (1963) etc. Sinatra collapsed during a concert in Richmond, Virginia, in March 1994 and was in deteriorating health afterward, last seen in public in January 1997 when he suffered a coronary. He died at 82 in Cedars Sinai Medical Center, Los Angeles, after suffering a heart attack at 82 in his Beverly Hills home. Not only were flowers and tributes piled on his star on the Hollywood Walk of Fame and outside his gated estate, but around the star marking his birthplace in Hoboken. Ultimate tributes included the top of the Empire State Building lit up in blue, a moment of silence at Yankee Stadium, the strip going dark in Las Vegas, and the top of the Capitol Records Building in L.A. draped in black bunting, a first. A vigil was held May 19 and the private funeral mass held May 20 at the Church of the Good Shepherd in Beverly Hills. Private burial was with his parents. Marked by September, the simple epitaph is the title of one of his standards *The best is yet to come.* His father **Anthony Martin Sinatra** (1891–1969) was removed from Holy Name Cemetery in Jersey City, New Jersey, and reburied at Palm Springs to entice Sinatra's mother **Natalie "Dolly" Sinatra** (Dec. 25, 1894–Jan. 6, 1977) to move west with him. She died in a plane crash a few years later. Sec B-8, 148–151, Desert Memorial Park, Cathedral City (Palm Springs), CA.

8449. Sinclair, Gordon (Allen Gordon Sinclair, June 3, 1900–May 17, 1984) Canadian writer, journalist and broadcaster from Toronto whose fame in the United States rested on his editorial *The Americans,* which he broadcast June 5, 1973, in the wake of withdrawal from Vietnam and the midst of the Watergate scandal. He later recorded it. Sinclair died at 83 in Etobicoke, six miles from Toronto. Park Lawn Cemetery, Etobicoke, Toronto, Ontario.

8450. Sinclair, Harry (July 6, 1876–Nov. 10, 1956) Founder of the Sinclair Oil Co. in 1916 and part owner of the St. Louis Browns. During the Harding administration 1921–3 he was given a lease to search for oil on U.S. Navy lands held as oil reserves, the basis of the Teapot Dome scandal. Mausoleum, block 354, crypt E6, Calvary Cemetery, east Los Angeles.

8451. Sinclair, Madge (April 28, 1938–Dec. 20, 1995) Kingston, Jamaica, born school teacher turned actress appeared in *Conrack* (1974), as Bell in the TV miniseries *Roots*, several others including the voice of the Lion Queen in *The Lion King* (1994). She died from leukemia, which she had had 13 years, in L.A. at 57. Ashes to residence in Pasadena.

8452. Sinclair, Ronald (Jan. 21, 1924–Nov. 22, 1992) Actor in films as a child (including young Scrooge in *A Christmas Carol* 1938), died at Sagus, California. Ashes to residence in Sagus, reportedly to spread at New Zealand.

8453. Sinclair, Upton (Sept. 20, 1878–Nov. 25, 1968) Baltimore born writer and reformer of the Muckraking period best known for his work *The Jungle* (1906), a gripping expose of the working conditions in the Chicago stockyards. He later moved to California and continued to champion left wing causes such as EPIC (End Poverty in California). He died at Bound Brook, New Jersey. Service at St. Paul's Episcopal Church there. Sec. 17, lot 45, Rock Creek Cemetery, Washington, D.C.

8454. Singer, Isaac Bashevis (July 14, 1904–July 24, 1991) Polish born author chronicled the lives of ghetto Jews in Eastern Europe and Jewish immigrants in America. He wrote entirely in Yiddish, his frankly sexual and often grim works not translated to English until the 1950's. Nobel Prize in Literature 1978 for his body of work including *Yentl the Yeshiva Boy*. He died in a Miami nursing home at 87. Epitaph notes *His greatest joy was work*. Block 10, lot 429, grave 2, Beth El Cemetery, Paramus, NJ.

8455. "The Singing Nun" (Jeanne Deckers/Souer Sourire aka Sister Luc Gabrielle, Oct. 17, 1933–March 31, 1985) Dominican nun at Fichemont Convent, Waterloo, Belgium, had a hit recording with *Dominique* (1963). She changed her name to Luc Dominique in 1967 and was increasingly outspoken in her criticism of church doctrine, leaving the convent by 1968. When she and her companion Anne Pecher, by then running a children's school in Wavre, were pressed by the Belgian government for $63,000 in back taxes for money earned during her singing career — which she had donated to the convent, they committed double suicide with sedatives in their home. Dark monument inscribed *Jai vu volver son amel A Travers les Nuages* curves around the head of their slab, bearing a white cross, in the town cemetery at Wavre, Belgium.

8456. Singleton, Penny (Dorothy McNulty, Sept. 15, 1908–Nov. 12, 2003) Philadelphia born actress on Broadway in the late 1920's and in films from 1930, played fuzzy brained Blondie Bumstead to Arthur Lake's Dagwood in over twenty-five films at Columbia based on the Chic Young comic strip, beginning with *Blondie* (1938) and running until 1950. She later appeared in *The Best Man* (1964) and was the voice of Jane Jetson in *The Jetsons* from 1962. Her second husband, Robert Sparks, died in 1963, forty years before her death at 95 in Sherman Oaks. Service at St. Francis de Sales Church there. Unmarked beside June E. Flin McNulty (marked). Sec. C, lot 349, grave 5, San Fernando Mission Cemetery, Mission Hills, CA.

8457. Singstad, Ole (June 29, 1882–Dec. 8, 1969) Norwegian engineer built the Holland Tunnel 1925–28 under the Hudson River, connecting New Jersey with Manhattan. Sec. 130, lot 37084, Greenwood Cemetery, Brooklyn, N.Y.C.

8458. Siodmak, Curt (Aug. 10, 1902–Sept. 2, 2000) Screenwriter, novelist and occasional director from Dresden, Germany, the younger brother of director Robert Siodmak. He wrote film scripts in Germany 1928–1935 before coming to Hollywood and turning out several evergreen horror-fantasy tales, including *The Invisible Man Returns, Black Friday, The Wolf-Man, Invisible Agent, Frankenstein meets the Wolf-Man, Son of Dracula* (co written with Eric Taylor), *I Walked With A Zombie, House of Frankenstein, The Lady and The Monster, The Climax, The Beast With Five Fingers* and *Donovan's Brain* (1953, from his novel of the same name, and his best known story other than *The Wolf Man*). He was a longtime resident of Three Rivers, Tulare County, California, where he died at 98, survived by Henrietta, his wife of over seventy years. His autobiography, *Wolf-Man's Maker*, was published posthumously in early 2001. Cremated with no services through Miller Memorial Chapel in Visalia, his son took the ashes to their home, to be buried with Siodmak's wife, upon her death, where a marker was already in place. Three Rivers Public Cemetery, Three Rivers, CA.

8459. Siodmak, Robert (Aug. 8, 1900–March 10, 1973) Dresden born (not Memphis as he claimed — his father had lived there a decade before) German director and brother of writer Curt Siodmak, considered a master of film noir with his U.S. films 1943–1949, including *Son of Dracula, The Suspect, Phantom Lady, The Strange Affair of Uncle Harry, The Spiral Staircase, The Killers, The Dark Mirror, Cry of the City, Criss Cross*, and *The File on Thelma Jordan*. He returned to Germany after 1953, directing *Die Ratten* (1955), *Nachts wenn der Teufel kam* (1957) and otherwise less notable films until 1968, living out his days with his wife on the shore of Lake Maggiore at Ascona, Switzerland, near the Italian border. He died from a heart attack at 72 in Locarno just weeks after his wife's death. She was cremated January 22 and he on March 13 at Crematorio Obitorio Communale, Bellinzona, Locarno, at a ceremony at the crematory attended by his brother Curt. The urns are no longer there, and there is no record of them in the Ascona cemeteries, according to the town council and Cultura-Ascona. Herve Dumont at the Swiss Film Archive was told by Curt Siodmak that his brother's ashes were mixed with those of his wife Babs (Bertha). If not buried in the cemetery, they were likely buried on their property or over Lake Maggiore, Ascona, Switzerland.

8460. Sir Lancelot *see* **Lancelot.**

8461. Sirica, John (John Joseph Sirica, March 19, 1904–Aug. 14, 1992) Federal judge presided over the Watergate hearings 1973–74, ordering President Nixon to turn over the White House tapes to the House Judiciary Committee considering impeachment, which eventually forced his resignation. Sirica died at 88 in a Washington, D.C. hospital. Sec. CGIV, lot 227, Gate of Heaven Cemetery, Silver Spring, MD.

8462. Sirk, Douglas (Claus Detlev Sierk, April 26, 1900–Jan. 14, 1987) Danish born stage and film director in Germany until 1937. American films include *Hitler's Madman* (1943), *Summer Storm* (1944), *Sleep My Love* (1948), *Magnificent Obsession* (1954) and *Imitation of Life* (1959). He retired in 1959 and settled for many years in Munich prior to his death at 86 in Lugano, Switzerland. Ashes interred in a crypt with his wife Hildegard in the cemetery at Castagnola/Lugano, Switzerland.

8463. Siskel, Gene (Eugene Kal Siskel, Jan. 26, 1946–Feb. 20, 1999) Chicago native and Yale graduate, the film critic for the *Chicago Tribune* from September 1969 was known for his pairing and contentious debates with *Chicago Sun Times* critic Roger Ebert, beginning in 1975, moving to PBS in 1978 and expanded to commercial stations in 1982. Their weekly reviews, popularizing "two thumbs up" (or down), lasted 24 years, until just before Siskel's death at 53 from a brain tumor in Evanston Hospital. He had undergone surgery the previous May but had returned to the program with Ebert and continued his column at the *Tribune*. Funeral at North Suburban Synagogue Beth-El, Highland Park, with private burial. Bronze flat headstone with the epitaph *Blessed is one who lived with a good name.* Memorial sec., street marker 22–24 and 17 back from Gloria Loden Martin marker, Westlawn Cemetery, Norridge, (Chicago), IL.

8464. Sisler, Dick (Richard Allen Sisler, Nov. 2, 1920–Nov. 20, 1998) First baseman and outfielder for the St. Louis Cardinals 1946–8, the Phillies as an outfielder 1948–52 and one of the 1950 Whiz Kids, with the Reds briefly in early 1952 and back with the Cardinals 1952–3. The son of Hall of Famer George Sisler, he had a .275 batting average, coached several National League teams and helmed the Cincinnati Reds in 1964 and '65. Cross Mausoleum, first floor, 57-B, Woodlawn Memorial Park, Nashville, TN.

8465. Sisler, George (March 24, 1893–March 26, 1973) First baseman for the St. Louis Browns, later with the Senators and the Braves, pitched, hit and fielded with skill 1915–1930, reaching a .341 average. Record for the most hits in a season with 257 in 1920. Gorgeous George, or the Sizzler, was among the original group inducted into the Hall of Fame (1939).

Buried originally at Oak Grove Cemetery, St. Louis, Missouri, the ashes were removed in 1990 and placed in a niche at the historic Des Peres (Old) Presbyterian Church Cemetery, Clayton near Geyer Road, Frontenac, St. Louis, MO.

8466. Sissle, Noble (July 10, 1889–Dec. 17, 1975) Song writer long in association with Eubie Blake. At their peak in the 1920's, they wrote *(I'm Just) Wild About Harry* and *You Were Meant For Me* as well as the Broadway revues *Shuffle Along* and *Chocolate Dandies.* Sissle, also an orchestra leader, was the unofficial mayor of Harlem, succeeding Bill Robinson in 1949, concerning himself with civic improvements and with homeless boys from the state school at Warwick. He died in Tampa at 86. Service at St. Mark's United Methodist Church at 55 Edgecombe Ave. in Harlem. Sec. L, grave 23323-A, Long Island National Cemetery, Farmingdale, Long Island, NY.

8467. Sitka, Emil (Emil Josef Sitka, Dec. 22, 1914–Jan. 16, 1998) Actor known for his Three Stooges shorts from 1947 managed to appear with all of them, including Curly (in his last two reeler) and all three of his replacements. He died at 83 in Camarillo, California. Best known as the justice of the peace in the Stooges' *Brideless Groom* (1947), his epitaph is taken from the short's wedding scene, his notoriously inappropriate (and hilarious) line *Hold hands, you lovebirds.* The plaque also has the notation *He danced all the way.* Santa Cruz lot 139, Conejo Mountain Memorial Park, Camarillo, CA.

8468. Sitting Bull (Tatanka Iyotake, 1831–Dec. 15, 1890) After defeating Custer and the 7th Cavalry at Little Big Horn, the Chief of the Sioux was exiled to Canada until the Sioux were returned to South Dakota. When he ordered his warriors to resist arrest, he was shot in the back of the head, after which the Sioux were massacred at Wounded Knee. The chief's remains were removed to Fort Yates, North Dakota, where a boulder with a plaque still marks the grave. When a dam was slated to cover the area in water in the 1960's, and after unsuccessful petitioning, the bones were secretly removed without authorization (though this is disputed by some) by his nephew Grey Eagle on April 8, 1953 and reburied on a bluff near the site where he died, marked by a monument and bust of him, at Mobridge, SD.

8469. Sjostrom, Victor *see* **Seastrom.**

8470. Skaggs, Jimmie (Dec. 20, 1944–July 6, 2004) Actor from Hot Springs, Arkansas, raised in Elyria, Ohio, in films (*Lethal Weapon, Catch Me if You Can*) and television (*Monk*) from the 1970's. He died in Highland Park, California, from lung cancer at 59, survived by his wife, Virginia Morris. Cremated through Forest Lawn, Glendale. Ashes to his Highland Park residence.

8471. Skakel, Rushton, Sr. (Oct. 5, 1923–Jan. 2, 2003) Business executive, brother of Ethel Kennedy, and father of Michael Skakel, convicted in 2002 of having killed fifteen year old Martha Moxley in 1975.

Skakel, Sr. suffered from frontal lobe dementia upon his death at 79 in Hope Sound, Florida. St. Mary's Cemetery, Greenwich, CT.

8472. Skelly, Hal (May 31, 1891–June 16, 1934) Dancer had been with the circus and light opera before joining Dockstader's Minstrels and subsequently appearing on Broadway in *Fidler's Tree* (1918) and *Burlesque*, filmed as *Dance of Life*. Skelly died when the car in which he was riding was hit by a train at a crossing. Old Block 6, lot 110A, Mt. Calvary Cemetery, Davenport, IA.

8473. Skelton, Red (Richard Bernard Skelton, July 18, 1913–Sept. 17, 1997) Red headed comedian from Vincennes, Indiana, in films from 1941, known for his TV show 1951–71and his down-and-out tender hearted characters including Freddie the Freeloader and Clem Kadiddlehopper. He died in Rancho Mirage at 84. **Richard Skelton, Jr.,** his son, died from leukemia May 10, 1958, ten days before his 10th birthday. Skelton's wife, **Georgia Davis Skelton** (born Sept. 17, 1922), was a suicide on the eighteenth anniversary of their son's death. Family room, left side, Sanctuary of Benediction, Memorial Terrace, Great Mausoleum, Forest Lawn, Glendale, CA.

8474. Skinner, B.F. (Burrhus Frederic Skinner, March 20 1904–Aug 18 1990) Primary psychologist of the 20th century at Harvard, espoused the theory of modification of behavior to create happiness in *Walden Two* (1948). He was ridiculed for his Skinner Boxes in which rats or pigeons were taught through repetition to push levers, play a sort of ping pong, etc. Resigned to death while ill with leukemia, Skinner said that he regretted being remembered only for his cold and often amusing research. He added what his daughter said she most remembered about him was his talking to her and tucking her in as a child, often taking her hand with tears in his eyes. "I'd hate," he added (to have people remember only) "he's the man who taught pigeons to play ping pong." Ashes buried beneath a flush plaque. Willow Pond sec., Mt. Auburn Cemetery, Cambridge, MA.

8475. Skinner, Cornelia Otis (May 30, 1899–July 9, 1979) Author of *Our Hearts Were Young and Gay* and other novels, plays and screenplays. Stage actress in selected films, including *The Uninvited* (1944, as Miss Holloway). Daughter of stage great Otis Skinner. The wife of Alden Sanford Blodget, she died from a stroke in New York. Ashes buried along Walnut Ave., lot 816, Oak Grove Cemetery, Fall River, MA.

8476. Skinner, Edna (May 23, 1921–Aug. 8, 2003) Actress from Washington, D.C., played Maggie on TV's *Topper* (1954–55) and Kay Addison on *Mr. Ed* (1961–63). Films include *The Long Long Trailer* and *Friendly Persuasion*. Retired from acting in 1964 and a champion angler, she wrote for fishing and related sports magazines prior to her death in North Bend, Oregon. Ashes scattered at sea.

8477. Skinner, Frank (Frank Chester Skinner, Dec. 31, 1897–Oct. 9, 1968) Composer from Mere-

dosia, Illinois, at Universal from 1937 (*Destry Rides Again, Son of Frankenstein, Tower of London, The Egg and I, The Suspect, Abbott & Costello Meet Frankenstein, Man of A Thousand Faces*). He died in Los Angeles at 70. The bandstand in his home town is dedicated to his memory. Oakland Cemetery, Meredosia, IL.

8478. Skinner, Otis (June 28, 1858–Jan. 4, 1942) Dean of American stage actors of his era known for *Othello* and as the beggar Haj in *Kismet, The Honor of the Family* and *A Hundred Years Old*. President of the Episcopal Actors Guild and Vice President of the Players Club. His wife, actress **Maud Skinner**, died in 1936. He died in New York at 83 and was buried with his wife beneath a family monument and two flush stones, next to a wooded area, in the town where they had their summer home. River Street Cemetery, Woodstock, VT.

8479. Skipworth, Alison (Alison Groom, July 25, 1863–July 5, 1952) Portly London born actress and comedienne long on the stage and screen as haughty, affected matrons, in *Outward Bound* (1930), *If I Had a Million* (1932), *Satan Met a Lady* (1936, a gender altered *Maltese Falcon*) etc. She died at her home, 202 Riverside Drive in Manhattan, leaving no survivors. Actors Fund of America plot, Kensico Cemetery, Valhalla, NY.

8480. Skolsky, Sidney (May 5, 1905–May 3, 1983) Hollywood columnist. Epitaph (from his book) is *Don't Get Me Wrong. I Loved Hollywood*. Maimonides 2, lot 9840, Mt. Sinai Memorial Park, Los Angeles.

8481. Skouras, Spyros (March 28, 1893–Aug. 16, 1971) Greek film executive took over 20th Century Fox in 1935, best known for developing Cinemascope in the 50's. He died in Mamaroneck, Long Island. Plot marked by a statue of Mary holding the dying body of Christ. Sec. 10, lot 93, Gate of Heaven Cemetery, Hawthorne, NY.

8482. Slaton, John Marshall (Dec. 25, 1866–Jan. 11, 1955) Governor of Georgia pressured into reexamining Leo Frank's conviction in the 1913 Mary Phagan murder case examined the evidence himself and commuted Frank's death sentence to life in June 1915, destroying his own chances for the senate. Two thousand years before, he said, a governor had thrown a Jew to a mob and he would not repeat the act. The death of his wife, a descendant of Gov. and Sen. James Jackson, in February 1945, made the *New York Times*, but his death a decade later did not. Grant mausoleum, block 57, Oakland Cemetery, Atlanta, GA.

8483. Slattery, Richard X. (June 26, 1925–Jan. 27, 1997) Actor in tough roles in TV's *The Gallant Men, Mr. Roberts, CPO Sharkey*, etc. Service at Pierce Brothers Valhalla mortuary, North Hollywood, California. Ashes to family, reportedly to be scattered at sea.

8484. Slaughter, Enos "Country" (April 27, 1916–Aug. 12, 2002) Right fielder and clutch hitter with St. Louis 1938–1953 batted .300 in nineteen seasons, thirteen with the Cardinals; he played in ten consecutive all star games and had his best year in 1946, when he hit .391 and led the N.L in RBIs with 130, as well as his Mad Dash in game seven of the World Series, when he hit a single, then managed to make it safely home for the winning run on a ball hit by Harry Walker. His spiking of Jackie Robinson in a close play at first base in August 1947 fed the image of the Cardinals and Slaughter in particular as opposing the integration of baseball. Until his death, he insisted he was pictured that way in the press "because I was a southern boy" and his being painted as opposing Robinson's inclusion was "a lot of baloney," though it allegedly delayed his election to the Hall of Fame from his eligibility in 1964 until 1985 He died at 86 in Duke University Medical Center, Durham, North Carolina. Black monument with him swinging away on the front, and a bat with cardinals on the back. Allensville United Methodist Church Cemetery, Denny's Store/Dirgie Mine Road, Allensville, east of Roxboro, NC.

8485. Slaughter, Frank G. (Feb. 25, 1908–May 17, 2001) Best selling novelist and doctor wrote 56 books, most revolving around medicine, beginning in 1941 with *That None Should Die* about socialized medicine and never out of print, and ending with *No Greater Love* in 1984. He died in Jacksonville, Florida, at 93. Evergreen Burial Park, Roanoke, VA.

8486. Slayton, Deke (Donald K. Slayton, March 1, 1924–June 13, 1993) One of the original Mercury Seven astronauts, from 1959, was scheduled to fly the second Mercury orbital mission but was grounded by an irregular heartbeat. He stayed with NASA as a supervisor, flew on the Apollo-Soyuz Test Program with Russia in 1975, and oversaw the space shuttle program until his retirement in 1982. He died from cancer at his home at League City, Texas, at 69. His ashes were scattered in three places: on his family farm at Leon, Wisconsin, six miles from his birthplace at Sparta; over the family plots at Leon Valley Cemetery, and in Texas.

8487. Slezak, Walter (May 3, 1902–April 22, 1983) Vienna born former romantic lead in Germany was the son of German actor, tenor and comedian **Leo Slezak** (Aug. 18, 1872–June 6, 1946). In America from 1930, in films from 1942, often as crafty Nazis or German agents (*Lifeboat, Farewell My Lovely, The Inspector General*). In 1955 he won the Tony and New York Drama Critics Award in the Broadway musical *Fanny* and in 1957 sang in *The Gypsy Baron* at the Met. Ill with a heart ailment, he killed himself with a .38 in his home at Flower Hill, Long Island, N.Y. Mass at St. Malachy's Church in Manhattan. Cremated by the Long Island Crematory at Babylon, New York, the ashes were returned through Fairchild mortuary in Manhasset, Long Island, for burial with his parents. Monument with bust in the Catholic village cemetery at Rotach-Egern, Bavaria, Germany.

8488. Sloan, Alfred P. (May 23, 1875–Feb. 17, 1966) President of General Motors from 1923 immensely boosted the auto industry and spent a vast sum in philanthropy including the Sloan-Kettering Cancer Research Fund, hospital and research center. Flat slab in separated lot, St. John's Memorial Cemetery, Cold Spring Harbor, Long Island, NY.

8489. Sloan, Norm (June 25, 1926–Dec. 9, 2003) Indiana four sport athlete graduated from Lawrence Central in 1944, went on to coach at Florida 1960–66, and led North Carolina State's Wolfpack for fourteen seasons to the NCAA title in 1974, but left in 1980 to coach the Florida Gators for nine seasons, amid scandals and probation, until 1989. He died of pulmonary fibrosis in Duke Hospital at 77. Cremated through Brown-Wynne mortuary, Raleigh. Ashes to family.

8490. Sloane, A. Baldwin (Aug. 28, 1872–Feb. 21, 1926) Prolific turn-of-the-century songwriter wrote *When You Ain't Got No More Money well You Needn't Come Round* (1888, lyrics by Clarence Brewster) for May Irwin, *Heaven Will Protect the Working Girl* (1903), *On the Boardwalk* (1910), several others. He died from acute alcoholism. Sec. 6, grave 71, Fairview Cemetery, Middletown, NJ.

8491. Sloane, Everett (Oct. 1, 1909–Aug. 6, 1965) Character actor from Orson Welles' Mercury Theatre in *Citizen Kane* (1941), *The Lady From Shanghai* (1948), in Rod Serling's *Patterns* (1956), many others and much on TV (*Twilight Zone* episode *The Fever*). He was losing his eyesight when he died from an overdose of sleeping pills, a suicide, in his west L.A. home. Niche in mausoleum, FNW-122, Rosedale Cemetery, Los Angeles.

8492. Sloane, Florence Adele (Florence Adele Sloane Burden Tobin, 1873–Jan. 10, 1960) New York City socialite and diarist, granddaughter of William Henry Vanderbilt, son of the commodore. Her diaries from 1892–1896 were excerpted and published by her granddaughter's husband, Louis Auchincloss, as *Maverick in Mauve*, a first hand portrait of the Gilded Age and turn of the century elitist life. Though she had always lived in New York City, her first husband James Burden's family, and their ironworks, had been at Troy, where she was buried. Burden plot, Oakwood Cemetery, Troy, NY.

8493. *General Slocum* Disaster (Victims) The *General Slocum* was an excursion steamer carrying a boat load of passengers for a Sunday outing from East Third in Manhattan to Locust Grove, Long Island, on June 14, 1904. They never reached their destination, as the boat caught fire and burned at North Brother Island in the East River, with 1,031 fatalities. A monument was later erected in the Brooklyn City Grounds section of the Cemetery of the Evergreens, Brooklyn, and a large one unveiled June 15, 1905 where 61 unidentified, and some 200 of the victims, were buried at the Lutheran Cemetery (now All Faiths Lutheran Cemetery), several blocks east of Linden Hill Cemetery, Maspeth/Ridgewood, Queens, NYC.

8494. Slovak, Hillel (April 13, 1962–June 25, 1988) Original member of the Red Hot Chili Peppers. Guitar engraved on plaque. Maimonides 6, lot 4613, Mt. Sinai Memorial Park, Los Angeles.

8495. Slovik, Eddie (Feb. 18, 1920–Jan. 31, 1945) The only American soldier executed for desertion during World War II was buried at Oisne-Aisne American Cemetery in France unmarked. Until her death in 1979 his wife attempted to have him returned to Detroit. The reburial finally took place privately beside his wife's grave on December 6, 1987. On her marker is inscribed *Compassion and justice unto this moment unfulfilled*. His reads *Honor and Justice Prevailed*. Ferndale sec., approximately 25 feet in, near right rear corner area, Woodmere Cemetery, Detroit, MI.

8496. Smalley, Phillips (Aug. 7, 1865–May 2, 1939) Actor in films from 1909 with his then wife Lois Weber in Rex Productions, later directed (and with Weber) before moving to supporting film roles. His ashes were kept until the death of his last wife in 1965, when they were inurned in the Columbarium of Remembrance (right), niche 60750, Courts of Remembrance, Forest Lawn Hollywood Hills, Los Angeles.

8497. Smalls, Robert (April 5, 1839–Feb. 22, 1915) Slave delivered the gunboat Planter from Charleston to Union forces. South Carolina representative 1875–87. Historical marker and bust near grave. Tabernacle Baptist Church Cemetery, Beaufort, SC.

8498. Smart, Gregory (Sept. 4, 1965–Aug. 1, 1990) Twenty-four year old Derry, New Hampshire, insurance agent whose wife of less than a year, Pamela, a media director at the high school in nearby Hampton, conspired with her fifteen year old student and lover, Billy Flynn, to murder her husband, shooting him with a handgun execution style as he entered their condominium. The case produced a sensational murder trial, later the basis for the obligatory TV movie. She was sentenced to life without parole. Forest Hill Cemetery, East Derry, NH.

8499. Smith, Adam (June 5, 1723–July 17, 1790) Scottish philosopher and economist often called the father of modern economics, published his masterwork *An Inquiry into the Nature and Causes of the Wealth of Nations* (1776), of immense long term influence and a basis in part for varying laissez-faire practices hence. Canongate churchyard, Edinburgh.

8500. Smith, Alexis (Gladys Smith, June 8, 1921–June 9, 1993) Actress from Penticton, British Columbia, in films primarily at Warner Brothers in the 1940's generally as cool and aloof beauties, in *The Adventures of Mark Twain, The Horn Blows at Midnight, Conflict, Night and* Day, *The Two Mrs. Carrolls, The Woman in White*, etc. In 1971 she starred on Broadway in Stephen Sondheim's musical *Follies* and won a Tony Award. Married from 1944 to actor Craig Stevens, she died in Los Angeles from cancer a day after her 72nd birthday. Cremated by the Neptune Society. Ashes buried at sea June 17 three miles off San Pedro, CA.

8501. Smith, Alfred E. (Dec. 30, 1873–Oct. 5, 1944) Irish Catholic governor of New York 1919–1928 with one term out was a colorful figure, known for his jaunty brown derby and his adopted song *The Sidewalks of New York*. Dubbed the Happy Warrior, he was the Democratic candidate for the presidency in 1928, defeated by Hoover in large part because of his Irish Catholicism. Stone marked Smith-Glynn. Sec. 45, lot 10, (1st) Calvary Cemetery, Woodside, Queens, N.Y.C.

8502. Smith, Andrew (c. 1836–Oct. 29, 1895) and **William** (July 1, 1830–Nov. 15, 1913) The cough drop manufacturing Smith Brothers from Poughkeepsie, whose pictures have graced their boxes of cough drops for a century, and frequently mis-identified them as Trade and Mark. Andrew is in sec. F, William in sec. 13, Poughkeepsie Rural Cemetery, Poughkeepsie, NY.

8503. Smith, Art (Arthur Gordon Smith, March 23, 1899–Feb. 24, 1973) Actor on Broadway and with New York's Group Theater acclaimed in Clifford Odets' *Rocket to the Moon,* for which he won the New York Critics Award. He also appeared in the Group Theater's documentary *Native Land*, narrated by Paul Robeson. His many films include *South Sea Sinner, Red Hot and Blue, Brute Force* (1947, as Dr. Walters), *In a Lonely Place* (1950, as Bogart's agent Mel). Blacklisted for his political affiliations, he made no films for a decade after 1952. He died of a heart attack at 73 in a nursing home at West Babylon, Long Island, New York. Ashes to family.

8504. Smith, Bessie (April 15, 1894–Sept. 26, 1937) Blues singer of the 1920's whose growling, earthy tones have grown more popular with time and earned her the title Queen of the Blues. She was injured when the car in which she was riding crashed into the back of a truck on route 61 near Clarksdale, Mississippi. Denied admission to a hospital that accepted whites only, the delay in transporting her to a free ward contributed to her death from increased loss of blood. Her grave just outside Philadelphia was unmarked until July 1970, when a stone was erected, half of it paid for by blues-rock singer Janis Joplin. Inscribed *The greatest blues singer in the world will never stop singing*. Though the stone lists her birth as 1895, most sources give 1894. Fifty feet from road, sec. C, lot 12, range 26, Mt. Lawn Cemetery, Sharon Hill (Darby Township), PA.

8505. Smith, Betty (Dec. 15, 1896–Jan. 17, 1972) Author of *A Tree Grows in Brooklyn*, based in part on her childhood in Brooklyn. She lived at Chapel Hill, North Carolina. Married name Finch. Sec. B-73-D, (New) Chapel Hill Memorial Cemetery, Chapel Hill, NC.

8506. Smith, C. Aubrey (Charles Aubrey Smith, July 21, 1863–Dec. 20, 1948) Knighted (1944) most English of Englishmen in Hollywood's so-called British Colony of the 1930's and 40's in countless roles as crusty, kindly, authoritative parts, as soldiers, judges, uncles, grandfathers, ministers, etc (*Tarzan* the Ape Man, Bombshell, Queen Christina, Morning Glory, Lives of A Bengal Lancer, The Florentine Dagger, China Seas, Little Lord Fauntleroy, Wee Willie Winkie, Rebecca, Waterloo Bridge 1940, Dr. Jekyll & Mr. Hyde 1941, Flesh and Fantasy, The White Cliffs of Dover, And Then There Were None, many others). He sponsored the British Hollywood Cricket team and other pro–English causes in Los Angeles, where he died from heart failure at 85. Cremated at Chapel of the Pines Crematory. Ashes returned nine months later in September 1949 for burial in his mother's grave in the family plot. The slab over the graves has his name and dates with the epitaph taken from Lincoln's second inaugural *With malice toward none. With charity for all.* St. Leonard's Churchyard, Hove, Sussex.

8507. Smith, Caleb Blood (April 16, 1808–Jan. 7, 1864) Lincoln's Secretary of the Interior 1861–63, former Indiana state legislator, Speaker of the House and Senator, was replaced in the cabinet two years into Lincoln's first term. He died the next year and was to be buried in a mausoleum to be constructed at Crown Hill Cemetery, Indianapolis. His widow Elizabeth bought the plot at the original sale of lots there June 8, 1864, and the mausoleum was the first one constructed in Crown Hill. He was buried in Greenlawn Cemetery, Indianapolis, until the late 1860's, when he was removed from Greenlawn (formerly the major city cemetery), but his whereabouts once he was disinterred from Greenlawn remain a mystery. His wife did not put him in the mausoleum in Crown Hill, though it has his name over the door; *she* was entombed there in 1878, along with a daughter and son. Caleb Smith's family were in the City Cemetery at Connersville, Indiana, where a sign states that he is believed to be buried there in an unmarked grave, never located. The reasons for the secrecy and confusion were never determined.

8508. Smith, Charles (Sept. 12, 1920–Dec. 26, 1988) Thin, gangling actor from Flint, Michigan, cast in many bit to supporting roles — usually as wide eyed innocents — in films from 1939, including *The Shop Around the Corner* (1940, as Rudy), the leader of the jive talking teens in *Yankee Doodle Dandy*, a memorable scene as Sanderson, the homesick G.I. in *A Guy Named Joe* (1943), as Dizzy Stevens in the *Henry Aldrich* series 1941–44, many others. He died in Burbank from a heart attack at 68. Cremated January 10 at Pierce Bros. Chapel of the Pines, Los Angeles. Ashes buried in the channel between Long Beach and Catalina.

8509. Smith, Cheryl "Rainbeaux" (June 6, 1955–Oct. 25, 2002) Actress whose stage nickname reportedly came from her frequent presence around the Rainbow Room in Los Angeles as a teen. She appeared in a long string of cheerleader, prison and horror films, several minor cult favorites from the early 1970s to 1984: *Phantom of the Paradise, The Swinging Cheerleaders, Farewell My Lovely, Revenge of the Cheerleaders, Massacre at Central High, The Choirboys, Melvin*

and Howard, Independence Day. Addicted to heroin from the mid 1970's, she died from complications of hepatitis at 47. Service and interment November 9. Acacia, lot 9826, space 3, Forest Lawn, Glendale, CA.

8510. Smith, Hal (Harold John Smith, Aug. 24, 1916–Jan. 28, 1994) Actor best known as Mayberry's happy drunk Otis Campbell on *The Andy Griffith Show* 1960–68. He died in Santa Monica at 77. Basement level, first row of crypts; Eternal Light 8, 10-J, Woodlawn Cemetery mausoleum, Santa Monica, CA.

8511. Smith, Hilton (Feb. 27, 1907–Nov. 18, 1983) Negro Leagues great from Giddings, Texas played from 1931, joining the Kansas City Monarchs in 1935 and was one of their top pitchers, winning twenty or more games in each of his twelve years with the team, including a 93–11 record consecutively from 1939 to 1942. A member of seven Monarch pennant winners and the 1942 world championship team, he often relieved the flamboyant Satchel Paige. In his later years he was a scout for the Chicago Cubs prior to his death in Kansas City at 76. Hall of Fame 2001. Block 25, lot 67, space 19, Mt. Moriah Cemetery, Holmes Rd., Kansas City, MO.

8512. Smith, Howard I. (Aug. 12, 1893–Jan. 10, 1968) Actor from Attleboro, Massachusetts, in films and TV often as jowl faced blowhards (*Kiss of Death, Call Northside 777* 1947, *I Bury the Living, Touch of Evil* 1958, *Murder, Inc.* 1960, *Twilight Zone* episode *A Stop at Willoughby* 1960). He died in Hollywood from a heart attack at 74. Actors Fund of America plot, Kensico Cemetery, Valhalla, NY.

8513. Smith, Howard K. (Howard Kingsbury Smith, May 12, 1914–Feb. 15, 2002) Newscaster from World War II reported from 1941 in Europe with Edward R. Murrow's group, remaining with CBS in Europe and the Middle East until 1957. He moderated the landmark 1960 presidential debate between Kennedy and Nixon and narrated a 1961 documentary *Who Speaks for Birmingham?*, in which he quoted Edmund Burke's warning "All that is necessary for the triumph of evil is for good men to do nothing." He moved to ABC shortly after, as correspondent, anchor, and co-anchor (with Frank Reynolds) of the *Evening News* until 1975, then served until 1979 as a commentator, when he retired. He died at 87 from pneumonia and congestive heart failure at his Bethesda, Maryland, home. Handled through Devol's mortuary in Georgetown. Oak Hill Cemetery, Georgetown, Washington, D.C.

8514. Smith, Jack *see* **Whispering Jack Smith.**

8515. Smith, James (Sept. 8, 1719–July 11, 1806) Irish born Pennsylvania judge, iron manufacturer and militia leader signed the Declaration of Independence from Pennsylvania. First Presbyterian Church Cemetery, York, PA.

8516. Smith, Jefferson "Soapy" (c. 1860–July 8, 1898) Con man and outlaw whose stay in Skagway, Alaska, was cut short by a vigilante committee. As burial honors, a pea and three shells were tossed into the grave after he had been shot and killed. Skagway town cemetery, Skagway (north of Juneau), AK.

8517. Smith, Jess W. (1872–May 30, 1923) Close friend of Attorney General Harry Daugherty from Washington Court House, Ohio, went to Washington with him in the Harding administration and was placed in charge of veterans' affairs. After two years of selling liquor permits and accepting various kickbacks, Smith shot himself in a Washington hotel room just months before the Teapot Dome and related administration scandals were about to break. Stone grave length slab, sec. 4, Washington Court House Cemetery, Washington Court House, OH.

8518. Smith, Jimmy (Dec. 8, 1928–Feb. 8, 2005) The Emperor of the Hammond B-3 made the electric organ a mainstream of jazz, beginning in the 1955 with his first trio, first in the Philadelphia area, moving to New York in 1956 at the Club Bohemia and Birdland. His recordings on Verve and Blue Note include *Groovin at Small's Paradise*, *The Cat*, some numbers with Wes Montgomery, and his 1965 rendition of *Got My Mojo Workin'*. He died in Phoenix at 76. Reynolds sec., lot 264, grave 6, Merion Cemetery, Bala Cynwyd, PA.

8519. Smith, John (c. 1580–June 21, 1631) English explorer, head of colonial Jamestown, Virginia, where his statue looks out to sea toward England. He returned there, and was buried at the Church of the Holy Sepulchre without Newgate, Holborn, London.

8520. Smith, Joseph (Dec. 23, 1805–June 27, 1844) Mormon founder and reported prophet from Palmyra, New York, began the Church of Jesus Christ of Latter Day Saints in 1830 after claiming to be shown gold plates buried in the woods which he translated to the Book of Mormon. The Mormons moved west to Nauvoo, Illinois, on the Mississippi. In 1844 he and his brother **Hyrum** were in jail at nearby Carthage for practicing polygamy. They were supposedly under protection from angry townspeople but were shot and killed by a mob which stormed the jail. A man was supposedly preparing to behead Joseph Smith when storm clouds parted and a ray of sun broke through, at which point the mob dispersed. After being hidden two other places, Joseph and Hyrum were found one hundred feet from the Mississippi in January 1928 and reburied atop the bank beside Joseph's legal wife **Emma**. The slab covering the graves is surrounded by an iron fence and the stone sculptures of the sun face are placed near by. Joseph Smith Historic Site, overlooking the Mississippi at Nauvoo, IL.

8521. Smith, Joseph (Nov. 6, 1832–Dec. 10, 1914) Son of the founder of the Mormon Church stopped on the trek west to Utah and remained in Missouri, splitting from the Brigham Young group as head of the Reorganized Church of Jesus Christ of Latter Day Saints beginning in 1860 and abandoning polygamy. Block 3, lot 102, Mound Grove Cemetery, Independence, MO.

8522. Smith, Joseph Fielding (Nov. 13, 1839–Nov. 19, 1918) Nephew of Mormon founder Joseph Smith worked to gain statehood for Utah (1896) and served as President of the Church of Jesus Christ of Latter Day Saints 1901–1918. Park 14-14-1-E, Salt Lake City Cemetery, Salt Lake City, UT.

8523. Smith, Kate (Kathryn Elizabeth Smith, May 1, 1907–June 17, 1986) Large, soft voiced singer on radio from the early 1930's, known for her theme *When the Moon Comes Over the Mountain* (1934) and for her rendition of *God Bless America*. She spent her later years in North Carolina, suffering from a variety of ailments including diabetes, which caused the loss of a leg. Her will stipulated that she be placed in a sealed bronze coffin in a mausoleum at St. Agnes Cemetery, Lake Placid, New York. A widely publicized dispute ensued after her death when St. Agnes officials prohibited above ground mausoleums, but Smith had been a summer resident since 1965 and a liberal contributor to St. Agnes's parish. By 1987 her wish was given the nod by the church. The pink granite mausoleum, made in Barre, Vermont, contains only her sarcophagus. Over the door is her full name and inside are inscribed the words of Franklin Roosevelt: *This is Kate Smith: This is America*. Her coffin was removed from a vault in North Elba Cemetery for the widely attended dedication ceremony November 14, 1987. St. Agnes Cemetery, Lake Placid, NY.

8524. Smith, Kent (March 19, 1907–April 23, 1985) Ernest faced leading man in quiet hero roles in Lewton's *Cat People* (1942) and *Curse of the Cat People* (1944), Robert Siodmak's *The Spiral Staircase* (1946), *Nora Prentiss* (1947), turning up twenty years later as Dr. Robert Morton on TV's *Peyton Place* as well as many other films through the 1970's. He died at 78 from congestive heart failure, survived by his wife since 1962, actress Edith Atwater. Ashes scattered at sea.

8525. Smith, Lane (Walter Lane Smith III, April 29, 1936–June 13, 2005) Actor from Memphis in considerable Off-Broadway work, many films including *The Final Days* (1989, as Richard Nixon), *The Mighty Ducks*, *My Cousin Vinny*, and as Perry White in TV's *Lois and Clark: The New Adventures of Superman*. He died at home in Northridge, California, from ALS (Lou Gehrig's Disease) at 69. Cremated by the Neptune Society. Ashes to family in Toluca Lake, CA.

8526. Smith, Lillian Eugena (Dec. 12, 1897–Sept. 28, 1966) Writer and civil rights literary pioneer co-founded *The North Georgia Review*, later *South Today*, the first journal of American southern whites to publish the work of blacks. Her novels include *Strange Fruit* (1944) and *Killers of the Dream* (1949). Her *One Hour* also took on the McCarthy hearings. Buried near the old theater chimney, Laurel Falls camp atop Screamer Mountain, Clayton, GA.

8527. Smith, Loring (Nov. 18, 1890–July 8, 1981) Actor from Stratford, Connecticut, did a few film and television roles, with his trademark all knowing con-man look (*Keep Em Flying, Shadow of the Thin Man, Pat and Mike, Twilight Zone* episodes *The Whole Truth* and *I Dream of Genie; The Cardinal, Hurry Sundown*). He lived at Norwalk and died at Fairfield, Connecticut, at 80. Burial through Raymond mortuary, Norwalk. Norwalk Cemetery, Norwalk, CT.

8528. Smith, Mamie (Sept. 16, 1883/1890–Oct. 30, 1946) Cincinnati born black female vocalist in vaudeville and clubs toured with her Jazz Hounds and was the first woman to make a blues record, with *Crazy Blues* in 1920. Frederick Douglass Memorial Park, 3201 Amboy Road, Staten Island, NY.

8529. Smith, Margaret Chase (Dec. 14, 1897–May 29, 1995) The Lady from Maine, Republican congresswoman known for her red rose, succeeded her husband Clyde Smith in congress in 1940 and served there 1940–49 and as senator 1949–1973. The first woman to serve in both houses, she was known for her common sense views, repudiating McCarthyism in 1950 and renewing her Declaration of Conscience in 1971 in tolerance of Vietnam protestors. Ashes at the Margaret Chase Smith Library, Skowhegan, ME.

8530. Smith, Merriman (Albert Merriman Smith, Feb. 10, 1913–April 13, 1970) UPI White House correspondent broke the story of President Kennedy's assassination and was aboard Air Force One when President Johnson was sworn in, won the Pulitzer Prize in 1964 and authored two books on his years covering the presidents. A suicide by gunshot at 57. Sec. 32, grave 823, Arlington National Cemetery, Arlington, VA.

8531. Smith, Michael (Michael John Smith, April 30 1945–Jan 28 1986) U.S. Navy pilot, astronaut on the space shuttle Challenger, which exploded sixty seconds after lift off at Cape Canaveral. The cabin was recovered from the sea in April. Sec. 7A, site 208-1, grid TU-23/24, Arlington National Cemetery, Arlington, VA.

8532. Smith, Michael "Smitty" (Michael Leroy Smith, March 27, 1942–March 6, 2001) Drummer with Paul Revere and the Raiders from 1962 played on their hits through the decade, later leaving the group and retiring to Hawaii to pursue peace and environmental causes. He died from natural causes at 58 on Kona, his home. Cremated through Dodo mortuary, Kona. A memorial gathering was held at the airport there March 18, and the ashes returned with the family to Portland, Oregon, and reportedly scattered at sea.

8533. Smith, O.C. (Ocie Lee Smith Jr., June 21, 1932–Nov. 23, 2001) Vocalist from Mansfield, Louisiana, sang with Count Basie's orchestra from 1961 before branching out as a single, recording hits with *Hickory Holler's Tramp* and the Grammy winning *Little Green Apples* in 1968. In 1985 he became a minister, founding the City of Angels Church of Religious Science in Los Angeles. He died suddenly at 69 in his home at Ladera Heights, California. Cremated through Inglewood Park mortuary, Inglewood. Ashes buried at sea December 1 off the coast of Los Angeles County.

8534. Smith, Ovid Wellford (a.k.a. James Smith, Nov. 9, 1844–Jan. 28, 1868) At 16, enlisted as James Smith in the 2nd Ohio Volunteer Infantry Regiment and volunteered for the famous Andrews Raid to destroy Confederate supply lines. The raiders captured the train *The General* at Big Shanty, Georgia, April 12, 1862. Though he did not actually participate, he was equally recognized and received the Medal of Honor July 6, 1864. An Ohio historical marker is near his flush bronze veteran's plaque in front of the original eroded stone. Sec. C, lot 84, Greenlawn Cemetery, Columbus, OH.

8535. Smith, Perry *see* **Clutter.**

8536. Smith, Pete (Sept. 4, 1892–Jan. 12, 1979) Producer of the *Pete Smith Specialty* Shorts, usually featuring Dave O'Brien 1936–1955. Two of the three hundred odd commentaries on American life won Academy Awards. Despondent over ill health, he jumped to his death from the roof of a Los Angeles convalescent hospital. Columbarium of Memory, niche 20102, Memorial Terrace, Great Mausoleum, Forest Lawn, Glendale, CA.

8537. Smith, Queenie (Sept. 8, 1898/1902–Aug. 15, 1978) New York born stage and screen actress 1934–78 (*Mississippi* [as Alabam], *The Killers* [Swede's beneficiary], *The Snake Pit, The Great Rupert, Sweet Smell of Success, Foul Play* [as Elsie], many others). She died from cancer in Burbank, California, at 75. Cremated August 22 at Pierce Bros. Chapel of the Pines, Los Angeles. Though friends in San Antonio say she was buried in L.A. Chapel of the Pines records show a Fairview Cemetery, San Antonio, TX.

8538. Smith, Red (Walter Wellesley Smith, Sept. 25, 1905–Jan. 15, 1982) Syndicated sports columnist for the *New York Herald*, the *New York Tribune* and the *New York Times*. Awarded the Pulitzer Prize in journalism in 1976. Among his reminiscences was his collection of farewells *To Absent Friends*. He died in New York. Funeral mass at St. Patrick's Cathedral. Long Ridge Union Cemetery, Erskine Road, north of Stamford, CT.

8539. Smith, Samantha (July 29, 1972–Aug. 25, 1985) U.S. school girl from Houlton, Maine, whose letter to Soviet Premier Andropov in 1983 asking for an end to communist aggression led to her being personally invited to visit Moscow and meet the party leader. Her plea for world peace and the response it engendered gained international attention. She and her father were killed in a plane crash two years later. A statue of her with a Russian bear cub, releasing a dove of peace, stands on the state capitol grounds in Augusta, with the words *Maine's young ambassador of goodwill*. Her ashes were returned to the family. Plot at Estabrook Cemetery, Amity, ME.

8540. Smith, Sammi (Jewel Fay Smith, Aug. 5, 1943–Feb. 12, 2005) Country singer and songwriter from Orange, California, earned a Grammy for her recording of Kris Kristofferson's *Help Me Make It Through the Night* in 1971. Guardian West mortuary, War Acres. Elmhurst Cemetery, Guymon, OK.

8541. Smith, Samuel F. (Oct. 21, 1808–Nov. 16, 1895) Baptist clergyman and poet wrote *America* while a student at Andover in 1832. Set to the music of *God Save the King*, it was later known by the first line *My Country 'Tis of Thee* as noted on his gravestone. Sec. M, Newton Cemetery, Newton Center, MA.

8542. Smith, Susan V. (murder case) Twenty three year old mother of two small boys, three and fourteen months, claimed a black man hijacked her car with the children in it October 25, 1994. After a ten day search expanding nationwide, she confessed on November 3 to having pushed her car down a boat ramp into John D. Long Lake at Union, South Carolina, with them in it, fully conscious. **Alex** and **Michael Smith** were buried November 6 at Bougansville United Methodist Church Cemetery, West Springs, SC.

8543. Smith, Thorne (James Thorne Smith, March 27, 1883/1892–June 21, 1934) Novelist and screenwriter fond of fun-loving ghosts wrote *Topper* (1926, first filmed in 1937), *Night Life of the Gods* (1931) and his last, unfinished work, *The Passionate Witch* (filmed in 1942 as *I Married a Witch*). He died from a heart attack in Sarasota, Florida. Sec. M, lot 5830, Mt. Olivet Cemetery, Maspeth, Queens, N.Y.C.

8544. Smith, Tom (Robert Thomas or Thomas Robert Smith, May 20, 1878–Jan. 23, 1957) Stoic horse trainer once known as The Lone Plainsman for breaking mustangs is best known for his patience and persistence in training the underdog Seabiscuit, small and crooked legged, into a champion. Sunrise Slope, lot 6121, space 4, Forest Lawn, Glendale, CA.

8545. Smith, Tillie (c. 1867–April 9, 1886) Nineteen year old whose body was found behind Centenary Collegiate Institute, later Centenary College, at Hackettstown, New Jersey, where she was a resident kitchen maid. Returning there after the 10 p.m. curfew, she was strangled during an attempted rape by the janitor, James Titus, who served nineteen years, his death sentence commuted. An area martyr to preserving maidenhood, Tillie Smith has allegedly become the college's resident ghost. A white marble monument was erected at the top of the cemetery with the inscription *She died in defense of her honor*. Union Cemetery, Hackettstown, NJ.

8546. Smith, Walter Bedell (Oct. 5, 1895–Aug. 9, 1961) Indianapolis born U.S. Army general, chief of staff to Eisenhower in World War II, signed the Treaty of Surrender with Germany in 1945 officially ending the war. He later served as Ambassador to Russia and Director of the CIA under Truman. Buried near his friend and mentor, George C. Marshall. Sec 7, grave 8197-A, Arlington National Cemetery, Arlington, VA.

8547. Smith, "Whispering Jack" (Jack Smith, May 31, 1897–May 13, 1950) The Whispering Bari-

tone, New York born song plugger and recording artist for Victor was a popular radio voice of the 1920's, half talking his songs (*Me and My Shadow, Cecilia*) in a soft voice. He died from a heart attack at 52 in his home at 204 Central Park South, Manhattan. Anna Schmidt stone. Sec. 11, range 27, plot 68, grave 2, (Old) St. Raymond's Cemetery, the Bronx, N.Y.C.

8548. Smith, William French (Aug. 26, 1917–Oct. 29, 1990) U.S. Attorney General under Ronald Reagan 1981–85. Garden of Honor, Little Garden of Tender Memories, Forest Lawn, Glendale, CA.

8549. Smith and Dale Joe Smith (Joe Sultzer, Feb. 16, 1884–Feb. 22, 1981) and **Charles Dale Marks** (Sept. 6, 1881–Nov. 16, 1971) Vaudeville team known for their corny jokes, together from 1898 and best known for the Dr. Kronkhite sketch, continuing routines through the 1950's when they appeared frequently on *Ed Sullivan*. They were reportedly the basis for the play and film *The Sunshine Boys* (1975) and, other than Olsen and Johnson, are the only comedy team in show business buried together. Their stone, also with Marks' wife, has under Smith's name the epitaph *Booked solid*. Rhododendron sec 171, Woodlawn Cemetery, the Bronx, N.Y.C.

8550. Smithson, James (1765–June 26, 1829) English nobleman died in Genoa in 1829 and left a fortune to his nephew, to be used after the nephew's death for an institution of higher learning in Washington, D.C., where he had never been. The nephew died in 1835 and in 1846 President Polk signed a measure to erect what became known as the Castle on the mall, the first building of the Smithsonian Institution. In 1903, when the English cemetery at Genoa was to be moved, Alexander Graham Bell went there to secure Smithson's bones. Sarcophagus, left side of the foyer, original "Castle" at the Smithsonian Institution, Washington, D.C.

8551. Smokey (the) Bear (May 3, 1950–Nov. 9, 1976) Two and a half month old black bear cub found in a charred tree after a fire at Capitan, New Mexico, lived in the National Zoo in Washington D.C. until his death. By then, in a cartoon with a ranger hat on, he had become the symbol for preventing forest fires. Buried under a boulder detailing his story at Smokey Bear Historical State Park, Capitan, NM.

8552. Smoot, Reed (Jan. 10, 1862–Feb. 9, 1941) Republican senator from Utah 1909–1933, co-author of the high Smoot-Hawley Tariff of 1930–31, a prelude to the increased U.S. and European economic depression of the 1930's. The names Hawley and Smoot came into use again in 1993 when their bill was pointed out as the antithesis of free trade with disastrous results, during NAFTA debates. Block 3, lot 75, Provo Burial Park, Provo, UT.

8553. Snead, Sam (May 27, 1912–May 23, 2002) Native of Hot Springs, Virginia, known for The Sweetest Swing in golf, joined the PGA Tour in 1937 and won a record 81 PGA Tour events over thirty years; he was the only player to win in six decades of sanctioned tournaments, from 1936 to the 1982 Legends of Golf. His seven wins in the majors numbered three Masters (1949, 1952, 1954), the British Open at St. Andrews in 1946, and three PGA wins, in 1942, 1949 and 1951) during the match play era. He was a runner up in the U.S. Open four times. Known for his straw hat and homespun humor, he appeared at the Masters as an honorary starter until shortly before his death in Hot Springs at 89. Burial at his home, Chestnut Rail Farm, Rte. 220 at Healing Springs/Carloover, just south of Hot Springs, VA.

8554. Snodgrass, Fred (Oct. 19, 1887–April 5, 1974) Outfielder from Ventura, California, with the New York Giants blew the 1912 world series against Boston when he muffed a fly ball after calling it. Though McGraw raised his salary, the error that cost a world series, as with Fred Merkle and the 1908 pennant, followed Snodgrass to the end of his days. Unit 1, sec. B, niche 1, Ivy Lawn Memorial Park mausoleum, Ventura, CA.

8555. Snodgress, Carrie (Oct. 27, 1945–April 1, 2004) Husky voiced actress from Barrington, Illinois, in *Rabbit Run,* nominated for an Oscar as best actress in *Diary of A Mad Housewife* (1970), left her profession and traveled for seven years with Neil Young, with whom she had a son, Zeke. Later roles included *Pale Rider* (1985), *Murphy's Law* (1986), *The Fury* (1987) and *Blueberry Hill* (1988). Last married in the early 1980's to painter Robert Jones, she died awaiting a liver transplant in Los Angeles at 60. Brotherly Love, lot 4317, space 1, Forest Lawn, Glendale, CA.

8556. Snow, Hank (Clarence Eugene Snow, May 9, 1914–Dec. 20, 1999) Country singer born in Liverpool, Nova Scotia, known for *I'm Movin On*, which stayed on the country-western charts for nearly a year in 1950. Other hits for The Rhinestone Ranger included *I've Been Everywhere.* A member of the Grand Ole Opry for nearly 50 years, he died in Nashville at 85. . His black oval stone has a landscape, with snow, and the words *Still movin on.* Hillcrest, lot 103A, grave 1, Spring Hill Cemetery, Gallatin Road, Madison, Nashville, TN.

8557. Snowden, Leigh (Martha Lee Estes, June 23, 1929–May 16, 1982) Blonde model from Tennessee in a few films of the 1950's made *Variety* after her sashay across the naval base at San Diego brought an ovation by thousands of sailors. Put to work at Universal, she appeared in *Kiss Me Deadly, All That Heaven Allows, The Creature Walks Among Us, Francis in the Navy, I've Lived Before* (all 1955–56) prior to marrying musician Dick Contino in 1956. She died from cancer in North Hollywood at 52. Cremated at Angeles Abbey through the Neptune Society. Ashes scattered at sea.

8558. Snyder, Jimmy (James L. Snyder, 1909– June 29, 1939) Indianapolis 500 driver in the 1930's hit a record 130 m.p.h. and placed second at 114 m.p.h. just behind Wilbur Shaw in the 1939 race. Killed a month later. Maple, lot 4, block 5, grave 1,

Cedar Park Cemetery, Calumet Park, (south of Chicago), IL.

8559. Snyder, Jimmy the Greek (Emetrios Synodinos, James George Snyder, Sept. 9, 1918–April 21, 1996) Colorful Las Vegas based oddsmaker picked eighteen of twenty-one Super Bowl winners, appeared on CBS's *NFL Today* 1976–1988, but was fired after making controversial comments about blacks in sports. He died in Las Vegas from heart failure at 76. Sent through Palm mortuary to Mosti mortuary. Mausoleum G-43, Union Cemetery, Steubenville, OH.

8560. Snyder, Mitch (Aug. 14, 1943–July 5, 1990) Advocate of the homeless lobbied for more shelters for those on the street and had undergone starvation diets to bring attention to the cause. A suicide by hanging. Ashes buried at Luther Place Memorial Church and N Street Village, Washington, D.C.

8561. Snyder, Moe (Martin Snyder, Dec. 6, 1893–Nov. 9, 1981) "The Gimp," racketeer nightclub owner, husband and promoter of Ruth Etting, shot her accompanist Meryl Alderman in a jealous confrontation in the 1930's, and did a year in prison. Alderman recovered and married the then divorced Etting. The subject of the 1955 film *Love Me or Leave Me* (1955). Sec. H, lot 48, upright stone along the road, Rosemont Park Cemetery, Chicago, IL.

8562. Snyder, Ruth Brown (c. 1894–Jan. 12, 1928) Wife of a magazine editor in a comfortable Queens home became bored, began an affair with corset salesman Judd Gray (*q.v.*) and persuaded him to murder her husband, Albert Snyder, on March 20, 1927. Things didn't go as planned and she ended up finishing him off herself by beating him on the head with a blunt weight. The trial overflowed with spectators and provided extra entertainment with the bickering between Snyder and Gray, by then blaming one another. Both were convicted and sentenced to death, dying in the electric chair at Sing Sing a few minutes apart. A camera strapped to a reporter's leg managed to record Snyder receiving the voltage. She was buried in the Brown family plot, her stone marked *May R.* Arbutus sec. 119, several rows up from Myosotis Avenue, Woodlawn Cemetery, the Bronx, N.Y.C. **Albert Snyder (Schneider)** was buried beside his parents Charles and Mary Schneider, his stone marked only *Brother.* Sec. K, lot 654, Mt. Olivet Cemetery, Maspeth, Queens, N.Y.C.

8563. Soble, Ron (Ronald Norman Soble, May 28, 1928–May 2, 2002) Actor from Illinois in films 1958–99 (*The Cincinnati Kid, True Grit, Chisum, Papillon*) and many television parts. He died at home in Mission Hills, California, of brain cancer at 69. Ashes through the Neptune Society of Burbank scattered at sea May 11 off Los Angeles County.

8564. Socarros, Carlos Prio (July 14, 1903 April 5, 1977) President of Cuba 1948–52, overthrown by Batista, a suicide by gunshot in Dade County, Florida. The Cuban flag, in color, is on his monument. Woodlawn Park Cemetery, Miami, FL.

8565. Söderbaum, Kristina (Sept. or Oct. 5, 1912–Feb. 12, 2001) Swedish actress from Stockholm in Germany during the 1930's, often in the works of her husband, director Veit Harlan, particularly controversial for the anti–Semitic *Jud Süss* (1940), in which she appeared. They continued to make films through 1958. Harlan died in April 1964. She died at 88 in Hitzacker, Lower Saxony. Seeshaupt friedhof, Seeshaupt am Starberger See (on Lake Starnberg), Bayern (Bavaria), Germany.

8566. Sokoloff, Vladimir (Dec. 26, 1889–Feb. 14, 1962) Russian actor in Hollywood from 1937 in Slavic and other foreign parts. Abbey of the Psalms/ Hollywood Forever Mausoleum, Corridor G-4 (Light), crypt 5245, Hollywood Forever Cemetery, Hollywood (Los Angeles), CA.

8567. Solari, Rudy (Dec. 21, 1934–April 23, 1991) Actor, director-producer founded the Solari Theatre in Beverly Hills. Originally from the Bay Area, he had been in L.A. and conducting acting classes since 1956. He died from cancer at 56. Vale of Peace, lot 3546, Forest Lawn Hollywood Hills, Los Angeles.

8568. Solter, Harry *see* **Harry Salter.**

8569. Soma, Ricki (Enrica Soma, May 9, 1929–Jan. 29, 1969) The fourth wife (1950–c.1960) of director John Huston was the daughter of Tony Soma, owner of Tony's Place in Manhattan, was a ballerina and model and the mother of Huston's children Tony (Walter Anthony) and Anjelica. She died in a car crash near Gray, France, at 39. Her ashes went to her father Tony's mantel in New York with those of her mother Anjelica — who died of pneumonia in 1932 — to be buried with him upon his death, which occurred in a fire at his home at Miller Place, Long Island, March 31, 1979 at 89. Cremated at Washington Memorial Park, Coram, Long Island, the ashes went to O.B. Davis mortuary and to his lawyer Peter Costigan, both in Port Jefferson Station, Long Island, New York. His widow Dorothy, 85, died in Seattle January 16, 1996. She was cremated and interred at Evergreen-Washelli Cemetery, Seattle. None of the others' ashes are there.

8570. Somers, Charles (Oct. 13, 1868–June 29, 1934) Financed the American League, founded and owned the first A.L. team in 1901. First Vice President of the A.L. 1901–1916. Sec. 11, lot 224, Lakeview Cemetery, Cleveland, OH.

8571. Sondergaard, Gale (Edith Holm Sondergaard, Feb. 15, 1899–Aug. 14, 1985) Dark eyed actress from Litchfield, Minnesota, in mysterious and sinister roles won an Oscar as best supporting actress in her first film *Anthony Adverse* (1936), subsequently portraying many mystics and villainesses (*The Cat and the Canary* 1939, a particularly menacing turn in *The Letter* 1940; *The Black Cat* 1941, *Sherlock Holmes* and *The Spider Woman* 1944, *The Spider Woman Strikes Back*, *The Time of Their Lives* 1946). Her husband **Herbert Biberman** (March 4, 1900–June 30, 1971) was a member of the "Hollywood Ten," sentenced to prison for refusing to testify before the House Un-American Activities Committee. Also blacklisted, she made no films 1948–69. When Biberman died in New York in 1971, his ashes were scattered at sea off the California coast. She died in Los Angeles at 86 fourteen years later. Cremated at Rosedale Cemetery in Los Angeles, her ashes were buried at sea in Los Alamos Bay.

8572. Sontag, Susan (Jan. 16, 1933–Dec. 28, 2004) New York born writer and philosopher wrote *The Benefactor* (1963), the essay *Notes on Camp* (1964), which chronicled and analyzed, ahead of its time, the pop-art generation which she was a part of. *On Photography* (1977) came from her talks with Edgar de Evia, and *Illness as Metaphor* (1978), looked at her own decades long struggle with cancer. She died from leukemia in Manhattan at 71. Div. 2, Cimetiere de Montparnasse, Paris.

8573. Soo, Jack (Goro Suzuki, Oct. 28, 1917–Jan. 11, 1979) Oakland born Japanese-American actor in the stage and screen versions of *Flower Drum Song* (1961) gained renewed popularity as Detective Nick Yamana, world weary maker of the twelfth precinct's legendary bad coffee, in TV's *Barney Miller* 1976–79. He died from cancer at 61 mid-way through the show's fourth season. In an unusual approach, the other actors in the ensemble stepped out of character to pay tribute to Soo in an episode devoted to his memory. Eternal Love sec., lot 3980, Forest Lawn Hollywood Hills, Los Angeles.

8574. Sopwith, Thomas Octave Murdoch (Jan. 18, 1888–Jan. 27, 1989) Knighted aviation pioneer developed the Sopwith Camel, a single seat biplane acclaimed as the most successful fighter plane in World War I. Little Somborne Church cemetery, near King's Somborne, Hampshire, England.

8575. Sordi, Alberto (June 15, 1920–Feb. 25, 2003) Rome born Italian film star from the late 1930's with a thick Roman accent was among Italy's best known post-war comic actors in films, including Fellini's *White Sheik* (1952), *An American in Rome* (1954), *A Farewell to Arms, Count Max* (1957), *Great War* (1959), *The Best of Enemies* (opposite David Niven, 1961), *Complexes* (1965). He also essayed drama, as in *An Average Little Man* (1977), and was an acclaimed director. Within a week of his death in Rome from a heart attack at 82, the mayor named a street for him. Cimitero Monumentale al Verano, Rome.

8576. Sorel, Cecil (Sept. 17, 1873–Sept. 3, 1966) Stage and screen actress known for *Les Perles de la Couronne* (*Pearls of the Crown* 1937). Div. 9, Montparnasse Cemetery, Paris.

8577. Sorin, Louis (Aug. 21, 1896–Dec. 14, 1961) New York born character actor unofficially known as the RCA Building's "mayor of the third floor," on stage from 1921, best known as Roscoe W. Chandler in the stage and screen versions of *Animal Crackers* (1930) with the Marx Brothers. He died at 65 from pulmonary edema at his home, 405 East Fifty-fourth Street in Manhattan. Cremated at Ferncliff Crematory December 17. Ashes buried in unidentifiable space, Ferncliff Cemetery, Hartsdale, NY.

8578. Sothern, Ann (Harriette Lake, Jan. 22, 1909–March 15, 2001) Blonde actress from Valley City, North Dakota, who took her name from E.A. Sothern, in many B films from 1934, including *Brother Orchid*, the *Maisie* series 1939–47, *Panama Hattie*, and in better fare including *Cry Havoc* (1943), *A Letter to Three Wives* (1949), *Lady in a Cage* (1963), *The Best Man* (1964), in her TV series *Private Secretary* 1952–53 and *The Ann Sothern Show* 1958–61, plus guest spots including *The Lucy-Desi Comedy Hour*. Last seen in *The Whales of August* (1987), for which she received an Academy Award nomination. Divorced from Roger Pryor and Robert Sterling, she was injured in a 1974 accident on stage and learned to walk again using a cane. She moved to Ketchum, Idaho, in 1984, near her daughter Tisha, where she died at 92. Mass through Wood River Chapel in Hailey at Our Lady of Snows Catholic Church in Sun Valley March 23. Pink headstone reading *Always in our hearts*. Northeast area, Ketchum Cemetery, Ketchum, ID.

8579. Sothern, E. A. (Edward Ashley Sothern, April 1, 1826–Jan. 20, 1881) English stage star and playwright known for his *David Garrick* and other characterizations. A stone cross marks his grave. Southampton Cemetery, Southampton, Hampshire, England.

8580. Sothern, Edward H. see **Julia Marlowe.**

8581. Soto, Freddy (June 22, 1970–July 10, 2005) Spanish-American comedian and actor from El Paso in numerous television appearances and a few films, including *The Three Amigos* and *Spanglish*, died in his sleep in Los Angeles at thirty-five. Mass at St. Patrick's Cathedral, El Paso. Mount Carmel Cemetery, El Paso, TX.

8582. Souders, George (Sept. 11, 1900–July 28, 1976) Winner of the 1927 Indianapolis 500 was one of only six drivers in Brickyard history to do so on their first try. As noted on his upright stone showing him in his racecar, Souder won at just over 97 m.p.h. in a Duesenberg Special Battle. Battle Ground Cemetery, Battle Ground (near West Lafayette), IN.

8583. Soule, Olan (Feb. 28, 1909–Feb. 1, 1994) Lanky, bespectacled actor with a powerful voice on radio in *Mr. First Nighter,* later in films and much TV of the 1960's and 70's, in *Dragnet* (as the lab technician), *Andy Griffith* (as John the choir director) etc. Enduring Faith sec., lot 3098, space 1, Forest Lawn Hollywood Hills, Los Angeles.

8584. Sousa, John Philip (Nov. 6, 1854–March 6, 1932) Bandleader and composer known for all American standard marches including *Semper Fidelis* (1888) and *Stars and Stripes Forever* (1897). Leader of the U.S. Marine Band 1880–1892. His monument, surrounded by a hedge, has a bench attached to it, with a slab over the grave bearing a carved wreath and bandmaster's baton. His own music was played at the burial. Range 77, site 163-S, Congressional Cemetery, Washington, D.C.

8585. Southern, Jeri (Aug. 5, 1926–Aug. 4, 1991) Jazz pianist and vocalist known for *You Better Go Now*, memorable versions of *When I Fall in Love, Remind Me,* and others, at her peak in the 1950's. She died from cancer a day before her 65th birthday. Garden of Heritage, third level, lot 1105, Forest Lawn Hollywood Hills, Los Angeles.

8586. Southern, Terry (May 1, 1924–Oct. 29, 1995) Offbeat writer from Alvarado, Texas, did the screenplay or contributed heavily to *Dr. Strangelove, or How I Learned to Stop Worrying and Love the Bomb* (1964), *The Loved One* (1965), appeared on the cover of the Beatles' LP *Sgt. Pepper's Lonely Hearts Club Band* (1967), wrote for *Barbarella* (1968), the novel and screenplay *Candy* (filmed in 1968), worked on *Easy Rider* (1969), wrote the novel *The Magic Christian* (1969), produced and appeared in *End of the Road* (1970), and wrote for *Saturday Night Live,* among other things. In his last days he remained hip, praising *Bevis and Butthead*. He died in New York City of respiratory failure at 71. Ashes scattered on his property in Canaan, CT.

8587. Southworth, Billy (William Harrison Southworth, March 9, 1893–Nov. 15, 1969) Outfielder with the Boston Braves, New York Giants, Pirates, Indians and Cardinals 1915–1929. He managed the Cardinals to world series wins in 1942 and 1944 over 1940–45, and the Braves 1946–51. Green Lawn Cemetery, Columbus, OH.

8588. Sovine, Red (Woodrow Wilson Sovine, July 7, 1918–April 4, 1980) County music singer-songwriter best known for his sentimental ballads, frequently about truckers. Good Shepherd sec., lot 111c, grave 1, Woodlawn Memorial Park, Nashville, TN.

8589. Spaggiari, Albert (Dec. 14, 1933–June 9, 1989) Colorful French bank robber led a group of international thieves in digging a tunnel for two months into the vault of the Societe Generale bank at Nice in July 1976. They took $10 million and left a trail taunting and embarrassing authorities in various cities. Captured, he bounded out of a window in the judge's office of the Palais de Justice in March 1977 and disappeared on the back of a friend's motorcycle, leaving for posterity his memoir *The Sewers of Paradise.* He lived in Argentina, Madrid and Geneva, giving interviews in the latter two, but was not recaptured. He died from lung cancer at 65. Laragne-Montéglin, France.

8590. Spahn, George (Feb. 11, 1889–Sept. 22, 1974) Owner of Spahn Ranch in the San Fernando Valley, made infamous by the Manson family's residence there in 1969. The owner was ignorant of their nocturnal activities. Whispering Pines, lot 150-G, Eternal Valley Memorial Park, Newhall, CA.

8591. Spahn, Warren (April 23, 1921–Nov. 24, 2003) Pitcher from Buffalo with the Braves 1942–1964 was the winningest left hander ever, with a record of 363–245 and a 3.09 ERA. He threw the Braves to National League pennant wins in 1948 (at Boston), 1957 and 1958 (Milwaukee), and the World Series in

1957. He won twenty games thirteen times, matching Christy Mathewson for the N.L. record, was a fourteen time All Star, led the league in victories eight times, consistently 1957–61, and pitched two no-hitters: against Philadelphia September 15, 1960, and against San Francisco April 28, 1961. His thirty five homers were a league record for pitchers, as were his 5, 243½ innings. Cy Young winner 1957. Elected to Cooperstown 1973. He died at 82 in Broken Arrow, Oklahoma. Floral Haven mortuary, Broken Arrow. Block 20, Elmwood Cemetery, North 9th St., Hartshorne, OK.

8592. Spalding, Albert Goodwill (Sept. 2, 1850–Sept. 9, 1915) Pitcher with Boston took twenty four straight wins in 1875, helping to organize the National League in 1876, the same year he founded the sporting goods business manufacturing the baseballs bearing his name. He later managed at Chicago. Elected to the Hall of Fame 1939. Though his family are all buried at Byron Cemetery, Byron, Illinois, where he was born, there is no record of him there. He died from a stroke at his home in Point Loma, California. The funeral was overseen by his second wife, Elizabeth Churchill, who after his death engaged in a legal battle with his son Keith over his estate. The son claimed undue influence was exerted over him by his wife and Mrs. Katherine Tingley, head of the Theosophical Society at Point Loma. It was settled in July 1917, with he receiving ⁵⁄₁₂ of the estate. Cremated at Greenwood Cemetery in San Diego, through Hambley-Smith mortuary (now out of business), Spalding's service was held privately at his home, with the ashes received from the crematory by "Point Loma homestead" for probable burial or scattering there or at sea.

8593. Spangler, Edman "Ned" (Aug. 10, 1825–Feb. 7, 1875) One of the group involved in John Wilkes Booth conspiracy, first to kidnap President Lincoln and finally to murder him as well as other leaders of the federal government. Four were hanged. Spangler was sentenced to six years in prison. His headstone notes that it was *Erected by the Surratt and Dr. Samuel A. Mudd Societies*. Left side rear near Pophill Road, St. Peter's Cemetery, Waldorf, Charles County, MD.

8594. Spanier, Muggsy (Francis Joseph Spanier, Nov. 9, 1906–Feb. 12, 1967) Jazz cornet great associated with the Chicago sound of the 1920's and 30's, with and without a plunger mute. He played with Ted Lewis's band and on his own, touring until 1964. Family stone. Sec. 19, block 4, lot 13, space 12, Mt. Carmel Cemetery, Hillside, IL.

8595. Spann, Johnny Micheal "Mike" (March 1, 1969–Nov. 25, 2001) The first U.S. combat casualty in Afghanistan, the ex marine from Winfield, Alabama, was with the CIA's covert Special Activities Division, interrogating pro–Taliban prisoners at Mazar-e Sharif when he was killed. Sec. 34, grave 2359, grid V-14, Arlington National Cemetery, Arlington, VA.

8596. Spann, Otis (March 21, 1930–April 24, 1970) Chicago Blues pianist, often backed up by Muddy Waters, his half brother. He died at 40. Unmarked other than a piece of plywood until funds were raised by *Blues Revue* magazine, and a bronze plaque was set June 6, 1999. Sec. 6, lot 13, row 8, grave 31, Burr Oak Cemetery, Alsip (south Chicago), IL.

8597. Sparks, Ned (Nov. 19, 1883–April 2 1957) Horse faced staccato speaking character actor, often chewing a cigar, in films of the 1930's (*Lady For a Day* 1932, *Gold Diggers of 1933, Imitation of Life* 1934). He died at 73 from an intestinal blockage in Apple Valley, California. Block A, sec. 11 ½, lot 3, Victor Valley Memorial Park, Victorville, CA.

8598. Speaker, Tris (Tristam E. Speaker, April 4, 1888–Dec. 8, 1958) The Gray Eagle, outfielder for the Boston Red Sox and the Cleveland Indians 1907–1926, the last seven years as manager of the Indians. A legend in the outfield and great hitter with a .344 lifetime batting average. In 1923, his best season, he tied Babe Ruth, batting .380 with RBI honors with 130. Hall of Fame 1937, an original member at the 1939 dedication. Sec. 1, block 2, Fairview Cemetery, Hubbard, TX.

8599. Spear, Sammy (Samuel Shapiro Spear, May 31, 1909–March 11, 1975) Orchestra leader, long with Jackie Gleason on his Miami based TV show. Carmel div. G, row 1, grave 42, Lakeside Memorial Park, Miami, FL.

8600. Speck, Richard (victims) The murder of eight student nurses in Chicago July 14, 1966, shocked the nation and brought the term "mass murderer" into the common American vocabulary. A drifter, alcoholic and sometime merchant marine cold-bloodedly entered the town house at 2319 100th Street where the nurses, weeks shy of graduation, lived, and one by one took them to separate rooms where they were stabbed, strangled, and or violated, killing eight, then calmly returned to his hotel room. One near victim, Corazon Amurao, hid under a bed for hours, and later identified her would-be killer in court. Five of the nurses were initially interred in the greater Chicago area: **Gloria Davy**, 22, at Holy Cross Cemetery, Calumet City; **Suzanne Farris**, 21, sec. L, block 10, lot 9, grave 1, Mount Carmel Cemetery, Hillside; **Merlita Gargullo**, 23, was returned to the Philippines, where she had grown up on Mindoro Island; **Mary Ann Jordan**, 21 and the sister of Suzanne Farris's fiancé, St. Mary's Cemetery, Evergreen Park; she was removed and reburied October 26, 1971, at Riverside Cemetery, Three Oaks, Michigan; **Patricia Matusek**, 20, sec. KC, lot 890, St. Mary's Cemetery, Evergreen Park; **Valentina Paison**, 24, was returned to Jones City, 150 miles north of Manila, The Philippines; **Nina Schmale**, 23, sec. C, lot 181, grave 1, Wheaton Cemetery, Wheaton; **Pamela Wilkening**, 20, had her wake held in Lansing, Illinois. Cremated through Schroeder-Lauer mortuary, Lansing, her urn went to the family.

Speck (Dec. 6, 1941–Dec. 5, 1991) escaped execution with the 1972 Supreme Court ruling abolishing capital punishment. Serving six consecutive terms of 50 to 150 years each at Stateville, Illinois, Correctional Center, he died from a heart attack one day before his 50th birthday. There is no record of his ashes at Woodlawn Cemetery, Joliet, Illinois, where he has been listed. He was cremated and the ashes held in the safe of the Will County coroner to be scattered over a rose garden or other location as (or if) requested by the family.

8601. Spector, Ben (dec. April 20, 1949) Father of record producer Phil Spector. His epitaph *"To know him was to love him"* inspired one of his son's many hits, slightly paraphrased, in the late 1950's. Beth David Cemetery, Elmont, NY.

8602. Speed, Joshua (Nov. 14, 1814–May 29, 1882) Louisville native moved to Springfield, Illinois, in the late 1830's, became a newspaper editor and friend of Abraham Lincoln for life. Speed was Lincoln's western affairs adviser during the Civil War and was offered the position of Secretary of the Treasury but declined, though Lincoln appointed his brother **James Speed** Attorney General. Both Speeds are at Cave Hill Cemetery, Louisville, KY.

8603. Speer, Albert (March 19, 1905–Sept. 2, 1981) Nazi party member from 1931 directed war production 1942–45 as minister of armaments. Sentenced to twenty years in Spandau at the Nuremberg trials in 1946, he was released with Baldur von Schirach in 1966. Speer died from a cerebral hemorrhage while in London. Tall family monument enclosed by a hedge. Field O, no. 7, A-B-C-D, Bergfriedhof, Heidelberg.

8604. Spellman, Francis, Cardinal (May 4, 1889–Dec. 2, 1967) Archbishop of New York, elevated to Cardinal in 1946, promoted schools and hospitals. Buried with an illuminated scroll, such as was used in medieval times, written in waterproof ink identifying him and recounting his biography, near the other bishops and cardinals beneath the high altar (no admittance), St. Patrick's Cathedral, Manhattan, N.Y.C.

8605. Spence, Ralph (Nov. 4, 1889–Dec. 21, 1949) Playwright and screenwriter best known for the play *The Gorilla* (1925), filmed as a silent, in 1931 and 1939. He also wrote *Sh! The Octopus,* filmed in 1937, and many film scripts, including Wheeler and Woolsey comedies. Memorial G, sec. 7723, lot 3, Valhalla Memorial Park, North Hollywood, CA.

8606. Spencer, Diana *see* **Diana, Princess of Wales.**

8607. Spencer, Douglas (William Henry Mesenkop, Feb. 10, 1910–Oct. 6, 1960) Tall, thin, bald actor appeared in *The Night Has a Thousand Eyes* (1948), *The Thing* (*From Another World,* 1951, as Scott, the zealous reporter), *The Diary of Anne Frank* (1958), several others. He died from a heart attack and diabetic condition at 50 in Los Angeles. Block 351/2, lot 3, grave 5, Oakland Cemetery, Princeton, IL.

8608. Spencer, Elizabeth (Elizabeth Dickerson, c. 1861–April 22, 1930) Edison's favorite soprano 1911–1926, with Walter Van Brunt and solo, lived at Denver, Colorado, and after 1916 at Montclair, New Jersey. Buried as Mrs. E.B. Southworth. Birch Lawn, lot 28, Mt. Hebron Cemetery, Montclair, NJ.

8609. Spencer, Herbert (April 7, 1905–Sept. 18, 1992) Chilean born film composer from 1935 received Oscar nominations for *Scrooge* (1970), *Jesus Christ Superstar.* Sec. C, urn garden, Westwood Memorial Park, Los Angeles.

8610. Spencer, John (John Speshock, Dec. 20, 1946–Dec. 16, 2005) New York born actor raised at Paterson, New Jersey, began as a boyfriend on *The Patty Duke Show* (1964–5) but by his early 40's was playing far older parts, in films including *Sea of Love, Presumed Innocent, Green Card, Forget Paris, The Rock, Cop Land, Twilight, The Negotiator,* and as a regular on television's *L.A. Law* (as Tommy Mullaney 1990–94) and *West Wing* (as Leo McGarrey from 1999). He died from a heart attack at 58 in Los Angeles. Sent through Pierce Bros. Westwood mortuary to Laurel Grove Cemetery, Totowa, NJ.

8611. Spencer, Len (Leonard G. Spencer, Jan. 12, 1867–Dec. 15, 1914) Early recording artist with Columbia and the U.S. Phonograph Co. specialized in minstrel songs. He also did drama, including the earliest surviving audio dramatization of *Dr. Jekyll and Mr. Hyde,* and impersonations — allegedly the voice advertised as McKinley at the Pan American exposition. Glenwood Cemetery, Washington, D.C.

8612. Spenser, Edmund (c. 1552–Jan. 13, 1599) London born poet. At Kilcoman in Ireland, where Queen Elizabeth conferred on him an estate, he wrote his greatest work *The Fairy Queen.* In 1598 rebellion broke out at Kilcoman, his castle was burned and his child killed in the fire. He returned to Westminster, depressed and ill, where he died the next year. At his funeral contemporaries, believed to have included Shakespeare, wrote elegies which they threw into the grave, along with the pens they had written them with. Near Chaucer in Westminster Abbey, London.

8613. Sperber, Wendie Jo (Sept. 15, 1958–Nov. 29, 2005) Actress in films from 1978 (*I Wanna Hold Your Hand, Corvette Summer, 1941,* as Marty McFly's sister Linda in the *Back to the Future* films), as on television as Amy on *Bosom Buddies* 1980–82, Stacy on *Private Benjamin* 1982–3, Mavis Davis on *Hearts Afire* 1992–93, etc. Diagnosed with breast cancer in 1997, she survived it for eight years and founded the weSPARK cancer support group before her death in Los Angeles at 47. Burial December 2. Ramah E Garden, R-5, Mount Sinai Memorial Park, Los Angeles.

8614. Spiegel, Sam (Nov. 11, 1901–Dec. 31, 1985) Polish born maverick producer who sometimes used the name S.P. Eagle among others, in Hollywood from 1941 (*Tales of Manhattan, The Stranger, We Were Strangers, The African Queen, On the Waterfront, The Bridge on the River Kwai, Suddenly Last Summer, Lawrence of Arabia*), died on the French Riviera at 82.

Burial through Frank E. Campbell mortuary, Manhattan. New Shearith Israel sec., Beth Olam Cemetery, Cypress Hills Street, Glendale-Ridgewood, Brooklyn-Queens, N.Y.C.

8615. Spigelgass, Leonard (Nov. 26, 1908–Feb. 14, 1985) Screenwriter (AA nom for *Mystery Street* 1950) worked with many greats as far back as Von Stroheim. T Building/Hall of David, corridor T-8-2, Beth Olam Cemetery adjacent Hollywood Forever Cemetery, Hollywood (Los Angeles), CA.

8616. Spilotro, Anthony (May 19, 1938–June 14, 1986) Chicago born organized crime figure was allegedly the model for Joe Pesci's character Nicky Santoro in Martin Scorsese film *Casino*. Spilotro and his brother were found executed gangland style and buried in an Indiana cornfield. The autopsies on the beaten bodies showed sand or earth in the lungs, indicating they were buried alive. Willow Hills Cemetery, Willow Springs, Cook County, IL.

8617. Spinell, Joe (Joseph J. Spagnuolo, Oct. 28, 1936–Jan. 13, 1989) New York born actor with the Theater of the Forgotten for nine years played tough, sarcastic and sometimes brutal roles in films 1972–89, beginning with soldier turned informer Willi Cicci in both *The Godfather* (1972) and *The Godfather II* (1974), *Farewell My Lovely* (1975, as Nick), *Taxi Driver* (1976, the dispatcher), *Rocky* (1976) and *Rocky II* (1979) as Gazzo, *Maniac* (1980, which he also wrote, as Frank Zito), *The First Deadly Sin* (1980, as Charles Lipsky the doorman, opposite Sinatra). John Wayne Gacy reportedly wanted Spinell to play him in a film, but he was found dead from a heart attack at 52 in his Sunnyside, Queens, apartment. Listed on light brown Spagnuolo stone. Sec. 51-106-61, (1st) Calvary Cemetery, Woodside, Queens, N.Y.C.

8618. Spink, J.G. Taylor (John George Taylor Spink, Nov. 6, 1888–Dec. 7, 1962) St. Louis journalist joined his father **Charles'** weekly *The Sporting News*, taking over as publisher upon Charles' death in 1914, functioning as publisher, editor, advertising manager, columnist and editorial writer. Called The Bible of Baseball, Spink provided it overseas for troops during both World War I and II, and was also credited, along with Ring Lardner, Hugh Fullerton and Christy Mathewson, with helping uncover the 1919 Black Sox scandal. He assumed publication of the *Official Baseball Guide* in the 1940's and authored both *Daguerreotypes* and *Judge Landis and Twenty Five Years of Baseball*. An award in his name is given yearly to sports writers. Mausoleum with his father, block 329, lot 5374, Bellefontaine Cemetery, St. Louis, MO.

8619. Spitalny, Phil (Nov. 7, 1890–Oct. 11, 1970) Musician, leader of Phil Spitalny's All Girl Orchestra, popular during the Big Band era, died in Miami at 79. Sent to Miller-Deutsch Chapel in Cleveland. 5' brown monument with his laminated picture, Old Warrensville Synagogue sec., a few rows behind and right of the (only) mausoleum, about half way down,

row 5, grave 6, Ridge Road #2 Cemetery, Ridge Road, Brooklyn, Cleveland, OH.

8620. Spivack, Murray (Sept. 6, 1903–May 8, 1994) New York born sound engineer in Hollywood 1930–1973 made his mark in *King Kong* (1933), creating the ape's roar from various animals as well as lending his own voice to Kong's more subdued grunts and quizzical utterances while studying Fay Wray. He worked on the music for several films at RKO (*Son of Kong, Flying Down to Rio, The Lost Patrol, The Gay Divorcee*) and later *Laura, Spartacus, West Side Story, Cleopatra, My Fair Lady, The Sound of Music, Patton,* and won an Oscar for *Hello Dolly* (1968). He died in Cedar-Sinai Hospital, Los Angeles, at 90. Handled through Glasband-Willen mortuary, West Hollywood (now out of business. Records at Home of Peace Memorial Park). Shipped east for burial. The family stone reads *Spivack* but his headstone says *Spivak*. Memorial Park sec., block 27, lot 575, south half lot 576, grave 6, Cedar Park Cemetery, Paramus, NJ.

8621. Spivak, Charlie (Feb. 17, 1907–March 1, 1982) Trumpet player with several of the Big Bands, later led his own orchestra. Identified with "Stardreams," among others. Plaque has a trumpet on it. Sec. C (Garden of the Cross), lot 109, near the cross, Grandview Memorial Gardens, Traveller's Rest (near Greenville), SC.

8622. Spock, Benjamin (May 2, 1903–March 15, 1998) Pediatrician and psychiatrist from New Haven changed the upbringing of a generation and their offspring with *The Commonsense Book of Baby and Child Care* in 1946, encouraging less rigid feeding schedules and discipline and more maternal tenderness. Later an anti war activist, his work was accused of promoting a permissiveness that bore the most rebellious generation in American history. He died in La Jolla, California, at 94. After a service at St. James By-the-Sea Episcopal Church, his coffin was driven around with jazz music and snake dancing New Orleans style, as he requested; the women carrying parasols, including his 54 year old widow, who danced atop the hearse. Cremated, his ashes were to be scattered or buried on his birthday, May 2, at the family plot near Camden, ME.

8623. Sprague, Kate Chase (August 13, 1840–July 31, 1899) Daughter of Salmon P. Chase was the belle of Washington society from the Lincoln years into the 1880's. Married to William Sprague of Rhode Island, she was known for her long running affair with New York Senator Roscoe Conkling, ending after Sprague threatened Conkling with a gun during a party at their R.I. estate. She and Sprague later divorced. Afterward she lived with her daughter in Washington, earning a modest income by selling poultry. Buried with her father and daughter on a hilltop overlooking the lake. Sec. 30, Spring Grove Cemetery, Cincinnati, OH.

8624. Spreckels, Adolph (Jan. 5, 1857–June 28, 1924) Son of **Claus Spreckels**, The Sugar King, shot *San Francisco Chronicle* editor Michael de Young over articles about his father he perceived to be libelous. De Young survived; Spreckels pleaded insanity and was eventually released. Family mausoleum, sec. L, Cypress Lawn Cemetery/Memorial Park, Colma, CA.

8625. Springfield, Dusty (Mary Isabel Catherine Bernadette O'Brien, April 16, 1939–March 2, 1999) Soulful vocalist from Hampstead, London, educated in a convent, brought the Motown sound to the UK with *I Only Want to Be With You* (1963). Dubbed the White Diva of Soul, later recordings include *You Don't Have to Say You Love Me* (1966), *The Look of Love*, her album *Dusty in Memphis* and the single *Son of A Preacher Man* (1968). After 15 years in L.A., she re-emerged in 1987 with the Pet Shop Boys and *What Have I Done to Deserve This*. She died at 59 after a five year struggle with breast cancer, in her home at Henley-on-Thames, the day she was to have been presented her OBE. Funeral March 12, her coffin in a carriage drawn by horses to St. Mary the Virgin Methodist Church, Hart St., Henley-on-Thames, Oxfordshire; the streets blocked off and the service — with her recordings, including *You Don't Have to Say You Love Me* and *Don't Forget About Me*, and eulogies including one by singer Lulu, broadcast outside and covered by the BBC on TV. Cremated afterward, her ashes were scattered at her favorite spots over Ireland. There is a cenotaph in her memory, a white headstone with gold lettering, her name, *O.B.E.* and dates, in the parish churchyard at Henley-on-Thames.

8626. Spruance, Raymond (July 3, 1886–Dec. 13, 1969) U.S. Admiral in World War II commanded at Midway, a turning point for the Allies in the Pacific, and at Tarawa, the Marshall Islands, Saipan and Guam. Sec C-1 gr 3, Golden Gate National Cemetery, San Bruno, CA.

8627. Spungen, Nancy *see* **Sid Vicious.**

8628. Spurgeon, Cock-Eyed Liz (Liz Spurgeon aka Elizabeth Enderlin, Jan. 28, 1857–Aug. 18, 1929) Operator of a sporting house called The Palace of Joy in Buena Vista, Colorado, from 1876. In 1897 she married Alphonse "Foozy" Enderlin and settled down. Double stone marked E. and A. Enderlin, surrounded by an iron pipe fence. Sec A, Mt. Olivet Cemetery, Co. Rd 321 (Rodeo St.), Buena Vista, CO.

8629. Spyri, Johanna (Johanna Heusser Spyri, June 12, 1827–July 7, 1901) Swiss author of *Heidi*, published in two volumes 1880–81 and translated into English 1884. Her stone bears the lines from Psalm 39;8: *Herr, wess soll ich mich/ trösten/ jch hoffe dich.* Grave 81210, Friedhof Sihlfeld, Zurich.

8630. Squire, Katherine (March 9, 1903–March 29, 1995) Actress from Defiance, Ohio, on stage, screen (*Song Without End, Studs Lonegan, The Days of Wine and Roses, Blade, Two Lane Blacktop, When Harry Met Sally*) and television (*Alfred Hitchcock Presents, Twilight Zones One More Pallbearer, In His Image*), adept at self righteous middle aged women. Married name Mitchell, she died at 92 in a rest home at Lake Hill, near her home in Woodstock, New York.

Cremated at Wiltwyck Cemetery through Simpson-Gaus mortuary, Kingston. Ashes to family.

8631. Stabile, Dick (Richard Stabile, May 29, 1909–Sept. 25, 1980) Big Band leader of the 1930's and 40's. Sec. EE, row 67, San Fernando Mission Cemetery, Mission Hills, CA.

8632. Stack, Robert (Robert Langford Modini, Jan. 13, 1919–May 14, 2003) Los Angeles born actor in films from 1939 (*The Mortal Storm, To Be or Not To Be, A Date With Judy*) known as the cryptic, unsmiling Elliot Ness on TV's *The Untouchables* 1959–1963 (a stereotype he kidded in *Airplane*, 1980) and later as the host of *Unsolved Mysteries* 1988–97. He died from a heart attack at 84, found in a chair at home by his wife Rosemarie. Book urn at eye-level, corner of glass case, Room of Prayer, Westwood Memorial Park, west Los Angeles, CA.

8633. Stafford, Jean (July 1, 1915–March 26, 1979) Writer won the Pulitzer Prize in 1970 for her collected works. Short stories include *In the Zoo.* Buried with her husband, *New Yorker* writer **Abbott J. Liebling** (Oct. 18, 1904–Dec. 28, 1963) beneath 18th century style slate markers in Green River Cemetery, East Hampton, Long Island, NY.

8634. Stafford, Terry (Nov. 22, 1941–March 17, 1996) Singer-songwriter born in Oklahoma and raised in Amarillo had a hit with *Suspicion* in 1964, co-wrote *Amarillo By Morning*, and wrote and recorded numerous other numbers, both pop and country. He died from a heart attack in Amarillo at 54. Sec. 1A, lot 60, space 3, Llano Cemetery, Amarillo, TX.

8635. Stagg, Amos Alonzo (Aug. 16, 1862–March 17, 1965) Football coach with the University of Chicago had five undefeated seasons, introduced several lasting aspects of the game including the huddle and various plays, and lived to 103. Uninscribed niche, Park View Crematorium and Mausoleum, Stockton, CA.

8636. Stahl, John (Jan. 21, 1886–Jan. 12, 1950) New York born actor turned director circa 1914 and worked through the 1940's. Sound films include *Strictly Dishonorable* (1931), *Back Street* (1932), *Only Yesterday* (1933), *Imitation of Life* (1934) *Magnificent Obsession* (1935), *The Keys of the Kingdom* (1944). Private mausoleum (room) 19, crypt B, Begonia Terrace, Great Mausoleum, Forest Lawn, Glendale, CA.

8637. Stainer, John (June 13, 1840–March 31, 1901) English professor of music at Oxford, author of the cantata *The Holy City* (*Jerusalem*). Stone cross. St. Cross (also called Holywell) Cemetery, Oxford, Oxfordshire.

8638. Stalin, Joseph (Dec. 21, 1879–March 5, 1953) Totalitarian Russian Communist dictator before, during and after World War II suffered a stroke in his Moscow apartment March 1, according to Moscow Radio, but in reality died at his dacha near Kuntsevo southwest of the city. According to his daughter, just before his death he stared at those in the room, lifted his hand and lowered it in what could've been interpreted as bringing down a curse. He was in the Lenin mausoleum in Red Square until 1956, when Khrushchev denounced his reign of terror and had him removed to a less exalted place, with other leaders of the State, with bust and slab outside the Kremlin Wall in Moscow. Stalin's wife **Nadezhda Alliluyeva Stalin** (1903–Nov. 8, 1932) lies beneath a white marble shaft with a white marble head of her atop it, now enclosed in glass, near their son, who died from a drug overdose in 1972. Hers is among the most popular monuments in Novodevichy Cemetery, Moscow.

8639. Stallings, George T. (Nov. 10, 1869–May 13, 1929) Manager of Boston N.L. in 1914 took the Miracle Braves from the cellar in July to the world championship in October. He died from a heart ailment in Haddock, Georgia, at 63. Honeysuckle sec., lot 2EE, Riverside Cemetery, Macon, GA.

8640. Stallings, Laurence (Laurence Tucker Stallings, Nov. 25, 1894–Feb. 28, 1968) World War I Marine captain from Macon, Georgia, who lost a leg in battle wrote the play *What Price Glory?*, filmed in 1946, and various war screenplays with a bitter edge (*The Big Parade, The Cock-Eyed World, Three Godfathers* [1948], *She Wore A Yellow Ribbon;* contributed to *Lives of a Bengal Lancer,* others). Found dead in Los Angeles from heart disease at 73. Cremated by Gates-Kingsley-Gates. Ashes buried Officers' sec., site 46A, Fort Rosecrans Cemetery, Point Loma (San Diego area), CA.

8641. Stander, Lionel (Jan. 11, 1908–Nov. 30, 1994) Gravel voiced actor in serio-comic to heavy parts, always with smiling sarcasm, in *Mr. Deeds Goes to Town* (1936) and *A Star is Born* (1937). Blacklisted in the 1950's, he worked as a Wall Street broker, returning to films in the 1960's in *The Loved One.* From 1979–84 he appeared as Max the chauffeur in TV's *Hart to Hart,* with five reprisals filmed in the year before his death. Garden of Honor (private), garden crypt 7246, Forest Lawn, Glendale, CA.

8642. Standing, Gordon (Nov. 24, 1887–May 21, 1927) English baritone on stage, nephew of Herbert Standing, appeared in nine films from 1919 before he died after being attacked by a lion at the Selig Zoo. Chapel of the Psalms, lower columbarium, east wall, tier 3, niche 30, Hollywood Forever Cemetery, Hollywood (Los Angeles), CA.

8643. Standing, Guy (Sept. 1, 1873–Feb. 24, 1937) Knighted London born actor in films of the 1930's, brother of Wyndham and Herbert Standing Jr., father of Kay Hammond. Films include *The Story of Temple Drake, The Eagle and the Hawk, Death Takes a Holiday, Lives of a Bengal Lancer.* He died from a heart attack reportedly brought on earlier by a rattlesnake or spider bite while in the Hollywood hills. Ashes buried sec. F, lot 288, Grandview Memorial Park, Glendale, CA.

8644. Standing, Herbert (Nov. 13, 1846–Dec. 5, 1923) English actor on stage and in American silent films 1914–1923 (*Stella Maris, The Squaw Man*). Fa-

ther of actors Sir Guy and Wyndham Standing. Vaultage, Chapel of the Pines Crematory, Los Angeles. His son **Herbert Standing Jr.** (1884–Sept 23 1955) is in the Actors Fund Plot, Kensico Cemetery, Valhalla, NY.

8645. Standing, Wyndham (Cecil Wyndham Standing, Aug. 24, 1881–Feb. 1, 1963) Brother of Guy Standing, in films from 1915, including *Hells Angels, A Study in Scarlet, Design For Living, Mary of Scotland,* later many smaller to bit roles. He died at the Motion picture Country Hospital at 81. Not at Valhalla in North Hollywood as sometimes listed. Cremated February 2 at Pasadena Crematorium, Altadena (no extant records), through White's mortuary (out of business).

8646. Standish, Burt L. (William Gilbert Patten, Oct. 25, 1866–Jan. 16, 1945) Writer from Corrina, Maine, created the mythical baseball hero Frank Merriwell, whose exploits graced 208 novels over eighteen years in the 1890's and 1900's, invariably winning the game, often with a home run in the bottom of the ninth. The works were published by the firm he worked for, Street and Smith. He also penned another 440 books, 648 full length novels in all. He earned no royalties, and by 1940 needed assistance, bringing contributions in from many long ago readers, including Wendell Willkie. He died at 78 in Vista, California. Cremated at Cypress Lawn Cemetery, San Diego. Ashes to his son at Vista, CA.

8647. Standish, Miles (c 1584–Oct. 3, 1656) Military leader of the Plymouth Colony in Massachusetts who, according to legend and Longfellow's poem *The Courtship of Miles Standish,* asked John Alden to propose marriage for him to Priscilla Mullins. The effort failed, and she married Alden. Standish died at South Duxbury and is buried with the others in the old burying ground, the grave marked with a boulder surrounded by a stone wall and cannon mounts encircling it. A large shaft nearby rises above the trees; a statue of him atop it. Old Burying Ground or Miles Standish Burying Ground, South Duxbury, MA.

8648. Stanford, Leland (March 9, 1824–June 21, 1893) California governor and senator founded Stanford University as a memorial to his son, who died in Italy of typhoid. The parents and son are in a mausoleum on campus, where they are known as the holy family. Stanford University campus, Palo Alto, CA.

8649. Stanford, Sally (May 5, 1903–Feb. 1, 1982) Head of a San Francisco brothel in the 1940's was mayor of Sausalito in the 1970's. Angeles Garden B, crypt 16, tier 2, at Mt. Tamalpais Cemetery, San Rafael, CA.

8650. Stanislavsky, Konstantin (Jan. 17, 1863–Aug. 7, 1938) Co-founder (1897) of the Moscow Art Theatre, designed to bring more realism to plays. Specializing in Chekhov, with less obvious drama and plot, he designed new acting techniques based on internalization by the actor, eventually termed Method Acting, not widely popular in America until the 1950's, but long stressed in the Actors Studio and the

Group Theatre of New York. Novodevichy Cemetery, Moscow.

8651. Stanky, Eddie (Sept. 3, 1915–June 7, 1999) Philadelphia born second baseman of the 1940's and 50's hit .268 and played in three world seasons in 11 seasons with the Dodgers (where he set the standing record with 148 walks in 1945), the Red Sox, and the New York Giants, leading the NL with 144 walks in 1950 and manning second in the series of 1951. He managed the Cardinals 1952–55, the White Sox 1966–68 and at South Alabama 1977–1983. He died from heart failure at Daphne, Alabama, east of Mobile. Catholic Cemetery, 1700 Martin Luther King Drive, Mobile, AL.

8652. Stanley, Florence (July 1, 1924–Oct. 3, 2003) Gravel voiced actress from Chicago, long on Broadway and in films, including *Up the Down Staircase, Outrageous Fortune, Atlantis: The Lost Empire,* best known as Detective Phil Fish's wife Bernice on TV's *Barney Miller* and *Fish* 1975–78. The wife of Martin Newman, she died in Los Angeles at 79. Garden of Ramah E, lot 6409, space 2, Mt. Sinai Memorial Park, Los Angeles.

8653. Stanley, Forrest (Aug. 21, 1889–Aug. 27, 1969) Actor in silent films from 1915 (*The Cat and the Canary* 1927, as Charlie Wilder; *Bare Knees, Arizona*), later showed up in a few roles on television. Sec. T, tier 35, grave 167, Holy Cross Cemetery, Culver City, CA.

8654. Stanley, Francis (June 1, 1849–July 31, 1918) and **Freeland O. Stanley** (June 1, 1849–Oct. 2, 1940) Identical twins developed the Stanley Steamer in 1897, the first automobile (1899) to make it to the top of Mount Washington, in two hours and ten minutes. Francis, killed in a car wreck, was buried in sec. B, Newton Center Cemetery, Newton, Massachusetts. Freeland is at Riverside Cemetery, Kingfield, ME.

8655. Stanley, Frank C. (William Stanley Grinsted, Dec. 29, 1868–Dec. 12, 1910) Pioneer recording artist was an alderman of West Orange, New Jersey. He died from pneumonia at 41. The stone lists only his real name and dates. Old sec., lot 798, Rosedale Cemetery, Orange, NJ.

8656. Stanley, George M. (George Maitland Stanley, April 26, 1903–May 11, 1970) Sculptor designed the first Academy Award statuettes, first presented at the Hollywood Roosevelt Hotel May 16, 1929 for the 1927–28 year, depicting a knight holding a sword, atop a reel of film, the reel containing five spokes, symbolizing the original five branches of the academy: actors, directors, writers, technicians, and producers. Columbarium of Independence, niche 33106, Freedom Mausoleum, Forest Lawn, Glendale, CA.

8657. Stanley, Henry Morton (John Rowlands, Jan. 28, 1841–May 10, 1904) Welsh born reporter for the *New York Herald* was sent by them in 1868 into Africa to locate Dr. Livingstone, which he did in Tanzania in 1871 with (so legend has it) the famed greeting "Dr. Livingstone, I presume?" He later circumnav-

igated lakes, established the basis of British East Africa. In Parliament 1895–1900. Knighted 1899. Rough hewn stone monument, St. Michael's Churchyard, Pirbright, Surrey, England.

8658. Stanley, Kim (Patricia Beth Reid, Feb. 11, 1925–Aug. 20, 2001) Actress from Tularosa, New Mexico, first acclaimed on Broadway as twelve year old Millie in *Picnic* (1952), as Cherie in *Bus Stop* (1954), several others. She received Emmys for a 1963 episode of *Ben Casey* and as Big Mama in the 1984 PBS version of *Cat on A Hot Tin Roof*. Her few but memorable films include *The Goddess* (1958), the uncredited narration of *To Kill A Mockingbird* (1962), *Seance on a Wet Afternoon* (1964), *Frances* (1982, as her mother) and as Pancho Barnes in *The Right Stuff* (1983). In later years she returned to New Mexico, teaching acting at the College of Santa Fe. She died in Santa Fe from uterine cancer at 76. A memorial service was held at the college. Cremated, her ashes were retained by family.

8659. Stanton, Edwin McMasters (Dec. 19, 1814–Dec. 24, 1869) Lincoln's Secretary of War, credited with the words "Now he belongs to the ages" upon the death of the president. After Reconstruction policy disputes with President Johnson, Stanton refused to leave his office and the Tenure of Office Act was used to bring about the impeachment trial of Johnson in March 1868. Stanton had just been appointed to the Supreme Court by Grant and walked to the White House to thank him when he caught a chill and died. An obelisk marks his grave, at an intersection of the descending sidewalk, crowded with Victoriana. Lot 675, Oak Hill Cemetery, Georgetown, Washington, D.C.

8660. Stanton, Elizabeth Cady (Nov. 12, 1815–Oct. 26, 1902) Advocate of women's rights, beginning with the Seneca Falls Convention of 1848, worked for decades for female suffrage and other legislation. Lake sec. 48, off Central Ave., Woodlawn Cemetery, the Bronx, N.Y.C.

8661. Stanwyck, Barbara (Ruby Stevens, July 16, 1907–Jan. 20, 1990) Screen star from Flatbush, Brooklyn could play sultry roles in *Baby Face* (1933), *Double Indemnity* (1944, AA nom.), *The Strange Love of Martha Ivers* (1946) or exude sincerity and warmth for drama or comedy, in *The Miracle Woman* (1931), *So Big* (1932), *Stella Dallas* (1937, AA nom.), *Golden Boy* (1939), *The Lady Eve, Ball of Fire* (AA nom.), *The Lady Eve, Meet John Doe* (all 1941), *Sorry Wrong Number* (1948, AA nom.). She made an easy transition to TV as the matriarch on *The Big Valley* 1965–69. Married to Frank Fay 1929–1935 and to Robert Taylor 1939–1952. Special Oscar 1982. She died at 82 from congestive heart failure complicated by pneumonia and emphysema in St. John's Hospital, Santa Monica. Cremated through Gates-Kingsley-Gates, the ashes went to her nephew in San Rafael and were to be scattered by her press agent Larry Kleno over Lone Pine, California, at her request.

8662. Stargell, Willie (Wilver D. Stargell, March 6, 1940–April 9, 2001) Pops, the leader of the Pittsburgh Pirates through the 1970's, hit 475 career home runs, twice leading the N.L., with 48 in 1971 and 44 in 1973. A native of Earlsboro, Oklahoma, known for his good nature and gentlemanly demeanor, he helped lead the team to six division titles and two world championships, in 1971 and 1979, when he shared the N.L. MVP with Keith Hernandez. Hall of Fame 1988. On Pittsburgh's opening day in 2001, when a new statue of him was unveiled at their new PNC Park, Stargell, long ill with a kidney disorder, died of a stroke in Wilmington, North Carolina, at 61. Outside right wall, far left, second from top. Oleander Memorial Gardens Mausoleum, adjacent Greenlawn Cemetery, Wilmington, NC.

8663. Stark, John (Aug. 28, 1728–May 8, 1822) Colorful colonial general at Bunker Hill and Saratoga best known for the Battle of Bennington, Vermont, which aborted British attempts to cut off New England. Statue and family graveyard in Stark State Park, Manchester, NH.

8664. Stark, Pauline (Pauline Starke, Jan. 10, 1901–Feb. 3, 1977) Silent screen actress from Joplin, Missouri, left films shortly after sound, in 1930. Married to producer George Sherwood. Ashes scattered at sea.

8665. Stark, Ray (Oct. 3, 1914–Jan. 17, 2004) Chicago born Hollywood literary and talent agent turned producer, made the Broadway hit *Funny Girl* and the subsequent film, about his mother-in-law Fannie Brice. Other works include the films *Night of the Iguana, Funny Lady, The Sunshine Boys, The Goodbye Girl, California Suite, Annie, Brighton Beach Memoirs.* Irving Thalberg Award 1980. He produced up to 1999, five years before his death in Holmby Hills at 88. With his wife Frances Brice Stark (d. 1992) and her mother, whose ashes he had moved from Home of Peace Memorial Park after his wife's death. Westwood Memorial Park, West Los Angeles.

8666. Starkweather, Charles (Nov. 25, 1938–June 25, 1959) Garbage man in Lincoln, Nebraska, began his killing spree in December 1957, and on January 28, 1958 killed the parents and baby sister of his girlfriend, fourteen year old Caril Ann Fugate. After a nationwide manhunt and eleven brutal murders, he was captured near Douglas, Wyoming, in early February. Fugate was given a life sentence and eventually paroled. Starkweather died in the electric chair at the Nebraska State Penitentiary. Flush stone. Sec. 28, grave 996, Wyuka Cemetery, Lincoln, NE.

8667. Starr, Belle (Feb. 5, 1848–Feb. 3, 1889) Bandit Queen of the Indian Territory stole horses and cattle. Shot in the back by an unknown assassin, Indian and white women dressed her for burial and placed in her hands a six shooter given her by Cole Younger. The grave was later robbed of her jewelry and gun. Her marker was inscribed *Shed not for her the bitter tear, nor give the heart to vain regret. Tis but the* casket that lies here. The gem that fills it sparkles yet. Belle Starr Cabin, reached by horseback, Youngers Bend, near Porum, OK.

8668. Starr, Edwin (Charles Edwin Hatcher, Jan. 21, 1942–April 2, 2003) Rhythm and Blues vocalist and songwriter from Nashville had hits in the mid to late 1960s with *Agent Double O Soul* and *Stop Her on Sight,* but was best known for War, which reached number one in summer 1970. Residing in England, he died from a heart attack at 61 in home near Nottingham. Black upright stone listing his real name. Southern (Wilford Hill) Cemetery and Crematorium, Nottingham, Nottinghamshire.

8669. Starr, Frances (June 6, 1881–June 11, 1973) Broadway actress from Albany, New York, famed as Juanita in David Belasco's *Rose of the Rancho* 1906–08 and as Laura Murdock in his *The Easiest Way* 1909–11 worked steadily on the New York stage to 1953, including the mother in *Claudia* (1941) and the headmistress in *The Young and the Fair* (1948). She made only four films, notably *Star Witness* (as Ma) and *Five Star Final* (as Nancy Voorhees), both 1931. The widow of Chicago lawyer Emil C. Wetten, her third husband, she died at 92 at her home, 10 Mitchell Place, Manhattan. Buried as Frances Starr. Headstone reads *Frances Grant Starr 1973.* Her mother was Emma Grant. Van Tuyl lot, sec. 122, lot 11, Albany Rural Cemetery, Albany, NY.

8670. Starr, Sally (Jan. 23, 1909–May 5, 1996) Screen actress from Pittsburgh formerly in the George White Scandals in films 1917–1936, especially busy in many 1930 talkies. Buried as Sally (Mrs. John F.) Kovacevich. Garden of Devotion, lot 111-D, space 4, Jefferson Memorial Park, Pleasant Hills (south of Pittsburgh), PA.

8671. Starrett, Charles (March 28, 1903–March 23, 1986) Actor from Athol, Massachusetts, was a football star at Dartmouth College. He did romantic leads (*The Mask of Fu Manchu*) before going into westerns by 1936, often as *The Durango Kid* and in numerous B's. He died at Borrego Springs, California. Cremated at Laguna Beach, the ashes were scattered on the campus at Dartmouth College, Hanover, NH.

8672. Starrett, Vincent (Oct. 26, 1886–Jan. 5, 1974) Writer and Sherlock Holmes scholar best known for *The Private Life of Sherlock Holmes,* first published in 1933 and updated several times. A charter member of the Baker Street Irregulars, a group of literati devoted to Holmes. Unmarked. Sec. C, lot 903, grave 4, Graceland Cemetery, Chicago, IL.

8673. Stassen, Harold (April 13, 1907–March 4, 2001) Liberal Minnesota Republican was elected to three two year terms as governor, in 1938, 1940 and 1942, his last successful campaign for office, though he became known as a perennial presidential candidate, losing the party's nomination in 1948 (to Dewey), making his mark in 1952 by swinging his delegates to Eisenhower and taking the prize from Robert Taft, and running in the primaries in 1964, 1968, 1976,

1980, 1984, 1988 and 1992. He died at 93 in a Minneapolis suburb. Acacia Cemetery, Mendota Heights (south St. Paul), MN.

8674. Stauffenberg, Graf (Count) Claus Philipp Maria Schenk Von (Nov. 15, 1907–July 20, 1944) German army officer since 1926 was a staff officer with the panzer division in Poland and northern France 1939–40. Later on the Russian front, however, he became disillusioned with the brutal policies toward the Slavs and Jews, and requested transfer to North Africa, where he was badly wounded in 1943. In July 1944 he was the chief of staff of the Reserve Army command when he headed the conspiracy to eliminate Hitler, placing a bomb in his headquarters at Rastenburg July 20. The bomb failed to kill the fuehrer, and Stauffenberg and his co-conspirators were summarily executed the same night. A-S 41/42, Kirchof St. Matthäus (aka Friedfof Matthai-Gemeinde), Grossgörschenstr. 12–14 (Schöneberg), Berlin.

8675. Stayner, Steven (April 18, 1965–Sept. 16, 1989) Kidnapped at seven in 1973 and held for seven years until at fourteen he escaped with another child in 1980, his first words to police inspired the TV movie about the case, *I Know My First Name Is Steven.* He died at twenty-four when his motorcycle crashed into a stalled car. Knee high monument, Garden of Peace, Merced District Cemetery, Merced, CA.

8676. Stearnes, Turkey (Norman Stearnes, May 8, 1901–Sept. 4, 1979) Negro Leagues outfielding great, born in Nashville, Tennessee. Died in Detroit. Hall of Fame 2000. Plaque with his picture and career summary. Sec. 1600, row 4, grave 20, Lincoln Memorial Park Cemetery, Mt. Clemens (north Detroit), MI.

8677. Stearns, Johnny (John A. Stearns, Oct. 23, 1916–Dec. 1, 2001) Co-star with his wife on television's first situation comedy, *Mary Kay and Johnny* 1947–50. He resided at Corona Del Mar, California. Westwood Memorial Park, west Los Angeles.

8678. Stedman, Lincoln (May 16, 1906–March 22, 1948) Actor son of Myrtle and Marshall Stedman, in many films from World War I into the 1930s. Unmarked. Sec. C, lot 303, grave 8, Holy Cross Cemetery, Culver City, CA.

8679. Stedman, Marshall (Aug 16, 1875–Dec. 16, 1943) Actor from Bethel, Maine, married to Myrtle Stedman; they were later divorced. He appeared in films 1910–15. Mausoleum, Magnolia crypt 43F, Melrose Abbey, Anaheim, CA.

8680. Stedman, Myrtle (Myrtle Lincoln, March 1, 1885–Jan. 8, 1938) Chicago born actress in silent films including *Hypocrites* (1915), directed by Lois Weber, *Sex* (1920), *Rich Man's Wives* and *Reckless Youth* (1922), *The Famous Mrs. Fear* (1923) and character parts in sound films up to her death from a heart attack at 52. Magnolia, lot 447, Inglewood Park Cemetery, Inglewood, CA.

8681. Steel, Dawn (Aug. 19, 1946–Dec. 20, 1997) Head of production at Paramount became the first female to head a studio, Columbia, in 1987. She later left to produce independently (*Cool Runnings* 1993). She died from a brain tumor in Los Angeles at 51. Psalms 9, lot 101, Mt. Sinai Memorial Park, Los Angeles.

8682. Steele, Bob (Robert Bradbury, Jan. 23, 1907–Dec. 21, 1988) Actor in many B westerns, small in stature and known for menacing, bullying parts, particularly in *Of Mice and Men* (1939, as Curley) and *The Big Sleep* (1946, as Canino). He turned up in many westerns through his later years (*Hang Em High,* etc.). Plaque lists his death as 1989. Columbarium of Remembrance (Right), niche 60722, until moved in early 2001 to Columbarium of Providence, niche 64689, Courts of Remembrance, Forest Lawn Hollywood Hills, Los Angeles.

8683. Steele, Freddie (Frederick Earle Steele, Dec. 18, 1912–Aug. 23, 1984) Tacoma born world middleweight champion 1936–38, in films 1941–48 (*The Miracle of Morgan's Creek, Duffy's Tavern, Black Angel*), memorable as Bugsy in Preston Sturges' *Hail the Conquering Hero* (1944) and as Warnicki in *The Story of G.I. Joe* (1945). He retired to Aberdeen, Washington, where he died from a stroke at 71. His stone notes his reign as middleweight champ. 10th addition, block L, grave 23, Fern Hill Cemetery, Aberdeen, WA.

8684. Steele, John Marvin (Nov. 29, 1912–May 16, 1969) Private with the 82nd Airborne, the barber for F company, whose parachute caught on the steeple of the church tower at St. Mere Iglese, the first town in France liberated by the Allies in the early hours of D-Day, June 6, 1944. Played by Red Buttons in the film *The Longest Day* (1962), he survived the war and died at 56 from lung cancer. As a lasting memorial to the liberation, a dummy chute is kept on the clock tower at St. Mere Iglese. Masonic Cemetery, Metropolis, IL.

8685. Stefansson, Vilhjalmur (Nov. 3, 1879–Aug. 26, 1962) Canadian explorer of the Arctic and expert on Eskimo life, aided by his forced 1906 stay with them for a year when his ship was stuck in the ice. He later taught at Dartmouth. Marked by a boulder with a plaque. Pine Knolls Cemetery, Hanover, NH.

8686. Steffens, Lincoln (April 6, 1866–Aug. 9, 1936) Journalist of the Muckraking era, editor of *McClure's,* wrote a series of articles published as *The Shame of the Cities* (1904), which, with the work of Ida Tarbell and Upton Sinclair, were major books of the decade as influential agents of reform. Family mausoleum, sec. F, Cypress Hills Cemetery, Colma, CA.

8687. Stehli, Edgar (July 12, 1884–July 25, 1973) Actor born in Lyons, France, settled at Montclair, New Jersey, as a boy. He appeared on radio (from 1933, as inventor Dr. Huer on *Buck Rogers in the 25th Century, Crime Doctor, Mr. Kean, Mr. and Mrs. North*), stage (as Osric to John Barrymore's *Hamlet,* in O'Neill's *The Fountain,* Dr. Einstein in *Arsenic and Old Lace*), film, and television (*Twilight Zone* episode *Long Live Walter Jameson*). Married to Emilie Greenough from 1923; they had a fifty acre summer home and tree preserve from 1928 at Vernon, New Jersey. He died at Upper Montclair, New Jersey, at 89. Cremated at Cedar Lawn Cemetery, Paterson, New Jersey, the day after his death. Ashes mailed to his wife in Upper Montclair.

8688. Steiger, Rod (Rodney Stephan Steiger, April 14, 1925–July 9, 2002) Intense, beefy method actor born in Westhampton and raised in Newark created the role of *Marty* on television, but became a film star opposite Marlon Brando in Elia Kazan's *On The Waterfront* (1954). Though he did many films, (*Oklahoma, The Harder They Fall, Al Capone, The Loved One, Dr. Zhivago*), he shone in *The Pawnbroker* (1965) and was a front-runner for the Best Actor Oscar, but won two years later as Chief Gillespie in *In The Heat of the Night* (1967). Later roles included a tour de force in *No way To Treat A Lady* (1968) but by the 1980's he was often ill with depression, yet re-emerged in several films in the 1990's prior to his death from pneumonia and kidney failure due to pancreatic cancer in St. John's Health Center, Santa Monica, at 77. He said his preferred tombstone epitaph would be *See you later*, and it is. Cremation July 11. Columbarium of Providence, niche G65094, Courts of Remembrance, Forest Lawn Hollywood Hills, Los Angeles.

8689. Stein, Gertrude (Feb. 3, 1874–July 27, 1946) Writer and Paris salon keeper from Allegheny, Pennsylvania, authored *Three Lives* (1905–6, published 1909), *The Making of Americans* (1906–8, published 1925) and, among other works, a collection of poems forming what are described as "cubist" still lifes, *Tender Buttons* (1941). She remained in Paris through the Nazi occupation of World War II. Her companion of many decades **Alice B. Toklas** (April 30, 1877–March 7, 1967), author of several cookbooks, returned home with her in December 1945. Stein had began suffering stomach pain in November and died the following summer following surgery for abdominal cancer. Buried October 22 (later joined by Toklas), beneath a polished gray stone with her name and dates in gold leaf. Div. 94, Pere Lachaise Cemetery, Paris.

8690. Stein, Herbert (Aug. 27, 1916–Sept. 8, 1999) Economist, Chairman of the Council of Economic Advisors during the Nixon administration. Father of economist and actor-comedian Ben Stein. King David Memorial Garden, Falls Church, VA.

8691. Stein, Jules (April 26, 1896–April 29, 1981) Los Angeles physician, later president of MCA, founded and helped finance the Hollywood Canteen for servicemen 1942–1945, co-founded with Bette Davis and John Garfield. Family enclosure (Little Garden), Garden of Memory (private), Forest Lawn, Glendale, CA.

8692. Steinbeck, John (Feb. 27, 1902–Dec. 20, 1968) Chronicler of the 20th century west in earthy portraits of migrant life including *Of Mice and Men* (1937), *The Grapes of Wrath* (1939, Nobel Prize), and *East of Eden* (1952). A native of Salinas, California, he set many of his stories in the area. Upon his death from heart disease in his Manhattan apartment, services were held at St. James Episcopal Church, with Psalms 46 and 121 read and Henry Fonda reading some of the author's favorite poems. His ashes are commemorated by a small bronze plaque set in concrete. Hamilton family plot, block 60, lot 5, Gardens of Memories/Oddfellows, Salinas, CA.

8693. Steinberg, Lisa (Elizabeth Lisa Launders, May 14, 1981–Nov. 4, 1987) The infant daughter of nineteen year old Michele Launders was turned over to New York lawyer Joel Steinberg with the assurance she would be given a good home with loving parents. Instead, he took her home. After six years, she was found on November 4, 1987, the victim of horrendous child abuse, filthy, beaten and bruised on their cold bathroom floor at 14 West 10th St., Greenwich Village. The (illegally) adoptive mother, Hedda Nussbaum, a one time editor at Random House and author of children's books, was equally battered yet had made no move to help the child. The six year old went into a coma and was deemed brain dead the same day. Nussbaum was acquitted. Steinberg received eight and a half to twenty-three years for manslaughter, the maximum allowed. Lisa was buried under her full real name. Flush stone, far up behind Anna Held's monument, near the road behind sec. 42, in sight of Jimmy Walker across the road, and blocked by the monuments to Manning, Moore, and Donnelly. Sec. 42, Gate of Heaven Cemetery, Hawthorne, NY.

8694. Steiner, Max (May 10, 1888–Dec. 28, 1971) Hollywood composer born in Vienna scored over 200 films, most at RKO and Warners, including *King Kong, The Informer* (1935, AA), *Gone With the Wind* (1939), *Now Voyager* (1942, Academy Award), *Casablanca* (1942), *Since You Went Away* (1944, AA), *The Treasure of the Sierra Madre* (1948), *The Caine Mutiny* (1954). Columbarium of Enduring Honor, niche 24046, Holly Terrace, Great Mausoleum, Forest Lawn Glendale, CA.

8695. Steinmetz, Charles Proteus (Karl August Rudolf Steinmetz, April 9, 1865–Oct. 26, 1923) German born electrical engineer in America discovered the law of hysteresis, leading to the ability to calculate loss of electrical power due to magnetism, improving the design of motors, generators and transformers. Consulting engineer with General Electric in Schenectady from 1893 until his death, studying alternating current and patenting over 100 inventions. Vale Cemetery, Schenectady, NY.

8696. Steinway, William (March 5, 1836–Nov. 30, 1896) Partner in the piano manufacturing business begun by his father **Henry Englehard Steinway** (Steinweg, Feb. 15, 1797–Feb. 7, 1871) in New York in 1853. The massive mausoleum, designed by William, is made of stone with a roof, the size of a large two story house. His brothers **Christian Frederick Theodore** (Nov. 6, 1825–March 29, 1889) and **Theodore Edwin** (Oct. 6, 1883–April 8, 1957) are also there.

Sec. 46/47 along Chapel Ave., Greenwood Cemetery, Brooklyn, N.Y.C.

8697. Sten, Anna (Annel Stenskaya Sudakevich, Dec. 3, 1908–Nov. 12, 1993) Russian born actress from Kiev known as Samuel Goldwyn's Folly, his failed attempt to duplicate Garbo in the early 1930's, starring her in *We Live Again* and *Nana* (both 1934) and *The Wedding Night* (1935). Widow of producer-director Eugene Frenke, she died in her Manhattan home. Cremated at Garden State Crematory through the Frank E. Campbell mortuary. Ashes scattered in the Pacific.

8698. Stendhal, Marie Henri Beyle (Jan. 23, 1793–March 23, 1842) Prolific French writer (*The Red and the Black* 1830, *The Charterhouse of Parma* 1839). Div. 30, Montmartre Cemetery, Paris.

8699. Stengel, Casey (Charles Dillon Stengel, July 30, 1890–Sept. 29, 1975) N.L. outfielder went on to manage, becoming a legend with the New York Yankees 1949–1960, winning ten pennants and seven world series in twelve years, the best managerial record ever. Hall of Fame 1966. The Ole Perfessor was known for his butchering of the English language and frequent incomprehensible sentences, one of which graces the bronze plaque with his likeness on the brick wall above his grave: *There comes a time in every man's life, and I've had plenty of them.* Court of Freedom, lawn crypt 6A, block 7060, Forest Lawn, Glendale, CA.

8700. Stennis, John (Aug. 3, 1901–April 23, 1995) U.S. Democratic senator from Mississippi 1947–88, chairman of the Armed Services Committee and the Defense Sub-committee of the Appropriations Committee in the 1970's. The oldest member of the senate on his retirement in 1988. Pinecrest Cemetery, DeKalb, MS.

8701. Stephens, Alexander Hamilton (Feb. 11, 1812–March 4, 1883) Former representative from Georgia, a small, sickly man, was elevated to the Vice Presidency of the Confederacy. Denied his seat in the U.S. Senate in 1866, he was again admitted as a representative from Georgia 1873–1882. Entombed for a year in the Cotting-Burke tomb, Oakland Cemetery, Atlanta. He was moved to his home Liberty Hall in 1884. On his monument is inscribed in Latin *Not for himself but for others.* Statue and grave at Liberty Hall, Alexander Stephens State Park, Crawfordsville, GA.

8702. Stephenson, D.C. (David Curtis Stephenson, Aug. 21, 1891–June 28, 1966) Grand dragon of the Ku Klux Klan in Indiana in the early 1920's boasted "I am the law in Indiana" and aspired to political greatness, leaving the Klan for politics by 1924, where he felt his ally and newly elected Governor Ed Jackson would protect his activities such as having been arrested for indecent behavior. In early 1925 he met and courted **Madge Oberholtzer** (1896–April 14, 1925) who worked in the Department of Public Instruction in Indianapolis and lived in Irvington on the east side of the city. On March 15, 1925, he and two other men abducted Oberholtzer and took her aboard a train for Hamilton, while Stephenson raped her. At Hamilton she was taken to a drugstore where she bought bichloride of mercury tablets and ingested six pills in a suicide attempt. Stephenson and his companions deposited her back at her parents house in Irvington March 17, telling them she had been in a car accident. She died April 14, and was buried at Memorial Park Cemetery, Indianapolis, Indiana. A diary she had kept and managed to continue recording in during her last weeks led to the arrest of Stephenson and his accomplices. They were acquitted, but he went to prison for 30 years, lived in Seymour, Indiana, from 1958, and was arrested for child molestation in 1961 at Independence, Missouri. He settled finally at Jonesboro in eastern Tennessee, where he married in 1964. He died two years later from a heart attack at 74. Sec. L, row 6, grave 9, Mountain Home National Cemetery, Mountain Home, Johnson City, near Jonesboro, TN.

8703. Stephenson, Henry (Henry Garroway, April 16, 1871–April 24, 1956) Character actor in dignified, kindly authoritative roles in films of the 30's and 40's including *Mutiny on the Bounty, Little Lord Fauntleroy, The Charge of the Light Brigade, Oliver Twist* (1946, as Mr. Brownlow), many others. He died at 85 in St. Luke's Hospital, San Francisco, while accompanying his wife Dorothy (**Ann Shoemaker**, Jan. 10, 1891–Sept. 18, 1978). He had become ill with nephritis and was unable to continue with her to Milwaukee. Not until her tour was finished was a funeral service held, on July 26 at the Church of the Transfiguration in Manhattan. Actors Fund of America Plot, Kensico Cemetery, Valhalla, NY.

8704. Stephenson, James (April 14, 1889–July 29, 1941) Suave, mustached actor from Yorkshire in U.S. films 1937–41 (*Confessions of a Nazi Spy, Beau Geste, Shining Victory*) nominated for a best supporting actor Oscar for *The Letter* (1940). Slated for the role of Dr. Tower in *King's Row* (played by Claude Rains), he died from a heart attack the next year at 52. Signature and year of death on his plaque. Whispering Pines, lot 1275, Forest Lawn, Glendale, CA.

8705. Sterling, Ford (George F. Stitch, Nov. 3, 1884–Oct. 13, 1939) Silent screen comic best known as the Chief of the original Keystone Kops appeared in many features including *Sally* (1929). He died from a heart attack at 58. Ashes in an unmarked communal wall niche (Dawn), colonnade at the Chapel of the Psalms, Hollywood Forever Cemetery, Hollywood (Los Angeles), CA.

8706. Sterling, Jan (Jane Sterling Adriance, April 3, 1921–March 26, 2004) New York born blonde aristocrat known for her roles as loose women in several films, "the original happy hooker," she said (*Ace in the Hole* 1951, which afforded her the line "I never go to church because it bags my nylons," *The High and the Mighty* 1954, AA nom., *The Incident* 1967, *First Monday in October* 1981, her last), and stage and television roles. The widow of actor Paul Douglas (*q.v.,* died 1959), she lived in London, the companion of actor

Sam Wanamaker (*q.v.*) until his death in 1993 and afterward, moving to the Motion Picture and Television Fund Home in Woodland Hills, California, shortly before her death there at 82 following several strokes. Her son Adams Douglas had died only three months before. Listed as Jan Sterling-Douglas. Cremated through Bastian and Perrott mortuary. Ashes April 2 to a sister in Palm Beach, FL.

8707. Stern, Isaac (July 21, 1920–Sept. 22, 2001) Russian born master violinist and teacher who saved Carnegie Hall from being destroyed in the late 1950's when Lincoln Center was being planned. Stern rallied benefactors enabling the city to acquire it for $5 million in 1960. Stern had made his debut there January 8, 1943. He toured around the world for decades, but as a strong supporter of Israel refused to play in Germany until 1999, though as he went there to teach, he noted "I forgive nothing." His services were handled by Mt. Sinai Chapel in East Brunswick, New Jersey. Stern and Linda Reynolds, his wife of five years, had a home near New Milford, Connecticut, where a gathering was held. His grave, in a twelve grave lot not far from his home, has a marker with the epitaph *Fiddler.* Rear of Morningside Cemetery, Gaylordsville, CT.

8708. Stettinius, Edward (Edward R. Stettinius, Jr., Oct. 22, 1900–Oct. 31, 1949) General Motors and U.S. Steel executive in the administration of Franklin Roosevelt as Lend Lease administrator and Under Secretary of State and Secretary of State 1944–45, playing a major role in the formation of the United Nations at Dumbarton Oaks in 1944 and at 1945 when Truman appointed him the first U.S. delegate to the U.N. Resigned 1946. Locust Valley Cemetery, Locust Valley, near Oyster Bay, Long Island, NY.

8709. Steuben, Friedrich Wilhelm Von, Baron (Sept. 17, 1730–Nov. 28, 1794) Prussian officer who became a Colonial hero in the American Revolution. He took charge of the men at Valley Forge and turned them into a disciplined army. In gratitude for his service there and later at Yorktown, America made him a citizen and voted to present him with a 16,000 acre farm north of Utica, New York, where he died. The grave, unmarked, was unearthed later by a former military aide when a road was to be constructed over it. The Baron was then buried in the forest, where a large monument and plaque, stating that his services were indispensable to the American cause, now marks the grave. Steuben Memorial, Remsen, NY.

8710. Stevens, Craig (Gail Shickles, Jr., July 8, 1918–May 10, 2000) Actor from Liberty, Missouri, in films from the mid 1940's, including *Night Unto Night, Since You Went Away, Night and Day, Abbott & Costello meet Dr. Jekyll & Mr. Hyde,* on TV as *Peter Gunn* 1958–1961. Married to actress Alexis Smith (d. 1993), his last appearance was in Blake Edwards' *S.O.B.* (1981). He died from lymphoma at 81. Like Smith, his ashes were scattered at sea, by the Neptune Society May 23 off Los Angeles County.

8711. Stevens, George (Dec. 18, 1904–March 8, 1975) Acclaimed Hollywood director, son of actor John L. Stevens and actress Georgie Cooper and father of producer-director George Stevens, Jr. Increasingly appreciated for his footage in and out of action during World War II, his works as director include *A Place in the Sun* (1951, Academy Award), *Shane* (1953), and *Giant* (1956, Academy Award). Low on output but a perfectionist with content, his films were usually set amid wide expanses of the great outdoors. He died from a heart attack at 70. Signature on plaque. Morning Light, lot 8034, Forest Lawn Hollywood Hills, Los Angeles.

8712. Stevens, Inger (Inger Stensland, Oct 18, 1934–April 30, 1970) Swedish actress in American films (*The World, Flesh and the Devil, Five Card Stud*) and TV from 1957, including *The Twilight Zone* episode *The Hitch-hiker* and a TV sitcom, *The Farmer's Daughter* 1963–65. A suicide attempt on New Years Day 1959 had failed, but eleven years later, the wife of Isaac Jones, she took a fatal overdose of barbiturates in her Laurel Canyon home and died on the way to the hospital at 35. Cremated through Angelus mortuary at Inglewood Park Cemetery. Ashes scattered at sea.

8713. Stevens, Morton L. (Sept. 30, 1887–Aug. 5, 1959) Actor starred on stage in *The Iceman Cometh* and *Finian's Rainbow.* Rocklawn Cemetery, Marlborough, MA.

8714. Stevens, Onslow (Onslow Stevenson, March 29, 1902–Jan. 5, 1977) Los Angeles born actor, son of actor Houseley Stevenson, appeared in varied parts in many films including numerous melodramas (*Secret of the Blue Room* 1933; *The Crosby Case* 1934; *The Monster and the Girl* 1941; *House of Dracula* 1945, as Dr. Edelman; *The Couch* 1960). His death at 74 while a resident of a nursing home was ruled a homicide, though no one was ever charged. Unmarked. Restland sec., block B, grave 328-B. Valhalla Memorial Park, North Hollywood, CA.

8715. Stevens, Thaddeus (April 4, 1792–Aug. 11, 1868) Republican representative from Pennsylvania led the fiery Radical faction in Congress 1865–68 pressing for harsh post-war treatment of the defeated south. He was so ill during Andrew Johnson's impeachment trial that he was carried in on a seat by four young black men, once remarking to them "Who's going to carry me in here when you boys die?" A staunch supporter of negro rights, he lived for years with a mulatto housekeeper, and was later the basis for the villain in Griffith's pro-southern *Birth of a Nation* (1915). He died in Washington, D.C. and lay in state in the capital rotunda, the photo of his coffin there for many years mistaken for that of Lincoln. Stevens was buried in a small graveyard surrounded by an iron fence. On the large stone oval shaped monument is inscribed his reason for his permanent location: *I repose in this quiet and secluded spot, not from any natural preference for solitude but, finding other cemeteries limited by charter rules as to race, I have chosen this that*

I might illustrate in my death the principles which I advocated through a long life — Equality of Man before his creator. Old Schreiner's (Concord) Cemetery, downtown Lancaster, PA.

8716. Stevens, Wallace (Oct. 2, 1879–Aug. 2, 1955) Noted poet from 1897 won the 1955 Pulitzer Prize for his *Collected Poems.* Sec. 14, Cedar Hill Cemetery, Hartford, CT.

8717. Stevenson, Adlai (Adlai Ewing Stevenson, Oct. 23, 1835–June 14, 1914) Illinois congressman, vice president on the Democratic ticket with Grover Cleveland 1893–97. Grandfather of the two time presidential candidate of the same name. He died in Chicago. Large stone monument marked Stevenson-Scott lists his career, in the same lot with his grandson. Sec. 11, lot 3, Evergreen Memorial Cemetery, Bloomington, IL.

8718. Stevenson, Adlai (Adlai Ewing Stevenson II, Feb. 5, 1900–July 14, 1965) Grandson of Cleveland's second vice president, the liberal minded governor of Illinois, branded an "egghead" by conservatives, had a wide following in his two campaigns for the presidency in 1952 and 1956, but was soundly defeated by Eisenhower both times. Appointed Ambassador to the United Nations by Kennedy, his finest moment came in October 1962 when he confronted the Russian representative before the entire body over Soviet missiles based in Cuba. Stevenson died from a heart attack on a London street at 65. Services in the National Cathedral. Buried in the lot with his grandfather, his 8' monument is perpendicular to that of the earlier Stevenson. Sec. 11, lot 3, Evergreen Memorial Cemetery, Bloomington, IL.

8719. Stevenson, B.W. (Louis C. Stevenson, Oct. 5, 1949–April 28, 1988) Country-western and pop singer-songwriter penned several hits including *Shambala* (for Three Dog Night) but recorded only one hit himself, *My Maria* (1973). He died in Nashville at 38. Sec. 14, lot 86, Laurel Land Memorial Park, Dallas, TX.

8720. Stevenson, Houseley (July 30, 1879–Aug. 6, 1953) English born character actor, father of actors Houseley Jr. and Onslow. His rubbery, expressive face was used to advantage in several films including *Dark Passage* (1947, as the back alley plastic surgeon), *All the King's Men* (1949, as Jack Burden's editor). Block (Memorial) J, sec. 9583, lot 4, Valhalla Memorial Park, North Hollywood, CA.

8721. Stevenson, McLean (Edgar McLean Stevenson, Jr., Nov. 14, 1927–Feb. 15, 1996) Actor from Bloomington, Illinois, related to Adlai, used his hometown as that of his character, Col. Henry Blake, in TV's *M.A.S.H.* from its premiere in September 1972 until he was written out at the end of the 1974–75 season. He died from a heart attack at 68 following surgery for cancer in Tarzana, California. Services at Bel Air Presbyterian Church, Van Nuys, February 21. Cremated by the Neptune Society in Burbank. Columbarium of Valor, niche G64649, Courts of Remembrance, Forest Lawn Hollywood Hills, Los Angeles.

8722. Stevenson, Robert Louis (Nov. 13, 1850–Dec. 3, 1894) Scottish writer from Edinburgh wrote most of his best known works in the 1880's, including *Treasure Island, Kidnapped, The Strange Case of Dr. Jekyll & Mr. Hyde, A Child's Garden of Verses* and *The Master of Ballantrae,* often while traveling to improve his health. He was frail and tubercular and by 1888 was seeking a better climate. He found it on the island of Samoa, six hundred feet up the slope of Vaea where he built his house, Vailima, three miles from the town of Apia. He was on the veranda with his wife Fanny just before dinner when he felt his head, said "What's that?" and sagged to his knees, caught by a servant. He died from the stroke later that evening at 44. The Samoans made a hardwood coffin and took it by relay teams to the summit of Vaea, where their Tusitala (Teller of tales) was buried with a Presbyterian service. A white sarcophagus was later built over the grave with a quotation from Stevenson: *Under the wide and starry sky, dig the grave and let me lie, and I laid me down with a will./ This be the verse you grave for me: Here he lies where he longed to be./ Home is the sailor, home from the sea, And the hunter home from the hill.* When his wife Fanny died in 1910, her ashes were placed at his grave. Summit of Vaea near Apia, on the western side of the island of Samoa in the south Pacific. There is also a cenotaph to Stevenson in the south aisle of the High Kirk of St. Giles, Edinburgh.

8723. Stewart, Alexander T. (Oct. 12, 1803–April 10, 1876) Scotch-Irish merchant in Manhattan. By 1862 the A.T. Stewart Dry Goods Co. was the largest in the world. He owned Niblo's Garden as well and founded Garden City, Long Island, as a community for families of moderate income. Though a philanthropist, he was known as a tight fisted miser, worth some $50 million. Buried in the western half of the churchyard at St. Mark's-in-the-Bowery in Manhattan, his body was stolen and held for ransom, which the widow paid. Presumably the correct body (from several that had been stolen) was returned. Re-interred in the basement, Church of the Incarnation, Garden City, Long Island, NY.

8724. Stewart, Anita (Feb. 17, 1902–May 4, 1961) Silent screen star 1912–1928 (*Mary Regan, Never the Twain Shall Meet*). Married name Converse (divorced), she died from an overdose of barbiturates, a probable suicide, at 59. Several sources list her birth as 1895, though the death certificate gives 1902. Sanctuary of Liberty, crypt 20737, Freedom Mausoleum, Forest Lawn, Glendale, CA.

8725. Stewart, Billy (March 24, 1937–Jan. 17, 1970) Washington, D.C. born rhythm and blues vocalist had hits with *I Do Love You, Sitting in the Park* and his scat version of Gershwin's *Summertime* that went to #10 in 1966. He and two members of his band died in a car wreck in North Carolina. Flat black marker with a record engraved in the corner. Adams sec., lot 160, grave 4, Harmony Memorial Park, Landover, MD.

8726. Stewart, Cal (Calvin E. Stewart, 1856–Dec. 7, 1919) Pioneer recording artist from Virginia played the folksy humorist Uncle Josh at the mythical Punkin Centre from the mid 1890's on wax cylinders to the year of his death, when he recorded an Uncle Josh bit with Ada Jones. He died after a stroke in Chicago. Buried in his wife's hometown. Stone monument with cross inscribed *Your Uncle Josh*. Fairview Cemetery, Tipton, IN.

8727. Stewart, Donald Ogden (Nov. 30, 1894–Aug. 2, 1980) Hollywood screenwriter from Columbus, Ohio, penned all or part of *The Barretts of Wimpole Street, Marie Antoinette, Love Affair, The Philadelphia Story* (1940, which won him an Oscar), *A Woman's Face, Keeper of the Flame, Without Love, Edward My Son*. He moved to England in 1951 after being blacklisted as a leftist and having his passport revoked while abroad. Cremated August 7, 1980, at Golders Green, along with his second wife Ella Winter. Ashes later removed by the family.

8728. Stewart, Henry Redd (Henry Ellis Stewart, May 27, 1923–Aug. 9, 2003) Ashland, Tennessee, born singer and songwriter with Pee Wee King's Golden West Cowboys co-wrote (with King) *The Tennessee Waltz* as well as *Slow Poke, You Belong to Me* and *Bonaparte's Retreat*. He died at 80, two weeks after the death of his wife Darlene. Garden of the Christus, lot 840, grave 1, Louisville Memorial Gardens East, Louisville, KY.

8729. Stewart, Horace aka **Nick O'Demus** (Horace Winfield Stewart, March 15, 1910–Dec. 18, 2000) Film and TV actor in over three dozen films 1936–88, played Lightnin' in the TV series *Amos 'n' Andy* 1951–53. Ashes to residence, Los Angeles.

8730. Stewart, James (James Maitland Stewart, May 20, 1908–July 2, 1997) Favorite son of Indiana, Pennsylvania, where a statue of him was dedicated in front of the court house on his 75th birthday. The most earnest persona in films from 1935, he made his mark in Frank Capra's *You Can't Take it With You* (1938) and *Mr. Smith Goes to Washington, Destry Rides Again* (1939) and *The Philadelphia Story* (1940, AA) before serving in Europe in World War II, officially retired as a Brigadier General in 1968. His first postwar film *It's A Wonderful Life* (1946) became both his and director Capra's best known work and a Christmas perennial after its rediscovery in the 1970's. Later trademark films include *Harvey* (1950), Anthony Mann westerns, four Hitchcock thrillers (*Rope, Rear Window, The Man Who Knew Too Much* and *Vertigo*), many others. Married from 1949 to **Gloria Hatrick McLean** (March 10, 1918–Feb. 16, 1994). She died from cancer at 75 and was buried beside her son **Ronald McLean**, who was killed at 24 in Vietnam June 8, 1969. His epitaph reads *He that dwelleth in the secret place of the most high shall abide under the shadow of the Almighty*. After his wife's death, Stewart's health and spirits declined rapidly; he died at 89 from a blood clot to the lung in Beverly Hills. Memorial service July 7 at Beverly Hills Presbyterian Church, where he was a member. Private burial with his wife and stepson. The epitaph from the *91st Psalm* were the chosen words of courage his father wrote him at the beginning of World War II, before Stewart embarked on bombing missions over Europe. Stewart carried the letter with him for the rest of his life: *For he shall give his angels charge over thee to keep thee in all thy ways*. Wee Kirk Churchyard, plot 8, Forest Lawn, Glendale, CA.

8731. Stewart, Jermaine (William Jermaine Stewart, Sept. 7, 1957–March 17, 1997) Singer and dancer on Chicago's *Soul Train* did backup vocals for various groups before recording with Arista in the 1980's, where he had three hits that played on both the pop and rhythm and blues charts. He died from liver cancer at 29. Unmarked. Garden of Devotion 10, lot 6, grave 41, Homewood Memorial Cemetery, Homewood, IL.

8732. Stewart, Mike (Mike G. Stewart, April 19, 1945–Nov. 13, 2002) Guitarist and vocalist on backup harmony with the We Five, who had a hit with *You Were On My Mind* in 1965. He later produced Billy Joel's top selling album, *Piano Man*, among others. Glass niche, Remembrance Mausoleum, Chapel of the Chimes, Sacramento, CA.

8733. Stewart, Paul (March 13, 1908–Feb. 17, 1986) Silver haired, dark browed actor from the Mercury Theatre played many an opportunist or heavy in films (*Citizen Kane, The Window*) and TV over four decades from 1941. Ashes scattered at sea.

8734. Stewart, Payne (William Payne Stewart, Jan. 30, 1957–Oct. 25, 1999) Popular golfer from Springfield, Missouri, known for his tam-o-shanter, knickers and exuberance, died at 42 when his Lear 35 lost pressure sometime after leaving Orlando, Florida, where he lived. The plane headed north with its passengers dead or unconscious until it ran out of gas and crashed near Mina, South Dakota, four hours later. Memorial service October 29 at the First Baptist Church in Orlando. Obelisk-cenotaph beside his father's headstone. Lot 99, E West between 7th and 8th, Hazelwood Cemetery, Springfield, Missouri. His plaque in Florida has his image and *The Champion of Our Hearts*. Doctor Phillips Cemetery, Orlando, FL.

8735. Stewart, Potter (Jan. 23, 1915–Dec. 7, 1985) Supreme Court justice raised in Cincinnati, appointed by Eisenhower in 1958 at 43. At his retirement in 1981, he was replaced by the first female Supreme Court member, Sandra Day O'Connor. Sec. 5, site 40–2, Arlington National Cemetery, Arlington, VA.

8736. Stiller, Mauritz (Moshe Stiller, July 17, 1883–Nov. 8, 1928) Influential film director in Stockholm in the 1920's brought Greta Gustafsen to Hollywood and launched her career as Greta Garbo in 1925. She became a star while his career floundered in the U.S. By 1928 he had returned to Stockholm, where he died from a lung ailment at 45. Jewish section, Norra Kyrkogarden (North Cemetery), Stockholm.

8737. Stilwell, Dick (Richard G. Stilwell, Jr., July 27, 1943–Nov. 23, 2002) Buffalo born son of **Richard Stilwell,** commander of United Nations forces in Korea, was a career army officer and decorated Vietnam veteran before he began appearing in roles in films, usually as police (*The Pelican Brief, L.A. Confidential*) and television. He died in an auto accident at 59. Sec. 5-R, row 10, site 2, Arlington National Cemetery, Arlington, VA.

8738. Stilwell, Joseph (March 19, 1883–Oct. 12, 1946) "Vinegar Joe," commander of the armies in the China-Burma-India theater 1942–44, removed from command because of differences in policy with Chiang-Kai-Shek. In 1945 he commanded forces at Okinawa. Cenotaph, sec. 2, row A, grave 12, West Point Post Cemetery, West Point, N.Y. His ashes were scattered by plane in the Pacific near his home at Carmel, CA.

8739. Stimson, Henry (Sept. 21, 1867–Oct. 20, 1950) U.S. statesman 1911–1950 in the cabinets of Taft, Hoover, Roosevelt and Truman. As Truman's Secretary of War, he was influential in the decision to drop the atomic bomb on Hiroshima and Nagasaki to expedite the end of World War II. Stone reads *Lawyer, soldier, statesman.* St. John's Memorial Cemetery, Cold Spring Harbor, Long Island, NY.

8740. Stockdale, Carl (Feb. 19, 1874–March 15, 1953) Actor in some 200 films. He provided an alibi for Charlotte Shelby in the 1922 William Desmond Taylor murder case. Chapel of the Psalms, colonnade north, tier 5, Hollywood Forever Cemetery, Hollywood (Los Angeles), CA.

8741. Stockdale, James (James Bond Stockdale, Dec. 23, 1923–July 5, 2005) U.S. Navy Vice Admiral from Abingdon, Illinois, shot down over North Vietnam September 9, 1965 and tortured by his captors, spending four years in solitary confinement; two in leg irons. The highest ranking naval officer in captivity. Rather than make a propaganda film for the enemy, he smashed his own face with a stool and cut his wrists, eventually convincing his captors to back off the brutal treatment, helping his fellow POWs and serving as a model for them. Among his many awards, including two Distinguished Flying Crosses, three Distinguished Service Medals, two Purple Hearts and four Silver Stars, was the Medal of Honor, awarded him in 1976. He was Ross Perot's seemingly out of place running mate in the 1992 presidential election, then remained retired at Coronado, California, where he died at 81. U.S. Naval Academy Cemetery, Annapolis, MD.

8742. Stockwell, Guy (Nov. 16, 1933–Feb. 7, 2002) Actor in films and much television. Brother of Dean Stockwell. He died at 68 in Prescott, Arizona, where he had lived for five years. Cremation through Hampton mortuary, Prescott. Ashes to family there.

8743. Stoker, Bram (Abraham Stoker, Nov. 8, 1847–April 20, 1912) Irish born playwright and long time stage manager of Sir Henry Irving, a civil servant prior to 1876 when he turned toward the theatre. His novel *Dracula* was published in 1897 and sealed his fame. Inurned with his son (1961), East Columbarium, third level, Golders Green Crematorium, London.

8744. Stokes, Carl (June 21, 1927–April 3, 1996) The first black mayor of a major American city defeated Republican Seth Taft in 1967 to serve two terms as mayor of Cleveland. Brother of Rep. Louis Stokes. His flush stone has his picture on it. Sec. 5C, near pond, Lakeview Cemetery, Cleveland, OH.

8745. Stokes, Frank (Jan. 1, 1888–Sept. 12, 1955) Early Blues recording artist, vocalist and guitarist made thirty eight sides for Paramount and Victor. Sec. 1, div. 6, row 19, grave 43, Hollywood Cemetery, Memphis, TN.

8746. Stokes, Maurice (June 17, 1933–April 6, 1970) Basketball great with the Royals in Rochester and Cincinnati 1954–58, formerly at St. Francis College, suffered brain damage to his motor control center after a fall in the last season game of 1958. His 12 year struggle with posttraumatic encephalopathy gained national attention. At his request he was buried on the St. Francis campus at Loretto, PA.

8747. Stokowski, Leopold (April 18, 1882–Sept. 13, 1977) English conductor, a U.S. citizen from 1915 and foremost symphony conductor 1912–1938 in Philadelphia, and in Cincinnati, New York, and Houston. He founded the New York Symphony Orchestra in 1944 and appeared in several films, notably *Fantasia* (1940), announcing the work accompanying the animation. He died at Hampshire, England, at 95. Grayish pink speckled stone inscribed *Music is the voice of the all.* St. Marylebone Cemetery, London.

8748. Stollenwerck, Logan Henry (March 11, 1902–April 30, 1971) SMU football great 1921–1924, quarterback of the Aerial Circus, with the first SWC team to utilize the forward pass. All SWC for three years and captain of the championship team. Court of Flowers, lot 362, space 5, (Sparkman) Hillcrest Memorial Park, Dallas, TX.

8749. Stoloff, Ben(jamin) (Oct. 6, 1895–Sept. 8, 1960) Philadelphia born director did nearly fifty films, mostly B's (*Soup to Nuts* 1930, *Destry Rides Again* and *Night Mayor* 1932, *Night of Terror* 1933) and produced several others. T Building/Hall of David, T-4, 5162, Beth Olam Cemetery adjacent Hollywood Forever Cemetery, Hollywood (Los Angeles), CA.

8750. Stoloff, Morris W. (Aug. 1, 1898–April 16, 1980) Philadelphia born musical director at Columbia from 1936 won Oscars for *Cover Girl* (1944), *The Jolson Story* (1946), *Song Without End* (1960). Other works included *From Here to Eternity* (1953) and *Lawrence of Arabia* (1962). Cremated at Angeles Abbey, Compton, California, through the Neptune Society. Ashes scattered at sea.

8751. Stoltz, Robert (Aug. 8, 1880–June 27, 1975) Austrian composer of opera and ballet. White monument with his face on it. Gruppe 32 C, nummer 24, Zentralfriedhof (Central Cemetery), Vienna.

8752. Stolze, Dorothy "Dottie" (May 1, 1923–July 19, 2003) All American Girls Professional Baseball star in the late 1940s and early 50s, spotted by a scout in Alameda, California, in 1946, played shortstop and various other positions except pitcher for the Muskegon Lassies, and later with the Peoria Redwings, until the AAGPBL folded in 1952. Only her nickname was used in the 1992 film *A League of Their Own*. She returned to Alameda, where she lived until her death at 80. New Tacoma Memorial Park, Tacoma, WA.

8753. Stompanato, Johnny (Oct. 19, 1925–April 4, 1958) Racketeer boyfriend of Lana Turner was stabbed to death by her fifteen year old daughter Cheryl Crane in Turner's Beverly Hills home while allegedly abusing Turner. World War II veterans marker beside his parents. Third addition, block 145, Oakland Cemetery, Woodstock, IL.

8754. Stone, Christopher (Thomas Edward Bourassa, Oct. 4, 1940–Oct. 29, 1995) Actor, husband of Dee Wallace, died from a heart attack at 55. Cremated through Praisewater Meyer-Mitchell mortuary. Ashes to residence.

8755. Stone, Ezra (Dec. 2, 1917–March 3, 1994) Voice of radio's Henry Aldrich from 1939, originally on Broadway in *The Aldrich Family* (1938). He later produced plays and from 1979 was director of the David Library of the American Revolution at Washington Crossing, Pennsylvania. Killed in an auto accident at Perth Amboy, New Jersey, his ashes were interred with his wife's on his property, Stone Meadows Farm, near Newtown, PA.

8756. Stone, Fred (Aug. 19, 1873–March 6, 1959) Vaudeville and stage star ranged from acrobatics to comedy and drama. Teamed on stage with David Montgomery, he also played the scarecrow in the 1902 film *The Wizard of Oz*. His last stage success was as the grandfather in *You Can't Take it With You* (1945). Films include *Alice Adams* (1935), many others. Enduring Faith, lot 4118, Forest Lawn Hollywood Hills, Los Angeles.

8757. Stone, George E. (George Stein, May 18, 1903–May 26, 1967) Polish born versatile character actor from talkies to television in supporting roles of all types (Italian henchmen, small time thugs, Jewish peddlers, womanizing choreographers) in *Little Caesar, Cimarron, The Last Mile, The Phantom of Crestwood, 42nd Street, The Face Behind the Mask, The Man With the Golden Arm,* many others. He died from a stroke in Woodland Hills, California. Moses 18, lot 5427, Mt. Sinai Memorial Park, Los Angeles.

8758. Stone, Grace Z. (Ethel Vance) (Jan. 9, 1891–Sept. 29, 1991) Authoress wrote *The Bitter Tea of General Yen* (1930, filmed in 1932) and *Escape* (1939, filmed in 1940) under the pen name Ethel Vance because her daughter was reportedly in Axis territory at the time. Stone was identified as the author in 1942, after the anti–Nazi tale had been filmed and her daughter was safe. Stonington Cemetery, Stonington, CT.

8759. Stone, Harlan Fiske (Oct. 11, 1872–April 22, 1946) Chief Justice of the U.S. Supreme Court 1941–46 espoused liberal viewpoints broadening individual freedoms, labor's bargaining power, etc. Sec. A, lot 55, Rock Creek Cemetery, Washington, D.C.

8760. Stone, Harold J. (Harold Hochstein, March 3, 1913–Nov. 18, 2005) New York born actor played dozens of detectives and military officers, often with unusual complexity, a mainstay in films (*The Harder They Fall, The Wrong Man, The Invisible Boy, Spartacus, The St. Valentine's Day Massacre*) and television 1954–80, particularly in the 50's and 60's (several *Alfred Hitchcock Presents* episodes, notably *Lamb to the Slaughter; Twilight Zone* episode *The Arrival, My World and Welcome to It, Bridget Loves Bernie*). He died at the Motion Picture and Television Country House and Hospital, Woodland Hills, Los Angeles, at 92. Canaan 3, lot 1108, space 2, Mount Sinai Memorial Park, Los Angeles.

8761. Stone, I. F. (Isador Feinstein, Dec. 24, 1907–June 18, 1989) Political journalist with a sharp wit and left wing sentiments espoused over a sixty five year span. In his newsletter *I.F. Stone's Weekly* 1953–1968, he jabbed tirelessly at the establishment with ever caustic observations. Ferreting inconsistencies from government documents and newspapers, among his disclosures was the Atomic Energy Commission's false assertion in 1957 that its first underground test could only be detected two hundred miles away (instead of the actual 2,600 miles). He defended the constitutional rights of communists, the Warren Report on the assassination of JFK, and denounced violence for any cause. Books include *The Truman Era, Underground in Palestine* and *The Hidden History of the Korean War*. He died at 81 from a heart attack in a Boston hospital. A resident of Washington, D.C., he was buried near his daughter's home. Flush plaque. Lot 163, grave 8, Walnut Ave., Mt. Auburn Cemetery, Cambridge, MA.

8762. Stone, Irving (Irving Tennenbaum, July 14, 1903–Aug. 26, 1989) San Francisco born novelist specialized in a popular blend of history and fiction, in *Lust For Life* (Van Gogh), *Love is Eternal* (Abe and Mary Lincoln), *Those Who Love* (John and Abigail Adams), *The President's Lady* (Andrew and Rachel Jackson), *The Agony and the Ecstasy* (Michelangelo), *Passions of the Mind* (Freud) and *Immortal Wife* (John C. and Jesse Fremont). The author was cremated through Malinow-Silverman mortuary in Los Angeles. Ashes returned to family. His wife **Jean Stone** (Jean Factor, Feb. 27, 1911–April 16, 2004), his research collaborator and "editor in residence" from 1934, died at 93 in Beverly Hills. Alcove of Love, crypt C135A, Hillside Memorial Park, Los Angeles.

8763. Stone, Jesse (Nov. 16, 1901–April 1, 1999) Rhythm and blues composer and musician from Atchison, Kansas, called the Father of Rock 'n' Roll wrote *Shake, Rattle and Roll*, recorded by Bill Haley and the Comets in 1953, a landmark in bringing black music to white audiences. He died at Altamonte Springs, Florida, at 97. Garden of Hope, plot M, row 43, grave 65, Pinelawn Memorial Park, Farmingdale, Long island, NY.

8764. Stone, Lewis (Lewis Sheperd Stone, Nov. 15, 1879–Sept. 13, 1953) Worcester, Massachusetts, born stage and silent screen lead went on to many austere or kindly authoritative, fatherly roles, many at MGM through the 1930's before his run as Judge Hardy in the *Andy Hardy* series 1939–1947. On the night of his death he was chasing adolescents that had thrown refuse on his property when he collapsed and died from a heart attack in front of his home on Lorraine Boulevard in Los Angeles. Cremated at Rosedale Cemetery in L.A., his ashes were listed as being sent to Kensico Cemetery, Valhalla, New York, where he purchased a lot in 1914 in sec. 174; his first wife and two daughters are buried there unmarked, but his ashes, according to his daughter Barbara Ion, were scattered over his ranch in Malibu.

8765. Stone, Lucy (Aug. 13, 1818–Oct. 18, 1893) Women's Rights advocate organized the convention at Worcester, Massachusetts, in 1850, chartered the Women's Suffrage Organization in 1869 and began publishing the *Women's Journal* in 1870. Among the first notables to maintain her maiden name after marriage, inspiring the beginning of the Lucy Stoner leagues across the country, which also became a term for free thinking 19th century women. She was the first person cremated in Massachusetts, just after the practice became legal. Crematory niche 3-A, gold urn, lower columbarium, Forest Hills Cemetery, Jamaica Plain, Boston, MA.

8766. Stone, Milburn (July 5, 1904–June 12, 1980) Universal second lead through the 1940's played leads, detectives and killers alike but gained his fame as crusty Doc Adams on TV's *Gunsmoke* 1955–75. He died at 75 from a heart attack in La Jolla, California. Vista Del Lago, 401 D, El Camino Memorial Park, La Jolla, CA.

8767. Stone, W. Clement (William Clement Stone, May 4, 1902–Sept. 3, 2002) Businessman, philanthropist and author built the Combined Insurance Company of North America in the 1920's, co-wrote three success-through-positive-attitude books in the 1960's and was a major contributor to Richard Nixon's presidential campaigns in 1968 and 1972. The $2 million contribution was part of the impetus to limit campaign spending. Known for his pencil mustache, suspenders and bow tie, Stone and his wife **Jesse V. Stone** gave some $275 million to mental health, Christian and patriotic organizations. Buried with his son and daughter. Sec. C, Lake Forest Cemetery, Lake Forest, IL.

8768. Stoneman, Ernest "Pop" (March 25, 1893–June 14, 1968) Early country-western recording artist on Okeh with *The Sinking of the Titanic* (1924), was Victor's top country artist in 1927. Sec. 27, lot 75, east ⅓, Mount Olivet Cemetery, Nashville, TN.

8769. Stoneman, Jimmy (Oscar James Stoneman, March 8, 1937–Sept. 22, 2002) Bass player with the Stoneman Family, son of Ernest, at the Grand Ole Opry from 1962. Sec. 27, lot 80, Mount Olivet Cemetery, Nashville, TN.

8770. Colonel Stoopnagle *see* **F. Chase Taylor.**

8771. Storey, Edith (March 18, 1892–Oct. 9, 1967) Silent screen actress in many exotic plots 1910–20. Some sources had formerly listed her death in 1955. She died at 75 (as Edith Storey) in Northport, Long Island. Room of Peace (main building), E-8, Fresh Pond Crematory, Middle Village, Queens, N.Y.C.

8772. Stossel, Ludwig (Feb. 12, 1883–Jan. 29, 1973) Short, squat Austrian actor from Lockenhaus in supporting roles, not always comical (*All Through the Night, House of Dracula*), later resurfaced on television in the Little Old Wine-Maker commercials of the 1960's. Cremated through Groman mortuary (their records were destroyed in the earthquake in the early 1990's)at Hollywood Memorial Park Cemetery, Hollywood (Los Angeles). Their records only show the ashes were picked up in February 1973, not by who or to where.

8773. Stothart, Herbert (Sept. 11, 1885–Feb. 1, 1949) Milwaukee born prolific composer co-wrote *Rose Marie* with Rudolph Friml on Broadway. At MGM in the 1930's and 40's his scores included *The Merry Widow, David Copperfield, A Tale of Two Cities, Naughty Marietta, Anna Karenina, Mutiny on the Bounty, A Night at the Opera, Rose Marie, Camille, San Francisco, Romeo and Juliet, Maytime, The Good Earth, The Wizard of Oz* (Academy Award), *Waterloo Bridge* (1940), *Mrs. Miniver, National Velvet*, many others. *Heart Attack, A Symphonic Poem*, was written in 1947 after he suffered a coronary. He died from cancer in Los Angeles two years later at 64. Everlasting Love, lot 982, space 2, Forest Lawn, Glendale, CA.

8774. Stotz, Carl (Carl E. Stotz, Feb. 20, 1910–June 4, 1992) Founder of Little League baseball. A lumberyard clerk in Williamsport, Pennsylvania, in 1939, he organized thirty boys on three teams. By the time of he died at 82 there were 2.5 million children on some 140,000 teams. West gateway, lot 500, grave 1, Twin Hills Memorial Park, Williamsport/Muncy, PA.

8775. Stout, Rex (Dec. 1, 1886–Oct. 27, 1975) Author from Noblesville, Indiana, wrote the Nero Wolfe series of mysteries 1927–1975. His ashes were spread at points around his home at West Redding, CT.

8776. Stowe, Harriet Beecher (June 14, 1811–July 1, 1896) Sister of Henry Ward Beecher and daughter of Lyman Beecher, her powerful novel *Uncle Tom's Cabin* (1852) contributed to the fiery abolitionist feelings in the north leading up to Civil War. Upon meeting her, Lincoln is said to have remarked "So this is the lady who wrote the book that started the war?" She lived with her husband at Cincinnati, at Brook Farm in Hartford, Connecticut, and in Maine. She died in Hartford at 85. A wreath from the black citizens of Boston signed "The children of Uncle Tom" lay upon her coffin, taken for burial to Philips Andover Academy, where her husband had taught. Her monument is a red scotch granite shaft and cross with the epitaph *Her children rise up and call her blessed.* Near her monument is a small stone marking her son, who drowned in the Conneaut River. Phillips Andover Academy Cemetery, Andover, MA.

8777. Stradivari, Antonio (1644–Dec. 18, 1737) Most famous of violin makers, whose works are known by the Latin equivalent of his name. In seventy years he made 1,116 violins, viols and violincellos. He was buried in the Dominican Church in Cremona, Italy, but the monastery was associated with the Inquisition and was very unpopular. Upon its eventual destruction in the 1890's, the site was turned into a park and Stradivari's burial stone was erected in one of the gardens.

8778. Stradtner, Gloria Marie (Gloria DeMartini, June 14, 1926–Dec. 22, 1998) Brooklyn born patron saint of homeless dogs and cats left abandoned in the many cemeteries of Brooklyn and Queens set traps throughout the cemeteries for fifty years or more, going back at night to rescue the creatures in one necropolis after another, then would take them home, feed them, and frequently find them homes through shelters. She died from cancer at 72. At her funeral mass at Blessed Sacrament Roman Catholic Church in Richmond Hill, the poem *Weep Not* (believed to be written by her) was read: *Do not weep for me when I am gone' For I have friends in the great beyond/ All the little ones I used to feed/ Will come to me in my time of need/ They will purr and bark in great delight/ And I will hold and hug them tight/ Oh what a great day that will be/ When my furry friends all welcome me.* Listed on DeMartini stone. Sec. 32, range N, #002, St. Charles Cemetery, Farmingdale, Long Island, NY.

8779. Straight, Beatrice (Aug. 2, 1914–April 7, 2001) Stage and screen thespian won an Oscar for best supporting actress in *Network* (1976), and later played the head of the parapsychology team in *Poltergeist* (1982). She died at her Beverly Hills home from cardio-pulmonary arrest at 86. Cremated through Forest Lawn Hollywood Hills. Ashes to residence in Santa Monica, CA.

8780. Strange, Glenn (Aug. 16, 1899–Sept. 20, 1973) Cowboy from Carlsbad, New Mexico, began working in films as a stuntman in 1929. He appeared in numerous B westerns at Universal and three times as the Frankenstein monster (*House of Frankenstein* 1944, *House of Dracula* 1945, *Abbott & Costello meet Frankenstein* 1948). Like fellow Universal contractee Milburn Stone, he settled down as a regular (Sam the bartender) on TV's *Gunsmoke* 1962–1973, until his death from lung cancer in St. Joseph's Hospital, Burbank, at 74. Churchyard, lot 4295, Forest Lawn Hollywood Hills, Los Angeles.

8781. Strange, Michael (Blanche Oelrichs Tweed, Oct. 1, 1890–Nov. 5, 1950) Playwright who wrote as Michael Strange was also a suffragette and the wife of John Barrymore 1920–1928. Their daughter Diana claimed her mother had a far greater affection for her stepbrother **Robin Thomas** (1915–1943) than for her. He died at 29 and was buried in Indianapolis in the plot of a close friend, but his mother had him removed to her family plot in the Bronx. On his stone was inscribed *My beloved spake and said unto me 'Rise up my fair one and come away. Blessed are the pure in heart for they shall see God.* Michael Strange died six years later from leukemia and has a matching stone beside her son's, inscribed *For lo, the winter is past. The rain is over and gone. And ye shall know the truth. And the truth shall make you free.* Both names are also on the Oelrichs obelisk in the center of the sloping lot, but no mention of Diana Barrymore, who was buried beside her mother in January 1960. Chapel Hill sec., Woodlawn Cemetery, the Bronx, N.Y.C.

8782. Strange, Robert (Nov. 26, 1881–Feb. 22, 1952) Mustached character actor in films from 1931 (*The Walking Dead, The Story of Vernon and Irene Castle*, dozens of others). Acacia Urn Garden, niche 18, Oakwood Memorial Park, Chatsworth, CA.

8783. "The Stranger" (c. 1840–1862) Civil War soldier arrived for burial in Gray, Maine, and to everyone's surprise was a Confederate. Rebel or not, with nowhere to send him back to, he was buried and a stone erected and inscribed *Stranger. A soldier of the late war. Died 1862. Erected by the Ladies of Gray.* Just like the Union soldiers, he receives a flag on Memorial Day. Gray Cemetery, Gray, ME.

8784. Strasberg, Lee (Nov. 17, 1901–Feb. 17, 1982) Austrian born acting coach and actor founded the Group Theatre in New York in 1930 and the Actors Studio in 1947, becoming the chief proponent of the Method Acting approach derived in part from Stanislavsky. Already a legend as a teacher, he made his screen acting debut as mobster Hyman Roth, loosely based on Meyer Lansky, in *The Godfather II* (1974), earning an Oscar nomination. His last appearance was in *Going in Style* (1979). He died in Los Angeles. Buried with his wife **Paula** (Paula Miller, 1909–April 29, 1966), his grave is marked by a white boulder from his California home with his name and dates cut into it. A bronze plaque was later placed near the top of it, and a few feet to its left a small flat cylinder on legs inscribed *We came to the theatre on the wings of a dream*, followed by his name and dates. His daughter, actress Susan Strasberg (May 22, 1938–Jan. 21, 1999) died from cancer at 60 in her Manhattan home, but is not with her father. Top drive on the right near the end.

Westchester Hills Cemetery, Hastings-on-Hudson, NY.

8785. Strasser, Arthur (Artur Strasser, Feb. 13, 1854–Nov. 8, 1927) Austrian sculptor noted for Oriental figures, particularly *Marc Anton mit Löwengespann* (1899–1900), next to the Secession Building in Vienna. Gruppe 32C, nummer 7, Der Zentralfriedhof (The Central Cemetery), Vienna.

8786. Strasser, Gregor (May 31, 1892–June 30, 1934) German chemist and politician from Geisenfeld in Bavaria was, with his brother Otto (1897–1934), a leading member of the National Socialist (Nazi) party in Germany from 1920. By 1933 he resigned because of leftist leanings causing disagreements with Hitler and was subsequently murdered in Berlin in the Blood Purge that also saw the murder of Ernst Roehm. The ashes were sent to his office at his chemical products factory.

8787. Stratemeyer, Edward (Oct. 4, 1862–May 10, 1930) Author of books for young people wrote the *River Boys* series 1899–1925 and founded the Stratemeyer Literary Syndicate in 1906, which later wrote and published the *Bobbsey Twins* books, and *The Hardy Boys*— ghost-written by Leslie McFarlane. His headstone is inscribed *With tender devotion we turn the last page.... The final chapter closes, leaving in young hearts the treasury of fine ideals.* Sec. E, lot 5122, Evergreen Cemetery, Hillside, NJ.

8788. Stratten, Dorothy (Dorothy Ruth Hoogstraten, Feb. 28, 1960–Aug. 14, 1980) Playmate of the Year for *Playboy* magazine, the Canadian model had been promoted by her husband Paul Snider but had become involved with director Peter Bogdonavich. Snider confronted Stratten in a meeting in his home that ended with his shooting her in the head before turning the gun on himself. She was buried beneath a brown marble tablet with an inscription from Hemingway's *A Farewell to Arms*: *If people bring so much courage to this world the world has to kill them to break them, so of course it kills them. It kills the very good and the very gentle and the very brave impartially. If you are none of these, you can be sure that it will kill you too, but there will be no special hurry.* Sec. D, lot 170, Westwood Memorial Park, west Los Angeles. **Paul Snider** was buried at Schara Tzedeck Cemetery, Vancouver, B.C.

8789. Stratton, Charles *see* **Tom Thumb.**

8790. Stratton, Monty (May 21, 1912–Sept. 28, 1982) Texas born pitcher for the Chicago White Sox in the mid 1930's lost a leg in a (self-inflicted) hunting accident in 1938. His comeback in the minor leagues was chronicled in the film *The Stratton Story* (1949). Sec. 4, lot 419, Memory Land Cemetery, Greenville, TX.

8791. Straus, Isidor (Feb. 6, 1845–April 15, 1912) and **Ida** (Feb. 9, 1849–April 15 1912) Former overseer of the china department at Macy's in New York City with his brother Nathan managed and later owned Macy's by 1896, the biggest department store in the world. Straus and his wife Ida died on the Titanic together after she refused to leave him and take her seat in a lifeboat. He was recovered; she was not. They are commemorated by a stone barge cut into the family monument-compound. The inscription reads *Many waters cannot quench our love— neither can the floods drown it.* Myosotis sec., along Myosotis Ave., Woodlawn Cemetery, the Bronx, N.Y.C. His brother and co-founder **Nathan Straus** (Jan. 31, 1848–Jan. 11, 1931) of the Abraham and Straus stores also worked later in life for a law enforcing the pasteurization of milk. Beth El Cemetery, Glendale-Ridgewood, Queens, N.Y.C.

8792. Strauss, Harry "Pittsburgh Phil" (Hershel Strauss, July 28, 1909–June 12, 1941) The heaviest hitter in Brooklyn's Murder Inc. in the 1930's, credited with 100 killings, Williamsburg born Strauss used both stabbing and strangulation but was particularly fond of ice picks. In one case, he set the body afire to watch it burn. As informant Abe Reles noted in his fluent testimony, "Pep was nuts." Through Reles' testimony seven members of Murder Inc. died in Sing Sing's electric chair 1941–44. Arrested in 1940 for the 1936 murder of Puggy Feinstein, Strauss feigned insanity by chewing on a leather strap but was convicted and executed with Martin "Bugsy" Goldstein. Sec. AA, block 1, row K, grave 321, Society Nathan Vlodinger, corner Beth Israel and Lincoln, Beth David Cemetery, Elmont, NY.

8793. Strauss, Johann (Oct. 25, 1825–June 3, 1899) The Waltz King, whose music symbolized the new and proud Vienna of 1888 penned *The Emperor Waltz* to honor Franz Josef's 40th year as Emperor of Austria. Among his other ever-popular favorites in three quarter time are *The Blue Danube, Artists Life, Voices of Spring* and *Tales from the Vienna Woods*. He died at his Vienna home while a concert was being given in the Volksgarten there. The music stopped and the band struck up *The Blue Danube,* understood to announce his passing after a long illness. His monument in the Central Cemetery in Vienna, has a sculpted marble maiden beneath an inset with his image in relief. The grave of he and his wife Adele in front of the monument is covered by a slab with a sculpted wreath on it. Gruppe 32A, nummer 27, Zentralfriedhof, Vienna. His father, composer **Johann Strauss the Elder** (March 14, 1804–Sept. 25, 1849) has a statue with his friend and former partner **Josef Lanner** (April 12, 1801–April 14, 1843), erected in 1915. Johann the Elder is at gruppe 32 A, nummer 15, and Lanner at 32 A, nummer 16, in the Zentralfriedhof (Central Cemetery). **Josef Strauss** (Aug. 20, 1827–July 22, 1870) and **Eduard Strauss** (March 15, 1835–Dec. 28, 1916), both accomplished composers, were sons of Johann the Elder and brothers of Johann the Waltz King. Josef, subject to depression and melancholy, like several other members of the family, died in Warsaw at 43 from a possible brain tumor. He was later buried in the Central Cemetery in Vienna with all three of his wives beneath a black monument with a white marble angel of sorrow leaning against it. Both are in gruppe 32 A, Josef at nummer 44, and Eduard at nummer 42, Zentralfriedhof (Central Cemetery), Vienna.

8794. Strauss, Joseph Baerman (Jan. 9, 1870–May 16, 1938) Noted architect built and designed the Golden Gate Bridge at San Francisco 1933–37. Sanctuary of Benediction, crypt 6281, right wall, Memorial Terrace, Great Mausoleum, Forest Lawn Glendale, CA.

8795. Strauss, Levi (Feb. 26, 1829–Sept. 26, 1902) Creator in 1850 of work pants made of blue canvas with increased durability. Later using denim, "Levis" or blue jeans gained widespread use by farm and city laborers, cowboys and eventually a majority of society. Family mausoleum, plot C, sec. 2, Home of Peace Cemetery, Colma, CA.

8796. Strauss, Pittsburgh Phil *see* **Harry Strauss.**

8797. Strauss, Richard (June 11, 1864–Sept. 8, 1949) Eminent German composer-conductor, originally at Munich and Weimar, wrote tone poems (*Don Juan* 1888, *Thus Spake Zarathustra* 1896, *Don Quixote* 1897, *A Hero's Life* 1898) and opera, primarily from 1900, including *Elektra* (1909) and *Der Rosenkavalier* (1911). Later symphonies *The Alpine Symphony* (1915) and *Frau ohne Schatten* (1919). He also founded the Salzburg Festivals and was co-director of the Vienna Opera. He became controversial during World War II in making a deal with the Nazis for the protection of his Jewish daughter-in-law and grandsons. Later "rehabilitated," he wrote mellow opera and string compositions in post war London. Garmisch Cemetery, Garmisch-Partenkirchen, Bavaria, (southern) Germany.

8798. Strauss, Robert (Nov. 8, 1913–Feb. 20, 1975) Actor in *Stalag 17* (1953) and other films and TV as pushy salesmen, menacing thugs, etc. He died from a stroke at New York University Medical Center in Manhattan. No services. Cremation and ashes to family.

8799. Stravinsky, Igor (Igor Fedorovich Stravinsky, June 17, 1882–April 6, 1971) Polish composer born in Russia whose works include three ballets for the *Ballets Russes* of Serge Diaghilev in Paris (*Firebird* 1910, *Petrushka* 1911, and *The Rite of Spring* 1913) using repetitive folklike melodic motives, mixed meters, polyrhythms and ostinatos, all distinguishing traits throughout his career. His only full length opera was *The Rake's Progress* (1951). In Paris through the 1920's and afterward in New York City, where he died. A U.S. citizen from 1945. Greco sec., Cimetero of San Michele, Venice, Italy.

8800. Strawser, Neil (Aug. 16, 1927–Dec. 31, 2005) CBS newsman from Rittman, Ohio, with the network 1952–86, the only television journalist allowed in the Guantanamo Bay naval base during the Cuban Missile Crisis, also anchored their radio coverage of the 1963 Kennedy assassination. He left in 1986 to serve as Democratic spokesman for the House Budget Committee. Congressional Cemetery, Washington, D.C.

8801. Streeter, Edward (Aug. 1, 1891–March 31, 1976) Author of *Father of the Bride*. Sec. 9, lot 11, Forest Lawn Cemetery, Buffalo, NY.

8802. Streicher, Julius *see* **Goering.**

8803. Strickfaden, Kenneth (May 23, 1896–Feb. 29, 1984) Special effects and electrical wizardry expert at Universal who staged the creation of life in the Frankenstein monster by lightning in the original *Frankenstein* (1931). Still in possession of the lab apparatus over forty years later, he donated the equipment for use in Mel Brooks' *Young Frankenstein* (1974). He died in Inglewood, California. Block 17, lot 139, grave E, Woodlawn Cemetery, Santa Monica, CA.

8804. Strickland, David (Oct. 14, 1969–March 22, 1999) Young actor from Glen Cove, New York, in films and on TV's *Suddenly Susan* hanged himself in a Las Vegas motel. Service at the Church of the Recessional at Forest Lawn, Glendale. Ashes to his mother in Pacific Palisades, CA.

8805. Strickland, William (1788–April 6, 1854) Early 19th century Greek Revival architect designed the first Bank of the United States and the U.S. Mint in Philadelphia as well as the tomb of President James Knox Polk (1849) and the state capitol in Nashville, where he is entombed. Tennessee State Capitol, Nashville, TN.

8806. Stricklett, Elmer (Aug. 29, 1876–June 7, 1964) Pitcher with the Chicago White Sox introduced them to his particularly effective spitball c. 1904, later used on the mound effectively by Big Ed Walsh. Cremated I.O.O.F. Crematory, Santa Cruz, CA.

8807. Strickling, Howard (Aug. 25, 1897–July 15, 1982) Publicity agent at MGM from the early 30's until 1969 was known as the prime fixer during any of the studio's embarrassing moments when stories to the press needed tidying up for the good of MGM and its stars. Closely associated with both Irving Thalberg and Louis B. Mayer, he was later studio vice president. He retired to Chino, California, and died in Pomona at 82. Acacia, lot 95, Bellevue Memorial Park, Ontario, CA.

8808. Striker, Fran (Francis Hamilton Striker, March 17, 1903–Sept. 4, 1962) Radio writer authored the original radio screenplay *The Lone Ranger*, first broadcast in January 1933, and penned nearly 2400 scripts from 1929–1941. Sec. 1, grave 86–94, Arcade Rural Cemetery, Arcade, NY.

8809. Stringer, Korey (May 8, 1974–Aug. 1, 2001) Right tackle for the Minnesota Vikings died from a heat-stroke while practicing with the team in 100 plus degree heat. Estate between exterior maus. A and B, Pineview Memorial Gardens, Warren, OH.

8810. Strode, Woody (Woodrow Strode, July 25, 1914–Dec. 31, 1994) Los Angeles born black athlete and actor educated at UCLA played pro football in Canada and worked as a professional wrestler before going into films, in small parts prior to meaty roles in John Ford's *Sergeant Rutledge* (1960) and *The Man Who Shot Liberty Valance* (1962). Last seen in *The Quick and the Dead* (1994). He died in his sleep at 80 in his home at Glendora, California. Epitaph reads *As long as the rivers flow.* Sec. 46, grave 283, Riverside National Cemetery, Riverside, CA.

8811. Stroh, Bernhard (Oct. 20, 1822–June 24, 1882) German born founder of the Stroh Brewing Company. He died in New Hampshire. Red sandstone obelisk. Sec. Q, lot 9, Elmwood Cemetery, Detroit, MI.

8812. Stromberg, Hunt (July 12, 1894–Aug. 23, 1968) Kentucky born former St. Louis sportswriter was a producer at MGM 1925–1943, turning out many films including *Red Dust, The Thin Man* series, the Jeanette MacDonald–Nelson Eddy musicals, *The Great Ziegfeld* (1936, Academy Award for best picture), *Night Must Fall,* many others. Sec. H, lot 477, Calvary Cemetery, east Los Angeles.

8813. Strong, George Templeton (1820–July 21, 1875) Manhattan lawyer, trustee of Columbia, vestryman at Trinity Church, a founder of the Union League Club, president of the Church Music Association and Philharmonic Society. His diary spans much of mid 19th century New York, with many observations on the Civil War and its affect on the north. He died at home at 111 E. 21st. Interred in the vault of his maternal great grandfather, William Brownjohn, in the southern section of Trinity Churchyard, lower Manhattan, N.Y.C.

8814. Stroud, Robert (Jan. 28, 1890–Nov. 21, 1963) The Birdman of Alcatraz ended up in prison for the murder of a man in Alaska, where he had been a pimp. In 1916 he stabbed and killed a prison guard at Leavenworth for no known reason, shortly before his upcoming release. He was saved from the gallows when his mother pleaded with Mrs. Woodrow Wilson, based on Stroud's expertise as a canary doctor. His sentence was commuted to life, which he served in solitary confinement with only his birds as company. His story was filmed with Burt Lancaster in 1962. Masonic Cemetery, Metropolis, IL.

8815. Strudwick, Shepperd (Sept. 22, 1907–Jan. 15, 1983) Actor from Hillsborough, North Carolina, trained at the Actors Studio and long on the New York stage into the 1980's, nominated for a Tony opposite Eva Le Galliene in *To Grandmother's House We Go* (1980). He acted in films under the name John Shepperd in the early 1940's (*The Loves of Edgar Alan Poe, Dr. Renault's Secret* 1942). Later films under his real name include *Joan of Arc* (1948), *The Red Pony, All the King's Men* (1949), *A Place in the Sun* (1951), *Autumn Leaves* (1956) and much TV including daytime soap operas and *The Twilight Zone* episode *Nightmare as a Child.* He died in his Manhattan home from cancer at 75. Ashes buried with his parents. Hillsborough

Memorial (or Newtown) Cemetery, Hillsborough, NC.

8816. Strummer, Joe (John Mellor, Aug. 21, 1952–Dec. 22, 2002) British musician born in Turkey formed The Clash in 1976, best known for their 1980 LP *London Calling.* They broke up in 1986, after which Strummer recorded solo and worked on soundtracks before forming The Mescaleros in the late 90's. He died from heart failure at 50 after taking his dog for a walk. West London Crematorium, London.

8817. Struss, Karl (Nov. 30, 1886–Dec. 15, 1981) New York City born cinematographer used a special filter technique for changing facial appearance without stop motion in both *Ben Hur* (1926) and *Dr. Jekyll & Mr. Hyde* (1931). Co-Oscar winner (the first) for *Sunrise* (1927). With Paramount 1931–1949. Cremated at Chapel of the Pines, Los Angeles. Unmarked at head of Henry Struss grave, Hickory Knoll sec. 126, Woodlawn Cemetery, the Bronx, N.Y.C.

8818. Stuart, Charles (Dec. 18, 1959–Jan. 4, 1990) and **Carol Dimaiti Stuart** (March 26, 1959–Oct. 23, 1989) Boston couple supposedly attacked in their car in the Mission Hill section of Boston October 23, 1989. A black man was arrested and identified by Stuart as the man who fatally shot his pregnant wife in their car as they returned from a lamaze class. When Stuart jumped to his death from the Tobin Bridge on January 4, 1990, it became apparent, with his brother's testimony, that he had shot himself in the car and killed his wife in October, concocting the story of an attack by a black man. Her picture is engraved on the black polished Dimaiti stone, Holy Cross Cemetery, Malden, Massachusetts. Stuart is unmarked. Vanderwood sec., lot 1444, Woodlawn Cemetery, Everett, MA.

8819. Stuart, Emily Cowenhoven (July 1, 1914–April 2, 1989) The daughter of wealth and a publishing family was a mother and grandmother living alone on a quiet street in Princeton, New Jersey, when she was stabbed to death in her cellar, the motive unknown. Her death was the subject of the HBO special *My Mother's Murder.* Rocky Hill Cemetery, Route 518 off of 206 north out of Princeton, Rocky Hill, NJ.

8820. Stuart, Gilbert (Dec. 3, 1755–July 9, 1828) Colonial and early American portrait painter, best known for his painting of George Washington in 1796, originally an unfinished portrait and the basis for the picture on the $1 bill. Though the gravesite can no longer be pinpointed, Stuart was buried in the Old Central Burying Ground on Boston Common, Boston, MA.

8821. Stuart, Iris (Frances McCann MacKinnon, Feb. 2, 1903–Dec. 21, 1936) Wampas Baby Star in a few silent films 1926–27 died in New York City from TB at 33. Sec. 40, lot 136, grave 4, Gate of Heaven Cemetery, Hawthorne, NY.

8822. Stuart, J.E.B. (James Ewell Brown Stuart, Feb. 6, 1833–May 12, 1864) Confederate general known by Lee as "the eyes of the army" was late in arriving at Gettysburg but was otherwise a distinguished leader, particularly in the Virginia Campaign just before his death in battle at Yellow Tavern. Obelisk facing the road, east edge of sec. between D and E, Hollywood Cemetery, Richmond, VA.

8823. Stuart, Roy (July 17, 1935–Dec. 25, 2005) New York born actor in film and TV supporting roles, including Corporal Boyle on *Gomer Pyle U.S.M.C.* 1965–68. Eden Memorial Park, Mission Hills, CA.

8824. Stubbs, Harry (Sept. 7, 1874–March 9, 1950) Short, portly English character actor in blustery to hapless roles: *The Invisible Man* (1933, as Inspector Bird), *Werewolf of London* (1935, bobby with bad arches), *The Invisible Man Returns* (1940, Constable Dukesbury), *The Mummy's Hand* (1940, bartender), *The Wolfman* (1941, Rev. Norman), *Frankenstein meets the Wolfman* (1943, as Bruno). He died at the Motion Picture Country Home of a stroke. Ashes in vaultage, Pierce Brothers' Chapel of the Pines Crematory, Los Angles, CA.

8825. Stucker, Stephen (July 2, 1947–April 2, 1986) Actor who played the giddy, effeminate air traffic controller in *Airplane* (1980) and its sequel. He died from AIDS, was cremated through Pierce Bros. at Chapel of the Pines Crematory in Los Angeles and the urn given to his sister to scatter at sea.

8826. Studebaker, Clement (March 12, 1831–Nov. 27, 1901) and **John M. Studebaker** (Oct. 10, 1833–March 16, 1917) Carriage manufacturers; after Clement's death, John began producing the Studebaker automobile, which continued until 1963. He has a mausoleum in sec. J, with a marble maiden inside guarding the sarcophagus, and Clement is buried in the family lot along the road in sec. I, both in Riverview Cemetery, South Bend, IN.

8827. Stuhldreher, Harry A. (Oct. 14, 1901–Jan. 26, 1965) Quarterback at Notre Dame in Rockne's famed backfield of 1924, "across a gray October sky" with Miller, Layden and Crowley, dubbed The Four Horsemen by Grantland Rice. He coached for Villanova 1925–36 and Wisconsin 1936–47. Calvary Cemetery, Pittsburgh, PA.

8828. Stump, Bob (Robert Lee Stump, April 4, 1927–June 20, 2003) Congressman from Arizona 1977–2003, a major overseer of the national defense system, served twenty six years, as chairman of the Armed Services Committee from 2001, retiring in 2003. Sec. 9, 10 B-2-7, Greenwood Cemetery, Phoenix, AZ.

8829. Sturgeon, Theodore (Feb. 26, 1918–May 8, 1985) Pioneer writer of science fiction from 1949 (*Without Sorcery, More Than Human, Venus Plus X, Some of Your Blood* and *The Dreaming Jewels*). He died at Springfield, Oregon, at 67. Cremated through England mortuary in Eugene. Ashes to family.

8830. Sturges, John (John Elliot Sturges, Jan. 3, 1910–Aug. 18, 1992) Director from Oak Park, Illinois, in Hollywood 1945–1973. Films include *Mystery Street, The Magnificent Yankee, The People Against O'Hara* (1950), *Kind Lady, It's A Big Country* (1951), *Bad Day at Black Rock* (1955), *The Old Man and the Sea* (1958), *The Magnificent Seven* (1960), *The Great Escape* (1963) and *Ice Station Zebra* (1968). He retired to San Luis Obispo, California, where he died from a heart attack at 82. Cremation through Reis Chapel. Ashes scattered at sea 3 miles off Avila Beach, CA.

8831. Sturges, Preston (Edmund P. Biden, Aug. 29, 1898–Aug. 6, 1959) Chicago born film director, a supreme individualist, wrote and directed polished, sophisticated comedy including *The Great McGinty* (1940), *Sullivan's Travels* (1941), *The Miracle of Morgan's Creek* (1944) and *Hail the Conquering Hero* (1944). After he left Paramount he went to work for Howard Hughes but was removed from *Vendetta* by Hughes and went to Europe in a self imposed exile. He died in New York from a heart attack. Maplewood, grave 74, Ferncliff Cemetery, Hartsdale, NY.

8832. Sturgis, Frank (Dec. 9, 1924–Dec. 4, 1993) Philadelphia born ex-policeman and private investigator received a 1–4 year prison term for the burglary of the Democratic party headquarters in the Watergate complex June 17, 1972. He served thirteen months and was denied a pardon by President Carter. The Watergate burglary brought about the long and involved cover-up by the Nixon administration that led to the president's resignation August 9, 1974. Sturgis died in a Miami veterans hospital of lung cancer at 68. Unmarked grave. Sec. B, tier 7, lot 1344, grave 5, Miami Memorial Park, Miami, FL.

8833. Stutz, Harry C. (Sept. 12, 1876–June 26, 1930) Manufacturer of the Stutz Bearcat, a pioneer motor car, beginning his company in 1913. Unmarked. Sec. 47, lot 334, Crown Hill Cemetery, Indianapolis, IN.

8834. Stuyvesant, Peter (c 1610–Feb. 1672) Heavy handed, peg legged Dutch governor of New Netherland was its last, surrendering to the English in 1664, when it was renamed for the Duke of York and called New York. He died on his bowerie (farm) and was carried into the chapel adjacent his house for services and burial. The chapel and crypts still stand beneath St. Marks-in-the-Bowery, erected in 1799 after a fire destroyed the original church. It is the oldest church, excepting St. Paul's on lower Broadway, standing in Manhattan. Stuyvesant's ghost allegedly haunts the church, according to a column by Meyer Berger, and was believed to occasionally ring the bell in the tower. A bust of Stuyvesant on a pedestal, given by the Queen of Holland in 1915, dominates the eastern part of the churchyard near the plaque on the exterior east wall of the church marking the crypt. St. Mark's Church-in-the-Bowery, East 10th St. and 2nd Ave., Manhattan, N.Y.C.

8835. Styka, Jan (April 8, 1858–April 28, 1925) Polish born painter depicted the Polish struggle for freedom and in several religious works, notably *The Crucifixion*. Elaborate tablet in a line with those of Rudolph Friml, Gutzon Borglum, Robert Millikan,

Carrie Jacobs Bond, has a palette with splashes of color on it. Court of Honor below the Last Supper Window, Memorial Terrace, Great Mausoleum, Forest Lawn, Glendale, CA.

8836. Styne, Jule (Dec. 31, 1905–Sept. 20, 1994) British born prolific composer of the American stage and screen, once piano accompanist for Jolson, Ruth Etting and Sophie Tucker, won an Oscar for *Three Coins in the Fountain* (1954) and a Tony for *Hallelujah, Baby!* (1968). Broadway works include *Gentlemen Prefer Blondes* (1949), *Bells Are Ringing* (1956), *Gypsy!* (1959) and *Funny Girl* (1964), each providing signature tunes for Marilyn Monroe, Ethel Merman, Barbra Streisand and several for Frank Sinatra. He died in Manhattan at 88. Sec. 35, row H, Mt. Ararat Cemetery, Farmingdale, Long Island, NY.

8837. Sugerman, Danny (Oct. 11, 1954–Jan. 5, 2005) Avid Doors fan hired by Jim Morrison to put together a scrapbook kept up with the other members of the band, eventually serving as their manager, and later for Iggy Pop. He co-wrote *No One Gets Out of Here Alive* (1980), was a consultant on the 1991 film *The Doors,* authored *Wonderland Avenue: Tales of Glamour and Excess* reflecting his own addictions, and a book on the group Guns 'n' Roses. Married to Oliver North's former secretary Fawn Hall, he died from lung cancer at 50. Westwood Memorial Park, Los Angeles.

8838. Suhr, Gus (August Richard Suhr, Jan. 3, 1906–Jan. 16, 2004) Star with the San Francisco Seals in the Pacific Coast League played with the Pirates for ten years through the 1930's, was traded to the Phillies, and returned with the Seals during World War II before retiring. His best year was 1936, when he hit .312, drove in 118 runs and made the National League All Star team. The second oldest living ball-player and the oldest surviving Pirate, he died in Scottsdale, Arizona, at 98. Garden of Memory, unit 5, tier 4, number 8A-B, Olivet Memorial Park, Colma, CA.

8839. Sukeforth, Clyde (Nov. 30, 1901–Sept. 3, 2000) Baseball player, coach and scout from Washington, Maine, was a catcher in the majors for ten years, hitting .354 for Cincinnati in 1929, but is best known as the scout for Branch Rickey's Brooklyn Dodgers who spotted Jackie Robinson with the Kansas City monarchs in 1945 and encouraged Rickey to sign him the next year, elevating him to the Dodgers in 1947. Sukeforth was also the pitching coach in the 1951 N.L. race against the New York Giants. With Sukeforth reporting that Carl Erskine was bouncing his curveball, Dodger manager Charlie Dressen chose Ralph Branca, who then delivered Bobby Thompson's pennant winning run. Dressen blamed Sukeforth, who abruptly quit. He died at 98 in Waldoboro, Maine. Brookland Cemetery, Friendship Road, Waldoboro, ME.

8840. Sullavan, Margaret (May 16, 1909–Jan. 1, 1960) MGM actress in sensitive roles in *Three Comrades* (1938), *Shopworn Angel* (1939), *The Shop Around the Corner* and *The Mortal Storm* (1940). Divorced from Leland Hayward, and long beset by emotional instability and substance abuse, she was appearing in *Sweet Love Remembered* in New Haven, Connecticut, prior to Broadway, when she was found dead in her room at the Taft Hotel there at 48 from an overdose of prescription drugs. Lot 83, St. Mary's Whitechapel Trinity Episcopal Churchyard, Routes 201 and 354, Lively, Lancaster County, VA.

8841. Sullivan, Ann *see* **Helen Keller.**

8842. Sullivan, Arthur Seymour (May 13, 1842–Nov. 22, 1900) Knighted composer with W.S. Gilbert of the definitive musical satires of Victorian England. The operas of Gilbert and Sullivan remain popular today. St. Paul's Cathedral, London.

8843. Sullivan, Barry (Thomas Barry Sullivan, July 5, 1821–May 3, 1891) Premier Irish 19th century thespian. A statue of him as Hamlet, holding the skull of Yorick, is at his grave. Glasnevin Cemetery, Dublin.

8844. Sullivan, Barry (Patrick Barry Sullivan, Aug. 29, 1912–June 6, 1994) New York City born actor in films from 1943 (*Lady in the Dark, The Bad and the Beautiful*), much on TV. Service and cremation through Forest Lawn Hollywood Hills, Los Angeles. Ashes to residence.

8845. Sullivan, Ed (Edward V. Sullivan, Sept. 28, 1902–Oct. 13, 1974) Broadway columnist in a few films began as host of television's *Toast of the Town* in 1948, later changed to *The Ed Sullivan Show* on CBS, a national Sunday night mainstay through 1971. Famous for his stiff stance and speech, more widely imitated with the years, he introduced many top acts to American audiences, including Broadway numbers sung by the original performers as well as Elvis Presley, the Beatles, and endless others. He died from cancer at 72. Mass at St. Patrick's Cathedral. Though Irish Catholic, his wife Sylvia was Jewish, so (as with George Burns and Gracie Allen) he was interred in a non-sectarian cemetery. Unit 8, alcove G, side comp. 122 (beside the elevator), main mausoleum, Ferncliff Cemetery, Hartsdale, NY.

8846. Sullivan, Francis L. (Jan. 6, 1903–Nov. 19, 1956) Heavy, thick browed character actor of English ancestry with bass voice adept at stuffy or officious characters, including the lawyer in both the 1934 and 1946 versions of *Great Expectations, The Mystery of Edwin Drood, The Citadel, Oliver Twist* (as Mr. Bumble, 1948) *Joan of Arc* (also 1948), *Christopher Columbus,* and as Phil Nosseross in Jules Dassin's *Night and the City* (1950). He was also cast as Hercule Poirot in Agatha Christie plays on stage, and won a Tony on Broadway in *Witness for the Prosecution* 1954–56. A U.S. citizen, Sullivan died from a lung ailment in Mt. Sinai Hospital, New York City, his family then residing in London. Sec. 69, lot 126, grave2, (4th) Calvary, Woodside, Queens, N.Y.C.

8847. Sullivan, Fred (Frederic Richard Sullivan, July 18, 1872–July 24, 1937) London born character actor, short and stout with a walrus mustache, in small official roles in Paramount talkies including *Murder*

By the Clock (1931, as the coroner), *If I Had a Million* (1932), *Duck Soup* (1933). He died in Los Angeles from a heart ailment. No markers on family lot, including his wife and mother-in-law. Block P, lot 20, grave 2, San Gabriel District Cemetery, San Gabriel, CA.

8848. Sullivan, John L. (Oct. 15, 1858–Feb 2, 1918) The last bare knuckle heavyweight boxing champion, taking the title from Paddy Ryan and defending it for ten years, including the last bare knuckle fight (75 rounds, defeating Jake Kilrain) in 1889. A man of immense popularity, he was defeated by Gentleman Jim Corbett in 1892. Corbett who, like Sullivan, went on to become a cohort of political figures and show business people alike, remained a good friend of Sullivan's and served as a pallbearer after Sullivan's death from a heart attack at 59. Sullivan-Lennon family plot with names on a polished gray granite obelisk. Sec. 3 at Honeysuckle and Maple, Mt. Calvary Cemetery, Roslindale, Boston, MA.

8849. Sullivan, Liam (William Edward Sullivan, May 18, 1923–April 19, 1998) Actor from Jacksonville, Illinois, on Broadway and in film and TV, particularly in many series of the 1960's, including *The Twilight Zone* episodes *The Silence, The Changing of the Guard* and *Star Trek* (*Plato's Stepchildren*), many others. He died from a heart attack in Los Angeles at 74. Memorial service at the Church of Religious Science in Burbank. Cremated by Pierce Bros Cunningham and O'Connor. Sec. L, 23 west, Diamond Grove Cemetery, Jacksonville, IL.

8850. Sullivan, Louis Henri (Sept. 3, 1856–April 14, 1924) Founder of the Chicago School of Architecture in partnership with Dankmar Adler, designed many noted Chicago buildings as well as the Getty Tomb in Graceland Cemetery, where he is also buried. Lakeside sec., Graceland Cemetery, Chicago, IL.

8851. Sullivan, Mary (Jan. 1944–Jan. 4, 1964) The last confirmed victim of the Boston Strangler was a 19 year old nursing assistant from Hyannis who had moved only three days before to 44A Charles St., Beacon Hill. Found propped up in bed by her two new roommates, she had been violated with a broomstick and was considered the most gruesome of the crime scenes, with three different scarves tied in bows around her neck and a Happy New Year card propped against her foot. Thirty-six years later, her nephew along with the DeSalvo family, believing he was not the actual strangler, had her body exhumed October 13, 2000, for potential DNA evidence. St. Francis Xavier Cemetery, Centerville, MA. See De Salvo.

8852. Sullivan, Niki (June 23, 1937–April 6, 2004) Original member of Buddy Holly and the Crickets, and from 1958 The Crickets. He died unexpectedly at home in Kansas City at 66. Cremated through Speaks Suburban Chapel, Independence, MO.

8853. Sullivan, Big Tim (Timothy D. Sullivan, July 23, 1862–Aug. 31, 1913) The first Tammany Hall boss from the notorious Five Points and Tenderloin area of Manhattan, a former member of the Whyos, ruled over and enabled his crime ridden district from the 1890's to 1912, installing Tom Foley in power by 1901 to insure various gambling and prostitution operations were not disturbed. His one positive legacy, the Sullivan Law, making it a crime to carry a concealed weapon, was passed in 1911, though enforced only at the discretion of the police. By 1912 paresis had started to erode his mind, and he was institutionalized, escaped, and was fatally injured the next year at 50 when hit by a train on the New York, New Haven and Hartford railroad near Pelham Parkway. His body lay in the Fordham Morgue unidentified for nearly two weeks, narrowly escaping transport to Hart's Island and Potter's Field. His services were held at Old St. Patrick's Cathedral on Mott St. in Manhattan. Calvary Cemetery, Woodside, Queens, N.Y.C.

8854. The Five Sullivans Five brothers from Waterloo, Iowa, enlisted in the U.S. Navy in World War II, requesting they be kept on the same ship, despite general practices to the contrary. Torpedoed and sunk at Guadalcanal November 13, 1942, the U.S.S. *Juneau* went down and all five, **George, Frank, Joseph, Madison** and **Albert**, were lost. George alone survived the initial impact, but died awaiting rescue. Since then, U.S. Armed Forces do not station siblings in the same unit. Their loss was the subject of the 1944 film *The Fighting Sullivans*, which was pulled from many theatres because of heavy losses in the communities during the war. A statue of them stands at the school in Waterloo, and they are listed on their parents' stone. Calvary Cemetery, Waterloo, IA.

8855. Sully, Frank (Frank Thomas Sullivan, June 17, 1908–Dec. 17, 1975) Character actor (*The Grapes of Wrath*, etc.). Gardenia, lot 54, Forest Lawn Sunnyside, Long Beach, CA.

8856. Sully, Thomas (June 8, 1783–Nov. 5, 1872) English born painter came to the U.S. as a leading portrait painter in Philadelphia, though his best known work was *Washington Crossing the Delaware* (1818). Obelisk. Sec. A, lot 43, Laurel Hill Cemetery, Philadelphia, PA.

8857. Madame Sul-Te-Wan (Nellie Connelly, March 7, 1873–Feb. 1, 1959) Actress from Louisville known by her exotic name in films from silents, notably as Tituba in *Maid of Salem* (1937). Block L, sec. 943, lot 19, Valhalla Memorial Park, North Hollywood, CA.

8858. Summers, Hope (Sara Hope Summers Witherell, June 7, 1901–June 22, 1979) Stage producer and actress in several films (ranging from *Inherit the Wind* and *The Ghost and Mr. Chicken* to *Foul Play*) and TV during her last twenty years played Clara Edwards on TV's *The Andy Griffith Show* 1960–68. She died from heart failure in Woodland Hills, California. Ashes interred block 18, First and Cypress, Mountain View Cemetery, Walla Walla, WA.

8859. Summersby, Kay (later Kay Morgan, Nov.

23, 1908–Jan. 20, 1975) Irish born driver for the Supreme Allied Commander, U.S. General Dwight D. Eisenhower in Europe 1942–45. Eisenhower reportedly wanted to divorce his wife and marry Summersby but was discouraged by General George C. Marshall, who told him it would ruin his career. Others who knew Eisenhower, including his son John, refute the story and say Summersby was never more than a close friend. Ashes scattered at County Cork, Ireland.

8860. Summerville, Slim (George J. Somerville, June 10, 1892–Jan. 5, 1946) Tall, lanky actor in good natured hayseed roles, ranging from Tjaden in *All Quiet on the Western Front* (1930) to *Captain January* (1935) and a series of comedies with ZaSu Pitts. He died from a stroke at 53 in his home at Laguna Beach, California. Services through Laguna Beach (now Ray) mortuary, with cremation at Long Beach Crematory. The ashes were buried under the name George J. Somerville, 53, January 21, 1946, in the lot of Thomas Somerville (1939). Unmarked. Utopia plot, lot 217, grave C, Inglewood Park Cemetery, Inglewood, CA.

8861. Sumner, Charles (Jan. 6, 1811–March 11, 1874) Boston born Republican senator from Massachusetts was a leading abolitionist. Beaten half to death on the senate floor by South Carolina Representative Preston Brooks after an anti-slavery speech in 1856, it took Sumner three years to recover, after which he became a leading Radical Republican reconstructionist following the Civil War. His funeral procession was the largest in Mt. Auburn's history of impressive corteges and famous occupants. Rectangular monument with pillars at the corners. Arethusa Path, lot 2447, hillside just off Walnut Ave., Mt. Auburn Cemetery, Cambridge, MA.

8862. Sumner, J. D. (Nov. 19, 1925–Nov. 15, 1999) Gospel bass singer performed with the Stamps as well as Elvis Presley from 1971 until Presley's death. He died in Nashville at 74. N Cross Mausoleum, 3rd floor, 383 B-B1, Woodlawn Memorial Park, Nashville, TN.

8863. Sumner, William Graham (Oct. 30, 1840–April 12, 1910) Sociologist and economist at Yale from 1872 until his death espoused the Darwinian theory of economic survival of the fittest and formed a basis for the so called laissez faire policy that was followed by the Republican party primarily from the late 19th century until the stock market crash. His study *Folkways* was published in 1906. Alderbrook Cemetery, Guilford, CT.

8864. Sunday, Billy (William A. Sunday, Nov. 18, 1862–Nov. 6, 1935) Baseball player turned Presbyterian minister in 1903, famed for his fundamentalist hell-fire and damnation style in personal appearances at chautauquas and over the radio. The epitaph on his monument is from II Timothy 4:7: *I have fought a good fight. I have finished my course. I have kept the faith.* Sec. 32, lot 106, Forest Home Cemetery, Forest Park, IL.

8865. Sunderland, Nan *see* **Walter Huston.**

8866. Sun Ra *see* **Herman Blount.**

8867. Suppe, Franz Von (April 18, 1819–May 21, 1895) Austrian composer of the *Poet and Peasant* overture. Draped white marble monument featuring carved cherubs in the folds of the drapes and a bronze bust of Suppe on the carved pedestal in front. Gruppe 32 A, nummer 31, Zentralfriedhof (Central Cemetery), Vienna.

8868. Suratt, Valeska (June 28, 1882–July 3, 1962) Terre Haute born stage actress in vamp roles, in films 1915–17 in Theda Bara type vehicles, at her peak in vaudeville c 1920. She later lived in Manhattan and died, out of touch with reality, in Washington, D.C. Unmarked, next to her mother Mary (1914). Sec. 14, lot 32, Highland Lawn Cemetery, Terre Haute, IN.

8869. Surratt, John (John Harrison Surratt, Jr., April 13, 1844–April 21, 1916) Son of Mary Surratt carried messages for the Confederacy during the Civil War. He was almost certainly involved in the initial pot to kidnap Lincoln, if not the later and final one to murder him, planned in large part at his mother's boarding house. When the president was assassinated, he had fled to Canada. Later captured in Egypt, he was tried in a civil court, the jury was deadlocked, and he went free. He died at 72 years and 8 days of age. Marked by a stone cross with his last name on the base. Sec. J, lot 264, New Cathedral Cemetery, Baltimore, MD.

8870. Surratt, Mary (May 1823–July 7, 1865) Owner of the house where John Wilkes Booth and his band of conspirators, including her son, met several times prior to the night Lincoln was assassinated and Secretary of State Seward attacked. Although she did not participate in the murder or attack and no evidence ever proved she had knowledge of the plot to kill the president, she was nonetheless hanged with Lewis Paine, David Herold and George Atzerodt in the Washington, D.C. prison yard, the first woman in America to suffer death by hanging as a legal sentence. Her daughter went to the White House on the morning of the execution to plead with President Johnson for her mother's life but was turned away by Preston King of New York (who six months later tied a bag of shot around his neck and stepped off a Hoboken ferry into the Hudson). Stanton was also said to have claimed "That Surratt woman haunts me." The bodies of she, David Herold and George Atzerodt were removed from the arsenal prison yard by their families before Booth's was allowed to be removed in 1869. Later that of Capt. Henry Wirz was also removed, while that of Paine (Powell) was kept by the government, unclaimed or not located, until Paine's skull was released to his family and buried in 1994. Mary Surratt is buried beneath a small white stone, often with a rosary placed over it, inscribed only *Mrs. Surratt*. A small bronze tablet placed against it is inscribed *To the memory of Mary Eugenia Jennings Surratt 1823–1865, widow from Surrattville, Prince George's*

County, Maryland, swept by events and emotions surrounding the assassination of Lincoln from obscurity to the limelight of a military trial and inglorious death on a scaffold and whose guilt in the conspiracy is still questioned. Below is the original stone. Sec. 12-F, lot 31, Mount Olivet Cemetery, Washington, D.C.

8871. Surtees, Robert L. (Aug. 9, 1906–Jan. 5, 1985) Cinematographer from Covington, Kentucky, former assistant to Gregg Toland, won Oscars for *King Solomon's Mines* (1950), *The Bad and the Beautiful* (1952) and *Ben Hur* (1959). Other works include *Our Vines Have Tender Grapes, Oklahoma, Mutiny on the Bounty* (1962), *Same Time Next Year*. Father of cinematographer Bruce Surtees. He died in Carmel, California, at 78. Cremated January 9 through Paul mortuary, Pacific Grove. Ashes scattered at sea three miles west of Point Lobos.

8872. Susann, Jacqueline (Aug. 20, 1921–Sept. 21, 1974) Popular novelist of erotic romances including *Valley of the Dolls* and *Once is Not Enough*. Also a popular and lively talk show personality, she died from cancer at 53. Ashes inurned in a book shaped container with her name and dates on the spine, kept on a shelf with her first editions by her husband at their home.

8873. Susskind, David (Dec. 19, 1920–Feb. 22, 1987) Producer (*Requiem for a Heavyweight, A Raisin in the Sun, All the Way Home*) and TV interviewer hosted *Open End* from 1958, later *The David Susskind Show*. Upper drive on right, Westchester Hills Cemetery, Hastings-on-Hudson, NY.

8874. Sutcliffe, Stuart (June 23, 1940–April 10, 1962) The fifth Beatle, an art student and friend of John Lennon's, died from head injuries believed to have resulted from an incident three years before in Hamburg when the (then) Silver Beatles were accosted by a group of "teddy boys" after their night's playing. The beating took place in the parking lot of the Lilherland Town Hall and all escaped but Sutcliffe, who was severely beaten and kicked about the head. His mother donated his body to medical research where, two years later, a small tumor in the brain, believed to have been caused by the beating, was found. Sec. 1939, no. 552, Huyton Parish Church Cemetery, Huyton, East Liverpool, England.

8875. Sutherland, A. Edward (Jan. 5, 1897–Dec. 31, 1973) London born film director in the U.S., formerly acted in vaudeville and silents from 1914, began directing in 1924. Best known for several W.C. Fields vehicles and others at Paramount as well as for RKO and Goldwyn in the 1930's, including *Palmy Days, Secrets of the French Police* (1931), *Murders in the Zoo, International House* (1933), *Mississippi* (1935), *Poppy* (1936), *The Invisible Woman* (1941, a last film with his crony John Barrymore), *Abie's Irish Rose* (1946). Married for a time to Louise Brooks. Sec. B-17, lot 326, Desert Memorial Park, Cathedral City (Palm Springs), CA.

8876. Sutherland, David (April 4, 1949–June 6,

2005) Artist of Dungeons and Dragons and the fantasy worlds of M.A.R. Barker's Tékumel helped create the basic look and intricacies of the role playing game industry, beginning in 1974. He died at 56 in Sault Sainte Marie, Michigan. Sec. 20-B, grave 80, Fort Snelling National Cemetery, Minneapolis, MN.

8877. Sutherland, Dick (Archie Thomas Johnson, Dec. 23, 1881–Feb. 3, 1934) Silent and talkies film actor, died at 52 from heart disease related to Acromegaly. Memorial lot 84, grave 3, Inglewood Park Cemetery, Inglewood, CA.

8878. Sutherland Sisters Grace (1854–Jan. 13, 1946), **Isabella** (1852–Dec. 1, 1914), **Mary** (died May 12, 1939), **Naomi** (1858–July 13, 1893), **Sarah** (1845–Sept. 9, 1919), and **Victoria** (1849–May 25, 1902) were six sisters from upstate New York who appeared in vaudeville and chautauqua shows in the 1870's and 1880's, displaying their excessively long hair, with tresses below their dresses. Five of the sisters are at the Castlemaine vault, Glenwood Cemetery, Lockport, New York. Victoria is at Forest Lawn Cemetery, Buffalo, NY.

8879. Sutter, John (Feb. 15, 1803–June 18, 1880) Owner of the California land where gold was discovered became one of Americana's hard luck stories. The loss of his employees to hunt for gold left his ranch bankrupt. Lacking funds to recover the land in court, Sutter's Mill made many others rich while he returned to Pennsylvania and died without funds in Washington, D.C. Grave marked by a block surrounded by a stone curb. Moravian Cemetery, Lititz, PA.

8880. Suttles, Mule (George Suttles, March 31, 1900–July 9, 1966) Negro Leagues slugger and first baseman from Blocton, Alabama, played twenty-three seasons from 1921, with the Newark Eagles, Chicago American Giants (including their 1933 championship), and Birmingham Black Barons. 327 lifetime batting average. He died in Newark at 66. Hall of Fame 2006. Glendale Cemetery, Bloomfield, NJ.

8881. Sutton, Frank (Frank Spencer Sutton, Oct. 23, 1923–June 28, 1974) Tennessee born actor in many tough roles in films (*Marty* 1955, *Town Without Pity* 1962) and TV before gaining rerun immortality as Sgt. Carter on *Gomer Pyle U.S.M.C.* 1964–1970. He was appearing in summer stock in *Luv* at a Shreveport, Louisiana, dinner theatre when he died from a heart attack at 50. Memorial service at Chapel of the Psalms, Hollywood Memorial Park Cemetery (now Hollywood Forever), Hollywood (Los Angeles), California. Spencer-Sutton lot, sec. 12, lot 180, Greenwood Cemetery, Clarksville, TN.

8882. Sutton, Grady (April 5, 1906–Sept. 17, 1995) Chubby actor from Chattanooga in films as slow-witted or innocent, good natured yokels, a particular favorite of W.C. Fields, who used him in several films including *The Man on the Flying Trapeze* (1936), *The Bank Dick* (1940) and *You Can't Cheat an Honest Man* (1941). He also appeared in *Alice Adams* (1935), *Stage Door* (1937), many others. He died at

89 at the Motion Picture Country Home in Woodland Hills, California, with no survivors and wishing no services. Cremated through Pierce Bros.-Cunningham and O'Connor mortuary, the ashes were scattered at sea September 29, three miles off Newport Beach, CA.

8883. Sutton, John (Oct. 22, 1908–July 10, 1963) English technical advisor on many films involving the British Empire in India, where he was born. Cast usually as suave characters, with a pencil thin mustache, he entered films as a second lead, appearing with Vincent Price in *Tower of London* (1939), *The Invisible Man Returns* (1940) and later *The Bat* (1959). He died at Cannes, France. Reportedly cremated or buried in the Protestant Cemetery at Cannes.

8884. Sutton, Willie (June 30, 1901–Nov. 2, 1980) Lone wolf bank robber known as The Actor because of the many effective disguises and other ruses he used in numerous escapes over the years. Most active in New York City in the 1940's and 50's, he finally served his sentence 1951–1969, authoring his memoirs *Where the Money Was*, and retiring to Spring Hill, Florida, where he died at 79. Unmarked. Bowles lot, St. Stephen's sec., range G, lot 19, Holy Cross Cemetery, Brooklyn, N.Y.C.

8885. Sutton-Vane (Vane Hunt Sutton-Vane, Nov. 9, 1888–June 15, 1963) British actor and playwright achieved his fame and success with his play *Outward Bound* on the London stage in 1923, filmed in Hollywood in 1930. He died at 74 in Hastings on the southeast coast of England. Service through Banfield and Pomphrey mortuary there. Cremation and the ashes placed in the Garden of Remembrance. No marker. Hastings Crematorium, Hastings, Sussex.

8886. Swain, Mack (Feb. 16, 1876–Aug. 25, 1935) Heavy, often bearded comedian in silent films, best known as Charlie Chaplin's prospecting partner in *The Gold Rush* (1925). He died in Tacoma, Washington. Cremated at Oakwood Crematory in Tacoma. Ashes scattered at sea.

8887. Swanson, Gloria (Gloria May Josephine Swanson, March 27, 1899–April 4, 1983) Chicago born silent screen star worked for Mack Sennett, often opposite Bobby Vernon, before becoming glamour personified at Paramount 1917–1927 (*Male and Female, The Affairs of Anatol, Sadie Thompson*). She was married to her third husband, a Marquis, by 1928 when Joseph Kennedy bankrolled her in Erich Von Stroheim's *Queen Kelly*, scrapped before completion. Her most memorable role came in 1950 as aging silent star Norma Desmond in Billy Wilder's *Sunset Boulevard* (1950), which won her a third Oscar nomination. A long time advocate of health food, she maintained her good looks into her 70's. Her last film was *Airport 1975*. She died at 84 in a New York Hospital. Cremated by Trinity Cemetery Crematory the next day without ceremony. Columbarium of the Church of the Heavenly Rest, 2 East 90th St., Manhattan, N.Y.C.

8888. Swarthout, Gladys (Dec. 25, 1904–July 7, 1969) Singer and actress began with the Chicago Opera Company in 1924 and joined the New York Metropolitan Opera in 1929. Her mezzo-soprano voice was cast in a few mid 1930's films at Paramount. She died from a rheumatic heart ailment in her villa at Florence, Italy. She was cremated there with a memorial service held at St. James American Church. Epitaph *And is He dead whose soul lifts thine on high?* Chapman plot, lot 110 (corner), Brookside Cemetery, Englewood, NJ.

8889. Swayze, John Cameron (April 4, 1906–Aug. 15, 1995) Broadcaster with clipped tones from Wichita, Kansas, went from NBC's *Camel Caravan* to the news, replaced by Huntley and Brinkley in 1956, but best known for his Timex watch commercials. A resident of Greenwich, Connecticut, he died at his winter home in Sarasota, Florida. Cremated through Workman Brothers mortuary in Sarasota, the ashes were sent to his family at Bedford, NY.

8890. Sweat, Isaac Payton (July 19, 1944–June 23, 1990) Singer, guitarist and drummer, played with Blazer Trail, The Continentals, Johnny Winter's Black Plague Band. Songs include *Cotton Eye Joe* and *The Race is On*. A suicide at 45. Sec. 407, lot 18, space 1, Forest Park Westheimer, Houston, TX.

8891. Sweeney, Bob (Oct. 19, 1918–June 7, 1992) Part of radio's *March and Sweeney* with Hal March went on to TV acting in *The Brothers, Fibber McGee & Molly, The Burns & Allen Show* and *Our Miss Brooks*. Films include *The Last Hurrah* (as the undertaker), *Toby Tyler*, before going into full time directing with *The Andy Griffith Show* 1960–68, later producing *Hawaii Five-O*. He died from cancer at 73. Cremated through Pierce Bros. Valley Oaks mortuary, Westlake Village, California. Ashes to residence in Westlake Village.

8892. Sweeney, Charles W. (Dec. 27, 1919–July 15, 2004) Lowell, Massachusetts, born pilot of the B-29 *Bock's Car* which dropped the second atomic bomb, Fat Man, on Nagasaki, Japan, August 9, 1945, effectively forcing the Japanese surrender and ending the Second World War. Their original target, Kokura, was obscured by clouds. Sweeney retired a brigadier general in 1956. He lived in Milton, Massachusetts, until his death in Boston at 84. Flush military marker notes *Silver Star* and *Air Medal*. Sec. 38, gravesite 404, Massachusetts National Cemetery, Bourne, MA.

8893. Sweet, Blanche (June 18, 1896–Sept. 6, 1986) Blonde silent film star from Chicago began at Biograph in 1909, working for D.W. Griffith until 1915 and starring in *Judith of Bethulia* (1914). At Famous Players-Lasky in the 1920's she starred in *Anna Christie* (1923) and *Tess of the D'Urbervilles* (1924) directed by Marshal Neilan, her first husband. Her career faded with sound. Married to actor Raymond Hackett from 1936 until his death in 1958, the year of her last film appearance (in *The Five Pennies*). Upon her death at 91 in New York City, her body was donated to science with no services held. Cremated at Garden State Crematory, North Bergen, New Jersey, in April 1988, the ashes were returned to her friend Martin Sopocy, while a drive was organized to dedicate a flower in her name at the Brooklyn Botanic Garden. The Blanche Sweet Lilac was dedicated there April 28, 1990, and the ashes spread around the base of the plant by a group of her friends September 19, 1990.

8894. Sweet, Dolph (Adolphus Sweet, July 18, 1920–May 8, 1985) Burly Broadway, film and TV actor from New York City was starring in the TV sitcom *Gimme a Break* when he died from cancer in Los Angeles at 64. Cremated at Grandview Memorial Park in Glendale, California, his ashes were scattered from Hampton Bay, Suffolk County, Long Island, NY.

8895. Swenson, Karl (July 23, 1908–Oct. 8, 1978) Brooklyn born character actor in many films (the doomsayer in *The Birds* 1963) and television, ranging from Eddie Haskell's father on *Leave it to Beaver* in 1958 to Lars Hanson from 1974 until his death from a heart attack while visiting at Torrington, Connecticut. Cremated at Pittsfield, Massachusetts, through Newkirk mortuary, Canaan, Connecticut (no records). A resident of Laguna Niguel, California. Ashes returned to family. His wife, actress **Joan Tompkins** (July 9, 1915–Jan. 29, 2005), lived at Laguna Niguel, until her death at 89. Cremated by the Neptune Society of Orange County at Costa Mesa.

8896. Swenson, May (May 28, 1913–Dec. 4, 1989) Poet published eleven volumes of verse; her work appeared in *The Atlantic Monthly, The New Yorker, The Paris Review, Parnassus and Poetry* and elsewhere. Bench monument. Block 41A, lot 1, Logan City Cemetery, Logan City, UT.

8897. Swickard, Josef (June 26, 1866–March 1, 1940) German born stage and screen actor, brother of actor-director Charles Swickard, in films from 1912; with Mack Sennett 1914–17, best known as Rudolph Valentino's father, Marcelo Desnoyers, in *The Four Horsemen of the Apocalypse* (1921), though he appeared in smaller parts through the 1930's. A year before his death, his wife, actress Margaret Campbell (*q.v.*) was murdered by their son. Sec. 1, lot 411, Hollywood Forever Cemetery, Hollywood (Los Angeles), CA.

8898. Swift, Gustavus (Jan. 24, 1839–March 29, 1903) Founder of the Chicago based meat processing company. Sec. 9, lot 3, Mt. Hope Cemetery, Worth Twp., Chicago, Illinois. **Edward Swift** is in a family room in the mausoleum at Rosehill Cemetery, Chicago, IL.

8899. Swift, Jonathan (Nov. 30, 1667–Oct. 19, 1745) Irish satirist and author of *Gulliver's Travels* (1726). An ordained Anglican priest, he became Dean of St. Patrick's in Dublin in 1713. Thirty two years later, paralyzed and declared insane, he died in Dublin. His tomb is marked by a dark plaque in the floor, with a plaque on the wall in Gaelic beside a marble bust in his memory. St. Patrick's Cathedral, Dublin.

8900. Swigert, Jack (John L. Swigert, Jr., Aug. 30, 1931–Dec. 27, 1982) Denver born astronaut on the back-up team stepped into the crew of Apollo 13 in April 1970 when Thomas Mattingly was exposed to German measles. The mission, intended to be the third moon landing, was forced to abort and use lunar gravity to angle them toward earth with reduced power in a crisis that riveted world attention, as chronicled in the 1995 film *Apollo 13*. Swigert was elected to congress on the Republican ticket a month prior to his death from cancer at 51 in Georgetown University Hospital, Washington, D.C. His rose monument has above his name, dates, and designation as both *Astronaut Apollo 13* and *Congressman,* in a circle the Greek logo of Apollo, and *Apollo XIII Ex Luna Scientia*. Sec. 17, block I, lot 15, grave 9, Mount Olivet Cemetery, Denver, CO.

8901. Swinburne, Algernon (April 5, 1837–April 10, 1909) Considered the greatest English poet after the death of Tennyson, Swinburne was cared for during the last thirty years of his life by an admirer, Theodore Watts. Strongly anti-religious, he made Watts promise to have no service read over the grave. To compromise, the vicar read a brief service as the coffin was carried from the hearse to the grave at St. Boniface Church, Bonchurch, Isle of Wight.

8902. Switzer, Carl "Alfalfa" (Aug. 7, 1927–Jan. 21, 1959) Alfalfa in the Hal Roach *Our Gang* comedies, later known as *The Little Rascals*, sported an ever-present cowlick, squeaking voice and love for the *Our Gang* sweetheart Darla (Hood). His parts as a young adult were fewer and smaller (*It's a Wonderful Life* and as the century old Indian in *Track of the Cat*). By the time of his death he was training hunting dogs, one of which was lost. He posted and paid the $50 reward but when the owner declined to reimburse him he went to the man's house at 10400 Avenue in Mission Hills, where an argument ensued and Switzer allegedly drew a knife, after which he was fatally shot at 31. His flat plaque has the image of a hunting dog engraved beside his name and dates. Sec. 6, lot 26, grave 6, Hollywood Forever Cemetery, Hollywood (Los Angeles), CA.

8903. Swope, Herbert Bayard (Jan. 5, 1882–June 20, 1958) St. Louis born journalist moved to Chicago papers and then to New York as a celebrated crime reporter with the *New York World* beginning in 1909, becoming its executive editor by 1920. When he left in 1929, the *World* had won three Pulitzer Prizes and had a reputation for its crusades, among them an expose of the Ku Klux Klan. In later years Swope, among the noted journalistic and literary alumni of the Algonquin Round Table of the 1920's, served in a number of capacities including chairman of the New York State Racing Commission and advisor to the Roosevelt administration in economics as well as to the War Department. He retired to his estate at Sands Point, Long Island, New York, where he died. Cremation and inurnment in Fresh Pond Crematory, Middle Village, Queens, N.Y.C.

8904. Symington, Stuart (June 26, 1901–Dec. 14, 1988) High profile Democratic senator, born in Amherst, Massachusetts, served four terms from Missouri. First elected in 1952, he sponsored the B-52 and was a contender in the 1960 Democratic presidential primaries, resigning December 27, 1976. He died at New Canaan, Connecticut. Ashes with Evelyn Wadsworth Symington. National (Washington) Cathedral (Cathedral of Saints Peter and Paul), Mt. St. Albans, Washington, D.C.

8905. Szell, George (June 7, 1897–July 30, 1970) Budapest born pianist and conductor in Vienna, Germany, and throughout Europe, became musical director and conductor of the Cleveland Orchestra in 1946 and over twenty-four years built it into one of the leading orchestras in the world. He died there from cancer at 73. Cleveland Crematory. Urn given to a private party to go to Zurich, Switzerland (not recorded in cemeteries there).

8906. Szilard, Leo (Feb. 11, 1898–May 30, 1964) Nuclear physicist at the University of Chicago worked with Enrico Fermi on the first chain reaction in 1942 and was instrumental in the development of the Manhattan Project. Columbarium of Apostles, room 1 west, sec. E, niche 17, Cypress View Crematory, San Diego, CA.

8907. Szokoll, Carl (Oct. 15, 1915–Aug. 25, 2004) Austrian film producer and screenwriter who was the link man in Vienna for those plotting to assassinate Hitler July 20, 1944; a captain with the Austrian army absorbed into the Wehrmacht since 1938, he was ordered to implement Valkyrie, the Nazi plan for dealing with civil insurrection, as the assassins planned to use it to restore order after Hitler's presumed death at Rastenburg, east Prussia. While the colonel who gave him the order was executed, Szokoll, who in fact had been the last to speak to head coup leader Claus von Stauffenberg on an untapped phone line, pleaded that he was only obeying orders in rounding up Nazi officers in Vienna and was spared. He became further known as the savior of Vienna for his pleas that the Red Army treat it as an open city and not destroy it, which were heeded. Gruppe 33G, nummer 33 (honor grave), Zentralfriedhof, Vienna.

8908. Szpilman, Wladyslaw (Dec. 5, 1911–July 6, 2000) Classical pianist from Sosnowiec played on Polish radio in Warsaw until the Nazi invasion in 1939, lived in the Jewish ghetto created there and after its abolition hid in various places throughout the city, managing to elude capture and survive the war. He continued playing and composing afterward, and published a memoir, *Smierc Miasta* (*Death of a City*), censored by the Communist government until 1998, and dramatized in the 2002 Roman Polanski film *The Pianist*. Dark charcoal stone and slab. Powazki Cemetery, Warsaw, Poland.

8909. Tabakin, Ralph (Sept. 22, 1921–May 13, 2001) Baltimore based character actor turned up in several Barry Levinson films and others, including *Diner, The Natural, Good Morning Vietnam, Avalon,* and, most notably, as the mordant medical examiner Dr. Scheiner on TV's *Homicide: Life on the Street* 1995–99. A resident of Silver Spring, he died from heart disease at 79. Judean Memorial Gardens, Olney, MD.

8910. Tabor, Horace Austin Warner (Nov. 26, 1830–April 10, 1899) Vermont born prospector became a millionaire with the Leadville and Matchless silver mines in Colorado. For ten years he and his second wife, **Elizabeth McCourt Doe Tabor** (1854–March 7, 1935), nicknamed "Baby Doe," giddily tried to spend their fortune until they were ruined in the 1893 panic and the 1896 devaluation of silver. At his death, he urged Baby Doe not to abandon the Matchless Mine in any event. She moved into a shack near the mine where she lived in poverty for thirty five years until she was found frozen to death in her heatless cabin in 1935. An opera, *The Ballad of Baby Doe,* was written and performed in 1956, twenty one years after her death. Their monument has his profile engraved on it, and the notation *Unknown to fame until approaching the age of fifty, chance suddenly brought him considerable wealth and reputation. A few years later and the throw of the dice quickly returned him to his former obscurity but left in the wake a colorful character in the annals of Colorado history.* Sec. 18, block 6, lot 16, Mt. Olivet Cemetery, Denver, CO.

8911. Tafler, Sydney (July 31, 1916–Nov. 8, 1979) English character actor in films from 1947 (*The Lavender Hill Mob, Passport to Pimlico, The Birthday Party, The Spy Who Loved Me*). Buried with his wife, actress Joy Shelton (*q.v.*). Rear area, row 83, Golders Green Jewish Cemetery, north London.

8912. Taft, Alphonso (Nov. 5, 1810–May 21, 1891) Vermont born Secretary of War and Attorney General under Hayes 1877–81, his former Cincinnati law associate. Father of William Howard Taft and patriarch of a long line of Cincinnati Republican politicians. Sec. 52, lot 114, Spring Grove Cemetery, Cincinnati, OH.

8913. Taft, Lorado (Lorado Zadoc Taft, April 29, 1860–Oct. 30, 1931) Noted sculptor worked and wrote against modernism. Works include the neo-Renaissance fountain at the Washington, D.C. railroad station and *Time* in Chicago's Washington Park. Ashes scattered at his parents' graves in Elmwood Cemetery, Elmwood, IL.

8914. Taft, Robert Alphonso (Sept. 8, 1889–July 31, 1953) Mr. Republican, son of William Howard Taft and long time senator from Ohio, co-author of the 1947 Taft-Hartley labor act and three time unsuccessful contender for his party's nomination to the presidency, in 1944, 1948 and 1952. After being diagnosed with cancer in New York, he came back to the senate briefly but returned to a Manhattan hospital shortly afterward, where he died at 63. Unlike his father, who had a simple Unitarian service, Senator Taft had a full Washington funeral in the U.S. capitol. He was flown back to Cincinnati and buried behind the then new parish church, his grave marked by a wall with a bronze plaque with his image on it and quotes on either side, built into the hill. Episcopal Presbyterian Church of Indian Hill Cemetery, Cincinnati, OH.

8915. Taft, William Howard (Sept. 15, 1857–March 8, 1930) Twenty-seventh President of the United States (1909–1913), rotund and mustached Cincinnati born son of Alphonso Taft, held the dubious distinction of being the heaviest man to occupy the White House. He was also the only man ever chosen to head both the executive and judicial branches of government. Married to **Helen Herron** (Jan. 2, 1861–May 22, 1943), daughter of Rutherford B. Hayes' one time Cincinnati law partner. His term as president was an unhappy four years following that of his friend Theodore Roosevelt. Happy to be rid of the office, Taft returned to his alma mater, Yale, to teach law until his appointment as Chief Justice of the Supreme Court by President Harding in 1921, his true ambition from the outset. His health declined in 1929, rapidly after the funeral of his brother Charles in Cincinnati in December. He was forced to resign in February 1930, shortly before his death from a stroke and heart disease at 72 in his home at 2215 Wyoming Ave. in Washington, D.C. His flag covered coffin drawn through the streets on a caisson, after a simple Unitarian service, he was buried in Arlington, the only American president there for thirty three years. The grave is marked by a pink shaft of Stoney Creek granite sculpted by James Earl Frazier, surmounted by a carved ornamental acroteria design, with benches on either side, the lot surrounded by a hedge and near the grave of General Omar Bradley. Sec. 30, grave S-14, grid YZ-39/40, Arlington National Cemetery, Arlington, VA.

8916. Taggart, Ben (April 5, 1889–May 17, 1947) Character actor from Ottawa in American films from 1915. Sec. 261, row E, grave 2, Los Angeles/Sawtelle National Cemetery, Westwood, west Los Angeles.

8917. Talbot, Lyle (Lyle Henderson, Feb. 8, 1902–March 3, 1996) Actor in varied tough guy detective and thug roles in films of all sorts from the early 30's (*The 13th Guest, Three on a Match, 20,000 Years in Sing Sing*) moved with TV to amiable parts, notably as Ozzie's neighbor Joe Randolph on *The Adventures of Ozzie and Harriet* 1956–66. He died in San Francisco at 94. Private memorial service. Cremated by the Neptune Society of Northern California. Ashes scattered at sea March 6 off the Marin County coast.

8918. Talbott, Gloria (Feb. 7, 1931–Sept. 19, 2000) Actress from Glendale, California, starred in a handful of B movies in the late 1950's, notably *The Cyclops, Daughter of Dr. Jekyll* and *I Married A Monster From Outer Space*. She retired after *An Eye For An Eye* (1966). Married three times, she died at 69 in her native Glendale. Entombed as Gloria Talbott Mul-

lally. Mausoleum, sec. 112, crypt B-7, San Fernando Mission Cemetery, Mission Hills, CA.

8919. Talley, Marion (Dec. 20, 1906–Jan. 3, 1983) Opera singer from Kansas City made her debut at the New York Metropolitan Opera as Gilda in 1926, but was widely criticized for having no flair with the music, and for having brought her family there from Kansas City. She went on to a concert career and appeared in the film *Follow Your Heart*. Sanctuary of Remembrance, crypt 39, Westwood Memorial Park, west Los Angeles.

8920. Talleyrand-Perigord, Charles Maurice (Feb. 2, 1754–May 17, 1838) French politician known for his quick maneuvering to best advantage. He at first sided with the French Revolution but later went into hiding during the Reign of Terror. At the Congress of Vienna in 1815, he led the French government's negotiations under Louis XVIII. Later Minister to England under Louis Philippe. The family has a large lot in div. 31, Pere Lachaise Cemetery, Paris. He is on the grounds of his chateau at Valencay, France.

8921. Tallichet, Margaret (March 13, 1915–May 3, 1991) Dallas born actress married to director William Wyler from 1938 until his death in 1981. Her best known film role was in the minor classic *Stranger on the Third Floor* (1940), shortly before her retirement from films. She died from cancer at 76 in Indio, California. Cremated through Fitzhenry mortuary, her ashes were scattered at sea.

8922. Talmadge, Constance (April 19, 1899–Nov. 23, 1973) Brooklyn born actress, primarily comedic, sister of Norma and Natalie, came to stardom as the spirited gamin in D.W. Griffith's *Intolerance* (1916). She retired with sound shortly before Norma. Married four times, lastly to Walter Giblin, a New York stockbroker (died 1964). After his death she returned to L.A., where she died at 74 from hepatitis and pneumonia. Her death certificate lists her year of birth as 1903 and her age as 70. Abbey of the Psalms/Hollywood Forever Mausoleum, top of four crypts, family room, corridor G-7 (Eternal Love), Hollywood Forever Cemetery, Hollywood (Los Angeles), CA.

8923. Talmadge, Herman (Aug. 9, 1913–March 21, 2002) Georgia Governor 1948–1955 and Senator 1957–1980, the son of fiery Governor **Eugene "Genie" Talmadge** (1884–1946), was a segregationist southern Democratic governor but as a senator gradually came to draw a considerable amount of the Black vote, with improved roads and schools and the Rural Development Act. On the Senate Watergate Committee in 1973 his profile rose, particularly when quizzing John Erlichman about the illegal entry of Daniel Ellsberg's psychiatrist's office. In 1979 however, the Senate Ethics Committee investigated his campaign funding, his fellow senators denounced him, and he lost his bid for re-election in 1980. He died at his Hampton, home at 88. Eugene Talmadge is at Oak Grove Cemetery, McRae, Georgia. Herman was buried at

Talmadge Cemetery, Lovejoy, Henry County (near Hampton), GA.

8924. Talmadge, Natalie (April 29, 1898–June 19, 1969) Youngest of three sisters made only a few silents; better known for her marriage to Buster Keaton, later divorced. Crypt above Norma and below Constance. Abbey of the Psalms/Hollywood Forever Mausoleum, family room, corridor G-7 (Eternal Love), Hollywood Forever Cemetery, Hollywood (Los Angeles), CA.

8925. Talmadge, Norma (May 26, 1893 or 1895–Dec. 24, 1957) Eldest of three actress sisters from Brooklyn pushed into stardom by their mother Peg, beginning at Vitagraph in 1910. She married producer Joseph Schenck in 1916 and he molded her career with a long string of tearful melodramas featuring her as the suffering heroine. She made a few talkies and retired by 1930. Married to George Jessel in the 1930's and later to Dr. Carvel James, who survived her. They lived in later years in Las Vegas, where she was in a wheelchair with arthritis and remained primarily in seclusion. She died there in her sleep on Christmas Eve 1957 from a stroke complicated by pneumonia at 62 or 64. Her death certificate lists her birth as May 2, 1897 and her age as 60, though most sources give May 26 either two or four years earlier. Removed by Palm mortuary to Forest Lawn Glendale, but interred above her mother **Peg** (Margaret, 1934). Abbey of the Psalms/Hollywood Forever Mausoleum, family room, corridor G-7 (Eternal Love), Hollywood Forever Cemetery, Hollywood (Los Angeles), CA.

8926. Talman, William (Feb. 4, 1915–Aug. 30, 1968) Actor played the ever losing but never discouraged prosecutor Hamilton Burger on TV's *Perry Mason* 1957–1966. He was the first celebrity to do a commercial broadcasting his terminal illness, lung cancer, showing his small daughter and warning against cigarette smoking. The spots aired in the summer of 1968, just prior to and after his death at 53. Buried near Ray Collins. Court of Liberty, lot 833, Forest Lawn Hollywood Hills, Los Angeles.

8927. Tamiroff, Akim (Oct. 29, 1899–Sept. 17, 1972) Actor from Baku, Russia; a member of the Moscow Art Theater, his thick accent was generally used for sly villainy but he was adept at broad comedy as well. Films include *The General Died at Dawn* (1936, AA nomination), *For Whom the Bell Tolls* (1943), *Touch of Evil* (1958). He died in Palm Springs. Cremated through Wiefel and Sons mortuary. Ashes were scattered at sea.

8928. Tandy, Jessica (June 7, 1909–Sept. 11, 1994) London born actress on Broadway 67 years won Tonys for *A Streetcar Named Desire* (1948), *Foxfire* and *The Gin Game*. Married to actor Hume Cronyn from 1942, earlier films included *The Seventh Cross* (1943, with Cronyn) and *The Birds* (1963), but her career centered on the stage, where she teamed with Cronyn in plays beginning in 1951 with *The Four Poster*. Her renown expanded in her last decade with films: *Foxfire* (TVM 1983), *Cocoon* (1985), *batteries not included* (1987), all with Cronyn, *Driving Miss Daisy* (AA, 1989), *Fried Green Tomatoes* (1991), *To Dance With the White Dog* (TVM, 1993, with Cronyn), *Used People* and *Nobody's Fool*, several others. The Cronyns received the Kennedy Center Life Achievement Honors in 1986 and Academy Awards for their lifetime of work in 1994. She died at her home in Easton, Connecticut, after a five year battle with ovarian cancer. Cremated at Ferncliff Cemetery, Hartsdale, New York through Magner mortuary, Norwalk, Connecticut. Ashes to her residence, Easton, CT.

8929. Taney, Roger Brooke (March 17, 1777–Oct. 12, 1864) Chief Justice of the Supreme Court 1836–1864 favored leaving more power and discretion to the states than to the central government. His most famous and lamented opinion, The Dred Scott Decision in 1857 said a slave was property, not a citizen with constitutional rights, and could be returned to their "masters" after having reached free northern territory, denying their protection by the federal government. A newer upright monument has been placed at the head of his eroding white slab, with an historical marker at its foot. St. John's Cemetery, Frederick, MD.

8930. Tanguay, Eva (Aug. 1, 1878–Jan. 11, 1947) Immensely popular risqué vaudeville star known as the *I Don't Care* Girl, after the popular song she used as a theme, and for her temper and independence off stage. She was for a time the most sought after performer in vaudeville, her entrance always announced by blaring trumpets. Abbey of the Psalms/Hollywood Forever Mausoleum, corridor D-1 (Hope), top tier, Abbey of the Psalms, Hollywood Forever Cemetery, Hollywood (Los Angeles), CA.

8931. Tanney, Vic (Feb. 18, 1912–June 11, 1985) Founder of fitness programs and salons. Crypt inscribed *Father of Fitness*. Mausoleum crypt 12-C, Valley Oaks Memorial Park, Westlake Village, CA.

8932. Tarbell, Ida (Nov. 5, 1857–Jan. 6, 1944) Leading "muckraker" of the Progressive movement in the first decade of the twentieth century wrote for *McClure's* but was known for *The History of the Standard Oil Company* (1904), which helped to bring about the breakup of the Rockefeller monopoly in 1911. Buried in the rich oil country that boomed through the 1880's. Woodlawn Cemetery, Titusville, PA.

8933. Tarkington, Booth (July 29, 1869–May 19, 1946) Hoosier author of *The Gentleman from Indiana, Penrod* (1914), *Alice Adams* (1919) and *The Magnificent Ambersons* (1922), the last two winning Pulitzers. A native of Indianapolis, he set many of his stories there, including the Amberson saga. Mausoleum near the Benjamin Harrison lot. Sec. 13, Crown Hill Cemetery, Indianapolis, IN.

8934. Tarleton, Banastre (Aug. 21, 1754–Jan. 16, 1833) British Cavalry officer from Liverpool, infamous in the American Revolution for practicing ruthless, total war. Chasing Buford's Virginia patriots to

The Waxhaws, his horse was shot just as the colonists waved a flag of truce, and thinking their commander killed, his British Legion killed the colonials, who had surrendered, thus earning his reputation as The Butcher. Cornwallis put Tarleton on the trail of the elusive Francis Marion in November 1780 but he failed to capture The Swamp Fox. He was later promoted to major general, was made a Baronet, and served seven terms as a Whig in the House of Commons. Buried at Leintwardine in northernmost Herefordshire, on the border of Shropshire and Wales. Leintwardine Churchyard, Herefordshire.

8935. Tarnower, Herman (March 18, 1910–March 10, 1980) Physician who authored *The Scarsdale Diet* was shot and killed by his lover, Jean Harris, in White Plains, New York. She served twelve years for the murder. Larchmont Temple sec., Mt. Hope Cemetery, Hastings-on-Hudson, NY.

8936. Tartikoff, Brandon (Jan. 13, 1949–Aug. 27, 1997) New York born President of NBC 1980–1991developed many popular series, including *Hill Street Blues, Cheers, Family Ties, L.A. Law, The Cosby Show.* He died at 48 after a 23 year battle with Hodgkin's Disease. Gardens of Ramah 12, lot 2056, Mt. Sinai Memorial Park, Los Angeles.

8937. Tashman, Lilyan (Oct. 23, 1899–March 21, 1934) Silent and talkies actress in cool, sophisticated roles, often devious, known as the best dressed woman in Hollywood, in *Bulldog Drummond* (1929), *The Cat Creeps* (1930), *Millie* and *Murder by the Clock* (1931). Last seen as Nellie Bly in *Frankie and Johnny*, shot at Astoria in Queens and completed March 8, 1934. Operated on for cancer in Doctors' Hospital, Manhattan, on March 16, she died there five days later, survived by her husband, actor Edmund Lowe. Services at the Universal Chapel in Manhattan had a eulogy by Eddie Cantor. Crowds rushed and crowded the burial, knocking over the stone of her sister Annie (1929) and forcing the rabbi from Temple Emanu-El to read the committal service quickly and have the coffin lowered. As of 1988, the cemetery still withheld the location. Washington Cemetery, Brooklyn, N.Y.C.

8938. Tate, Sharon (Jan. 24, 1943–Aug. 9, 1969) Actress wife of director Roman Polanski less known for her films (*The Fearless Vampire Killers* 1967, *Valley of the Dolls* 1968) than for the savage murder of she and her unborn child along with four others at her home, 10050 Cielo Drive in Beverly Hills, on a hot Friday night in August 1969. The killers, later identified as members of the Charles Manson "family," inflicted multiple stab wounds on Tate, who was in her third trimester. She was buried in St. Anne's Garden, Holy Cross Cemetery, Culver City, California, the plaque replaced by a new one after her mother **Doris** was buried with her in 1992. Replacing Doris Tate at all parole hearings was the actress's younger sister **Pattie Tate Ford**; she died from breast cancer at 40 June 3, 2000, was cremated and her urn buried with her mother and sister. Also killed were hair stylist **Jay Se-**

bring (Thomas Kummer, born Oct. 10, 1933). Services at the Wee Kirk of the Heather chapel in Forest Lawn, Glendale, California. Sec. 24, lot 281, grave 12, Holy Sepulchre Cemetery, Southfield, Michigan; **Abigail Folger** (born Aug. 11, 1943), coffee heiress, and her companion, Polanski's friend and fellow Pole **Voytek (Wojciech) Frykowski** (born Dec. 22, 1936). She was entombed in sec. N-205 at hall 14, mausoleum at Holy Cross Cemetery, Colma, California. He was cremated at Forest Lawn, Glendale, and the ashes sent to St. Josef Cemetery at Lods, Poland. Not at the house with the other four but in his car as the murderers approached the house was eighteen year old **Steven Earl Parent** (born Feb. 12, 1951), also fatally shot. Sec. B, tier 11, grave 32, Queen of Peace Cemetery, Rowland Heights, California. One member of the Manson "family" (not a part of the Tate-LaBianca killings), **John Philip Haught** (April 20, 1947–Nov. 5, 1969), nicknamed Christopher Jesus or Zero, shot himself, or was shot, in the head three months after the murders. USN veterans' marker, Two Ridge Cemetery, Wintersville, OH. *See also* **Hinman, Hughes, LaBianca, Spahn.**

8939. Tati, Jacques (Jacques Tatischeff, Oct. 9, 1908–Nov. 4, 1982) French actor-comedian and director known as Mr. Hulot in *Mr. Hulot's Holiday* (1953) and *Mon Oncle* (1958), which won an Oscar. His inscription is at the upper left of the family slab-monument, with a stone cross recumbent on top and at its base a replica of his cinema awards. Ancien Cimetiere, St. Germain-en-Laye, outside Paris.

8940. Tatischeff, Sophie (Oct. 22, 1946–Oct. 27, 2001) Film editor daughter of Jacques Tati worked in French films 1971–1986, and restored much of her father's work. Her name is on the front base of their family slab. Ancien Cimetiere, St. Germain-en-Laye, outside Paris.

8941. Tatum, Art (Oct. 13, 1909–Nov. 4, 1956) Jazz pianist from the 1930's acclaimed for his improvisational style. Buried in Rosedale Cemetery, Los Angeles, with a bar from *Someone to Watch Over Me* and the epitaph *Though the strings are broken, the melody lingers on* on his flush black plaque. He was removed in 1992 to Forest Lawn, where his name, dates, a silhouette of him at the piano, and the line *Someone to Watch Over Me* are now inscribed on his crypt. Sanctuary of Peaceful Rest, crypt 16107, Jasmine Terrace, Great Mausoleum, Forest Lawn, Glendale, CA.

8942. Tatum, Goose (Reece Tatum, May 3, 1921–Jan. 18, 1967) Star of the Harlem Globetrotters through the 1940's and 50's. Sec. D, grave 2668, Fort Bliss National Cemetery, El Paso, TX.

8943. Taurog, Norman (Feb. 23, 1899–April 7, 1981) Chicago born film director 1923–1968 whose prolific output included *Lucky Boy* (1929), *Skippy* (1931, AA), *Huckleberry Finn* (1931), *If I Had A Million, We're Not Dressing, Mrs. Wiggs of the Cabbage Patch* (1934), *College Rhythm, Boys' Town* (AA nom., 1938), several Martin and Lewis comedies in the

1950's and more Elvis Presley films (nine) than any other director. Cremated by Weifel and Sons, Palm Springs, April 10. Ashes scattered at sea.

8944. Taussig, Joseph Knefler (Aug. 30, 1877–Oct. 29, 1947) 5th Naval District commander in 1940 told a U.S. senate committee that events pointed to war with Japan. Repudiated for "poor judgment" by the Navy, he was retired three months before Pearl Harbor was bombed. Sec. 30, grave 724, Arlington National Cemetery, Arlington, VA.

8945. Tayback, Vic (Victor Tayback, Jan. 6, 1930–May 25, 1990) Burly, balding actor played intimidating characters before his role as Mel in the 1975 film *Alice Doesn't Live Here Anymore* and the much lighter TV series *Alice* that followed. He died from a heart attack at 60. Sheltering Hills, lot 3813, Forest Lawn, Hollywood Hills, Los Angeles.

8946. Taylor, Ben (Benjamin Harrison Taylor, July 1, 1888–Jan. 24, 1953) Negro Leagues great, first baseman and manager, had a lifetime batting average of .334. Hall of Fame 2006. Sec, K, Arbutus Memorial Park, Pikesville, Baltimore, MD.

8947. Taylor, C. I. (Charles Isham Taylor, June 20, 1875–Feb. 23, 1922) Player and manager helped found the Negro National League in 1920 and the National Association of Colored Professional Baseball Clubs, managing the Birmingham Giants from 1904, which became the West Baden Sprudels in 1910, and the powerful Indianapolis ABCs from 1914, named for their sponsor, the city's American Brewing Company. Brother of Ben, Johnny and Candy Jim Taylor. Crossed bats on either side of his stone. Sec. 53, lot 555, Crown Hill Cemetery, Indianapolis, IN.

8948. Taylor, Candy Jim (James A. Taylor, Feb. 1, 1884–April 3, 1948) Third and second basemen, later manager in the Negro Leagues, brother of Ben (*q.v.*), Johnny and C.I. Taylor, all players. He played from 1904, at his peak in 1916 with C.I.'s Indianapolis ABC's, the black world champions, when he batted .478 in a five game series with the New York Lincoln Stars and .360 in seven of ten BWS games. As manager, he won pennants with the St. Louis Stars in 1928 and the Homestead Grays in 1943 and 1944, going on to win the BWS both years. A plaque was placed in memory of him, Jimmie Crutchfield and John Donaldson, September 26, 2004. Burr Oak Cemetery, Alsip, IL.

8949. Taylor, Charles see **John I. Taylor.**

8950. Taylor, Charles E. (May 24, 1868–Jan. 30, 1956) Assistant to the Wright Brothers in building the first engine and flying machine used in their famed 1903 flight at Kitty Hawk. His plaque, noting his work and bearing the spread wings, is near those of fellow aerial pioneers Roy Knabenshue and John Moisant in the Portal of the Folded Wings, Valhalla Memorial Park, North Hollywood, CA. Also buried in the Portal of the Folded Wings are several other aviation pioneers including **Bertrand Blanchard Acosta** (Jan. 1, 1895–Sept. 1, 1954), pilot on the 1927 Byrd trans–Atlantic flight, **Walter R. Brookins** (July 11, 1889–April 29, 1953), instructor for the Wright Brothers, **John F. B. Carruthers** (1889–1960), chaplain of the Portal of the Folded Wings and air historian (*At the grave when my warfare is ended, tho no flowers emblazon the sod, may a prayer mark the good I intended, leaving all decoration to God*), **Francis O. Dalton** (1915–1980), Distinguished Flying Cross, **Warren S. Eaton** (June 12, 1891–June 22, 1966), flying school pioneer, built the first acrobatic airplane and invented the radio direction finder, **W. B. "Bert" Kinner** (Dec. 16, 1882–July 4, 1957), inventor of the compound folded wing, Amelia Earhart's first plane, etc., **Elizabeth Lippincott McQueen** (Sept. 25, 1878–Dec. 25, 1958), founder of the Women's International Assn of Aeronautics, **James Floyd Smith** (Oct. 17, 1884–April 18, 1956), inventor of the free type manually operated parachute, **Carl B. Squier** (April 17, 1893–Nov. 5, 1967), co-founder of Lockheed, distinguished flyer and air salesman.

8951. Taylor, Derek (May 7, 1932–Sept. 7, 1997) Liverpool born publicist and spokesman for the Beatles, particularly visible during their last two, strife filled years 1968–70, left Apple in 1970 but remained on good terms with all four and worked on the Anthology shortly before his death from cancer of the esophagus at 65. Service at Sudbury, Suffolk.

8952. Taylor, Don (Dec. 13, 1920–Dec. 29, 1998) Actor, writer and director from Freeport, Pennsylvania, had pivotal roles in *Winged Victory, The Naked City* (1948), *Father of the Bride* (1951), *Stalag 17* (1953), etc. He later directed various films and TV (Emmy nomination for *The Night They Tore Down Tim Riley's Bar*). He died at 78, survived by his wife, actress Hazel Court. Plaque in Urn Garden (right), Westwood Memorial Park, Los Angeles.

8953. Taylor, Dub (Walter Claude Dub-Taylor, Jr., Feb. 26, 1907–Oct. 3, 1994) Virginia born comic actor in hundreds of appearances beginning with Frank Capra's *You Can't Take it With You* (1938). His familiar goofy, fox-wise smile showed up in over three hundred films, many of them westerns, including *Bonnie and Clyde, The Wild Bunch* and *Back to the Future III*, as well as many TV appearances. Father of actor Buck Taylor. He died at 85 in Westlake Village, California. Cremated through Forest Lawn Hollywood Hills, his ashes were returned to his home and reportedly scattered near there.

8954. Taylor, Eric (Eric Whitmore Taylor, July 16, 1894–Sept. 9, 1952) Prolific screen-writer of B thrillers born in England (according to cemetery records) turned out plots 1936–1952, including the *Ellery Queen* series (seven films 1940–42), the *Crime Doctor* series (four from 1943–46), Universal horrors *Black Friday, The Black Cat* 1941, *Ghost of Frankenstein, Son of Dracula, The Spider Woman Strikes Back*, as well as *The Whistler, Dick Tracy Meets Gruesome*, and had done several westerns and *Big Jim McLain* when he died in a San Francisco hotel at 58. Cremated September 10 at Cypress Lawn Cemetery, Colma, his wife Virginia took the ashes on the 11th to the "Santa Barbara Chapel." Ashes buried Montecito sec., lot 134, grave 3, Santa Barbara Cemetery, Santa Barbara, CA.

8955. Taylor, Estelle (Estelle Boylan, May 20, 1899–April 15, 1958) Silent screen actress married in the 1920's to heavyweight champion Jack Dempsey, starred with him in *Manhattan Madness* (1925), with John Barrymore in *Don Juan* (1926, as Lucretia Borgia), *Where East is East* (1929, with Lon Chaney), *Street Scene* and *Cimarron* (1931), the year she and Dempsey divorced. After the September 1926 fight in which he was bested by Gene Tunney, it was to Taylor's question "What happened Ginsberg?" (her nickname for him) that Dempsey responded "Honey, I forgot to duck." The line was later attributed to President Ronald Reagan as original after the attempt on his life in March 1981. Her last appearance was in 1945. She died from cancer at 58. Sec. 2, lot 402, Hollywood Forever Cemetery, Hollywood (Los Angeles), CA.

8956. Taylor, F. Chase ("Col. Lemuel Stoopnagle") (Oct. 4, 1897–May 29, 1950) Part of radio and film's comedy team Col. Stoopnagle and Bud, in the 1930's appeared in a few films including *International House* (1933). Sec. AA, lot 74, Forest Lawn Cemetery, Buffalo, NY.

8957. Taylor, Fred R. (Dec. 3, 1924–Jan. 6, 2002) Ohio State University baseball All Star and member of the 1950 Big Ten championship basketball team played for the Washington Senators, then coached hoops at OSU 1958–1976, winning the championship in 1960 and runner-up in 1961 and '62, with seven Big Ten championships. Union Cemetery, Olentangy River Road, Columbus, OH.

8958. Taylor, George (Sept. 11, 1716–Feb. 23, 1781) Signer of the Declaration of Independence from Pennsylvania. St. John's Lutheran Church Cemetery, Easton, PA.

8959. Taylor, Harry (James Harry Taylor, May 20 1916–Nov. 5, 2000) Pitcher for Brooklyn and Boston 1946–1952, died in West Terre Haute, Indiana. Along south drive of horseshoe one third of the way in and three lots back on right. Shepherd's Cemetery, Shepherdsville (on 63 between Terre Haute and Clinton), Vigo County, IN.

8960. Taylor, John ("of Caroline") (Dec. 19, 1753–Aug. 21, 1824) Virginia born politician and political philosopher was designated John Taylor of Caroline to identify him with Caroline County, Virginia, where he lived and farmed and to distinguish him from others with the common name. He served in the Virginia House of Delegates and in the senate, filling unexpired terms. Chiefly noted as a staunch states' rights advocate who opposed ratification of the Constitution and any strong federal governing. He published several works which still define the Democratic agrarian liberal strain in American politics. Related to both presidents Madison and Taylor. He died at

his plantation and was buried there in the Taylor burial ground, Hazelwood, Caroline County, VA.

8961. Taylor, John I. (Jan. 14, 1875–Jan. 26, 1938) Son of **Gen. Charles Taylor** (July 14, 1846–June 22, 1921), editor and publisher of *The Boston Globe* 1880–1921. His father bought the Boston American League baseball team for him, and he took it over in April 1904, changing their name from the Pilgrims to the Red Sox in 1907, and moving them from the Huntington Avenue Grounds to his new Fenway Park in April 1912. John's brother **William Osgood Taylor** (Jan. 8, 1871–July 15, 1956) continued as publisher of *The Globe*. All three Taylors are at the intersection of White Oak and Chestnut Ave., Forest Hills Cemetery, Jamaica Plain, Boston, MA.

8962. Taylor, Johnnie (May 5, 1938–May 31, 2000) Arkansas born, Dallas based rhythm and blues vocalist dubbed The Philosopher of Soul, best known for *Who's Makin Love (To Your Old Lady)?* and later for *Disco Lady* (1976). He died from a heart attack in Dallas at 62. Entombment at Forest Hill (Abbey) Mausoleum, Forest Hill Cemetery, Kansas City, MO.

8963. Taylor, June (Dec. 14, 1917–May 16, 2004) Chicago born choreographer whose June Taylor Dancers graced The Jackie Gleason Shows variety shows from 1952 in their various incarnations through 1971, moving with the program to Miami Beach, where she remained with her husband, attorney Sol Lerner. Her sister Marilyn, a former June Taylor Dancer, became Gleason's last wife. From 1978–1990 she choreographed the Miami Dolphin's Starbrites. Our Lady of Mercy Cemetery, Miami, FL.

8964. Taylor, Kent (Louis Weiss, May 11, 1906–April 11, 1987) Mustached leading man from Iowa in Hollywood in the 1930's (*Mrs. Wiggs of the Cabbage Patch, Death Takes a Holiday, Five Came Back*) drifted to generally shady parts. Niche in the Sanctuary of Remembrance, Westwood Memorial Park, west Los Angeles, CA.

8965. Taylor, Laurette (Helen Laurette Magdalene Cooney, April 1, 1884–Dec. 7, 1946) Leading Broadway actress known for her starring role in *Peg O My Heart* in the 1910's and 20's, filmed in 1922, and later *The Glass Menagerie*. After several years of hard times, she appeared again in the 1940's prior to her death from a heart attack in her New York home. Unmarked. Cooney family plot and stone, Butternut sec. along Butternut Ave., Woodlawn Cemetery, the Bronx, N.Y.C.

8966. Taylor, Marshall "Major" (Marshall W. Taylor, Nov. 26, 1878–July 6, 1932) Indianapolis born bicycle racing champion had broken two world records by 1896, though because he was Black, he was banned from the Capital City Track. By 1898 he held seven world records, winner of the one mile race in 1898 and breaking his own record the next year. He competed in Europe in 1902, defeating every bicycle racing champion there. Retired in 1910, by 1930 he was impoverished and moved to Chicago, where he attempted to sell his 1928 autobiography *The Fastest Bicycle Racer in the World*. He died at 53 in Cook County Hospital and was buried in an unmarked grave. In May 1948 several pro bike racers, sponsored by Frank Schwinn, had him removed to a grave other than Potters Field and a bronze marker placed, inscribed *World champion bicycle rider who came up the hard way without hatred in his heart. An honest, courageous and God-fearing, clean living, gentlemanly athlete. A credit to his race who always gave out his best. Gone but not forgotten.* Mount Glenwood Cemetery, Glenwood, IL.

8967. Taylor, Maxwell (Aug. 26, 1901–April 19, 1987) U.S. Army general was chairman of the joint chiefs of staff 1962–64 and U.S. Ambassador to Vietnam 1964–65, during which he backed substantial escalation of U.S. involvement there. Sec. 7A, grave 20, Arlington National Cemetery, Arlington, VA.

8968. Taylor, Mel (Sept. 24, 1933–Aug 11 1996) Drummer for The Ventures (*Walk Don't Run* 1964, etc.) Lot 3708, sp 2, Maimonides 30, lot 3708, space 2, Mt. Sinai Memorial Park, Los Angeles.

8969. Taylor, Richard "Dick" (Jan. 27, 1826–April 12, 1879). Son of U.S. President Zachary Taylor, military secretary to his father during the Mexican War, later commanded a Confederate brigade under Ewell in Jackson's Shenandoah Valley Campaign, fought at Seven Days, commanded the District of Western Louisiana and fought at Red River, Mansfield, Pleasant Hill. Tomb in sec. 1, Metairie Cemetery, New Orleans, LA.

8970. Taylor, Robert (Spangler Arlington Brugh, Aug 5, 1911–June 8, 1969) MGM lead from Filley, Nebraska, for twenty years evolved from the boyish medical student the studio recruited to star opposite Garbo in *Camille* (1936) to tougher roles in *Three Comrades, Escape* and *Waterloo Bridge* (1940), later in more jaded and tough roles in many war films, westerns and costume epics (*Ivanhoe*) but never losing his trademark widows' peak hair style. Married to Barbara Stanwyck 1939–51. TV series *The Detectives*. He died from lung cancer at 57 in St. John's Hospital, Santa Monica. After his name and dates is the epitaph *And a lifetime to go.* Columbarium of Evening Star, lower right beside marble statue, Garden of Honor (private), Forest Lawn, Glendale, CA.

8971. Taylor (Davis), Sarah Knox *see* **Zachary Taylor.**

8972. Taylor, William Desmond (William C. Deane-Tanner, March 26, 1872–Feb. 1, 1922) Silent film director known today for his murder and the ensuing outcry against immorality in the film colony. He was found dead from a gunshot wound in his bungalow at 404½ South Alvarado in Hollywood. Investigations revealed lingerie belonging to actress Mary Miles Minter, until then the picture of innocence, and Mabel Normand, though cleared of suspicion, removed several personal effects from the bungalow before the police were called. No one was charged, but the popular theory laid the murder on Minter's mother, Charlotte Shelby, helped along by a 1967 reinvestigation by silent film director King Vidor, published in 1986 as *A Cast of Killers.* Taylor turned out to be an Irishman who had left a wife and daughter in New York and was reunited with his daughter in the last year of his life. It was she who had the plaque placed on his crypt, listing his birth name. His birth is variously given as April 26, 1877 and 1872, though his death certificate lists March 26, 1872. Cathedral Mausoleum, corridor C, crypt 594, Hollywood Forever Cemetery, Hollywood (Los Angeles), CA.

8973. Taylor, Zachary (Nov. 24, 1784–July 9, 1850) 12th President of the United States (1849–1850), Old Rough and Ready was a career military man who gained fame in the Mexican War. His term was cut short by death when, after a long and hot July 4th celebration at the base of the incomplete Washington monument, he returned to the White House to swill iced milk and cherries. He died five days later from what was deemed a form of cholera morbus. An 1884 account of his burials had him buried first at Washington, then at the Taylor estate in Louisville, then to Cave Hill Cemetery in Louisville where it was marked by a slab, and then to the State Cemetery at Frankfort. Actually, Taylor was interred in a vault in Congressional Cemetery, Washington, D.C., taken from there to the family cemetery on the Taylor land at Louisville in October 1850 and placed in a stone vault set in a hillside, a few yards from the grave of his mother and father, Lt. Colonel **Richard Taylor** (April 3, 1744–Jan. 19, 1829) and **Sarah Dabney Strother Taylor** (Dec. 14, 1760–Dec. 13, 1822). There it remained with the coffin of his wife **Margaret Smith Taylor** (Sept. 21, 1788–Aug. 18, 1852) until 1926, when they were removed from the old vault into a new mausoleum erected just in front of it and facing the front of the cemetery. In 1883 a monument to Taylor listing his military victories and topped by a statue of him above a towering shaft was dedicated at the front of the small graveyard. In 1928 the surrounding land remaining from the family estate became a national cemetery. The original family home, Springfield, a short distance away, remains in the hands of Taylor relatives, who also maintained the title to the burial ground. The original tomb is still in the hillside with the marble tablet over the door, inscribed *Z. Taylor* with his dates of birth and death. The monument and tomb at Louisville remain Zachary Taylor's only shrine; he is the only U.S. president without a home or museum open to the public. Zachary Taylor National Cemetery, 4701 Brownsboro Road, Louisville, Kentucky. Based on biographer Clara Rising's theory that Taylor was assassinated by arsenic poisoning, the family and U.S. Dept. of Veterans' Affairs allowed the Jefferson County coroner to exhume the body at Louisville on Monday, June 17, 1991. It was taken downtown, examined by forensics experts and returned to the cemetery later that afternoon. On

Wednesday, June 26, toxicology experts announced that their findings from hair and nail samples were consistent with death from gastroenteritis, as had been listed at and since the death, concluding that he was not poisoned by arsenic. The president's daughter, **Sarah Knox Taylor Davis** (March 6, 1814–Sept. 15, 1835) married soldier (and future Confederate president) Jefferson Davis against her father's wishes. She contracted malaria and died at 21. Marble box type marker, Locust Grove plantation cemetery, Bains Road, north of St. Francisville, LA. *See also* **Richard "Dick" Taylor.**

8974. Taza (Tahzay) (d. Sept. 26, 1876) Son of Cochise, chief of the Chiricahua Apaches, was brought to Washington in 1876 by an agent with no money, who forced the Indians to dance and exhibited them along the way. After their arrival, Tahzay was fatally stricken with pneumonia. A stone erected by the American Indian Society was placed September 26, 1971. On the back is his sculpted face. Range 2, site 125, Congressional Cemetery, Washington, D.C.

8975. Tchaikovsky, Peter Ilyich (May 7, 1840–Nov. 6, 1893) Russian composer whose works often reflected his long battle with melancholia: *None But the Lonely Heart, Romeo and Juliet* (1869), *Piano Concerto No. 1* (1874–75), *Swan Lake* (1875–76), *The Nutcracker* and the *1812 Overture* (1880). His death at 53 was apparently due to drinking unboiled water from a tap during the cholera season in St. Petersburg. Contrary to the health laws regarding cholera, he lay in state and was touched and kissed by many filing past the bier. Speculation has abounded that he actually took arsenic, either by his own wish or under pressure from government officials accusing him of sexual misconduct, with the contaminated water being used to attempt to hide the poison. No proof was ever established of any of this. After services at Kazan Cathedral, his wish was to be buried in the tiny village of Frovlovskoe, but he was instead placed beneath a monument with his bust and sculpted angels in Tikhvin Cemetery, St. Petersburg.

8976. Tead, Phil (Phillips or Phillip Tead, Sept. 29, 1893–June 19, 1974) Actor from Somerville, Massachusetts, a near double for Walter Brennan — whose origins and life span were near to his as well — appeared in many films, usually in small or unbilled parts. Among his more prominent roles was as Wilson, one of a group of reporters in *The Front Page* (1931). Ashes scattered at sea.

8977. Teagarden, Jack (Aug. 29, 1905–Jan. 15, 1964) Texas born trombone player, vocalist and band leader at his peak in the 1930's and 40's played with several bands made many records, including *Ain't Misbehavin* (1935) and his trombone solo *Mighty Like a Rose*. Epitaph reads *Where there is hatred let me sow love*. Hillside sec., lot 3821, space 4, Forest Lawn Hollywood Hills, Los Angeles.

8978. Teal, Ray (Jan. 12, 1902–April 2, 1976) Familiar mustached character actor in many small memorable roles (*The Best Years of Our Lives, Judgment at Nuremburg*) played the sheriff on TV's *Bonanza* 1959–1972. His plaque lists his year of birth as 1908. Sec. H, lot 595, Holy Cross Cemetery, Culver City, CA.

8979. Tearle, Conway (Frederick Levy, May 17, 1878–Oct. 1, 1938) New York born actor on stage from 1892 in England, and the in U.S. from 1905, films from 1914. Among his last was *Romeo and Juliet* (1936) as the Prince of Verona. Half brother of Sir Geoffrey Tearle. Chapel of the Pines Crematory, Los Angeles. Ashes returned to his widow in Van Nuys, CA.

8980. Teasdale, Sara (Aug. 8, 1884–Jan. 29, 1933) Reclusive St. Louis poet noted for her eccentricity and sensitive themes. She considered herself an invalid, and during a period of depression took all of her sleeping pills prior to taking a bath in her New York home. Though divorced since 1929, her stone is inscribed *Sara Teasdale Filsinger,* as she wished. Block 166, lot 2693, Bellefontaine Cemetery, St. Louis, MO.

8981. Teasdale, Verree (March 15, 1904–Feb. 17, 1987) Actress from Spokane, married to actor Adolphe Menjou. Films include *Payment Deferred* (1932) and as Hyppolita, Queen of the Amazons, in *A Midsummer Night's Dream* (1935). Buried beside Menjou. Sec. 8/Garden of Legends, lot 11, Hollywood Forever Cemetery, Hollywood (Los Angeles), CA.

8982. Tebaldi, Renata (Feb. 1, 1922–Dec. 19, 2004) Italian operatic soprano from Pesaro, praised for her performances particularly singing Puccini or Verdi, at her peak in the 1950's, a mainstay at La Scala in Rome, she also made 270 appearances at the New York Metropolitan Opera 1955–1973. Throughout her career, a rivalry and feud with Maria Callas (*q.v.*) was alleged, fueled largely by the press. She died at her home in San Marion in north central Italy at 82. Langhirano Cemetery, Parma, (Emilia Romagna), Italy.

8983. Tebbetts, Birdie (Nov. 10, 1912–March 24, 1999) Four time All Star catcher 1936–52 with the Tigers, Red Sox and Indians, a member of the 1940 world champion Detroit Tigers, and managed 1953–65, with the Reds, Braves and Indians, then scouted from 1968–1994. St. Bernard Catholic Church Cemetery, Holmes Beach, FL.

8984. Tebeau, "Patsy" (Oliver Wendell Tebeau, Dec. 5, 1864–May 15, 1918) Brawling St. Louis born first baseman and manager with the Cleveland Spiders in the 1890's known for his fighting and bad temper, silenced by an 1898 league resolution, played and managed the Cardinals 1899–1900 before quitting, believing he was being edged out by his third baseman, John J. McGraw. He ran a saloon in St. Louis until his suicide by gunshot there at 53. Buried at Calvary Cemetery there, according to the St Louis Globe Democrat; he was instead sent to Cleveland and interred June 26. Mangan-TeBeau flat stone is the only marker on the lot. Sec 10, lot 134 (a few yards from Ed Delehanty), Calvary Cemetery, Cleveland, OH.

8985. Tecumseh (March 1768–Oct. 5, 1813) Shawnee leader in the Northwest Territory during the earliest days of white settlement there. With his brother, The Prophet, he had battled forces under William Henry Harrison at Tippecanoe, near what is now Lafayette, Indiana, in 1811. The British were turned back by Oliver Perry at the Battle of Lake Erie in 1813 and Harrison pursued the English and the Indians, under British commander H.A. Proctor, to the Thames River, where he was killed, allegedly by future Vice President Richard Mentor Johnson, and buried somewhere in the area by his braves, the exact site unknown. Both Harrison and Perry searched for the body to no avail. In September 1941, bones were disinterred, reassembled and reburied in a cairn on Walpole Island Indian Reservation, Ontario.

8986. Tedrow, Irene (Aug. 3, 1907–March 10, 1995) Actress in films and TV, played Mrs. Elkins on TV's *Dennis the Menace* 1961–63. Below her name and dates her plaque reads *The play's the thing.* Sec. D, ground niche (Kent), Westwood Memorial Park, west Los Angeles.

8987. Teilhard de Chardin, Pierre (May 1, 1881–April 10, 1955) French paleontologist made several missions to China between 1923 and 1945, known for his discovery of the fossilized skull of Peking Man. Author of *Le Phenome Humain* (1938–1940) and other texts on the subject. In later years he worked in New York City, where he died from a heart attack. Buried in the Jesuit Novitiate cemetery of St. Andrews (later the Culinary Institute of America), Rte. 9 between Hyde Park and Poughkeepsie, NY.

8988. Tell, Alma (March 27, 1898–Dec. 29, 1937) Silent screen and stage actress, sister of Olive Tell. Married name Blystone. Block (memorial) H, sec. 9170, lot 4, Valhalla Memorial Park, North Hollywood, CA.

8989. Tell, Olive (Sept. 27, 1894–June 8, 1951) Stage and silent screen actress, sister of Alma Tell, died in Bellevue Hospital in Manhattan at 55 from a fractured skull suffered in a fall at the Dryden Hotel where she lived. Walter B. Cooke mortuary to Garden State Crematory. Ashes to her husband Henry M. Hobart.

8990. Tellegen, Lou (Isador Louis von Dammeler, Nov. 26, 1881–Oct. 29, 1934) Dutch stage star appeared opposite Sarah Bernhardt both on tour and in three films. He settled in Hollywood by 1916, starring in silent films as sophisticated leading men. Married for several years to opera and screen star Geraldine Farrar. Reduced to bit parts and ill with cancer, he committed suicide by stabbing himself with, or falling on, a pair of scissors. His ashes were scattered at sea, as he wished, on November 5, 1934.

8991. Telvi, Abraham (Sept. 12, 1934–July 25, 1956) Thug allegedly hired by mobster Johnny Dio to throw acid in journalist Victor Riesel's face, blinding him for life. Telvi was killed within the year to assure his silence. Old Montefiore Cemetery, Queens, N.Y.C.

8992. Templeton, Alec (July 4, 1910–March 28, 1963) Welsh born blind pianist made several recordings in the 1940's and 50's and was a regular on radio. Sec. L 4, Putnam Cemetery, Greenwich, CT.

8993. Templeton, Fay (Dec. 25, 1865–Oct 3, 1939) Musical stage star of the turn of the century, best known in George M. Cohan's *Forty Five Minutes From Broadway* (1905). She died in San Francisco at 73. Under her married name Patterson, she shares a plaque with Wendy Barrie. Actors Fund of America plot, Kensico Cemetery, Valhalla, NY.

8994. Ten Boom, Corrie (April 15, 1892–April 15, 1983) Youngest of three sisters in Amsterdam was the first licensed female watchmaker in Holland (1923) and organized a girls club that became the Triangle Club in the 1930's. From 1940 her family was active in the Dutch underground. Arrested in 1944, they were sent to Ravensbruck but were liberated at war's end, though her sister Betsie died. After the war she went to Germany and elsewhere to preach. Her 1971 book *the Hiding Place* brought her fame and was filmed in 1975. In 1977 she moved to the United States, and died eight years later on her 91st birthday. Her rose headstone reads *Jesus is victor.* Lawn A, lot 501, grave A, Fairhaven Memorial Park, Santa Ana, CA.

8995. Tennyson, Alfred, Lord (Aug. 6, 1809–Oct. 6, 1892) English poet laureate, author of *The Charge of the Light Brigade* (1855) and *Crossing the Bar,* among the best known and most often recited poems in English history. He died at his home Aldworth, near Haslemere, Hampshire. Buried next to Robert Browning, holding a copy of *Cymbeline,* which he had clasped at the time of his death. Poets' Corner, Westminster Abbey, London.

8996. Mother Teresa (Agnes Gonxha Bojaxhu, Aug. 27, 1910–Sept. 5, 1997) Macedonian born Albanian builder's daughter became a novitiate in 1928 with the Loretto Order which ran mission schools in India, becoming a nun in 1937. In 1947 she left the order for the slums of Calcutta, setting up schools and known to her students as "Mother." She founded the order of Missionaries of Charity in 1950, and continued for the rest of her life reaching out, comforting, bringing medicine, feeding and educating the poorest of the poor. She was awarded the Nobel Peace Prize in 1979 and the U.S. Medal of Freedom in 1985. She had at least two heart attacks and various other health problems when she died from a sudden heart attack at 87 in Calcutta, her eventual elevation to sainthood a near certainty. The plaque later set on her tomb quotes appropriately from John 15;12: *Love one another as I have loved you.* After a state funeral there September 13, an honor usually reserved for heads of state, she was buried at the Missionaries of Charity in Calcutta.

8997. Terhune, Max (Feb. 12, 1891–June 5, 1973) B western actor from Franklin, Indiana, in The Three Mesquiteers and Range Buster series. His stone bears the nickname *Alibi.* Sec. C, lot 44 E ½, Valleyview Cemetery, Clarkdale, AZ.

8998. Terranova, Ciro (1889–Feb. 20, 1938) New York gangster was a capo in the Joe Masseria family dubbed The Artichoke King for his control of artichoke imports into the city. After Masseria's killing in 1931, Terranova's power was decreased by the new confederation run by Lucky Luciano, Meyer Lansky, and others. Brother-in-law of Black Handers Lupo the Wolf— buried later in his lot — and the Morello brothers. He died of natural causes at 49. Sec. 35, (3rd) Calvary Cemetery, Woodside, Queens, N.Y.C.

8999. Terrell, Tammi (Thomasina Montgomery, April 29, 1945–March 16, 1970) Rhythm and blues, soul and pop singer from Philadelphia teamed on several recordings with Marvin Gaye (*Ain't No Mountain High Enough, If I Could Build My Whole World Around You, Ain't Nothin Like the Real Thing, You're All I Need to Get By*) for Motown 1967–68. She collapsed on stage while performing with Gaye in Virginia in 1967, and for three years fought the brain tumor that took her life at 24 in Graduate Hospital, Philadelphia. Section A2-21-29-1, along the front and behind the office, Mt. Lawn Cemetery, Sharon Hill (southwest of Philadelphia), PA.

9000. Terry, Alice (Alice Taafe, July 24, 1899–Dec. 22, 1987) Silent screen actress from Vincennes, Indiana, in films from 1916 with Triangle, best known in the work of her husband, director Rex Ingram (*The Four Horsemen of the Apocalypse* 1921, *The Arab* 1924, *The Magician* 1926). After sound ended their careers, they moved to the French Riviera, later returning to Hollywood. Though his ashes were interred at Forest Lawn, Glendale, she was not. Block (memorial) D, sec. 3347, lot 5, Valhalla Memorial Park, North Hollywood, CA.

9001. Terry, Bill (William Harold Terry, Oct. 30, 1898–Jan. 9, 1989) Top flight first baseman and hitter with the New York Giants from 1923. Beginning in 1927 he batted .320 or more nine years in a row, succeeding John J. McGraw as manager and winning three pennants during his reign 1932–1941. Hall of Fame 1954. Garden Cloister (exterior) mausoleum F, unit 3, Evergreen Cemetery, Jacksonville, FL.

9002. Terry, Bill H. Jr. (Feb. 23, 1949–July 3, 1969) Black American serviceman killed in Vietnam was refused burial in an Alabama cemetery because of his race. The family, supported by the NAACP, successfully sued and won, allowing his interment there in January 1970. It was the first suit of its kind. Block 45, lot N ½ 218, Elmwood Cemetery, Birmingham. AL.

9003. Terry, Don (Donald Prescott Loker, Aug. 8, 1902–Oct. 6, 1988) 1924 Olympic boxer from Natick, Massachusetts, entered films in 1928, best known as *Don Winslow of the Navy*. Decorated for bravery in World War II while serving with amphibious forces. Mausoleum, Cypress 3, plot 58, space (crypt) C, Green Hills Memorial Park, Ranch Palos Verdes (San Pedro area), CA.

9004. Terry, Ellen (Feb. 27, 1848–July 21, 1928) Distinguished British stage actress associated with Sir Henry Irving also made several silent films. Her ashes rest in a silver casket within a black marble case on the south wall of The Actors Church (St. Paul's, Covent Garden), London.

9005. Terry, Ethel Grey (Oct. 2, 1882 or 1891–Jan. 6, 1931) Silent screen actress from Oakland, California, appeared in films 1914–1928, including *The Sign of the Cross* (1914, as Berenice), *Intolerance* (1916), opposite Lon Chaney in *The Penalty* (1920, as Rose), *Peg o' My Heart* (1922), *Wild Bill Hickok* (1923, as Calamity Jane). She died from breast cancer in Hollywood, listed as 39, the wife of Carl Gerard. Urn Interred (death certificate in the Herrick Library file) with her mother, actress Lillian Lawrence (*q.v.*). Her inscription reads *Ethel Grey Terry Gerard Jan. 6, 1931* (*ashes*). Building A, crypt 308N, Hollywood Forever Cemetery, Hollywood (Los Angeles), CA.

9006. Terry, Phillip (Frederick Henry Kormann, March 7, 1909–Feb. 23, 1993) San Francisco born actor married to Joan Crawford 1942–45. Films include *The Parson of Panamint* (1941), the minor classic *The Monster and the Girl* (1941, reincarnated as a gorilla) and as Ray Milland's brother in *The Lost Weekend* (1945). Ill with a series of strokes from 1978, he died from pneumonia fifteen years later at 83. Ashes scattered at sea off Santa Barbara, CA.

9007. Terry, Tex (Edward Earl Terry, Aug. 22, 1902–May 18, 1985) B cowboy actor. Monument with cowboy hat and crossed six shooters, and military marker. Coxville Cemetery, Coxville (north of Terre Haute), IN.

9008. Tessier, Robert (June 2, 1934–Oct. 11, 1990) Burly actor with shaved head from Lowell, Massachusetts, of Algonquin Indian ancestry, in films from the late 1960's (*The Born Losers, The Longest Yard, The Deep*) also did motorcycle stunts, and by the 1980's appeared in various commercials. A decorated veteran of the Korean War, he died from cancer at 56. St. Joseph's Cemetery, Chelmsford Center, MA.

9009. Tesla, Nikola (July 9, 1856–Jan. 7, 1943) Croatian scientist and inventor patented, among other things, a system for the electrical transmission of power, a regulation system for alternating current motors, and a method for operating arc lamps. His work is considered the foundation for the development of radio, and later television. He died in the Hotel New Yorker, was cremated through Frank E. Campbell mortuary, and the ashes interred in a gold sphere at the Tesla Museum, Belgrade, Serbia.

9010. Tevis, Lloyd (March 20, 1824–July 24, 1899) San Francisco tycoon competed with and bought Wells Fargo in the 1870's, serving as president of the company until the 1890's. He also owned the famed San Francisco streetcar system. His monument features an ornately carved bronze angel, inset in a long monument with benches and angels in bas-relief, kneeling on either side of the central bronze. Sec. F, lot 11, Cypress Lawn Cemetery, Colma, CA.

9011. Tex, Joe (Joseph Arlington, Jr., Aug. 8, 1933–Aug. 13, 1982) Rhythm and blues soul singer won a talent contest at the Apollo in 1954, later had hits with *You've Got to Hold What You've Got* (1964), *Skinny Legs and All* (1967), *I Gotcha* (1972) before retiring. He died from a heart attack at 49. Gray granite monument, in the circle. Dennis Bryant Cemetery, county road 415 east of Navasota, TX.

9012. Texarkana Phantom (murders) The scene of one of America's better known unsolved serial killer crime sprees was Texarkana, straddling the Arkansas-Texas border, in the spring of 1946. Beginning on the moonlit night of February 22, when Mary Jeanne Lary and Jimmy Hollis, 24, were attacked while parking in a lovers' lane off Richmond Road, the town became increasingly paralyzed with fear of the hooded killer and sexual predator. While the first two escaped alive due to the lights of an oncoming car, the second couple did not. **Richard Griffin**, 29 and recently a Navy SeaBee, and **Polly Ann Moore** were found in his 1941 Oldsmobile on the rainy morning of March 24 in a grove off Robinson Road in Bowie County, Texas, shot through the head with a .32. Both were natives of Atlanta, Cass County, Texas. She was returned there through Hanner mortuary in Atlanta and buried at Bryans Mills Cemetery, Bryans Mills, Texas. He was returned through Texarkana (Texas) mortuary, with services at the United Methodist Church in Atlanta. Union Chapel Cemetery, Douglassville, Cass County, Texas. In the early morning hours of April 14, following their attendance at a dance at the VFW Hall where **Betty Jo Booker** played saxophone, **Paul Martin**'s car was found at the entrance to Spring Lake Park; his body was found a mile and a half away and Booker's in a patch of woods two miles away, near Fernwood. She had been molested and both were killed by revolver shots. Martin (born May 8, 1929) was buried in sec. B, lot 150, space 3, Hillcrest Memorial Park, Texarkana, Texas. Booker (born June 5, 1930) was buried in the "Woodlawn section of State Line Cemetery," now Woodlawn Cemetery, 3000 County Ave., Texarkana, Arkansas. The final victim was **Virgil Starks** (born April 3, 1909), shot twice in the back of the head May 3, 1946 through the living room window of his house off 67 southeast of the city in Miller County, Arkansas. His wife Katy, though shot twice in the face, survived and escaped. Starks was buried in sec. D, lot 460, space 1, Hillcrest Memorial Park, Texarkana, Texas. Though in the midst of the case, local authorities were overshadowed by the entrance of the famed "Lone Wolf" Texas Ranger **Manuel Gonzaullas** (July 4, 1901–Feb. 13, 1977), the killer, known over the decades only as The Phantom, was never definitely caught. The case was the basis for the 1977 film *The Town That Dreaded Sundown.* The only real suspect, based on the testimony of his wife and later confirmed by those he was imprisoned with, was **Youell Swinney** (March 9, 1917–Sept. 15, 1994) who was sentenced to life for

auto theft and assorted crimes, but was paroled in 1974. He died at 77 in a Dallas nursing home in September 1994. Gonzaullas died in Dallas at 75. His ashes were returned to the residence.

9013. Thackery, William Makepeace (July 18, 1811–Dec. 24, 1863) English author of *The Luck of Barry Lyndon* (1844) and *Vanity Fair* (1847–48), among others, having recently patched up a feud with Charles Dickens, retired to his room in his home at Palace Green, Kensington, two days before Christmas, complaining of feeling unwell. He was found dead in his bed the next morning with his hands gripping the rail above his head, a cerebral effusion listed as the cause of death. Kensal Green Cemetery, London.

9014. Thalberg, Irving (Irving Grant Thalberg, May 30, 1899–Sept. 14, 1936) Brooklyn born boy wonder producer at Universal moved to the new Metro-Goldwyn-Mayer in 1924 and served as head of production until his death twelve years later, making many of the studio's showcase films under his own guidance and supervision, often at odds with studio chief Louis B. Mayer. With a long list of titles to his credit, Thalberg was more involved in the making and quality of his pictures than most producers. Married to actress Norma Shearer from 1927, he starred her in several plum A films, from *The Divorcee* (1930) and *A Free Soul* (1931) to *The Barretts of Wimpole Street* (1934) and *Romeo and Juliet* (1936), his last major project. Unlike many producers, Thalberg also had the respect of the entire industry, and his death was keenly felt. Born with a heart defect, he was working on *The Good Earth* when he died from pneumonia at 37. Services at B'nai B'rith Temple in Los Angeles were topped off by Wallace Beery dropping flowers on the crowd from his small plane overhead. The Irving Thalberg Award for excellence by an individual producer in the art of film, given at the annual Oscar ceremonies, was established in his honor. Sarcophagus below Shearer's crypt, marble family room next to that of Jean Harlow, far end on the right, Sanctuary of Benediction, Memorial Terrace, Great Mausoleum, Forest Lawn, Glendale, CA.

9015. Thanhouser, Edwin (Nov. 11, 1865–March 21, 1956) Pioneer film executive, head of the Thanhouser Film Co. c. 1910–1920. Bench and plaque. Sec. 161, lot 12019, grave 1, Kensico Cemetery, Valhalla, NY.

9016. Thaw, Harry Kendall (Feb. 12, 1871–Feb. 22, 1947) Pittsburgh bon vivant, socialite and playboy shot and killed architect Stanford White on the night of June 25, 1906, during a dinner party on the rooftop of Madison Square Garden in Manhattan, incensed over White's past relationship with Thaw's wife, showgirl Evelyn Nesbit. Judged insane, he was imprisoned in a relatively luxurious cell for several years and released in 1915, dying decades later in Miami. His 3' upright marker bears the Biblical epitaph *And now abideth faith, hope and charity, these three, but the* *greatest of these is charity.* Sec. 16, circular family lot (119), Allegheny Cemetery, Pittsburgh, PA.

9017. Thaw, John (Jan. 3, 1942 — Feb. 21, 2002) West Gorton, Manchester, born English actor best known as British television's popular *Inspector Morse* from 1985–2000. He died at 60 from cancer of the esophagus at his home in Wiltshire, survived by his wife, actress Sheila Hancock. He was cremated in a private funeral attended by his family at Westerleigh, Gloucestershire. Ashes buried or spread in a garden of his home at Luckington, Wiltshire.

9018. Thaxter, Phyllis (Phyllis Thaxter Schuyler, Feb. 13, 1892–July 31, 1966) Actress from Portland, Maine. Not to be confused with the stage, screen and TV actress of the same name (born November 1921), also from Portland. Evergreen Cemetery, Portland, ME.

9019. Thayer, Ernest Lawrence (Aug. 14, 1863–Aug. 21, 1940) Lawrence, Massachusetts, born writer, poet and journalist published *Casey at the Bat* in the *San Francisco Daily Examiner* June 3, 1888, written in Worcester, Massachusetts, and published under the alias Phinn. It was almost immediately adopted by DeWolf Hopper for his reciting repertoire. As late as 2004, the towns of Holliston, Massachusetts, where the author lived, and Stockton, California, whose team Thayer covered for the Hearst papers, both claim to have been home to the Mudville Nine and The Mighty Casey. Thayer died in Santa Barbara, California. Ashes scattered.

9020. Thayer, Lorna (Aug. 16, 1919–June 4, 2005) Boston born actress in films over forty years (*The Lusty Men, The Beast With A Million Eyes, Nothing in Common, Frankie and Johnny*), best known as the unrelenting waitress encountering an adamant Jack Nicholson in *Five Easy Pieces* (1970). Formerly married to actor George Neise, she died at the Motion Picture Retirement Home in Woodland Hills, California, at 85. Pierce Bros. Valhalla Memorial Park, North Hollywood, CA.

9021. Theby, Rosemary (Rose Masing, April 8, 1885–June 10, 1973) St. Louis born actress with Vitagraph from 1910 specialized in vamps prior to Theda Bara, continuing in silents and smaller roles in sound films to 1940. She remarried in 1938 to Truitt Hughes and retired to Kansas City. She died in Los Angeles at 88. Ashes buried without record (unidentifiable space), Westwood Memorial Park, Los Angeles.

9022. Thesiger, Ernest (Jan. 15, 1879–Jan. 14, 1961) London born stage actor with sharp, skeletal features appeared in several English and American film roles of a devious or evil nature, in James Whale's *The Old Dark House* (1932) and *Bride of Frankenstein* (1935, as Dr. Pretorious), *The Ghoul* (1933), *The Man Who Could Work Miracles* (1937), *They Drive By Night* (1938), *Caesar and Cleopatra* (1945, as Theodotus), *Scrooge/A Christmas Carol* (1951, as the undertaker). His favorite role was on the stage as Polonius in *Hamlet,* including a tour of Moscow with the play in 1956.

C.B.E. 1960, the year prior to his death a day before his 82nd birthday. Buried in the lot of his parents, marked by a long slab of stone with a cross; his name and dates are on the side. His father **Alfred Thesiger** (1838–1880), Lord Justice of Appeal, died from blood poisoning at 42. Brompton Cemetery, Old Brompton Road, London.

9023. Thigpen, Lynne (Cherlynne T. Thigpen, Dec. 22, 1948–March 13, 2003) Actress from Joliet, Illinois, on the New York stage from *Godspell* (1973) won a Tony for *An American Daughter* (1997), appeared in strong, sometimes aggressive and abrasive roles in films (*The Warriors* 1979, *Tootsie* 1982, *Lean on Me* 1989, *The Paper* 1992, *Just Cause* 1995, *Shaft* 2000) and was familiar on television both in her Emmy winning role as The Chief on the PBS children's program *Where in the World is Carmen Sandiego?* from 1991 and as Ella Mae Farmer on CBS's *The District*, the role in which she was still appearing at the time of her unexpected death at the home she shared with Larry Aronson in Marina Del Ray at 54, attributed to acute cardiac dysfunction resulting in a brain hemorrhage. Never married. Interred beside her parents. Level E, crypt 33, mausoleum (east side), Elmhurst Cemetery, Joliet, IL.

9024. Thimig, Helene (June 5, 1889–Nov. 6, 1974) Austrian actress married to Max Reinhardt, appeared in over twenty films: *Strangers in the Night* (1944), *Isle of the Dead* (as Madame Kyra), *Hotel Berlin* (1945), *The Locket* (1946, as Mrs. Monks), *Cloak and Dagger, Cry Wolf.* Triangular plaque reads *Helene Thimig-Reinhardt.* Left archway (Arkaden Links), nummer 152, Friedhof Feuerhalle Simmering, Vienna.

9025. Thomas, Arlene Tichy Mosel (Aug. 27, 1921–May 15, 1996) Author of children's books including *The Funny Little Woman* (1973 Caldecott Medal). Sec. 5, Lakeview Cemetery, Cleveland, OH.

9026. Thomas, Brandon (Walter Brandon Thomas, Dec. 24, 1850–June 19, 1914) English actor and playwright, author of *Charley's Aunt.* Family monument of polished black granite. Brompton Cemetery, Old Brompton Road, London.

9027. Thomas, Danny (Amos Muzyad Jahoob, Jan. 6, 1912–Feb. 6, 1991) Actor-singer-producer raised in Toledo, Ohio, the son of Catholic immigrants from Lebanon, the background used for his character Danny Williams in his TV series *Make Room For Daddy* 1953–1971, cumulatively. As producer he developed *The Andy Griffith Show* and several others. Father of actress Marlo Thomas. He was founder and chief promoter and fund raiser for St. Jude's Children's Cancer Research Hospital in Memphis, opened in 1962. At his death from a heart attack at 79, services were held at the Church of the Good Shepherd in Beverly Hills. Interred in the chapel at St. Jude's Children's Hospital, Memphis, TN.

9028. Thomas, Dave (July 2, 1932–Jan. 9, 2002) Atlantic City born restaurateur dropped out of high school in Fort Wayne in 1948 to work at Hobby

House Restaurant, moved to Columbus, Ohio, in 1962 to take over four Kentucky Fried Chicken stores, sold eight of them back to KFC for a fortune in 1968 and opened his first Wendy's there in November 1969, named after his then eight year old daughter Melinda, nicknamed Wendy. Thomas made his first TV commercial in 1977, and over 24 years endeared himself to viewers with his sense of humor. A tireless advocate of adoption, he raised millions for various programs to aid agencies and adopted children like himself prior to his death from liver cancer at 69 in Fort Lauderdale, Florida. Chapel B, crypt 1-B, Union Cemetery, Olentangy River Road, Columbus, OH.

9029. Thomas, Dylan (Oct. 27, 1914–Nov. 9, 1953) Welsh poet, author of *Do Not Go Gentle Into That Good Night*, was known for his increasingly abysmal behavior when drinking, which was almost constant by the time of his death at 39. In 1950–53 he lived off and on in New York. Suffering from delirium tremens at the last, a doctor was called to his room at the Chelsea Hotel and injected him with a half grain of morphine sulfate. He sank into a coma and was admitted to St. Vincent's Hospital, where he died. The cause was listed as bronchopneumonia with fluid on the brain and a diseased liver. The morose poet had had his picture taken standing in a hole in the same cemetery where he was buried November 24. Marked by a white cross; his wife **Caitlin Macnamara** is beside him, unmarked. St. Martin's Churchyard, Laugharne, Dyfed, on the south coast of Wales.

9030. Thomas, Erwin Ross (Nov. 3, 1850–Sept. 13, 1936) Auto manufacturer produced the Thomas Flyer with which George Schuster won a 1907 race from New York to Paris, going westward. Sec. 26, lot 40, Forest Lawn Cemetery, Buffalo, NY.

9031. Thomas, George Henry (July 31, 1816–March 28, 1870) Union general in the Civil War known as the Rock of Chickamauga for his staunch defense there. He also commanded at Atlanta, Franklin and Nashville. Virginia born, he died in San Francisco. White marble monument topped by an American Eagle and surrounded by an iron railing. Sec. I-1, Oakwood Cemetery, Troy, NY.

9032. Thomas, Jameson (March 24, 1888–Jan. 10, 1939) Actor in films of the 1920's and 30's (*Lives of a Bengal Lancer, The Last Outpost, The Man Who Cried Wolf*) died from tuberculosis at 50. Sec. 1, lot 1024 (urn garden), Hollywood Forever Cemetery, Hollywood (Los Angeles), CA.

9033. Thomas, John Charles (Sept. 6, 1887–Dec. 13, 1960) Baritone with the New York Metropolitan Opera and in concerts; among his many recordings was *The Green Eyed Dragon* (1933). He died in Apple Valley, California. Cremated at Mountain View Cemetery, San Bernardino, the ashes were sent, according to crematory records, through the O'Donnell mortuary in Victorville for burial with his family in Easton Cemetery, Easton, Maryland. Only Spring Hill Cemetery is at Easton, and they have no record of him.

9034. Thomas, Lowell (April 6, 1892–Aug. 29, 1981) Newscaster and world traveler from Woodington, near Greenville, Ohio, penned his adventures with Lawrence of Arabia but was best known for his newsreel narrations as the voice of Fox Movietone News from 1935 and on CBS 1930–1976, with the sign-off "So long until tomorrow." He also made many documentaries and travelogues, covering nearly every major event from World War I. In World War II he covered both the Pacific and Europe, flying over Berlin in flames. After the war he penetrated into the forbidden city of Tibet and met with the Dalai Lama, bringing a message back to President Truman on parchment. He died from a heart attack at his home in Pawling, New York, at 89. The grave of he and his wife is marked by a boulder with a plaque on it and their two headstones. Christ Church of Quaker Hill Cemetery, Pawling, NY.

9035. Thomas, Martha Carey (Jan. 2, 1857–Dec. 2, 1935) Professor of English, Dean of Bryn Mawr College and president 1894–1922 sponsored the National College Equal Suffrage League and campaigned for increased women's education, persuading Johns Hopkins Medical School to admit the first females. Ashes marked by a tablet inscribed *M.C.T. 1857–1935*. The Cloisters, Bryn Mawr College, Bryn Mawr, PA.

9036. Thomas, Michelle (Sept. 23, 1969–Dec. 22, 1998) Boston born, New York raised actress played Justine on TV's *The Cosby Show* 1988–90 and Myra on *Family Matters* 1992–98. She died in New York from stomach cancer at 29. Only her nickname "Choo-Choo" and the dates appears on the stone with her family. Sec. 43, row 2, grave 10, Rosedale Cemetery, Orange, NJ.

9037. Thomas, Olive (Olive R. [birth certificate] or Olive Elaine Duffy, Oct. 20, 1894–Sept. 10, 1920) Showgirl from McKees Rocks, Pennsylvania, left home and a teenage marriage to become a star of the *Ziegfeld Follies* and *Midnight Frolics* of 1915 and 1916. She left Ziegfeld in 1917 for Hollywood and silent films, signing with Triangle and later with film producer Myron Selznick. From 1917 she was married to Jack Pickford, traveling with him to Paris in 1920 on what was called a second honeymoon. According to Pickford, she accidentally swallowed a bottle of bichloride of mercury in their room at the Hotel Ritz on September 5, mistaking it for sleeping tablets. She died in the American Hospital in Neuilly five days later. Speculation abounded that it was a suicide and that she was taking the mercury as a treatment for syphilis given her by Pickford, or that she took her life after failing to make a drug buy for Pickford, with and without whom she had been frequenting champagne and cocaine parties in Montmartre. Her name was found on the list of customers of a convicted drug dealer, a U.S. Army captain named Spalding, shortly after her death. There was also a foul play angle in that Pickford had just taken out an insurance policy on her, but how and why she swallowed the poison remains unknown. Her body was released and sent on September 18 to New York aboard the Mauritania. Services, organized by Ziegfeld but not attended by him — he had a reported fear of any atmosphere of death, were held at St. Thomas Episcopal Church at 5th Ave. and 53rd St. in Manhattan on September 28, a swelling crowd at the church causing several to faint. Though her name has long faded into oblivion, Thomas was the first major scandal in the film industry. Her body was placed in a receiving vault at Woodlawn until September 25, 1921, when it was interred in a small two tiered mausoleum with just the name *Pickford* over the door. The bottom tier remains empty; at his death in 1933, Jack Pickford, by then twice re-married and divorced, was interred with his mother at Forest Lawn, Glendale, California. Wintergreen sec. 108/121, lot 14851, two rows back from Park Ave., Woodlawn Cemetery, the Bronx, N.Y.C.

9038. Thomas, Rufus (March 26, 1917–Dec. 15, 2001) Mississippi Rhythm and Blues great known for *Walkin the Dog, Bear Cat* on Sun Records, *Cause I Love You* (with his daughter Carla) and (much later) *The Funky Chicken*. Film appearances include *Great Ball of Fire* (1989) and *Cookie's Fortune* (1999). He died in Memphis at 84. Service through R.S. Lewis mortuary at Mississippi Boulevard Christian Church. New Park Cemetery, Memphis, TN.

9039. Thomas, Seth (Aug. 19, 1785–Jan. 28, 1859) Connecticut clock maker whose name became synonymous with quality mantle clocks. He set up his business in 1812 in what became Thomastown. Hillside Cemetery, Thomaston, CT.

9040. Thomas, Terry- (Terry-Thomas Hoar Stevens, July 14, 1911–Jan. 8, 1990) London born comedian in both British and American films from 1949, usually as bombastic or exaggerated villains (*tom thumb, The Wonderful World of the Brothers Grimm, It's A Mad, Mad, Mad, Mad World*). Long ill with Parkinson's Disease, he died at Busbridge Hall Nursing Home. Service at St. John the Baptist Church, Busbridge, Surrey. Cremated at Guildford Crematorium, Surrey.

9041. Thomas, Vivia (d. Jan. 7, 1870) Disguised as a soldier, she followed her former lover, according to legend, to Fort Gibson, Oklahoma, where she killed him, infuriated by his rejection. The Indians were blamed for his death and her gender not discovered until her death. Officers Circle 2119, by flag pole, Fort Gibson National Cemetery, Fort Gibson, OK.

9042. Thomas, William "Buckwheat" (March 12, 1931–Oct. 10, 1980) One of the *Little Rascals* of Hal Roach's *Our Gang* two reelers of the 30's and 40's, among the most popular of the group. He lived a quiet life in L.A. until his death from natural causes at 49. A bizarre postscript occurred when the program *20/20* interviewed and gave credence to a man posing as Buckwheat in 1990, a decade after the death of the real one. His World War II veteran's marker presents the problem that he was by those dates 14 when the war

ended. Acacia Slope, lot 773, grave 1, Inglewood Park Cemetery, Inglewood, CA.

9043. Thomashefsky, Boris (Bores Thomashefsky, May 12, 1868–July 9, 1939) A force behind the Yiddish Theater and director of the Anglo-Jewish Theater unit of the Federal Theater. He produced works by Goldfadn including *Shmendrick and the Fanatic*, the name Shmendrick becoming synonymous with bumbler. Silent film appearances include *The Jewish Crown* (1915), *Here Ye, Israel* (1915) and *Period of the Jew* (1915). Married to Bessie-Baumfeld Kaufman 1891. Uncle of Paul Muni. Sec. 67, Yiddish Theatrical sec., Mt. Hebron Cemetery, Flushing, Queens, N.Y.C.

9044. Thompson, Ben (Nov. 11, 1842–March 11, 1884) English born gunfighter, the most fearless and dangerous in Texas, ended his career as the iron fisted marshal of Austin. He was ambushed in a San Antonio variety theatre as he sat watching a song and dance program, shot by three old enemies with a grudge, and widely mourned by the citizens of Austin. Sec. 1, lot 71, Oakwood Cemetery, Austin, TX.

9045. Thompson, Bobby (Robert C. Thompson, July 5, 1937–May 18, 2005) Musician from Spartanburg, South Carolina, pioneered the five string banjo and was a mainstay in Nashville's elite session musicians dubbed The A Team, played on pop as well as country recordings, and was a regular on television's *Hee Haw*, playing alongside both Roy Clark and Buck Owens. Ill with multiple sclerosis from the 1980's, when he retired. Willow Grove (or Rickman) Cemetery, Honeysuckle Lane or Wolf Hollow Road near Browning Road (264), northwest of Hartsville, TN.

9046. Thompson, Dorothy (July 9, 1894–Jan. 30, 1961) Syndicated columnist of the 1920's and 30's was the second wife (1928–1942) of Sinclair Lewis. She died in Lisbon, Portugal. Upright white marble stone with finely cut lettering. Town cemetery, Barnard, VT.

9047. Thompson, Edith (Edith Jessie Thompson, Dec. 25, 1893–Jan. 9, 1923) English housewife and milliner whose lover, Frederick Bywaters, murdered her husband. Found innocent of murder, she was hanged at Holloway for adultery at the same time Bywaters was hanged for murder at Pentonville. When Holloway prison was rebuilt, she was removed and reburied April 1, 1971, at Woking along with three other women, hanged in 1903 and 1954. The case was the subject of the book *Criminal Justice* and the 2001 film *Another Life*. Her black grave length slab, dedicated November 13, 1993, reads *Sleep on Beloved. Her death was a legal formality.* Plot 117, Brookwood Cemetery, Woking, Surrey.

9048. Thompson, Edward Lee (March 14, 1914–July 16, 1979) Left handed Negro Leagues pitcher with the Winona (Minnesota) Monarchs, the Kansas City Monarchs, and the Chicago American Giants. Sec. E, block 1, lot 16, space 1, East Linwood Cemetery, Galesburg, IL.

9049. Thompson, Hal (Harold Edward Thompson, Aug. 28, 1899–March 3, 1966) Canadian singer and actor on stage from the 1920's and in films of the 30's, best known as the romantic lead opposite Lillian Roth in *Animal Crackers* (1930). Never married. He died from severe burns and carbon monoxide suffered in a fire at 1229 North Mansfield Avenue, Los Angeles, at 66. Ashes buried Meditation sec., lot 751, space 2, Forest Lawn, Glendale, CA.

9050. Thompson, Hunter S. (Hunter Stockton Thompson, July 18, 1937–Feb. 20, 2005) Writer from Louisville, Kentucky, a correspondent from 1959 with various news services, pioneered "gonzo" journalism, involving the teller of the tale as an integral part of the story — exemplified in his coverage of the 1972 national political conventions. He served as *Rolling Stone's* national affairs editor 1970–84 and *High Times* global affairs correspondent 1977–82, among other positions, but was best known for his 1972 book *Fear and Loathing in Las Vegas.* An advocate of both drugs and firearms, the latter was freely used on his Colorado ranch, where he fatally shot himself at 67. As he wished, his ashes were blasted from a cannon across the ranch at Woody Creek, Pitkin County, CO.

9051. Thompson, J. Lee (John Lee Thompson, Aug. 1, 1914–Aug. 30, 2002) Diminutive English director from Bristol acclaimed for *The Guns of Navarone* (1961) and *Cape Fear* (1962), both with Gregory Peck, later directed two *Planet of the Apes* sequels, *Death Wish 4*, etc. He died at 88 in Sooke, Vancouver Island, British Columbia. Cremated September 5 at Royal Oak Burial Park Crematorium, Victoria, Vancouver Island. The ashes were picked up by McCall Bros. mortuary the next day.

9052. Thompson, James "Uncle Jimmy" (1848–Feb. 17, 1931) The first performer on the Grand Ole Opry. Monument with fiddle erected in 1975. Laguardo Cemetery, Laguardo, TN.

9053. Thompson, John Taliaferro (Dec. 31, 1860–June 21, 1940) U.S. Army Brigadier General in World War I invented the Thompson sub-machine gun c. 1921, too late for the war but intended for use by law enforcement. He became melancholy in later years over its ascendancy by 1925 as the "Chicago Typewriter." He did not live to see it used as originally intended in World War II. Sec. S, site 120, West Point Military Academy Post Cemetery, West Point, NY.

9054. Thompson, Kay (Nov. 9, c. 1903–July 2, 1998) St. Louis born author of the *Eloise* books about a precocious six year old living at the Plaza in New York, beginning in the 1950's. She was previously a classical pianist, an arranger and songwriter, sang with the Mills Bros., Fred Waring, and the Williams Bros., and acted in dramas of the early 30's (*Madame Satan, Thirteen Women, Of Human Bondage*) and later worked in stage and screen musicals (*Funny Face* 1957). She died at the home of her goddaughter on Manhattan's upper east side, or en route to Lenox Hill Hospital, her age listed as between 92 and 95. Cremated at Garden State Crematory July 12, her ashes were sent through the Nagle Funeral Home in Manhattan to her sister in California.

9055. Thompson, Marshall (James Marshall Thompson, Nov. 27, 1925–May 18, 1992) Actor in films (*Bad Bascomb, Mystery Street, My Six Convicts*), later a TV actor-director, did *Daktari* 1966–68 as Dr. Marsh Tracy. He later resided in Africa, returning in his last years to Birmingham, Michigan. He died at nearby Royal Oak of heart failure at 66. Cremated at Evergreen Cemetery in Detroit May 20, the ashes were picked up May 22 by Wm. R. Hamilton Co. of Birmingham and returned to the family in an urn, to be taken to California. The *L.A. Times* obituary listed burial at Westwood.

9056. Thompson, Mickey (Dec. 7, 1928–March 16, 1988) Race car driver and designer of several engines including Slingshot Draggers. He and his wife **Trudy Feller** were shot and killed in their Bradbury, California, home. Garden of Reflection, lot 1576, Rose Hills Memorial Park, Whittier, CA.

9057. Thompson, Sam (Samuel Luther Thompson, March 5, 1860–Nov. 7, 1922) Powerful hitter and outfielder from the handlebar mustache days with Detroit N.L. and Philadelphia N.L. 1885–1898. Lifetime average .336; he topped .400 twice. Hall of Fame 1974. Sec. 2, lot 22, Elmwood Cemetery, Detroit, MI.

9058. Thompson, Will Lamartine (Nov. 7, 1847–Sept. 20, 1909) Hymn writer penned the words and music to *Jesus is All the World To Me, Lead Me Gently Home, Father,* and *Softly and Tenderly Jesus is Calling,* several others. Sec. 2, lot 243, Riverview Cemetery, East Liverpool, OH.

9059. Thompson, William Hale "Big Bill" (May 14, 1868–March 19, 1944) Boston born mayor of Chicago during the Prohibition era served non-consecutive terms 1915–1923 and 1927–1931. Known for keeping the city "wide open," the 1926 victory was ensured by mobsters patrolling the polls. Spire near the lake. Sec. I, div. 2, lot 57, Oakwoods Cemetery, Chicago, IL.

9060. Thomson, Fred (Feb. 26, 1890–Dec. 25, 1928) A World War I chaplain recovering from wounds when he met and married screenwriter Frances Marion; by the 1920's he had left the ministry and become a top cowboy star at FBO with his horse, Silver King. He died from pneumonia following a gallstone operation at 38 on Christmas night 1928. Whispering Pines sec., lot 163, Forest Lawn, Glendale, CA.

9061. Thoreau, Henry David (July 12, 1817–May 6, 1862) Leading voice of transcendentalism lived his theory of civil disobedience and spent two years in the wilderness at Walden Pond near Concord, Massachusetts, communicating only with nature and chronicling his thoughts and experiences in *Walden,* published in 1854. He made the last entry in his journal in November 1861, terminally ill with tuberculosis. Attended by his mother and sister, he died in his

Concord home, reportedly with total peace and res-ignation. He was buried in the then new cemetery in the town hollow, his grave on a bluff later called Authors' Ridge, joined there in the ensuing years by Hawthorne, Emerson, and the Alcotts. There is a family monument, and a small weathered headstone marked *Henry*. Sleepy Hollow Cemetery, Concord, MA.

9062. Thorndike, Sybil (Oct. 24, 1882–June 9, 1976) British stage great acclaimed as Saint Joan in the 1920's. Dame Commander of the British Empire 1931. Sporadic film appearances (*Major Barbara* 1941, Hitchcock's *Stage Fright* 1950). Married to actor-producer Lewis Casson. At her death from a heart attack at 93, she was the only actress honored by burial in Westminster Abbey. Her plaque in The Actor's Church (St. Paul's, Covent Garden) bears her epitaph, from Shaw's *Saint Joan*: *My head was in the skies and the glory of God was upon me*. Her tomb is marked with a plaque ending in the lines *...And now the scripts lie fading on the shelf. We celebrate your finest role—yourself; The calls, the lights grow dim but not this part. The Christian spirit. The great generous heart*. South choir aisle, Westminster Abbey, London.

9063. Thornhill, Claude (Aug. 10, 1909–July 1, 1965) Bandleader known for his soft instrumental theme *Snowfall*. Unmarked grave next to his parents, Mr. and Mrs. Charles Thornhill. Sec. C, lot 78, grave 6, Roselawn Memorial Park, Terre Haute, IN.

9064. Thornton, Barbara (Jan. 6, 1950–Nov. 8, 1998) Singer and medieval musicologist from Summit, New Jersey, founded the Sequentia medieval music ensemble in Cologne, Germany, where she died from complications from a brain tumor at 48. Burial in Ascona, Switzerland.

9065. Thornton, Daniel (Jan 31 1911–Jan. 18, 1976) Governor of Colorado 1951–55 has a sculpted cowboy hat and boots at the base of his monument. Sec. 62, Gunnison Cemetery, Gunnison, CO.

9066. Thornton, Harry (1883–1918) Classical pianist entertained troops in France during World War I. After his death from influenza in 1918, his wife erected a stone piano at his grave, built to scale with upraised lid, later stolen. Along the side is inscribed (from Puccini) *Sweet thou art sleeping, cradled in my heart. Safe in God's keeping while I must weep apart.* East sec., Highgate Cemetery, London.

9067. Thornton, Matthew (Sept. 9, 1714–June 24 1803) One of three signers of the Declaration of Independence from New Hampshire presided over the provincial congress in 1775, later was in the state senate and an associate justice of the Supreme Court. Historical marker, monument and grave. Thornton's Ferry Cemetery, Merrimack, NH.

9068. Thornton, Melanie (May 13, 1967–Nov. 24, 2001) Pop vocalist fronted the group La Bouche, with hits including *My Lover* and *Sweet Dreams*. She died at 34 in a plane crash in Switzerland. Mount Pleasant Memorial Gardens, Mount Pleasant, SC.

9069. Thornton, Teri (Sept. 1, 1943–May 2, 2000) Detroit born jazz singer known for *Somewhere in the Night*, the theme of the television series *The Naked City*, her LP *Devil May Care* with an ensemble line-up of musicians, and her 1998 recording of *I'll Be Easy to Find*, which had won the Thelonius Monk International Jazz Competition award for best vocal in 1996. Detroit Memorial Park, Warren (north Detroit), MI.

9070. Thornton, Willie Mae "Big Mama" (Dec. 11, 1926–July 25, 1984) Black blues shouter did *Hound Dog* and *Ball and Chain*. The former was toned down by Elvis Presley, but Janis Joplin's version of the latter was closer to Thornton's sound. Sec M, lot 2486, grave B, near the fence, Inglewood Park Cemetery, Inglewood, CA.

9071. Thorpe, Jim (May 28, 1888–March 28, 1953) All American Indian athlete won several gold medals in the 1912 Olympics in Stockholm. He was later stripped of the medals for having played semi-pro baseball. In later years he played both major league baseball and pro football. The medals were returned to his descendants nearly forty years after his death. When he died in California in 1953 the Pennsylvania towns of Mauch Chunk and East Mauch Chunk decided to claim the body, merge together and become Jim Thorpe, in the hope of attracting a lucrative tourist trade, which never materialized. Thorpe is interred in a $15,000 pink granite sarcophagus on a small lot near the edge of town. On it are inscribed the words of the King of Sweden in 1912: *Sir, you are the greatest athlete in the world*. Jim Thorpe Tomb, Jim Thorpe, PA.

9072. Thorpe, Richard (Feb. 24, 1896–May 1, 1991) Director from Hutchinson, Kansas, helmed western and action films from 1923, including *Secret of the Chateau, Tarzan Escapes, Night Must Fall, Tarzan Finds A Son, Tarzan's Secret Treasure, Tarzan's New York adventure, The Sun Comes Up, The Black Hand, Ivanhoe, Jailhouse Rock*. Ashes scattered at sea.

9073. Thorson, Ralph "Papa" (Ralph Edgar Thorson, Jr., July 11, 1924–Nov. 17, 1991) Modern day bounty hunter dramatized in Steve McQueen's last film *The Hunter* (1980) appeared in a cameo as a bartender. He died in Los Angeles. Cremated through Pierce Brothers Valhalla mortuary in North Hollywood, the ashes were picked up by his daughter December 6, 1991 for transport to Arlington National Cemetery but never interred there.

9074. Thorson, Russell (Oct. 14, 1906–July 6, 1982) Weathered-faced actor from Minnesota on several radio programs turned to television with the 1950's, appearing in many westerns and crime programs, with regular roles on *The Detectives* (1959–61) as Lt. Detective Otto Lindstrom, and as Sheriff Evans on *The Virginian* (1962–3). Films include *I Want to Live, Good Day For A Hanging, My Blood Runs Cold, Two on A Guillotine, Hang 'Em High, Walking Tall*. He died in Van Nuys, California, at 75. Cremated at

Forest Lawn, Glendale. Ashes to residence in Studio City, CA.

9075. Thrash, Catherine *see* **Jim Jones** (Jonestown).

9076. Thumb, Tom (Charles S. Stratton, Jan. 4, 1838–July 15, 1883) Circus midget promoted by P.T. Barnum. His wedding to **Lavinia Warren**, also a midget, was a major event, photographed by Matthew Brady. Buried down and across the road from Barnum, a plaque on the base of Stratton's monument notes his fame as Tom Thumb and relates that a statue, erected before his death atop his parents' monument, was smashed by vandals in 1959. It was replaced, atop the newly added spire, by the Barnum Festival Society and Mountain Grove Cemetery Association in 1961 through public subscription. His wife died in 1918 and is buried there beneath a small marker. Sec. 8, Mountain Grove Cemetery, Bridgeport, CT.

9077. Chief Thunderbird (Richard Davis, Aug. 6, 1866–April 6, 1946) Native American actor in films of the 1930's and 40's. Eventide, lot 2221, space 2, Forest Lawn, Glendale, CA.

9078. Chief Thundercloud (Victor Daniels, April 12, 1899–Dec. 1, 1955) Stuntman and actor from the late 1920's, played the original Tonto in *The Lone Ranger* entries. He died after surgery for stomach cancer at 55. Corridor of Mercy, crypt 7355, Fuchsia Terrace, Great Mausoleum, Forest Lawn, Glendale, CA.

9079. Thurber, James (Dec 8, 1894–Nov. 2, 1961) Noted humorist from Columbus whose stories and drawings were high points of the *New Yorker* magazine for many years, including *The Secret Life of Walter Mitty*, filmed in 1947. He lived at Cornwall, Connecticut, in his last years becoming abusive to his wife and others. After a fight in their suite at the Algonquin in Manhattan, he collapsed and was taken to Doctors Hospital, where he was found to have suffered several strokes and hardening of the arteries. He died just over a month after being admitted, and though he had expressly wished not to be buried in Columbus, "in which my once bickering but now silent family occupies a good square mile of space," his ashes were interred there on the snowy morning of November 8, 1961, marked by a small headstone in the family's corner lot near the lake. Sec. 50, Greenlawn Cemetery, Columbus, OH.

9080. Thurman, Maxwell (Maxwell Reid Thurman, Feb. 18, 1931–Dec. 1, 1995) U.S. Army Vice Chief of Staff and commander of the United States Southern Command, dubbed Mad Max and the Maxatollah, led the 1989 invasion of Panama to oust Manuel Noriega, and was the primary author of the all volunteer army. Epitaph *Be all that you can be.* Sec. 30, grave 416-A-LH, Arlington National Cemetery, Arlington, VA.

9081. Thurmond, Strom (Dec. 5, 1902–June 26, 2003) The oldest and longest serving U.S. senator in history, the Edgefield, South Carolina, native had landed a glider behind enemy lines at Normandy on D-Day, and first gained national attention when he headed the Dixiecrats, a group of southern Democrats who broke with the party over civil rights and ran Thurmond as a third party candidate in 1948. He entered the senate as a write-in Democratic candidate from South Carolina in 1954, the only senator ever to do so — was reelected in 1956 and seven more times, retiring in 1999. He also held the record for a filibuster (to kill part of a civil rights bill), at 24 hours and 18 minutes, on August 28, 1957. In 1964 he switched to the Republican party, the first southern senator to do so. Neither that nor his second marriage, at 66 in 1968 to a 24 year old former intern, cost him his seat or his popularity. Increasingly he reached out to black constituents as well, and in 1981 became Senate president pro tem, subsequently chairing the Judiciary Committee and serving as senior member on both Armed Services and Foreign Affairs. He died at Edgefield, where he was born, six months after his 100th birthday, and was buried, after the state's largest funeral in memory, beside his daughter Nancy, who was hit by car at 22 in April 1993. After his death, an African-American daughter he had acknowledged and supported but kept secret came forward, casting his reputation as a reformed segregationist into further controversy. Willowbrook Cemetery, Edgefield, SC.

9082. Thurston, Howard (July 20, 1869–April 13, 1936) Magician toured the world beginning in 1903. He died in Miami at 66. The large and old mausoleum he is in is at the corner of Greenlawn Cemetery but is not a part of it or operated by it. Always locked, the key is kept by Columbus Art Memorials next door, though there is no admittance without proof of relationship. Greenlawn Abbey (1927), up a dirt drive on the right off Greenlawn at Greenlawn and Harmon, Columbus, OH.

9083. Tibbett, Lawrence (Nov. 16, 1896–July 15, 1960) California born operatic baritone acclaimed for *Porgy and Bess* and as Falstaff at the New York Metropolitan Opera from 1923. He also sang in several films and was nominated for an Oscar for *The Rogue's Song* (1931). Whispering Pines, lot 794, Forest Lawn, Glendale, CA.

9084. Tieri, Frank "Funzi" (Feb. 22, 1904–March 31, 1981) Underboss in the Genovese crime family. Couch crypt in Cloister Mausoleum, St. John's Cemetery, Middle Village, Queens, N.Y.C.

9085. Tierney, Gene (Nov 19, 1920–Nov. 6, 1991) Brooklyn born film star of the 1940's, best known as *Laura* (1944). Other films include *Leave Her to Heaven* (1946, Oscar nomination), *Dragonwyck* (1946), *The Ghost and Mrs. Muir* (1947), *The Left Hand of God* (1955), *Advise and Consent* (1962). She underwent treatment for depression for several years, retiring from films by 1965. Formerly married to Oleg Cassini, she was the widow of Texas oil magnate W. Howard Lee when she died in Houston at 70. Lee lot, corner sec. E-1, Glenwood Memorial Park, Houston, TX.

9086. Tierney, Lawrence (March 15, 1919–Feb. 26, 2002) New York born tough guy actor, brother of actor Scott Brady, known to be just as formidable a drinker and fighter off screen as on, starred in *Dillinger* (1945). Forty years later his career had a renewal with *Prizzi's Honor* (1985) and *Silver Bullet* (1986) before he gained a new following with Quentin Tarantino's *Reservoir Dogs* (1992) and other appearances through the 1990's. He died in a Los Angeles nursing home at 82 following several strokes and pneumonia. Cremated, his ashes were held at Abbott and Hast mortuary, Silver Lake, until returned to family at the end of March.

9087. Tiffany, Charles Lewis (Feb. 15, 1812–Feb. 18, 1902) Connecticut born founder of a fancy-goods shop in New York City in 1837; it soon gained an international reputation for its finery, including sterling silver. Branches were later opened in Paris, London and Geneva. The most prominent jeweler in America, he received the French Legion of Honor in 1878 and founded the New York Society of Fine Arts. Sec. 66 near Central and Valley, Greenwood Cemetery, Brooklyn, N.Y.C.

9088. Tiffany, Louis Comfort (Feb. 18, 1848–Jan. 17, 1933) Son of store founder and jeweler Charles Tiffany was renowned for his stained glass. He first opened a factory to design it in 1878. At the 1900 Paris Exhibition he was recognized as the master of the Art Nouveau style. Among his other works were the Favrille glass which became popular in the 1890–1915 period and again after the 1960's. Family lot, sec. 66 near Central and Valley, Greenwood Cemetery, Brooklyn, N.Y.C.

9089. Tilbury, Zeffie (Nov. 20, 1863–July 24, 1950) London born character actress in many films as earthy old women (*Werewolf of London, The Mystery of Edwin Drood, The Last Days of Pompeii*—all 1935, *Maid of Salem* 1937, *The Grapes of Wrath* 1940, as Grandma, *Tobacco Road* 1941), acted under her maiden name. Married name Woodthorpe. Memory Hall, sec. G, niche L-10, Pierce Brothers' Chapel of the Pines Crematory, Los Angeles.

9090. Tilden, Bill (William Tatem Tilden, Jr., Feb. 10, 1893–June 5, 1953) Tennis great Big Bill Tilden dominated the game in the 1920's, winning ten Grand Slam singles titles, seven U.S. and three at Wimbledon. In 1945 at 52 he teamed with Vincent Richards to win a doubles championship. He died in Hollywood, California, at 60. Sec. D, lot 65, Ivy Hill Cemetery, Germantown section of Philadelphia, PA.

9091. Tilden, Samuel J. (Samuel Jones Tilden, Feb. 9, 1814–Aug. 4, 1886) Reform governor of New York whose reputation was made for having put William Marcy "Boss" Tweed behind bars. He ran for president in 1876 on the Democratic ticket in what came to be regarded as the Stolen Election; not decided until February 1877, when Republican Ohio Governor Rutherford B. Hayes was given the White House by one electoral vote based upon a commission study-

ing the tally from four disputed southern states. Most studies show that Tilden actually won. He retired without dispute to his New York City law practice and died in his Yonkers mansion at 72. He never married, and his estate went to form, along with the Astor and Lenox Libraries, the New York Public Library in Manhattan. His body was returned upstate to his birthplace and interred alone in an ornate monument with a stone sarcophagus complete with gargoyles and a walkway around the top, a block away from the Presbyterian church where he attended services. Large circular lot, Evergreen Cemetery, New Lebanon, NY.

9092. Tilghman, William T. "Big Bill" (July 4, 1854–Nov 1, 1924) Marshall in Dodge City and the (Oklahoma) Indian Territory, former Buffalo hunter and scout. He was shot through the back in Cromwell, Oklahoma. Lot 18, block 16, Oakpark Cemetery, Chandler, OK.

9093. Till, Emmett Louis (July 25, 1941–Aug. 28, 1955) The unofficial catalyst for the exploding Civil Rights movement in the American south of the 1950's was a 14 year old Chicago black youth who, while visiting relatives in Mississippi, remarked "Bye, Baby" to a white woman. Her husband and his brother-in-law took Till from his relatives to the Tallahatchie River where they beat him, gouged out an eye, and shot him in the head before dumping his body, attached to a 75 lb. fan, into the river. Recovered, his condition required a quick burial, but his mother insisted he be returned to Chicago and the body shown in an open coffin. A picture of the body was published in *Jet* magazine, and the killers were acquitted, igniting unrest and fury in the Black community. His mother, **Mamie Till Mobley**, kept the case and his memory alive until her death at 81 on January 6, 2003. Both are at Burr Oak Cemetery, Alsip, IL.

9094. Tillman, Georgeanna (Feb. 6, 1944–Jan. 6, 1980) Original member of The Marvelettes from Inkster, Michigan, formed in 1960, had hits from 1961–66 beginning with *Please Mr. Postman*. She left the group in the late 1960's, after *Don't Mess With Bill*, their last hit. Married to Billy Gordon of The Contours, she died from lupus and complications at 35. Garden of Faith E, sec. 55 C, grave 3, Metropolitan Memorial Gardens, Willow Road, Belleville, MI.

9095. Tillstrom, Burr (Oct. 13, 1917–Dec. 6, 1985) Puppeteer created the Kuklapolitan Players in 1936, evolving into radio's *Kukla, Fran and Ollie*, with Fran Allison as host 1948–1957. He died in Palm Springs at 68. His stone has only his name on it. Sec. 16, lot 80, sub-lot 5, Rosehill Cemetery, Chicago, IL.

9096. Tilyou, George Cornelius (Feb. 3, 1862–Nov. 30, 1914) Builder of Brooklyn's Coney Island (originally Steeplechase Park) in the 1890's; he designed some of the rides as well. Monument surmounted by a statue. Sec. 62, plot 29049, Greenwood Cemetery, Brooklyn, N.Y.C.

9097. Tincher, Fay (April 17, 1884–Oct. 11, 1983)

Silent screen actress. Died at 99 in Long Island College Hospital, Brooklyn. Silver Mount Cemetery, Staten Island, N.Y.C.

9098. Tindley, Charles Albert (July 7, 1851–July 26, 1933) One of the founders of gospel music was the son of slaves and illiterate until self-taught to read and write at seventeen. A Methodist Episcopal minister, he wrote over forty hymns including *We'll Understand It Better By and By*. Unmarked. Celestine, lot 717, grave 2, Eden Cemetery, Upper Darby Township, Philadelphia, PA.

9099. Tinker, Joe (July 27, 1880–July 27, 1948) Chicago Cubs shortstop 1902–1913, the first ⅓ of the famed double play, Tinker-to-Evers-to-Chance, immortalized by the Franklin P. Adams poem that helped put all three into the Hall of Fame in 1946. He hit .421 in 1908. Later managed. Sec. L, lot 101, Greenwood Cemetery, Orlando, FL.

9100. Tinney, Frank (March 29, 1887–Nov. 27, 1940) Vaudeville comedian, star of the Follies of 1910 and the Music Box specialized in cornball blackface humor with no dialect. His career faded in 1924 when he was accused of beating up showgirl Imogene Wilson (Mary Nolan). A nervous breakdown and divorce from Edna Davenport preceded his retirement by 1926. He died at the Veterans Hospital at Northport, Long Island. Family stone to Mary Tinney only. Sec. 53, Holy Cross Cemetery, Yeadon, Philadelphia, PA.

9101. Tiny Tim (Herbert Khaury, April 12, 1932–Dec. 1, 1996) Entertainer with long frizzy hair and piercing falsetto built a concert career out of his 1968 rendition of *Tiptoe Through the Tulips*, his 1969 marriage on *The Tonight Show* drawing an audience of 40 million. Off stage, he was an ardent historian of American music and musical artists, particularly the Tin Pan Alley period c. 1890–1930. He was performing his theme in Minneapolis when he collapsed from a heart attack. Room 117, tier 2, crypt F, Lakewood Cemetery mausoleum, Minneapolis, MN.

9102. Tiomkin, Dimitri (May 10, 1899–Nov. 11, 1979) Russian born composer in Hollywood received twenty two Academy Award nominations, and won for *High Noon* (1952), *The High and the Mighty* (1954), *The Old Man and the Sea* (1958). He died in London. Columbarium of Memory, niche 19425, Memorial Terrace, Great Mausoleum, Forest Lawn, Glendale, CA.

9103. Tippit, J. D. (Sept. 18, 1924–Nov. 22, 1963) The second victim of Lee Harvey Oswald was Dallas police officer Tippit, who had stopped him on a side street and attempted to detain him when Oswald pulled a gun from his jacket and fired, killing him instantly. Sec. 62, lot 1, Laurel Land Memorial Park, Dallas, TX.

9104. Tipton, Billy (Dorothy Lucille Tipton, Dec. 29, 1914–Jan. 12, 1989) Jazz singer and musician, born female, became Billy at 19 in 1933 and maintained the ruse, not discovered until her death in Spokane, Washington, nearly 55 years later. There is no grave. Cremated in Spokane, the ashes were divided into two boxes for those close to him, according to the biography *Suits Me* by Diane Middlebrook.

9105. *Titanic* (dramatis personae) One of the most compelling and emotional stories in recorded history is the fate of the White Star liner *Titanic,* the largest and most luxurious steamer in the world when it was launched from Belfast in May 1911. On her maiden voyage from Southampton in April 1912, she carried 2,227 passengers with only twenty lifeboats and rafts, equipped for approximately fifty persons each. On Saturday night, April 14, at 11:40 p.m., the ship veered to avoid an iceberg in the North Atlantic at 41.46 N long., 50.14 W. lat. Its side was seared, allowing water to fill one bulkhead after another and dooming the ship to sink. It was one of several ironies that had the burg been struck head on, the ship would probably have stayed afloat. Evacuation procedures began, with four of the lifeboats destroyed in launching, leaving the survival capacity at about 928, yet only 711 were set afloat in the boats, 705 of them surviving. Many of the second and particularly third class/steerage passengers were kept below until too late to abandon ship. Despite radio signals and distress rockets fired into the air, the ship *Californian* did not respond. The *Titanic* sank at 2:20 a.m. on the 15th, carrying 1,522 persons to their deaths. The survivors were picked up by the liner *Carpathia* and taken to New York, while four vessels searched the 750 miles due east from Halifax to search for victims. App. 209 were recovered and brought to Halifax, where a morgue was set up at the Curling Rink. Of these, 150 were buried in Halifax, most of them (121) in Fairview Lawn Cemetery, where a large sign is marked *Titanic* and long rows in semi-circles feature stone after stone reading only *Died April 15, 1912* and an identifying number. These include a single unknown child long thought to be a member of the Paulson family, and Mrs. Paulson (#206), but the unknown child was identified by DNA in 2001 as Eino Panula, 13 months, from Finland. Several monuments to known victims there bear lines from the hymn *Nearer My God to Thee*, which, along with *Autumn*, a small group of musicians played on deck as the evacuations were taking place. Of the bodies recovered, some 119 were buried at sea due to limited embalming capacity, with the 121 in Fairview (Lawn), 19 more beneath a large walnut tree in Mt. Olivet Catholic Cemetery, and 10 in Baron Von Hirsch Jewish Cemetery (only 2 of these identified), all in Halifax. In all 328 bodies were recovered and 124 remained unidentified. Stories were told by the rescue parties of women afloat with their white skirts billowing in the wind, at least one of these clutching her dead dog. The tales have remained hauntingly effective in books, films, documentaries and through the Titanic Memorial Society. Of the notables and known figures who died, **John Jacob Astor IV** (*q.v.*) was returned to New York. Among the handful of the last survivors who became increasingly the chief first hand accounts of the sinking, **Ruth Becker Blanchard** (Oct. 28, 1899–July 6, 1990), the daughter of missionaries in India, was en route home to America with her mother, sister and brother. Though separated briefly, all were saved. She was in her later years interviewed frequently about her memories of the ship's sinking. Upon her death, her ashes were scattered in the Atlantic at the site where the *Titanic* went down. Her mother **Nellie E. Baumgartner Becker** (June 19, 1876–Feb. 15, 1961), then 35, and sister **Marion Louise Becker** (Dec. 28, 1907–Feb. 15, 1944) then 4, are in block 74, lot 12, Oakland Cemetery, Princeton, Illinois. Fourth Officer **Joseph G. Boxhall**'s ashes were scattered over the site of the sinking upon his death in 1967. **Harold Bride**, telegrapher, survived the sinking; his colleague **Jack Phillips** was lost afterward. Upon Bride's death, his ashes were scattered outside Glasgow Crematorium, north Glasgow, Scotland. The so-called "Unsinkable" **Molly Brown** (*q.v.*), survived in a lifeboat, buoying the spirits of others and lived another twenty years before her burial at Holy Rood Cemetery, Westbury, Long Island, New York. President Taft's aide, Major **Archibald Butt** (*q.v.*), was not recovered. A memorial fountain was dedicated in his memory by Taft near the White House, and a cenotaph to him placed in Arlington National Cemetery, Arlington, Virginia. After the success of the 1998 film *Titanic*, interest mounted in grave 227 at Fairview Lawn Cemetery, Halifax, marked *J. Dawson*; for a time, it was romanticized to be the basis for the male lead in the film named Jack Dawson. Investigation of White Star records showed however that it was an Irish born crew member, **Joseph Dawson**, last residing at Southampton. **Frederick Fleet** (1887–1965), the lookout who spotted the iceberg, was commemorated by a white marble stone at his grave with the *Titanic* on it, dedicated by the Titanic Historical Society of Indian Orchard, Massachusetts, at Hollybrook Cemetery, Shirley (near Southampton), England. **Archibald Gracie** (*q.v.*), who survived to relate the details of the sinking died within the year from the effects of the exposure. He lies across the walk from Herman Melville in Woodlawn Cemetery, the Bronx, N.Y.C. **Benjamin Guggenheim** (*q.v.*), son of the New York millionaire, also not recovered, declined his life jacket and, with his valet, asked to be remembered as having died like gentlemen. The family mausoleum is at Salem Fields Cemetery, Brooklyn, N.Y.C. **Edith Haisman** (Oct. 27, 1896–Jan. 20, 1997), fifteen years old when the ship went down, likewise lost her father, **Thomas William Solomon Brown**. In 1993, four years before her death at 100 in Southampton, England, she received a watch thought to be his, retrieved by salvage efforts. Her ashes were placed in St. Mary's Extra Church cemetery in Sholing, Southampton. **Eva Hart**, seven years old and on her way to a new life in Canada when she was put into a lifeboat, lost her father on the *Titanic*.

She was among the last eight survivors of the voyage, and the one with the clearest memory of the sinking, when she died at 91 in London February 14, 1996. She has a memorial plaque at Chadwell Heath, Bromford. Her ashes were scattered in nearby St. Chad's Church cemetery, Bromford, Essexshire, England. All of the band members playing on deck near the last were lost. Bandmaster **Wallace Henry Hartley**, 33, was recovered and buried at Colne, Lancashire, England, a sculpted violin on the base of his monument. **Albert Edward James Horswell** (March 26, 1879–April 7, 1962), able bodied seaman, in his bunk when the *Titanic* hit the iceberg, helped organize passengers into the boats before going into the water as the ship went down. He was rescued in Emergency Lifeboat 1. Sec. A, lot 362, space 3, Rosewood Memorial Park, Humble, TX. Violinist **John Law "Jack" Hume** has a stone (#193) at Fairview Lawn Cemetery in Halifax. The manager of the White Star Line, **J. Bruce Ismay** (*q.v.*), managed to survive and came under much criticism for the shortage of lifeboats and consequent loss of life. He lived to old age but was haunted the rest of his life by the experience, as reflected in the engraved sea vessels and inscriptions on his monument in Putney Vale Cemetery, London. Stewardess **Violet Jessop** (died May 5, 1971) wrote a memoir *Titanic Survivor*, published posthumously. She is buried in the local (not parish) cemetery at Hartest, Suffolk, England. **Charles Lightoller** (1874–Dec. 8, 1952) Second officer of the *Titanic*, the only senior officer to survive, was a principal witness and defender of the White Star line. He lived to rescue 130 men at Dunkirk with his unarmed yacht during World War II. Ashes commemorated by a white card and rosebush. Mortlake Crematorium, London. **Captain Stanley Lord** (dec. 1962) of *The Californian*, who failed to heed the *Titanic*'s distress rockets or to speed to her aid until it was too late, died in 1962, protesting his image as portrayed in *A Night to Remember*; he claimed a mystery ship was in between the *Californian* and the *Titanic*. Rake Lane Cemetery, New Brighton (the Wirral), Cheshire. **Marjorie Newell** (Feb. 12, 1889–June 11, 1992), later Marjorie Newell Robb, a founder of the New Jersey Symphony Orchestra, was rescued in lifeboat number 6, the last of *Titanic*'s first class passengers to die, at 103. Orient Path, lot 6191, Mount Auburn Cemetery, Cambridge, Massachusetts. Thirteen month old **Eino Panula** from Finland was for ninety years buried in the *Titanic* section at Fairview Lawn Cemetery in Halifax under a small obelisk inscribed *Erected to the memory of an unknown child whose remains were recovered after the disaster to the Titanic April 15, 1912*. He and his mother were reportedly offered a seat in a lifeboat but she refused to go without her other four children. All six drowned. When exhumed in 2001, scientists postulated that a copper medallion marked *Our Babe* and placed in the coffin by sailors may have helped preserve the bone fragments from oxidation so that the DNA tests could be made which proved the child's identity. Of the 150 still buried in Halifax's three cemeteries, 45 remain unidentified. Among the hundreds who survived, **Charles Hallis Romaine** a.k.a. **Harry Romine**, was one of three gamblers who made it into a lifeboat (#15). He died Jan. 18, 1922 and is buried in sec. 12, Maplewood Cemetery, Anderson, Indiana. **Captain (Sir) Arthur Rostron** (1869–Nov. 4, 1940), captain of the *Carpathia* and rescuer of hundreds of survivors, is buried in the small West End Cemetery at West End Road and High St. in the west end section of Southampton, England. **Captain Edward John Smith**, R.D., R.N.R., who went down with the ship, has a cenotaph at Etruria Methodist Church, Stoke-on-Trent, England. A statue of him was also erected at Litchfield. **Mr. and Mrs. Isador Straus** (*q.v.*) died together, she refusing to get in a lifeboat and leave him. A stone barge commemorates their fate in Woodlawn Cemetery, the Bronx. He was recovered; she was not. First class passenger **John B. "Jack" Thayer**, second vice president of the Pennsylvania Railroad, was lost, though his son John III and his wife survived. He is memorialized on the stone of his remarried wife, Church of the Redeemer Cemetery, Bala Cynwyd, Pennsylvania. A diarist in steerage from Norway, **August Wennestrom** a.k.a. **Anderson**, settled in Culver, Indiana, and is buried in Culver Cemetery there. In September 1985, the wreck was finally located on the ocean floor by Robert Ballard after years of searching, and the ship was explored and photographed. It was shown to have split in two as it went down. It's location also revealed the *Californian* had been closer than had been reported and could probably have reached the *Titanic* had she responded to the distress rockets.

9106. Tobey, Kenneth (Jesse Kenneth Tobey, March 23, 1917–Dec. 22, 2002) Actor from Oakland in many films from 1947–1993, particularly ubiquitous as officers of one brand or another in science fiction and military-action pictures (*Twelve O'Clock High, The Wings of Eagles, The Beast from 20,000 Fathoms* 1953, *It Came from Beneath the Sea* 1955) and television (co-starring in *The Whirlybirds* 1957–9), best known as Capt. Pat Hendry in Howard Hawks' *The Thing [from Another World]*, (1951). He later turned up in *Airplane!, The Howling, Gremlins,* many others, and remained active at film conventions until shortly before his death at 85 in Eisenhower Memorial Hospital, Rancho Mirage, California. Cremated by the Neptune Society of Riverside, his ashes went into an urn purchased by his daughter Tina and taken December 30 to her home, Palm Springs, CA.

9107. Tobias, George (July 14, 1901–Feb. 27, 1980) New York born character actor in amiable roles at Warner Brothers in the late 1930's and 40's, frequently supporting James Cagney or Errol Flynn, later played Mr. Cravits on TV's *Bewitched*. He died from cancer at 78. Service at Mt. Sinai Memorial Park, Los Angeles. Flat plaque, Brodsky plot, sec. B, path 21,

(Old) Mount Carmel Cemetery #1, Glendale, Queens, N.Y.C.

9108. Tobin, Dan (Oct. 19, 1910–Nov. 26, 1982) Slight character actor in films from the mid 40's (*The Big Clock*), much on TV. Sanctuary of Tranquility, Westwood Memorial Park, west Los Angeles.

9109. Tobin, Genevieve (Nov. 29, 1899–July 31, 1995) New York born actress 1923–41 (*One Hour With You* 1932, *The Petrified Forest* 1936) married to director William Keighley, lived for years in Paris. She died at 95, listed as 93, in Las Encinitas, California. Niche with her family and Keighley, Columbarium of Memory, niche 20184, Memorial Terrace, Great Mausoleum, Forest Lawn, Glendale, CA.

9110. Toch, Ernst (Dec. 7, 1887–Oct. 1, 1964) Composer in Hollywood scored films at Paramount in the 1930's and 40's (*Peter Ibbetson, The Cat and the Canary, The Ghost Breakers, Dr. Cyclops, The Unseen*). Sec. D, lot 167, Westwood Memorial Park, west Los Angeles.

9111. Tocqueville, Alexis de (July 19, 1805–April 16, 1859) French politician and writer renowned for *Democracy in America* (1835–1840) came to the U.S. in 1831 to study the Democratic system of government, which primarily elicited his praise, though he feared "the tyranny of the majority" over the taste and creativity he valued within his own aristocracy. Double sarcophagus outside the church dans le village du meme nom, A l'est de Cherbourg, Tocqueville, France.

9112. Todd, Ann (Jan. 24, 1909–May 6, 1993) British actress in films from talkies, including *The Ghost Train* (1931), *Things To Come* (1936) and particularly known for being abused by James Mason in *The Seventh Veil* (1946) and opposite Gregory Peck in *The Paradine Case* (1948). Divorced three times, including from Victor Malcolm and David Lean, she appeared in British films and television until her death in London from a stroke at 82. Handled through J.H. Kenyon, 49 Marloes Road, Kensington. Funeral and cremation May 14 at Mortlake Crematorium, Richmond, Surrey.

9113. Todd, Mabel (Aug. 13, 1907–June 2, 1977) Blonde actress in light roles in films 1937–1946 (*Hollywood Hotel, Gold Diggers in Paris, The Cowboy and the Lady, The Mystery of the White Room, The Talk of the Town*). Divorced (married name *Doss*), she died from cancer at 69 in Queen of Angels Hospital, Los Angeles, and was buried unembalmed by the County–USC Medical Center. Sec. E, tier 19, grave 95-M, Queen of Heaven Cemetery, Rowland Heights, CA.

9114. Todd, Michael (Avram Goldbogen, June 22, 1907 (stone says 1909)–March 22, 1958) Film producer-promoter (*Around the World in 80 Days* 1956) had been Elizabeth Taylor's (third) husband less than a year when he flew to accept a Showman of the Year Award from the Friars' Club, leaving her at home because of a cold, and died when the plane crashed in New Mexico. In late June 1977, shortly after Taylor had visited the grave, it was robbed, the bones found intact nearby in a sack and re-buried. Silverman and Weiss Cemetery, near gate 66, Waldheim Jewish Cemeteries, Forest Park (Chicago), IL.

9115. Todd, Thelma (July 29, 1906–c. Dec. 15, 1935) Ice cream blonde actress-comedienne from Lawrence, Massachusetts, in Hal Roach two reelers played spirited parts in numerous films of the 1920s and 30's, including *Seven Footprints to Satan* (silent, 1929), *The Maltese Falcon/Dangerous Female* (1931), *Monkey Business* and *Horse Feathers* with the Marx Brothers, two comedies with Wheeler and Woolsey, *Fra Diavolo* and *The Bohemian Girl*, her last film, with Laurel and Hardy. On Saturday night, December 14, 1935, English actor Stanley Lupino gave a party for her at the Trocadero in Hollywood. She shared separate quarters with director Roland West above the cafe on the Pacific Coast Highway bearing her name, and though he was notified she was coming home, she never arrived. Her body was found Monday morning in her garage on Posetano Road above the Palisades, dead apparently from carbon monoxide poisoning. A ruling of accidental death was reached, though several people claimed to see her the following day, Sunday, and her face was bruised and bleeding from a force possibly greater than that incurred from falling against the wheel or dashboard, indicating a struggle. Speculation has continued for seventy years that she may have been a mob hit, but no hard evidence was ever produced to substantiate the theory. Cremated at Forest Lawn, Glendale, the ashes were retained by her mother, Alice Todd, who kept the urn with her at all times until her death in December 1969, when it was buried with her. Rose granite family stone, sec. 19, lot 5548, hillside right of the Jennings Street entrance, Bellevue Cemetery, Lawrence, MA.

9116. Todman, Bill (July 31, 1916–July 29, 1979) Co-producer, with Mark Goodson, of several successful TV game shows from the 1950's through the 70's. Family monument and flush plaque. Jewish Community Center of White Plains sec., Mt. Hope Cemetery, Hastings-on-Hudson, NY.

9117. Tojo Hideki (Dec. 30, 1884–Dec. 23, 1948) World War II Japanese Prime Minister was considered by the Allies to be the third (with Hitler and Mussolini) major villain of the war, begun by the Japanese attack on Pearl Harbor. Arrested in the Tokyo suburb of Setagaya in September 1945, he shot himself just above the heart when he saw American officers coming, but recovered and was hanged at Sagamo Prison three years later. General MacArthur refused to return the remains to the widow. Tojo was cremated with six others hanged at the same time. By some accounts, Japanese workers secretly scooped up some of the ashes and on August 17, 1960, a new tomb containing them was unveiled at Hazu with the inscription *The Tomb of the Seven Martyrs*. The urn with most or all of Tojo's ashes, however, was placed about 1978 in the inner sanctum of the Yasukuni (Jinja)

Shrine (1871) at Kudanshita, atop Kudan Hill, Chiyoda Ward, Tokyo. Some of the ashes were also placed in Zoshigaya Cemetery, Tokyo.

9118. Toklas, Alice B. *see* **Gertrude Stein.**

9119. Toland, Gregg (May 29, 1904–Sept 28, 1948) Acclaimed Hollywood cinematographer lauded for his deep focus work in *Citizen Kane* (1941) won an Academy Award for *Wuthering Heights* (1939). He died from a heart attack at 44. Book shaped urn. Chapel of the Psalms, lower columbarium, column 2/H, tier 4, Hollywood Forever Cemetery, Hollywood (Los Angeles), CA.

9120. Toler, Sidney (April 28, 1888–Feb. 12, 1947) Actor and playwright from Warrensburg, Missouri, and raised in Wichita, Kansas, in films from 1919. He took over the role of *Charlie Chan* at Fox upon Warner Oland's death in 1938, moved with the series to Monogram and continued in the part until 1946, doing twenty two *Chan* films in all. He died at his Beverly Hills home from uremia related to prostate cancer at 58. Cremated through Pierce Brothers Chapel of the Pines Crematory, Los Angeles. Ashes sent to Flanagan mortuary in Wichita for burial with his family. The monument lists his birth year as 1874. Sec. 4, lot 145, Highland Cemetery, Wichita, KS.

9121. Tolkien, J.R.R. (John Ronald Reuel Tolkien, Jan. 3, 1892–Sept. 2, 1973) English scholar, linguist and author best known for his trilogy *The Lord of the Rings*, written between 1954–1968, in which he created the world of Middle Earth, a monumental work with an immensely wide following, described by many as having allegorical meanings applicable to good and evil. It followed *The Hobbit* (1937). Neither work was intended for children, according to the author-illustrator, a professor at Oxford 1925–1959. He died at 81 in Bournemouth. Service at Oxford Catholic Church with burial in the Catholic section of Wolvercote Cemetery, Oxford.

9122. Tolson, Clyde (Clyde Anderson Tolson, May 22, 1900–April 14, 1975) Associate in the FBI with J. Edgar Hoover as well as his long time personal associate and (by some accounts) companion. Congressional Cemetery, Washington, D.C.

9123. Tolstoy, Leo (Sept. 9 [Aug. 28 O.S.], 1828–Nov. 20 [Nov. 7 O.S.], 1910) Russian novelist and Count, author of *War and Peace* (1869) and *Anna Karenina* (1877), left his home at age 82 because of constant trouble with the Countess Sonya over his unorthodox views on religion and unconventional trends of thought. He left his estate at Yasnaya Polyana, a hundred miles south of Moscow, but was ill and had to disembark at Astapovo, where he died from pneumonia. He had refused the rites of the Catholic Church and was returned for burial as he had requested on the edge of the Zakaz Forest on his estate. A grave length dark stone covers the grave, situated down a densely wooded path at Yasnaya Polyana.

9124. Tomack, Sid (Sept. 8, 1907–Nov. 12, 1962)

Brooklyn born actor in films from 1944 and several television shows, including Gillis in *The Life of Riley* from 1949. He died from a heart ailment in Palm Springs at 55. Sec. A-9, lot 14, Desert Memorial Park, Cathedral City (Palm Springs), CA.

9125. Tombaugh, Clyde William (Feb. 4, 1906–Jan. 17, 1997) Discoverer of the ninth planet Pluto, while a twenty four year old without a degree, at Lowell Observatory in Arizona, in 1930. He later confirmed Mercury's thirty three day rotation period on its axis and the vortex nature of Jupiter's large red spot. Cremated through Grahams mortuary, Las Cruces, New Mexico, part of his ashes were scattered over a mountain at Mesilla Park near Las Cruces. Part were sent with an unmanned spacecraft *New Horizons* launched from Cape Canaveral in January 2006 to photograph Pluto and send data back. Pluto was demoted to a dwarf planet in 2006.

9126. Tombes, Andrew (June 29, 1885–March 17, 1976) Bald actor from Ashtabula, Ohio, in films for twenty years from 1934, often playing shady characters with a genial veneer: *Charlie Chan at the Olympics* (chief of homicide), *Meet John Doe* (as Spencer), *Hellzapoppin, It Ain't Hay, The Mad Ghoul* (undertaker), *Phantom Lady* (bartender), *Murder in the Blue Room* (Dr. Carroll). He died in New York at 90. Sec. 178, 188–439, Kensico Cemetery, Valhalla, NY.

9127. Tomlin, Pinky (Truman Tomlin, Sept. 9, 1907–Dec. 12, 1987) Bandleader of the early 1930's on radio and recordings known for the song *The Object of My Affection*. Murmuring Trees, lot 1458, Forest Lawn Hollywood Hills, Los Angeles.

9128. Tomlinson, David (May 7 1917–June 24, 2000) English actor from Henley-on-Thames on stage and in films 1933–1980, usually in amiable roles. Best known as Mr. Banks in Disney's *Mary Poppins* (1964), *The Love Bug* (1969), *Bedknobs and Broomsticks* (1971) etc. Buried, as he wished, in the garden of his home at Buckinghamshire.

9129. Tompkins, Daniel D. (June 21, 1774–June 11, 1825) Governor of New York 1807–1817 and Vice President of the U.S. under James Monroe 1817–1825. By the time of his vice presidency, he was deeply in debt to both New York and the federal government for loans he had taken out while governor, which *he* felt were owed to him. Increasingly bitter, he spent his last years at his home on Staten Island, beset by depression and alcoholism, despite holding the second highest office in the land. He died at 51. A bust of him on a pedestal is in the (locked) western half of the churchyard, but he is buried beneath a grave length slab near the vault of Peter Stuyvesant in the eastern section of the churchyard of St. Mark's Church in the Bowery, E. 10th St. and 2nd Ave on the lower east side of Manhattan, N.Y.C.

9130. Tone, Franchot (Stanislas Pascal Franchot Tone, Feb. 27, 1905–Sept. 18, 1968) Actor at MGM in the 1930's played earnest to cocky leads or second leads in *Bombshell, Gabriel Over the White House,* *Mutiny on the Bounty, Lives of a Bengal Lancer, Three Comrades.* Later films offered more cold blooded characters (*Phantom Lady, The Man on the Eiffel Tower*). Known for his marriage to Joan Crawford as well as his off screen drinking and brawls — which were still occurring as late as 1961 when he filmed the *Twilight Zone* episode *The Silence*— he was active in theatre in New York until shortly before his death there from lung cancer. Though he and Crawford had been divorced since 1939, they remained friends to the extent that she stated she saw to it that his wish was carried out in having his ashes spread over Mustoka Lake in Canada. His biographer however, was told that his ashes were never scattered but were stored at Ferncliff Cemetery, Hartsdale, New York (though they find no record), for a time after his cremation there, and shipped eventually to his son's home outside Boston, in a mahogany box kept on a shelf in the library, surrounded by Shakespeare.

9131. Tong, Sammee (April 21, 1901–Oct. 27, 1964) Chinese-American actor from San Francisco in sporadic films from the 1930's, best known as Peter the houseboy in the TV series *Bachelor Father* 1957–1962. He committed suicide with pills in Palms, California, at 63. Freedom Courtyard, lot 2339, Forest Lawn, Glendale, CA.

9132. Tonge, Philip (April 26, 1897–Jan. 28, 1959) Mustached actor on stage and in films (*Miracle on 34th St.* 1947, *O. Henry's Full House* 1952, the drunken father in William Wellman's *Track of the Cat,* 1954). Sec. 8/Garden of Legends, lot 15, Hollywood Forever Cemetery, Hollywood (Los Angeles), CA.

9133. Toole, John Kennedy (Dec. 17, 1937–March 26, 1969) Author from New Orleans wrote the novel *A Confederacy of Dunces* in 1961 while a soldier stationed in Puerto Rico. Toole tried throughout the decade to get the book published without success. He committed suicide by carbon monoxide poisoning with a hose in a garage in Biloxi, Mississippi, in 1969. For another decade his mother pushed the novel, until it came to the attention of Walker Percy in 1976. Published in 1980, it won a posthumous Pulitzer Prize in fiction in 1981. Ducoing family tomb, 19 Latainer between Magnolia and Hawthorne, Greenwood Cemetery, New Orleans, LA.

9134. Toomey, Regis (Aug. 13, 1898–Oct. 12, 1991) Pittsburgh actor of Irish descent in over 150 films from 1929, in occasional leads but usually as uniformed cops or detectives, with and without the Irish brogue, ranging from *Murder By the Clock* (1931) to *The Big Sleep* (1946). He lived in later years at the Motion Picture Country Home in Woodland Hills, California. He died at 93. Service at St. Mel's Catholic Church in Los Angeles. Ashes scattered at sea off Marina Del Rey, CA.

9135. Toones, Fred "Snowflake" (Fred Toomes, Jan. 5, 1906–Feb. 13, 1962) Black actor in nearly two hundred films 1932–47, usually in walk-ons in shorts (*Woman Haters*), many serials and westerns at Republic from 1936. He died from a cerebral hemorrhage at 56. Burial February 13 through J.S. Williams mortuary. Lincoln Memorial Park, Compton, CA. No record.

9136. Torén, Märta (May 21, 1926–Feb. 19, 1957) Swedish actress from Stockholm in films of the late 1940's appeared in a few films in Hollywood (*Casbah* 1948, *One Way Street* 1950, *Sirocco* 1951, *Puccini, Assignment in Paris* 1952, *The Man Who Watched the Trains Go By* 1953) returned to Europe to act in Italy but died from leukemia at 30 in Stockholm. Grave 13A, 237, Norra Begravningsplatsen, Stockholm, Sweden.

9137. Torme, Mel (Melvin Howard Torme, Sept. 13, 1925–June 6, 1999) Chicago born vocalist, pianist and composer dubbed The Velvet Fog, known for his smooth interpretations of numbers ranging from ballads to jazz scat singing, where he was considered on a par with Ella Fitzgerald. A juvenile radio actor writing songs by age 13, his best known composition was *The Christmas Song*, recorded by Nat King Cole in 1946. He made numerous albums and performed up until 1996, when he suffered a stroke from which he never recovered. He died at UCLA Medical Center three years later at 73. His service at Pierce Bros. Westwood was public; speakers included Donald O'Connor, Charlton Heston and Cliff Robertson. Grave length red plaque in the area in front of Truman Capote and Heather O'Rourke in the northwest corner of the cemetery. Sec. B, lot 114, Westwood Memorial Park, west Los Angeles.

9138. Torquemada, Tomas de (1420–Sept. 16, 1498) Grand Inquisitor of Spain (1483–1498), though probably of Jewish descent, influenced and oversaw the expelling of the Jews from Spain in 1492 under Ferdinand and Isabella, and was associated with much of the torture and cruelty synonymous with the Spanish Inquisition. Tomb in the sacristy of the Monasterio de Santo, Avila, Spain.

9139. Torre, Janice (Aug. 17, 1914–Feb. 21, 1985) Songwriter for several Hollywood films including *Night Song, Song of My Heart, Tom Thumb*. Married name Perky. Sec. 41, lot A, Metairie Cemetery, New Orleans, LA.

9140. Torrence, David (Jan. 17, 1865–Dec. 26, 1951) Scottish born actor, brother of Ernest Torrence. Tall, stern and menacing in many parts like his brother, primarily in films of the 1920's and 30's (*The Tower of Lies, Disraeli, Five Star Final, Smilin Through, The Mask of Fu Manchu, Berkeley Square*). Alcove of the Pines, niche 7, Golden West Mausoleum, Inglewood Park Cemetery, Inglewood, CA.

9141. Torrence, Ernest (June 16, 1878–May 15, 1933) Better known of two Scottish actor brothers made numerous silent films, first seen in *Tol'able David* in 1921, often cast as the villain, he also turned up in *The Hunchback of Notre Dame* (1923), *Peter Pan* (1924, as Captain Hook), and several talkies, last in *I Cover the Waterfront* (1933). He died in New York at 54. Columbarium of Prayer, niche 10677, Memorial Terrace, Great Mausoleum, Forest Lawn, Glendale, CA.

9142. Torres, Raquel (Paula Marie Osterman, Nov. 11, 1908–Aug. 10, 1987) Mexican born actress in *White Shadows in the South Seas* (1928), *The Sea Bat* (1930), *Duck Soup* (1933). Her crypt plaque (Ames) lists her birth year as 1916. Hall of Celestial Peace, crypt 13283, Holly Terrace, Great Mausoleum, Forest Lawn, Glendale, CA.

9143. Torriente, Carlos (Cristobal Torriente, Nov. 16, 1893–April 11, 1938) Cuban outfielder from Cienfuegos with the Negro Leagues seventeen seasons, with a lifetime batting average .339; he hit .432 in 1920. Hall of Fame 2006. He died in New York City at 42. Interred at Calvary Cemetery in Queens, he was removed to Cuba. Cenotaph at Cemeterio de Cristobal Colon, Havana, Cuba.

9144. Torrio, Johnny (Feb. 1882–April 16, 1957) Naples born gang leader was operating brothels in connection with New York's Five Points Gang by 1904. He went to Chicago and by 1918–19 had called Al Capone to work for him there. Despite engineering the murder of Big Jim Colosimo in May 1920, Torrio's rule in Chicago was talk before guns, but after his hand was forced into allowing the killing of Dean O'Banion in 1924, Chicago exploded in machine gun warfare. Torrio, carrying packages into his house after shopping with his wife, was ambushed, shot and left for dead in 1925 by north-siders avenging O'Banion's death. He recovered and turned over his Chicago business operations to Capone, served a jail term and went to Italy. He later returned to New York in the liquor business and real estate, serving a term in Leavenworth 1939–1941 for tax evasion, then returned to New York and a quiet life. When he died from a heart attack at 75 in a barber's chair, the death went unreported in the papers for several days as being a well known person. He was buried in the same nonsectarian cemetery where another New York gangland figure, Albert Anastasia, was buried later the same year after he too died in a Manhattan barber's chair, though much less quietly. Family mausoleum, Hemlock Ave. just off Border Ave., sec. 130, Greenwood Cemetery, Brooklyn, N.Y.C.

9145. Toscanini, Arturo (March 25, 1867–Jan. 16, 1957) Italian conductor with the New York Metropolitan Opera 1926–1936 died at his home in the Riverdale section of the Bronx. Service at St. Patrick's Cathedral in Manhattan, after which the body was flown to Milan for a service at La Scala Opera House and a mass at Duomo Cathedral. At his burial a 400 voice choir sang the music of Verdi, upon whose work he had built his career and legend as a conductor of tremendous force and energy. In 1989 his son-in-law, Russian pianist Vladimir Horowitz, was interred in his mausoleum. Cimitero Monumentale, Milan.

9146. Tose, Leonard (March 6, 1915–April 15, 2003) Owner of the Philadelphia Eagles bought them for $16 million in 1969; known for his high stakes lifestyle, he eventually lost much of his fortune gambling. Tiferes Beth Israel Cemetery, Fairfield Road, Norristown, PA.

9147. Totheroh, Rollie (Roland Totheroh, Nov. 29, 1890–June 18, 1967) San Francisco born cinematographer for Charles Chaplin photographed all of his best known work from 1915 through *Monsieur Verdoux* (1947). One row up and over from Frank Lackteen. Mem. G, Valhalla Memorial Park, North Hollywood, CA.

9148. Touhy, Roger (Roger Towey, Sept. 18, 1898–Dec. 16, 1959) Bootlegger in Des Plaines, Illinois, in the 1920's produced a superior beer and posed a challenge to the Capone outfit in Chicago. Threatened by them, Touhy bluffed it out, standing up to Capone through a feud lasting several years. By 1934 he was imprisoned on kidnapping charges. Involved in a prison break in 1942, his sentence at Stateville was extended. Released in November 1959, he was gunned down on a Chicago street less than a month later. Unnamed in family plot. Sec. Q, lot 20, block 8, grave 5, Mt. Carmel Cemetery, Hillside, IL.

9149. Toulouse-Lautrec, Henri de (Nov. 24, 1864–Sept. 9, 1901) French artist who suffered from an abnormal growth pattern had a head and torso of normal size but the rest underdeveloped. His work depicted the wilder night life of Montmartre, of which he partook regularly. For the last two years of his life he suffered from syphilis as well as delirium tremens caused by alcoholism. After a stroke in early 1901, he lived with his mother at Malrome, Gironde. Shortly before his death, he told the attending priest that he was happier to see him then than he would be when he came soon with his "little bell." He was buried in St. Andre-du-Bois Cemetery but his mother had him moved to the village churchyard of Verdelais, two miles from Malrome, Gironde.

9150. Tourneur, Jacques (Nov. 12, 1904–Dec. 19, 1977) Paris born son of director Maurice Tourneur, in the U.S. from 1914–28 and from 1935, working extensively in America 1939–1963. A protégé of Val Lewton, he directed from 1942, several literate suspense and horror films during the film noir era, notably *Cat People* (1942), *I Walked With A Zombie, The Leopard Man* (1943), *Days of Glory, Experiment Perilous* (1944), *Out of the Past* (1947) and *Curse of the Demon* (*Night of the Demon*, 1958). His last work in the genre was *A Comedy of Terrors* (1963). He died at Bergerac, France, at 73. Cimetière Beylive, Bergerac, Dordogne Province, France.

9151. Tourneur, Maurice (Maurice Thomas, Feb 2 1873–Aug. 4, 1961) French film director in the U.S. from 1914, known for his stylishness, subtlety and maintenance of mood, with *Poor Little Rich Girl* (1917), *Treasure Island* and *The Last of the Mohicans, While Paris Sleeps* (1920), *The Brass Bottle* (1923). He returned to France after a dispute during *The Mysterious Island* (1929). He directed until 1949, when he

lost a leg in a car accident, and later translated American novels to French prior to his death in France at 83. Div. 71, Pere Lachaise Cemetery, Paris.

9152. Toussaint, Pierre (c. 1788–June 30, 1853) Former slave obtained his freedom and removed to New York City in the period after the American Revolution. Now being considered for sainthood, his remains were removed in 1990 from Old Saint Patrick's Church Cemetery on Mott St. in Manhattan to the crypts below the high altar of St. Patrick's Cathedral, Manhattan, N.Y.C.

9153. Towalski, (Li'l) Richard (Dec. 6, 1942–March 28, 2001) Li'l Richard and His Polka All Stars toured all over the world and recorded extensively. He had been on Chicago radio for twenty years, beginning at age twelve. Sec. 45, block 25, lot 10, grave 5, St. Adalbert Cemetery, Niles (Chicago area), IL.

9154. Tower, John (Sept. 29, 1925–April 5, 1991) Four term conservative Republican Senator from Texas chaired the Armed Services Committee until 1984 and headed the Iran-Contra investigation panel in 1987. His 1989 appointment as Secretary of Defense was blocked due to allegations of drinking and womanizing, the first senator to be rejected for a spot in a new administration. He and his daughter were among twenty three killed in the crash of their plane near Brunswick, Georgia. Southeast corner, Providence Monument Garden, (Sparkman) Hillcrest Memorial Park, Dallas, TX.

9155. Townes, Harry (Sept. 18, 1914–May 23, 2001) Actor from Huntsville, Alabama, on Broadway and in films made many TV appearances through the 1950's and 60's, including *Studio One, Alfred Hitchcock Presents, Gunsmoke, Bonanza, The Twilight Zone* (episodes *The Four of Us Are Dying* and *Shadow Play*), *Mannix, Star Trek, Quincy,* many others. An ordained Episcopal priest, he returned to Huntsville to live by the 1980's. His last film was in 1986. Buried at his birthplace. Block 13, lot 4, space 3, Maple Hill Cemetery, Huntsville, AL.

9156. Townsend, Ed (April 16, 1929–August 13, 2003) Singer-songwriter from Fayetteville, Tennessee, penned over two hundred numbers, but made his mark when he recorded his romantic ballad *For Your Love* in 1958. His controversial *Let's Get it On,* a hit for Marvin Gaye in 1973, was not about sex, he insisted, but about getting on with life. A resident of Sun City, California, he died from heart failure in a San Bernardino hospital at 74. Service at the Riverside Salvation Army chapel through Miller-Jones mortuary, Sun City. Ashes to wife and interred the next month. Niche in new columbarium. BA, row C, site 213, Riverside National Cemetery, Riverside, CA.

9157. Townsend, Peter (Nov. 22, 1914–June 19, 1995) British Group Captain, the one time intended of Princess Margaret. She renounced him for duty at her elder sister's urging. He made his home in "exile," where he was buried, at St. Leger-en-Yvelines, France.

9158. Townson, Ron (Jan. 29, 1933–Aug. 2,

2001) St. Louis born vocalist had a background in opera and spirituals and had worked with Nat Cole and Dorothy Dandridge prior to co-founding The 5th Dimension, originally called the Versatiles, and serving as its center point, with hits 1967–69 including *Up Up and Away, Stoned Soul Picnic, Sweet Blindness, Aquarius/Let the Sunshine In,* and *Wedding Bell Blues,* several written by Laura Nyro. The group dissolved in the early 1970's as the members pursued solo careers; Townson performed up to 1997. He died in Las Vegas at 68 from kidney disease. Memorial service at the Jehovah's Witness Centennial Kingdom Hall, North Cimarron Road. Cremated through Palm Mortuary, Las Vegas. Ashes buried or stored in an unmarked, undisclosed location at Palm Memorial Park, Las Vegas, NV.

9159. Toynbee, Arnold (April 14, 1889–Oct. 22, 1975) British historian and philosopher authored the 12 volume *A Study of History* (1934–1961). Village churchyard, Terrington, North Yorkshire.

9160. Trace, Al (Dec. 25, 1900–Aug. 31, 1993) Bandleader-writer of the 1930's and 40's (*Mairsy Doats, If I Knew You Were Coming Id've Baked a Cake*). Haven of Dedication, crypt 17-A, Sunland Memorial Park, Sun City, AZ.

9161. Tracy, Arthur (Abba Tracovutsky, June 25, 1899–Oct. 5, 1997) The Street Singer, on radio and records (*Marta*) from 1931. He died in NY. at 98. Sec. A-3, plot 496, grave 3, Beth Kehillah Cemetery, Cardiff, Egg Harbor Township, near Pleasantville, NJ.

9162. Tracy, Lee (William Lee Tracy, April 14, 1898–Oct. 18, 1968) Actor in films of the early 1930's as fast talking reporters or agents with rapid fire nasal delivery, in *Doctor X, Dinner at Eight, Bombshell, Turn Back the Clock,* etc. He was replaced on *Viva Villa* (1934) after a drunken incident involving his urinating off a balcony while on location in Mexico. A veteran of World War I, he served again in World War II and re-surfaced in films afterward. Oscar nomination as the dying U.S. President in *The Best Man* (1964). He died from liver cancer in St. John's Hospital, Santa Monica, California. Buried with his wife and parents. Center Lawn, half way up hill, Evergreen Cemetery, Shavertown (north of Wilkes-Barre), PA.

9163. Tracy, Spencer (April 5, 1900–June 10, 1967) Milwaukee born actor in films 1930–1967, regarded by many critics, peers and film historians as the most natural and arguably the best to grace the movies. He won back to back Oscars as best actor for *Captains Courageous* (1937) and *Boys Town* (1938) and was nominated posthumously for *Guess Who's Coming to Dinner* (1967), his ninth film with Katherine Hepburn and his last. By then, his heart was so weak no insurance company would cover him, so director Stanley Kramer took the gamble, with production wrapping just two weeks before Tracy died at 67 in his kitchen. A requiem mass was held June 12 at Immaculate Heart of Mary Catholic Church in Hollywood, conducted by Monsignor John O'Donnell, who had been the technical advisor on *Boys' Town.* Hepburn and a friend had helped carry the casket from the mortuary into the hearse before the service, then left after following a short way toward the church. The graves of Tracy and his wife Louise (d. 1983) are in the narrow grassy area on either side of the walk, the only inscription the name *Tracy* on the wall, with a tree and bench in the center of their corner garden enclosure. Garden of Everlasting Peace, right of the entrance off the Freedom Courtyard, Forest Lawn, Glendale, CA.

9164. Tracy, William (Dec. 1, 1917–June 18, 1967) Actor from Pittsburgh in films 1938–1959, often as cocky characters, beginning as savvy juveniles in *Angels With Dirty Faces* (Jerry as a boy), Pepi Katona in *The Shop Around the Corner* (1940) and as Terry Lee in *Terry and the Pirates* (1940); in the 1952 television series he played Hot Shot Charlie. Tracy died in Hollywood at 49. Memorial C, sec. 2124, lot 5, Valhalla Memorial Park, North Hollywood, CA.

9165. Trafficante, Santo, Sr. (May 28, 1886–Aug. 10, 1954) Head of the Mafia in Tampa from 1950 until his death from stomach cancer four years later. He was succeeded by his son **Santo Trafficante, Jr.** (Nov. 15, 1914–March 17, 1987), named the leader of the Mafia in Cuba, and allegedly involved, with the Chicago mob, in a conspiracy to murder President Kennedy in 1963. Trafficante Jr. died during heart surgery at 72. A picture of him is on his crypt. Mausoleum, L'Unione Italiana cemetery, Tampa, FL.

9166. Traubel, Helen (June 20, 1899–July 28, 1972) Singer from St. Louis with the New York Metropolitan Opera doing Wagner, later on Broadway in *Pipe Dream* (1955) and a few films including *Deep in My Heart* (1954), *Ladies Man* (1961). Niche (Bass), Sanctuary of Remembrance, Westwood Memorial Park, west Los Angeles.

9167. Traven, B. (Berick Traven Torsvan, March 5, 1890–March 27, 1969) Chicago born author of a dozen novels written in German, known for *The Treasure of the Sierra Madre* (1927, translated in 1934) was a notorious recluse whose identity even remained a mystery until after his death. He lived in Germany during World War I and afterward moved to Mexico, where he died. Cremated in Mexico, his ashes were reportedly scattered by plane over the jungle at Chiapas.

9168. Travers, Bill (Jan. 3, 1922–March 29, 1994) British actor and animal rights activist from Newcastle-on-Tyne, younger brother of Linden Travers, starred in *(Wee) Geordie, Footsteps in the Fog, The Barretts of Wimpole Street* (1957), *Gorgo, The Green Helmet,* and with his wife Virginia McKenna, with whom he starred as game warden George Adamson in *Born Free* (1966); they also formed the animal campaign "Elefriends." He died in his sleep at 72 at their home on Leith Hill, South Holmwood, near Dorking, Surrey. Coldharbour churchyard, Coldharbour, Surrey.

9169. Travers, Henry (Travers Hagerty, March 5, 1874–Oct. 18, 1965) Actor born in England to Irish parents came to Hollywood in the early 30's as various kind little old men, in *The Invisible Man* (1933), *On Borrowed Time* (1939), *Ball of Fire* (1941), *Mrs. Miniver* (1942 AA nom), *Shadow of A Doubt* (1943) *The Bells of St. Mary's* (1945), but most enduring as angel Clarence Oddbody in Frank Capra's *It's a Wonderful Life* (1946). Columbarium of Nativity, Hall of Inspiration, Holly Terrace, Great Mausoleum, Forest Lawn, Glendale, CA.

9170. Travers, Linden (Florence Lindon-Travers, May 27, 1913–Oct. 23, 2001) English actress from Durham with deep set eyes in films 1935–1949, in roles varying from evil and conniving to steadfast (*The Lady Vanishes* 1938, *The Ghost Train* 1941, *Christopher Columbus* 1949). Married to James Holman from 1948 until his death in 1974, in later years she studied psychotherapy and qualified as a hypnotist. She retired to St. Ives, Cornwall, where she died at 88. Burial through W.J. Winn undertakers. Her grave overlooks the sea and bears the epitaph *Soothed by every azure breath that under heaven is blown*. Barnoon Cemetery, St. Ives, Cornwall.

9171. Travis, Bill (William Barrett Travis, Aug. 9, 1809–March 6, 1836) Lawyer and soldier from Edgefield, South Carolina, helped in the capture of San Antonio during the Texas Revolution in December 1835 and at twenty-six led the official army troops, joined with the volunteers under the ailing (with pneumonia) Jim Bowie, in holding out during the siege of the Alamo from February 23 to March 6, 1836, when all 180 Texans at the garrison but six — who surrendered and then were shot, possibly including Davy Crockett — were over-run by the Mexicans and massacred. Bowie, who had written a message to Santa Anna inquiring about a willingness to parley, may have been comatose or dead by the final onslaught. The probable remains of Travis, Bowie and Crockett were later buried in a peach orchard nearby on the orders of Sam Houston. They went then to the sanctuary of the Old San Fernando Church until they were exhumed July 28, 1936, exposed to public view for a year, and entombed May 11, 1938, in the sarcophagus at the historic site. The Alamo, San Antonio, TX.

9172. Travis, Sister Helen (Helen C. Travis, Aug. 31, 1930–Feb. 15, 2000) The subject of the independent film *Sister Helen* was fifty six years old and had lost her husband to a heart attack at 55, a son who was stabbed to death, and a second son with a drug overdose, when she gave up her former life of drinking and became a Benedictine nun at age 56, and founded a safe house for recovering addicts in Mott Haven at 142nd Street in the South Bronx. Loud, vivacious, frequently funny and sometimes profane, but dedicated to making her charges stay clean, she operated the city owned building until her death from a heart attack at 69. Our Saviour sec., range 81, grave 83, (New) St. Raymond's Cemetery, the Bronx, N.Y.C.

9173. Traynor, Pie (Harold Traynor, Nov. 11, 1899–March 16, 1972) Third base great for the Pirates from 1920 through the 30's managed them to 1939. Hall of Fame 1948. Sec. 20, lot 16-E, Homewood Cemetery, Pittsburgh, PA.

9174. Treacher, Arthur (A. T. Veary, July 21, 1894–Dec. 14, 1975) Tall English actor played butlers with caustic, condescending asides, in films of the 1930's (*Remember Last Night, David Copperfield, Heidi, The Little Princess*). By the 1960's he was the sidekick on *Merv Griffin*'s talk show, with Treacher's silence and expressions often the most entertaining part of the program. Later associated with the fast food fish and chips chain bearing his name. A resident of Douglastown, Queens, N.Y.C., he died at North Shore University Hospital in Manhasset, Long Island. Cremated at Fresh Pond Crematory, Middle Village, the ashes were returned for storage at the Frederick mortuary, Douglastown, Queens, N.Y.C.

9175. Tree, Dorothy (Dorothy Estelle Triebitz, May 21, 1906–Feb. 12, 1992) Actress from Brooklyn in many small and supporting parts, including *Dracula*'s "wife" (the one on the left as the trio move into the shot) in the 1930 film, *Madame DuBarry, Three Godfathers* (the 1936 version, as Blackie), *Charlie Chan in the City of Darkness, Abe Lincoln in Illinois* (as Elizabeth Edwards), *Knute Rockne, All American* (as Martha), *The Asphalt Jungle* (as Louis Calhern's reclusive wife) and *The Men* (1950, as Ellen's mother). A founder of the Screen Actor's Guild, Dorothy Tree (Uris) died at 85 in Englewood, New Jersey. Cremated at Cedar Lawn Cemetery in Paterson through Wien and Wien mortuary (now Gutterman-Musicant) in Hackensack, the ashes were sent to Gramercy mortuary in Manhattan and picked up by her son.

9176. Tree, Herbert Beerbohm (Dec. 17, 1852–July 2, 1917) Knighted British thespian came to America briefly to grace Griffith's *Macbeth* (1916) with Constance Collier, the earliest name from the English theatre to give Hollywood a hint of respectability. He died the next year. The father, by his mistress, of Carol Reed, and grandfather of Oliver Reed. Cremated at Golders Green Crematorium, the ashes are marked by a stone sculpted statue, behind the stone of actress Kay Kendall. St. John's Cemetery, Church Row, Hampstead, London.

9177. Treen, Mary (Mary Louise Treen or Summers, March 27, 1907–July 20, 1989) Actress from St. Louis played numerous good natured friends, secretaries, switchboard operators, club members, etc., including Cousin Tilly in *It's A Wonderful Life* (1946), in a long list of films from 1930 through 1983. Married name Pearson (widowed). Ill with cancer, she died from cardiorespiratory arrest at 82 in her home at Balboa, Orange County, California. Cremated by the Neptune Society of Orange County, her ashes were buried at sea by them July 28, 1989.

9178. Tremayne, Les (April 13, 1913–Dec. 19, 2003) Balham, England, born radio actor from 1930 starred in *The Thin Man* and *The Falcon* but is best known for *The First Nighter* from 1936, replacing Don Ameche at "the little theatre off Times Square." Through the 1930's, he was at times doing forty five radio shows a week. He announced and narrated many programs on both radio and television, and appeared in films 1949–1968 including *The Blue Veil, It Grows on Trees,* as General Mann in *The War of the Worlds* 1953, narrated *Forbidden Planet* (1956), *North By Northwest* (1958, as the auctioneer), *The Angry Red Planet* (1960), *Say One For Me, The Gallant Hours, The Fortune Cookie,* etc. He died at 90 in St. John's Health Center, Santa Monica. Memorial service January 7 at Pierce Bros.' Westwood Memorial Park, west Los Angeles. Pending construction of a new mausoleum at Westwood, he was taken to Westminster Memorial Park, Westminster, CA.

9179. Trenet, Charles (May 18, 1913–Feb. 18, 2001) French singer and songwriter dubbed by Jean Cocteau as "France's last troubadour" wrote *Douce France* while in uniform in 1943, and was known for his 1946 ballad *La Mer,* popularized in English as *Beyond the Sea,* and *Que Reste-Il de Nos Amours (I Wish You Love).* He resided in New York for several years after World War II before returning to France in 1951, wrote nearly 1,000 songs in all, and was decorated with the Legion of Honor in 1998. He died at 87 in Creteil, southeast Paris. Funeral at Paris' La Madeleine Church. Cremated at Pere Lachaise Cemetery and the ashes buried with his parents. Cimetiere de L'ouest, Narbonne, in southern France.

9180. Trenier, Claude (July 14, 1919–Nov. 17, 2003) A leader of the Fabulous Treniers formed in southern New Jersey in 1948 with his twin brother Clifford (died 1984) and friend Don Hill. They became a mainstay on the Las Vegas strip, a favorite of the so-called Rat Pack and other top names, and appeared in films including *Calypso Heat Wave* and *The Girl Can't Help It.* He died from cancer at 84 in Las Vegas. Sec. W, tier 65, grave 18, Holy Cross Cemetery, Culver City, CA.

9181. Trent, Sybil (Sybil Nieporent, Sept. 22, 1926–June 15, 2000) Radio actress on *Let's Pretend* 1935–1954, also appeared in several shorts and feature films as a child in the 1930's. She died in New York at 73. Ferncliff Cemetery, Hartsdale, N.Y.

9182. Treptow, Martin (Jan. 19, 1894–July 29, 1918) World War I U.S. Army private killed in France was an unknown name until the 1981 inauguration of Ronald Reagan, when he quoted from a letter Private Treptow had written home, talking about his willingness to sacrifice for America's freedom. Reagan was thought to have mistakenly said Treptow lay across the Potomac in Arlington; his actual words were "...Under such a marker..." (as those in Arlington) "...lies a young man, Martin Treptow, who left his job in a small town barber shop in 1917 to go to France with the famed Rainbow Division." Block 21, lot 1, along gravel drive, Bloomer City Cemetery, Bloomer, WI.

9183. Treves, Frederick (Feb. 15, 1853–Dec. 7, 1923) Surgeon at the Royal London Hospital famed for his discovery of and care for Joseph (John) Merrick, dubbed The Elephant Man. His esteem grew after the successful appendectomy he performed on Edward VII, after which he received a knighthood. Ashes buried Dorchester Abbey cemetery, Dorchester, Oxfordshire.

9184. Trevor, Claire (Claire Wemlinger, March 8, 1910–April 8, 2000) Blonde actress from Brooklyn known for memorable film performances as cynical, hard used women, in *Dead End* (1937, AA nom.), *Stagecoach* (1939), *Murder My Sweet* (1944, without the heart of gold) *Key Largo* (1948, Academy Award) and *The High and the Mighty* (1954, AA nom.). She also did theatre and TV, winning an Emmy for "Dodsworth" (1956). The widow of Milton Bren (1979), she died from a respiratory ailment at 90 near Newport Beach, California. Cremated through Pacific View mortuary. Ashes scattered in the Pacific April 12 off the coast of Orange County, CA.

9185. Triangle Shirtwaist Co. Fire (Victims) Although previous New York City conflagrations such as the 1876 Brooklyn Theatre Fire or the 1904 General Slocum explosion took more lives, the Triangle Sweatshop Fire, like the *Titanic* disaster, occasioned great interest and sympathy because so many were lost due to negligence. One hundred forty five victims, mostly young women, were trapped in the ten story factory in Greenwich Village when it caught fire on Saturday afternoon, March 25, 1911. Not only did most other factories close at noon on Saturday, but the doors were locked to keep the employees from leaving their work stations except at breaks. The women on the top three floors were trapped by the locked doors; many held hands and jumped to their death as policemen, fireman and onlookers stood on the street and wept. There is a monument to the victims at the mass gave where most of the unidentified were buried, in the Workmen's Circle section at Mt. Zion Cemetery, Maspeth, Queens. The smaller stone is inscribed *Dedicated to the memory of the workers who lost their lives in the Triangle Shirt Waist Co Fire on March 25, 1911. Out of their martyrdom came new concepts of social responsibility and labor legislation that have helped make American working conditions the finest in the world. International Ladies Garment Workers Union.* In April 2004 an obelisk was dedicated at the site of the monuments in Workmen's Circle, inscribed *Triangle Shirtwaist Factory Fire/ March 25, 1911/ We remember the victims of this tragic event and strive to achieve safe working conditions and dignity for all in In A shenere un a besere velt— better and more beautiful world.* Mt. Zion Cemetery, Maspeth, Queens, N.Y.C. Six of the unidentified were buried in the Cemetery of the Evergreens, marked by a stone monument featuring a profile in relief of a woman kneeling in prayer. Beneath her is inscribed *In sympathy and sorrow, citizens of New York raise this monument over the graves of* *unidentified women and children who, with one hundred and thirty nine others, perished by fire in the Triangle Shirtwaist Factory, Washington Place, March 25, 1911.* Others unidentified were buried on Hart's Island in the East River. Cemetery of the Evergreens, Bushwick, Brooklyn, N.Y.C. The next to last survivor, **Bessie Gabrilowich Cohen** (Dec. 25, 1894–Feb. 21, 1999) then 19, found her way down the stairs and escaped. She died in Los Angeles at 104. Everlasting Peace, block 11, lot 345, grave 2, Hillside Memorial Park, Los Angeles. The last one was Vienna born **Rose Freedman** (March 27, 1893–Feb. 15, 2001), who went to the roof with her dress over her head and was helped to another building. After her husband died in 1952, she made a career at the Mark Cross Pen Company in New York and later at Metropolitan Life Insurance. She went to Mexico at 100 to study Spanish, and died at 107 at the home of her daughter in Beverly Hills, California. Service at Port Chester, New York, through Parkside Chapel, Flushing, Queens. Mt. Zion Cemetery, Maspeth, Queens, N.Y.C.

9186. Trieste, Leopoldo (May 3, 1917–Jan. 25, 2003) Italian actor, playwright, screenwriter and director from Calabria wrote *La Frontiera* (*The Frontier*) and *Cronaca* (*Hot News*), focusing on the deportation of Jews from Rome. While his films as a director went barely noticed, he was acclaimed for his roles in Fellini's *The White Sheik* and *I Vitelloni,* in the 1961 *Germi's Divorzio Ali'Italiana* (*Divorce Italian Style*) and as the landlord persuaded by the young Vito Corleone to be kinder to his tenant in *The Godfather II* (1974). Never married, he died at 85 and was buried January 28 in Rome. The Jewish Cemetery was presumed by the Italian consulate in Chicago, but the burial, per the magazine *Passed On*, was in the Cimitero de Campo Verano, Rome.

9187. Trigger (1932–July 3, 1965) Among the most famous horses of the screen, the Palomino loyally carried Roy Rogers through 87 B westerns and 101 television programs. He was stuffed after his death and is displayed at the Roy Rogers Museum, Victorville, California. After Dale Evans' death, the museum was moved to Branson, MO.

9188. Trilling, Lionel (July 4, 1905–Nov. 5, 1975) Literary critic wrote studies of various personalities, as well as *The Liberal Imagination* (1950). His wife, **Diana Trilling** (July 21, 1905–Oct. 23, 1996) also wrote biographies, of Jacqueline Kennedy Onassis and Jean Harris, among others. Plots 653/665, St. James sec., Ferncliff Cemetery, Hartsdale, NY.

9189. Trintignant, Marie (Jan. 21, 1962–Aug. 1, 2003) Parisian born actor-daughter of French actor Jean-Louis and director Nadine Trintignant, in films and television from age four in 1967. Her over fifty films include *Betty* (1992), *Harrison's Flowers* (2000), *Lost Seamen* (2003) and the title role in *Janis Et Joplin* (2003). She sustained brain damage from a beating by her boyfriend, Noir Desir singer Bertrand Cantat, in a hotel room in Vilnius, Lithuania, on July 26,

2003, and died in a hospital at Neuilly-sur-Seine six days later at 41. Pere Lachaise Cemetery, Paris.

9190. Trist, Nicholas (Nicholas Philip Trist, June 2, 1800–Feb. 11, 1874) Virginia born diplomat, married to Thomas Jefferson's granddaughter who, though recalled by President Polk, ignored the recall order and negotiated with Mexico the Treaty of Guadalupe Hidalgo on February 2, 1848, ending the Mexican War and gaining for the United States the control of Texas, California, and the southwest, although his defiance of Polk cost him his career. Sec. B, lot 42, site 5, Ivy Hill Cemetery, Alexandria, VA.

9191. Troisi, Massimo (Feb. 19, 1953–May 4, 1994) Italian actor, director and writer noted for *Il Postino* (*The Postman*) released just after his death from a heart attack. Cimitero di San Giorgio, Cremona, Italy.

9192. Trollope, Anthony (April 24, 1815–Dec. 6, 1882) English writer claimed to have invented the pillar box for posting letters. After his father lost his money in a Cincinnati business venture, his mother Francis supported them by writing novels, some 114 books in all. Trollope died in Hastings, Sussex. His autobiography was published posthumously. Upon meeting him in 1875, Henry James had referred to him in a letter as "the dullest Briton of them all." Kensal Green Cemetery, London.

9193. Trotsky, Leon (Nov. 7 [Oct. 26 O.S.], 1879–Aug. 21, 1940) One time Soviet leader and rival of Stalin was expelled from the U.S.S.R. in 1929 and lived the last three years of his life in the Coyoacán, a suburb of Mexico City on the Avenide Viena. Ramon Mercader was a twenty six year old follower of Stalin who ingratiated himself with Trotsky, his family, and guards as a loyal friend named Jacques Mornard. In the early evening of August 21, 1940 he walked into Trotsky's study with him, carrying an overcoat. They were supposedly to discuss an article, but Mercader/Mornard pulled an ice axe from under the coat and buried it in Trotsky's skull. The victim was able to attack back and prevent further injury but died just over twenty four hours later. The killer spent twenty years in prison, then returned to Russia, where he died from bone cancer in October 1978. The U.S. State Department refused to receive Trotsky's body. He was cremated and the ashes buried on the grounds of the house, beneath a an upright stone with his name and the communist symbol, the hammer and sickle. Trotsky home, Avenida Viena, Coyoacán, Mexico.

9194. Trotter, John Scott (June 14, 1908–Oct. 29, 1975) Orchestra leader closely associated with Bing Crosby on Decca in the 1930's and 40's. Sec. 1, lot 113, Sharon Memorial Park, Charlotte, NC.

9195. Troup, Bobby (Robert William Troup Jr., Oct. 18, 1918–Feb. 7, 1999) Composer-actor wrote *Route 66* and later played Dr. Joe Early on NBC's *Emergency* 1972–77. He died at 80 in Sherman Oaks, California, three days after a heart attack. Columbarium of Providence, niche 64815; moved in 2003 to niche 64716, Courts of Remembrance, Forest Lawn Hollywood Hills, Los Angeles.

9196. Trout, Dizzy (Paul Howard Trout, June 29, 1915–Feb. 28, 1972) Detroit pitcher 1939–52. In 1944 he won twenty-seven games, starting forty and relieving in nine more. Garden of the Good Shepherd, block 2, lot 96A, grave 1, Homewood Memorial Gardens, Homewood, IL.

9197. Trowbridge, Charles (Jan. 10, 1882–Oct. 30, 1967) Actor in many films 1931–1958 showed up seemingly everywhere in the 1930's and 40's as dignified judges, doctors or lawyers (*Nancy Drew Detective, Each Dawn I Die, The Man They Could Not Hang, Johnny Apollo, Our Town* [the minister], *The Mummy's Hand* [Dr. Petrie], *The Man With Nine Lives, The Letter,* dozens more). Remembrance sec., lot 233, Forest Lawn Hollywood Hills, Los Angeles.

9198. Troy, Doris (Doris Higgensen, Jan. 6, 1937–Feb. 16, 2004) Rhythm and Blues vocalist, a gospel singer from Harlem, had a hit with *Just One Look* in 1963, later covered by The Hollies, Linda Ronstadt and others. Unlike most female vocalists of the time, she wrote her own hit, and others, using the name Payne. She sang back-up for many artists and groups, was an ordained minister, and in 1983 was the subject of the Off Broadway musical *Mama I Want to Sing,* written by her sister Vy Higgensen and starring Troy as her own mother. She died in Las Vegas from emphysema at 67. Funeral at Williams Institutional CME Church, Manhattan. Sec. T, lot 189C, grave 3, George Washington Memorial Park, Paramus, NJ.

9199. Trueblood, D. Elton (Dec. 12, 1900–Dec. 20, 1994) Quaker theologian from Pleasantville, Iowa, served as chaplain at Harvard 1935, editor of *The Friend* 1935–45, chaplain at Stanford 1936–1945, and at Earlham College, Richmond, Indiana, from 1945 as professor of philosophy, opening the Earlham School of Religion c.1960. In 1964 he delivered the funeral eulogy for his friend, fellow Quaker and Iowan Herbert Hoover. Retired 1966, he remained at Earlham as professor at large, moving in 1988 to the Philadelphia area, where he died at 94. Ashes near a bench where he liked to sit. Garden of the Bethany Theological Seminary adjacent Earlham College, Richmond, Ind.

9200. Trudeau, Pierre Elliot (Oct. 18, 1919–Sept. 28, 2000) Canada's charismatic, flamboyant fifteenth prime minister 1968–1984. He promoted French as the official language in Canada as well as the metric system, was known for dating celebrities, for making obscene hand gestures at protesters, for his young and free spirited wife Margaret, and for the Charter of Rights in a new Canadian Constitution in 1982. St. Remi-de-Napierville Cemetery, St. Remi, Quebec.

9201. Truex, Ernest (Sept. 19, 1890–June 27, 1973) American actor starred in impish, improbable hero roles, several opposite Mary Pickford, later in timid or henpecked middle aged to elderly roles, including the *Twilight Zone* episodes *What You Need* and *Kick the Can.* He was married to former stage actress

Sylvia Field (died at Fallbrook Ca. July 31, 1998 at 97), later Mrs. Wilson on TV's *Dennis the Menace* 1959–63. Truex died from a heart attack at Fallbrook, California, where he lived. His family are buried in section 9, Flushing Cemetery, Flushing, Queens, N.Y.C., with a monument bearing only the family name. He was cremated and his ashes spread over Phillips Ranch, a private estate at Valley Center, CA.

9202. Truffaut, Francois (Feb. 6, 1932–Oct. 21, 1984) French New Wave pioneer director, former critic, first famous with *Les Quatre Cents Coups* (*The 400 Blows*), released in 1959 and said to be semi-autobiographical, followed by many films over twenty years, influenced by the styles of both Hitchcock and Renoir. Truffaut played a scientist in *Close Encounters of the Third Kind* (1977). He died at 52 from cancer. Grave length polished black slab inscribed *La terre te cache mais mon coeur te voit toujours* (*The earth covers you up but my heart will see you always*). Div. 21, Montmartre Cemetery, Paris.

9203. Truman, Harry S (May 8, 1884–Dec. 26, 1972) 33rd U.S. President 1945–1953, the former Democratic senator from Missouri had been vice president only three months when FDR died suddenly at Warm Springs, Georgia, April 12, 1945, leaving him the responsibility for deciding whether or not to drop the Atomic Bomb on Japan to end the Second World War, still raging in the South Pacific. After warnings failed, the city of Hiroshima was nearly leveled, as was Nagasaki, forcing the Japanese surrender and ending the war in August. Feisty and pugnacious, he also battled with the 88th congress, won an improbable re-election in 1948, and fired Gen. Douglas MacArthur during the Korean War. He retired in 1953 to Independence, Missouri, and lived nearly twenty years in the white frame home on North Delaware St. that had belonged to the parents of his wife, **Bess (Elizabeth Virginia) Wallace** (Feb. 13, 1885–Oct. 18, 1982). He died in a Kansas City hospital at 88. Full honors were accorded him in Washington, D.C., before being flown back home for burial. A grave length stone slab lists his full name (the "S" stood for nothing, he said; his parents just put it there), dates and offices held. He is buried, as he wanted, next to his wife in the courtyard, near his office. Harry S Truman Library and Museum, Independence, Missouri. Truman's parents, **John Anderson Truman** (Dec. 5, 1851–Nov. 3, 1914) and **Martha Ellen Young Truman** (Nov. 25, 1852–July 26, 1947) are buried in Forest Hill Cemetery, Kansas City, Missouri. Bess Wallace Truman's parents, **David Willock Wallace,** a suicide by gunshot at 43 June 17, 1903, and **Madge Gates Wallace,** are in separate sections of Woodlawn Cemetery, Kansas City, MO.

9204. Trumbauer, Frankie (May 30, 1901–June 11, 1956) Outstanding jazz saxophonist from St. Louis at his peak in the 1920's and 30's with the Paul Whiteman Orchestra 1927–1936, with Bix Beiderbecke and on his own. He left concert tours after 1940 and worked as a test pilot at the North American B-25 plant in Kansas City, Missouri, later joining the Civil Aeronautics Authority. He collapsed and died at 55 just inside the door of St. Mary's Hospital in Kansas City after leaving work. Cremated June 13 through the D.H. Newcomber mortuary and Chapel of the Paseo at Brush Creek in Kansas City, the ashes were returned to the widow in a temporary urn and later scattered by plane over the grounds of the Unity Society of Practical Christianity 15 miles south of Kansas City.

9205. Trumbo, Dalton (Dec. 19, 1905–Sept. 10, 1976) Screen writer of the 1940's (*Kitty Foyle, The Remarkable Andrew, Our Vines Have Tender Grapes*) in Hollywood became the first of the so-called Hollywood Ten in 1947, blacklisted by the film industry and sentenced to a jail term for refusing to testify before congress about alleged members of pro-communist organizations within the industry. He was also the first to work his way back into films; his story *The Brave One* (1956) won an Academy Award for the fictional Robert Rich, much to the embarrassment of the Academy. At the insistence of Otto Preminger and Kirk Douglas he was given screen credit for *Spartacus* and *Exodus* in 1960 and '61, and turned out several more screenplays, notably *Johnny Got His Gun* (also directed, 1971) before his death from cancer sixteen years later. Body donated to science.

9206. Trumbull, John (June 6, 1756–Nov. 10, 1843) Son of Jonathan Trumbull, governor of Connecticut, John Trumbull was a noted colonial and early American painter, best known for his *Declaration of Independence*. He donated his paintings to Yale University, establishing the first college art museum in the United States in 1831 for one thousand dollars a year and the stipulation that he be buried beneath the art gallery. The tablet reads *Colonel John Trumbull, patriot and artist, friend and aide of Washington. To his country he gave his sword and pencil.* New Yale University of Fine Arts, New Haven, CT.

9207. Trumbull, Jonathan (Oct. 12, 1710–Aug. 17, 1785) Governor of Connecticut during the Revolution and father of painter John Trumbull and **Jonathan Trumbull II** (March 26, 1740–Aug. 7, 1809), Connecticut congressman and governor 1797–1809. All but John the painter are buried in the Trumbull Burial Ground, Lebanon, CT.

9208. Truth, Sojourner (Isabella Van Wagner, 1797–Nov. 26, 1883) Black evangelist and reform leader, a former slave who was freed in New York, was a strong voice for abolition, speaking with Frederick Douglass and on her own, also a champion of women's suffrage. Lot 634, rounded spire near C.W. Post monument, Oak Hill Cemetery, Battle Creek, MI.

9209. Tryon, Tom (Jan. 14, 1926–Sept. 4, 1991) Actor from Wethersfield, Connecticut, left acting after working for Otto Preminger in *The Cardinal* and *In Harm's Way*. With the success of his first novel, *The Other* (1971), the film version later produced by him,

he worked only as a writer, including *Harvest Home, All That Glitters* and a posthumously published *By the Rivers of Babylon*. He died at 65 from stomach cancer in L.A. Cremated by Aftercare Cremation Society. Ashes scattered in the Pacific along the Long Beach coastline.

9210. Tse, Ray A detailed Mercedes in stone marks the landmark gravesite in Rosedale Cemetery, Linden, NJ.

9211. Tsongas, Paul (Paul Efthemios Tsongas, Feb. 14, 1941–Jan. 18, 1997) Democratic senator from Massachusetts 1979–85, diagnosed with non–Hodgkin's lymphoma in 1984, came back briefly as a party centrist front runner for the presidency in 1992. He died from pneumonia and a liver ailment in Boston at 55. His stone is situated on a shaded hillside above the water. Woodbine Path, lot 1699, Lowell Cemetery, Lowell, MA.

9212. Tubb, Ernest (Feb. 9, 1914–Sept. 6, 1984) Popular country singer and composer of over 200 songs including *I'm Walking the Floor Over You* (1940), with the Grand Ole Opry from 1942. He also recorded *The Big Rock Candy Mountain*. Unmarked until 1998, when a plaque for him was set. His son, country songwriter **Justin Tubb** (Aug. 20, 1935–Jan. 24, 1998) is buried with him. Garden of Peace, sec. A, lots 28 and 29, spaces 2. Hermitage Memorial Gardens, Hermitage (Old Hickory), TN.

9213. Tubman, Harriet (c. 1821–March 10, 1913) Most famous of the "conductors" of the Underground Railroad helped some 300 slaves escape the south to freedom, including her own parents. She escaped in 1849 and became known as the Moses of her people. After the 1850 Fugitive Slave Act she made several raids, possibly as many as nineteen, into the south to bring out slaves. During the Civil War she served as both scout and nurse with Union forces, but was not brought to national attention until a biography by Sarah Bradford appeared in 1869. She retired to Auburn, New York, where she established a home for aged freedmen and other blacks, which still stands at the edge of town. Her stone notes her life and work *well done*. Small upright stone, West Lawn C, Fort Hill Cemetery, Auburn, NY.

9214. Tuchman, Barbara (Jan. 30, 1912–Feb. 6, 1989) Pulitzer Prize winning historian for *The Guns of August* (1962) and *Stilwell and the American Experience in China 1911–1945* (1971). Other works include *The Proud Tower, A Portrait of the World Before the War 1890–1914*. Though she did not have a graduate degree, her writing was considered among the most compelling and readable of American historians. A native New Yorker, she died from a stroke at 77 in Greenwich, Connecticut. Burial in the Maurice Wertheim plot, on left around curve uphill. Temple Israel Cemetery, Hastings-on-Hudson, NY.

9215. Tucker, Dan (Daniel Tucker aka "Old Dan Tucker," Feb. 14, 1744–April 7, 1818) Revolutionary soldier, planter, and minister from Virginia took up a land grant in Elbert County, Georgia, and settled there, naming the estate Point Lookout. After his death, a rhyme about him, reportedly composed by area Negroes who held him in high esteem, sent him into American folklore with *"Old Dan Tucker was a good ole man, washed his face in a fryin' pan, combed his hair with a wagon wheel, and died with a toothache in his heel."* Tucker graveyard near Point Lookout, Elbert County, GA.

9216. Tucker, Forrest (Feb. 12, 1919–Oct. 25, 1986) Husky voiced, burly actor from Plainfield, Indiana, began in films of the 1940's playing bullies and heavies, moving on to heroic parts (*The Abominable Snowman of the Himalayas*), and lighter fare including the TV sitcom *F Troop*. Given a star on Hollywood Boulevard, he was ill with throat cancer and died soon after. Columbarium of Radiant Dawn, Courts of Remembrance, Forest Lawn Hollywood Hills, Los Angeles.

9217. Tucker, George Loane (June 12, 1872–June 20, 1921) Chicago born film director from 1910, beginning at IMP, became well known with *Traffic in Souls* (1913). He directed in England the next few years, married to actress Elizabeth Risdon (*q.v.*), before returning to Hollywood for his best known film *The Miracle Man* (1919), which advanced the careers of Lon Chaney, Betty Compson and Thomas Meighan. He died at 49 in L.A. Flush metal marker inscribed *G.L.T.* Sec 19/Secret Gardens, lot 237, Hollywood Forever Cemetery, Hollywood (Los Angeles), CA.

9218. Tucker, Karla Faye (Nov. 18, 1959–Feb. 3, 1998) Pickaxe murderer long on death row in Texas died by lethal injection in Huntsville at 37 despite claims that she had been redeemed by religion. It was the first execution of a woman in Texas since 1863. Forest Park Lawndale, Houston, TX.

9219. Tucker, Lorenzo (June 27, 1907–Aug. 19, 1986) Actor known as the Black Valentino. Sec. 19, lot 2661, Riverside National Cemetery, Riverside, CA.

9220. Tucker, Preston (Sept. 21, 1903–Dec. 26, 1956) Failed auto magnate devised the Tucker Car in the 1940's; his life was the subject of the film *Tucker, the Man and His Dream*. Flat plaque with his Tucker Car on it. Block 41, sec. 1121, grave 4, Michigan Memorial Park, Flat Rock, MI.

9221. Tucker, Richard (Aug. 28, 1913–Jan. 8, 1975) Brooklyn born tenor with the New York Metropolitan Opera was originally promoted by Toscanini. He died while on tour in Michigan and was returned to New York, the first singer to have his services held at the Metropolitan Opera House. In October 1975, Cardinal Cooke, a close friend, conducted at St. Patrick's Cathedral in Manhattan the first mass said there for a Jew. Sec. A, Mt. Lebanon Cemetery, Glendale, Queens, N.Y.C.

9222. Tucker, Sophie (Sophia Abuza, Jan. 13, 1887–Feb. 9, 1966) Vaudeville and Broadway star of Russian-Jewish descent. Known as The Last of the Red Hot Mamas, she was at her peak during World War I and the 1920's, known for her risqué songs and tough, heart of gold persona, and *Some of These Days*, her theme song. She died from a lung and kidney ailment in New York City at 79. Sec. 6, lot 189, grave 10, Temple Emmanu-El Cemetery, Wethersfield, CT.

9223. Tucker, Tommy (Gerald Duppler, May 18, 1903–July 11, 1989) Light band leader from 1929 with Tommy Tucker and His Californians, used "It's Tommy Tucker Time," and had a hit in 1941 with *I Don't Want to Set the World on Fire*, more closely identified with The Ink Spots. Married to Virginia Dare. A resident of Osprey, Florida, he died in Sarasota at 86. Southeastern Cremation Service through the National Cremation Society, Sarasota.

9224. Tucker Sisters Singing trio from Dallas, popular from the 1936 Centennial state fair, when Betty Jane was seven. They recorded, headlined in clubs from New York to Hollywood, did USO shows and performed on CBS radio through the 1940's and 50's. Betty Jane declined a contract with MGM in the late 40's in order to remain part of the trio. **Sammie Lee** (Sammie Magee, Aug. 15, 1920–June 18, 1994), older of the three, is in the Masonic sec., lot 35, block J, space 4, near **Betty Jane** (Oct. 7, 1928–June 4, 2004), youngest member, with a long bronze plaque and the epitaph *Love never dies as long as the heart remembers*. Masonic sec., Restland Memorial Park, Dallas, Texas. **Ernestine** (Ernestine Tucker Ryan, Aug. 11, 1924–Sept. 17, 2004) died at Northfield, Ohio, three months after Betty Jane, and is buried at Whitehaven Memorial Park, Mayfield Heights (Cleveland), OH.

9225. Tufts, Sonny (Bowen Charleston Tufts III, July 16, 1911–June 5, 1970) Member of a prominent Boston banking family, kept out of World War II by a football injury, went to Hollywood as a briefly popular leading man in the 1940's, also doing many radio dramas. By the 1950's his name had become a camp joke, aided by bad publicity. He died from pneumonia at 58. Cremated at Pierce Brothers' Chapel of the Pines Crematory in Los Angeles. Ashes buried lot 417, head of grave 8, Munroe Cemetery, Lexington, MA.

9226. Tugwell, Rexford (July 10, 1891–July 21, 1979) Member of Franklin Roosevelt's "Brain Trust" from Sinclairville, New York, and proponent of constitutional reform served as Under Secretary of Agriculture and advisor on political and other subjects. Professor of Political Science at the University of Chicago 1946–57. Books include a biography of *Grover Cleveland, The Brains Trust* (1968) and *In Search of Roosevelt* (1972). He died in Santa Barbara at 88. Cremated through McDermott-Crockett mortuary there. Ashes returned to family.

9227. Tulane, Paul (May 10, 1801–March 27, 1887) Merchant from Princeton, New Jersey, established a university in New Orleans in 1834 and willed his land to the school, which was later named for him. He returned to Princeton, where he died. Although the quiet town cemetery holds the graves of such names as Grover Cleveland, Aaron Burr and John O'Hara, the statue of Tulane at his grave is among the most prominent of monuments. Princeton Cemetery, Witherspoon Street, Princeton, NJ.

9228. Tullar, Grant Colfax (Aug. 5, 1869–May 20, 1950) Bolton, Connecticut, born publisher of hymns was a Methodist minister briefly in Dover, Delaware, before becoming an evangelist and cofounding, with Isaac Meredith, the Tullar-Meredith music publishing house in New York. Their output included *Joy Dispels Our Sorrow, The Lord of the Harvest, People That in Darkness Walked, We Will Follow Jesus, He Did Not Die in Vain, All the World for Jesus,* and *Nailed to the Cross.* Birch lot 3, grave 8, Restland Memorial Park, Hanover, NJ.

9229. Tully, Tom (Aug. 21, 1908–April 27, 1982) Actor in tough roles including the first captain in *The Caine Mutiny* (1954, Oscar nomination as best supporting actor). TV series *Lineup.* Suffering from arthritis and other ailments, he had lost a leg in 1970. He died in Newport Beach, California, at 85. With no services, he was cremated at Pacific View Memorial Park, Newport Beach. Ashes scattered at sea.

9230. Tumblety, Francis J. (1833–May 28, 1903) Canadian born doctor in the east end of London in the autumn of 1888 was the subject of the 1995 book *The Lodger, The Arrest and Escape of Jack the Ripper,* naming him as the notorious Whitechapel murderer. He spent his later years in St. Louis but was buried in Rochester, where he lived as a boy. Family obelisk, sec. 13, lot 73, Holy Sepulchre Cemetery, Rochester, NY.

9231. Tunney, Gene (James Joseph Tunney, May 25, 1897–Nov. 7, 1978) Most unusual of heavyweight boxing champions was a Shakespearian scholar from a wealthy family, but less colorful than the more pugnacious personalities of the ring. He won the heavyweight title from Jack Dempsey in 1926 and kept it in the controversial rematch the next year, when the long count allowed him extra time to recover from a blow by Dempsey that many felt should have ended the fight. Tunney defended his title only once, defeating Tom Heeney in 1928 and retiring undefeated. He died in Greenwich, Connecticut. Cremated at Ferncliff Cemetery, Hartsdale, New York. In France with the Marines in World War I, he has a flush veterans marker in the lot of his wife's family. Long Ridge Union Cemetery, Erskine Road, north of Stamford, CT.

9232. Turich, Rosa (Rosa Sinohui, May 19, 1903–Nov. 20, 1998) Actress from Tucson in films (*Hondo, Lonely Are the Brave*) and TV (*I Love Lucy*). Wife of comedian Felipe Turich. She died in Santa Ana at 95. Mausoleum, block 102, crypt C-1, San Fernando Mission Cemetery, Mission Hills, CA.

9233. Turkus, Burton (Dec. 2, 1902–Nov. 22, 1982) Member of the Brooklyn District Attorney's Office who prosecuted Murder Inc. in the late 1930's and early 40's, sending seven of its members, including the leader Lepke Buchalter, to the electric chair at Sing Sing between 1941–44, largely on information provided by Abe Reles. Leaving in 1945, he was appointed by Governor Dewey to the State Board of Mediation. He died suddenly at 79, listed as 80, in his Manhattan home. Service and burial through Frank E. Campbell mortuary. Friars Club lot, Kensico Cemetery, Valhalla, N.Y.

9234. Turnbull, Julia Anna (June 18, 1822–Sept. 11, 1887) Acclaimed ballerina of the 19th century. Sec. 91, plot 12057, Greenwood Cemetery, Brooklyn, N.Y.C.

9235. Turner, Curtis Morton "Pops" (April 12, 1924–Oct. 4, 1970) "The Babe Ruth of stock car racing," as noted on his grave length tablet, died in a plane crash at Punxsutawney, Pennsylvania. Garden of Devotion, lot 65, D-1, Blue Ridge Memorial Gardens, Roanoke, VA.

9236. Turner, Florence (Jan. 6, 1887–Aug. 28, 1946) Stage and vaudeville actress starred on the silent screen as The Vitagraph Girl from 1907 and under her own name from c. 1910. She died in Woodland Hills, California. Ashes in vaultage, Chapel of the Pines Crematory, Los Angeles.

9237. Turner, Frederick Jackson (Nov. 14, 1861–March 14, 1932) Harvard professor and historian whose thesis drew a line with the ending of the frontier, c. 1890, as bringing about drastic alterations in the socio-economic and political development of America. He authored *The Frontier in American History* (1920) and *Sections in American History,* which won the Pulitzer Prize posthumously in 1933. Cremated at Mountain View Cemetery, Pasadena, California. Ashes buried April 23, 1932. Sec. 30, lot 36 west 32 ft., grave 5, Forest Hill Cemetery, Madison, WI.

9238. Turner, Jack (John E. Turner, Feb. 12, 1920–Sept. 12, 2004) Race driver dubbed "Cactus Jack" at Indianapolis six times survived three spectacular flips in the 1961, 1962 and 1963 Memorial Day classics, was badly injured with burns and a crushed vertebrae the third time, and retired after the 1963 race. He died at 84 in Renton, Washington. Ashes scattered at sea.

9239. Turner, Big Joe (Joseph Vernon Turner, May 18, 1911–Nov. 24, 1985) The Boss of the Blues, Rhythm and Blues great from Kansas City dating to the 1920's was a major inspiration for what became rock and roll. Signed by Atlantic in the early 50's, he recorded *Shake, Rattle and Roll,* several others, with his style soon mimicked by Haley, Presley, etc. Other hits included *Corrina Corrina* and *Flip, Flop and Fly.* He died at 74 from kidney failure in Los Angeles. His flush black plaque has his picture to the right of the names and dates. Lot 4, grave 3358, Roosevelt Memorial Park, Gardena, CA.

9240. Turner, Lana (Julia Jean Mildred Turner, Feb. 8, 1921–June 29, 1995) Idaho born, L.A. raised actress first noticed in *They Won't Forget* (1937), reigned as a Hollywood glamour queen through the 1940's and 50's (*The Postman Always Rings Twice* 1946,

The Bad and the Beautiful 1952, *Peyton Place* 1957, *Madame X* 1966). Her career survived her daughter's fatal stabbing of Turner's boyfriend John Stompanato in 1958. She died from cancer of the nasopharynx in her Century City home at 74. No services. Cremated through McCormick mortuary, her ashes were returned the next day to her daughter in Los Angeles. Reportedly she was to be scattered at Hawaii, where she had a home.

9241. Turner, Nat (c. Oct. 1800–Nov. 11, 1831) Leader of a murderous uprising of slaves in 1831 terrorized the south until his capture and hanging. A graphic depiction of the revolt is told in William Styron's Pulitzer Prize winning *The Confessions of Nat Turner* (1966). The bodies of the slaves captured and executed were buried with the exception of Turner. His body was reportedly delivered to doctors who skinned it and made grease of the flesh; a Mr. R.S. Barham's father owned a money purse said to be made from his hide. His skeleton was for many years in the possession of a Dr. Massenburg but has since been misplaced. Other sources have it given to medical students in Virginia.

9242. Turner, Roscoe (Sept. 29, 1895–June 23, 1970) Stunt pilot from Corinth, Mississippi, the model for the comic strip *Smilin' Jack*, set coast to coast and transcontinental speed records through the 1930's. Crypt in the Community mausoleum, 2K, D-10, Crown Hill Cemetery, Indianapolis, IN.

9243. Turner, William Thomas (Oct. 23, 1856–June 23, 1933) Liverpool born captain of the ill-fated *Lusitania* had, at 29 in 1885, received a Human Service Medal for saving a boy from drowning who had fallen from a dock, but he was to be remembered for sailing his armed passenger ship (the arming of the liners forced the cessation of Germany's former policy of searching the vessel and setting its passenger off before firing a torpedo) into a war zone, though warned against doing so by Germany. He was told by Lord of the Admiralty Churchill that the *Juno* would be off the south coast of Ireland to meet the *Lusitania*, but the *Juno* was not sent; Turner's ship was torpedoed and sank in under twenty minutes, taking over 1200 people, among them 124 Americans. Only 6 of 48 lifeboats were successfully launched, and while Turner was the last to leave his ship, he survived and was rescued. With the cloud left over him, largely by Churchill, he retired to the Crosby area of Liverpool, where he died. Buried with his parents at Rake Lane Cemetery, Wallasey, on the Wirral, across the River Mersey from Liverpool.

9244. Turpin, Ben (Sept. 19, 1869–July 1, 1940) Cross eyed comedian from New Orleans in dozens of silent films from 1907 gained his true fame after joining Mack Sennett in 1917, particularly when playing dignified types or lampooning idols of the day, the crossed eyes insured with Lloyds of London against uncrossing. He died from heart disease at 70, survived by his wife **Babette Dietz** (1886–1978), now en-

tombed above him. Crypt in family room, Azalea Corridor, private mausoleum (family room) 9B, Azalea Terrace, Great Mausoleum, Forest Lawn, Glendale, CA.

9245. Tussaud, Marie (Dec. 1, 1761–April 16, 1850) Artist in wax set up her famed museum in Baker Street, London, in 1802, after touring for many years. Two commemorative family wall plaques. St. Mary's Catholic Church, Cadogan Street, Chelsea, London.

9246. Tutin, Dorothy (April 8, 1930–Aug. 6, 2001) English actress noted on the stage from 1953 as Rose in Graham Greene's *The Living Room* (Variety Club of Great Britain Actress of the Year), later did *I Am A Camera, The Lark, Peter Pan* 1971–2, *A Month in the Country* 1974–5 (a second Variety Club Award), *A Little Night Music* 1989, and Shakespearean roles with Peter Hall's Royal Shakespeare Company from 1960. Films include *The Importance of Being Earnest* (1952), *The Beggar's Opera, Cromwell, The Shooting Party* (1984), *Savage Messiah* and *Indian Summer* (1996). Named a C.B.E. in 1967 and D.B.E. 2000. Married from 1963 to Derek Waring. She died from leukemia at 71 in King Edward VII Hospital, Midhurst, Sussex. Ashes to funeral director at Cunnington.

9247. Tuttle, Lurene (Aug. 29, 1906–May 28, 1986) Character actress in many roles in films and TV, most prominent in the 1950's and 60's, with a soft, motherly voice, ranging from *Psycho* (1960) — in which she notes that she helped Norman pick out the dress his mother was buried in ("periwinkle blue") — to *The Ghost and Mr. Chicken* (1966), many others. Whispering Pines, lot 1570, Forest Lawn, Glendale, CA.

9248. TWA Flight 800 A 4' by 8' memorial tablet to the 230 persons lost when TWA 747 flight 800 exploded twelve miles beyond Long Island as it began a New York to Paris flight on the night of July 17, 1996 is beside fifteen individual markers over eighteen lots donated for the memorial area. All but fifteen of the passengers were recovered. Twelve caskets filled with the victims' personal items were buried here December 4, 1996. Pinelawn Memorial Park, Farmingdale, Long Island, NY.

9249. Twain, Mark (Samuel Langhorne Clemens, Nov. 30, 1835–April 21, 1910) American humorist and novelist from Hannibal, Missouri, where he set the stories of *Tom Sawyer* (1876) and *Huckleberry Finn* (1884). By the 1870's he lived at Quarry Farm in his wife's home town, Elmira, New York, with his octagonal study, a riverboat cabin, set on a quiet bluff, and at his mammoth brick mansion at Brook Farm in Hartford, Connecticut. Though known for his witty and often insightful commentary on man and his folly, by the 1890's his personal life was one sorrow after another. In 1872 his two year old only son **Langdon** died from diphtheria and was buried in the Langdon plot at Woodlawn Cemetery in Elmira. Their daughter **Suzy**, a particularly bright girl and promising scholar, died from spinal meningitis in the Nook Farm house August 18, 1896, at 24. Thus continued a line of stones down two sides of the Langdon plot, the two rows facing each other and bearing inscriptions chosen by Clemens. On Suzy's is *Olivia Susan Clemens, March 18 1872–Aug 18 1896. Warm summer sun, shine kindly here. Warm southern wind, blow softly here; Green sod above, lie light. Lie light. Good night, dear heart. Good night. Good night.* This verse, often used as an epitaph, was erroneously attributed to Clemens. When he was made aware of this he had the name of the Australian poet, Robert Richardson, cut into the stone. His wife, **Olivia** Langdon, died from heart failure eight years later in Florence, Italy. On her stone he inscribed *In this grave rest the ashes of Olivia Langdon, the beloved and lamented wife of Samuel L. Clemens, who reverently raises this stone to her memory. Gott sie der gnadding, O meine wonne! (God be merciful to you, O my joy!).* In his last year, he lived at his home Stormfield at Redding, Connecticut, with his daughter **Jean**, who died from an epileptic seizure in her bath on Christmas Eve morning, 1909, age 29. Having stated he would never look on another grave of a loved one, he saw her taken from the house for burial in Elmira. For her stone he had inscribed *In memory of Jean Lampton Clemens, a most dear daughter. Her desolate father sets this stone. After life's fitful fever she sleeps well. July 26, 1880–Dec. 24, 1909.* His autobiography concludes with this depressing account and the reference to her death with the words "In the grave! If I can believe it! God rest her sweet spirit!" He lived only four months after her death, dying from heart disease at Stormfield as he had predicted, with the coming of Haley's Comet, which had ushered in his birth in 1835. He was survived by one daughter, Clara Clemens Gabrilowitsch. His body was taken to New York and on to Elmira, with the services held in the Langdon home in which he had been married, and buried in his characteristic white suit, the grave lined with laurel leaves. On his marker is only his real and pen name and his dates of birth and death. No epitaph is inscribed on the front as with his wife and daughters. At the front of the lot is the Langdon family obelisk, and at the rear is the joint monument to Clemens and his son-in-law, Clara's husband Ossip Gabrilowitsch, with bronze cameo profiles of both men on the shaft, which she had erected upon the latter's death in 1936 when he died in Detroit, his wish to be buried at Clemens' feet carried out by his wife. **Clara** died in 1962 and was buried in the lot as well. Sec. G, lot 40, Woodlawn Cemetery, Elmira, NY.

9250. Tweed, Blanche Oelrichs *see* **Michael Strange.**

9251. Tweed, William Marcy "Boss" (April 3, 1823–April 12, 1878) Infamous head of New York's Tammany Hall was convicted of organizing and engineering the theft of $200 million from the city of New York between 1865–1871. Tweed came to symbolize the outrageous political corruption of the Gilded Age. His undoing was expedited by the cartoons of

Thomas Nast and the follow-up investigations of Governor Samuel Tilden, who took all the credit. In one of history's ironies, Governor Tilden was then elected to the presidency, but had the result reversed by political corruption. Boss Tweed died after a year in the Ludlow Street jail. The family plot has relatively modest monuments in it, surrounded by an iron railing. Sec. 55, lot 6447, facing intersection, Greenwood Cemetery, Brooklyn, N.Y.C.

9252. Twelvetrees, Helen (Helen Jurgens, Dec. 25, 1907–Feb. 13, 1958) Blonde talkies star in films 1929–39 (*The Cat Creeps, Millie, Bad Company, The Spanish Cape Mystery*). The name Twelvetrees, too good to discard, was retained from a former marriage. Her last was to USAF Capt. Conrad Payne. They lived near Olmstead Air Force Base at Middletown, near Harrisburg, Pennsylvania, when she died from an overdose of drugs taken for a kidney ailment at 50. Unmarked. Middletown Cemetery, Middletown, PA.

9253. Twitty, Conway (Harold Lloyd Jenkins, Sept. 1, 1933–June 5, 1993) Country music star formerly had pop hits with *It's Only Make Believe* (1958), *Lonely Blue Boy, Mona Lisa.* He won a 1971 Grammy for *After the Fire is Gone.* Named for silent screen comedian Harold Lloyd, the stage name was a mixture of Conway, Arkansas, and Twitty, Texas. He died at 59 from an abdominal aneurysm while on tour in Springfield, Missouri. Exterior crypt with his real name, bottom tier, left rear, Memory Chapel Mausoleum, Sumner Memorial Gardens, Gallatin, TN.

9254. Tyler, Beverly (Beverly Jean Saul, July 5, 1927–Nov. 23, 2005) Actress from Scranton, Pennsylvania in films 1943–58 (*The Green Years, The Beginning or the End, My Brother Talks to Horses, The Fireball, Voodoo Island*) and television appearances, on *Death Valley Days, Bonanza, The Andy Griffith Show, Hazel.* She married **James Jordan, Jr.,** son of the Fibber McGee and Molly team, in 1962 and moved with him to Reno, where she died from a pulmonary embolism at 78. Cremated through Ross, Burke and Knobel mortuary. Urn to Our Mother of Sorrows Cemetery, Reno, NV.

9255. Tyler, John (March 29, 1790–January 18, 1862) 10th President of the United States 1841–45 was the first to succeed to the office on the death of a sitting president (William Henry Harrison). Tyler, part of the 1840 rallying cry "Tippecanoe and Tyler Too!" was actually a southern states' rights Democrat placed on the Whig ticket to garner national support. By the end of his term in 1845, his entire cabinet had resigned. He retired to his Virginia estate "Sherwood Forest" (a wry allusion to his standing as a political outlaw) in Charles City County. Elected to the Confederate Congress in Richmond in 1861, he died in the Exchange Hotel in Richmond from a coronary thrombosis; considered a traitor, his death was not mentioned in the northern papers. Though he wished a simple funeral, his coffin, covered by a Confederate flag, lay in state in the capitol at Richmond with services at St. Paul's Episcopal Church. Burial was just a few yards from James Monroe, the only case of two non-related American presidents buried within yards of one another. His second wife, **Julia Gardiner Tyler** (May 4, 1820–July 10, 1889) was buried beside him upon her death twenty seven years later, also in the Exchange Hotel in Richmond. For decades the grave was marked only by a magnolia tree, and for a time by a small headstone, until in 1911 congress authorized a monument and appropriated $10,000 for it. A granite obelisk topped by a bronze bell with eagles, with a bust of Tyler on a pedestal at the front, was dedicated October 12, 1915 by their daughter **Pearl Tyler Ellis** (June 20, 1860–June 30, 1947), one of his fourteen children who is in the lot. Others include **Lachlan** (Dec. 2, 1851–Jan. 26, 1902), **Robert Fitzwater** (March 12, 1856–Dec. 30, 1927), **Julia Spencer** (Dec. 25, 1849–May 8, 1871) and **Lyon Gardiner Tyler** (Aug. 1853–Feb. 12, 1935), historian and president of William and Mary College. Presidents' Circle, Hollywood Cemetery, Richmond, Virginia. Another son **David Gardiner Tyler** (July 12, 1846–Sept. 5, 1927) was a member of the Virginia state legislature, U.S. representative from Virginia 1893–97, and a state court judge. Sec. Q, lot 37, Hollywood Cemetery, Richmond. Their son **John Alexander Tyler** (April 7, 1848–Sept. 1, 1883), who served with the Confederacy in the Civil War and fought in the Franco-Prussian War, is buried with the Gardiners (see Gardiner) at South End Burying Ground, East Hampton, Long Island, N.Y. John Tyler's first wife, **Letitia Christian** (Nov. 12, 1790–Sept. 10, 1842) suffered several paralytic strokes and did not serve as hostess in the White House. She died there at 51 and was buried at her birthplace, Cedar Grove plantation, route 106 three miles south of I-64 (sign to cemetery), New Kent County, VA.

9256. Tyler, Judy (Judith Marie Hess, Oct. 9, 1932–July 3, 1957) Actress from Milwaukee played Princess Summerfall Winterspring on the *Howdy Doody* TV show with Buffalo Bob 1951–53, appeared on Broadway in *Pipe Dream* (1955), and opposite Elvis Presley in the film *Jailhouse Rock* (1957). She died with her second husband Greg Lafayette in a car wreck at Billy the Kid, Wyoming. Urn in Nisonger room, unit 8, first floor, main mausoleum, Ferncliff Cemetery, Hartsdale, NY.

9257. Tyler, Tom (Vincent Markowski, Aug. 9, 1903–May 1, 1954) B film actor with sharp, chiseled features and piercing eyes in westerns played *Captain Marvel* in the 1941 feature and the serials, as well as Kharis, the first wrapped, strangling mummy on film, in *The Mummy's Hand* (1940) and memorable parts in John Ford westerns including *Stagecoach* (1939) and *She Wore A Yellow Ribbon* (1948). A former prize fighter and weight lifter, he was stricken by a gradually crippling arthritic condition in 1943 and died nine years later at 50 from a heart attack at his home in Hamtramck, Michigan, a Detroit suburb. His flush

plaque has his image in a cowboy hat engraved beside the name and dates. Slepski plot, sec. 15, lot 51, Mount Olivet Cemetery, Detroit, MI.

9258. Tynan, Kenneth (April 2, 1927–July 26, 1980) British theatre critic and dramatist. St. Cross (Holywell) Churchyard, St. Cross Road, Oxford, Oxfordshire.

9259. Typhoid Mary *see* **Mary Mallon.**

9260. Tzara, Tristan (April 4, 1896–Dec. 24, 1963) Founder of Dadaism, the early 1920's literary and artistic movement steeped in nonsense, including reading the phone book as poetry and *The Vaseline Symphony*. Div. 8, Montparnasse Cemetery, Paris.

9261. Udall, Morris K. (June 15, 1922–Dec. 12, 1998) Arizona representative familiarly known as Mo, in congress 1961–1991, was a vocal liberal Democrat. During the 1970's, he failed in two tries to win the speakership or to gain his party's nomination in the 1976 presidential primaries. Known for his self deprecating humor, the father of a well known political family penned the 1988 book *Too Funny to be President*. Unable to speak since the 1991 fall that ended his career, he died after a long battle with Parkinson's Disease at 76 in Washington, D.C. Ashes scattered over the Catalina Mountains, north of Tucson, AZ.

9262. Udet, Ernst (April 26, 1896–Nov. 17, 1941) World War I German air ace credited with sixty-two downed planes became Director General of the Nazi Luftwaffe, in charge especially of long range bombing and transportation problems. Largely over the failure of the Blitz over England, he was forced to suicide by his former colleague and friend Göring. His grave is marked with an upright stone. Invalidenfriedhof, Scharnhorstr. 33 (Mitte), Berlin.

9263. Uhse, Beate (Oct. 25, 1919 – July 16, 2001) Grande dame of German erotica, called Europe's first erotic stock when she put her company on the Frankfurt exchange in 1999. A pilot from age 18, she flew fighter planes as a captain in the Luftwaffe during World War II. At the war's end she removed to Flensburg in Schleswig-Holstein, at the northern tip of Germany, and by 1951 was marketing sexually oriented material. At her death in Switzerland from pneumonia at 81, her company had 93 stores and over 100 franchises across Europe. Burial at Glücksburg (near Flensburg), Schleswig-Holstein, Germany.

9264. Ulmer, Edgar G. (Sept. 17, 1904–Sept. 30, 1972) Imaginative Vienna born director best known for the dark and stylish horror cult classic *The Black Cat* (1934). Subsequent poverty row features were ignored until the French declared him a minor auteur who left his distinctive mark on *Bluebeard* (1944) as well. Epitaph reads *Talent Obliges*. His wife, writer and script supervisor **Shirley Kassler** (June 12, 1914–July 6, 2000), who wrote as **Shirley Castle**, is interred with him. New Beth Olam Mausoleum/Hall of David, T-9-2, crypt 1587, Hollywood Forever Cemetery, Hollywood (Los Angeles), CA.

9265. Ulric, Lenore (Lenore Ulrich, July 21,

1892–Dec. 30, 1970) Stage actress from a German immigrant family in Minnesota. Film appearances include *Camille* (1937). She died in an Orangeburg, New York, sanitarium. Cremated at Ferncliff Cemetery, Hartsdale, New York. Ashes returned to a sister.

9266. Umberto I (March 14, 1844–July 29, 1900) King of Italy from January 9, 1878, and Duke of the House of Savoy, led Italy out of isolation into a period of nationalism, entering into the Triple Alliance with Germany and Austria-Hungary, while failing to establish a colonial hold in northeast Africa. Assassinated by an anarchist after twenty-two years on the throne. Elevated tomb, with **Queen Margherita,** second chapel on the left, The Pantheon, Rome.

9267. Underhill, Wilbur (March 16, 1901–Jan. 6, 1934) The Tri-State Terror, robber and killer in the Midwest with Ford Bradshaw in the early 1930's, known for his cold-bloodedness, killing one man during a holdup for not raising his hands fast enough. While on his honeymoon in Shawnee, Oklahoma, he was surrounded by federal agents and shot a dozen times, though he managed to hold them off and break through their cordon before he passed out and died five days later in a hospital at McAlester. Over 2,000 people attended the funeral. Sec. 10, block 4 NW ¼, lot 3, space 1, Memorial Park Cemetery, Joplin, MO.

9268. Underwood, Oscar W. (May 6, 1862–Jan. 25, 1929) Congressman and senator from Alabama 1914–1927 authored the Underwood Tariff during Wilson's term, lowering the rates. He was among the Democratic contenders for the White House in 1912 and 1924. Block 14, lot 123, Elmwood Cemetery, Birmingham, AL.

9269. Unitas, Johnny (John Unitas, May 7, 1933–Sept. 11, 2002) Pittsburgh born quarterback defined his Baltimore Colts, the greatest qb of his era, from 1956–1972. A three time MVP, he led the Colts to four NFL championships, set NFL records by throwing touchdowns in forty-seven consecutive games and passing for over 300 yards in twenty three games, completed 2,830 of 5,186 attempted passes, and had a career total of 290 touchdowns, a record when he retired in 1973. In his most fabled game in 1958, he led the Colts on an 80 yard drive to beat the New York Giants 23–17, a game that marked the advent of the modern televised football era. Hall of Fame 1979. He died from heart attack at 69 while exercising at a physical therapy center in Timonium, Maryland. Mass conducted by the Archbishop of Baltimore at the Cathedral of Mary Our Queen in north Baltimore. Cremation through Ruck Tow and Son mortuary. Dulaney Valley Memorial Gardens, Timonium, MD.

9270. Unknown Confederate Soldier The subject of the Alexander Gardner photograph titled *The Home of a Rebel Sharpshooter, Gettysburg, July, 1863* was, by many accounts and theories, arranged in the position for the photograph. Gardner also claimed his skeleton and musket remained in the spot when he returned for Lincoln's speech in November, although he was almost certainly buried (as noted by William A. Frassanito in *Gettysburg, A Journey in Time*) in a mass grave of unknowns and removed later, as were the Confederate dead of Antietam, to Confederate Hills Cemetery near Hagerstown, MD.

9271. Unknown Soldier (Tomb of the Unknown Soldier) On March 4, 1921, the new U.S. congress passed a joint resolution to not only bestow Medals of Honor on the grave of the Unknown British Soldier in Westminster Abbey and on that of the Unknown French Soldier at the Arch de Triomphe, but also to return to the U.S. an American unknown then buried in France for interment at the memorial amphitheatre in Arlington National Cemetery. On October 22 one American was exhumed from four cemeteries (Belleau Wood, the Somme, St. Mihiel, and the Meuse-Argonne). All four coffins were taken to Chalons and randomly shuffled, after which an American sergeant chose one by placing a spray of flowers on it. The soldier was buried on soil brought from France with military honors on Armistice Day, November 11, 1921. When President Harding dedicated the tomb, Taft, Wilson (though ill) and future presidents Coolidge and Hoover were present as well, along with General Pershing. On the white marble sarcophagus, dedicated in 1926, is the inscription *Here rests in honored glory an American soldier known but to God.* The tomb is guarded 24 hours a day, 365 days a year, by a soldier from the U.S. Army's 3rd Infantry, the Old Guard. Since the original dedication in 1921, three more men have been interred there, marked by flat slabs in front of the original sarcophagus. Those from World War II and Korea were interred in a joint ceremony dedicated by President Eisenhower May 30, 1958. The unknown serviceman from Vietnam was interred between the previous two on Memorial Day 1984, eulogized by President Reagan. The Changing of the Guard at the Tomb of the Unknown Soldier is conducted every hour October through March and every half hour April through September. Sec. 26, grid QR-32/33, Arlington National Cemetery, Arlington, VA. On May 14, 1998, the casket of the Vietnam Unknown Soldier was exhumed for DNA testing to determine if the remains could be positively identified; the most probable identity of the soldier had been narrowed to **Lt. Michael Blassie** (April 4, 1948–May 11, 1972) of St. Louis, whose plane went down near An Loc during the Easter offensive of 1972. On June 29, 1998 the remains were formally identified as Blassie's and he was sent home, where a cenotaph for him had long been set, and buried July 11 in sec. 85, grave 1, Jefferson Barracks National Cemetery, St. Louis, Missouri. Whether the Vietnam Unknown's grave would remain empty was not immediately decided.

9272. Unser, Jerry (Jerry Unser, Jr., Nov. 15, 1932–May 17, 1959) Formula One race driver, brother of four time Indianapolis 500 winner Al, three time winner Bobby, and uncle of multiple winner Al Jr. Injured in the 1958 500 in the crash that killed Pat O'-Connor, Jerry Unser was hurt in practice at the Brickyard on May 2 of the following year and died two weeks later at 26. His plaque reads *He died as he lived.* Block 18, sec. 44, grave 1, Sunset Memorial Park, Albuquerque, NM.

9273. Untermyer, Samuel (June 6, 1858–March 16, 1940) Renowned trial lawyer framed the 1913 Income Tax law. He has a striking monument with ascending figure and mourners in the Cliff sec. 54, Woodlawn Cemetery, the Bronx, N.Y.C.

9274. Upjohn, Richard (June 22, 1802–Aug. 17, 1878) Architect designed Trinity Church in lower Manhattan facing Wall Street, a nationally recognized landmark, as well as the gothic sandstone gates of Greenwood Cemetery, where he lies. Sec. 121 along Atlantic Ave., Greenwood Cemetery, Brooklyn, N.Y.C.

9275. Upjohn family   Manufacturers of pharmaceuticals. Sec. 43, lot 24, Rosedale Cemetery, East Orange, NJ.

9276. Urecal, Minerva (Sept. 22, 1884–Feb. 26, 1966) Character actress with sharp features in a variety of roles from the mid 1930's to the 60's; a rather frightening version of Marjorie Main. The last name she took from the town of Eureka, California. Abbey of the Psalms/Hollywood Forever Mausoleum, corridor E-1 (Serenity), tier 3, niche 8, Hollywood Forever Cemetery, Hollywood (Los Angeles), CA.

9277. Urich, Robert (Dec. 19, 1946–April 16, 2002) Actor from Toronto, Ohio, appeared as generally amiable characters in several television series: as Peter Campbell in *Soap,* as Detective Dan Tanna in *Vega$* and as *Spenser: For Hire* 1985–88. He announced in 1996 that he suffered from synovial cell sarcoma, a cancer attacking the joints. When his series *The Lazarus Man* was dropped because of his illness, he sued, but stayed busy raising money for cancer research and speaking about the disease. As likeable off screen as on, Urich died from his cancer at a hospital in Thousand Oaks, California, at 55. Service April 19 at St. Charles Borromeo Catholic Church, North Hollywood. His family, including his father, are buried at Toronto Union Cemetery, Toronto, Ohio. His ashes are marked by a monument with a cross at the family's cottage in southern Ontario.

9278. Uris, Leon (Leon Marcus Uris, Aug. 3, 1924–June 21, 2003) Novelist, a marine on Guadalcanal in World War II, chronicled the many facets of various wars and their glories as well as tragedies, including *OB VII, Trinity, Battle Cry* (World War II), *Mila 18* (the Warsaw Ghetto uprising), *Exodus* (Israel), *The Haj* (Palestine), several others. His self composed epitaph is *American soldier. Jewish writer.* Sec. 18, site 635, Quantico National Cemetery, Quantico, VA.

9279. Urry, Lewis F. (Jan. 29, 1927–Oct. 19, 2004) Canadian born developer of the Alkaline battery at Parma Laboratories in the 1950's, far outlast-ing others. A chemical engineer for Energizer 1950–2004, by his death at 77 in Middleburg Heights, Ohio, it sold billions and was enshrined near Edison's light bulb in the Smithsonian. Burial through Bogner family mortuary, North Ridgeville. Butternut Ridge Cemetery, Eaton Township, North Ridgeville, OH.

9280. Ustinov, Peter (April 16, 1921–March 28, 2004) British born actor, playwright and author, the son of part Russian parents, won best supporting actor Oscars for *Spartacus* (1960) and *Topkapi* (1964), appeared in over ninety films (*We're No Angels, The Sundowners, Death on the Nile* as Hercule Poirot), won three Emmys (for *Dr. Johnson, Barefoot in Athens* and *A Storm in Summer*), a Grammy for narrating *Peter and the Wolf,* and worked for decades with UNICEF as a goodwill ambassador for the U.N. agency and an advocate for the United Nations Educational, Scientific and Cultural Organization (UNESCO). Knighted 1990. He died at 82 in a Geneva clinic, near his home overlooking Lake Geneva at Bursins, (canton of) Vaud, Switzerland, where he had lived since 1980 (and in Switzerland since 1957). Burial April 3 in the Bursins village cemetery, Bursins, Switzerland.

9281. Vadim, Roger (Roger Vadim Plemiannikov, Jan. 26, 1928–Feb. 11, 2000) French film director best known for showcasing beautiful women, including his wives, in such works as *And God Created Woman* (1956, with wife Brigitte Bardot) and *Barbarella* (1968, with wife Jane Fonda). His last wife was actress Marie Christine Barrault, from 1990 until his death from cancer at 72 in Paris. All five wives attended his burial February 18 at the family vault in the cemetery on the Mediterranean at Saint Tropez, France.

9282. Vail, Lester (Lester Lee Seib, June 29, 1899–Nov. 28, 1959) All purpose actor (*Dance Fools Dance, Murder by the Clock* 1931) later a director. Ashes in vaultage at Pierce Brothers Chapel of the Pines Crematory, Los Angeles.

9283. Valachi, Joseph (Sept. 22, 1904–April 3, 1971) The first member of the mafia to break the blood oath of La Cosa Nostra and relate much of its secrets and history, before senate hearings in September and October 1963. Valachi claimed Vito Genovese had him marked for death, so he opted for federal protection. A $100,000 contract was reportedly put out on him, but some 200 federal marshals protected Valachi, the most heavily guarded prisoner in the federal penitentiary system. He was moved several times before going to La Tuna Institute in 1968, where he died from a heart attack, listed as 67, although the birth date on his stone is 1904, making him 66. Buried secretly May 7, 1971. St. Matthew, lot 64, Gate of Heaven Cemetery, Lewiston (Niagara Falls area), NY.

9284. Vale, Vola (Violet Irene Smith, Feb. 12, 1897–Oct. 17, 1970) Silent screen actress born in Buffalo and raised in Rochester, New York, in films 1916–28, including *The Silent Man, Soul of the Beast* and *Little Annie Rooney.* Married from 1932 to Lawrence McDougal, who died a few months before her death in Hawthorne, California, at 73. Mausoleum niche A-4, Roosevelt Memorial Park, Gardena, CA.

9285. Valens, Ritchie (Richard S. Valenzuela, May 13, 1941–Feb. 3, 1959) Young Mexican-American rock and roll singer died at 17 in a plane crash near Council Bluffs, Iowa, with Buddy Holly and The Big Bopper en route to Fargo on tour with the Winter Dance Party. Though only 17, he had hits with *La Bamba, Donna* and *Come On Let's Go*, the latter title inscribed on his plaque, replaced with a more elaborate one with pictures on it of both he and his mother when she was buried beside him in 1987. Sec. C, lot 248, grave 2, three rows in, San Fernando Mission Cemetery, Mission Hills, CA.

9286. Valentine, Joseph A. (Giuseppe Valentino, July 24, 1903–May 18, 1949) New York born cinematographer in Hollywood from 1924, photographed, among others, *Night of Terror* and *Man Hunt* (1933), *Remember Last Night?* (1935), *The Moon's Our Home* and *Three Smart Girls* (1936), *One Night in the Tropics* (1940), *The Wolf Man* (1941), *Saboteur* (1942), *Shadow of A Doubt* (1943), *Tomorrow is Forever* (1945), *Joan of Arc* (for which he won an Oscar) and *Rope* (both 1948), the latter famous for its unique lack of cuts. Valentine died at 45 from a heart attack in Cheviot Hills, California. Sec. B, lot 36, grave 3, Holy Cross Cemetery, Culver, CA.

9287. Saint Valentine (dec. Feb. 14, 270 A.D.) Christian martyr, a Roman bishop who maintained his faith despite persecution by Claudius Caesar II, who ordered his death because Valentine had overseen the marriage of Roman soldiers who were to remain single. Although there is debate over whether his heart was left at the Blessed John Duns Scotus Church in Glasgow, Scotland, and other body parts kept at his home town in Italy, the shrine reputed to contain his remains is at Whitefriars Street Catholic Church, Dublin, Ireland.

9288. Valentino, Rudolph (Rodolfo Alfonzo Raffaele Pierre Philibert Guglielmi, May 6, 1895–Aug. 23, 1926) Silent screen matinee idol from Castelleneta in southern Italy whose career was launched by writer June Mathis in Rex Ingram's *The Four Horsemen of the Apocalypse* (1920). He became the idol of millions, particularly women, as the tango dancer in the Ingram film, then with his portrayal of *The Sheik* (1921), the matador in *Blood and Sand* (1922), and the Zorro-like hero of *The Eagle* (1925), reprising his Arab role in *Son of the Sheik* (1926). First married to actress Jean Acker, he was far more enamored of his second wife Natacha Rambova (*q.v.*), and built his mansion "Falcon Lair" for the two of them on a summit in Beverly Hills, but she left him and for the last two years of his life he lived there alone. He became ill in New York City on August 14, 1926 and was taken to Polyclinic Hospital, where he underwent surgery for a ruptured appendix and perforated ulcer. On the 21st, after steady recovery, his temperature rose and he developed peritonitis, which proved fatal. He was 31. What

followed has been equaled in the annals of American mass hysteria only by the death of Elvis Presley in Memphis in 1977; the outpouring of emotion over the deaths of Presidents Roosevelt and Kennedy was more orderly and controlled. Valentino's viewing remains New York's largest funeral. Over 10,000 people jammed the Frank E. Campbell Funeral Church where he lay on a "couch" in the Gold Room, lately occupied by Anna Held, Vernon Castle, Olive Thomas, Lillian Russell, etc. After a plate glass window was broken in the ensuing pushing and shoving, the body was moved into a smaller room and placed in a glass coffin. Some versions have the body replaced with a wax dummy for the duration of the mass viewing. Police did their best to maintain order in a line estimated at 30,000, stretching (eight abreast at some points, and in the rain) from Broadway and 66th east toward Columbus Avenue, north two blocks to 68th and Campbell's entrance. Shortly after the police ordered Campbell's to close the doors, a group of Fascist guards sent by Mussolini were admitted, followed by a confrontation with anti–Fascists after which both groups were barred. Rambova wanted him cremated and buried with her family in the Hudnut plot in Woodlawn in the Bronx, but this was negated. The actor's brother Alberto Guglielmi agreed with William Randolph Hearst that the place for him was Hollywood. On Monday morning, August 30, the coffin was taken from Campbell's to St. Malachy's Catholic Church, with a side show of exaggerated grief exceeding her screen performances by his self proclaimed fiancée, actress Pola Negri, and other loudly sobbing actresses. The body was taken by train to Chicago and on to Los Angeles, where a service was held at the Church of the Good Shepherd September 6. The previous February crowds at Hollywood Cemetery had overrun the interment of actress Barbara LaMarr to the exclusion of the family. Consequently, Valentino was interred secretly in a crypt provided by his friend and mentor June Mathis in a rear alcove of the Cathedral Mausoleum. A more impressive memorial for him was planned, but he was never moved far. When June Mathis died the next year and her crypt was needed, her husband Sylvano Balboni hired a lawyer to get the family to move Valentino's body. He was moved into Balboni's crypt above her, which his brother Alberto eventually paid Balboni for, and there he remains. A memorial to him with a bronze statue titled *Aspiration* was unveiled in Hollywood's DeLongpre Park in 1930. After repeated vandalism it was removed in 1954 but reinstated in 1976 with a bronze bust of Valentino on a pedestal. One dubious memorial was the nasal musical ode *There's A New Star in Heaven Tonight,* written by Jimmy McHugh and sung at the committal service. At 12:10 p.m. each August 23, a memorial service is held at the crypt, with an actress mimicking the once real "Lady in black" (Ditra Flame), who would appear grief stricken with a heavy veil at the crypt. Like the annual ceremony at the crypt of Marilyn Monroe, it has become a part of the Hollywood tourist's list of things to see. Corridor A, crypt 1205, Cathedral Mausoleum, Hollywood Forever Cemetery, Hollywood (Los Angeles), CA.

9289. Valk, Frederick (June 10, 1895–July 23, 1956) German actor from Hamburg, long on the stage, in British films 1940–1956, among them *Dead of Night* (1946, as Dr. Van Straaten). He died suddenly at home in London at 61. His funeral, attended by representatives of the Piccadilly Theatre, the Old Vic, and the German Embassy, as well as Peter Ustinov, was at Golders Green. Ashes spread at sec. 3V, Golders Green Crematorium, north London.

9290. Vallandingham, Clement L. (July 29, 1820–June 17, 1871) Ohio Democratic congressman since 1857 opposed the Civil War and led the so-called Copperheads in the north. Accused of being anti-Union, he was arrested in 1863 and banished by Lincoln to the Confederacy. He left the south for Canada and eventually returned to Dayton, Ohio, to practice law. Edward Everett Hale's story *The Man Without A Country* was based on Vallandingham's banishment. Back in Dayton, he was demonstrating how a gun his client allegedly used to shoot a man could not have been the weapon, when he accidentally picked up the wrong gun and fatally shot himself in the chest. His grave is marked by a marble shaft with his profile in relief on it. Sec. 28, Woodland Cemetery, Dayton, OH.

9291. Vallee, Rudy (Hubert Prior Vallee, July 28, 1901–July 3, 1986) Singing idol from the University of Maine known for his megaphone, nasal voice and trademark songs of the 1928–1930 period (*My Time is Your Time, I'm Just a Vagabond Lover, The Stein Song*). He appeared in early musicals and later turned to straight roles, often stuffy, in *I Remember Mama*, several others. He died from a heart attack in his Beverly Hills home while watching the centennial celebration of the Statue of Liberty on TV. Cremated by the Neptune Society at Angeles Abbey, Compton, Ca. Family monument with columns; his individual grave was unmarked for many years. A flush footstone was eventually set, removed, and replaced. Sec. G toward B near Hyacinth Ave., Mt. Hyacinth Catholic Cemetery, Westbrook, ME.

9292. Valli, Virginia (Virginia McSweeny, June 10, 1898–Sept. 24, 1968) Chicago born actress in silents and talkies 1915–1931, retired as the wife of actor Charles Farrell, long time mayor of Palm Springs in the 1950's, and is buried with him. Sec. 10–3, lot F, Wellwood Murray Cemetery, Palm Springs, CA.

9293. Valvano, Jim (March 10, 1946–April 28, 1993) New York City born athlete and colorful NCAA coach led the North Carolina State Wolfpack in an uphill battle to the miracle championship of 1983, symbolized by Jimmy V's often quoted credo "Don't give up! *Never* give up!" He left in 1990 and later broadcast with Dick Vitale on ESPN. The flashy and quick witted Valvano died after a year long battle with

bone cancer at 47 in Duke University Medical Center. Hillside south sec., Oakwood Cemetery, Raleigh, NC.

9294. Van, Billy B. (Aug. 3, 1878–Nov. 16, 1950) Turn of the century stage comedian participated in the formation of Metro-Goldwyn-Mayer, toured in vaudeville with former heavyweight champion James J. Corbett. A founder of Equity in 1915. He retired to New England in 1927 as a soap manufacturing executive. Pine Grove Cemetery, Newport, NH.

9295. Van, Bobby (Robert King, Dec. 6, 1928–July 31, 1980) Song and dance star of the cabaret revue circuit, musicals, films (*The Affairs of Dobie Gillis* 1953) and TV variety shows. His popularity declined in the 1960's but revived with *No No Nanette*, co-starring Ruby Keeler, in 1971. He also choreographed a few films before his death from cancer at 51. Maimonides 20, lot 5729, Mt. Sinai Memorial Park, Los Angeles.

9296. Van, Gloria (Lucille Fanolla, Aug. 17, 1920–Dec. 24, 2002) Big Band singer with Johnny "Scat" Davis, Gene Krupa, Hal McIntyre, associated with *Embraceable You,* appeared on television in *Windy City Jamboree* and *The Wayne King Show.* Married to singer Johnny Allison, brother of Fran Allison, she died in Elk Grove, Illinois, of kidney failure at 84. St. Michael the Archangel Cemetery, Palatine, IL.

9297. Van, Gus (August Von Glahn, Aug. 12, 1887–March 12, 1968) Vaudeville partner of Joe Schenck, long time songwriters and performers. New York City born, he outlived Schenck by 38 years. He died in Miami Beach. Cremated at Grove Park Crematory through Riverside Chapel, Miami, FL.

9298. Van Alstyne, Egbert (March 5, 1878 [often listed as 1882]–July 9, 1951) Composer and lyricist from Marengo, Illinois, wrote or co-wrote roughly four hundred songs, notably *In the Shade of the Old Apple Tree, Memories,* and *Pretty Baby,* which he is credited with co-writing, though many listings say it was written by Tony Jackson. He wrote songs for various films including *Manhattan Melodrama, Midnight, Castle on the Hudson,* several others. Chapel floor, wall L, crypt 1228-B, mausoleum, Memorial Park Cemetery, Skokie, IL.

9299. Van Buren, John (Feb. 10, 1810–Oct. 13, 1866) The second son of President Martin Van Buren, "Prince John" was himself a politician and a leader of the Barn Burner faction of the Democratic party in the 1848 elections. He died at sea at 56 and in the ensuing storms many wanted to throw his body overboard, a common belief being that a corpse brought bad luck to a vessel at sea. He was returned to New York and buried beneath a stone cross with his name, dates and places of birth and death on the base. Circular lot on an overgrown bluff. Sec. 62, Albany Rural Cemetery, Menands, Albany, NY.

9300. Van Buren, Martin (Dec. 5, 1782–July 24, 1862) 8th President of the United States 1837–1841 was a political wizard of the Democratic party known as "The Red Fox of Kinderhook," the small Hudson River town where he was born, lived, died and is buried. Trusted advisor of Andrew Jackson, he served as his vice president 1833–37, succeeding to the White House in 1837, where his administration was soon mired in a financial depression. He retired to his home Lindenwald at Kinderhook in May 1841, traveling extensively through Europe in the 1840's and 50's. He died at Lindenwald and was buried at Kinderhook Cemetery, a rural graveyard outside the town. The tall gray obelisk to he and his wife is identifiable from the road. Behind it are four flat marble tablets, comprising the original grave marker for the president's wife **Hannah Hoes Van Buren** (March 8, 1783–Feb. 5, 1819). The inscriptions read *Sacred to the memory of Mrs. Hannah Van Buren, wife of Martin Van Buren, who departed this life the 5th of Feb. A.D. 1819 in the 36th year of her age. She was a sincere Christian, dutiful child, tender mother and most affectionate wife. Precious shall be the memory of her virtues.* These tablets and one with a Biblical quotation are beside a fourth which states they mark the tomb of the first person buried in the cemetery *"removed to this place from Albany 1855."* Yet other burials date much farther back, including the president's parents, **Abraham Van Buren** (Feb. 17, 1737–April 8, 1817) and **Maria Goes Hoes Van Alen Van Buren** (Jan. 1747–Feb. 6, 1817). Hannah Van Buren died in Albany, probably from pneumonia, but is believed to have been buried in Kinderhook Cemetery at that time. To whom the "first person interred" refers is unclear. The president's name, office and dates are on the obelisk. Kinderhook Cemetery, Kinderhook, NY.

9301. Van Cleef, Lee (Jan. 9, 1925–Dec. 16, 1989) New Jersey born actor, navy veteran of World War II, moved on to films from his theater group, usually cast as western villains with his sharp features and narrow, icy eyes (*High Noon, The Man Who Shot Liberty Valance*) but later known for several Sergio Leone spaghetti westerns with Clint Eastwood (*For A Few Dollars More; The Good, the Bad and the Ugly*) in the 1960's. Epitaph reads *Best of the bad.* Serenity, lot 156, Forest Lawn Hollywood Hills, Los Angeles.

9302. Van der Lubbe, Marinus (Jan. 13, 1909–Jan. 10, 1934) Dutch born Communist in Germany from 1933, protesting the new Third Reich and its chancellor. Found at the burning Reichstag February 27, 1933, he confessed under torture by the Gestapo and was convicted, then beheaded. The Reichstag fire gave the Nazi government a reason to declare martial law and employ increasingly brutal practices. Südfriedhof, Leipzig, Germany.

9303. Van Devanter, Lynda (May 7, 1947–Nov. 15, 2002) Army nurse from Arlington, Virginia, served in the operating room with the 71st Evacuation Hospital at Pleiku in Vietnam from 1969–70, and published a memoir of her experiences and their after effects, *Home Before Morning*, in 1983, the model for the later television series *China Beach*. The founding executive director of the Women's Project of the Vietnam Veterans of America 1979–84, she was the wife of Charles T. Buckley and a nursing supervisor at Reston Hospital upon her death at 55 in Herndon, Virginia, from systemic collagen vascular disease, which she attributed to exposure to Agent Orange. Chestnut Grove Cemetery, Herndon, VA.

9304. Van Doren, Carl (Sept. 10, 1885–July 18, 1950) Pulitzer Prize winning historian, editor and teacher. Ashes scattered at Wickshire, his home at Cornwall, CT.

9305. Van Doren, Mark (June 13, 1894–Dec. 10, 1972) Pulitzer Prize winning poet, editor and teacher, father of Charles, brother of Carl. Buried at Cornwall Hollow, CT.

9306. Van Druten, John (June 1, 1901–Dec. 19, 1957) Playwright penned *Voice of the Turtle* (1943) as well as the stage and screen hit *I Remember Mama* (1944). Block 1, unit 4, lot 16, Coachella Valley Cemetery, Coachella, CA.

9307. Van Dyke, W.S. "Woody" (Woodbridge Strong Van Dyke II, March 21, 1890–Feb. 5, 1943) Seattle born stylish film director at MGM in the 1930's, "One Take Woody" wrapped under budget and on time without his films suffering in quality. Directing from 1916, his works include *Trader Horn* (1931), *Tarzan the Ape Man* (1932), the Jeanette MacDonald–Nelson Eddy operettas, *Manhattan Melodrama* (1934), the *Thin Man* series, *San Francisco* (1936), *It's A Wonderful World* (1939) and *Journey For Margaret* (1942). Ill with cancer, he died in his Brentwood home in Los Angeles from an overdose of medication at 52. Columbarium of Sanctuary, niche 10202 (second from top, far right), Memorial Terrace, Great Mausoleum, Forest Lawn, Glendale, CA.

9308. Van Enger, Charles (Charles James Van Enger, Aug. 29, 1890–Jan. 4, 1980) Port Jervis, New York, born cinematographer 1920–1965. Works include *The Last of the Mohicans* (1920), *Salome* (1923), *The Phantom of the Opera* (1925), *Night Monster* (1942), *Sherlock Holmes Faces Death* (1943), *The Spider Woman* (1944), many Abbott and Costello films at Universal 1942–50 including *Abbott and Costello meet Frankenstein.* He died in Woodland Hills, California, at 89. Cremated at Pierce Bros. Chapel of the Pines Crematory. Ashes scattered at sea.

9309. Van Fleet, James (March 19, 1892–Sept. 24, 1992) Four star U.S. Army general led forces on D Day, at the Battle of the Bulge, and was credited by President Truman with driving the communist guerillas from postwar Greece, as well as holding the Chinese communists at the 38th Parallel in the Korean War. Retired 1953. He died at 100 in Polk City, Florida. Sec. 7, grave 8195-A, Arlington National Cemetery, Arlington, VA.

9310. Van Gogh, Vincent (March 30, 1853–July 29, 1890) Dutch painter with a distinctive, readily identifiable style utilizing swirls in both landscapes and portraits. He was also remembered for his mad acts such as sending his severed ear to his love, as well as for his botched suicide. He shot himself in the stomach at Auvers, France, having intended to shoot himself in the head. He slipped as the bullet fired and so suffered a lingering death. Buried beside his brother, their small stones along the wall, in the cemetery at Auvers-sur-Oise, north of Paris.

9311. Van Heusen, Jimmy (Edward C. Babcock, Jan. 26, 1913–Feb. 6, 1990) Composer from Syracuse, New York, scored many films, winning Oscars for *Swinging on a Star* (from *Going My Way* 1944) and *High Hopes* (from *A Hole in the Head* 1959). He also collaborated with James Burke and Sammy Cahn on many others. His plaque has a piano, musical notes and the epitaph *Swinging on a Star.* Sec. B-8, lot 63, Desert Memorial Park, Cathedral City (Palm Springs), CA.

9312. Van Meter, Homer (Dec. 3, 1905–Aug. 23, 1934) Henchman of John Dillinger, an ace machine gunner, took up with the Indiana bandit after Harry Pierpont and Charlie Mackley were imprisoned in Ohio in 1934. He took part in the shootout at the Little Bohemia Lodge in northern Wisconsin and participated in several bank robberies. On the FBI's most wanted list, he survived Dillinger by only a few weeks. Recognized on a street in downtown St. Paul, Minnesota, he was pursued into an alley, engaged in a gun battle with St. Paul police and was killed just as his more famous cohort had been in Chicago a month earlier. Van Meter's brother took the body back to Fort Wayne, where there was no room for him in the family plot, so he was buried in a single graves area, beneath a light rose-brown headstone. Sec. 4, block A, row 2, space 10, Lindenwood Cemetery, Fort Wayne, IN.

9313. Van Ronk, Dave (June 30, 1936–Feb. 10, 2002) Raspy voiced blues-folk vocalist influential in the folk music revival in New York in the early and mid 1960's, a mentor to Bob Dylan. Columbarium, First Presbyterian Church, Manhattan, N.Y.C.

9314. Van Sloan, Edward (Edward Van Sloun, Nov. 1, 1882–March 8, 1964) Character actor born in Minnesota of Dutch descent and raised in San Francisco, known for his all knowing professors, battling the supernatural in *Dracula* (both the New York stage run and the 1931 film, as Dr. Van Helsing, reprised in *Dracula's Daughter* 1936), *Frankenstein* (1931, as Dr. Waldman), *The Mummy* (1932, as Dr. Muller), less stellar characters in *Behind the Mask* (1932), *The Death Kiss* (1933), *The Crosby Case* (1934), and many smaller and bit roles through dozens of films of the 1930's and 40's. He retired to San Francisco by the late 1940's, where he died in his Stanyan St. home at 81, unmentioned in any papers including San Francisco. Cremated at Olivet Memorial Park, Colma, California, the ashes were sent for burial with those of his wife Myra (1960) in the Jackson-Roop lot of her family outside Philadelphia. There was no more room on the front of the stone for his name and dates, so a small headstone

for him was placed at the back of the larger monument on the lot, near a day-care playground at the edge of the cemetery. Boehm Dutch Reformed Church Cemetery, Blue Bell (northwest of Philadelphia), PA.

9315. Van Tien Dung (May 2, 1917–March 17, 2002) North Vietnamese general was Hanoi's military chief of staff by 1953, fought the French and the Americans and oversaw the fall of the south and Saigon in 1975, as chronicled in his memoir, *The Great Spring Victory*, considered a relatively objective and accurate account of the end of opposition to Communist rule there. Mai Dich Cemetery, Hanoi, Vietnam.

9316. Van Vechten, Carl (June 17, 1880–Dec. 21, 1964) Author whose writing, compared in style to Art Deco, chronicled the New York of the1920's in his novels. Ashes scattered over the Shakespeare Gardens in Manhattan's Central Park, N.Y.C.

9317. van Vogt, A. E. (Albert Elton van Vogt, April 26, 1912–Jan. 26, 2000) Science fiction writer of the 1930's forward. His works include *The Silkie,* the novella *The Weapon Shops of Isher,* and *The Rull.* Sec. F, tier 33, grave 85, Holy Cross Cemetery, Culver City, CA.

9318. Van Zandt, Townes (March 7, 1944–Jan. 1, 1977) Country singer and songwriter penned *Pancho and Lefty* (went to #1 in 1983), *If I Needed You,* many others. His hits were all recorded by others, though he made several albums on independent labels. Some of his ashes were laid beneath a headstone in the Van Zandt plot in Dido Cemetery, Dido (outside Fort Worth), TX.

9319. Van Zant, Ronnie (Jan. 15, 1948–Oct. 20, 1977) Lead singer and writer with the rock group Lynrd Skynrd died in the crash of their small plane at Gillsburg, Mississippi, along with band members **Steve Gaines** (born Sept. 14, 1949), guitarist, and his sister **Cassie** (Jan. 9, 1948), a back up singer. Van Zant was interred in a two tiered mausoleum at Jacksonville Memory Gardens, Orange Park (Jacksonville), Florida — the same cemetery as the Gaineses — until the June 29, 2000, disturbance of both his tomb and Steve Gaines's ashes. Gaines was re-interred in an undisclosed location there. Cassie is marked by a bench with her mother, behind the office. Van Zant was removed and reburied in an underground vault at the lot of his parents Lacy and Marion Van Zant in Riverside Memorial Park Cemetery, Jacksonville, FL.

9320. Vance, Clarice (Clara Ella Black, March 14, 1871–Aug. 24, 1961) Vaudeville singer known for her recordings (*I'm Wise, He's a Cousin of Mine* 1907), the Southern Songbird was a star from the 1890's to 1913. Appeared in *Daughters of the Night* (1924).She died in a mental hospital in Napa, California, from senility and cancer at 90. County grave sec., lot 31 (marker has only "31" on it), St. Helena Public Cemetery, St. Helena, CA.

9321. Vance, Cyrus R. (March 27, 1917–Jan. 12, 2002) Secretary of State under President Jimmy Carter

1977–1980, he resigned in April 1980 over the president's decision to attempt a military rescue of the hostages held in Tehran. Ill with Alzheimer's Disease, he died in New York at 84. Funeral at The Church of the Heavenly Rest in Manhattan. Sec. 64, grave 6551, Arlington National Cemetery, Arlington, VA.

9322. Vance, Dazzy (Arthur Charles Vance, March 4, 1891–Feb. 16, 1961) Pitcher with the Dodgers, first in the N.L. to lead strikeouts seven consecutive years 1922–28, the Dazzler was considered the finest pitcher to grace Ebbets Field; he threw a no hitter against the Phillies in 1924. MVP N.L. 1925. Hall of Fame 1955. Family monument, grave length slab, and bench. Sec. 4, Stage Stand Cemetery, Homosassa Springs, FL.

9323. Vance, Vivian (Vivian Roberta Jones, July 26, 1909–Aug. 17, 1979) Although she made a few films and was a busy stage actress, the Cherryvale, Kansas, native, later of Albuquerque, became indelibly stamped as Lucille Ball's perennial sidekick Ethel Mertz in *I Love Lucy* 1951–1957 and *The Lucy-Desi Comedy Hour* 1958–1960, reappearing as Viv on *The Lucy Show* 1962–65. Married to actor Philip Ober in the 1950's, she lived for years in Connecticut but died at her last home in Belvedere, California, from cancer at 70, though listed as 64, survived by her husband John Dodds. Cremated by the Neptune Society at Bahia Valley Memorial Park Crematory, Novato, Marin County, California. Her ashes were picked up August 28 and scattered by air at sea off Marin County.

9324. Vandegeer, Richard (Jan. 11, 1948–May 17, 1975) Helicopter pilot killed trying to rescue crew members of a merchant ship seized by the Khmer Rouge became the last name on the Vietnam Memorial (panel 01W, line 132). Not recovered until 1991, he was buried in October 2000. Sec. 66, grave 6027, Arlington National Cemetery, Arlington, VA.

9325. Vandenburg, Arthur (March 22, 1884–April 18, 1951) Republican senator from Michigan 1928–1951 was a major opponent of the New Deal in the 1930's and was discussed as a Republican presidential nominee but never received the nod. He did support the U.N. and NATO at the conclusion of World War II, though formerly a strict isolationist. Lot 45, block 2, grave 8, Oak Hill Cemetery, Grand Rapids, MI.

9326. Vanderbilt, Amy (July 22, 1908–Dec. 27, 1974) Syndicated columnist wrote *Amy Vanderbilt's Etiquette* 1954–1974. She also did several books. Buried under her married name, Kellar. Sumachs 55, Cemetery of the Evergreens, Brooklyn, N.Y.C.

9327. Vanderbilt, Consuelo (March 2, 1877–Dec. 6, 1964) Daughter of William Henry and Alva Vanderbilt Belmont was forced by her mother into a marriage with Winston Churchill's brother, the 9th Duke of Marlborough, thus sending much of their fortune to England and electing Alva "the most hated mother in America." Consuelo Vanderbilt Balsan,

noted on her stone as the mother of the 10th Duke of Marlborough, is in the same cemetery as Winston Churchill. St. Martin's Churchyard, Bladen, Oxfordshire.

9328. Vanderbilt, Cornelius (May 27, 1794–Jan. 4, 1877) New York steamboat and railroad tycoon first monopolized the Hudson River transportation by charging lower fares. The Commodore was a millionaire by 1847, continuing to drive out competitors. His philanthropy included donating a ship for use in the Civil War, refurbishing broken down vessels as warships, building Grand Central Station in Manhattan, creating thousands of jobs during the panic of 1873, and creating Vanderbilt University in Nashville, Tennessee. Upon his death his son William Henry inherited his empire. The Commodore was interred in the palatial family mausoleum in Moravian Cemetery on Staten Island. The cemetery dates to the early 18th century. The church was given fifty three and a half acres by the Vanderbilts, whose massive mausoleum is at the rear of the cemetery, carved from "living rock," commissioned by the Commodore and completed in 1886, nine years after his death. It is the largest family mausoleum in the United States. Twenty five Vanderbilts are entombed in the structure, situated on a thickly wooded, twenty two acre property. Extensive damage and disrepair has occurred over the past century. The fifteen foot gate to the Vanderbilt mausoleum, which fell off the hinges and killed a woman in 1967, is always locked and the isolated site has intermittently become a haven for vandals. Expensive stained glass has been removed and replaced with cement so that light no longer streams in, and the bushes and trees landscaped by Frederick Law Olmstead have become overgrown, where from the ornate vaulted entrance was once a clear view of the Atlantic. Moravian Cemetery, New Dorp, Staten Island, N.Y.C.

9329. Vanderbilt, Gloria Morgan (Aug. 23, 1904–Feb. 13, 1965) and **Thelma, Viscountess Furness** (Aug. 23, 1904–Jan. 29, 1970) Twin sisters known as the Magical Morgans. Gloria was the widow of Reginald Vanderbilt and lost a custody battle over the younger Gloria to her sister-in-law Gertrude Whitney, detailed in the book *Little Gloria, Happy at Last*. The sisters are buried together. Sec. D, lot 176, Holy Cross Cemetery, Culver City, CA.

9330. Vanderbilt, William Henry (May 8, 1821–Dec. 8, 1885) **and Descendants** Son of the Commodore inherited the family fortune and business interests. His brother, the wayward **Cornelius Jeremiah**, was left little by contrast and fatally shot himself in April 1882. William Henry suffered much public displeasure when he remarked "The public be damned" in October 1882 regarding their interest in one of his railroads and its service. The next year, having been snubbed as "new money" and denied a box at the Astor Theatre, he built and opened the New York Metropolitan Opera House. At his death in 1885 he was interred in the new $300,000 family mausoleum on Staten Island, with guards who checked every fifteen minutes to make sure the body was not stolen and held for ransom, as had been done with A.T. Stewart. **Cornelius Vanderbilt II** (Nov. 27, 1843–Sept. 12, 1899), who took over at the death of William Henry. Cornelius's son **Alfred Gwynne Vanderbilt** (1877–May 7, 1915) died when the *Lusitania* was sunk by a German torpedo in the Irish Sea. Eyewitness accounts laud him as having been selfless during the panic, helping others with their lifejackets before his death; some said his life-jacket, like many, had been hastily put on backwards, hastening his drowning. He was never recovered. Among the other noted Vanderbilts within are **George Washington Vanderbilt** (Nov. 14, 1862–March 6, 1914), founder of Biltmore Industries in North Carolina, **William Kissam Vanderbilt** (Dec. 12, 1849–July 22, 1920) and his son **William Kissam Vanderbilt Jr.** (Oct. 26, 1878–Jan. 8, 1944). Moravian Cemetery, New Dorp, Staten Island, N.Y.C.

9331. Vander Meer, Johnny (Nov. 2, 1914–Oct. 6, 1997) Left hander from Midland Park, N.J., with the Cincinnati Reds 1937–43 and 1946–49 threw back to back no-hitters, against the Boston Braves at Crosley Field on June 11 and against the Brooklyn Dodgers at Ebbets Field's first night game on June 15, 1938. He led the N.L. in strikeouts in 1941, '42 and '43. He died in Tampa at 82. Sec. J, block E, west space 15, Garden of Memories (adjacent Myrtle Hill Cemetery), Tampa, FL.

9332. Vander Pyl, Jean (Oct. 11, 1919–April 12, 1999) The voice of Wilma on TV's *The Flintstones* 1960–66 and later of Rosie the Robot and Mrs. Spacely on *The Jetsons* was the last of the original cast of the "modern stone age family" to die, from lung cancer at 79 in Dana Point, Orange County, California. Mass at Our Lady of Fatima Catholic Church, San Clemente. Her plaque has her picture, and the figure of Wilma Flintstone, with the epitaph *Traveling Mercy*. Sec. A, near statue, tier 34, grave 350, Ascension Cemetery, Lake Forest, near El Toro, CA.

9333. Vandross, Luther (April 20, 1951–July 1, 2005) New York born four time Grammy winning vocalist from 1981 known for romantic ballads combined rhythm and blues, soul and pop in *Here and Now, Any Love, Your Secret Love,* and his last LP, *Dance With My Father* (2003). He suffered a stroke in his Manhattan home April 16, 2003, and died two years later at 54 in John F. Kennedy Medical Center, Edison, New Jersey. Service at Frank E. Campbell mortuary and the Riverside Church, Manhattan. Block X, lot 123, sec. A, grave 3, George Washington Memorial Park, Paramus, NJ.

9334. Vanel, Charles (Aug. 21, 1892–April 15, 1989) French character actor in films 1920–1988, including *Le Salaire de la Peur* (1953), *To Catch A Thief* (1954), *Les Diaboliques* (1955, as the sly investigator), *Cadaveri Eccellenti* (1976). He was cremated and part of his ashes buried at Cimetiere Paysager de Mougins,

(provence of) Alpes Cote d-Azur (Maritimes), France. Part were scattered in the Mediterranean.

9335. Vann, Joey (Joseph Canzano, April 3, 1943–Feb. 28, 1984) Lead singer from Jersey City with the Duprees; they used the Glenn Miller sound on their ballads 1961–63, notably *You Belong to Me* (1962) and *Have You Heard, Gone With the Wind, My Own True Love.* McLaughlin mortuary, Jersey City. He died from a heart attack at 40. Monument with family name only, Sec. B, block 2, grave 53, Holy Cross Cemetery, North Arlington, NJ.

9336. Vanzetti, Bartolomeo *see* **Sacco and Vanzetti.**

9337. Varconi, Victor (Mihaly Varkonyi, March 31, 1891–June 16, 1976) Hungarian actor on stage and screen in Hungary and Germany before coming to America in continental parts in silent films. Among his appearances was as Pontius Pilate in DeMille's 1927 *King of Kings.* Others include *The Black Camel* (1931), etc. Sec. M, tier 6, grave 139, Calvary Cemetery, Santa Barbara, CA.

9338. Varden, Evelyn (June 12, 1893–July 11, 1958) Actress from Adair, Oklahoma, on stage and screen. specialized during her last decade in playing nosey and domineering neighbors and relatives. Stage roles ranged from Mrs. Gibbs in *Our Town* to *Candle in the Wind* and *Family Portrait.* Films include *Pinky* (1949), *Hilda Crane, Night of the Hunter* (1955) and *The Bad Seed* (1956). She died at her residence in New York City, survived by her husband, William J. Quinn. Ashes from the Frank E. Campbell mortuary to the residence at the Gorham Hotel, Manhattan.

9339. Varden, Norma (Jan. 20, 1898–Jan. 19, 1989) English born actress in many bubbly or snobbish matron roles played Jack Benny's mother in the 1950's TV series, the victim (in flashbacks) in *Witness for the Prosecution* (1957), many others (*Waterloo Bridge, Casablanca, Strangers on a Train*). She died at Santa Barbara a day before her 91st birthday. Cremated through Welch-Ryce-Haider mortuary. Room 3, group F, row 14, niche 74, Santa Barbara Cemetery mausoleum, Santa Barbara, CA.

9340. Varney, Jim (James Howard Varney, June 15, 1949–Feb. 10, 2000) Actor from Lexington, Kentucky, gained notoriety in commercials for various products by the 1980's as Ernest P. Worrell, the inept neighbor of the never seen Vern, recipient of his trademark line "Know what I mean, Vern?" Varney, trained in Shakespearian theatre, went on to do several *Ernest* films as well as *The Beverly Hillbillies* and *Daddy and Them.* He died at home in White House, Tennessee, from lung cancer at 50. Black upright stone with the masks of tragedy and comedy. Sec. C-1, Lexington Cemetery, Lexington, KY.

9341. Varotta, Joseph (1916–June 1, 1921) Five year old boy kidnapped from in front of his home on E. 13th St., Manhattan, on May 24, 1921, by Black Hand members demanding ransom. The money could not be raised, and the child's body washed ashore in the Hudson River at Piermont, New York, June 11, 1921. Three Black Handers were convicted, though Governor Al Smith commuted their death sentences to life in prison. The child's stone tells the story: *Here rest the remains of Joseph Varotta, age 5 years, who was kidnapped by the Blackhands at 354 East 13th St., New York, May 24, 1921, was found June 11, 1921, at Piermont, New York.* Sec. 51, plot 38, grave 8, (1st) Calvary Cemetery, Woodside, Queens, N.Y.C.

9342. Varsi, Diane (Feb. 23, 1938–Nov. 19, 1992) Blonde actress from San Mateo, California, nominated for an Oscar at 19 for her role as Alison MacKenzie in *Peyton Place* (1957). Other films include *Ten North Frederick* and *Compulsion* before she walked out on her contract with Fox and moved to Vermont. She re-appeared in a few films in the 1960's and 70's, and died in Los Angeles from respiratory failure and lyme disease at 54. Marked by a tree, right of Martha Ames Black. Sec. M, Mt. Tamalpais Cemetery, San Rafael, CA.

9343. Vassar, Matthew (April 29, 1792–June 23, 1868) English born businessman ran a brewery and other businesses and speculated in land in the U.S. Founder of Vassar Women's College (1861). Monument with an urn shaped dome. Sec. L, Poughkeepsie Rural Cemetery, Poughkeepsie, NY.

9344. Vassar, Queenie (Oct. 28, 1870–Sept. 11, 1960) Stage actress born in Glasgow, Scotland, married to actor Joseph Cawthorn (*q.v.*). Her few film appearances were as unpleasant characters: as Grandma in *The Primrose Path* (1940) and as the head of the thieves in *None But the Lonely Heart* (1944). Entombed with Cawthorn. Abbey of the Psalms/Hollywood Forever Mausoleum, Sanctuary of Refuge, crypt 2085, Hollywood Forever Cemetery, Hollywood (Los Angeles), CA.

9345. Vaughan, Arky (Joseph Floyd Vaughn, March 9, 1912–Aug. 30, 1952) Shortstop from Clifty, Arkansas. His lifetime batting average of .318 was second only to Honus Wagner among shortstops. He hit .385 for the Pirates in 1935, unequalled in the N.L. Vaughn drowned at 40 with a friend when their boat capsized in Lost Lake near Eagleville, California, in the northeast corner of the state. Hall of Fame 1985. Eagleville Community Cemetery, Eagleville, CA.

9346. Vaughan, Frankie (Francis Abelson, Feb. 3, 1928–Sept. 16, 1999) Liverpool born crooner had hits in the late 1950's with *Give Me the Moonlight, The Green Door, Kisses Sweeter Than Wine* and *Garden of Eden* and appeared in the 1960 film *Let's Make Love.* He died at his home High Wycombe from a heart related ailment and was buried the same day. Rose brown stone in cement covered area. Bushey Jewish Cemetery, Bushey, Hertfordshire.

9347. Vaughan, Sarah (March 27, 1924–April 3, 1990) Jazz vocalist from Newark began with singing *Body and Soul* at the Apollo Theatre in Harlem in 1942, launching a long and fruitful recording and concert career. Mainstream hits included *Broken Hearted Melody* (1954), but she was best known for her jazz numbers with a complete control over her voice, maintaining range and pitch. She died from cancer in the San Fernando Valley north of Los Angeles at 66. Her polished black upright stone has a piano etched on it and the name inscribed *Sassy Sarah Vaughan.* Northeast corner Crestwood 2, Glendale Cemetery, Bloomfield, NJ.

9348. Vaughan, Stevie Ray (Stephen Ray Vaughan, Oct. 3, 1954–Aug. 27, 1990) Blues guitarist with trademark black felt hat died in a helicopter crash shortly after headlining a concert with Eric Clapton and Robert Cary. The burial was attended by more than a thousand mourners. His long bronze plaque bears a shining star and the sentiment *Thank You … for all the love you passed our way.* At first in sec. 25, lot 194, space 4, he was moved to the Vaughan Estates near sec. 11, Laurel Land Memorial Park, Dallas, TX.

9349. Vaughn, Alberta (July 27, 1904–April 26, 1992) Silent screen and talkies comedienne from Ashland, Kentucky, a Mack Sennett bathing beauty and WAMPAS Baby Star (1924), appeared in *Rough and Ready, Nip and Tuck, The Going of Cumming, The Fast Male, The Big Charade,* etc., retiring in 1936. Unmarked. Block J, sec. 9994, lot 3, Pierce Bros. Valhalla Memorial Park, North Hollywood, CA.

9350. Vaughn, Billy (April 13, 1919–Sept. 26, 1991) Kentucky born vocalist, bandleader and composer best known for *Melody of Love* (1955) and *Sail Along Silvery Moon.* Sec. 11, lot 437, Oak Hill Memorial Park, Escondido, CA.

9351. Vaughn, Hilda (Hilda W. Strouse, Dec. 27, 1898–Dec. 28, 1957) Deadpan actress from Baltimore in films 1929–40, including *Susan Lennox, Her Fall and Rise* (1931), *Ladies of the Big House, The Phantom of Crestwood* (1932, as Karen Morley's maid), *Dinner at Eight* (1933, as Jean Harlow's opportunistic maid), *Anne of Green Gables, Chasing Yesterday* (1934), *Nothing Sacred* (1937), *Charlie Chan at the Wax Museum* (1940). She died in Baltimore, listed as Hilda Strouse, the day after her 59th birthday. Oheb Shalom Cemetery, 6130 O'Donnell St., Baltimore, MD.

9352. Veblen, Thorstein (July 30, 1857–Aug. 3, 1929) American economist, author of *The Theory of the Leisure Class* (1899), so enraged the business community that he was forced to resign his post at the University of Chicago. He later taught at Stanford and authored several more books. He died in his cabin retreat at Palo Alto, California. Ashes scattered at sea.

9353. Veeck, Bill (Feb. 9, 1914–Jan. 2, 1986) Baseball impresario enjoyed a colorful career as owner and promoter of the Cleveland Indians, the St. Louis Browns and the Chicago White Sox (twice, from 1959–61 and 1975–80, when he kept the team from leaving the city). Veeck, a veteran who lost a leg in World War II, was a legend at staging crowd pleasing events, the most memorable on August 19, 1951, when he signed midget Eddie Gaedel for $100 to bat once for the losing Browns against the Detroit Tigers. The

3'6" batter was walked on four high pitches. Veeck authored two memoirs, *Veeck as in Wreck* and *The Hustler's Handbook*. He died from a heart attack at 71 in Masonic Medical Center in Chicago, where he had returned to live after several years in Easton, Maryland. A memorial service was held at St. Thomas the Apostle Church in Chicago. He donated his body to science at the Masonic Medical Center. His ashes were later scattered on consecrated ground by his wife and a priest at Oakwoods Cemetery, Chicago, IL.

9354. Veidt, Conrad (Jan. 22, 1893–April 3, 1943) Lean star of the German cinema of the 1920's in several classics: as Cesare the somnambulist in *The Cabinet of Dr. Caligari* (1919), *The Hands of Orlac*, *Waxworks* and *The Student of Prague*. In Hollywood in *The Beloved Rogue* (1926) and *The Man Who Laughs* (1928), he returned briefly to Germany, fled the Nazi regime and worked in England through the 1930's (*F.P.1.* 1933, *Jew Suss* 1934, *Dark Journey* 1937) before coming to America late in the decade, where for the last few years of his life he portrayed assorted villains (Jaffar in *The Thief of Baghdad*), primarily sinister German agents and officers (*Escape*, *Whistling in the Dark*, *A Woman's Face*, *All Through the Night* and *Casablanca*, as Major Strasser). He died a few months after *Casablanca*'s release from a heart attack at 50 while playing golf. The ashes were interred at Hollywood Memorial Park Cemetery until 1950, when his wife Lily had them removed and reinterred in unit 6, tier AC, col. A, niche 1, main mausoleum, Ferncliff Cemetery, Hartsdale, New York. In December 1980, after Lily Veidt's death, they were removed, mixed with her ashes and sent to her nephew in Los Angeles. He in turn turned them over to a Veidt enthusiast in Sacramento, who in turn relinquished them when in November 1997 as the Conrad Veidt Society organized the purchase of a niche for the mixed inurned ashes of he and his wife, formally placed at a dedication ceremony April 3, 1998. First floor columbarium off Cloisters, Golders Green Crematorium, north London.

9355. Velázquez, Consuelo (Aug. 21, 1916–Jan. 22, 2005) Mexican composer of many popular tunes best known for *Bésame Mucho*, translated into over thirty languages and recorded all over the world. She died at 88 in Mexico City. Cremated in Panteón Español. Ashes interred Iglesia de Santo Tomás Moro, Mexico City.

9356. Velez, Lupe (Guadeloupe Velez de Villalobos, July 18, 1908–Dec. 14, 1944) The Mexican Spitfire, petite actress-singer-comedienne in films from 1926, known for her series of *Mexican Spitfire* comedies with Leon Errol and her often stormy marriage to Johnny Weissmuller. Her secretary found her in her bed, clad in pajamas and carefully propped up on pillows, dead from an overdose of sleeping pills at 36. A suicide note accused her French lover of planning to marry her out of pity because she was pregnant. Tomb with a marble angel in an arch at its head. Panteon Delores Cemetery, Mexico City, Mexico.

9357. Venable, Evelyn (Oct. 18, 1913–Nov. 16, 1993) Cincinnati born actress in films of the 1930's with a notably deep voice (*Death Takes a Holiday* 1934, as Grazia; *Mrs. Wiggs of the Cabbage Patch* 1934, *Alice Adams* 1935). Married to cinematographer Hal Mohr. A lifelong vegetarian, she died at Lost Falls, Idaho, at 80. Cremated through English chapel at Coeur D'Alene. Ashes scattered over the mountains in Idaho.

9358. Venuti, Joe (Sept. 16, 1903–Aug. 14, 1978) Jazz violinist from New Orleans prominent in the 1920's recorded with Paul Whiteman, Benny Goodman and extensively on his own. Rediscovered in his last years, he was touring jazz festivals and nightclubs up to 1977, the year before his death in Seattle at 74. Sec. 27, range 5, lot 59, Holy Cross Cemetery, Yeadon, Philadelphia, PA.

9359. Vera-Ellen (Vera Ellen Westmeyer Rohe, Feb. 16, 1921–Aug. 30, 1981) Cincinnati born singer and dancer, former Radio City Rockette, in films of the 1940's and 50's. Films include *On the Town* and *Love Happy* (1949), *Three Little Words* (1950) and *White Christmas* (1954). She died from cancer at 60. Her plaque has the white silhouette of a ballerina beside her name and dates. Roselawn, lot 188, grave B, Glen Haven Memorial Park, Sylmar, CA.

9360. Verdi, Giuseppe (Oct. 10, 1813–Jan. 27, 1901) Italian composer from Roncole studied at Milan, composed *Umberto*, *Nabucco*, *I Lombardi* and *Ernani* in the 1839–1844 period, after which the operas established him as the foremost Italian composer. His more famous works of later years were *Il Trovatore* and *La Traviata* (1852), the more dramatic *Aida* (1871), *Monzoni Requiem* (1874), *Otello* (1887) and *Falstaff* (1893). He suffered a stroke at the Grand Hotel in Milan January 21, 1901 and died there six days later. Buried in the Cimitero Monumentale, he was soon removed and reburied, inside and marked by a tablet in the floor, at his home he established for retired musicians. Casa di Riposa, Verdi estate, Milan.

9361. Verdon, Gwen (Jan. 13, 1925–Oct. 18, 2000) Dancer-actress from Culver City, California, gained fame on Broadway, winning Tonys for *Can-Can* (1953), as Lola in *Damn Yankees* (1955, reprised on film in 1958), *New Girl in Town* (1957) and *Redhead* (1959). Other stage triumphs were *Sweet Charity* (1966) and as Roxie Hart in *Chicago* (1975). From 1960 she was married to Bob Fosse, who choreographed her dances in most of her musicals; though they later separated, she was with him when he died on a Washington street during a revival of *Sweet Charity* in 1987. Other than *Damn Yankees*, her few films include *The Cotton Club*, *Cocoon*, and *Marvin's Room*. She died in her sleep at the home of her daughter in Woodstock, Vermont. Cremated by Cabot mortuary, there, the ashes were taken to New York City.

9362. Verlaine, Paul (Paul Marie Verlaine, March 30, 1844–Jan. 8, 1896) French symbolist poet whose life ranged from bohemia to fervent Catholicism, celebrated for his lyricism. An alcoholic, he died in a public infirmary at 51. Div. 20, Batignolles Cemetery, Paris.

9363. Vermeer, Jan (Johannes Vermeer van Delft, Oct. 30, 1632–Dec. 15, 1675) Dutch genre artist, the "painter of light" produced sensitive and poetic figures in interiors with detail (*The Procuress, The Milkmaid, Woman With a Water Jug, Young Woman Standing at a Virginal, The Love Letter*). A flat plaque in the floor marks the vicinity of his grave in his mother-in-law's family vault. Oude Kerk (Old Church), Delft, Holland (The Netherlands).

9364. Verne, Jules (Feb. 8, 1828–March 24, 1905) French novelist like H.G. Wells predicted varied fantastic means of transportation. Verne's fantasies came much closer to later fact. Written in the 1860's and 70's, *Around the World in Eighty Days, Five Weeks in a Balloon, A Journey to the Center of the Earth* and particularly *From the Earth to the Moon* and *Twenty Thousand Leagues Under the Sea* foresaw the future. The last of his works published in his lifetime was *Master of the World* in 1904. He spent his final years at 44 Boulevard Longueville in Amiens, where he died at 78 from diabetes and other ailments. He was buried at Amiens in a tomb designed in 1907 by his son Michael and done by Albert Roze. It depicts Verne with his hair tossed by the wind, breaking free of the tomb in a magnificent sweep. Above it are cut the words *Jules Verne — Onward to Immortality and Youth.* Cimitiere de la Madeleine, Amiens, France.

9365. Verne, Kaaren (April 6, 1918–Dec. 23, 1967) German leading lady in Hollywood from 1940 in *King's Row* (1941), *All Through the Night* (1942), *Sherlock Holmes and the Secret Weapon* (1942), *The Seventh Cross* (1944), *Ship of Fools* (1965). Married to actor Peter Lorre 1942–1950, and to businessman James Powers at the time of her death at 52, a suicide. She took an overdose of Phenobarbital and ethanol in her Hollywood home, slit her wrists and got into the bathtub, where she drowned (the actual listed cause of death) at 49. Her flat plaque lists her name with the American spelling *Karen.* Powers lot, block 49, range 14, lot 11, grave 6, Calvary Cemetery, St. Paul, MN.

9366. Verneuil, Henri (Achod Malakian, Oct. 15, 1920–Jan. 11, 2002) Oscar nominated Turkish born director and writer of French films from 1952. Cimetiere St. Pierre, Marseille, Bouches-du-Rhone (13), France.

9367. Vernon, Bobby (March 9, 1897–June 28, 1939) Chicago born stage and screen writer and comedian in comedy shorts of the silent screen, including several with Mack Sennett and Triangle teaming him with Gloria Swanson and a dog named Teddy (*Teddy at the Throttle* 1917). Son of actress Dorothy Vernon. He died from a heart attack at 42. Sanctuary of Harmony, crypt 8174, Gardenia Terrace, Great Mausoleum, Forest Lawn, Glendale, CA.

9368. Vernon, Dorothy (Nov. 11, 1875–Oct. 28, 1970) Screen actress in many comedies including the Three Stooges' first Columbia short *Woman Haters* (1934). Mother of comedian Bobby Vernon. Sec. 13 (Pineland), lot 518, Hollywood Forever Cemetery, Hollywood (Los Angeles), CA.

9369. Vernon, Inez Jolivet (c. July 19, 1915) Sister of actress Rita Jolivet, a violinist who had played with the Met, was found by the owner of her apartment at 31 West Eleventh St., Manhattan, dressed in black and kneeling at the foot of her bed with her head in her hands and her right temple shattered by a bullet from an automatic pistol, found under the body. It was ruled a suicide and that she had been dead three days. She was planning on going to Europe and had her trunks ready and purchases made, but had been depressed since the death of her husband of eight years, film manufacturer **George L. Vernon**, on the *Lusitania* May 7, in the company of Charles Frohman and her sister Rita Jolivet, who survived the disaster. Winterbottom and Sons mortuary, 75 West 47th St., Manhattan. Initially to be buried at Marble Cemetery, that is crossed out on the death certificate in place of cremation at New York–New Jersey Crematory July 25.

9370. Vernon, Jackie (March 29, 1924–Nov. 10, 1987) New York born comedian in nightclubs and on TV. Ashes scattered at sea.

9371. Vernon, John (Adolphus Raymundus Vernon Agopsowicz, Feb. 24, 1932–Feb. 1, 2005) Canadian actor from Zehner, Saskatchewan, with piercing eyes, on stage decades before he landed in films as usually villainous authority figures, best known as Dean Wormer in *Animal House* (1978), as well as *Point Blank* (1967), *Topaz* (1969), *Dirty Harry* (1971, as the mayor), *The Outlaw Josie Wales* (1976, the head bounty hunter). He died in Van Nuys, California, from a heart ailment at 72. Cremated through Praisewater-Meyer-Mitchell mortuary. Ashes February 8 to family in Van Nuys.

9372. Vernon, Wally (May 27, 1904–March 7, 1970) Actor and frequent comic in many films from the 1930's (the postman in *He Walked by Night*) died at 65 after he was struck by a car in a hit and run accident. Vale of Peace, lot 4897, grave 3, Forest Lawn Hollywood Hills, Los Angeles.

9373. Versace, Gianni (Dec. 2, 1946–July 15, 1997) Acclaimed Italian fashion designer shot in the head without warning or motive in front of his Miami Beach home. The subsequent nationwide hunt for the murderer, **Andrew Cunanan** (b. Aug. 31, 1969) ended after eight days when he was found shot to death, a suicide, on a houseboat off Miami July 23. Versace's ashes were taken to a family vault at Moltrasio near Lake Como, Italy. Cunanan was cremated in Fort Lauderdale. Niche 24-C, Holy Rosary Chapel, Holy Cross Cemetery, San Diego, CA.

9374. Vestine, Henry (Dec. 25, 1944–Oct. 20, 1997) Guitarist and a founding member of Canned

Heat in the 1960's, died in Paris at 52. Oak Hill Cemetery, Eugene, OR.

9375. Vetsera, Marie (Mary), Baroness *see* **Rudolf.**

9376. Vetter, David (Sept. 21, 1971–Feb. 22, 1984) Born with no immune system and forced to wear a space suit type garment to protect him from germs, he was known as the Boy in the Plastic Bubble. Flat plaque with *He never touched the world but the world touched him* later replaced by upright stone, family monument. Conroe Cemetery, Conroe, TX.

9377. Vian, Boris (March 10, 1920–June 23, 1959) French writer, poet, musician and vocalist whose works include *J'irai Ctacher sur vos Tombes* (*I Shall Spit on Your Graves*), *L'Automne á Pékin, Les Morts ont tous la Même Peau, Chroniques de Jazz.* He died from a heart attack at 39. Unmarked. Cimitiére de Ville d'Avray, Hauts de Seine, France.

9378. "Vicious, Sid" (John Simon Ritchie, May 10, 1957–Feb. 2, 1979) English born bass player with the Sex Pistols from 1977 stabbed to death his companion and fellow drug seeker **Nancy Spungen** (Nancy Laura Spungen, Feb. 27, 1958–Oct. 12, 1978) at the Chelsea Hotel in Manhattan October 12, 1978. Arrested for murder, he was bailed out, and died from "acute intravenous narcotism" less than four months later at 63 Bank St., Manhattan. Cremated at Garden State Crematory February 7 through Walter B. Cooke mortuary, 234 8th Ave. Ashes returned to his mother Anne Beverly, London, and reportedly scattered on Spungen's grave (they refused his burial there). Flat plaque along walk, sec. B-B, King David Memorial Park, Bensalem, PA.

9379. Vickers, Martha (Martha MacVicar, May 28, 1925–Nov 2, 1971) Model first on film at Universal as a murder victim in *Frankenstein Meets the Wolfman*, ailing patient in *Captive Wild Woman* (both 1943), student in *The Mummy's Ghost* (1944) made memorable her portrayal of the seductive younger sister Carmen Sternwood in *The Big Sleep* (1946). In films to 1960. Three times divorced, first from Mickey Rooney in 1951. She died at 46 from cancer and was buried under her last married name Rojas. Block IJ, sec. 10648, lot 2, Valhalla Memorial Park, North Hollywood, CA.

9380. Victor, Henry (Oct. 2, 1892–May 15, 1945) Tall British born lead in England from silents switched to character parts with his German accent. In films in the U.S. including *Freaks* (1932), *The Mortal Storm* (1940), *To Be or Not to Be* (1942) and *Sherlock Holmes and the Secret Weapon* (1942), he died from a stroke or brain tumor at 52. Cremated at Pierce Brothers Chapel of the Pines, Los Angeles. Ground plaque. Sec. F, lot 225, space 2, Oakwood Memorial Park, Chatsworth, CA.

9381. Victor, Kathrin aka **Kathrin Leichliter** (Katena Ktenavea, Aug. 18, 1923–Oct. 22, 2004) New York born actress in Jerry Warren's low budget horror movies 1953–66 and sporadically afterward, at first as

Katina Vea, in *Mesa of Lost Women, Teenage Zombies, Cape Canaveral Monster, Creature of the Walking Dead, House of Black Death,* etc. She worked later in animation. Buried under the name Leichliter. Hillside sec., lot 6432, space 3, Forest Lawn Hollywood Hills, Los Angeles.

9382. Victoria (May 24, 1819–Jan. 22, 1901) Queen of England, Scotland and Ireland from 1837 until her death, ascending just as England became the greatest power in Europe and reigning through the long period of colonialism and expansion around the world. The period of stiff social customs, both quaint and intolerant, that marked much of 19th century England, has come to be referred to as Victorian, encompassing three quarters of a century, eighteen U.S. Presidents, and several generations. When her husband Albert died in 1861, she entered a long period of mourning that was not overcome until her Golden Jubilee in 1887. She left off keeping her diary on January 14, 1901, for the first time in sixty-nine years and, with her numerous descendants around her, died eight days later at Osborne House near Cowles on the Isle of Wight. Dressed all in white with her wedding veil over her face, after a wide public tribute she was interred February 4 in the mausoleum at Frogmore, where the words *Vale desideratissime (Farewell most beloved. Here at length I shall rest with thee. In Christ I shall rise again)* had been ordered placed over the door upon Albert's death forty years earlier. The recumbent white figure of Victoria done at that time was located at Windsor, where it had been walled up for security since 1863, and placed over her, next to the prone sculpture of Albert over his tomb. Open to visitors only on a specified date during the year. Royal Mausoleum, Frogmore, Windsor.

9383. Vidal, Henri (Nov. 26, 1919–Dec. 10, 1959) Rugged French leading man in films from 1941, best known for the Italian production *Fabiola* (1948). Married to French actress Michele Morgan. He died from a heart attack at 40. Buried at Pontgibaud, France.

9384. Vidor, Charles (July 27, 1900–June 4, 1959) Hungarian director from Budapest worked at UFA in Berlin before coming to America in 1924. Films range from *The Double Door* (1934) to *Gilda* (1946). He died in Austria while shooting *Song Without End.* Married to Harry Warner's daughter Doris, he was interred in the Harry Warner mausoleum, sec. D, Home of Peace Memorial Park, east Los Angeles.

9385. Vidor, Florence (July 23, 1895–Nov. 3, 1977) Silent screen star married to King Vidor 1915–23 appeared in the sophisticated light films of Ernst Lubitsch and Mal St. Clair, ending her career after one 1929 talkie *Chinatown Nights.* She died 48 years later in Pacific Palisades. Cremated through Memory Garden Cemetery, Brea, California, her ashes were later returned to the family and (reportedly) scattered at sea.

9386. Vidor, King (Feb. 8, 1894–Nov. 1, 1982) Director of *The Big Parade* (1925), *The Crowd* (1928),

The Champ (1931), *Our Daily Bread* (1934) worked up to 1980, when he made a thirty minute documentary on Andrew Wyeth. His 1967 research on the William Desmond Taylor murder case led to *A Cast of Killers* published in 1986. He died at 88 from heart failure at his home, Willow Creek Ranch, in the Diabolos mountains just west of Paso Robles, California. A memorial service was held at the home of his long time close friend, actress Colleen Moore, at Paso Robles. Cremated at the Chapel of the Roses in Atascadero, through Kuehl-Nicolay mortuary, the ashes were returned to his grandson for reported scattering or burial at his at Willow Creek Ranch.

9387. Viertel, Berthold *see* **Salka Viertel.**

9388. Viertel, Salka Steurmann (1889–Oct. 20, 1978) Polish born actress and writer, wife of Swedish director **Berthold Viertel** (June 28, 1885–Sept. 24, 1953) collaborated on the screenplays of several of Garbo's Hollywood films of the 1930's (and appeared with her in the German version of *Anna Christie*). Parents of writer Peter Viertel. He returned to Europe and died in Vienna. Gruppe O, reihe 1, nummer 104, Central Cemetery (Zentral Friedhof), Vienna. Salka Viertel stayed in Los Angeles until her later years and died in Switzerland. Evangelischel churchyard, Klosters, Switzerland.

9389. Vigran, Herb (June 5, 1910–Nov 29, 1986) All purpose comedic character actor in films ranging from *Stranger on the 3rd Floor* (1940) to *Angel in My Pocket* (1968) and much TV through the 50's and 60's, including several *I Love Lucy* episodes. Ashes scattered.

9390. Villa, Pancho (Doroteo Arango, June 5, 1878–July 20, 1923) Mexican bandit and revolutionary was a Robin Hood type folk hero and social reform advocate. A fugitive wanted for murder since 1894, he backed the reform government of Madero over Diaz in 1911. In 1913 he joined Venustiano Carranza in a revolt against General Huerta, later breaking with Carranza and occupying Mexico City with Emilio Zapata. In 1915 he withdrew to Chihuahua, where guerilla raids into New Mexico led President Wilson to send General Pershing looking for him in 1916. After Carranza was killed in 1920 he was given amnesty and lived in retirement until assassinated at Parral by supporters of Carranza's General Obregon. He was not taken to the ornate mausoleum he had purchased at Chihuahua City but to a grave at Parral, where in 1926 his body was unearthed and his skull stolen.

9391. Villard, Henry (April 10, 1835–Nov. 12, 1900) German born journalist in America became president of the Northern Pacific Railroad and owner of the *New York Evening Post*. He died at Thorwood, Dobbs Ferry, New York. His monument is by Karl Bitter, of a sculpted laborer with a sledge hammer and anvil, resting wearily against an arched wall. It may signify his railroad development; on the rear is a bronze cameo profile of him. His five year old son **Hilgard**, who drove the golden spike in 1883, is also buried here, as is his son **Oswald Villard** (March 13, 1872–

Oct. 1, 1949), who did editorials for the *New York Post* 1897–1918, owned the *Nation* 1918–1932 and was a founder of the NAACP in 1910. Their lot, in view of their home at Dobbs Ferry, is not far from another famous German immigrant, Carl Schurz. Westminster sec. 62, Sleepy Hollow Cemetery, Tarrytown, NY.

9392. Villechaize, Herve (April 23, 1943–Sept. 4, 1993) 3'11" French actor best known as the comic sidekick Tattoo on the TV series *Fantasy Island* in the 1970's and 1980's. He died at 50 in North Hollywood from a self inflicted gunshot wound to the chest. Ashes buried at sea off the Los Angeles coast by the Neptune Society September 14, 1993.

9393. Vincent, Gene (Eugene Vincent Craddock, Feb. 11, 1935–Oct. 12, 1971) Rock and roll star of the late 1950's had his biggest hit with *Be-Bop-a-Lula* in 1958. In the accident in London two years later which killed Eddie Cochran, he was badly injured and later had a leg amputated. On his plaque is a bar of music and a picture of him, microphone in hand. Garden of Repose, A-91, Eternal Valley Memorial Park, Newhall, CA.

9394. Vincent, Strong (June 17, 1837–July 7, 1863) Union Brigadier general killed at Gettysburg holding Little Round Top, as noted on his marker. Circular lot, sec. 1, lot 6, Erie Cemetery, Erie, PA.

9395. Vine, Dave (1890–April 17, 1955) Vaudeville and burlesque performer for over thirty five years on the RKO and Pantages circuits. Father of performer **Billy Vine** (Dec. 23, 1914–Feb. 10, 1958). Billy is entombed in unit 1, tier A, crypt 12; Dave in unit 7, private alcove N, tier A, crypt 52, main mausoleum, Ferncliff Cemetery, Hartsdale, NY.

9396. Vinson, Fred (Frederick Moore Vinson, Jan. 22, 1890–Sept. 8, 1953) Former Kentucky congressman, judge and Secretary of the Treasury under Truman 1945–46 was appointed Chief Justice of the Supreme Court in 1946, succeeding Harlan Fiske Stone. He was a liberal constructionist in civil rights matters but felt the court should refrain from intervening between the legislative and executive branches. He died in Washington, D.C. Monument on a hillside above a curve in the drive, Pine Hill Cemetery, Louisa, KY.

9397. Vinson, Gary (Robert Gary Vinson, Oct. 22, 1936–Oct. 15, 1984) TV actor in *The Roaring Twenties* 1960–62 and as Christy in *McHale's Navy* 1962–66, died from a self inflicted gunshot wound at 47. Cremated by Angeles Abbey, Compton, California. Ashes reportedly scattered at sea.

9398. Vinson, Helen (Helen Rulfs, Sept. 17, 1905–Oct. 7, 1999) Actress from Beaumont, Texas, in some 40 films from 1932–1945, including *I Am A Fugitive From A Chain Gang (1932), The Power and the Glory* (1933), *The Kennel Murder Case, In Name Only* (1939), and *The Thin Man Goes Home* (1945), her last. Married for a time to tennis pro Fred Perry; her last married name was Hardenbrook. She died at 94 in the Carol Woods Retirement Center, Chapel Hill,

North Carolina. Cremated through Walker mortuary there, the ashes were sent for burial with the Rulfs beneath a flush marker listing her real and stage names. Second addition, lot 54, Oak Grove Cemetery, Nacogdoches, TX.

9399. Vinton, Victoria (Aug. 23, 1912–found June 12, 1980) New Jersey born dancer and actress in films of the 1930's and 40's, usually in bit parts other than B westerns (*Pals of the Prairie, The St. Louis Kid, Cheyenne Tornado, Ambush Valley, Vengeance of Rannah, The Singing Buckaroo*). Found by her son Victor Yates, she was a suicide at 67 from an overdose of barbiturates. Gardens of Victory, lawn crypt 600-B, Forest Lawn Hollywood Hills, Los Angeles.

9400. Virgilio, Nicholas A. (June 28, 1928–Jan. 3, 1989) Acclaimed Haiku poet. His monument forms a lectern at the top, on which is inscribed (on three lines) *Lily:/ out of the water... / out of itself.* 125A Ridge Lawn, Harleigh Cemetery, Camden, NJ.

9401. Visaroff, Michael (Nov. 18, 1892–Feb. 27, 1951) Russian born actor familiar as the mustached villager of the Carpathian Mountains, replete with long pipe and ominous warnings of vampires, in *Dracula* (1931) and *Mark of the Vampire* (1935). Married to actress **Nina Visaroff** (c. 1888–Dec. 14, 1938). He died from pneumonia. Beth Olam Mausoleum/Hall of Solomon; she is in corridor P/9, crypt 131; he is in corridor M-5, crypt 2231, Beth Olam Cemetery adjacent Hollywood Forever Cemetery, Hollywood (Los Angeles), CA.

9402. Visconti, Luchino (Nov. 2, 1906–March 17, 1976) Italian stage and screen director and screenwriter also directed opera, working with Maria Callas and others. He wrote and directed *Rocco e i suoi fratelli* (Rocco and His Brothers, 1960), *Gottopardo (The Leopard*, 1963), *La Caduta degli dei* (The Damned, 1969), *Morte a Venezia* (*A Death in Venice*, 1971), *Gruppo di famiglia in un interno* (Conversation Piece, 1975). His ashes are buried in the park of the villa where he spent his last days, on the Island of Ischia in the Bay of Naples, Italy.

9403. Viterelli, Joe (March 10, 1941–Jan. 28, 2004) Bronx born heavy-set actor for the last fourteen years of his life, typed as gangsters from his first film at 49, *State of Grace* (1990) and subsequently in *Mobsters, Ruby, The Firm, Bullets Over Broadway, Analyze This* (and the sequel, *Analyze That*), *Mickey Blue Eyes, A Walk in the Park, Shallow Hal, Serving Sara*. He died in Las Vegas of a stomach hemorrhage at 62. Sec. BB, tier 48, grave 56, Holy Cross Cemetery, Culver City, CA.

9404. Vivaldi, Antonio (March 4, 1678–buried July 28, 1741) Italian composer from Venice was a major figure in Baroque music and the development of the concerto, a primary influence on Bach. Among his best known works, including many violin compositions, was *The Gloria Mass*. He died a pauper in Vienna, at Satler's house by the Karner gate, St. Stephen's Parish, and was interred in the "Hospital

Burial Ground." The house, situated between Ring Karntnerstrasse, Krugerstrasse and Walfischgasse, was demolished in 1858, and the burial ground taken over, when work was started on Ringstrasse. There is a plaque near St. Charles Church.

9405. Vivyan, John (May 31, 1915–Dec. 20, 1983) TV star of *Mr. Lucky* 1959–60 appeared sporadically in films. Urn in Room of Prayer, south wall, Westwood Memorial Park, west Los Angeles, CA.

9406. Voegele, Charles (d. 1926) Alsatian aboard the U-20 who protested the German sinking of the passenger liner *Lusitania* May 7, 1915, and was imprisoned at Kiel for three years. He died at 32 from unknown reasons and is buried at Strasbourg.

9407. Vogel, Janet (Janet Vogel Rapp, June 10, 1941–Feb. 21, 1980) First tenor with the Pittsburgh based vocal group The Skyliners, with hits *Since I Don't Have You* (1959) and *This I Swear* (1960). A suicide at 38 by carbon monoxide poisoning. St. Wendelin Catholic Church Cemetery, Carrick, Pittsburgh, PA.

9408. Volk, Leonard (Nov. 7, 1828–Aug. 19, 1895) Noted sculptor of Lincoln did the bust in front of the tomb and at the Illinois state house at Springfield, the fireman's monument and soldiers and sailors' monument in Rosehill Cemetery, Chicago, and his own detailed seated figure of himself atop his own grave there. Island between sections M and N, Rosehill Cemetery, Chicago, IL.

9409. Volstead, Andrew J. (Oct. 31, 1860–Jan. 20, 1947) Conservative Republican congressman from Minnesota who drafted and whose name was attached to the act making consumption of alcohol illegal in America 1920–1933. The Volstead Act accomplished little beyond widespread contempt for the loosely enforced law and the creation of bootlegging competition with subsequent gangland murders. It was repealed shortly after Roosevelt took office in 1933. Lot near the front. City cemetery outside Granite Falls, MN.

9410. Voltaire, Francois (Nov. 21, 1694–May 30, 1778) French writer and philosopher of the Age of Enlightenment was denied a Christian burial. He had asked to die a Catholic but refused to renounce his writings, so a mass and burial in an abbey at Scellieres were forbidden and he was put there without the church's knowledge. During the French Revolution, his body was brought to the Pantheon in Paris by a procession of 100,000 citizens. A great deal of the remains were later removed, most by reactionary Royalists and priests in 1814. A foot, two teeth and the brain were seized as relics. His heart was placed beneath his statue in the National Library in Paris in 1924 when it was rediscovered. The statue and tomb remain near the tombs of Rousseau, Hugo and Zola, in the Pantheon, Paris.

9411. Von Braun, Wernher (March 23, 1912–June 16, 1977) German rocket expert and technical director considered one of the top minds in the field came to the United States after World War II and worked on the development of space rocketry, up to and including the moon landing. Buried before the announcement of his death from cancer. Flush bronze plaque. Ivy Hill Cemetery, Alexandria, VA.

9412. Von Eltz, Theodore (aka Julius Theodore Von Eltz, Nov. 5, 1893–Oct. 6, 1964) Stage, radio, film and TV actor in many roles 1920–1956, including *The Sea Wolf* (1926), *Sergeant York* (1941), *Rhapsody in Blue* (1946) and *The Big Sleep* (1946, as Geiger). Columbarium of Dawn, niche 30853, Holly Terrace, Great Mausoleum, Forest Lawn, Glendale, CA.

9413. Von Erich Brothers　Chris Von Erich (Chris Adkisson, Sept. 30, 1969–Sept. 12, 1991), **David Von Erich** (July 22, 1958–Feb. 9, 1984), **Kerry Von Erich** (Kerry Adkisson, Feb. 3, 1960–Feb. 18, 1993) and **Mike Von Erich** (Michael Adkisson, March 2, 1964–April 13, 1987), four WWF wrestlers, sons of Fritz, all died young, David from inflammation of the intestines in Japan; Mike (sleeping pills), Chris (gunshot) and Kerry (gunshot) were suicides. Their father, **Fritz Von Erich** (Jack Adkisson, Aug. 16, 1929–Sept. 10, 1997), died from cancer at 68. He is in the Hilltop sec., lot 530; the sons are in Hilltop, lot 535, Grove Hill Memorial Park, Dallas, TX.

9414. Von Fallersleben, August Heinrich Hoffmann (April 2, 1798–Jan. 19, 1874) German poet and literary historian penned the poem *Deutschland, Deutschland über Alles* in 1841, a patriotic homage to his country, set to the music of Franz Josef Haydn and adopted as the German national anthem after World War I. It is still the national anthem, though only the last verse is sung. Friedhof an der Klosterkirche (cemetery at the monastery church), Corvey Castle, Höxter, Germany.

9415. Von Harbou, Thea (Dec. 27, 1888–July 1, 1954) German author of *Metropolis*, filmed in 1926 and first published in English in 1927. Married in Germany to Rudolph Klein-Rogge and to Fritz Lang; they were later separated. When Hitler came to power, he left and she remained. Friedhof Heerstrasse, Trakehner Allee (Charlottenburg), Berlin.

9416. Von Hoene, Dick (July 17, 1940–Feb. 4, 2004) Cincinnati broadcaster, popular as The Cool Ghoul on WXIX TV's "Scream In" movies from 1970 into the 1980's. He died from a heart attack at 63 while shopping. Spring Grove Cemetery, Cincinnati, OH.

9417. Von Karajan, Herbert (April 5, 1908–July 16, 1989) Acclaimed Salzburg born Austrian conductor with various symphonies, including the Vienna State Opera, the Berlin Philharmonic, numerous others over some sixty years. Village church cemetery at Anif, near Salzburg, Austria.

9418. Von Kleinsmid, Rufus B. (June 27, 1875–July 9, 1964) Chancellor at the University of Southern California for twenty-six years oversaw its growth from a small debt ridden school to an internationally known institution. Rectangular plaque with his image

and a tribute from President Eisenhower. Memorial Court of Honor below the Last Supper Window, Memorial Terrace, Great Mausoleum, Forest Lawn, Glendale, CA.

9419. Von Schirach, Baldur (May 9, 1907–Aug. 8, 1974) Colleague of Adolf Hitler from 1925 became the Reichsjugendfuhrer—the leader of the Hitler youth—from 1931–1940, and leader of the NSDAP in Wien/Austria. He received a twenty year sentence at the 1946 Nuremburg trials and with Albert Speer was released at midnight October 1, 1966, leaving only Rudolf Hess at Spandau Prison. A boulder marks the grave. Krov Friedhof, Krov, the Rhineland-Palatinate.

9420. Von Seyffertitz, Gustav (Aug. 4, 1863–Dec. 25, 1943) Austrian born character actor, tall and lean with sharp features, in films in America from 1914 (when he used the name G. Butler Clonbough). Films include silent screen villains in *Sherlock Holmes* (1922, as Moriarty), *The Wizard* and *Sparrows* (1926). With sound he moved to supporting roles in the 1930's, often as psychiatrists, with a heavy Austrian accent (*Remember Last Night, Mr. Deeds Goes to Town, Son of Frankenstein*). He died at 80 in the Motion Picture Country Home in Woodland Hills, California. Cremated at Chapel of the Pines Crematory, Los Angeles. Columbarium of Fidelity, niche 16237, Gardenia Terrace, Great Mausoleum, Forest Lawn, Glendale, CA.

9421. Von Sternberg, Josef (May 29, 1894–Dec. 22, 1969) Austrian film director considered a master of the American cinema 1927–1935, specializing in the films of Marlene Dietrich (*The Blue Angel* in Germany, 1930, and in the U.S. *Morocco, Dishonored, Shanghai Express, Blonde Venus, The Scarlet Empress, The Devil is A Woman*). Other works include *Crime and Punishment* (1935). Known for his dictatorial temperament, complete with beret and megaphone. He died at 75 from a heart ailment. Niche in Sanctuary of Remembrance, Westwood Memorial Park, west Los Angeles.

9422. Von Stroheim, Erich (Sept. 22, 1885–May 12, 1957) Vienna born director and actor, a perfectionist who invariably went miles beyond his budget, with *Foolish Wives* (1922), *Merry-Go-Round* (1923), notably *Greed* (1923–25; his version ran nine hours before it was trimmed), *The Merry Widow* (1925, completed by Rupert Julian) and *Queen Kelly* (1928) with Gloria Swanson, from which he was fired by the backer, Joseph Kennedy. In the 1930's and 40's he acted in many villainous roles, as well as the complex German officer in *La Grande Ilusion* (1937). Among his last appearances was as Gloria Swanson's loyal butler in Billy Wilder's *Sunset Boulevard* (1950), for which he was nominated for an Oscar. He died in Paris from a spinal ailment at 71. Buried with his companion, French actress **Denise Vernac**; only their names are on the long polished black slab between two high hedges. Maurepas Cemetery, Les Yuelines, Maurepas, some 30 km. west of Paris.

9423. Von Tilzer, Albert (Albert Gumm, March 29, 1878–Oct. 1, 1956) and **Harry Von Tilzer** (Harry Gumm, July 8, 1872–Jan. 10, 1946) Indianapolis natives were longtime New York songwriters. Albert was a lyricist who helped compose several standards, including *Take Me Out to the Ball Game* (with Jack Norworth), *Shine on Harvest Moon* and *(I'll Be With You) In Apple Blossom Time*. Harry was in New York from 1892 and penned dozens of well known tunes ranging from *Only a Bird in A Gilded Cage* and *In the Sweet Bye and Bye* (to Bryan's lyrics), to *Wait til the Sun Shines Nellie* (1905), *I Want a Girl (Just Like the Girl That Married Dear Old Dad)*, *All Alone*, many other primarily sentimental numbers. It was he who stuffed paper between piano strings to create a tinny sound he liked, reputedly (and arguably) giving rise to the term Tin Pan Alley. The brothers are both in the family lot. Block B, path 16, on left, (Old) Mt. Carmel Cemetery (#1), Glendale-Ridgewood, Queens, N.Y.C.

9424. Von Trapp, Georg (Baron) (April 4, 1880–May 30, 1947) and **Maria (Baroness)** (Jan. 26, 1905–March 28, 1987) Austrian patriarch of the Von Trapp Family Singers married his children's governess, who organized her stepchildren into a singing group upon fleeing Austria with the Nazi invasion, eventually settling in the Green Mountains of Vermont. Their life in the Alps before and during their escape was the subject of *The Sound of Music* on Broadway and in the 1965 film. Family cemetery, Von Trapp Family Lodge (ski resort), Mountain Road (Luce Hill), Stowe, VT.

9425. Von Wangenheim, Gustav (Feb. 18, 1895 or April 11, 1895–Aug. 5, 1975 [per IFN] or Oct. 14, 1975 [per IMDB]) German actor from Bremen or Weisbaden appeared in films to 1931, best known as Thomas Hutter, the character based on Jonathan Harker and later incorporated into the 1931 Hollywood switch to Renfield, in F.W. Murnau's *Nosferatu* (1922), the first, most gruesome and artistic filming of *Dracula*. Von Wangenheim died in New York at 80. He shares a lot with his father, **Eduard von Winterstein (Eduard Freiherr von Wangenheim)** 1871–1961. Zentralfriedhof Friedrichsfelde, Gudrunstr. (Lichtenberg), Berlin.

9426. Von Zell, Harry (July 11, 1906–Nov. 21, 1981) Radio announcer and occasional TV and film actor in light comedy (*The Burns and Allen Show*) once formally introduced the President of the United States on a national microphone as "Hoobert Heever." He died from cancer at 75. Cremated at Angeles Abbey, Compton, California, through the Neptune Society. Ashes reportedly scattered at sea.

9427. Voorhees, Daniel W. (Sept. 26, 1827–April 10, 1897) Indiana Democratic congressman and senator known as The Tall Sycamore of the Wabash favored free silver coinage until President Grover Cleveland's patronage gifts supposedly changed Voorhees' mind. Obelisk, sec. 3, lot 136, Highland Lawn Cemetery, Terre Haute, IN.

9428. Voorhis, Jerry (Horace Jeremiah Voorhis, April 6, 1901–Sept. 11, 1984) Democratic U.S. Representative from California 1937–47, defeated by Richard Nixon in 1946, the beginning of his political career. Lot 2537, space 2, Mountain View Cemetery, Altadena, CA.

9429. Voris, Roy "Butch" (Roy M. Voris, Sept. 19, 1919–Aug. 9, 2005) Los Angeles born U.S. Navy captain assembled the daredevil Blue Angels aerial exhibition group after service in World War II. They trained in secret over the Florida Everglades in 1946, first performing at Jacksonville in June, and specializing in three plane blind rolls, flying in close V formation and executing a 360 degree roll in unison. Voris served as their first leader 1946–48 and again from 1952, surviving a mid-air collision at Corpus Christi that year. Later a spokesman for NASA, he died in Monterey, California, at 85. Cremated by Paul mortuary at the Little Chapel By the Sea. Ashes scattered in the Pacific.

9430. Vukovich, Bill (Dec. 13, 1918–May 30, 1955) "The Mad Russian," winner of the 1953 and 1954 Indianapolis 500 was in the running to take a record three in a row when his car rammed into a pile-up at 150 miles per hour, flew over the wall and burst into flames. Block 13, sec. 1605, space 4, Belmont Memorial Park, Fresno, CA.

9431. Vukovich, Billy III (Aug. 31, 1963–Nov. 25, 1990) Grandson of the two time Indy 500 winner ran in three 500s and others before his death in a crash at Mesa Marin near Bakersfield at 27. Garden of the Apostles, sec. 520, space 2, Belmont Memorial Park, Fresno, CA.

9432. Vye, Murvyn (Marvin Wesley Vye, July 16, 1913–Aug. 16, 1976) Yale educated actor from Quincy, Massachusetts, with a baritone singing voice originated the role of Jigger in *Carousel* on Broadway and appeared in several films 1945–65, including *Golden Earrings* (1947, as Zoltan), *Pickup on South Street*, *The Road to Bali*, *River of No Return*. The dates of birth and death are according to the death certificate. He died in Pompano Beach, Florida, at 63 of natural causes, though the police investigated. His body was shipped to Armand G. Erpf Cemetery (private), Arkville, NY.

9433. Waddell, Rube (George Edward Waddell, Oct. 13, 1876–April 1, 1914) Lefthanded pitcher from Bradford, Pennsylvania, in both leagues gained fame with the Philadelphia Athletics, where Connie Mack said he was the best lefthander he ever saw. He was known for his off the field antics, including chasing fire engines, and Mack sold him to St. Louis in 1908, having tired of his behavior. He died from pneumonia complicating tuberculosis at 38 after helping victims in a flood. Hall of Fame 1946. Rough hewn stone monument. Block 5, lot 182, grave 2, Mission Burial Park, San Antonio, TX.

9434. Wade, Benjamin F. (Oct. 27, 1800–March 2, 1878) Republican abolitionist senator from Ohio backed President Andrew Johnson after the death of

Lincoln until it was clear Johnson would not support the radical reconstructionists' policy toward the south. Wade, as president pro-tem, was prepared to take over the White House in 1868 upon Johnson's impeachment, but one vote saved Johnson and Wade's hopes were dashed. Squat obelisk, right rear area, sec. A, lot 53, Oakdale Cemetery, Jefferson, OH.

9435. Wade, Henry M. (Nov. 11, 1914–March 1, 2001) Dallas County district attorney for thirty-six years never lost a case he prosecuted; he sought the death penalty successfully twenty-nine of thirty times. He prosecuted Jack Ruby and sent him to prison, and in 1970 was the first named defendant in a suit by pregnant carnival worker Norma McCorvey, denied an abortion by Texas' 100 year old ban on abortions. The case eventually went to the Supreme Court and resulted in the legalization of abortion *Roe v. Wade* in January 1973. He died at 86 of complications from Parkinson's Disease. Meadow of Reflection, east end, Sparkman-Hillcrest Memorial Park, Dallas, TX.

9436. Wade, Jennie (Mary Virginia Wade, May 21, 1843–July 3, 1863) The only civilian in Gettysburg, Pennsylvania, to be killed by gunfire during the fierce battle that took place there between the Union and Confederate troops during the first three days of July 1863. She was baking bread in the McClellan house, her sister's home, when a stray bullet passed through two doors and killed her. She was buried by Union soldiers in the garden, having died unaware that her sweetheart, Jack Skelly, was killed in battle at about the same time. The McClellan House, now called the Jennie Wade house, still stands in Gettysburg as a free attraction. She was reburied beneath a substantial monument. Sec. A, Evergreen Cemetery, Gettysburg, PA.

9437. Wade, Jeptha Homer (Aug. 11, 1811–Aug. 9, 1890) Entrepreneur built telegraph lines through the Midwest that became part of Western Union. He donated land for both Wade Park in Cleveland and Case Western Reserve University. Spire in sec. 3, lot 4, Lakeview Cemetery, Cleveland, OH.

9438. Wadlow, Robert (Robert Pershing Wadlow, Feb. 22, 1918–July 15, 1940) The tallest man in the world stood 8'11" tall. He was exhibited at various carnivals, shows and newsreels until his death from a foot infection in Michigan at 22. His grave is somewhat raised to show the length of the burial, in the town where he was born. Sec. 4, W22, space 2, along Cole Drive, Oakwood/Upper Alton Cemetery, Upper Alton, IL.

9439. Wadsworth, Henry (Joseph Henry Wadsworth, June 18, 1903–Dec. 5, 1974) Actor from Maysville, Kentucky, in leads and second leads chiefly in films of the 1930's (*Applause 1929, Ghost Train, Dangerous Corner, The Thin Man, Mark of the Vampire*). He died in New York City. Sec. 4, lot 96, grave 14, Maysville Cemetery, Maysville, KY.

9440. Waggner, George (Sept. 7, 1894–Dec. 11, 1984) New York born producer-director, formerly screenwriter and actor, appeared in *The Sheik* (1921) and *The Iron Horse* (1923, as Buffalo Bill). He was later known for the horror films he directed at Universal 1940–45, including *Man Made Monster, Horror Island, The Wolfman, The Climax,* many others. He also co-scripted or directed many action films through the 1950's. Ashes in Dawn of Tomorrow, crypt 342, Forest Lawn, Glendale, CA.

9441. Wagner, George *see* **Gorgeous George.**

9442. Wagner, Honus (John or Johannes Peter Wagner, Feb. 24, 1874–Dec. 6, 1955) Barrel chested star of the Pittsburgh Pirates 1900–1917 was considered the greatest shortstop in baseball history. When he retired, The Flying Dutchman had scored more runs, hits and stolen more bases than anyone else in the N.L. An original inductee into the Hall of Fame (1936), he was born and died at Carnegie, Pennsylvania, outside Pittsburgh. The cemetery has sculpted hedges in the shape of religious symbols adorning its several hills. Flush plaque, lower left area at the bottom of the hill. Garden of the Cross, lot 327C, Jefferson Memorial Park, Pleasant Hills, south of Pittsburgh, PA.

9443. Wagner, Richard (May 22, 1813–Feb. 13, 1883) The greatest composer of German opera, born in Leipzig; his works were later associated with German nationalism, *Lohengrin, Tristan and Isolde, Tannhauser* and *Die Meistersinger*, as well as symphonies. He also wrote literary compositions which were as controversial as his music, referred to as an abandoning of opera for a dramatic poem set to highly charged music. Wagner was in Venice working on an essay when he suffered a heart attack and died. There is a cenotaph to him there. He was buried in a tomb he had designed in the garden of his home. Haus Wahnfried, Bayreuth, Bavaria.

9444. Wagner, Robert F., Sr. (June 8, 1877–May 4, 1953) German born U.S. senator from New York 1927–1949 authored the Wagner Act (National Labor Relations Act) in 1935 to aid unions in combating unfair practices by employers. Passed during FDR's Second Hundred Days, it was the most far reaching of their work other than the Social Security Act, which Wagner also worked on. His son **Robert Wagner, Jr.** (April 20, 1910–Feb. 12, 1991) was mayor of New York 1954–1965. Both are in sec. 45, lot 79, (1st) Calvary Cemetery, Woodside, Queens, N.Y.C.

9445. Wagner, Roger (Jan. 16, 1914–Sept. 17, 1992) Head of the Roger Wagner Chorale. Oak Knoll Mausoleum, room 21F, Valley Oaks memorial Park, Westlake Village, CA.

9446. Wainwright, Jonathan M., Jr. (Aug. 23, 1883–Sept. 2, 1953) American general commanding troops in the Philippines after MacArthur was forced out was captured by the Japanese in May 1942 and held as a prisoner of war for three years until MacArthur returned, as promised. Wainwright, liberated in August 1945, became a symbol of hope and perseverance to the Allies. He died from a stroke in San

Antonio eight years to the day after the Japanese surrender. Sec.1, grave 358-B, Arlington National Cemetery, Arlington, VA.

9447. Waite, Morrison R. (Morrison Remick Waite, Nov. 29, 1816–March 23, 1888) A founder of the Republican Party in the 1850's, the former Ohio lawyer was appointed Chief Justice of the Supreme Court by President Grant in 1874 and served until his death. Sec. 42, lot 1, above the lake, Woodlawn Cemetery, Toledo, OH.

9448. Waitkus, Eddie (Edward Stephen Waitkus, Sept. 4, 1919–Sept. 15, 1972) First baseman for the 1950 Philadelphia Phillies, the Whiz Kids, was shot in the chest in Chicago in 1949 while there to play the Cubs—the basis for Bernard Malamud's *The Natural* and the subsequent film. He recovered and returned the next year to help Philadelphia win the pennant. World War II lot, tier 22, grave 31, City of Cambridge Cemetery, Cambridge, MA.

9449. Wakely, Jimmy (Feb. 16, 1914–Sept. 23, 1982) Soft voiced country and popular vocalist (*Moon Over Montana*) made several duets with Margaret Whiting as well as recording on his own. In films as a singing cowboy. Homeward sec., lot 8010, space 2, Forest Lawn Hollywood Hills, Los Angeles.

9450. Walbrook, Anton (Adolph Wohlbrueck, Nov. 19, 1896–Aug. 9, 1967) Vienna born film star first in Germany, in *The Student of Prague* (1935), *The Soldier and the Lady/Michael Strogoff* (Hollywood, 1937) and in England in *Gaslight* (*Angel Street*, 1940), *Dangerous Moonlight* (1941), *The Life and Death of Colonel Blimp* (1943), *The Red Shoes* (1948) and *The Queen of Spades* (1949). He died in Bavaria but was returned for burial to London. His upright stone, near that of George Du Maurier, bears the epitaph *Our Dearest Friend.* St. John's Churchyard, Church Row, Hampstead, London.

9451. Walburn, Raymond (Sept. 9, 1887–July 26, 1969) Actor from Plymouth, Indiana, on stage and screen from 1912 (*Mr. Deeds Goes to Town, Hail the Conquering Hero, The Sin of Harold Diddlebeck, State of the Union,* scores of others), essaying roles ranging from butlers to crooked businessmen or politicians and everything in between. He died in New York City at 81. Cremated at Ferncliff Cemetery, Hartsdale, New York. Ashes returned to the Frank E. Campbell mortuary, Manhattan.

9452. Walcott, Jersey Joe (Arnold Raymond Cream, Jan. 31, 1914–Feb. 25, 1994) New Jersey born boxer tried twice to win the heavyweight title from Joe Louis in 1947 and 1948 and lost his first try at Ezzard Charles but took the title from him in Pittsburgh in July 1951, the oldest heavyweight champion. He held it for eleven months, losing to Rocky Marciano in June 1952. He spent his life in Camden, New Jersey, where he worked with the juvenile division of the department of public safety. Hillcrest sec. B, lot 414, Sunset (Memorial Park) Cemetery, Pennsauken, NJ.

9453. Wald, Jerry (Jerome Irving Wald, Sept. 16, 1911–July 13, 1962) Brooklyn born screenwriter and producer said to be the basis for Budd Schulberg's *What Makes Sammy Run?* He worked as a writer for Warner Bros. and was second in charge of production at Columbia before forming his own production company in 1956, releasing through Fox. Winner of the 1948 Irving Thalberg Memorial Award, his works included *Johnny Belinda, The Glass Menagerie* and *Young Man With a Horn.* He collaborated on many scripts without receiving screen credit. An indefatigable worker, he died from a heart attack at 50. Niche G2146, Columbarium of Honor, Garden of Honor (private), Forest Lawn, Glendale, CA.

9454. Waldoff, Claire (Oct. 21, 1884–Jan. 22, 1957) German burlesque star, notably in *Roland von Berlin* (1907) and at Unter den Linden, where she was the chief attraction and a recording artist, popular through the 1920's. With the advent of the Nazis, her career was stopped, and she retired to Bad Reichenhall, Upper Bavaria. White wall niche, rounded at the top, with Olga Frehn v Roeder. Der Prager Friedhof, Stuttgart.

9455. Waldron, Charles D. (Dec. 23, 1874–March 4, 1946) Stage and screen actor in the theatre prior to silent films and then in both during the 1920's, moving on to talkies. His later appearances included *Crime and Punishment* (1935), *Stranger on the Third Floor* (1940, as the district attorney), *The Devil and Daniel Webster* (1941), *Dragonwyck* and *The Big Sleep* (1946, as General Sternwood). Some sources list his birth in 1877. Columbarium of Memory, niche 19479, Memorial Terrace, Great Mausoleum, Forest Lawn, Glendale, CA.

9456. Walker, Madam C. J. (Sarah Breedlove Walker, Dec. 23, 1867–May 25, 1919) Pioneer Black business woman from Louisiana founded the Walker method of straightening hair, based in Indianapolis. A millionaire and philanthropist. Butternut sec. 141, south part 14052, four from Park, three east of walk, Woodlawn Cemetery, the Bronx, N.Y.C.

9457. Walker, Charlotte (Dec. 29, 1876–March 23, 1958) Silent screen actress from 1915 through the 1940's. Mother of actress Sara Haden. Appearances include *The Trail of the Lonesome Pine* (1916), *The Midnight Girl* (1925), *Millie* (1931), etc. City Yard(s) Cemetery, Galveston, TX.

9458. Walker, Cheryl (Aug. 1, 1918–Oct. 24, 1971) Actress in films through the 1940's, the 1938 Pasadena Tournament of Roses queen resembled Larraine Day; her biggest role was the lead character Eileen in the all star *Stage Door Canteen* (1943). The wife of T.W. Andrews, she died from cancer at 53. Block Z, lot 481, grave 2, curb B-24, San Gabriel District Cemetery, San Gabriel, CA.

9459. Walker, Curt (William Curtis Walker, July 3, 1896–Dec. 9, 1955) Outfielder for the New York Yankees 1919, Giants 1920–21, Philadelphia Phillies 1921–24, and the Cincinnati Reds 1924–30, with a .304 batting average. Glenwood Cemetery, Beeville, TX.

9460. Walker, Fred "Dixie" (Sept. 24, 1910–May 17, 1982) Georgia born outfielder for the Yankees and the Dodgers 1931–49, known in Brooklyn in the 40's as the "people's cherce." Block 26, lot 311, Elmwood Cemetery, Birmingham, AL.

9461. Walker, Harry "The Hat" (Oct. 22, 1916–Aug. 8, 1999) Outfielder with the Cardinals whose left handed double drove in Enos Slaughter's series winning run in 1946. Brother of Fred "Dixie" Walker. Cedar Grove Cemetery, Leeds, AL.

9462. Walker, Helen (July 17, 1920–March 10, 1968) Leading lady of the 1940's and early 50's, her films include *Lucky Jordan* (1942), *The Man in Half Moon Street* (1944), *Brewster's Millions* (1945), *Cluny Brown* (1946), *Call Northside 777* and *Nightmare Alley* (1947). Injured in a car accident in 1946, her career declined and she retired from the screen in 1955. She died from cancer at 47 in North Hollywood and was buried at her birthplace. Sec. A, lot 403, grave 3, Oak Hill Cemetery, Sterling, MA.

9463. Walker, James J. (June 19, 1881–Nov. 18, 1946) Flamboyant mayor of New York 1926–1932 seemed to go with the image of the Roaring Twenties, said to wear the city in his buttonhole like a flower. State supreme court hearings in 1931 revealed that the city government under his loose management was guilty of considerable financial mishandling. He resigned the next year and married showgirl Betty Compton, who later divorced him. Always colorful, he had also been the composer of *Will You Love Me in December as You Do in May?* (1906). Walker died from a blood clot in the brain at Doctors Hospital in Manhattan after slipping into a coma in his east end apartment. Requiem mass at St. Patrick's Cathedral, Manhattan. Polished rose-brown stone. Sec. 41, lot 246, Gate of Heaven Cemetery, Hawthorne, NY.

9464. Walker, Johnnie (Jan. 7, 1894–Dec. 5, 1949) New York born silent screen and talkies actor, once a matinee idol, appeared in several sound films including *Up the River* (1930). He died from a stroke in Brooklyn at 55. Sec. H, grave 10367, Long Island National Cemetery, Farmingdale, Long Island, NY.

9465. Walker, June (June 14, 1900–Feb. 3, 1966) New York born stage actress in a few films (*War Nurse* 1930, as Babs, *Through Different Eyes* 1942, *The Unforgiven* 1960, *A Child is Waiting* 1963). Mother of actor John Kerr (her married surname). She died in Sherman Oaks, California, at 65. North wall, bottom row, Room of Prayer, Westwood Memorial Park, west Los Angeles.

9466. Walker, Junior (Autry DeWalt Mixon, Jr., June 14, 1931–Nov. 23, 1995) Motown's premier alto sax player of the 1960's, from Blytheville, Arkansas, had hits with *Shotgun* and *What Does it Take?* with his All Stars. He had been touring with Motown All-Stars shortly before his death from cancer at 64 in Battle Creek. Rounded upright stone with a saxophone on it, 5th section back along Oak Ave. on left. Oak Hill Cemetery, Battle Creek, MI.

9467. Walker, Kim (June 19, 1968–March 6, 2001) Young actress in television and films including *Say Anything*, best known as Heather Chandler in the black comedy *Heathers* (1989). She died from cancer related to a brain tumor at 32. Sec. 40, block 1, range 4, plot E, grave 421, Pinelawn Memorial Park, Farmingdale, Long Island, NY.

9468. Walker, Mary Edwards (Nov. 26, 1832–Feb. 21, 1919) Female surgeon in the Civil War and feminist was the first and only woman to date awarded the Medal of Honor. Known for her preference for bloomer outfits and in later years for men's suits. When the Medal of Honor Board tried to remove her from the honored in 1917, she refused to turn in her medals (both old and new) and was buried with them pinned to her Prince Albert coat. Oswego Town Rural Cemetery, Oswego, NY.

9469. Walker, Moses "Fleetwood" (Oct. 7, 1857–May 11, 1924) Black baseball player briefly in the major leagues in 1887 was treated so badly he was driven from the game, later publishing the black newspaper *Our Own Country*. Integration of baseball took another sixty years. A stone was placed on his grave in October 1990. Sec. P, lot V, Union Cemetery, Steubenville, OH.

9470. Walker, Nancy (Ann Swoyer Barto, May 10, 1922–March 25, 1992) Actress-comedienne long on TV as Rosie in Bounty Paper Towel commercials and as Rhoda's mother in *Rhoda* in the 1970's. Later on *True Colors* until shortly before her death from lung cancer in Studio City, California, at 69, survived by her husband David Craig. No funeral or memorial service per her wishes; she was cremated by the Neptune Society and her ashes scattered at sea.

9471. Walker, Nella (March 6, 1886–March 22, 1971) Stage actress from Chicago appeared in films 1929–1954, often in matronly roles (*Seven Keys to Baldpate, The Vagabond Lover, Captain January, Stella Dallas, The Crime of Dr. Hallett, Kitty Foyle, Hellzapoppin, Buck Privates, Murder in the Blue Room, In Society, The Locket, Sabrina*). Crypt 21170B, Sanctuary of Allegiance, Freedom Mausoleum, Forest Lawn, Glendale, CA.

9472. Walker, Robert (Robert Hudson Walker, Oct. 13, 1918–Aug. 28, 1951) Leading man in films of the 1940's and early 50's, the son of a Salt Lake City newspaper editor, in wholesome serviceman roles in *Since You Went Away, The Clock, Till the Clouds Roll By* during World War II. He underwent treatment for alcohol and drug abuse from 1948, with the end of his marriage to Jennifer Jones. A well publicized escape from a clinic in Topeka resulted in his smashing up a police station there. His best known role, as Bruno in Hitchcock's *Strangers on a Train* (1951) was released the year of his death at 32 in his Sunset Boulevard home. He had received an injection of sodium amytal from his doctor, but the death was considered unusual since Walker had received a considerably higher dosage on several occasions. Rosehill, row 23, space 109, Washington Heights Memorial Park, Ogden, UT.

9473. Walker, Robert (June 19, 1888–March 4, 1954) Actor in silents and talkies, a generation before the later, better known actor of the same name. Block (memorial) A, sec. 405, lot 3, Valhalla Memorial Park, North Hollywood, CA.

9474. Walker, Rube (Albert Walker, May 16, 1926–Dec. 12, 1992) Catcher for the Cubs and Dodgers. Blue Ridge Memorial Park, Lenoir, NC.

9475. Walker, Stuart (March 4, 1888–March 13, 1941) Cincinnati born stage actor, director and occasional producer and playwright, originally with David Belasco and managing repertory companies. He produced *Five Flights Up* and the series of Portmanteau plays. Beginning in Hollywood in 1930, he directed several atmospheric films, including *The Eagle and the Hawk* (1933), *Great Expectations* (1934), *The Mystery of Edwin Drood* and *Werewolf of London* (1935). He died from a heart attack in Los Angeles at 53. Headstone with his name and death date. Sec. 104, lot 27, Spring Grove Cemetery, Cincinnati, OH.

9476. Walker, Sydney (May 4, 1921–Sept. 30, 1994) Philadelphia born stage actor with various repertory companies, the San Francisco Conservatory Theatre from 1974. One of his last roles was in the 1992 film *Prelude to a Kiss*. Like the projected future of his character in the film, he died from lung cancer in San Francisco at 73, unreported by the press for four weeks. Ashes scattered at sea off Marin County through the Neptune Society.

9477. Walker, T-Bone (Aaron T. Walker, May 28, 1910–March 16, 1975) Hard driving blues guitarist and vocalist began with Cab Calloway, recorded several blues numbers on his own, later appeared with Count Basie and toured Europe extensively. He died at 65, three months after suffering a stroke. Capistrano Gardens, crypt 1815, Inglewood Park Cemetery, Inglewood, CA.

9478. Walker, Vernon L. (May 2, 1894–March 14, 1948) Special effects artist and cinematographer in Hollywood, long at RKO, shot *King Kong, Son of Kong,* and oversaw the special effects in *She, The Last Days of Pompeii* (both 1935), *The Hunchback of Notre Dame* and *Gunga Din* (both 1939), *The Spiral Staircase* (1946), as well as the lengthy and imaginative nightmare sequences in the film noir prototype *Stranger on the Third Floor* (1940). Four Oscar nominations 1940–44 (*Swiss Family Robinson, The Navy Comes Through, Bombardier, Days of Glory*). Mignonette plot, lot 222, grave C, Inglewood Park Cemetery, Inglewood, CA.

9479. Walker, William (July 1, 1896–Jan. 27, 1992) The grandson of slaves, actor Bill Walker was on the Board of Directors of the Screen Actors Guild 1951–1971, urging the use of more realistic black roles in films. His acclaimed roles included the doctor in the all black version of *The Well* (for which he was later honored by President Reagan on behalf of the black press) and the Rev. Sykes in *To Kill a Mockingbird* (1962). Sec. 32, grave 631, Riverside National Cemetery, Riverside, CA.

9480. Wallace, Beulah Sippie (Nov. 1, 1898–Nov. 1, 1986) Blues singer from Houston began recording on Okeh in Chicago in the 1920's, but by decade's end left the blues world for the Leland Baptist Church in Detroit, working as organist and singer, still making occasional appearances and "rediscovered" in the 1960's; she made several appearances, including *Late Night With David Letterman,* prior to her death on her 88th birthday. Trinity Cemetery, Detroit, MI.

9481. Wallace, Bobby (Roderick J. Wallace, Nov. 4, 1873–Nov. 3, 1960) Baseball great spent sixty years in the majors playing several positions but known as Mr. Shortstop, with Cleveland, St. Louis, and Cincinnati 1894–1918, afterward managing, umpiring and scouting. Hall of Fame 1953. Evergreen plot, div. A, lot 226, Inglewood Park Cemetery, Inglewood, CA.

9482. Wallace, Edgar (April 1, 1875–Feb. 10, 1932) English writer of 172 books (*The Four Just Men, The Ringer*) and 16 plays, most often associated with *King Kong,* which he never lived to write. While in Hollywood during the embryonic stages of the ambitious project, Wallace died from pneumonia complicated by diabetes. Producer Merian C. Cooper had promised him credit for the story, which he received. Wallace's name appears on the book and the 1933 film although he did little more than outline the animated scenes Cooper had devised with Willis O'Brien. Returning from Hollywood by train, English actor Ivor Novello was shocked to find Wallace's name tagged to a crate bound for England in the baggage car, having recently met him in the film colony. There is a memorial plaque to Wallace in Ludgate Circus, London, inscribed *He knew poverty yet had walked with kings and kept his bearing.* His funeral took place February 25, with burial beneath a white stone cross bearing his name and dates. Fern Lane churchyard, Little Marlow, England.

9483. Wallace, George (George Corley Wallace, Aug. 25, 1919–Sept. 13, 1998) Four time Democratic Governor of Alabama elected in 1962, 1970, 1974 and 1982, gained national attention in 1963 when he stood in the door to prevent black students from entering the University of Alabama but yielded eventually to the National Guard. He ran for president as a third party candidate on the American Independent ticket in 1968, and again in the Democratic primary in 1972, until he was shot in a parking lot in Laurel, Maryland, on May 15 in an assassination attempt and was left paralyzed from the waist down. By the mid 70's he had renounced his segregationist policies, winning his last gubernatorial race with a populist coalition of blacks and whites. He died from a heart attack in a Montgomery hospital at 79. Burial with his wife Lurlene, who succeeded him as governor from 1966–68. Circle of Life, sec. 12, lot 4, Greenwood Cemetery, Montgomery, AL.

9484. Wallace, Henry (Oct. 7, 1888–Nov. 18, 1965) Secretary of Agriculture in the first two terms of Franklin Roosevelt's administration 1933–1940 was put on the ticket in 1940 as vice president, but the Iowa Democrat, known for his interests not only in agriculture but in mysticism, was replaced on the ticket in 1944 by Missouri Democrat Harry Truman, and missed becoming president by only three months. Secretary of Commerce under Truman 1945–46, he later split from the party and ran unsuccessfully for president as a Progressive in 1948. Sec. 31, Glendale Cemetery, Des Moines, IA.

9485. Wallace, Irving (March 19, 1916–June 29, 1990) American novelist with several bestsellers in the 1960's. He has two plaques on his crypt. The top one lists his name and dates, the bottom one bears the lines *Life is not a daily dying, not a pointless end, but a soaring and blinding gift snatched from eternity.* Courts of the Book, Isaiah V, crypt 136, Hillside Memorial Park, Los Angeles.

9486. Wallace, Jean (Oct. 12, 1923–Feb. 14, 1990) Actress wife of Franchot Tone and later of Cornel Wilde, appeared in several films from the 1940's including *The Man on the Eiffel Tower* with Tone (1949). Corridor G-4 (Light), crypt 6253, Abbey of the Psalms/Hollywood Forever Mausoleum, Hollywood Forever Cemetery, Hollywood (Los Angeles), CA.

9487. Wallace, Lew (April 10, 1827–Feb. 15, 1905) Union General from Brookville, Indiana, later lived at Crawfordsville. He served in diplomatic positions in the Republican administrations of Hayes and Garfield/Arthur, and wrote the campaign biography of his fellow Hoosier, Benjamin Harrison, elected to the White House in 1888. Wallace is best known for *Ben Hur* (1880), his epic historical novel and a pioneer in that form of literature. His study is still on display at Crawfordsville, Indiana. Obelisk, sec. 7, Oak Hill Cemetery, Crawfordsville, IN.

9488. Wallace, Lurleen B. (Sept. 19, 1926–May 7, 1968) Governor of Alabama succeeded her husband George Wallace in 1967. Her term was cut short, beset from the outset by the discovery that she was suffering from cancer. She died the following year at 41. Joined by her husband over 25 years later, a two columned monument marks their lot and white headstones. Circle of Life, Greenwood Cemetery, Montgomery, AL.

9489. Wallace, Morgan (Morgan Weill, July 26, 1881–Dec. 12, 1953) Tall, bald character actor from Lompoc, California, resembled Fred Stone somewhat, in many films (*Orphans of the Storm*, as the Marquis de Praille, *Up the River, Smart Money*, as Prosecutor Black, *The Maltese Falcon* aka *Dangerous Female* 1931, *It's A Gift, Fury*, as Fred Garrett). Meditation sec., lot 25, grave 5A, Forest Lawn, Glendale, CA.

9490. Wallace, Ray L. (April 21, 1918–Nov. 26, 2002) Logger and adventurer in northern California, Oregon, and Washington, was a renowned practical joker and, as confirmed by his family after his death in a Centralia, Washington, nursing home at 84, he had created in the late 1950's much of the evidence — including photos and footprints — that there was a creature dubbed Bigfoot in the Pacific Northwest. Lone Hill Cemetery, Toledo, Lewis County, WA.

9491. Wallant, Edward Lewis (Oct. 19, 1926–Dec. 5, 1962) Author whose acclaimed works *The Human Season* (1960), *The Pawnbroker* (1961) and *The Tenants of Moonbloom* brought his comparison to Bernard Malamud and Philip Roth among premier Jewish American authors. He died at 36 from a stroke in Norwalk Hospital, Norwalk, Connecticut, where he lived, and was buried the next day. Independent Hebrew Cemetery, Norwalk, CT.

9492. Wallenda, Karl (Jan. 21, 1904–March 22, 1978) German born high wire performer, the founder and star of the Flying Wallendas, continued doing dangerous tricks after the deaths of two family members while performing in Detroit in 1962 and the death of his son-in-law in West Virginia in 1972. The 73 year old Wallenda fell to his death from a wire stretched between two hotels in San Juan, Puerto Rico, when a gust of wind caused him to lose his balance. Buried with several other members of the family, his marker has a laminated photo of him on it. Sec. L, lot 51, Manasota Memorial Park, Bradenton, FL.

9493. Waller, Charlie (Charles O. Waller, Jan. 19, 1935–Aug. 18, 2004) Texas born, Louisiana raised founder of The Country Gentlemen, based in Washington in 1957, called the voice and rhythmic soul of modern Bluegrass music, he sang and played guitar, recording over fifty albums, and credited with bring Bluegrass from the front porches of Appalachia to college campuses as well as D.C. nightclubs. He died from a heart attack at home in Gordonsville, Virginia, at 69. Maplewood Cemetery, Gordonsville, VA.

9494. Waller, Eddy C. (June 14, 1889–Aug. 19, 1977) Character actor, in many small parts at Universal in the 1940's, usually as country bumpkins (*The Mummy's Tomb, Night Monster* etc.) Columbarium of Remembrance, niche 60409, Forest Lawn Hollywood Hills, Los Angeles.

9495. Waller, Fats (Thomas Waller, May 21, 1904–Dec. 15, 1943) New York born jazz pianist, composer and bandleader, an American original, was known for his impromptu and outrageous vocalizing with the lyrics of the numbers. His recordings and compositions include *Honeysuckle Rose, Your Feet's Too Big, Ain't Misbehavin, It's a Sin to Tell A Lie*, etc. He died from a heart attack at 39 in his berth just as his train pulled into Kansas City to be held over during a blizzard. Louis Armstrong, also at the depot, was incredulous and unable to stop crying when told that Waller, three years his junior, had died. He was cremated and his ashes scattered over Harlem.

9496. Walley, Deborah (Aug. 12, 1941–May 10, 2001) Perky actress from Bridgeport, Connecticut, succeeded Sandra Dee as Gidget in *Gidget Goes Hawaiian* in 1961, followed by several 1960s beach films, *Spinout, Benji,* etc. She died from cancer of the esophagus at 57 in Sedona, Arizona. Ashes to residence.

9497. Wallis, Hal B. (Sept. 14, 1899–Oct. 5, 1986) Chicago born film producer since the 1920's was at Warner Brothers 1933–1944 and responsible for many of their best films during that period, the driving force behind *Casablanca* and several other genuine classics. He worked as an independent afterward, releasing through Paramount and Universal. Married for many years to Louise Fazenda, he later married actress Martha Hyer. He died at 87. Sanctuary of Truth, private room 49, crypt D, Memorial Terrace, Great Mausoleum, Forest Lawn, Glendale, CA.

9498. Walpole, Hugh (March 13, 1884–June 1, 1941) Writer from New Zealand settled in England, where he penned *The Cumberland Family Saga,* including *Rogue Herries, Judith Paris, The Fortress, Vanessa.* Knighted 1938. Celtic cross, corner of the south side of the church. St. John's Churchyard, Keswick, Cumbria.

9499. Walsh, Adam (Dec. 4, 1901–Jan. 12, 1985) Center for Notre Dame, the captain of Knute Rockne's famed 1924 team. St. John's Cemetery, Brunswick, ME.

9500. Walsh, Adam (Nov. 14, 1974–July 27, 1981) Six year old boy disappeared at a shopping mall across from a Hollywood, Florida, police station. Two weeks later, part of his remains were found in a canal 120 miles away. The boy's father John Walsh, who went on to host *America's Ten Most Wanted,* believes the murderer of his son was a serial killer now serving five consecutive life terms. Nothing else was recovered. An empty casket was buried in the area after a service at St. Maurice's Catholic Church, Hollywood, FL.

9501. Walsh, Arthur (Feb. 26, 1896–Dec. 13, 1947) Violinist with Edison from 1915 made many recordings after service in World War I, and played *I'll Take You Home Again, Kathleen* at Edison's funeral in 1931. Vice President of Edison, Inc. from 1931, later Commissioner of the Port of New York and Senator from New Jersey 1943–44, appointed by the governor, Edison's son. He died from cancer in New York City at 51. Sec. 8, block R, tier 5, grave 2, Gate of Heaven Cemetery, East Hanover, NJ.

9502. Walsh, Delphine (1908–May 31, 1929) Stage actress with the Franchon and Marco Players and Hollywood Scandals died from a probable botched abortion, termed an illegal operation, in which two doctors were held for questioning. Unmarked. Sec. 2, lot 113, Hollywood Forever Cemetery, Hollywood (Los Angeles), CA.

9503. Walsh, "Big Ed" (Edward Arthur Walsh, May 14, 1881–May 26, 1959) Spitball pitcher at his peak with the Chicago White Sox 1906–1912. Hall of Fame 1946. Palm Garden 1, right front corner area, across from office. Forest Lawn Memorial Park, Pompano Beach, FL.

9504. Walsh, George (George Frederick Walsh, March 16, 1889–June 13, 1981) New York born actor, brother of Raoul Walsh, in films from 1914–1936 (bridegroom of Cana in *Intolerance,* John L. Sullivan in *The Bowery* 1933, etc.), originally cast in the lead in *Ben Hur* but replaced by Ramon Navarro. He died in Pomona, California, at 92. Flat plaque with his wife **Winifred Craven** (1911–1966). Block W, lot 82, grave 1, San Gabriel District Cemetery, San Gabriel, CA.

9505. Walsh, J. T. (James Patrick Walsh, Sept. 28, 1943–Feb. 27, 1998) San Francisco born character actor from age 31 appeared in over 60 films, usually as cowardly villains, including *Good Morning Vietnam, A Few Good Men, Needful Things, Hoffa, Backdraft, Silent Fall, Crime of the Century, Sling Blade* and *Breakdown.* He died from a heart attack at 54 while vacationing in San Diego. Service at Forest Lawn Hollywood Hills, Los Angeles, where the ashes were held briefly until sent home.

9506. Walsh, Jim (Ulysses Walsh, July 20, 1903–Dec. 4, 1990) Musicologist and foremost expert on American recordings 1895–1920. A newspaperman at Roanoke, Virginia, he was better known for his *Favorite Pioneer Recording Artists* articles in *Hobbies* magazine 1942–1985, written from his home in Vinton, Virginia. His recordings and memorabilia from forty five years of research were donated to the National Archives. His body was donated to science.

9507. Walsh, Raoul (March 11, 1887–Dec. 31, 1980) Noted film director, former actor and assistant to D.W. Griffith, played John Wilkes Booth in *Birth of a Nation* (1915). Married to actress Miriam Cooper; they divorced in 1927. In 1929 while filming the first outdoor talkie *In Old Arizona,* Walsh lost an eye and, like John Ford, was recognizable for his eye patch. Among his many films were the gangster sagas *The Roaring Twenties* (1939), *High Sierra* (1941) and *White Heat* (1949). He stopped directing in 1964, nearing blindness in his other eye. New single plaque. Sec. B, tier 28, grave 40, Assumption Cemetery, Simi Valley, CA.

9508. Walsh, Sean Fallon (Oct. 9, 1934–March 6, 2000) Irish-American actor on TV soaps and a few films and TV spots of the 1970's. He died in suburban Cleveland of prostate cancer at 65. Holy Cross Cemetery, Brookpark, Cleveland, OH.

9509. Walsh, Stella (Stella Walasiewiczowna, April 3, 1911–Dec. 4, 1980) 1932 Olympic Gold and Silver medalist for Poland. It was not discovered until after her death, murdered in the parking lot of a Cleveland discount store, that she had male sex organs as well as female. Sec. 95, lot 2003, grave 1, Calvary Cemetery, Cleveland, OH.

9510. Walsh, Thomas Francis Morgan (Sept. 19, 1908–Oct. 21, 1984) Journalist with the *Baltimore Sun* and its U.S. Historical branch retired in 1939 to write mystery novels, including *Nightmare in Manhattan* (1955, filmed in 1961 as *Union Station*), *Dark Window, Dangerous Passenger* and *Eye of the Needle.* Enfield Street Cemetery, Enfield, CT.

9511. Walsh, Thomas James (June 12, 1859–March 2, 1933) Democratic senator from Montana 1912–1933 prominent during the Teapot Dome investigations 1923–24. He died on a train in North Carolina en route to Washington to accept an appointment as attorney general in the new Roosevelt administration. St. John's Garden, Resurrection Cemetery near Helena, MT.

9512. Walston, Ray (Herman Ray Walston, Nov. 2, 1914–Jan. 1, 2001) Mississippi born, New Orleans raised actor famed for his TV role as *My Favorite Martian* 1963–66 won a Tony Award as the devil in *Damn Yankees* on Broadway 1955–56, appeared in numerous films including *Kiss Them For Me, South Pacific, Damn Yankees, The Apartment, The Sting, Fast Times at Ridgemont High* (as Mr. Hand), and won two Emmys as the blunt Judge Henry Bone on CBS's *Picket Fences* 1992–96. He died unexpectedly at 86 in his Beverly Hills home. Service at Westwood Memorial Park, west Los Angeles. Cremated by the Neptune Society of Burbank, the ashes were returned January 11 to his family.

9513. Walter, Bruno (Bruno Walter Schlesinger, Sept. 15, 1876–Feb. 17, 1962) Conductor from 1893, at Munich, with the Berlin Opera, the New York Metropolitan Opera, the Los Angeles and New York Philharmonic as well as the NBC Symphony. St. Abbondio Church Cemetery, Montagnola, Switzerland.

9514. Walters, Larry (April 19, 1949–Oct. 6, 1993) The Lawn Chair Pilot, with 45 weather balloons took his seat into flight, until he was arrested over LAX for violating their air space. "A man can't just sit around," he said. A suicide at forty-four, he shot himself in the heart. Columbarium of Valor, niche G64493, Forest Lawn Hollywood Hills, Los Angeles.

9515. Walthall, Henry B. (Henry Brazeale Walthall, March 16, 1878–June 17, 1936) Silent screen actor played the Little Colonel in *Birth of a Nation* (1915). He aged quickly and moved on to character roles and kindly old men, in *The Road to Mandalay* (1926), *A Tale of Two Cities* (1935), *The Devil Doll* and *China Clipper* (1936, he died during its filming). Only his name is on his crypt plaque. Sanctuary of Hope (now closed), crypt 370, Abbey of the Psalms/Hollywood Forever Mausoleum, Hollywood Forever Cemetery, Hollywood (Los Angeles), CA.

9516. Walton, Douglas (J. Douglas Duder, Oct. 16, 1910–Nov. 15, 1961) Artist and screen actor from Toronto in *Bride of Frankenstein* (as Shelley), *Mary of Scotland* (as Darnley), *The Picture of Dorian Gray.* He taught painting in California after service in World War II before moving to New York in 1958, where he died from a heart attack, listed as 51. Ferncliff Crematory, Hartsdale, New York. Ashes to Frank E. Campbell mortuary, N.Y.C.

9517. Walton, George (1749/1750–Feb. 2, 1804) Signer of the Declaration of Independence from Georgia, buried with Lyman Hall in vaults beneath a shaft called The Signers' Monument on the courthouse grounds at Augusta, GA.

9518. Walton, Gladys (April 13, 1903–Nov. 15, 1993) The Darling of the Five Reelers acted in over thirty eight silents at Universal 1919–1925 (*La La Lucille, Rich Girl Poor Girl, Risky Business, Second Hand Rose, A Little Girl in a Big City*). She retired 1925, married (Herbel) and moved to Chicago. She later removed to her home at Morrow Bay, California, called Gladys's Castle, with a backyard lighthouse and elevator, where she died at 90. Ashes buried sec. 4, block 3, lot 5, plot 10, Cayucos Morrow Bay Cemetery, Highway 1, Cayucos, CA.

9519. Walton, James "Bud" (Dec. 20, 1921–March 21, 1995) Brother and co-founder with Sam Walton of the Wal-Mart stores built his fortune in real estate and outlet construction, his worth estimated at $1 billion. Sec. B, estate 1-1, Memorial Park Cemetery, Columbia, MO.

9520. Walton, Sam (Samuel Moore Walton, March 29, 1918–April 4, 1992) Founder of Wal-Mart, Sam's Clubs, etc. The homespun tycoon was among the richest men in America. Block 9, lot 15, Bentonville Cemetery, Bentonville, AR.

9521. Walton, Sam (Samuel Thaw Walton, Jan. 3, 1943–May 12, 2002) Right tackle with the New York Jets during their 1968–69 Super Bowl season. He ended his days as a homeless vagrant in Memphis nicknamed Boonie. Found dead at 59 on May 12 after several days in a vacant apartment, he was identified by fingerprints. The cause was listed as a heart attack. Union Cemetery, Memphis, TN.

9522. Wanamaker, John (July 11, 1838–Dec. 12, 1922) Founder of the leading men's clothing store in the nation, opened in his native Philadelphia in the 1860's. Wanamaker family tower (locked) crypt, Churchyard of St. James the Less, 3227 West Clearfield St., Philadelphia, PA.

9523. Wanamaker, Sam (June 14, 1919–Dec. 18, 1993) Chicago born actor on Broadway after World War II left the U.S. over his leftist politics. Lead role in *Give Us This Day* (1949) before being placed on the far reaching Hollywood blacklist. He appeared in British theatre and films from the 1960's, directing several features in the 70's. Active in rebuilding the Globe Theatre, which had stood on the south bank of the Thames in Shakespeare's day, he worked at organizing its reconstruction approximately 100 yards from the original site. Later appearances in U.S. films include *Private Benjamin* (1980) and the TV miniseries *The Holocaust.* He died after a five year struggle with cancer. Ashes reportedly divided between the cornerstone of the Globe Theatre and Southwick Cathedral, London, where he has a plaque.

9524. Wanderone *see* **Minnesota Fats.**

9525. Waner, Lloyd James "Little Poison" (March 16, 1906–July 22, 1982) Brother of Paul "Big Poison" Waner, from Harrah, Oklahoma, he was considered a complete player, good at fielding, throwing and batting. The nicknames were Brooklynese for the big and little persons, both Waners, in the Pirates' outfield 1927–1940. He began with Pittsburgh in 1927, later with Boston, Cincinnati, Philadelphia and Brooklyn. He batted over .300 in ten of his first twelve seasons. Lifetime average .316. Hall of Fame 1967. Sec. 11, 2 nwc, 186, Rose Hill Memorial Park, Oklahoma City, OK.

9526. Waner, Paul Glee "Big Poison" (April 16, 1903–Aug. 29, 1965) One of baseball's finest hitters, he was one of seven players with over 3,000 hits. With Pittsburgh from 1926, he topped .300 for twelve seasons, dominating the Pirates' outfield with his brother Lloyd. Hall of Fame 1952. Sec. L, lot 164, space 1, Manasota Memorial Park, Bradenton, FL.

9527. Wanger, Walter (July 11, 1894–Nov. 18, 1968) San Francisco born producer. A former Army Intelligence officer during World War I, he served on President Wilson's staff at the Paris Peace Conference in 1919. His films ranged from *The Cocoanuts* (1929) to *Gabriel Over the White House* (1933), *Stagecoach* (1939), *I Want to Live* (1958) and *Cleopatra* (1963). He suffered a financial disaster with *Joan of Arc* (1951), and in April 1952 was sentenced on a reduced charge to four months at an honor farm for shooting Jennings Lang, whom he accused of trying to destroy his marriage to actress Joan Bennett; he had revitalized Bennett's career in 1945 by remaking her screen image into that of a sultry brunette. They were divorced in 1962. He died in his sleep six years later in his New York apartment. Mausoleum, Emmanu-El crypt 44–1, Home of Peace Cemetery, Colma, CA.

9528. Ward, Amelita (d. 1987) Brunette actress in B films 1943–49 (*The Falcon in Danger, The Falcon and the Co-Eds, Gildersleeve's Ghost, Jungle Captive, Smuggler's Cove, Slattery's Hurricane, Rim of the Canyon*) married and divorced from Leo Gorcey. Cremated in Alexandria, Virginia, in 1987.

9529. Ward, Artemas (Nov. 26, 1727–Oct. 28, 1800) Continental major general at the beginning of hostilities in the American Revolution, before George Washington took command after the battles of Lexington and Concord in April 1775. Above ground family vault with inscriptions in cut light brick. Mountain View Cemetery, Shrewsbury, MA.

9530. Ward, Carrie Clarke (Jan. 9, 1862–Feb. 6, 1926) Stage actress from Virginia City, Nevada, in silent films, including *Penrod* with Jack Pickford (1922), *The Eagle* with Valentino (1925, as Aunt Aurelia), and *The Only Thing* with Joan Crawford (1925). Crypt 121, bottom tier, Corridor (Bldg.) C — closed since an earthquake in the early 1990's — Hollywood Forever Cemetery, Hollywood (Los Angeles), CA.

9531. Ward, Clara (April 21, 1924–Jan. 16, 1973) Flamboyant gospel singer, daughter of evangelist **Gertrude Ward** (1901–1981) expanded her audience to the Newport Jazz Festival by 1957. Film appearances include *It's Your Thing* (1969) and *A Time to Sing* (1970). Entombed with her mother. Front left at eye level. Sanctuary of Commandments, crypt 20051, Freedom Mausoleum, Forest Lawn, Glendale, CA.

9532. Ward, Edward (April 3, 1900–Sept. 26, 1971) Composer worked on over 200 films from the mid 1920's to the late 1950's, including the scores for *Great Expectations* (1934), *The Mystery of Edwin Drood* (1935), *Dracula's Daughter* (1936), *Night Must Fall* (1937), *The Phantom of the Opera* (1943). He died in Los Angeles from a stroke at 71. Cremated through Pierce Bros. Westwood. Ashes sent (per the death certificate) to St. Paul's Churchyard, Affton (southwest of St. Louis), St. Louis County, MO.

9533. Ward, Jay (Sept. 20, 1920–Oct. 12, 1989) TV animator behind *Rocky and His Friends* in the early 1960's. The jokes were often far over the children's heads but did not diminish the popularity of Rocky and Bullwinkle, Boris and Natasha, *Aesop's Fables, Fractured Fairy Tales*, etc. Garden of Remembrance, lot 2359A, against wall, Forest Lawn, Glendale, CA.

9534. Ward, John Montgomery (March 3, 1860–March 4, 1925) Pioneer baseball pitcher from Bellfonte, Pennsylvania, in the 1870's and 80's pitched a perfect game for Providence, N.L., in 1880. Later a shortstop and manager of New York and Brooklyn. President of the Boston Red Sox 1911. He organized the short lived Players League in 1890. Hall of Fame 1964. He died suddenly a day after his 65th birthday while on vacation in Georgia. Taken to the Higby receiving vault in the village rural cemetery at Babylon, Long Island, New York, he was buried June 2, 1925. Sec. 2, lot 185, grave 2, Greenfield Cemetery, Hempstead, NY.

9535. Ward, John Quincy Adams (June 29, 1830–May 1, 1910) Sculptor from Champaign County, Ohio. Best known works were *The Indian Hunter* (1867, now in Central Park), *The Good Samaritan* in the Public Gardens at Boston, statues of Gen. John Reynolds at Gettysburg and of Israel Putnam at Hartford, Connecticut. In 1883 he unveiled his statue of Washington at the Federal Building on Wall Street in Manhattan. Others include sculpted statues of Peter Cooper and Horace Greeley in Manhattan. He served as president of the National Academy of Design, founded the National Sculpture Society in 1899 and was its first president. At his death in New York City, he was returned for burial, marked by a replica of *The Indian Hunter*, to Oakdale Cemetery, Urbana, OH.

9536. Ward, Montgomery (Aaron Montgomery Ward, Feb. 17, 1843–Dec. 7, 1913) Chicago business magnate began his mail order catalogue service aimed at farmers who could obtain goods at a lower price while Ward saved the overhead costs of a store. By 1888 his annual sales ran to a $1,000,000. He retired from active leadership in 1886. The bulk of his fortune eventually went to Northwestern University. His family room, with an ornately sculpted bronze door, is near that of Sears at the extreme right front of Rosehill mausoleum, Rosehill Cemetery, Chicago, IL.

9537. Ward, Rodger (Jan. 10, 1921–July 5, 2004) Race driver from Beloit, Kansas, a World War II Air Force fighter pilot, appeared at the Indianapolis 500 from 1951 to 1966, nearly retiring in 1955 when Bill Vukovich ran into him and was killed. He won in 1959 and 1962, and promoted the front engine car which finished ninth in 1961 and marked the end of rear engine roadsters. He failed to qualify in 1965, and retired upon leaving the race in 1966. He resided in Lake Forest, California, and died in a hospice in Anaheim at 83. Memorial service at the San Diego Auto Club. Cremated through Inland Memorial mortuary. Ashes July 16 to family.

9538. Ward, Samuel A. (Dec. 28, 1847–Sept. 28, 1903) Organist from 1880 at Grace Episcopal Church in Newark, New Jersey, where he was born and died, also founded a music store there. His song *Materna* became the music for *America the Beautiful*. A plaque in his memory was placed on the church parish house in 1934. Mt. Pleasant Cemetery, Newark, NJ.

9539. Ware, Herta (June 9, 1917–Aug. 15, 2005) Actress, former wife of Will Geer involved in the labor movement from the 1930's co-founded the Theatricum Botanicum in Topanga, California, in the 1950's when Geer was blacklisted. Among her film roles was as Jack Gilford's dying wife in *Cocoon* (1985). Later married and divorced from David Marshall, she was with Geer when he died. She died at their home in Topanga at 88. Cremated through Callanan mortuary and her ashes returned to her family. Memorial service Theatricum Botanicum, Topanga Canyon, Los Angeles.

9540. Ware, Irene (Irene A. Ahlberg, Nov. 6, 1910–March 11, 1993) New York born actress in films of the 1930's, primarily melodramas (*Chandu the Magician* 1932, *The Raven* 1935). Long retired, as Irene Campbell she died at 82 in Santa Ana Medical Center from pneumonia and severe dementia. Ashes returned through Saddleback Chapel to her family in Encinitas, CA.

9541. Warfield, David (Nov. 28, 1866–June 27, 1951) Star of vaudeville and Broadway was with Weber and Fields until David Belasco made him a star in *The Auctioneer* (1901), featuring him as Solomon Levi, his best known role. He died a millionaire fifty years later in his Central Park West apartment. A bench inscribed with his last name marks his grave in a private enclosure in a row of similar hedge enclosed lots. Front of St. Paul sec., plot 180, Ferncliff Cemetery, Hartsdale, NY.

9542. Warfield, William (Jan. 22, 1920–Aug. 25, 2002) Bass-baritone and pianist from West Helena, Arkansas, best known for his rendition of *Old Man River* in the 1951 film version of *Show Boat*. He toured Europe the next year in *Porgy and Bess* with Leontyne Price, his wife from 1952–72. In 1975 he sold out Carnegie Hall, in 1984 received a Grammy nomination for his narration of Aaron Copland's *A Lincoln Portrait*, chaired the voice department at the University of Illinois and in his last years taught music at Northwestern. He died in Chicago at 82 while recovering from a broken neck suffered at his southside home. Headstone with World War II veteran's plaque

at the head of a grave length slab with his name and dates, a show boat at the bottom, and above it *Uncle Bill*. *"Old man river. He just keeps rollin' along."* Sec. AA, lot 2, Mt. Hope Cemetery, Rochester, NY.

9543. Warhol, Andy (Aug. 6, 1928–Feb. 22, 1987) Acclaimed pop artist and underground film maker also managed the Velvet Underground. He was perennially controversial and his motives remained intentionally obscure. Whatever his work or intentions, he gained his greatest fame for his painting of a Campbell's Soup can and for his statement that everyone would be "famous for fifteen minutes." He died in a Manhattan hospital at 58 following complications from a routine gall bladder operation. His upright stone, which almost appears as a drawing, has a Russian Orthodox cross above his name and dates, with praying hands below it. Warhol plot with his parents, atop a steep hill just outside Pittsburgh. St. John the Baptist Byzantine Catholic Church Cemetery, Bethel Park/Castle Shannon, PA.

9544. Waring, Fred (June 9, 1900–July 29, 1984) Bandleader popular in the late 1920's with his Pennsylvanians, with whom he entertained for nearly seven decades. The first electronic recording of a song was their version of *Collegiate* (1927) followed by the first all musical film *Syncopation* and other hits including *Sleep*. He also invented the Waring Blender. In the last year of his life he was still performing at 84; his last concert was at Pennsylvania State University (which houses the Fred Waring Collection) on Friday July 27, 1984. He suffered a stroke the next day at State College, his summer home. Buried near his 600 acre winter residence east of Stroudsburg, his stone notes that he was the recipient of the Congressional Gold Medal in 1983. Presbyterian Church Cemetery, Shawnee-on-Delaware, PA.

9545. Warmerdam, Cornelius "Dutch" (June 22, 1915–Nov. 13, 2001) The most dominant pole vaulter in history set a world indoor record in 1939 and broke the 15' barrier in 1940. He cleared 15'7¾" in 1942, a record that lasted fifteen years, and 15'8½" in 1943, which lasted sixteen. When he retired he had recorded the forty three highest vaults of all time. He coached track at Fresno State University 1947–1980. Garden of Valor, 503-A-3, Fresno Memorial Gardens, Fresno, CA.

9546. Warner, Albert (July 23, 1884–Nov. 26, 1967) One of the two older founders of Warner Brothers film studios, Albert and Harry were born in Poland, relocated to Ontario and then to Youngstown, Ohio, where they began showing films, joined by younger brothers Sam and Jack. They went to Pittsburgh, then New York, landing in Hollywood as Warner Bros. by 1918. Albert lived to retire from active leadership but remained on the studio board of directors until 1966. He died in Miami Beach and is the only one of the four interred in New York. Family mausoleum, rear of Salem Fields Cemetery, Brooklyn, N.Y.C.

9547. Warner, Anna Bartlett (Aug. 31, 1827–Jan. 22, 1915) Poet who wrote as Elizabeth Wetherell, including the hymn *Jesus Loves Me*, taught cadets at West Point for many years. Sec. 30, lot Q, grave 587, Post Cemetery, West Point Military Academy, West Point, NY.

9548. Warner, H. B. (Henry Byron Warner, Oct. 26, 1876–Dec. 24, 1958) Silent screen star of stately demeanor played Christ in DeMille's epic *King of Kings* (1927). He went on to sound films with memorable parts in *Five Star Final, Supernatural, A Tale of Two Cities*, and several Frank Capra pictures including *Mr. Deeds Goes to Town* (1936), *Lost Horizon* (1937, Academy Award nomination) and *It's A Wonderful Life* (1946, as Mr. Gower the druggist). Ashes in vaultage at Pierce Brothers' Chapel of the Pines Crematory, Los Angeles.

9549. Warner, Harry (Dec. 12, 1881–July 25, 1958) The elder of the Warner Brothers and cofounder, with Albert, was originally the president and remained in that position, though it was Sam behind the experiment with sound and Jack who ran the studio. Harry and Jack quarreled before the former's death when Jack kept his stock and took over the company once Harry and Albert sold out. Father in law of director Charles Vidor. Family mausoleum, Home of Peace Memorial Park, east Los Angeles.

9550. Warner, Jack L. (Aug. 2, 1892–Sept. 9, 1978) The youngest of twelve children of Jewish immigrants from Poland joined his brothers Albert, Harry and Sam in the formation of Warner Brothers film production in 1912 in Youngstown, Ohio. In Hollywood from 1918, they averted bankruptcy through *The Jazz Singer* (1927). From that point on, Jack Warner ran the studio in Burbank, a prime Hollywood mogul legendary for his long running battles with his various stars, including Bette Davis, James Cagney, Humphrey Bogart and Errol Flynn. In 1957 he gained complete control when his brothers sold their shares, selling his interest to Seven Arts in 1967. A polished black marble fountain and grave length tablet, with the inscription *In Memory of years of devotion*, marks his grave. Sec. C, Home of Peace Memorial Park, east Los Angeles.

9551. Warner, Marvin (June 8, 1919–April 8, 2002) U.S. diplomat, Ambassador to Switzerland under Carter was a corporate baseball owner and horse breeder who headed Home State Savings in Cincinnati until its collapse in 1985. Convicted of fraud, he was sentenced to twenty eight months in prison. He died while watching the launch of the space shuttle *Atlantis*. Lakeside Memorial Park, Miami, FL.

9552. Warner, Pop (Glenn Scobey Warner, April 5, 1871–Sept. 7, 1954) Football coach 1896–1938, at Cornell, Carlisle and later at Pittsburgh, Stanford and Temple Universities. He retired with 313 victories, one fewer than Amos Alonzo Stagg. His name was given to football leagues for boys across the country. Maplewood Cemetery, Springville, NY.

9553. Warner, Sam L. (Aug. 10, 1887–Oct. 5, 1927) Third of four Warner Brothers was vice president of the company, including Vitaphone, at the time of his death at 40 in Los Angeles from pneumonia. It was he who became interested in the possibilities of synchronizing screen action and sound, and pressured his partner brothers into buying Vitaphone in May 1927. The resulting pioneer film *The Jazz Singer* saved the studio from bankruptcy, opening to record crowds and changing film history — the week of Sam Warner's premature death. Warner mausoleum with iron grating over the crypt fronts, sec. D, Home of Peace Memorial Park, east Los Angeles.

9554. Warren, Charles (Feb. 7, 1840–Jan. 21, 1927) Knighted English soldier, served in the Boer War and founded the Boy Scout movement but is best remembered as the unpopular London police commissioner 1886–88 who presided over the Bloody Sunday riots in Trafalgar Square in November 1887 and failed to find the Whitechapel murderer dubbed Jack the Ripper the following autumn. Long at odds with Home Secretary Matthews, he resigned November 10, 1888, following the most savage of the Whitechapel murders. Funeral at Canterbury Cathedral. Burial at Westbere.

9555. Warren, E. Alyn (Edward Alyn Warren, June 2, 1874–Jan. 22, 1940) Actor from Richmond, Virginia, in films from 1915, sometimes cast as sinister Orientals; appearances include *Outside the Law, The Unholy Three* (prosecutor), *The Bells, Abraham Lincoln* (Stephen Douglas), *A Free Soul, Daughter of the Dragon* (Lu Chong), *The Hatchet Man, The Mask of Fu Manchu* (messenger), *Tarzan the Fearless, The Devil Doll, They Won't Forget, Miracles For Sale*. Vaultage, (Pierce Bros.) Chapel of the Pines Crematory, Los Angeles.

9556. Warren, Earl (March 19, 1891–July 9, 1974) Governor of California 1943–1953 was considered a safe Republican choice when President Eisenhower appointed him Chief Justice of the Supreme Court in 1953, but Warren surprised the administration with a series of liberal decisions, notably the landmark *Brown v. the Board of Education* in 1954, forcing school integration, and *Miranda v. Arizona* (1966), requiring the reading of Constitutional rights to all suspects taken into custody by police. He also chaired the commission named for him, appointed by President Johnson to investigate and report on the assassination of President Kennedy. Because of his strong support of civil liberties, Warren was the most controversial chief justice of the 20th century. He resigned in June 1969, maintaining an office in Washington, D.C., where he died five years later. He was the first person other than a president to lie in state on a catafalque that had held Lincoln. Buried on a knoll a few yards from his contemporary, Eisenhower's Secretary of State John Foster Dulles. Sec. 21, site S-32, grid M-20/21, Arlington National Cemetery, Arlington, VA.

9557. Warren, Harry (Dec. 23, 1894–Sept. 22,

1981) Prolific composer of Hollywood film numbers won Academy Awards for *Lullaby of Broadway* (from *Gold Diggers of 1935*), *You'll Never Know* (from *Hello, Frisco, Hello* 1943) and for *The Atchison, Topeka and the Santa Fe* (from *The Harvey Girls* 1946). He also wrote the music for *42nd St.* (1933), *Gold Diggers of 1933*, many more. Sanctuary of Tenderness, Westwood Memorial Park, west Los Angeles.

9558. Warren, James (Sept. 28, 1726–Nov. 28, 1808) American Revolutionary General and President of the Provincial Congress of Massachusetts. Husband to Mercy Otis, sister of James Otis. A bronze monument with his image was erected by the Sons of the American Revolution in 1923. Old Burial Hill, Plymouth, MA.

9559. Warren, John May (May 14, 1930–July 27, 1938) Child whose homely and pugnacious 1933 toddler-baby picture taken in Westport, Connecticut, was found to have been retouched and falsified as Hitler's, bringing complaints from Berlin. Five years later, age 8, the boy was riding his bicycle in Lakewood (Cleveland), Ohio, when he fell while holding a glass milk bottle, a shard of which pierced his heart. He was sent from William and Roy Daniels mortuary in Cleveland to (unspecified on the d.c. or mortuary records) Chicago, IL.

9560. Warren, Katherine (July 12, 1905–July 17, 1965) Detroit born actress in films from 1949, often as proper society wives (*All the King's Men*, as Jack Burden's mother; *Night Into Morning, Scandal Sheet, The People Against O'Hara, The Caine Mutiny*, as Willie Keith's mother; *The Violent Men, Inside Detroit, Jailhouse Rock*). She died at her home, 3281 South Sepulveda, Los Angeles, from a heart attack at 60. A widow, her married name was Chesney. Cremated July 20 through Moeller-Murphy-Moeller at the Chapel of the Pacific, Woodlawn Cemetery. Urn in undersized permanent storage crypt. Unit 1, 95-X, sec. C, mausoleum, Woodlawn Cemetery, Santa Monica, CA.

9561. Warren, Mercy Otis (Sept. 14, 1728–Oct. 19, 1814) Poet and historian of the American Revolutionary era, sister of James Otis and the first American literary figure. Her plays, written at home in Plymouth, include *The Adulateur* (1773), *The Group* (1775) and her better known *Poems Dramatic and Miscellaneous* (1790). Her 1805 history of the war is of interest for its first hand views of the figures of the day. Buried with her husband, Gen. James Warren. Old Burial Hill, Plymouth, MA.

9562. Warren, Robert Penn (April 24, 1905–Sept. 15, 1989) Guthrie, Kentucky, born author and poet graduated from Vanderbilt, a member of the literary group known as The Fugitives, embodying a southern literary renaissance. Best known for *All the King's Men* (1946), which won the Pulitzer Prize in 1947 and was made into an Oscar winning film in 1949, though it deleted the narrator Jack Burden's interwoven Ph.D. thesis about a Civil War figure, Cass

Mastern. Warren won the Pulitzer Prize again in 1958 for *Promises: Poems 1954–56, 1957*, the first writer to win in both literature and poetry. He was buried where he lived and wrote the last thirty years of his life. Upright stone, Willis Cemetery, Stratton, VT.

9563. Warrick, Ruth (June 29, 1916–Jan. 15, 2005) Actress from St. Joseph, Missouri, played Emily Monroe Norton Kane — Kane's first wife — in *Citizen Kane* (1941), and later had roles in the soap operas *Peyton Place, As the World Turns,* and for three decades from 1970 was Phoebe Tyler Wallingford on the soap opera *All My Children* prior to her death from pneumonia at 88 in New York City. Ashes interred in the Church of the Transfiguration (the Little Church Around the Corner), Manhattan, N.Y.C.

9564. Warwick, Robert (Robert T. Bien, Oct. 9, 1878–June 6, 1964) Sacramento born matinee idol of the silent screen in character roles with sound, many as detectives, exhibiting his baritone voice in *So Big, Doctor X* (both 1932), *The Murder Man* and *A Tale of Two Cities* (both 1935), *The Private Lives of Elizabeth and Essex* (1939), dozens of others. Not to be confused with the older actor Robert Warwick (1868–1944), buried at Hollywood Cemetery (Hollywood Forever). Flush rose colored double plaque. Sec. N, lot 399, Holy Cross Cemetery, Culver City, CA.

9565. Washburn, Bryant (April 28, 1889–April 30, 1963) Chicago born actor in silents at Essanay, later moved to Hollywood, often as a villain. Sec. T, tier 51, grave 70, Holy Cross Cemetery, Culver City, California. **Bryant Washburn, Jr.** (Oct. 12, 1915–Dec. 3, 1960), also an actor, is in sec. O, grave 410, Santa Fe National Cemetery, Santa Fe, NM.

9566. Washburn, Edward Payson (Nov. 17, 1831–March 26, 1860) Artist best known for *The Arkansas Traveller* and *The Turning of the Tune*. Willow 580, Mount Holly Cemetery, Little Rock, AR.

9567. Washington, Blue (Edgar Washington Blue aka Edgar Hughes Washington, Feb. 12, 1898–Sept. 15, 1970) Black actor often cast in racist stereotypes, in films 1919–1957 (*Haunted Spooks* with Harold Lloyd, *Beggars of Life, Prisoner of Shark Island, Tarzan's Revenge,* many others). He died of liver failure in Lancaster, California, at 72. Sec. E, lot 4377, Evergreen Cemetery, Los Angeles.

9568. Washington, Booker T. (April 5, 1856–Nov. 14, 1915) A former slave, the first head of Tuskegee Institute for the education of blacks stressed higher education and economic independence as the crux of true freedom, accepting racial segregation until their economic progress would eventually break down color barriers. He established the National Negro Business League and wrote several books, including *Up From Slavery* (1901). Marked by a large rough hewn monument, both he and George Washington Carver are buried in the small cemetery on the campus of Tuskegee Institute, thirty five miles east of Montgomery, AL.

9569. Washington, Dinah (Ruth Jones, Aug. 29,

1924–Dec. 14, 1963) Queen of the Blues also recorded mainstream hits such as *September in the Rain* (1961) and *What a Difference a Day Made.* She died from an accidental drug overdose, combining pills and alcohol, at 39. On her flush red plaque are both her names and musical notes. Elm Grove sec., lot 155, grave 4, Burr Oak Cemetery, Alsip (Chicago area), IL.

9570. Washington, Ford Lee (March 21, 1907–Jan. 31, 1955) Buck of Buck and Bubbles, black comedic dancing duo of vaudeville and Broadway, a few films. Sec. 16, block C, row J, grave 14, Cypress Hills Cemetery, Brooklyn, N.Y.C.

9571. Washington, Fredi (Dec. 23, 1903–June 28, 1994) Actress best known as Louise Beavers' light skinned daughter intent on "passing" in the 1934 *Imitation of Life.* She died at 90 in Stamford, Ct. Cremated through Gallagher mortuary in Stamford (married name Bell). No disposition available.

9572. Washington, George (Feb. 22, 1732–Dec. 14, 1799) Commanding general of the Colonial Army in the Revolution and the first President of the United States (1789–1797), popularly known as the Father of His Country. In life Washington endured much hardship and defeat during the war with England. As president, he urged neutrality amid possible foreign entanglements, presiding quietly over the struggles between the agrarian Democrat Jefferson and the Federalist Hamilton. He retired to his estate Mount Vernon on the Potomac below Alexandria, Virginia, where he regularly rode his horse around inspecting his estate; on December 12, 1799 he did so in the hale and snow for five hours. The cold this produced quickly turned to what modern study has termed acute inflammatory edema. A tracheotomy, then new and dangerous, might have relieved the problem but was not tried. In dying, Washington asked that his body not be put into the tomb until two days after death, then thanked the doctors, saying that he was going and there was nothing more they could do. His body was placed in a red brick tomb on the estate, half way down the slope behind the mansion, where his wife **Martha Dandridge Custis Washington** (June 2, 1731–May 22, 1802) was placed beside him two and a half years later. Though this original tomb still stands, the coffins were removed when the present tomb was constructed farther down toward the Potomac in 1831–32, and placed there along with many other family members. On a white tablet over the gateway is inscribed *Within this enclosure rest the remains of Gen. George Washington.* The sarcophagi of he and his wife were placed behind the inner wall of the enclosure until October 7, 1837, when they were removed to their present location in the ante-room, visible behind high iron gates. On the president's white marble, coffin shaped sarcophagus, constructed in 1837 to contain his lead coffin, is inscribed only *Washington.* On his left, his wife's simpler one is inscribed *Martha, Consort of Washington.* The tomb and surrounding monuments are at the foot of a long hill, only a short distance from the Potomac. Nearby a monument to many slaves and free blacks buried in their own graveyard but unmarked was dedicated in 1983 on the site of the graveyard. Mount Vernon itself fell into disrepair, like most subsequent presidential estates, until the Mount Vernon Ladies Association was formed in 1858 and began meticulous care of the grounds. Mount Vernon, near Alexandria, Virginia. Washington's mother **Mary Ball Washington** (1708–Aug. 25, 1789) is marked by a towering obelisk inscribed *Mary, the mother of Washington,* at Kenmore Plantation and Gardens, Fredericksburg, VA.

9573. Washington, Grover, Jr. (Dec. 12, 1943–Dec 18, 1999) Buffalo born pioneer jazz saxophonist mastered tenor, alto and soprano and blended pop with jazz. First celebrated for his 1970 LP *Inner City Blues,* his most successful album was *Limelight,* featuring *Just the Two of Us,* his best known work, with vocals by Bill Withers. Washington died at St. Luke's–Roosevelt Hospital in Manhattan at 56, having collapsed earlier after taping four songs for *the Saturday Early Morning Show.* Franconia Island, West Laurel Hill Cemetery, Bala Cynwyd, PA.

9574. Washington, Harold (April 15, 1922–Nov. 25, 1987) Chicago's first black mayor had easily won a second term in office in April 1987. He died from a heart attack suffered in his office shortly before Christmas. Interred in a mausoleum with a bench and plantings, and a stone with the epitaph *He loved Chicago.* Sec. 1, div. 2, south part along the road, Oakwoods Cemetery, Chicago, IL.

9575. Washington, Lloyd (March 23, 1921–June 22, 2004) Ink Spot vocalist 1945–60. Ashes were at the Ernie K-Doe Lounge until placed in the Barbarin tomb, renamed the New Orleans Musicians' Tomb in October 2004. St. Louis I Cemetery, New Orleans, LA.

9576. Washington, Ned (Edward Washington, Aug. 15, 1901–Dec. 20, 1976) Lyricist wrote for Broadway and film, including the songs *Smoke Rings, I'm Getting Sentimental Over You,* and *My Foolish Heart.* Mausoleum, block 4, crypt E3, Holy Cross Cemetery, Culver City, CA.

9577. Wasserman, Lew (Lewis Robert Wasserman, March 15, 1913–June 3, 2002) Cleveland native was a Hollywood agent before becoming the chairman and CEO of MCA, Universal's parent company. With them for over fifty years and controlling over fifteen percent of their stock, he was renown for his friendships with presidents and other world leaders. Among his many expansions at Universal was the now traditional studio tour. Buried the day after his death. Small family garden enclosed in a hedge. Canaan, block 4, plot 8A, space 1B, Hillside Memorial Park, Los Angeles.

9578. Waterman, Ida Shaw (March 10, 1852–May 22, 1914) Stage actress in elder roles in silent films 1914–26, including *The Enchanted Cottage* (1924), *Stella Maris,* and *The Swan* (1926), died in Cincinnati at 90. Buried as Ida Francoeur. Ashes interred sec. 104, lot 101, grave 5C, Spring Grove Cemetery, Cincinnati, OH.

9579. Waterman, Willard (Aug. 29, 1914–Feb. 2, 1995) Radio veteran of over twenty years prior to replacing Harold Peary as *The Great Gildersleeve* 1950–1955, then continuing in the part on TV. Afterward he appeared as Upson in the film version of *Auntie Mame*, etc. A founder of the American Federation of Radio Artists. He died at Burlingame, California, at 80. Ashes interred Cypress Circle, lot 506, sec. A, space 4, Skylawn Memorial Park, San Mateo, CA.

9580. Waters, Ethel (Oct. 31, 1896–Sept. 1, 1977) Black stage and film actress grew up in poverty in Philadelphia before beginning her stage career in New York in the 1920's, recording jazz numbers including *Am I Blue* and *Dinah*. She appeared in the stage and film versions of the musical *Cabin in the Sky* (1943) and in dramatic roles in *Pinky* (AA nom. 1949) and *Member of the Wedding* (both stage and screen, 1952). In later years she lived on her Social Security check, having spent or given away what she had made. Deeply religious, she said a star could "receive roses and go home and cry alone" but she could call on the Lord and was never alone. Her best selling inspirational autobiography *His Eye is on the Sparrow* was reprinted many times. In a speech shown at the time of her death, she told a crowd of her assurance of Heaven, concluding with "I'll be looking for you all there." She died at 80 at the home of friends in Chatsworth, California, from diabetes and cancer complicating heart and kidney failure. Services at the Church of the Recessional at Forest Lawn, Glendale. The epitaph on her plaque is *His eye is on the sparrow.* Garden of Ascension, lot 7152, Forest Lawn, Glendale, CA.

9581. Waters, Muddy (McKinley Morganfield, April 4, 1915–April 30, 1983) Mississippi born blues singer and musician was a major influence on Chicago blues of the 40's. He formed the first electric blues band, recorded thirty years with the Chess Brothers. His flush marker lists his real name with a guitar and the epitaph *The mojo is gone... The master has won.* Sec. H, Restvale Cemetery, Alsip (Chicago area), IL.

9582. Watkin, Pierre (Dec. 29, 1887–Feb. 3, 1960) Character actor in many films, including Mr. Skinner the bank president (with the hardy hand clasp) in *The Bank Dick* (1940). Unmarked, mausoleum block L, sec. 998, lot 15, Pierce Bros. Valhalla Memorial Park, North Hollywood, CA.

9583. Watkins, Sam R. (June 26, 1839–July 20, 1901) A private from Columbia, Tennessee, in Co. H of the Army of the Tennessee, Watkins' insightful and often humorous narrative of his service through the Civil War was printed as *A Confederate Soldier's Memoirs* in the 1880's, later titled *Co. Aytch.* It remains a favorite of the first hand remembrances of Civil War soldiers, and the primary memoir from the southerner's point of view. He served throughout the war and fought in all of his company's major battles including Shiloh. Zion Presbyterian Church Cemetery, Columbia, TN.

9584. Watson, Bobs (Nov. 16, 1930–June 26, 1999) Child actor from age two, adept at crying on cue, as Pee Wee in *Boys Town* (1938), *In Old Chicago*, as Pud in *On Borrowed Time* (1939), *Dodge City* etc. In films sporadically to 1967, he became an ordained minister the next year. He appeared in *Deadly Delusions* (1998) prior to his death from prostate cancer at 68 in Laguna Beach. A memorial mass was held for him at Boys Town, Nebraska, where Father Flanagan had helped inspire Watson's ministry. Behind the Cathedral Mausoleum/Court of the Apostles, unit 9, crypt 6593, H6, Hollywood Forever Cemetery, Hollywood (Los Angeles), CA.

9585. Watson, Harry (Aug. 31, 1921–June 8, 2001) Brother of Bobs Watson, one of nine children of Coy and Golda, several of whom were in show business. In films including *The Barber Shop* with W.C. Fields and *Mr. Smith Goes to Washington*, he became a news photographer in his father's press photo business, as his brothers did, later working for the Los Angeles Daily News and for KTTV, known for a sense of dry humor he sometimes used on his subjects. Tribute sec., lot 2792, space 1, Forest Lawn Hollywood Hills, Los Angeles.

9586. Watson, Johnny "Guitar" (Feb. 3, 1935–May 17, 1996) Rhythm and blues composer and musician, suffered a heart attack while touring in Japan. Guitar on plaque. Sanctuary of Enduring Honor, crypt 14267, Great Mausoleum, Forest Lawn, Glendale, CA.

9587. Watson, Lucille (May 27, 1879–June 24, 1962) Quebec born stage and screen actress, in Hollywood from 1934 as various society matrons and dowagers, both haughty and kind hearted (*Waterloo Bridge* 1940, *Watch on the Rhine* 1942, Oscar nomination). Widow of playwright Louis Shipman. Unmarked in the lot of her husband's family, where Louis Evan Shipman has an 18th century stone. Sec. 37, lot 153, Mount Hope Cemetery, Hastings-on-Hudson, NY.

9588. Watson, Minor (Dec. 22, 1889–July 28, 1965) Character actor in many films, usually as benevolent lawyers, in *Huckleberry Finn* (1931), *Our Betters* (1933), *Babbitt* (1934), *Dead End* (1937), *Boys Town* (1938), *Yankee Doodle Dandy* (1942, as E.F. Albee), *Mr. 880* (1949), many others. Headstone next to his wife, along the road. Block 13, lot 2, Alton Cemetery, Alton, IL.

9589. Watts, Charlie (Oct. 30, 1912–Dec. 13, 1966) Actor from Clarksville, Tennessee, a graduate of Vanderbilt and an M.A. from Peabody, in theatre and a regular in films from 1950, often as back slapping good old boys (*An Affair to Remember, Giant, Billy Rose's Jumbo, Dead Ringer*). He died from cancer in Nashville at 52. Tartley (now Neal-Tartley) mortuary, Clarksville. Sec. 11, Greenwood Cemetery, Clarksville, TN.

9590. Watts, Isaac (July 17, 1674–Nov. 25, 1748) English composer of hymns, notably *O God Our Help in Ages Past*. Rectangular sarcophagus shaped monument. Bunhill Fields, London.

9591. Watts, John (Aug. 27, 1749–Sept. 3, 1836) Speaker of the New York Assembly, congressman, and the first judge of Westchester County, New York (1806). His large statue in judicial wig and robes, commissioned by a descendant in 1893, dominates the south end of Trinity Churchyard in downtown Manhattan, N.Y.C.

9592. Waugh, Evelyn (Oct. 28, 1903–April 10, 1966) English novelist, author of *The Loved One*, a satirical look at the Hollywood sanitization of death by mortuaries and cemeteries, particularly Forest Lawn, through the beautifying of everything in name as well as landscaping. It was filmed in 1965, a year before his death from a heart attack at 62. Stone slab, St. Peter and Paul's Churchyard, Combe Florey, Somerset.

9593. Waxman, Al (Albert Samuel Waxman, March 2, 1935–Jan. 17, 2001) Toronto born actor in much Canadian theatre, TV and various films — often as detectives — from the early 1970's, best known as shopkeeper Larry King on the CBC's *The King of Kensington* 1975–80 and as Lieutenant Samuels on CBS's *Cagney and Lacey* 1981–88. He died of complications during bypass surgery in Toronto at 65. Service at Holy Blossom Temple. Upright black stone. Community Sec., Pardes Shalom Cemetery, Richmond Hill, (near Toronto), Ontario.

9594. Waxman, Franz (Franz Wachsmann, Dec. 24, 1906–Feb. 24, 1967) Composer left Germany in 1934 after a beating by anti-Semites. In the U.S. from 1935, his scores include *Bride of Frankenstein* (1935), *The Invisible Ray* (1936), *A Day at the Races* and *Captains Courageous* (1937), *A Christmas Carol* (1938), *Dr. Jekyll & Mr. Hyde* (1941), many others, including Academy Awards for *Sunset Boulevard* (1950) and *A Place in the Sun* (1951), several other nominations. In 1947 he founded the Los Angeles Music Festival. Waxman died from cancer at 60. Beth Olam Mausoleum/Hall of Solomon, foyer O, tier 5, niche 1, Beth Olam Cemetery adjacent Hollywood Forever Cemetery, Hollywood (Los Angeles), CA.

9595. Waymire, Kellie (Kellie Suzanne Waymire, July 27, 1967–Nov. 14, 2003) Actress born in Columbus, Ohio, appeared in theatre, films, and television, where she was best known, on *One Life To Live*, as Crewman Elizabeth Cutler on *Enterprise* 2001–02 and as Melissa on *Six Feet Under*. While appearing in the play *Kate Crackernuts*, she died at 36 in her Venice, California, home, reportedly from cardiac arrhythmia. Initially to be buried at West Milton, Ohio, her ashes went to her father in Houston, TX.

9596. Wayne, Anthony (Jan. 1, 1745–Dec. 15, 1796) Leading Colonial general in the Revolutionary War called Mad Anthony Wayne because of his tactical boldness bordering on recklessness throughout the war. He was recalled to service in the Ohio Valley by Washington in 1792, ending with his pacification of several tribes and the Treaty of Greenville in 1795. He died the next year at Presque Isle, now Erie, Pennsylvania, while taking control of forts being abandoned by the British in accordance with the Jay Treaty. He was buried, as he requested, at the foot of the flagstaff in the military garrison at Presque Isle. His son Isaac went to retrieve the body in 1809 and bring it back to St. David's Churchyard at Radnor, now Wayne, Pennsylvania, west of Philadelphia. The flesh, according to legend, was boiled from the bones so they would fit into Isaac's saddlebags. The boiling bowl is on display in the Erie Historical Society. The saddlebags with the bones, by some accounts, were stolen. Still a service took place at Wayne in 1809 and something of Mad Anthony was buried there, where a monument to him now stands near his birthplace at Waynesboro. The flesh was supposedly returned to the original grave, no longer identifiable, at what is now the Soldiers and Sailors Home, 560 3rd St. in Erie, making Wayne the only noted American historical figure with two graves.

9597. Wayne, Bernie (Bernie Weitzner, March 6, 1919–April 18, 1993) Composer best known for *Blue Velvet*, as noted on his stone (*He made all our days Blue Velvet*). He also wrote the *Miss America* theme. Sec. CC, tier 64, grave 49, Holy Cross Cemetery, Culver City, CA.

9598. Wayne, Carol (Sept. 6, 1942–Jan. 13, 1985) Actress, skater and showgirl from Chicago did several bit parts in television before gaining attention as the Teatime Lady on *The Tonight Show* with Johnny Carson. She drowned at 42 while vacationing at Manzanillo, Mexico. Cremated.

9599. Wayne, David (Wayne McKeekan, Jan. 30, 1913–Feb. 9, 1995) 5'7" actor from Traverse County, Michigan, won Tonys for *Finian's Rainbow* (1947) and *Teahouse of the August Moon* (1954). Films include *Adam's Rib, Portrait of Jennie, Wait til the Sun Shines Nellie*, many others. Much TV, including the *Twilight Zone* episode *Escape Clause* (1959) and the series *House Calls*. He died from lung cancer at 81 in Santa Monica. Cremated by Pierce Brothers Westwood Village mortuary, the ashes were returned to the residence through his executor.

9600. Wayne, John (Marion Robert Morrison, May 26, 1907–June 11, 1979) The consummate film hero, born at Winterset, Iowa, was a USC student when he began working as a prop man at Fox, starring by 1930 in *The Big Trail* and other westerns but not achieving his status as the ultimate no nonsense, All American cowboy until John Ford's *Stagecoach* (1939). Gradually perfecting his slow swagger and measured, self confident speech, he stepped out of cowboy gear only occasionally, starring for Ford in *Fort Apache* (1948), *Three Godfathers, She Wore a Yellow Ribbon* (1949), *The Quiet Man* (1952), *The Searchers* (1956), and *The Man Who Shot Liberty Valance* (1962). Other signature Wayne roles, through his peak in the 50's and 60's, include *Red River* (1948), *Rio Bravo* (1959), *McClintock* (1963), *Rio Lobo, Hondo, The Sons of Katie Elder* (1965), *True Grit* (1969, Academy Award), *Rooster Cogburn* (1975, with Katherine Hepburn) and his swan song, Don Siegel's *The Shootist* (1976), his most in depth character study, about a gunfighter dying of cancer. He had lost a lung during cancer surgery in 1964 but survived and for over a decade was free of the disease. Shortly after undergoing heart surgery in Boston, he checked into UCLA Medical Center in Los Angeles for further cancer surgery. A week after congress authorized a special gold medal in his honor, he died in the hospital with his seven children present. True to his tough screen image, he frequently refused pain medication in order to be conscious while his family was there. His last appearance was on April 9, 1979 at the Oscar ceremonies when he presented the Oscar for best picture to *The Deer Hunter.* Though he had requested cremation and as an epitaph *Feo, fuerte y formal* (*Tough, ugly and dignified*), his secret committal service was held at dawn on June 15, 1979 in Newport Beach next to the grave of Chic Iverson's son Charles IV, who died in a motorcycle wreck in 1973, but the location was not given out and the grave remained unmarked until March 1998. The bronze plaque shows a profile of Wayne on horseback, a mission and a mesa in the distance below a western sky with clouds, bordered by a lasso and inscribed *Tomorrow is the most important thing in life/Comes unto us at midnight very clear/ It's perfect when it arrives and puts itself in our hands/ It hopes we've learned something from yesterday. JOHN WAYNE 1907–1979.* Bayview Terrace, adjacent lot 573, Pacific View Memorial Park, Newport Beach, CA.

9601. Wayne, Johnny (May 28, 1918–July 11, 1990) Comedian with the team Wayne and Shuster, on radio before and during World War II; they were the first to entertain troops at Normandy after the D Day invasion. Always dependent on a live audience, they had a popular show on the CBC and appeared frequently on U.S. TV, with a record sixty seven appearances on the Ed Sullivan Show. Wayne died from cancer at 72. Large polished black stone, Holy Blossom Cemetery, Toronto, Ontario.

9602. Wayne, Michael (Nov. 23, 1934–April 2, 2003) Eldest son of actor John Wayne became a producer on several of his father's later films, including *The Alamo, McLintock, The Green Berets, Chisum, Big Jake, Cahill U.S. Marshal, McQ* and *Brannigan.* He died at 68 from heart failure related to Lupus. Mass at St. Charles Borromeo Catholic Church, North Hollywood. Courts of Remembrance, wall crypt 2230, Forest Lawn Hollywood Hills, Los Angeles.

9603. Wayne, Thomas (Thomas Wayne Perkins, July 22, 1940–Aug. 15, 1971) Battsville, Mississippi, born brother of Johnny Cash's guitarist Luther Perkins had a hit as Thomas Wayne with *Tragedy* in 1959, which went to number 5, and was soon covered by

The Fleetwoods. He died in a car crash at 31. Buried near his brother, who died in a fire three years before. Sermon on the Mount sec., 54B, space 2, Woodlawn East Memorial Park, Hendersonville, TN.

9604. Weatherwax, Rudd (Sept. 23, 1907–Feb. 26, 1985) Trainer and owner of several generations of collies that starred as "Lassie." Block (memorial) IJ, sec. 1040, lot 2, Valhalla Memorial Park, North Hollywood, CA.

9605. Weaver, Buck (George Weaver, Aug. 18, 1890–Jan. 31, 1956) The Ginger Kid from Stowe, Pennsylvania, played third base and shortstop with the Chicago White Sox 1912–1920. He was one of the eight so-called Blacksox banned from baseball for life by Commissioner Kenesaw Mountain Landis for having thrown the 1919 world series to Cincinnati, though Weaver (who asked for but was denied a separate trial) and Jackson were believed to be innocent of taking money or laying down during games. Weaver applied for reinstatement several times to no avail. He died in Cook County, Illinois, at 65. Sec. 35, lot 258, grave 1, Mt. Hope Cemetery (adjacent Mt. Olivet), Worth Twp. (Chicago), IL.

9606. Weaver, Charley (Cliff Arquette, Dec. 28, 1905–Sept 23, 1974) Radio and TV comic from Toledo, Ohio, sported a porkpie hat, mustache, suspenders, wire rims and homespun humor. In later years a regular on *Hollywood Squares.* Arquette died in Burbank, California, of a heart attack at 68. Ashes scattered.

9607. Weaver, Doodles (Winstead Sheffield Weaver, May 11, 1912–Jan. 15, 1983) Film and TV comic actor of the 1940's to 60's. A suicide by gunshot in Burbank at 68 after years of illness and heart surgery, listed as 71. Avalon Cemetery, Avalon, Catalina Island (Santa Catalina), CA.

9608. Weaver, Sylvester "Pat" (Sylvester Weaver, Jr., Dec. 21, 1908–March 15, 2002) Pioneer television executive at NBC in the early 1950's revolutionized both morning and late night TV with *The Today Show* in 1952 and *Tonight* in 1954. He also eliminated the control of the programs by the sponsors, selling them air time instead. Brother of Doodles Weaver and father of Sigourney Weaver. He died in Santa Barbara at 93. Ashes to family.

9609. Webb, Chick (William Webb, Feb. 10, 1909–June 16, 1939) 4'11" drummer and bandleader from Baltimore led the Harlem Stompers in the late 1920's and rose in popularity with his discovery of vocalist Ella Fitzgerald in the late 1930's. He died at 30. Sec. F, lot 691, space 1, Arbutus Memorial Park, Baltimore, MD.

9610. Webb, Clifton (Webb Parmalee Hollenbeck, Nov. 19, 1891–Oct. 13, 1966) Indianapolis born actor flourished in the New York theatre of the 1920's but gained fame in films after playing the acidic Waldo Lydecker in *Laura* (1944). Subsequent roles featured him in typically abrasive, pompous and sarcastic parts such as Mr. Belvedere. In fragile health and devastated by the death of his mother Maybelle (1960), he died from heart failure in his home at 1005 N. Rexford Drive home in Beverly Hills. His shade supposedly stayed a while, and was formally exorcised in 1970. Entombed beside his mother. Abbey of the Psalms/Hollywood Forever Mausoleum, Corridor G-6 (Peace), crypt 2350, Hollywood Forever Cemetery, Hollywood (Los Angeles), CA.

9611. Webb, J. Watson, Jr. (James Watson Webb, Jr., Jan. 9, 1916–June 10, 2000) Film editor at 20th Century Fox on *The Lodger, Sunday Dinner for A Soldier, State Fair, The Dark Corner, Kiss of Death, Call Northside 777, A Letter to Three Wives, Jackpot, Cheaper By the Dozen, Love Nest, Don't Bother to Knock,* also headed from 1960–1977 the Museum of Americana headed by his family at Shelburne, Vermont. A grandson of sugar tycoon Henry Osborne Havemeyer and great-grandson of William H. Vanderbilt. He died in Brentwood, California, at 84. Webb family cemetery, Shelburne, VT.

9612. Webb, Jack (April 2, 1920–Dec. 23, 1982) Director and star of *Dragnet* on radio and TV 1952–59 and 1967–1970 remains indelibly identified as Detective Joe Friday, working the day watch out of the L.A.P.D., with the tight smile and request for "just the facts." He died from a heart attack at 62. Sheltering Hills, lot 1999, Forest Lawn Hollywood Hills, Los Angeles.

9613. Webb, Richard (Sept. 9, 1915–June 10, 1993) Star of the *Captain Midnight* TV series in the 1954–58 and some sixty films (*The Remarkable Andrew, West Point Widow, Out of the Past, The Big Clock*) and many television roles. Despondent over poor health, a suicide by gunshot. Cremated through Pierce Bros. Meyer-Mitchell. Ashes to family.

9614. Webb, Roy (Oct. 3, 1888–Dec. 10, 1982) Composer scored many films at RKO from c. 1935 (*Alice Adams, Journey Into Fear, Kitty Foyle, Cat People, I Walked With A Zombie, The Seventh Victim, The Leopard Man, The Curse of the Cat People, The Body Snatcher, Murder My Sweet, Notorious, The Spiral Staircase, Out of the Past*). Unmarked. Whispering Pines, lot 1864, space 1, Forest Lawn, Glendale, CA.

9615. Webber, Charles (Nov. 15, 1944–Jan. 17, 2003) Co-founder and trumpet player with the Swingin' Medallions, who had a hit with *Double Shot (of My Baby's Love)* in 1966. He left music in 1969 for law enforcement in South Carolina, where he died from cancer in Greenwood, his hometown since 1950, at 58. Oakbrook Memorial Park, Greenwood, SC.

9616. Weber, Joe (Aug. 11, 1867–May 10, 1942) Half of the vaudeville team of Weber and Fields, he and Lew Fields performed together from the 1880's through the 1920's in caricatures using primarily Jewish humor. They were immensely popular and their long partnership was an unusually amiable one. They died just a year apart. Ashes in a crypt with his wife. Friedman-Weber mausoleum, path A, Hungarian Union Field Cemetery, Glendale-Ridgewood, Queens, N.Y.C.

9617. Weber, Lois (June 13, 1881–Nov. 13, 1939) Concert pianist and actress from Pittsburgh was one of the first female directors (1913) of the silent screen. She dealt openly and honestly with birth control in *Where Are My Children?* (1913) and advanced the careers of Billie Dove, Anita Stewart and others. Divorced from actor Phillips Smalley and Army Captain Harry Gantz, she died in Los Angeles at 58 from a gastric ulcer. Cremated at Pierce Brothers' Chapel of the Pines Crematory, the ashes were sent in June 1940 to H.O. Gould Co. (no longer in existence) for interment in "Hinsdale Cemetery, Riverside, Illinois." There is a Fullersburg Cemetery on the edge of Hinsdale, and a small older cemetery within the town. To date her ashes have not been located at either, or at a pet cemetery (the only cemetery) in Hinsdale.

9618. Weber, Louise (July 13, 1866–Jan. 29, 1929) Parisian dancer known as **La Goulue** (The Glutton), famed for popularizing the Can-Can and dancing with Valentin le Désossé (Jacques Renaudin, a wine merchant by day) at the Moulin Rouge in Montmartre in the late 1880's to early 90's. The nickname came from her draining the glasses dry in bars. She was more notorious as the queen of Parisian sensuality, her world immortalized in the paintings of Toulouse-Lautrec. She retired with her fortune by 1895, but once out of the Moulin Rouge, she fell upon hard times. Homeless, white haired and toothless, by 1928 she returned to Montmartre selling peanuts and cigarettes. Transferred from Cimitiere de Pantin. Sarcophagus below wall plaque. Div. 31, Cimetiere de Montmartre, Paris.

9619. Weber, Max (April 18, 1881–Oct. 4, 1961) Abstract Russian born painter at his peak in the 1920's. His style varied over the years from Impressionism to Cubism, and Fauvism to Abstract. Weber was the first living painter honored with a one man show of his work at the Museum of Modern Art in New York (1930). 81-G-20, Mt. Ararat Cemetery, Farmingdale, Long Island, NY.

9620. Webster, Ben *see* **May Whitty.**

9621. Webster, Ben (Benjamin Francis Webster, March 27, 1909–Sept. 20, 1973) Kansas City born tenor saxophone jazz great, began with Lester Young and worked with a string of bands before joining Duke Ellington for three years beginning in 1940. Among his later associations was with Art Tatum, Oscar Peterson as well as working with kindred greats Coleman Hawkins and Charlie Parker. He moved to Europe in 1964, continuing to record until his death (*No Fool, No Fun* 1970). He died in Amsterdam at 64. Assistens Cemetery, Copenhagen, Denmark.

9622. Webster, Daniel (Jan. 18, 1782–Oct. 24, 1852) Influential congressman from New Hampshire (1813–17) and from Massachusetts beginning in 1823, was elected to the senate from there in 1826. "The God Like Daniel" was, with Clay as compromiser and Calhoun for the south, the strongest of voices in pre

Civil War Washington. The voice of the north for thirty years, his eloquence in debate was considered unequalled, particularly after his celebrated reply to Robert Hayne in 1830 concerning the rights of states over those of the union ("Liberty and Union, now and forever, one and inseparable"). He, Calhoun and Clay also died within two years of one another at the outset of the turbulent 1850's. Webster died at his home at Marshfield, Massachusetts (southeast of Boston and north of Plymouth). He lay in state in an open coffin on his front lawn and was buried in nearby Governor Winslow Burying Ground. A white marble block atop a knoll in the center of the small, secluded graveyard, is inscribed with his name, while a small stone obelisk with a religious inscription chosen by Webster marks the grave. There is also a memorial bronze plaque placed there by Dartmouth College. In Stephen Vincent Benet's story *The Devil and Daniel Webster*, it was said that if one went to the graveyard and called the name of the great orator, the ground would shake and his voice could be heard inquiring "Neighbor, how stands the Union?" Governor Winslow Burying Ground, Winslow Cemetery Road, near Marshfield, MA.

9623. Webster, Margaret *see* **May Whitty.**

9624. Webster, Mike (March 18, 1952–Sept. 23, 2002) Football Hall of Famer (1997) with the Pittsburgh Steelers from 1975–1986, helped take them to four Super Bowls, had 150 consecutive starts and more games (220) than any other player in Pittsburgh. In later years he was homeless and troubled by substance abuse. The last of the late 70's dynasty to leave the team, he was the first of them to die, in Pittsburgh at 50. Cremated through Somma Funeral Home, Pittsburgh.

9625. Webster, Noah (Oct. 16, 1758–May 28, 1843) Known for his 1828 *Dictionary of the English Language*; continually updated, it made his surname a household word. Obelisk in his family lot inside an iron fence, adjacent those of Eli Whitney and Lyman Beecher. Grove Street Cemetery, New Haven, CT.

9626. Wedekind, William Jennings (1866–1945) Dubbed the world's greatest horse-shoe craftsman at the 1892 Chicago World's Fair, he developed various types of horse shodding, including rubber. Boulder with sculpted anvil. Westlawn Cemetery, Hagerstown, IN.

9627. Weed, Thurlow (Nov. 15, 1797–Nov. 22, 1882) Influential Whig publisher of the *Albany Evening Journal* from 1830 was a major party leader in New York, a leader of the anti–Masonic faction, and with William H. Seward helped elect both Harrison in 1840 and Taylor in 1848. The first Republican ticket they formed (1856) was defeated, in large part by the defection of the Know Nothings who ran Millard Fillmore. The Republicans won in 1860 with Lincoln, however, who Weed stayed in touch with and advised throughout the war. In his last days he was delirious and having conversations with Lincoln about the war;

his last words were to order a carriage to take him home. Marked by a spire, corner lot, sec. 109, lot 1, Albany Rural Cemetery, Menands, Albany, NY.

9628. Weeghman, Charles (Charles Henry Weeghman, March 8, 1874–Nov. 2, 1938) Owner of the ill fated Federal League's Chicago entry 1914–16, the ChiFeds, at his new Weeghman Field on Chicago's north side at Clark and Addison. The first game was played there April 23, 1914, beginning ninety plus years in the neighborhood. The ChiFeds became The Whales, and finally The Cubs, while Weeghman Field became Wrigley Field. Headstone, (second) sec. 1, lot 76, facing Klute monument. Lutherania Cemetery, Richmond, IN.

9629. Weeks, Anson (Feb. 14, 1896–Feb. 7, 1969) San Francisco born band leader popular in the early 1930's, at his peak during the early depression years when *Dancin with Anson* was broadcast from the Top of the Mark (the Mark Hopkins Hotel) in San Francisco. He featured and promoted several musicians and vocalists including Tony Martin, Dale Evans and later bandleader Bob Crosby. Weeks died in Sacramento. Ashes buried in plot 48, lot 151, grave 2, Mountain View Cemetery, Oakland, CA.

9630. Weems, Mason Locke "Parson" (Oct. 11, 1759–May 23, 1825) Early American writer whose fanciful biography of George Washington gave birth to the story of the honest boy who could not tell a lie about chopping down the cherry tree. Family cemetery on his estate Bel Air, near Dumfries, VA.

9631. Weems, Ted (Wilfrid Theodore Weems, Sept. 26, 1901–May 6, 1963) Bandleader whose hits included *I Wonder Who's Kissing Her Now* (1939, with Perry Como) and his composition *Heartaches* (1947, with whistling Elmo Tanner). Block 11, lot 409, site 4, Fort Lincoln Cemetery, Brentwood, MD.

9632. Wegener, Paul (Dec. 11, 1874–Sept. 13, 1948) Bischdorf, Prussia, born actor, producer and director in Germany, best known for his starring roles in fantasy films before and during the period of the Weimar Cinema in the 1920's, including *Der Student von Prag* (1913), *Der Rattenfanger von Hamelin* (1916), three filmings of the ancient Jewish legend *Der Golem* (1914, 1917 and 1920), *Alraune* (1927) and the starring role in Rex Ingram's 1926 release *The Magician*, filmed in France. He collapsed on stage at the Deutschen Theatre in July 1948 and died in his sleep two months later. A Chinese temple-stone marks the grave, guarded by a marble Buddha from his garden. Friedhof Heerstrasse, Trakehner Allee 1 (Charlottenburg), Berlin.

9633. Wegman, Marie "Blackie" (April 30, 1925–Jan. 20, 2004) Baseball player with the All American Girls Professional League in the postwar years played primarily third base with Rockford, Fort Wayne, Muskegan and Grand Rapids. Sec. 26, lot 23, grave 3, St. Joseph's (New) Cemetery, Cincinnati, OH.

9634. Weidler, Virginia (March 21, 1926–July 1,

1968) Child star at Paramount and MGM in films including *Mrs. Wiggs of the Cabbage Patch* (1934), *Maid of Salem* (1937), *The Great Man Votes, The Women* (1939), and *The Philadelphia Story* (1940). She died from heart failure at 42 in her Pacific Palisades home. Cremated Oddfellows Cemetery. Ashes scattered at sea.

9635. Weill, Kurt (March 2, 1900–April 3, 1950) German composer best known for his *Threepenny Opera* (1928) in collaboration with Bertolt Brecht and featuring his wife, singer Lotte Lenya, mentioned in the song later popularized as *Mack the Knife.* They came to the U.S. in 1935, where he composed for Broadway musicals. Sec. B, lot 1009-1010, Mount Repose Cemetery, Haverstraw, NY.

9636. Weinberg, George (1901–Jan. 29, 1939) A member of Dutch Schultz's organization and the brother of the Dutchman's right hand man **Bo Weinberg** (Abraham Weinberg, 1897–Sept. 9, 1935), who disappeared during Schultz's last weeks, allegedly executed by his boss for disloyalty, although this scenario was not proven. Bo Weinberg's body was never found. His brother George, influenced by the vanishing of his brother and the murder of his boss and associates in Newark in October 1935, turned informer, but while at a safe house guarded by police in White Plains, lifted a firearm from an officer and shot himself in the head at 37. Sec. 8, Beth Olam Synagogue, New Mt. Carmel Cemetery (Mt. Carmel #2), Glendale-Ridgewood, Queens, N.Y.C.

9637. Weinshank, Albert *see* **St. Valentine's Day Massacre.**

9638. Weir-Cook, Harvey (June 30, 1893–March 24, 1943) Combat ace in World War II from Wilkinson, Indiana, credited with seven victories while with the 94th Aero Squadron. He was killed while flying a P-40 fighter over New Zealand. For decades what is now Indianapolis International was Weir-Cook Airport. There is still a memorial to him there. Sec. O, grave 440, National Memorial Cemetery of the Pacific (The Punchbowl), Honolulu, HI.

9639. Weiss, Alta (Feb. 9, 1890–Feb. 12, 1964) Doctor's daughter at Ragersville, Ohio, pitched from age 14, joining a men's semi-pro team at 17 in 1907 and in 1908 forming the barnstorming Weiss All Stars. Later a physician, she retired to Ragersville. Buried with her parents in Westlawn Cemetery, Winesburg, OH.

9640. Weiss, Carl (Dec. 18, 1905–Sept. 8, 1935) Baton Rouge doctor shot and killed Louisiana Senator Huey Long in the hall of the state capitol building for reasons unknown. The theory was he felt Long responsible for widespread political corruption and was willing to be a martyr to political idealism. He died at the scene, riddled with bullets by Long's bodyguards. In 1991 he was exhumed from section E, lot 53, Rose Lawn Memorial Park, Baton Rouge, Louisiana. Sections needed for study, in an effort to determine if Long's bodyguards may actually have killed the sen-

ator and set Weiss up, were retained by the Smithsonian Institution. The rest of the remains were cremated and returned to the family but were not re-interred in the family lot as of 1995.

9641. Weiss, George (June 23, 1894–Aug. 13, 1972) Baseball executive 1919–1966, Yankee farm club manager 1932–1947 and general manager 1947–60, winning ten flags and seven series. President of the Mets 1961–66. Hall of Fame 1971. Lot 39, Catalpa Ave., Evergreen Cemetery, New Haven, CT.

9642. Weiss, Hymie (Earl J. Weiss, 1898–Oct. 11, 1926) Chicago gangster of the 1920's inherited the O'Banion northside bootlegging outfit in opposition to the Gennas and Capone. Through 1925 the vengeful Weiss disposed of three Genna brothers and badly wounded Johnny Torrio, who left Chicago to Capone. He was credited with the original term "Take him for a ride" and with a brazen attempt on Capone's life on September 26, 1926, when a parade of autos lined up in front of Capone's restaurant haunt in Cicero and let the machine guns spray. Weiss was gunned down three weeks later by ten shots as he crossed North State Street in front of Holy Name Cathedral, where both he and O'Banion had attended mass as boys. The bullets that cut he and his henchmen down from a second story room across the street chipped off much of the inscription on the corner of the church; the disseminated cornerstone remained that way until a 1969 renovation. Interred in what was deemed unconsecrated ground, his family mausoleum, with his name over the door, faces the road. Sec. K, Mt. Carmel Cemetery, Hillside, IL.

9643. Weiss, Mendy (Emmanuel) *see* **Buchalter.**

9644. Weissmuller, Johnny (Peter John Weissmuller, June 2, 1904–Jan. 21, 1984) Olympic athlete from Windber, Pennsylvania, winner of over fifty swimming titles in the 20's, won five gold medals, dominating the 1924 and 1928 Olympics and setting sixty seven world records. His fame as Tarzan came in 1932 with *Tarzan the Ape Man* at MGM, followed by seventeen sequels. He suffered a series of strokes in 1977 and was an invalid at his home in Acapulco, where he moved in 1979. He died five years later from a cerebral thrombosis at 79. About 100 friends and neighbors and his widow Maria attended the burial, where two of his favorite Mexican songs were sung by a choir and a recording of his well known Tarzan cry was played as the coffin was lowered. A tall stone monument along the road commemorates the area of his grave, marked by a slab with a cross and open book. Valle de la Luz (Valley of Light) Cemetery, seven miles east of Acapulco, Mexico.

9645. Welch, Elisabeth (Feb. 27, 1904–July 15, 2003) New York born vocalist on Broadway from 1922, launched the Charleston the next year, was in *Liza, Runnin Wild,* and *The New Yorkers* (1931) in which she sang *Love For Sale.* She migrated to Paris and settled in London, where she remained popular for seventy years in the West End, from Cole Porter's *Nymph Errant* in 1933 to *A Time to Start Living* in 1992 and including film appearances in *Dead of Night* (1946) and notably as the Goddess, singing *Stormy Weather*, in Shakespeare's *The Tempest* (1979). She introduced both *Stormy Weather* and Edith Piaf's *La Vie en Rose* to England, and was associated with the works not only of Porter but of Lorenz Hart, Ivor Novello and others. She died in Northolt, Middlesex, at 99. Breakspear Crematorium, Ruislip, Middlesex.

9646. Welch, Joseph Nye (Oct. 22, 1890–Oct. 6, 1960) Army counsel from the Boston law firm of Hale and Dorr faced down Sen. Joseph McCarthy in a dramatic confrontation before the Senate Permanent Subcommittee on Investigations June 9, 1954. Having accused the Army of communist infiltration, his exchanges with Welch included the implication of a young lawyer with Hale and Dorr, prompting Welch's response. McCarthy was put on the defensive and censured shortly afterward. Welch subsequently became a celebrity, appearing as the judge in Otto Preminger's *Anatomy of a Murder* (1959). He died in Hyannis, Massachusetts, from a heart attack at 69, near his residence at Walpole. Cremated at Forest Hills Cemetery, Boston, the ashes were picked up by Doan and Beal mortuary at Harrichport, near Walpole, and returned to the family.

9647. Welch, Smiling Mickey (Michael Francis Walsh or Welch, July 4 1859–July 30 1941) Brooklyn born baseball pitcher of the 1880's. Known for his unusual smile, he had pitched over 300 victories, a feat only matched then by Pud Galvin and Tim Keefe, with Troy 1880–83 and with the Giants 1883–1892, including the first game at the Polo Grounds, a win over Boston, May 1, 1883. He teamed with Tim Keefe to win the N.L. pennant in 1888 and '89. He died in a sanitarium at Nashua, New Hampshire. Hall of Fame 1973. Buried as Michael F. Walsh. Sec. 4, range 17, plot 5, grave 6, (1st) Calvary Cemetery, Woodside, Queens, N.Y.C.

9648. Weldon, Ben (Ben Weinblatt, June 12, 1901–Oct. 17, 1997) Toledo born balding, chubby character actor in many roles on stage and in films from the 1930's through television in the 60's, often as thugs (*Marked Woman* 1937, *City For Conquest* 1940, *All Through the Night* 1942, *The Big Sleep* 1942). He died in Woodland Hills, California, at 96. Ashes in the rose garden, Pierce Bros. Chapel of the Pines Crematory, Los Angeles.

9649. Welk, Lawrence (March 11, 1903–May 17, 1992) Bandleader of German descent from the German speaking hamlet of Strasburg, North Dakota. Known for his Champagne Music, complete with bubbles, his biggest hit was *Josephine* in the 1930's prior to his Saturday night music and dance program, a mainstay from 1955–1971, later on independent stations. He died from pneumonia at 89 in St. John's Hospital, Santa Monica. Sec. Y, tier 9, grave 10, Holy Cross Cemetery, Culver City, CA.

9650. Welles, Gideon (July 1, 1802–Feb. 11, 1878) Hartford newspaper editor was Secretary of the Navy 1861–69 in Lincoln's cabinet during the Civil War and in the subsequent administration of Andrew Johnson. The candid diary of "Old Neptune" gives much first hand insight and primary source material on the characters and events of his day. Obelisk, sec. 3, Cedar Hill Cemetery, Hartford, CT.

9651. Welles, Orson (George Orson Welles, May 6, 1915–Oct. 10, 1985) First known for his Halloween 1938 radio broadcast of *War of the Worlds*, the legendary independent maverick director released his films through RKO in the early 1940's, most featuring his Mercury Players, beginning with his masterpiece *Citizen Kane* (1941), followed by *The Magnificent Ambersons* (1942), badly cut from his original version, after which he took several film roles (*Tomorrow is Forever* 1945, *The Stranger* 1946) before financing *The Lady from Shanghai* (1948), appearing in *The Third Man* (1949), and his last creative effort with Hollywood, *Touch of Evil* (1958). American Film Institute's Life Achievement Award 1975. Heavy and bearded, he was still appearing in Paul Masson wine commercials on TV when he died in his sleep at his home in L.A. from a heart attack at 70. Cremated in Los Angeles, his ashes were kept by his daughter Beatrice until May 6, 1987, his 72nd birthday, when they were taken by her to the farm of his bullfighter friend Antonio Ordonez in Spain and buried at his request, as a priest intoned a prayer at their lowering, in a dry well. A plaque in the form of a scroll with his name and dates was later placed on the well, and a rosebush planted in it. Ordonez farm, Ronda, west of Malaga on the southern coast of Spain.

9652. Welles, Sumner (Oct. 14, 1892–Sept. 24, 1961) Diplomat and author, in Tokyo and Buenos Aires under Wilson was chief of the division of Latin American affairs of the Department of State and commissioner of the Dominican Republic in the 1920's. He served under FDR as Assistant Secretary of State and ambassador to Cuba and later as Under-secretary of State 1937–42 and delegate to several Pan-American conferences. Sec. 8, Rock Creek Cemetery, Washington, D.C.

9653. Wellington, Arthur Wellesley, 1st Duke of (May 1, 1769–Sept. 14, 1852) British soldier and statesman became the toast of Europe upon his defeat of Napoleon at Waterloo in 1815. He subsequently served as Prime Minister from 1828 and drew criticism over his modification of Catholic and dissenters' voting laws and his pronouncement of the British electoral system as flawless. He was later foreign secretary and an adviser to Queen Victoria. His monument, designed by Alfred Stevens, was not completed until 1894. It faces Lord Nelson across the main crypt aisle of St. Paul's Cathedral, London.

9654. Wellman, William (Feb 29, 1896–Dec. 9, 1975) Pugnacious and colorful American film director had flown in France during World War I, was shot down behind the lines and received the Croix de Guerre with four gold palm leaves and five U.S. citations. His fame came with *Wings* (1927), the first Academy Award winning film, *The Public Enemy* (1931), *A Star is Born* (1937), *The Ox Bow Incident* (1943) and *Track of the Cat* (1954). He died at 79 from leukemia. Cremated by Gates Kingsley and Gates at Woodlawn Cemetery, Santa Monica, his ashes were scattered at sea by plane as he requested.

9655. Wells, H.G. (Herbert George Wells, Sept. 21, 1866–Aug. 13, 1946) English author of science fiction and history forecast with considerable accuracy many future events as well as such ideas as time travel and invisibility. His works, most written in the 1890's, deal often with world chaos and destruction through scientific advancement, including *The Time Machine, The War of the Worlds, The Invisible Man, The Island of Dr. Moreau, The Food of the Gods* and *When the Sleeper Wakes*. In 1920 he published his *Outline of History*. His hopes for the future were greatly depressed with World War II; he stayed in London during much of the Blitz, afterward becoming increasingly pessimistic about both religion and the future of mankind. He died from cancer of the liver at 70. Cremated at Golders Green Crematorium in north London August 16, his ashes were scattered by air over the English Channel, just west of the Isle of Wight, by his two sons Anthony West and Gip Wells.

9656. Wells, Henry (Dec. 12, 1805–Dec. 10, 1878) Express delivery magnate with William Fargo ran the Wells-Fargo stages in the west until forced to sell out the majority of stock to Lloyd Tevis. He funded Wells College in upstate New York. Oak Glen Cemetery, Aurora, NY.

9657. Wells, Herman B (June 7, 1902–March 18, 2000) President from 1938, Chancellor until the 1960's, and President Emeritus of Indiana University until his death at 97. A widely loved figure and a fixture in Bloomington. Headstone with parents, near right front of north entrance. I.O.O.F. Cemetery, Jamestown, Boone County, IN.

9658. Wells, Jacqueline *see* **Julie Bishop.**

9659. Wells, Junior (Amos Blakemore, Dec. 9, 1934–Jan. 15, 1998) Bluesman from the Muddy Waters era sang and played harmonica, first gaining attention in 1946 with Sonny Boy Williamson, Little Walter and others. Works include *Hoodoo Man Blues*. He died in Chicago, in a coma since September following a heart attack. Oak Woods Cemetery, Chicago, IL.

9660. Wells, Mary (May 13, 1943–July 26, 1992) Detroit born singer known for her Motown hits 1961-4 including her trademark *My Guy*. Diagnosed with cancer of the larynx in 1990, she died two years later at 49. Service at the Hall of Liberty, Forest Lawn Hollywood Hills. Columbarium of Patriots, Freedom Mausoleum, Forest Lawn, Glendale, CA.

9661. Wells, Willie (Aug. 10, 1906–Jan. 22, 1989) Shortstop and hitter in the Negro Leagues from 1924, with ten .300 plus seasons, after which he managed ten Negro League teams. He died in Austin at 80. Hall of Fame 1997. His grave had a flush plaque at sec. J, lot 135, space 13, Evergreen Cemetery, Austin, Texas. The only athlete to be so honored, and one of few people of color there, he was moved to the Texas State Cemetery, where a new monument with a bronze plaque bearing his likeness and accomplishments was dedicated October 5, 2004, in a ceremony attended by some one hundred people, including his daughter Stella, Texas Governor Rick Perry, and longtime Monarchs manager John "Buck" O'Neil. The effort at first to give him a more prominent marker, and then to place him in the State Cemetery, was spearheaded by *The Round Rock Express* earlier in 2004. Statesman's Meadow sec. 2, row G, number 33, Texas State Cemetery, Austin, TX.

9662. Wellstone, Paul (July 21, 1944–Oct. 25, 2002) Democratic senator from Minnesota served from 1991, favoring left wing causes and legislation, but known for his integrity and honesty, and for voting his conscience, including siding with conservative Senators Jesse Helms and Sam Brownback on issues regarding free trade with China and the trafficking of women overseas, respectively. He voted against the Gulf War in 1991 and was opposed to a strike against Iraq at the time of his death at 58. While campaigning in northern Minnesota and en route to a funeral with his wife Sheila, daughter Marcia, and longtime aides, his small plane crashed about two miles from the airport at Eveleth. His death left the party's prospects of maintaining control of the senate precarious; the campaign was turned over to Walter Mondale. Sec. 1, lot 13, Lakewood Cemetery, Minneapolis, MN.

9663. Welty, Eudora (April 13, 1909–July 23, 2001) Jackson, Mississippi, based writer known for loving depictions of small town southern Mississippi. Among her works were *A Curtain of Green* (1941, featuring her celebrated stories *A Worn Path* and *Why I Live at the P.O.*, *The Golden Apples* (short stories, 1949, her favorite work), *The Ponder Heart, Losing Battles* and *The Optimist's Daughter*, for which she won the Pulitzer Prize in 1973. She lived her life in the home in Jackson her father built in the 1920's, and died in Baptist Medical Center from pneumonia at 92. She lay in state at the Old Capitol Museum. Service at Galloway Memorial United Methodist Church. Greenwood Cemetery, Jackson, MS.

9664. Wences, Senor (Wenceslao Moreno, April 17, 1896–April 20, 1999) Spanish ventriloquist from Penarada came to the U.S. in 1934 and was well known through his many appearances on *Ed Sullivan* for Pedro, a head inside a box of whom he would inquire "S'awright?" "S'awright," or Johnny, a face painted on his hand (who could blow smoke rings). He died in his New York City home at 103. Memorial service and burial at Salamanca, Castilla y Leon, Spain.

9665. Wendell, Bill (William Joseph Wenzel Jr.,

March 22, 1924–April 14, 1999) Radio and TV announcer whose career ranged from serving as Ernie Kovacs' foil in the 1950's to announcer on NBC's *Late Night With David Letterman* 1982–93 and for two more years when the show moved to CBS, until his retirement in 1995. He died from cancer at 75 in Boca Raton, Florida. Garden of Peace, wing 6, corridor N, crypt 43E, Gate of Heaven Cemetery, Hawthorne, NY.

9666. Wenrich, Percy (Jan. 23, 1880–March 17, 1952) The Joplin Kid, composer of *When You Wore a Tulip* (1914), *On Moonlight Bay* (1915), *Put on Your Old Gray Bonnet*, many others. A plaque was placed on the gate around his family lot June 29, 1973, listing his famous songs and a quote: *The feeling for home ... gave me the music* and *The playing of his music is the true memorial.* West Division, block 172, lot 4 NW, Fairview Cemetery, Joplin, MO.

9667. Wentworth, John (March 5, 1815–Oct. 16, 1888) Early Chicago newspaper publisher known as Long John was the first Chicago mayor (1857–1863), in between terms in congress, to have enough influence to make things run his way. He was the precursor of many ultra powerful Chicago mayors and aldermen. His 72' obelisk and lot occupies an entire half a section (91), Rosehill Cemetery, Chicago, IL.

9668. Werefkin, Marianne (1860–1938) Russian born artist lived at Ascona, with the Ticino people in the Swiss-Italian region, the last twenty years of her life. Her paintings, described as spiritual and reflecting life's transitory nature, include *The Red Tree* (*Albero rosso*), *Atmosfera Tragica*, and *Scuola d'autunno* and the later *The Evening of Life.* Russian Orthodox cross and slab. Ascona town cemetery, Ascona, Switzerland.

9669. Werfel, Franz (Sept. 10, 1890–Aug. 26, 1945) Screenwriter, author of *The Song of Bernadette*, filmed in 1943. While fleeing Nazi Germany, he and his wife, the widow of Gustave Mahler, stopped at Lourdes, where Werfel vowed to write the story of Bernadette if they evaded capture, and was true to his word. Gruppe 32C, nummer 39, Zentralfriedhof (Central Cemetery), Vienna.

9670. Werner, Ilse (June 11, 1921–Aug. 8, 2005) Actress born in Batavia, now Jakarta, in Germany at Ufa, popular from 1938 and during World War II in *Bel Ami, U-Boote westwärts* (1941), *Münchhausen* (1943). Dubbed Die Frau mit Pfiff (The Whistling Singer), among her last films was *Alles wegen Robert De Niro* (1996). She died in Luebeck, Germany, at 84. Friedhof Goethestraße, Potsdam, Germany.

9671. Werner, Oskar (Oskar Josef Bschließmayer, Nov. 13, 1922–Oct. 23, 1984) Vienna born actor in German films from 1938, later in England (*Eroica* 1949, *Decision Before Dawn* 1951, *Mozart* 1955, *Jules et Jim* 1962 for Francois Truffaut, *Ship of Fools* 1965, *Fahrenheit 451* 1966 — again for Truffaut, *Shoes of the Fisherman* 1968). He died from a heart attack at Marburg an der Lahn, Germany, at 61. The grave was due in 2004 to be removed and re-used, the twenty year lease having expired. His children planned to honor his wish against an honor grave in Vienna. Town cemetery at Triesen, Liechtenstein.

9672. Wernerius, Matthias (1873–1931) Pastor of the Holy Ghost Parish in Dickeyville, Wisconsin, 1918–1931 constructed 1925–1930 a stone grotto encrusted with mortar and bright colored objects of all shapes, sizes and material. He is interred there, at the grotto, Dickeyville, WI.

9673. Wernicke, Otto (Sept. 30, 1893–Nov. 7, 1965) Stout German actor in films 1930–1959 played the police inspector Lohmann in Fritz Lang's *M* (1931) as well as (by then Commissioner Lohmann) in *The Testament of Dr. Mabuse* (1933). Other films include *Peer Gynt* (1934). He died in Munich at 72. Feld 115, reihe 1, nummer 17, Nordfiedhof, Munich.

9674. Werrenrath, Reinald (Aug. 7, 1883–Sept. 12, 1953) Brooklyn born baritone with the New York Metropolitan Opera was known for his *Pagliacci*. Among his recordings was *Duna*, many others. He taught music and supervised at NBC. Upright stone. Sec. 161, 13005, Greenwood Cemetery, Brooklyn, N.Y.C.

9675. Wertz, Vic (Victor Woodrow Wertz, Feb. 9, 1925–July 7, 1983) Power hitting outfielder with Detroit 1947–52 and 1961–63, and Cleveland 1954–58. His apparent sure fire run in the 1954 world series off Don Liddle became Willy Mays' most famous catch. Sec. 33, lot 311, grave 11, Holy Sepulchre Cemetery, Southfield, MI.

9676. Wesley, John (June 28, 1703–March 2, 1791) Fifteenth son of a Methodist minister was the founder of Methodism. Garden at rear, graveyard of Wesley Chapel, City Road, London.

9677. Wessel, Dick (Richard Michael Wessel, April 20, 1913–April 20, 1965) Burly dark haired actor in bits and supporting roles, often as sarcastic, usually comical or bullying characters, in films from 1935 (*They Made Me A Criminal, Brother Orchid, The Strawberry Blonde, Gentleman Jim*, a few turns as *Blondie*'s hapless mailman, *Harvey* 1950, as Mr. Cracker the bartender; *An American in Paris, Gentlemen Prefer Blondes, No Time for Sergeants, The Gazebo, Pocketful of Miracles*). He died of a heart attack in Studio City, California, on his 52nd birthday. Cremated at Chapel of the Pines, Los Angeles. Ashes buried sec. PS-3, lot 370E, Fort Rosecrans National Cemetery, Point Loma, (San Diego area), CA.

9678. Wessel, Horst (Sept. 9, 1907–Feb. 23, 1930) German low life bohemian student joined the Nazi party in 1926 and became a member of the Strom Troopers (SA). He died in a brawl, possibly with Communists, in his room in the Berlin slums. Elevated to martyrdom by Goebbels, he was celebrated in the song *Horst Wessel Lied*, adopted as an anthem by the party. Sec. 1, row 11, grave 2, Nikolaifriedhof in Prenzlauer Berg, Prenzlauer Allee/Mollstr. (Prenzlauer Berg), Berlin.

9679. Wessely, Paula (Jan. 20, 1907–May 11,

2000) Acclaimed Austrian stage actress in Vienna's Volkstheater from 1924, The Wessely was known for her particular manner of speaking German, but her exploitation by the Nazi propaganda machine under Goebbels brought her accusations of being a tool of the Third Reich. She regained her national fame and approval and became Austria's foremost actress in the postwar era, with the Burgtheater from 1951. Gruppe 6, reihe 3, nummer 3, Grinzinger Friedhof, Vienna.

9680. West, Benjamin (Oct. 10, 1738–March 11, 1820) Massachusetts born painter studied in Italy and went to England, where he became president of the British Royal Academy in 1792. Loyal to America during and after the Revolution, he was respected through the war and afterward. St. Paul's Cathedral, London.

9681. West, Billy (June 18, 1853–Feb. 15, 1902) 19th century minstrel star. His wife commissioned the monument at his grave, with a bronze bust of him and a banjo above the rose granite monument, benches on either side and burial space within the curbed lot for members of his troupe. Sec. 196 along Border Ave., near the Fort Hamilton Parkway entrance, Greenwood Cemetery, Brooklyn, N.Y.C.

9682. West, Claudine (Ivy Claudine West, Jan. 10, 1884–April 11, 1943) Script writer at MGM, particularly adept at European themes and settings, frequently co-written (*The Barretts of Wimpole Street, Marie Antoinette, Goodbye Mr. Chips*, AA nom., *Random Harvest*, AA nom). She won an Oscar for *Mrs. Miniver* (1942). Vale of Memory, lot 1854, space 4, Forest Lawn, Glendale, CA.

9683. West, Dottie (Dorothy Marie Marsh West, Oct. 11, 1932–Sept. 4, 1991) Country singer won the first Grammy for a country and western song, *Here Comes My Baby* (1964), and later recorded *Country Sunshine* (1974) and many hits with Kenny Rogers. She died at 58 in Vanderbilt University Hospital from liver damage sustained in an auto accident August 30 en route to perform at the Grand Ole Opry. Her charcoal monument has her picture, name and dates, and *Our Country Sunshine*. On the back are her words *"I was born a country girl..."* Mount View Cemetery, McMinnville, TN.

9684. West, Jessamyn (Mary Jessamyn West, July 18, 1902–Feb. 23, 1984) Author from North Vernon, Indiana, drew on her Quaker ancestry for *Friendly Persuasion*. From age seven she lived at Yorba Linda, California, a distant relative of Richard Nixon and a graduate of Whittier College. Among her other books was *The Woman Said Yes*, a study of dealing with terminal illness within her own family. She died from a stroke at her home of forty years at Napa, California. Ashes returned to her husband.

9685. West, Mae (Aug. 17, 1893–Nov. 22, 1980) Brooklyn born stage and film star with endless comic double entendres and innuendos, many of which she wrote. On stage from 1898, she was arrested for a lewd show (*Sex*, 1926) and served a short time at Riker's Island. Her best known play was *Diamond Lil* (1928),

followed by films through the 30's (*Night After Night, She Done Him Wrong*). She emphasized that she had brought sex to films and peppered it with humor, but deplored the explicit material later on the screen. She died at 87 in the Ravenwood Apartments in Los Angeles after a three month hospitalization for a stroke. Her body was shipped November 25 from Forest Lawn Hollywood Hills, and entombed in New York with her parents, an iron gate with the family name over the crypt fronts, in the second floor hallway of a mausoleum that was without power for some time, so that visitors were shown through with a flashlight. The lake the building once faced was filled in and covered, for a time (1988) with a mound of earth. Crypt 1 (top), aisle EE, Cypress Hills Abbey, Cypress Hills Cemetery, Brooklyn, N.Y.C.

9686. West, Nathaniel (Nathaniel Weinstein, Oct 17 1903–Dec. 22, 1940) Screenwriter penned *Miss Lonelyhearts* (1933) and *Day of the Locust* (1935), among others. He was killed in a California auto accident the day after F. Scott Fitzgerald's funeral when he turned in front of an oncoming car. His wife **Eileen McKenney** (born April 3, 1913), the model for *My Sister Eileen*, died in the crash with him. He was returned for burial and her ashes buried in his coffin. Path 23, Mt. Zion Cemetery, Maspeth, Queens, N.Y.C.

9687. West, Rebecca (Cicily Isabel Fairfield Andrews, Dec. 25, 1892–March 15, 1983) Irish feminist, novelist, journalist, critic and political essayist. Works include *Black Lamb and Grey Falcon, The Meaning of Treason* and *A Train of Powder*. She lived for a decade with H.G. Wells (after trashing his 1912 novel *Marriage*). Upright stone. Brookwood Cemetery, Woking, Surrey.

9688. West, Roland (Feb. 20, 1885–March 31, 1952) Silent screen producer-director of *The Monster* 1925, *The Bat* 1926, and its sound remake *The Bat Whispers* 1930; several vehicles with his then wife Jewel Carmen. He was questioned regarding the death of his business partner Thelma Todd in 1935 after she was found dead in his garage. He owned the property afterward, which later went to his surviving wife, actress Lola Lane. Buried beside Lola's sisters Leota and Rosemary. Acacia Slope 5130, space 5, Forest Lawn, Glendale, CA.

9689. West, Sandra (1939–March 10, 1977) Remarkable for her grave with its auto motif. She was buried May 19, 1977, in a blue negligee in her blue 1964 Ferrari. Sec. 1, lot 2, Alamo Masonic Cemetery, San Antonio, TX.

9690. West, Vera (June 26, 1900 [CA Death Index lists 1898]–June 29, 1947) Designer at Universal in the 1930's and 40's; nearly every set of their film credits read "gowns ... Vera West." A suicide, she was found in her swimming pool with a note lamenting her long time blackmailing by an unknown person. Columbarium of Inspiration, niche 14614, Holly Terrace, Great Mausoleum, Forest Lawn, Glendale, CA.

9691. Westcott, Gordon (Nov. 6, 1903–Oct. 30,

1935) Utah born actor, second lead at Paramount and Warner Brothers 1931–35 (*Love Me Tonight, Voltaire, Footlight Parade, Fog Over Frisco*). His death at 31 occurred in a polo accident. Father of actress Helen Westcott. Columbarium of Graces, niche 11016, Dahlia Terrace, Great Mausoleum, Forest Lawn, Glendale, CA.

9692. Westcott, Helen (Myrthas Helen Hickman, Jan. 1, 1928–March 17, 1998) Actress daughter of Gordon Westcott, in film leads of the 1940's and 50's (*The Gunfighter* 1950, *Abbott & Costello meet Dr. Jekyll & Mr. Hyde* 1953, *The Last Hurrah* 1958). Former child actress (*A Midsummer Night's Dream* 1935). She died from cancer at 70 in Edmonds, Washington. Cremated through Beck mortuary in Edmonds. Ashes to her guardian, likely scattered.

9693. Westerfield, James (March 22, 1913–Sept. 20, 1971) Heavy, bald character actor with bushy brows in gregarious, frequently self serving film roles, often as bumpkins. *On the Waterfront* (1954), *Birdman of Alcatraz* (1963), *True Grit* (1969). Sec. B, lot 1113, grave 9, San Fernando Mission Cemetery, Mission Hills, CA.

9694. Westerfield, Stephanie (Oct. 8, 1943–Feb. 15, 1961) Figure skater placed second at the 1961 National Championships and was a member of the 1961 U.S. world figure skating team, killed at seventeen when their Sabina Airlines flight crashed in Brussels, Belgium. Evergreen Cemetery, Colorado Springs, CO.

9695. Westinghouse, George (Oct. 6, 1846–March 12, 1914) One of two brothers from Central Bridge, New York, invented the air brake for trains but is better known for the development of the AC (alternating current) system of electrical transmission, forming the Westinghouse Electric Co. in 1882, later Westinghouse Broadcasting. Sec. 2, grave 3418, Arlington National Cemetery, Arlington, Virginia. His brother **Henry Westinghouse** (Nov. 16, 1853–Nov. 18, 1933), inventor of the single action steam engine, is in Whitewood sec. 133, Woodlawn Cemetery, the Bronx, N.Y.C.

9696. Westley, Helen (Henrietta Meserole Manney, March 28, 1875–Dec. 12, 1942) Brooklyn born stage actress was a founder of the Theatre Guild in 1918, remaining on the New York stage 1900–1934, until she went to Hollywood and was cast most often as cranky to snippy old women, in *Death Takes a Holiday* and *Anne of Green Gables* 1934. She became ill early in 1942 and retired to the home of her daughter in Middlebush, Franklin Township, New Jersey, where she died ten months later. Divorced from John Westley, her last married name was Conroy. Cremated at Rose Hill Cemetery in Linden, New Jersey, the ashes were picked up by a neighbor for return to her daughter in Middlebush, NJ.

9697. Westman, Nydia (Feb. 19, 1902–May 23, 1970) Actress-comedienne in many nervous and fluttery film parts: *The Invisible Ray, The Cat and the Canary, The Late George Apley, The Ghost and Mr.* *Chicken* ("And they used Bon-Ami!"), many others. Oakdale sec., plot 312-A, Oakwood Memorial Park, Chatsworth, CA.

9698. Westmore, Bud (Hamilton Adolph Westmore, Jan. 13, 1918–June 23, 1973) Youngest of the family of make-up artists known as the House of Westmore was at Universal in the postwar years, where he developed the *Creature from the Black Lagoon* and several other monstrosities and mutations. Like three earlier brothers, he died from a heart attack. Block (mausoleum) L, sec. 931, lot 4, Valhalla Memorial Park, North Hollywood, CA.

9699. Westmore, Ern (Ernest Henry Westmore, Oct. 29, 1904–Feb. 1, 1967) Twin brother of Perc, worked at RKO in the 1930's. He died from a heart attack in a New York hotel lobby. Sec. 8/Garden of Legends, lot 78, Hollywood Forever Cemetery, Hollywood (Los Angeles), CA.

9700. Westmore, George (June 28, 1879–July 12, 1931) English born make-up artist, father of nineteen children from which five sons became noted make-up artists in Hollywood, each at a separate studio. George Westmore committed suicide at 52 by drinking bichloride of mercury. Vale of Memory, lot 1070, Forest Lawn, Glendale, CA.

9701. Westmore, Monte (Montague George Westmore, June 12, 1902–March 30, 1940) The second Westmore into the make-up business worked for Selznick on *Gone With the Wind* and others. He died from a heart attack at 37. Buried near his parents. Vale of Memory, lot 978, Forest Lawn, Glendale, CA.

9702. Westmore, Perc (Percival Westmore, Oct. 29, 1904–Sept. 30, 1970) Twin brother of Ern worked primarily for Warner Bros. He created Paul Muni's makeup in *The Story of Louis Pasteur* and Bette Davis as Queen Elizabeth in *The Private Lives of Elizabeth and Essex* (1939). Like his brothers he suffered from a congenital heart defect and died from a coronary at his home. Garden of Remembrance, lot 1751, off the Court of the Christus, Forest Lawn, Glendale, CA.

9703. Westmore, Wally (Walter Westmore, Feb. 12, 1906–July 3, 1973) Paramount's make-up wizard for many years; among his creations was the Hyde makeup on Fredric March in *Dr. Jekyll & Mr. Hyde* (1931). He died after a series of strokes. Meditation sec., lot 763, Forest Lawn, Glendale, CA.

9704. Westmoreland, William (William Childs Westmoreland, March 26, 1914–July 18, 2005) U.S. Army general from Spartanburg, South Carolina, veteran of World War II, Korea, and superintendent at West Point, commanded American military operations, MACV, in Vietnam 1964–68, oversaw the introduction of ground troops and urged a stronger military buildup, but was recalled and further build-up limited after the 1968 Tet Offensive. Army Chief of Staff 1968–72. Maintaining the U.S. held the line and did not lose the war, but did not make good its commitment to South Vietnam, he died at 91 in Bishop Gadsden Retirement Home, Charleston, South Carolina. Sec. 18, site 66, Post Cemetery, West Point Military Academy, West Point, NY.

9705. Weston, Paul (March 12, 1912–Sept. 20, 1996) Orchestra leader married to Jo Stafford from 1952, with Capitol through the 1940's. Mausoleum E4, block 289, Holy Cross Cemetery, Culver City, CA.

9706. Westover, Winifred (Nov. 9, 1899–March 19, 1978) American silent screen actress, married to cowboy star William S. Hart. Sanctuary of Remembrance, Westwood Memorial Park, Los Angeles.

9707. Wettling, George (Nov. 28, 1907–June 6, 1968) Dixieland and jazz drummer from 1920's Chicago, adept at altering his playing to fit and best showcase whoever he was backing up. Cypress NW ¼ lot 5, block 5, grave 3, Cedar Park Cemetery, Calumet Park (south Chicago), IL.

9708. Wexler, Paul (May 23, 1929–Nov. 21, 1979) Tall, lanky actor in films and much television from 1952 (*Suddenly,* as Deputy Slim Adams, *The Four Skulls of Jonathan Drake*). He died from leukemia at 50 in Daniel Freeman Hospital, Inglewood, California. Cremated at Grandview Memorial Park, Glendale. Canaan 8, lot 2564, space 1F, Mt. Sinai Memorial Park, Los Angeles.

9709. Whale, James (July 22, 1889–May 29, 1957) Stylish English director in Hollywood from 1930 filmed his stage success *Journey's End,* followed by *Waterloo Bridge* and *Frankenstein* in 1931. His dark, macabre sense of wit mixed with foreboding was used in subsequent studio chillers *The Old Dark House* (1932), *The Invisible Man* (1933) and *Bride of Frankenstein* (1935). He made several offbeat films (*The Kiss Before the Mirror* 1933, *One More River* 1934, *Remember Last Night* 1935) and the spectacle *Show Boat* (1936). By the late 1940's he retired to his home in Pacific Palisades, a recluse. By 1956 he had suffered several strokes. His body was found fully clothed in the shallow end of his swimming pool, with a cut on his head. A suicide note was left, but was not made public until nearly thirty years later. According to his wishes he was cremated, at the Chapel of the Pacific, Woodlawn Cemetery, Santa Monica. His niche lists his birth as 1893, the updated year he often gave. Columbarium of Memory, niche 20076, Memorial Terrace, Great Mausoleum, Forest Lawn, Glendale, CA.

9710. Whalen, Grover (June 2, 1886–April 20, 1962) Grover the Greeter held the position of official greeter for the city of New York in the 1920's, following a term as police commissioner. Sec. 9, lot 783, grave 9/10, (1st) Calvary Cemetery, Woodside, Queens, N.Y.C.

9711. Wharton, Edith (Jan. 24, 1862–Aug. 11, 1937) New York born writer raised in affluent circles and married into a wealthy Boston family, wrote considerably on the stratified society and the reaction, particularly of the aristocracy, to social change. Her most acclaimed novel, *The Age of Innocence,* was published in 1920 and won the Pulitzer Prize for literature.

Other works and short stories include *Tales of Men and Ghosts* (1910), many others, over fifty books in all. She lived in France from 1907, divorced from Edward Wharton in 1913. Although her last visit to the U.S. was in 1923, her home in Washington Square in Manhattan and the Wharton estate The Mount at Lenox, Massachusetts, in the Berkshires remain tourist attractions. She died at St. Brice-sous-foret near Paris and was buried (near the grave of Walter Berry) beneath a white marble slab of her own design with a cross and the inscription *O crux spes unica.* Cimitiere des Gourds, Versailles.

9712. Wheat, Zach (Zachariah Davis Wheat, May 23, 1888–March 11, 1972) Baseball star outfielder with the Brooklyn Dodgers 1909–1926, the best the team ever saw in the opinion of both Branch Rickey and Casey Stengel. As a hitter, only "Buck" mastered Christy Mathewson's fadeaway at the Polo Grounds. Hall of Fame 1959. Flat plaque. Block 101, lot 137, grave 7, Forest Hills Cemetery, Kansas City, MO.

9713. Wheatcroft, Stanhope (May 11, 1888–Feb. 13, 1966) Stage and screen actor in silent films and talkies. Block (memorial) G, sec. 6501, lot 2, Valhalla Memorial Park, North Hollywood, CA.

9714. Wheatley, Dennis (Jan. 8, 1897–Nov. 11, 1977) Prolific English author of over sixty books of mystery, fantasy and adventure over a forty year period. Two of his characters were the Duke de Richelieu and Gregory Sallust, often involved with the occult, in *The Devil Rides Out, The Haunting of Toby Jugg.* Science fiction and adventure themes dominated *Black August, The Secret War, Sixty Days to Live, Star of Ill Omen* and *The Man Who Missed the War.* Brookwood Cemetery, Woking, Surrey.

9715. Wheatley, Phillis (c.1753–Dec. 5, 1784) The first recognized African-American poet was brought to America as a slave and took the name of her master, merchant John Wheatley. Her publication *Poems on Various Subjects, Religious and Moral* (1773) was widely praised. Specific gravesite unknown; somewhere at the Central Burying ground on Boston Common, Boston, MA.

9716. Wheeler, Bert (April 7, 1895–Jan. 18, 1968) Half of the comedy team of Wheeler and Woolsey 1928–1938. First teamed with Robert Woolsey in *Rio Rita* on the stage and in the 1930 film, Wheeler was the light, simple half, often paired in romantic subplots with Dorothy Lee. Never noticed by the critics, they were popular money makers for RKO 1930–37. Wheeler performed intermittently after Woolsey's death in 1938 but never regained the limelight they shared in the 30's. He died in New York from emphysema. Mass at St. Malachy's Catholic Church. Catholic Actor's Guild of America plot, sec. 47, lot 46, grave 29, (1st) Calvary, Woodside, Queens, N.Y.C.

9717. Wheeler, Burton K. (Feb. 27, 1882–Jan. 7, 1975) Influential Republican senator from Montana 1922–1946 was an isolationist in accord with the administrations of the 1920's but strongly at odds with

Roosevelt over involvement in European conflicts. His senate career ended after the Second World War. Sec. 30, lot 27, Rock Creek Cemetery, Washington, D.C.

9718. Wheeler, William A. (June 30, 1819–June 4, 1887) New York Republican congressman served as vice president under Hayes 1877–1881. He was born, lived, died and is buried in the same town. His white marble monument incorrectly lists the years of his vice presidency as 1876–1880. Sec. K, lot 5, Morningside Cemetery, Malone, NY.

9719. Whelan, Tim (Francis Timothy Whelan, Nov. 2, 1893–Aug. 12, 1957) Director from silents did several Harold Lloyd comedies including *Safety Last* (1923). Later works include *The Murder Man* (1935), *The Thief of Baghdad* (1940), *The Mad Doctor* (1941). Sec. D, lot 224, Holy Cross Cemetery, Culver City, CA.

9720. Whipper, Leigh (Oct. 29, 1876–July 26, 1975) Black actor from Charleston, South Carolina, on the stage and in a few films including *Of Mice and Men* (1939, as Crooks), *The Ox Bow Incident* (1943, as Sparks). A resident of New York City from 1907, he died at 98 in Harlem Hospital Center. Cremated at Ferncliff Cemetery, Hartsdale, New York, the ashes were returned to his son through Trumbo funeral chapel in Manhattan, N.Y.C.

9721. Whipple, William (Jan. 14, 1730–Nov. 28, 1785) Representative from New Hampshire at the Continental Congress in Philadelphia signed the Declaration of Independence and served as a general in the American Revolution. North Cemetery, Portsmouth, NH.

9722. Whistler, James Abbott McNeill (July 10, 1834–July 17, 1903) American painter from Lowell, Massachusetts, best known for his painting *Mrs. George Washington Whistler* (1872), commonly known as *Whistler's Mother*. In his later years he lived at Paris and London, where he died. Sarcophagus by the north wall in the new section of St. Nicholas Churchyard, Chiswick Mall, London. Whistler's celebrated mother, **Anna Matilda McNeill Whistler** (Sept. 27, 1804–Jan. 3, 1881), his famous subject, is buried at Hastings, England. Whistler's father, **George Washington Whistler** (May 19, 1800–April 7, 1849) was from Fort Wayne, Indiana. He died in Russia when the artist was too young to immortalize him on canvas. He has a cenotaph in sec. 94, plot 1673, Greenwood Cemetery, Brooklyn, N.Y.C., and an obelisk at his grave in Evergreen Cemetery, Stonington, CT.

9723. White, Alice (Alva V. White, Aug. 25, 1904–Feb. 19, 1983) Script girl for Josef Von Sternberg cast in vivacious parts in late silent and early sound films, from *The Sea Tiger* (1927) through the 1930's. Ashes scattered at sea.

9724. White, Barry (Sept. 12, 1944–July 4, 2003) Rhythm and Blues vocalist from Galveston, raised in south central Los Angeles, known for his deep, rumbling baritone voice, as often talking as singing, used on several seductive records through the 1970's (*I'm*

Gonna Love You Just a Little More, Baby; It's Ecstasy When You Lay Down Next to Me, You're the First, the Last, My Everything; Love Serenade, Can't Get Enough of Your Love Babe), primarily directed at his second wife (from 1974–1988), singer Glodean James. With a resurgence in popularity through the 1990s, he won two Grammys in 1999. On dialysis and ill with high blood pressure, he suffered a stroke in September 2002 and was hospitalized from then until his death ten months later from kidney failure in Los Angeles at 58. Services through Angelus-Rosedale Cemetery and mortuary, Los Angeles. Ashes scattered in the Pacific from a yacht off the California coast.

9725. White, Byron "Whizzer" (Byron Raymond White, June 8, 1917–April 15, 2002) Jurist earned his nickname as a football star at the University of Colorado in the mid 1930's and played one year of pro ball in 1938 before going to England as a Rhodes Scholar, where he met John Kennedy, who in 1962 appointed the Denver lawyer and deputy attorney general an Associate Justice on the Supreme Court. White, who was JFK's only appointment other than Arthur Goldberg later that year, voted increasingly with the conservatives. He retired in 1993 and was replaced with Ruth Bader Ginsberg. White died in Denver at 84, leaving no living former Supreme Court justices. Ashes in All Souls Walk (columbarium), B-78, St. John's Episcopal Church, 1350 Washington St., Denver, CO.

9726. White, Clarence (June 7, 1944–July 14, 1973) Country and pop guitarist first with the Country Colonels did session work with many; with the Byrds 1968–73. He was run down by a drunk driver in Palmdale, California. Corridor of Reverie 88E, Joshua Memorial Park, Lancaster, CA.

9727. White, Daniel (Sept. 2, 1946–Oct. 21, 1985) San Francisco city supervisor who was enraged over his ouster in a partisan political move assassinated Mayor George Moscone and Supervisor Harvey Milk in City Hall in November 1978. Based on the so-called "Twinkie defense" that too much sugar contributed to his extreme stress, White served only a short term in prison, was released after less than a decade and took his own life by running his car engine in a closed garage. Sec. 2C, grave 5064, Golden Gate National Cemetery, San Bruno, CA.

9728. White, David (Daniel David White, April 6, 1916–Nov. 27, 1990) Actor from Colorado on Broadway, in films (*Sweet Smell of Success* 1962) and TV, best known as Larry Tate, Darren Stephens' boss on TV's *Bewitched* 1964–1972. Two years after his son Jonathan was killed in the terrorist bombing of Pan Am Flight 103 over Lockerbie, Scotland, White died from a heart attack in Los Angeles at 74. Cremated through the Alpha Society, his ashes were in a communal niche (up to 70 urns), unmarked and inaccessible, in a basement at Grandview Memorial Park, Glendale, California. They were moved by July 2004 to a glass front niche with his bust and photos. Valentino Columbarium, Cathedral Mausoleum, Hollywood Forever Cemetery, Hollywood (Los Angeles), CA.

9729. White, E. B. (Elwyn Brooks White, July 11, 1899–Oct. 1, 1985) New York born writer originally with the *New Yorker* displayed extensive versatility. Works include *Is Sex Necessary?* (1929, written with James Thurber), *One Man's Meat*, a column for *Harper's Weekly* 1938–1943, *The Lady is Cold* (1929, a collection of poems), satires on world government, on Hemingway, *The Second Tree From the Corner* (1953) and his best known work, the children's book *Charlotte's Web* (1952). Buried with his wife, *New Yorker* editor **Katherine Sergeant Angell** (dec. 1977). Brooklin Cemetery, Brooklin, ME.

9730. White, Edward D. II (Nov. 3, 1845–May 19, 1921) Senator from Louisiana and associate justice on the Supreme Court was appointed Chief Justice by President William Howard Taft in 1910. Taft truly wanted the job instead of the presidency. When White died in 1921, Taft was appointed Chief Justice by President Harding. Chief Justice White is buried in lot 600 East, Oak Hill Cemetery, Georgetown, Washington, D.C. His father, Louisiana Governor **Edward D. White** (1794–April 18, 1847) is in a family tomb in sec. 8, lot 54, St. Joseph's Cemetery, Thibodaux, LA.

9731. White, Edward H. (Nov. 14, 1930–Jan. 27, 1967) The names McDivitt and White became well known in 1965 when the two NASA astronauts manned a space flight in which White, attached to the capsule, walked in space. He died in a fire on the launch pad at Cape Canaveral with Virgil Grissom and Roger Chaffee, a disaster in the U.S. space program unequalled until the Challenger explosion nineteen years and one day later. Grissom and Chaffee were buried side by side in Arlington National Cemetery. Sec. 18, row G, grave 80, Post Cemetery, West Point Military Academy, West Point, NY.

9732. White, Ethel Lina (1876–Aug. 13, 1944) Mystery writer from Abergavenny, Monmouthshire, Wales, best known for *Some Must Watch* (1933, filmed as *The Spiral Staircase*), *Wax* (1935), *The Wheel Spins* (1936, filmed as *The Lady Vanishes*) and *Midnight House/Her Heart in Her Throat* (1942, filmed as *The Unseen*). She moved to London at the end of World War I and worked for the Ministry of Pensions while publishing fourteen mystery novels from 1931 until the year of her death. Never married, she died at 2 Arlington Park Mansions, Chiswick, at 68. Cremated at Mortlake Crematorium August 16, her ashes were spread in the Garden of Remembrance, Mortlake Crematorium, Richmond, Surrey, at the edge of London.

9733. White, Frank (Durward Frank Kyle, June 4, 1933–May 21, 2003) Republican Governor of Arkansas 1981–83, one of only two to defeat Bill Clinton, ousted him in 1980 and was in turn defeated by Clinton in 1982. White was known for passing a law allowing "creation science" to be taught along with evolution, though it was later overturned as unconsti-

tutional. He died from a heart attack in Little Rock at 69. Mt. Holly Cemetery, Little Rock, AR.

9734. White, George (March 12, 1890–Oct. 10, 1968) New York producer of *George White's Scandals* from the World War I era into the mid 1930's, featuring many of the top composers of the day, with film versions in 1934, 1935 and 1945. Unmarked. Block G (Graceland), sec. 7280, lot 6, Valhalla Memorial Park, North Hollywood, CA.

9735. White, Hal (Harold White, March 18, 1919–April 21, 2001) Major league pitcher with the Detroit Tigers 1941–52, then spent a year with the St. Louis Cardinals. Sec. 411, grave 776, Florida National Cemetery, Bushnell, FL.

9736. White, Jesse (Jesse Marc Weidenfeld, Jan. 3, 1917–Jan. 9, 1997) Buffalo born, Akron raised actor in the Broadway and 1950 film version of *Harvey* (as the male nurse), many later film and TV roles, including the Maytag repairman in commercials 1967–89. Moses 25, lot 4391, Mt. Sinai Memorial Park, Los Angeles.

9737. White, Joseph M. (Oct. 14, 1891–Feb. 28, 1959) The Silver Masked Tenor, popular on early radio and recordings through the 1920s and 30s. Sec. T, grave 2044, Long Island National Cemetery, Farmingdale, Long Island, NY.

9738. White, Josh, Sr. (Feb. 11, 1915–Sept. 5, 1969) Folk and blues singer known for protest ballads, including *Strange Fruit*. His upright stone bears the lines *May the road rise with you and the wind be ever at your back. And may the Lord keep you in the hollow of his hand*. Mapleview East, sec. 118, Cypress Hills Cemetery, Brooklyn, N.Y.C.

9739. White, Jules (Sept. 17, 1901–April 30, 1985) Director of many Three Stooges shorts died from Alzheimer's Disease at 83. Beth Olam Cemetery/Hall of Solomon, M-7, crypt 1377, Beth Olam Cemetery adjacent Hollywood Forever Cemetery, Hollywood (Los Angeles), CA.

9740. White, Marjorie (July 22, 1908–Aug. 20, 1935) Blonde actress in several talkies (*Sunny Side Up, Just Imagine, Women of All Nations, Charlie Chan Carries On, The Black Camel*) and the Three Stooges' first short *Woman Haters* (1934). She died in a car accident at 27. Buried (and marked) under her married name, Tierney. Sec. 13, lot 538, Hollywood Forever Cemetery, Hollywood (Los Angeles), CA.

9741. White, Pearl (March 4, 1889–Aug. 4, 1938) Actress from Green Ridge, Missouri, was the undisputed queen of the silent serials, in which she was left hanging from a cliff or tied to the railroad tracks by such dependable pioneer villains as Paul Panzer and Warner Oland. Most of her films were made in New York and New Jersey 1911–1925, the most famous *The Perils of Pauline* (1914). She did her own stunts and made the harrowing escapes believable, but retired to France by 1923. Her retirement, depending on the story, was due to her looking for her last husband or because of the death of stunt man John Stevenson during the making of her thriller *Plunder* in New York, after which she suffered a breakdown. In France she spent much of her time at the Riviera amid the casinos. Her death in the American Hospital in Neuilly at Paris supposedly resulted from an old spinal injury. She specified a strictly private and simple service. Grave marked by a polished black slab with a cross. Div. 13, Passy Cemetery, Paris.

9742. White, Reggie (Reginald Howard White, Dec. 19, 1961–Dec. 26, 2004) NFL great from Chattanooga dubbed the Minister of Defense played fifteen years, setting a record (since passed) 198 sacks, with the Philadelphia Eagles, the Green Bay Packers — helping them to the 1997 Super Bowl victory, and the Carolina Panthers. He retired in 2000 to his home and ministry at Cornelius, North Carolina, where he died unexpectedly at 43 from a respiratory ailment thought related to sleep apnea. Funeral at University Park Church, Charlotte, through A.L. Jinwright mortuary. Glenwood Memorial Park, Mooresville, NC.

9743. White, Ruth (Ruth Godfrey White, April 24, 1914–Dec. 3, 1969) Actress from Perth Amboy specialized in offbeat, often crabby and whiny middle aged and elderly woman on stage from 1949 (*The Birthday Party*), screen (*Edge of the City, To Kill A Mockingbird, Midnight Cowboy, The Reivers*) and television (*Twilight Zone* episode *The Incredible World of Horace Ford*, 1963). Never married, she died from cancer at 55. Sec. E, plot 2, lot 8, St. Mary's Cemetery, Amboy Ave., Perth Amboy, NJ.

9744. White, Ryan (Dec. 6, 1971–April 8, 1990) Kokomo, Indiana, boy diagnosed with Acquired Immune Deficiency Syndrome in December 1984 when he was 13. The reaction of many of his fellow students and their parents to his AIDS, acquired through blood transfusions for hemophilia, drove he and his mother to Cicero, a smaller town northeast of Indianapolis. In the ensuing five years he became a national symbol for understanding and tolerance. He died at 18 in Indianapolis, where his services at the Second Presbyterian Church brought an overflow crowd including Elton John, who performed *Skyline Pigeon*. An elaborate monument with his picture and numerous tributes engraved on it, has the words *Kid of courage* above his name and a pigeon, soaring skyward. Cicero Cemetery, Cicero, IN.

9745. White, Slappy (Melvin White, Sept. 20, 1921–Nov. 7, 1995) Baltimore born actor-comedian on *Laugh In,* played Melvin on *Sanford and Son,* appeared on *Amazing Grace* (1974) and various game shows. He died of a heart attack in Brigantine, New Jersey, at 73. King Memorial Park, Baltimore, MD.

9746. White, Sol (King Solomon White, June 12, 1868–Aug. 26, 1955) Infielder from Bellaire, Ohio, with various black ball clubs from 1887, co-founded the Philadelphia Giants in 1902, later managed and wrote columns on the Negro Leagues. He died at 87 in Central Islip, New York. Hall of Fame 2006. Frederick Douglass Memorial Park, Staten Island, N.Y.C.

9747. White, Stanford (Nov. 9, 1853–June 25, 1906) New York born architect was the most sought after designer of structures in his day, particularly in New York, where his work included the Washington Square Arch, the *New York Herald* Building, and Madison Square Garden (1889). In the latter he kept an elaborate apartment where he had once entertained showgirl Evelyn Nesbit. After much brooding over White's past attentions to his (by then) wife Nesbit, Pittsburgh socialite Harry K. Thaw fatally shot White on the rooftop of Madison Square Garden during a performance of *Mamzelle Champagne*. The case was later dramatized in the film *The Girl in the Red Velvet Swing* and in E.L. Doctorow's book *Ragtime,* filmed in 1981. St. James Episcopal Churchyard, St. James, Long Island, NY.

9748. White, Thelma (Thelma Wolpa, Dec. 4, 1910–Jan. 4, 2005) Blonde actress from Lincoln, Nebraska, in sporadic B films and shorts of the 1930's and 40's achieved dubious notoriety for her role as the party giver in the now camp 1936 effort *Reefer Madness*, a low budget, unintentionally hilarious anti-drug offering written by a religious group warning of, and picturing, the instant madness stemming from the use of marijuana. Re-released in the 1970's, it became a cult favorite, but made the retired actress, later an agent, shudder with embarrassment. Widowed (Millard), she died from pneumonia at 94 in the Motion Picture and Television Hospital, Woodland Hills, California. Ashes buried column niches, south base, space 511, Valhalla Memorial Park, North Hollywood, CA.

9749. White, Theodore H. (May 6, 1915–May 15, 1986) News correspondent first prominent in his coverage of General Stilwell and the China-Asia theatre after World War II, Teddy White became a national fixture with his *The Making of the President 1960*, a meticulous study of the processes and events leading up to the election. *The Making of the President* was repeated in 1964, 1968 and 1972, winning the Boston born Harvard graduate the Pulitzer Prize. In 1978 he published his memoirs *In Search of History*. White died from a stroke at 71 in Manhattan. A memorial service was held at Temple Beth El in New York, attended by many luminaries including Jacqueline Onassis, Larry O'Brien and Sen. Daniel Patrick Moynihan, who delivered the eulogy. Cremated at Garden State Crematory in North Bergen, New Jersey, his ashes were scattered.

9750. White, William Allen (Feb. 10, 1868–Jan. 29, 1944) Owner and editor of the *Emporia Gazette* in Emporia, Kansas, from 1895 until his death. His wry editorials won a Pulitzer Prize in 1923, as did his autobiography, published posthumously in 1947. His several books include *A Puritan in Babylon*, a biography of Calvin Coolidge. Usually a loyal Republican, White first gained attention in the 1896 campaign with a pro-McKinley piece titled *What's the Matter With Kansas?* He split from the party and joined the Progressives in 1912, associated with the Muckrakers that gave fire to the movement. However, the best known work by the Sage of Emporia was his eulogy to his young daughter, who died when thrown by a horse as she struck a tree limb while distracted. *Mary White* was published in 1921 and reprinted in papers and collections across the country. White, his wife **Sallie Lindsay** (Dec. 3, 1869–Dec. 19, 1950) and daughter **Mary** (June 18, 1904–May 13, 1921), are marked by white tablets set in red brick and the lot enclosed by a hedge. Their son **Bill** (1973) and his wife (1988) are also there. South edge block 25, lot 47, Maplewood Cemetery, Emporia, KS.

9751. Whitehead, John (July 10, 1948–May 11, 2004) Rhythm and Blues singer-songwriter with a comedic bent, called the driving force behind the Sound of Philadelphia from the late 1960's through the 80's, recorded with the Epsilons, toured with Otis Redding, and penned with Gene McFadden (*q.v.*) the unofficial city anthem, *Ain't No Stoppin' Us Now*, used by the Eagles and Phillies. He was shot in the neck and killed at 55 outside his house while having a hose installed in his vehicle by the man believed to have been the target of the drive-by. Sec. M, lot 1, row 10, Mount Moriah Cemetery, 62nd Street and Kingsessing Ave., Philadelphia, PA.

9752. Whitehead, O.Z. (Oothout Zabriskie, March 1, 1911–July 29, 1998) New York born actor made sporadic appearances in films 1935–1992, including *The Grapes of Wrath* (1940, as Al), *Beware My Lovely* (1952, as Mr. Franks), *The Last Hurrah* (1958, as Norman Cass, Jr., "The Commodore"), *The Man Who Shot Liberty Valance* (1962, as Herbert Carruthers), *The Lion in Winter* (1968, as the Bishop of Durham). He died in Dublin from cancer at 87. White Baha'i stone inscribed *Blessed is he who is faithful to my covenant—Baha'ullah*. Mt. Jerome Cemetery, Dublin, Ireland.

9753. Whiteman, Paul (March 28, 1891–Dec. 29, 1967) "The King of Jazz," Pops Whiteman was the most popular mainstream dance band leader of the 1920's; his style, including the use of a banjo and oboe and dramatic flourishes at the finish, is immediately recognizable. He developed his symphonic orchestrations from the tinny dance styles of 1919–20, introduced George Gershwin's *Rhapsody in Blue* at the Aeolian Hall in New York in Feb 1924, and among several other later stars he developed, the Rhythm Boys (Bing Crosby, Harry Barris and Al Rinker) sang with him at his peak 1927–1930, including the 1930 color film *The King of Jazz*. Bix Beiderbecke, Frankie Trumbauer, the Dorsey Brothers and many others were featured in his orchestra before organizing bands of their own. Whiteman appeared as himself in several films. He died in Bucks County, Pennsylvania, and is interred with his wife, silent screen actress Margaret Livingston (*q.v.*), in their rough hewn mausoleum, the lot long secluded by shrubbery. First Presbyterian Church of Ewing Cemetery, Trenton, NJ.

9754. Whiting, Barbara (May 19, 1931–June 9, 2004) Actress daughter of Richard Whiting and sister of singer Margaret Whiting, in films of the 1940's and early 50's, including *Home Sweet Homicide, Centennial Summer,* and *Beware My Lovely,* as well as radio and several television roles. She married Gail Smith, General Motors director of advertising, in 1959 and moved to Detroit. She died from cancer in Pontiac, Michigan, at 73. Mass at Holy Name Church, Birmingham. Greenwood Cemetery, Birmingham, MI.

9755. Whiting, Richard (Nov. 12, 1891–Feb. 19, 1938) Popular song writer from the World War I era until his death penned *Till We Meet Again* (1918), many others. Father of vocalist Margaret Whiting. Whispering Pines, lot 1897, Forest Lawn, Glendale, CA.

9756. Whiting, William (Nov. 1, 1825–May 3, 1878) London born minister composed the words of the *Navy Hymn* (*Eternal Father, Strong to Save*), set to music by English composer John Bacchus Dykes. St. James Cemetery, Winchester, Hampshire.

9757. Whitley, Keith (April 1, 1955–May 9, 1989) Kentucky born country singer married to country western vocalist Lori Morgan, died from alcohol poisoning at 33. Double stone. Crestview sec., Spring Hill Cemetery, Madison, Nashville, TN.

9758. Whitman, Charles (June 24, 1941–Aug. 1, 1966) Texas sniper killed his wife and mother August 1, 1966, then climbed atop a tower above the University of Texas at Austin where he shot forty-six people, killing sixteen. He was finally overcome and riddled with bullets in an over-the-top charge by Austin policemen. He had sought psychiatric help over the headaches, ideas and impulses he had been having; an autopsy showed a brain tumor. The basis of the 1968 film *Targets*. Buried beside his mother **Margaret Whitman** (Oct. 26, 1922–Aug. 1, 1966). Sec. 16, lot 97, space 3, Hillcrest Memorial Park, West Palm Beach, Florida. His wife, **Kathleen Frances Leissner Whitman** (July 12, 1943–Aug. 1, 1966) was a twenty three year old biology teacher. Sec. H, lot 42, space 5, Davis-Greenlawn Memorial Park, Needville, TX.

9759. Whitman, Walt (May 31, 1819–March 26, 1892) Unorthodox free thinker from Long Island worked on the *Brooklyn Eagle* as a young man. His lifelong work *Leaves of Grass* was begun in 1855 and not completed until shortly before his death. It's most celebrated poem was *Song of Myself,* in which his awareness of all humankind as links in nature's chain was best displayed. Two other poems, *O Captain, My Captain!* and *When Lilacs Last in the Dooryard Bloom'd* were odes on the death of Lincoln. He lived with his brother in Camden, New Jersey, until 1884, when he bought a house on Mickle St. in downtown Camden and lived there the rest of his life. He died at 71 from TB and pulmonary emphysema after a series of strokes. He carefully designed his tomb, and after it was built sent photos of himself beside it to his friends while making regular inspections of it. His parents were brought from Long Island and interred there, joined later by several other family members. It is of rough hewn rock with a pointed rooftop, built into the side of a hill in Harleigh Cemetery, Camden, NJ.

9760. Whitney, Art (Arthur W. Whitney, Jan. 16, 1858–Aug. 15, 1943) Major league baseball player, primarily at third base and shortstop 1880–1891, with the Grays, Wolverines, Alleghenys, Giants and Browns. Lot 388 (Locke), Edson Cemetery, Lowell, MA.

9761. Whitney, Eli (Dec. 8, 1765–Jan. 8, 1825) Inventor of the Cotton Gin (1793) and interchangeable parts for guns began America's industrial growth while an infant nation. *In the social relations of life a model of excellence, while private affection weeps at his tomb, his country honors his memory* is inscribed on his red sandstone sarcophagus in the family lot, enclosed by an iron fence along Cedar Avenue, adjoining the lots of Noah Webster and Lyman Beecher. Grove Street Cemetery, New Haven, CT.

9762. Whitney, John Hay (Aug. 17, 1904–Feb. 8, 1932) Business magnate, grandson of John Hay, inherited two family fortunes. Minister to Britain under Eisenhower 1957–1961. As New York based chairman of Selznick International, having financed it, he bought the rights to *Gone With the Wind.* Aside from investment houses, he founded the John Hay Whitney Foundation to provide fellowships and later community development grants. He also published and edited the *New York Herald Tribune* from the late 1950's until it folded in 1966. At his death in Manhasset, Long Island, his fortune was estimated at over $200 million. Christ Episcopal Church Cemetery, Manhasset, Long Island, NY.

9763. Whitney, Myron (Myron William Whitney, Sept. 5, 1836–Sept. 17, 1910) Premier oratorio bass soloist in 19th century America, known for his outstanding volume, toured extensively. Encircled Celtic cross. Bayview Cemetery, Sandwich, Buzzards Bay, Cape Cod, MA.

9764. Whitney, Peter (Peter King Engle, May 24, 1916–March 30, 1972) Portly actor in films from the 1940's (*Murder He Says* 1945, *Three Strangers,* as twins, *Key Largo*) often as a thug, with varying levels of intelligence. TV series *The Rough Riders* 1958–9. He died from heart disease at 55 in Santa Barbara, California. Cremated at Valley Oaks Memorial Park, Westlake Village, through McDermott-Crockett mortuary, Santa Barbara. Ashes scattered at sea.

9765. Whitson, Beth Slater (Dec. 1, 1879–April 26, 1930) Lyricist (*Meet Me Tonight in Dreamland* 1909, *Let Me Call You Sweetheart* 1910), both with music by Leo Friedman. Sec. N, Spring Hill Cemetery, Nashville, TN.

9766. Whittaker, Johnson (Aug. 23, 1858–1931) South Carolina born slave who became a cadet at West Point, the only black there. On April 6, 1880, he was tied up and assaulted, cut with a knife and his life threatened unless he left. When reported, the white cadets were judged innocent. Whitaker was branded a liar, court martialed as a trouble maker and a fake,

his dream of being a U.S. Army officer ended. In 1994, Sen. Ernest Hollings pushed for the restoration of Cadet Whittaker's honor and his reinstatement with the U.S. Army posthumously. He was buried in an all Black cemetery in Orangeburg, SC.

9767. Whittier, John Greenleaf (Dec. 17, 1807–Sept. 7, 1892) Quaker poet from the "flowering of New England" was, like his colleagues, a staunch abolitionist, best known today for his mellow and thoughtful sonnets on all aspects of life, death and the hereafter. Among his poems were *Snowbound, The Last Eve of Summer* (1890) and *To O. W. Holmes,* his last poem, written only two weeks before his own death. *At Last* (1882) was recited to him as he was dying, at Hampton Falls, New Hampshire, at 84. Buried near his birthplace; his grave is in a long line of small and identical simple stones, in the Friends' tradition, surrounded by a high hedge. A sign at the entrance on the road proclaims *Here Lies Whittier.* Union Cemetery, Amesbury, MA.

9768. Whitty, May (June 19, 1865–May 29, 1948) English character actress on stage from 1881, made Dame Commander in 1918. In both England and Hollywood through the 1930's and 40's she played many cranky, often soft hearted, dowagers (*Night Must Fall* 1937, *The Lady Vanishes* 1938, *Mrs. Miniver* 1942, *Lassie Come Home, Flesh and Fantasy* 1943, *The White Cliffs of Dover, Gaslight* 1944, and *The Return of October* 1948, her last film). Her husband, stage actor and director **Ben Webster** (June 2, 1864–Feb. 26, 1947) had died the year before her death in Los Angeles at 82. Cremated at Pierce Brothers' Chapel of the Pines Crematory, her ashes were sent February 6, 1950 to St. Paul's Covent Garden, London, "The Actors' Church." A plaque commemorates she and her husband with the epitaph *They were lovely and pleasant in their lives and in their deaths they were not divided.* Their daughter, actress **Margaret Webster** (1905–1972), has a plaque below theirs with the epitaph *She served God right merrily.* St. Paul's Church (The Actor's Church, Covent Garden, London.

9769. Whorf, Richard (Richard Baker Whorf, June 4, 1906–Dec. 14, 1966) Character actor in *Blues in the Night* (1940, as Jigger), *Yankee Doodle Dandy* (1942, as Sam Harris), many others, later directed in both film and TV. Hillside sec., lot 5145, Forest Lawn Hollywood Hills, Los Angeles.

9770. Wian, Bob (Robert Charles Wian, June 15, 1914–March 31, 1992) Founder of Bob's Big Boy, the original double decker hamburger variation, beginning with a diner he purchased in Glendale, California, in 1936, turned into a 1,000 outlet franchise, owned by various companies, such as Frisch's in the Midwest, and sold his interest to Marriott in 1977. He later served in Glendale government and was the mayor. Bayview Terrace, lot 959, grave E, Pacific View Memorial Park, Newport Beach, CA.

9771. Wickersham, Ruby (Jan. 14, 1914–Feb. 17, 2001) Winchester, Indiana, cook ran a restaurant with her husband from the 1940's, providing pies to the Muncie and Anderson areas by and 1959 and expanding within a decade to concentrate on their bakery, providing Wick's Old Fashioned Pies, ranked among the nation's top ten. Double sarcophagus, reserve 15, northwest corner sec. 15, Fountain Park Cemetery, Winchester, IN.

9772. Wickes, Mary (Mary Isabella Wickenhauser, June 13, 1916–Oct. 22, 1995) St. Louis born actress in comedic roles with sarcastic asides, including Miss Preen the nurse in *The Man Who Came to Dinner* on stage and in the 1942 film. On TV in *I Love Lucy* (the ballet teacher), as Miss Carthcart in *Dennis the Menace*, *The Father Dowling Mysteries* and films ranging from *Now, Voyager* (1942) to *Sister Act* and its sequel. She died at UCLA Medical Center at 85. Cremated through Pierce Bros. Westwood mortuary. Ashes buried November 18 in the J.R. Thomas lot. Approximately 300' in main drive, beyond oak trees on left. Shiloh City Cemetery, Shiloh, IL.

9773. Wienlawski, Henryk (July 10, 1835–March 31, 1880) Noted Polish concert violinist and composer was a child prodigy at the Paris Conservatory from age eight to eleven, a record young age for graduation. Sec. 11, row 4, Powazki Cemetery, Warsaw, Poland.

9774. Wierzynksi, Kazimierz (Aug. 27, 1894–Feb. 13, 1969) Polish poet of the Skamander movement, celebrated life through the singing of athletic glory, in *Olympic Laurel* (1927); later darker works include *The Bitter Crop* (1933) and *Forgotten Battlefield* (1944). Sec. 9, rows 3–4, Powazki Cemetery, Warsaw, Poland.

9775. Wiesenthal, Simon (Dec. 31, 1908–Sept. 20, 2005) Noted Nazi hunter had been in the Janwska concentration camp at Lvov, Poland, with his wife **Cyla Mueller** (died Nov. 10, 2003), who escaped in 1942 using fake papers he prepared for her, and passed as a non–Jewish Pole in Warsaw and the Rhineland during the remainder of the war. Simon Wiesenthal was liberated from Mauthausen in 1945 and settled with his wife in Vienna the next year. Between them they lost some 89 relatives in the Holocaust. Credited with bringing some 1100 Nazis to justice, the Simon Wiesenthal Center was established in 1977. Cyla Wiesenthal was buried November 12, 2003, in Vienna. Arcades, tomb no. 18, Neuer Jüdischer Friedhof, Zentralfriedhof, Vienna. Her husband died in Vienna at 96 within two years. She was to be exhumed and buried with him. Pinsker Cemetery, Herzliya, north of Tel Aviv, Israel.

9776. Wiggins, Charles (July 15, 1897–March 11, 1979) The Negro Speed King, race driver and mechanic won the 1926 Gold and Glory Sweepstakes, black racers then being barred from the Indianapolis 500, although 1934 winner Bill Cummings credited him with an integral part of his victory. Wiggins was listed as a janitor, not part of the pit crew. He lost a leg in the 1936 Sweepstakes and retired. His grave went unmarked until a May 2003 article on a documentary about him caused anonymous donors to erect a granite headstone June 4, 2003, with an image of he and his wife Roberta and the title of the documentary, *For Gold and Glory*. Sec. 100, lot 244, Crown Hill Cemetery, Indianapolis, IN.

9777. Wiggins, Charles Edward (Dec. 3, 1927–March 2, 2000) U.S. Representative from California 1967–1979, former mayor of El Monte, was one of the last holdouts, along with David Dennis of Indiana, supporting President Nixon during the House Judiciary Committee's Watergate impeachment inquiry in 1974. Sec. 7A, grave 155-E, Arlington National Cemetery, Arlington, VA.

9778. Wiggins, Thomas "Blind Tom" (May 25, 1849–June 13, 1908) Former slave from Columbus, Georgia, blind and mentally handicapped, played piano by ear and began touring in 1859, playing for President Buchanan, among others. He later toured the south and raised money for the Confederacy, and composed over one hundred pieces of music. Unmarked. Pleasant Hill, plot D, Cemetery of the Evergreens, Brooklyn, N.Y.C.

9779. Wigglesworth, Michael (Oct. 18, 1631–June 10, 1705) Author of the epic poem *The Day of Doom* (1662) used in catechism. Bell Rock (Colonial) Cemetery, Malden, MA.

9780. Wightman, Hazel Hotchkiss (Hazel Virginia Hotchkiss, Dec. 20, 1886–Dec. 5, 1974) "Lady Tennis" Helen Hotchkiss entered the U.S. championships in 1909, winning all she entered: women's singles, women's doubles, and mixed doubles, repeating the feat in 1910 and 1911. After marrying George Wightman in 1912 and becoming a mother, she returned, winning the woman's championship in 1919. Holder of two Olympic Gold Medals, and forty-five titles in all. Sec. A North, UGP 187, Newton Cemetery, Newton, MA.

9781. Wilberforce, William (Aug. 24, 1759–July 29, 1833) English philanthropist worked to abolish the slave trade, with specific results in England. His death was attributed to influenza. A memorial to him is at the Chapel of St. John's College, Cambridge. A seated statue is near the black plaque marking his grave in Statesman's Corner, Westminster Abbey, London.

9782. Wilbur, Crane (Nov. 17, 1886–Oct. 18, 1973) Silent screen actor was Pearl White's leading man in several of her serials including *The Perils of Pauline* (1914). By the mid 20's he turned to writing for stage and screen and by the 30's was directing (*The Bat*, 1959). Scripts include *The Monster* (the play, 1925), *House of Wax* (1953) and *The Mad Magician* (1954). Married to actress Lenita Lane (*q.v.*), who is buried with him. Lincoln Terrace, lot 4229, Forest Lawn Hollywood Hills, Los Angeles.

9783. Wilburn, Teddy (Thurman Theodore Wilburn, Nov. 30, 1931–Nov. 24, 2003) Half of the country-western duo The Wilburns, with his brother

Doyle, sang harmonies on some thirty hits such as *Hurt Her Once For Me*, and helped launch the careers of many including Loretta Lynn. Sec. X, grave 166, Nashville National Cemetery, Nashville, TN.

9784. Wilcox, Daeida Hartell (1861–Aug. 7, 1914) The then wife of **Harvey Wilcox** (1832–March 19, 1891), a Kansas prohibitionist who had settled in Los Angeles in 1883, Mrs. Wilcox so liked the name "Hollywood" in a conversation she had on a train with a woman from Hollywood, Illinois, that she named their Los Angeles estate Hollywood. The Wilcox ranch was filed with the county recorder on February 1, 1887, as Hollywood, California. After her husband's death, she married Philo Beveridge, managing her real estate carefully and giving parcels of land to churches in what would in forty years be referred to as Sin City. Crypts in Corridor C, crypts 989 and 990, Cathedral Mausoleum, Hollywood Forever Cemetery, Hollywood (Los Angeles), CA.

9785. Wilcox, Frank (Frank R. Wilcox, March 13, 1907–March 3, 1974) Mustached character actor from DeSoto, Missouri, in hundreds of films and television roles from 1939, played endless businessmen, lawyers, judges, detectives, but may have been best known as oil company president John Brewster in TV's *The Beverly Hillbillies* 1962–66. World War II flat military plaque. Sec. BB, tier 9, grave 19, San Fernando Mission Cemetery, Mission Hills, CA.

9786. Wilcox, Harlow (Harlow M. Wilcox, March 12, 1900–Sept. 24, 1960) Long time radio announcer on *Fibber McGee and Molly* appeared as announcer and actor on other programs and television. Columbarium of Dawn, niche 30308, Holly Terrace, Great Mausoleum, Forest Lawn, Glendale, CA.

9787. Wilcox, Howdy (Howard Wilcox, June 24, 1889–Sept. 4, 1923) Winner of the 1919 Indianapolis 500, the first since 1916 because of World War I. He was killed in a race four years later in Altoona, Pennsylvania. Sec. 56, lot 240, Crown Hill Cemetery, Indianapolis, IN.

9788. Wilcox, Robert (Robert Wesley Wilcox, May 19, 1911–June 11, 1955) Actor in B films (*Blondie Takes A Vacation, The Man They Could Not Hang* 1939, *Island of Doomed Men* 1940) from the mid 30's. At the time of his death he was married to Diana Barrymore, both of them by then alcoholics nursing faded brief careers. He died from a heart attack at 45 in his sleep on the train back to Rochester. Riverside Cemetery, Rochester, NY.

9789. Wilcoxon, Henry (Sept. 8, 1905–March 6, 1984) Actor from the West Indies on the London stage imported by Cecil B. DeMille to play Marc Antony to Claudette Colbert's *Cleopatra* (1934). He later produced for DeMille and appeared in many films (up to *Caddyshack* 1978) and much TV. Married to actress Joan Woodbury. Ashes to family.

9790. Wilde, Cornel (Oct. 13, 1915–Oct. 17, 1989) Actor in films of the 1940's forward, played Mendoza the hotel heist insider in *High Sierra* (1940),

was nominated for an Oscar as Chopin in *A Song to Remember* (1945) and appeared in *Centennial Summer* (1946), *Forever Amber* (1947), many costume dramas and adventures. Married to actress Jean Wallace. He died from leukemia at Cedar-Sinai Medical Center in L.A. Urn garden west, Westwood Memorial Park, west Los Angeles.

9791. Wilde, Oscar (Oct. 16, 1854–Nov. 30, 1900) Irish born author of *The Importance of Being Earnest* and *The Picture of Dorian Gray* (1890) was imprisoned in Reading gaol 1895–97 for what were termed homosexual offenses. He lived in Paris afterward, his death possibly due to an ear injury suffered in prison, leading to the cerebral meningitis which killed him. Buried in Bagneaux Cemetery on the outskirts of Paris, he was removed in July 1909 to Pere Lachaise by his friend Robert Ross. His monument was designed by Jacob Epstein and dedicated in 1914, though cemetery officials made Epstein cover the formerly exposed testicles on the modernistic statue with a fig leaf. By 1922 however the leaf had been chipped away. Div. 89, Pere Lachaise Cemetery, Paris.

9792. Wilde, Ted (1889–Dec. 17, 1929) Writer-director in silent films, worked extensively with Harold Lloyd vehicles including *Girl Shy, The Freshman, For Heaven's Sake, Speedy* before his death from a stroke at 39. Sunrise Slope, lot 3112, space 2, Forest Lawn, Glendale, CA.

9793. Wilder, Billy (Samuel Wilder, June 22, 1906–March 27, 2002) Austrian film writer (*Menschen an Sontag/People on Sunday*, 1929) fled Nazi Germany and landed in Hollywood as a writer in the 1930's, working with Charles Brackett (*Ninotchka* 1939, *Ball of Fire* and *Hold Back the Dawn* 1941, all three Oscar nominated) and then as a director, leaving his mark with several acknowledged classics, blending liveliness and humor with suspense, in *Double Indemnity* (1944, AA nom), *The Lost Weekend* (1945, AA), *Sunset Boulevard* (1950, AA nom), *Stalag 17* (1953, AA nom), *Sabrina* (1954, AA nom), *Love in the Afternoon* and *Witness for the Prosecution* (1957, AA nom), *Some Like It Hot* (1959, AA nom), the first of seven collaborations with Jack Lemmon including *The Apartment* (1961, AA), *Irma la Douce* (1963) and *The Fortune Cookie* (1968) before his retirement in 1981. He died from pneumonia in his Los Angeles home at 95, the same day as both Dudley Moore and Milton Berle. No services. Cremation by Pierce Bros. Westwood April 3. Ashes interred April 8. His stone reads *Billy Wilder/ I'm a writer, but then nobody's perfect.* Garden of Serenity, Westwood Memorial Park, west Los Angeles.

9794. Wilder, Laura Ingalls (Feb. 7, 1867–Jan 10, 1957) Author of the *Little House* series of children's adventures set in the opening middle west and based on her girlhood in Wisconsin, Minnesota, and South Dakota. *Little House on the Prairie* (1935) was transferred into a popular TV series in the 1970's. She died just before her 90th birthday. Buried with her husband **Almanzo Wilder** (1857–1949) in Mansfield, Missouri, their home for many years. Their rose brown stone is next to that of their daughter **Rose Wilder Lane** (Dec. 5, 1886–Oct. 30, 1968), a feminist and writer. As with the lot of her family in DeSmet, South Dakota, a chain surrounds their frequently visited lot. Mansfield Cemetery, Mansfield, MO. *See also* Charles Ingalls.

9795. Wilder, Thornton (April 17, 1897–Dec. 7, 1975) Novelist and playwright won a Pulitzer Prize for the novel *The Bridge of San Luis Rey* (1927) and for two plays, *Our Town* (1937) and *The Skin of Our Teeth* (1942). He is buried, not on a New England hilltop as with Grovers' Corners, New Hampshire in *Our Town,* but in his family lot, his name on the center obelisk and his flat grave marker, at the rear of a relatively flat cemetery along a busy thoroughfare. Mt. Carmel Cemetery, Hamden, CT.

9796. Wilding, Michael (July 23, 1912–July 8, 1979) English actor primarily in British theatre and film in patrician roles (*Stage Fright* 1949, as Ordinary Smith). The second husband (1952–57) of Elizabeth Taylor and father of two of her children, his fourth and final marriage was to actress Margaret Leighton, with whom he lived in a cottage at Batchmore, Chichester, Sussex. He died after a fall in his home at 64. Service through Edward White and Sons mortuary, attended by Alec Guinness, Elizabeth Taylor and their son on 14 July 1979. Memorial plaque at The Actors Church, St. Paul's Covent Garden, London. Cremation and scattering; reference 51/k, Chichester Crematorium, Chichester, Sussex.

9797. Wiley, Jan (Jan-Harriet Wiley, Feb. 23, 1916–May 27, 1993) Blonde actress from Marion, Indiana, in films 1937–1946, including *Stage Door, Dick Tracy vs. Crime Inc., The Strange Case of Dr. RX, The Living Ghost, So Proudly We Hail, A Fig Leaf for Eve, She-Wolf of London* and *The Brute Man.* She retired after 1946. Divorced (married name *Greene*), she died at 77 from cancer in a Rancho Palos Verdes retirement home, Los Angeles. Cremated by the Neptune Society. Ashes buried at sea June 3 three miles off San Pedro.

9798. Wilhelm, Hoyt (James Hoyt Wilhelm, July 26, 1922–Aug. 23, 2002) Pitcher from Huntersville, North Carolina, with the majors 1952–72, played with nine teams, beginning with Leo Durocher's New York Giants, and amassed 143 wins—123 in relief—and 227 saves in a then record 1,073 games. Considered the finest knuckleball thrower ever, he was the first relief pitcher elected to the Hall of Fame, in 1985, yet his best game came as a starter, a no hitter for Baltimore against the Yankees September 20, 1958. He moved to Sarasota in 1975, where he died at 80. Field of Honor east 132-D1, Palms Memorial Park, Sarasota, FL.

9799. Wilhelmina *see* **William of Orange.**

9800. Wilkeson, Leon (April 2, 1952–July 27, 2001) Bass player with Lynyrd Skynyrd from 1972, leaving briefly and then returning, survived the 1977 plane crash that killed three of the band's members. He died at 49 in Jacksonville. Riverside Memorial Park Cemetery, Jacksonville, FL.

9801. Wilkins, Roy (Aug. 30, 1901–Sept. 8, 1981) Executive secretary and director (1965–1977) of the NAACP. Heritage Garden III, range 11, grave 19, Pinelawn Memorial Park, Farmingdale, Long Island, NY.

9802. Wilkinson, Bud (Charles Burnham Wilkinson, April 23, 1916–Feb. 9, 1994) University of Oklahoma football coach 1947–1963, with a record 145 wins out of 178 games. Undefeated 1954–56 with forty seven consecutive wins, fourteen conference and three national championships. He later broadcast and coached at St. Louis (NFL) 1978–79. Mausoleum, unit B, chapel floor, Oak Grove Cemetery, St. Louis, MO.

9803. Wilkinson, J. L. (James Leslie Wilkinson, May 14, 1878–Aug. 21, 1964) Innovative (white) Negro Leagues owner of the Kansas City Monarchs 1920–1948. Hall of Fame 2006. Garden Mausolem 1, view 5, crypt C, tier 49, Mount Moriah Cemetery, Kansas City, MO.

9804. Willard, Archibald (Aug. 22, 1836–Oct. 11, 1918) Artist known for *Spirit of '76.* Sec. 11, lot 1520, Greenwood Cemetery, Wellington, OH.

9805. Willard, Frances (Sept. 28, 1839–Feb. 17, 1898) President of the Women's Christian Temperance Union, a strong advocate of prohibition and women's suffrage, did not live to see both passed into law by constitutional amendments 1919–20. Rough hewn monument. Sec. F, Rosehill Cemetery, Chicago, IL.

9806. Willard, Jess (Dec. 29, 1881–Dec. 15, 1968) Heavyweight boxing champion 1915–1919 took the title from Jack Johnson, who had held it since 1908, and lost it to The Manassa Mauler, Jack Dempsey, in an outdoor match at Toledo, Ohio, four years later. He died at 86 in Pacoima, California. Homeward, lot 3859, Forest Lawn Hollywood Hills, Los Angeles.

9807. Willard, John (Nov. 28, 1885–Aug. 31, 1942) Playwright from San Francisco best known for *The Cat and the Canary,* first filmed in 1927 and again in 1930, 1939 and 1979. He also wrote *Channing of the Northwest* (1922), *Fog* (filmed as *Black Waters* 1929), worked on the screenplay for *The Mask of Fu Manchu* (1932) and had appeared in a few silent films, including *Sherlock Holmes* (1922, as Inspector Gregson). He died in Los Angeles at 56 from myocarditis and bronchial asthma. Sanctuary of Seclusion, crypt 8006, Gardenia Terrace, Great Mausoleum, Forest Lawn, Glendale, CA.

9808. William I, Prins of Orange (April 24, 1533–July 10, 1584) William the Silent, prince of Orange, led the Dutch revolt against the Spanish from 1568 until his assassination in 1584, including the declarations of independence of the northern provinces of the Netherlands in 1579 and 1581. He and his descendants of the House of Orange, including **William II** (1626–1650), and, descended from **John The Old,**

Duke of Nassau (1535–1606): **William I** (1772–1843), **II** (1792–1849), **III** (1817–1890) and his daughter **Queen Wilhelmina** (Aug. 31, 1880–Nov. 28, 1962), are interred beneath the Nieuwe Kerk (New Church), Delft, Holland (the Netherlands).

9809. William II (Kaiser Wilhelm of Germany, Jan. 27, 1859–June 4, 1941) King of Prussia and Emperor of Germany, grandson of Britain's Queen Victoria, ascended to the throne in 1888. Imperialistic policies and saber rattling for two decades had antagonized his enemies when war was declared with his backing of Austria in 1914. Removing himself to army headquarters, he lost touch with the German people and identified himself with the monarchy, contributing to defeat with annexation policies and unrestricted submarine warfare which brought the U.S. into the war in 1917. He lost authority to part leaders in the Reichstag, fled to the Netherlands after the Armistice in November 1918 and abdicated his throne. He died in exile at Doorn in the Netherlands and was buried in a tomb on the estate there. Schlosspark Charlottenburg. His death was ignored by the press in Berlin, though the Nazi government sent flowers and representatives.

9810. William, Warren (Warren William Krech, Dec. 2, 1895–Sept. 24, 1948) Leading man in suave roles on Broadway and in film from 1931, including *Three on A Match* (1932), *Lady For a Day, Golddiggers of 1933, Cleopatra* (1934, as Caesar), *Imitation of Life* (1934), *Satan Met a Lady* (1936), *The Wolfman* (1941) and many B films as *Philo Vance, Perry Mason* or the *Lone Wolf.* He died at 52 in his Encino, California, home from multiple myeloma after five years illness. Cremated at Pierce Brothers' Chapel of the Pines Crematory in Los Angeles, his ashes were given to his wife for intended burial with his mother and father, newspaper publisher **Freeman Krech** (1856–1931), in Nassau Knolls Cemetery, Port Washington, Long Island, New York. According to his wishes however, his ashes were scattered in Long Island Sound. A cenotaph to him is attached to the niche of his wife Helen, who died the next year from a heart ailment, in the Columbarium of Memory, Memorial Terrace, Great Mausoleum, Forest Lawn, Glendale, CA.

9811. Williams, Barney (July 20, 1823–April 25, 1876) Irish born 19th century theatre comic. A white marble bust of him graces his monument. Sec. 111, Greenwood Cemetery, Brooklyn, N.Y.C.

9812. Williams, Bert (Egbert Austin Williams, Nov. 12, 1874–March 4, 1922) The only black vaudeville star on the major circuits from the turn of the century until his death was considered among the finest pantomimists and comedians of his era, accorded a command performance before Edward VII in 1904. He starred in the *Ziegfeld Follies* 1910–1919, leaving in 1920. Touring with the Shuberts in *Under the Bamboo Tree,* he collapsed on stage in Detroit and died at his home on 7th Ave. in Manhattan just over a week later from pneumonia at 47. Spirea sec. 186, near the intersection of Spirea and Laurel Avenues, Woodlawn Cemetery, the Bronx, N.Y.C.

9813. Williams, Charlie (Charles Williams, Dec. 12, 1943–Sept. 10, 2005) First black umpire to work behind home plate during a world series, between Philadelphia and Toronto in 1993 — game 4 the longest in series history, at four hours, fourteen minutes. In the majors from 1982, he also called two All Star games and two National League playoffs. He died at 61 from complications of diabetes in Oak Lawn, Illinois. Homewood Cemetery, Pittsburgh, PA.

9814. Williams, Clark (Leander Crowe, May 14, 1906–Feb. 13, 1989) Nova Scotia, born stage actor, writer and director, made a few films as "Clark Williams" at Universal 1933–38, with featured parts in *Secret of the Chateau* (as Paul), *WereWolf of London* (Hugh Renwick) and starring in *Tailspin Tommy in the Great Air Mystery* (1935). He moved to Carmel, California, in 1936 and remained until his death there at 83 over fifty years later, retaining his real name. Cremated by Paul mortuary and Chapel By the Sea, Monterey. Ashes sent to Truro Cemetery, Truro, Nova Scotia.

9815. Williams, Claude "Lefty" (March 9, 1893–Nov. 4, 1959) Pitcher with the Chicago White Sox in the 1919 world series threw two games as did Eddie Cicotte, giving the win to Cincinnati for a fee of $10,000. Indicted but acquitted, the eight participants were banned from the majors for life and were given the sobriquet "Black Sox." Williams died at Laguna Beach at 66. Ashes stored where he was cremated, in a common storage sealed crypt (no markers). Gardenia Hall, Melrose Abbey, Anaheim, CA.

9816. Williams, Cleveland "Big Cat" (June 30, 1933–Sept. 10, 1999) Heavyweight boxing contender lost in the third round to Muhammad Ali in 1966. He was later shot during an altercation with a state trooper, resulting in lifelong kidney problems. Inducted into the World Boxing Hall of Fame in 1997, he died two years later from injuries suffered in an auto-pedestrian accident. Unmarked. Block 11 ½, lot 136s, grave 3, Paradise Cemetery North, Houston, TX.

9817. Williams, Cootie (Charles Williams, July 10, 1911–Sept. 15, 1985) Jazz trumpeter with Duke Ellington at the Cotton Club replaced Bubber Miley in late 1928 and remained to 1941; he led his own band for twenty years and rejoined Ellington in 1961. His flush plaque has a trumpet beside his name. Alpine Hill, Woodlawn Cemetery, the Bronx, N.Y.C.

9818. Williams, David "Carbine" (Nov. 13, 1900–Jan. 8, 1975) Imprisoned in 1921 for killing a policeman, he designed the M1 rifle while incarcerated. Pardoned by Herbert Hoover in 1929, his life was the subject of a 1952 film. Old Bluff Presbyterian Church Cemetery, Godwin, NC.

9819. Williams, Earle (Earle Rafael Williams, Feb. 28, 1880–April 26, 1927) Silent screen star from 1910 at Vitagraph, died from bronchial pneumonia at

47. Corridor of the Daffodil, crypt 2525 (top row), Begonia Terrace, Great Mausoleum, Forest Lawn Glendale, CA.

9820. Williams, Emlyn (George Emlyn Williams, Nov. 26, 1905–Sept. 25, 1987) Welsh actor, playwright and director from Mostyn, Flintshire, authored the theatrical hits *Night Must Fall* and *The Corn is Green,* both later filmed, and appeared in several plays and films, later performing a one man show as Charles Dickens. He died in his London home at 81. Cremated at Golders Green Crematorium, north London.

9821. Williams, Frances (Frances Jellinek, Nov. 3, 1901–Jan. 27, 1959) St. Paul born blonde actress on stage in the 1920's in *Mary, George White's Scandals, Artists and Models, The Cocoanuts,* introduced *As Time Goes By* in *Everybody's Welcome* (1932), recorded several songs including *Sunny Disposish* (unreleased for fifty years) and appeared in a few films (*Broadway Through A Keyhole, Hollywood Party*) of the 1930's and 40's. She died at Lenox Hill Hospital in Manhattan from cancer at 57. Cremated at Ferncliff through Universal Chapel January 29. Unmarked, Prospect sec., grave 1016, Ferncliff Cemetery, Hartsdale, NY.

9822. Williams, Gaar (1880–June 15, 1935) Satirical cartoonist lampooned small town life at the turn of the century, in the *Chicago Tribune* 1921–1935 and in syndication. He published two books *How to Keep From Growing Old* and *Among Folks in History.* Buried in his home town, where much of his material had been generated. Boulder with hand lettered plaque. Sec. 8 at the point, lot 490, east of Shiveley monument, Earlham Cemetery, Richmond, IN.

9823. Williams, Garth (April 16, 1912–May 8, 1996) New York born illustrator acclaimed for his children's books, including E.B. White's *Charlotte's Webb* and *Stuart Little,* Laura Ingalls Wilder's *Little House on the Prairie* and George Selden's *The Cricket in Times Square.* He died at Marfil in Gunajuato state in Mexico, where he had lived for much of 35 years. Obituaries listed burial at Aspen, Colorado, where he had lived in the 1950's.

9824. Williams, Grant (John Grant Williams, Aug. 18, 1931–July 28, 1985) Actor in B films of the 1950's and 60's, best known as *The Incredible Shrinking Man* (1957). TV series *Hawaiian Eye* 1959–63. He died from peritonitis at 54. Cremated by Pierce Brothers' Chapel of the Pines Crematory in Los Angeles. Sec. C-218, site 83, Sawtelle/Los Angeles National Cemetery, Westwood village, Los Angeles, Ca.

9825. Williams, Guinn "Big Boy" (April 26, 1900–June 6, 1962) Burly character actor with a gravel voice nicknamed "Big Boy" by Will Rogers. The son of a Texas congressman, he played pro baseball before entering films in 1919, a frequent cowboy heavy in the 1920's and many a sidekick in westerns, war and adventure films of the 30's and 40's at MGM and Warner Bros. TV series *Circus Boy* in the late 50's. Enduring Faith, lot 1694, Forest Lawn Hollywood Hills, Los Angeles.

9826. Williams, Gus (July 19, 1848–Jan. 16, 1915) Nineteenth century stage, minstrel and vaudeville star and producer. Among his songs was *Keep the Grass Green on My Grave.* Apparently due to a lack of bookings and ill health, he shot himself in the Yonkers, New York, railroad station. A triangular shaped four sided polished gray stone marks his grave, looking across the lake (or earth pile) at the DeWolf Hopper lot. Sec. 47/48, lot 22246, Greenwood Cemetery, Brooklyn, N.Y.C.

9827. Williams, Guy (Armand Catalano, Jan. 14, 1924–May 7, 1989) New York born leading man played *Zorro* at Disney in 1957, later appearing in *The Sign of Zorro* and *Zorro the Avenger* (1960), *The Prince and the Pauper* (1962), *Captain Sinbad* (1963) and on TV's *Lost in Space* 1965–68 as Professor John Robinson. He was found dead of a brain aneurysm in his room in Buenos Aires, Argentina. Ashes scattered off Malibu. On August 2, 2003, a bench in his memory was dedicated at Mission San Luis Rey Cemetery in Oceanside where parts of the series *Zorro* had been filmed 1957–59. Just inside the gate, the bench is inscribed *In loving memory of Guy Williams/ The One and Only "Zorro"/ You carved a "Z" on our hearts and changed our lives forever.* Mission San Luis Rey Cemetery, Oceanside, CA.

9828. Williams, Hank (Sept. 17, 1923–Jan. 1, 1953) Country and western legend known for *Your Cheatin' Heart* and others died in the back seat of a limo from chronic alcoholism complicating a back ailment while on tour. His elaborate monument, matched decades later by a twin one for his wife Audrey, features a poem by her, a granite cowboy hat and a guitar on the grave slab. Over a plaque with Williams' image on his monument is the line from his song, *Praise the Lord, I Saw the Light.* Bear right from entrance; monuments visible on the left. Oakwood Cemetery annex, Montgomery, AL.

9829. Williams, Hosea (Jan. 5, 1926–Nov. 16, 2000) Civil Rights activist organized marchers in Selma in 1965, served as advance man at numerous other rallying points through the years, was with Rev. King when he was assassinated in Memphis in 1968, served as head of the Southern Christian Leadership Conference, and organized holiday dinners for the poor and homeless in Atlanta, feeding thousands each year. He died from cancer at 74. Seating behind his family at the funeral was appropriately reserved for the homeless. Like King and Ralph Abernathy, he was drawn on a wagon by mules to his grave. St. Matthew Mausoleum, Lincoln Cemetery, Atlanta, GA.

9830. Williams, Hugh (Hugh Anthony Glanmoor Williams aka Brian Williams, March 6, 1904–Dec. 7, 1969) British actor and playwright in English and American films, often as cads, from 1930 (*Charley's Aunt* 1930, *David Copperfield* 1935, as Steerforth, *Wuthering Heights* 1939, *Dark Eyes of London*). He died in London at 65. Cremation, with the ashes sprinkled in the Crocus Lawn, sec. A4, at Golders Green. There is a five line entry in the Book of Remembrance and until November 1992, when relinquished by the family, there was a memorial wall tablet, no 47, bay 29, East Boundary Wall, inscribed *Hugh Williams. 6th March 1904—7th Dec. 1969. Actor and playwright. Loved and remembered always.* Golders Green Crematorium, London.

9831. Williams, Jim (James Arthur Williams, Dec. 11, 1930–Jan. 14, 1990) Savannah antique dealer and socialite known for his annual parties at Mercer House of the city's Who's Who was tried four times for the shooting death of Danny Hansford in the mansion May 2, 1981. John Berendt's best seller *Midnight in the Garden of Good and Evil* chronicled the more colorful life in Savannah from just prior to Hansford's death until Williams' death from a heart attack in Mercer House at 59. Buried next to his mother **Blanche Brooks Williams** (Jan. 22, 1907–Jan. 31, 1997). Ramah Church Cemetery, Highway 57, Gordon, GA.

9832. Williams, "Smokey" Joe (Joseph Williams, April 6, 1885–Feb. 25, 1951) Seguin, Texas, born Negro Leagues pitching great 1910–1932 with the Pittsburg Grays and the Lincoln Giants, "Cyclone" had a .624 winning percentage. Hall of Fame 1999. He died in New York City, though there is no death record located under his name. The location was a point of considerable confusion until clarified by baseball historian Bob Lord. Sec. D, lot 543, site 8, Lincoln Memorial Cemetery, Suitland Rd., Capitol Heights, MD.

9833. Williams, Joe (Joseph Goreed, Dec. 12, 1918–March 29, 1999) Jazz and blues singer from Cordele, Georgia, popularized the phrase *Every Day I Have the Blues.* He had performed with Count Basie, later in Las Vegas, and appeared as Grandpa Al on *The Cosby Show.* He won a Grammy in 1985 for his LP *Nothin' But the Blues.* He died at 80 after leaving a Las Vegas hospital for treatment of a respiratory ailment and walking several miles. Memorial service April 7 at the First Church of Religious Science. Cremated by Palm Mortuary Eastern. Lake View Mausoleum Columbarium, Palm Valley Memorial Park, Las Vegas, NV

9834. Williams, John (April 15, 1903–May 5, 1983) British actor in droll, wry parts in American films by the 1950's, including *Dial M For Murder* (as Inspector Hubbard) and *It Takes A Thief* (both 1954), *Witness For the Prosecution* (1957), many more, also turned up with great regularity on TV's *Alfred Hitchcock Presents.* He died at La Jolla, California at 80. Cremated by the Telophase Society. Scattered at sea.

9835. Williams, Joseph P. (Feb. 12, 1915–Nov. 8, 2003) Bank of America executive in the 1950's developed the first of all national bank credit cards. Gold Coast Crematory through Babione funeral home, Boca Raton, Florida. Ashes to residence in Atlantis, FL.

9836. Williams, Kathlyn (Kathlyn Williams Eyton, May 31, 1884/1887–Sept. 23, 1960) Silent screen actress from Butte, Montana, in films from 1908 (*The Adventures of Kathleen* [serial] 1913, *Our Dancing Daughters* 1928). Deodora Hall South, sec. O, niche 85, Chapel of the Pines Crematory, Los Angeles.

9837. Williams, Kim (Sept. 21, 1923–Aug. 6, 1986) Naturalist, writer and radio commentator popular on National Public Radio with *All Things Considered,* extolled the virtues of natural foods and a wide variety of topics. She announced her terminal cancer on the radio during her last program, with Susan Stamber, July 16, 1986. She died at her home in Missoula, Montana, three weeks later. Ashes returned to her residence.

9838. Williams, Larry (May 10, 1935–Jan. 2, 1980) Rhythm and blues/rock n roll singer of *Boney Morony* fame, later in films including *Just For the Hell Of It, The Klansman,* etc. A suicide at 44. Unmarked next to his sister Julia Ann Williams (1994). Parkview plot, lot 425, grave C, Inglewood Park Cemetery, Inglewood, CA.

9839. Williams, Marion (Aug. 29, 1927–July 2, 1994) Miami born gospel singer first with the Clara Ward Gospel Singers 1945–59, and her own group the Stars of Faith 1959–66. She recorded extensively, turning down large sums offered for her to do blues. In 1993 she won the $374,000 MacArthur Foundation Fellowship, the first singer to receive the "genius" award as well as the Kennedy Center Honors. She died from vascular disease in Philadelphia, where she had lived since 1947. Sec. P, lot 279, grave 2, Ivy Hill Cemetery, Philadelphia, PA.

9840. Williams, Mary Lou (Mary Elfrieda Winn, May 8, 1910–May 28, 1981) Atlanta born jazz and pop pianist and composer, with Andy Kirk's Orchestra 1929–1942. She later formed various groups in America and Europe. Her stone notes *Pianist-composer.* Sec. K, lot 586, grave 6, Calvary Cemetery, Pittsburgh, PA.

9841. Williams, Michael (Michael Leonard Williams, July 9, 1935–Jan. 11, 2001) English actor of Irish descent and raised in Liverpool, with the Royal Shakespearian Company 1963–1977. There he met and eventually put his career on hold for (later Dame) Judi Dench, who he married in 1971. They worked in the BBC series *Love in A Cold Climate* and on screen in *A Fine Romance,* as well as plays, television plays and radio. He died at 65. Funeral at the village church at Outwood, Surrey. Red-brown memorial plaque in the garden of St. Paul's Covent Garden, The Actor's Church, London.

9842. Williams, Paul (July 2, 1939–Aug. 17, 1973) Founding member of the original five Temptations 1964–1970 was called the soul of the group by founder Otis Williams, and was responsible for much of their famed choreography. He had developed a drinking problem and ceased performing three years before he was found dead from a self inflicted gunshot wound to the head in his car on a Detroit street. Service at Tried Stone Baptist Church, where the other four original Temps sang and served as pallbearers. Sec. G, lot 275, grave 4, Lincoln Memorial Park Cemetery, 21661 14 Mile Road, Mt. Clemens (northwest of Detroit), MI.

9843. Williams, Ralph Vaughan (Oct. 12, 1872– Aug. 26, 1958) British composer produced nine symphonies as well as opera, ballet, hymns and songs, forming national music in the 20th century from choral works of the Tudor era. He was best known for *Fantasia on a theme by Thomas Tallis* and *Sea Symphony.* Cremated at Golders Green Crematorium, his ashes are in the north choir aisle, Westminster Abbey, London.

9844. Williams, Rhys (Dec. 31, 1897–May 28, 1969) Portly, balding Welsh actor of memorable presence in *How Green Was My Valley* (1941, on which he also served as dialogue coach), *The Corn is Green, The Bells of St. Mary's* (1945), *The Spiral Staircase* (1946), *Tenth Avenue Angel* (1948), *The Sons of Katie Elder* (1965), many others. Columbarium of Remembrance right, niche 60467, Courts of Remembrance, Forest Lawn Hollywood Hills, Los Angeles.

9845. Williams, Robert (Sept. 12, 1894–Nov. 3, 1931) Stage and screen actor from North Carolina had just gained prominence in *The Iron Man* and opposite Jean Harlow in *Platinum Blonde* in 1931 when he died later in the year from blood poisoning resulting in a ruptured appendix. Whispering Pines, lot 783, Forest Lawn, Glendale, CA.

9846. Williams, Roger (c 1603–Jan. or March 1683) English born founder of the colony of Rhode Island had left Great Britain for Massachusetts as a Separatist, preaching religious freedom, separation of church and state and the rights of native American Indians. In 1635 he was banished from the colony and moved south where he purchased land from the Indians and named his settlement Rhode Island. He was buried near his home at Benefit and Bower Streets, marked by a circular slab. Unearthed in 1860, an apple tree had formed a human shape and left little else, prompting a pamphlet titled *Who Ate Roger Williams?* What they had was reinterred and a monument erected at the approximate site as a WPA project in the 1930's. It forms a large stone square arch over a statue of Williams on a bluff overlooking the center of the city and state capitol. Roger Williams Park, Providence, R.I.

9847. Williams, Roy (July 29, 1907–Nov. 7, 1976) The oldest, biggest and toughest looking, mousketeer on *The Mickey Mouse Club* in the 1950's was also a gag man and cartoonist who designed numerous uniform insignias during World War II. His plaque reads *The Big Mooseketeer.* Sanctuary of Remembrance, crypt 22902, Courts of Remembrance, Forest Lawn Hollywood Hills, Los Angeles.

9848. Williams, Spencer, Jr. (July 14, 1893–Dec. 13, 1969) Black actor and director prolific in African American films from the 1920's played Andy on the TV series *Amos 'n' Andy* in the early 1950's. He died

from a kidney ailment at 76. Sec 209, row 7, grave 3, Sawtelle/Los Angeles National Cemetery, Westwood village, Los Angeles.

9849. Williams, Stanley Tookie (Dec. 29, 1953– Dec. 13, 2005) Co-founder of the Crips, Los Angeles based street gang, was convicted in 1981 of four murders in 1979. His impending execution twenty-six years later brought celebrities and activists out with petitions to commute the sentence, based on anti-gang literature and children's books he had written. California Governor Arnold Schwarzenegger upheld the jury's decision, and Williams was executed at San Quentin by lethal injection. He requested his ashes be scattered over South Africa.

9850. Williams, Ted (Theodore Samuel Williams, Aug. 30, 1918–July 5, 2002) San Diego born slugger with the Boston Red Sox 1939–1960 was their greatest player and, as he wished, the greatest hitter who ever lived. The last man to hit over .400, his record .406 in 1941 still stands. Despite taking five years out of his career to serve as a flyer in the Marines in World War II and again in Korea, the Splendid Splinter led the American League in batting, total bases and runs scored six times, in slugging percentage nine times, and bases on balls eight times. He hit 521 home runs with a lifetime batting average of .344, was twice A.L. MVP, twice won the Triple Crown, and was named Player of the Decade 1951–60. In a photo finish to his career, he hit a home run in his last at bat, September 28, 1960, at Fenway Park, captured in John Updike's article for *The New Yorker*, "Hub Fans Bid Kid Adieu." As he had vowed twenty years before when fans had booed him, he did not tip his hat to the fans, until 1991 and the 50th anniversary of his .400 plus season. Retired to Florida, where for decades he not only fished but wrote about fishing, his last public appearance, to a tumultuous standing ovation, was to throw out the first ball of the 1999 All Star game. Frail from strokes since the early 1990's, he declined after heart surgery in January 2001 and died from a heart attack at 83 the next year at Citrus County Memorial Hospital, near his home in Crystal River, Florida. Williams wished no funeral services, to be cremated, and — according to a friend — to have his ashes sprinkled off the Florida Keys where he had fished. However, although it was opposed by his estranged eldest daughter, who sought a legal injunction, his son John Henry had his body removed from Hooper mortuary in Inverness the day of his death and flown to Arizona for freezing in a cryonics center. John Henry Williams died from leukemia at 35 March 6, 2004, and received the same disposition as his father. The suit by his daughter was dropped when funds were depleted by June 2004. Alcor Life Extension Foundation, Scottsdale, AZ.

9851. Williams, Tennessee (Thomas Lanier Williams, March 26, 1911–Feb. 25, 1983) Mississippi born playwright grew up in the slums of St. Louis, taking his name from his Tennessee ancestors. His work usually dealt with tensions of a neurotic and or sexual nature, most often in southern settings. Acclaimed plays include *The Glass Menagerie* (1941), *A Streetcar Named Desire* (1947, Pulitzer Prize), *The Rose Tattoo* (1950), *Summer and Smoke* (1948), *Cat on a Hot Tin Roof* (1955, Pulitzer Prize), *Sweet Bird of Youth* (1959), all later filmed, the screenplay for *Suddenly Last Summer* (1959) and the novel *The Roman Spring of Mrs. Stone* (1950). His death in New York City at 71 reportedly resulted from choking on a nose spray bottle cap that dropped into his mouth as he was using the spray. His monument, erected over seven years after his death, bears the epitaph *The violets in the mountains have broken the rocks.—Carmino Read*. The playwright's sister **Rose Williams** (Nov. 19, 1909–Sept. 4, 1996), the model for the sister in *The Glass Menagerie*, was a schizophrenic who underwent a prefrontal lobotomy in the 1930's and was institutionalized the rest of her life, dying at 86 in Tarrytown, New York, thirteen years after her brother. Her flush stone next to his monument bears the epitaph *Blow out your candles, Laura*. West edge sec. 15, near intersection, Calvary Cemetery, St. Louis, MO.

9852. Williams, Tex (Sollie Paul Williams, Aug. 23, 1917–Oct. 11, 1985) Country western singer best known for his recording *Smoke That Cigarette*. Zane Grey Garden, lot 139-C, Eternal Valley Memorial Park, Newhall, CA.

9853. Williams, Tony (Samuel Williams, April 5, 1928–Aug. 14, 1992) Lead singer with the Platters 1955–1960 through sixteen gold records including *Only You, My Prayer, I'm Sorry, Smoke Gets in Your Eyes, The Great Pretender, Harbor Lights, Twilight Time*. He died in New York City at 64. Services at St. Peters' Church in Manhattan by Rev. John Garcia Gensel, "The Jazz Pastor." Sec. 15, grave 1594, Calverton National Cemetery, Calverton, Long Island, NY.

9854. Williams, Walter Washington (Nov. 14, 1842–Dec. 19, 1959) Last surviving soldier of the Civil War died at 117, buried in his Confederate uniform with military honors. Mt. Pleasant Church Cemetery, Franklin, TX.

9855. Williams, William B. (Aug. 6, 1923–Aug. 3, 1986) Radio personality of forty years specialized in standards on his *Make Believe Ballroom* program from WNEW in Manhattan. It was allegedly he who first referred to Frank Sinatra as the Chairman of the Board. Friars Club lot, Kensico Cemetery, Valhalla, NY.

9856. Williamson, John (John L. Williamson, Nov. 10, 1951–Nov. 30, 1996) Basketball guard 1973–81 tagged Super John and known for his jump shot teamed with Julius Erving to lead the New York Nets to two ABA championships in the 1970's. He moved with the Nets to the NBA after 1976, briefly with the Pacers and back with the Nets in New Jersey in 1977–78. His number 23 was retired by the Nets; he had been on dialysis eight years prior to his death from kidney failure at 44 in New Haven, Connecticut. Upright brown stone with his picture and *Above the rim*

over next to en engraving of him dunking a shot. Hamden Plains Cemetery, Hamden, CT.

9857. Williamson, Sonny Boy (#1) aka **John Lee Williamson** (John Lee Williamson, March 30, 1914–June 1, 1948) Blues harpist from Madison County, Tennessee, emerged in the mid 1930's, the era of the "Bluebird Beat," first recording in 1937 with *Good Morning Little Schoolgirl* and with Bluebird to 1945, then with Victor. He played for a time with a group featuring Big Bill Broonzy; other accompanists included Yank Rachell, Eddie Boyd and Willie Dixon. Returning from work at the Plantation Club in Chicago, he was fatally mugged at 34. Old Blairs Chapel CME Cemetery, Madison County (near Jackson), TN.

9858. Williamson, Sonny Boy (#2) aka **Willie Williamson** ([Aleck] Rice Miller, Dec. 5, 1899–May 25, 1965) Mississippi born blues singer and harp player, a legend and precursor of many that followed. The Blues' first radio star, he broadcast from KFKA in Helena, Arkansas, for the King Biscuit Flower Company and by the late 1940's began calling himself Sonny Boy, after the popularity of the earlier, younger blues harpist John Lee Williamson. He wrote several tunes but first recorded with Elmore James on *Dust My Broom* in 1951. Miller died in Helena at 65. His upright monument has his photo at the top and is usually decorated with harmonicas along with beer bottles. Whitfield Church Cemetery, Tutwiler, MS.

9859. Willingham, Noble (Aug. 31, 1931–Jan. 17, 2004) Actor from Mineola, Texas, a teacher at Baylor, began in films in 1970 when *The Last Picture Show* filmed in Texas, and went on to appear in *Norma Rae, The Howling, Good Morning Vietnam, Pastime* (1991, as the skipper), *City Slickers* and *City Slickers II, Ace Ventura Pet Detective, Walker Texas Ranger 3* and many TV roles, notably as the bar-keep C.D. Parker on *Walker, Texas Ranger* 1993–99, which he left to run as the 2000 Republican candidate from East Texas' Congressional District 1, losing to Max Sandlin. Found dead of natural causes at his Palm Springs home at 72, he was cremated through Wiefels and Sons mortuary there. Sec. B-A, row C, niche 124, Riverside National Cemetery, Riverside, CA.

9860. Willis, Chuck (Harold Willis, Jan. 31, 1928–April 10, 1958) Atlanta born rhythm and blues singer of the 1950's, a forerunner of soul, made several recordings at Okeh 1951–54 but was better known at Atlantic 1956–58 with *It's Too Late, What Am I Living For?* and *Hang Up My Rock n Roll Shoes*. He died from a stomach ailment at 30. Buried as Harold Willis. Upright stone by tree along road. Southview Cemetery, Atlanta, GA.

9861. Willis, Matt (Marion Willis III, Oct. 26, 1913–March 30, 1989) Actor prominent in the Fredericksburg, Virginia, Little Theatre, made a few films, notably *Return of the Vampire* (1943, as Andreas the werewolf). He died at 75 and donated his body to medical research.

9862. Willis, Vic (Victor Gazaway Willis, April 12, 1876–Aug. 3, 1947) Pitcher with Boston N.L. 1898–1905, Pittsburgh 1906–1909 and St. Louis 1910. Born in Cecil County, Maryland, he died there at Elkton. Hall of Fame 1995. Upright headstone along drive. St. John's Cemetery, Newark, DE.

9863. Willkie, Wendell (Wendell Lewis Willkie, Feb. 18, 1892–Oct. 8, 1944) Republican presidential candidate in 1940 was a New York corporation lawyer but emphasized his birth and boyhood in Elwood, Indiana, locating his headquarters in the Durbin Hotel at his wife's hometown, Rushville, Indiana. Though soundly defeated, he was Roosevelt's closest race and, in FDR's view, his most worthy opponent, traveling to Europe and to Asia to garner support for the war effort on behalf of the president. His book *One World* advocated peace through united cooperation. Willkie suffered the first of several heart attacks in Rushville in 1944. He returned to New York and was admitted to Lenox Hill Hospital, where he suffered thirteen more coronaries before succumbing at 52. Lot enclosed by a hedge and dominated by a large cross; an open granite book has quotations from his book *One World*. His wife and son are also buried there, with simple stones along the sides. Right area of cemetery beyond bridge. East Hill Cemetery, Rushville, IN.

9864. Willock, Dave (Aug. 13, 1909–Nov. 12, 1990) Actor in films and TV 1939–1976 in some 200 appearances, generally in amiable roles (*Four Jills in a Jeep, The Fabulous Dorseys,* TV series *Margie* 1961–2, among others; as the father in *Whatever Happened to Baby Jane?, Hush Hush Sweet Charlotte*). Ashes scattered in the rose garden, with memorial niche. Valhalla Memorial Park, North Hollywood, CA.

9865. Wills, Bob (James Robert Wills, March 6, 1905–May 13, 1975) Fiddler and composer known as The King of Western Swing wrote and recorded both *San Antonio Rose* and *Faded Love.* On his plaque is the first line from the former, *Deep within my heart lies a melody.* Sec. 15, lot 560, space 2, Memorial Park Cemetery, Tulsa, OK.

9866. Wills, Chill (July 18, 1902–Dec. 15, 1978) Texas born actor's deep voice was used as *Francis the Talking Mule* in a series of comedies. He was in many westerns, usually in gregarious parts (*Giant*) and received an Oscar nomination for *The Alamo* (1960). Ashes in Garden of Devotion (ground plaque), Grandview Memorial Park, Glendale, CA.

9867. Wills, Frank (Feb. 4, 1948–Sept. 27, 2000) The Watergate security guard who discovered the break-in at Democratic National Committee offices early on June 17, 1972, alerted by consecutive pieces of gray tape placed over the lock. He left the job soon after and worked in security at Georgetown University. In the 1976 film *All the President's Men,* he played himself. Eventually he moved to North Augusta to care for his ailing mother. When she died in 1992, he could not afford to bury her, so he donated her body to science. Wills died in Augusta at 52 from a brain

tumor. Mount Transfiguration Baptist Church, 350 Blanchard Rd., North Augusta, SC.

9868. Wills, Helen (Helen Newington Wills Moody Roark, Oct. 6, 1905–Jan. 1, 1998) Poker faced tennis great from Centerville, California, won Wimbledon singles titles eight times 1927–30, 1932–33, 1935 and 1938, a record until broken by Martina Navratilova in 1990. She also won the U.S. title seven times 1923–5, 1927–29 and 1931, and the French four times. She died at 92 in Carmel, California, leaving no survivors. Her estate was willed to her alma mater USC-Berkeley, and her ashes scattered at sea.

9869. Wills, Nat (Louis McGrath Wills, July 11, 1873–Dec. 9, 1917) Vaudeville star with Ziegfeld known as The Happy Tramp, also an early stage union organizer, was working on his car in his garage at Woodcliff, New Jersey, with the door closed because of the cold, and was asphyxiated by the exhaust fumes after the door stuck. He was 44; the death ruled an accident. Flush plaque inscribed *Nat M. Wills 1873–1917. The Happy Tramp.* Wisteria sec. along Fern Ave. near Filbert Ave., Woodlawn Cemetery, the Bronx, N.Y.C.

9870. Willson, Meredith (May 18, 1902–June 15, 1984) Broadway and film composer penned *The Unsinkable Molly Brown* and *The Music Man* (1957), filmed in 1962. He died in Santa Monica at 82 but was returned to Mason City, Iowa, and the small town life he celebrated in the Music Man's fictional River City. As his cortege passed his birthplace, a barbershop quartet serenaded his widow with *Lyda Rose, I'm home again Rose.* The marble family monument has a sundial beside one end of it and a birdbath at the other. On his stone is a bronze plaque inscribed *Meredith, The Music Man, May the Good Lord Bless and Keep You 1902–1984.* Greenwood, lot 59, Elmwood Cemetery, Mason City, IA.

9871. Wilmot, David (Jan. 20, 1814–March 16, 1868) Democratic congressman authored the Wilmot Proviso in 1846 to prohibit slavery in the territory acquired in the Mexican War. The amendment passed the House twice but was defeated in the Senate. He later joined the Free Soil party. The epitaph on his marble stone is from the proviso: *Neither slavery nor involuntary servitude shall ever exist in any part of said territory, except for crime whereof the party shall first be duly convicted.* Upright white marble stone along the front of Riverside Cemetery, Towanda, PA.

9872. Wilson, Alan C. "Blind Owl" (Alan Christie Wilson, July 4, 1943–Sept 2, 1970) Guitarist and vocalist with Canned Heat was found dead from an overdose of barbiturates in his sleeping bag in Topanga Canyon. The death certificate shows cremation through Gates-Kingsley-Gates at the Chapel of the Pacific, Woodlawn Cemetery, Santa Monica. Ashes sent to Woodlawn Cemetery, Everett, Massachusetts. No record of them there. Memorial service at Arlington, MA.

9873. Wilson, August (Frederick August Kittel, April 27, 1945–Oct. 2, 2005) Poet and playwright co-founded the Black Horizons Theater in Pittsburgh, and wrote a ten play cycle including *Jitney, Gem of the Ocean, Joe Turner's Come and Gone, The Piano, Ma Rainey's Black Bottom*, which ran on Broadway, and *Fences,* which won both a Tony and the Pulitzer Prize. He died in Seattle of liver cancer at 60. Funeral through White Memorial Chapel, Thomas Boulevard, at the Soldiers and Sailors National Museum and Memorial, Pittsburgh. Greenwood Memorial Park, Lower Burrell, O'Hara Township, Pittsburgh, PA.

9874. Wilson, Ben F. (Benjamin Franklin Wilson, July 7, 1876–Aug. 25, 1930) Silent film actor from Corning, New York, in many westerns and serials, appeared in 133 films and directed 115. Last co-starring with Neva Gerber, he died from heart disease at 54. No marker. Colonnade, north wall, tier 2, niche P, Hollywood Forever Cemetery, Hollywood (Los Angeles), CA.

9875. Wilson, Carl (Carl Dean Wilson, Dec. 21, 1946–Feb. 6, 1998) Co-founder of the Beach Boys in Hawthorne, California, in 1961, with brothers Brian, the writer, and Dennis, who devised their surfing image. Carl played lead guitar and later took over a majority of the vocals, including *God Only Knows* (1966). Married to Dean Martin's daughter Gina, he was the acknowledged cohesive force in the band. Diagnosed with lung and brain cancer in the spring of 1997, he continued to perform throughout the year at over one hundred tour dates until his death at 51 in Los Angeles. Ashes interred February 11, with his charcoal toned marker set within six weeks, inscribed *The heart and voice of an angel. Carl Dean Wilson* (and dates) *The world is a far lesser place without you.* Sec. D, Westwood Memorial Park, west Los Angeles.

9876. Wilson, Clarence (Clarence Hummel Wilson, Nov. 17, 1876–Oct. 5, 1941) Short, thin, bald actor in many films of the 1930's (*The Front Page, The Penguin Pool Murder*) usually as mousy or ill tempered would-be authoritarian figures. A native of Cincinnati, he died in Hollywood. Columbarium, West mausoleum, room A, niche 227, Grandview Memorial Park, Glendale, CA.

9877. Wilson, Dennis (Dec. 4, 1944–Dec. 28, 1983) Drummer for the Beach Boys with brothers Brian and Carl founded the group in Hawthorne, California, in 1961, singing the praises of surfing, cars, romance and summer in general. The most popular American group 1962–66, they toured into the 90's. Drinking heavily and performing only sporadically in his last years, he drowned while drinking and diving off the coast of Los Angeles County at 39. At first entombed January 3 at Inglewood Park Cemetery, where his father **Murray** was buried, he was removed and, through special permission from President Reagan, was given a full burial at sea by the Coast Guard January 4, 1984.

9878. Wilson, Don (Sept. 1, 1900–April 25, 1982) Heavy, bass voiced announcer for Jack Benny over many years on radio, films (*Niagara*) and TV also did commercials and hosted a talk show produced by his wife, Lois Corbet. He died at 81 after collapsing at his home in Cathedral City, California. Cremated through Wiefel and Son mortuary, his ashes were scattered in the California desert.

9879. Wilson, Don (Donald E. Wilson, Feb. 12, 1945–Jan. 5, 1975) Pitcher with the Houston Astros 1966–74 hurled two no hitters in his short career. He died from fumes in his locked garage. Crypt with his son Alexander, who died in the same mishap. Sanctuary of Prayer, crypt 26742, Forest Lawn Memorial Park, Covina, CA.

9880. Wilson, Dooley (Arthur Wilson, April 3, 1886–May 30, 1953) Black minstrel, vaudeville and stage actor from Tyler, Texas, got his nickname doing whiteface Irish mimicry as a youth. He later appeared in the Federal Theatre productions of John Houseman and Orson Welles in the 1930's and starred in the stage production of *Cabin in the Sky* before finding his place in film history as Sam the piano player (he could not play the piano but was a drummer), singing *As Time Goes By* in *Casablanca* (1942). Sec. D, lot 6, grave 5 NE, Rosedale Cemetery, Los Angeles.

9881. Wilson, Dorothy (Dorothy Harmie, Nov. 14, 1908–Jan. 7, 1998) Actress from Minnesota in films 1929–37 (*Lucky Devils, Before Dawn, The Last Days of Pompeii, In Old Kentucky, The Milky Way*), many at RKO. Married to writer-director **Lewis R. Foster** (1898–1974). She died at 89 in Lompoc, California. Whispering Pines sec., lot 810, space 8, Forest Lawn, Glendale, CA.

9882. Wilson, Earl (Harvey Earl Wilson, May 3, 1907–Jan. 16, 1987) Syndicated columnist chronicled the New York show business world. A native of Rockford, Ohio, he began work with the *Piqua Daily Call*, later with the *Washington Post* and *New York Post*. He also authored *My Sister Eileen*. His death in Yonkers came less than a year after his wife. Service and cremation through Frank E. Campbell mortuary in Manhattan. Unit 5, col. E, tier M, niche 5, main mausoleum, Ferncliff Cemetery, Hartsdale, NY.

9883. Wilson, Edith (Sept. 2, 1896–March 31, 1981) Black actress in vaudeville, best known as Aunt Jemima for Quaker Oats for eighteen years, was also a jazz and blues vocalist with Duke Ellington at the Cotton Club, with Bill Robinson on tour in England. Also played the Kingfish's mother on radio in *Amos 'n Andy*. Films include *To Have and Have Not*. Mt. Glenwood Cemetery, Glenwood, IL.

9884. Wilson, Flip (Clerow Wilson, Dec. 8, 1933–Nov. 25, 1998) Black comedian from Jersey City did stand-up on TV from 1965 on *The Ed Sullivan Show* and *Laugh-In* before taking his landmark sassy character Geraldine to *The Flip Wilson Show* on NBC 1970–74, winning two Emmys. Wilson died from liver cancer in his Malibu home at 64. Cremated December 8 through Pierce Bros. Westwood Village mortuary. Ashes to his daughter at Santa Cruz, CA.

9885. Wilson, Francis (Feb. 7, 1854–Oct. 7, 1935)

Son of Philadelphia Quakers formed his own theatrical company in 1889, staging operettas (*Erminie*) and acting comic roles. Biographer of Joseph Jefferson and the first president of Actors Equity, he died in his Gramercy Park home in Manhattan, and had asked to be buried beside the humblest of his profession. Actors Fund of America plot, Kensico Cemetery, Valhalla, NY.

9886. Wilson, Hack (Lewis R. Wilson, April 26, 1900–Nov. 23, 1948) Stocky N.L. center fielder 1923–1934 with N.Y., Chicago, Brooklyn and Philadelphia hit a record 190 RBI's in 155 games and 56 runs in 1930, a N.L. high .307 batting average in over twelve seasons, with four home run titles. Hall of Fame 1979. He died without funds, his funeral paid for by N.L. President Ford Frick. The grave was unmarked for several years until a monument was erected with crossed bats and the notation *One of baseball's immortals* (with his name and dates) *rests here.* A bronze plaque with his image and stats was attached to the rear of the monument May 30, 1988. Sec. E, lot 60, Rose Hill Cemetery, Martinsburg, WV.

9887. Wilson, Harold (March 11, 1916–May 24, 1995) British prime minister led the Socialist Labour party governments 1964–1970 and 1974–76. Knighted 1976, created a Life Peer, Baron Wilson of Rievaulx, 1983. He died in London at 79. Churchyard of St. Mary the Virgin, St. Mary's in the Scilly Isles.

9888. Wilson, Henry (Jeremiah Jones Colbath, Feb. 16, 1812–Nov. 22, 1875) Vice President in the second term of U.S. Grant (1873–77), the former Republican senator from Massachusetts died in office in Washington. A descendant, Sen. Lloyd Benson of Texas, was the vice presidential candidate on the Democratic ticket in 1988, someone in the family line having switched parties. Old Dell Park Cemetery, South Natick, MA.

9889. Wilson, J. Frank (John Frank Wilson, Dec. 11, 1941–Oct. 4, 1991) Singer and one time hospital orderly from Lufkin, Texas, with his Cavaliers recorded the 1964 evergreen hit *The Last Kiss*, originally written and recorded by Wayne Cochran and based on the death of **Jeanette Clark** in Barnesville, Georgia, a few years before. Wilson died in Parkwood Nursing Home in Lufkin at 49 from the effects of diabetes. His flush bronze plaque reads *Last Kiss will be remembered long even though you're afar.* Last Supper sec., block H, lot 36, space 3, Garden of Memories Cemetery, Lufkin, TX.

9890. Wilson, Jackie (June 9, 1934–Jan. 21, 1984) Soul and pop singer of the 1960's with a wide vocal range and a stage presence that earned him the sobriquet "Mr. Excitement" had hits with *Higher and Higher* and *Lonely Teardrops,* several others. After a heart attack in fall 1975 while performing, he remained paralyzed in a New Jersey nursing home for nine years. He was buried in an unmarked grave until a subscription drive for a marker netted an unexpected $18,000, so an above ground mausoleum was built

and dedicated on his 53rd birthday, June 9, 1987. There is the notation *Mr. Excitement* and the epitaph *No More Lonely Teardrops.* On a bench in front of the double vault, where his mother Eliza is also interred, are the words *Jackie the complete entertainer.* Behind the office, Westlawn Cemetery, Wayne (west of Detroit), MI.

9891. Wilson, James (Sept. 14, 1742–Aug. 21, 1798) Native of St. Andrews, Scotland, delegate to the Continental Congress from Pennsylvania and to the Constitutional Convention, signed both the Declaration of Independence and the Constitution. Later an Associate Justice of the Supreme Court. He died at Edenton, North Carolina, and was buried there for over a century, until his removal November 22, 1906, near Robert Morris along the wall and marked by a stone slab, in historic Christ Church Cemetery at 2nd and Arch Streets, Philadelphia, PA.

9892. Wilson, Jud (Ernest Judson Wilson, Feb. 28, 1894–June 24, 1963) Negro Leagues player from Remington, Virginia, with various teams 1922–45 had a .351 lifetime batting average. World War I veteran, he died in Washington, D.C., at 69. Hall of Fame 2006. Sec. 43, grave 1114, Arlington National Cemetery, Arlington, VA.

9893. Wilson, Justin (April 24, 1914–Sept. 5, 2001) Cajun cook with a flair for comedy put out five cookbooks and hosted several cooking shows on PBS (with his signature endorsement "I ga-ron-tee") as well as albums of stories. A native of Amite, Louisiana, he lived in Summit, Mississippi, for six years prior to his death at 87 in Baton Rouge. St. Williams Catholic Church Cemetery, Port Vincent, LA.

9894. Wilson, Kemmons (Charles Kemmons Wilson, Jan. 5, 1913–Feb. 12, 2003) Entrepreneur from Osceola, Arkansas, founded the Holiday Inn hotel chain in 1952, taking the name from the 1942 Bing Crosby film, after he was insulted on a trip to Washington, D.C. the previous year by high rates and poor accommodations. Imitated by many chains. Also the chairman of several other ventures, he died at 90 in Memphis. Service at Christ United Methodist Church. Sec. 6, lot 76, grave F, Forest Hill Cemetery Midtown, Memphis, TN.

9895. Wilson, Lois (June 28, 1894–March 3, 1988) Pittsburgh born actress starred in silent films beginning in 1916, including *The Covered Wagon* (1923), *Monsieur Beaucaire* (1924) and *The Great Gatsby* (1926, as Daisy). She died in Reno, Nevada, at 93. Sunrise Slope, lot 3565, Forest Lawn, Glendale, CA.

9896. Wilson, Margery (Sarah Baker Strayer, Oct. 31, 1896–Jan. 21, 1986) Silent screen actress from Gracey, Kentucky, in many films, notably as Brown Eyes in the French segment of D.W. Griffith's *Intolerance* (1916), was also a pioneer female film-maker, acting in, writing and directing *Insinuation* and producing and directing *The Offenders*, both 1922, after which she left films. She died at 89, a widow (last name Bushnell) in Arcadia (California) Convalescent Hospital. Cremated January 27 at Rosedale Mortuary and Cemetery, Los Angeles. Ashes inurned with her daughter Elizabeth Bushnell Magyar (1966) as she arranged. Niche CWW 126, mausoleum, Rosedale Cemetery, Los Angeles.

9897. Wilson, Marie (Katherine Elizabeth Wilson/White, Aug. 19, 1916–Nov. 23, 1972) Actress in films from 1939 as dumb blondes starred in *My Friend Irma* (1949) and on radio and TV. Married from 1951 to **Robert Fallon**, she died from cancer at 56. Columbarium of Remembrance, niche 61274, Courts of Remembrance, Forest Lawn Hollywood Hills, Los Angeles.

9898. Wilson, Mary Louise Roberta (Sept. 18, 1914–Nov. 19, 2001) The Angel of Anzio cared for some 73,000 patients while overseas with the 56th Army Hospital in Italy. Awarded the Silver Star for valor February 18, 1944, she was the first woman to receive the medal and was part of Tom Brokaw's book *The Greatest Generation* (1999). Good Shepherd, lot 178, space 10, Laurel Land Memorial Park, Dallas, TX.

9899. Wilson, Meri (June 15, 1949–Dec. 28, 2002) Pop rock singer-songwriter was a child prodigy with a degree at IU and a masters in education from Georgia State, modeling and singing in Dallas clubs in the 1970's when her novelty song *Telephone Man* was recorded in 1977 and sold over a million. Later similar records followed, as well as the serious number, *My Heart Walkin'*, written with pianist Ray Kennedy. She died at 53 when she lost control of her car on highway 377 in Sumter County, Georgia. Buried as Meri Wilson Edgemon. Oak Grove Cemetery, Americus, GA.

9900. Wilson, Michael (Franklin Michael Wilson, July 1, 1914–April 9, 1978) Screenwriter from McAlester, Oklahoma, in Hollywood from 1940 won an Oscar for *A Place in the Sun* (1951). Blacklisted by the HUAC the same year. He died from a heart attack in Beverly Hills at 63. Cremated at Angeles Abbey through the Neptune Society. Ashes buried at sea April 14.

9901. Wilson, Samuel "Uncle Sam" (Sept 16, 1766–July 31, 1854) The original Uncle Sam was a meat packer from Massachusetts who sent crates of food for soldiers during the War of 1812 with "U.S." stamped on them, giving way to the nickname representing the federal government. The face was created for World War I enlistment posters by James Montgomery Flagg in 1917. The original's grave has a rough hewn rock with a bronze plaque attached and a flag which is raised and lowered daily. Sec. F, Oakwood Cemetery, Troy, NY.

9902. Wilson, Sloan (May 8, 1920–May 25, 2003) Harvard graduate from Connecticut and World War II Coast Guard veteran penned some fifteen postwar novels, including *The Man in the Gray Flannel Suit* and *Summer Place*, both filmed. He died from Alzheimer's Disease at 83 in Colonial Beach, Virginia. Ashes scattered from his former home, the Coast Guard cutter U.S.S. *Tampa*.

9903. Wilson, Teddy (Theodore Wilson, Nov. 24, 1912–July 31, 1986) Influential jazz pianist from Austin, in Detroit by 1929 and Chicago by 1931 played with various groups including Benny Goodman 1936–39. Also an arranger and composer, he worked with Art Tatum, Earl Hines, Fats Waller, many others, and later formed his own band and sextet, doing primarily studio work. In later years he taught and toured with his trio including his son Teddy Jr. His stone, "*dedicated by Japanese friends,*" has a piano above his name and the designation *Mozart of Jazz.* Sec. 8A, Fairview Cemetery, New Britain, CT.

9904. Wilson, Terry (William T. Wilson, Sept. 3, 1923–March 30, 1999) Western actor from Huntington Park, California, in many films, best known as assistant wagonmaster Bill Hawks on TV's *Wagon Train* 1957–65. He died at 75 in West Hills, California. Ebensteiner Family 16, Valley Oaks Memorial Park, Westlake Village, CA.

9905. Wilson, Theodore R. "Ted" (Dec. 10, 1943–July 21, 1991) Black TV and film actor began with the Negro Ensemble Company in New York before going to Washington and to Los Angeles, where his TV series appearances included *That's My Mama* and the short lived *Sanford Arms* (1977). Films include *A Fine Mess, The River Niger* and Mel Brooks' *Life Stinks,* his last appearance, released at the time of his death from a stroke at 47. Service and cremation through Forest Lawn, Glendale. Ashes returned to family.

9906. Wilson, William G. (Bill W.) (Nov. 26, 1895–Jan. 24, 1971) Co-founder of Alcoholics Anonymous in 1935. His grave is regularly decorated with tributes from recovering alcoholics, particularly chips and tokens denoting time sober and notes of gratitude. East Dorset Cemetery, East Dorset, VT.

9907. Wilson, Woodrow (Thomas Woodrow Wilson, Dec. 28, 1856–Feb. 3, 1924) 28th President of the United States (1913–1921) grew up in the south, the son of a Presbyterian minister. He was president of Princeton and the reform Governor of New Jersey before his election on the Democratic ticket in 1912. In his first term he pushed through considerable reform legislation but (like Roosevelt with World War II and Johnson with Vietnam) was later bogged down in war and international involvements. His proposal for American entry into the League of Nations with his Fourteen Points program was adamantly blocked by isolationist Republicans in the Senate led by Henry Cabot Lodge. While touring the country on behalf of ratification, Wilson suffered a stroke at Pueblo, Colorado, in September 1919. Studies by historian Arthur Link and others have indicated the debilitating stroke played a major part in his refusal to acquiesce to any of Lodge's alterations. For whatever reasons, neither man gave in and entry into the League was defeated.

Wilson only recovered partially from his stroke. He was seen little and lost the drive and spirit that had been predominant up to 1919. Reading mystery novels and going regularly to movies, he retired to a three story house on S Street southwest in Washington, taking little interest in the isolationist Harding administration. A large crowd gathered outside his house as death approached, many kneeling in the snow at the indication of his passing. Lodge, who would himself die the following November, was specifically asked by the widow not to attend the services. The president's parents, **Joseph R.** (Feb. 28, 1822–Jan. 21, 1903) and **Jessie Janet Woodrow Wilson** (Dec. 20, 1826–April 15, 1888), were buried at Columbia, South Carolina, where the plot was full. Saying he disliked burial, his widow ruled out Arlington, and although Princeton Cemetery wanted him buried in their University president's section, she chose the National Cathedral in Washington for his entombment, after a service at his home, by candlelight in the Bethlehem Chapel. It remained in a gated chapel recess below for 32 years. At the centennial of his birth, December 28, 1956, he was moved up to the newly completed Wilson Bay along the south side of the main floor of the cathedral. His widow **Edith Bolling Galt Wilson** (Oct. 15, 1872–Dec. 28, 1961) was buried below his sarcophagus. Her name and dates are inscribed in the wall above it. The National Cathedral (Cathedral of Saints Peter and Paul), Mt. St. Albans, Washington, D.C. Wilson's first wife, **Ellen Louise Axson Wilson** (May 15, 1860–Aug. 6, 1914), served as first lady for a year and a half, until her death in the White House at 54. She was buried with her family beneath a white marble monument with a profile of a maiden in bas-relief. The tribute from her husband reads *A traveller between life and death, the reason firm, the temperate will. A perfect woman, nobly planned, to warn, to comfort and command. And yet a spirit still and bright, with something of angelic light.* Myrtle Hill Cemetery, Rome, Georgia. The president's eldest of three daughters by his first wife, **Margaret Woodrow Wilson** (April 30, 1886–Feb. 12, 1944) never married. She died a recluse at an Eastern mystical retreat at Pondicherry, India, from uremia at 57, and was buried in the Christian Cemetery there. Their second daughter, **Jessie Woodrow Wilson Sayre** (Aug. 28, 1887–Jan. 15, 1933), died from appendicitis at 45 and was buried in her husband **Francis Sayre**'s family plot in Nisky Hill Cemetery, Bethlehem, Pennsylvania. Sayre (April 30, 1885–March 29, 1972) was later rector of the National Cathedral in Washington (as was their son) and is interred there, as is his father-in-law, although he also has a cenotaph in the plot at Nisky Hill. The Wilsons' youngest daughter, **Eleanor Randolph Wilson McAdoo** (Oct. 16, 1889–April 5, 1967) married Democratic politician and later cabinet member William Gibbs McAdoo in May 1914 at the White House. They were later divorced. She died in Montecito, California, at 77. Central sec., block E,

grave 173, Santa Barbara Cemetery, Santa Barbara, CA.

9908. Winchell, Paul (Paul Wilchin, Dec. 21, 1922–June 24, 2005) New York City born ventriloquist popular on children's television from the 1950's with his dummies Jerry Mahoney and Knucklehead Smiff became the voice of Tigger in *Winnie the Pooh and the Blustery Day* (1968) and subsequent *Pooh* films, and earned a Grammy in 1974 for the song *The Most Wonderful Thing About Tiggers*. In later years he devoted time to innovative medical devices as well, and won a 1986 lawsuit over the destruction of the tapes of his early live performances. He died in Moorpark, Ventura County, California, at 82. Service through Rose Family Funeral Home and Cremation, Simi Valley. Ashes scattered at sea.

9909. Winchell, Walter (April 7, 1897–Feb. 20, 1972) Influential gossip columnist and radio commentator from New York whose rapid fire delivery was familiar on radio for decades, narrated various documentary shorts and Desilu's TV hit *The Untouchables* 1959–1963. His broadcasts from World War II onward began with the trademark "Good Evening Mr. and Mrs. America and all the ships at sea." He died in Los Angeles at 74. Sec. 17, lot 6, 11–3, Greenwood Cemetery, Phoenix, AZ.

9910. Winchester, Oliver (Nov. 30, 1810–Dec. 11, 1880) Manufacturer of arms from 1857 created the Brown repeating rifle and later the sideloading Winchester rifle. His daughter-in-law **Sarah Lockwood Winchester** (Sept 1837–Sept. 5, 1922) became an eccentric, guided by a spiritualist to atone for those killed by Winchester rifles; to do so she constructed her "mystery house" in San Jose, California, and adding rooms to confound the spirits and stave off death, resulting in some 160 rooms in all. Both are in the family lot. Large boulder-monument with the Winchester name on an angled cross. Highland sec., lot 64, Evergreen Cemetery, New Haven, CT.

9911. Winde, Beatrice (Beatrice Lucille Williams, Jan. 5, 1924–Jan. 3, 2004) Actress who formerly toured with Yale's "colored" choir, on stage and in films including *The Autobiography of Miss Jane Pittman* (1974, as Lena), *The Taking of Pelham One Two Three, Oliver's Story, The Super, It Could Happen to You, Jefferson in Paris, Simon Birch, Mickey Blue Eyes, The Hurricane*. She died from cancer in New York two days before her 80th birthday. Ashes scattered in Chicago by her family.

9912. Windsor, Claire (Clara Viola Cronk, April 14, 1898–Oct. 24, 1972) Blonde, blue eyed star of Hollywood silents noted for her roles in the films of Lois Weber (*What's Worth While?* 1920, *What Do Men Want?* 1921). She retired with sound but for a few appearances. Divorced from actor Bert Lytell, she died in Los Angeles at 75. Across the road and down from the *Finding of Moses* statue. Kindly Light sec., lot 298, Forest Lawn, Glendale, CA.

9913. Windsor, Marie (Emily Marie Bertelsen,

Dec. 11, 1919–Dec. 10, 2000) Actress from Marysvale, Utah (population 300) in tough roles on radio, Broadway and films, excelling in 1940's and 50's film noir, including John Garfield's faithless wife in *Force of Evil,* as well as *The Narrow Margin, The Killing* (1956, directed by Stanley Kubrick), several others. Honored for her work with the Screen Actors Guild and the Motion Picture and Television Fund, she died at 80 in her Beverly Hills home, survived by her husband of forty-six years, Jack Hupp. Cremated, her ashes were later to be buried in the town cemetery, Marysvale, UT.

9914. Winfield, Paul (Paul Edward Winfield, May 22, 1941–March 7, 2004) Los Angeles born actor played Diahann Carroll's boyfriend in the television series *Julia* (1968), was nominated for an Oscar for *Sounder* (1972), for Emmys in the miniseries *King* (1978) and *Roots: The Next Generation* (1979), and won an Emmy in 1995 as a federal judge facing a challenge to his ruling on busing in CBS's *Picket Fences.* He also narrated *City Confidential* up to his death from a heart attack at 62 in Los Angeles, just after the passing of his companion Chuck Gillan, with whom he is buried. Epitaph *I, if the birds do not come, will sing to you/ Will you, who are seeing and flight and all music, Will you sing to me, if the birds do not come?* Court of Liberty, lot 1475, space 2B, Forest Lawn Hollywood Hills, Los Angeles.

9915. Wing, Toby (Martha Virginia Wing, July 14, 1915–March 23, 2001) Blonde actress from Virginia in films of the 1930's, including *Palmy Days, The Kid From Spain, 42nd Street* (in the *Young and Healthy* number with Dick Powell), and *True Confession* (1937). She retired to Virginia by 1943, the wife of aviator and Eastern Airlines Captain Henry "Dick" Merrill, where she died in Mathews at 85. Ashes interred at Christ Episcopal Church, Mathews, VA.

9916. Wininger, Bo (Francis G. Wininger, Nov. 16, 1922–Dec. 7, 1967) Golfer in the 1960's, a mainstay in the PGA. Stone has crossed clubs. Block 31, lot 22, Summit View Cemetery, Guthrie, OK.

9917. Winninger. Charles (Karl Winninger, May 26, 1884–Jan. 27, 1969) Chubby character actor in endearing roles in *Show Boat* (as Captain Andy in both the 1929 and 1936 film versions), *Nothing Sacred, Three Wise Fools, Sunday Dinner for a Soldier* (1944), *State Fair* (1945). Enduring Faith, lot 1075, Forest Lawn Hollywood Hills, Los Angeles.

9918. Winslowe, Paula (Winifred Reyleck, March 21, 1910–March 7, 1996) Radio actress from North Dakota played Peg Riley on *The Life of Riley* 1944–1951, plus many other program appearances, dubbed the voice of Jean Harlow, then deceased, in *Saratoga* (1937), that of *Bambi*'s ill fated mother in the 1942 Disney film, played Mrs. Conklin on TV's *Our Miss Brooks* 1953–58, and made numerous appearances in television dramas up to 1965. Divorced from John Sutherland, she died at 85 in the Motion

Picture Country Home, Woodland Hills. Sec. BB/St. Joseph, tier 17, grave 116, Holy Cross Cemetery, Culver City, CA.

9919. Winstead, Charles (May 25, 1891–Aug. 3, 1973) FBI agent fired a majority of the bullets that killed John Dillinger as he exited the Biograph Theatre in Chicago July 22, 1934. Fairview Crematory through Strong-Thorne mortuary, Albuquerque, New Mexico. Ashes to family.

9920. Winter, Dale *see* **Big Jim Colosimo.**

9921. Winter, Edward (June 3, 1937–March 8, 2001) Actor from Ventura, California, in numerous roles from 1964, nominated for a Tony for *Cabaret* and *Promises, Promises,* also appeared in films and much television, but was best known as the paranoid army intelligence officer Col. Flagg in seven episodes of *M.A.S.H.* between 1973–1979. He died from Parkinson's disease — the death certificate lists primary degenerative dementia — at 63 in the Motion Picture and Television Hospital, Woodland Hills, California. Cremated by the Neptune Society of Burbank. Ashes March 16 to his family.

9922. Winterhalter, Hugo (Aug. 15, 1909–Sept. 17, 1973) RCA musical director made several recordings including *Oh My Papa* and both an instrumental and vocal version of *Canadian Sunset,* both in the 1950's, many others. Died in Greenwich, Connecticut. Rockland Cemetery, Sparkill, NY.

9923. Winters, Don (April 17, 1929–Aug. 17, 2002) South Georgia raised country music singer dubbed The Yodeling King began recording in Nashville in the 1950's and with Bobby Sykes joined Marty Robbins to form the Marty Robbins Trio, continuing until Robbins' death in 1982. He died from liver cancer at 73 in his home in Nolensville, Tennessee. Nolensville Cemetery, Nolensville, TN.

9924. Winters, Jesse "Nip" (April 29, 1899–Dec. 12, 1971) Top flight Negro Leagues pitcher 1920–1933, the best in the Eastern Colored League's history. Sec. FF, lot 45, Union Hill Cemetery, Kennett Square, PA.

9925. Winters, Ralph (June 17, 1909–Feb. 26, 2004) Oscar winning film editor in Hollywood over seventy years, nominated six times, won for *King Solomon's Mines* and *Ben Hur.* Garden Mausoleum of Truth, CC wall, first row, crypt 33, Hillside Memorial Park, Los Angeles.

9926. Winters, Roland (Nov. 22, 1904–Oct. 22, 1989) Boston born actor was the third, last, and least of the screen's Charlie Chans, at Monogram 1947–49. He died at the Actors Fund Nursing Home at Englewood, New Jersey, at 84. Cremated at Cedar Lawn Cemetery in Paterson, the ashes were picked up by Wien and Wien mortuary, Englewood. Their records show they then went to the Gramercy Funeral Chapel in Manhattan, which has records only seven years.

9927. Winthrop, John (Jan. 22 [Jan. 12 O.S.] 1588–April 5 [March 26 O.S.] 1649) Governor of the Massachusetts Bay Colony intermittently 1629–1648, espousing the Puritan doctrine. He removed to Boston at the end of his life and established the Congregational Church there. King's Chapel Burying Ground, Tremont Street, Boston, MA.

9928. Winwood, Estelle (Estelle Goodwin, Jan. 24, 1883–June 20, 1984) English actress from Lee on stage and screen for 75 years in both the UK and Hollywood (*The Swan* 1956; *23 Paces to Baker Street* 1956; *Alive and Kicking* UK 1958; *Darby O'Gill and the Little People* 1959; *Dead Ringer* 1964; *Camelot* 1967; *The Producers* 1968; *Murder By Death* 1976) in many supporting roles, an inveterate scene stealer. She died at 101. Ashes in untitled, unidentifiable space at Westwood Memorial Park, west Los Angeles.

9929. Wirz, Henry (Nov. 25, 1823–Nov. 10, 1865) Swiss born Confederate commandant of the notorious Andersonville prisoner of war camp for Union soldiers during the Civil War at Andersonville, Georgia. Because of the inhumane conditions there, Wirz was arrested as a war criminal after the war. He was hanged at the old Capitol Prison and buried there for a time near the Lincoln assassination conspirators but was later removed for reburial. An older stone has only *Wirz* on it but a newer flush plaque is inscribed *Capt. Henry Wirz, C.S.A. Confederate hero-martyr.* Center sec. 27, Mount Olivet Cemetery, Washington, D.C.

9930. Wise, Robert (Sept. 10, 1914–Sept. 14, 2005) Film director born in Winchester, Indiana, and raised in Connersville, was first an editor at RKO, working on *The Devil and Daniel Webster,* Orson Welles' *Citizen Kane* and *The Magnificent Ambersons,* and producer Val Lewton's thrillers before taking over *Curse of the Cat People* (1944) for Lewton and directing *The Body Snatcher* the same year. He went on to receive four Oscars and seven nominations, and amass credits including *The Set Up, The House on Telegraph Hill, The Day the Earth Stood Still, Executive Suite, Tribute to A Bad Man, Run Silent Run Deep, I Want To Live* (AA nom., 1958), *Odds Against Tomorrow, West Side Story* (AA with Jerome Robbins and as producer, 1961), *The Haunting, The Sound of Music* (AA as producer and director, 1965), *The Sand Pebbles, The Andromeda Strain, Audrey Rose,* and *Star Trek The Movie* (1979), *A Storm in Summer* (TV, 2000). Irving Thalberg Award 1966. AFI Life Achievement Award 1998. He died unexpectedly at UCLA Medical Center, Los Angeles, just after his 91st birthday. Cremated by Pierce Bros. Westwood mortuary. Ashes September 22 to his family in Los Angeles.

9931. Wise, Stephen S. (March 17, 1874–April 19, 1949) Budapest born New York rabbi founded the Zionist Organization of America and the Stephen Wise Free Synagogue and Jewish Institute of America in New York 1922. Stephen Wise Free Synagogue mausoleum, Westchester Hills Cemetery, Hastings-on-Hudson, NY.

9932. Wise, Tom (Thomas A. Wise, March 23, 1865–March 21, 1928) Stage actor from Faversham,

Kent, went first to California and then to Broadway in June 1888 in a variety of roles over four decades, including Falstaff. He died in Manhattan from a cardiac-asthma related illness at 62. He was Shepherd of the Lambs Club, which organized his funeral at the Church of the Transfiguration (the Little Church Around the Corner), with a eulogy by Walter Hampden. Cremated at Fresh Pond Crematory, Middle Village, Queens, the urn was to be kept at the Lambs Club in Manhattan.

9933. Wister, Owen (July 14, 1860–July 21, 1938) Novelist and historian from Philadelphia best known for *The Virginian* (1902). Sec. J, lot 206, Laurel Hill Cemetery, Philadelphia, PA.

9934. Withers, Grant (June 17, 1904–March 27, 1959) Actor in films from the late 1920's moved to serials, melodramas and westerns with the 30's and 40's (*Billy the Kid, My Darling Clementine, Fort Apache, Wake of the Red Witch*). Married to Loretta Young 1930–1931. A suicide by overdose of sleeping pills at 54. Corridor of Springtime, crypt 15161, Jasmine Terrace, Great Mausoleum, Forest Lawn, Glendale, CA.

9935. Witherspoon, Cora (Cora Bell Witherspoon, Jan. 5, 1890–Nov. 17, 1957) Actress often in shrewish or nagging wife parts (*Libeled Lady, The Bank Dick*). Sec. 1, Metairie (Lake Lawn-Metairie) Cemetery, New Orleans, LA.

9936. Witherspoon, John (Feb. 5, 1723–Nov. 15, 1794) Signer of the Declaration of Independence from New Jersey was a Presbyterian minister and the president of Princeton College 1768–1794. The words on his stone sarcophagus marker are in Latin and badly eroded, but like many graves around it, including Aaron Burr, Sr., it has a new bronze plaque affixed to it noting the occupant and his achievements. Presidents' sec., enclosed by an iron railing, Princeton Cemetery, Princeton, NJ.

9937. Witter, Dean (Aug. 2, 1887–May 25, 1969) Founder of the investment company bearing his name. Boulder surrounded by flush plaques. Palm 3, lot 52, Sunset View Cemetery, El Cerrito, near Berkeley, CA.

9938. Wittgenstein, Ludwig (April 26, 1889–April 29, 1951) Austrian philosopher taught at Cambridge, analyzing language and meaning, espousing the picture theory stating simple objects exist and form more complex ones, the relationships of which are represented in language. For him the problems of philosophy dissolved with failure to understand the picture relationships, which could not be articulated. Grave length flush slab with name and dates. St. Giles Cemetery, Cambridge, England.

9939. Wodehouse, P.G. (Pelham Grenville Wodehouse, Oct. 15, 1881–Feb. 14. 1975) Knighted English writer specialized in British caricatures. Residing in America at Remsenburg, Long Island, he died in Southampton Hospital at 90. Ashes buried beneath a monument with engraved quill and ink well, an open book listing "Jeeves," "Blandings Castle," "Leave it to

Smith" and "Meet Mister Mullner," and the notation *He gave joy to countless people.* Remsenburg Cemetery, Remsenburg, Long Island, NY.

9940. Wolcott, Oliver (Dec. 1, 1726–Dec. 1, 1797) Signer of the Declaration of Independence from Connecticut commanded a regiment in the Revolution and served as Governor 1796-7. His son **Oliver Wolcott** (Jan. 17, 1760–June 1, 1833) was Secretary of the Treasury 1795–1800 and Governor 1817–1827. East Cemetery, Litchfield, CT.

9941. Wolf, Hugo (March 13, 1860–Feb. 22, 1903) Austrian composer ranked with Schubert as master of the German lied. His work, primarily from the late 1880's, included music to poems by Morike and fifty songs from Goethe. His one completed opera was *Der Corregidor* (1896). He died in a mental hospital from syphilis at 42. His monument has his image in relief. Gruppe 32 A, nummer 10, Zentralfriedhof (Central Cemetery), Vienna.

9942. Wolf-Ferrari, Ermanno (Jan. 12, 1876–Jan. 21, 1948) Italian composer known for his comic operas *I Quattro Rusteghi* and *Il Segreto di Susanna.* Monument with bust at the head of his grave length tablet. Cimitero di San Michele, Venice.

9943. Wolfe, Glynn "Scotty" (July 25, 1908–June 10, 1997) The world's most married man acquired 29 wives but no one to pay his funeral expenses, covered by Frye Chapel and Palo Verde Cemetery, Blythe, CA.

9944. Wolfe, Ian (Nov. 4, 1896–Jan. 23, 1992) Character actor in hundreds of films from the 1920's through TV sitcoms prior to his death at 95. His issued epitaph read *If employers call, tell them I'm on location in some other world.* Cremated by Pierce Bros. Westwood mortuary, Los Angeles. Ashes to residence in Sherman Oaks, CA.

9945. Wolfe, James (Jan. 2, 1727–Sept. 13, 1759) English Major General opposing French General Montcalm in the battle over Quebec City on the Plain of Abraham. At the point of the British victory in routing the French, Wolfe was mortally wounded, as was Montcalm. He was embalmed and transported to England for burial at Greenwich. There is also a memorial to Wolfe at Westminster Abbey, where Canadian soldiers left their native flags to fight with the British in World War II, retrieving their colors prior to their return to Canada. Crypt below St. Alfege's Church, Greenwich, England.

9946. Wolf, Johanna (June 1, 1900–June 5, 1985) Adolf Hitler's secretary for twenty years longer than any other; he came to address and refer to her with the familiar "Wolfin" (She-wolf). Feld 36A, reihe 2, nummer 10, Ostfriedhof, Munich.

9947. Wolfe, Thomas (Oct. 3, 1900–Sept. 15, 1938) Author of *Look Homeward, Angel* (1929) and *You Can't Go Home Again* (published posthumously in 1940) from Asheville, North Carolina. The former was a literal autobiography of himself, family and way of life in Asheville, which offended many there at the time. He became ill with pneumonia on a trip from Seattle to Vancouver, activating an old TB lesion which traveled to his brain. He died at 37 in Johns Hopkins Hospital in Baltimore. Inscribed on his upright stone in the family plot is *Tom, son of W.O. and Julia E. Wolfe, a Beloved American Author,* the dates, and the quotations *The last voyage, the longest, the best*—(from) *Look Homeward Angel* and *Death bent to touch his chosen son with mercy, love and pity, and put the seal of honor on him when he died*—(from) *The Web and the Rock.* Sec. Q, Riverside Cemetery, Asheville, NC.

9948. Wolff, Albert (Albert Harris Wolff, March 1, 1903–March 21, 1998) The last of Eliot Ness's fabled Untouchables, the federal agents in Chicago in the 1920's who were incorruptible and instrumental in sending Al Capone to prison for income tax evasion. He died in a Mason, Ohio, nursing home at 95. Westlawn Memorial Park, Norridge (Chicago), IL.

9949. Wolfman Jack (Robert Weston Smith, Jan. 21, 1938–July 1, 1995) Brooklyn born disc jockey whose gravel voice and howls over 250,000 watt XERF over the Mexican border in the early 1960's made him a staple in rock and roll history, topped off by his appearance in the 1973 film *American Graffiti.* He later hosted *The Midnight Special* and other TV musical programs and was the subject of several records. His death at 57 came with a sudden heart attack in his Belvidere, North Carolina, home. Cremated July 8 through Evans mortuary in Edenton, the service on his estate was conducted by Rev. Robert Schuller, as he had requested, and a large marker erected immediately over his ashes buried there. The gray stone has *Wolfman Jack* above his full name and dates, beneath that *One more time* and around the base *Clap for the wolfman,* a howl, etc. Belvidere Plantation, Belvidere, NC.

9950. Wolheim, Louis (March 28, 1881–Feb. 18, 1931) Burly, rugged faced actor acclaimed for his role in Eugene O'Neill's *The Hairy Ape* and specialized in other coarse, brutish parts, usually amiable, ranging from the dance hall proprietor in *Dr. Jekyll & Mr. Hyde* with John Barrymore (1920) to Lew Aires' comrade in arms in *All Quiet on the Western Front* (1930). He died early the following year from stomach cancer at 49. His rectangular urn bears the inscription from Keats: *When through the old oak forest I am gone, let me not wander in a barren dream. But when I am consumed in the fire, give me new phoenix wings to fly at my desire.* Chapel of the Psalms, lower columbarium, column D, tier 2, niche 5, Hollywood Forever Cemetery, Hollywood (Los Angeles), CA.

9951. Wolpe, Stefan (Aug. 25, 1902–April 4, 1972) German born composer in the U.S. from 1944, wrote for piano, chamber music and trumpet, in modified serial method. Epitaph reads *A thousand birds will fly out of my mouth when I die.* Boulder with plaque. Green River Cemetery, East Hampton, Long Island, NY.

9952. Womack, Harry (Harris Womack, June 25, 1945–March 7, 1974) Bassist with The Valentinos, formerly the gospel singing Womack Brothers, brother of Bobby, was fatally stabbed by his girlfriend. Garden of Everlasting Peace, garden crypt 5036, Forest Lawn, Glendale, CA.

9953. Wong, Anna May (Wong Liu Tsong, Jan. 3, 1905–Feb. 3, 1961) Chinese American actress born in Los Angeles' Chinatown, in heavy dramatic roles in silents and talkies, including *The Thief of Baghdad* (1924), *Mr. Wu* (1927), *Daughter of the Dragon* (1931), *Shanghai Express* (1932), *Limehouse Blues* (1934), *Island of Doomed Men* (1940), many films in the UK through the 30's. She died in her Santa Monica home from a heart attack at 56. Cremated at the Chapel of the Pacific, Woodlawn Cemetery, Santa Monica, her ashes are marked by a rose granite monument with Chinese characters reading *Lee Toy Wong*, an Americanization of her real name. Sec. 5, lot 136, grave 3 ne, Rosedale Cemetery, Los Angeles.

9954. Wood, Ed (Edward D. Wood, Jr., Oct. 10, 1924–Dec. 10, 1978) Cult film director whose low budgets seldom impaired his enthusiasm. He gave work to an aged and ailing Bela Lugosi in his last years, but became increasingly famous for pictures so bad they were good, including *Glen or Glenda* aka *I Led Two Lives* (1952, his avant garde pro-transvestite venture), and the notorious *Plan 9 From Outer Space* (1959), often tagged the worst picture ever filmed. The 1994 film *Ed Wood* recounted his life. He died from heart disease at 54. Cremated through Utter-McKinley mortuary at Memory Gardens Crematory, Brea, California. Ashes scattered at sea.

9955. Wood, Evelyn (Evelyn Nielsen Wood, Jan. 8, 1909–Aug. 26, 1995) Teacher from Logan, Utah, developed speed reading courses, beginning Evelyn Wood Reading Dynamics in Washington in 1959, growing to 150 schools around the U.S. She died in Tucson at 86. Cypress Hill, lot 174, grave 4, tier W, Wesatch Lawn Memorial Park, Salt Lake City, UT.

9956. Wood, Fernando (June 14, 1812–Feb. 14, 1881) Mayor of New York 1854–59 served in congress 1863–65 and 1867 until his death in 1881. He was believed to be the head of New York's Copperheads during the Civil War when Confederate terrorists burned several hotels there. White family obelisk, eastern section, Trinity Cemetery, 155th and Riverside, Manhattan, N.Y.C.

9957. Wood, Grant (Feb, 13. 1892–Feb. 12, 1942) Iowa artist whose paintings of Midwestern rural life resembled elaborately colored drawings; most focused on his own area, including a landscape overview of Herbert Hoover's birthplace at West Branch, Iowa, and his signature work *American Gothic* (1930). He died at Iowa City at 49. His name is engraved in the steps to his family lot on a hillside, where his simple rose headstone sits in the shade looking up at an angle toward the family monument, surmounted by a stone lion. Three fifths around horseshoe drive on left, Riverside Cemetery, Anamosa, Iowa. The subjects staring out of Wood's 1930 *American Gothic* were Dr. **Byron H. McKeeby** (July 10, 1867–Jan. 6, 1950), Wood's dentist, and the artist's sister **Nan Wood Graham** (July 19, 1889–Dec. 14, 1990). McKeeby is buried at Oak Hill Cemetery, Cedar Rapids, Iowa, and Nan Graham, like her brother, is at Riverside Cemetery, Anamosa, IA.

9958. Wood, Guy (July 24, 1911–Feb. 23, 2001) Songwriter penned not only *Shoo-Fly Pie and Apple Pan Dowdy* but music for Radio City Music Hall and TV's *Captain Kangaroo, Music of Love* (*The Bell Waltz*) and both *Till Then* and *My One and Only Love*. Cremated through Yardley and Pinto mortuary, Sag Harbor, Long Island, New York. Ashes to the family until buried later in their plot. Cedar Lawn Cemetery, East Hampton, Long Island, NY.

9959. Wood, Jimmie (Feb. 1, 1898–Sept. 7, 1972) Composer and actor. Plaque reads *The Greatest*. Serenity, lot 413, Forest Lawn Hollywood Hills, Los Angeles.

9960. Wood, Smokey Joe (Howard Ellsworth Wood, Oct. 25, 1889–July 27, 1985) Kansas City born Boston Red Sox pitching great at his peak in 1912. His arm gave out by the end of the 1910's. He died at 95 in West Haven, Connecticut. Per town historian George Fluhr and grandson David Wood, he was buried ½ mile into his (private) property; four to six graves enclosed by a stone wall in a field. Wood family cemetery (private property), Shohola Township, between Milford and Shohola, PA.

9961. Wood, Leonard (Oct. 9, 1860–Aug. 7, 1927) Co-founder of the Rough Riders with TR in the Spanish American War was the commanding general and later military governor of Cuba and the Philippines. Army Chief of Staff 1910–1914. Sec. 21, grave S-10, Arlington National Cemetery, Arlington, VA.

9962. Wood, Marvin (Jan. 21, 1928 Oct. 13, 1999) Coach at the Milan, Indiana, high school from 1952–54 led the team to its historic 1954 state championship over powerful Muncie Central 32–30, capped by Bobby Plump's winning shot at Hinkle Fieldhouse in the most dramatic David and Goliath story in the 86 year history (1911–1997) of Indiana's fabled one class basketball system. The basis for Gene Hackman's character in the 1986 film *Hoosiers*. Wood died at 71 from bone cancer in South Bend. Sec. 7, left side near center, Absury Cemetery, Morristown, IN.

9963. Wood, Natalie (Natasha Gurdin, July 20, 1938–Nov 29, 1981) Child actress in *Miracle on 34th Street* (1947) went on to teenage stardom opposite James Dean in *Rebel Without a Cause* (1955, AA nomination) and many romantic leads of the 1960's and 70's including two other Oscar nominations, for *Splendor in the Grass* (1961) and *Love With the Proper Stranger* (1963). Married to actor Robert Wagner 1957–1963 and again from 1972 until her death, she had been filming *Brainstorm* when she was reported missing from Wagner's boat "Splendor" off Catalina Island. She had taken a dinghy out into the ocean at night and drowned, though in a recent interview she had expressed a fear of "dark water." Buried in a Russian orthodox ceremony, her grave is generally identifiable by its many potted plants and flowers, near that of Donna Reed. Sec. D, Westwood Memorial Park, west Los Angeles.

9964. Wood, Peggy (Margaret Wood, Feb. 9, 1892–March 18, 1978) Brooklyn born stage actress and soprano on Broadway from 1910 introduced the title song in *Maytime* (1917), starred in *Bitter Sweet* (1929), and *Blithe Spirit* in London (1929) and New York (1941). Her few films include *Handy Andy* (1934), *The Right to Live* (1935, as Nurse Wayland), *The Story of Ruth* (1960), and *The Sound of Music* (AA nom., 1965, as Mother Abbess). Married to John V.A. Weaver (d. 1938). She died in Stamford, Connecticut, at 86. Cremated at Ferncliff Crematory, Hartsdale, New York. Ashes to family at Stamford, CT.

9965. Wood, Sam (July 10, 1883–Sept. 22, 1949) Director from Philadelphia at MGM made *A Night at the Opera*, *A Day at the Races*, *Our Town* (1940), and received Oscar nominations for *Goodbye Mr. Chips* (1939), and *Kitty Foyle*, *King's Row* and *For Whom the Bell Tolls*. Garden of Memory (private), lawn crypt 640, Forest Lawn, Glendale, CA.

9966. Woodbury, Levi (Dec. 22, 1789–Sept. 4, 1851) Democratic statesman from New Hampshire served in congress from the 1820's through the 1840's in between appointments as Secretary of the Navy under Jackson and Secretary of the Treasury under Van Buren, who appointed him Associate Justice of the Supreme Court, where he served ten years until his death. Harmony Grove Cemetery, Portsmouth, NH.

9967. Woodhull, Victoria (Victoria Claflin Woodhull, Sept. 23, 1838–June 9, 1927) Spiritualist, suffragist, social reformer, founded a brokerage firm on Wall Street in 1870, reportedly funded by Cornelius Vanderbilt, who was also interested in spiritualism. She also announced her candidacy for President in 1870, the first female to do so, published a paper espousing socialism and free love, went to jail in 1872 for sending obscenity through the mails (reports of a philandering stockbroker). She and Elizabeth Cady Stanton were the first women to address congress, in 1871, although Stanton and Susan B. Anthony later withdrew support from Woodhull, who they felt was too radical. She married several times, finally to English banker John Biddulph Martin. She has a cenotaph at Tewksbury Abbey, noting she *Devoted herself unsparingly to all that could promote the great cause of Anglo-American friendship*. Ashes scattered at sea from New Haven, Sussex.

9968. Woodley, David (David Eugene Woodley, Oct. 25, 1958–May 4, 2003) The youngest starting quarterback in NFL history starred at Louisiana State before joining the Miami Dolphins in 1980, completing 176 his first year, still the team record. He started in the 1983 Super Bowl, a loss to the Redskins, and was succeeded by Dan Marino that fall. Woodley had a

liver transplant in 1992 and died from liver and kidney failure in Shreveport at 44. First concrete road to right after entrance; grave along road on right after c. 200 yards. St. Joseph's Cemetery, Shreveport, LA.

9969. Woodruff, Eleanor (Eleanor Stark Woodruff, Sept. 12, 1891–Oct. 7, 1980) Broadway and silent screen actress from Towanda, Pennsylvania, at Pathé in two reelers 1913–14 (*The Two Mothers*, *The Perils of Pauline* with Pearl White, *Big Jim Garrity* with Robert Edeson), at Vitagraph from 1915 (*The Island of Surprise* with William Courtenay), and at World in 1916, returning to Broadway in starring and supporting roles through 1931, when she married stock broker Dorsey Richardson. She died at 89, a year before her husband. (Researched by Billy Doyle for *Classic Images* Jan. 1991). Trinity All Saints Cemetery, Princeton, NJ.

9970. Woods, Donald (Ralph L. Zink, Dec. 2, 1904 or 1909–March 5, 1998) Canadian actor in films from 1934: *The Florentine Dagger*, *A Tale of Two Cities* (1935, as Charles Darnay), *The Black Doll*, many others. Later films include *Thirteen Ghosts* (1960) and much TV. Also a real estate broker, he died at 93 (or 88, as reported) in Palm Springs. Cremated through Wiefels and Sons mortuary. Ashes buried at sea.

9971. Woods, Edward (Edward Alexander Woods, July 5, 1903–Oct. 8, 1989) Actor in early sound films was originally cast in the lead in *The Public Enemy* (1931) but exchanged roles with supporting player James Cagney and was relegated to relative obscurity after his role as Tom Powers' pal Matt. Lesser roles followed in *Broadminded*, *Dinner at Eight*, *Tarzan the Fearless*. He died at 86 in Salt Lake City. Burial through Larkin mortuary there. His purplish brown monument, curved upward on top, is engraved in English script, with the epitaph *Thank you Lord for the privilege of seeing your world. Its beauty and grandeur, for love, music and art—the great adventure and challenge of living.* On the rear is inscribed, above engraved pine trees, *Paradise is open to all kind hearts.* West sec. 7-132-1 east, Salt Lake City Cemetery, Salt Lake City, UT.

9972. Woods, Granville T. (April 23, 1856–Jan. 30, 1910) The Black Edison, African-American inventor from Ohio, had his own electric company in Cincinnati by 1884 and moved to New York by 1890. He held sixty patents in all, developed the railway telegraph system in 1877, enabling crew members on moving trains to communicate with one another, as well as inventing the telephone transmitter (1844), galvanic battery (1888), and automatic circuit breaker device (1890). Lot 5, range 3, grave 144, St. Michael's Cemetery, Astoria, Queens, N.Y.C.

9973. Woods, Harry MacGregor (Nov. 4, 1896–Jan. 14, 1970) Songwriter of the 1920's wrote *Paddlin' Madelyn Home* (1925), *When the Red Red Robin Comes Bob Bob Bobbin' Along* (1926), *Side By Side* (1927) and had a second career as an actor in westerns, often playing the heavy. His large flush gray tablet notes his work. Pembroke Center Cemetery, Pembroke, MA.

9974. Woods, Rose Mary (Dec. 26, 1917–Jan. 22,

2005) President Richard Nixon's secretary from his election to the senate in 1950 until two years after he resigned the presidency, in 1976, became a famous name after the controversial erasure of eighteen minutes of White House tapes came under scrutiny during the 1973–4 Watergate hearings. Woods said she had accidentally erased a few minutes by hitting the wrong button while answering the phone, but denied having erased the entire eighteen minutes. She returned to Sebring, Ohio, twenty miles south of Youngstown, where she was born, and died at a nursing home in nearby Alliance at 87. Burial from Gednetz-Ruzek mortuary. Grandview Cemetery, Sebring, Ohio.

9975. Wooldridge, Henry G. (Nov. 29, 1822–May 30, 1899) Kentucky colonel who had his entire family sculpted in sandstone and marble — his mother, brother, sisters and himself, all facing forward in a strange "procession to nowhere" over their graves in the family plot, now enclosed by a chain link fence. Maplewood Cemetery, Maplewood, KY.

9976. Wooley, Sheb (Shelby F. Wooley, April 10, 1921–Sept. 16, 2003) Former cowhand from Erick, Oklahoma, in western films from the late 1940's, notably as one of Frank Miller's three henchmen in *High Noon* (1952). He also appeared in *Giant* (1956), as scout Pete Nolan on TV's *Rawhide* from 1959, and intermittently in later pictures, including *The War Wagon, The Outlaw Josie Wales* and *Hoosiers.* After his 1958 hit novelty record *Purple People Eater,* he worked more in the music business than as an actor, recording parodies as Ben Colder (*Talk Back Blubbering Lips, Don't Go Near the Eskimos, Fifteen Beers Ago*). Ill with leukemia for five years, he died at 82 in Nashville. Crypt, north wall area, Woodlawn East Memorial Park, Hendersonville, TN.

9977. Woolf, Edgar Allan (April 5, 1886–Dec. 9, 1943) New York born playwright; his *Mme. Champagne* was playing at the Madison Square Roof Garden the night Harry K. Thaw shot Stanford White in 1906. Later in Hollywood, he wrote screenplays for several mystery and fantasy pictures, including *The Mask of Fu Manchu, Freaks, Flesh, This Side of Heaven* and *The Wizard of Oz.* He died at 57 when he tripped over his dog's leash and fell down a flight of stairs. Sent through Gates-Kingsley-Gates, Los Angeles. East Side Cemetery, Chateaugay, NY.

9978. Woolf, George "The Iceman" (George Monroe Woolf, May 31, 1910–Jan. 4, 1946) Racehorse jockey from Cardstown, Alberta, whose nickname came from his solid nerves. He rode relatively few mounts 1928–1946 and suffered from diabetes, yet won 97 major U.S. race stakes, his favorite with *Seabiscuit,* first in the 1938 Hollywood Gold Cup, coming from fourteen lengths back to win the race, and most notably at Pimlico later in the same year, upsetting the Triple Crown winner War Admiral. He had won all major races but the Kentucky Derby when at 35 he fell from W.W. Taylor's horse *Please Me* at

Santa Anita on January 3, 1946, and never regained consciousness. Sanctuary of Providence, crypt 9707, Gardenia Terrace, Great Mausoleum, Forest Lawn, Glendale, CA.

9979. Woolf, John (March 15, 1913–June 28, 1999) British director from Cricklewood, north London, earned the U.S. Bronze Star during World War II, then returned to England and formed Romulus Films, producing *The African Queen* (1951). Other works include *Richard III, Moulin Rouge, Beat the Devil, Room at the Top* and *Oliver!* (1968). Knighted 1975. In all, his films won 13 Oscars. He died in London at 86. Sec. P, row 6, Willesden (Jewish) Cemetery, northwest London.

9980. Woolf, Virginia (Jan. 25, 1882–March 28, 1941) English novelist with a bent toward suicide, which she eventually accomplished by drowning herself in the Ouse River at her estate at Rodmell, Sussex, between Lewes and Newhaven. Her husband Leonard buried her ashes at the foot of an elm tree in their garden; the tree was blown down in January 1943. Monk's House, Rodmell, Sussex.

9981. Woollcott, Alexander (Jan. 19, 1887–Jan. 23, 1943) Acid tongued Broadway theatrical critic of the 1920's and 30's was a chief organizer of the Algonquin Round Table, collected wits of the New York literary and theatrical circle of the day. He hosted the *Town Crier* radio program in later years and was the basis for the central character in *The Man Who Came to Dinner.* The night of his death he was a guest on radio's *People's Platform* on CBS and had exchanged insults with fellow panelist Marcia Davenport shortly before air time; a short way into the discussion he scrawled "I am sick" on a piece of paper and pushed it toward fellow panelist Rex Stout. Stout said he knew immediately it was serious or the proper and waspish Woollcott would have written "I am ill." He was taken to Roosevelt Hospital with a massive heart attack, after which he suffered a stroke and died at 56. His service was held at the McMillan Academy Theater at Columbia University, where Paul Robeson sang The 23rd Psalm and Ruth Gordon delivered the eulogy. His ashes were to be sent to Hamilton College at Clinton, New York, but were mistakenly sent to Colgate University at Hamilton, New York. They were then forwarded on to Hamilton College, where they arrived with 67 cents postage due. The marble urn was buried in the college cemetery in a service held July 15, 1943. Woollcott himself was an incurable wanderer through cemeteries, according to Harpo Marx, particularly during his famed summers on Neshobe Island at Lake Bomoseen in Vermont, when he would go on expeditions traversing the country cemeteries and writing down epitaphs. His small stone near the rear of the cemetery has his name and complete dates in raised letters. Hamilton College Cemetery, Clinton, NY.

9982. Woolley, Monty (Edgar Montillion Woolley, Aug. 17, 1888–May 6, 1963) The son of a proprietor of fashionable hotels in Manhattan and Saratoga Springs gained his greatest fame as an actor in 1942 when he starred as Sheridan Whiteside, a takeoff on Alexander Woollcott, in the film version of Kaufman and Hart's *The Man Who Came to Dinner*, after many years of teaching drama at Yale. From 1942 he was a popular film star, known for his snow white beard and generally haughty roles. He died at 74 of heart and kidney ailments in an Albany, New York, hospital. Family plot with a large family monument and a row of individual headstones. Sec. A, lot 4, Greenridge Cemetery, Saratoga Springs, NY.

9983. Woolrich, Cornell (Cornell George Hopley Woolrich, Dec. 4, 1903–Sept. 25, 1968) New York born writer, sometimes using the pseudonyms George Hopley and William Irish. A dialogue and later *film noir* screenwriter from 1928, his works include *The Black Curtain* (filmed as *Street of Chance*, 1942), *Black Alibi* (*The Leopard Man*, 1943), *Phantom Lady* (as William Irish, 1944), *The Night Has A Thousand Eyes* (1948), *The Window* (1949), *It Had To Be Murder* (filmed as *Rear Window*, 1954). He died in New York City. Entrance 3, 1G-102, Shrine of Memories Mausoleum, Ferncliff Cemetery, Hartsdale, NY.

9984. Woolsey, Robert (Aug. 14, 1889–Oct. 31, 1938) Comedian teamed with Bert Wheeler from Ziegfeld's *Rio Rita* on stage in 1927 through numerous RKO comedies 1930–1937, with thick round glasses, chewing a cigar and spouting lines so corny they were funny. The team remained popular though ignored by the critics; part of their appeal was in how much they seemed to be enjoying the gags, whether the audience was or not. Ill for some time, Woolsey died at 49 from a chronic kidney ailment. Whispering Pines, lot 1906, space 5, Forest Lawn, Glendale, CA.

9985. Woolworth, F. W. (Frank Winfield Woolworth, April 13, 1852–April 8, 1919) Founder of the chain of five and ten cent stores bearing his name opened his first stores in Utica, New York, and Lancaster, Pennsylvania, in 1879, selling slightly damaged goods at low prices. By his death he had a thousand stores and a fortune estimated at $65 million. He died at Glen Cove, New York, from septic poisoning at 67 after refusing to go to a dentist. His mammoth mausoleum has an Egyptian motif, complete with large breasted sphinxes guarding either side of the steps. Many Woolworths are interred within, including his granddaughter Barbara Hutton. Across and up the road from the more parsimonious vault of J.C. Penny. Pine sec. along Central Ave., Woodlawn Cemetery, the Bronx, N.Y.C.

9986. Worden, Hank (Norton Earl Worden, July 23, 1901–Dec. 6, 1992) Former bronco rider from Rolfe, Iowa, was in 116 films, including *Red River* and several John Ford westerns, notably as the spectral dimwit Mose Harper in *The Searchers* (1956). Final appearances included the room service waiter in TV's *Twin Peaks* (1990). Eulogy by Pat Buttram. Columbarium of Victory, niche 32616, Freedom Mausoleum, Forest Lawn, Glendale, CA.

9987. Worden, John Lorimer (March 12, 1818–Oct. 18, 1897) Union naval officer commanded the ironclad ship *Monitor* in its celebrated battle with the C.S.S. *Virginia*, originally the U.S.S. *Merrimack*, at Hampton Roads, Virginia, March 9, 1862. Temporarily blinded in battle, command was passed to his first officer Samuel D. Greene, who continued to a stalemate, though a tactical northern victory, as the south was prevented from dispersing the northern blockade. Promoted to rear admiral, Worden was later superintendent of the U.S. Naval Academy. His family monument bears an anchor on it, and there is a boulder with a bronze plaque commemorating him straight in the cemetery from route 22. Pawling Cemetery, Pawling, NY.

9988. Wordsworth, William (April 7, 1770–April 23, 1850) English poet known for *Ode: Intimations of Immortality from Recollections of Early Childhood* (1804). Poet laureate from 1843. He died at his home Rydal Mount and was buried nearby, in the Lake district near the Irish Sea and a short distance south of the Scottish border. Buried with his sister **Dorothy** (Dec. 25, 1771–Jan. 25, 1855), a major influence on his work. St. Oswald's Churchyard, Grasmere, Cumbria.

9989. Worlock, Frederick (Dec. 14, 1886–Aug. 1, 1973) Stage actor in films from 1939. Unmarked. Block G, sec. 6602, lot 6, Valhalla Memorial Park, North Hollywood, CA.

9990. Worsley, Wallace (Dec. 8, 1878–March 26, 1944) American director of silent films whose work included the Lon Chaney vehicles *The Penalty* (1920) and *The Hunchback of Notre Dame* (1923). Columbarium of Memory, niche 19512, Memorial Terrace, Great Mausoleum, Forest Lawn, Glendale, CA.

9991. Worth, Irene (Harriet Abrams, June 23, 1916–March 10, 2002) Stage actress from Fairbury, Nebraska, raised in California and long a fixture in London theatre, she won Tony Awards for *Tiny Alice* (1965), *Sweet Bird of Youth* (1976) and as the stern and icy Grandma Kurnitz in *Lost in Yonkers* (1991), a role she repeated on film in 1993. She suffered a stroke in a New York post office March 8, 2002, and died two days later in Roosevelt Hospital at 85. Burial through Frank E. Campbell mortuary March 18. Flush plaque with the remembrance *She brought to life/ beauty of language/ Consummate actress/ Dear friend, loving sister.* Kensico Gardens, lot 188, grave 1, Kensico Cemetery, Valhalla, NY.

9992. Worth, William Jenkins (March 1, 1794–May 7, 1849) Major General in the War of 1812, Seminole insurrections and the Mexican War, after whom Fort Worth was named. He died in San Antonio but was buried in Manhattan at the tip of a block facing the Flatiron building, his 50' obelisk the work of James G. Batterson in 1851. Once surrounded by plantings and enclosed by a cast iron fence, it fell into disrepair until subscribers financed its restoration, cleaning and upkeep, leading to the rededication in November 1995. Broadway and 5th Ave. at W. 25th St., Manhattan, N.Y.C.

9993. Wray, Fay (Vina Fay Wray, Sept. 15, 1907–Aug. 8, 2004) Brunette actress born near Cardstown, Alberta, Canada, in Los Angeles from age twelve and in films from the mid 1920's, became indelibly known as the blonde leading lady opposite *King Kong* (1933) despite her many other films (*The Wedding March, The Finger Points, Dr. X, The Most Dangerous Game, The Mystery of the Wax Museum, The Vampire Bat, One Sunday Afternoon, Viva Villa, The Clairvoyant, The Affairs of Cellini*). Married to writer John Monk Saunders (*q.v.*) 1928–1939, whom she divorced; to Frank Capra's lead writer Robert Riskin (*q.v.*) from 1942 until his death in 1955, and from 1971 until his death in 1991 to neurosurgeon Sanford Rothenberg. Retired from films in 1958, she died in her Fifth Avenue apartment in Manhattan at 96. The lights of the Empire State Building were dimmed in her honor. Buried by herself, her white bench and a flush gray plaque, placed within a month, are near the Hattie McDaniel cenotaph. Garden of Legends (sec. 8), lot 2300, Hollywood Forever Cemetery, Hollywood (Los Angeles), CA.

9994. Wray, John (John Griffith Malloy, Feb. 13, 1887–April 5, 1940) Philadelphia born silent screen director whose work included *Anna Christie* (1923) with Blanche Sweet and Dorothy Davenport Reid's *Human Wreckage*. With sound he turned to acting, in *All Quiet on the Western Front* (1930, as Himmelstoss), *Dr. X* (1932), *The Miracle Man* (1932), many others. He died from a liver ailment at 52 in St. Vincent's Hospital, Los Angeles. Buried by the Actors Fund. Unmarked. Sec. N, lot 246, grave 5, along the road, Calvary Cemetery, East Los Angeles.

9995. Wray, Link (Frederick Lincoln Wray, Jr., May 2, 1929–Nov. 5, 2005) Guitarist from Dunn, North Carolina, whose pioneering use of the thundering power chord, first at a sock hop in Fredericksburg, Virginia, produced his 1958 record *Rumble* and others, and influenced generations of rock and roll musicians including Pete Townshend, Jimmy Page, Bruce Springsteen, Bob Dylan, Steve Van Zandt and beyond. Residing in Denmark from 1978, he died at 76 in his home at Copenhagen. Entombed in the Christians Church (Christians Kirk), Copenhagen.

9996. Wren, Christopher (Oct. 20, 1632–Feb. 25, 1723) English architect is entombed in his finest work, with the inscription (roughly) in Latin, *If you seek his monument, look around*. St. Paul's Cathedral, London.

9997. Wright, Edythe (May 14, c.1907/1917–Oct. 27, 1965) Vocalist from Bayonne, New Jersey, sang with Tommy Dorsey's orchestra 1935–39. A Democratic state committeewoman before moving to Manasquan in 1950. The wife of John T. Smith, she died at Point Pleasant Hospital, listed as 45 — though her big band career indicates she was eighteen to twenty-eight when recording with Dorsey by 1935. Mass at St. Denis Church, Manasquan, through Meehan mortuary, Spring Lake Heights. Sec. 6R, range I, plot 16, St. Catherine's Cemetery, Spring Lake, NJ.

9998. Wright, Frank Lloyd (June 8, 1869–April 9, 1959) Master of modern architecture, the Wisconsin born Wright designed organic structures, very controversial at the time, which are functional though often abstract in appearance. Works include the Guggenheim Museum in New York and the Imperial Hotel in Tokyo. He designed his own homes, Taliesin at Spring Green, Wisconsin, and Taliesin West at Scottsdale, Arizona. He was buried in the Lloyd-Jones Cemetery near Taliesin at Spring Green, Wisconsin. The metal letter embedded in rock bears his name, with the epitaph *Love of an idea is Love of God*. Removed on orders from his wife in 1985 (though the marker remained), he was taken to Taliesin West and the ashes scattered on a hillside there or buried. There is a grave marker there. Taliesin West, Scottsdale, AZ.

9999. Wright, George (Jan. 28, 1847–Aug. 31, 1937) Among the earliest baseball standouts, proficient at everything, a star of the 1869 Cincinnati Red Stockings organized by his brother Harry, he moved with them to Boston and helped win four pennants there in the 1870's, batting over .330 each year. Hall of Fame 1937. Field of St. Mary, Holyhood Cemetery, Brookline, MA.

10000. Wright, Harold Bell (May 4, 1882–May 24, 1944) Novelist from Rome, New York, authored *The Shepherd of the Hills* and *The Winning of Barbara Worth*. His small cenotaph in a garden court is in the form of a book, with a quote on a tablet above it *And the desert shall rejoice and blossom as the rose.1.35.1.* Garden Court memorial, Greenwood Memorial Park, San Diego, CA.

10001. Wright, Harry (William Henry Wright, Jan. 10, 1835–Oct. 3, 1895) Baseball's first organizer of a professional team (the Cincinnati Red Stockings in 1869), called (along with Chadwick and Cartwright) The Father of Baseball. Brother of George Wright. Hall of Fame 1953. A statue of him on a pedestal marks his grave. Greenlawn sec., lot 10, West Laurel Hill Cemetery, Bala Cynwyd, PA.

10002. Wright, Orville (Aug. 19, 1871–Jan. 30, 1948) and **Wilbur** (Aug. 16, 1867–May 30, 1912) Famed aviation pioneers grew up in Henry and Wayne County, Indiana, and at Dayton, Ohio, where they operated a bicycle shop prior to their experiments with flying, culminating in the test flight at Kitty Hawk, North Carolina, December 17, 1903. Wilbur died from typhoid at their boyhood home on Hawthorn St. in Dayton at 45. Orville later stopped his manufacturing interests; their papers show Wilbur to have been the dominant engineer in the planning of air flight. Orville died from a heart attack at 76 and was buried beside his brother in the family lot. Sec. 101, Woodland Cemetery, Dayton, OH.

10003. Wright, Richard (Sept. 4, 1908–Nov. 28, 1960) American novelist born on a plantation near Natchez, Mississippi, drew on his own experiences with racial injustice for his writings, including *Native Son* (1940), *Black Boy* (1945), *The Outsider* (1953), *Black Power* (1954), and *The Long Dream* (1958). He moved to Paris in the early 1950's and died there at 52. Columbarium, div. 87, niche 848, Pere Lachaise Cemetery, Paris.

10004. Wright, Robert C. (Sept. 25, 1914–July 27, 2005) Songwriter long in collaboration with George Forrest had many Broadway credits including *Song of Norway, Gypsy Lady* and *Kismet*, for which they won Tonys, and numerous songs in films including Oscar nominations for *It's A Blue World, Always and Always* and *Pennies For Peppino*. Others include *The Donkey Serenade, Stranger in Paradise* and *Baubles, Bangles and Beads*. Wright died in Miami at 90. Ashes from Cofer-Kolski-Combs mortuary, Miami, to his executor.

10005. Wright, Ruby (Jan. 8, 1914–March 9, 2004) Vocalist from Anderson, Indiana, with Barney Rapp's New Englanders, married him in 1936, opened the Sign of the Drum nightclub with him in Cincinnati, and when she became pregnant was replaced by Doris Kappelhoff, later Day. She recorded her best known song *Let's Light the Christmas Tree*, left over from World War II, in 1957, and *Three Stars* in 1959. A regular on Ruth Lyons' *Fifty-Fifty Club* and with WLW 1953–1969, she ran the Barney Rapp Travel Agency until 1991, and died at 90 in Jewish Hospital, Cincinnati. Entombed beside Rapp. Memorial Mausoleum, sec. E-28, D-1, Spring Grove Cemetery, Cincinnati, OH.

10006. Wright, Silas (May 24, 1795–Aug. 27, 1847) New York congressman 1827–30, senator 1832–34, and governor 1845–47 was a prospective anti-slavery Democratic candidate for president. Gone home and tending his farm all summer at Canton in upstate New York, he suffered a heart attack at the town post office, went home and died. Silas Wright (Miner Street) Cemetery, Miner St. at West St., Canton, NY.

10007. Wright, Syreeta (Rita Wright aka Syreeta Wright Muhammad, Aug. 3, 1946–July 6, 2004) Motown songwriter and artist, collaborated with her then-husband Stevie Wonder on *Signed, Sealed, Delivered* and *If You Really Love Me*, among others. Lakeview Estates, lot 23, grave B, Inglewood Park Cemetery, Inglewood, CA.

10008. Wright, Teresa (Muriel Teresa Wright, Oct. 27, 1918–March 6, 2005) New York City born actress raised in Maplewood, New Jersey, played wholesome, conscientious roles in *The Little Foxes* (1941), *Mrs. Miniver* (AA 1942), *Pride of the Yankees, Shadow of A Doubt* (1943), *The Best Years of Our Lives* (1946), *Pursued* (1947), *The Men* (1950) *Track of the Cat*

(1954), hired by Samuel Goldwyn in 1941, and let go by him in 1948 for her refusal to do glamour and cheesecake shots. Married and divorced from writer Niven Busch and playwright Robert Anderson, whom she re-married, she reappeared in later years in films (*The Good Mother* 1988, *The Rainmaker* 1997) and had recently moved from Rowayton, Connecticut, where she had lived from 1985, to East Haven upon her death at 86 from a heart attack in Yale-New Haven Hospital. Donated to Yale Medical School, New Haven, CT.

10009. Wright, Wilbur *see* **Orville Wright.**

10010. Wright, Will (William Henry Wright, March 26, 1894–June 19, 1962) Character actor from San Francisco with enormous ears, in many films from 1940 and television in the 1950's and early 60's, often as grouchy and miserly old men, always colorful (*Shadow of the Thin Man, The Hoodlum Saint, The Blue Dahlia, Act of Murder, Mrs. Mike, All the King's Men, Adam's Rib, Niagara, Johnny Guitar, River of No Return, The Man With the Golden Arm, Not As a Stranger, The Court Martial of Billy Mitchell, Inherit the Wind, Cape Fear*) and many television roles, including Ben Weaver on *The Andy Griffith Show* 1960–62. He died from cancer in Hollywood at 68. Methodist sec., plot 106, Suisun Fairfield Cemetery, Fairfield, CA.

10011. Wrigley, Philip K. (Dec. 5, 1894–April 12, 1977) Son of the founder of the chewing gum empire and owner of the Chicago Cubs was the last major league owner to hold out for day baseball only, forbidding lights in Wrigley Field. Ashes in a bronze urn interred April 16, 1977. Private mausoleum 54 (family room), niche D, Sanctuary of Gratitude, Memorial Terrace, Great Mausoleum, Forest Lawn, Glendale, CA.

10012. Wrigley, William, Jr. (Sept. 30, 1861–Jan. 26, 1932) Founder of the chewing gum company owned the Chicago Cubs from 1920— their park was renamed Wrigley Field in 1922 — and invested in the development of Catalina Island off the California coast. Interred in the Wrigley Memorial on Catalina Island, he was removed and reinterred December 14, 1946. Private mausoleum 54 (family room), Sanctuary of Gratitude, Memorial Terrace, Great Mausoleum, Forest Lawn, Glendale, CA.

10013. Wrixon, Maris (Dec. 28, 1917–Oct. 6, 1999) Blonde actress in the late 1930's and 40's. Films include *Jeepers Creepers, Knute Rockne All American, The Ape*, and *Waterfront*. Married to film editor Rudi Fehr. Sec. B, lot 926, grave 8, San Fernando Mission Cemetery, Mission Hills, CA.

10014. Wuornos, Aileen (Feb. 29, 1956–Oct. 9, 2002) The first so-named female American serial killer was a native of Rochester, Michigan, who dropped out of school at fifteen and was committing armed robbery by 1981. By 1989, she was stopping men on Florida highways with stories of broken down cars and waiting children, offering prostitution, and shooting them multiple times. The first of seven, Richard Mallory of Clearwater, was found in a junkyard December 13, 1989. The next, David Spears, found June 1 along Highway 19 in Citrus County; Charles Carskadden, found June 6 in Pasco County; Tony Burresa, found July 31 in Marion County; Dick Humphreys, also found in Marion County; Walter Antonio, found November 19 in Dixie County, and Peter Siems, whose body was never found. Arrested in a bar in Port Orange January 9, 1991, she confessed initially so her companion would not be blamed, she said. Stories of her abuse by the victims varied over the years. Finally requesting death, she was executed by lethal injection at Starke, her last words a bizarre declaration of coming back with Jesus on June 6, just like the film *Independence Day*. A friend from her home state, Dawn Botkins, claimed the body with plans to scatter the ashes in Michigan

10015. Wurlitzer, Rudolph (Dec. 30, 1873–May 27, 1948) Cincinnati based organ manufacturer produced the "Mighty Wurlitzer," the finest in theater and other organs from the turn of the century into the 1930's. He also made pianos and player pianos and promoted early concerts before and during the World War I era. Bench and plaque on hillside. Sec. 80, lot 24, Spring Grove Cemetery, Cincinnati, OH.

10016. Wycherly, Margaret (Oct. 26, 1881–June 6, 1956) London born actress on stage from the late 1890's known for *The Thirteenth Chair* (1917, filmed in Hollywood in 1929) and *Tobacco Road* (1933). In films she played the mother of Gary Cooper in *Sergeant York* (1941, Oscar nomination) and of James Cagney in *White Heat* (1949). She died in Manhattan, divorced from playwright Bayard Veiller. Her ashes were sent for burial in Bepton-Midhurst West Cemetery at Bepton, Midhurst, England.

10017. Wyeth, N.C. (Newell Convers Wyeth, Oct. 22, 1882–Oct. 19, 1945) Painter and illustrator of the novels of Stevenson, James Fenimore Cooper and others, also painted murals for the National Cathedral in Washington, D.C. Father of Andrew Wyeth. Birmingham Meetinghouse Cemetery, Chadds Ford, PA.

10018. Wyler, William (July 1, 1902–July 27, 1981) German American film director of prolific output from the 1920's made several classics, including *Dodsworth* (1936), *Wuthering Heights* (1939), and three Oscar winners: *Mrs. Miniver* (1942), *The Best Years of Our Lives* (1946) and *Ben Hur* (1959). He received the Irving Thalberg Award in 1965 and the American Film Institute's Life Achievement Award in 1976. Married to actress Margaret Tallichet. Eventide sec., lot 2998, Forest Lawn, Glendale, CA.

10019. Wymark, Patrick (July 11, 1926–Oct. 20, 1970) British actor from Cleethorpes, Lancashire, in films 1959–1970, including *The League of Gentlemen, Children of the Damned, Operation Crossbow* (as Churchill), *Repulsion* (landlord), *The Witchfinder General* (*The Conqueror Worm*), *Where Eagles Dare* (Col.

Wyatt Turner). He died from a heart attack in Melbourne, Australia, at 44. Square upright stone. west sec., Highgate Cemetery, London.

10020. Wynette, Tammy (Virginia Wynette Pugh Richey, May 5, 1942–April 6, 1998) Country singer from Itawamba County, Mississippi, best known for her 1968 number one hit *Stand By Your Man*. She was known as the First Lady of Country Music by the time of her death from a blood clot to the lung at 55 during a nap in her Nashville home. At the request of her children, her body was exhumed for an autopsy a year later, on April 14, 1999. Cross Mausoleum, 3rd floor, 274-275 B, Woodlawn Memorial Park, Nashville, TN.

10021. Wynn, Early (Jan. 6, 1920–April 4, 1999) Major league pitcher from Hartford, Alabama, threw from 1939–1963 with Washington, Cleveland, and the Chicago White Sox. He had 164 wins for Cleveland, won the Cy Young Award at 39 in 1959 with Chicago, and earned his 300th and final win four years later. Known for his fierceness, he dropped four batters in 1949 in retaliation for Detroit's knocking down Cleveland's outfielder Larry Doby, the first black player in the American Leagues. "If they hurt him, they hurt me," Wynn said, "I've got to teach them manners." Hall of Fame 1972. He died at 79 after suffering a stroke in Venice, Florida. Service through Ewing mortuary, Venice. Ashes to family. Per *The Cleveland Plain Dealer* of August 3, 2005, his daughter, accompanied by team spokesman Bob DiBasio, scattered his ashes in 1999 on the pitcher's mound at Jacobs' Field, Cleveland.

10022. Wynn, Ed (Isaiah Edwin Leopold, Nov. 9, 1886–June 19, 1966) Philadelphia born lisping vaudeville, radio and television comedian known for befuddled silliness found a second career in the 1950's and 60's in semi-dramatic roles, including the 1956 Rod Serling teleplay *Requiem For a Heavyweight*, the 1959 film *The Diary of Anne Frank* and two *Twilight Zone* episodes (*One For the Angels* and *Ninety Years Without Slumbering*). He had undergone surgery for cancer in his neck prior to his death at 79 in Beverly Hills. His gold niche plaque, in the center of a marble wall, is inscribed *Dear God—Thanks* and his signature. Columbarium of Dawn, niche 30706, Holly Terrace, Great Mausoleum, Forest Lawn, Glendale, CA.

10023. Wynn, Keenan (July 27, 1916–Oct. 14, 1986) Actor son of comedian Ed Wynn in films from 1942, adept at mustached heavies and bullies as well as light material, appearing in films and TV into the 1980's. He died from cancer at 70. Ashes inurned with his family, Ed Wynn niche, Columbarium of Dawn, niche 30706, Holly Terrace, Great Mausoleum, Forest Lawn, Glendale, CA.

10024. Wynn, Nan (father Abraham Vatz, May 8, 1918–March 23, 1971) Brunette singer and actress from Wheeling, West Virginia, briefly in films 1938–1947 (*Million Dollar Baby, A Shot in the Dark, Pardon*

My Sarong, Princess O'Rourke, Is Everybody Happy?).
Widowed (married name Small), her death at 52 was
ruled a suicide by barbiturate overdose in her home at
101 Ocean Avenue, Los Angeles. Cremated at Odd
Fellows Crematory through Wilshire mortuary. Ashes
sent (according to the death certificate and the crematory) to Riverside Cemetery, Miami Beach, Florida,
which doesn't exist. They may have gone to Riverside
Chapel, Miami Beach. No records extant.

10025. Wynters, Charlotte (Dec. 4, 1899–Jan. 7,
1991) Actress from Wheeling, West Virginia, first with
David Belasco, worked in films 1931–57 (*Nancy Drew
Trouble Shooter, High Sierra, The Great Lie, Dr. Kildare's
Victory, Now Voyager*). Married to Barton MacLane
from 1939, they owned a cattle ranch in the Nevada
foothills of Madera County until her death. Buried
beside MacLane. Mem. F, sec. 5460, lot 4, Pierce
Bros.' Valhalla Memorial Park, North Hollywood, CA.

10026. Wynyard, Diana (Dorothy Cox, Jan. 16,
1906–May 13, 1964) London born stage and screen
star. Films include *Rasputin and the Empress* (1932),
Cavalcade (1933), *One More River* (1934), *Gaslight*
(*Angel Street*, 1940). Divorced from Sir Carol Reed
and remarried to Dr. Tibor Csato, she died from a
kidney ailment in London at 58. Ashes spread on the
Crocus Lawn at 4E, Golders Green Crematorium,
north London.

10027. Wythe, George (1726–Jan. 8, 1806) Member of the Virginia House of Burgesses and Continental Congress, signed the Declaration of Independence
and helped amend Virginia's laws to adhere to the regulations required for statehood. President of William
and Mary from 1779. He adhered to the principles of
republicanism, helping to ratify the Constitution. St.
John's Church Cemetery, Richmond, VA.

10028. Xavier, Francis (April 7, 1506–Dec. 2,
1552) Catholic saint went to Goa in India, among
other places, where he founded a missionary college
and baptized some 30,000 people. From there he went
to Japan, where he died, was returned to India and
interred at Old Goa. At intervals, the Lord of Goa
and Apostle of the Indies is removed from his silver
casket and displayed in a glass case, when both Christians and Hindus make a pilgrimage to the now largely
deserted ancient city. Jesuit Church of Bom Jesus in
Goa, India.

10029. Yablonski, Joseph "Jock" (March 3,
1910–Jan. 5, 1970) Head of the United Mine Workers was murdered in an explosion at home in Clarksville, Pennsylvania, along with his family, after he contested the fixed win of Tony Boyle as UMW president.
Boyle died in prison. Washington Cemetery, Washington, PA.

10030. Yale, Elihu (April 5, 1649–July 8, 1721)
Boston born benefactor of Yale University died in
London. His monument is inscribed *Born in America. In Europe bred. In Africa travell'd and in Asia wed.
Where long he lived and thriv'd; in London dead. Much
good, some ill, he did; so hope all's even and that his soul
thro' mercy's gone to Heaven. You that survive and read
this tale, take care, For this most certain exit to prepare.
Where blest in peace, the actions of the just, Smell sweet,
and blossom in the silent dust.* St. Giles Church Cemetery, Wrexham, Wales.

10031. Yale, Frankie (Frank Ioele or Uale, 1893–
July 1, 1928) Brooklyn born gang leader, head of the
Unione Sicilione from 1918. He befriended Torrio and
Capone, sent Capone to Torrio in Chicago in 1919
and reputedly carried out various executions for them
there, including (arguably) the firm handshake that
sealed Dean O'Banion's fate in 1924. His relationship
with Capone deteriorated after Yale shorted him on alcohol shipments. When Capone sent James DeAmato
to New York to watch Yale and the spy was killed, Yale
was fingered for execution. He was mowed down in his
speeding car by machine gun fire, the auto crashing
onto a stoop at 924 44th St. in Borough Park, Brooklyn, the first New York gangland casualty by machine
gun (three years behind Chicago). His funeral featured a $12,000 casket followed by 28 truck loads of
flowers, with one wreath inscribed "We'll See them,
kid," though no one was indicted for the murder. Ioele
family stone. Range 14, plot 9, St. Edmund's sec. (near
the fence), Holy Cross Cemetery, Brooklyn, N.Y.C.

10032. Yamamoto, Isoruko (April 4, 1884–April
18, 1943) Commander-in-chief of the combined Japanese fleet during World War II suffered a major defeat
at Guadalcanal, evacuating the island in January 1943.
At 59 and with snow white hair, his plane was sighted
by U.S. intelligence, so that eighteen American P-38s
were waiting for the first ambush by air of an enemy
commander-in-chief, shot down near Kahili in southern Bouganville. On June 5, his ashes were interred in
a full state ceremony at Tama Reien (Cemetery), Harjuku Ward, Tokyo.

10033. Yankovic, Frankie (Frank R. Yankovic,
July 28, 1915–Oct. 14, 1998) Accordion playing Polka
King from the late 1940's had hits with *Just Because,
Blue Skirt Waltz, In Heaven There Is No Beer, Beer Barrel Polka,* and *Pennsylvania Polka,* winning four Grammys. He died in Tampa, Florida, at 83. Sec. 114, lot
507, Calvary Cemetery, Cleveland, OH.

10034. Yarborough, Barton (William Barton
Yarborough, Oct. 2, 1900–Dec. 19, 1951) Texas born
actor in many B films of the 1940's (*Ghost of Frankenstein* as Dr. Kettering) including Abbott & Costello
pictures and as Doc, with an exaggerated southern
drawl, in the *I Love a Mystery* films. He had just started
as Joe Friday's partner on TV's *Dragnet* when he died
from a heart attack at 51. Resurrection Slope, lot 243,
Forest Lawn, Glendale, CA.

10035. Yarborough, Ralph Webster (June 8,
1903–Jan. 27, 1996) Democratic senator from Texas
1957–70 was riding in the limousine with Vice President Lyndon Johnson when President Kennedy was
assassinated in Dallas. JFK was in Texas initially to
mend a widening feud between the liberal Yarborough and the conservative John Connally. Yarborough

practiced law until he was 90. His reddish brown monument has an American eagle in the inset. Republic Hill, sec. 2, row G, plot 10, State Cemetery, Austin, TX.

10036. Yarborough, William P. (May 12, 1912–Dec. 6, 2005) Lieutenant General, U.S. Army, helped develop airborne forces during World War II, leading several parachute assaults and helping liberate Rome and Genoa, served as Provost Martial of the post-war American sector of Vienna, and was head of the Center for Special Warfare 1961–65, expanding the Special Forces unit to encompass counterinsurgency and with President Kennedy's approval authorizing their signature green berets in 1961. Retired 1971. He died in Southern Pines, North Carolina, at 93. Sec. 4, grave 3099D, Arlington National Cemetery, Arlington, VA.

10037. Yarbrough, Jean (Jean Wilkes Yarbrough, Aug. 22, 1900–Aug. 2, 1975) Film director from Marianna, Arkansas, in Hollywood from 1936 helmed a long list of B's (*In Society, The Naughty Nineties, Here Come the Co-Eds, House of Horrors, She-Wolf of London, The Brute Man, Master Minds, Jack and the Beanstalk*) and television through the 1950's and 60's (*Beulah, The Abbott and Costello Show, Death Valley Days, The Guns of Will Sonnett, Adam 12*). He died from cancer at 74 in Los Angeles. Cremated August 5 at Rosedale Cemetery through the Neptune Society. As specified by him in June 1974, the ashes were released to the Neptune Society of San Pedro and buried at sea off Point Fermin.

10038. Yasgur, Max (Dec. 15, 1919–Feb. 9, 1973) Owner of the diary farm near Woodstock, New York, lent his land to what became the best known of all rock concerts, "Woodstock," in August 1969, the voice of the era of protest and student unrest. He died three years later at 54 in Marathon, Florida. Ahavath Israel Cemetery, near Liberty, Sullivan County, NY.

10039. Yates, Herbert John (Aug. 24, 1880 Feb. 3, 1966) Brooklyn born tobacco sales executive set up a film processing laboratory in 1912 that grew into Republic Pictures. Married from 1952 to actress Vera Hruba Ralston, who he tried unsuccessfully to promote to stardom in the 1940's. He died in Los Angeles at 85. Family mausoleum, First Ave., Oakwood Cemetery, Bay Shore, Long Island, NY.

10040. Yaw, Ellen Beach (Sept. 14, 1869–Sept. 9, 1947) "Lark Ellen," soprano with the New York Metropolitan Opera. El Portal De La Plaz, Rose Columbarium, Rose Hills Memorial Park, Whittier, CA.

10041. Yawkey, Tom (Feb. 21, 1903–July 9, 1976) Owner of the Boston Red Sox for 44 years poured a fortune into winning a world championship that never came. Unable to shake the curse of Harry Frazee's trading Babe Ruth in 1919, they missed three times in three seven game world series (1946, 1967 and 1975) while Yawkey was owner. Hall of Fame 1980. Cremated at Cambridge, Massachusetts. Ashes scattered in Winyah Bay, SC.

10042. Yearsley, Ralph (Oct. 6, 1896–Dec. 4, 1928) London born actor in Hollywood silents from 1922 (*Tom Mix in Arabia, Anna Christie, Peter Pan, The Kid Brother, The Little Shepherd of Kingdom Come, Show Boat*), married to actress **Grace Yearsley** (1895–1967). A suicide at 32, his ashes were later interred with hers. Columbarium of Remembrance, niche 60150, top tier, Courts of Remembrance, Forest Lawn Hollywood Hills, Los Angeles.

10043. Yeaton, Hopley (1740–May 12, 1812) Continental captain from New Hampshire served on the Brigates Deane and Raleigh, later joining the land campaign against the British in Rhode Island. His early coastal patrols qualify him as father of the American Coast Guard. Tomb at the U.S. Coast Guard Academy, New London, CT.

10044. Yeats, William Butler (June 13, 1865–Jan. 28, 1939) Irish poet and writer founded the Dublin Hermetic Society for the study of the occult in 1885. His works focus often on Irish life and myth in *The Rose* (1893), *The Wind Among the Reeds* (1899), the patriotic play *Cathleen ni Houlihan* (1902), the poem *An Irish Airman Foresees His Death*, and the mystical related work *A Vision* (1925). Nobel Prize for Literature 1923. He authored several volumes of poems as well and work regarding the Irish Free State and was president from 1902 of the National Theatre Society, later the Abbey Theatre. He was buried in the churchyard at Roqueburne, France, overlooking Cape Martin and Monaco. He was to have been moved to Ireland but the war prevented it until several years later. His upright gray stone is inscribed *Cast a cold eye on life, on death. Horseman, pass by.* Drumcliffe Churchyard, Sligo-Bundoran Road, County Sligo, Ireland.

10045. Yeaworth, Irvin "Shorty" (Irvin Shortess Yeaworth, Feb. 14, 1926–July 12, 2004) Director of a few horror and science fiction films, notably *The Blob*, filmed in summer 1957 at Yellow Springs and Phoenixville, Pennsylvania, as well as *Dinosaurus* (1960), *Way Out* (1967), went on to do educational, motivational and religious films, served as director of music at Phoenixville Presbyterian Church 1954–1975 and at Church of the Saviour in Wayne 1976–1988, where his funeral was held. He died at 78 when his vehicle went off the side of the road between Amman and Petra, Jordan. Great Valley Presbyterian Church Cemetery, Paoli, PA.

10046. Yerkes, Charles Tyson (June 25, 1837–Dec. 29, 1905) Financier, the model for Theodore Dreiser's trilogy, *The Financier* (1912), *The Titan* (1914) and *The Stoic*. He was jailed for misappropriating municipal funds in Philadelphia, was pressured to leave Chicago in 1900 and went to London to build a subway system, also funding Yerkes Observatory. Sec. 151, lot 26866, Greenwood Cemetery, Brooklyn, N.Y.C.

10047. Yogananda, Paramhansa (Jan. 5, 1893–March 7, 1952) The first Yoga master from India to settle in the United States, in 1920, and tour with "spiritual campaigns," teaching Kriya Yoga, which he dubbed the "jet airplane route to God." He published *Yogananda's Autobiography of a Yogi* in 1946, six years before his death at 59. Sanctuary of Golden Slumber, crypt 13857, Holly Terrace, Great Mausoleum, Forest Lawn, Glendale, CA.

10048. Yohannan, Francis (March 9, 1922– March 17, 2001) The basis for the character Yossarian, ever trying to avoid combat with an insanity designation in Joseph Heller's *Catch 22*. In real life, Yohannan was a longtime friend of Heller's. During a career in the U.S. Air Force, he served with Heller in the 57th Bomb Wing stationed in Corsica in 1944 and acquired over 9,000 air hours prior to his retirement in 1974. He died in Spokane at 79. Sec. 2, grave 574, Gettysburg National Cemetery, Gettysburg, PA.

10049. Yohe, May (April 6, 1869–Aug. 28, 1938) Stage actress and contralto from Bethlehem, Pennsylvania, a controversial figure of the 1890's married Lord Francis Hope, the possessor of the Hope Diamond, in 1894. He divorced her after she eloped in with a commoner from New York in 1901; she later divorced and re-married for the last time, to Captain John Smuts. She died in Boston from heart failure at 69. Ashes scattered from a boat over the Atlantic.

10050. York, Alvin C. (Dec. 13, 1887–Sept. 2, 1964) Backwoods Tennessee man called up for duty in France in World War I was an expert shot from years of hunting. Originally a conscientious objector, he claimed to have received divine guidance to go ahead and fight the Germans as it was a just cause, as heavily dramatized in *Sergeant York* (1941). York led seven men to wipe out a machine gun nest and capture 132 prisoners. Awarded the Medal of Honor and the Croix de Guerre. A flag flies at his marble angel, cross, slab and bench, Wolf River Cemetery near Pall Mall, TN.

10051. York, Dick (Richard York, Sept. 4, 1928– Feb. 20, 1992) Actor from Fort Wayne, Indiana, best known as Darrin Stephens on TV's *Bewitched* 1964– 69. Previous appearances included *Inherit the Wind* and *They Came to Cordura*, in which he received a permanent spinal injury while filming in 1958 that led to his retirement ten years later. He lived at Rockford, Michigan, near Grand Rapids, increasingly ill with emphysema, finally requiring oxygen. Despite his ailments, he was active in raising money for charity groups nationwide to benefit the destitute, including "bodybags for the homeless" etc., working from his home. He died in Blodgett Memorial Hospital in Grand Rapids at 63. His headstone is near the side entrance, Plainfield Township Cemetery, Rockford, MI.

10052. Yorty, Sam (Samuel William Yorty, Oct. 1, 1909–June 5, 1998) California congressman and "Maverick Mayor" of Los Angeles 1961–1973, a Democrat turned conservative, reduced city property taxes and oversaw the building of freeways, the city zoo and convention center, but was damaged by the Watts riots of 1965. Yorty did not support either John or Robert Kennedy's bids for the presidency; in his final speech just after winning the California primary, thirty years to the day before Yorty's death and only moments before his own assassination, Robert Kennedy remarked with good natured sarcasm in his last moments at the podium in the Ambassador Hotel, "Mayor Yorty has just sent me a message that we've been here too long already." Yorty died at 88 from a stroke complicated by pneumonia. There were no services. His ashes were scattered at sea by the Neptune Society June 11 off the coast of Los Angeles.

10053. Youmans, Vincent (Sept. 27, 1898–April 5, 1946) American composer from New York wrote the music for several Broadway shows including *No No Nanette* (1924), which introduced *Tea For Two* and *I Want to Be Happy*. Often in collaboration with lyricists Oscar Hammerstein II and Irving Caesar. He died in Denver at 47. Ashes scattered in the Atlantic, 25 miles from the Ambrose Light Ship off New York.

10054. Young, Brigham (June 1, 1801–Aug. 29, 1877) Leader of the Mormon religion or Church of Jesus Christ of Latter Day Saints, led the church in 1846 from Nauvoo, Illinois (where the founder Joseph Smith had been killed) westward to Salt Lake City, where they settled by 1848. He served as Governor of Utah 1850–57 and headed the Mormon community until his death, having taken up to twenty seven wives. He died from probable cholera and was buried behind the Lion House at Salt Lake City in the presence of a large gathering including sixteen of his wives and forty-four of his children. The graveyard now bears his name, his grave enclosed by an iron fence. Brigham Young Cemetery, Salt Lake City, UT.

10055. Young, Carleton (Carleton G. Young, May 26, 1907–July 11, 1971) Actor in films of the 1940's and 50's (*Abbott and Costello in Hollywood, His Kind of Woman, The Blue Veil*) and television. Alcove of Revelations, niche 29, Del Prado Mausoleum, Inglewood Park Cemetery, Inglewood, CA.

10056. Young, Carleton (Carleton S. Young, Oct. 21, 1905–Nov. 7, 1994) Actor from 1936 in many films, numerous westerns, several John Ford works (*The Last Hurrah, The Horse Soldiers, Sergeant Rutledge, The Man Who Shot Liberty Valance*, as the reporter who chooses to "print the legend"). His wife, dancer **Noel Toy**, kept his ashes until her own death in 2004, when they were interred together. Glass niche with photos and mementos. Chapel Columbarium, second floor, south wall, Hollywood Forever Cemetery, Hollywood (Los Angeles), CA.

10057. Young, Chic (Murat B. Young, Jan. 9, 1901–March 14, 1973) Cartoonist, creator of *Blondie*, which he drew from 1930 until his death. His stone with his wife Athel gives both his real and nick-name. Plot next to a pond, Sylvan Abbey Memorial Park, Clearwater, Pinellas County, FL.

10058. Young, Clara Kimball (Clara Kimball, Sept. 6, 1890–Oct. 15, 1960) Raven haired actress from Chicago at her peak in silents c. 1914 and with

Lewis Selznick productions from 1915 into the early 20's, where she starred in dramas featuring her in worldly parts. Her popularity faded with the late 20's when her second husband took over managing her career. She returned to vaudeville and to character parts in a few films, retiring in 1941. She died from a stroke at 70. Cremated through Chapel of the Pines Crematory, Los Angeles. North Mausoleum, columbarium unit A, niche 41, Grandview Memorial Park, Glendale, CA.

10059. Young, Clarence Upson (Oct. 14, 1895–Jan. 22, 1969) Screenwriter from Michigan penned B mysteries, adventures and westerns 1936–1956 (*Sky Raiders* 1941, *North to the Klondike, The Strange Case of Dr. RX, Night Monster* 1942, *The Ghost That Walks Alone* 1944, *Showdown at Abilene* aka *Gun Shy* 1956). He died from respiratory failure at South Coast Community Hospital, South Laguna, California, at 73. Cremated at Pacific View Memorial Park, Newport Beach, his ashes were held in storage there until interred in a niche in 1994. Alcove of Horizon (exterior), niche 322, Pacific View Memorial Park, Newport Beach, CA.

10060. Young, Coleman (May 24, 1918–Nov. 29, 1997) Detroit's first black mayor ran the city for twenty years 1974–1994, integrating the police force, promoting black based businesses, and winning election five times. Hazel Dell area, Elmwood Cemetery, Detroit, MI.

10061. Young, Cy (Denton True Young, March 29, 1867–Nov. 4, 1955) Baseball pitcher (the nickname either was short for cyclone, or for Cyrus, referring to his rural origins) threw a record 22 years, with Cleveland N.L., St. Louis N.L., Boston A.L., Cleveland A.L. and Boston N.L. 1890–1911. He held the record for most career wins as well as losses, pitching 874 games, with three no hitters (the first to pitch one in both leagues) and one perfect game. The premier pitcher in both leagues each year receives the award named in his honor. Hall of Fame 1937, an original inductee at the dedication. A baseball with eagle wings attached to it and his career achievements are noted on his monument. Peoli Cemetery, Peoli, OH.

10062. Young, Faron (Feb. 25, 1932–Dec. 10, 1996) Country singer and songwriter from Baton Rouge, dubbed The Singing Sheriff, had a hit with *Hello Walls* (1961). He wrote and recorded extensively, and did some acting, in *Daniel Boone,* etc. He died at 64 in Nashville a day after a self inflicted gunshot wound. His ashes were scattered over Old Hickory Lake outside Nashville, and according to Johnny Cash, blew back into the yard over the mourners.

10063. Young, Gig (Byron Ellsworth Barr, Nov. 4, 1913–Oct. 19, 1978) Actor from St. Cloud, Minnesota, in handsome lead roles from the early 50's took the name of his character in the 1942 film *The Gay Sisters* and kept it. He won an Oscar for *They Shoot Horses, Don't They?* (1969) and was nominated for his

roles in *Come Fill the Cup* (1951) and *Teacher's Pet* (1958). He and his fifth wife were found dead November 5, 1978 in their suite at the Osborne Apartments on 57th St. in Manhattan, an apparent murder-suicide. The ruling was that Young had fired one bullet from a .38 into her head and then done the same to himself. Cremated through Walter B. Cooke mortuary, his ashes were buried under a stone inscribed with his real name in the family plot in North Carolina, where the family had moved during his last year in high school. Green Hill Cemetery, Waynesville, NC.

10064. Young, Harold (Nov. 13, 1897–March 3, 1972) Portland, Oregon, born film editor (*The Strong Man* 1926, *The Private Life of Henry VIII* 1933) turned director (*The Scarlet Pimpernel* 1934, *The Mummy's Tomb* 1942, *The Frozen Ghost, I'll Remember April, Jungle Captive,* all 1945). Retired with the early 1950's. He died from a heart attack at in the Motion Picture Hospital, Woodland Hills, at 74. Sec. V, tier 1, (lower part of) grave 216, Holy Cross Cemetery, Culver City, CA.

10065. Young, Lester "Prez" (Aug. 27, 1909–March 15, 1959) Jazz great with tenor sax and cornet, played with Count Basie's orchestra in the 1930's. Associated with the Cool Jazz movement and known for his considerable work with vocalist Billie Holiday. His single upright stone bears the epitaph *Till we shall meet and never part.* Redemption, lot 11418, Cemetery of the Evergreens, Brooklyn, N.Y.C.

10066. Young, Loretta (Gretchen Young, Jan. 6, 1913–Aug. 12, 2000) Best known of four acting sisters, with Polly Ann, Elizabeth (known as Sally Blane) and Georgiana, played romantic leads in films 1927–1953, including *Laugh Clown Laugh* 1928, *Platinum Blonde* 1931, *Taxi* 1932, *Man's Castle* 1933, *The Call of the Wild* 1935, and later in more rewarding roles in *The Stranger* 1946, *The Bishop's Wife* and *The Farmer's Daughter* (AA 1947), *Rachel and the Stranger* (1948), *Come to the Stable* (AA nom. 1949) and *Cause For Alarm* (1951). Married to Grant Withers briefly in 1931 and to Thomas Lewis from 1940; they were long separated when she divorced him in 1969. Her third marriage in 1993 was to Jean Louis, who died in 1997. She left films to host TV's *The Loretta Young Show* 1953–60 and another version until 1963 when she retired, other than the 1986 TV movie *Christmas Eve.* She died at 87 from ovarian cancer at the home of her half sister Georgiana (Mrs. Ricardo) Montalban. Mass at St. Louis Catholic Church, Cathedral City. Cremated afterward as she directed, her ashes were buried October 7 in the grave of her mother, Gladys Belzer, and left unmarked. Sec. F, tier 65, grave 49, Holy Cross Cemetery, Culver City, CA.

10067. Young, Noah (Feb. 2, 1887–April 18, 1958) Nebraska born silent film foil in over one hundred pictures from 1918, primarily comedies, including *Safety Last* (as "The Law"), did many unbilled parts in talkies up to 1935. Sec. M, lot 435, space 4, Forest Lawn, Glendale, CA.

10068. Young, Polly Ann (Polly Ann Hermann, Oct. 25, 1908–Jan. 14, 1997) Actress sister of Loretta Young and Sally Blane retired early. Sec. F, tier 60, grave 49, Holy Cross Cemetery, Culver City, CA.

10069. Young, Robert (Robert George Young, Feb. 22, 1907–July 21, 1998) Chicago born actor in films from 1931, often in amiable romantic leads including *The Black Camel, The Sin of Madelon Claudet, Strange Interlude, Today We Live, Remember Last Night, Three Comrades, The Canterville Ghost,* with occasional forays into villainy (*Secret Agent* 1936, *The Mortal Storm* 1940) and more complex roles in *Journey For Margaret* (1942), *The Enchanted Cottage* (1945) and *Crossfire* (1947). Yet he was best known for his two TV series, as the perfect dad Jim Anderson in *Father Knows Best* 1954–60 and as *Marcus Welby M.D.* 1969–76. In his last decade he revealed a lifelong struggle with depression and alcoholism, and in 1991 attempted suicide. Betty Henderson Young, his wife of 60 years, died in 1994. Young died from general old age at 91 in his home at Westlake Village, California. Graceland sec. lot 5905, Forest Lawn, Glendale, CA.

10070. Young, Rodger (April 28, 1918–July 31, 1943) Medal of Honor recipient was a sergeant in the National Guard demoted himself because of deafness. He lost his life attacking a machine gun nest in the Solomon Islands, saving his platoon and inspiring a folk song, as noted on the historical marker near his grave. Re-interred from the Solomons July 22, 1949. McPherson Cemetery, Clyde, OH.

10071. Young, Roland (Nov. 11, 1887–June 5, 1953) London born actor on stage from 1908, in many films from the beginning of sound (*The Unholy Night, The Bishop Murder Case*). Out of character as Uriah Heep in *David Copperfield* (1935), he usually played whimsical little men, in *Ruggles of Red Gap* (1935), *The Man Who Could Work Miracles* (1936), *Topper* (1937, AA nomination, and two sequels), *The Young in Heart* (1938), *The Philadelphia Story, And Then There Were None* (1945), many others. He died in his sleep at his home, 61 West 9th St., New York City, at 65. Cremated at Ferncliff Cemetery through Frank E. Campbell mortuary in Manhattan. Ashes returned to his widow Dorothy Patience May at their West 9th St. home in Manhattan.

10072. Young, Skip (Ronald Plumstead, March 14, 1930–March 17, 1993) Actor played Wally Plumstead, Dave and Rick's cheerful buddy, on *The Adventures of Ozzie and Harriet* 1957–1966. Later a radio announcer, he died in Apple Valley, California, at 63. A veteran of Korea. Ashes buried sec. 13A, grave 332, Riverside National Cemetery, Riverside, CA.

10073. Young, Waldemar (July 1, 1878–Aug. 30, 1938) Grandson of Brigham Young, a prolific screenwriter in Hollywood 1917–1938, penned several Lon Chaney-Tod Browning collaborations 1925–9, including *The Unholy Three, The Blackbird, The Unknown, London After Midnight, The Big City, West of Zanzibar,* and *Where East is East.* Other scenarios or adaptations include *Dorothy Vernon of Haddon Hall, Sally, The Miracle Man* (1932), *Love Me Tonight, The Sign of the Cross, Island of Lost Souls, Cleopatra, Peter Ibbetson, The Lives of A Bengal Lancer* (1935, AA nom.), and *Test Pilot.* He died from pneumonia in Hollywood at 70. Sec. I-1-8-E5, Salt Lake City Cemetery, Salt Lake City, UT.

10074. Young, Whitney (July 31, 1921–March 11, 1971) Black civil rights leader, head of the National Urban League from 1968 until he drowned in Africa while there for a Ford Foundation Conference. His grave has a flush ground plaque with name and dates and behind it a bronze tablet on a stone wall inscribed *Every man is our brother and every man's burden our own. Where poverty exists all are poorer. Where hate flourishes all are corrupted. Where injustice reigns all are unequal.* The shaded grave and garden area is uncharacteristic at Ferncliff, where most are in open manicured lawns, with red flowers the only decorations. Knollwood Garden 2, plot C, grave 5, Ferncliff Cemetery, Hartsdale, NY.

10075. Younger, Bob (Robert Ewing Younger, Oct. 29, 1853–Sept. 16, 1889) Brother of Cole, Jim and John, wounded and captured in the Northfield, Minnesota, raid. Sentenced to life in prison, he died of TB at Stillwater, Minnesota. Buried next to his mother, Cole, and Jim. Lee's Summit Cemetery, Route 291, Lee's Summit, MO.

10076. Younger, Cole (Jan. 15, 1844–March 21, 1916) Bandit of the American West was a member of Quantrill's Raiders during the Civil war and of the James gang afterward, a cousin to Frank and Jessie James. Wounded and captured with Jim and Bob in the Northfield, Minnesota, raid; like Frank, he was free later and eluded further capture until after enough years had gone by that he was no longer wanted. Beside his gravestone, next to his mother and brothers Jim and Bob outside Kansas City, is a C.S.A. military stone listing him as a member of Quantrill's raiders. Northeast corner area, Lee's Summit Cemetery, Route 291, Lee's Summit, MO.

10077. Younger, Jim (Jan. 15, 1848–Oct. 19, 1902) Wounded and captured in the Northfield, Minnesota, raid, he was paroled in 1901. A suicide the next year. Buried with his mother, Cole and Bob. Lee's Summit Cemetery, Lee's Summit, MO.

10078. Younger, John (1851–March 16, 1874) Member of the James and Younger gang was killed in a fight with a Pinkerton detective. His grave was marked for many years by a metal rod. An inscribed granite tombstone was placed there in 1991. Old Yeater Cemetery, Clalk Level and Osceola Roads, near Roscoe, MO.

10079. Youngman, Henny (March 16, 1906–Feb. 24, 1998) New York rapid fire comic, the king of the one liners could do 50 or more jokes in an 8 minute routine, none exceeding 24 seconds. Best known for the line "Take my wife... Please!" She was Sadie

Youngman (1905–1987) and is interred beside him. He died at 91 in Manhattan. Sec. 9, block 9, Mt. Carmel (New) Cemetery #2, Glendale, Queens, N.Y.C.

10080. Youngs, Pep (Ross Middlebrook Youngs, April 10, 1897–Oct. 22, 1927) Right fielder with the champion New York Giants 1921–24 had a lifetime batting average of .322; he hit .300 nine of ten seasons until his death at 30 from a kidney ailment. Hall of Fame 1972. Block 3, lot 89, Mission Burial Park, San Antonio, TX.

10081. Yule, Joe (April 30, 1984–March 30, 1950) Scottish born vaudeville and burlesque performer, father of Mickey Rooney. He was signed by MGM in 1930 in a series of character roles, later playing Jiggs in several *Maggie and Jiggs* films at Monogram in the 1940's. Graceland sec., lot 6598, Forest Lawn, Glendale, CA.

10082. Yung, Victor Sen *see* **Sen Yung.**

10083. Yurka, Blanche (June 18, 1887–June 6, 1974) Czech born Broadway actress began her sporadic film career in 1935 as Madame DeFarge in *A Tale of Two Cities*. Many other but less impressive parts followed. She died in Mt. Sinai Hospital in Manhattan at 86. Cremated at Ferncliff Cemetery, Hartsdale, New York, her ashes were buried beneath a plaque shared with Florence Reed in the Actors Fund of America plot at Kensico. A spire dominates the center of the large lot of flush plaques, many with two names on them, with a portrait in relief of Shakespeare on the spire and the epitaph for all: *The play is done. The curtain drops, Slow falling to the prompter's bell.* Near left edge, Actors Fund of America plot, Kensico Cemetery, Valhalla, NY.

10084. Yuro, Timi (Rosemarie Timotea Aurro Yuro, Aug. 4, 1940–March 30, 2004) Chicago born, San Francisco raised vocalist of Italian parentage, made several recordings 1961–65, but had a major hit only with her first, *Hurt* (1961). Cancer in her larynx spread to an inoperable brain tumor, from which she died in Las Vegas at 63, married name Selnick. Ashes to be spread over the graves of her parents at Cicero, IL.

10085. Yussupov, Felix (March 23, 1887–Sept. 27, 1967) Russian prince and nephew of Czar Nicholas of the House of Romanov, along with the Czar's cousin Grand Duke Dimitri and other right wing activists conspired to assassinate Rasputin in December 1916. The poison failing, they shot him and threw the body in the Neva River. Sent into exile, Yussupov escaped the fate of his relatives. Plan II, tomb 391, St. Genevieve-des-Bois Cemetery, Paris.

10086. Zacharias, Helmut (Jan. 27, 1920–Feb. 28, 2002) German violinist and composer, acclaimed for his popular and lively renditions of classical music as well as jazz and popular numbers. He died from Alzheimer's Disease at 82. Ohlsdorfer Friedhof, Hamburg.

10087. Zachary, Tom (Jonathan T. Zachary, May 7, 1896–Jan. 24, 1969) Southpaw pitcher with the Washington Senators sent Babe Ruth his record setting 60th home run in the world series of 1927. Alamance Memorial Park, Burlington, NC.

10088. Zaharias, Babe Didrikson (Mildred Didrikson, June 26, 1914–Sept. 27, 1956) Champion 1932 Olympic star and golfer from Texas, won the U.S. Open in 1948, 1950 and 1954. She died from cancer at 42 in Galveston. Her monument is in the shape of a polished granite open book on a pedestal within a private hedge enclosure. Her flat headstone lists her birth in 1911 and notes *World's greatest woman athlete.* Island at intersection of blocks C, I and K, with a Texas historical marker placed nearby. Forest Lawn Cemetery, Beaumont, TX.

10089. Zaharias, George (Theodosios Vetoyanis, Feb. 27, 1908–May 22, 1984) The son of Greek immigrants was a pro wrestler whose named was changed by a promoter c. 1928 to Zaharias, Greek for sugar. Married to Babe Didrikson from 1937, the film *Pat and Mike* was reportedly based loosely on their story. Upright dark stone with a drawing of him. Block 18, lot 1A, Roselawn Cemetery, Pueblo, CO.

10090. Zale, Tony (Anthony Florian Zaleski, May 29, 1913–March 20, 1997) Middleweight boxing champion 1941–47, the Man of Steel was known for his three bouts with Rocky Graziano 1946–8, losing the title to him in 1947 and taking it back briefly in 1948. Flush bronze veterans' plaque near road. Sec. E, lot 29, Calvary Cemetery, Portage, IN.

10091. Zangara, Giuseppe or **Joseph** (c. Sept. 7, 1900 or 1902–March 20, 1933) Italian born communist attempted to kill President elect Franklin D. Roosevelt in Miami in early 1933 and missed, but managed to fatally wound Chicago Mayor Anton Cermak. Expressing no remorse and saying he would promptly do it again if given the opportunity, he died in Florida's electric chair two weeks after Cermak's death. Buried in the prison cemetery unofficially tagged Gopher Hill, marked by a license plate in cement with name and number as are the others. Zangara is grouped illogically with 1926 burials. Union Correctional Institute, Raiford, FL.

10092. Zanuck, Darryl Francis (Sept. 5, 1902–Dec. 22, 1979) Hollywood studio executive from Wahoo, Nebraska, worked for Warner Bros. in 1931 and for Fox 1935–52, where he was renowned as a powerful and effective studio head, the last of the Hollywood moguls, taking charge of 20th Century Fox again 1963–1971. Cremated, he has a memorial plaque with an elaborate and lengthy tribute from his daughter beside that of his wife **Virginia Fox Zanuck**. Sec. D, lot 41, Westwood Memorial Park, west Los Angeles.

10093. Zappa, Frank (Dec. 21, 1940–Dec. 4, 1993) Free spirited rock musician with the Mothers of Invention in the late 1960's, many of their compositions (*Don't Eat the Yellow Snow, Jewish Princess*) were controversial. Hits included *Dancing Fool* and (later)

Valley Girl, with his daughter Moon Unit. He prided himself on material not on the popularity charts, often with meanings undetectable from the outlandish titles. Dead at 52 from prostate cancer, he was buried the next day before the announcement of his death was made. Unmarked. Sec. D, lot 100, Westwood Memorial Park, west Los Angeles.

10094. Zapruder, Abraham (May 15, 1905–Aug. 30, 1970) Dallas citizen who unknowingly made what would become the most studied home movie in history, graphically depicting the fatal shooting of President Kennedy. The film was not released to the public until 1975, though Zapruder sold it to *Life Magazine* in 1963. It has been used endlessly to support both conspiracy and single gunman theories. Never involved in the investigation, Zapruder died from heart disease seven years after he filmed the scene, unaware his effort was to become a national curiosity. Block 52, BB east ½ (fourth row from rear of sec.), (Temple) Emmanu-El Cemetery, Dallas, TX.

10095. Zaslow, Michael (Nov. 1, 1944–Dec. 6, 1998) TV actor portrayed the villainous Roger Thorpe on CBS's *The Guiding Light* 1972–97 until fired due to the debilitation caused by Lou Gehrig's Disease (amyotrophic lateral sclerosis). He emerged in 1998 on ABC's *One Life to Live*, reviving his old character (1983–86) David Renaldi, but with the character suffering from ALS and using a wheelchair and voice synthesizer. Handled through Riverside Chapel, Manhattan, the family accompanied the body to Garden State Crematory, North Bergen, NJ.

10096. Zbyszko, Stanislaus (Stanislaus Cyganiewicz Zbyszko, April 1, 1879/1881–Sept. 23, 1967) Polish born wrestler from 1909 was the world heavyweight champion three times. He also spoke six languages, and played the part of Gregorius, proponent and practitioner of Greco-Roman wrestling, in Jules Dassin's *Night and the City* (1950). He died in St. Joseph, Missouri. Bhonython Circle, Laurel Hill Cemetery, 293 Beach St., Saco, ME.

10097. Zelig, Big Jack (Selig Harry Lefkowitz, May 13, 1888–Oct. 5, 1912) Head of a faction of Monk Eastman's New York gang, it was Zelig's assassins who reputedly killed Herman "Beansie" Rosenthal earlier in 1912 on the orders of police Lieutenant Charles Becker. He had also killed gunman Julie Morrell the past December at a dance hall, aborting Morrell's killing of him, sent by rivals. Zelig was on a Second Avenue trolley car northbound at 14th St. in Manhattan when he was shot and killed by Red Phil Davidson, allegedly because he had robbed Davidson, the killer said. Zelig was due to testify in Becker's trial however. His monument reads *Selig Harry Lefkowitz*, shows his age as 24, and adds *May his soul rest in peace.* Sec. 4, post 396, row 3, grave 4, Washington Cemetery, Brooklyn, N.Y.C.

10098. Zenger, John Peter (1697–July 28, 1746) Colonial American printer in New York was arrested for sedition in 1734 after printing criticisms of the governor. He was acquitted in 1735 in a trial at St. Paul's Church, now a historic site in Mt. Vernon, New York. Zenger's trial and acquittal were a precursor to the freedom of the press guaranteed over fifty years later in the Constitution. The exact gravesite is lost, in Trinity Churchyard, downtown Manhattan, N.Y.C.

10099. Zeppelin, (Count) **Ferdinand Von** (July 8, 1838–March 8, 1917) Titled, retired Lieutenant General with the German army designed and constructed airships, subsequently named for him. The first was launched July 2, 1900. Monument with cross. Abt. 8, reihe 5, folge 16, bis 18, Der Prager Friedhof, Stuttgart.

10100. Zevon, Warren (Warren William Zevon, Jan. 24, 1947–Sept. 7, 2003) Songwriter turned singer, Chicago born and California raised, known for many macabre numbers, generally with a touch of humor. He had played keyboard for the Everly Brothers, written songs for the Turtles as well as *Carmelita, Hasten Down the Wind,* and *Poor Poor Pitiful Me,* a hit for Linda Ronstadt in 1977 before his first recording made it big with *Werewolves of London* in 1978. Other favorite if ominous numbers included *Roland the Headless Thompson Gunner, Excitable Boy,* the later albums *Detox Mansion, The Envoy, Sentimental Hygiene, Mr. Bad Example* and *My Ride's Here,* much of his work with an eye on death, both tongue-in-cheek and with resignation. A year before his death, he announced he had terminal lung cancer, then went on to record his last album, *The Wind,* featuring *Disorder in the House* and the poignant *Keep Me in Your Heart.* He died at home in Los Angeles at 56, was cremated and his ashes scattered in the Pacific.

10101. Zhukov, Georgi Konstantinovich (Dec. 1, [Nov. 19 O.S.] 1896–June 18, 1974) Soviet military commander, chief of staff of the Red Army, a marshal from 1943 involved in every major battle of the war, including the invasion and later occupation of Germany. He was first supported and later ousted from political power by Stalin and finally by Khrushchev in November 1957. Grave with other honored ones at the Kremlin Wall, Moscow.

10102. Ziegfeld, Florenz (March 21, 1867–July 22, 1932) Chicago born theatrical producer on Broadway 1907–1931 introduced many later stars of stage and screen in his lavish musicals "glorifying the American girl." The yearly Ziegfeld Follies began in 1907 and ran for twenty one years, along with the Midnight Frolics. Particularly in the 1910–20 period, they showcased many major names including Al Jolson, Eddie Cantor, Fannie Brice, W.C. Fields, Will Rogers and Marilyn Miller. He produced many other stage musicals as well. Married to Anna Held from c. 1897–1913 and from 1915 to stage beauty and later character actress Billie Burke. He died in Los Angeles at 63, having been under nursing care for pleurisy in both lungs. An Episcopal service was held at Pierce Brothers mortuary. Interred in a crypt, right wall, room 1, Sanctuary of Vespers, Memorial Terrace, Great Mausoleum, Forest Lawn, Glendale, California. On June 8, 1974, his body was reburied with his widow (d. 1970) and her mother beneath a weeping willow and bronze statue in memory of Burke's mother. His original faded plaque, removed from the crypt in California, was replaced in 1993 with his complete birth and death dates and the former moved from 1869 back to 1867. Sec. 78, Powhatan plot, Kensico Cemetery, Valhalla, NY.

10103. Ziegler, Ron (Ronald Ziegler, May 12, 1939–Feb. 10, 2003) Press secretary for President Richard M. Nixon was born in Covington, Kentucky, and raised in Cincinnati; once a guide on the jungle tour at Disneyland, he worked for H.R. Haldeman and followed him into the Nixon White House in 1969, where his premier spot made him the most beleaguered ever of presidential spokespersons facing the fourth estate after the June 17, 1972, Watergate break-in which he termed "a third rate burglary." He remained loyal to Nixon, accompanying him on the plane to San Clemente the day the president resigned. Ziegler died from liver and kidney failure related to alcoholism at 63 in Coronado, California, a San Diego suburb. Cremated the day after his death by the Telophase Cremation Society of San Diego, his ashes went to his wife in Alexandria, VA.

10104. Zimbalist, Efrem (April 9, 1890–Feb. 22, 1985) Concert violinist from Rostov, Russia, in America from 1911, composed suites for violin, orchestra and piano. Married to opera singer Alma Gluck (*q.v.*) from 1914 until her death in 1938. He lived to 94 and was buried beside his wife in their immaculate lot of identical stones with individual inscriptions. His reads *In the night his song shall be with me,* from the Book of Psalms, and has an engraved violin. Old Town Hill Burying Ground, New Hartford, CT.

10105. Zimbalist, Sam (March 31, 1904–Nov. 4, 1958) New York born film editor from the 1920's turned producer (*Tortilla Flat, Thirty Seconds Over Tokyo, King Solomon's Mines, Quo Vadis, Mogambo, The Catered Affair, The Barretts of Wimpole Street* [1957]), died in Rome while making *Ben-Hur;* he was awarded an Oscar posthumously. Sunset Slope, block 7, plot 102, grave 4, Hillside Memorial Park, Los Angeles.

10106. Zimmerly, Eileen (Henrikson) (Sept. 22, 1904–March 6, 1923) Silent film bathing beauty was murdered at 18, found shot in the head in her Venice, California, apartment. Sec. 6, lot 7, Rosedale Cemetery, Los Angeles.

10107. Zimmerman, Joseph James, Jr. (Aug. 23, 1911–March 31, 2004) Milwaukee born inventor of the answering machine came up with the idea because he could not afford a secretary for his heating and air conditioning company in 1949, the year he patented the device. Answering recordings appear in films by 1955 (*Kiss Me Deadly*) and by 1957 there were 6,000 machines in use. With the U.S. Army Signal Corps, Zimmerman had been among the first on Omaha Beach at Normandy on D-Day. He died at 92. St. Mary's Cemetery, Elm Grove, WI.

10108. Zola, Emile (April 2, 1840–Sept. 29, 1902) French novelist and champion of the working classes. His series of novels 1871–1893 intended to follow scientifically the effects of heredity and environment on one family, considered the chief monument of the French Naturalist movement. The series of twenty novels, *Les Rougon-Macquart* contains such social epics as *Nana* (1878) and *Germinal* (1885). Zola was equally famous for championing the cause of Captain Alfred Dreyfus, imprisoned for treason due to anti-Semitism, until Dreyfus was freed. The writer was 62 when he and his wife went to sleep with the fire lit and the windows tightly closed. She recovered but he died from smoke inhalation caused by the blocked chimney. A monument with his bust is at his original grave in div. 24, Montmartre Cemetery, Paris. Removed in 1908, his tomb is among the honored, near that of Hugo, Rousseau and Voltaire. The Pantheon, Paris.

10109. Zucco, George (Jan. 11, 1886–May 28, 1960) Actor from Manchester, England, known for his wild eyed villains in many a horror film and melodrama 1939–46, including *The Adventures of Sherlock Holmes* (1939, as Moriarty), *The Mummy's Hand* (1940), *Dr. Renault's Secret* (1942), *The Mad Ghoul* (1943), *Sherlock Holmes in Washington* (1943, again as Moriarty), a string of poverty row chillers at Monogram and PRC and numerous smaller roles in A films. He retired in 1951 and spent his last days in a sanitarium after suffering several strokes, at south San Gabriel, California, where he died at 74. His daughter **Frances Zucco** (1932–March 15, 1962) also an actress, died from cancer just under two years later and is inurned with him. Unmarked. Columbarium of Remembrance, niche 60353, Courts of Remembrance, Forest Lawn Hollywood Hills, Los Angeles. His widow **Stella Zucco,** (Stella Francis, March 9, 1900–April 7, 1999), a former actress he married in 1929, requested her ashes be placed with those of her friend Justine Johnstone (in the Rose Garden of Pierce Bros. Chapel of the Pines Crematory, Los Angeles). They were spread, however, in the rose garden of a friend at her home above Malibu, CA.

10110. Zukor, Adolph (Jan. 7, 1873–June 10, 1976) Hungarian immigrant came to New York in 1892 and formed Famous Players film company in 1913. He merged with Jesse Lasky and by the 1920's was president of Paramount Pictures. He lived on a 760 acre estate "The Dells" in Rockland County, New York, where he spent most of his time until his wife's death in 1956. Unlike other studio heads, Paramount's top mogul stayed behind the scenes, remaining in New York except for annual trips to Hollywood. In later years he spent the winters there at his Century City apartment, where he died during a nap at 103. Buried beside his wife, close to the road near the top of a steep hillside. Temple Israel Cemetery, Hastings-on-Hudson, NY.

10111. Zumwalt, Elmo (Nov. 29, 1920–Jan. 2, 2000) U.S. Admiral commanded Navy forces during the Vietnam War 1968–1970. Chief of Naval Operations until 1974, he was noted for his Z-Grams, which made naval careers more attractive by relaxing many restrictions. His use of Agent Orange in defoliation contributed to the eventual death of his son, Elmo III, in 1986, but his son did not blame him, and Zumwalt continued to feel the use of the chemical was justified in saving the lives of American servicemen. He died from complications after surgery for a stomach tumor at Duke University Medical Center, Durham, North Carolina. Sec. 3, lot 382 (replatted), U.S. Naval Academy Cemetery, Annapolis, MD.

10112. Zuta, Jack (John Zoota, Feb. 15, 1888–Aug. 1, 1930) Russian immigrant allied with Chicago's north side gangs in the 1920's, running gambling and prostitution operations and known for his savvy with figures, until his alliance with George "Bugs" Moran (*q.v.*) and a suspect in the murder of Capone friend and Unione Sicilione president Antonio Lombardo and of *Tribune* reporter Jake Lingle made him a target for assassination. He was shot and killed in the dance pavilion of the Lake View Resort near Delafield, Wisconsin, where he had gone into hiding. Obelisk, Hebrew Cemetery, near Middlesboro, Bell County, KY.

10113. Zwillman, Abner "Longy" (July 27, 1899/1904–Feb. 27, 1959) Newark born head of the New Jersey underworld from the 1920's (the nickname came from an alias, George Long, used in an early arrest) was linked with Murder, Inc. and appeared before the Kefauver hearings in Washington in 1951. He operated several legitimate businesses but was under investigation for his vending machine operations when he was found hanged in his West Orange, New Jersey, home at 54. Flat plaque near white bench toward rear of center, one section from the rear. B'Nai Abraham Memorial Park, Route 22, Union, NJ.

Bibliography

Allen, Hervey. *Israfel: The Life and Times of Edgar Allan Poe*. New York: Farrar & Rinehart, 1934.

Allen, Maury. *Roger Maris: A Man for All Seasons*. New York: Donald I. Fine, 1986.

Alsberg, H.G., ed. *The American Guide*. New York: Hastings House, 1949.

American Cemetery Magazine.

The American Heritage Books of Presidents and Famous Americans. Vols. I–XII. New York: American Heritage, 1967.

Andrews, Deborah, ed. *The Annual Obituary 1980–1989*. Chicago: St. James, 1990.

Anger, Kenneth. *Hollywood Babylon*. New York: Dell, 1975.

_____. *Hollywood Babylon II*. New York: Dutton, 1984.

Arbeiter, Jean, and Linda D. Cirino. *Permanent Addresses*. New York: M. Evans, 1983.

Arce, Hector. *Gary Cooper*. New York: Bantam, 1979.

_____. *Groucho*. New York: Putnam, 1979.

Auburn State Prison. Compiled by Michael Pettigrass, Historical Records, Auburn Correctional Facility, Auburn, NY.

Auchincloss, Louis. *Persons of Consequence*. New York: Random House, 1979.

Bahn, Paul G. *Map to the Stars' Graves*. Final Curtain, 1986.

Baldock, Robert. *Pablo Casals*. Evanston, IL: Northwestern University Press, 1993.

Beauchamp, Cari. *Without Lying Down: Frances Marion and the Powerful Women of Early Hollywood*. New York: Scribner, 1997.

Beeson, Trevor. *Westminster Abbey*. 5th ed. London: Fisa, 1985.

Begg, Paul, Martin Fido and Keith Skinner. *The Jack the Ripper A to Z*. London: Headline, 1991.

Behn, Noel. *Lindbergh: The Crime*. New York: Atlantic Monthly Press, 1994.

Benoit, Tod. *Where Are They Buried? How Did They Die?* New York: Black Dog and Leventhal, 2003.

Berger, Meyer. *Meyer Berger's New York*. New York: Random House, 1953.

Beyern, Bertrand. *Guide des Tombes D'hommes Celebres*. Paris: Cherche-Midi, 1998.

Bielski, Ursula. *Chicago Haunts: Ghostly Lore of the Windy City*. Chicago: Lake Claremont, 1997.

Bigler, Philip. *In Honored Glory*. Arlington, VA: Vandermere, 1987.

Binder, John J. *The Chicago Outfit (Images of America)*. Charleston, SC: Arcadia, 2003.

Blum, Daniel. *Great Stars of the American Stage*. New York: Greenburg, 1952.

Bogle, Joanna. *Who Lies Where*. London: Marshall, Morgan & Scott, Lamp Press, 1989.

Bommersbach, Jane. *The Trunk Murderess: Winnie Ruth Judd*. New York: Berkeley, 1994.

Bradley, James, with Ron Powers. *Flags of Our Fathers*. New York: Bantam, 2000.

Brandon, Jim. *Weird America*. New York: Dutton, 1978.

Brooks, Patricia. *Permanently New Yorkers: Final Digs of the Notable and Notorious*. Guilford, CT: Globe Pequot, 2006.

Brooks, Tim. *The Complete Directory to Prime Time TV Stars*. New York: Ballantine, 1987.

Brown, Peter, and Steven Gaines. *The Love You Make*. New York: Signet, 1983.

Browning, James A. *Violence Was No Stranger*. Stillwater, OK: Barbed Wire, 1994.

Brunas, Michael, John Brunas and Tom Weaver. *Universal Horrors: The Studio's Classic Films, 1931–1946*. Jefferson, NC: McFarland, 1990.

Bugliosi, Vincent. *Helter Skelter*. New York: Bantam, 1978.

Burns, Walter Noble. *The One Way Ride*. Garden City, NY: Doubleday, Doran, 1931.

Butterfield, Roger. *The American Past*. New York: Simon & Schuster, 1947.

The California Death Index. Online at: http://vitals.rootsweb.com/ca/death/search.cgi.

Camden History Society. *Hampstead Cemetery Tomb Trail*. London, 1994.

Capote, Truman. *In Cold Blood*. New York: Signet, 1965.

Carmen, Karen, and Georg Gaston. *Robert Shaw: More Than a Life*. Lanham, MD: Madison, 1994.

Castellucio, Frank, and Alvin Walker. *The Other Side of Ethel Mertz: The Life Story of Vivian Vance*. New York: Berkley, 2000.

Catton, Bruce. *The Civil War*. New York: McGraw, 1971.

Chellel, Michael. *Michael's Memory Map*. Hollywood, CA.

Chronicle of the Cinema. New York: Dorling Kindersley, 1995.

The Cincinnati Post.

Clark, James. *The Murder of James A. Garfield*. Jefferson, NC: McFarland, 1993.

Classic Images Magazine. May 1984.

Cohen, Rich. *Tough Jews: Fathers, Sons and Gangster Dreams*. New York: Vintage, 1999.

Collier, Peter, and David Horowitz. *The Kennedys: An American Drama*. New York: Warner, 1984.

Comden, Betty. *Off Stage*. New York: Simon & Schuster, 1995.

Conan Doyle, Sir Arthur. *The Annotated Sherlock Holmes*. Ed. William Sabine Baring-Gould. New York: Clarkson-Potter, 1977.

Costello, Peter. *Jules Verne*. New York: Scribners, 1978.

Cremer, Robert. *Lugosi: The Man Behind the Cape*. Chicago: Harry Regnery, 1976.

Crivello, Kirk. *Fallen Angels*. Secaucus, NJ: Citadel, 1988.

Cross, David, and Robert Bent. *Dead Ends: An Irreverent Guide to the Graves of the Famous*. New York: Plume, 1991.

Culbertson, Judi, and Tom Randall. *Permanent Californians*. Chelsea, VT: Chelsea Green, 1989.

_____, and _____. *Permanent Italians*. New York: Walker, 1996.

_____, and _____. *Permanent Londoners*. Chelsea, VT: Chelsea Green, 1991.

_____, and _____. *Permanent New Yorkers*. Chelsea, VT: Chelsea Green, 1987.

_____, and _____. *Permanent Parisians*. Chelsea, VT: Chelsea Green, 1986.

Cullen, Tom A. *When London Walked in Terror*. New York: Avon, 1965.

Curtis, James. *Between Flops: A Biography of Preston Sturges*. New York: Limelight, 1982.

_____. *James Whale*. Metuchen, NJ: Scarecrow, 1982.

D'Antonio, Dave. *Invincible Summer: Traveling America in Search of Yesterday's Baseball Greats*. South Bend, IN: Diamond Communications, 1997.

Delaney, John J., and James Edward Tobin. *Dictionary of Catholic Biography*. Doubleday.

Del Re, Gerard and Patricia. *History's Last Stand*. New York: Avon, 1993.

Dickerson, Robert B., Jr. *Final Placement*. Algonac, MI: Reference Pub., 1982.

Dictionary of American Biography and Comprehensive Index through Supplement 8. New York: Scribner, 1990.

Donaldson, Norman and Betty. *How Did They Die?* New York: Crown, 1980.

Douglas, Helen Gahagan. *A Full Life*. New York: Doubleday, 1982.

Druxman, Michael. *Basil Rathbone: His Life and Films*. New York: A.S. Barnes, 1977.

Duff, David, ed. *Queen Victoria's Highland Journals*. Exeter, England: Webb & Bower, 1983.

Easton, Carol. *No Intermissions: A Biography of Agnes DeMille*. New York: Little, Brown, 1996.

Eaton, John P., and Charles Haas III. "Footsteps in Halifax, Footnotes to History." In *The Titanic Commutator*, 1983.

Eaton, Quaintance. *The Miracle of the Met*. New York: Meredith, 1968.

Edwards, Anne. *Vivien Leigh*. New York: Simon & Schuster, 1977.

Edwards, Bob. *Fridays with Red: A Radio Friendship*. New York: Simon & Schuster, pp. 30, 223.

Eels, George. *Ginger, Loretta and Irene Who?* New York: Putnam, 1976.

Eliot, Marc. *Death of a Rebel*. Garden City, NY: Anchor/Doubleday, 1979.

Ellenberger, Allan R. *Celebrities in Los Angeles Cemeteries: A Directory*. Jefferson, NC: McFarland, 2001.

Ellis, Nancy Brewer, and Parker Hayden. *Here Lies America*. New York: Hawthorn, 1978.

The Encyclopedia of American History. Guildford, CT: Dushkin, 1973.

Everton, George K. Sr. *The Handy Book for Genealogists: Vital Records Sources*. 6th ed. Logan, UT: Everton, 1971.

Ewen, David. *American Composers: A Biographical Dictionary*. New York: Putnam, 1982.

Exton, Peter, and Dorsey Kleitz. *Milestones Into Headstones*. McLean, VA: EPM, 1985.

Eyman, Scott. *Mary Pickford: America's Sweetheart*. New York: Donald I. Fine, 1990.

Fernicola, Richard G., M.D. *Twelve Days of Terror: A Definitive Investigation of the 1916 New Jersey Shark Attacks*. Guilford, CT: Lyons, 2001.

Filmfax Magazine.

Find-A-Grave website at: http://www.findagrave.com/. Maintained by Jim Tipton and A.J. Marik.

Forma, Warren. *They Were Ragtime*. New York: Grosset & Dunlap, 1976.

Fowler, Gene. *Beau James: The Life and Times of Jimmy Walker*. New York: Viking, 1949.

Frank, Gerold. *The Boston Strangler*. New York: Signet N.A.L., 1967

Fraser-Cavassoni, Natasha. *Sam Spiegel*. New York: Simon & Schuster, 2003.

Frassanito, William A. *Gettysburg: A Journey in Time*. Gettysburg, PA: Thomas, 1996.

Gabler, Neal. *An Empire of Their Own: How the Jews Invented Hollywood*. New York: Anchor/Doubleday, 1988.

Gaines, James R. *Wit's End: Days and Nights at the Algonquin Round Table*. New York: HBJ, 1977.

Gay, John, and Felix Barker. *Highgate Cemetery, Victorian Valhalla*. London: John Murray, 1984.

Gelman, Woody, and Barbara Jackson. *Disaster Illustrated: 200 Years of American Misfortune*. New York: Harmony, 1976.

Gilbert, Julie. *Opposite Attraction: The Lives of Erich Maria Remarque and Paulette Goddard*. New York: Pantheon, 1995.

Girardin, G. Russell, with William J. Helmer. *Dillinger: The Untold Story*. Bloomington: Indiana University Press, 1994.

Giuliano, Geoffrey. *Blackbird: The Life and Times of Paul McCartney*. New York: Dutton, 1991.

Golden, Eve. *Anna Held and the Birth of Ziegfeld's Broadway*. Lexington: University Press of Kentucky, 2000.

Google Groups alt.obituaries online at: http://groups.google.com/group/alt.obituaries?gvc=2&hl=en.

Gould, Stephen Jay. *Triumph and Tragedy in Mudville: A Lifelong Passion for Baseball*. New York: Norton, 2003, pp. 223–230.

Grace, Kevin, and Tom White. *Images of America: Cincinnati Cemeteries, the Queen City Underground*. Charleston, SC: Arcadia, 2004.

Greenwood, Douglas. *Who's Buried Where in England*. London: Constable Books, 1982.

Haining, Peter, ed. *The Edgar Allan Poe Scrapbook*. New York: Schocken Books, 1978.

Halliwell, Leslie. *The Filmgoer's Companion*. New York: Avon, 1984.

Hampton, William Judson. *Presidential Shrines from Washington to Coolidge*. Boston: Christopher, 1928.

Harrington, Chris. "Paint Him Black." *The Nashville Flyer*. Dec. 1997.

Harrison, Ben. *Undying Love*. New York: St. Martin's, 2001.

Harrison, Shirley, narr. *The Diary of Jack the Ripper*. Hyperion, NY: Smith-Gryphon, 1993.

Haskins, James. *Mabel Mercer: A Life*. Atheneum, NY, 1987.

Hatzl, Johann. *Ehrengraber am Wiener Zentralfriedhof (Guide to the Central Cemetery, Vienna)*. Vienna: Compress Verlag.

Haycroft & Kunit, ed. *Twentieth Century American Authors*. New York: Wilson, 1942.

Hayman, Ronald. *Hitler and Geli*. New York: Bloomsbury, 1997.

Hoidas, Ken, and Mari Allyn Huff. *The Incomplete Listing of Dead Gangsters*. Chicago, 1995. Adapted from William J. Helmer. *Chicago Beer Wars and Bootlegger Body Count*. Chicago: Mad Dog, 1990.

Hoover, Dwight W. *A Pictorial History of Indiana*. Bloomington: Indiana University Press, 1980.

Hucke, Matt, and Ursula Bielski. *Graveyards of Chicago*. Chicago: Lake Claremont, 1999.

Hyams, Joe. *Bogie*. New York: Signet, 1965.

The Indianapolis Star.

The Internet Movie Database (IMDb) at: http://us.imdb.com/.

Israel, Lee. *Kilgallen*. New York: Dell, 1979.

James, Bill. *Stats — All Time Major League Handbook*. 2nd ed. Morton Grove, IL: Stats Inc., 2000.

Jarvis, Everett G. *Deaths of Noted Movie and TV Personalities*. 4th ed. Baltimore, MD: Wisdom for Youth, 1990.
_____. *Final Curtain*. Secaucus, NJ: Citadel, 1993.

Jerome, Robert A., and Herbert A. Wisbey, Jr. *Mark Twain in Elmira*. Elmira, NY: Elmira Quality Printers, 1977.

Joachimsthaler, Anton. *The Last Days of Hitler: The Legends, the Evidence, the Truth*. Trans. Helmut Bogler. London: Brockhampton, 1999.

Jockle, Clemens. *Memento Mori, Friedhofe Europas*. Munich: Parkland, Germering, 2001.

Jones, Neal T., ed. *A Book of Days of the Literary Year*. London: Thames & Hudson, 1984.

Jordan, David M. *Roscoe Conkling of New York*. Ithaca, NY: Cornell University Press, 1971

Kane, Joseph Nathan. *Facts About the Presidents*. New York: Ace, 1976.
_____. *Facts About the Presidents*, 6th ed. New York: Wilson, 1993.

Kaplan, Justin. *Walt Whitman: A Life*. New York: Simon & Schuster, 1980.

Katz, Ephraim. *The Film Encyclopedia*. New York: Putnam, 1979.

Kazan, Elia. *A Life*. New York: Alfred A. Knopf, 1988.

Kear, Lynn, and John Rossman. *Kay Francis: A Passionate Life and Career*. Jefferson, NC: McFarland, 2006.

Keefe, Rose. *Guns and Roses: The Untold Story of Dean O'Banion, Chicago's Big Shot Before Al Capone*. Nashville, TN: Cumberland House, 2003.

Kellow, Brian. *The Bennetts: An Acting Family*. Lexington: University Press of Kentucky, 2004.

Kelly, Susan. *The Boston Stranglers*. New York: Kensington, 1995, 2002.

Kerrigan, Michael. *Who Lies Where: A Guide to Famous Graves*. London: 4th Estate, 1995.

Ketchum, Richard N. *Will Rogers: The Man and His Times*. New York: Touchstone, 1973.

Keylin, Arleen, ed. *Hollywood Album 2*. New York: Arno, 1979.

Keylin, Arleen, and Suri Fleischer, ed. *Hollywood Album*. New York: Arno, 1977.

Kilduff, Peter. *The Illustrated Red Baron: The Life and Times of Manfred Von Richtofen*. London: Arms and Armour, 1999.
_____. *Richthofen: Beyond the Legend of the Red Baron*. New York: Wiley, 1994.

Kimmel, Stanley. *The Mad Booths of Maryland*. New York: Dover, 1967.

Kirkpatrick, Sidney D. *A Cast of Killers*. New York: Penguin, 1986.

Knight, Stephen D. *Jack the Ripper: The Final Solution*. London: Grafton/Collins, 1986.

Kobler, John. *Capone: The Life and World of Al Capone*. New York: Fawcett Crest, 1971.

Kort, Michele. *Soul Picnic: The Music and Passion of Laura Nyro*. New York: St. Martin's, 2002.

Kotsilibas-Davis, James. *The Barrymores*. New York: Crown, 1981.

Koykka, Arthur S. *Project Remember*. Algonac, MI: Reference Pub. Inc., 1986.

Kraft, Stephanie. *No Castles on Main Street*. New York: Penguin, 1979.

Lahr, John. *Notes on a Cowardly Lion*. New York: Limelight, 1984.

Lamb, Brian, and the C-SPAN staff, with Richard Norton Smith and Douglas Brinkley. *Who's Buried in Grant's Tomb? A Tour of Presidential Gravesites*. National Cable Satellite Corp., Washington, D.C. Distributed by Johns Hopkins University Press, Baltimore, MD, 2000.

Lamparski, Richard. *Lamparski's Hidden Hollywood*. New York: Fireside/Simon & Schuster, 1981.
_____. *Whatever Became Of*. New York: Ace, 1967.
_____. *Whatever Became Of Vol. II*. New York: Ace, 1970.
_____. *Whatever Became Of Vol. III*. New York: Ace, 1971.
_____. *Whatever Became Of*, 4th Ed. Bantam, 1975.
_____. *Whatever Became Of*, 5th Ed. Bantam, 1976.
_____. *Whatever Became Of*, 6th Ed. (1st annual). Bantam, 1976.
_____. *Whatever Became Of*, 7th Ed. (2nd annual). Bantam, 1977.
_____. *Whatever Became Of*, 8th series. New York: Crown, 1982.
_____. *Whatever Became Of*, 9th series. New York: Crown, 1985.
_____. *Whatever Became Of*, 10th series, New York: Crown, 1986.
_____. *Whatever Became Of*, 11th series, New York: Crown, 1989.

Lanchester, Elsa. *Elsa Lanchester, Herself*. New York: St. Martin's Press, 1982.

Lanctot, Barbara. *A Walk Through Graceland Cemetery*. Chicago: Chicago Architecture Foundation, 1988.

Langguth, A.J. *Saki: A Life of Hector Munro*. New York: Simon & Schuster, 1981.

Larson, Erik. *The Devil in the White City: Murder, Magic and Madness at the Fair That Changed America*. New York: Crown, 2003.

Lash, Joseph P. *Eleanor and Franklin*. New York: Signet, 1973.

Leamer, Laurence. *As Time Goes By: The Life of Ingrid Bergman.* New York: Onyx/American Library, 1987.

Lederer, Joseph, and Arley Bondarin. *All Around the Town.* New York: Scribner, 1975.

Lewis, Paul. *Queen of the Plaza: A Biography of Adah Isaacs Menken.* New York: Funk & Wagnalls, 1964.

Life Magazine, The Year in Pictures 1972–1977 and 1981–1999. New York: Time-Life.

The Lincoln Library of Essential Information. 16th ed. The Frontier Press Co., 1946.

Lindbergh, Reeve. *No More Words: A Journal of My Mother Anne Morrow Lindbergh.* New York: Simon & Schuster, 2001.

Litsky, Frank. *Superstars (of Sports).* Secaucus, NJ: Derbibooks, 1975.

Lorant, Stefan. *Lincoln: A Picture Story of His Life.* New York: Norton, 1969.

The Los Angeles Times online at http://latimes.com/gp/homepage.html/.

Lottman, Herbert R. *Albert Camus: A Biography.* Garden City, NY: Doubleday, 1979.

Lotz, David. TBL: Collected Data including birth and death dates and places, cemetery and plot locations. Plano, Texas, 1993–2005.

Louvish, Simon. *Monkey Business: The Life and Legend of the Marx Brothers.* New York: St. Martin's/Griffin, 1999.

Lovell, Mary S. *The Sisters: The Saga of the Mitford Family.* New York: Norton, 2001.

Lynch, Thomas. *The Undertaking: Life Studies from the Dismal Trade.* New York: Penguin, 1998.

Madden, W.C. *Images of America: Crown Hill Cemetery.* Charleston, SC: Arcadia, 2004.

Mank, Gregory William. *The Hollywood Hissables.* Metuchen, NJ: Scarecrow, 1989.

_____. *It's Alive.* San Diego: A.S. Barnes, 1981.

_____. "The Mystery of Lionel Atwill" in *Monsters from the Vault,* Vol. 10, no. 20, summer 2005.

_____. *Women in Horror Films, 1930s.* Jefferson, NC: McFarland, 1999.

_____. *Women in Horror Films, 1940s.* Jefferson, NC: McFarland, 1999.

Maples, William R., and Michael Browning. *Dead Men Do Tell Tales: The Strange and Fascinating Cases of a Forensic Anthropologist.* New York: Doubleday, 1994.

Marion, John Francis. *Famous and Curious Cemeteries.* New York: Crown, 1977.

Marks, Paula Mitchell. *And Die in the West.* New York: Morrow, 1989.

Marshall, Peter, Adrienne Armstrong, and Alex Trebek. *Backstage with the Original Hollywood Square.* Nashville, TN: Rutledge Hill, 2002.

The Marshall Cavendish Illustrated History of Popular Music. 20 vols. Long Island, NY: Marshall Cavendish, 1989.

Martin, Mary. *My Heart Belongs.* New York: Morrow, 1976.

Martin, Percy E. "On the Trail of George Atzerodt (Adventures with Mr. Hall on the Trail of George Atzerodt)" in *The Surratt Society News.* Clinton, MD, July, 1984.

Martin, Ralph G. *Cissy.* New York: Simon & Schuster, 1979.

Marx, Arthur. *My Life with Groucho: A Son's Eye View.* London: Robson, 1988.

Massie, Robert K. *The Romanovs: The Final Chapter.* New York: Ballantine, 1995.

May, Allan. "Late for the Opera: Samoots Amatuna," on *AmericanMafia.com,* 1999.

Maynard, Mary. *Dead and Buried in New England.* New York: St. Martin's Press, 1993.

McCullough, David. *Mornings On Horseback.* Beaverton, OR: Touchstone, 1982.

McLaren, Angus. *A Prescription for Murder: The Victorian Serial Killings of Dr. Thomas Neill Cream.* Chicago: University of Chicago Press, 1993.

McMichael, N.H., ed. *Westminster Abbey Official Guide,* 1977.

Medved, Michael. *The Shadow Presidents.* New York: Times Books, 1979.

Mee, Charles L., Jr. *The Ohio Gang.* New York: M. Evans, 1981.

Meller, Hugh. *London Cemeteries: An Illustrated Guide and Gazetteer.* 3rd ed. Aldershot, England: Scolar Press, 1994.

Merrill, Boynton, Jr. *Jefferson's Nephews: A Frontier Tragedy.* New York: Avon, 1978.

Milton, Joyce. *Loss of Eden: A Biography of Charles and Anne Morrow Lindbergh.* New York: HarperCollins, 1993.

Morley, Sheridan. *Tales from the Hollywood Raj.* New York: Viking, 1983.

Morton, Frederic. *A Nervous Splendor.* Boston: Atlantic Monthly Press/Little, Brown, 1979.

Mosley, Charles, comp. *American Presidential Families.* New York: Macmillan, 1993.

Mosley, Leonard. *Disney's World.* New York: Stein & Day, 1986.

Murphy, Edwin. *After the Funeral: the Posthumous Adventures of Famous Corpses.* New York: Citadel Press, 1995.

Nash, Jay Robert. *Bloodletters and Badmen.* 3 vols. New York: Warner Paperback Library, 1975.

_____. *Encyclopedia of World Crime.* 6 vols. Wilmette, IL: Crime Books, 1989.

_____. *People to See, an Anecdotal History of Chicago's Makers and Breakers.* Piscataway, NJ: New Century, 1981.

National Baseball Hall of Fame Guide. Cooperstown, NY: National Hall of Fame.

Nationwide Gravesite Locator at: http://gravelocator.cem.va.gov/j2ee/servlet/NGL_v1.

The New York Times obituaries and funeral notices, indexed 1858–1968 and 1968–1978, with yearly supplements 1979–2006.

Nichols, Roy Franklin. *Franklin Pierce: Young Hickory of the Granite Hills.* Philadelphia: University of Philadelphia Press, 1958.

Okuda, Ted. *The Columbia Comedy Shorts.* Jefferson, NC: McFarland, 1986.

Parish, James Robert. *The Hollywood Celebrity Death Book.* Las Vegas: Pioneer, 1993.

Parkman, Francis. *Montcalm and Wolfe* (1884). London: Collier-Macmillan, 1969.

Pearson, Lynn F. *Discovering Famous Graves.* Buckinghamshire, England: Shire, 1998.

Père Lachaise Cemetiére website at http://www.wikipedia.org/wiki/Le_P%25E8re_Lachaise_Cemetery.

Perry, George. *The Life of Python.* Boston: Little, Brown, 1983.

Perry, Jim. *The Stars Beyond.* Hollywood: J.E. Perry, 1978.

Persico, Joseph E. *Nuremburg, Infamy on Trial*. New York: Penguin, 1994.

Peters, James Edward. *Arlington National Cemetery: Shrine to America's Heroes*. Rockville, MD: Woodbine House, 1986.

Peters, Margot. *Mrs. Pat*. New York: Alfred A. Knopf, 1984.

Petit, Ira S. *The Diary of a Dead Man*. Ed. J.P. Ray. New York: Acorn, 1969, 1976.

Petrova, Ada, and Peter Watson. *The Death of Hitler: The Full Story with New Evidence from Secret Russian Archives*. New York: Norton, 1995.

Pictorial Forest Lawn. Glendale, CA: The Forest Lawn Memorial Association, 1944.

Pike, Jeff. *The Death of Rock n Roll*. Boston: Faber and Faber, 1993.

Pitkin, Thomas M. *The Captain Departs: Grant's Last Campaign*. Carbondale: Southern Illinois University Press, 1973.

Plath, Sylvia. *Letters Home*. Ed. Aurelia Plath. New York: Bantam, 1977.

Preston, Diana. *Lusitania: An Epic Tragedy*. New York: Walker, 2002.

Price, Victoria. *Vincent Price: A Daughter's Biography*. New York: St. Martin's, 1999.

Profumo, David. *Bringing Down the House: A Family Memoir*. London: John Murray Publishers, 2006.

Raggsdale, Grady, Jr. *Steve McQueen: The Final Chapter*. Ventura, CA: Vision House, 1983.

Rees, Dafydd, and Luke Crampton. *Encyclopedia of Rock Stars*. New York: DK, 1996.

Rhodes, Elisha Hunt. *All for the Union*. Ed. Robert Hunt Rhodes. New York: Orion, 1985.

Riordan, William L. *Plunkitt of Tammany Hall*. New York: Dutton, 1963.

Rosenstone, Robert A. *Romantic Revolutionary: A Biography of John Reed*. New York: Alfred A. Knopf, 1975.

Ross, N.L. *Lon Chaney: Master Craftsman of Make Believe*. Quality R.J., 1987.

Rouse, Parker, Jr. *Virginia*. New York: Scribner, 1975.

Rubin, Barbara, Robert Carlton, and Arnold Rubin. *L.A. in Installments: Forest Lawn*. Santa Monica, CA: Westside, 1979.

Sann, Paul. *The Lawless Decade*. New York: Fawcett, 1971.

Scheibmayr, Erich. *Graber in Oberbayern Ausserhalb von München*. Munich: Windeckstrasse, 1995.

_____. *Letzte Heimat*. Munich: Erich Scheibmayr.

_____. *Wer? Wann? Wo?* Munich: Erich Scheibmayr, 1989.

_____. *Wer? Wann? Wo? Teil 2*. Munich: Erich Scheibmayr, 1997.

_____. *Wer? Wann? Wo? Teil 3*. Munich: Erich Scheibmayr, 2002.

Scheinin, Richard. *Field of Screams: The Dark Underside of America's National Pastime*. R. Scheinen, 1994.

Schessler, Ken. *This Is Hollywood*. La Verne, CA: Ken Schessler, 1989.

Schlesinger, Arthur, Jr. *The Age of Jackson*. Boston: Little, Brown, 1945.

Scott, Tony Luke. *The Stars of Hollywood Forever*. Culver City, CA: Tony Scott, 2001.

Seager, Robert, II. *And Tyler Too*. New York: McGraw-Hill, 1963.

Shaara, Michael. *The Killer Angels*. New York: Ballantine, 1974.

Sharkey, Terence. *Jack the Ripper: 100 Years of Investigation*. New York: Dorset, 1992.

Shaughnessy, Dan. *At Fenway: Dispatches from Red Sox Nation*. New York: Three Rivers, 1996.

Sherman, William Tecumseh. *Memoirs of Gen. W.T. Sherman*. New York: Library of America, 1990.

Sievers, Harry. *Benjamin Harrison, Hoosier Statesman*. New York: University Pub., 1959.

Slater, Scott, and Alec Solomita. *Exits*. New York: Dutton, 1980.

Slide, Anthony. *The Idols of Silence: Stars of the Cinema Before the Talkies*. Cranbury, NJ: A.S. Barnes, 1976.

_____. *The Vaudevillians*. Westport, CT: Arlington House, 1981.

Sloane, Florence Adele. *Maverick in Mauve*. Garden City, NJ: Doubleday, 1983.

Slominsky, Nicholas. *Baker's Biographical Dictionary of Musicians*. 6th ed. New York: Schirmer, 1978.

Smith, Gene. "The Haunted Major." *American History Magazine*, Feb.-March, 1994.

_____. *The Life and Death of Serge Rubinstein*. New York: Doubleday, 1962.

_____. *When the Cheering Stopped: The Last Years of Woodrow Wilson*. New York: Morrow, 1964.

The Social Security Death Index online at: http://ssdi.genealogy.rootsweb.com/cgi-bin/ssdi.cgi.

Southern, Eileen. *A Biographical Dictionary of Afro-American and African Musicians*. Westport, CT: Greenwood, 1982.

Southwick, Leslie. *Presidential Also-Rans and Running Mates, 1788 Through 1996*, 2d ed. Jefferson, NC: McFarland, 1998.

Spencer, Thomas E. *Where They're Buried*. Baltimore, MD: Clearfield, 1998.

Spiering, Frank. *Lizzie*. New York: Random House, 1984.

The Sporting News.

Srebnick, Amy Gilman. *The Mysterious Death of Mary Rogers*. New York: Oxford University Press, 1997.

Stanton, Doug. *In Harm's Way: The Sinking of the U.S.S. Indianapolis*. New York: Henry Holt, 2000.

Stanton, Scott. *The Tombstone Tourist*. Portland, OR: 3T, 1998.

Steen, Michael F. *Celebrity Death Certificates*. Jefferson, NC: McFarland, 2003.

Stern, Philip Van Doren. *Robert E. Lee*. Bonanza, 1973.

Stewart, William T., Arthur F. McClure, and Ken D. Jones. *The International Film Necrology*. New York: Garland, 1981.

Stone, Irving. *They Also Ran*. New York: Signet, 1968.

Stuart, Gloria. *I Just Kept Hoping*. Boston: Little, Brown, 1999.

Styron, William. *The Confessions of Nat Turner*. New York: Signet, 1968.

Taylor, Ina. *The Edwardian Lady: The Story of Edith Holden*. Winston, NY: Holt, Rinehart, 1980.

Thorne, J.O., and T.C. Collocott. *Chambers Biographical Dictionary*. Rev. ed. New York: Press Syndicate of the University of Cambridge, 1984.

Tipton, Jim. *Find-A-Grave* website at http://www.findagrave.com/.

Torrence, Bruce T. *Hollywood: The First Hundred Years*. New York: New York Zoetrope, 1982.

Tranberg, Charles. *I Love the Illusion: The Life and Career of Agnes Moorehead*. Boalsberg, PA: Bearmanor Media, 2005.

Truitt, Evelyn Mack. *Who Was Who on Screen*. New York: Bowker, 1983 (3rd ed.) and 1984 (4th ed.).

Turkis, Burton B., and Sid Feder. *Murder Inc.* (1951). New York: Da Capo, 1992.

Underwood, Peter. *Karloff*. New York: Drake, 1982.

Updike, John. *Memories of the Ford Administration*. New York: Alfred A. Knopf, 1992.

Vidal, Gore, *1876*. New York: Ballantine Books, 1976.

_____. *Lincoln*. New York: Random House, 1984.

Von Drehle, David. *Triangle: The Fire That Changed America*. New York: Atlantic Monthly Press, 2003.

Walsh, Jim. "Favorite Pioneer Recording Artists" in *Hobbies* Magazine 1951–1973.

Ward, Geoffrey C. *Before the Trumpet: Young Franklin Roosevelt*. New York: Harper & Row, 1986.

Ward, Geoffrey C., and Ken Burns. *Baseball, an Illustrated History*. New York: Alfred A. Knopf, 1994.

Ward, Geoffrey C., Ric Burns, and Ken Burns. *The Civil War, an Illustrated History*. New York: Alfred A. Knopf, 1995.

Warren Commission. *Report of the Warren Commission on the Assassination of President Kennedy*. New York: McGraw-Hill, 1964.

Watkins, Sam R. *Co. Aytch*. New York: Collier, 1962 and 1970.

Wayne, Jane Ellen. *Crawford's Men*. New York: St. Martin's, 1988.

Weaver, G.S., D.d. *The Lives and Graves of Our Presidents*. Columbus, OH: Potts & Leech, 1884.

Webster's American Biographies. Ed. Charles Van Doren. Springfield, MA: Merriam-Webster, 1984.

Weicchman, Louis J. *A True History of the Assassination of Abraham Lincoln and the Conspiracy of 1865*. Ed. Floyd Risvold. New York: Alfred A. Knopf, 1975.

Westmore, Frank, and Muriel Davidson. *The Westmores of Hollywood*. Philadelphia: J.P. Lippincott, 1976.

Weymouth, Lally. *America in 1876*. New York: Vintage/Random House, 1976.

White, Barbara Erlich. *Renoir: His Life, Art and Letters*. New York: Morrow, 1984.

White, Theodore H. *In Search of History*. New York: Warner, 1978.

White, William Allen. *A Puritan in Babylon*. New York: Macmillan, 1938.

Whitfield, Eileen. *Pickford: The Woman Who Made Hollywood*. Lexington: The University Press of Kentucky, 1997.

Whitman, Alden. *Come to Judgment*. New York: Penguin, 1981.

Wilk, Max. *The Wit and Wisdom of Hollywood*. New York: Warner Paperback Library, 1973.

Williams, T. Harry. *Huey Long*. New York: Bantam Books, 1970.

Williamson, David. *Kings and Queens of Great Britain*. London: Webb & Bower, 1986.

Wilson, Vincent. *The Book of Distinguished American Women*. Brookeville, MD: American Historical Research Associates, 1983.

_____. *The Book of the Founding Fathers*. Brookeville, MD: American Historical Research Associates, 1974.

Wolf, Marvin J., and Katherine Mader. *Fallen Angels*. New York: Ballantine, 1986.

Worth, Fred L. *Rock Facts*. New York: Facts on File, 1985.

Yankee, Luke. *Growing Up with Eileen Heckart*. New York: Back Stage Books, 2006.

Yonover, Neal S. *Crime Scene U.S.A.* Book soup publishing through Hyperion, N.Y., 2000.

You're Outta Here website at http://www.cjnetworks.com/~roryb/outta.html Maintained by Eric Rohr.

Index